LA CUISINE

Raymond Oliver

LA CUISINE

Secrets of Modern French Cooking

Photographs by
Charles Affif

Translated and edited by
Nika Standen Hazelton
with
Jack Van Bibber

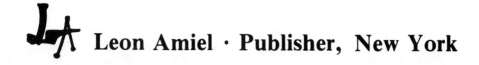 Leon Amiel · Publisher, New York

ACKNOWLEDGMENTS

The photographs in this book are by *Charles Affif*. The establishments and societies which have put their facilities at the disposition of Raymond Oliver in the preparation of the photographs are:
La Porcelaine de Paris, Les Cristalleries de Baccarat, Le Pyrex-Sovirel, Le Creuset, E. Dehillerin, Les Cristalleries de Saint-Louis.
La boucherie Marbeuf, la poissonerie Ch. Queyroy & Fils, la charcuterie Pignot.
The pâtisseries were photographed under the technical direction of G. Lenotre, pâtissier à Paris.

* * * * *

The original chapter on wines as well as the charts, maps, list of appellations contrôllées, etc., were edited and established with the cooperation of *Henry Clos-Jouve*, of the Académie Rabelais, Président de l'Association des Chroniqueurs Gastronomiques Français, *M. Eylaud,* Secrétaire Général du Comité Médical International pour l'Étude Scientifique du Vin, and *Marcel Lugan,* Secrétaire Général de la Confédération Nationale des Producteurs de Vins et Eaux-de-vie à Appellations d'Origine Contrôlées.
The chapter on cheese was edited with the cooperation of *Jean Richard,* Grand Chancelier de la Confrérie Nationale de Taste-Fromage.

CONTENTS

INTRODUCTION

It is a widely held misconception that our ancestors were, in their day, incomparable gastronomes. This deeply rooted error has also made them all into authentic gargantuas. The truth of the matter is very different. It is true that certain holidays were the occasion of sumptuous feasts, but it is no less true that these holidays were rare, and we may even say, exceedingly rare. Moreover these holidays always had symbolic aspects, the significance of which has been lost along with the traditions themselves. Gastronomy was long the privilege of the very few, at least in the elaborate form popularized by Brillat-Savarin. However, today cookery has become democratic, vulgarized, to use the true meaning of that word. What was the moving force of this evolution? Essentially two factors: transportation and equipment. One may be fond of cooking on the hearth, even of food prepared in a dinner pail; one may also appreciate learned preparations simmered in earthenware pots; one is no less a perfectly respectable gastronome for that.

But are we being really serious? Isn't our nostalgia for the past just a little fanciful, creating a seductive image, letting us see only the good side?

I have the same nostalgia as each of you. I too have "played with fire," and have used earthenware pots and ceramic platters. It is probable that a restaurant which returned to the traditions of our grandmothers would excite the warm and well-deserved enthusiasm of its clients. These guests would have the same reasons to go into ecstasies as they do over the sumptuous décor of hydrangeas at the "Coq Hardi" or the refined atmosphere of the "Moutière."

Cooking, divested of its décor, seems mutilated, or reduced. Such settings may seem highly artificial, yet they are no less indispensable to the culinary art of which they are, moreover, an aspect.

Cooking is like the fruit of a great love: a strong and slightly egotistical love on the part of the men, altruistic and sensitive on the part of the women. Be it one or the other, it is always present, demanding its share of gratitude and recognition. Isn't this natural?

Such is the problem. What solutions can I propose?

Doubtless, I can give much advice, the best of which is the most elementary, and a little knowledge of technique. Technique can improve, just as experience can be acquired. Nothing can replace this last quality, not even talent, though talent must not be neglected for it is un-

doubtedly, in large measure, the source of genius. Just as technique tends to supplement our at times deficient senses, so the ancient customs such as firemaking and its rituals are lost in a past which will never return. For today equipment has come to our rescue.

It seems necessary to clarify certain points, even at the risk of causing laughs from the younger generation for whom these things are gone forever. I have known and used wood fires, charcoal, and bakers' ovens also heated with wood; so it must not be thought that these are ancient methods. Today a ten-year-old child can use a gas or electric range quite well. Ask him to light a fire for a spit or an oven and he will do less well. Fifty years ago the opposite would have been the case. The same is true in what concerns smaller equipment. A child can, without great risk, manipulate an aluminum or enamelware casserole, but an adolescent, even an adult, will be hard put to use an earthenware casserole or a country oven. This observation may appear obvious, but it really isn't; for to these simple factors—transportation and equipment—may be ascribed all the reasons for the evolution in cooking.

When I say: "If a dish is better reheated, it is because it was not cooked the night before," it is, of course, a joke. There are some dishes, such as the terrines, the ragouts or the stews, which do not attain their full flavor until after a sort of "osmosis." But besides those how many can you reheat with conviction, when there is absolutely no need to do so? A comparison might be *drawn with certain white wines—the Sauternes for example—which are almost automatically subjected to three years of aging in barrels. How many "years" justify such homage and, on the contrary, how many others might deserve a treatment just as flattering? Let us admit that, generally speaking, for every three "years" there are two which would be better off bottled after only fourteen months. In the same fashion, how many stews have become stuck to the bottom of the pan during unjustified "reheatings"?*

There is no such thing as the art of fixing leftovers; there are only tricks, and often a great deal of indulgence on the part of the guests. Once again we are on the fringe of gastronomy. By what outward signs may we judge this period of transition?

We are confronted with a group of conditions: the giving up of a certain type of cooking, the refusal of the older people to recognize this, the search for procedures to replace it, the desire to evade the issue, and the curiosity which is its cause. We may say that outside of Paris concierges (last vestals of miroton*), there is no more simmering in the farmhouses. Many writers on gastronomy are tearing their hair out in a morass of lamentations. The barbecue, be it Apache or Japanese, is everywhere, from garden to living room. Exotic cooking is savored with pleasure on condition that it be colorful and "hot." Chinese, Japanese, Vietnamese restaurants are happily multiplying in the cradle of Escoffier and Prosper Montagné. This is a truth which it would be* *futile to deny. Should we rejoice or lament? There are some currents which cannot be bucked.*

I have traveled the world over, with my culinary knowledge my only baggage, and I have found the same welcome in Tokyo, Mexico, Montreal or Johannesburg. No! French cuisine is not in danger, it is unlikely that it ever will be: it is simply undergoing a transition, a moulting, an evolutionary crisis. This situation, which is not clearly apparent to everyone, does however disturb great numbers of our contemporaries. "But where are the snows of yesteryear?"

I believe it is time to take a look at the past.

The Romans were surprised by the gastronomy of the Gauls. Nothing is new under the sun. They found expert cheeses, such as Cantal or Bleu made of ewes' milk; they found fattened geese and pigs; cultivated broad beans, grains, roots, oysters, sea fishing. They took home recipes and techniques; they quickly monopolized the bay-leaf sauces to the increase of their own glory. The kings did not add much, for Saint Louis knew of no more than three sauces. Charlemagne was supposed, nevertheless, to have introduced a gastronomy already qualified as exotic. "The Béarnais" had to marry a Medicis before, once again, the Florentine cooks came back for a new harvest af bay leaves. Louis XIV had an appetite which Louis XVI called that of a pig, and Napoleon was only fond of chicken with olives, garlic and anchovies. Napoleon III, as aware of his epicurean role as he was of his role of emperor, had to bring some order out of the complicated mess of a gastronomy encumbered with "sauçailles." All the great French cooks who were to make our colors shine the world over were born during this period, therefore not at all long ago. People have often been mistaken in considering the cooking of this period as weighed down by complicated techniques, learned research, and the perpetual presence of truffles and foie gras.

This cuisine, which was that of my apprenticeship, is probably the basis without which nothing is possible. Even though François Mauriac may be telling the truth when he asserts that Picasso is conscious of the mystification which emanates from his work, it is no less exact that we possess some real proof of the qualities of the painter. Divested of his first period, deprived of his exceptional line, it is probable that what would be left of him would be merely the capers of a practical joker. We can, without risking too much, draw a parallel between painting and cooking. To innovate in cooking, it is more difficult to attack a boiled egg than a pheasant mousse. It is those dishes without possible recourse that remain the challenge of the great cooks. Experience, control, calm, are the first qualities of the great chefs. When some say that cookery is dying, it is because they refuse to see reality. Never has cookery had as many lovers as it has today. Rudyard Kipling was once asked how he was able to draw such an accurate picture of the centurion in Puck of Pook's Hill. *"I simply watched ane of our soldiers living on the Indian frontier," he replied. It is probable that if the cooks of the last half of the 19th century had been able to write they would have used the same arguments that I am using. Cleopatra's cook was as aware of the fortune of his masters as is the cook of Brezhnev or of Mao Tse Tung. The shape of the pot may change, the nature of the food may be different, the intention must remain the same.*

For therein lies a basic principle. Cooking cannot, without risk, be stripped of its intentions, of its rites, of its symbols. It must create happiness at any price. There can be no happiness without love, that goes without saying, whatever the form of the latter.

In our lives the form of love of which we are the most aware, which is available to everyone, is it not that of Eros or of Cupid? Many are the symbols which point in this direction, not that we need to look for erotism in aphrodisiacs, but rather in the most simple, at times the most humble gesture: the offering. To cook for oneself is always boring in the end; to cook for others, or better still for the one other, that is certainly an act of faith and love. Believe me, there is no cuisine without love.

What is the reason for this book, to whom is it addressed, what does it contain? That is what I would now quickly like to indicate.

Cooking is governed by a certain number of very strict laws; one must be familiar with the main points of these. It is the A B C *of all art or of all technique. It is perfectly true that some gifted people can rely success-*

fully on their guesswork in a few preparations, but for this they must be in a "state of grace." Moreover, inspired poets are not, in any case, the most fruitful.

But cooking is a daily affair, if not twice- or thrice-daily. It is well known that specialization is to be feared (if specialization is anything but monotony), and that imagination has its weaknesses.

I have known restaurateurs who created great food by finding inspiration in cookbooks, others in walking through Les Halles. Those who create with slippered feet may be doing the most elaborate work.

This cookbook, whatever its intrinsic value, has two meanings: first, it represents a sum of knowledge and everyone can, from this point of view, usefully consult it. Second, it is an escape, an open door to adventure, even if it is not necessarily the most audacious. A work of art is always an adventure; the omelet does not escape this rule.

This cookbook is therefore a necessity, just as a dictionary is; there are few homes which do not have a dictionary and a cookbook. If the solvers of crossword puzzles leaf through Littré, the gastronomes find their inspiration in Escoffier or in Ali Bab. Nonetheless these two remarkable works are both very different. One is precise and functional: that is the Escoffier. The other is inspired and full of fantasy, and is unfortunately very difficult to follow.

In writing this book I was not able to divorce myself entirely from the idea I have of the "cooking lesson." The word is not enough, we must have the picture.

The photograph indicating the position of the hands, the shape of the knife, the place to stick in the fork, and a thousand other details, becomes an absolute necessity. For in cooking, the technical lecture which is not accompanied by a demonstration is totally useless.

Color with its precision has completely changed the uses of photography; photographs have now become suggestive and appetizing, if one may say that; they are in any case favorable to inspiration.

A modern cookbook, if it is to be practical and functional, must be faithful to its destination. I desire this book to be useful and practical, without ceasing to be attractive and amusing. I wish it to be for you the guide to a fascinating and infinitely varied game, and often capable of repaying you a hundredfold for the effort you will have spent on it.

If gastronomy is an art with well-defined rules, the same is true of its presentation. To tell the truth these are only two aspects of the same thing, concurring to make the perfection which is perhaps not, after all, beyond the grasp of human nature. The art of table setting is, by anticipation, that of making the guest appreciate all the more the dishes which will be presented to him; for it would be out of the question to expect from him graceful behavior if one had neglected to put him in a "state of receptivity" by an immaculate tablecloth, crystal with the reflections of a dream, silverware in the best taste, flowers which appeal to the nose as well as the eye, etc. It may be compared to feminine beauty. What attractions can bring about the birth of desire, if they have not been judiciously put to their best advantage by the artifices of which the feminine sex has the secret? It even would seem that it is decidedly the ladies who know the best, along with the art of "make up," that no less difficult art of "making up" a festive table.

You may be a cook without equal, perhaps, but please leave to your wife the care of creating with love the showcase that is to set off your work.

Before going into all this art of cookery we have shown a few tables arranged by some of our friends who are well known for their good taste and the warmth of their welcome. Let them be thanked for allowing us thus to place this book under the sign of elegance and courtesy.

Remarks on Entertaining

THE INVITATIONS

The first duty of the hostess is to take care of the invitations.

If the occasion involves only close friends, she may invite them by telephone, at the last minute if necessary, but she won't be surprised if her friends are not always available on a particular day. But if she wishes to arrange her table, it would be better to start at least ten days ahead, so as to assure herself that the friends she wishes to assemble will be able to come.

If the occasion involves more or less important acquaintances, or people to whom one owes consideration and regard, one should send invitations at least fifteen days ahead.

If you wish particularly to have such and such persons and you want to arrange your party around them, telephone them to suggest two or three dates so that they can make a choice. The date thus determined is the one you will send to the other people you invite. In any case you must still send out a card, as a reminder, but without the notation "R.S.V.P." For a dinner you must indicate the dress: street dress, black or white tie.

If you are sending out cards you might consider the following formula:
On a standard-sized visiting card:

Mr. and Mrs. Louis X
request the pleasure of Mr. and Mrs. John Y's company
for dinner at home on January 2 at 8 o'clock.
Black tie   *R.S.V.P.*
                                               (address)

or more simply:

                                               (address)

Mr. and Mrs. Louis X
Dinner, January 2, 8 o'clock
Black tie   *R.S.V.P.*

You must write "request the honor" and not "request the pleasure" for a reception including important personnages.

The words "a reminder" at the top right of the card are used to confirm a spoken invitation. If the invitation was not extended this way, one uses the formula R.S.V.P., placed at the bottom of the card at the right, above the address.

Always mention titles, for example:

"request, etc., His Excellency the Ambassador to Portugal and Mrs. X";

"request, etc., His Honor the Senator and Mrs. X";

"request, etc., the Count and Countess of X."

If the dinner is given in honor of a famous person, it is customary to write at the top of the card: "On the occasion of the visit of Mr. Y" or: "To celebrate the award of the Legion of Honor to Mr. Z." In cases like these the invitations are generally engraved or printed and "Monsieur" and "Madame" are spelled out.

In the case of a tea party only the hostess invites. You may use either of two types of cards:

Mrs. John X

with the name placed in the center of the card; this type must not have a printed or engraved address.

Or:

(address)

Mrs. John X

The invitation will in this case read as follows:

Mrs. John X
Tea
Thursday, October 16

R.S.V.P.   *4 o'clock*

If you use the first formula, you write your address by hand underneath the R.S.V.P.

It is also the hostess who invites to a bridge party; you will mention, according to the hour: tea, bridge or bridge dinner.

For a cocktail party, there are two possible situations: either you are receiving friends whom you know well and Mrs. X invites alone:

Mrs. Jacques X
will receive Wednesday, February 26

R.S.V.P.   *7 o'clock*

Or if you are inviting mostly your husband's acquaintances (business club or sporting friends), the invitations may be sent by both host and hostess.

The invitation should be for 7 o'clock; the guests will have no reason to be late; 6 o'clock has become too early, for the men leave their offices later and later.

For a baptism or a first communion, if you send out invitations, which is not always necessary for a strictly family lunch, you should use the same formula as for a luncheon invitation.

For an invitation to an engagement party the wife should invite:

> *Mrs. Jean X*
> *will receive, on the occasion of the engagement of her*
> *daughter Odile to Mr. Pierre X, Thursday, October 11,*
> *1964, from 5 to 8 o'clock.*
> *R.S.V.P.*   *(address)*

or:

> *On the occasion of the engagement of her daughter*
> *Odile to Mr. Pierre Y*
>   *Mrs. Jean X*
> *will receive Thursday, October 11, 1964, from 5 to*
> *8 o'clock.*
> *R.S.V.P.*   *(address)*

In the case of a marriage, it is now customary for the two families to get together to receive. You may write:

In the case of a luncheon:

> *Mrs. Jean X (mother of the bride)*
> *Mrs. Pierre Y (mother of the groom)*
> *will receive after the religious ceremony or the celebra-*
> *tion of the marriage*
>   *at the Hôtel George-V.*
>   *R.S.V.P.*

In case of a reception from 5 to 8 o'clock:

>   *Mrs. Jean X*
>   *Mrs. Pierre Y*
> *will receive on October 5*
>   *at the Hôtel George-V*
> *5 to 8 o'clock*   *R.S.V.P.*

These cards are to be included in the wedding announcement in which the homes of the two families have already been mentioned.

For a dance, you must use the following formula if you are receiving for the coming out of your daughter:

> *Mrs. Jacques X*
> *will receive on the occasion of the coming out*
>   *of her daughter Anne.*
> *R.S.V.P.*   *from 10 o'clock*
> *Black or white tie*   *(address)*

In principle, it is not correct to put R.S.V.P. on any invitation. In former times this was not even permitted, but today one may mention it; the hostess must know how many people to expect. As it is, there already is far too great a tendency not to reply to invitations; it is therefore a good thing to stress the necessity for doing this.

If the invitation is for lunch or dinner, one has an obligation to reply either with an acceptance or a refusal. For all other parties it is obligatory to reply, and to do so as soon as possible, if you intend to refuse the invitation.

WHAT THE HOST AND HOSTESS SHOULD WEAR

The basic rule for you, the mistress of the house, is to be dressed with sobriety, which in no way excludes elegance. Moreover your appearance must be such that it never places one of your guests in a state of inferiority.

For a luncheon you should wear a tailored dress or suit, little jewelry (a pin, a pearl necklace, a ring). Your husband will wear a plain dark suit with a white shirt, a plain tie, dark socks and black shoes. Yellow shoes are out of the question unless it is a country party, in which case your appearance can be a little more relaxed.

For a dinner of eight to twelve persons, your dress will be short but elegant. It could be, in the American style, a long hostess gown. But if the occasion is a dinner involving protocol, to which you have invited important people, the hostess gown will not do unless your invitation specified black tie and long dress.

If the dinner is informal, your husband will dress as for luncheon, but he is obliged to wear a white shirt. If your invitation mentions black tie, he will wear a dinner jacket, a white shirt with a soft collar, a black or garnet-colored bow tie, black socks and patent-leather shoes. At home, at least if it is not an official dinner, he may wear a dinner jacket to his own taste. Except at official dinners one can wear a white jacket with a white vest and black trousers, or a midnight blue jacket, and a silk cummerbund.

As for the hostess, her dress will remain the same, as it is now customary for the short dress, called a "cocktail dress," to accompany a dinner jacket, at least when the invitation has not specified "long dress."

THE GREETING

When you give a party you should always be ready in good time. Remind your husband in the morning that you are giving a lunch or dinner party. Do not hesitate to telephone his secretary, if he has one, so that she may remind him again.

If your guests are met at the door by a butler or a maid, either should take the guests' coats, umbrellas and hats. You must reserve a good deal of room to handle all these clothes. Your friends may wish to wash their hands or comb their hair: if you do not have a special guest bathroom, make certain that your bathroom to which they are taken is ready to receive them (soap, clean hand towels, comb, clothes brush, etc.).

Once your guests are ready they will be brought into the living room by the butler or the maid, who will be careful not to knock at the door: they must only knock at the doors of the bedrooms or bathrooms, or the study if you or your husband are working there.

If you have no servants you or your husband will open the door, and it is you who will take care of the coats of your guests. You will suggest that they wash their hands and will then take them to the living room.

You must stand up at the arrival of each of your guests and move towards them to welcome them. Your husband will kiss the hands of the married ladies (but not the single girls) if this custom is familiar to him.

You must introduce all the guests to each other if they do not know each other. You will introduce a man to a woman, the least important person to the most important, the younger to the older, taking care to cite with the name the titles of your guests, for example:

"Madame, let me introduce Monsieur X, senator of the Loir-et-Cher——la comtesse de. . . ."

or:

"My good friend, Monsieur Pierre Louis, Ingénieur civil des Mines—Monsieur Fabre, Président de la Sociéte Z."

If you do not know one of your guests, your husband should introduce him to you and add: "My wife." The converse is also true; you must say: "My husband," and not: "Mr. Dupont." Say: "My son," "my daughter," except if you are introducing your married daughter: "my daughter, Mrs. Jacques Martin."

If you are introducing an ambassador say: "His Excellency the Ambassador of Y." You must introduce civilians to clerics.

But above all use a clear and intelligible voice in pronouncing the names and titles. There is nothing more disagreeable than to sit at table next to someone whom we cannot place. You must initiate the first arrivals by saying to them: "I am happy to be able to introduce the Y's and X's who. . . ." As soon as you sit down to dinner the atmosphere will have been created and your role simplified.

It is customary to offer a drink before dinner. Don't say "offer an apéritif" because it sounds disagreeably like a bar. Don't bring out too many bottles. Offer sherry or port and whisky, and don't forget the sparkling water and ice. You can also offer champagne, but it must be dry, well chilled, and served by preference in tumblers, not in *coupes,* which are used only at dessert or for a buffet. Other apéritifs are possible, but they have their place in the country or at more intimate meals.

The drink can be accompanied by salted crackers, almonds, olives and other tidbits. The hostess will serve these drinks herself except when the occasion is a large reception or one involving protocol; at the latter occasions she will be assisted by a butler and maid.

THE TABLE

For a dinner for six to eight persons, a round table is the ideal solution. Above this number a rectangular table, with the narrow ends slightly rounded, is the most convenient. Above all your guests must be comfortable; they must be able to move their arms without having to go in for gymnastics. If your table is not big enough for ten people, only invite eight! Twelve inches of space between places is ideal.

For a luncheon you may use white or colored tablecloths or American table mats (a mat is a cloth rectangle; they are now also made in cork or artistically decorated plastic materials). If the table top is pretty, these individual mats enable you to show it off to advantage. For a dinner it is preferable to use a white or embroidered tablecloth.

You must not forget the filled salt cellars and pepper shakers. Use wine coasters only if you have no one to serve the wine.

The place setting comprises one plate for a soupless meal (soup is only served at dinner, unless it is a fish soup). This plate will be changed after each course.

For a dinner with soup, you will place a soup bowl on top of a serving plate. You may also use cups, called bouillon cups, which you may place directly on the serving plate, or on matching saucers if you have them. The dessert and cheese plates will be set out on a sideboard as will all the other plates.

The place settings are arranged on either side of the plate, generally facing inward, with the initials or engraving showing except if one is using English silver which is engraved in the inside face. To the right of the plate goes the soup spoon, if there is to be soup, and the knife. To the left, the fork. One does the same with the fish knife and fork if fish is on the menu.

In principle one changes the place setting with every course; the necessary utensils for the next course will be placed on the new plate, which will have been warmed if the next course is a hot dish.

Dessert silver is arranged on appropriate plates: the cheese knife at an angle with the handle to the lower right of the cheese plate; the dessert silver crossed, with handles to the lower side, on the dessert plate.

At the same time that one presents the cheese plate, the finger bowls are presented, placed on the cheese plates. These bowls, which may be more or less valuable, are filled with tepid water in which you have placed a round slice of lemon, a mint leaf, or a rose petal. One presents finger bowls also after any dish which required the use of fingers, such as shellfish, crustaceans, artichokes, asparagus.

At each place there will be glasses; the number will vary according to the wines which accompany the menu; there will be at least two, a large one for water and a medium-sized one for wine. If there are several wines, the glasses should be arranged according to height from left to right, as many wineglasses as you need. Use a medium-sized glass for Burgundy, a smaller glass for Bordeaux, and an even smaller glass for dessert wine such as Madeira. For champagne one places a *coupe* or *flûte* to the right of the other glasses.

Water, and the principal wine if it's *vin ordinaire*, are on the table so that each guest may serve himself as he pleases, even when the service of drinks is to be taken care of by the staff. Water must be presented in a carafe, but wine, to be strict about it, should be presented in its bottle, especially if it is a great growth of a particular year. The wine carafe is more attractive, and in some very fine homes the wine is decanted, that is to say, it is poured very gently into a carafe about an hour ahead of time, making sure that any sediment remains in the bottle.

On each plate a napkin is placed, one that matches the cloth if you are using a cloth, and it is folded into a cone or an envelope. A roll or a piece of bread can be placed within the fold of the napkin unless you follow the American style of using a special bread and butter plate, which is placed above the dinner plate and to the left. On leaving the table, each guest leaves his napkin on the table without refolding it; it is never used a second time.

As for the decoration of the table, let it be very simple for lunch, more deliberately elegant for dinner. Flowers, fruits, vegetables, shellfish—all that your imagination suggests as good, as long as the effect is happy. A centerpiece is a minimum, but it should never be so impressive, either in height or extension, that it hides people from one another or inconveniences the guests. On the other hand, it is not against the rules to arrange several matching bouquets on the table, or decorative objects, or even garlands.

For a dinner, especially for an intimate dinner, candlelight is always agreeable. It makes people look beautiful and it gives to silver and crystal a luster that is full of charm and mystery. But it is good to provide electric light in the dining room as well so that it will not be too dark to permit the meal to be served.

The menu should be made up taking into account the tastes of your guests if you know them, but although its composition may be varied according to the importance of the meal or with the seasons, its unfolding, on the other hand, follows precise rules.

A classic meal is made up of an hors-d'oeuvre, an entrée, a saltwater or freshwater fish, a meat or poultry with a garniture of vegetables, a salad, plus the cheese tray, the desserts and the fruits. If it is not indispensable to have all these dishes, it is in any event necessary to respect the order in which they are served.

For a luncheon an entrée or a fish course, a main dish, cheese, dessert or fruits are sufficient.

For a dinner you may add a consommé or soup, or oysters.

Do not serve too many dishes; the quality should surpass the quantity. If you have no one to serve at table, plan a hot dish to start, followed by a cold one. In this way you will not have to get up since you will bring in the hot dish when you sit down and you will have at hand the cold dish, the salad, cheeses and desserts. At a large dinner avoid serving lobster *à l'américaine,* for it is too difficult to eat; also avoid dishes based on garlic, which does not agree with everyone. If among your guests you have a Moslem or a Jew, do not serve pork. Serve fruit juice and not alcohol to the Moslem.

Do not forget to jot down the composition of your menus so that you will not repeat the same meal with the same guests. They might doubt your culinary talents.

For a meal among close friends or for a few guests it is unnecessary to put menus on the table. When you do, place one hand-written menu at each end of the table: your guests will pass them around.

Do not mention the wines, for they will be revealed when the host or hostess serves them, unless one of them happens to be a noble bottle; otherwise silence is golden.

THE SEATING

You must preside at the center of the table, with your husband opposite you. Or you may, following the English method, seat yourselves at either end of the table: this allows you not to seat two people on the end. However, if the table is the long one, this formula has the inconvenience of preventing your leading the general conversation.

Alternate ladies and gentlemen if you have an equal number of men and women. It is always possible to do this and still seat host and hostess opposite to one another if the number of persons at the table is a multiple of four plus two extra persons. However, if you have eight, twelve, or sixteen at the table, it will not be possible to seat men and women alternately and still have host and hostess opposite to one another. In such a case, you the hostess will preside at the end of the table according to the plans below.

For a table of eight persons, let us list the guests by couples and according to their importance: Mr. A and Mrs. a, Mr. B and Mrs. b, Mr. C and Mrs. c. Here are two ways of seating your guests:

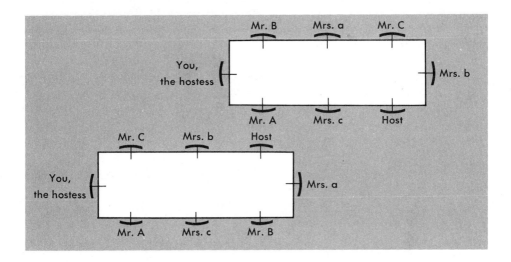

If you are having a ladies' luncheon, seat facing yourself the lady you wish to honor. If your husband is having only men he will do the same. If you are single you may ask your nearest relative or the eldest person or the most representative to be seated opposite yourself. This is equally true for a single man.

If you are using two tables, which is often a solution to adding to the number of seats of honor, you and your husband can preside, one at each table, seating opposite you the most distinguished guests.

If you are having more than eight for dinner, place a little card on top of one of the glasses at each place (format: half of a visiting card) with the name of the guest written very legibly.

For a very large dinner, to avoid having your friends look all around the table, place a plan of the seating arrangement on a small table or chest of drawers in the entrance hall. Knowing where their seats are, they will go directly to them.

The problem of the seating arrangement is often very difficult to resolve. Give this serious thought before sending out your invitations, and avoid inviting two couples or two persons both of whom merit the seat of honor. It is better to give two dinners or two luncheons. If you must have several important persons and you do not know how to seat them, you may use the protocol service of the State Department. This service will look up in the official bulletin which regulates the ranks and precedences, and will give you all useful information. But, happily, you will not always be faced with such great difficulties and you will usually be able to solve your problems alone.

You will seat at your right and continue by order of precedence:
the person whom you are honoring;
an ecclesiastic;
a foreigner (unless he is a friend of your son's);

a foreign officer before a French officer, even if his rank is lower;

a prefect (in his department he represents the government).

Age does not come before function or titles; it can only be used to decide between two persons having the same function or the same title. Be careful about decorations; a commander of the Legion of Honor goes before a knight of the Legion of Honor. If you must invite a Bishop, ask him to preside with you. A government official always goes before a professional man. A woman is seated according to the seat reserved for her husband, unless by reason of her profession or her decoration she has a more important place.

If your guests have neither rank nor titles, it is then according to their age that you must seat them. You must honor a person whom you are receiving for the first time, especially if the other guests are regularly invited to your table.

Avoid having your children at an important dinner, but plan, nevertheless, on having one at your service in case a guest should cancel at the last minute. This will also enable you to avoid thirteen at table, and to have a balanced table. If you have no children, have recourse to a single friend, but be careful that it does not happen too often, or he will become hurt after a while by this role of stopgap! Also avoid placing couples across from each other, and do not separate newlyweds.

THE SERVICE

If you have a butler to serve, he should wear a white jacket and white gloves for a formal dinner. If it is a maid, she should wear black with a long-sleeved dress or blouse and a white apron.

When the dinner is ready, the server announces at the living-room door, "Dinner is served" or "Madame is served," or "Monsieur is served" if your husband is entertaining alone. If you have an important guest, a diplomat or a Bishop presiding at table with you, the server must address him: "His excellency is served."

You will be the first to go into the dining room, and you ask the guest to your right to take his seat; your husband will do the same with his right-hand neighbor. You should be the first one seated.

The server must present the plates from the left and begin with the woman seated to the right of the host, then go on to the woman seated on his left, and so on, finishing with you; he will begin again with the man at your right, and end with the host. When the first course is finished, he will take a clean plate from the sideboard, take away the used plate with the left hand, and place the clean one from the other side. If there is soup, he takes away the soup bowl with the plate which is underneath it.

In a large dinner the server must change the plates for each course and you yourself must indicate the time for changing by leaving your knife and fork on your plate. In a more intimate meal you may keep your silver, but if a guest has left them on his plate the butler must bring back others on a clean plate. If in bringing the silver a piece falls on the floor, he must pick it up and remove it; he will take another one from the sideboard and bring it on a plate to the table. The silver is taken away from the right.

The courses should be passed twice except for the soup, salad, cheese and fruits (of course it's understood that if one of your guests compliments the cheese, one should pass it again). Before passing the cheese the server must take away the salt cellars, pepper shakers and mustard pots and remove any bread crumbs, either with a crumber or with the napkin he uses in carrying the plates, and collect them in a plate. He brings in the dessert plates (with spoon, fork and knife) and, after the cheese, removes the plate with the soiled knife and presents a clean plate, with a knife if there are fruits for dessert.

The server must serve the wines from the right, hold the bottle by the body and not the neck, and be very careful not to soil the tablecloth. He should begin by putting a little wine in the glass of the host, so that he may taste it. He continues to serve around the table; with wines it is alright to serve the guests around the table just as they are seated. The large glass already being filled with water, the red wine should be poured into the medium-sized glass, the white wine into the smallest glass, and the champagne into the champagne glass. If you serve two kinds of red wine, one with the roast and another with the cheese, it is preferable to plan on an extra glass to avoid mixing them.

The butler should watch out during the entire meal that your guests do not want for anything: bread, water, wine.

If you have more than ten guests it is preferable to have two people to serve. Each will pass one dish. The service will be more rapid and the food will still be hot when it is placed on the plates.

Do not leave the table until all your guests have finished and the butler has opened the door to the living room.

If you have no servants, you will ask your friends to sit down at the table and you will preside, preferably at the end of the table, so that you will be able to place near yourself a serving table on which you will have arranged everything you will need during the meal; plates, silver, bread, water. Your friends will help.

You will also have the wines placed near you. Your husband will serve them or else, if you are alone, you will ask one of your friends to do it. Do not forget to set out wine coasters.

If the dining room and the living room are the same room, once the dinner is over, clear the table quickly, put everything on the serving table, and take it to the kitchen; it is very disagreeable to spend the evening near soiled dishes.

When the meal is over you return to the living room. Have a tray ready with coffee cups and tea cups. Unless they are close friends do not ask: "Do you take coffee?" Serve it; your guests will take it if they desire it. But have tea ready just the same.

After the coffee, you will offer liqueurs and brandies in appropriate glasses. See that the conversation remains general.

At about eleven o'clock you will have refreshments served, or bring them out yourself: fruit juice, mineral water, whisky.

ADVICE FOR THE GUESTS

As a general rule accept an invitation only if you intend to return it; there are two cases in which you may be excused from doing so. If you are single you may acquit yourself of this debt by sending flowers or a box of candy, etc. The other case is if you have been invited by an important person such as a minister or priest, or the president of a business, and the small size of your apartment or the lack of personnel prevents your entertaining at home. After a party you have attended you must then send a thank-you note, accompanied by, if you feel the occasion warrants, either flowers or candy.

If you are invited by telephone and do not know if the date is convenient for your husband, give an answer within 24 hours. Do not ask the names of the other guests; the hostess will tell you if she deems it appropriate. On the other hand do not forget to ask the time, the address and what to wear, in case you do not receive a confirmation card.

If the invitation was sent to you on a visiting card, answer in the same manner, writing in ink. Answer as soon as possible, especially if it is a luncheon or a dinner, for the hostess must know the number of persons on whom she can count. It is usual to answer within 48 hours. Following is the usual formula:

> *Mr. and Mrs. X*
> *send Mr. and Mrs. Y the expression of their most dis-*
> *tinguished sentiments and thank them for their amiable*
> *invitation which they accept with the greatest pleasure.*

or should it be a single man invited by a woman:

> *John X*
> *pays his respectful homage to Mrs. Z and thanks her, etc.*

A single young lady sends "her respectful sentiments."

But if you are on a footing of intimacy with the person who has invited you, you can, less ceremoniously, use only the formula of thanking the host.

If you are unable to accept, always begin with the polite formula and add "to which they regret they are unable to attend, being busy that day" or "being absent at that date." It is polite to be precise about the reason for your refusal, even if the reason is a white lie.

Wear the dress mentioned on the invitation. If nothing is said, wear street clothes to a luncheon: an elegant suit or a dress. Take off your coat in the hall, but keep your hat on unless the hostess asks you to take it off, should you be the only one to have one on. Carry your gloves in your hand.

Your husband should wear a dark suit, a conventional tie, black shoes, dark socks and a white shirt or one of a discreet color. He should never enter a living room with his coat or his hat in hand; he should put them down of his own accord, even if no one asks him to.

For a dinner you should wear a dressier dress; you will thus honor the hostess, who will be delighted that her dinner is an elegant one. If the invitation mentions "black tie," you wear a short dress known as a "cocktail dress" and your husband a dinner jacket. If "white tie" is stipulated, you should wear a long evening dress; take off your gloves before sitting down at table. Your husband will be in tails.

Be prompt, especially if you are asked to a lunch or a dinner. If the invitation says 8 o'clock, try to be there at 8. Do not be early; you would embarrass the hostess who might not be ready. But do not be late, and foresee the time it will take you to get there and any possible traffic problems. If for any reason you cannot be on time, telephone to warn of your delay and ask the hostess not to wait for you to sit down to the meal. She will sometimes be obliged to start dinner and you will be personally much less embarrassed on arrival; it is extremely disagreeable to enter a room where eight or ten people await only you to go into the dining room.

If at the last minute it should happen that you feel too tired or have some imperative hindrance, telephone immediately; the hostess will be grieved, but if the excuse is valid, she will understand your reasons. On the following day you should send a note and flowers to be completely forgiven.

Do not arrive two hours late to a cocktail party; do not think that it is "chic." If the invitation says 6 o'clock, the hostess will await you from that moment on. Your husband may be delayed by an appointment. In that case do not wait for him to come and pick you up, but meet in front of your friend's house. In this way you will both gain time.

When you go to a party your husband must wait for you to enter the living room. You will approach the hostess to greet her. Then you should approach the guests whom you know, and your hostess will introduce those whom you have never met. Say: "How do you do Monsieur, or Madame," without adding "enchanted." If it is someone whom you want very much to know you may add: "I am delighted to meet you." If the hosts forget to introduce someone, behave simply and introduce yourself; a woman introduces herself to another woman by saying: "Simone X"; and not "Mrs. X." A man always introduces himself as "John X" and not "Mr. X."

You may sit down as soon as the hostess asks you to and only get up again to greet an older woman, an official, or an ecclesiastic. Your husband should stand up for everyone. You shake hands with younger women and with men.

When you go into the dining room, look for your place at the table discreetly, if it has not been indicated to you previously. Wait to sit down until the hostess has done so.

If you are served bouillon in a cup, do not use the spoon. Cut and eat the tender parts of asparagus with a fork. Do not cut your salad with a knife. Eat cheese with bread and not with a fork. Do not begin to taste a dish until the hostess has done so. Do not leave your silverware on your plate if your hostess has not done so. If, per chance, you are missing a piece of silver, say so quietly to the person who is serving, or to the hostess if there is no servant.

When the hostess gets up from the table, do the same, leaving your napkin unfolded next to your plate. If you take coffee or tea, do not leave your spoon in the cup but in the saucer. Do not powder your nose at the table, but do it discreetly when returning to the living room.

If you are seated to the right of the host, at the end of the evening do not forget that this place gives you the duty to signal the departure. If not, wait for the guest of honor to leave before doing so yourself, unless you are obliged to leave for some very important reason. In this case you might want to take French leave: at a dinner for eight or ten people, it is very difficult. In a larger dinner or some other party you should go up to the hostess, explain your reasons and your regret at leaving, and ask her permission to go without saying goodbye to the other guests. She will be agreeable. If the evening is pleasant, the departure of one person or of a couple can break up the ambiance. Do not go, however, without taking leave of at least one of your hosts and ask him to give your excuses to the others.

When you intend to return a dinner by a dinner, you should send neither flowers nor candy, unless it is a dinner given for a special reason such as a birthday, baptism, engagement, marriage, or other special occasion. If you want to give flowers do not bring them yourself as you would place the hostess in a difficult situation, for she will not have time to arrange them and she will give them to the butler or the maid who will, at that moment, have other things to do. Have them sent, either in the morning, which will please your hostess and give her time to redecorate her rooms, or on the following day. Send a visiting card with your "thanks for a pleasant evening."

A single man must always send flowers; a single lady can dispense with this, but she must send a thank-you note. A hostess will always be pleased if you telephone her the following day to tell her how much you have enjoyed her party. If you spend a weekend or a visit with friends, bring a gift: a box of candy or, if you know each other well enough, something to decorate the house, or a personal gift for your hostess if you know her tastes.

If you are invited to the country never bring flowers unless it happens to be in the dead of winter.

We have not discussed here different types of meals: the party to observe the baptism, the first communion, the engagement party, the wedding reception, an anniversary; nor those other parties which are outside of the limits of this book: tea, bridge, cocktail party, balls, etc. We refer our readers to the witty little book of M. d'Amécourt, *Savoir-vivre.*

LA CUISINE

Chez Louise de Vilmorin

Chez Madame Nicole Mourlot

Chez Madame de N.

Chez Madame A. Wilson

Chez Madame Nicolas de Vilmorin

Chez Louise de Vilmorin

Chez Raoul Guiraud

Chez Monsieur F. Eisenkopf

Chez Madame Nicole Mourlot

Chez Madame T.

Chez le Peintre Chapelain-Midy

Table Rustique

Déjeuner sur la Terrasse

Pour un Repas de Chasse

Chez Madame Nicole Mourlot

Chez Madame la Baronne Alix de Rothschild

I

TRICKS OF THE TRADE

Les Tours de Main

EDITORS' INTRODUCTORY NOTE

In translating and editing M. Oliver's book, we have tried our utmost best to preserve the personal style and flavor of the author's language and recipes, so that the American cook may come as close as possible to M. Oliver's ways of doing things. We have kept the authenticity of M. Oliver's recipes and only adjusted them to American kitchen techniques and circumstances when this could not be avoided, but these adjustments have been kept to a minimum. Any other course would have been impertinent considering M. Oliver's stature. The Tricks of the Trade which follow, however, present a unique opportunity for the American cook to observe a great chef at work. We have therefore completely preserved their original approach, even when it conflicted with standard American kitchen practices.

Our thanks to Inez Krech, copyeditor of this book, for her invaluable suggestions, which went far beyond the call of duty and for which we are most grateful.

NIKA STANDEN HAZELTON
JACK VAN BIBBER

ABAISSE—ABAISSER

To roll out a piece of dough with a rolling pin to the required thickness.

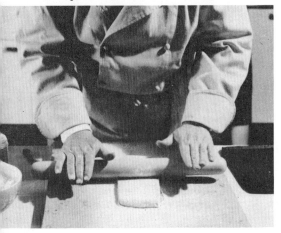

The piece of dough thus rolled out is called *une abaisse*.

ABATS

Secondary cuts of butcher's meat. These are the heads and ears of veal and pork; *les amourettes,* the spinal marrow of beef and veal; the sweetbreads of lamb and veal; beef lungs; *la fressure,* the liver, heart and spleen of lamb and mutton; beef and veal hearts; lamb and beef tongue; the brains of beef, lamb and mutton; beef, calf's and pork liver; beef kidneys; beef and veal tripe; *la fraise,* a calf's intestinal casing; oxtail; pig's blood and beef marrowbones.

ABATIS

The innards of poultry, which include the head, neck, gizzard, liver, heart, feet and wing tips of poultry, as well as cocks' combs and kidneys *(crêtes et rognons du coq).*

HOW TO CLEAN POULTRY INNARDS

Singe the neck, head, wing tips and feet.

Rub the feet with a kitchen towel to remove the skin; cut off the spurs.

Trim the liver very carefully to remove and discard the gall bladder.

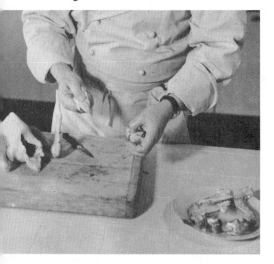

Be careful not to cut into or break the gall bladder, because the gall it contains produces a bitter taste.

Cut the gizzard in two and discard the crop (it contains grit, seeds, etc.).

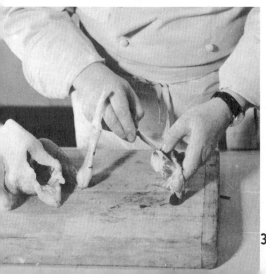

ABRICOTER

Apricot jam is used extensively in the preparation of cakes and pastries as a glaze and as decoration. *Abricoter* means to coat a cake with apricot jam.

Cook down the apricot jam until it is very thick; then apply it to the cake with a brush.

ADOUCIR

1. To reduce the saltiness of a food by adding water, milk or a light broth.
2. To reduce the bitterness of vegetables by cooking them in water. Fruits are sweetened in syrup.

AGNEAU

Lamb, or *agneau,* comes from a sheep less than a year old. When very young, *agneau de lait* or milk-fed lamb, the meat is insipid, for these lambs have not yet grazed. Milk-fed lamb is eaten by preference in the spring. When a little older (Pauillac or *pré-salé),* the meat becomes one of great delicacy. *Agneau de pré-salé,* salt-marsh lamb, has grazed on meadows flooded periodically by salt water or irrigated with salt water.

Good-quality lamb is recognized by the width of its hindquarters and the whiteness of its fat. The best lamb kidneys are pale pink in color.

Lamb can be cooked by the same general methods used for other meats, and also by some of those used for poultry. Although a *blanquette* of mutton is out of the question, because the flavor of mutton is too strong, a *blanquette* of lamb is highly esteemed; and so are fricassees of *fressures*—the heart, spleen, liver and lungs—and other lamb dishes in cream sauces.

Editors' Note: M. Oliver's following suggestions for cooking lamb and mutton are naturally based on French cuts, which are considerably different from American cuts. The English terms used for these French cuts are their nearest American equivalents.

CUTS FOR ROASTING
The *baron,* comprising both the loins and both hind legs; the *carré,* the rib section or rack; the shoulder; a whole baby or milk-fed lamb.

CUTS FOR BROILING
Rib chops, shoulder chops and kidneys.

CUTS FOR COOKING IN A SAUCE
Shoulder, breast and neck.

CUTS FOR BOILING
Leg (*à l'anglaise,* that is, in the English style).

AIGUILLETTES

Thin strips of the white meat of chicken. To obtain *aiguillettes* of duck, remove the second joints, drumsticks and the wings, since they are usually skinny. Cut the thick part of the breast meat on both sides into thin strips, cutting lengthwise and parallel with the breastbone.

The term is also used for thin slices of butcher's meat and to describe a special cut of beef rump or sirloin roast.

AIGUISER

1. To season a food highly.
2. To point up the flavor of a drink or a sauce with lemon juice or a dash of vinegar.

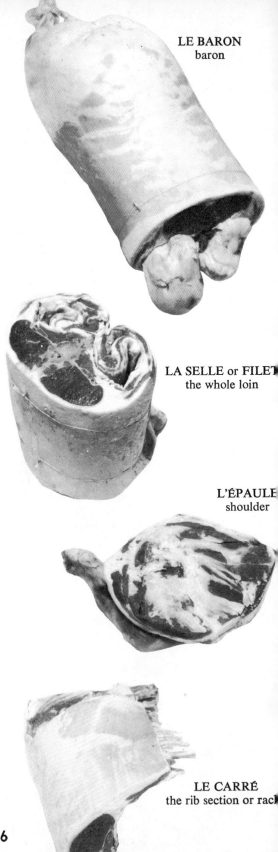

LE BARON
baron

LA SELLE or FILET
the whole loin

L'ÉPAULE
shoulder

LE CARRÉ
the rib section or rack

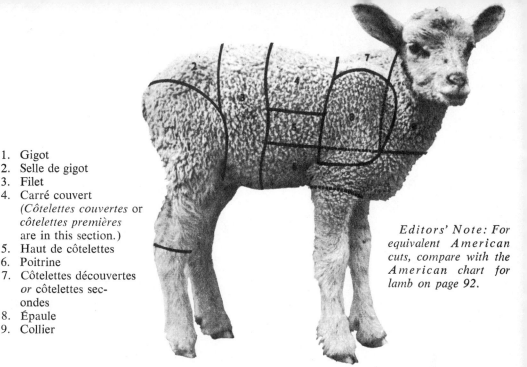

1. Gigot
2. Selle de gigot
3. Filet
4. Carré couvert
   (*Côtelettes couvertes* or
   côtelettes premières
   are in this section.)
5. Haut de côtelettes
6. Poitrine
7. Côtelettes découvertes
   or côtelettes sec-
   ondes
8. Épaule
9. Collier

Editors' Note: For equivalent American cuts, compare with the American chart for lamb on page 92.

LE BARON, the baron, includes both the loins and both hind legs. It is a highly prized cut, always roasted whole, and served only on special occasions.

LA SELLE is the sirloin or rump; FILET D'AGNEAU is the loin extending up to the first rib chop. These cuts are usually prepared with young spring vegetables.

L'ÉPAULE, the shoulder blade and arm, is an economical cut. It may be prepared in the same way as the leg, roasted whole. It may also be boned and rolled.

LE CARRÉ, the rib section or rack, goes from the end of the loin to the neck. *Côtes premières* or *couvertes* are in this section (rib chops); *côtes secondes* or *découvertes* are in the shoulder section of the rack (shoulder chops). The rack is usually roasted whole and served with young spring vegetables.

LE GIGOT ENTIER, or whole leg, consists of the main leg bones plus the hip bone or sirloin *(selle);* it does not include the loin.

LE GIGOT RACCOURCI, or French leg, has had the hip bone or sirloin removed.

Lamb and mutton are prepared with all varieties of beans—*lingots, chevriers,* wax, Soissons, dried white beans and green flageolets. Only the chops are suitably accompanied by potatoes. As far as other vegetables are concerned, care should be taken to choose only the youngest.

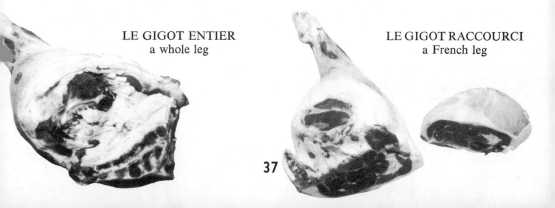

LE GIGOT ENTIER
a whole leg

LE GIGOT RACCOURCI
a French leg

For 1 egg: 1 tablespoon water, 1 tablespoon oil, ½ teaspoon salt and 1 grating or pinch of pepper.

APPAREIL

The prepared ingredients needed to make a particular dish. For instance: *crêpe* batter is the *appareil* for *crêpes*.

ARROSER

Basting a food (meat, fowl or fish) with its own juice or fat over the whole surface of the food at regular intervals during the process of cooking.

ASPIC

Aspic stocks (pp. 166-167) are extensively used for coating cold foods (fish, chicken, meats, vegetables, etc.) to enhance both the flavor of the food and the appearance of the dish. Before attempting to coat the food in question, the food itself should be very cold and the aspic should also be cold but still barely liquid (see NAPPER, p. 114). Several coatings with aspic stock are often necessary to cover the food (a whole chicken, for example) completely, and the food should be chilled in the refrigerator between coatings.

Many foods are also completely molded in aspic stock, in a wide variety of plain or decorative molds; the filled molds are chilled until the aspic is completely set, then unmolded on a cold serving dish.

Set the mold into a bowl containing cracked ice. Spoon a small amount of liquid aspic stock into the mold to coat the inside. Turn the mold in the ice to let the aspic stick to the sides.

When the aspic layer is set, place the food in the mold and fill the mold with more cold aspic stock.

ALLUMETTES

Hors-d'oeuvre or small entrées. Here, puff paste is cut into thin ½- to 1-inch strips, like matchsticks.

ANGLAISE

A mixture of egg, water, oil, salt and pepper, used for dipping foods that are then breaded before being sautéed or deep-fried. The purpose is to make the bread crumbs adhere well to the food during the frying process.

Water is added to the mixture to make it thinner and simply to increase the volume of the *anglaise*.

To make the *anglaise,* beat the ingredients together, as if making an omelet, until they are foamy and well blended. There should always be the same amount of water as of oil. The *anglaise* will keep well in the refrigerator for several days.

Chill the mold in the refrigerator until the aspic is completely set; then unmold.

ATTELET

A metal skewer topped with a decorative design. Nowadays, *attelets* are scarcely used other than for terrines.

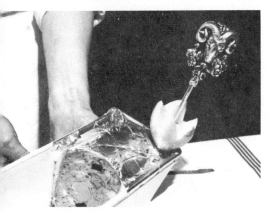

A meat terrine with its *attelet*.

BAIN-MARIE

A cooking method in which two pots are used; the bottom one holds hot water. Few things are actually cooked in a *bain-marie,* but it is frequently used to keep hot or to reheat certain delicate foods, such as scrambled eggs, *sauce béarnaise,* etc.

BARDE—BARDER

A thin sheet of fresh pork fat used to wrap around (to bard) meat, poultry or fish before cooking.

HOW TO BARD A ROAST

Wrap the roast lengthwise in a single sheet of fresh pork fat.

Arrange narrow strips of pork fat on the sides. Then tie the roast securely (see FICELER, p. 89).

BARQUETTE

A small, oval-shaped tart shell made from puff paste (p. 715) or *pâte brisée* (p. 713).

HOW TO MAKE BARQUETTES

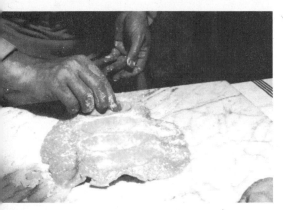

Several *barquette* molds are first covered with a sheet of dough which is allowed to settle into the molds. It may be lightly pressed into the molds with the fingers.

Run the rolling pin over the tops of the mold to cut off excess dough. Then lift the lined molds away from the rest of the dough.

BÂTONNET (see COUPER, p. 57).

BEIGNETS

Various fritters or foods, coated with a frying batter, which are cooked in deep fat.

BEURRE

In France, cooking butter is sold loose, by weight. The best sweet table butter (such as that served with hors-d'oeuvre, for instance) is usually prepackaged. Lightly salted butter is generally considered to be suitable for every kind of cooking.

HOW TO MAKE A BUTTER SAUCE
(see LIER, p. 109).

BEURRE NOISETTE

Butter which is heated until it turns golden brown, the color of hazelnuts *(noisettes)*.

BEURRE CLARIFIÉ
(See CLARIFIER, p. 53)

BEURRE EN POMMADE
Butter softened to spreading consistency.

To make *beurre en pommade*, all that is needed is to beat barely soft butter with a spoon to the desired consistency.

BEURRE MANIÉ

Butter that is kneaded with an equal quantity of flour (or sometimes with potato starch or cornstarch) and used to thicken sauces. In order to be quickly absorbed into a sauce, the mixture must be blended into a smooth paste.

Put softened butter into a bowl and beat the mashed anchovies gradually into the butter until the mixture is a smooth paste.

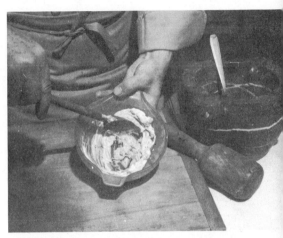

Editors' Note: For purposes of convenience, throughout this book 1 tablespoon beurre manié is used to mean 1 tablespoon each of butter and flour blended together.

A blender may also be used for making compound butters.

BEURRES COMPOSÉS

These are compound butters, butters that have been blended with various ingredients, such as mashed anchovies, mustard, etc. They are used in some sauces and as garnish for cold or hot dishes. See the section on Compound Butters beginning on page 792. For instance, Anchovy Butter: Mash anchovies in a mortar with a pestle.

BEURRER

Coating with butter is most conveniently done by melting the butter and spreading it on with a brush.

Brushing a tart pan with melted butter.

Brushing a paper-lined baking sheet with butter.

Dessert creams may be brushed with melted butter to prevent formation of a skin on the surface while the cream cools. Thickened sauces may be buttered in the same way.

BISCUIT

1. A *biscuit* dough takes its name from its final use; for instance, one speaks of a dough *(pâte)* for *biscuit de Savoie* (Savoy Spongecake).
2. Some *biscuit* pastries or cakes are baked twice; the second baking serves to dry out the pastry thoroughly.
3. Some ice creams are called *biscuits* because of their shape.

BISQUE

A type of soup made from shellfish. Originally the term referred to a way of making any kind of soup, but today it refers only to soups made from shellfish. A white *bisque*, without tomatoes, lends itself well to various subtle flavorings. The fish stock that forms the basis of a *bisque* must be very strong so that other seasonings will not overpower its flavor. The essentials of a *bisque* are its smoothness, and its delicacy of flavor which results from using live shellfish in the preparation.

BLANC

1. The white meat of fowl: wings and breasts.
2. Cooking *au blanc* means to cook in a *court bouillon,* that is, in a seasoned liquid.

CUIRE À BLANC

To bake a shell (for a tart, for instance) "blind," that is, without filling. The shell will be filled after baking.

Note: Do not confuse the *cuire au blanc* and the *cuire à blanc* cooking techniques.

BLANCHIR

To blanch a food means to plunge it into boiling water. Blanching is a brief preliminary process and should not fully cook the food. It has a variety of purposes: to cook partially foods that are then finished off by a different process; to remove excessively strong flavor from certain foods; and sometimes to firm foods that would otherwise be too soft.
HOW TO BLANCH DRIED VEGETABLES
Start blanching dried vegetables in *cold* water and drain them as soon as the water reaches the boiling point. It is not necessary to rinse them under running cold water.
HOW TO BLANCH FRESH VEGETABLES
Plunge the vegetables into boiling water for about 3 minutes, or sometimes longer, depending on the vegetable; drain them and rinse under running cold water.

HOW TO BLANCH SHALLOTS
Place the shallots in a cloth or a fine sieve. Drop them into cold water and remove them when the water starts boiling.

HOW TO BLANCH ORANGE OR LEMON ZEST
Put the zest (the rind without any of the white peel) into a saucepan of cold water and bring to the boiling point. Then drain immediately.

HOW TO BLANCH SPRIGS OF PARSLEY OR OTHER HERBS
Fill a saucepan three-quarters full of water and bring to the boiling point.

Put the herb sprigs into a strainer and sprinkle them generously with coarse (Kosher) salt. Plunge the strainer into boiling water and bring again to the boiling point.

Remove the strainer immediately and plunge it into cold water to firm the sprigs. Keep the sprigs in cold water until they are used.

Certain vegetables and fruits, such as tomatoes, almonds, peaches, etc., are also blanched briefly so that they may be more easily peeled.

BOEUF

Beef is the best and most wholesome of all meats. The word *biftek* has become synonymous for any piece of meat that can be cooked and eaten as is, whether it comes from the broiler, the roasting pan, or the skillet.

Editors' Note: M. Oliver's following suggestions for cooking beef are naturally based on French cuts, which are considerably different from American cuts. The English terms used for these French cuts are their nearest American equivalents.

CUTS FOR ROASTING
Aloyau (le filet et le faux filet), or the whole loin (tenderloin and loin strip); *entrecôte non désossée,* or rib roast.

CUTS FOR BROILING
The *filet* cut into slices *(tournedos* and *médaillons);* the small end of the *filet* cut into *filets mignons;* the *entrecôte* sliced into rib steaks; a *rumsteak,* that is, sirloin sliced into steaks (if the meat is too tough to be broiled or sautéed, it may be braised).

CUTS FOR BRAISING
Collier, the neck or upper vertebrae section of the shoulder; *culotte,* the rump; *tranche,* top round *(tende de tranche); rond,* sirloin tip or knuckle *(tranche grasse ou rond);* and *paleron,* shoulder-blade part.

CUTS FOR BOILING AND STEWING
Culotte, rump; *gîte à la noix,* bottom round; *queue,* tail; *plat de côtes,* short ribs; *pointe de culotte,* rump; *rumsteak,* sirloin tip; and *crosse,* shank.

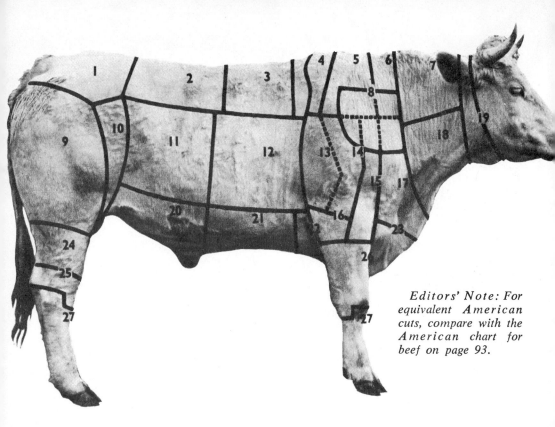

Editors' Note: For equivalent American cuts, compare with the American chart for beef on page 93.

1. Rumsteak
2. Contre-filet et filet
3. Milieu de train de côtes
4. Pointe de paleron
5. Milieu de paleron
6. Premier talon
7. Second talon
8. Pièce parée
9. Globe
10. Aiguillette baronne
11. Bavette
12. Plat de côtes couvert
13. Noix de macreuse

14. Macreuse à pot-au-feu
15. Jumeau de pot-au-feu
16. Charolaise
17. Grille
18. Veine grasse
19. Salière
20. Blanchet
21. Tendron
22. Poitrine
23. Gros bout
24. Milieu de gîte
26. Gîte
27. Crosse

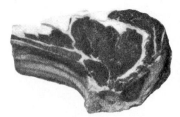

CÔTE DE BŒUF
for two, to grill over a wood fire.

Excellent *pot-au-feu* is made with *plat de côtes,* short ribs; *jarrets,* shanks; *bavette,* part of the flank opposite the loin; *poitrine,* brisket; and *collet,* neck.

The other cuts, *macreuse,* shoulder; *jumeau,* shoulder; *aiguillette,* a special cut of the sirloin; *culotte,* rump; and *gîte,* foreshank, may be stewed, provided the quality of the beef is superior.

ENTRECÔTE À GRILLER
cut from the ribs, for grilling.

Le FILET DE BŒUF is the underpart of the loin, the tenderloin, from tail end of vertebrae to rib section.

Aiguillette de RUMSTEAK a special cut of the sirloin, prepared for roasting.

FAUX FILET
the other part of the loin, the loin strip, ready to roast.

FILET DE BŒUF
the tenderloin, prepared for *tournedos.*

FILET DE BŒUF
trimmed for Chateaubriand.

TRAIN DE CÔTES DÉSOSSÉ
boned ribs, to cut into *entrecôtes minutes,* minute steaks.

TRAIN DE CÔTES NON DÉSOSSÉ, CÔTE DE BŒUF, or ribs not boned, to roast in the oven.

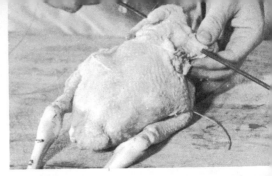

BOUCHÉE

Literally, a mouthful. These little puff-paste pastries are used for a number of recipes, especially for hors-d'oeuvre, patties, quenelles, etc. (see CROUSTADE, p. 60).

BOUILLON

1. The liquid part of a *pot-au-feu*.
2. A synonym for White Stock (see p. 165).

BOUQUET GARNI

A *bouquet garni* is made with various herbs, most frequently thyme, bay leaf and parsley. Fresh sprigs of herbs may be tied together with string, or the herbs may be tied in a cloth bag for easy removal.

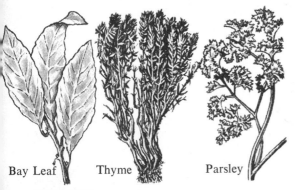

Bay Leaf   Thyme   Parsley

BRAISER

Le braisage, or braising, is cooking with very little liquid in a closed container in the oven.

BRIDER

To truss a fowl with string in order to preserve its shape during cooking. It is also called *trousser.*

Editors' Note: The chickens in the photographs have been prepared for trussing in the French manner (see How to Prepare a Chicken, p. 147, in PRÉPARATION DES VIANDES ET VOLAILLES), with the leg tendons cut to make it easier to tie the legs close to the breast of the bird. In the United States decades of breeding have produced a smaller, chunkier bird, with shorter legs; also, a great proportion of chickens come to market in the United States with more of the wing left on the bird and more of the leg cut off. You may find it difficult to truss an American chicken exactly as M. Oliver describes; it may be easier to tie the legs close to the lower part of the body.

HOW TO TRUSS A CHICKEN WITH ONE THREAD

Run a threaded trussing needle through one wing tip, the skin of the neck, the backbone, and the other wing tip. Move the thread down the side of the bird and run the needle through the thigh on one side.

And then through both legs.

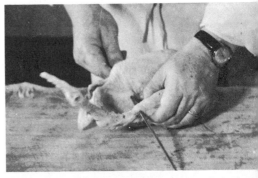

Run the needle through the thigh on the other side and pull up the thread.

Cross the two ends of the thread and tie around the body, tying the legs tightly to the breast.

The chicken is trussed.

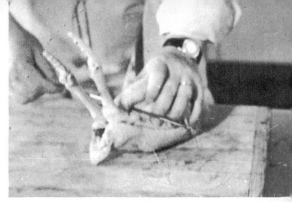

Pass this thread over the legs.

HOW TO TRUSS A CHICKEN
WITH TWO THREADS

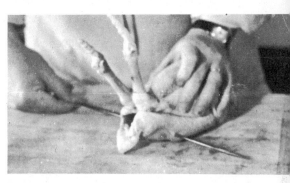

Run the thread again through the carcass under the legs. Fasten that thread.

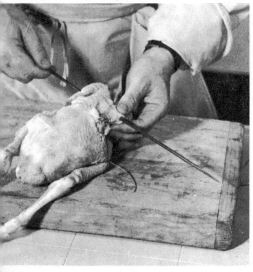

Run the thread through the wing tips and the backbone.

Pull the legs up and run another thread through the carcass where the second joint and drumstick meet.

Tie the legs to the breast with the first thread. The chicken is trussed.

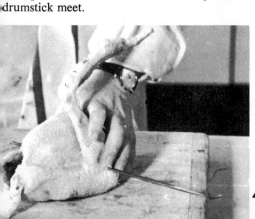

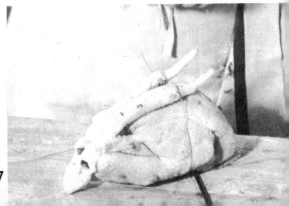

The skewered tongue is ready.

BROCHE

A mechanism used for roasting foods. Today, electric spits are used more and more frequently, with results that are as satisfying as those achieved with the old-fashioned spits turned by hand over a wood fire (see EM-BROCHER, p. 83).

BROCHETTE

A long skewer used for threading small foods or pieces of food (birds, kidneys, crayfish tails, etc.) that are to be broiled or deep-fried.

HOW TO PREPARE SKEWERED TONGUE

HOW TO PREPARE SKEWERED CRAYFISH TAILS

Run both ends of each of the crayfish tails onto the skewer.

Cut the tongue into even pieces of medium size and thread alternate pieces of tongue and bay leaf on the skewer.

Roll the skewered crayfish tails in a mixture of herbs, such as thyme, basil and marjoram.

BRUNOISE   (see COUPER, p. 57).

48

CAISSE

Small containers, also called *cassolettes, caissettes* and *cocottes,* used for preparing many hors-d'oeuvre.

CANAPÉ

Slices of bread cut into different shapes, depending on the use to which they are to be put. The appearance of canapés depends largely on the taste of the cook. The base is bread, which may be toasted or not, and softened butter. The bread must be firm. The butter may be mixed with other ingredients such as mustard, etc., as a compound butter. It may be tinted with food coloring, vegetable juices, etc. The butter may be simply spread on the bread, or used for decoration. In the latter case, a pastry bag is used to pipe it on in a decorative pattern.

HOW TO CUT AN UNSLICED LOAF OF BREAD FOR CANAPÉS

Cut off the crust on all four sides and both ends of the bread. Cut the bread lengthwise into very thin slices.

Depending on the use, cut the slices into squares,

ovals,

or rounds. There are special cutters to ease this job.

HOW TO MAKE A CANAPÉ

(for example, a sausage canapé)
Cut bread into small rounds, butter it, and top with sliced sausage, but remove the skin of the sausage first. Pipe a thin lattice of softened butter on the sausage and place half of a pitted olive in the center of each canapé.

49

CANNELER

To flute or score a vegetable or a fruit lightly with a special knife. Sometimes, this word is wrongly used instead of *chiqueter* (see CHIQUETER, p. 52).

HOW TO FLUTE A MUSHROOM

Turn the mushroom and, with the scoring knife, cut off small strips of the skin.

The mushroom is fluted.

How to flute a lemon.

CARAMEL

Melted sugar used for coloring soups, sauces, gravies, etc.

HOW TO MAKE CARAMEL

Put the sugar into a hot copper saucepan. Stir it, as it melts, with a wooden spatula so that it will color evenly.

After a few minutes of cooking over low heat (do not allow the sugar to burn), remove the caramel from the heat. Stir in a very small amount of water. The caramel must be of an amber-reddish color.

CASSOLETTE (see CAISSE, p. 49).

CASSONNADE

Raw or partially refined sugar. In pastry making, raw cane sugar is used because its aroma is reminiscent of that of rum.

CAVIAR

Salted or marinated sturgeons' roe.

Iranian caviar is by far the most highly prized because of its appearance. It is gray-green, and all the more precious as the grains are fairly large.

Russian caviar is of many qualities. The variety having closely packed dry black grains is excellent. There are also Russian and Turkish pressed caviars.

French caviar: M. Jean Barnagaud, of the Maison Prunier, is responsible for the use of caviar from the Garonne. This variety is more perishable than the others.

False caviars: When caviar is to be used only for decoration, one may use salmon roe (called pink caviar) or the roes of cod or pike. The specialty from Provence, called La Poutargue or Boutargue, is made from dried and pressed mullet, a local fish.

CHAMPIGNONS

HOW TO PREPARE MUSHROOMS

Wash them very carefully to remove any trace of earth. Drain and dry them carefully so as not to break them. If necessary, cut off the stems.

Editors' Note: This would apply far more to the many wild mushrooms, popular in France, than to our cultivated mushrooms that require only the briefest of rinses or a quick wiping with a damp towel.

HOW TO COOK MUSHROOMS

The recipes in this book dealing with mushrooms do not give exact cooking times because these depend on the variety of mushrooms used. Generally speaking, count on 8 to 10 minutes for wild mushrooms and somewhat less for cultivated ones. Water or other liquid in which mushrooms have been cooked is called mushroom stock and is frequently used to flavor soups and sauces (see also CANNELER, p. 50, COUPER, p. 57, and TOURNER, p. 158).

CHAPELURE

These are two kinds of bread crumbs:

Fresh white bread crumbs, made from firm white bread finely grated or blended in an electric blender. These are used for breading foods *à l'anglaise* before frying them.

Dry, golden bread crumbs, made by drying the crusts of French bread in the oven and then crushing them with a rolling pin or in a mortar. Dry bread crumbs should be sifted to obtain even-sized crumbs. They will keep for a long time, provided they are stored in an airtight container.

CHAPONS

Small crusts of bread rubbed with garlic, which may be added to salads, especially those made with dandelion or chicory (curly endive).

CHAUD-FROID

A dish that is cooked, but served cold. One speaks, for instance, of a *chaud-froid* of chicken (see Chaud-Froid Sauce, pp. 764, 776).

CHEMISER

To line the insides of a mold, a terrine, or another container.

HOW TO LINE A MOLD FOR PÂTÉ EN CROÛTE

This is a rather delicate operation because pâté molds often have no bottoms, and one has to be made from pastry dough.

Roll out a rather thick layer of dough on a floured board and dust it well with flour. Fold the dough in half and pull up the edges in order to form a kind of pouch.

51

The pouch is shaped.

Fit this pouch into the mold and pat it on so that it will cling tightly to the sides.

CHINOIS

A chinois is a funnel-shaped strainer of very fine mesh.

CHIQUETER

To score a pastry made from puff paste, such as a *vol-au-vent*, in order to facilitate its baking.

CISELER

1. To make small regular cuts with the point of a knife to facilitate even cooking, or to let seasonings penetrate the food.
2. For vegetables: see COUPER, p. 57.

How to *ciseler* a fish.

The mold is lined.

CITRONNER

To rub certain vegetables with a cut lemon in order to prevent their discoloring.

CHIFFONNADE (see COUPER, p. 57).

CLARIFIER

To clarify, that is, to make a food or liquid completely clear by removing impure elements. In general, liquids are clarified by filtration or by decanting.

HOW TO CLARIFY STOCK

For about 1 quart: Make sure that the stock is absolutely free of any grease. Scrape or mince as finely as possible about ¼ cup (2 ounces) of absolutely lean beef, enough of the green top of a leek to make ¼ cup, enough parsley sprigs to make 2 tablespoons, and 2 sprigs of fresh tarragon or chervil. Combine these ingredients and blend them with 2 unbeaten egg whites.

Heat gently just to the simmering point, and agitate the casserole gently so that the mixed ingredients will be in touch with all of the liquid. Keep at this simmering point, and no more than that, for about 20 minutes.

Beat everything together.
Trickle the lukewarm stock gently into this mixture.
Mix well.
Pour everything into a casserole.

Pour through a ladle with very fine holes, a fine sieve, or a strainer lined with a damp cloth.
Note: In the case of chicken stock, use minced chicken rather than beef. For fish stock, omit the meat and herbs and use only the leek and the egg whites.

In one glass, the cloudy unclarified stock; in the other, the stock after clarification.

53

It should be noted that the addition of minced meat depends on the flavor of the stock. Only by tasting can one determine whether adding minced meat is necessary and, if so, how much.

HOW TO CLARIFY ASPICS

Aspics are clarified like stocks, but with about half of the minced meat, since the liquid aspic should already be well reduced and of strong flavor.

HOW TO CLARIFY BUTTER

Melt the butter over very low heat and skim off the foam. Strain the clear yellow liquid into a bowl, taking care to leave all the milky residue in the bottom of the pan.

HOW TO CLARIFY SUGAR

While sugar is cooking, the impurities in it rise and stick to the sides of the saucepan. This scum may ruin the sugar, and it must be removed quickly with the fingers.

A bowl of ice water should be at hand to cool the fingers before and after the removal of the sugar scum, also to dissolve the scum. This operation is also called "washing" *(lavage)* the sugar.

Editors' Note: Instead of using your fingers, a brush dipped into cold water may be used to wash the sides of the saucepan.

HOW TO CLARIFY THE YOLKS OF EGGS

Break the eggshell into halves over a bowl and transfer the egg yolk from one half of the shell to the other, back and forth, until all the egg white has dropped into the bowl.

CLOUTER

To insert into a food such as a piece of meat or fish, or a vegetable, other small strips or pieces of foods (truffles, tongue, pickles, etc.). An onion stuck with cloves.

COLLER

To add dissolved gelatin to a food so that it will jell firmly after it is chilled.

COLORANTS

These are the most frequently used food colorings in France:

Caramel gives sauces and stocks a brown color.

Spinach juice is made from squeezing chopped spinach, straining it through a fine strainer, and diluting it with a little water colored green.

Bicarbonate of soda restores the natural color of fresh vegetables.

Cochineal dyes foods red.

A beaten egg, when baked or cooked, gives a golden color (see DORER, p. 82).

The coral, or eggs, of the lobster, crushed raw with the back of a spoon or a rubber spatula, provides an ideal and unsurpassed way to tint *béchamels* and white-wine sauces for fish.

HOW TO CRUSH LOBSTER CORAL

Mash the coral.

CONCASSER (see COUPER, p. 57).

CONSOMMÉ (See this section of Soups and Stocks, p. 167).

CONTISER

To insert a truffle slice cut in the shape of a cock's comb into the flesh of chicken or game, or to insert pieces of truffles into fillets.

Hold the living lobster with firm hands. Split open the underside of the tail. Remove the coral by scraping it off with a fork.

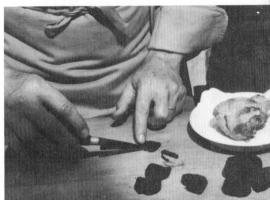

Cut the truffle into the shape of a cock's comb. Make an incision in the food that is to be treated, and push in the truffle, with the help of a knife.

COQUILLE

Certain kinds of foods may be served in a cleaned scallop shell. One also speaks of a *coquille* of crab served in a crab shell. *Coquille* shells may also be made of porcelain, metal or pastry.

HOW TO MAKE A COQUILLE FROM PASTRY DOUGH

To make a shell of pastry dough, 2 scallop shells of the same size are needed as molds.

Cut all around the shell.

Butter the inside of one of the shells and the outside of the other.

Place the buttered bottom of the other shell on top of the layer of dough.

Roll out puff paste to ¼-inch thickness. Line the shell that is buttered on the inside with this dough. Make it stick well.

Weight the concave side of the top shell with any convenient small weight. Bake in the oven. Unmold the shells after baking.

CORRIGER

To modify or change the flavor of a particular food by adding some other substance to it.

CORSER

To emphasize the flavor or to strengthen the taste or the aroma of a food or a sauce.

COUCHER

To pipe dough, or a filling, or a purée, onto a baking sheet, using a pastry bag fitted with a fluted or plain tube (see DÉCORER, p. 66).

COULIS

The juice that drains during cooking from meat, or from some vegetables such as tomatoes.

COUPER

To cut or slice vegetables or other foods into squares, lengths, rounds, etc., means, in culinary terms, to mince, chop, or slice them into *mirepoix, julienne, rondelles,* etc.

The pieces should all be cut into the same size for their aesthetic appearance and also for the practical purpose of allowing them to cook evenly in the same amount of time.

In order to cut vegetables properly, it is essential to anchor them firmly by cutting off a first slice (as in the case of potatoes) or by cutting them into halves (as in the case of onions). Put the cut side on the chopping board and hold it down firmly, gripping it with the finger tips so that the flat side of the knife slides against the knuckles, thus minimizing the risk of cutting oneself.

CONCASSER

To cut a food into rather large pieces.

Soles that have been *concassées.*

ÉMINCER

To cut into thin slices. The term does *not* correspond to the English term "to mince."

CUTTING AN ONION INTO THIN SLICES

Cut the onion into halves.

Put the onion half on the chopping board and cut it into thin slices.

The onion, thinly sliced or *émincé.*

CUTTING CARROTS INTO THIN SLICES

Hold the tail end of the carrots in the fingertips of the left hand.

Cut into thin slices. The knife must be very sharp.

CUTTING MUSHROOMS INTO THIN SLICES

After cleaning them, cut them into thin slices.

CUTTING ROUELLES

Rouelles are thin rounds, as for instance the *rouelles* of carrots (above).

CISELER

This term is used at times in the same sense as *émincer*.

CUTTING DARNES

The term *darnes* applies to thick slices of fish only.

CUTTING BÂTONNETS

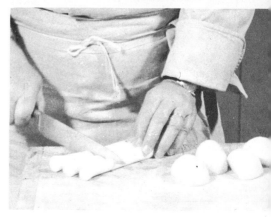

Leeks cut *en bâtonnets,* or sticks.

Pastry *bâtonnets,* or narrow strips.

CUTTING EN JULIENNE

This means cutting a food into fine strips.

CUTTING LEEKS EN JULIENNE

Cut the white part of leeks into 3-inch lengths and then split them lengthwise. Flatten out the halves and then cut them lengthwise into very fine strips.

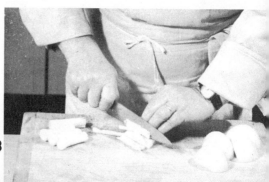

CUTTING POTATOES EN JULIENNE

Cut the potatoes into thin slices. Pile 6 or 7 of these slices on top of each other and cut them into very thin strips.

CUTTING EN CHIFFONNADE

The term means to cut delicately textured foods, such as lettuce leaves, into thin strips.

First wash and dry the leaves and remove the hard ribs. Pile about 10 leaves on top of each other, roll them up in the shape of a cigar, and cut them crosswise into very thin strips.

EFFILER

To cut into extremely thin julienne strips.

CUTTING EN MIREPOIX

To cube foods.

First cut the carrots, leeks, turnips or other vegetables into thick rounds and then into small cubes. If the vegetables are very large or thick, first cut them lengthwise into quarters.

CUTTING EN BRUNOISE

To cut into extremely small dice (to mince).

Cut the vegetables lengthwise, into 4 parts if necessary. Then mince them into tiny dice.

HACHER

To chop vegetables or herbs into small pieces, without making them necessarily of exactly equal size.

COURT-BOUILLON

A seasoned liquid used mainly to poach and cook fish (see POISSON, p. 131).

CRÈME

The word encompasses the natural cream coming from milk, as well as some cheeses, and thickened soups and desserts made with eggs, milk and a flavoring. In Desserts there are recipes (p. 672) for the dessert creams most frequently used for cream puffs, éclairs and other pastries.

CROQUETTE

A food prepared with a variety of *salpicons* (a *salpicon* is a mixture of ground or diced foods, bound together with a sauce), which is formed into any desired shape, dipped into an *anglaise,* breaded, and then fried in deep fat. Croquettes are served as hors-d'oeuvre or as a garnish, unless they are sweet or dessert croquettes.

CROUSTADE

A pastry shell made from puff paste or *pâte brisée,* or from crustless bread or the small rolls called *empereurs* in France.

HOW TO MAKE A PASTRY CROUSTADE

Lightly score the center of one of the rounds, using a plain round pastry cutter smaller than the fluted one.

Cut out 2 rounds of dough with a fluted pastry cutter.

Cut out the center of the second round of dough, using the same smaller round cutter. Brush the scored round with water.

Place the round with the hole on top of the scored one. The pieces that have been cut out can be baked along with the *croustades* and used as lids or toppings for them. Bake the *croustades* as indicated in the recipe used.

HOW TO MAKE A CROUSTADE FROM BREAD

Trim all the crusts from an unsliced loaf of firm white bread. Cut off a slice, ½ to 1 inch thick, depending on the use to which the *croustade* will be put.

Smooth the bottom.

HOW TO MAKE A CROUSTADE FROM ROLLS

Leaving an edge of about ¼ inch on all sides, cut into the bread to the depth of about ½ inch, depending on the thickness of the *croustade*. Cut out the inside; this is best done by using bias cuts.

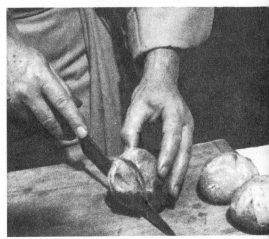

Cut the top off the roll.

Scoop out the inside.

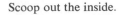

CROUTON

Small cubes of firm bread fried in butter and used in soups, scrambled eggs, and certain kinds of omelets.

Croutons used for garnish are made from firm white bread fried in butter and they may be small cubes or fairly large slices cut into any desired shape.

Croutons of aspic are pieces of firm aspic cut into different shapes with a pastry cutter.

CRUSTACÉS

LES CRABES

Among the crabs eaten in France, there are:

The *tourteau,* which has a very delicate flavor; this is caught on the Channel and Atlantic seacoasts. It has an oval shape and it may weigh as much as 4 pounds, or more.

The *araignée de mer,* which is eaten only at the place where it is caught. Cooking turns it a bright red color.

The common crab, or *enragé,* is smaller than the *tourteau;* this is the usual kind of crab sold live in the fish markets.

Portunes, also called *étrilles,* and *dormeurs,* are equally edible.

Crabs, even the *tourteau,* have very little edible meat, which makes crabmeat dishes very expensive.

HOW TO CUT UP A RAW CRAB
FOR PILAFF

Break off the pointed apron on the underside and pull off the top shell.

Discard the spongy part and the stomach under the eyes.

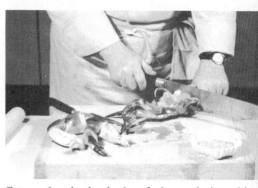

Cut or break the body of the crab into big pieces. Cut the claws into big pieces by heavy blows with the heel of a knife.

Break off the claws.

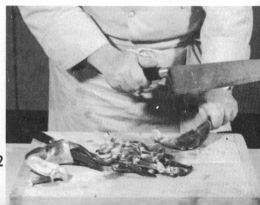

62

LES ÉCREVISSES

Écrevisses, or crayfish, are small freshwater shellfish. The intestinal tubes have to be removed before cooking or else the meat may taste somewhat bitter. Serve about 8 medium-sized crayfish to each person. Poaching time is about 12 minutes.

HOW TO CLEAN CRAYFISH

Hold the live crayfish firmly by the back and tail with the left hand.

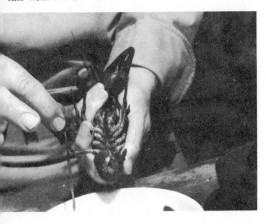

Remove the intestinal tube.

LES CREVETTES

There are three kinds of *crevettes,* or shrimp.

Gray shrimp are small, their flesh is rather soft, and their shell very thin. They cook quickly and become spotted with red when cooked.

Pink shrimp, somewhat larger than gray shrimp, have a clear shell which becomes pink in cooking. Since their shell is extremely thin, they may be eaten without shelling.

Bouquets are large pink shrimp, which may reach a length of 5 inches. Their pink color after cooking is very pronounced. Their flesh is much firmer than that of the other varieties.

HOW TO COOK SHRIMP

Prepare a very concentrated and well-salted *court bouillon* (see p. 131); it should be as salty as sea water. Count on about 2 ounces of salt for 2 quarts of water.

LES SCAMPIS

These are big shrimp from the Adriatic Sea, which have a pronounced flavor of iodine. They are either grilled or broiled in their shells *(scampi al ferri)* or fried in batter *(scampi fritti).* In France, the tails of *langoustines,* prepared like scampi, are sometimes called scampi.

LES LANGOUSTINES

These small spiny lobsters are small crustaceans (similar to the prawns of the United States), orange in color but for the ends of the legs and the claws, which are white. *Langoustines* never turn red during cooking, and they are cooked like *bouquets,* or large shrimp.

HOMARDS and LANGOUSTES

Lobsters are large crustaceans, which may reach a considerable size and have the general shape of *écrevisses.* The shell of *langoustes* (or rock lobsters) is rounder than that of *homards.* (*Langoustes* from Morocco, also called *langoustes royales,* are flatter than those fished on the French coasts.) *Homards* have 2 fairly large claws. *Langoustes* have none.

The taste of the flesh of female *homards* and *langoustes* is preferable to that of the males. Female lobsters may be recognized by the roe or coral that they carry, but there is also another way of distinguishing them from the males. All lobsters have a pair of short feelers on the underside, at the point where the tail meets the upper body. If these are short and atrophied, they belong to a male lobster. If they are of a good size, it is a female.

HOW TO DRAIN CRUSTACEANS

As soon as the lobster is cooked, cleave the lobster deeply between the eyes and, holding it up by the tail, let it drain.

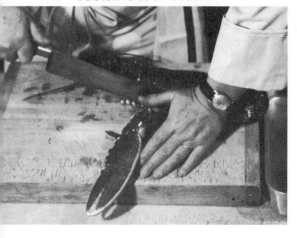

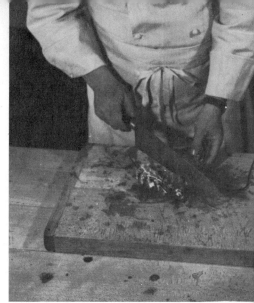

Using a heavy knife or a cleaver, remove the claws and the feelers or legs of a large lobster.

Cut the upper body of the lobster lengthwise into halves.

Cut the claws into two pieces.
Note how the heel of the knife should strike the claw.

Cut the tail into thick slices, following the ring design on the lobster.

Remove the coral and reserve it.

HOW TO PREPARE A LIVE LANGOUSTE

Plunge the tip of the knife into the back of the live *langouste*.

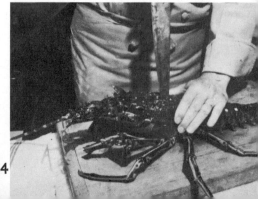

Split the *langouste*.

CUISSON

The term indicates the process of cooking a food, the cooking time, and also certain liquids in which various foods are cooked, as, for instance, the liquor *(cuisson)* of mushrooms.

DARNE

A thick slice of raw fish.

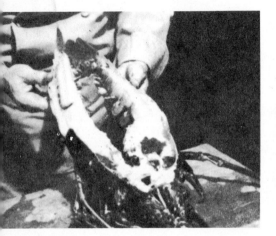

Open it up.

A *darne* of fresh cod.

DAUBE

The cooking of fresh meats, fowl or game in a well-seasoned stock that is usually made with wine.

DÉCANTER

To pour a liquid from one container into another, leaving the sediments of the liquid behind in the bottom of the first container. To make quite sure that they do stay behind, pour through a fine cloth.

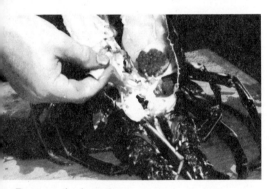

Remove the intestine.

Scoop out the coral and reserve it.

How to decant oyster liquid to rid it of sand.

DÉCORER

To decorate dishes and pastries, use a pastry bag or a paper decorating cone.

HOW TO FILL A PASTRY BAG

Hold it firmly and open it wide.

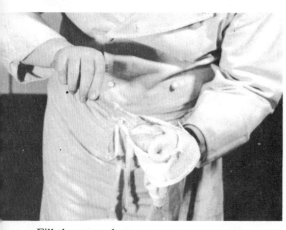

Fill the pastry bag.

Close it.

HOW TO MAKE A DECORATING CONE FROM PAPER

Roll a triangular piece of firm paper into a cone. Cut off the tip. In order to make a rose decoration, cut the tip of the cone crosswise into four.

HOW TO MAKE A BORDER OF DUCHESS POTATOES

Note the position of the hands and see how close the pastry bag is to the dish.

HOW TO DECORATE A GÉNOISE

Start making roses or rosettes by slightly twisting the pastry bag as you press out each mound of cream.

Pipe along the edge of the cake in a continuous flow, making roses at ½-inch intervals.

HOW TO MAKE A MARBELIZED DESIGN

Frost the cake and then pipe thin bands of fondant of a different color across it.

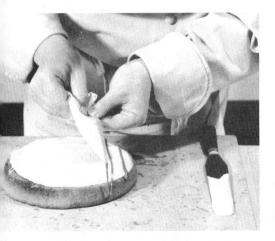

Lightly score each of these bands with the tip of a knife, first from left to right and then from right to left, alternately.

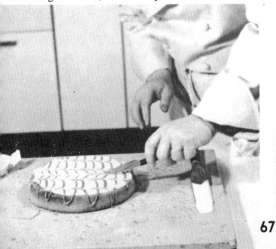

DÉCOUPER

CARVING RAW MEATS

Before being carved or cut into pieces, meats, birds and game must be cleaned, drawn and, if necessary, plucked. All of these steps will be found under the heading PRÉPARATION (p. 140).

HOW TO CUT A CHICKEN INTO PIECES

Using a sharp knife, cut into the joint where the thigh is attached to the body.

Sever the thigh, with the leg attached to it, from the body of the chicken.

Cut into the thigh joint on the other side in the same manner.

Remove the wings; note the position of the knife.

Cut off the second thigh.

Slice off the breasts on either side of the breast bone.

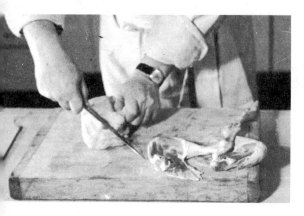

Insert the knife at the wing joint.

Remove the bones from the two thighs, but leave in the leg bones to serve as handles.

Finally, cut the chicken carcass into halves.

HOW TO CUT A HARE FOR STEW

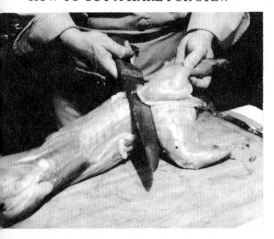

Cut off the shoulders and forelegs.

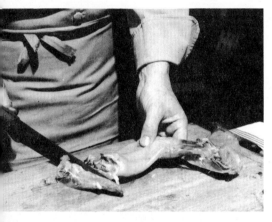

Cut each shoulder into halves on either side of the bone.

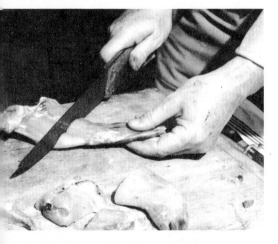

Cut each shoulder crosswise into 3 pieces.

Remove the liver.

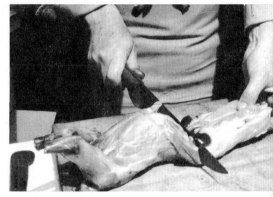

Cut off the saddle near the kidneys.

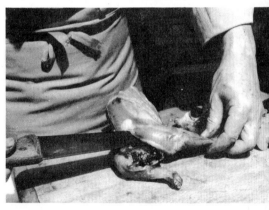

Take off the hind legs.

Cut them into 2 or 3 pieces.

69

Cut the body into pieces.

Then cut off the leg and thigh.

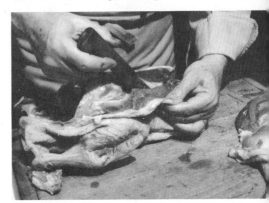

Cut the saddle into pieces.

Do the same with the wing and leg on the other side.

HOW TO CUT A GOOSE FOR CONFITS

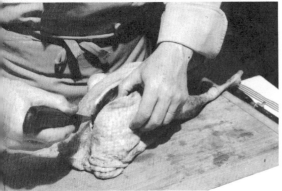

Cut along the breast bone and remove the skin.

Cut the wing off the body on one side.

Cut off the breast meat on both sides of the breastbone.

Note the naked carcass on the left.

HOW TO CUT A PIGEON OR SQUAB

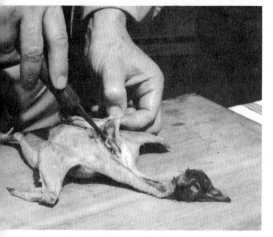

Cut along the backbone.

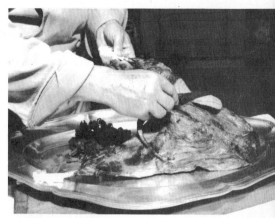

Start high up on one side of the leg and cut rather thick slices.

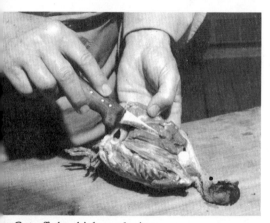

Cut off the thighs and wings.

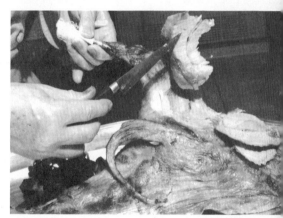

Continue carving down in even slices. When one side is finished, start on the other.

HOW TO CARVE A SADDLE OF LAMB

Make a deep perpendicular incision into the center of the roast.

Remove the meat along the breastbone and cut off the neck.

Cut off a slice horizontally from one side.

Or else, make vertical slices (this is the French method).

Continue in the same way.

HOW TO CARVE A LEG OF LAMB

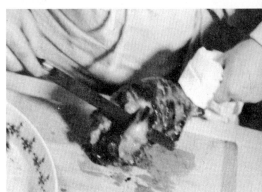

Turn the leg over and carve the other side.

Place the carved meat on a hot platter.

Discard any trussing strings.

Slice the thick side of the leg horizontally (this is the English method).

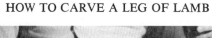

HOW TO CARVE A SHOULDER OF LAMB

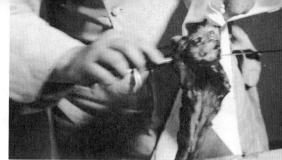

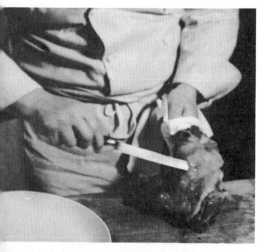

Cut off a first slice across the grain.

Slice the meat around the bone joint.

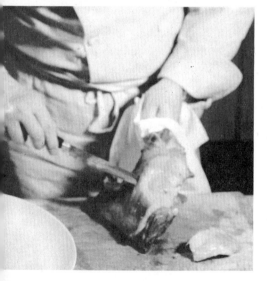

Slice off all the meat in the same manner.

The carved shoulder.

HOW TO CARVE A HARE

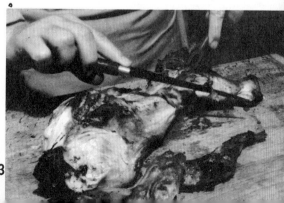

Remove the forelegs and the hind legs.

73

Cut the saddle into thick slices.

Cut the remaining meat into pieces.

Cut the meat into slices.

HOW TO CARVE A DUCK

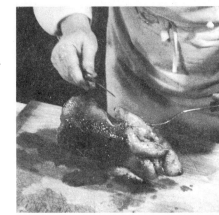

HOW TO CUT A SADDLE OF HARE

Cut off the leg and second joint from one side.

Cut along the backbone and cut off the meat on either side.

Then remove them from the other side.

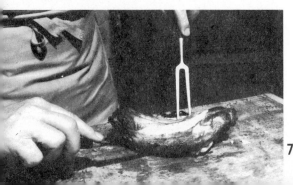

HOW TO CARVE A TURKEY

Slice the breast meat into long thin slices. Remove the wings by cutting them off at the shoulder joint. Remove the legs by inserting the carving fork into the thigh and plunging the knife into the joint.

HOW TO CARVE A PIGEON OR SQUAB

The bird is cut lengthwise into halves (see how to cut a raw pigeon, above).

HOW TO CARVE A ROAST CHICKEN

Proceed as in cutting a chicken into pieces (above), or simply cut it into quarters.

Note: For directions for carving or boning fish, see DÉSOSSER (p. 77). For lobster, *langoustes* and crabs, see CRUSTACÉS (p. 62).

Hold the duck firmly

and cut the breast meat lengthwise into long strips.

DÉGLACER

To deglaze the food particles that stick to the bottom of a pan during cooking by stirring them with liquid. These particles are called *glaces*.

How to deglaze.

DÉGORGER

To soak vegetables to lessen their bitter flavor or to allow them to release some of their juices.

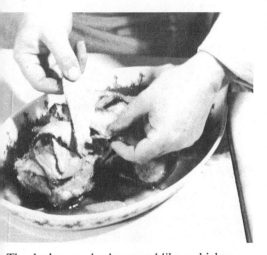

The duck may also be carved like a chicken.

HOW TO DÉGORGER A CUCUMBER

Peel the cucumber and cut it into large dice. Put these into a strainer and set the strainer over a bowl. Sprinkle the cucumbers with salt and let them rest until they *dégorge* their juices.

HOW TO DÉGORGER SNAILS

Sprinkle them with salt and vinegar.

DÉGRAISSER

This means to degrease, or to skim off the fat that covers a stock, a sauce, or the pan juices of foods.

HOW TO SKIM OFF THE FAT FROM STOCK

Pass absorbent paper over the top of the stock. The paper will absorb the grease, like a blotter, without altering the stock.

To discard the fat from a dish, it is usually enough to pour off the fat quickly before it has a chance to get cold and set.

DÉPOUILLER

1. To *dépouiller* a sauce means to rid it of its impurities while it is cooking. The tool used is an *écumoire,* a ladle with small holes, or a slotted spoon.
2. To *dépouiller* game, see PRÉPARATION DES VIANDES ET VOLAILLES (p 140).

How to *dépouiller* a sauce.

DÉS

These are small dice for *mirepoix* or *brunoise* (see COUPER, p. 57).

DÉSOSSER

Editors' Note: The French word for fish-bones is arête, *plural* arêtes.
Since the verb *désarêter* does not exist, we always speak of *désosser*, that is, to bone.

HOW TO BONE A WHITING

Use the kind of knife ordinarily used for filleting sole. Cut into the fish just below the head, down to the backbone.

Cut into the top or back of the fish, cutting from the head towards the tail, and loosen the backbone.
The backbone is loosened.

Cut under the fillet and detach it from the tail.

Cut in the opposite direction, and cut off the fillet at the head end.

One fillet is removed. Turn the fish over and repeat, as above, removing the second fillet. Slide the blade of the knife between the skin and the fillet.

77

Peel off the skin, working from the tail towards the head. The fillet is ready.

Using a knife with a very flexible blade, called a *couteau à filet de sole,* cut horizontally along the backbone.

HOW TO BONE A SOLE

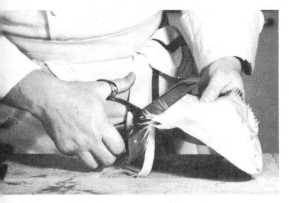

Cut off the tip of the tail with scissors.

Loosen the skin slightly with the point of a knife so that it is easy to hold the tail between the thumb and the first finger.

Loosen the fillet, working lengthwise, inserting the knife like a spatula between the backbone and the fillet.

Peel off the skin. Do the same on the other side of the fish.

Cut off the fillet completely.

On the left, the trimmings; in the middle, the bones; and on the right, the boned and trimmed fillets, which may be cooked flat, or folded over, or twisted or rolled, *en paupiettes*.

and tie it.

HOW TO BONE A COLINEAU

Editors' Note: A colineau *is a hake, a fish with flaky white flesh related to the cod, but regarded in Europe as belonging to a separate fish family. It is an important food fish.*

To roll up a fillet, roll it lengthwise along the nerve (the white streak along the middle). During cooking, the nerve tightens and keeps the rolled-up fillet, or *paupiette,* in shape.

Using a knife with a very flexible blade, cut into the fish lengthwise, along the top or back, in order to loosen the backbone.

To fold the fillet, score the nerve in the shape of a cross. Fold the fillet over this cross

The backbone is loosened.

Cut it off at both the head and tail ends.

Facilitate the removal of the bone by cutting with scissors.

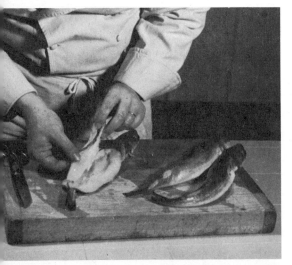

Pull out the bone.

The hake is boned. The same method may be used for similar fish, such as whiting.

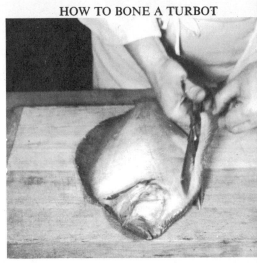

Cut off the barbels with large scissors and then cut off the gills with a knife having a very flexible blade (*couteau à filet de sole*).

Feel the position of the backbone under the skin and make an incision along it, lengthwise. Detach the backbone from the flesh, by holding the knife very flat against the backbone.

Gently pull the flesh back on both sides, exposing the backbone.

Cut off the backbone at both the head and tail ends.

Remove it entirely by cutting it off at the sides with large scissors.

The boned turbot is ready to be stuffed.

Some cooks do not bone the fish; they think, and rightly so, that it will be more flavorful if unboned. The inconvenience of this is that it is neither very pleasant nor easy to eat a fish full of bones, and that a stuffing cannot be spread out evenly in an unboned fish.

HOW TO BONE ANY OTHER FLAT FISH

Soles and other flat fish are boned like turbot. For a sole Colbert or a sole Hermitage only one side of the fish needs to be boned. The fish is then breaded in the case of sole Colbert, or left as is for sole Hermitage.

HOW TO BONE A POACHED SOLE

Remove the cooked fish with a spatula, and place it on an overturned oval dish.
Cut the top fillet into halves, cutting along the center of the backbone.

Cut off the barbels.

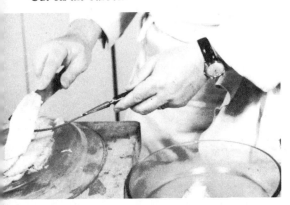

Detach half of the top fillet and put in on a plate; do the same for the other half.

Remove the backbone.
Cut the bottom fillet into halves and lay the halves over the top halves, to reassemble the fish.

HOW TO BONE MEAT, POULTRY, OR GAME

See PRÉPARATION DES VIANDES ET VO-LAILLES (p. 140).

DESSÉCHER

To *dessécher,* or dry out, means to keep foods over high heat in order to let their excess moisture evaporate.

How to dry out mashed potatoes.

The potatoes must be stirred constantly to prevent their sticking to the bottom of the saucepan and scorching.

DÉTREMPE   (see PÂTES, p. 123).

DORER

Dorer means to gild or to make a food golden, especially a pastry, by painting it with beaten egg yolk, using a pastry brush. The egg turns golden during baking.

Gilding with a pastry brush.

DRESSER

To place any food, meat, fowl, etc., in a neat arrangement on a plate, in a timbale, or on any serving piece. It is absolutely necessary to handle the food with utmost care, so that its appearance will not suffer.

A simple *dressage*.

A *dressage en accolade*.

DUXELLES

A mushroom mixture used to thicken or augment a stuffing or a sauce and to intensify its flavor. To make *duxelles*, mince ¼ medium-ized onion and 2 shallots, and cook them in 2 tablespoons oil and 4 tablespoons butter, combined and heated, until they are just soft and transparent. Finely chop ½ pound mushrooms and press them through a sieve to remove their moisture. Add the mushrooms to the butter and onion mixture, and let them cook until they almost form a paste. Stir constantly and cook slowly until there is no moisture left. Season to taste with salt and pepper. Mushroom stems and peeling may be used for *duxelles*.

Duxelles can be used immediately or stored in the refrigerator for later use.

ÉBARBER

To cut off the barbels and fins of fish with scissors.

ÉCAILLER

To scale fish, for which one may use a special scaling knife, an ordinary sharp knife, or even the edge of a scallop shell. The fish should be scraped vigorously, working from the tail towards the head.

ÉCHAUDER

This term means to scald, that is, to drop a food into boiling water. This culinary technique allows fruits and vegetables, tomatoes,

for instance, to be peeled without too many difficulties.

Eels are also scalded prior to removing the *limon,* the slimy substance that coats them and certain other fish.

ÉCORCHER

This means removing the skin of a fish (see DÉSOSSER, p. 77).

EFFILER (see COUPER, p. 57).

EMBROCHER

To thread meat, fowl or game on a skewer or spit.

HOW TO SKEWER A CHICKEN

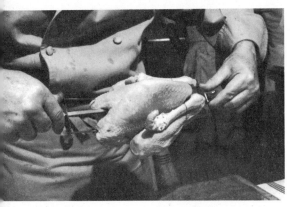

Introduce the spit or skewer into the cavity of the chicken and push it through the other end.

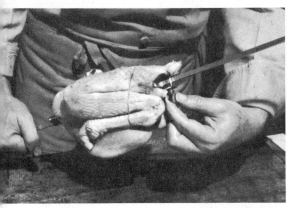

Push the fasteners on the spit into the flesh of the chicken and tighten them. The chicken is now ready.

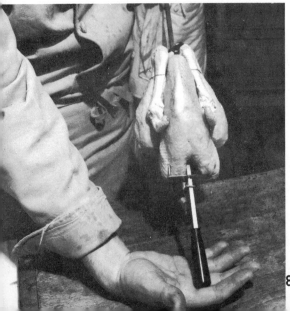

ÉMINCER (see COUPER, p. 57).

ÉMONDER

To remove or peel off the skin or filament which covers some fruits, vegetables and meats. Chestnuts may be peeled by dropping them into hot fat; peppers and pimientos by broiling them or baking them in a hot oven until the outer skin blisters and can be scraped and washed off; tomatoes and brains are skinned by dipping them into boiling water.

HOW TO SKIN BRAINS

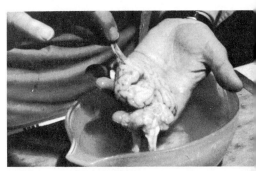

Plunge the brains briefly into boiling water, remove them from the water, and carefully peel off the filament which encloses them.

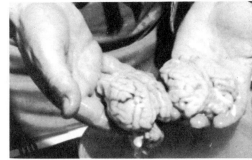

On the left, skinned brains, on the right, brains *au naturel*.

HOW TO SKIN TOMATOES

Place the tomatoes in a strainer and dip them briefly into boiling water.

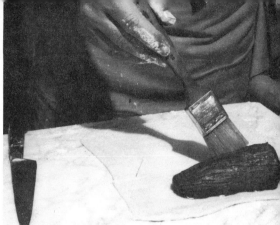

Plunge the tomatoes into cold water and peel off the skins.

Put the meat on one of the pieces and paint it with beaten egg yolk, using a pastry brush.

Note: This process is sometimes erroneously called *limoner.*

Cover the meat with the second piece of dough and press the edges tightly together. Paint the whole top with beaten egg yolk. Score the dough in a few places and then bake.

ENROBER

To coat one food with another, such as wrapping a food with a pastry crust which hardens during baking, or coating with an aspic which hardens in chilling.

HOW TO COAT A BEEF TENDERLOIN WITH A PASTRY CRUST

Roll out the pastry to the thickness of ⅛ inch. Cut the dough into 2 equal-sized lengths.

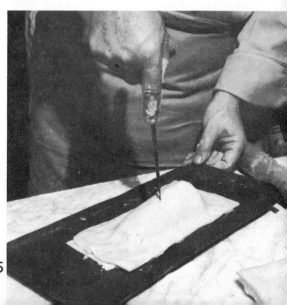

ÉPLUCHER À VIF

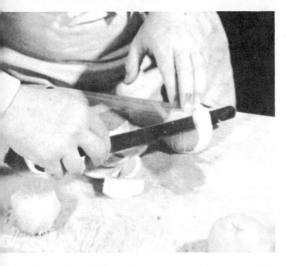

To peel a fruit, such as an orange, completely, removing both the outer rind and peel and the inner skin. Observe the orange on the left, which has been completely peeled.

To section an orange, carefully cut along both sides of the membranes that hold each section. A very sharp knife is needed for this.

ÉPONGER

To put vegetables which have been cooked in water on a cloth so that any surplus moisture may drain off completely.

ESCALOPER

To cut meats, fish, chicken and other fowl into thin slices.

HOW TO CUT MEATS INTO SCALLOPS

Cut the meat across the grain into slices that are ¼ inch thick. Note how the fingers are held away from the knife.

HOW TO CUT FISH INTO SCALLOPS

Cut into the cod below the backbone. Cut the slice lengthwise into halves.

An *escalope,* or scallop, of cod.

HOW TO CUT CHICKEN INTO SCALLOPS

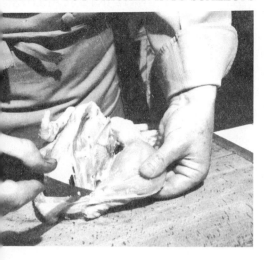

Cut off the breast. Note the way of holding the knife and the position of the fingers on the left hand.

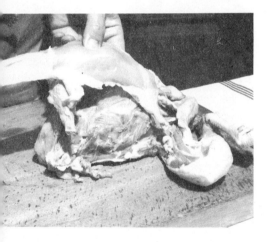

Skin the meat by firmly pulling off the skin. You now have a *filet*. Cut it horizontally into halves.

Flatten the scallop with the flat side of a cleaver.

ESCARGOTS

Most prized are the *escargots,* or snails, from Burgundy, and the kind called *petits-gris.*

PREPARATION

Let the snails starve, that is, do not feed them for 48 hours. Then feed them bran. Wash the snails. Purge them once only, and rapidly, by sprinkling them with salt and vinegar. Rinse them under running cold water. Blanch the snails by plunging them into boiling salted water and keeping them there until they can easily emerge from their shells. Throw away any snails that do not emerge. Remove the snails from their shells with the help of a two-tined fork.

Remove the snails' intestines: Hold a snail with the thumb and first finger of the left hand. Using a small sharp knife, score the snail. Remove the intestinal tube (which will be swollen) by pulling it out.

Note: It is necessary to starve snails because they may have previously fed on poisonous vegetable matter (see *Editors' Note,* p. 289).

HOW TO MAKE SNAIL BUTTER

Beurre d'escargots, that is snail butter (see p. 795), is prepared with softened butter mixed with garlic, parsley, salt and pepper. This butter cannot be made much in advance because the chemical composition of the garlic will deteriorate the butter. To slow up this deterioration, garlic may be crushed between 2 pieces of cloth before being mixed with the butter. Even then, it must not be kept for more than 2 or 3 days, even in the refrigerator.

ESSENCES

Highly concentrated liquids made from plants, meats, fish, etc., used to flavor certain dishes.

ÉTOFFER

This term, meaning to stuff, is sometimes used instead of *farcir* (below).

ÉTOUFFÉE, ÉTUVÉE

Cooking in the *étouffée* or *étuvée* manner means to cook with no liquid at all, or with very little, in a tightly covered pot.

EXPRIMER

To extract the juice of a fruit, such as a lemon, or of a meat, etc.

FARCIR

This is stuff a fowl, fish, vegetable, etc., with a mixture called a *farce,* or stuffing.

A *farce* must be inspired by the use to which it will be put. There are no very strict rules about it, but we must bear in mind that the stuffing must be lighter and smoother than the food in which it is stuffed. Furthermore, in most cases the stuffing must contain fat. When stuffings are too lean, pork or ham fat may be added to them. The addition of heavy cream also will make a stuffing richer, and softer.

It is essential to season a stuffing well: spices, *fines herbes* of every kind and spirits are all wonderfully suited to the purpose. The stuffing of a meat that is to be poached or boiled must always be more heavily spiced than might seem necessary, whereas the stuffing of a roast should be rather underseasoned.

An excellent stuffing, and one that can be used almost always, is made from one third minced or ground chicken, one third minced or ground veal and one third minced or ground pork. Fresh white bread crumbs soaked in milk and squeezed dry, and *foie gras* sprinkled with brandy, may also be used in a stuffing.

A *mousseline* (and *mousselines* are not necessarily *farces*) is made from ground fish mixed with cream. The whites of eggs are blended into this mixture to firm it.

FARINER

To dust a food lightly with flour before frying or roasting.

HOW TO FLOUR A GOUJONNETTE OF SOLE

Roll the *aiguillettes,* or strips of sole, in the flour. Tap the strips lightly with the finger tips so that the flour will stick to them.

FICELER

To tie with string certain cuts of meats and
fowl such as roasts, *paupiettes,* other meat
rolls, etc., so that they may be cooked without
coming apart or losing their shape.

HOW TO TIE A ROAST

Tie the barded roast (see **BARDE,** p. 39)
twice or three times lengthwise, depending on
its width. Then tie it crosswise at close intervals.

Note the position of the fingers to enable the
cook to hold the roast correctly while tying it.

FILET

A *filet* or fillet is the loin section of meats; the
word is also used sometimes for the breast
meat of domestic fowl or game birds. A *filet* is
also a piece of boned fish (see **DÉSOSSER,** p.
77).

FINES HERBES

The *fines herbes,* or aromatic herbs, most commonly used are (1) celery, (2) chervil, (3)
chives, (4) tarragon, (5) fennel or finocchio,
(6) parsley, (7) basil, (8) rosemary, (9)
thyme and (10) bay leaf.

FIXER AU REPÈRE

(see **LUTER,** p. 111).

FLAMBER

To sprinkle a food with alcohol (Cognac, Armagnac, etc.) and to set it aflame in order to enhance the flavor of the food.

Domestic fowl and game birds are also held over a flame in order to burn off the pinfeathers and to clean the outsides of the birds completely.

HOW TO FLAME A CHICKEN

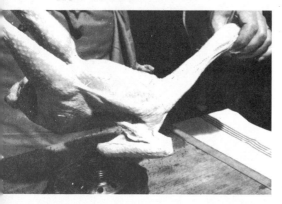

Move the wings quickly over the flame.

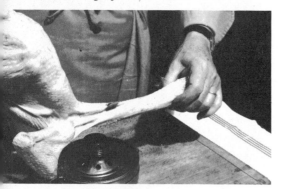

Then do the same for the legs and the neck.

FONCER

To line the bottom of a casserole, a mold, a terrine, or any other container, with a layer of dough, with sheets of fresh pork or ham fat, or with other foods.

PASTRY DOUGH FOR LINING

This dough, *pâte à foncer,* is made according to the method described in *Pâtes à Froid* (p. 125). Use the following proportion of ingredients: 4½ cups flour, 1⅛ cups butter, 2 teaspoons salt, ¾ cup water.

A finer dough is made by increasing the butter by ¼ cup and by adding 1 egg. In this case, the water should be reduced by half, to 6 tablespoons.

FONDANT

This is sugar cooked to the *petit boulé,* or soft-ball, stage, (234° to 240° F.) and worked with a spatula until it is very white and smooth (see SUCRE, p. 154).

HOW TO MAKE FONDANT

Editors' Note: There are many ways of making fondant, and all of them require a skilled hand and much practice. The following recipe testifies to M. Oliver's expertise and it is not recommended for beginners. A more detailed recipe for fondant, supplied by the editors, is on page 668.

First Method: 2 pounds sugar, 1 cup very pure water (preferably distilled), 1 teaspoon lemon juice.

Coat a marble slab very lightly with oil, using a cloth lightly dipped into oil. Cook the sugar to the soft-ball stage and pour it onto the marble. Cool the sugar slightly and then push it together and fold it over with a wooden spatula to make the smallest possible mass. Work the sugar by pushing it out and folding it over again, working towards the middle of the marble slab. The sugar, which at first was shiny and soft, grows white and opaque bit by bit until it suddenly becomes dull-looking and dry. Stop working the sugar, cover it with a damp cloth, and let it rest for about 2 minutes. Scrape the sugar free from the slab with a metal spatula, knead it into a ball, and put the ball on a plate. Cover it with a damp cloth until it will be used.

Second Method: 2 pounds sugar, 1 cup very pure water, ¼ cup light corn syrup.
Put the cooked sugar in a wide-mouthed metal container and work it, following the same principles as for the first method.

Note: In both these recipes, the fondant may be found hard to knead. It helps to add a few drops of water or flavoring essence to it and to reheat it gently in the top part of a double boiler over hot, not boiling, water. Fondant that is too warm loses its characteristic shininess; the temperature is right when the fondant can be tolerated by the fingertips or lips. See GLACER (p. 99).

FONDRE

The term *faire fondre* means to cook vegetables in a mixture of oil and butter over low heat until they are soft.

HOW TO COOK VEGETABLES IN BUTTER

Pour the oil, the butter and the vegetables into a heated casserole.

Stir the vegetables as they cook to prevent sticking.

FONDS

Fonds are the basic stocks used in sauces and soups. See the section on stocks beginning on page 164.

Cooking a fish stock over low heat.

Straining the cooked stock through a sieve with very fine holes (a *chinois*).

91

Editors' Note: Since French meat cuts vary considerably from American cuts, the following American chart for lamb may prove helpful for substitutions. Compare with French cuts on pages 36-37.

LAMB CHART

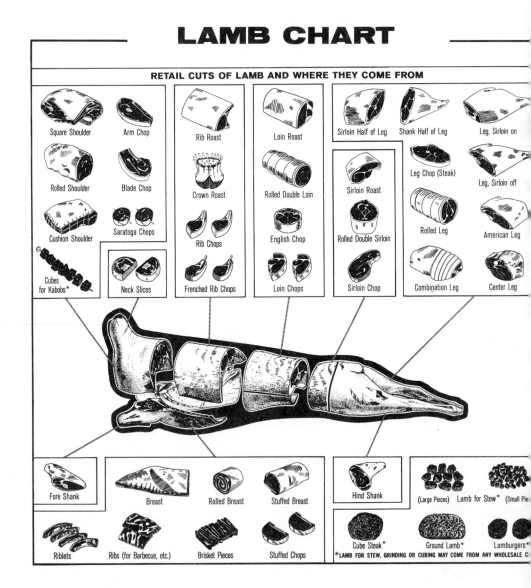

RETAIL CUTS OF LAMB AND WHERE THEY COME FROM

Square Shoulder | Arm Chop | Rib Roast | Loin Roast | Sirloin Half of Leg | Shank Half of Leg | Leg, Sirloin on

Rolled Shoulder | Blade Chop | Crown Roast | Rolled Double Loin | Sirloin Roast | Leg Chop (Steak) | Leg, Sirloin off

Cushion Shoulder | Saratoga Chops | Rib Chops | English Chop | Rolled Double Sirloin | Rolled Leg | American Leg

Cubes for Kabobs* | Neck Slices | Frenched Rib Chops | Loin Chops | Sirloin Chop | Combination Leg | Center Leg

Fore Shank | Breast | Rolled Breast | Stuffed Breast | Hind Shank | (Large Pieces) Lamb for Stew* (Small Pie

Riblets | Ribs (for Barbecue, etc.) | Brisket Pieces | Stuffed Chops | Cube Steak* | Ground Lamb* | Lamburgers*

*LAMB FOR STEW, GRINDING OR CUBING MAY COME FROM ANY WHOLESALE C

(Courtesy of the National Live Stock and Meat Board)

Editors' Note: Since French beef cuts vary considerably from American cuts, the following American chart for beef may prove helpful for substitutions. Compare with French cuts on pages 44-45.

BEEF CHART

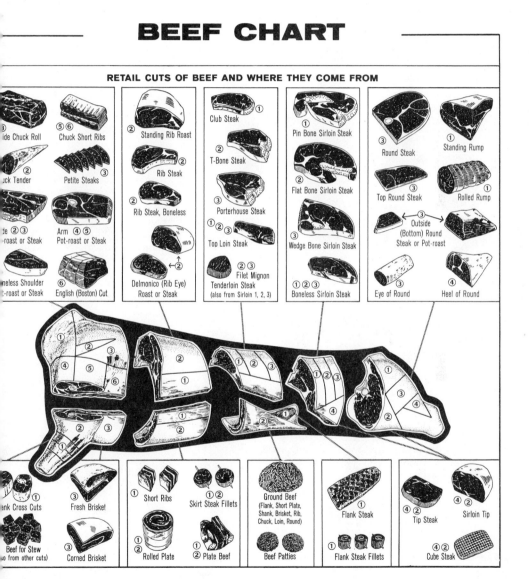

RETAIL CUTS OF BEEF AND WHERE THEY COME FROM

ide Chuck Roll

Chuck Short Ribs

uck Tender

Petite Steaks

de ②③
-roast or Steak

Arm ④⑤
Pot-roast or Steak

neless Shoulder
-roast or Steak

English (Boston) Cut

Standing Rib Roast

Rib Steak

Rib Steak, Boneless

Delmonico (Rib Eye)
Roast or Steak

Club Steak

T-Bone Steak

Porterhouse Steak

Top Loin Steak

Filet Mignon
Tenderloin Steak
(also from Sirloin 1, 2, 3)

Pin Bone Sirloin Steak

Flat Bone Sirloin Steak

Wedge Bone Sirloin Steak

Boneless Sirloin Steak

Round Steak

Standing Rump

Top Round Steak

Rolled Rump

Outside
(Bottom) Round
Steak or Pot-roast

Eye of Round

Heel of Round

ank Cross Cuts

Fresh Brisket

Beef for Stew
o from other cuts)

Corned Brisket

Short Ribs

Skirt Steak Fillets

Rolled Plate

Plate Beef

Ground Beef
(Flank, Short Plate,
Shank, Brisket, Rib,
Chuck, Loin, Round)

Beef Patties

Flank Steak

Flank Steak Fillets

Tip Steak

Sirloin Tip

Cube Steak

(Courtesy of the National Live Stock and Meat Board)

FONTAINE

A culinary term indicating the well *(fontaine)*, or hollow, that is made in the center of a quantity of flour piled on a baking board; eggs, liquid, sugar and other ingredients are put into this well, prior to mixing all the ingredients together.

FOUETTER

To beat a sauce, a *crème,* eggs, etc., with a beater or wire whisk. More and more foods are beaten with electric beaters of all kinds.

How to beat a sauce. Hold the whip so that it is easy to beat with it.

FRAISER

To firm a dough by pressing it with the palms of the hands, by kneading and slapping it, until it becomes smooth. Puff paste, however, is never treated in this manner.

FRAPPER

To cool a bottle of champagne, a *crème,* or other foods, very rapidly over crushed ice. This may also be done in the freezing compartment of a refrigerator.

Note: No salt is used with the ice when cooling in this fashion. However, salt is always used with ice when cooling in the *sangler* manner (see SANGLER, p. 153).

FRÉMIR

This term describes the state that water reaches just before boiling. For instance, poaching in water requires water that barely "shudders," the literal translation of the term *frémir.*

FRITURE

To fry in deep fat that is hot but not boiling. The most important factor in frying is the temperature to which a fat can be heated without smoking. Some fats, such as butter and goose fat, have a low smoking point. Others, especially the combination of equal parts of peanut and olive oil, are excellent for the purpose (and so are the hydrogenated shortenings used in the United States). A temperature of around 375° F. is suited for frying of most foods.

Three rules must be observed in frying: the fat must not smoke; it must be absolutely clear and clean; the temperature must be kept steady while the food is frying. One way to keep the temperature constant is to take care not to fry too large a quantity of food at one time, for this lowers the temperature too much.

HOW TO DEEP-FRY A GOUJONNETTE

Cut the fish into strips *(goujonnettes)* and then flour (see FARINER, p. 88).
Put the strips into a frying basket and plunge them into the hot fat. Cook until they are golden brown.

FRUITS DE MER

Fruits de mer, literally "fruits of the sea," include shellfish, mollusks, sea urchins, etc.

LES HUÎTRES

Oysters may grow wild, but more and more they are commercially bred in oyster beds. The oysters most prized in France are the green oysters of Marennes, the oysters of Belon, Cancale, Courseulles, Arcachon and Rochefort; Portuguese oysters are like these of Marennes. The freshness of oysters can be told from the way they resist being opened (see below). Oysters are considered wholesome when their flesh is shiny and their liquid clear. They are usually eaten raw, as a first course.

LES MOULES

Mussels, like oysters, may grow wild on natural rocky beds or they may be commercially bred on wooden stacks. There are several kinds of mussels: *moules communes,* or common mussels, which are smaller than the mussels from Provence; the *caïeu d'Isigny* is a large mussel, which can reach a length of 4 inches. Mussels should never be gathered in harbors, or from the hulls of ships, or in muddy waters, since they will not be wholesome after breeding in those places. Prior to cooking, mussels must be thoroughly scrubbed in many changes of water. Except sometimes in Provence, mussels are nearly always eaten cooked. They are ready to eat when they have opened after cooking, but throw away any that remain closed.

OTHER SEAFOOD

Many other shellfish, mollusks and bivalves are found in French waters, but not all of them are found in American waters. Found both in France and the United States are *coquilles Saint-Jacques* or scallops, *palourdes* or clams, *coques* or *boucardes,* that is, cockles, *bigorneaux* or winkles, *couteaux* or razor shells, and *bernicles* or limpets. With no accurate equivalents in American waters are *praires, lavignons, fléons, pétoncles, amandes de mer, vernis, ormiers* and others, which are eaten raw or cooked and are most frequently combined on a seafood platter. In order to free them of sand, they must be soaked in heavily salted water for 1 hour. They will open and discharge the sand.

MOLLUSKS

These include *la seiche* or cuttlefish, *poulpe* or octopus, and *calamar* or squid. Their regional names are *encornet, tantonnet* or *suppion.* In cleaning some of these mollusks, the ink sac which contains a dark fluid must be carefully removed.

HOW TO OPEN OYSTERS

Wear a thick leather glove on the left hand to hold the well-scrubbed oysters, or wrap a folded kitchen cloth around the oyster. Hold the oyster flat side up.

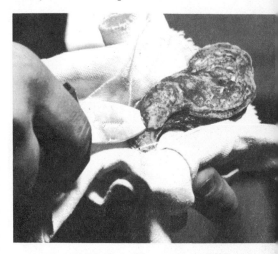

Use a heavy knife or a special oyster knife.

Insert the knife in the hinge of the shell.

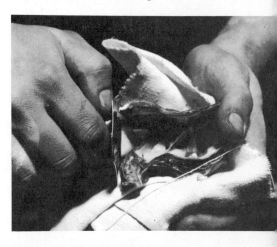

Twist the knife to lift the upper shell sufficiently to insert the knife further into the oyster shell, and cut through the hinge muscle. Slide the knife between the shell halves, pushing them apart.

Force open the upper shell.

HOW TO OPEN AND CLEAN SCALLOPS

Editors' Note: In France, and in most other countries, scallops come to market still in their shells, so it is important to know how to open and clean them. In the United States, however, almost all scallops are opened and cleaned on board the fishing boats which gather them; the only part of the creature which is retained is the white muscle which we find in the fish store. The coral, which M. Oliver speaks of here and in the recipes, is about one third of the mollusk and looks like an orange tongue; it is actually the roe of the scallop. Unfortunately this too is discarded by the fishermen who supply American markets. If you are fortunate enough to have any unopened scallops, you will discover that the coral has a taste similar to that of the white muscle, but is more delicate in texture; cook it along with the white muscle, for it will add to the appearance of the dish.

Insert a sharp knife between the valves.

Trim and clean the oyster, removing all little bits of broken shell. Just before serving, strain the oyster liquid through a kitchen cloth and pour the strained liquid back onto the oyster. This removes sand and any remaining bits of shell (see DÉCANTER, p. 65).

Sever the edible muscle where it joins one valve. Remove the muscle from the shell. Wash the muscle in cold water and trim it.

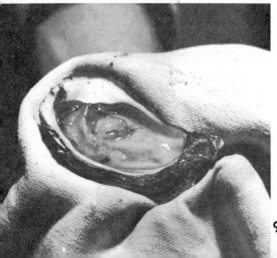

The edible muscle and the coral are ready for use.

HOW TO CLEAN SQUID

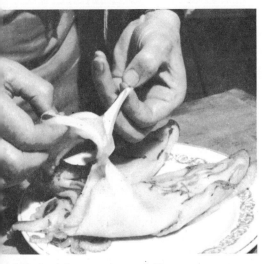

Lift the ink sac very carefully.

Cut it off.

Remove the inner shell, which is transparent.

Cut off the tentacles as part of cleaning the squid.

HOW TO OPEN AND CLEAN OURSINS OR SEA URCHINS

Editors' Note: Sea urchins, members of the marine species Echinus, *are shaped somewhat like a tangerine, with flattened tops and bottoms. The common variety found in France has a thin shell, all in one piece, which is covered with sharp spines. Sea urchins are eaten by themselves either raw, or lightly boiled like eggs, or used as an ingredient in other dishes. Their strong taste of the sea is highly prized throughout the Mediterranean.*

Wear leather gloves when handling the sea urchins, or protect your hands against their spines with folded kitchen towels. Wash the sea urchins under running cold water. Insert one blade of a pair of scissors or poultry shears on the concave side, where the sea urchin's mouth is located, and cut all around to remove the top. Tap the sea urchin twice and throw out the liquid, emptying the shell of everything but the coral, which will remain in the shell. Spoon out the coral as when eating a boiled egg, or dunk little pieces of bread into it. Or use the coral in recipes. The sea urchin may also be opened by holding it on its side and cutting off the side where the mouth is located with one cut of a sharp knife.

FUMET

A strong liquid stock used to thicken and flavor fish soups, sauces, etc. See the section on stocks, beginning on page 164.

97

GARDE-MANGER

Some foods lose their flavor when chilled and they are better kept in a cool larder, a *garde-manger*. Among them are cheeses and fruits, cold meat dishes that would dry out when too cold, and some delicate vegetables. Even fish and shellfish may be stored this way, provided they lie on a bed of crushed ice.

GARNITURES

Decorative garnishes or vegetables served with a dish, either on the same platter or on the side.

GASTRIQUE

A liquid which has been reduced to form a glaze is called a *gastrique*. Most frequently this is done by putting the liquid and its flavoring into a saucepan and cooking it over high heat until all the liquid has evaporated.

The most common *gastriques* have a base of vinegar and pepper, vinegar and *fines herbes,* or caramel and vinegar; there are all sorts of similar combinations. *Gastriques* are indispensable for certain sauces, for instance Sauce Béarnaise (p. 779).

GÉLATINE

Gelatin, in France, is sold either in sheets or powdered. Sheet gelatin must be soaked in cold water for 10 minutes, until it is soft.

Drain the sheets and stir them, over gentle heat, into the liquid in which they'll be used until the gelatin has completely dissolved. Soften powdered gelatin for 3 to 4 minutes in the cold liquid in which it will be used, or in a little water (about ¼ cup for each envelope of American gelatin). Dissolve the softened gelatin over gentle heat, or proceed according to

package directions. One sheet of French gelatin equals 2 grams; 4 sheets or 8 grams correspond to 1 envelope of American gelatin, which weighs 8 grams or measures 1 scant tablespoon.

GELÉE

A *gelée,* or aspic, may be made naturally by chilling a liquid in which the gelatinous parts of meats and fish have liquified during cooking. Calf's feet and chicken feet are ideally suited for making jellies and aspics.

Commercial gelatin is made from bones and is much used since it considerably simplifies the making of these preparations. All jellies and aspics must be made very carefully and served as soon as possible after they have set.

When jelly is made with ingredients that contain blood, it will be very clear. Otherwise, it must be clarified (see CLARIFIER, p. 53). Jellies and aspics, with the exception of fish jellies, are generally flavored with fortified wines and other spirits such as port, sherry, Madeira, Armagnac and brandy. See ASPIC (p. 38) for the method of lining molds with aspic.

GIBIER

This word, translated into English as game, includes all edible wild animals that are hunted by man. A distinction is made between furred game *(le gibier à poil)* and feathered game *(le gibier à plumes).*

Editors' Note: The list below refers to the game found and cooked in France. In several instances this is different from American game or is game not found or not hunted in the United States.

FURRED GAME

Hares: the most prized are those of the flatlands. They live in the underbrush and feed upon thyme and other herbs which flavor their flesh. An excellent wild hare (not to be confused with a commercially raised rabbit) is aged approximately 8 months, weighs about 7 pounds, and sports a round and firm saddle. This kind of hare may be cooked in any desired way: it may be roasted, broiled on a spit, braised with wine, jugged and stewed, or prepared *à la royale.* One may prepare rabbits in the same way, but their flesh is often tasteless.

Big game, such as chamois, ibex, izard (a species of chamois), deer, doe, stag (the red deer) and hind (the female red deer), are good only when young. As soon as they begin to age, their meat is tough. In this case, they may be marinated. Venison must be eaten when it is 1 to 3 years old. Young wild boar are cooked like pork or venison.

FEATHERED GAME

There are two kinds: game birds which live either in the uplands or in woods or on the plains, and shorebirds and waterfowl.

The game birds include upland birds such as *le coq de bruyère* and the *grand tétras* (varieties of grouse); they must not be hung too long; these birds weigh from 2 to 6 pounds. *Gélinotte* and the *petit coq de bruyère* (other grouse varieties) and pheasants are birds that live in the woods; the indication of their youthfulness (up to 15 months) is the softness and pliability of the breastbone.

The common partridge *(perdrix grise)* is smaller than the red-legged partridge *(perdrix rouge* or *bartavelle)*. As these birds grow older, their feet turn black and wrinkled. A *perdreau* is a young partridge. The *perdrix blanche*, or ptarmigan, is an upland bird.

Thrush, quail (and the quail known as *râle des genêts* or *roi de caille),* lark (also called *mauviette),* ortolans, the *bec-figue* and the *béguinette,* a warbler, are birds of the plains.

Shorebirds include the woodcock, which lives in swamps; it may be hung until it is somewhat high. Snipe are smaller birds and often cooked like woodcock. Wild ducks, coots and teal have very lean flesh, and they have the advantage of being considered by the Catholic Church as suitable fare for meatless days. Wild goose is cooked in the same manner as domestic goose. Lapwing and plover are prepared like woodcock.

All waterfowl and shorebirds may taste of fish. Since this fishiness is found in the fat of these birds, it is necessary to remove as much fat as possible before cooking.

To be of good quality, a woodcock, lapwing, teal, etc., should be plump, but not too fat, with meat that is on the light side.

MARINADE FOR GAME

Generally speaking, game that is old, or very big, such as wild boar and stag, must be marinated before cooking. A marinade is a seasoned liquid.

Put the game that is to be marinated into a large bowl (do not use aluminum) together with onion and carrot rounds, peppercorns, thyme, bay leaf, whole cloves, minced shallots, red wine, brandy and coarse (Kosher) salt. Turn the meat frequently so that all sides may soak in the marinade. The marinating game must be kept in a cool place or, covered, in the refrigerator. Marinating time depends on the kind and age of the game and the recipe you plan to use.

GLACER

One may *glacer,* or freeze, for instance, dessert creams. One may also *glacer,* or glaze, meats, fish and other foods in a hot broiler oven, or by using a salamander.

The word *glace* can mean a frozen cream, or the juices of meats which have been reduced.

GLAÇAGE IN THE OVEN

Glazing a dish of fillets of sole *à la crème,* for instance, in a hot broiler oven, or with a salamander, takes but a few seconds; the glazing results from the combined action of the heat and the steam. In the case of ovens used for home cooking (as compared to restaurant ranges) it may be advisable to place a pan full of water on the bottom of the oven. Put the food to be glazed into the oven when the steam begins to rise.

Note: This technique is also called *lustrer à chaud,* to shine up the surface of a food with heat.

GLAÇAGE OF SAUCES

Glazing sauces that do not contain flour is difficult. If the sauce includes cream in its ingredients, one may beat egg yolks into the cream before adding it to the dish (2 egg yolks for 4 people).

There are also several other ways. One may add another, thickened sauce *(béchamel, velouté)* to the sauce when it has been reduced. Generally speaking, and depending on the kind and quantity of the sauce, for 4 persons, 2 tablespoons of *béchamel* or *velouté* will do the trick. Then the butter is added and the sauce is finished. Hollandaise, about 1 tablespoon for each person, may also be added to a sauce at the last moment to glaze it.

GLAÇAGE OF VEGETABLES

First cut the vegetables into even sizes, then put the pieces into a saucepan with cold water and bring just to the boiling point; drain. Then put the vegetables into a small saucepan, barely cover them with water, and add 1 teaspoon of sugar, a little salt and a little butter. Cook the vegetables without a cover until the pan liquid has evaporated completely.

Note: Tiny white onions and leeks cut into strips are cooked in the same manner, but in a 350° F. oven, in order that they may get an even color.

GLAÇAGE OF A CAKE WITH FONDANT

Spread it with a metal spatula.

Take enough fondant (pp. 90, 668), stir in a few drops of water or flavoring essence, and warm it (do not heat) slightly to lukewarm, stirring constantly. The fondant must not get too hot or it will become opaque and brittle.

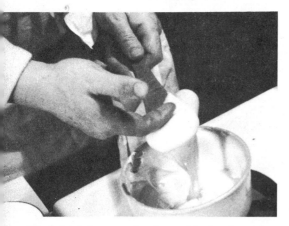

Lift up the cake immediately after icing it, or excess fondant will stick to the pastry board.

DECORATING THE CAKE

Test the lukewarm fondant with the fingertips. Note the position of the fingertips.

Pour the fondant over the cake.

Once the cake has been iced, warm a small quantity of fondant to lukewarm. Stir in a few drops of water and any desired food coloring. Fill a pastry tube with the fondant and pipe the decorations onto the cake.

DÉCOR MARBRÉ (see DÉCORER, p. 66).

GRATIN

The crust formed on top of a food by the heat of an oven or a broiler. By analogy, *gratin* is the name given to any dish so finished, such as a *gratin* of cauliflower, potatoes, etc.

GRENOUILLES

Frogs, or *grenouilles*, are now sold ready to cook, but it might be pointed out that only their legs are edible, provided the leg meat is white and that the legs have been skinned. Living frogs must first be killed by dashing their heads against a stone and cutting off the body with scissors. Then the legs are skinned, washed, dried, and cooked.

GRILLADE

Cooking on a grill, over embers, or over a lively fire, or over charcoal.

HACHER (see COUPER, p. 57).

INCISER (see CISELER, p. 52).

JARDINIÈRE DE LÉGUMES

This is a vegetable medley, composed of green peas, green or other fresh beans, turnips and carrots, all cooked in salted water. The green beans are cut into 1-inch pieces, and the turnips and carrots into small dice.

JULIENNE

The name given to a mixture of vegetables that have been cut into fine strips (see COUPER, p. 57).

LAPIN

(see VOLAILLE, p. 160).
Editors' Note: M. Oliver places the domestic rabbit in the same category as barnyard fowl, therefore recipes for rabbit will be found in the poultry chapter and general information on rabbits on page 160.

LARDER

To lard, that is, to insert strips of fat or other foods into a piece of meat, chicken or any other food, with the help of a larding needle.

HOW TO LARD A PIECE OF MEAT

Cut the fat into long thin strips.

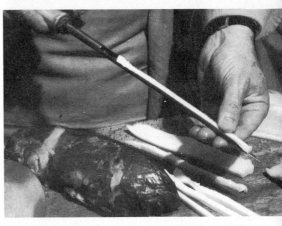

Place the strips of fat into the hollow of the larding needle.

Insert the larding needle into the meat.

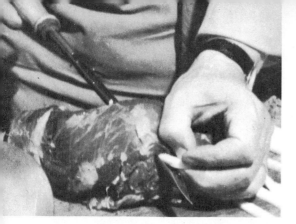

Grip the end of the strip of fat with the fingers and pull the larding needle back out of the meat.

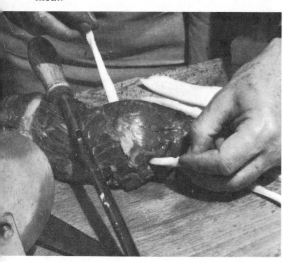

The meat is larded.

LÉGUMES

Vegetables, or *légumes,* include a number of edible plants.

L'AIL

In the spring, the shoots of fresh garlic may be cut into snippets and used in a green salad or in a soup. In winter, the bulbs, garlic cloves, must be firmly covered by their skin, which is thin and may be white or pink.

LES ARTICHAUTS

In France, the most appreciated artichokes are the big green artichokes of Laon, the big *camus* and the smaller Perpignan. *Carciofini* are small Italian artichokes. Good-quality artichokes are never spotted gray or black, and their leaves are of an even green. They are eaten from May to October.

HOW TO PREPARE ARTICHOKE BOTTOMS

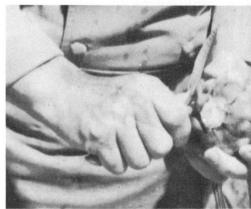

Do not cut off the stalk, but break it off.

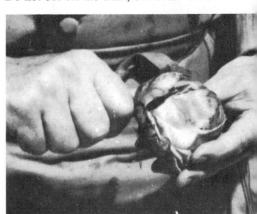

Cut off the leaves around the base.

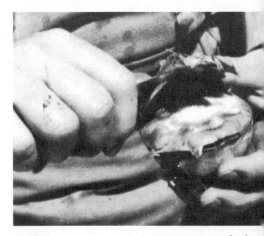

Cut off the bottom part which was attached to the stalk.

102

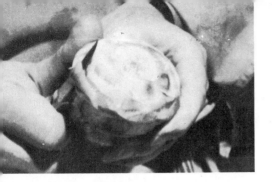

Finish trimming the new bottom of the artichoke by cutting around it evenly, cutting off any leaves that are sticking out.

LES ASPERGES

Asparagus is a delicate spring vegetable. Among the best-known French asparagus varieties are those of Sauternes and Argenteuil. There is also a kind of white asparagus coming from Germany, and a small green variety known as *pointes d'asperges,* or asparagus tips. Asparagus is a very fragile vegetable, which does not travel well. Truly fresh asparagus may be recognized by the purplish color of the heads, which must be tightly closed and snap off easily.

HOW TO PREPARE AND COOK ASPARAGUS

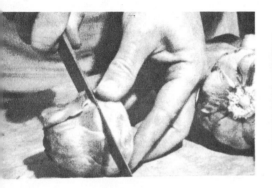

Rub the cut bottom with a cut lemon half in order to prevent any discoloration. Slice off all of the top leaves just above the base.

Peel off the thin outer skin of the asparagus (do not scrape it); use a sharp knife or vegetable peeler, and work from the top to the base.

Scoop out the chokes, the fuzzy central part, with a small melon scoop. Rub the cut surface once more with the lemon.

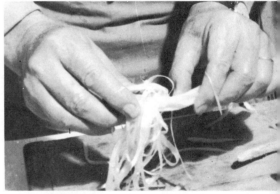

Break off the base of the stem with the fingers, at the point where it becomes woody.

Bring water to the boiling point in a big saucepan. Plunge the asparagus into the boiling water; the heat must be high so that the water will resume boiling as soon as possible. Add salt to the water after putting in the asparagus.

LES AUBERGINES

Eggplant is eaten in the spring and the summer, when the vegetables are smooth and shiny; the flesh should be firm. Eggplant is never cooked in water. For some recipes, it is not even necessary to peel it.

Cut off both ends.

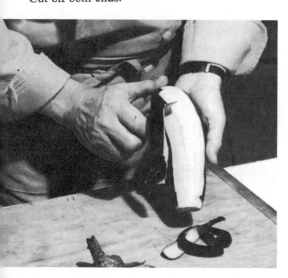

Peel the eggplant.

LES BLETTES

Swiss Chard is a summer and fall vegetable grown especially in the country around Lyon. It is first blanched and then cooked like cardoons and spinach.

LES CARDONS

The best cardoons come from Tours. They are an autumn vegetable in the shape of a giant bunch of celery, of which the ribs and the leaves are eaten.

HOW TO PREPARE AND COOK CARDOONS

Cut off the leaves and the wilted outer stalks, keeping only the tender ones. Cut the stalks into 3- to 4-inch pieces. Pare off the outer fibers with a vegetable peeler or a knife. Drop the trimmed pieces immediately into acidulated water in order to prevent their darkening. (Use the juice of 1 lemon or 2 to 3 tablespoons vinegar to 3 cups of water.) Cook *au blanc* (see p. 42) until the cardoons are tender. Or cook them in boiling salted water until tender. Cooking time may vary from 30 or 40 minutes to 2 hours, depending on the toughness of the vegetable.

LES CAROTTES

Different kinds of carrots can be found in the vegetable markets at different seasons; they in-

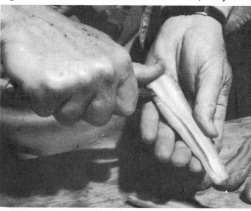

HOW TO CUT OUT THE INNER CORE OF A CARROT

Cut the carrot lengthwise into halves. Cut on the bias along both sides of the tough inner core. Remove the core.

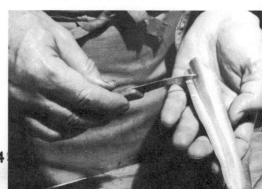

clude the round short carrots (called *grelots),* medium-long and long carrots. In the spring, when they are very tender, they need only be scraped before cooking. In the winter, on the other hand, the tough inner core must be removed. Only the orange part of the carrot is used, and this is blanched before cooking.

LE CÉLERI EN BRANCHES

This is the kind of celery cultivated in such a way that only the stalks and leaves will develop. It is a year-round vegetable, often prepared like cardoons. The stalks are eaten raw or cooked, and the leaves are sometimes used for soups.

To prepare celery, cut off the base, separate the stalks, cut off the leaves, and wash the stalks. Pare off the outer fibers with a vegetable parer or a small knife. Cut the stalks into 4- to 6-inch pieces and blanch them in boiling salted water for about 10 minutes, depending on the thickness of the stems. Remove the celery with a slotted spoon and drain it in a strainer or on a kitchen cloth.

LE CÉLERI-RAVE

This is a kind of celery cultivated for its large root; the stems and leaves are small and undeveloped. It is called celery root, celeriac, or knob celery. It is a winter vegetable, and far more common in France than branch celery.

To prepare celery root peel off the thick skin; wash the peeled root and cut it into quarters, slices or slivers. Blanch it in boiling salted water for 5 minutes and drain. Celery root may be cooked like celery.

LES CHAMPIGNONS (see p. 51). LES CHOUX

Among the best-known cabbage varieties are Savoy cabbage, broccoli, green cabbage and red cabbage. Cabbage is eaten the year round. Sometimes, in cooking, cabbage gives off a very characteristic smell; an easy way to counteract this is to put a kitchen cloth wrung out in vinegar on the lid of the saucepan in which the cabbage is cooking.

To prepare cabbage, cut off the stump; remove the outer leaves that are wilted and any that are too thick ribbed. Wash the cabbage and blanch it in boiling water for a few minutes.

LES CHOUX-FLEURS

Cauliflower is a cabbage variety eaten the year round, except in winter. Buy only cauliflower that still has some of its green leaves; these are a sign of the cauliflower's freshness.

To prepare cauliflower, separate the flowerets and cut off the tough part of their stems. Blanch the flowerets, so that they will not smell too strongly during cooking, in boiling salted water until barely tender. Rinse the flowerets quickly under running cold water to firm them and drain in a strainer.

HOW TO TRIM A CAULIFLOWER

Cut off the stump.

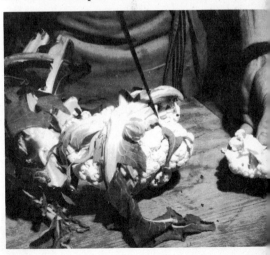

Loosen the flowerets and cut them off.

LES CHOUX DE BRUXELLES

Brussels sprouts are the small green shoots of some varieties of the cabbage family. They are eaten in the autumn and winter.

To prepare Brussels sprouts, remove the wilted outer leaves and cut off the stems. Drop the trimmed sprouts into a basin filled with cold water. Wash and drain them. Heat a large amount of salted water to the boiling point and add the sprouts. Cook them until barely tender. Remove them with a slotted spoon, rinse them quickly under running cold water to firm them, and drain them in a strainer.

Cut into pieces and drain in a strainer.

LES CONCOMBRES

Cucumbers are eaten in spring and summer. Since they contain a great deal of water they must be drained (see DÉGORGER, p. 75).

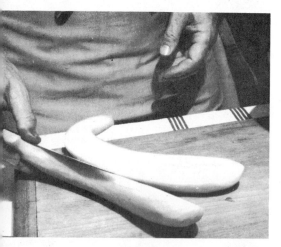

To prepare cucumbers, peel off the green skin, taking care that no trace of it is left. Cut the cucumber lengthwise into halves. Remove the center part which contains the seeds.

LES COURGES ET COURGETTES

These are pumpkin and the squash known in America as zucchini. Among the types of pumpkin the varieties called *potiron* and *citrouille* are the best.

To prepare zucchini, wash them, for like eggplant they are seldom peeled. Most often they are sliced and deep fried. There is no need to remove the seeds unless they are very big.

LES CROSNES

Chinese artichokes come from the Far East; they were first cultivated in France at Crosnes, in Seine-et-Oise, hence the name. It is a very delicate winter vegetable.

To prepare Chinese artichokes, first wash them. Put them into a thick kitchen cloth and sprinkle them with coarse (Kosher) salt. Twist the ends of the kitchen cloth and shake it. The skins will come loose. When the skins are removed, blanch the vegetables in boiling salted water for a few minutes. Then they may be cooked in butter, or in the pan gravy from a roast.

LES ENDIVES

Belgian endives are a rich and delicate fall and winter vegetable.

To trim them, cut off the base and remove any spotted leaves. Wash the whole endive in cold water and dry carefully with a kitchen cloth or kitchen paper. Belgian endives may be eaten raw or cooked.

LES ÉPINARDS

The two spinach varieties best known in France are English spinach and the spinach from Viroflay.

To prepare spinach, cut off the roots and wash the leaves very carefully in at least 3 changes of cold water to remove every trace of sand. Blanch as quickly as possible in boiling water. Rinse under running cold water and carefully squeeze out all excess moisture with the hands. Whole spinach leaves may be eaten raw, as a salad.

LE FENOUIL

Fennel, or finocchio, is a winter vegetable. The stalks alone are eaten, and they are often served like celery.

To prepare fennel, cut off the long fingerlike tendrils, trim the base, and remove the tough outer stalks.

LES FÈVES

The best broad or fava beans are those from Seville and the variety called *juliennes.*

To prepare broad beans, shell them and remove the skins of the beans if they are tough.

LES GOMBOS

Okra is a South American plant; the pods are served like green beans.

To prepare okra, cut off the stem ends, but trim carefully so as not to cut into the pods. Fresh okra must be blanched in water acidulated with lemon juice or vinegar for a few minutes. Dried okra must be soaked in cold water for several hours, then blanched like fresh okra. Save the water in which the vegetable was soaked for the stock of a *pot-au-feu.*

LES HARICOTS

There are many kinds of beans: green beans, flageolet beans, red and white beans, and *mange-tout* or snow peas, of which both pods and peas are eaten.

To prepare green beans, cut off both ends, and string them if necessary. Wash the beans in cold water. Cook them in boiling water for 10 to 15 minutes.

Flageolet beans are small and greenish;

when fresh they are cooked in the usual fashion; when dried, they are cooked after soaking in cold water like all dried beans. All recipes for dried beans may be used for flageolet beans with the exception of *cassoulet,* which must be made with small white beans.

Fresh or dried red beans are cooked like white beans.

LES LAITUES

Various kinds of lettuces are eaten in France the year round except in winter. These include romaine, Batavia and the *reine de mai.*

To prepare lettuces, cut off the stem ends and wash them very carefully in several changes of water.

LES LENTILLES

The small green lentils from Puy are preferred. They are cooked like dried white beans.

LES MARRONS

Chestnuts may now be bought already peeled, which saves a great deal of time and trouble.

To peel chestnuts, make an incision in the flat side of the chestnut, using a pointed small knife. Put the chestnuts into a preheated 350° F. oven for 10 minutes. Peel them while they are hot. The scored chestnuts may also be dropped into hot deep fat for 2 to 3 minutes, drained, and then peeled while hot. See page 582 for the method of peeling chestnuts by boiling them briefly.

LES NAVETS

Turnips are eaten the year round; the varieties include the turnips from Meaux (as a garnish for rich meats), the yellow turnips from Montmagny, the white turnips from Croissy. They are only worth eating when very fresh and young, that is, when they are firm, but tender.

LES OIGNONS

The best-known onions include the white onions from Paris, the pale red onions from Niort and those from Mulhouse. They are a year-round vegetable.

To prepare onions without the usual tears caused by onion juices, peel them under running water. To slice or mince them, see COUPER (p. 57).

LES POIVRONS

Bell peppers are wrongly called sweet peppers. They can be red or green. They may be eaten raw or cooked.

To prepare bell peppers, cut a hole into the top or slice off the top and remove the membranes and seeds.

LES POIREAUX

The leeks known as *gros du Midi* are a summer vegetable and those called *longs de Paris* are a winter vegetable.

To trim them, cut off the roots and the faded and wilted parts of the green tops, as well as any wilted outer leaves.

LES POIS

The best peas are Prince Albert peas and the varieties called *téléphone, sabre blanc* and *ridés de Knight.* To recognize peas of good quality, look for shiny green pods and peas.

The dried green peas eaten in France are always split green peas.

LES POIS CHICHES

Ceci beans, or chick-peas or garbanzos, are usually prepared and cooked like dried white beans.

LES POMMES DE TERRE

The potato is an all-purpose vegetable that comes in endless varieties. Generally speaking, the skin of good-quality potatoes should be thin and range from a beige to a purplish color. The inside should be white, and at times pinkish at the edges.

Here are a few desirable varieties: *la belle de Fontenay,* the longish yellow potatoes from Holland, the long red potatoes from Holland, the Marjolin, the *saucisse,* the *quarantaine,* etc.

To prepare potatoes, it is only necessary to peel them and to remove completely all the eyes and any spots, so that the potatoes will be spotless. If potatoes are peeled before being used, it is absolutely necessary to blanch them immediately to avoid discoloration. The uncooked potatoes are put into cold water which is then brought to the boiling point. Then drain the potatoes and set them aside for cooking.

LES SALSIFIS

Oyster plant, or salsify, is a winter vegetable. The best-known varieties are the white oyster plant, and the black one also known as *scorsonère.* They are cooked like cardoons.

To prepare oyster plant, scrape it with a knife and drop the scraped vegetable immediately into water acidulated with lemon juice or vinegar; this prevents discoloration. Cut the oyster plant into 3-inch strips. Wash them and cook them in boiling salted water until tender.

LES TOMATES

There are many kinds of tomatoes: the Marmande, Chemin, round and oval tomatoes.

HOW TO PREPARE TOMATOES

To prepare tomatoes, cut into the blossom end and remove the stem. Drop the tomatoes into hot water. Bring the water to the boiling point, remove the tomatoes, put them into cold water; then peel them.

Cut the tomato crosswise into halves.

Squeeze the tomato gently with the hands.

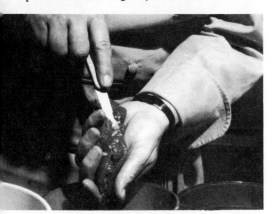

Scrape out the seeds.

LES TRUFFES

A truffle is a kind of fungus that grows underground, especially in the Périgord and Lot regions; it is related to the mushroom. The white truffles of Piedmont in Italy, which carry a slight scent of garlic, are usually eaten raw.

To prepare truffles, choose firm symmetrical round truffles. Wash and brush them under running cold water to remove any trace of earth which may cling to them. If the truffles are not to be used immediately, it is better to preserve them in their earth, in a cool place. One may also store them, after brushing and washing, by putting them into a small container, not a plastic one but a preserving jar that shuts very tightly, indeed hermetically. Sprinkle a little salted water over the truffles and seal the jar. Set the jar in a deep kettle filled with cold water. Bring to the boiling point and keep at the boiling point for 1 hour. Remove the kettle from the heat and cool the water before removing the jar. Truffles prepared in this manner may be stored for several years.

LEVER

1. To cut out a fillet from a fish, for instance from a sole (see DÉSOSSER, p. 77).
2. *Lever* also means to rise, and a dough that rises is a dough in the process of fermenting.

LIER

This means to bind or to thicken sauces, creams, soups, etc., by adding either a starch or another thickening ingredient. There are about as many *liaisons,* or thickening mixtures, as there are recipes; a few follow here:

LIAISON WITH EGG YOLKS AND CREAM

This is the most popular *liaison.* Egg yolks and cream are beaten together first. Then a few spoonfuls of the liquid that is to be thickened are stirred into the mixture to heat it a little, but without cooking it, since the egg yolks, once cooked, will no longer thicken a food.

Then the egg-yolk mixture is stirred into the food that is to be thickened. One can also thicken a food with cream alone, or with beaten egg yolk alone.

LIAISON WITH BEURRE MANIÉ

Beurre manié is a mixture of butter kneaded together with flour or cornstarch (see p. 41); it is used exclusively to thicken sauces. The blended mixture is stirred into the sauce in small pellets.

LIAISON WITH CORNSTARCH OR POTATO STARCH

Thin the cornstarch or potato starch with a liquid suited to the sauce or the liquid to be thickened. These may include water, wine, spirits, port wine, etc. The liquid used for thinning the starch must be cold, but the liquid that is to be thickened with this starch mixture must be at the boiling point. Stir constantly during cooking.

LIAISON WITH BUTTER

Beat the sauce while it is cooking. Melt the butter.

Remove the sauce from the heat and add the melted butter, little by little, until the sauce has the desired consistency.

Note: This technique is also called *monter une sauce* with butter.

LIMONER

The *limon* is a slimy substance that covers the body and scales of certain kinds of fish. *Limoner* means to remove this substance.

HOW TO LIMONER AN EEL

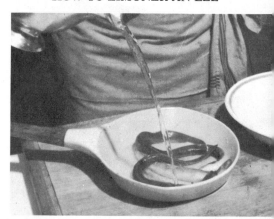

Pour boiling water over the live eels.

Scrape off the *limon* with the nails.

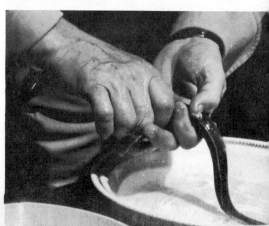

Note the position of the fingers; this position allows a firm grasp on the eel.

Note: The word *limoner* is sometimes erroneously used for cleaning brains (see ÉMONDER, p. 84).

LUTER

This term means sealing a casserole in an absolutely airtight manner, using strips of dough made from flour and water. *Fixer au repère* or *souder,* to solder, are other expressions for the same technique.

HOW TO SEAL A CASSEROLE

Put the lid on the casserole, pressing it down.

Pinch the dough with a pastry pincher.

MACÉDOINE

A mixture of vegetables or fruits cut into pieces of different shapes and sizes. A *macédoine* of vegetables might consist, for instance, of peas, diced carrots, diced green beans and diced artichoke hearts.

Arrange a band of dough all around the edge of the casserole. Paint the dough with water.

HOW TO PREPARE A MACÉDOINE OF FRUITS

Cut an orange into quarters, peel it *à vif,* that is, completely, removing both the orange zest and the white inner skin, as well as the membranes between the sections. Drop the cut fruit into a bowl.

Only the membranes are left.

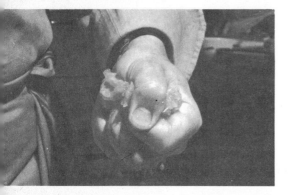

Squeeze out these membranes over the bowl to get the last drops of juice.

Peel, pit and slice a peach. Cut a banana into rounds. Naturally, there are many other fruits which may be used, according to the season.

MACÉRER

To soak a meat, a fish, or other foods in a seasoned liquid (see MARINER, below).

MALAXER

To work any food, such as butter or pastry, in order to soften it.

MANIER

Kneading with the hands (see BEURRE MANIÉ, p. 41).

MARINER

To soak a food, such as meat, game or fish, in a seasoned liquid which is called a marinade. The reason for this is to tenderize meats that are tough (such as venison), or to make foods more aromatic.

MARINADE FOR HERRING

Score the carrots and cut them into rounds. Slice the onions.

Put the herring with the carrots and onions into a terrine. Cover with oil.

MARINADE FOR GAME

(see GIBIER, p. 98).

MARQUER

To pre-prepare a food to the last detail, so that it is ready for immediate cooking.

MASQUER

To mask a food or cover it completely with a thick substance such as aspic, sauce, cream, etc.

MÉDAILLON

A usually round, or sometimes oval, shape (medallion) into which foods are cut, such as *tournedos,* veal scallops, etc.

Cutting *médaillons* for *tournedos.*

Cutting *médaillons* of lobster.

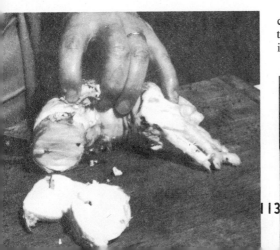

HOW TO CUT FOIE GRAS INTO MÉDAILLONS

Dip the knife into hot water before cutting.

Cut the *foie gras* into slices.

MIGNONNETTE

Peppercorns, coarsely crushed, are called *mignonnette.*

To prepare a *mignonnette,* spread peppercorns on a board and crush them with the bottom of a heavy saucepan or any other suitable implement, such as a filled can.

113

The peppercorns crushed into *mignonnette*. Note how coarsely they are crushed; *mignonnette* should not be confused with ground pepper.

MIREPOIX (see COUPER, p. 57).

MONDER (see ÉMONDER, p. 84).

MONTER

To beat a sauce, or white of egg, etc., to make it foamy.

MORTIFIER

To age meats (venison, for instance) in order to tenderize them. This is done by hanging the meat in a very dry place.

MOUILLER

To add liquids, such as stock, to foods. Lobster bisque is *mouillé* with fish stock, for instance.

The liquid used in cooking a given dish is called *mouillement,* a synonym for *cuisson* (p. 65).

How to add liquid to a food.

MOUTON (see AGNEAU, p. 36).

Editors' Note: Mutton is the meat of sheep, either wethers or ewes, that are over 20 months old. Mutton is used more in Europe than in the United States. The cuts of mutton are the same as those of lamb. However, they will be larger, less tender, and less delicate in flavor; the preparation must be chosen accordingly.

NAPPER

This means to coat one food with another and rather thick one, such as aspic, sauce, cream.

How to coat an omelet with sauce.

HOW TO COAT WITH GELATIN

Pour liquified aspic stock into a bowl and set it in another one filled with crushed ice.

Place the cold food to be coated on a rack and spoon the aspic stock over it when the stock is very cold and just at the point of jellying.

NOISETTE

Noisette butter is butter that has been heated until it is browned; the color should be like the color of hazelnuts (*noisettes*).

On the other hand, a *noisette* of butter is a piece of butter the size of a hazelnut.

OEUFS

OEUFS À LA COQUE

These are eggs cooked in their shells, called soft-boiled or soft-cooked eggs. Use fresh, but not newly laid, eggs. Eggs that have been stored in a cool place for 8 days are excellent; if used the day it has been laid, an egg might jolt the liver.

There are two ways of cooking eggs *à la coque*.

First Method: Put sufficient water into a saucepan so that it will cover the eggs, and bring it to the boiling point. Slide the eggs into the water with the help of a spoon. If the eggs were refrigerated, let them first stand at room temperature for 5 to 10 minutes, or the shells will crack when plunged into the boiling water. If several eggs are to be cooked, put them quickly into the water one after the other, so that the water will not cool too much. Cooking time depends on the size of the eggs. A 2-ounce egg will take 3 minutes of cooking. In order to solidify fully the white of the egg, cook it a little longer.

Second Method: Fill a casserole with cold water and put the eggs into it. Bring to the boiling point. When the water begins to boil,

the eggs will be ready. Take care not to use too large a saucepan, nor too much water, and to bring the water to the boiling point neither too quickly nor too slowly. If the water takes too long to boil, the egg will be prematurely hard-cooked.

OEUFS MOLLETS

Oeufs mollets are eggs cooked in their shells until the whites are completely firm, but the yolks are still soft. Slide the eggs into a casserole full of boiling water and let them boil for 6 minutes. Drain the eggs and peel them under cold water. If the eggs are to be eaten warm, peel them as quickly as possible, or else the yolks will harden, and they will no longer be eggs *mollets*.

OEUFS DURS

These are eggs cooked in their shells until hard, called hard-cooked eggs. Cook the eggs in a saucepan full of boiling water for a minimum of 10 and a maximum of 15 minutes. The water must boil constantly. Peel the eggs under cold water.

OEUFS EN COCOTTE, CASSOLETTE, CAISSETTE

These are shelled eggs baked in individual baking dishes. Butter the dishes and add a little heavy cream and salt.

Break 1 egg into each dish and season with salt and pepper.

115

Set the baking dishes in a pan full of hot water and bake them, preferably in the oven, for about 6 minutes. More hot cream may be spooned over the eggs. These baked-egg dishes are often garnished in different ways. Depending on the garnish, the baking dish may have to be first heated, then lightly buttered, and finally lined with the garnish, for instance, a purée. Then the egg is added. In other cases, the baking dish needs only to be buttered and not heated at all. If the garnish is a very simple one, it is simply put into the buttered dish before the addition of the egg.

OEUFS SUR LE PLAT

These are shelled eggs, cooked in shallow heat-proof dishes in which they are also served. They are cooked on top of the stove or in the oven. First Method:

Heat an individual shallow baking dish, melt a little butter in it, sprinkle a little salt over the butter, and remove the dish from the heat. Break the eggs carefully into the butter.

Cook over high heat until the white has almost, but not completely, set; almost set, because the heat of the dish will go on cooking the egg after it has been removed from the stove. Season with a turn of the peppermill.

Second Method: Butter an individual shallow baking dish—which must be cold—very heavily, sprinkle salt over the butter, and break the eggs into the dish. Put the baking dish into a preheated 350° F. oven. When the egg is warm, season the yolk with a turn of the peppermill and then bake until the white is set.

OEUFS BROUILLÉS

These are scrambled eggs.
First Method: Break the whole eggs into a saucepan and cook them, beating them constantly with a wire whisk. Add a little heavy cream, beat some more, remove from the heat, and stir in a little softened butter.

Second Method: Beat the eggs as for an omelet and pour them into a small saucepan which contains a little melted warm butter.

Cook slowly *au bain-marie* (over barely simmering water), or over low heat, stirring constantly with a wooden spoon. When the eggs are beginning to set, stir in a little heavy cream, but this is optional. Remove the eggs from the heat and stir in a few pieces of butter the size of hazelnuts.

Third Method: Heat a saucepan and melt some butter in it, but do not let it brown. The saucepan should be very hot. Break the whole eggs into the pan. Cook the eggs over high heat for a few minutes, beating all the time with a small wire whisk. Remove from the heat as soon as the eggs are beginning to set, and go on beating them until they are done, but still soft. If necessary, put them briefly back over the heat for a moment or more, to help their cooking. If you want to, you may add a little heavy cream when you are putting the eggs back over the heat. Away from the heat, add a few pieces of softened butter the size of hazelnuts.

You may add a garnish to the scrambled eggs. Add it to the beaten raw eggs before cooking them, or add it to the cooked eggs at serving time.

OEUFS POCHÉS

These are poached eggs. Choose very fresh eggs. It is better to poach only a few eggs at a time.

Use a heavy and rather flat saucepan. Add water and vinegar, in the proportions of 1 part vinegar to 5 parts water. Do not add salt. Bring to just below the boiling point; the water should barely simmer.

Break each egg and slide it into the barely simmering water, without breaking the yolk. Cook for about 3 minutes. Carefully remove the eggs with a slotted ladle.

If the poached eggs are to be served cold, have ready a bowl filled with salted cold water. Carefully drop the poached eggs into the cold water. Take them out with the slotted ladle and drain them on a kitchen towel.

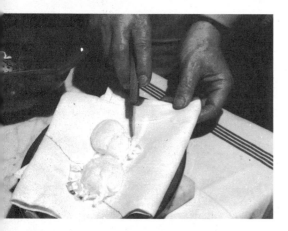

Trim the eggs.

If the eggs are to be served hot, have ready a bowl filled with lukewarm salted water. Carefully drop the eggs into it, remove them, and drain them, as described above. Use the eggs immediately.

OEUFS FRITS

These are fried eggs. Eggs are fried, one at a time, in two ways. In the English way, the yolk is exposed; in the French way, the yolk is covered with a layer of the white.

Heat about ¼ inch of salad oil in a skillet that is neither too large nor too deep. Prop up the skillet with one of the burners of the stove, or with a round mold, so that the skillet will rest at a slight angle, with the oil collected at one side. Keep the hands free. Remove the skillet from the heat and slide an egg into the hot oil. Return the skillet to the heat; heat a spatula.

If the egg is to be fried in the English manner, push the white around the yolk with the spatula.

If the egg is to be fried in the French way, spread some of the egg white over the yolk to cover it; with the spatula push the remaining egg white around to give the egg a neat shape.

To the left, an egg fried in the English manner; to the right, in the French way.

While the egg is frying, the oil must always be very hot, but not smoking or burning, so that the egg white becomes crisp and golden. Cooking time: about 2½ minutes.

Note: If there is no stove burner or mold handy to prop up the skillet while the egg is frying, break the egg into a saucer, hold the skillet at an angle, so that the hot oil will flow to one side, slide the egg into the oil, and fry.

Or by cutting off the top, like a hat.

OEUFS FARCIS

Stuffed eggs are first hard-cooked in boiling water for 10 to 15 minutes. They may be cut in 3 different ways:

Remove the yolks and push them through a sieve.

Lengthwise.

Stir the yolks together with some mayonnaise.

Or by cutting a lengthwise wedge into the egg.

Add *fines herbes* and blend well.

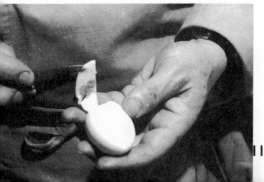

Fill a pastry bag with the mixture of egg yolk, mayonnaise and *fines herbes* and pipe it into the whites.

Immediately stir the eggs with a fork over high heat. Cook the omelet according to taste: very moist, medium or well done. While the omelet is cooking, tap the skillet against the stove from time to time so that the omelet will not stick to the pan.

Note the different shapes of the stuffed eggs.

OMELETTE

A 5-egg omelet is a good serving for 2 persons.

Break the eggs into a porcelain or glass bowl. Season the eggs with salt and pepper; it is better to season each egg separately. Add 1 tablespoon of cold water and beat the eggs with a fork. The eggs must be beaten just sufficiently to be well blended, but no more than this. Do not overbeat.

Heat a good-sized piece of butter in a skillet, but do not let it brown. Pour the beaten eggs into the butter and shake the pan, holding it with one hand.

Roll up the omelet; fold over one third of the omelet, working from the side of the pan with the handle, toward the open side. Fold the other edge in reverse over the first fold.

Roll over the omelet onto a hot serving dish with the fold underneath.

Omelets can also be made by beating the yolks and whites separately. The yolks should be beaten with a fork; the whites should be beaten with an egg beater until stiff. Or whole eggs may be beaten with a wire whisk. These two methods are more suited to dessert omelets.

Omelets that will be served cold must always be thoroughly cooked, almost overcooked, and peppered more freely than those to be eaten hot.

HOW TO ADD A FILLING TO AN OMELET WHILE IT IS COOKING

Let the omelet set a little and then spoon the filling across the middle.

Roll up the omelet in the usual way; if necessary, tap the skillet handle in order to shape the omelet. You don't see the stuffing while the omelet is cooking.

HOW TO FILL A COOKED OMELET

Make the omelet in the usual manner and put it on a hot serving dish.

Make a lengthwise cut into the omelet and push the sides apart slightly.

Slide the stuffing into the omelet.

On the left, an omelet stuffed during cooking; on the right, one stuffed after cooking.

PANER

Paner means to bread a food, that is, to dip a food first into flour, then into an *anglaise* (see p. 38), and finally into bread crumbs. *Paner* also means to coat a food with bread crumbs only.

HOW TO BREAD A CUTLET

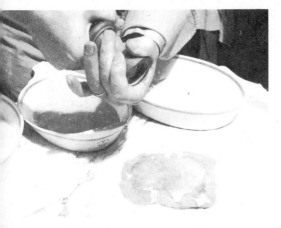

Season the meat with salt and pepper.

Dip the meat into the flour and pat it on.

Dip the meat into the *anglaise* mixture.

Finally, dip it into the bread crumbs (see CHAPELURE, p. 51).

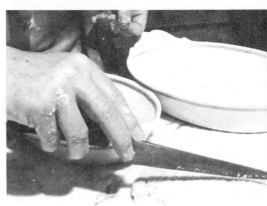

Score the edges of the meat lightly with a knife so that the cutlet will not curl during cooking.

PANIER

HOW TO MAKE ORANGE AND LEMON PANIERS, OR BASKETS

Mark the outlines of a basket handle on an orange by cutting from the stem end down to the

middle on either side of the fruit, leaving a strip, which will be the handle, in between the two cuts.

Cut away the parts of the orange on either side of the handle, in a pointed or zigzag pattern.

Scrape the underside of the handle and scoop out the inside of the orange. Use the same method for lemons.

PAPILLOTE

1. A garnish made from frilled paper put on the bones of cutlets, steaks and roasts.
2. The term is used also for a technique of cooking and serving a food in a packet of parchment paper, for instance, calf's sweetbreads *en papillote*.

PARER

To trim and pare a food, removing unnecessary parts of it, to give the food a pleasing appearance. The trimmed-off parts are called *parures*.

PASSER

1. A term used to describe putting a food into melted butter for just a moment and then taking it out.
2. It also refers to straining and filtering: for instance, *passer un consommé* means to strain a consommé.

PÂTES

There are far too many kinds of doughs and batters to describe them all. Doughs used for specific pastries and cakes will be found in the chapter on desserts. For the rest, let us describe just a few.

Originally, doughs were a mixture of nothing but flour and water, called *détrempe*. This mixture is still the basis of puff paste.

LA DÉTREMPE

Spread flour on the baking board in the shape of a ring, making a well in the middle. Add a few pinches of salt.

Pour 1 or 2 tablespoons of cream into the well in the ring of flour.

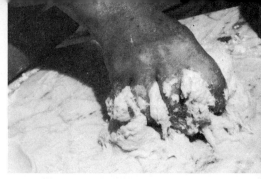

Gather the dough together and form a ball. Note how dough spreads between the fingers.

Add water.

In order to clean the hands of surplus dough, dip them into flour and rub.

Mix. Note the position of the fingers.

From time to time, push the flour from the rim towards the middle, covering the well.

The *détrempe* ball. Using a sharp knife, score the top in the shape of a cross to let the dough "breathe."

GENERAL METHOD OF MAKING PÂTES À FROID

(pâte brisée, pâte à pâté, pâte sablée, etc.)

Spread the flour in the middle of the baking board in the shape of a ring, making a well in the middle. Put into this well the eggs, salt, water or cream, the softened butter or lard, all the ingredients needed to make the pastry.

Gradually push and sprinkle the flour over the well, mixing thoroughly with the hands.

Knead thoroughly. It is essential to hold the hands and fingers as shown in the picture.

Fraisant, or pushing out the dough (see FRAISER, p. 94); note the position of the right hand.

The dough is ready, and shaped into a ball. This kind of dough must not be too firm and hard; if it is, the dough is called *cordée*.

HOW TO MAKE PUFF PASTE

For a detailed recipe for puff paste, see page 715.

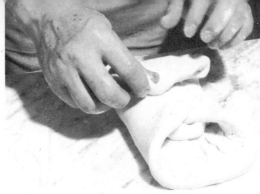

Make a *détrempe* (see above), and roll it out on a floured board.

Put the butter in the middle of the sheet of dough and fold the dough over, first on one side,

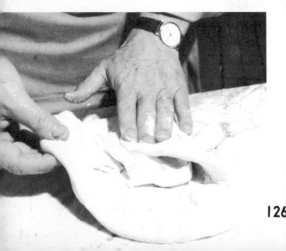

then on the other side,

and finally at both ends, sealing the butter in firmly since it absolutely must not ooze out. Roll out the dough into an oblong and fold again. This operation is called *donner un tour à la pâte,* or to give the dough a "turn." Let the dough rest in a cool place and repeat the operation six times, resting the dough between each two turns.

HOW TO MAKE PÂTE À CHOUX

For a detailed recipe for *pâte à choux,* see page 710.
Combine the butter, salt and sugar in a saucepan. Over high heat, bring to the boiling point.

When the mixture is boiling, dump in the flour all at once.

Beat in the eggs, two at a time, and blend quickly.

Mix well and stir with a wooden spatula until the mixture clears the sides of the saucepan and forms a ball. This operation is called *dessécher,* that is, to dry out the paste.

Dump the paste into a bowl.

The finished dough must be somewhat shiny, thick and smooth.

HOW TO MAKE CRÊPE BATTER

For a detailed recipe for *crêpe* batter, see page 740.

Combine the milk, salt, sugar and butter in a saucepan, and heat the mixture.

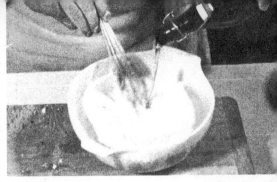

Put the flour into a bowl and make a well in the middle. Pour the oil and the eggs into this well. The number of eggs may vary, but the flour must absorb the eggs completely.

Measure the volume of this batter as closely as possible, and stir in half of its volume of beer. The final batter must be a little thicker than water.

Mix well.

Strain the batter through a very fine sieve.

HOW TO MAKE GÉNOISE PASTRY

For a detailed recipe for *génoise*, see page 683. Put the sugar and the eggs into a saucepan or flameproof bowl.

When the butter has melted in the milk, pour this mixture into the batter. Beat with a wire whisk to blend thoroughly.

Beat the mixture over hot water or over the lowest possible heat, without heating it too much since it must not cook.

On the left, note the flan ring that balances the round-bottomed bowl as it stands over the heat.

Remove the mixture from the heat when it is heated through, and continue beating until it has doubled in volume and drops from the beater in the shape of a ribbon.

Fold in the flour and then the melted butter. Once the *génoise* dough is ready, pour it into a buttered pan and bake.

PÂTÉ EN CROÛTE

Pâtés en croûte, that is, pâtés covered with pastry, are made with unsweetened pastry. Instead of molding the pâté in a terrine, it is molded, or encased, in pastry.

These pastries may vary considerably, according to the filling and the taste of those who will eat them. A pâté of *foie gras,* for instance, may well be encased in puff paste or *brioche* dough, but a pâté made from calf's feet will benefit from more substantial pastry.

Pâtés en croûte are molded in special tin molds with detachable sides. If no such mold is available, the filling may be encased in the pastry in the form of a roll and thus this pâté resembles a galantine, with the pastry dough taking the place of the cloth in which a galantine is cooked. This kind of pâté is called a *pâté moulé,* or molded pâté.

One must always bear in mind that the pâté will be eaten sliced. In order that each serving contain a little of all of the ingredients in the filling, such as truffles or cocks' combs for instance, care has to be exercised in distributing these ingredients evenly through the pâté. A simple way of solving this problem is to place these ingredients in even rows throughout the mixture. See also CHEMISER (p. 51) and FONCER (p. 90).

PAUPIETTE

A thin slice of meat or fish, rolled over a stuffing.

HOW TO PREPARE PAUPIETTES

Season the slices of meat with salt and pepper.

Place a spoonful of stuffing in the middle of each slice.

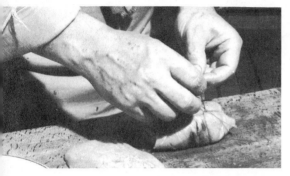

Roll up each slice and tie it with string.

Or fasten it closed with wooden food picks; use one where the edges come together and another on each side if necessary.

PAVÉ

1. A big aspic in the shape of a block.
2. The term is also used for a dessert pastry in the same block shape.

PELER

To peel, or to remove the skin of a vegetable or a fruit (see ÉMONDER, p. 84). The word is also used for boning a fish (see DÉSOSSER, p. 77).

HOW TO SKIN AN EEL

Cut into the skin around the two fins close to the gills. Insert the knife under the skin and loosen it as much as possible. Pull off the skin, working from the head towards the tail. Cut off the head, discard the fins, and draw the eel. Finally, cut the eel into slices.

PELURES

Peelings, or pieces of the skin of a peeled fruit or vegetable, which are sometimes used in cooking, for instance, mushroom peelings or truffle peelings.

PERSIL FRIT

Persil frit is parsley quickly fried in deep hot (375° F.) fat and used as a garnish. Before frying, the parsley should be as dry as possible.

PERSILLADE

A mixture of parsley and, usually, garlic, which are finely minced.

PILAW

The name pilaw or pilaf is given to dishes in which a chief ingredient is rice cooked in the pilaf way (see Rice Pilaf, p. 659).

PILER

To crush a food with a heavy wooden pestle or with any other weighty object. The results may be twofold: *en pommade*, when the crushed food has the consistency of softened butter, or *en purée*, or puréed.

PINCER

To make slits or folds in the edges of pastry with a special tool called a *pince-pâte*.

PIQUER (see LARDER, p. 101).

PLUCHES

Stemless little leaves of herbs used in the kitchen (see BLANCHIR, p. 42).

Pluches of parsley, chervil and watercress.

POCHER

To poach is to cook a food gently in a large quantity of water, stock or *court bouillon*.

The liquid used for poaching must never boil; it must barely shudder (*frissonner*), that is, it must stay just below the full boiling point.

POÊLER

To cook in butter or fat in a skillet, or *poêle*.

POINTE

A tiny amount of a powdered food, as much as can be held on the point of a kitchen knife; for instance, a *pointe* of cayenne pepper.

POISSON

THE FRESHNESS OF FISH

The freshness of fish can be recognized by the scarlet hue of the gills, the lustrous scales, and the shiny and somewhat protruding eyes.

HOW TO MAKE COURT BOUILLON FOR FISH AND SHELLFISH

Peel the vegetables and cut them into very fine slices. Put water or Fish Stock (p. 166) into a kettle, together with dry white wine (if the *court bouillon* will be used for cooking fish) or vinegar (if it is to be used for shellfish). Add the spices and herbs. Bring to the boiling point and simmer until the vegetables are very tender.

Proportions: 1 cup dry white wine or vinegar, 1 quart water or light fish stock, 2 carrots, 2 medium-sized onions, 2 shallots, 3 parsley roots, 1 teaspoon salt, 1 sprig of fresh thyme or ½ teaspoon dried thyme, ½ bay leaf, 6 peppercorns.

Note: Ways of using *court bouillon* will be found in the chapter on Fish and Shellfish (p. 337).

Editors' Note: The following fish, reproduced for the interest of the readers, are commonly used as food fish in France. Not all of them are to be found in American waters, and even when found here, they may belong to a different branch of the same fish family.

SALTWATER FISH

LE SAINT-PIERRE, John Dory, is a good-quality fish which is eaten the year round. It is often used in *bouillabaisse* and other fish soups.

LA SOLE, Cha nel or Dover So is fished all ye. This is an excelle fish, and the ki fished off t French coast is t most highly prize *Editors' Not American so-cal sole is usua flounder or ot flatfish. The tr sole is not fou here.*

LE TURBOT is eaten from May to July. It is a very fine fish.

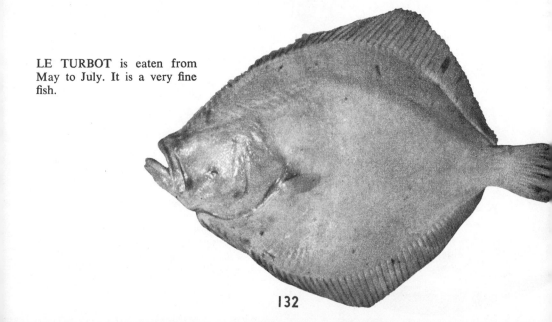

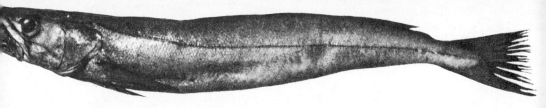

LE COLIN or MERLU, hake, is a delicate fish, eaten between May and July.

L'ÉGLEFIN or LIEU NOIR, haddock, is not a very delicate fish, though its flesh is of quite a good quality.

LE BAR or LOUP, sea bass or sea perch, does not have a very distinctive flavor, and it is best eaten seasoned with fennel.

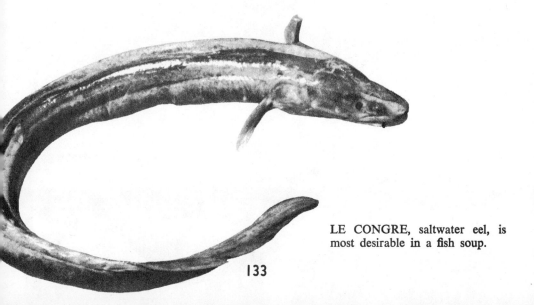

LE CONGRE, saltwater eel, is most desirable in a fish soup.

133

LE MAQUEREAU, mackerel, is fished between May and August. It is a very fatty fish.

LA VIVE, weaver, is usually filleted, and its flavor resembles that of sole. The fish is especially used for fish soups and *bouillabaisse*.

LE ROUGET-BARBET, red mullet, tastes strongly of iodine. Its quality is quite good; it is eaten only in the spring.

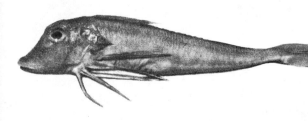

LE ROUGET-GRONDIN, red gurnet, which must not be confused with red mullet, is used in *bouillabaisse*.

LE HARENG, herring, is a seasonal fish, fished several times during the year. It is mostly eaten smoked or salted.

LE MERLAN, whiting, i prized for the delicacy of it flesh. It is a year-round fish.

LE MULET, gray mullet, is a common fish with a delicate flesh.

FRESHWATER FISH

L'ANGUILLE DE RIVIÈRE, freshwater eel, is especially used in *matelotes* or fish soups.

LA CARPE, carp, is eaten between November and March. Mirror carp is especially prized.

LE BROCHET, pike, is the most popular freshwater fish. Its flesh is very delicate.

LA TRUITE D'ÉLEVAGE is trout raised in tanks or pools and it embodies all the virtues of the finest fish.

PORC

The pig is the only animal of which literally every part is eaten, including the blood, which is used to make puddings. Pork is eaten fresh, salted, or smoked.

CUTS FOR ROASTING OR BRAISING

Carré, loin; *échine*, the shoulder-chop end o the loin; *épaule*, whole shoulder (blade an arm); *palette*, (shoulder-blade section); *jam bon*, ham.

CUTS FOR BROILING OR SAUTÉING

Côtes, rib chops; *échine détaillée*, shoulde chops; *filet*, tenderloin, loin strip, or loi chops.

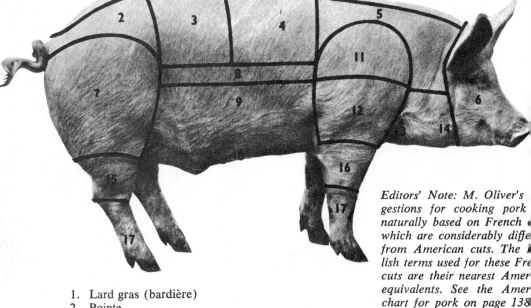

1. Lard gras (bardière)
2. Pointe
3. Filet
4. Carré de côtes
5. Échine à 5 côtes
6. Tête
7. Jambon
8. Travers de côtes
9. Lard maigre
10. Poitrine
11. Palette
12. Épaule
13. Plat de côtes
14. Gorges
15. Jambonneau arrière
16. Jambonneau avant
17. Pieds

Editors' Note: M. Oliver's gestions for cooking pork naturally based on French which are considerably diffe from American cuts. The lish terms used for these Fr cuts are their nearest Amer equivalents. See the Amer chart for pork on page 138

Le JAMBONNEAU
boned hind knuckle

Le JAMBON DE PARIS

canned, frequently otherwise boiled an pressed into shape in mold.

Pork cookery, that is, most of it, is usually called *charcuterie*. Certain regions of France, such as Alsace, Corsica, the Massif Central and the Southwest, are especially famous for their pork cookery.

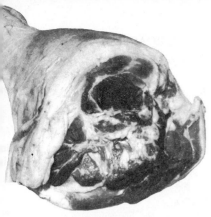

L'ÉPAULE ROULÉE, a rolled fresh shoulder roast, is flavorful and less expensive than ham.

Le JAMBON FRAIS, fresh ham—shank half, is used especially for making the so-called York and Paris hams.

La POITRINE or LARD MAI-GRE, bacon, is used fresh, smoked, or salted. The part on the left is the *plat de côtes,* spareribs, which is used lightly salted and boiled, or fresh and broiled or grilled.

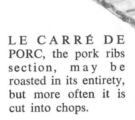

LE CARRÉ DE PORC, the pork ribs section, may be roasted in its entirety, but more often it is cut into chops.

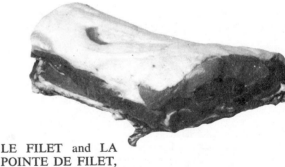

Le FILET DÉSOSSÉ, a boned loin, ready to be roasted.

LE FILET and LA POINTE DE FILET, the loin, bone-in, and its sirloin end, is also used for loin chops.

LA POITRINE FU-MÉE, b o n e l e s s smoked breast, is used especially for *chou-croûte.*

L'ÉCHINE, or chop end of the loin, seen here cut in two, is used especially for *chou-croûte,* goulash and stew.

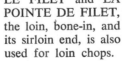

137

Editors' Note: Since French meat cuts vary considerably from American cuts, the following American chart for pork may prove helpful for substitutions. Compare with French pork cuts on pages 136-137.

PORK CHART

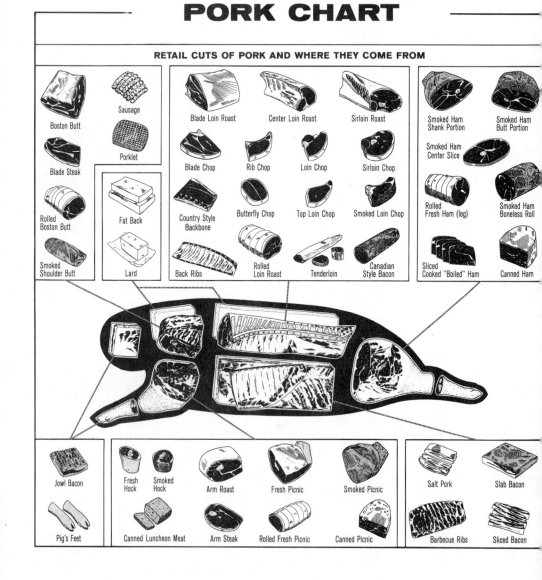

RETAIL CUTS OF PORK AND WHERE THEY COME FROM

Boston Butt

Sausage

Porklet

Blade Steak

Rolled Boston Butt

Fat Back

Smoked Shoulder Butt

Lard

Blade Loin Roast

Center Loin Roast

Sirloin Roast

Blade Chop

Rib Chop

Loin Chop

Sirloin Chop

Country Style Backbone

Butterfly Chop

Top Loin Chop

Smoked Loin Chop

Back Ribs

Rolled Loin Roast

Tenderloin

Canadian Style Bacon

Smoked Ham Shank Portion

Smoked Ham Butt Portion

Smoked Ham Center Slice

Rolled Fresh Ham (leg)

Smoked Ham Boneless Roll

Sliced Cooked "Boiled" Ham

Canned Ham

Jowl Bacon

Pig's Feet

Fresh Hock

Smoked Hock

Canned Luncheon Meat

Arm Roast

Arm Steak

Fresh Picnic

Rolled Fresh Picnic

Smoked Picnic

Canned Picnic

Salt Pork

Barbecue Ribs

Slab Bacon

Sliced Bacon

(Courtesy of the National Live Stock and Meat Board)

Editors' Note: Since French veal cuts vary considerably from American cuts, the following American chart for veal may prove helpful for substitutions. Compare with French cuts on page 159.

VEAL CHART

RETAIL CUTS OF VEAL AND WHERE THEY COME FROM

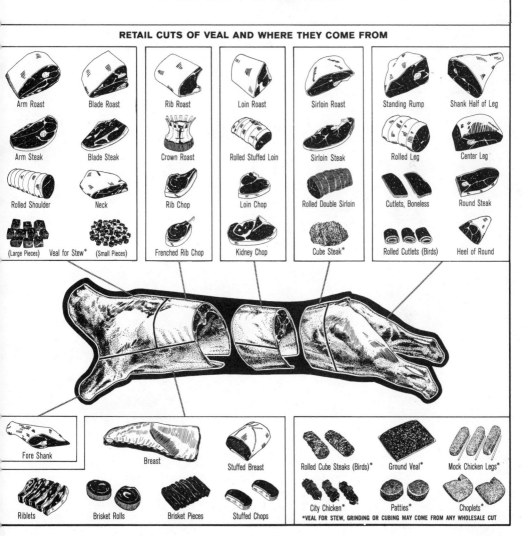

Arm Roast | Blade Roast | Rib Roast | Loin Roast | Sirloin Roast | Standing Rump | Shank Half of Leg

Arm Steak | Blade Steak | Crown Roast | Rolled Stuffed Loin | Sirloin Steak | Rolled Leg | Center Leg

Rolled Shoulder | Neck | Rib Chop | Loin Chop | Rolled Double Sirloin | Cutlets, Boneless | Round Steak

(Large Pieces) Veal for Stew* (Small Pieces) | Frenched Rib Chop | Kidney Chop | Cube Steak* | Rolled Cutlets (Birds) | Heel of Round

Fore Shank | Breast | Stuffed Breast | Rolled Cube Steaks (Birds)* | Ground Veal* | Mock Chicken Legs*

Riblets | Brisket Rolls | Brisket Pieces | Stuffed Chops | City Chicken* | Patties* | Choplets*

*VEAL FOR STEW, GRINDING OR CUBING MAY COME FROM ANY WHOLESALE CUT

(Courtesy of the National Live Stock and Meat Board)

PRÉPARATION DES VIANDES ET VOLAILLES
Preparing meats and poultry.

HOW TO CUT AND TRIM A RACK OF LAMB

Hold the meat in a vertical position and cut into it with one blow of a cleaver.

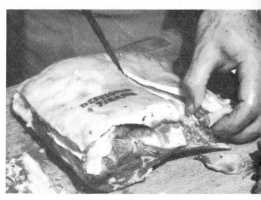

Trim the meat, that is, remove all surplus fat and tissue.

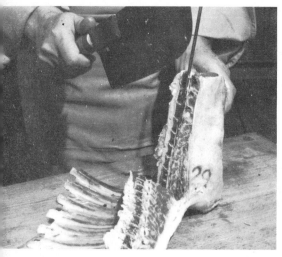

Free the chine on either side.

Insert a skewer as a guide line into the chine and with the cleaver finish cutting the rack into halves.

Using a sharp knife, cut off the fat from the ends of the ribs.

The rib bones are exposed. Scrape off all the fat from the ends of the rib bones.
The rack of lamb is trimmed.

HOW TO BONE A SHOULDER OF LAMB

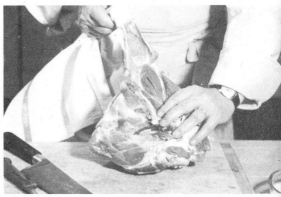

Pull back the meat and grip the shoulder blade joint with the hand wrapped in a towel.

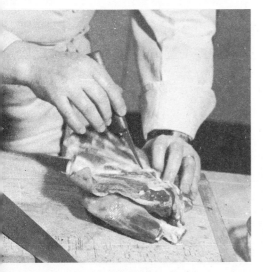

Cut into the shoulder alongside the bone.

Twist the towel around the joint and pull it back, removing the shoulder blade bone.

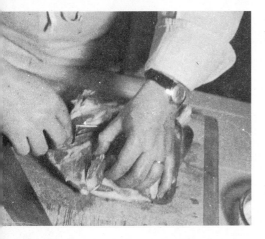

Pull back the meat and free first the shoulder blade joint and then the shoulder blade proper.

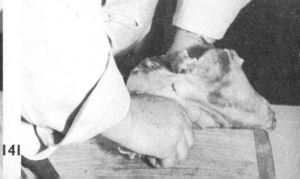

Free the main bone and cut into the joint. Loosen it by pulling.

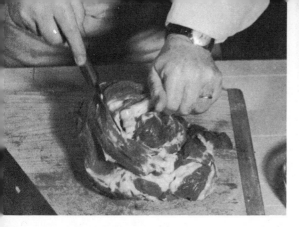

Cut around the bone.

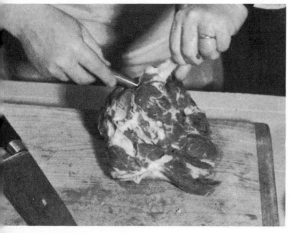

Remove the bone.

HOW TO PREPARE A LEG OF LAMB

Cut the meat all around the end of the leg bone.

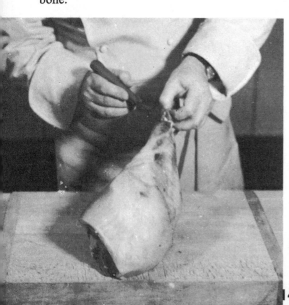

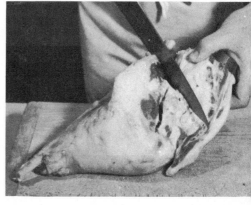

Shorten the leg by cutting off the hipbone o sirloin end of the leg.

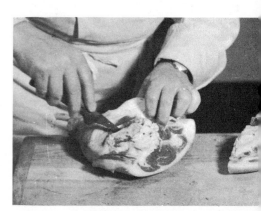

Trim the cut end neatly.

Season the trimmed leg with salt and insert slivers of garlic into it.

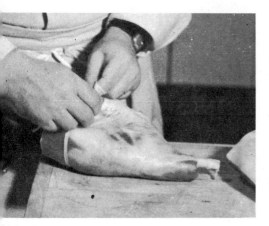

The leg of lamb is ready. Tie it with string.

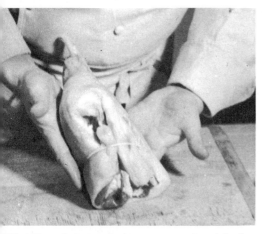

The French leg, or *gigot raccourci*, ready for roasting.

Cut off the feet and wings of the duck.

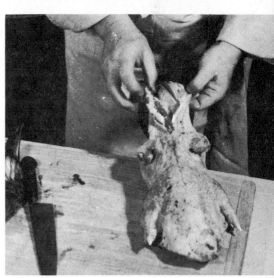

Make an incision into the skin of the neck and take out the lungs from the chest cavity.

Open the bird by the rump.

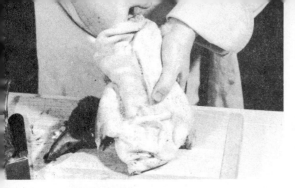

Draw the innards.

Remove the liver and tear off the bile sac.

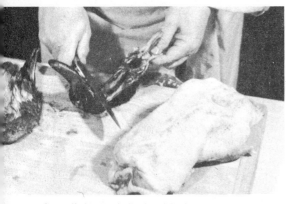

Cut off the neck flush with the carcass.

Truss the duck.

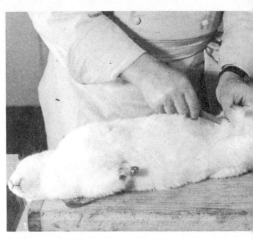

To skin the hare, cut into the skin between

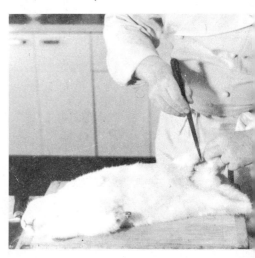

the hind thighs and legs. Free the skin of th hind legs.

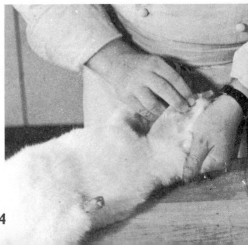

Cut off the tail.

Remove the head by cutting it off back of the ears.

Pull off the skin, starting from the hind legs, using the knife as necessary to facilitate the job.

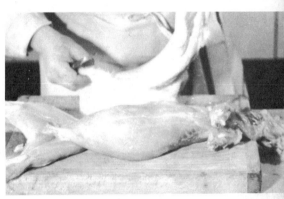

The skinned rabbit.

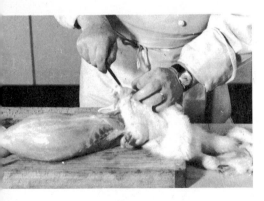

Cut into and all around the skin of the forelegs. Pull the skin off entirely.

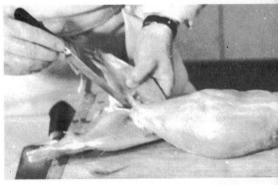

To draw the rabbit, cut around the pelvic bone. Cut into the skin without touching the intestines.

Cut into the neck and shake out the whole intestinal tract.

Cut around the bones of the saddle to free it.

Remove the liver and lungs, and tear the bile sac off the liver.

The saddle is freed.

Discard any entrails which may be left.

To bone the rabbit, gash the upper part of the chest.

Cut the loins away from the backbone. Loosen the backbone.

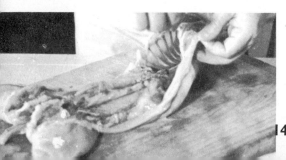

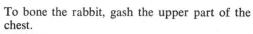

Take out the entire backbone.

Take out the shoulder bones.

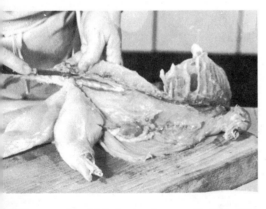

Take out the thigh bones from each side. The rabbit is completely boned.

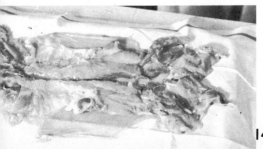

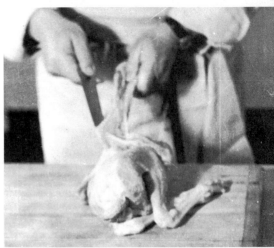

Make an incision in the skin of the neck.

Pull back the skin all around the neck. Loosen the skin around the crop and discard the crop.

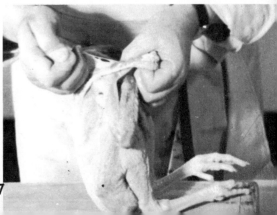

Cut off the excess neck skin.

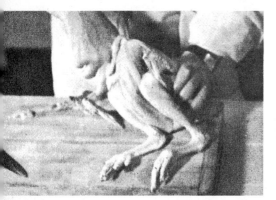

Insert the fingers into the neck cavity in order to take out the lungs.

Cut off the neck flush with the carcass.
Cut the chicken open at the rump and remove the innards.

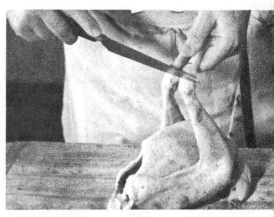

Trim the feet, leaving the long central toe on each foot as an extension of the leg.

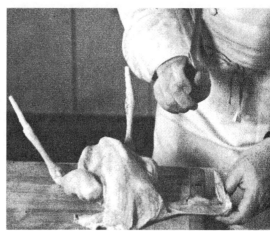

Cut off the wing tips.

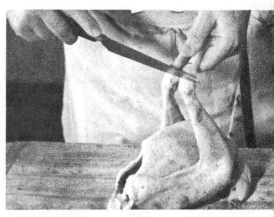

Score the joints to cut the tendons to simplify trussing. Then truss the chicken (see BRIDER, p. 46).

HOW TO BONE A CHICKEN

There are two ways to bone a chicken. This is the first method.

Split the chicken along the backbone.

Cut and scrape the flesh away from the carcass bones on one side of the chicken. As you cut,

Stop cutting when you reach the ridge of the breastbone.

Then cut very closely against the breastbone ridge to free it from the carcass.

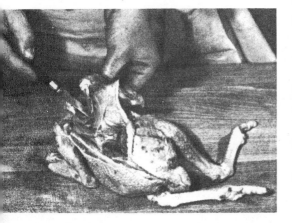

pull the flesh from the bones. Sever the ball joints that connect wing and thigh to carcass.

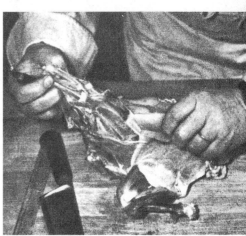

Both sides having been boned, pull off the carcass.

Scrape and cut the flesh from the thigh bones. Scrape the flesh away from the wing-bones and pull them out.

Do the same for the other side, the cutting side of the knife always facing the bones. Free the chicken breast on each side from the carcass up to the top ridge of the breastbone.

Sever the thigh bones from the ball joints of the legs. Then cut off part of the leg bones, leaving the tip ends in. These tip ends of the

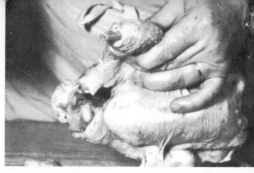

Force the flesh of the legs up toward the thighs, exposing the leg bones, so that, in cooking, the flesh will shrivel, leaving the leg bones completely exposed.

leg bones will help to keep the shape of the leg and will serve for decoration (see PAPIL-LOTE, p. 123).

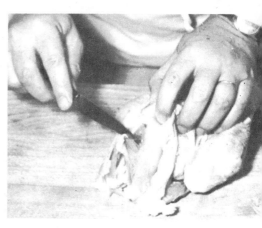

Force back the skin and flesh at the front of the breast cage to expose the wishbone.

Here is a second method.

Cut off the wing tips between the first and second joints.

Cut off the legs just above the first joint.

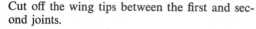

Free the wishbone and cut it off with a small sharp knife. Finish boning the chicken, following in general the steps described in the first method, but leave the bird whole, without splitting it along the backbone.

QUATRE ÉPICES

Quatre épices is a standard mixture of four spices used extensively in French cooking. The usual proportions are: 4 ounces ground white pepper, ⅓ ounce ground cloves, 1 ounce ground ginger, and 1¼ ounces grated nutmeg. This mixture makes approximately 1½ cups and can be used as needed.

QUENELLE

A mixture or *farce* made from finely ground meat, poultry, fish, etc., mixed with egg whites and cream, or sometimes with whole eggs. The mixture is usually shaped like tiny sausages and cooked by poaching. A typical *quenelle* mixture would be ½ pound finely ground meat or fish into which 1 egg white is blended by pounding in a mortar with a pestle; 1 cup heavy cream is then gradually worked into the mixture. The absorption of the cream is facilitated if the ground meat or fish is kept very cold; set the bowl containing the mixture in a larger vessel containing cracked ice.

RAFRAÎCHIR

To put a food into cold water to freshen and firm it. For instance, fresh vegetables are *rafraîchis* in cold water after blanching.

RÉDUIRE

To reduce liquids, such as stocks and sauces, means to boil them so that part of the liquid content will evaporate. This is done to thicken the stock or sauce and to intensify the flavor.

RELEVER

To intensify the flavor of a food. *Remonter* is another word used for this.

REPÈRE

1. A dough made from flour and water, used to seal casseroles hermetically (see LUTER, p. 111).
2. A mixture of flour and egg whites used to glue a garnish on a dish.

REVENIR

Faire revenir means to cook a food in butter, oil, or any other fat, until it barely turns golden, before this food is finished off according to the recipe. In other words, it is a preliminary step in a recipe.

RISSOLER

Faire rissoler a meat, or a vegetable, means to cook it in very hot fat until it turns golden brown.

RIZ

Rice is a starchy cereal; in France, it does not enjoy the popularity it has in other parts of the world; nevertheless, there are several excellent varieties on the market. Generally speaking, short, round-grained rice (such as rice from Piedmont), which cooks quickly and does not largely increase in volume during cooking, is one of the common varieties, whereas long-grained rice (such as the rice from Java, the Camargue and Madagascar) cooks longer and increases considerably in size during cooking.

HOW TO COOK RICE

Editors' Note: Washing rice is not always necessary in the United States, where rice is usually sold prepackaged, whereas in France it is largely sold loose.
Rice must be washed quickly before cooking. Under no circumstances should rice be left soaking in water before cooking, for this would make it sticky. There are two basic ways of cooking rice: the first one is to cook rice in hot fat until barely golden and then add a boiling liquid. The second method is to cook it in liquid without fat; this is the way to prepare rice *à la créole*.
Note: No matter which way it is cooked, rice must not be stirred. To stop the cooking, add a ladleful of cold water to the boiling rice.

RÔTI

A food cooked or roasted in the oven or on a spit.

ROUELLES

Round slices of foods, such as crosswise slices of carrots (see COUPER, p. 57).

ROUX

A mixture of flour and butter, usually of equal proportions, which is cooked until it reaches a desired color. The color then defines the kind of *roux:* a brown *roux,* a blond or golden *roux* and a white *roux.* Brown sauces need a dark brown *roux,* whereas white sauces require a white or blond *roux.*

Note: Strictly speaking, a white *roux* should be very white, but it is possible to let it cook a little longer until it turns barely golden. Aesthetically, the *roux* should be as white as possible, but on the other hand, it also must not have a floury taste—and this can only be eliminated with longer cooking.

RUBAN

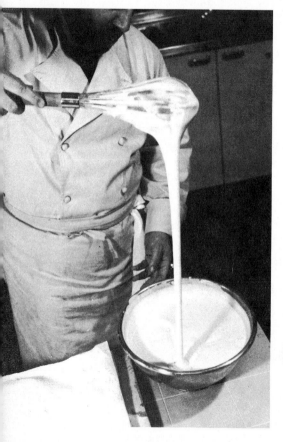

A dough (or any other mixture of foods) is said to *faire un ruban,* or make a ribbon, when it will pour smoothly and thickly, without breaking, in the manner of a ribbon.

SAISIR

To sear a piece of meat or game by cooking it over very high heat at the very beginning of the cooking process.

SALADE

There is an almost unlimited number of mixtures of vegetables, meats, fish and other foods which might be called salads. They can be either raw or cooked. These salads are usually dressed with a French dressing, or *vinaigrette,* or with mayonnaise; or sauceboats of these dressings may be served as accompaniment.

Salad proper is eaten raw and seasoned. It is essential that the greens be very carefully trimmed, washed and drained. The salad must be seasoned at the last moment and not tossed, so that it will not be bruised. Among the best-liked salad greens are romaine, escarole, chicory, endives, field salad and various lettuces such as Batavia lettuce.

Note: Fruits are also used for salads (see MACÉDOINE, p. 111).

SALPICON

A mixture of foods generally cut into dice and bound together with a sauce.

HOW TO MAKE A SALPICON OF TONGUE

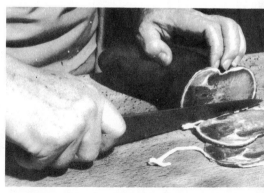

Cut the tongue into rather thick slices.

Trim the slices and cut them into lengthwise strips.

Cut the strips crosswise to make dice.

SANGLER

This term means to surround a mold, or other container that is to be frozen, with crushed ice that has been mixed with coarse salt or saltpeter. For instance, *sangler* a sherbet mold.

SAUCE

Sauces, whatever their nature, are the seasoned liquids that accompany raw or cooked foods.

The *fonds de sauce,* or sauce bases, are very concentrated stocks or consommés made for using in sauces. The most frequently used are the *fonds bruns,* or brown stocks, used to prepare brown sauces, and the *fonds blancs,* or white stocks, used for white sauces (see the section on Stocks, p. 164). A *jus de cuisson,* or pan juice, that has been *lié,* or thickened, becomes a sauce. The most common *jus de cuisson* are the pan juices of roasts and those from *fonds de cuisson,* obtained from any cooked foods.

HOW TO THICKEN A JUS DE CUISSON FROM A ROAST

Transfer the roast to a hot serving plate. Deglaze the pan in which it was cooked with any kind of liquid, such as water, consommé, dry white wine, Madeira, sherry, etc., scraping up all the brown bits at the bottom of the pan with a wooden spoon. Strain the liquid through a fine sieve and return it to the pan. Bring it to the boiling point. In another small bowl, thin a little flour, cornstarch or potato starch with cold water, dry white wine, Madeira, etc., until it is a smooth paste. Stir this mixture into the boiling pan liquid, bring again to the boiling point, stirring all the time until thickened, and remove from the heat.

SAUTER

To sauté foods means to cook them in shallow hot fat. *Sauter* is similar to REVENIR (p. 151), but there is a difference: in sautéing, the pieces of food must not touch each other, and they are cooked over higher heat.

SINGER

This means simply to add a little flour to a sauce in order to thicken it. The amount of flour depends on the nature of the sauce and the way it will be used eventually.

SOUFFLÉ

Soufflés are dishes made from purées that have been thickened with egg yolks; then stiffly beaten egg whites are added to the mixture before it is baked in the oven.

Note: The word soufflé, by extension, is also used to refer to dishes prepared with *mousselines.*

SOUPE DE POISSONS

Fatty fish such as mackerel, herring and skate are not suited for fish soups. Neither are salmon and salmon trout, which are considered too good for it. Eel, however, which is a fatty fish, lends itself well to excellent fish soups, but if other fish are to be added to the eel soup it is better to omit the eel altogether since its flavor would dominate all others.

There are two ways of making fish soups:

CLEAR FISH SOUP

Heat oil and butter in saucepan (about ⅔ oil to ⅓ butter) and cook minced onions and carrots in it until they are very soft, but not brown (see FONDRE, p. 91).

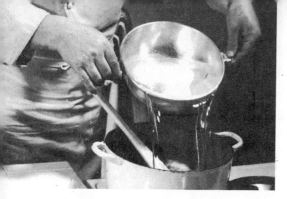

Add dry white wine and water (about ⅕ wine to ⅘ water).

Pasta may be substituted by bread slices. Line the tureen with the bread slices and pour the soup over them.

For 4 persons: ¼ cup oil, 2 tablespoons butter, 2 medium-sized onions, minced, 2 carrots, minced, ¾ cup dry white wine, 3 cups water, 1 pound (or more) fish, 1 *bouquet garni* (p. 46), salt and pepper.

Add the fish, herbs such as parsley and celery, and salt and pepper. Cook over high heat for 15 to 20 minutes.

THICK FISH SOUP

Cook the vegetables in hot oil and butter in the same manner as in the clear fish soup (above). Stir in a little flour, cook for a minute or two, then add the dry white wine, water, salt, pepper, the fish and the *bouquet garni*. Cook for 15 to 20 minutes. Strain the soup through a coarse sieve into another saucepan. Beat together the egg yolks and cream, stir them into the soup, and strain through a fine sieve.

For 4 persons: the same ingredients as in the clear fish soup (above), plus 1 tablespoon flour, 2 egg yolks and ½ cup heavy cream.

SUCRE

Editors' Note: In the cooking of sugar, the different degrees of crystallization which occur at certain temperatures are organized differently in France from the way they are in the United States. The following illustrations refer to the French terminology. So that the reader may compare, the American sugar terminology follows the French one. Furthermore, the French method of boiling sugar, described below, requires the skill of a chef, such as M. Oliver. We recommend home cooks to use a standard candy thermometer to gauge sugar temperatures and to follow the simpler methods outlined in standard American cookbooks. These are more apt to prevent the failures that so easily occur in this tricky technique that requires both skill and very fast work.

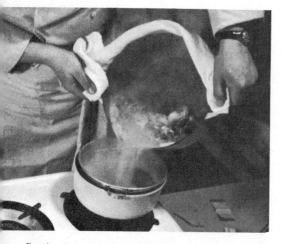

Strain the soup through a coarse sieve into another saucepan. Bring again to the boiling point and add elbow macaroni, noodles, or other suitable pasta. Serve as soon as the pasta is tender.

HOW TO COOK SUGAR

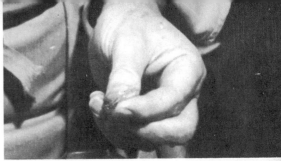

Sugar cooked *au filet*, or thread (first stage), when it may be pulled without breaking.

Boiling sugar is very difficult, because the various stages are gauged with the fingers. The

The *grand soufflé*, or large thread (second stage).

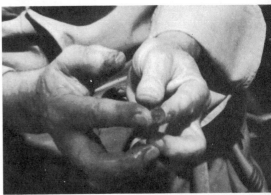

thumb and forefinger must therefore be dipped into cold water before seizing a little of the sugar, and immediately dipped again into cold water in order to prevent burning.

Use an unlined copper kettle or an enamelware cast-iron saucepan.

Sugar cooks to various stages, which depend on its temperature.

The *petit boulé*, or small pearl (third stage), when the sugar can be rolled into a small ball.

The *grand boulé*, or large pearl (fourth stage), when the sugar forms a distinctly larger ball.

Le petit cassé (fifth stage), when the sugar can no longer be rolled into a ball, but will crack.

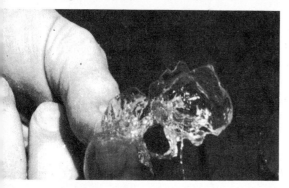

Le grand cassé (sixth stage).

Finally the sugar caramelizes (see CARAMEL, p. 50).

AMERICAN SUGAR TERMINOLOGY

Thread 230° to 234° F. The sugar syrup, dropped into ice water, forms a coarse thread.
Soft Ball 234° to 240° F. The sugar syrup, dropped into ice water, forms a ball but flattens out when picked up with the fingers.
Firm Ball 242° to 248° F. The sugar syrup, dropped into ice water, will form a ball that holds its shape unless pressed.
Hard Ball 250° to 268° F. The sugar syrup, dropped into ice water, will form a ball that holds its shape, but is still malleable.
Soft Crack 270° to 290° F. The sugar syrup, dropped into ice water, will divide into hard threads, which will still bend.
Hard Crack 300° to 310° F. The sugar syrup, dropped into ice water, will divide into hard and brittle threads.
Caramelized Sugar 310° to 338° F. The sugar syrup turns golden between these two temperatures, but blackens at 350° F.

SUER

Faire suer is to cook meat, poultry or game in a tightly closed container until it "sweats," that is, the first drops of moisture appear on it.

TAMISER

This means to strain a food. The strainer used for flours and for puréeing fine fruits is made with a silk netting *(tamis en soie)*. For other foods, coarser metal strainers are used.

Shake the strainer to and fro over paper to let the powdered particles of food fall through.

How to strain a solid food through a metal strainer set over a plate.

Very little of the strained food drops into the plate. It must be scraped off from the underside of the strainer.

TAPISSER

The term *tapisser* means literally "to paper," that is, to cover a food with slices of pork fat or any other similar ingredient.

TERRINE

A container, usually made from earthenware, in which various foods such as meats, game, poultry, etc., are cooked.

By extension, the word *terrine* is also applied to the food itself, for instance, a *terrine of chicken*.

TOAST

Editors' Note: In French, the word "toast" does not necessarily mean only a slice of toasted bread, but also bread cases used to hold different mixtures of foods.

HOW TO MAKE TOASTS

Use firm, white and somewhat stale unsliced bread. Slice it into any desired thickness. Trim off the crusts.

Leaving a ½-inch edge, make a ½-inch cut into the 4 sides of the bread.

Remove the inner part by cutting bias slices. Smooth out the bottom with the point of the knife.

TOMATES, PURÉE DE

Commercially canned tomato paste is often too strong in flavor to be used in certain sauces or dishes. Fresh tomato purée can be easily made by the following method: Peel, seed, and coarsely chop any desired quantity of tomatoes. Put them in a heavy enamelware saucepan and let them slowly reduce over low heat until they form a paste, stirring frequently. Season to taste with sugar, salt and pepper. The purée may also be more highly flavored by cooking the tomatoes with onions, garlic, any desired herbs, etc. It should finally be puréed through a very fine strainer.

TOMBER

Faire tomber (or *faire tomber au beurre*) means to cook vegetables very slowly and gently in hot fat, over low heat, until they are tender but still light colored. On no account must the vegetables be allowed to brown.

TOURNER

This means to cut and trim a vegetable into neat, even-sized pieces so that they may cook evenly. *Tourner* also means to flute and to decorate a vegetable.

HOW TO TRIM OLIVES

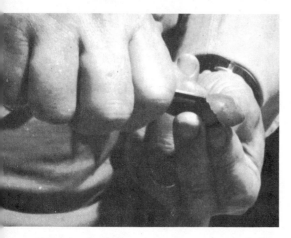

Cut into the olive on the bias, reaching down to the pit.

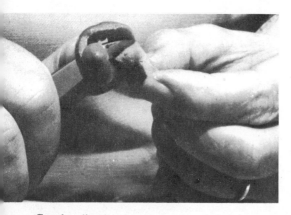

Cut the olive into a spiral, around the pit. The trimmed olive, put back into its original shape.

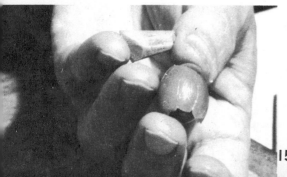

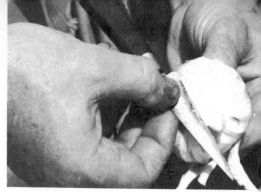

To flute mushrooms, use a small sharp knife and make shallow cuts from the center to the edge of the cap, twisting the mushroom around as you do so.

TRAVAILLER

Travailler means to work a liquid by stirring it until it becomes perfectly smooth.

To *travailler* a stuffing or a dough means to work it with the hands, a spatula, or a wooden spoon until it is absolutely smooth.

A dough which *travaille,* or is working, describes a dough that is rising.

TROUSSER

The term means to truss a chicken or other poultry, that is, to tie its legs and wings with string so that the bird will keep its shape during cooking (see BRIDER, p. 46).

VANNER

The word is used to describe stirring or shaking a sauce to make it smooth and to prevent formation of a skin on top while it cools.

VAPEUR

The word means steam, and cooking *à la vapeur* is to place food into a steaming basket or on a rack and set this over boiling water. The rising steam cooks the food. The saucepan is usually covered during steaming.

VEAU

The veal most prized in France is between 2 and 3 months old, with white meat that has a pinkish tinge to it. The fat of veal is white and smells slightly of milk. Normandy specializes in raising veal.

Editors' Note: The following suggestions for cooking veal are based on French cuts, which are different from American cuts. The terms used for the French cuts in the translations are their nearest American equivalents. Because of the difference in cutting and dressing the meat, the cut identified by the American term may not be quite the same as the French cut.

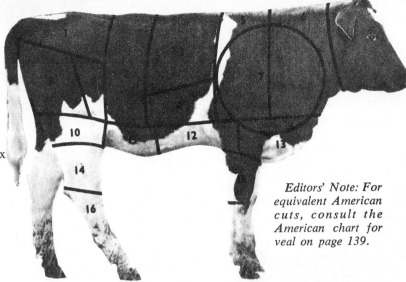

1. Quasi
2. Longe
3. Carré raccourci
4. Haut de côtelettes
5. Côtes découvertes
6. Collier
7. Épaule
8. Sous-noix
9. Noix pâtissière
10. Nerveux de sous-noix
11. Flanchet
12. Tendron
13. Poitrine
14. Jarret
15. Jarret de devant
16. Crosse

Editors' Note: For equivalent American cuts, consult the American chart for veal on page 139.

CUTS TO BE COOKED WITH A SAUCE

Collet, neck; *poitrine*, breast; *pieds*, calf's feet; *jarret*, shank.

CUTS TO BE BOILED

Jarrets, shanks; *pieds*, calf's feet; *tête*, head.

LA NOIX PÂTISSIÈRE is a part of the leg corresponding to the sirloin tip or knuckle in a leg of beef. Comparing with cross cuts of leg of beef, you have: top round (*noix de veau*); bottom round (*sous-noix de veau*); sirloin tip or knuckle (*noix pâtissière*). The *noix pâtissière* may be roasted as a whole or cut into chops and scallops.

LE QUASI, the hip section with aitchbone, the sirloin, is cooked like the *noix pâtissière*.

LE CARRÉ DE VEAU, the rib section with the first rib chops showing in front; 4th to 9th vertebrae, the best piece.

CUTS TO ROAST AND BRAISE

Noix, top round; *longe,* loin; *quasi,* sirloin; *rouelles,* cross-cut rounds of the leg; *poitrine,* breast; *selle,* loin.

CUTS TO GRILL OR BROIL OR PAN-FRY

Côtes, rib chops; *noix,* top round—the fleshy upper part of the leg, and the *longe,* loin, cut into scallops; the *filet,* fillet, cut into *médaillons* and *noisettes.*

LA SOUS-NOIX, the bottom round including the eye, the upper part at the right, may be roasted in its entirety. Usually this cut is made into scallops. The *sousnoix* is excellent when larded and braised as a *fricandeau.*

LE CARRÉ or FILET consists of covered ribs (upper part of the cut) and the open ribs (lower part of the cut). This is the loin section, usually, with fillet and loin strip, but sometimes the rib section as shown here. The *filet* is the piece including the 8th to 13th vertebrae, going up to the neck.

VENAISON

This Frenchified version of the English word "venison" designates animals of the chase that are edible: stag, deer, wild boar, etc. Wild rabbits and hares are called *basse-venaison*, or minor venison.

VOLAILLE

The word designates barnyard fowl. It includes rabbits since they are usually raised along with the birds.

Editors' Note: The following specifications apply to French poultry.

Poulardes are hens or roasting chickens that weigh from 3 to 6 pounds. They are fatter than spring chickens and are also somewhat less flavorful. *Poulardes* are appreciated when poached, but they may also be roasted or pot-roasted. They may also be prepared in the *chaud-froid* way, made into loaves, pâtés and terrines.

Poulets are spring chickens. Various regions of France prepare their various parts differently: in the Chalosse and in the Landes, their *tripes* are cleaned and fricasseed.

In the countryside, the blood is used to make *la sanguette,* which, with the addition of vinegar to prevent coagulation, is used to thicken wine sauces. The neck, wing tips, combs and kidneys are also used.

It is very difficult to recognize a good bird. Yardsticks differ; some birds, such as those from Bresse or Houdan, must have blue-gray feet. Others must have a pliable beak and breastbone. The appearance of the birds is also important: thin drumsticks and thin skin speak of a poor quality. The best kinds of chickens are the Crèvecoeur, Mans, Bresse *(poulet-reine),* Houdan (which weigh as much as 7 pounds), Faverolles, Chalosse, etc.

Chapons, capons, are castrated young roosters which have been fattened.

OTHER POULTRY

These include ducks, trukeys, pigeons, guinea hens and geese. Ducks *(canards)* from Rouen or Nantua are well suited to delicate dishes served with young vegetables. Their flesh is tender and flavorful. Ducks from Nantua are smaller than those from Rouen, and they may be roasted, provided they are young and tender. Older ducks may be turned into ragouts, pâtés or galantines.

Turkeys *(dindons),* also called *dindes* (hens), or *dindonneaux* (young turkeys), are prepared like *poulardes* or *poulets.*

Pigeons (the varieties called *biset* and *pa-lombe)* are called squab on menus and must without fail, be young and tender.

Guinea hens *(pintades,* also called at time *faisan de Bohême,* Bohemian pheasant) are cooked like *poulardes* and *poulets.* A young guinea hen (called *pintadeau)* is prepared like pheasant or young partridge.

Ordinary geese (which weigh up to just over 8 pounds) are cooked like any other birds, but geese from Toulouse (which may weigh up to 20 pounds) are used for *confits* or potted goose; *foie gras* comes from this kind of goose.

LE LAPIN

Rabbits *(lapins)* at the age of 3 months are young and tender, with a thick-set body and forelegs that are rather thin and very flexible. The claws are short. An older rabbit may be used for making terrines. A freshly killed rabbit cannot be cooked for two days, but it may be marinated.

HOW TO ROAST A CHICKEN

Salt the bird only on the inside, in the cavity. If skin is salted, the butter used to coat the skin will take the salt along when it drips into the pan and make the pan juices too salty. Butter or grease the bird generously and put it over high heat if it is to be cooked on a spit, or into a preheated 375° F. oven. Brown the bird without basting it. As a matter of fact, basting should begin only when the bird is three-quarters cooked; basting produces a layer of air between skin and meat, and this layer of air puffs up the skin. Also, continuous basting opens up the pores of the bird, thus letting the richest juices ooze out.

HOW TO POACH A CHICKEN

This method preserves the full flavor. After the bird has been stuffed and trussed, put it into a fresh or water-freshened pig's caul. Tie the caul tightly with string to close it. Put the wrapped chicken into a large saucepan and cover it with hot chicken stock or consommé. Cook over medium heat, with the liquid at a simmer, until it is done, and take it out of the pot. Let it cool in the pig's caul if it is to be served cold, or take it out of the caul immediately, carve and serve.

ZESTER

To cut off the orange or yellow part of the skin of an orange, lemon or other similar fruit. This is done with a knife or a vegetable parer, and every trace of the white membrane must be scraped off the *zeste* or rind, the outer part of the skin of the fruit.

II

GOOD DISHES
GOOD RECIPES

Bons Plats
Bonnes Recettes

1
SOUPS AND STOCKS
Potages et Fonds

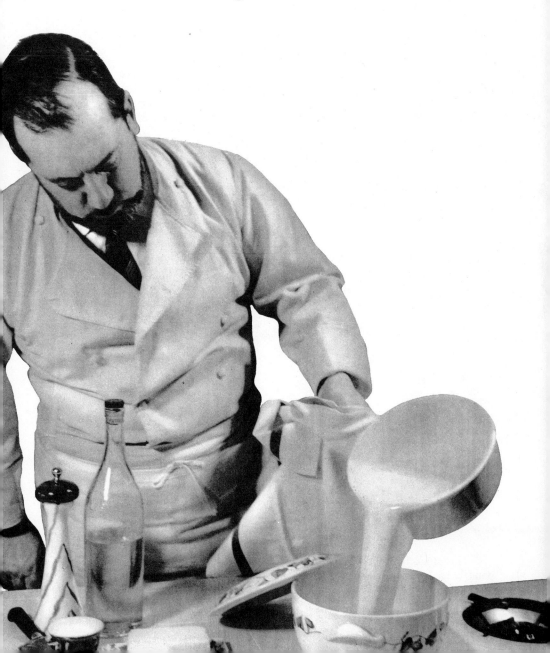

STOCKS

Fonds

Fonds de cuisine, that is, kitchen stocks, are used for braising or stewing meats, fish or vegetables; or as the base for sauces, soups, etc.

Brown Stock / LE FOND BRUN

Put the meat, bones and vegetables into a roasting pan and roast them in a preheated 450° F. oven for about 15 minutes, until they are browned in color. Take care that the vegetables do not scorch; remove them before the meat and bones if they brown too quickly. Transfer all three to a deep kettle. Add the garlic, thyme, bay leaf, parsley, wine, water and tomato paste. Bring very, very slowly to the boiling point and simmer over low heat for 4 hours or longer without seasoning. The more slowly the stock cooks, the clearer the final broth will be. Any scum that rises to the surface should be continually removed throughout the cooking. When the stock is reduced and of a good flavor, strain it through a coarse sieve and then through a fine sieve or damp cheesecloth. It may be seasoned with salt, if desired, but remember that it is frequently reduced in preparing various sauces and that the seasoning can easily be done later on.

FOR ABOUT 2 QUARTS:

2 **pounds lean beef (brisket or shin), cut into cubes**	½ **teaspoon dried thyme**
2 **pounds beef bones**	1 **bay leaf**
1 **veal knuckle**	3 **parsley sprigs**
2 **carrots, sliced**	1 **cup dry white wine**
2 **large unpeeled onions, sliced**	4 **quarts cold water**
2 **celery stalks, sliced**	2 **tablespoons tomato paste**
1 **garlic clove**	**Salt**

How to thicken (*lier*) a brown stock:

Bring 2 quarts of strained stock to the boiling point over high heat. Combine 3 tablespoons of cornstarch with 3 tablespoons of cold water and stir them into the boiling stock. Blend well. Let the stock simmer for a few minutes and remove it from heat, or let it stand over very low heat without boiling it.

Brown Poultry Stock /

This stock is prepared like ordinary brown stock (above), but use 3 pounds of poultry backs, necks, and giblets in place of the beef meat and bones. The veal knuckle may be used for added flavor if desired.

/ *Brown Veal Stock*

Prepare in the same way as ordinary brown stock (p. 164), substituting shoulder of veal and veal bones for the beef meat and bones.

LE FOND BLANC / *White Stock*

It is possible to make a white stock in the same manner as a brown stock, without browning the meat, bones and vegetables, although beef is never used in a white stock —only veal or chicken. Another way of making it is to follow the procedure for *sauce espagnole* (p. 760), by first sautéing the chopped vegetables gently in the butter. When they are soft and barely golden, add the meat and bones, the *bouquet garni,* clove and the water. Bring very slowly to a simmer and then cook gently for 4 hours or longer. Veal releases a great deal of scum and as it rises to the surface even greater care should be taken to remove it from a white stock than from a brown one. When the stock is reduced and of a good flavor, strain it through a coarse sieve and then through a fine one or through cheesecloth. Season, if desired, with a little salt.

FOR ABOUT 2 QUARTS:

3 to 4 pounds shoulder of veal, cut into cubes	2 large onions, peeled and sliced
1 veal knuckle	2 celery stalks, sliced
2 pounds veal bones	1 Bouquet Garni (p. 46)
2 carrots, sliced	1 clove
2 leeks (white part only), sliced	4 quarts cold water
	Salt

/ *White Poultry Stock*

Prepare in the same manner as a white stock (above), but use 3 pounds of chicken or other poultry backs, necks and giblets in place of the veal meat and bones. Or use a 4-pound stewing fowl. If desired, the veal knuckle may be retained for added flavor.

LE FOND (OU FUMET) DE GIBIER / *Game Stock*

Prepare in the same manner as an ordinary brown stock (p. 164), substituting 4 pounds of cracked bones, meat trimmings and lights of any desired game for the beef meat and beef and veal bones. A game stock should be additionally seasoned with a *bouquet garni* of 5 or 6 juniper berries and a sprig of fresh sage or ½ teaspoon dried sage.

Fish Stock / LE FOND (OU FUMET) DE POISSON

First Method:

Omit the butter and oil and put all the other ingredients into a large saucepan. Bring to the boiling point, lower the heat, and simmer for about 30 minutes, or until the stock is reduced and has a good flavor. Strain through a fine sieve.

Second Method:

Heat the butter and the oil in a large saucepan and add the vegetables. Sauté gently until the vegetables are tender and slightly golden. Add the fish trimmings and bones and all the other ingredients. Simmer over medium heat for about 30 minutes, skimming frequently. When the stock is reduced and has a good flavor, strain it through a very fine sieve or through a triple layer of cheesecloth. If desired season very lightly with salt.

FOR ABOUT 3½ CUPS:

2 tablespoons butter
1 tablespoon peanut oil
1 large onion, peeled and sliced
1 celery stalk, sliced
1 carrot, sliced

2 pounds fish bones and trimmings
  (flounder, whiting, or halibut;
  do not use fat fish)
1 cup dry white wine
4 cups cold water
1 Bouquet Garni (p. 46)
Salt

Brown Stock for Aspics / LE FOND DE GELÉE

Make a brown stock (usually a brown stock is preferred to a white one for aspics because of its color) as described above. If possible use a calf's foot in making the stock. Salt the stock sparsely. Simmer it over medium heat until it is reduced by about one third and has a strong flavor. Every trace of fat must be removed from the stock before using it for an aspic.

To find out if the stock has the necessary consistency for jellying, pour a little of it into a saucer and chill it. If it jells satisfactorily in 10 or 15 minutes, clarify it by the method described on page 53. It is then ready to use.

If it does not jell satisfactorily, it may be reduced further and tested again, or a little unflavored gelatin may be softened in cold water and added to the hot stock; then test again. The exact amount of gelatin depends on how well the stock jells without the gelatin. Remember that 1 tablespoon or commercial package of gelatin will jell 2 cups of any liquid; thus, if the stock seems to half-jell when tested, use no more than ½ tablespoon of gelatin for each 2 cups of stock. Avoid using too much gelatin, even to be safe, since excess gelatin gives an aspic a rubbery and unpleasant texture.

Frequently a stock for aspic is flavored with sherry or Madeira. Use about 2 tablespoons of wine for each cup of stock.

Generally speaking, clarifying (p. 53) a stock for aspic should be the final step before using it, since even the addition of salt can cloud the stock slightly and the objective, of course, is to have it crystal clear.

LE FOND DE GELÉE DE POISSON / *Fish Stock for Aspics*

Prepare in the same manner as a brown stock for aspics, using, of course, a fish stock (p. 166) in place of the brown stock.

SOUPS

Potages et Soupes

Unless otherwise noted, each of the soups in this section will serve 4 persons.

Consommés

There are three kinds of basic consommés: clear beef consommé, chicken consommé; and *pot-au-feu*.

CONSOMMÉ BLANC DE VIANDE / *Beef Consommé*

Put the water, meats and bones in a big earthenware pot *(marmite)* or a deep kettle. Bring slowly to the boiling point, skim, season with the salt, and skim again.

Prepare the variety of vegetables, chopping them: carrots, turnip, celery and leeks. Add all of these to the pot, together with the whole unpeeled head of garlic, the *bouquet garni,* and the onions stuck with cloves. Add more water if necessary; all the ingredients should be well covered.

Bring slowly to the boiling point, skim, and simmer very slowly for 4 hours, skimming as necessary. It should reduce to about 6 cups and be of a good strong flavor.

At the end of the cooking time, correct the seasoning and strain through a fine sieve. In order to obtain a very clear consommé, degrease it as described on page 76, and if the consommé is not sufficiently clear, clarify it as described on page 53.

FOR ABOUT 6 CUPS:

3 quarts (or more) cold water
1 pound lean beef (brisket or shin), cut into cubes
1 pound veal shoulder, cut into cubes
2 pounds beef bones, cracked
1 veal knuckle and/or 1 or 2 other veal bones
1 teaspoon salt

2 carrots
1 turnip
3 celery stalks
3 leeks
1 garlic head, unpeeled
1 Bouquet Garni (p. 46)
2 large onions, each stuck with 1 clove

EDITORS' NOTE: *In older French classical cooking a* bouillon *became a* consommé *when it was clarified. Nowadays we tend to think of* consommé *as a very strong* bouillon *or* bouillon-double. *In any case, the soup above will be splendidly flavored and, if properly clarified, sparkling clear.*

Chicken Consommé / CONSOMMÉ BLANC DE VOLAILLE

Prepare in the same manner as the beef consommé (above), but substitute about 2 pounds of chicken parts—backs, necks, and giblets—or a 3- to 4-pound fowl—for the lean beef and beef bones. If a whole fowl is used, more water will be necessary to cover it. When the fowl is tender, after about 1½ hours, remove the meat from the bones, reserving it for another use; return the bones to the pot and continue cooking until the broth is well reduced and has a good flavor.

Pot-au-Feu / LE POT-AU-FEU

A *pot-au-feu* is a consommé that is somewhat richer than clear beef consommé.

Put the water in a large earthenware pot *(marmite)* and bring it to the boiling point. Add the beef shin, rump, beef bones and veal knuckle. As soon as the water boils again, skim off any scum that rises to the surface, season with salt, and skim again.

Add the vegetables: 1 large unpeeled onion which has been roasted in the oven until it is almost black (this gives a fine color to the broth); another, peeled and stuck with cloves; the leeks, celery, carrots, turnip, *bouquet garni* and garlic. Add more water if necessary; all ingredients should be well covered.

Simmer very gently for 3 to 4 hours, or until the beef is tender. Remove the beef and serve it with a little of the broth or reserve it for any desired use.

Continue simmering the broth until it is reduced to about 4 cups and has a good strong flavor. Strain it through a fine sieve, degrease it (p. 76) and, if desired, clarify it (p. 53).

FOR ABOUT 6 CUPS:

3 quarts (or more) water	2 cloves
1 pound lean beef (brisket or shin)	2 leeks, sliced
2 pounds rump of beef	2 celery stalks, sliced
2 pounds beef bones	2 carrots, sliced
1 veal knuckle	1 turnip, sliced
2 teaspoons salt	1 Bouquet Garni (p. 46)
2 large onions	1 garlic head, unpeeled

COMMENT LIER LES POTAGES / *How to Thicken Soups*

Soups may be thickened with flour, cornstarch, potato flour, egg yolks, or cream. It is possible to thicken soups with one or more mashed potatoes, but potatoes do not take well to reheating and they may also give a coarse taste to the soup. If the soup is to be used at a later time than when being made, such as in the evening or the next day, do not use potatoes on any account.

Proportions:

Potatoes: ½ cup mashed potatoes for 4 cups soup.

Flour: 1 to 1½ tablespoons for each cup of soup. (Generally, it's necessary to make a *roux* or *beurre manié* using these proportions.)

Cornstarch: 1 teaspoon for each cup of soup.

Potato flour: 1 teaspoon for each cup of soup.

Egg yolks: 1 egg yolk for each cup of soup.

Cream and egg yolks: about ¼ cup heavy cream and 1 egg yolk to each cup of soup.

COMMENT GARNIR LES POTAGES / *How to Garnish Soups*

There are any number of soup garnishes: royal garnish, poached eggs, fine noodles, pastas, vegetables, croutons, flowerets, leaves of herbs, *quenelles* and *profiteroles.*

Royal garnish: beat together 1 small whole egg, 1 egg yolk, and 6 tablespoons heavy cream and season with salt and grated nutmeg. Strain through a fine sieve. Pour the mixture into a buttered small flat baking dish so that it is about ½ inch deep in the dish. Bake in a preheated 350° F. oven for about 15 minutes. Unmold, cool, and cut into dice.

For deviled toast, croutons, and other garnishes made with toasted bread: sprinkle small rounds of bread with a mixture of cayenne pepper and grated cheese, and bake in a preheated 400° F. oven until golden brown.

Profiteroles: these are small cream puffs (see p. 711) which may be filled, depending on taste, with a *sauce velouté,* a purée of vegetables, or a *sauce Mornay.*

Consommé Borghese | CONSOMMÉ BORGHÈSE

Prepare the chicken consommé and clarify it as described on page 53.

Simmer the asparagus tips in boiling salted water until they are tender, about 5 minutes, and drain them. Simmer the chicken breast in the stock in a covered saucepan for about 8 minutes, drain it, and cut the meat into julienne strips.

A few minutes before serving time, bring the consommé to a boil and add the asparagus and chicken strips.

4 cups Chicken Consommé (p. 168)   **½ chicken breast, boned**
20 asparagus tips   **½ cup White Stock (p. 165)**

Consommé Célestine |

Use a clarified beef or chicken consommé which you'll serve with *crêpes* cut into thin strips.

When you are making the *crêpes,* add a handful of finely shredded parsley and chervil to the batter. Make very thin *crêpes* and cut them into small strips as soon as they have been sautéed. Put the *crêpes* into 4 soup plates, and pour the very hot consommé over them.

4 cups Beef or Chicken Consommé   **1 tablespoon chopped parsley**
(p. 167), clarified   **1 tablespoon chopped chervil**
4 Crêpes (p. 740)

Jellied Consommé | CONSOMMÉ EN GELÉE

The simplest and the best way to make a consommé of jellying consistency is to use chicken feet—one for each cup of consommé—if you can find them.

The chicken feet are added to the other ingredients when you are making the chicken consommé, which is then clarified as described on page 53. If you can't find chicken feet, use unflavored gelatin, instead, in the proportions and manner described for Brown Stock for Aspics (p. 166).

4 cups Chicken Consommé (p. 167)
Unflavored gelatin

Consommé Florence |

Clarify some *pot-au-feu* broth to make consommé as described on page 53. Pour it boiling hot into a tureen containing peeled whole cooked chipolata sausages, that is, cooked tiny link sausages. Sprinkle with the chervil.

4 cups Pot-au-Feu (p. 168)   **2 tablespoons chopped chervil**
4 chipolata or tiny link sausages

CONSOMMÉ CÉLESTINE

Cut the crêpes *into fine strips in this fashion: pile up the* crêpes, *one on top of the other, hold them lightly so they will not slip, and cut them with a very sharp knife.*

Then all you do is pull them apart gently with the fingers and put the strips into the soup plates.

JELLIED CONSOMMÉ
LE CONSOMME EN GELEE

Make the aspic with chicken feet or with unflavored gelatin. If you use gelatin, soak it in cold water to soften it before adding it to the hot consommé.

Double Consommé | CONSOMMÉ DOUBLE

This is a consommé made like any other: beef, chicken or *pot-au-feu,* but with double strength, that is, with additional lean meat or poultry, as well as vegetables. The consommé is then simmered with these additional ingredients for 1 hour, or even longer, to reduce it to very strong flavor. It is then strained and clarified as described on page 53.

Sherry or Madeira is added to this consommé after clarification.

At the very last moment, at serving time, you may also add the juice of 1 lemon.

6 cups Beef or Chicken Consommé (p. 167) or Pot-au-Feu (p. 168)
1 pound very lean raw beef or chicken meat, ground
1 carrot, sliced
1 leek, sliced
1 celery stalk, sliced
½ cup sherry or Madeira
Juice of 1 lemon

Consommé Flavored with Celery |

CONSOMMÉ AU FUMET DE CÉLERI

Prepare a Double Consommé (above), but without adding sherry or Madeira. Before you clarify it, add a generous cup of finely sliced celery and several sprigs of fresh tarragon or any other herbs.

Consommé Madrilène |

This is a basic consommé which is clarified, as described on page 53, together with the tomatoes, beef and leek. But you must be careful: too much tomato will dilute the consommé and thus lower its quality while too little tomato will neither flavor nor color. The trick is to use tomatoes which have been chopped fine and well drained. This has also the advantage of not making the consommé too acid.

4 cups Beef or Chicken Consommé (p. 167)
½ pound tomatoes, peeled, seeded, drained and chopped
½ pound lean beef, ground
1 small leek, sliced

Consommé Printanier |

To 4 cups of Beef or Chicken Consommé (p. 167) add a mixture of finely diced vegetables such as green snap beans, baby carrots, turnips, sorrel and also peas. Precook the vegetables in lightly salted water; you'll need about 2 tablespoons of each.

Cream Soups

Soupes à la Crème

VELOUTÉ DE VOLAILLE / *Cream of Chicken Soup*

Prepare the chicken consommé and add the giblets to it. Let it cool to luke-warm.

Prepare a white *roux* with the butter and flour and gradually add the luke-warm consommé to it. Simmer it over low heat for about 30 minutes. Strain it through a very fine sieve.

At serving time, stir in the cream; or mix the cream with the optional egg yolks, add it to the soup off the heat, and then stir it constantly over low heat until slightly thickened. Season to taste with salt and pepper.

5 cups Chicken Consommé (p. 168)	½ cup heavy cream
½ pound chicken giblets	Optional: 2 egg yolks
4 tablespoons butter	Salt
4 tablespoons flour	Freshly ground white pepper

Note: When using this soup as the base for cream of asparagus, carrot, or other soups, either omit the egg yolks, or add them only at the very last as described above.

/ *Cream Soup with Chicken Wings*

POTAGE CRÉMÉ AUX AILERONS DE VOLAILLE

Heat 4 tablespoons of the butter over low heat and cook the onion, carrot, celery, turnip and parsley roots in it until they are very soft but not golden or browned. Mash the chicken wing tips and add them to the vegetables. Sauté gently for 5 minutes. Add the cream of chicken soup and the *bouquet garni* and season lightly with salt and a very little pepper, or even no pepper at all. Cover the saucepan and cook the soup over low heat for about 30 minutes. Remove the chicken wing tips and discard the *bouquet garni*.

Strain the soup through a very fine sieve or purée briefly in a blender. Make a white *roux* with the remaining butter and the flour and gradually add the puréed soup to it, stirring until thickened. Bring it again to the boiling point, check the seasoning, and add a dash of cayenne.

6 tablespoons butter	4 cups Cream of Chicken Soup
1 onion, chopped	(above)
1 carrot, chopped	1 Bouquet Garni (p. 46)
1 celery stalk, chopped	Salt
½ turnip, chopped	Freshly ground white pepper
2 parsley roots, chopped	2 tablespoons flour
12 chicken wing tips or the giblets of 2 chickens	Cayenne pepper

Note: One can make this kind of soup with giblets excepting the liver, wing tips, necks, feet, or the hearts or gizzards alone, but wing tips give a more delicate flavor and since they are readily available one can easily indulge in this sort of a recipe.

Cream of Asparagus Soup I / CRÈME ARGENTEUIL

Peel the asparagus and cut off the tips. Blanch the tips, that is, cook them in boiling salted water until barely tender, about 5 minutes. In the same way, blanch the peeled asparagus stalks. Simmer the stalks with the cream of chicken soup in a covered saucepan for about 30 minutes. Purée the asparagus stalks and soup in a blender or food mill and stir in the *crème fraîche* or cream. Put the mixture back into the saucepan and return it to the heat. Add the asparagus tips and simmer the soup slowly until very hot. Season to taste with salt and pepper.

2 pounds asparagus	⅔ cup Crème Fraîche (p. 666) or
4 cups Cream of Chicken Soup	heavy cream
(p. 173)	Salt
	Freshly ground white pepper

Cream of Asparagus Soup II / CRÈME D'ASPERGES

Peel the asparagus. Cut off the tips, the very tender ends only, and cook them in boiling salted water for 10 minutes. Drain them and rinse under running cold water. Reserve them.

Cook the peeled asparagus stalks in the boiling consommé in a covered casserole for about 20 minutes, or until the asparagus is very tender. Force the asparagus with the consommé through a food mill or purée briefly in a blender.

Make a *roux* with the butter and flour, gradually add the asparagus purée, and cook for about 10 minutes, or until the mixture is smooth and thick. Stir frequently.

While the soup is cooking, make a *liaison,* that is, beat together the egg yolks and the *crème* and bind the soup with them: stir one fourth of the soup into the beaten egg and *crème,* stirring constantly with a wooden spoon. Then stir this mixture into the remaining soup and heat it gently, stirring constantly, until it is slightly thickened. Season to taste with salt and pepper. Add the asparagus tips. Pour the soup into a heated tureen and serve very hot.

1½ pounds asparagus	4 egg yolks
4 cups Chicken Consommé (p. 168)	½ cup Crème Fraîche (p. 666)
3 tablespoons butter	Salt
3 tablespoons flour	Freshly ground white pepper

Cream of Avocado Soup / CRÈME D'AVOCATS

Pour the cream of chicken soup into a saucepan and bring it to the boiling point. Purée the avocado by first pressing it through a food mill and then through a fine sieve. Bind this purée with the egg yolk. Stir one fourth of the hot soup into the avocado purée and blend well. Pour this mixture back into the saucepan and heat gently. Season it rather heavily with salt and pepper. This soup may be served with fried croutons.

4 cups Cream of Chicken Soup
  (p. 173)
1 medium-sized avocado
1 egg yolk

Salt
Freshly ground white pepper
Croutons (p. 62)

CRÈME DE CAROTTES / *Cream of Carrot Soup*

Peel the carrots and cut the orange part only into small dice; reserve the inner yellow parts. Cook the dice in boiling salted water for about 10 minutes, or until they are tender.

Cook the yellow parts of the carrots in the cream of chicken soup for about 30 minutes. Press the carrots and the soup through a food mill and stir in the *crème fraîche* or cream. Reheat it just until very hot and then add the cooked diced carrots. Season to taste with salt and pepper.

12 medium-sized carrots
4 cups Cream of Chicken Soup
  (p. 173)

⅔ cup Crème Fraîche (p. 666) or
  heavy cream
Salt
Freshly ground white pepper

CRÈME DE CRESSON / *Cream of Watercress Soup*

Trim the watercress, wash it, and shake it dry. Reserve about ¼ cup of leaves and blanch them in boiling water for 1 minute.

Simmer the rest of the watercress and the butter in a covered saucepan over low heat for about 10 minutes. Add the cream of chicken soup, bring to the boiling point, and simmer gently for 10 minutes. Purée the mixture through a fine sieve or in a blender and then return to the saucepan.

Add the chicken consommé or milk and bring the soup once more to the boiling point. Season to taste with salt and pepper. Pour the soup into a tureen, stir in the cream, and add the blanched watercress leaves.

2 bunches of watercress
3 tablespoons butter
3½ cups Cream of Chicken Soup
  (p. 173)
¾ cup Chicken Consommé (p. 168)
  or milk

Salt
Freshly ground white pepper
¾ cup Crème Fraîche (p. 666) or
  heavy cream

VELOUTÉ DE CHOU-FLEUR / *Cream of Cauliflower Soup*

Blanch the cauliflower: break the head into flowerets and put them in a saucepan with cold water to cover. Bring it to the boiling point, cook for 1 minute, drain, and rinse the flowerets under running cold water.

Wash the leek, slice it into small rounds, and cook them in the butter until they are soft. Stir in the flour, cook for a few minutes until it is golden, and add the boiling water. Add the blanched cauliflower, season to taste with salt and pepper, and simmer for 20 minutes.

Strain the soup through a food mill or purée it in a blender. Stir in the *crème fraîche,* correct the seasoning, and serve with the croutons.

1 small head of cauliflower	Salt
1 large leek, white part only	Freshly ground white pepper
2 tablespoons butter	½ cup Crème Fraîche (p. 666)
2 tablespoons flour	1 cup Croutons (p. 62)
3½ cups boiling water	

Cream of Chicken Soup with Tapioca /
VELOUTÉ DE VOLAILLE AU TAPIOCA

Prepare the chicken stock and let it cool to lukewarm. Make a white *roux* with the butter and flour and gradually add the lukewarm chicken stock to it. Simmer the soup over low heat for 30 minutes. Strain it through a very fine sieve. Add 1 teaspoon of tapioca for each person. Bring the soup to the boiling point, and let it stand in a warm corner of the kitchen stove without boiling. At serving time add the cream and season to taste with salt and pepper.

5 cups White Poultry Stock (p. 165)	4 teaspoons tapioca
	¼ cup heavy cream
3 tablespoons butter	Salt
3 tablespoons flour	Freshly ground white pepper

Cream of Curry Soup / CRÈME AU-CURRY

Heat the chicken consommé in a saucepan and bring it to the boiling point. Remove from the heat.

Prepare a *liaison,* that is, blend together the cream, egg yolks, curry powder and lemon juice. Beat a ladleful of hot consommé into this *liaison* and then beat the mixture into the remaining consommé in the saucepan. Return to low heat and stir constantly without boiling until slightly thickened. Season to taste with salt and pepper.

4 cups Chicken Consommé (p. 168)	1 tablespoon curry powder (or more to taste)
¼ cup Crème Fraîche (p. 666) or heavy cream	1 tablespoon lemon juice
4 egg yolks	Salt
	Freshly ground white pepper

Cream of Herb Soup / CRÈME AUX HERBES

Blanch a small *bouquet* of *fines herbes* in boiling water for 2 minutes; tarragon, parsley and chervil should be the prevailing ones. The tarragon and chervil leaves may be left whole, that is, unchopped, if desired.

Tomato Consommé with Fines Herbes

Consommé au Fumet d'Herbes Fines

Tomato Consommé with Fines Herbes

Consommé au Fumet d'Herbes Fines

MAKE A GOOD beef consommé, using three of the tomatoes in the preparation to give it a light tomato flavor, and add to the usual ingredients the special herbs listed below. Cut the rest of the tomatoes into tiny dice or balls. They should be the size of salmon's eggs. Pour the consommé into soup bowls and serve the tomato balls separately in a bowl.

The consommé should be boiling hot because the tomatoes will always cool it a little.

For 4 persons:

4 cups Beef Consommé (p. 167)
8 ripe tomatoes
1 tablespoon each of freshly chopped rosemary, savory
and tarragon, or ½ teaspoon of each dried

Night Owls' Onion Soup

Soupe à l'Oignon des Noctambules

Night Owls' Onion Soup

Soupe à l'Oignon des Noctambules

COOK THE ONIONS in the combined oil and butter until they are beginning to turn golden. Sprinkle the flour over the onions and cook them, stirring constantly, until they are light brown. Stir in the hot consommé and simmer for 10 minutes. Season to taste with salt and pepper.

Now you may do one of two things:

1. Strain the soup and discard the onions. Bind the soup with half of the thick *sauce béchamel* and spread the remaining *béchamel* over the sautéed bread slices.

2. Leave the onions in the soup and serve it just as it is.

In either case, put a few of the sautéed bread slices in each serving of soup, sprinkle with grated cheese and cayenne, and brown under the broiler.

For 8 persons:

6 medium-sized onions, minced
2 tablespoons peanut oil
6 tablespoons butter
3 tablespoons flour
8 cups boiling Chicken
    Consommé (p. 168)
Salt
Freshly ground white
    pepper

Optional: 2 cups thick
    Sauce Béchamel (p. 761)
1 loaf of French bread,
    cut into slices and
    sautéed in butter until
    golden
2 cups grated Swiss or
    Parmesan cheese
Cayenne pepper

German Beer Soup

Soupe Allemande à la Bière

German Beer Soup
Soupe Allemande à la Bière

MELT THE BUTTER in a casserole, stir in the flour, and cook for 2 minutes, stirring constantly. Cool the mixture. Stir in the beer. Mix well and season with the nutmeg, salt to taste, the ginger and the cinnamon. Return to high heat and cook for 15 minutes, stirring constantly.

Make a *liaison* by beating together the egg yolks, the wine, sugar and grated lemon rind. Stir a few spoonfuls of the hot soup into the *liaison*, beating vigorously. Then add the mixture to the soup in the casserole, which should be barely simmering. Stir over very low heat for 3 minutes, but do not allow to boil.

Serve the soup in a tureen, with the toast on the side.

For 4 persons:

3 tablespoons butter	2 egg yolks
3 tablespoons flour	2 tablespoons dry white
4 cups light or dark beer	wine
Pinch of grated nutmeg	1 tablespoon sugar
Salt	Grated rind of ½ lemon
1 teaspoon ground ginger	8 to 10 slices of toast
¼ teaspoon ground	
cinnamon	

Japanese Soup

Soupe Japonaise

Japanese Soup

Soupe Japonaise

PROPERLY SPEAKING, THIS is not a soup. Fondues being much in fashion, this dish should really be called a "soup-fondue." I am not going to give you the exact Japanese recipe. What I am going to give you is a French adaptation.

First of all, prepare the chicken consommé. Cut all of the meat of the chicken into slices or large dice.

Have your butcher cut the sirloin across the grain into the thinnest possible slices.

Slice the mushrooms.

Portion out the chicken slices, the sirloin slices and the mushrooms on 4 individual serving plates. Put the blanched spinach and the softened Chinese noodles in separate serving bowls.

Put a fondue pot filled with a little of the hot consommé in the middle of the table. Light the flame under it. Pour the remaining hot consommé into a pitcher and stand it also on the table.

Give each guest a soup bowl and one of the dishes of meat and mushrooms. Also give each guest a small container of soy sauce and some horseradish mustard.

Each guest cooks his own meat, vegetables and noodles in the fondue pot. They should be cooked for only a minute or so. The cooked food is put into the bowl with a few spoonfuls of consommé from the fondue pot. As the consommé runs low in the pot, replenish it with some from the pitcher.

The soy sauce and horseradish mustard may be used to season the consommé or used for dipping.

For 4 persons:

6 to 8 cups Chicken
    Consommé (p. 168), made
    with a 3-pound whole
    chicken
1½ pounds boneless
    sirloin
½ pound mushrooms
2 pounds spinach, blanched
    in salted water for 5
    minutes and well drained

½ pound Chinese (rice)
    noodles, barely softened
    in lukewarm water
Soy sauce
Horseradish blended with
    mustard to taste

Spring Salad with Asparagus Tips

Salade Printanière aux Pointes d'Asperges

Spring Salad with Asparagus Tips
Salade Printanière aux Pointes d'Asperges

THIS SALAD IS served to each person on 2 plates.

Braise the artichoke heart (see p. 545) and cook the asparagus in boiling salted water until barely tender. Line 2 plates with the lettuce.

In the center of one of the plates put the artichoke heart, topped with the slice of *foie gras* and the slice of truffle. Around it, arrange the asparagus tips, the pine nuts and the Belgian endive.

On the other plate place the strips of celery heart, the red cabbage salad and the truffles and walnuts. Sprinkle with the parsley. Scoop out a lemon, fill it with mayonnaise, and put it in the middle of the plate. Serve both with a French dressing on the side.

For each person:

1 large artichoke heart
6 large asparagus tips, peeled
6 leaves of Boston or
   other lettuce
1 thin slice of foie
   gras
1 thin slice of black
   truffle
2 tablespoons pine nuts
6 leaves of Belgian
   endive, cut into strips
1 small celery heart, cut
   into thin strips

½ cup red Cabbage Salad
   (p. 208)
¼ cup coarsely chopped
   truffles
¼ cup shelled walnuts
1 tablespoon chopped
   parsley
1 lemon
Mayonnaise (p. 782)
¼ cup Simple French
   Dressing (p. 787)

Avocado Salad Acapulco

Salade d'Avocats Acapulco

Avocado Salad Acapulco

Salade d'Avocats Acapulco

MIX THE DICED lobster with the shredded romaine and the capers; bind the salad with mayonnaise and season with salt and pepper.

Cut the desired number of avocados lengthwise into halves and remove the pits. Fill each cavity with lobster salad, sprinkle with the lemon juice, and top with the round of lobster meat. Sprinkle with the chopped parsley and the lobster coral. Serve well chilled.

For each person:

¼ cup diced cooked
   lobster meat
¼ cup shredded heart of
   romaine lettuce
1 teaspoon capers
2 tablespoons Mayonnaise
   (p. 782)
Salt

Freshly ground black
   pepper
½ large avocado
Juice of ½ lemon
1 round slice of lobster
   meat, from the tail
1 teaspoon chopped parsley
½ teaspoon lobster coral

Pizza à la Garibaldi

Pizza à la Garibaldi

Editors' Note: In France uncooked bread dough may often be bought in neighborhood bakeries, and thus M. Oliver has not provided us with his own recipe. Use your own favorite one, or the one we have suggested in Pissaladière (p. 266).

ROLL OUT THE dough into a 12-inch round, leaving the outer rim a little thicker than the center. Generously oil a baking sheet and put the dough on it. Sprinkle the dough with a little olive oil and with the grated cheese. Place the stuffed green olives, the black olives and the anchovy fillets in an orderly manner on the dough. Top with *sauce tomate;* sprinkle with a little ground marjoram and a little more olive oil. Bake in a preheated 400° F. oven for 25 minutes.

For 4 persons:

Uncooked bread dough, sufficient for 1 medium-sized loaf
½ cup olive oil
1 cup grated Swiss cheese
2 cups stuffed green olives
1 cup black olives, pitted
12 anchovy fillets, drained
2 cups Sauce Tomate (p. 769)
3 tablespoons chopped fresh marjoram, or 1 tablespoon
      dried marjoram

Fritters Samurai

Beignets Frits des Samouraï

Fritters Samurai

Beignets Frits des Samouraï

FIRST MAKE THE *pâte à choux,* as described on page 710, but postpone adding the eggs.

Scald the other cup of milk in a saucepan, and gradually stir in the tapioca. Cook, stirring constantly, for about 8 minutes, or until the mixture is thick and smooth. Remove from the heat. Let the *choux* paste and the tapioca cool for a few minutes.

Heat together the oil and the butter in a skillet over fairly high heat and sauté the shellfish in it for about 5 minutes, or until tender. Drain. Purée the shellfish in a blender, or in a mortar with a pestle.

Mix together the *choux* paste, the tapioca and the shellfish purée. Beat in the eggs, one at a time, beating well after each addition. Season with a little salt and cayenne and the *quatre épices.*

Fry the mixture by tablespoons, a few at a time, in deep fat heated to 375° F. on a frying thermometer. The fritters will expand and turn upside down while frying. When they have puffed up and are golden on all sides, drain them on kitchen paper. Pile them on a hot serving plate lined with a napkin and serve very hot.

For 4 persons:

For the pâte à choux:
- ½ cup butter
- 1¾ cups flour
- 1 cup milk
- 1 teaspoon salt
- ½ teaspoon sugar
- 6 eggs
- 1 cup milk
- ¼ cup quick-cooking tapioca

- 2 tablespoons peanut oil
- 2 tablespoons butter
- ½ pound shelled shrimp, lobster or crabmeat
- Salt
- Cayenne pepper
- ¼ teaspoon Quatre Épices (p. 667)
- Fat for deep frying

Make a *liaison,* that is, blend the cream, egg yolks and lemon juice. Thicken the hot consommé with it, as in cream of curry soup (above), season to taste with salt and pepper, and garnish the soup with the mixed blanched herbs.

3 tablespoons chopped Fines Herbes (p. 89)	Juice of 1 lemon
¼ cup Crème Fraîche (p. 666) or heavy cream	4 cups hot Chicken Consommé (p. 168)
4 egg yolks	Salt
	Freshly ground white pepper

VELOUTÉ DE POTIRON / *Cream of Pumpkin Soup*

Cook the minced onion in the butter until it is soft and just turning golden. Add the water and the pumpkin pieces. Season lightly with salt, cover the saucepan, and simmer over very low heat for 30 minutes.

When the pumpkin is very tender, strain it through a food mill or purée it in a blender. Rectify the seasoning and bring the soup to the boiling point. Wash the rice in lukewarm water and add it to the soup. Simmer for about 30 minutes, or until the rice is tender.

Pour the soup into a heated soup tureen and add the milk.

1 onion, minced	Salt
2 tablespoons butter	Freshly ground white pepper
1 cup water	2 tablespoons uncooked rice
4 cups coarsely chopped pumpkin, without seeds	½ cup milk

Note: To vary the taste of this soup, you may add a minced hot pepper, or minced basil or fennel leaves, and season it with cayenne pepper. A small rib of fresh fennel, minced, may also replace the onion.

/ *Cream Soup à la Saint-Germain*

POTAGE CRÉMÉ SAINT-GERMAIN

Heat the butter in a saucepan and cook all of the chopped vegetables in it until they are soft, about 10 minutes. Add the boiling water, season lightly with salt and pepper, and add the dried peas or beans together with the ham or veal bone. Simmer for about 45 minutes, or until the beans are very tender. Discard the bone and purée the mixture through a food mill or in a blender. Return it to the saucepan, add the diced fresh vegetables, correct the seasoning, and simmer for 2 minutes. Just before serving add the *crème fraîche.*

4 tablespoons butter	¾ cup dried vegetables, such as peas or beans, soaked in water for 12 hours
1 onion, chopped	
1 carrot, chopped	
1 celery stalk, chopped	1 small veal or ham bone, cracked
½ turnip, chopped	1 cup mixed cooked fresh vegetables, diced (carrots, green snap beans, celery, turnips, etc.)
2 parsley roots, chopped	
4 cups boiling water	
Salt	½ cup Crème Fraîche (p. 666)
Freshly ground white pepper	

Cream of Sorrel Soup / CRÈME GERMINY

This soup may be described as a consommé thickened with egg yolk and garnished with sorrel.

Make a purée of the sorrel by boiling it in salted water for about 10 minutes, draining it, and then pressing it through a sieve.

Bring the consommé to the boiling point and remove from the heat. Make a *liaison* by blending the egg yolks and the cream, and dribble one fourth of the consommé into it, mixing well. Gradually beat the rest of the consommé into this mixture. Return the soup to the saucepan and heat without bringing it to the boiling point until it is slightly thickened. While the soup is warming through, add the sorrel purée. Season to taste with salt and pepper. Pour the soup into cold soup dishes.

½ pound sorrel
3 cups Chicken or Beef Consommé
  (p. 168)
2 egg yolks

¼ cup Crème Fraîche (p. 666) or
  heavy cream
Salt
Freshly ground white pepper

Note: All consommés may be thickened like cream of sorrel soup. All you need to do is to replace the sorrel purée with any other puréed greens.

Cream of Dried Vegetable Soup /
CRÈME DE LÉGUMES SECS

The dried vegetable may be split peas, white beans, chick-peas, or fava beans. They must first be blanched in boiling water for 2 minutes, cooled for 1 hour in the cooking liquid, and then drained. Put them into a casserole or a cocotte and add the hot consommé. Cover them and cook in a preheated 350° F. oven for about 45 minutes, or until they are soft. Purée them in a food mill and then force them through a very fine sieve, or blend the soup briefly in a blender. Season to taste with salt and pepper, add the cream, and serve.

1 cup dried vegetable
4 cups Beef or Chicken Consommé
  (p. 167)

Salt
Freshly ground white pepper
½ cup heavy cream

Vichyssoise /

This is a thick vegetable soup, served cold, of the kind popular in Russian cooking.

First of all, mince the leeks and cook them slowly in the butter. They must remain white and be limp. Add the stock and the potatoes. Simmer, covered, over very low heat on the top of the stove or in a preheated 300° F. oven for about 40 minutes.

When the vegetables are very tender, strain them first through a food mill and then through a fine sieve, or purée in a blender. Season with salt, pepper and cayenne; the seasonings should be generous in view of the amount of cream which will be added later. Cool the soup, stirring it occasionally, or cover it with a piece of buttered wax paper while it is cooling to prevent formation of a skin.

The soup should now be chilled, as should the cream that is to go into it. The cups in which it will be served should also be chilled. Blend the soup and the cream together; the proportions should be about ⅔ purée to ⅓ cream. Taste for salt and pepper. Add the blanched chervil leaves. Pour the soup into the cups.

With the addition of the cream, the soup will be somewhat more substantial. Also, since it is chilled, the taste will be milder, since extreme cold has a tendency to diminish flavors rather than to enhance them. A slice of truffle may be added to each cup of soup; this is an ideal garnish, and adds to the flavor as well.

FOR 6 PERSONS:

5 to 6 leeks, white part only, minced	Cayenne pepper
4 tablespoons butter	2 cups (more or less) Crème Fraîche (p. 666) or heavy cream
4 cups White Poultry Stock (p. 165)	4 tablespoons fresh chervil leaves, blanched in boiling water for 1 minute
4 medium-sized potatoes, sliced	
Salt	
Freshly ground white pepper	Optional: 6 slices of truffle

A Few Classic French Soups

SOUPE À L'OIGNON GRATINÉE / *Onion Soup Gratinée*

Cook the minced onions in the butter until they are very soft; add the consommé or boiling water and simmer for 30 minutes. Season to taste with salt and pepper.

Line the bottom of an ovenproof casserole or soup tureen with the toasted slices of French bread, sprinkle them with the cheese, and pour the boiling soup over the bread. Put the casserole into a preheated 400° F. oven until the top is bubbly.

4 medium-sized onions, minced	Salt
3 tablespoons butter	Freshly ground black pepper
4 cups boiling Beef Consommé (p. 167) or boiling water, lightly salted	8 slices of French bread, toasted
	1 cup grated Gruyère cheese

SOUPE À LA QUEUE DE BOEUF / *Oxtail Soup*

Cut the oxtail into 8 pieces, and each pig's trotter into 4 pieces. Put the meat into a big earthenware pot (*marmite*) or deep kettle and add cold water to cover. Add the pig's ear cut into halves. Bring the soup to the boiling point, skim when needed, and season lightly with salt and pepper; simmer, covered, for about 2 hours.

Add the vegetables, bring back to the boiling point, and simmer, covered, for another 2 hours. Correct the seasoning.

Broil the sausages in a hot oven or under a broiler.

When the meats and vegetables are very tender, cut the pig's ear into thin strips and return to the soup. Serve the soup in a heated tureen. Slice the sausages and arrange them in a circle on top of the soup.

FOR 8 PERSONS:

1 oxtail	1 small cabbage, coarsely chopped
2 pig's trotters	10 small white onions
1 pig's ear	2 carrots, sliced
Salt	2 small turnips, diced
Freshly ground black pepper	8 chipolata or tiny link sausages

Petite Marmite Henry IV

Put the water or the consommé into a big earthenware pot (*marmite*) or a big kettle. Add the meat, the marrowbone (for which you've made a stopper with a piece of carrot so that the marrow won't ooze out since it will be needed later), the chicken and the giblets. If necessary, add more water so that the meat is well covered. Bring slowly to the boiling point and skim as needed. Season the soup with salt if you are using water. Add the vegetables except the cabbage and add the *bouquet garni;* bring again to the boiling point and lower the heat. Simmer for 1½ to 2 hours, or until the meat is tender. If necessary remove the chicken earlier, or as soon as it is tender.

From time to time, take the fat off the top of the soup with a small ladle; put it into a saucepan and reserve it for later use. In between all these operations, keep the *marmite* covered.

Blanch the cabbage in boiling salted water for 5 minutes, drain it, and cook it in the reserved fat over low heat for 20 minutes. Strain the soup and put it back into the *marmite,* or pour it into individual *marmites* or soup bowls. Cut the beef into cubes and remove the chicken meat from the bones; add them to the soup. Add the cabbage. Spread a few slices of toast with the marrow from the marrowbone and add them to the soup. If desired, sprinkle the soup with grated cheese.

FOR 8 PERSONS:

3 quarts water or Chicken Consommé (p. 138)	3 carrots, chopped
	2 turnips, chopped
1 pound fresh beef brisket, plate or shin	1 celery heart, chopped
	1 Bouquet Garni (p. 46)
1 marrowbone	1 small cabbage, chopped
1 chicken (3 pounds)	6 slices of toast
Giblets from the chicken	Optional: ½ cup grated Gruyère
Salt	cheese
1 large onion, stuck with 4 cloves	

Pistou Soup / SOUPE AU PISTOU

Trim the green beans and cut them into 1-inch pieces. Peel the potatoes and dice them.

Bring the water to the boiling point in a deep kettle, add the salt and pepper, the green beans and the potatoes; bring the soup to the boiling point and cover the kettle. Simmer the soup over low heat for 10 minutes. Add the tomatoes and the haricot beans. If you are using dried beans, first blanch them by boiling in water for 2 minutes, cooling for 1 hour in the water, and then draining them.

Let the soup boil up again, lower the heat, and simmer until the haricot beans are nearly tender. Add the zucchini and about 5 minutes before they are fully cooked, when you are sure that everything will be ready together, add the vermicelli. The total cooking time will be about 40 minutes.

Just before serving time, pound the basil leaves and garlic together in a mortar to make a smooth paste. Gradually add the oil, a little at a time, mixing it into the garlic mixture first with the pestle, and then, as it becomes more liquid, with a small wire whisk. The mixture should have the consistency of softened butter. Put it into a heated tureen, stir in a little of the broth with a wooden spoon, and then add the rest of the soup. Check the seasoning and serve immediately.

FOR 8 PERSONS:

1 pound green snap beans	4 small zucchini, cut into large
4 large potatoes	dice
2 quarts water	1 cup fine noodles (vermicelli),
2 teaspoons salt	broken up
Freshly ground black pepper	½ cup packed fresh basil leaves
4 tomatoes, peeled, seeded and	3 garlic cloves
chopped	¼ cup olive oil
1½ cups fresh or 1 cup dried	
haricot beans	

Note: One can reverse the order of cooking the beans and start with the haricot beans. It all depends on how long it will take to cook them. One can use summer squash or pumpkin in place of the zucchini.

POTAGE À L'OSEILLE / *Sorrel Soup*

Trim, wash, and drain the sorrel. Simmer it in the butter in a covered casserole for about 15 minutes, or until it is very tender. Add the boiling water and season to taste with salt, pepper and nutmeg. Bring it to the boiling point and simmer for about 5 minutes.

Beat the egg yolks with the *crème fraîche* in a bowl. Stir one fourth of the soup into the cream and egg mixture, and then pour it back into the remaining soup. Heat very gently, stirring constantly with a wire whisk, until it is slightly thickened. Serve very hot with the croutons.

½ pound sorrel	Grated nutmeg
3 tablespoons butter	3 egg yolks
4 cups boiling water	¼ cup Crème Fraîche (p. 666)
Salt	1 cup Croutons (p. 62)
Freshly ground black pepper	

SOUPE DE TOMATES I / *Tomato Soup I*

Cook the minced onion in the oil and 2 tablespoons of the butter until it is soft and golden. Stir in the flour, cook the mixture until the flour is golden, and then add the tomatoes, water and *bouquet garni*. Season with salt and pepper. Simmer the soup for 30 minutes, remove the *bouquet garni,* stir in the remaining butter, and pour the soup into a heated tureen.

1 onion, minced
1 tablespoon peanut oil
4 tablespoons butter
3 tablespoons flour
6 medium-sized tomatoes, peeled,
   seeded, drained and chopped

4 cups boiling water
1 Bouquet Garni (p. 46)
Salt
Freshly ground black pepper

Tomato Soup II / SOUPE DE TOMATES II

Proceed as in Tomato Soup I (above), but add 2 medium-sized potatoes, peeled and chopped, to the soup when you are adding the tomatoes. Strain the soup through a food mill or purée in a blender (after removing the *bouquet garni*) before reheating and adding the butter.

Thick Tomato Soup / TOURING À LA TOMATE

Heat the lard, goose fat or butter in a large casserole and cook the onions in it until they are barely golden. Add the tomatoes. Season generously with salt and with a good deal of pepper. Add the water and bring the soup to the boiling point. Simmer it for 10 minutes. Strain the soup through a food mill and return it to the heat; let it boil up again and add the noodles. Cook until the noodles are tender, 7 or 8 minutes, and serve immediately.

2 tablespoons lard, goose fat or
   butter
2 onions, minced
4 ripe tomatoes, peeled, seeded and
   chopped

Salt
Freshly ground black pepper
3½ cups water
½ cup thin noodles, broken up

Velouté Aurore /

Heat the butter and cook the minced onions and garlic in it until they are very soft and barely golden. Add the water, bring to the boiling point, and simmer over low heat for about 20 minutes. Add the tomatoes. Season generously with salt and pepper and add a little cayenne. Simmer without a cover for 15 minutes longer. While the soup is simmering, peel the avocado, purée it through a food mill, and blend this purée with the egg yolks in a bowl.

Strain the soup through a fine sieve or blend it briefly in a blender and return it to the saucepan. Bring it to the boiling point. Pour one fourth of it into the avocado-egg purée and then stir this mixture into the remaining soup. Heat very gently, stirring constantly, until it thickens slightly. Be very careful not to boil, as this soup will curdle easily.

3 tablespoons butter
3 onions, minced
2 garlic cloves, minced
3 cups boiling water
4 tomatoes, peeled, seeded, drained
   and chopped

Salt
Freshly ground white pepper
Cayenne pepper
1 ripe avocado
4 egg yolks

VELOUTÉ AUX AVOCATS / *Velouté of Avocado*

Heat the butter and cook the onions and garlic in it until they are soft. Add the water and cook for 10 minutes. Purée through a fine sieve or blend briefly in a blender. Bring the soup again to the boiling point and stir in the unbeaten egg whites. Press the flesh of the avocado through a sieve and blend it with the egg yolks. Pour one fourth of the soup into the avocado mixture, and then pour it back into the remaining soup. Heat the soup very gently, stirring constantly, until it thickens slightly. Season to taste with salt and pepper. Pour it into a heated tureen and serve it immediately with the croutons.

2 tablespoons butter	1 large very ripe avocado
2 onions, minced	Salt
2 garlic cloves, minced	Freshly ground white pepper
4 cups water	½ cup Croutons (p. 62)
3 eggs, separated	

POTAGE DE CRESSON / *Watercress Soup*

Wash the watercress and set aside ¼ cup of the leaves for garnishing.

Put the rest of the watercress into a saucepan with the boiling salted water, season lightly with pepper, and add the sugar and potatoes. Simmer for 20 minutes. Strain the soup through a food mill or purée in a blender. Bring it back to the boiling point and add the reserved watercress leaves. Simmer the soup for 1 minute longer.

Pour the soup into a heated tureen and stir in the *crème fraîche*.

1 bunch of watercress	1 lump of sugar
4 cups boiling water, lightly salted	2 medium-sized potatoes, diced
	¼ cup Crème Fraîche (p. 666)
Freshly ground white pepper	

TOURING BLANCHI / *White Soup*

Heat the lard or the goose fat in a casserole and cook the mashed garlic in it until it is golden. Add the water and thyme, and season with salt and pepper. Simmer, covered, for 10 minutes.

Strain the soup, put it back on the stove, bring it to the boiling point, and stir in the egg white. Lower the heat so that the soup is not boiling.

Blend the egg yolk with the vinegar. Put a little of the hot soup into the mixture and blend well. Pour this *liaison* back into the soup. Remove the soup from the heat.

Line the bottom of a heated tureen with the slices of bread, season the bread lightly with pepper, and pour the hot soup over it.

2 tablespoons lard or goose fat	Salt
6 garlic cloves, peeled and mashed	Freshly ground white pepper
4 cups water	1 egg, separated
1 sprig of fresh thyme or ½ teaspoon ground thyme	1 tablespoon vinegar
	4 slices of French bread

VELOUTÉ OF AVOCADO
LE VELOUTÉ AUX AVOCATS

On the left: *How to sieve the flesh of an avocado: Cut the avocado lengthwise into halves, remove the pit, and take out the flesh with a spoon. Mash the flesh through a sieve and remove the particles clinging to the bottom of the sieve with your hands.*

On the right, above: *The* liaison: *Take one fourth of the soup and stir it into the avocado purée beaten with the egg yolks.* Below: *Stir the mixture back into the remaining soup.*

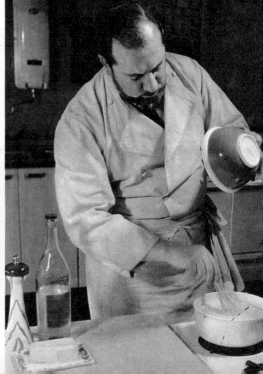

A Few Regional Soups

SOUPE AUVERGNATE / *Soup from the Auvergne*

Put the pig's head into a large deep kettle and add cold water to cover. Add the leeks, carrots, turnips, potatoes and cabbage, as well as the soaked lentils.

Simmer the soup over low heat for about 2 hours, or until the meat of the pig's head almost falls from the bones. The soup will be ready at this time. Take out the pig's head, remove the meat from the bones, and dice it. Season to taste with salt and pepper.

Line the bottom of a heated tureen with slices of dark bread, top them with the diced meat, and pour the boiling soup over everything.

FOR 6 TO 8 PERSONS:

1 small pig's head	½ head of cabbage, chopped
2 to 3 quarts water	½ pound dried lentils, soaked in
5 leeks, white and green parts, chopped	water
	Salt
3 carrots, chopped	Freshly ground black pepper
3 turnips, chopped	12 slices of black bread
3 medium-sized potatoes, chopped	

SOUPE CHAMPENOISE / *Champenoise Soup*

Traditionally, this soup is prepared at grape harvest time in the Champagne region in a cast-iron pot called a *chaudière* which holds at least 25 quarts; of necessity, so large an amount of soup needs simmering for a whole day.

To adapt the soup to household proportions, take a 5- to 6-quart kettle and fill it half full with cold water. Put the lean bacon and the smoked pork butt into it. Bring to the boiling point, cover the kettle, and simmer for 1½ hours before adding the whole carrots and turnips. Cook the soup over medium heat for about 20 minutes. Add the cabbage, the whole potatoes, and the leeks cut into halves. Simmer for another 20 minutes, or until all of the vegetables are tender. Should the pork butt be tender before the vegetables, take it from the kettle and keep it hot. Season to taste with salt and pepper; it will need little or no salt.

Cut the meats into pieces, cut the whole vegetables into halves, and put them in a heated soup tureen. If necessary, degrease the soup. Pour the boiling soup over everything.

You may also put a few slices of bread into the tureen.

FOR 6 TO 8 PERSONS:

3 (or more) quarts water	6 medium-sized potatoes, peeled
1-pound piece of lean bacon	3 leeks, cut into halves
1 smoked pork butt (2½ to 3 pounds)	Salt
3 carrots, scraped	Freshly ground black pepper
3 small turnips, scraped	
1 medium-sized cabbage, coarsely chopped	

Dumpling Soup from the Périgord /

MIQUES DU PÉRIGORD

Put the water in a very large earthenware pot (*marmite*) or a deep kettle—it should be only about half full—and add the slab bacon; if the bacon is very salty, blanch it in boiling water for 5 minutes to remove excess salt. Bring to the boiling point, skim, cover the pot, and simmer over low heat for 2 hours, skimming from time to time.

While the bacon is simmering, make the dumplings. Mix the compressed yeast with ¼ cup of lukewarm (80° to 90° F.) water in a bowl, or use ⅓ cup warmer (105° to 115° F.) water if using dry yeast, and gradually add about ¾ cup of the flour to make a soft dough. Shape the dough into a ball and let it stand in a warm place for about 20 minutes. This is the sponge. Put the rest of the flour on a pastry board, make a well in the center, and put the eggs and the softened butter into the well. Mix thoroughly and then knead in the sponge. Knead for about 10 minutes, or until the dough is elastic. Shape the dough into a ball and put it into a floured bowl. Let it rest in a warm place until doubled in bulk.

If desired you may knead ¼ cup of chopped bacon into the dough before setting it to rise.

When the soup has cooked for 2 hours, degrease it. Then add the vegetables. Both the meat and the vegetables should be well covered with liquid. If necessary, add a little hot water. Cover the soup and simmer it for 30 minutes.

Punch the dough down and shape it into dumplings of even size. Remember, they will more than double in size when they are steamed. Check again to see if the soup needs more hot water since the dumplings must not sit on top of the vegetables. Remove the bacon and keep warm. Add about half of the dumplings to the simmering soup and cover the pot tightly. Steam them for 10 minutes. The exact cooking time depends on the size of the dumplings. To test for doneness, stick a knitting needle, a cake tester or a thin skewer into one of the dumplings; if it comes out clean, they will be done. Remove the dumplings, put them in a bowl with a little of the broth, and keep warm. Repeat the process with the remaining dumplings. Put the dumplings in the middle of a large serving dish. Arrange the vegetables and the bacon, sliced, around them. Pour the broth into a heated tureen.

Each serving will consist of a piece of bacon, a few dumplings, a few vegetables, and a little soup.

Variations:

1. Cook the vegetables in the broth until they are barely tender. Remove them and keep warm in a little of the broth. Do not make small dumplings, but put the whole ball of dough into the simmering broth. After about 15 minutes of steaming, the big dumpling will come to the surface of the soup. Turn it over with a slotted spoon and allow it to cook for about 30 minutes longer. Test for doneness. Remove the big dumpling from the soup, drain it, and cut it into 8 pieces. Put the pieces in the middle of a big serving dish, and surround them with the vegetables and the sliced meat, as described above.

2. Once the small dumplings are cooked, they may be cut into rather thin slices and sautéed in a little hot butter and oil until they are golden. Put these slices into the

heated tureen and pour the soup over them. Place only the vegetables and the sliced meat on the serving dish.

FOR 8 PERSONS:

3 quarts water
2 pounds lean slab bacon

For the dumplings:
  1 ounce compressed yeast or 2
    packages active dry yeast
  4 cups sifted all-purpose flour
  4 eggs
  ½ cup butter, softened
  Optional: ¼ cup chopped cooked
    bacon

4 whole carrots
2 whole turnips
2 whole onions
4 leeks, cut into halves
1 small cabbage, quartered
8 small "new" potatoes
2 celery stalks, sliced

/ Garbure Béarnaise

Sometimes, this soup from the Béarn is served with grated Gruyère on the side, but this is not part of the old Béarnaise tradition.

If you are using a very salty smoked ham, follow the packer's instructions about presoaking it.

Blanch the ham, pork butt or bacon by bringing it to the boiling point in cold water to cover and then draining it.

Put the blanched meat into a deep kettle with the water, bring to the boiling point, and add the blanched dried beans. Then add the onion, fava or lima beans, carrots, turnip, leeks and cabbage, as well as the whole head of unpeeled garlic and the whole hot peppers. Season with salt and bring to a quick boil. Let the soup boil rapidly for 5 minutes, then lower the heat and let it simmer for about 1½ hours. After the first hour add the pumpkin, potatoes, basil and mint. Before serving, remove the onion, the garlic head, and the hot peppers. Taste the soup and rectify the seasoning. The *garbure* should be reduced and very thick with vegetables when ready to serve. Usually, the meat is removed from the bones and cut into pieces and then put back into the soup, but it may be served separately, if desired.

FOR 6 PERSONS:

1 center slice (2 pounds) smoked
  ham, or a 2-pound pork butt, or a
  2-pound piece of lean bacon
3 quarts water
1 pound dried white beans, blanched
  in boiling water for 2 minutes
  and cooled in the blanching
  liquid for 1 hour
1 onion, stuck with 4 cloves
1 pound fava or broad beans, or
  lima beans
3 carrots, chopped fine

1 turnip, chopped fine
3 leeks, white and green parts,
  thinly sliced
1 medium-sized head of cabbage,
  coarsely chopped
1 whole garlic head, unpeeled
3 hot peppers, fresh or dried
Salt
2 cups coarsely chopped pumpkin
3 potatoes, cut into large dice
3 tablespoons chopped fresh basil
2 tablespoons chopped fresh mint

Grape Picker's Soup | SOUPE DU VENDAGEUR (CHABROT)

EDITORS' NOTE: *This is a traditional thick soup from the Bordeaux country eaten at grape harvesttime.*

Fill a very large earthenware pot (*marmite*) or kettle about half full with cold water (you'll need 6 or 7 quarts) and add the brisket of beef and the veal bones. Bring very slowly to the boiling point, and skim carefully.

Add the green parts of the leeks, the celery leaves, parsley sprigs, turnips, the whole unpeeled garlic heads, and 1 onion peeled and stuck with the 3 cloves. Brown the other onion, unpeeled, in a hot oven until it is very dark, and add it to the soup to give it a rich color. Bring the soup slowly back to the boiling point, skim, and cook over low heat for 1 hour, uncovered.

Add the veal and skim any scum that rises to the surface from time to time.

Make a stuffing with the chicken livers, bread crumbs, *fines herbes* and egg and season it lightly with salt and pepper. Stuff the chicken with this mixture, sew the opening so that the stuffing won't ooze out during cooking, and truss the bird. Add the chicken after the veal has cooked for 1 hour. Make a bag with a triple layer of cheesecloth, put the white parts of the leeks and the halved carrots into it, and sew it closed. Add it to the soup. Bring the soup slowly back to the boiling point and skim again. Season lightly with salt and pepper. Skim very frequently so that the bouillon will be perfectly clear at the end of its cooking time. Begin testing the chicken and the meat after another hour to see whether they are tender. Remove each as soon as it is done.

When the meats and chicken are very tender, put them into a large bowl, with a few spoonfuls of broth to prevent their drying out. Remove the leeks and carrots from the bag in which they were cooked and add them to the bowl. Keep everything warm.

Simmer the bouillon for another hour, removing the top layer of fat from time to time with a ladle. Put a little of this fat on top of the meat and vegetables.

Slice the meats, disjoint the chicken, and put the pieces on a hot platter, together with the vegetables. Spoon a little hot bouillon over them and keep them warm.

Cut a loaf of stale bread into thin slices, and line the bottom of a soup tureen with the slices. Season with plenty of freshly ground pepper and strain the broth over the bread. Cover the tureen and keep it hot.

Heat the tomato purée with a little of the broth and check the seasoning.

This is the traditional way of eating this soup in the Southwest of France: fill a deep soup plate with the broth and the bread, sprinkled with a little grated cheese. Eat this first.

Refill the plate about one third full of bouillon and then fill it up with a young red Bordeaux wine (a Saint-Émilion or a Pomerol). The amount of wine depends on the diner's taste. This second plateful is called *chabrot,* and it is drunk from the plate rather than spooned.

Now fill the plate as you wish with the sliced meats and vegetables. Sprinkle with a little broth and season with the tomato purée, capers and pickles.

3 pounds brisket of beef
3 veal bones
4 leeks, green and white parts
   separated
½ cup packed celery leaves
3 parsley sprigs
2 turnips, sliced
2 whole garlic heads, unpeeled
2 onions
3 cloves
3 pounds shank of veal
4 chicken livers, chopped
2 cups fresh bread crumbs, soaked
   in 1 cup milk and squeezed dry

2 tablespoons fresh Fines Herbes
   (p. 89)
1 egg
Salt
Freshly ground black pepper
1 chicken (3 pounds)
8 carrots, cut into halves
1 loaf of stale French bread
1 cup fresh Tomato Purée (p. 157)
2 cups grated Gruyère cheese
1 bottle red Bordeaux wine
½ cup capers
3 cups sour pickles

/ *Potée Toulousaine*

EDITOR'S NOTE: *A* potée *is a soup, traditionally cooked in an earthenware pot, which contains pork and vegetables, especially cabbage and potatoes.*

Bring the water to a boil in a large earthenware pot (*marmite*) or a deep kettle.

Cut the meat lengthwise and crosswise into 8 pieces and put them into the boiling water. Add the haricot beans; if you are using dried beans, blanch them first for 2 minutes in boiling water, cool them in the water for 1 hour, and then drain. Season the soup lightly with salt, and simmer it over low heat for about 1½ hours.

Prick the sausages with a fork to prevent their splitting while they are being cooked. Put the sausages into a shallow baking dish greased with a little oil, and let them cook in a preheated 400° F. oven for about 15 minutes, or until they are nicely browned. Remove them and keep warm.

Heat the lard in a very large casserole or saucepan and cook the onions in it until they are golden. Add the cabbage, leeks, carrots, turnips, celery and *bouquet garni*. Stir the vegetables and sauté gently for about 15 minutes. Drain the meat and the beans, reserving the liquid. Add them to the vegetables together with the potatoes and enough of the reserved liquid so that all the ingredients are well covered. Cover the casserole and simmer for 15 minutes. Add the sausages, cut into halves, and, if desired, more of the reserved liquid to give the soup any desired consistency. Simmer for 5 minutes longer and then pour the soup into a hot tureen. Serve the soup in large deep plates; each serving should consist of a piece of meat, a piece of sausage, and some vegetables and broth.

FOR 8 PERSONS:

4 quarts water
1 pork shoulder butt (about 4
   pounds)
3 cups fresh or 2 cups dried
   haricot beans
Salt
4 Toulouse sausages or 4 sweet
   Italian sausages
1 tablespoon peanut oil
4 tablespoons lard

3 onions, chopped
1 small cabbage, shredded
5 leeks, white and green parts,
   sliced
3 carrots, sliced
2 turnips, diced
3 celery stalks, sliced
1 Bouquet Garni (p. 46)
4 medium-sized potatoes, quartered

Fish Soups

Soupes de Poissons

Bouillabaisse /

EDITORS' NOTE: *There are probably as many recipes for* bouillabaisse *as there are villages in and around the coast of southern France near Marseilles. What should or should not go into a true* bouillabaisse *is a passionately debated subject. This is as it should be, for it is a fine dish. The varieties of fish that go into it, combined with its traditional oil, saffron and tomatoes, give it an unmistakable flavor. Unfortunately, almost none of the fish that traditionally are used in a* bouillabaisse *are to be found in American waters. Splendid substitutes can be found, however, to give an American* bouillabaisse *its own character. We have suggested a few of these below, but almost any kind of fish may be used, whatever is locally available, provided only that there is a good contrast in the flavors and textures.*

I learned to make *bouillabaisse* from one of the most famous cooks in Marseilles. I made it for several years in the same place where La Mère Salvador practiced her art and often have even caught my own fish for a *bouillabaisse*.

The recipe that follows is my own. Where the original inspiration came from is not really important. This recipe is *grande cuisine*, and once you've mastered it, you can yourself modify it, making it either more complicated or simpler. The reaction of your friends will tell you if you've done right. The paper on which a recipe has been written down isn't worth the saucepan in which it is cooked!

Good, strongly flavored fish are essential: *racasse, Saint-Pierre, galinette, vives, lottes* or *merlans* (substitute mackerel, cod, sea bass or haddock). More delicate, tender-fleshed fish are also traditional, such as *rouquiers, cigales,* or *girelles* (substitute sole, flounder, whiting, mullet or red snapper). Lobster and eels are a must. While almost any combination of fish is allowed, eels and a strongly flavored fish (*racasse*) are always in a good *bouillabaisse*.

As for making the *bouillabaisse*, you can use your own imagination or you can follow the rules of the old masters. If the fish is truly fresh, you'll succeed wonderfully; the freshness of the fish is probably the greatest secret of a *bouillabaisse*.

Now let us make an inventory of all the necessary ingredients.

FISH STOCK / LE FOND OU FUMET

EDITORS' NOTE: *M. Oliver makes a stock from* rouquiers, sarans *and* girelles. *Since none of these fish is available here, we are substituting flounder or sole bones.*

Heat the oil and the butter in an enamelware pot (do not use aluminum) and gently sauté the vegetables and herbs until they are soft but not browned. All sorts of herbs are suitable, such as thyme, bay leaves, savory and rosemary, provided that none of the herbs dominates the flavor of the *bouillabaisse*. No salt or pepper is needed.

LA BOUILLABAISSE (1)

The success of the bouilla-baisse *depends on the fish stock. Contrary to what has sometimes been said, this stock should not have too many vegetables: for 2 pounds of fish bones and heads, 2 onions, 2 celery stalks and 2 carrots are sufficient.*

Use as many herbs as you like, providing that their taste does not dominate the bouillabaisse. *Above all, do not use any spices or salt or pepper.*

"Melt" the vegetables, that is, cook them over very low heat until they are soft. The trick of this is to cook the vegetables thoroughly, but without letting them lose their taste.

Add the mixture of water and wine when the vegetables are soft. I suggest white wine because it gives excellent results; practically all the Provençal cooks add wine to their stock for the *bouillabaisse*. The wine should be a very good one, so that it will not become acid while it is cooked. The best wine to choose is the one that will be drunk before and during the meal.

After you've added the liquid to the vegetables, add the fish bones, bring to a boil, and cook over high heat for 20 minutes. Strain through a fine sieve and reserve this stock. It should be boiling when added to the *bouillabaisse*.

THE FISH / LES POISSONS

The fish should be cut into 2-inch-thick slices, unless, of course, some of the fish that you have chosen are very small, ½ pound or less in size.

Put the cut-up fish into a deep china dish and season them lightly with salt and pepper. Add the saffron, a pinch each of thyme, savory and rosemary, the anise liqueur and the olive oil. Marinate the fish in a cool place for 1 hour, turning it occasionally.

THE LOBSTER/ LES CRUSTACÉS

In Marseilles, it is traditional to cook the lobster in the *bouillabaisse*. But it should be pointed out that besides the appearance, lobster adds little to the soup. I don't care particularly for lobster cooked in a *bouillabaisse;* the meat loses its flavor because the seasoning in a *bouillabaisse* is so much stronger than a normal *court bouillon* in which lobster is cooked. Here is my way of making the most of the lobster flavor.

Cut the lobsters lengthwise into halves, heat 3 tablespoons of the olive oil in a very large skillet, and cook the lobster halves in it until the shells turn bright red. Cover the skillet and simmer for 10 minutes over very low heat. Then add the lobsters to the *bouillabaisse* as described below. Pour a little of the fish stock into the skillet in which the lobsters were cooked, swish it around, and add it to the *bouillabaisse*.

THE LEEKS / LES POIREAUX

The traditional julienne of leeks is seldom put into a *bouillabaisse* nowadays, perhaps because cutting the leeks into julienne strips bores housewives since it means a little more work. Don't misunderstand me—I really don't think that the way the leeks are cut affects the taste of the soup. What is important is that their flavor is essential and they must not be omitted. If you don't feel like cutting them into julienne strips, cut them into thin slices, but only after you've washed them very carefully.

THE TOMATOES / LES TOMATES

Peel, seed, and drain the tomatoes. Then chop them or press them through a food mill.

THE POTATOES / LES POMMES DE TERRE

Whether to use potatoes or not depends on your own taste. If you decide to use them, peel them and cut them into ½-inch dice.

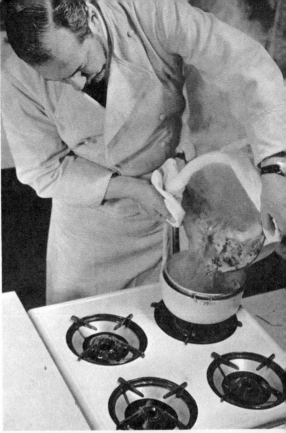

LA BOUILLABAISSE (2)

…wever good a fish stock, it alone does not …ke *the* bouillabaisse. *All the other ingredi*- …*s have a role to play, and each is in*- …*pensable. This is especially true of the* …*getables—leeks, tomatoes, and potatoes.*

…*n't cook the lobsters in the* bouillabaisse, …*atever the Marseillais say. They are far* …*re flavorful when cooked separately.*

…*rve the* bouillabaisse *by pouring it over* …*ces of stale bread.*

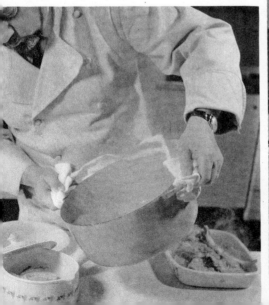

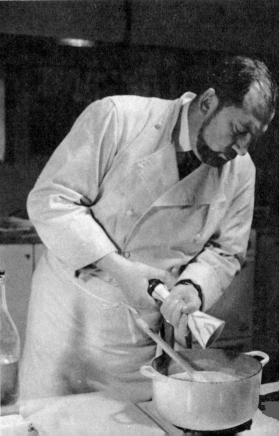

FINAL PREPARATION / PRÉPARATION FINALE

Use a big enamelware pot. Heat the remaining 2 tablespoons of oil, add the leeks cut into julienne strips, and cook until they are barely golden, stirring frequently with a wooden spoon. If you are including potatoes, add them now. Then add the strongly flavored fish, the fish marinade, the lobster, the lobster juices, and the hot fish stock. Now add enough boiling water to cover the fish. Season lightly with salt and pepper. Add the dried orange rind and the chopped tomatoes. Bring to the boiling point and cook, uncovered, over high heat for 5 minutes. Add the remaining tender fish and boil for 10 minutes longer. After the 15 minutes of cooking time, you may check any of the thicker pieces of fish to make sure they are done. Also make sure the potatoes are tender; they are sometimes slower to cook than the fish. It is, perhaps, better not to use potatoes in a *bouillabaisse,* but this is a matter of personal taste. I, myself, like *bouillabaisse* with or without potatoes. Remove the *bouillabaisse* from the heat, and serve as quickly as possible.

ROUILLE SAUCE / LA ROUILLE

If you like the flavor of hot red peppers, make the *rouille*. This sauce is easy to make, being composed of hot red peppers, garlic and fish liver. Cod liver would do well, or really any fish liver that your fish dealer will save for you.

Dried red peppers should be soaked in cold water for a few hours to soften. Mash them and the garlic together in a mortar. Add a little olive oil if you wish; I don't think the oil absolutely necessary because it affects the taste of the condiment. Mash the fish liver with the potato; you may use a few pieces of potato from the *bouillabaisse.* Gradually beat in some stock from the *bouillabaisse,* about 1 cup, or enough to give the *rouille* a consistency of heavy cream, and strain it through a fine sieve.

HOW TO SERVE THE BOUILLABAISSE / LA PRÉSENTATION

Line the bottom of a hot soup tureen with slices of stale bread, fill it with the *bouillabaisse*, and serve immediately. Serve the *rouille* separately, in a sauceboat.

Or else, you may divide the fish into soup bowls, pour the soup into the tureen, and give each guest another bowl for the soup.

FOR 6 PERSONS:

For the fish stock:

- 2 tablespoons olive oil
- 2 tablespoons butter
- 2 onions, chopped
- 2 celery stalks, chopped
- 2 carrots, chopped
- 1 tablespoon each of chopped fresh savory, thyme and rosemary, or ½ teaspoon each of dried
- 1 bay leaf
- 3 parsley sprigs
- 2 quarts water
- 2 cups dry white wine
- 2 to 3 pounds raw sole or flounder bones and heads
- 1 pound eel
- 2 pounds strongly flavored fish, such as mackerel, sea bass, cod or haddock
- 2 pounds delicate, tender-fleshed fish, such as sole, flounder, whiting, mullet or red snapper

For the marinade:
  Salt
  Freshly ground black and white
    pepper
  1 teaspoon ground saffron
  1 pinch to ½ teaspoon each of
    ground thyme, savory and
    rosemary
  1 tablespoon anise liqueur
  ¼ cup olive oil

3 lobsters (1 to 1½ pounds each)
5 tablespoons olive oil
3 leeks
4 ripe tomatoes

Optional: 3 potatoes
Salt
Freshly ground black pepper
½ teaspoon chopped dried orange
  rind

For the Rouille Sauce:
  2 small hot red peppers
  2 garlic cloves
  Optional: 1 teaspoon olive oil
  2 tablespoons fish liver
  ½ boiled potato

12 slices of stale French bread

COTRIADE DE MAQUEREAUX / *Cotriade of Mackerel*

A Breton fish soup.

Heat half of the butter and oil in a skillet and gently cook the mushrooms, shallot and the white part of 1 leek in it for about 10 minutes, covered. Shake the skillet occasionally so that the mixture cooks evenly.

Heat the remaining oil and butter in a large enamelware pot and cook the onions and the remaining leeks in it until they are tender. Stir in the flour and cook a little longer. Add the mushroom mixture, the water, wine and *bouquet garni*. Season lightly with salt and pepper, cover, and cook over low heat for 15 minutes. Add the garlic and the curry blended with the lemon juice. Mix well and then add the mackerel fillets. Cook over medium heat for 15 minutes and then transfer the fillets to a hot serving platter.

Taste the soup for seasoning and, if desired, reduce slightly over high heat to concentrate the flavor.

Line the bottom of a heated tureen with the toasted bread, discard the *bouquet garni*, and pour the soup over the toast. Serve the fillets separately, sprinkled with the parsley.

FOR 6 PERSONS:

3 tablespoons butter
3 tablespoons peanut oil
½ pound mushrooms, sliced
1 shallot, minced
5 leeks, white part only, minced
4 medium-sized onions, thinly
  sliced
5 tablespoons flour
3 cups water
3 cups Muscadet or other dry
  white wine

1 Bouquet Garni (p. 46)
Salt
Freshly ground black pepper
3 garlic cloves, minced
½ tablespoon curry powder
Juice of 1 lemon
6 mackerel fillets, each halved
6 slices of French bread, toasted
3 tablespoons chopped parsley

Fish Soup from Dieppe / SOUPE DIEPPOISE

Heat 2 tablespoons of the butter and the oil in a skillet and gently sauté the onions, leeks and celery in them until they are soft.

Scrub the mussels, put them into a saucepan with the water and ½ cup of the white wine, and cook them, tightly covered, over high heat for 7 or 8 minutes, or until they open. Drain the mussels and reserve the liquid after straining it through damp cheesecloth.

Put the fish stock in a saucepan; add the liquid from the mussels, the sautéed vegetables, *bouquet garni* and mashed garlic. Bring to the boiling point and simmer, covered, for about 20 minutes. Strain through a fine sieve and rectify the seasonings.

Place the fish fillets and the whole fish in a buttered very large enamelware baking dish. Season them with salt and pepper and add the strained fish stock. Bring to a boil on top of the stove, cover with buttered wax paper, and place the dish in a preheated 350° F. oven for 10 minutes; the liquid must barely simmer. Test for doneness and, if necessary, remove the sole fillets if they are done before the whole fish. Place 1 piece of fillet and 1 whole fish in each of 6 large hot soup plates and keep warm.

Pour the poaching liquid into a saucepan and bring to a boil. Mix the cornstarch with the remaining ½ cup of white wine. Stir this mixture into the hot stock to thicken it. Remove the soup from the heat and stir in the remaining butter. Correct the seasoning.

Remove the mussels from their shells and sprinkle over the fish in the soup bowls. Pour the hot soup over them and sprinkle with the chervil or parsley.

Serve the thinly sliced fried bread on the side.

FOR 6 PERSONS:

6 tablespoons butter	Salt
2 tablespoons vegetable oil	Freshly ground white pepper
2 medium-sized onions, minced	3 small gray sole fillets, cut
3 leeks, minced	into halves
1 celery stalk, minced	6 very small (less than 1 pound)
2½ pounds mussels	whole fish (pike, perch, etc.)
1 cup water	1 tablespoon cornstarch
1 cup dry white wine	2 tablespoons minced chervil or
3 cups Fish Stock (p. 166)	parsley
1 Bouquet Garni (p. 46)	6 thin slices of bread, fried in
1 garlic clove, mashed	butter and oil

Fish Soup Ferrecapienne / FERRECAPIENNE

As a contrast to *bouillabaisse*, this soup is made with one kind of fish* only.

Make a marinade with the thyme, grated lemon rind, oil, lemon juice, salt and pepper. Put the fish fillets into the marinade and marinate for 1 hour. Incidentally, the marinade may be as varied in its flavors as your taste is inclined. Fennel, bay leaves, savory, and rosemary may go into it, as well as a combination of mint, basil, coriander, nutmeg and cloves.

Cook all the vegetables in the heated butter and oil until they are soft and golden; stir in the flour, cook for a minute longer, and then gradually add the wine and the water. Season with salt and pepper and add the fish trimmings. Cook over medium heat for about 20 minutes and strain through a fine sieve.

Remove the fish fillets from the marinade and place them in a large skillet. Add the strained fish stock and poach the fillets for about 10 minutes, covered, over medium heat. Transfer them to a heated tureen (they may be cut into smaller pieces, if desired); put the tureen in a bowl of hot water to keep the fish hot.

Beat the egg yolks and the cream together. Bring the fish stock back to the boiling point. Add a little of it to the eggs and cream, stir this mixture into the hot stock, and heat very gently, stirring constantly, until the soup is slightly thickened.

Pour the soup into the tureen over the fish, add a few thin slices of bread fried in butter and oil, sprinkle with *fines herbes,* and serve immediately.

For the marinade:
½ **teaspoon ground thyme**
Grated rind of 1 lemon
¼ **cup olive oil**
Juice of 1 lemon
Salt
Freshly ground white pepper

4 **fillets (¾ pound each) of sea bass or red snapper***
2 **tablespoons butter**
2 **tablespoons olive oil**
1 **large onion, minced**
2 **carrots, minced**
1 **turnip, minced**

1 **celery stalk, minced**
1 **small rib of fennel, minced**
3 **tablespoons flour**
1 **cup dry white wine**
4 **cups water**
Salt
Freshly ground white pepper
***Trimmings and heads from the fish**
3 **egg yolks**
1 **cup heavy cream**
4 **slices of French bread, fried in butter and oil**
2 **tablespoons fresh Fines Herbes (p. 89)**

EDITORS' NOTE: **M. Oliver suggests a Mediterranean fish called* merlu *for this soup. We suggest you try a sea bass or red snapper, since* merlu *is unknown here.*

SOUPE DE SARDINES / *Sardine Soup*

Put the water, onions, garlic, tomatoes and *bouquet garni* into a large earthenware pot (*marmite*). Bring to the boiling point; season lightly with salt and pepper, and add the saffron, grated orange rind and olive oil. Boil for 10 minutes. Add the sardines to the pot and cook over medium heat for about 15 minutes.

Remove the fish to a bowl and keep them warm. Discard the *bouquet garni.* Strain the stock through a food mill into a large saucepan over medium heat.

Make the *ailloli*: pound together in a mortar the mashed garlic cloves, one of the egg yolks and the salt. Gradually add the oil as if you were making a mayonnaise. Beat energetically until the *ailloli* is thick and then beat in the remaining egg yolks. Add a little of the hot stock to the *ailloli* and then stir the mixture back into the rest of the stock. Heat the soup very gently for a few minutes longer.

Line the bottom of a heated tureen with the bread slices. Pour the thickened soup over the bread and top with the fish.

FOR 6 PERSONS:

1½ quarts water
2 onions, minced
2 garlic cloves, minced
2 tomatoes, peeled, seeded and
   chopped
1 Bouquet Garni (p. 46)
Salt
Freshly ground black pepper
1 teaspoon ground saffron
Grated rind of 1 orange

2 tablespoons olive oil
2 pounds fresh sardines, boned or
   not, as desired

For the ailloli:
4 garlic cloves, mashed
3 egg yolks
1 teaspoon salt
¾ cup olive oil
12 slices of French bread

Shad Soup / SOUPE D'ALOSE

Heat the butter and the olive oil in a large saucepan and gently sauté the onions, carrots and herbs in it until they are soft. Add the red wine and the water and the shad bones and heads. Season lightly with salt and nutmeg and simmer for 20 minutes. Strain the soup and pour it over thin slices of bread seasoned with freshly ground pepper in a hot tureen. Sprinkle with parsley.

2 tablespoons butter
1 tablespoon olive oil
2 onions, chopped
3 carrots, chopped
2 tablespoons minced fresh Fines
   Herbes (p. 89)
4 cups dry red wine

1 cup water
2 pounds raw shad bones and heads
Salt
Grated nutmeg
4 slices of French bread
Freshly ground black pepper
2 tablespoons chopped parsley

Bisques

It was the custom in the 18th and 19th centuries to thicken bisques with rice. By the beginning of the 20th century, while keeping to the same method, the rice was replaced by cream of rice. Finally in the last few years rice is often ignored altogether without anyone noticing the omission.

Lobster Bisque / BISQUE DE HOMARD

The method for making this soup is a personal one. I did not learn it from any chef or any writer, and I take the full responsibility for it.

Cut the lobster into sections as for lobster *américaine* (p. 381): cut the tail into 4 pieces and the body into halves. Save any lobster juices, and discard the sac behind the head.

Heat the butter in a very large skillet and cook the lobster pieces in it over high heat until they are bright red. Pour all of the butter in the skillet into a bowl. Flame the lobster pieces with half of the brandy, and turn the contents of the skillet out into another bowl. Return the butter to the skillet and add the onion, garlic, carrots, celery, parsley sprigs and shallots. Gently sauté the vegetables until they are soft. Add the *bouquet garni,* tomato purée, white wine, fish stock and the lobster pieces with their juices; season lightly with salt and cayenne pepper. Simmer, covered, for 20 minutes.

Remove the lobster pieces from the pot; remove the meat from the tail sections and the claws, and reserve the meat. Pound all of the lobster shells and the body sections in a mortar until they are thoroughly crushed. Add the pounded shells to the mixture in the skillet and simmer for 10 minutes.

Strain the soup first through a food mill or a coarse sieve, and then through a very fine sieve or damp cheesecloth into a saucepan. Bring it back to the boiling point. Mix together the egg yolks, cream and cornstarch. Add a little of the hot soup to this mixture, and then pour it back into the rest of the soup. Stir constantly over low heat until thickened. Correct the seasoning.

Cut the reserved lobster meat into small dice and stew them gently over hot water with the remaining ¼ cup of brandy. Add the lobster dice to the bisque at serving time.

FOR 6 PERSONS:

1 lobster (4 pounds)
6 tablespoons butter
½ cup brandy
1 large onion, minced
1 garlic clove, minced
2 carrots, minced
2 celery stalks, minced
6 parsley sprigs
3 large shallots, minced
1 Bouquet Garni (p. 46)

2 tablespoons Tomato Purée (p. 157)
2 cups dry white wine
4 cups Fish Stock (p. 166)
Salt
Pinch of cayenne pepper
4 egg yolks
1 cup heavy cream
1 tablespoon cornstarch

BISQUE D'HUÎTRES / *Oyster Bisque*

Prepare a lobster bisque as described above, but do not thicken with the egg yolks, cream and cornstarch until after the oysters have been cooked in this manner:

Open the oysters and carefully reserve all of their juice. Strain the juice to remove any traces of sand. Simmer the oysters in their liquid and the fish stock over low heat for 3 minutes. Drain them and add the poaching liquid to the bisque. Reduce the bisque rapidly by about one third. Then thicken it with the cornstarch, egg yolks and cream, as described in the lobster bisque recipe.

Add the oysters to the bisque, or serve them separately threaded on a skewer.

FOR 6 PERSONS:

1 recipe Lobster Bisque (above)
18 oysters

1 cup Fish Stock (p. 166)

Shrimp Bisque / BISQUE DE CREVETTES

Heat the butter and the oil in a saucepan and add the shelled shrimp with the celery, onions, carrots, and the prosciutto or Canadian bacon. Stir over medium heat for 5 minutes. Add the thyme, bay leaf and wine. Simmer, covered, for 10 minutes. Remove the bay leaf. Purée the mixture through a food mill. Put the purée into a saucepan and add the fish stock. Bring to the boiling point and simmer for 5 minutes. Season with salt and freshly ground pepper, strain through a fine sieve, and return to the heat. Bring to the boiling point again.

Make the *liaison* (thickening): blend the cornstarch with the cream and egg yolks. Remove the soup from the heat, stir one fourth of it into the egg-yolk mixture, and then pour it back into the remaining soup, stirring constantly with a small wire whisk. Return the saucepan to low heat and stir constantly until thickened. Strain again through a very fine sieve or triple layer of cheesecloth. Reheat, pour into a hot tureen, and serve immediately.

2 tablespoons butter	½ teaspoon ground thyme
1 tablespoon vegetable oil	1 bay leaf
1½ pounds raw shrimp, shelled and deveined	1 cup dry white wine
1 celery stalk, minced	4 cups Fish Stock (p. 166)
2 onions, minced	Salt
2 carrots, minced	Freshly ground white pepper
¼ cup finely minced prosciutto or Canadian bacon	2 teaspoons cornstarch
	½ cup heavy cream
	4 egg yolks

Cold Shrimp Bisque / BISQUE DE CREVETTES FROIDE

Cook the unpeeled shrimp in the hot oil and butter in a large skillet over low heat, together with the celery, onions, carrots, ham, thyme and bay leaf. Cover the skillet and cook for about 15 minutes. Stir occasionally as the shrimp cook.

When the shrimp are bright pink, shell them and reserve half of them. Mix the other half of them and all of the shells with the vegetables. Pound this mixture in a mortar until it is thoroughly crushed and then purée through a food mill. Add the fish stock to the purée and force through a fine sieve or blend it in an electric blender.

Bring the soup back to the boiling point, remove it from the heat, and stir in the *crème fraîche*, lightly whipped. Season with salt and freshly ground pepper.

Cut the reserved shrimp into dice, put them into a tureen, and pour the soup over them. Chill in the refrigerator and serve very cold.

1½ pounds shrimp, unpeeled	2 sprigs of fresh thyme or ½ teaspoon ground thyme
1 tablespoon vegetable oil	
3 tablespoons butter	1 bay leaf
1 celery stalk, minced	4 cups Fish Stock (p. 166)
2 onions, minced	¼ cup Crème Fraîche (p. 666)
2 carrots, minced	Salt
¼ cup minced prosciutto or Canadian bacon	Freshly ground white pepper

2
HORS-D'OEUVRE
Les Hors-d'Oeuvre

COLD HORS-D'OEUVRE

Hors-d'Oeuvre Froids

Cold Vegetable Hors-d'Oeuvre
Hors-d'Oeuvre Froids de Légumes

Artichokes with Anchovy Sauce /
ARTICHAUTS À L'ANCHOÏADE

EDITORS' NOTE: *The artichokes used in France for eating raw are much smaller and much more tender than our own artichokes. Baby artichokes of this kind can sometimes be found in vegetable markets catering to people of Mediterranean descent. Or else, use the smallest and freshest artichokes you can find. Allow 1 artichoke and 1 to 2 tablespoons of sauce for each serving.*

Break off the small bottom leaves of the artichokes and cut off the stems. Wash them in plenty of water and stand them up on the dish from which they will be served. Drain the oil from the can of anchovy fillets and mash them with 2 tablespoons of vinegar. Season lightly with pepper and gradually beat in the olive oil, using enough to make a sauce with the consistency of mayonnaise. Pour the sauce into a sauceboat and serve with the artichokes.

FOR 6 PERSONS:

6 **very small young artichokes**
1 **can (2 ounces) anchovies preserved in oil**

2 **tablespoons wine vinegar**
Freshly ground black pepper
5 **(or more) tablespoons olive oil**

Artichokes with Sauce Poivrade /
ARTICHAUTS À LA POIVRADE

Proceed as directed in Artichokes with Anchovy Sauce (above), substituting about ½ cup of Sauce Poivrade (p. 765) for the anchovy sauce.

/ *Artichokes with French Dressing*

ARTICHAUTS À LA VINAIGRETTE

Cook the artichokes in salted water, as described on page 543. When they are tender, drain and cool them.

Prepare the French dressing and serve it separately in a sauceboat.

FOR 6 PERSONS:

6 large artichokes
1 double recipe Simple French
Dressing (p. 787)

/ *Artichokes with Mustard Sauce*

ARTICHAUTS À LA MOUTARDE

Proceed as directed in the previous recipe. Serve the well-drained artichokes from a serving dish.

Prepare a recipe of Cream Mustard Sauce (p. 789), and serve it separately in a sauceboat.

/ *Artichokes with Sauce Tartare*

ARTICHAUTS SAUCE TARTARE

Cook the artichokes in salted water as described on page 543. When they are tender, turn them upside down and drain them on a rack. Squeeze them gently with the fingers to drain off all the cooking water. Allow them to cool completely.

Prepare the *sauce tartare* and serve it separately in a sauceboat.

FOR 6 PERSONS:

6 artichokes   **1 cup Sauce Tartare (p. 785)**

/ *Artichoke Hearts and Asparagus Salad*

FONDS D'ARTICHAUTS ET POINTES D'ASPERGES EN SALADE

Cook the two vegetables separately in salted water until tender—the asparagus tips will take 8 to 10 minutes, the artichoke hearts 20 to 30 minutes—and drain them on a rack.

Place the asparagus tips in the middle of a serving dish. Cut the artichoke hearts into fine slices and place them around the asparagus. Sprinkle with the French dressing with *fines herbes* and serve.

FOR 6 PERSONS:

1 pound asparagus tips   **1 double recipe French Dressing**
6 artichoke hearts   **with Fines Herbes (p. 788)**

Artichoke Hearts with Foie Gras /

FONDS D'ARTICHAUTS GARNIS

Poach the artichoke hearts as directed on page 549. Drain them, let them cool, and arrange them on a serving dish.

Wash the head of romaine lettuce and shred it into fine strips. Pour the French dressing over it and toss to mix.

Cut the *foie gras* into small cubes and add them to the salad. Mix well. Fill each artichoke heart with a little salad and garnish the top with a few pieces of coarsely chopped nuts.

Pile any remaining salad in the center of the dish and top with the rest of the chopped nuts.

FOR 6 PERSONS:

6 artichoke hearts
1 small head of romaine lettuce
½ cup Simple French Dressing
  (p. 787)

¼ cup (about 2 ounces) foie gras
¼ cup chopped walnuts

Artichoke Hearts à la Grecque /

FONDS D'ARTICHAUTS À LA GRECQUE

Cut the carrots and onions into small dice and sauté them gently in 2 tablespoons of the olive oil in a casserole for about 15 minutes. When they are soft, add the raw artichoke hearts, the *bouquet garni,* the wine and water. Season with salt and a few crushed peppercorns. Add the whole coriander seeds and the lemon.

Cover and simmer gently for about 30 minutes.

When the artichoke hearts are tender, remove the casserole from the heat, cool, and add the remaining 6 tablespoons of olive oil. Let stand for 2 hours.

Remove the artichoke hearts, carrots and onions with a slotted spoon and place in a deep vegetable dish. Discard the *bouquet garni.* Strain the cooking liquid, boil it down rapidly to about 1½ cups, and allow it to cool. Pour it over the vegetables and serve chilled.

FOR 4 PERSONS:

2 carrots
2 onions
½ cup olive oil
8 raw artichoke hearts
1 Bouquet Garni (p. 46)
2 cups dry white wine

1 cup water
Salt
Crushed peppercorns
6 coriander seeds
1 lemon, peeled and sliced

Asparagus with Mayonnaise /

ASPERGES À LA MAYONNAISE

Make sure that the asparagus is not overcooked but is very well drained. At serving time, add the whipped *crème fraîche* and the stiffly beaten egg white to the mayonnaise. Check the seasoning; if necessary, add a little salt and pepper.

Arrange the asparagus on the serving dish and serve the sauce separately.
Or else, coat the asparagus with the sauce.

FOR 4 PERSONS:

1½ pounds cooked asparagus
2 tablespoons Crème Fraîche (p. 666), whipped
1 egg white, stiffly beaten

1 cup Mayonnaise (p. 782)
Salt
Freshly ground white pepper

/ *Asparagus with Mustard Sauce*

ASPERGES À LA SAUCE MOUTARDE

Arrange the chilled asparagus on a serving dish and serve the mustard sauce on the side.

FOR 4 PERSONS:

1½ pounds cooked asparagus, chilled

1 cup Cream Mustard Sauce (p. 789)

/ *Asparagus with Sauce Tartare*

ASPERGES À LA SAUCE TARTARE

Arrange the chilled asparagus on a serving dish and serve the sauce on the side.

FOR 4 PERSONS:

1½ pounds cooked asparagus, chilled

1 cup Sauce Tartare (p. 785)

AVOCATS VINAIGRETTE / *Avocados with French Dressing*

Cut the avocados lengthwise into halves, remove the stones, sprinkle them lightly with freshly ground pepper, and put into each half 2 tablespoons of French dressing. Arrange them on a large platter or on individual plates.

Each avocado half may be filled with crab salad (crabmeat sprinkled with a little French dressing). This is a classic dish of the Pacific coast.

FOR 4 PERSONS:

2 avocados
½ cup Simple French Dressing (p. 787), made with lemon

Optional: 1 cup crab salad

CRÊPES AUX AVOCATS / *Avocado Crêpes*

Put the cornmeal into a bowl, add the boiling water, and let the mixture rest for 10 minutes. Add the eggs, 1 teaspoon salt, a little pepper, the vegetable oil and the butter; beat thoroughly. Then gradually add sufficient milk to make a pancake batter about as thick as heavy cream.

Let the batter rest for 2 hours.

Meantime, cut the avocados into halves, remove the stones, and then spoon out the flesh. Purée the flesh in a blender. Beat the olive oil into the purée and season with cayenne pepper, salt and black pepper to taste. Add the tarragon.

Make about 12 *crêpes* in the usual manner and let them cool. Fill them with the avocado mixture and roll them up. If necessary, secure them with food picks. Serve cold.

FOR 6 PERSONS:

½ cup cornmeal	2 tablespoons butter, melted
½ cup boiling water	½ cup lukewarm milk, approximately
2 eggs	4 medium-sized avocados
Salt	3 tablespoons olive oil
Freshly ground black pepper	Cayenne pepper
1 tablespoon vegetable oil	2 tablespoons minced fresh tarragon

Broad or Fava Beans with Coarse Salt /
FÈVES FRAÎCHES À LA CROQUE-AU-SEL

Choose very fresh young broad or fava beans, shell them, and put them into a serving dish. Serve them with coarse salt, fresh French bread and sweet butter on the side.

This isn't really a recipe, but a very popular way of eating broad or fava beans at the time of the first seasonal beans, when they're still small and tender.

Green-Bean Salad / HARICOTS VERTS EN SALADE

Cook the green beans in boiling salted water until barely tender, 8 to 10 minutes. Drain and cool them in a strainer.

Make the French dressing, pour it over the cold beans in a bowl, and toss. Depending on your taste, you may add a minced garlic clove.

FOR 4 PERSONS:

1½ pounds green snap beans	Optional: 1 garlic clove, minced
½ cup French Dressing with Fines Herbes (p. 788)	

White-Bean Salad / HARICOTS BLANCS FRAIS EN SALADE

Cook the shelled fresh white beans in boiling salted water for about 15 minutes, or until they are just tender. Drain them, put them into a serving dish, and let them cool.

AVOCADO CRÊPES
LES CRÊPES AUX AVOCATS

You must let the crêpe *batter rest for 2 hours before making the* crêpes, *even if you are in a hurry!*

If you don't have a blender for puréeing the avocado, press the flesh through a fine sieve.

Fry the avocado crêpes *carefully—they are somewhat fragile.*

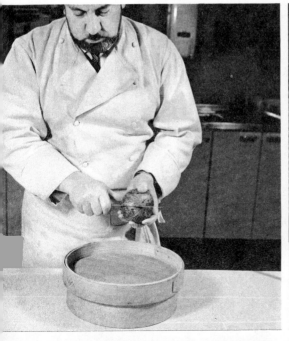

Make the French dressing with *fines herbes,* pour it over the cooled beans, and toss.

FOR 4 PERSONS:

4 cups shelled fresh white beans
¾ cup French Dressing with Fines
Herbes (p. 788)

Beet Salad / BETTERAVES EN SALADE

Cook the beets in salted water for about 40 minutes, peel them, and cut them into thin slices or small dice. Chill them and put them into a salad dish.

Sprinkle the beets with the French dressing, minced *fines herbes* and garlic. Toss well and serve cold.

Incidentally, I would not advise you to decorate Raw Vegetables Vinaigrette (p. 220) with beets. They are apt to bleed and to destroy the appearance of a well-arranged platter.

FOR 4 PERSONS:

6 medium-sized beets
½ cup Simple French Dressing
(p. 787)

2 tablespoons minced Fines Herbes
(p. 89)
1 garlic clove, minced

Beet Salad à la Crème / BETTERAVES À LA CRÈME

Boil the beets in salted water for about 40 minutes.

Peel them, cut them into thin slices, and arrange them on a long flat serving dish. Chill well.

Mix the mustard with the *crème fraîche* in a bowl, thin the mixture with the lemon juice, and season with salt and pepper to taste. Pour the dressing over the beets. Decorate with the chopped hard-cooked eggs and sprinkle with a little grated horseradish.

FOR 4 PERSONS:

6 medium-sized beets
3 tablespoons French mustard
½ cup Crème Fraîche (p. 666)
Juice of 1 lemon

Salt
Freshly ground black pepper
2 hard-cooked eggs, chopped
1 teaspoon grated horseradish

Cabbage Salad / CHOU ROUGE OU VERT EN SALADE

Choose a red or green cabbage that is very firm and remove the stalk and the wilted outer leaves. Cut it into halves, cut out the tough center, and then shred it fine.

Make the French dressing in a serving dish, add the shredded cabbage, and toss. Let it stand in the refrigerator for 48 hours.

At serving time, sprinkle with finely minced *fines herbes*.

FOR 6 PERSONS:

1 medium-sized red or green cabbage
1 cup Simple French Dressing
   (p. 787)

2 tablespoons finely minced Fines
   Herbes (p. 89)

CARDONS À LA GRECQUE / *Cardoons à la Grecque*

EDITORS' NOTE: *Cardoons are a vegetable belonging to the thistle family, found in the United States in Italian vegetable markets. The plant resembles a giant bunch of celery and may be more than 4 feet tall. However, the smaller the cardoon, the better the taste. Their color is greenish white, and their taste delicate and slightly bitter. They must be precooked before being put in a salad or finished with a sauce.*

If the cardoons are very large, use only about 12 inches of the stalks from the bottom up since the tops will be tough. To prepare the cardoons, trim off the tops and tough outer stalks. Pare them with a vegetable parer, as you would celery. Cut them into 2-inch pieces. Since cardoons discolor in the air as soon as they are cut up, and since they should be kept snowy white, drop the prepared pieces into a bowl of acidulated water (1 quart cold water to the juice of 1 large lemon) until cooking time.

Cook the carrots and onions gently in 2 tablespoons of the oil in a covered casserole for about 10 minutes, or until they are half tender. Add the prepared cardoons, the wine and the water. Season with salt and slightly crushed peppercorns; add the *bouquet garni,* the coriander seeds and the lemon slices. Simmer, covered, over low heat for about 1½ hours. When the cardoons are tender, add the remaining olive oil and let them cool in their stock for about 2 hours. Discard the *bouquet garni.*

Chill the cardoons and serve them with the carrots and onions and as much of the cooking liquid as desired.

FOR 4 PERSONS:

1 large or 2 medium-sized cardoons
2 carrots, diced
2 onions, sliced
¼ cup olive oil
2 cups dry white wine
1 cup water

Salt
4 peppercorns, slightly crushed
1 Bouquet Garni (p. 46)
6 coriander seeds
1 lemon, peeled and thinly sliced

CARDONS EN SALADE / *Cardoon Salad*

Heat the water together with the butter, lemon juice and salt. When the water is boiling, add the prepared cardoons. Simmer, covered, for about 1½ hours, or until the cardoons are tender. Drain the cardoons and dry them on kitchen toweling. Let them cool and arrange them in a serving dish.

Pour the French dressing over them and sprinkle with *fines herbes*. Serve chilled.

FOR 4 PERSONS:

4 cups water
3 tablespoons butter
Juice of 1 lemon
2 teaspoons salt
2 medium-sized cardoons, prepared
    for cooking as in the preceding
    recipe

½ cup Simple French Dressing
    (p. 787)
2 tablespoons minced Fines Herbes
    (p. 89)

Carrot Salad | CAROTTES RAPÉES

Pare the carrots and either cut them into very thin julienne strips or grate them coarsely.

Pile the carrots in the shape of a dome on a serving dish, and sprinkle them with the French dressing and the parsley. Surround the carrots with the sliced hard-cooked eggs and the sardines.

FOR 4 PERSONS:

1 pound small young carrots
⅓ cup Simple French Dressing
    (p. 787)

2 tablespoons minced parsley
2 hard-cooked eggs, sliced
8 small sardines, preserved in oil

Cauliflower Mayonnaise |

SALADE DE CHOU-FLEUR MAYONNAISE

Trim the cauliflower, wash it, and separate it into flowerets. Cook these in boiling salted water to cover for about 10 minutes, or until they are barely cooked and still very firm. Drain, rinse under running cold water, and drain on toweling.

Meantime, prepare the French dressing with *fines herbes*.

Place the flowerets in a serving dish and pour the dressing over them. Toss them lightly and then thinly coat with mayonnaise. Serve chilled.

FOR 4 PERSONS:

1 medium-sized cauliflower
½ cup French Dressing with Fines
    Herbes (p. 788)

½ cup Mayonnaise (p. 782)

Cauliflower à la Pimpernel | CHOU-FLEUR PIMPRENELLE

Wash the cauliflower and separate it into flowerets. Cook them in boiling salted water to cover for about 10 minutes, or until the cauliflower is barely tender, but still very firm. Drain, rinse under running cold water, and drain again thoroughly.

Marinate the cooked flowerets in the French dressing for 2 hours.

Make the mustard sauce and add the *crème fraîche* to it. Drain the cauliflower from the dressing, put it into a serving dish, and coat it with the mustard sauce. Sprinkle with the *fines herbes* and serve chilled.

FOR 4 PERSONS:

1 medium-sized cauliflower	2 tablespoons Crème Fraîche
½ cup Simple French Dressing	(p. 666)
(p. 787)	2 tablespoons minced Fines Herbes
1 cup Cream Mustard Sauce (p. 789)	(p. 89)

Note: Cauliflower may be prepared *à la Grecque* following the recipe for Mushrooms and Onions à la Grecque (p. 216), substituting cauliflower for the mushrooms and onions. The cooking time will have to be shortened; cook only as long as necessary for the flowerets to be tender but firm.

CHOU-FLEUR VINAIGRETTE / *Cauliflower Vinaigrette*

Proceed as in the preceding recipe, but do not use any mustard sauce. Instead, sprinkle the finely minced *fines herbes* over the cauliflower after it has marinated in the French dressing.

SALADE DE CÉLERI / *Celery Salad*

Trim the celery, cut off the green leaves, and remove any coarse outer stalks. If necessary, pare the stalks with a vegetable parer. Cut the tender white stalks into 3-inch pieces and slice the heart. Wash and drain the celery and dry it in kitchen towels.

Pour the French dressing into a serving bowl, add the celery, and toss well.

Prepare this salad a few hours in advance so that the celery has time to marinate in the dressing. Keep it chilled until serving time.

FOR 4 PERSONS:

1 large bunch of white celery
½ cup Simple French Dressing
(p. 787)

CÉLERI-RAVE À LA GRECQUE / *Knob Celery à la Grecque*

EDITORS' NOTE: *Knob celery, also known as celeriac or celery root, is a dark, coarse root vegetable of the celery family. Only the root is eaten. Knob celery is very popular in Europe and far more common than our branch celery.*

Peel the knob celery, cut it into ¾-inch dice, and sprinkle it with lemon juice. Let it stand for 15 minutes.

Cook the carrots and onions gently in 2 tablespoons of the oil in a casserole for about 10 minutes. Add the knob celery and stir well. Add the wine and the water.

Season lightly with salt and slightly crushed peppercorns. Add the coriander seeds, the *bouquet garni* and the lemon slices. Cook, covered, over medium heat for about 15 minutes, or until the celery is barely tender.

Drain the vegetables and discard the *bouquet garni.* Boil the cooking liquid over high heat until it is reduced to about 1 cup. Add the remaining olive oil and marinate the vegetables in this reduced liquid for 2 hours. Chill and then serve in a suitable dish.

FOR 4 PERSONS:

2 large celery knobs
Juice of 1 lemon
2 carrots, diced
2 onions, diced
5 tablespoons olive oil
2 cups dry white wine

1 cup water
Salt
4 peppercorns, slightly crushed
6 coriander seeds
1 Bouquet Garni (p. 46)
1 lemon, peeled and sliced

Knob Celery Rémoulade | CÊLERI-RAVE EN RÉMOULADE

Peel the knob celery, cut it into thin julienne strips, and sprinkle it with ½ teaspoon of salt and the vinegar. Let it rest for 15 minutes.

Drain the celery, toss it with the *sauce rémoulade,* and put it in a serving dish. Sprinkle it with the *fines herbes* and chill.

FOR 4 PERSONS:

2 large celery knobs
Salt
½ cup vinegar

¾ cup Sauce Rémoulade (p. 789)
2 tablespoons minced Fines Herbes
    (p. 89)

Stuffed Knob Celery | CÉLERI-RAVE FARCI

Peel the knob celery and cut each knob into halves. Cut out the center to form a hollow. Rub all the surfaces with sliced lemon to prevent discoloring. Cook the pieces in boiling salted water for about 30 minutes, or until they are tender. Drain well and cool them.

Prepare a vegetable *macédoine* (see p. 111) with the peas, carrots, turnip and green beans. Let these vegetables cool and toss them with the mayonnaise.

Fill the knob celery halves with this mixture and chill until serving time. Sprinkle with the *fines herbes* just before serving.

FOR 4 PERSONS:

2 large celery knobs
1 lemon, sliced
½ cup cooked peas
2 cooked carrots, finely diced
1 cooked turnip, finely diced

½ cup cooked green snap beans,
    slivered
1 cup Mayonnaise (p. 782)
4 tablespoons minced Fines Herbes
    (p. 89)

CONCOMBRES À LA GRECQUE / *Cucumbers à la Grecque*

Peel the cucumbers and cut them into large dice.

Cook the minced onion and carrot gently in 1 tablespoon of the olive oil and the peanut oil in a casserole for about 10 minutes, or until they are tender.

Add the diced cucumbers, the *bouquet garni,* the wine and water. Season with salt and pepper; add the coriander seeds and the sliced lemon. Bring to the boiling point and simmer for about 10 minutes, depending on the size of the diced cucumbers. They must keep their shape and remain firm. Drain the vegetables and discard the *bouquet garni.* Boil the cooking liquid until it is reduced to about ¾ cup.

Remove the liquid from the heat and cool. Add the remaining 2 tablespoons of olive oil and marinate the vegetables in this liquid for 2 hours. Serve cold.

FOR 4 PERSONS:

2 large cucumbers	2 cups dry white wine
1 onion, minced	1 cup water
1 carrot, minced	Salt
3 tablespoons olive oil	4 peppercorns, crushed
1 tablespoon peanut oil	6 coriander seeds
1 Bouquet Garni (p. 46)	1 lemon, peeled and sliced

CONCOMBRES EN SALADE / *Cucumber Salad*

Peel the cucumbers and cut them lengthwise into quarters; remove the seeds, and slice them as thinly as you like. Sprinkle the cucumbers generously with the salt and put them into a strainer for several hours so that their excess water will drain off.

Make the French dressing in a serving dish. Add the drained cucumbers, toss, and chill for about 15 minutes before serving.

FOR 4 PERSONS:

2 large cucumbers	⅓ cup Simple French Dressing
1 handful coarse salt	(p. 787)

Note: You may add minced tomatoes (first peeled, seeded, and drained) to the cucumbers. Also, instead of a French dressing, you may dress them with Crème Fraîche (p. 666), diluted with a little lemon juice.

AUBERGINES EN SALADE / *Eggplant Salad*

Peel the eggplants and chop into medium dice. Put them on a dish, sprinkle with coarse salt, and let them draw water for 10 minutes. Drain, squeeze dry in a kitchen towel, and arrange them on a serving dish.

Sprinkle the eggplant with the French dressing and with finely minced chervil and tarragon.

FOR 4 PERSONS:

2 small eggplants
2 tablespoons coarse salt
½ cup Simple French Dressing
(p. 787)

1 tablespoon each of minced fresh
chervil and tarragon

Endives with Anchovy Dressing /
ENDIVES CRUES À L'ANCHOÏADE

Choose fresh, solid Belgian endives. Trim, wash, and dry them, but do not separate the leaves. Mash the anchovies, stir in the mustard, season lightly with pepper, add the vinegar, and blend thoroughly. Finally, add the oil gradually, beating constantly, until the sauce has the consistency of very heavy cream.

Serve the sauce separately, so that each diner may help himself, dipping each endive leaf into the sauce.

FOR 4 PERSONS:

4 large Belgian endives
16 anchovy fillets, drained
1 teaspoon (or more, to taste)
French mustard

Freshly ground black pepper
2 tablespoons vinegar
½ cup olive oil

Fennel à la Grecque / FENOUIL À LA GRECQUE

Trim the fennel stalks, wash them, cut them into quarters, and dry them.

Put the fennel, lemon rind, thyme, bay leaf and the tomato paste mixed with the wine into a casserole (*cocotte*). Season with salt and pepper and add the coriander seeds and the oil.

Simmer over low heat for about 30 minutes. If desired, the cooking liquid now may be strained, reduced over high heat for a stronger flavor, and then poured back over the fennel. Cool.

Pour everything into a deep serving dish and chill before serving.

FOR 4 PERSONS:

4 large bulbs of fennel
Grated rind of 1 lemon
½ teaspoon ground thyme
1 bay leaf
4 tablespoons tomato paste

3 cups dry white wine
Salt
Freshly ground black pepper
8 coriander seeds
4 tablespoons olive oil

Leeks à la Grecque / POIREAUX À LA GRECQUE

Choose small leeks, trim off the green ends and the roots, and wash them very thoroughly. If they are at all large, cut them lengthwise into halves. Put them side by side in a casserole.

Pour the wine over the leeks and add the tomato paste mixed with the water. Season lightly with salt and add the peppercorns, coriander seeds, thyme, bay leaf, lemon rind and oil.

Cover the casserole and simmer for about 20 minutes, or until the leeks are tender.

Strain the cooking liquid into a saucepan and reduce it over high heat to about 1 cup.

Place the leeks in a serving dish, pour the reduced liquid over them, and chill before serving.

FOR 4 PERSONS:

16 small leeks	6 coriander seeds
3 cups dry white wine	1 sprig of thyme, or ¼ teaspoon
2 tablespoons tomato paste	dried thyme
1 cup water	1 bay leaf
Salt	Grated rind of 1 lemon
4 peppercorns	4 tablespoons olive oil

POIREAUX FARCIS / *Stuffed Leeks*

Generally, in stuffing vegetables such as tomatoes or squash, they are cut into halves, then the halves are scooped out and filled with a stuffing. However, the following recipe is a little more complicated.

Trim the leeks by cutting off the roots and the green ends and wash them thoroughly. Blanch them in boiling salted water for barely 10 minutes; they must remain firm. Remove the leeks with a slotted spoon and drain them in a sieve or on kitchen toweling.

Put the rice into a bowl. Add the sausage meat, bread crumbs, *fines herbes* and the egg; season with a little salt and cayenne pepper and the nutmeg. Mix well.

Core each of the cooked leeks with a vegetable parer or a marrow knife in order to make an opening in the center. Fill each opening with a little of the stuffing. Put the leeks side by side in an oiled flat baking dish, sprinkle with a little more oil, and cover the dish with aluminum foil which you have oiled on the side facing the leeks. Cook in a preheated 350° F. oven for 35 to 40 minutes. Cool the leeks before serving them.

Note: You can make a salad with the cored parts of the leeks. Cook them in boiling salted water until tender and serve them with a French dressing.

FOR 4 PERSONS:

12 large leeks	1 egg
1 cup cooked rice	Salt
¼ pound cooked sausage meat,	Cayenne pepper
finely crumbled	Pinch of grated nutmeg
¼ cup soft bread crumbs	⅓ cup olive oil
1 tablespoon Fines Herbes	
(p. 89)	

Melon /

You may serve melon as an hors-d'oeuvre, with very thin slices of Bayonne ham, or prosciutto, or with equally thinly sliced smoked salmon, or with powdered sugar or with Port wine.

Formerly, the melon used to be sliced, but nowadays small melons are popular and are simply cut into halves and seeded, and a half is presented as an individual serving. They are then eaten with a spoon, rather than with a knife and fork.

Another excellent way of serving melon is to cut it into little balls with a melon cutter, then marinate the little balls in Port. The melon balls may be served in sherbet glasses or they may be put back into the shells.

Mushrooms à la Grecque / CHAMPIGNONS À LA GRECQUE

Prepare in the same manner as Artichoke Hearts à la Grecque (p. 204), substituting 2 pounds of small mushrooms for the artichoke hearts. Trim off the ends of the mushrooms, but leave them whole. Reduce the cooking time for the mushrooms to about 15 minutes.

Marinated Mushrooms / CÈPES MARINÉS

EDITOR'S NOTE: Cèpes (Boletus) *are but one of the many mushrooms available in France. Their preparation can be applied to our own mushrooms.*

Blanch the mushrooms by cooking them in boiling salted water to cover for 3 minutes. Drain them well and put them into a deep bowl.

Combine the marinade ingredients, that is, the oil, garlic, thyme sprig, bay leaf, peppercorns, coriander, fennel seeds and parsley or parsley roots. Simmer them, covered, over very low heat for 15 minutes.

Pour the simmering marinade over the mushrooms, let them cool, and then chill the mushrooms for 3 to 4 days. Toss them occasionally. Drain them before serving and serve them drizzled with a little of the marinade.

FOR 4 PERSONS:

2 pounds small white mushrooms	½ bay leaf
¾ cup olive oil	6 peppercorns, slightly crushed
1 garlic clove, minced	½ teaspoon ground coriander
1 sprig of thyme, or ½ teaspoon dried thyme	½ teaspoon fennel seeds
	4 parsley roots, or 6 parsley sprigs

Mushrooms and Onions à la Grecque /

CHAMPIGNONS ET OIGNONS À LA GRECQUE

Put the mushrooms and the onions into a casserole together with the grated lemon rind, the thyme, bay leaf and the tomato paste mixed with the wine. Season lightly with salt and pepper; add the coriander seeds and the olive oil. Simmer, uncovered, for about 15 minutes, and cool. If desired, the cooking liquid may be strained, reduced over high heat to about 1½ cups, and then poured back over the vegetables.

FOR 4 PERSONS:

1 **pound very small mushrooms**	4 **tablespoons tomato paste**
½ **pound tiny white (pickling)**	3 **cups dry white wine**
onions, peeled	**Salt**
Grated rind of 1 lemon	**Freshly ground black pepper**
1 **sprig of thyme or ½ teaspoon**	6 **coriander seeds**
ground thyme	4 **tablespoons olive oil**
1 **bay leaf**	

CHAMPIGNONS EN SALADE / *Mushroom Salad*

Cut the mushrooms into very thin slices and put them into a deep serving dish.

Make the dressing and pour it over the mushrooms. Toss well and chill for about 1 hour before serving.

FOR 4 PERSONS:

1 **pound very white mushrooms**
½ **cup Simple French Dressing**
 (p. 787), made with lemon juice

/ *Mushroom and Truffle Salad*

CHAMPIGNONS ET TRUFFES EN SALADE

Proceed as in the preceding recipe and add finely sliced fresh white or black truffles to taste.

OLIVES FARCIES / *Stuffed Olives*

Olives complement any hors-d'oeuvre. Green or black olives may be served without any further preparation.

Perfect black olives may be marinated for a few days in olive oil, with the addition of crushed garlic, ground or dried thyme and crushed dried or fresh rosemary leaves. Toss frequently to insure uniform coating.

Green olives, as their name indicates, are unripe but very appetizing. Choose large ones, and if not already pitted, pit them (a mechanical gadget does this neatly) and stuff their cavities with one of the compound butters (pp. 792 to 795), such as anchovy or mustard butter.

OIGNONS À LA GRECQUE / *Onions à la Grecque*

Prepare in the same manner as Artichoke Hearts à la Grecque (p. 204), substituting about 1½ pounds of peeled tiny white onions for the artichoke hearts. Reduce the cooking time for the onions to about 15 minutes; the onions must remain whole and be barely tender.

Sweet Pepper Salad | PIMENTS DOUX GRILLÉS EN SALADE

Trim, wash, and dry the sweet peppers.

Turn them under a broiler or simply over an open flame on top of the stove until the outer skin is completely black and blistered. Scrape the skin off under running cold water, cut off the tops of the peppers, and remove seeds and membranes. Cut the peppers into thin julienne strips, arrange them in a serving dish, and pour the French dressing over them.

FOR 4 PERSONS:

6 large sweet peppers
¼ cup Simple French Dressing
(p. 787)

Pickles | PICALLILIS

They may be bought ready to eat. I personally do not consider them an hors-d'oeuvre, but as an accompaniment for boiled meats or fish.

Red Radishes | RADIS ROSES

Choose very firm radishes and wash them in cold water. Cut off their stems and tips and scrape them clean with a sharp little knife.

Wash the radishes again, drain them well, and put them into a serving dish.

Serve the radishes with salt and very fresh sweet butter.

I can't specify the number of radishes you'll need since radishes, eaten this way, are something to while away the time in a pleasant and appetizing manner.

Black Radishes | RADIS NOIRS

Trim and wash black radishes and cut them into thin rounds. Sprinkle them with salt and let them stand for a few minutes.

Drain the black radishes, dry them with kitchen toweling, and serve them with fresh sweet butter and salt.

Tomatoes Antiboise | TOMATES À L'ANTIBOISE

Choose small, firm, very ripe tomatoes. Cut off the tops and scoop out the insides. Sprinkle each of the tomato cavities with a little salt and pepper, 1 tablespoon of oil and 1 teaspoon of vinegar. Let them marinate for 2 hours.

Mince the hard-cooked eggs and mash them with the tunafish, capers, parsley, tarragon and chervil to make a smooth paste. Blend with the mayonnaise and the anchovy paste.

Pour the marinade out of the tomatoes and reserve. Fill each of the tomatoes with some of the stuffing and place them on a serving dish. Top each with a slice of lemon and a parsley sprig. Sprinkle a little of the reserved marinade over each and chill until serving time.

FOR 4 PERSONS:

8 small ripe tomatoes
Salt
Freshly ground black pepper
½ cup olive oil
3 tablespoons vinegar
4 hard-cooked eggs
1 cup tunafish, drained and flaked
1 tablespoon capers

1 tablespoon minced parsley
1 tablespoon minced tarragon
1 tablespoon minced chervil
1 cup Mayonnaise (p. 782)
1 tablespoon anchovy paste
8 slices of lemon
8 parsley sprigs

/ *Tomatoes Stuffed with Mussels*

TOMATES FARCIES AUX MOULES

Choose small ripe tomatoes. Cut off the tops and scoop out the insides. Sprinkle the cavities with salt and pepper.

Prepare the mussels *marinières,* using about 2 pounds of mussels. Remove the mussels from their shells and cool them in the liquor in which they cooked, which you have carefully strained.

Prepare a rather stiff mayonnaise and thin it slightly with a little of the strained mussel cooking liquid. Add the cooled mussels to the mayonnaise.

Depending on their size, stuff each tomato with 3 or 4 mussels. Sprinkle the tops with the *fines herbes* and put them into a serving dish. Garnish with lemon slices and parsley sprigs.

FOR 4 PERSONS:

8 small ripe tomatoes
Salt
Freshly ground black pepper
1 recipe Mussels Marinières
(p. 389)

1½ cups Mayonnaise (p. 782)
2 tablespoons minced Fines Herbes
(p. 89)
2 lemons, sliced
6 parsley sprigs

/ *Stuffed Tomatoes Provençale*

TOMATES FARCIES À LA PROVENÇALE

Choose very large firm tomatoes. Cut them horizontally into halves, remove the seeds, and sprinkle them with salt and pepper. Heat 3 tablespoons of the oil in a casserole, put the tomatoes, cut side down, into the hot oil, and cook them over low heat for 10 minutes. Cool.

In another saucepan, heat the remaining oil and cook 2 tablespoons of the parsley, the onion and the garlic in it until they are soft. Stir in the bread crumbs and anchovy paste and stir over low heat for 5 minutes. Cool.

Put the tomatoes, cut side up, into a serving dish and coat them with the stuffing. Sprinkle with the remaining parsley and serve immediately.

FOR 4 PERSONS:

4 large firm tomatoes	1 onion, minced
Salt	4 garlic cloves, minced
Freshly ground black pepper	1 cup soft bread crumbs
6 tablespoons olive oil	2 tablespoons anchovy paste
¼ cup minced parsley	

Raw Vegetables Vinaigrette | ASSIETTE DE CRUDITÉS

Any kind of vegetable that can be eaten raw may be used, such as: tomatoes, peeled, seeded, and chopped fine; carrots, cut into thin julienne strips; thinly sliced very white mushrooms; coarsely grated green cabbage, or fennel (finocchio), or red cabbage; raw or cooked artichoke hearts, finely chopped; peeled cucumber, thinly sliced; sweet peppers, cut into fine strips; celery stalks, cut into even pieces; and finely chopped onions.

Arrange all the prepared vegetables on a big platter, in a decorative and harmonious fashion.

Coat the vegetables with Simple French Dressing (p. 787), without tossing them, and sprinkle them with a generous amount of minced *fines herbes*.

Gazpacho Hors-d'Oeuvre | GAZPACHO

Peel the cucumbers, cut them into small dice, sprinkle them with coarse salt, and let them drain in a strainer for several hours.

Peel, seed, and drain the tomatoes; then cut them into the same size dice as the cucumbers.

Cut off the tops of the sweet peppers, remove their membranes, and cut them into tiny strips.

Dice the onion.

Choose a serving dish 4 to 5 inches deep. Put in alternate layers of cucumbers, tomatoes, onions, a few anchovy fillets and black olives. Sprinkle the layers lightly with salt and pepper.

Mash the garlic in a mortar, add the cuminseed and vinegar, and then beat in the oil. Pour this dressing over the vegetables and sprinkle with minced *fines herbes* and shallots.

Chill for several hours. Serve very cold; just before serving add the lemon juice.

FOR 4 PERSONS:

2 medium-sized cucumbers	4 garlic cloves
Coarse salt	1 pinch of ground cuminseed
4 tomatoes	3 tablespoons vinegar
2 sweet peppers	½ cup olive oil
1 onion	3 tablespoons minced Fines Herbes
8 anchovy fillets, drained	(p. 89)
12 black olives	2 teaspoons minced shallots
Salt	Juice of 1 lemon
Freshly ground black pepper	

/ *Ratatouille*

Heat the oil in a casserole. Add the onions and cook them gently until they are very soft, stirring often so that they will not brown.

Trim off the ends of the peppers, cut out the membranes, remove the seeds, and cut them into fine julienne strips. Peel, seed, and chop the tomatoes. Peel the zucchini and the eggplant and cut them into good-sized pieces. Add all these vegetables to the onions in the casserole. Season generously with salt and pepper and cook over low heat for about 30 minutes, stirring occasionally. Do not cover the casserole.

When the vegetables are tender, let them cool, put them into a serving dish, and sprinkle them with *fines herbes*.

FOR 4 PERSONS:

4 tablespoons olive oil	1 medium-sized eggplant
2 large onions, chopped	Salt
4 sweet peppers	Freshly ground black pepper
4 tomatoes	¼ cup minced Fines Herbes
1 pound zucchini	(p. 89)

Note: In Nice, the birthplace of *ratatouille,* the zucchini is not peeled.

SALADE RUSSE I / *Russian Salad I*

Shell the peas; trim the beans; peel the turnip and the potatoes. Cook each of these vegetables separately in boiling salted water until they are barely tender.

Meantime, clean and prepare the cucumber, carrots, celery and mushrooms. Cut these vegetables into either thin slices or julienne strips. Reserve a few pieces for later decoration.

When the first vegetables are cooked, thinly slice the potatoes and turnips and cut the green beans into small pieces. Cool.

Arrange the cooked and the raw vegetables in a serving dish any way you like: in mounds, or strips, separately or mixed. Top with the tongue, salami, diced lobster, anchovy fillets and minced truffle. Sprinkle with capers and minced sour pickle.

Coat the salad with mayonnaise and decorate the mayonnaise with the reserved vegetables. Chill until serving time.

FOR 6 PERSONS:

½ pound peas, shelled	4 slices of salami, diced
½ pound green snap beans	1 small cooked lobster, diced
1 turnip	4 anchovy fillets, drained and cut
2 potatoes	into strips
1 large cucumber	1 truffle, minced
2 carrots	1 tablespoon capers
2 celery hearts	1 sour pickle, minced
¼ pound mushrooms	2 cups Mayonnaise (p. 782)
4 slices of cooked or smoked tongue, diced	

Russian Salad II / SALADE RUSSE II

Cut the meat of the roast chicken into bite-size pieces.

Cook the potatoes in boiling salted water, peel, and slice them thinly.

Put all the cooked and raw meats and vegetables into a salad bowl and mix them well. Coat the salad mixture with the mayonnaise.

The salad bowl may be lined with lettuce and the salad may be decorated with sliced hard-cooked eggs and minced *fines herbes*.

Chill until serving time. Then, and not before, toss the salad with the mayonnaise.

FOR 6 PERSONS:

1 roast chicken (3 pounds), cooled
6 medium-sized new potatoes
1 celery heart, sliced
4 slices of cooked or smoked
 tongue, diced
4 slices of salami, diced
2 slices of York ham, diced

1 sour pickle, chopped
2 cups Mayonnaise Chantilly
 (p. 784)
1 head of lettuce
2 hard-cooked eggs, sliced
2 tablespoons minced Fines Herbes
 (p. 89)

Salade Niçoise I /

Trim the green beans and peel the potatoes. Cook them separately in boiling salted water until barely tender.

Peel the tomatoes and slice them. Arrange three quarters of the slices all around the edge of a serving dish. Chop the remaining slices and reserve.

Make the French dressing.

Drain the cooked green beans and potatoes. Cut the beans into pieces and slice the potatoes. Cool them.

Pile the vegetables in the center of the serving dish. Decorate the pile with anchovy fillets, olives and little heaps of the reserved chopped tomatoes. Sprinkle with the chopped fresh chervil and tarragon and the capers. Pour the French dressing over all and chill in the refrigerator until serving time.

FOR 6 PERSONS:

1 pound green snap beans
1 pound potatoes
6 tomatoes
¾ cup Simple French Dressing
 (p. 787)

8 anchovy fillets, drained
8 pitted green or black olives
1 tablespoon chopped fresh chervil
1 tablespoon chopped fresh tarragon
1 tablespoon capers

Salade Niçoise II /

Cook the rice in lightly salted water.

Trim and seed the hot red pepper and the sweet peppers. Cut the hot red pepper into thin strips and slice the sweet peppers into rounds.

When the rice is cooked, drain it, rinse it under running cold water, drain it again, and dry it on a clean kitchen towel.

Chop the hard-cooked eggs.

Put the rice in a serving dish. Add the hot and sweet peppers, the pitted black and green olives, the chopped eggs and the flaked tunafish. Mix well and toss with the French dressing. Chill in the refrigerator until serving time.

FOR 4 PERSONS:

1 cup uncooked rice	½ cup pitted green olives
1 hot red pepper	1 cup flaked tunafish
3 sweet peppers	½ cup Simple French Dressing
3 hard-cooked eggs	(p. 787)
½ cup pitted black olives	

/ *Salade Niçoise III*

Cook the rice in lightly salted water.

Scrape the carrots, peel the onions, and cut both into thin slices.

Peel the eggs and crush them with the anchovy fillets in a mortar. Add the mustard, mix well, and season lightly with salt and pepper. Add the olive oil very gradually, beating constantly, until the sauce has the consistency of mayonnaise.

Drain the rice, rinse it under running cold water, drain it again, and dry it on a clean kitchen towel. Put it in a deep serving dish. Top the rice with the sliced carrots and onions, the herring, hot and sweet peppers, and pitted black and green olives.

Pour the sauce over all, toss to blend, and chill until serving time.

FOR 4 PERSONS:

1 cup uncooked rice	1 cup (or slightly more) olive oil
2 carrots	4 pickled herrings, cut into small
2 onions	pieces
3 hard-cooked eggs	1 hot red pepper, seeded and diced
10 anchovy fillets, drained	2 sweet peppers, seeded and sliced
1 tablespoon French mustard	½ cup pitted black olives
Salt	½ cup pitted green olives
Freshly ground black pepper	

Cold Meat Hors-d'Oeuvre

Hors-d'Oeuvre Froids de Viandes et Volailles

BOEUF EN SALADE / *Boiled Beef Salad*

This is a good way to use beef left over from a *pot-au-feu*.

Cut the beef into small slices or pieces.

Add the potatoes, onion, sour pickles, tomatoes, sweet pepper cut into julienne strips and garlic. Toss lightly with the French dressing and sprinkle with the minced *fines herbes*. Chill in the refrigerator for a few hours before serving.

FOR 4 PERSONS:

1 pound boiled beef	1 sweet pepper
2 cooked potatoes, diced	½ garlic clove, minced
1 large onion, chopped	½ cup Simple French Dressing
5 small sour pickles, chopped	(p. 787)
2 tomatoes, peeled, seeded and chopped	3 tablespoons minced Fines Herbes (p. 89)

Ham Mousse / MOUSSE DE JAMBON

Cut the ham (it should be very lean) into pieces and mince it, using the finest blade of the meat grinder.

Coat the inside of a cold 6-cup mold on all sides with the cup of liquid aspic stock (see p. 38) for a description of the method).

Combine the ½ cup of boiling stock with the softened gelatin, stir until the gelatin is completely dissolved, and then stir in the *velouté*. Add the ham to this mixture, let it cool, and then set it in a bowl of cracked ice. Stir the mixture until it becomes syrupy and then stir in the *crème fraîche*.

Check the seasoning; if necessary, add a little salt and pepper. Stir over ice until the mixture is smooth and on the point of setting.

Pour the mixture into the lined mold and chill for 6 hours. At serving time unmold onto a serving dish.

FOR 4 PERSONS:

1 pound lean smoked ham	¾ cup warm Sauce Velouté for Chicken (p. 762)
1 cup liquid Brown Stock for Aspics (p. 166)	1½ cups Crème Fraîche (p. 666)
½ cup boiling Brown Stock for Aspics (p. 166)	Salt
1 tablespoon (1 envelope) unflavored gelatin, softened in ¼ cup water	Freshly ground white pepper

Headcheese / FROMAGE DE TÊTE

Have the butcher remove the snout of the pig's head and reserve the tongue and brains.

The head must be extremely well cleaned, including the teeth and ear. Soak it and the tongue in cold water to cover for 12 hours, changing the water several times.

Put the pork shoulder, veal shoulder, pork rind, tongue and the pig's head into a large kettle. Add enough water to cover, bring to the boiling point, and blanch for 5 minutes.

Drain and change the water. Add the bay leaf, onions, carrot and cloves. Season very lightly with salt and white pepper. Bring to a boil and simmer for about 1½ hours, or until the tongue is tender. Remove the tongue to a bowl with a little of the broth. Continue simmering the other meats for about 2½ hours longer, or until very tender. Simmer the brains in a little of the broth for 15 minutes and then drain.

Remove all of the meats from the kettle. Reduce the cooking liquid over high heat to about 3 cups and strain it.

Cut all of the meats except the sheets of pork rind into 1-inch pieces; discard the rind and bones of the pig's head. Line 1 large or 2 smaller loaf pans (the exact size will depend on the amount of meat on the pig's head) with the sheets of pork rind. Arrange alternate layers of fat and lean meat in the pans, sprinkling each layer with a pinch of the *quatre épices* and a little of the reduced cooking liquid, using about 1 cup of the liquid in all.

Set the pans in another one containing 1 inch of hot water and bake them in a preheated 400° F. oven for about 20 minutes.

Or instead of molding the headcheese, shape the cut-up pieces of meat after they cool slightly into a sausage and wrap it first in the pork rind and then in a triple thickness of cheesecloth. Tie the ends and simmer it over low heat in the broth in which the meats were cooked.

After this final cooking, weight the headcheese until it is cool and then chill it for several hours. At serving time, cut it into slices and serve it with sour pickles.

FOR ABOUT 10 SERVINGS:

½ **pig's or boar's head**
2 **pounds pork shoulder**
1 **pound veal shoulder**
3 **large pieces of pork rind**
   (see Note)
1 **bay leaf**
3 **onions, chopped**

1 **carrot**
6 **whole cloves**
Salt
Freshly ground white pepper
½ **teaspoon Quatre Épices**
   (see p. 667)

Note: Scraped fresh pork rind is available in butcher shops which specialize in pork products, or your own butcher can quite likely order it for you. It usually comes in fairly large sheets and it requires long slow cooking to tenderize it.

/ *Lambs' Trotters Vinaigrette*

PIEDS D'AGNEAU VINAIGRETTE

Clean the lamb trotters by first scraping them, then flaming them, and finally blanching them in lightly salted boiling water. Of course, if you can buy ready-to-cook lambs' trotters, this preliminary cleaning is unnecessary.

Cook them in water to cover in a casserole with the *garniture* specified below for about 1½ hours, or until they are tender.

When they are cooked, remove all the bones, cut the meat into small dice, and put it into a serving dish. Pour the French dressing over the meat and sprinkle with minced *fines herbes* and onion.

Chill for a few hours before serving.

FOR 4 PERSONS:

8 **lambs' trotters**
Cooking garniture:
   1 **onion**
   1 **garlic clove**
   2 **whole cloves**
   Grated rind of 1 lemon
   Juice of 2 lemons

Salt
Freshly ground black pepper
1 **cup Simple French Dressing**
   (p. 787)
1 **tablespoon minced Fines Herbes**
   (p. 89)
1 **tablespoon minced onion**

Above: *Put the ingredients in the mold in this order: first a layer of filling, then th*
wrapped pork liver, then more filling, and then the chicken breasts.

Below: *Top with a last layer of filling, put a bay leaf in the middle, and sprinkle wit*
a few thyme leaves and the brandy. Cover with the top layer of pastry and crimp th
edges together tightly. It is essential to put a funnel in the middle of the top; the pastr
completely encloses the pâté and the funnel provides the only opening for the stea
to escape while cooking.

PÂTÉ EN CROÛTE

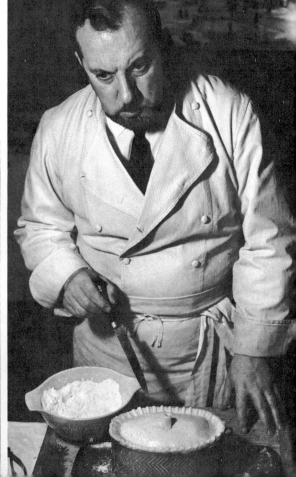

Pâté en Croûte /

Prepare a *pâte brisée* with the flour, eggs, lard and salt (see p. 713). Chill in the refrigerator.

Prepare the filling: mince the veal and the pork, using the finest blade of the meat grinder. Season with a teaspoon of salt, a little pepper, the spices and the minced *fines herbes;* stir in the eggs.

Roll out three quarters of the *pâte brisée* to a thickness of ¼ inch and then carefully line the insides of a 2-quart pâté mold (or any 2-quart round or oblong spring-form metal pan will do) with the pastry, allowing the pastry to overhang the top edge of the mold by 1 inch (see illustration p. 226). Put a generous layer of the filling in the bottom and top this with the slices of pork liver, each wrapped in a thin slice of fatback. Spread more filling over them, pressing it firmly between and around the slices of liver. Lay the chicken breasts over the filling and finally cover the breasts with all of the remaining filling. Press the bay leaf into the center of the filling and sprinkle with the thyme and the brandy.

Now roll out the remaining *pâte brisée* to approximately the size of the pâté mold; this will be the top. Brush the overhanging edge of the pastry in the pâté mold with a little of the beaten egg, carefully lay the pastry top over the mold, and trim off any surplus pastry with scissors. Pinch the edges together and then crimp them with a pastry crimper or a fork (see illustration).

Make a cylinder from a piece of heavy white paper or foil and put it through a hole in the middle of the top (see illustration). Brush the top with the remaining beaten egg.

Bake in a preheated 350° F. oven for about 2 hours (roughly about 30 minutes per pound). The pâté is done when the fat which rises in the funnel is absolutely clear and no longer rosy. Cool the pâté at room temperature and then chill before serving.

FOR 6 PERSONS:

For the pâte brisée:
3 cups flour
2 eggs
¾ cup lard
½ teaspoon salt
¾ pound lean veal
¾ pound lean pork
Salt
Freshly ground black pepper
1 teaspoon Quatre Épices (p. 667)
2 tablespoons minced Fines Herbes (p. 89)
3 eggs

¾ pound pork liver, cut into long narrow slices
6 or more large slices of pork fatback or blanched salt pork (about ⅛ inch thick)
4 small chicken breast halves, boned and skinned
1 bay leaf
1 tablespoon chopped fresh thyme, or ½ teaspoon dried thyme
1 tablespoon brandy
1 egg, beaten

Molded Pâté / PÂTÉ MOULÉ

Make the pastry by blending the flour, salt, egg and lard together until they form a smooth paste. Sprinkle with the ice water and blend it in very lightly and quickly. Let the pastry rest for 1 hour.

Cut one third of the veal and one third of the pork into ½-inch dice and mari-

MOLDED PÂTÉ

Put the filling— veal, pork and ham —on the rolled-out dough. Smooth it out so that the filling is distributed evenly. Roll up the pastry.

Enclose the pâté completely by turning under both ends of the pastry and sealing the top with a width of dough. The beaten egg yolk works like a glue and after baking it gives the pastry a fine glaze.

nate them and the ham in the wine with the onion and carrot for 1 hour. Then drain, discarding the onion and carrot.

Mince the remaining veal and pork, using the finest blade of the meat grinder. Mix this ground meat with 2 teaspoons of salt, a little pepper, a pinch of nutmeg, the 3 eggs, brandy and Port.

Roll out three quarters of the pastry into a large oblong about ⅛ inch thick. Lay a filling along the center of this oblong, alternating layers of the ground and diced meats. Press the bay leaf into the mixture and sprinkle with the thyme. Completely enclose the filling with the pastry (see illustration p. 229).

Roll out the remaining pastry into a long narrow oblong about 4 inches wide, and brush one side of it with egg yolk and cream. Reverse this strip of pastry on top of the wrapped pâté so that it covers the seam and press the edges together firmly to make a tight seal. Now brush the whole surface of the dough with egg yolk and cream.

Stick 2 small chimneys the size of a cigar, made from rolled-up firm white paper, into the top of the pâté (see illustration). They will allow the steam to escape during baking so that the pâté won't burst.

Cook in a preheated 350° F. oven for about 1½ hours. When the fat that rises in the chimney is absolutely clear, the pâté is done.

FOR 6 PERSONS:

For the pastry:
  4 cups sifted all-purpose flour
  1½ teaspoons salt
  1 egg
  ¾ cup lard
  ½ cup ice water

  1½ pounds lean veal
  1½ pounds lean pork
  ⅔ pound smoked ham, diced

For the marinade:
  1 cup dry white wine
  1 onion, sliced
  1 carrot, sliced

Salt
Freshly ground black pepper
Pinch of grated nutmeg
3 eggs
2 tablespoons brandy
2 tablespoons Port
1 bay leaf
1 tablespoon chopped fresh thyme,
  or ½ teaspoon dried thyme
2 egg yolks, mixed with 3
  tablespoons heavy cream

Terrine of Calf's Liver | TERRINE DE FOIE DE VEAU

Mince the calf's liver, using the finest blade of the meat grinder, together with the veal, the ½-pound piece of pork fat, the onion and the anchovies. Put the mixture into a bowl and add the flour, beaten eggs and cream. Season with 2 teaspoons of salt and a little pepper. Beat energetically to blend thoroughly.

Line a 1½- to 2-quart terrine or loaf pan completely with the slices of pork fatback, reserving a few slices for the top. Fill the lined mold about three quarters full with the ground mixture and top with slices of fatback; cover tightly with a piece of aluminum foil. Bake the terrine in a pan of hot water in a preheated 350° F. oven for about 2 hours. Cool with a weight on top of the pâté at room temperature for 24 hours. Unmold, cut into slices, and serve them as the topping of open-faced sandwiches, garnished with cucumber and tomato slices.

FOR 6 PERSONS:

1 pound calf's liver
½ pound lean veal
1 piece of fresh pork fatback or
     blanched salt pork (½ pound)
1 large onion
8 anchovy fillets, drained
4 tablespoons flour
3 eggs, beaten

⅓ cup heavy cream
Salt
Freshly ground white pepper
¾ pound fresh pork fatback, or
     blanched salt pork, sliced very
     thin
2 tomatoes, sliced
2 cucumbers, sliced

TERRINE DE VOLAILLE / *Terrine of Chicken*

Make a marinade with the wine, the chopped onion and carrots, the bay leaf, thyme, peppercorns and the ½ cup of brandy. Cut the veal and pork into long narrow strips and marinate them in the marinade for 3 hours. Drain and dry on kitchen toweling.

Make a stuffing, or *farce,* with the ground veal and pork, the eggs, brandy and Port; season with the salt and a little pepper.

Sauté the chicken livers in the butter over high heat for about 3 minutes and season with a little salt and pepper.

Line a 2½-quart terrine or loaf pan completely with thin slices of the pork fatback. Let the pork fatback overhang both of the long sides of the terrine so that the filling can later be covered. Now make layers of the stuffing, the chicken livers, a few slices of the pork fatback, the marinated veal and pork strips, and the chicken breasts. Use about half of each of the meats for a layer and make sure the stuffing is pressed firmly around the meats. Finally end with a layer of the stuffing. Cover the mixture with the overhanging slices of pork fat. Cover the terrine with a tight lid or with aluminum foil.

Set the terrine in a baking pan filled with about 1 inch of boiling water and bake in a preheated 350° F. oven for 2 hours. Remove the covering and let the pâté cool with a weight placed on it. Chill before serving.

FOR 6 PERSONS:

For the marinade:
  1 cup dry white wine
  1 onion, chopped
  2 carrots, chopped
  1 bay leaf
  2 sprigs of fresh thyme, or
       ½ teaspoon dried thyme
  6 peppercorns
  ½ cup brandy

⅓ pound lean veal
½ pound lean pork

For the stuffing:
  ⅔ pound lean veal, finely
       ground

1 pound lean pork, finely
     ground
3 eggs
2 tablespoons brandy
2 tablespoons Port
2 teaspoons salt
Freshly ground black pepper

½ pound chicken livers
3 tablespoons butter
Salt
Freshly ground black pepper
1½ pounds fresh pork fatback,
     or blanched salt pork, sliced very
     thin
4 small chicken breast halves,
     boned

Terrine of Chicken Livers / TERRINE DE FOIE DE VOLAILLE

Heat the 4 tablespoons of butter in a skillet and sauté the chicken livers in it with the thyme and bay leaf. Season them with salt and pepper and cook them over high heat for about 2 minutes. Add the minced shallots and cook for about 2 minutes longer. Remove the thyme (unless using dried thyme) and bay leaf and reserve six of the chicken livers. Put the remaining livers into a bowl, sprinkle them with the verbena liqueur or Port, and let them stand for 1 hour.

Mash the livers into a smooth paste in a mortar and then press the paste through a fine sieve. With a wooden spoon, beat the softened butter into this paste. Taste for seasoning, and add salt and pepper if necessary. Beat the egg whites until they are stiff and fold them into chicken-liver mixture.

Line a 1½-quart terrine or loaf pan with the slices of fresh pork fat, put half of the chicken-liver mixture into it, distribute the whole chicken livers on top, and cover with the remaining chicken-liver mixture. Cover with more fresh pork fat and then with a lid or aluminum foil. Chill for 24 hours. Remove the top slices of pork and spoon out the pâté with a spoon dipped into warm water.

FOR 6 PERSONS:

4 tablespoons butter
1 pound chicken livers
2 sprigs of thyme, or ½ teaspoon dried thyme
1 bay leaf
Salt
Freshly ground black pepper
1 tablespoon minced shallots

¼ cup verbena liqueur from the Velay, or Port wine
¾ cup butter, softened
3 egg whites
¾ pound fresh pork fatback, or blanched salt pork, sliced very thin

Terrine of Duck Livers / TERRINE DE FOIE DE CANARD

EDITORS' NOTE: *The very large duck livers of which M. Oliver speaks below are virtually unknown in the United States, and hence we suggest that one follow his second method, as being better adapted to the smaller duck livers that are available here.*

A rich fat duck liver is similar to goose liver, though it has a more delicate flavor. Smaller lean duck liver is more like chicken liver, although softer. The preparation of a duck-liver terrine varies somewhat, according to which type of duck liver is available.

First recipe, for large rich duck livers:

Sprinkle the rich duck livers generously with coarse salt and let them stand for 24 hours, rubbing the salt in occasionally. Wash and dry them and then rub them with the spices and paprika. Sprinkle them with the Armagnac and the Madeira. Let them marinate in this mixture for 12 hours, basting frequently.

Make a stuffing, or *farce*, with the ham and ham fat. Season with salt and pepper and add the marinade from the duck livers.

Line a 1½-quart terrine or loaf pan with the slices of fresh pork fat. Put a bay leaf and the thyme sprigs on the bottom. Spread half of the stuffing in the bottom of the terrine, top with the duck livers, spread the remaining stuffing over them, and cover with fresh pork fat. Set the terrine in a pan containing 1 inch of boiling water, and cook in a preheated 350° F. oven for about 1½ hours. Cool and then chill.

Second recipe, for lean duck livers:

Cook the minced shallots in the butter, add the duck livers, and sauté them over medium heat for about 5 minutes. Season them lightly with salt and pepper. Cool. Mash them to a smooth paste in a mortar. Add the spices, Armagnac, Madeira and the ham fat. Mix together thoroughly and strain through a fine sieve.

Line a 1½-quart terrine or loaf pan with the slices of pork fat and place the bay leaf and thyme in the bottom. Add the duck-liver mixture and cover with more pork fat. Cover the terrine tightly and set it in a pan containing 1 inch of boiling water. Cook in a 350° F. oven for about 1½ hours. Cool and then chill.

FOR 6 PERSONS:

2 tablespoons minced shallots (omit for 1st recipe)	2 tablespoons Madeira
4 tablespoons butter (omit for 1st recipe)	½ pound fresh ham, finely ground (omit for 2nd recipe)
1 pound duck livers	½ pound fresh ham fat, finely ground
Salt (or coarse salt for 1st recipe)	¾ pound fresh pork fatback, or blanched salt pork, sliced very thin
Freshly ground black pepper	1 bay leaf
1 teaspoon Quatre Épices (p. 667), or allspice	2 sprigs of thyme, or ½ teaspoon dried thyme
1 teaspoon paprika	
2 tablespoons Armagnac	

/ Terrine of Pork and Veal

TERRINE DE PORC ET DE VEAU À LA GELÉE

Put the meats into a large kettle of cold water and bring to the boiling point. Drain, rinse under running cold water, and return the meats to the kettle with all the other ingredients except the gelatin. Add water to cover and simmer over low heat for about 2 hours. Remove the meat and cut it into 1-inch cubes or chop it coarsely. Boil the broth until it is reduced to 4 cups and strain it through a strainer. Add the meat, simmer for 15 minutes, and correct the seasoning. Soften the gelatin in a little water and add it to the kettle. Rinse a 2-quart mold with cold water and chill it in the refrigerator. Pour the meat and broth into it and chill. Unmold and cut into slices.

FOR 8 PERSONS:

2 pounds lean pork	1 large carrot, chopped
2 pounds shoulder of veal	2 bay leaves
2 teaspoons salt	1 onion, stuck with 5 whole cloves
Freshly ground black pepper	2 cups dry white wine
1 teaspoon Quatre Épices (p. 667), or allspice	2 tablespoons (or envelopes) unflavored gelatin

Terrine of Hare | TERRINE DE LIÈVRE

What on earth do you do with a 9- to 10-pound wild hare with pronounced claws that bespeaks its old age, a hare that has been ravaged by the gun and is right there, on the kitchen table, so that something has to be done with it?

The answer is: pâté. If the hare has been poorly killed, if it has no more blood, if the meat is stringy, a pâté will give you the opportunity to show off your cleverness since you will have to create the elements of flavor and texture that are missing.

The hare must be skinned and dressed. Reserve the head and scraps, as well as any blood. You must also reserve the liver, the heart, and the lungs.

Bone the meat of the hare and set aside the larger, more presentable pieces, that is, the back (if not shot to pieces) and the part of the leg that is free of sinews. In any case, you'll have to remove the sinews from all these presentable pieces. There is only one sinew to the back, but it branches out almost entirely over the whole back and it should be removed. Chop fine or mince the remaining meat of the hare. Chop the reserved liver, heart and lungs coarsely.

With the bones and scraps make the following stock: Smash the bones, the head and the scraps and put them into a large heavy saucepan with the chopped onion and carrots, 2 teaspoons of salt, a little pepper and the *fines herbes.* Add the wine and enough water to cover the contents. Bring to the boiling point and skim as necessary. Cook without a cover over medium heat, until the liquid is very reduced and of a good strong flavor. Strain through a triple layer of cheesecloth. Bring again to the boiling point, skim, and degrease. Reserve.

Make a marinade with the sliced onion and carrot, the 2 teaspoons of spices, the rum and olive oil. Do not use any salt, pepper, or wine. Marinate all of the meat in this mixture.

In the Southwest of France, terrines are cooked in *pâtissières,* which are special molds made from glazed clay. Today, we have a choice of enamelware molds, fireproof glass molds, molds made from ovenproof china, and clay molds. These latter have the great disadvantage of being very fragile, but they impart a special taste to the foods cooked in them which we call *fréchin.* In any case, you will need a large terrine for this pâté; the exact size will depend on the size of the hare and the amount of the meat you can take from it. Line the terrine completely with slices of fresh pork fat.

Make a stuffing, or *farce,* with the ham, pork and veal. The meats may have a little fat, but not so much fat as to run liquid during cooking time; this would defeat the purpose. Season the stuffing with a little salt and pepper, the 1 teaspoon of spices and the Armagnac. Mix in the reserved minced hare meat and the chopped liver, heart and lungs. Add the reserved hare's blood and a little of the reserved stock, but be careful not to make the stuffing too wet. Blend everything thoroughly. Test the flavor of the stuffing by making a small patty and cooking it in a small skillet. Correct the seasoning, if necessary.

Wrap the larger, more presentable hare pieces, drained from the marinade, with fresh pork fat.

Spread half of the stuffing in the bottom of the terrine. Arrange the wrapped pieces of hare meat over the stuffing and top with the remaining stuffing. Cover with more fresh pork fat and then with a heavy lid. Set the terrine in a baking pan containing 2 inches of boiling water and bake in a preheated 350° F. oven for 2½ to 3 hours. Test for doneness by inserting a knitting needle or thin skewer in the middle of the pâté and pulling it out immediately. If the needle or skewer is hot (and this you find out with your tongue), the pâté is done. Cool the pâté at room temperature and remove the surplus fat. This pâté may be stored for some time in a cool place, but this is without any culinary merit. Far better to eat it within a week.

FOR 10 PERSONS:

1 wild hare (9 to 10 pounds)
1 large onion, chopped
2 large carrots, chopped
Salt
Freshly ground black pepper
2 tablespoons Fines Herbes
   (p. 89)
2 cups dry white wine

1½ pounds fresh pork fatback, or
   blanched salt pork, sliced very thin
½ pound ham, finely ground
½ pound pork, finely ground
½ pound veal, finely ground
1 teaspoon Quatre Épices (p. 667),
   or allspice
¾ cup Armagnac

For the marinade:
1 onion, sliced
1 carrot, sliced
2 teaspoons Quatre Épices
   (p. 667), or allspice
¾ cup rum
¾ cup olive oil

Cold Fish Hors-d'Oeuvre

Hors-d'Oeuvre Froids de Coquillages, Crustacés et Poissons

ANCHOIS / *Anchovies*

Usually canned anchovies are served very simply, with bread and butter. Anchovies that are packed in brine (available in some shops that cater to people of Mediterranean origin) are first thoroughly washed to remove all brine, then filleted. This kind of anchovy is better if marinated in a little olive oil before serving.

OEIL D'ANCHOIS / *Anchovy and Egg*

Use flat fillets of anchovies, drain them of their oil, and cut them into pieces. Mince the onions very fine.

On small individual plates arrange a circle of minced onions surrounded by a circle of anchovy pieces. Put a raw egg yolk in the middle. Serve very cold.

FOR 4 PERSONS:

16 anchovy fillets
4 small onions

4 egg yolks

Anchovy Salad / SALADE D'ANCHOIS

On a serving dish make rows of overlapping fillets of drained anchovies, thin slices of raw carrot, small rounds of white onion, the pulp of peeled lemons cut into small dice, sliced sour pickles and bay leaves.

Sprinkle with olive oil. Decorate with capers and quarters of hard-cooked eggs.

Clams on the Half Shell / CLAMS AU NATUREL

Open the clams and arrange them on the half shells on a platter filled with cracked ice. Garnish the platter with a few algae (seaweed), if available, or other greens, such as parsley.

Serve the French dressing with shallots, or the horseradish sauce, on the side.

Also, serve plenty of buttered black bread—the slices should be very thin—with the clams and have the lemon quarters on a separate dish.

FOR 4 PERSONS:

4 dozen clams
¾ cup Simple French Dressing
  (p. 787), made with 1 tablespoon
  minced shallots, or 1 cup
  Horseradish Sauce I (p. 790)

Algae or parsley
Thinly sliced black bread, buttered
2 lemons, cut into quarters

Crabs à l'Anglaise / CRABE FROID À L'ANGLAISE

EDITORS' NOTE: *Most types of French crabs (see p. 62) are larger than the hard-shell variety found on the East Coast of the United States and generally much smaller than the Dungeness crabs of the Pacific Coast. Thus, while 1 French crab is an adequate serving for 1 person, 3 American hard-shell crabs are about right for a serving since they will yield about ½ cup of meat.*

Cook the crabs in boiling salted water for about 15 minutes and let them cool. Remove the meat from the claws and shred it. Pull the shells apart; pick out all of the meat from the bodies and shred it. Reserve four of the top shells.

Mix the shredded crabmeat with the French dressing and toss well. Fill the four empty crab shells with the crabmeat and put them in a dish lined with a napkin. Garnish the top of each with a parsley sprig and the chopped hard-cooked eggs.

FOR 4 PERSONS:

12 hard-shell crabs
½ cup Mustard French Dressing
  (p. 788)

4 parsley sprigs
1 hard-cooked egg, chopped

/ *Crabmeat and Avocado Salad*

SALADE DE CRABE AUX AVOCATS

Cook the crabs in a flavorful *court bouillon* for 15 minutes. Let them cool and pick out all of the meat. Flake the crabmeat gently.

Cut the avocado lengthwise into halves, remove the seed, and take out the flesh with a spoon, taking care not to tear the avocado shell. Dice the avocado flesh and put it into a bowl with the crabmeat, tomato, sliced egg, lemon juice and ketchup. Season lightly with salt and pepper and fill the avocado shells with the mixture. Sprinkle with the *fines herbes* and serve chilled.

FOR 2 PERSONS:

6 hard-shell crabs
Court Bouillon for Shellfish
  (p. 131), made with vinegar
1 large avocado
1 small ripe tomato, peeled, seeded
  and diced
1 hard-cooked egg, sliced

1 teaspoon lemon juice
1 tablespoon ketchup
Salt
Freshly ground black pepper
2 tablespoons minced Fines Herbes
  (p. 89)

CRABE FROIDE MAYONNAISE / *Crabmeat Mayonnaise*

Simmer the crabs in the boiling *court bouillon* for 15 minutes. Remove from the heat and leave them in the *court bouillon* until almost lukewarm.

Shell the crabs, pick out all of the meat, and arrange it on a bed of lettuce leaves on a serving dish. Garnish with the meat of the legs and the claws, and with slices of hard-cooked eggs. Chill in the refrigerator until serving time and pass the mayonnaise separately, in a sauceboat.

FOR 4 PERSONS:

12 hard-shell crabs
Court Bouillon for Fish
  (p. 131), made with wine

Lettuce leaves
2 hard-cooked eggs, sliced
2 cups Mayonnaise (p. 782)

ÉCREVISSES / *Crayfish*

Crayfish are frequently used as an hors-d'oeuvre. They are poached in a Court Bouillon for Shellfish (p. 131), made with vinegar, for about 5 minutes, piled up in the shape of a pyramid in the serving dish, and garnished with curly parsley.

ANGUILLE FUMÉE / *Smoked Eel*

EDITORS' NOTE: *Smoked eel may be purchased in delicatessen and gourmet shops catering to a German and Scandinavian clientele.*

If the eel is not skinned, make an incision in the skin around the head with the point of a sharp knife, and carefully slip off the skin, with the right hand, holding the head of the eel with the left hand.

Cut the eel into thin slices, and arrange them in overlapping rows in a serving dish. Garnish the dish with lemon quarters and parsley.

FOR 4 PERSONS:

1 smoked eel (about 1½ pounds)	Parsley sprigs
2 lemons, cut into quarters	

Fish Aspic / ASPIC DE POISSON

Fish suited for this recipe must have firm flesh and easily removable bones, such as salmon, sea bass, sole or mackerel.

Make a fish stock with the bones and trimmings of the fish, the wine, water, salt, a little pepper, the thyme, bay leaf and *fines herbes*; boil it for 30 minutes.

Strain the stock and return it to the pot. Bring back to a boil and poach the fish in it until it is firm and will flake when tested with a fork. The exact time will depend on the thickness of the fish. Begin testing after about 15 minutes. Drain the fish, cool it, and then chill. Let the fish stock cool to lukewarm.

Dissolve the gelatin in a small amount of the stock, and then add it to the rest of the fish stock. Beat the egg whites until almost stiff and stir them into the stock. Bring back to the boiling point, without ceasing to beat. Remove from the heat and let it stand for 15 minutes. Strain through a triple layer of cheesecloth and cool. It should be perfectly clear.

Fill a large bowl with ice cubes and set a 2-quart mold in it. Pour a few spoonfuls of liquid aspic into the mold to coat the bottom and shake to and fro until it forms a thin jellied coating over the bottom. Arrange the cold shrimp, tomato slices and hard-cooked egg slices on the jelled aspic in an attractive pattern. Pour a few more spoonfuls of liquid aspic over the shrimp, tomato and egg layer and let it jell in a bowl of ice cubes or in the refrigerator. Then arrange on it the fish and the fronds of fennel, blanched if they are too green. Cover with the remaining liquid aspic and chill until jelled through.

FOR 4 PERSONS:

2 pounds boned fish, reserving the bones and trimmings	2 tablespoons (envelopes) unflavored gelatin
1 cup dry white wine, or ¼ cup white-wine vinegar	2 egg whites
4 cups water	12 cooked shrimp, shelled, deveined and chilled
2 teaspoons salt	1 tomato, sliced and chilled
Freshly ground white pepper	2 hard-cooked eggs, sliced and chilled
Pinch of dried thyme	
1 bay leaf	Several fronds of finocchio or fennel
2 tablespoons Fines Herbes (p. 89)	

COQUILLES DE POISSON / *Fish Coquilles*

Mix cold cooked shellfish, chopped or flaked, or leftovers of poached fish, also flaked, with mayonnaise. Line the scallop shells with a lettuce leaf and top them with the fish salad. Sprinkle with the *fines herbes* and serve very cold.

FOR 4 PERSONS:

2 cups cooked fish or shellfish
¾ cup Mayonnaise (p. 782)
4 scallop shells

4 tablespoons minced Fines
Herbes (p. 89)

SALADE QUIMPERLOISE / *Fish Salad Quimper Style*

Simmer the fish fillets in the *court bouillon* for about 10 minutes, or until barely done; drain and cool them and separate into large pieces. Put them into a salad bowl, together with the shrimp, lettuce, crabmeat, hard-cooked egg, capers, *fines herbes,* ketchup and the mayonnaise to which you've added the tomato paste. Season with salt and pepper to taste and mix well.

You may also include in this salad some shelled mussels and the meat of any crustaceans you like, even oysters, though these should be poached first.

Serve chilled; it is best to set the salad bowl into another dish filled with cracked ice.

FOR 4 PERSONS:

4 fish fillets (sole, whiting, etc.)
Court Bouillon for Fish
  (p. 131)
½ pound shrimp, cooked, shelled
  and deveined
1 small head of romaine lettuce,
  shredded
1 cup flaked crabmeat
1 hard-cooked egg, chopped

2 tablespoons capers
1 tablespoon minced Fines
  Herbes (p. 89)
2 tablespoons ketchup
¾ cup Mayonnaise (p. 782)
1 teaspoon tomato paste
Salt
Freshly ground black pepper

HADDOCK FUMÉ / *Smoked Haddock*

Smoked haddock may be served very simply with lemon quarters and thinly sliced buttered bread.

HARENG / *Herring*

Fresh herring may be prepared in the same manner as Mackerel in White Wine (p. 244).

However, commercially prepared herring fillets are far more widely used as hors-d'oeuvre. Canned rollmops are particularly good and need no further preparation; and then there is a variety of canned marinated herring.

Smoked herrings, of which in France there is a variety called *bouffis,* are usually prepared in the way described below, although they can also be lightly broiled and served with boiled potatoes dressed with olive oil.

The most popular way of preparing smoked herrings consists of removing their skin and bones, if they are not already filleted, and then soaking them in milk to cover for 24 hours to remove any excess salt. They are then drained, rinsed, and marinated in a generous amount of olive oil, sliced carrots, minced onions, bay leaves, peppercorns and sprigs of fresh or ground thyme for 48 hours.

At serving time, remove as many herring fillets as you need, and keep the remaining ones in the marinade. They will keep in the refrigerator for at least a week.

Herring Egyptienne | HARENGS FRAIS À L'ÉGYPTIENNE

Mince the onions and cook them in the hot oil until they are golden. Add the garlic, thyme and bay leaves. Mix well.

Peel, seed, and chop the tomatoes. Add them to the onions, together with the water and lemon juice. Season with salt and pepper to taste.

Clean the fresh herrings and add them to the sauce. Simmer over low heat for about 5 minutes. Cool. Serve the herrings in their sauce, warm or cold, depending on taste.

FOR 4 PERSONS:

2 medium-sized onions	1 cup water
2 tablespoons olive oil	Juice of 1 lemon
1 garlic clove, mashed	Salt
½ teaspoon ground thyme	Freshly ground black pepper
2 bay leaves, crumbled	8 small fresh herrings
1 pound tomatoes	

Herring Salad | SALADE DE HARENGS

Use herrings salted in brine and soak them in milk to cover for 24 hours to remove any excess salt.

Drain, skin, and bone the herrings. Cut the fillets lengthwise into slices. Arrange them in a deep serving dish in layers, alternating with the onions, potatoes, pickles and minced apple.

Garnish the dish with the hard-cooked eggs and pour the French dressing over the salad. Chill and toss well before serving.

FOR 4 PERSONS:

8 herrings salted in brine	2 sour pickles, sliced
Milk	1 apple, minced
2 medium-sized onions, minced	2 hard-cooked eggs, sliced
4 boiled and peeled potatoes, diced	¾ cup Simple French Dressing (p. 787)

SAINT-PIERRE À LA GRECQUE / *John Dory à la Grecque*

EDITORS' NOTE: *This odd-looking fish is oval, flat and thick-skinned, with large spines on its back. Its flesh is similar to turbot and sole. John Dory does not live in American waters, but the Atlantic porgy may be substituted.*

Combine in a saucepan the wine, tomato paste, oil, juniper berries, coriander, thyme, bay leaf, parsley, lemon rind, onions and some salt and pepper. Add about 3 cups of water, or enough to cover the fish fillets, and bring to the boiling point. Add the fish fillets, bring again to the boiling point, lower the heat, and poach the fish for about 5 minutes.

Remove the fillets from the pan and place them on a serving dish. Pour a little of the cooking liquid over them. Garnish with minced parsley, lemon slices and chopped hard-cooked eggs.

Chill in the refrigerator until serving time.

FOR 6 PERSONS:

1 cup dry white wine	Grated rind of 1 lemon
1 tablespoon tomato paste	3 small onions
2 tablespoons olive oil	Salt
2 juniper berries	Freshly ground black pepper
2 coriander seeds	12 small porgy fillets
1 sprig of fresh thyme, or ½ teaspoon ground thyme	2 tablespoons minced parsley
1 bay leaf	1 lemon, sliced
6 parsley sprigs	2 hard-cooked eggs, chopped

/ *Lobster Bellevue à la Parisienne*

LANGOUSTE EN BELLEVUE À LA PARISIENNE

EDITORS' NOTE: *European rock lobster is similar in appearance to the rock or spiny lobster found in southern waters of the United States and on the Pacific Coast. Unlike New England lobsters, they have no large front claws. The different kinds of lobsters are cooked in the same way, however, and may be used interchangeably.*

Cook the lobster in the *court bouillon* for about 20 minutes. Cool it in the *court bouillon* and drain. Using a pair of sharp scissors, cut out the under side of the lobster tail and remove all the meat in one piece without breaking the shell. Remove the meat from the front claws.

Cut the lobster meat into thick slices. Toss the *macédoine* of vegetables with 1 cup of the mayonnaise. Line the bottom of an oval serving dish with this salad. Put the lobster shell, empty side up, on the salad and arrange the lobster slices on it in overlapping rows.

This dish can be decorated according to one's own taste. Some of the possibilities are artichoke hearts garnished with tiny shrimp, or hard-cooked eggs cut into halves and spread with mayonnaise, or tiny tomatoes, or sliced truffles.

Serve chilled, with the rest of the mayonnaise in a sauceboat on the side.

FOR 4 PERSONS:

1 live 3-pound lobster
Court Bouillon for Lobster
   (p. 243)

2 cups cooked Macédoine of
   Vegetables (p. 111)
3 cups Mayonnaise (p. 782)

Lobster Catalane / ESCALOPES DE LANGOUSTE À LA CATALANE

Simmer the lobster in a boiling *court bouillon* for about 20 minutes and let it cool in the *court bouillon*. Remove all of the meat from the claws, tail and the front part of the body; reserve the meat from the claws and chop the remaining meat into coarse dice.

Cut the romaine into julienne strips and toss with the leaves of watercress. Cut the tops off the tomatoes, scoop out the insides, and turn them upside down on a rack so that they will drain completely.

At serving time, line the tomato shells with some of the salad greens. Combine the diced peppers and the lobster meat and bind them with the mayonnaise.

Pile the salad in the middle of an oval serving dish. Arrange the tomatoes on the dish. Top each tomato with the meat from one of the claws. Decorate the dish with remaining salad greens and the hard-cooked eggs.

FOR 4 PERSONS:

1 live 3-pound lobster
Court Bouillon for Lobster
   (p. 243)
1 small head of romaine lettuce
½ cup watercress leaves
4 ripe tomatoes

3 sweet red peppers, charred,
   scraped, seeded and cut into
   dice (see p. 619)
1 cup Mayonnaise (p. 782)
2 hard-cooked eggs, quartered

Lobster Coquille / COQUILLE DE LANGOUSTE

Cook the lobsters in the boiling *court bouillon* for about 20 minutes and let them cool in the cooking liquid until lukewarm.

Cut one of the romaine lettuces into julienne strips and toss with 1 cup of the mayonnaise.

Cut the lobsters lengthwise down the backs into halves. Remove the meat from the tail and pick out the meat from the forward part of the body and from the front claws. Cut the tail meat into slices and dice the meat from the body and the claws. Line the 4 lobster half shells with the romaine strips tossed with mayonnaise. Put a little of the diced meat in each shell and top with some of the sliced tail meat.

Line a serving plate with the remaining leaves of romaine, put the lobster on it, and chill in the refrigerator until serving time. Serve the remaining mayonnaise separately, in a sauceboat.

FOR 4 PERSONS:

2 live 3-pound lobsters
Court Bouillon for Lobster
   (p. 243)

2 heads of romaine lettuce
2 cups Mayonnaise (p. 782)

LANGOUSTE MAYONNAISE / *Lobster Mayonnaise*

Make the *court bouillon* first; there are various methods and combinations of ingredients, but they all serve one purpose; that is, to give the boiled lobster an aromatic flavor. Simmering in water alone does not do the job: the crustaceans will have an insipid flavor.

Use a big kettle with a tight-fitting lid. Put all the herbs, vegetables and seasonings into it and add the water. Simmer, covered, for about 30 minutes, then add the vinegar. Bring to the boiling point again. Plunge the rock lobsters head first into the *court bouillon.*

Count on the following simmering time: 15 minutes for a lobster weighing 1½ to 2 pounds, 20 minutes for a lobster weighing 2½ to 3 pounds, and 25 minutes for a lobster weighing 3½ pounds. Experience will teach how to cook a lobster that is very tender, yet thoroughly cooked through.

Cool the lobster in the *court bouillon,* but the best results are achieved by speeding the cooling. This is done by setting the kettle with the lobster into a bed of crushed ice.

When the lobster is cold, remove it from the *court bouillon* and break off the claws. Split the body lengthwise down the back into halves and remove the intestinal tubes with the point of a sharp knife. Remove the meat, keeping the shells intact. Cut the meat from the tail and claws into slices and pick out the meat from the claws and the front part of the body. Arrange the meat on a bed of romaine lettuce cut into julienne strips, or in the lobster shells. The mayonnaise is served separately, in a sauce-boat.

One hint about the preparation of the lobsters prior to cooking. Tuck the head feelers under the body, and tie the whole lobster to a small board so that it will stay flat while cooking. Sometimes there will be a lobster minus a claw or a feeler, leaving a cavity. Plug this cavity with a slice of carrot so that the lobster meat will not ooze out during cooking.

FOR 4 PERSONS:

Court Bouillon for Lobster:
  6 parsley sprigs
  2 or 3 parsley roots
  1 tablespoon chopped fresh
    chervil, or 1 teaspoon dried
  1 tablespoon chopped fresh
    tarragon, or 1 teaspoon
    dried
  ¼ teaspoon ground thyme
  1 bay leaf
  1 celery stalk, sliced
  1 medium-sized onion, sliced
  1 medium-sized onion, stuck
    with 4 cloves

  1 carrot, sliced
  1 garlic clove, crushed
  Zest of 1 orange and 1
    lemon
  4 peppercorns, crushed
  2 teaspoons salt
  5 to 6 cups water
  ½ cup vinegar

2 live 2-pound lobsters
Romaine lettuce
2 cups Mayonnaise (p. 782)

Lobster Parisienne | LANGOUSTE À LA PARISIENNE

Cook the lobsters as described in Lobster Mayonnaise (p. 243).

Cut the meat from the tail into slices, place them on a rack, season them lightly with salt and pepper, and glaze them with the jellied mayonnaise. Decorate each with a truffle slice. Chill.

Prepare a *salade Parisienne* by mixing together the *macédoine* of vegetables, the mayonnaise, and the chopped lobster meat from the claws and the front part of the body. Pile this salad into a mound on a serving dish and surround it with the lobster slices. Decorate with the hard-cooked eggs and the hearts of romaine.

FOR 4 PERSONS:

4 live 1½-pound lobsters
Court Bouillon for Lobster
   (p. 243)
Salt
Freshly ground white pepper
1½ cups Jellied Mayonnaise
   (p. 784)

2 truffles, sliced
2 cups cooked Macédoine of
   Vegetables (p. 111)
1 cup Mayonnaise (p. 782)
4 hard-cooked eggs, quartered
4 hearts of romaine lettuce

Lobster Salad | SALADE DE LANGOUSTE

Cook the lobster in a strong *court bouillon* as described in Lobster Mayonnaise (p. 243); let it cool in the *court bouillon* and then drain it.

Remove the meat from the tail, the front part of the body and the claws. Cut it into small dice, put it in a bowl, and toss it with the French dressing. Chill in the refrigerator for about 30 minutes.

Make the mayonnaise and hard-cook the eggs. Trim and wash the romaine, separate the leaves, and line a serving dish with them.

Drain the lobster meat, toss it with the mayonnaise, and pile it in the shape of a dome on the salad greens. Sprinkle with the *fines herbes*.

Slice the hard-cooked eggs and arrange them around the lobster in the serving dish.

FOR 4 PERSONS:

1 live 3-pound lobster
Court Bouillon for Lobster
   (p. 243)
1 cup Simple French Dressing
   (p. 787)

1 cup Mayonnaise (p. 782)
4 eggs
1 head of romaine lettuce
4 tablespoons minced Fines
   Herbes (p. 89)

Mackerel in White Wine | MAQUEREAUX AU VIN BLANC

Mince the onions and put them in a saucepan with the wine. Season with the salt, peppercorns, thyme and bay leaves. Bring to the boiling point and boil over high heat until the liquid is reduced by one third.

Put the mackerel fillets in an oiled skillet and top them with the lemon slices. Pour the boiling white wine and onions over the fish.

Put the skillet over medium heat, bring to the boiling point, and cook for 2 to 3 minutes. Cool in the skillet, and serve cold.

FOR 4 PERSONS:

3 medium-sized onions
3 cups dry white wine
1 teaspoon salt
6 peppercorns
½ teaspoon ground thyme

2 bay leaves
2 pounds mackerel fillets (4 to 8 fillets)
1 lemon, sliced

MOULES / *Mussels*

Raw mussels are often served on the half shell and may be seasoned with any of the French dressings on page 788.

Shelled mussels may be made into a salad, dressed with a French dressing, a mayonnaise, or any preferred seafood sauce.

Raw or steamed, they may also be combined with sliced cold boiled potatoes, sliced raw apples, green salad chiffonade style (cut into julienne strips), or rice boiled in plain water. Any suitable sauce may be used for seasoning.

SALADE DE MOULES AU RIZ / *Mussel and Rice Salad*

Scrub the mussels and put them into a large saucepan with the chopped shallots, the parsley, thyme, bay leaf, butter and wine. Cover the saucepan, bring to the boiling point, and cook for about 5 minutes, or until the shells open.

When the mussels are fully opened, drain them (reserving the liquid), shell them, and pile them in the center of a salad bowl. Sprinkle the mussels with half of the French dressing and chill in the refrigerator.

Cook the rice in boiling salted water for about 15 minutes, or until three-quarters done. Strain the *court bouillon* in which the mussels were cooked and add it to the cooking rice.

When the rice is tender, drain and cool it. Toss it with the remaining dressing and arrange it in a crown around the mussels. Serve chilled.

FOR 4 PERSONS:

2½ pounds mussels
2 shallots, chopped
1 parsley sprig
1 thyme sprig, or ½ teaspoon ground thyme
½ bay leaf

4 tablespoons butter
1½ cups dry white wine
1 cup French Dressing with Fines Herbes (p. 788)
1 cup uncooked rice
Salt

POULPE À LA PROVENÇALE / *Octopus Provençale*

Clean the octopus under running cold water and cut off the ends of the tentacles, the mouth and the eyes; remove and reserve the sac of ink; discard the intestines. Soak the octopus in cold water for 3 to 4 hours, so that the insides will be well cleaned; change the water a few times during the soaking. Drain the octopus, cut it into pieces, and beat these pieces with a wooden mallet to soften them.

Cut the pieces into big dice, all of the same size, and blanch them in slightly salted boiling water for a few minutes. Drain them and dry them with a kitchen cloth. Sprinkle the dice with flour.

Heat the oil in a casserole, add the onions, and cook them until golden; then add the diced octopus. Mix well, season with salt and pepper to taste, and simmer over low heat for 5 minutes. Add the tomatoes and cook until the pan liquid has thickened.

Add the wine and the water, the ink sac, the *bouquet garni,* and the garlic; check the seasoning. Cover the casserole, then simmer over low heat until the octopus is tender. The exact time will depend on the age and toughness of the octopus. Check to see if the octopus pieces are tender after 1½ hours.

Transfer to a serving dish, sprinkle with minced parsley, and cool.

This dish may be served warm or cold.

FOR 4 PERSONS:

2 pounds octopus	**2 cups dry white wine**
2 tablespoons flour	**1 cup water**
3 tablespoons olive oil	**1 Bouquet Garni (p. 46)**
2 medium-sized onions, minced	**1 garlic clove, mashed**
Freshly ground black pepper	**4 tablespoons minced parsley**
4 large tomatoes, peeled, seeded and chopped	**Salt**

Octopus Vinaigrette / POULPE À LA VINAIGRETTE

Proceed as in Octopus Provençale (above), but blanch the octopus pieces in salted water much longer, for about 2 hours, or until they are completely tender.

Drain them on a kitchen cloth. Cool them and put into a deep serving dish. Prepare a French dressing with *fines herbes* and pour it over the octopus pieces. Mix, chill, and serve.

FOR 4 PERSONS:

2 pounds octopus
½ cup French Dressing with Fines Herbes (788)

Note: You may surround the octopus with a crown of rice cooked in salted water with a pinch of saffron. You'll need ½ pound uncooked rice.

Oysters / HUÎTRES

Serve oysters on the half shell in the same manner as clams (see p. 236), with Shallot Vinegar (p. 788), buttered black bread and lemon quarters.

COCKTAIL D'HUÎTRES / *Oyster Cocktail*

The preparation is much the same as for Shrimp Cocktail (p. 250). Remove the oysters from their shells and prepare the cocktail sauce at the very last moment before serving time. Serve them in a glass embedded in cracked ice.

MOUSSE FROIDE DE BROCHET / *Cold Pike Mousse*

Cook the pike in the *court bouillon* until it is firm and flakes when tested with a fork. Drain it and remove the skin and bones.

Purée the fish in a blender, season lightly with salt and pepper, and blend in the *sauce béchamel*. Let it cool and fold in the whipped *crème*. Check the seasoning and add a little cayenne.

Pile the mousse onto a serving dish in the shape of a dome and smooth it out. Decorate with blanched tarragon leaves, chervil leaves, capers and sliced pickles.

Chill the dish and serve it very cold.

FOR 4 PERSONS:

1½ pounds pike
Court Bouillon for Fish
  (p. 131)
Salt
Freshly ground white pepper
½ cup Sauce Béchamel (p. 761)
¾ cup Crème Fraîche (p. 666), whipped

Cayenne pepper
2 tablespoons tarragon leaves, blanched
1 tablespoon chervil leaves, blanched
Capers
Sour pickles, sliced very thin

/ *Poutargue*

This recipe probably originates with Alexander the Great's Greek contemporaries, who brought it back with them from the Far East. It consists of mullet roe, the ancestor of caviar. The mullet roe is pressed together and completely dried in a somewhat lengthened and flattened shape. Cut the roe into thin slices and arrange them on a serving dish. Serve them with a Simple French Dressing (p. 787), or with fresh butter and lemon juice, or as a garnish for a platter of cold fish.

SALADE DE LANGOUSTINES / *Prawn Salad*

EDITORS' NOTE: *Shrimps may be substituted for the prawns, which are hard to find in the United States.*

Cook the prawns in a very strong *court bouillon* for about 8 minutes; drain and shell them. Cut the meat into small pieces, and toss them with the mayonnaise.

Cut romaine lettuce into julienne strips, and line a serving dish with the strips.

Cut the pepper into thin rounds, and mince the celery hearts. Pile the prawn salad in the center of the dish and garnish with the pepper rounds and the celery. Chill in the refrigerator until serving time.

FOR 4 PERSONS:

20 prawns or very large shrimp	1 head of romaine lettuce
Court Bouillon for Shellfish	1 green pepper
(p. 131), made with vinegar	1 celery heart
1 cup Mayonnaise Tyrolienne	
(p. 785)	

Smoked Salmon / SAUMON FUMÉ

Smoked salmon may be served *nature,* that is, simply cut into very thin slices, with a garnish of lemon slices. Or it may be served in a salad with mayonnaise and raw vegetables cut into small dice. The salmon slices may be also rolled up and filled with a little mixed vegetable salad bound with mayonnaise.

Another way of serving smoked salmon is with thin slices of melon.

Blini /

Blini are small *crêpes* made with a yeast dough.

Contrary to what is generally believed, Russians rarely use buckwheat flour for their *blini* except when wheat flour isn't available.

Put 2 cups of the flour, the egg yolks, sugar and salt into a big bowl. Dissolve the compressed yeast in 2 cups of the lukewarm milk (80° to 90° F.); if using dry yeast, have the milk slightly warmer (105° to 115° F.). Add this lukewarm milk to the bowl and make a soft dough. Cover the bowl and let the dough rise in a warm place until doubled in bulk.

When the dough has risen, beat in the remaining flour and then the remaining milk. Cover the bowl and let the dough rise again until doubled in bulk.

Beat the egg whites until they stand in stiff peaks and fold them into the dough. The dough must be smooth and have a batterlike consistency. If it is too thick, add a little more lukewarm milk before folding in the egg whites.

Butter or oil a skillet lightly and heat it. Drop in the batter by tablespoons. Cook the *blini* until they are golden on both sides.

The *blini* must be small and light. Serve them as an accompaniment for smoked salmon, caviar or any cold fish such as fillets of whiting or shad roe, with sour cream on the side.

FOR ABOUT 3 DOZEN *blini:*

4 cups flour	¼ ounce compressed yeast, or
3 eggs, separated	½ package active dry yeast
2 teaspoons sugar	3 cups lukewarm milk
½ teaspoon salt	Butter or oil for frying

Canned Sardines / SARDINES À L'HUILE

In France, there are various kinds of canned sardines—with bones or boneless, with skins or skinned, plain or with pickles. It is said that to be really good, sardines must have aged in their cans for 3 years. There are sardine lovers who insist that the cans' labels be marked with the year, as in vintage wines; in fact, they treat the sardines as if they were vintage wines. Even after 10 or 15 years, canned sardines are still excellent.

Serve sardines in a shallow hors-d'oeuvre dish, sprinkle them with the oil in which they were canned, and serve them with sweet butter.

ESCABÈCHE DE SARDINES / *Sardine Escabeche*

EDITORS' NOTE: *Since fresh sardines are rarely available in American fish markets, it is suggested that small fresh herrings or smelts or pilchards be used in their stead in any recipes calling for fresh sardines.*

Clean the sardines, season them lightly with pepper, and coat them on all sides with flour.

Heat 4 tablespoons of the oil in a large skillet and fry the sardines, a few at a time, until they are golden on both sides. Drain them and put them into a deep serving dish.

Add the remaining oil to the skillet; add the onion, carrot and mashed garlic, and sauté until golden. Add the water, wine, thyme, bay leaves, parsley and green pepper. Season with salt and pepper and cook for about 15 minutes.

Pour the stock over the sardines. They should be entirely covered. Cover and marinate them in the refrigerator for 24 hours. Serve chilled.

FOR 4 PERSONS:

2 pounds fresh sardines, fresh herrings or pilchards	2 cups water
Freshly ground black pepper	1 cup dry white wine
Flour	1 sprig of fresh thyme, or ½ teaspoon ground thyme
6 tablespoons olive oil	2 bay leaves, crumbled
1 onion, minced	6 parsley sprigs
1 carrot, minced	1 green pepper, minced
2 garlic cloves, mashed	Salt

SARDINES FRAÎCHES MARINÉES / *Marinated Sardines*

Clean the sardines and fillet them. Wash the fillets under running cold water and dry them on kitchen toweling.

In a glass or china salad bowl, make alternate layers of minced fennel and sardine fillets, beginning and ending with fennel.

To make the dressing, combine the salt, sugar, a little white pepper, the Dijon mustard, the olive oil, vinegar and water. Mix well and pour the dressing over the fish and fennel. Cover and marinate in the refrigerator for about 4 hours. Serve garnished with additional fennel sprigs.

FOR 4 PERSONS:

2 pounds fresh sardines, fresh
  herrings or pilchards
½ cup minced fresh fennel leaves
1 teaspoon salt
1 teaspoon sugar
Freshly ground white pepper

1 tablespoon Dijon mustard
½ cup olive oil
¼ cup white-wine vinegar
2 tablespoons water
Fresh fennel sprigs

Pickled Sardines or Smelts /

SARDINES FRAÎCHES OU ÉPERLANS FRAIS AU VINAIGRE

Clean the sardines or the smelts, wash them in running cold water, and dry them on kitchen toweling. Remove the backbones without cutting the fish entirely into two.

Put a sprig of fresh fennel leaves into each fish and lay them side by side in a shallow casserole or a skillet.

Combine the vinegar, water, peppercorns, spices, bay leaf, salt and sugar. Bring to the boiling point, cook for about 5 minutes, and pour over the fish. Cool and then refrigerate for 24 hours.

Serve chilled.

FOR 4 PERSONS:

2 pounds fresh sardines or smelts
Leaves from 1 head of fennel
  or finocchio
½ cup white-wine vinegar
1 cup water
6 white peppercorns

Pinch of ground cloves
Pinch of grated nutmeg
1 bay leaf
2 teaspoons salt
2 teaspoons sugar

Seafood Platter / PLATEAU DE FRUITS DE MER

EDITORS' NOTE: *A French seafood platter, of necessity, is composed of seafood different from an American selection, since some of the seafood mentioned below is not readily available in America.*

A *fruits de mer* platter is composed of the following seafood, served on a platter filled with cracked ice and decorated with a few algae: oysters on the half shell, clams, sea urchins, mussels, cockles, winkles, prawns, crabs, and other shellfish. Depending on taste, the seafood is seasoned with lemon juice or Shallot Vinegar (p. 788).

Shrimp Cocktail / COCKTAIL DE CREVETTES

Simmer the shrimp in boiling *court bouillon* for about 5 minutes. Drain, cool, shell, and devein them. Toss them with the mayonnaise. Add the paprika, cayenne pepper, a little black pepper and the cognac. Blend thoroughly and chill in the refrigerator.

At serving time, line 4 glass dishes with lettuce leaves and pile a few of the shrimp in each. Sprinkle with *fines herbes* and serve immediately.

FOR 4 PERSONS:

2 pounds large shrimp
   Court Bouillon for Shellfish
   (p. 131), made with vinegar
½ cup Mayonnaise (p. 782)
½ teaspoon paprika
Pinch of cayenne pepper

Freshly ground black pepper
¼ cup cognac
1 head of Boston lettuce
4 tablespoons minced Fines
   Herbes (p. 89)

SALADE DE CREVETTES / *Shrimp Salad*

Place the shelled shrimp on a serving dish and garnish the dish with slices of hard-cooked eggs. Sprinkle with the French dressing with *fines herbes*.

Keep the dish in the refrigerator until serving time.

FOR 4 PERSONS:

2 pounds cooked shrimp, shelled
   and deveined
4 hard-cooked eggs, sliced

½ cup French Dressing with
   Fines Herbes (p. 788)

SALADE TAHITIENNE / *Tahitian Salad*

Crack open the coconut, reserve the milk, and grate the white meat very fine.

Cut the bass or perch into big dice, put them in a deep bowl, and sprinkle with coarse salt. Let the fish marinate in the salt for 2 hours.

Remove the fish, sponge off the salt carefully with a clean cloth, and dry the fish thoroughly.

Pile the fish in the middle of a deep serving dish. Combine the lemon juice, onion, grated coconut meat, the coconut milk, hard-cooked egg and pepper; pour the mixture over the fish. Toss lightly, arrange the lemon quarters on top of the fish, and chill.

Set the serving dish into another filled with cracked ice when serving.

FOR 6 PERSONS:

1 coconut
2 pounds fillets of sea bass or
   ocean perch
2 tablespoons coarse salt
Juice of 2 lemons

1 medium-sized onion, minced
1 hard-cooked egg, chopped fine
¼ teaspoon freshly ground black
   pepper
2 lemons, quartered

Smoked Trout | TRUITES FUMÉES

Smoked trout should be skinned to make them more appetizing. Serve garnished with lemons cut into quarters and parsley sprigs. Sweet butter may be served on the side.

Tunafish in Oil | THON À L'HUILE

Tunafish, preferably canned in olive oil, is served with a garnish of romaine lettuce leaves and hard-cooked eggs cut into quarters, and accompanied by mayonnaise served in a sauceboat.

Winkles Cooked in a Court Bouillon |

BIGORNEAUX AU COURT BOUILLON

EDITORS' NOTE: *While winkles, or periwinkles, are not too popular in the United States, fancy fish markets will order them, especially markets in Spanish, Puerto Rican, Italian, or Greek neighborhoods. There are various types of winkles, but all of them are quite small, having a spiral shell only an inch or so long. They are simply scrubbed like mussels and then soaked in warm water to soften the limy membrane, called the operculum, that closes the opening in the shell.*

Soak the winkles in warm water for 1 hour to soften the membranes that close the shells.

Make the *court bouillon* as follows: Combine the water, wine, onion, carrot, spices, a little salt and pepper, the bay leaf and *fines herbes*. Bring it to the boiling point, add the winkles, and simmer for 5 minutes.

Meantime, make the French dressing and add the shallots to it.

Drain the winkles and let them cool; arrange them in a serving dish. Pass the French dressing separately in a sauceboat.

Winkles are loosened from their shells with a little fork or a nutpick.

FOR 4 PERSONS:

6 dozen small winkles	**Freshly ground black pepper**
4 cups water	**1 bay leaf**
1 cup dry white wine	**1 tablespoon Fines Herbes**
1 onion, stuck with 3 cloves	**(p. 89)**
1 carrot, cut into rounds	**1 cup Simple French Dressing**
1 teaspoon Quatre Épices	**(p. 787)**
(p. 667)	**2 shallots, minced**
Salt	

HOT HORS-D'OEUVRE

Hors-d'Oeuvre Chauds

Hot Vegetable Hors-d'Oeuvre

Hors-d'Oeuvre Chauds de Légumes

ARTICHAUTS À LA DIABLE / *Artichokes à la Diable*

Trim off the stems of the artichokes and cut off the sharp points of the leaves. Blanch them immediately in well-salted boiling water to which you have added the juice of 1 lemon for 10 minutes. Drain and cool. Gently spread the leaves apart and scoop out the chokes.

Now make the stuffing: Soak the bread crumbs in the milk, squeeze them dry, and then mix them with the crushed garlic and the minced capers and parsley. Season with salt and pepper.

Stuff each artichoke with a little of this stuffing. Put them in a small shallow baking dish, and sprinkle them with the oil and a little more salt and pepper.

Bake the artichokes in a preheated 425° F. oven for about 30 minutes, basting them occasionally with the oil in the dish. Halfway through the baking time, sprinkle them with the juice of the remaining lemon. They are done when one of the outside leaves can easily be pulled off the artichoke.

FOR 4 PERSONS:

4 large artichokes	4 teaspoons minced capers
2 lemons	2 tablespoons minced parsley
1 cup soft white bread crumbs	Salt
½ cup milk	Freshly ground black pepper
1 garlic clove, crushed	4 tablespoons olive oil

ARTICHAUTS À LA LYONNAISE / *Artichokes Lyonnaise*

Prepare the artichokes for stuffing as described in the previous recipe, using one of the lemons in blanching. To make the stuffing, cook the onion in 3 tablespoons of the butter until it is soft, then add the sausage meat and sauté for about 5 minutes. Remove from the heat, pour off the excess fat in the pan, and add the parsley.

Put a little of this stuffing into each artichoke.

Heat the remaining butter and the oil in a casserole and arrange the artichokes in it. Cook them in a preheated 425° F. oven for about 30 minutes. Baste frequently, and halfway through the baking sprinkle with the juice of the remaining lemon.

FOR 4 PERSONS:

4 large artichokes	½ pound sausage meat
2 lemons	2 tablespoons minced parsley
1 onion, minced	2 tablespoons olive oil
5 tablespoons butter	

Stuffed Artichokes Ménagère /

ARTICHAUTS FARCIS À LA MÉNAGÈRE

Prepare the artichokes for stuffing as in Artichokes à la Diable (p. 253), using one of the lemons in blanching. To make the stuffing, cook the minced beef and the chopped pork fat together in a heavy saucepan over low heat for 10 minutes; the mixture should not brown. Add the parsley and season with salt, pepper and nutmeg.

Put a little of this stuffing into each artichoke.

Heat the butter and oil in a casserole. arrange the artichokes in it, and cook them in a preheated 425° F. oven for about 30 minutes. Baste frequently during the baking, and halfway through sprinkle with the juice of the remaining lemon.

FOR 4 PERSONS:

4 large artichokes	5 tablespoons minced parsley
2 lemons	Salt
½ pound cooked beef (preferably boiled beef), minced very fine	Freshly ground black pepper Pinch of grated nutmeg
⅓ cup chopped fresh pork fat	3 tablespoons butter
	2 tablespoons olive oil

Asparagus Barquettes / BARQUETTES D'ASPERGES

Make the pastry and roll it out to the thickness of ⅛ inch. Line 12 *barquette* molds with the pastry and prick the bottoms with a small fork so that they will not puff up too much during the baking. Freeze in the refrigerator for 1 hour. Bake the pastry in a preheated 350° F. oven for 15 to 18 minutes. Let the shells cool slightly and then remove them from the molds.

Meantime, cook the asparagus tips in boiling salted water for 5 to 8 minutes, or until they are barely tender. Drain them well on a rack.

Place 3 asparagus tips in each of the tartlets shells; if necessary, cut them to fit the pastry. Top each with a generous tablespoon of *sauce Mornay* and sprinkle with the grated cheese and the bread crumbs. Bake in a preheated 425° F. oven for 3 minutes. Serve immediately on a hot serving plate.

FOR 12 BARQUETTES:

For the pastry:	1 cup hot Sauce Mornay
1 recipe Pâte Brisée	(p. 776)
(p. 713)	⅓ cup grated Swiss cheese
36 asparagus tips	¼ cup fine dry bread crumbs

CROÛTES D'ASPERGES GRATINÉES / *Asparagus Croûtes*

Trim the asparagus tips and cook them in boiling salted water for 5 to 8 minutes, or until they are barely tender. Drain them in a strainer for a few minutes.

Heat 2 tablespoons of the butter in a casserole, put the asparagus tips in it, and sauté very gently over low heat for 2 minutes.

Trim the crusts off the slices of bread and cut each slice into halves. Heat the remaining butter and the oil in a skillet and fry the slices on both sides until they are golden. Put them in a shallow baking dish. Arrange the asparagus tips neatly on the bread and sprinkle with the grated cheese and the bread crumbs.

Run under the broiler, or cook in a preheated 450°F. oven, until the tops are golden and bubbly. Serve immediately.

FOR 4 PERSONS:

36 asparagus tips
½ cup butter
4 slices of bread

2 tablespoons olive oil
⅓ cup grated Swiss cheese
¼ cup fine dry bread crumbs

SOUFFLÉ AUX AVOCATS / *Avocado Soufflé*

Heat the butter in a saucepan, add the flour, and stir with a wooden spoon until the *roux* is smooth; do not let it brown. Keep the heat as low as possible. Cool the *roux* slightly.

Heat the milk to the boiling point and pour it all at once into the cold *roux*. Beat rapidly with a wire whip. Season with the salt, a little pepper and the nutmeg.

Remove the pulp from the avocados and press it through a very fine sieve or purée it in a blender. Beat the egg yolks into the avocado purée. Stir this into the other mixture.

Heat the mixture over lowest possible heat, stirring constantly. Remove it from the heat before it comes to the boiling point.

Beat the egg whites until they stand in stiff peaks and fold them into the avocado mixture.

Pour the mixture into a buttered and floured 2-quart soufflé dish and bake in a preheated 375° F. oven for about 35 minutes. Or set the soufflé dish in a pan of boiling water and bake in a 375° F. oven for about 1 hour.

FOR 6 PERSONS:

5 tablespoons butter
6 tablespoons flour
2 cups milk
1 teaspoon salt
Freshly ground black pepper

Pinch of grated nutmeg
2 medium-sized avocados
5 egg yolks
6 egg whites

CROÛTES À LA DU BARRY / *Cauliflower Croûtes*

Wash the cauliflower and cook it in boiling salted water for about 12 minutes, or until it is tender.

Drain it and purée it in a blender. Mix the *sauce béchamel* with the cauliflower purée and season to taste with salt, pepper and nutmeg. Fold in the beaten egg white.

Fry the trimmed bread slices in 6 tablespoons of the butter and the oil until golden brown on both sides. Put them into a shallow baking dish. Top each with a little of the cauliflower mixture, sprinkle with the grated cheese and the bread crumbs, and dot with the remaining butter. Bake in a preheated 425° F. oven for about 5 minutes.

FOR 4 PERSONS:

½ medium-sized cauliflower,
   broken into flowerets
½ cup Sauce Béchamel (p. 761)
Salt
Freshly ground white pepper
Pinch of grated nutmeg

1 egg white, stiffly beaten
4 slices of firm white bread
½ cup butter
2 tablespoons olive oil
⅓ cup grated Swiss cheese
¼ cup fine dry bread crumbs

Celery Villeroy Canapés / CÉLERIS VILLEROY SUR CANAPÉ

Trim and peel the celery and cut the stalks into 3-inch lengths. Blanch them in boiling salted water for 10 minutes. Drain thoroughly.

Heat 3 tablespoons of the butter in a heavy saucepan, line the pan with a sheet of pork fat, add the celery pieces, and top them with another sheet of pork fat. Add the white stock and cook, covered, over low heat for 20 minutes.

Prepare the *sauce Villeroy*.

Remove the celery pieces from the pork fat, drain them in a strainer, and add them to the *sauce Villeroy*. Let them cool completely, and then chill in the refrigerator.

Mix the eggs with the oil and season with salt and pepper and the nutmeg.

Remove the celery pieces, one at a time, from the *sauce Villeroy* (each piece should be well coated), dip them first into the egg mixture, and then coat with the bread crumbs. Chill the coated pieces in the refrigerator for 1 hour.

Heat the oil to 375° F. on a frying thermometer and fry the celery pieces for 3 or 4 minutes, or until they are golden brown. Drain on kitchen toweling.

Trim the crusts from the bread slices and cut the slices into quarters. Fry the quarters in the remaining butter until they are golden.

Put the fried bread slices on a hot serving dish and top each with a piece of the fried celery. Serve immediately and very hot.

FOR 4 PERSONS:

1 large bunch of celery
9 tablespoons butter
2 large thin slices of fresh
   pork fat
½ cup White Stock (p. 165)
1 cup very thick Sauce Villeroy
   (p. 777)
2 eggs

1 tablespoon peanut oil
Salt
Freshly ground white pepper
Pinch of grated nutmeg
2 cups soft white bread crumbs
Oil for deep frying
4 (or more) slices of bread

CORNMEAL CROQUETTES

The sauce béchamel *should be thicker than usual. It is beaten into the* cornmeal mixture along with the egg yolks.

The oil used for frying should be very hot, 375° F., but not smoking.

Cornmeal Croquettes | CROQUETTES DE MAÏS

Bring the milk to the boiling point and pour it over the cornmeal in a saucepan. Cook, stirring constantly, until the mixture is smooth and thick.

Beat the *béchamel* and the 3 egg yolks into the cornmeal. Season with salt and pepper. Cool and then chill.

Mix together the 2 whole eggs and the oil and season with salt, pepper and nutmeg.

Put some flour in one bowl and the bread crumbs into another. Heat the frying oil to 375° F. on a frying thermometer. Shape generous spoonfuls of the cornmeal mixture into croquettes; dip them first into the flour, then into the egg mixture, and finally coat with the bread crumbs. Fry the croquettes until they are golden brown, about 3 minutes. Drain on paper towels before serving.

FOR 4 PERSONS:

3 cups milk	Salt
1 cup cornmeal	Freshly ground white pepper
1 cup Sauce Béchamel (p. 761)	Pinch of grated nutmeg
3 egg yolks	Flour
2 whole eggs	2 cups fine dry bread crumbs
1 tablespoon peanut oil	Oil for deep frying

Eggplant Fritters | ACRATS D'AUBERGINES

Peel the eggplants, cut them into pieces, and put them into an enamelware saucepan with cold salted water. Bring to the boiling point and boil for about 15 minutes, or until the eggplant pieces are tender. Drain and press them through a fine sieve or purée them in a blender.

Blend the flour and the eggs into this purée to make a drop batter. Beat it until it is light. Season with salt, pepper and a little cayenne. If the batter is not thick enough, add a little more flour.

Heat the fat to 360° F. on a frying thermometer. Drop the batter by tablespoons into the hot fat and fry until the fritters are puffed and golden.

Drain the fritters on kitchen toweling, put them on a hot serving dish, and sprinkle them with a little salt and the minced parsley. Serve immediately.

FOR 4 PERSONS:

2 medium-sized eggplants	Freshly ground black pepper
½ cup flour	Pinch of cayenne pepper
2 eggs, beaten	Fat for deep frying
Salt	¼ cup minced parsley

Leek Tart | TARTE AUX POIREAUX

Prepare the *pâte brisée,* roll it out to the thickness of ⅛ inch, and use it to line a 9-inch pie pan, or a flan ring placed on a baking sheet.

Trim off the roots and the green ends of the leeks and cut them into thin slices.

Blanch them in boiling salted water for 5 minutes. Drain and rinse under running cold water.

Heat the butter in a heavy saucepan and gently cook the leeks in it until they are soft but not brown.

Beat together the *crème fraîche,* the milk and the eggs. Season with a teaspoon of salt, a little pepper and the nutmeg. Spread the leeks in the tart, add the egg mixture, and sprinkle with the bread crumbs. Bake in a preheated 350° F. oven for about 30 minutes, or until a knife inserted in the custard comes out clean. Serve immediately.

FOR 4 PERSONS:

1 recipe Pâte Brisée (p. 713)
3 large leeks
3 tablespoons butter
1 cup Crème Fraîche (p. 666)
1 cup milk

4 eggs
Salt
Freshly ground white pepper
Pinch of grated nutmeg
¼ cup fine dry bread crumbs

CHAMPIGNONS EN AUMÔNIÈRE / *Mushrooms Aumônière*

EDITORS' NOTE: *An* aumônière *is a small bag used to hold alms. These little mushroom tidbits resemble their shape.*

Make the *crêpe* batter, omitting the sugar, and let it rest in the refrigerator for 3 hours.

Separate the mushroom caps and stems. Heat 1 tablespoon each of the butter and the oil in a heavy saucepan, add the mushroom caps, and gently sauté them over low heat until tender. Season with a little salt and pepper.

Mince the mushroom stems and gently sauté them in the remaining butter and oil in another skillet. Season with a little salt and pepper.

With the batter make 6 large *crêpes* 8 or 9 inches in diameter. Put each on a plate. In the center of each *crêpe* put a mushroom cap and a little of the minced mushrooms. Shape each *crêpe* into a bag enclosing the mushrooms, tie each loosely with string, and put them in a buttered shallow baking dish. Sprinkle them with grated cheese and the melted butter. Put them into a preheated 450° F. oven for about 10 minutes, or until the cheese is melted and golden.

Meanwhile, make the tomato sauce: cook the shallot in the butter until it is soft. Sprinkle with the flour and stir well. Add the tomato purée, the wine, bay leaf and sugar. Season with salt and pepper. Let the sauce simmer for about 10 minutes.

Take the *crêpes* from the oven and serve in the baking dish with the sauce on the side.

FOR 6 PERSONS:

½ recipe Crêpes batter (p. 740), without sugar
6 large mushrooms
2 tablespoons butter
2 tablespoons peanut oil
Salt
Freshly ground black pepper
¼ cup grated Swiss cheese
3 tablespoons melted butter

For the tomato sauce:
1 shallot, minced
2 tablespoons butter
1 tablespoon flour
¼ cup Tomato Purée (p. 157)
1 cup dry white wine
1 bay leaf
Pinch of sugar
Salt
Freshly ground black pepper

Mushroom Barquettes / BARQUETTES FORESTIÈRES

Make the pastry and roll it out to a thickness of ⅛ inch. Line 12 *barquette* molds with the pastry and prick the bottoms with a small fork so they will not puff up too much during the baking. Freeze in the refrigerator for 1 hour. Bake the pastry in a preheated 350° F. oven for 15 to 18 minutes. Let the shells cool slightly and then remove them from the molds.

Trim the mushrooms and cut them into halves or, if they are very large, into quarters. Heat the butter in a casserole, add the mushrooms, and cook them over low heat for 5 minutes. Add half of the *crème fraîche,* bring to the boiling point, and cook until the pan liquid has almost entirely evaporated.

Add the remaining *crème fraîche,* and toss with a wooden spoon. Season lightly with salt and pepper.

Distribute the mushroom halves or quarters in the *barquette* shells. Sprinkle some of the cooking juice and minced *fines herbes* over each *barquette* and serve immediately on a hot serving dish.

FOR 12 BARQUETTES:

1 recipe Pâte Brisée (p. 713)
12 large or 24 medium-sized mushrooms
3 tablespoons butter
1 cup Crème Fraîche (p. 666)
Salt

Freshly ground black pepper
2 tablespoons minced Fines Herbes (p. 89)

Mushroom Canapés / CANAPÉS DE CHAMPIGNONS GRATINÉS

Trim the crusts from the slices of bread. If desired, cut the slices into halves.

Heat 6 tablespoons of the butter in a skillet and fry the bread slices in it until they are golden on both sides.

Heat the remaining 4 tablespoons of butter in a heavy saucepan and gently sauté the minced mushrooms in it for about 5 minutes. Season with salt and pepper. Stir in the eggs and grated cheese and stir over the heat for a minute for the mixture to thicken, but not long enough to fully cook the eggs.

Put the fried bread slices into a shallow baking dish and spoon a little of the mushrooms and their sauce on each. Sprinkle with the bread crumbs and the melted butter.

Bake in a preheated 425° F. oven for 5 minutes, or place under a preheated broiler for about 3 minutes.

FOR 4 PERSONS:

4 slices of firm white bread, about 1 inch thick
10 tablespoons butter
½ pound mushrooms, minced
Salt

Freshly ground white pepper
2 eggs, beaten
½ cup grated Swiss cheese
¼ cup fine dry bread crumbs
3 tablespoons melted butter

CRÊPES AUX CHAMPIGNONS / *Mushroom Crêpes*

Prepare the *crêpe* batter and let it rest in the refrigerator for 3 hours.

Chop the mushrooms and purée them in a blender. Season them lightly with salt. Add the minced ham and the heavy cream.

Make about 12 *crêpes* in the usual manner and stuff each with a little of the mushroom filling. Put the stuffed *crêpes* side by side in a buttered shallow baking dish.

Sprinkle with the melted butter and grated cheese and cook in a 325° F. oven for 20 minutes. Serve immediately.

FOR 4 PERSONS:

½ recipe Crêpes batter (p. 740)
½ pound mushrooms
Salt
¼ cup minced prosciutto

2 tablespoons heavy cream
6 tablespoons butter, melted
½ cup grated Swiss cheese

CROÛTES AUX CHAMPIGNONS DE PARIS / *Mushroom Croûtes*

Finely mince the ¾ pound of mushrooms and the shallots.

Slice the mushroom caps thinly and sauté them in 2 tablespoons of the butter in a saucepan over low heat. Season them with salt and pepper.

Sauté the minced mushrooms and shallots in 2 tablespoons of butter for about minutes. Add the *crème fraîche* and season with salt and pepper.

Fry the trimmed bread slices on both sides in the remaining butter and the oil. Put them into a shallow baking dish, spoon some of the mushroom purée over each slice, and top each with sliced mushrooms. Sprinkle grated cheese on top of each. Bake in a preheated 400° F. oven for about 5 minutes, or run briefly under the broiler.

FOR 4 PERSONS:

¾ pound mushrooms
2 shallots
4 large mushroom caps
½ cup butter
Salt
Freshly ground white pepper

⅓ cup Crème Fraîche (p. 666)
4 slices of firm white bread,
  trimmed of crusts
2 tablespoons peanut oil
¼ cup grated Swiss cheese

BOUCHÉES FEUILLETÉES AUX CHAMPIGNONS / *Mushroom Patties*

Prepare and bake the patty shells, brushed with the egg yolk.

Heat the oil and the butter gently and sauté the sliced mushrooms and the minced onions and shallots in it over low heat for about 10 minutes. Season with salt and pepper.

Add the *sauce béchamel* to the mushrooms and season with a pinch of nutmeg. Mix thoroughly and cook for 1 or 2 minutes longer.

Fill each of the hot patty shells with a little of the mushroom mixture. Replace the tops of the shells and return to a 400° F. oven for 3 or 4 minutes.

FOR 4 PERSONS:

<table>
<tr><td>4 patty shells, 4-inch size
(see p. 717)</td><td>2 medium-sized onions, minced
2 shallots, minced</td></tr>
<tr><td>1 egg yolk, beaten</td><td>Salt</td></tr>
<tr><td>1 tablespoon peanut oil</td><td>Freshly ground white pepper</td></tr>
<tr><td>3 tablespoons butter</td><td>1 cup Sauce Béchamel (p. 761)</td></tr>
<tr><td>½ pound mushrooms, sliced</td><td>Pinch of grated nutmeg</td></tr>
</table>

Mushroom Tart | TARTE AUX CHAMPIGNONS

Make the *pâte brisée* and let it rest for 1 hour.

Heat the butter and the oil in a saucepan and cook the onion and shallot in it over low heat for about 5 minutes, or until they are soft.

Add the mushrooms. Season with salt, pepper and nutmeg, and add the lemon juice. Mix well and cook over medium heat, stirring frequently, until all the pan liquid has evaporated. Add the *crème fraîche*.

Roll out the *pâte brisée* to the thickness of ⅛ inch. Line an 8-inch pie pan with the dough, or line an 8-inch flan ring placed on a baking sheet. Pour the mushrooms and the sauce into the shell and spread them evenly. Sprinkle with the grated cheese and bread crumbs and bake in a preheated 350° F. oven for about 30 minutes. Serve immediately.

FOR 4 PERSONS:

<table>
<tr><td>1 recipe Pâte Brisée (p. 713)</td><td>Salt</td></tr>
<tr><td>3 tablespoons butter</td><td>Freshly ground white pepper</td></tr>
<tr><td>1 tablespoon peanut oil</td><td>Pinch of grated nutmeg</td></tr>
<tr><td>1 onion, minced</td><td>Juice of 1 lemon</td></tr>
<tr><td>1 shallot, minced</td><td>½ cup Crème Fraîche (p. 666)</td></tr>
<tr><td>¾ pound mushrooms, thinly
sliced</td><td>⅓ cup grated Swiss cheese
¼ cup fine dry bread crumbs</td></tr>
</table>

Onion Casserole | OIGNONS EN CASSEROLE

Mince the onions and cook them in the butter over medium heat for about 5 minutes, or until they are soft and golden.

Cut the pork and the veal into pieces and grind it, using the finest blade of the meat grinder. Add it to the onions, mix well, and stir in the bread crumbs, *crème fraîche* and lukewarm water. Season to taste with salt and pepper.

Put the mixture into a buttered baking dish and run under the broiler until bubbly. Serve very hot.

FOR 4 PERSONS:

<table>
<tr><td>4 large onions</td><td>½ cup Crème Fraîche (p. 666)</td></tr>
<tr><td>3 tablespoons butter</td><td>¼ cup lukewarm water</td></tr>
<tr><td>½ pound cooked lean pork</td><td>Salt</td></tr>
<tr><td>¼ pound cooked veal</td><td>Freshly ground black pepper</td></tr>
<tr><td>½ cup fresh white bread crumbs</td><td></td></tr>
</table>

TARTE AUX OIGNONS / *Onion Tart*

Make the *pâte brisée* and let it rest for 1 hour.

Cook the onions in the butter in a heavy saucepan over low heat for about 10 minutes, or until they are soft.

Beat the *crème fraîche* together with the milk, eggs and grated cheese. Season to taste with salt and pepper.

Roll out the pastry to a thickness of ⅛ inch and line a 9-inch pie pan with it, or line a 9-inch flan ring placed on a baking sheet. Spread the onions in the pastry and pour the egg mixture over the onions. Sprinkle with the bread crumbs. Bake in a preheated 350° F. oven for about 30 minutes. Serve immediately.

FOR 4 PERSONS:

1 recipe Pâte Brisée (p. 713)	4 eggs
4 large onions	1 cup grated Swiss cheese
3 tablespoons butter	Salt
1 cup Crème Fraîche (p. 666)	Freshly ground white pepper
1 cup milk	½ cup fine dry bread crumbs

BEIGNETS SOUFFLÉS À LA HONGROISE / *Hungarian Fritters*

Prepare the *pâte à choux,* omitting the sugar.

Mince the onions and cook them gently in the butter until they are soft but not brown. Season with salt and pepper and the paprika.

Beat the onions into the *choux* paste.

Heat the fat to 375° F. on a frying thermometer and drop the batter into it by generous spoonfuls, a few at a time. Fry them for about 5 minutes, or until they are puffed and golden brown.

Drain the fritters on paper towels and serve them sprinkled with a little salt on a hot dish lined with a napkin.

FOR 6 PERSONS:

1 recipe Pâte à Choux (p. 710) without sugar	Salt
6 medium-sized onions	Freshly ground white pepper
4 tablespoons butter	1 teaspoon paprika
	Fat for deep frying

SOUFFLÉ AUX PIMENTS DOUX I / *Sweet Pepper Soufflé I*

Heat the butter in a saucepan and add the flour. Mix with a wooden spoon until smooth and cook over low heat for 5 minutes. Plunge the bottom of the saucepan into cold water to cool the mixture.

Heat the milk to the boiling point and pour it all at once into the cooled *roux.* Beat thoroughly with a wire whisk. Season to taste with salt, pepper and nutmeg. Beat in the egg yolks.

Cut off the tops of the sweet peppers and remove the seeds and membranes. Use preferably 2 red and 2 green peppers. Cut a diamond-shaped piece about 1 inch across out of each pepper and finely mince the rest. Heat the oil in a heavy saucepan and cook the peppers in it over low heat for about 10 minutes, until they are soft. Season with salt and pepper. Reserve the diamond-shaped pieces and fold the minced peppers into the other mixture.

Butter and flour a 2-quart soufflé dish.

Beat the egg whites until they stand in stiff peaks, fold them into soufflé mixture, and pour it into the soufflé dish. Arrange the reserved diamond-shaped pepper pieces on the top in a design.

Bake in a preheated 375° F. oven for about 35 minutes, or set the soufflé dish in a pan of boiling water and bake in a 375° F. oven for about 1 hour.

FOR 6 PERSONS:

5 tablespoons butter	Pinch of grated nutmeg
6 tablespoons flour	5 egg yolks
2 cups milk	4 sweet peppers
Salt	3 tablespoons olive oil
Freshly ground black pepper	6 egg whites

Sweet Pepper Soufflé II / SOUFFLÉ AUX PIMENTS DOUX II

Cut off the tops of the peppers, remove the seeds and the membranes, and cut them into small strips.

Heat half of the oil and half of the butter in a heavy saucepan, add the peppers to it, and sprinkle with the thyme. Cook over low heat for about 10 minutes.

Separate five of the eggs. Add the remaining 2 whole eggs to the egg yolks. Season with salt and pepper and beat with a wire whisk or an egg beater until light.

Beat the egg whites until they stand in stiff peaks and fold them into the egg mixture.

Heat the remaining oil and butter in a very large skillet, pour the egg mixture into it, and top with the peppers. Mix quickly with a fork, cook like an omelet (see p. 120), and serve immediately on a hot serving dish.

You may reserve a few of the cooked pepper strips and decorate the top of the soufflé with them.

FOR 4 PERSONS:

4 sweet peppers	7 eggs
4 tablespoons olive oil	Salt
4 tablespoons butter	Freshly ground black pepper
2 tablespoons chopped fresh thyme, or ½ teaspoon dried thyme	

Potato Fritters / BEIGNETS DE POMMES DE TERRE

Cut the potatoes into fine julienne strips and sprinkle them with salt and pepper.

Make the batter: Beat the flour, milk and oil together with a wire whisk until very smooth. Fold in the egg white.

Pour the potatoes into the batter and mix thoroughly.

Heat the fat to 375° F. on a frying thermometer. Drop small quantities of the batter into the hot oil and cook until golden. Drain on paper towels.

Serve on a hot serving dish lined with a napkin; sprinkle with salt.

FOR 6 PERSONS:

6 medium-sized potatoes	1 cup milk
Salt	1 tablespoon peanut oil
Freshly ground white pepper	1 egg white
¾ cup flour	Fat for deep frying

CRÊPES AUX ÉPINARDS / *Spinach Crêpes*

Proceed as for Mushroom Crêpes (p. 261), but stuff the 12 *crêpes* with the following mixture:

Blanch the spinach in a large pot of boiling salted water for 4 minutes. Drain it, cool, and squeeze it completely dry. Purée it in a blender.

Cook the bacon dice in a skillet until they are not quite crisp and mix with the spinach purée. Add the softened butter and season to taste with salt and pepper.

FOR 4 PERSONS:

½ recipe Crêpes batter (p. 740)	Salt
1 pound spinach	Freshly ground black pepper
6 slices of bacon, diced	6 tablespoons butter, melted
4 tablespoons butter, softened	⅓ cup grated Swiss cheese

CROÛTES À LA FLORENTINE / *Croûtes Florentine*

Cook the spinach in a large quantity of boiling salted water for 5 minutes. Drain it and squeeze it completely dry. Purée it in a blender. Put it in a saucepan and add the *crème fraîche* and ¼ cup of the grated cheese. Cook over low heat until the cheese is melted.

Trim off the crusts of the bread slices and fry the bread in the oil and butter until golden. Place the slices in a shallow baking dish. Top each slice with a generous spoonful of spinach purée. Sprinkle with the remaining grated cheese and with bread crumbs.

Run under the broiler until brown and bubbly. Serve immediately.

FOR 4 PERSONS:

1 pound spinach	2 tablespoons olive oil
⅓ cup Crème Fraîche (p. 666)	4 tablespoons butter
½ cup grated Swiss cheese	¼ cup fine dry bread crumbs
4 slices of firm white bread	

CROÛTES À LA PROVENÇALE / *Croûtes Provençale*

Mince the onions and cook them in 3 tablespoons of hot olive oil until soft. Add the tomatoes. Season with salt and pepper, mix well, then add the thyme and the minced sweet pepper. Cook, stirring constantly, until all the liquid has evaporated and the mixture is thick.

Trim the bread; heat the remaining olive oil and the butter in a skillet and fry the bread slices in it until they are golden on both sides. Place them in a shallow baking dish. Spread some of the tomato mixture over each slice, and top with an anchovy fillet and a sliced olive. Sprinkle with grated cheese and bread crumbs and run under a hot broiler for 2 minutes.

FOR 4 PERSONS:

2 onions
5 tablespoons olive oil
4 tomatoes, peeled, seeded and
   chopped
Salt
Freshly ground black pepper
½ teaspoon dried thyme
1 sweet pepper, charred, scraped,
   seeded and minced (see p. 619)

4 slices of firm white bread
4 tablespoons butter
4 anchovy fillets
4 olives, pitted and sliced
⅓ cup grated Swiss cheese
¼ cup fine dry bread crumbs

Tart Andalouse | FEUILLETÉ À L'ANDALOUSE

Make the puff-paste tart shell and bake it as described on page 716.

Mince the onion and cook it in the oil and butter over low heat for about 10 minutes, or until it is soft. Add the sweet pepper and the tomatoes, season with salt and pepper, and cook, stirring constantly, until most of the moisture has evaporated.

Cut the celery into 1-inch lengths and boil the pieces in salted water for 20 minutes. Drain and add them to the other vegetables. Cook the mixture for about 10 minutes longer.

Cook the rice separately in lightly salted boiling water until tender. Drain.

Add the rice and the thyme to the other mixture and spread it in the baked tart shell. Top with the green and black olives. Bake the tart in a 400° F. oven for 7 or 8 minutes. Serve immediately.

FOR 4 PERSONS:

1 baked puff-paste tart shell,
   8-inch size (about ½ recipe,
   p. 716)
1 large onion
2 tablespoons olive oil
2 tablespoons butter
1 sweet pepper, seeded and
   minced
3 tomatoes, peeled, seeded and
   chopped

Salt
Freshly ground black pepper
1 small head of celery
¼ cup uncooked rice
1 tablespoon chopped fresh thyme,
   or ½ teaspoon dried thyme
10 green and black olives, pitted

Pissaladière |

Heat the oil and the butter in a heavy saucepan, add the minced onions, and cook over low heat for about 30 minutes, stirring frequently. The onions must not brown. Season with salt and pepper.

After the bread dough has risen, roll it out into a round about 12 inches in diameter, leaving the edges thicker than the center. Place the round on a well-oiled baking sheet. Spread it with the onions, anchovy fillets, tomatoes and black olives. Bake in a preheated 400° F. oven for 25 minutes, or until the outside edge of the bread is lightly browned.

FOR 4 PERSONS:

3 tablespoons olive oil	Bread dough (see below)
2 tablespoons butter	12 anchovy fillets, drained
1 pound onions, minced	3 very ripe tomatoes, peeled,
Salt	seeded and chopped
Freshly ground black pepper	10 pitted black olives, sliced

Note: The use of tomato in this recipe is a recent development, but today it is generally accepted.

> EDITORS' NOTE: *M. Oliver has not favored us with a recipe for bread dough. You may use your own favorite one, or ours that follows which is, simply, a recipe for French bread.*
>
> *Dissolve the compressed yeast in the lukewarm (80° to 90° F.) water, or use slightly warmer (105° to 115° F.) water if using dry yeast. Place the flour and salt in a bowl. Add the dissolved yeast and the oil; mix the ingredients together to make a soft dough. Add another tablespoon of water if the dough seems stiff; it must be fairly soft. Knead for 15 minutes, or until the dough is smooth and elastic. Form it into a ball, return it to the bowl, and set it in a warm place to rise until doubled in bulk, about 2 hours. Punch the dough down and it is ready to use. The proportions given below are sufficient for 1 medium loaf of French bread or 1* pissaladière *tart.*
>
> *½ package compressed or active dry yeast*
> *½ cup lukewarm water*
> *2 cups sifted flour*
> *1 teaspoon salt*
> *2 tablespoons olive oil*

SOUFFLÉ DE TOMATE / *Tomato Soufflé*

Heat the butter in a heavy saucepan and add the flour. Stir with a wooden spoon until the mixture is smooth and cook it over low heat for about 5 minutes. Remove from the heat and plunge the bottom of the saucepan into cold water to cool.

Heat the milk to the boiling point and pour it all at once into the cooled *roux.* Beat thoroughly with a wire whisk. Season to taste with salt, pepper and nutmeg.

Blend the tomato purée and the egg yolks together. Pour them, stirring constantly, into the hot white sauce. Stir it over very low heat and remove before it reaches the boiling point.

Beat the egg whites until they stand in stiff peaks and fold them into the other mixture.

Butter and flour a 2-quart soufflé dish. Pour the soufflé mixture into it and bake in a preheated 375° F. oven for about 35 minutes, or set the soufflé dish in a pan of boiling water and bake in a 375° F. oven for about 1 hour.

FOR 6 PERSONS:

5 tablespoons butter	Pinch of grated nutmeg
6 tablespoons flour	½ cup Tomato Purée (p. 157)
2 cups milk	5 egg yolks
Salt	6 egg whites
Freshly ground black pepper	

Truffle Fritters I / BEIGNETS DE TRUFFES

EDITORS' NOTE: *Fresh white or black truffles can be found in some food specialty shops in larger cities in the United States. Because of their cost, this and the following recipes are not ones you will be likely to try very often. However, canned truffles will make a poor substitute and we don't recommend them in these instances.*

Cut the truffles into thin slices. Blend together the brandy, ½ teaspoon of salt, a little pepper and a pinch of nutmeg; let the truffles marinate in this mixture for 2 hours.

Make the fritter batter: Beat together the flour, egg, oil and milk until the mixture is smooth. Season with a little salt and let it stand for 30 minutes.

Drain the truffles and dip each piece into the batter. Fry in hot oil, 360° F. on a frying thermometer, for 3 or 4 minutes, or until golden.

Drain and serve immediately on a hot serving dish lined with a napkin. Sprinkle with a little salt.

FOR 4 PERSONS:

6 medium-sized fresh truffles	½ cup flour
½ cup brandy	1 egg
Salt	1 tablespoon olive oil
Freshly ground black pepper	½ cup milk
Pinch of grated nutmeg	Oil for deep frying

Truffle Fritters II / BEIGNETS SOUFFLÉS DE TRUFFES

Make the *choux* paste.

Cut the truffles into tiny dice.

Heat the oil to 375° F. on a frying thermometer.

Put a little of the *choux* paste on a teaspoon and place a few truffle dice in the middle; enclose the dice in the paste. Drop the ball of paste into the hot oil and fry until it puffs up and is golden. Continue in this manner until all the paste has been fried.

Drain on kitchen paper and serve on a hot serving dish lined with a towel. Sprinkle with a little salt.

FOR 6 PERSONS:

½ recipe Pâte à Choux (p. 710)	Oil for deep frying
6 medium-sized fresh truffles	Salt

BOUCHÉES AUX TRUFFES / *Truffle Patties*

Prepare and bake the patty shells, brushed with the egg yolk.

Mince the truffles and sauté them in the hot butter over low heat for 5 minutes. Add the Madeira and bring to the boiling point. Stir in the *beurre manié,* blend well, and simmer for a few minutes longer. Season lightly with salt, pepper and nutmeg.

Fill each patty with a little of the truffle mixture, and bake in a preheated 400° F. oven for 5 minutes. Serve hot.

FOR 4 PERSONS:

4 baked patty shells, 3-inch size (see p. 717)	½ cup Madeira
1 egg yolk	2 teaspoons Beurre Manié (p. 41)
8 fresh truffles	Salt
3 tablespoons butter	Freshly ground black pepper
	Pinch of grated nutmeg

COURGETTES FARCIES EN BARQUETTES / *Zucchini Barquettes*

Make the pastry and roll it out to a thickness of ⅛ inch. Line 12 *barquette* molds with the pastry and prick the bottoms so that they will not puff up too much during the baking. Freeze or chill in the refrigerator for 1 hour.

Peel the zucchini, cut them lengthwise into halves, and remove the seeds. Cut 12 slices ¼ inch thick and about the size of the *barquette* shells from the zucchini. Blanch the slices in boiling salted water for 4 minutes, and drain them on a kitchen towel.

Heat the oil and the butter in a casserole, add the shallots and tomatoes, and sauté gently for about 15 minutes.

Soak the fresh bread crumbs in the milk, squeeze them dry, and add them to the casserole. Season lightly with salt, pepper and nutmeg, and add the minced parsley. Sauté for 5 minutes longer and then stir in the egg. Remove from the heat immediately.

Put the tartlet shells in a shallow baking dish and put a piece of zucchini into each. Top each with a little of the other mixture and sprinkle with dry bread crumbs and melted butter. Heat the *barquettes* under a broiler until the tops are brown and bubbly.

FOR 4 PERSONS:

1 recipe Pâte Brisée (p. 713)	⅓ cup milk
4 medium-sized zucchini	Salt
2 tablespoons peanut oil	Freshly ground black pepper
3 tablespoons butter	Pinch of grated nutmeg
3 shallots, minced	2 tablespoons minced parsley
3 tomatoes, peeled, seeded and chopped	1 egg, beaten
1 cup fresh white bread crumbs	½ cup fine dry bread crumbs
	¼ cup melted butter

Hot Cheese Hors-d'Oeuvre

Hors-d'Oeuvre Chauds de Fromage

Cheese Fritters / BEIGNETS AU FROMAGE

In a large bowl mix together the wheat flour, rice flour, two of the egg yolks and the milk.

Beat in the Swiss cheese, the Parmesan and the butter. Season with the salt, a little pepper and a pinch of nutmeg.

Butter a heavy saucepan and pour the cheese mixture into it. Cook over lowest possible heat, stirring constantly, until the mixture is thickened and smooth and the cheese has melted.

Oil a shallow baking dish or a jelly-roll pan and pour the mixture in it evenly, smoothing it with the blade of a knife or a spatula. Cool completely. Beat the remaining 3 egg yolks. Cut the dough into diamond shapes. Dip these into the beaten egg yolks and then into the bread crumbs mixed with the grated Swiss cheese.

Heat the frying fat to 375° F. on a frying thermometer and fry the fritters until they are golden. Drain them on kitchen toweling, and serve them in a hot serving dish lined with a napkin. Serve immediately.

FOR 4 PERSONS:

1 cup wheat flour	½ cup softened butter
⅓ cup rice flour	1 teaspoon salt
5 egg yolks	Freshly ground white pepper
2 cups milk, approximately	Pinch of grated nutmeg
½ pound Swiss cheese, cut into tiny dice	2 cups fresh white bread crumbs
	1 cup grated Swiss cheese
½ pound Parmesan cheese, cut into tiny dice	Fat for deep frying

Cheese Puffs / CHOUX AU FROMAGE

Heat the butter in a saucepan and add the water, salt and sugar. Bring the mixture to the boiling point, add the flour all at once, and stir vigorously with a wooden spoon until the mixture clears the sides of the saucepan.

Remove from the heat and beat in the eggs, one at a time, beating well after each addition. Then beat in the grated cheese. The dough should be smooth and shiny.

Heat the frying fat to 375° F. on a frying thermometer. Drop in the batter by tablespoons. Fry the puffs until they are golden and have turned upside down. Fry only a few puffs at one time; they should not be crowded.

Remove the cooked puffs with a slotted spoon, drain them on paper towels, and put them into a hot serving dish lined with a napkin. Keep hot until all are done.

FOR 6 PERSONS:

½ cup butter
1 cup water
½ teaspoon salt
Pinch of sugar

1¾ cups flour
6 eggs
⅓ pound Swiss cheese, grated
Fat for deep frying

CROÛTES AU FROMAGE CHAUDES / *Hot Cheese Sandwiches*

Heat the oil in a saucepan, add the bacon, and let it cook until transparent but not crisp. Add the cream cheese, Swiss cheese and cayenne. Cook over low heat, stirring constantly with a wooden spoon, until the mixture is smooth and thick.

Put the toast in a shallow baking dish and top with the cheese mixture. Run under the broiler until the top is bubbly. Serve immediately.

FOR 2 PERSONS:

1 tablespoon peanut oil
3 thin slices of bacon, diced
2 ounces cream cheese
¼ pound Swiss cheese, cut into
tiny dice

Pinch of cayenne pepper
4 slices of toasted white bread

Note: Instead of the cheese mixture described above, the toast may be spread with plain, Orange, or Beer Fondue (p. 272), and broiled until bubbly; these sandwiches may also be served cold. Instead of pouring the hot cheese mixture over the toast, pour it onto a sheet of wax paper and let it cool. Cut it into any desired shapes and put each piece on a piece of buttered toast cut to the same shape.

SOUFFLÉ AU FROMAGE / *Cheese Soufflé*

Melt the butter in a saucepan, add the flour, and stir constantly over medium heat for 2 to 3 minutes. Then add the cold milk. Season with the salt, cayenne and nutmeg; stir with a whisk until the mixture is smooth and thick. Remove from the heat and cool slightly.

Combine the egg yolks with the *crème fraîche* and beat them into the other mixture. Then stir in the grated cheese.

Beat the egg whites until stiff and fold them into the sauce.

Butter and flour a 2-quart baking or soufflé dish. Pour the soufflé mixture into it. Bake in a 375° F. oven for about 30 minutes. Serve immediately.

FOR 4 PERSONS:

4 tablespoons butter
3 tablespoons flour
1 cup milk
½ teaspoon salt
Pinch of cayenne pepper
Pinch of grated nutmeg

4 egg yolks
2 tablespoons Crème Fraîche
(p. 666), or heavy cream
½ pound Swiss cheese, grated
6 egg whites

Crêpes Chambourcy | CRÊPES À LA CHAMBOURCY

This recipe requires 3 separate preparations: a *crêpe* batter, the filling and a fritter batter.

1. Make about 24 *crêpes* from the batter on page 740.
2. Make a filling for the *crêpes*. Beat the cheese and the butter together. Season with the cayenne, a little salt and the nutmeg; beat in the egg.

½ pound Chambourcy cheese, or cream cheese	Pinch of cayenne pepper
	Salt
½ cup butter, at room temperature	½ teaspoon grated nutmeg
	1 egg

3. Prepare a batter for coating the *crêpes* before frying in deep fat. Beat the egg whites until they are foamy; they must not be stiff. In another bowl beat together the oil, egg yolks, flour, beer and salt. Stir in the egg whites. Beat with a wire whisk until all the ingredients are well blended.

4 eggs, separated	1 cup beer
1 tablespoon peanut oil	½ teaspoon salt
4 tablespoons flour	

Put a generous spoonful of filling in the middle of each *crêpe* and roll it up. Secure the ends with food picks so that the filling won't ooze out. Dip each *crêpe* into the batter for frying.

Heat a large quantity of frying fat to 375° F. on a frying thermometer. Fry a few *crêpes* at a time for about 3 minutes, or until they have puffed up. Drain on kitchen toweling and keep hot in a heated serving dish until all have been fried.

Beer Fondue | FONDUE À LA BIÈRE

Bring the beer to the boiling point in a saucepan and let it reduce by two thirds. Add the cheese, the tomato purée and the cayenne. Cook over lowest possible heat, stirring constantly, until the cheese has melted and the fondue is thickened and smooth. Blend together the kirsch and the cornstarch, and stir the mixture into the fondue. Cook for ½ minute longer, stirring constantly.

Eat in the usual way, dipping the bread cubes into the fondue.

FOR 2 PERSONS:

1⅓ cups beer	Pinch of cayenne pepper
¼ pound Swiss or Gruyère (natural, not processed) cheese, cut into tiny dice	1 teaspoon kirsch
	1 teaspoon cornstarch
1 tablespoon Tomato Purée (p. 157)	French bread, cut into bite-size cubes

Orange Fondue | FONDUE À L'ORANGE

With a vegetable peeler or a sharp knife, cut the zest (the orange part only) from the peel of an orange. Cut the zest into tiny julienne strips and blanch them in boiling water for 3 minutes. Drain thoroughly.

Crab à la Russe
Crabe à la Russe

Crab à la Russe

Crabe à la Russe

Editors' Note: In France, large crabs, similar to the variety found on the West Coast of the United States, are readily available. We have adapted M. Oliver's recipe to the smaller East-Coast variety, but by all means use only 4 larger ones if you live where they do.

HEAT THE WATER in a large kettle. Add the onions, carrots, *bouquet garni*, vinegar, a little salt and the peppercorns. Cook at a rolling boil for 5 minutes and add the crabs. Bring back to the boiling point and simmer for 15 minutes. Drain and cool the crabs. Open them and pick out all of the meat, reserving 4 of the shells. Flake the crabmeat and blend it with ½ cup of the mayonnaise.

Stuff the 4 crab shells with the crabmeat and sprinkle a few capers over each shell. Stir the tomato purée into the remaining mayonnaise and serve it in a sauceboat.

For 4 persons:

2 quarts water
2 onions, chopped
2 carrots, chopped
1 Bouquet Garni (p. 46)
¼ cup vinegar
Salt

6 peppercorns
12 hard-shelled crabs
1½ cups Mayonnaise (p. 782)
2 tablespoons capers
1 tablespoon Tomato Purée
(p. 157)

Shrimp Toast à la Rothschild

Toast de Crevettes à la Rothschild

Shrimp Toast à la Rothschild
Toast de Crevettes à la Rothschild

MAKE CROUSTADES FROM the slices of bread as described on page 61. Sauté them in 3 tablespoons each of the oil and butter over medium heat until they are crisp and golden on both sides. Drain on kitchen paper and then place in a baking dish.

Shell the shrimp and set them aside. Crush the shells in a mortar with a pestle until they are almost a paste; or blend them in a blender.

Heat the rest of the oil and 1 more tablespoon of the butter in a saucepan and cook the shallots, onion and carrot in it until they are golden. Add the paste made of the shrimp shells, mix well, and cook over low heat for about 3 minutes. Add the tomato paste, wine, fish stock and the *bouquet garni*. Cover and simmer over low heat for 20 minutes. Strain the sauce into another saucepan, return to the stove, and reduce over high heat to about ¾ cup. Season to taste with salt and pepper.

Cook the shrimp in 3 tablespoons of the remaining butter for 4 or 5 minutes (or less if they are tiny), transfer them to the sauce, and simmer for another minute, stirring constantly with a wooden spoon. Take out the shrimp with a slotted spoon and place them in the toast shells.

Stir the *crème fraîche* and the Cognac into the reduced sauce and bring to a final boil. Remove from the heat and stir in the remaining butter cut into pieces.

Spoon some of the sauce over the shrimp in each *croustade,* sprinkle with some of the grated cheese, and place a truffle slice on top of each. Brown quickly under the broiler.

For 4 persons:

4 slices of firm white
    bread, about 1½
    inches thick
4 tablespoons peanut oil
½ cup butter
1 pound small shrimp
2 tablespoons minced shallots
1 medium-sized onion, minced
1 carrot, minced
1 tablespoon tomato paste

½ cup dry white wine
¾ cup Fish Stock (p. 166)
1 Bouquet Garni (p. 46)
Salt
Freshly ground black pepper
2 tablespoons Crème Fraîche
    (p. 666), or heavy cream
2 tablespoons Cognac
¼ cup grated Swiss cheese
4 thin slices of truffle

Ballottines of Chicken with Lobster

Ballottines de Poulet au Homard

Ballottines of Chicken with Lobster
Ballottines de Poulet au Homard

MAKE A MOUSSELINE forcemeat. Cut the flesh of the smaller chicken into small chunks and put these into a blender container with the meat from the lobster claws and from the upper part of the lobster bodies. Blend until smooth. (Alternatively, the chicken and lobster meat may be pounded in a mortar with a pestle, but this is arduous labor.) Pour this mixture into a bowl placed over cracked ice and gradually work in the 2 egg whites. Season with the salt and beat in the heavy cream. Stuff the boned larger chicken with this forcemeat and reform it into its original shape. Simmer like any *ballottine* in the poultry stock for about 1½ hours.

Slice the meat when it is cooked and sprinkle it with the truffles. Cut the lobster tails into large dice and add them to the *sauce Américaine,* combined with the *velouté.* Pour some of the sauce over the *ballottine* and serve the rest separately.

For 10 persons:

1 chicken (1½ pounds),
    boned and skinned
2 lobsters (1½
    pounds each), cooked
    à l'Américaine (p. 381)
    with the sauce
2 egg whites
1 teaspoon salt

2 cups heavy cream
1 chicken (3½ pounds),
    boned but left whole
2 quarts White Poultry
    Stock (p. 165)
3 truffles, sliced
4 cups Sauce Velouté
    (p. 762)

Zakouski

Zakouski

THIS IS AN elaborate array of hors-d'oeuvre and may consist of *barquettes* filled with lobster salad, stuffed eggs on toast, caviar canapés, caviar canapés topped with stuffed eggs, salmon canapés topped with stuffed eggs, eggs stuffed with prunes and shrimp, sour pickle canapés, prune canapés, eggs stuffed with watercress and smoked salmon, eggs stuffed with red caviar, and eggs stuffed with anchovies and tomatoes.

The *barquettes* are best if made with Puff Paste (p. 715). The toasted bread should be cut into fancy shapes with cookie cutters. Butter tinted and flavored with paprika, spices, anchovy paste or puréed sardines may be used as added decoration.

Swiss Fondue

Fondue des Grands Crus de Gruyère

Swiss Fondue
Fondue des Grands Crus de Gruyère

RUB THE INSIDE of an earthenware casserole or a chafing dish with the garlic. Put the Swiss and Gruyère cheeses into the casserole and mix with the flour or cornstarch. Add the wine and the lemon juice, and season with cayenne and white pepper.

Simmer over low heat, stirring with a wooden spoon, until the cheese has melted. Stir in the kirsch. Transfer the casserole to the burner of a chafing dish or a fondue set and keep bubbling. Regulate the heat so that the fondue keeps hot without boiling, or the cheese will become stringy. Serve with Italian or French bread cut into bite-size cubes, each with a little crust.

To eat the fondue, spear a piece of bread with a long-handled fondue fork (or, if none is available, a skewer) and dip it into the fondue with a stirring motion until it is thoroughly coated with cheese. Serve the same wine used in the fondue.

For 4 persons:

1 garlic clove	2 cups dry white wine
1 pound Swiss and Gruyère cheese mixed, shredded or diced	1 tablespoon lemon juice
	Pinch of cayenne pepper
	Freshly ground white pepper
3 tablespoons flour, or 1½ tablespoons cornstarch	3 tablespoons kirsch

South American Omelet

Omelette Sud-Américaine

South American Omelet

Omelette Sud-Américaine

PEEL THE AVOCADO and discard the seed. Cut half of it into small dice and cut the other half into balls with a melon-ball cutter.

Beat the eggs with salt and pepper to taste and add the avocado dice. Melt the oil and the butter in a skillet, add the eggs, and make a flat omelet, like a *crêpe,* turning it over with a large spatula to cook the second side when the eggs begin to set.

Place the omelet on a hot serving dish. Garnish the omelet with the avocado balls.

For 2 persons:

1 large avocado, cut into halves
8 eggs
Salt
Freshly ground black pepper
1 tablespoon peanut oil
2 tablespoons butter

Eggs Meurette

Les Oeufs en Meurette

Eggs Meurette

Les Oeufs en Meurette

HEAT 3 TABLESPOONS of the butter in a casserole and add the bacon, the onion and the garlic. Cook until they are golden. Add the cloves, the wine, the consommé and the sugar. Season with salt and pepper to taste and add the *bouquet garni.* Simmer over low heat for about 25 minutes.

Fry the bread slices on both sides in the remaining butter until golden and put them on a hot serving dish.

Strain the sauce into a skillet. Reserve the bacon strips. Bring the sauce to the boiling point and poach the eggs in it, pushing the whites over the yolks with a spatula. Drain the eggs and put two on each slice of bread.

Thicken the sauce with the *beurre manié* and pour it over the eggs. Sprinkle with the reserved bacon strips and serve immediately.

For 4 persons:

½ cup butter
½ pound bacon, cut into
    thin narrow strips
1 onion, chopped
1 garlic clove, minced
2 whole cloves
2 cups dry red wine
½ cup Chicken Consommé
    (p. 168)
1 lump of sugar

Salt
Freshly ground black
    pepper
1 Bouquet Garni (p. 46)
4 slices of firm white bread,
    crusts trimmed off
8 eggs
2 tablespoons Beurre Manié
    (p. 41)

Fried Eggs en Aumônière

Oeufs Frits en Aumônière

Fried Eggs en Aumônière

Oeufs Frits en Aumônière

HEAT THE MILK to lukewarm. Melt the butter and dissolve the salt in it. Make a *crêpe* batter by putting the flour into a bowl and adding the eggs, the milk and the butter. Beat the batter thoroughly and stir in the beer. Let it rest in the refrigerator for 2 hours.

Cut four 3-inch rounds from the bread, the Swiss cheese and the ham. Heat 2 tablespoons of the oil and all of the butter in a skillet and fry the bread in it until golden on both sides. Drain and keep hot. Fry the ham on both sides in the same skillet. Put 1 round of Swiss cheese on each bread round and top it with a round of ham. Keep hot.

In a very small but deep skillet, heat the remaining oil. When it is very hot, break an egg into it. Tilt the skillet so that the egg will be covered with oil on all sides and with the help of a spatula, push the white over the yolk; the whole egg, when fried, should be an oval about the size of the bread, cheese and ham rounds. Drain the egg on kitchen toweling and quickly cook the other 3 eggs in the same manner.

Make 4 *crêpes* about 8 or 9 inches in diameter with the batter. Place them side by side on kitchen toweling. Put in the center of each a bread, cheese and ham round. Top each of these with a fried egg.

Tie up the *crêpes* with string or wire twists, as if making a pouch, and put them into a buttered baking dish. Brown quickly under the broiler and then serve very hot.

For 4 persons:

For the crêpe batter:	4 slices of French bread
¼ cup milk	2 slices of Swiss cheese
2 tablespoons butter	2 slices of ham
½ teaspoon salt	1 cup peanut oil
½ cup flour	3 tablespoons butter
2 eggs	4 eggs
¼ cup beer	

Make a classic cheese fondue and add the blanched orange rind to it just before adding the kirsch.

/ *Tian*

First make the pastry dough: put the flour into a large bowl or on a baking board and make a well in the middle of it; put two of the eggs, the lard and the milk into the well. Blend with a fork and knead into a ball. Let the dough rest for about 15 minutes.

Cut up the Swiss chard coarsely, discarding the tough center stems, and put it into a large saucepan with just the water that clings to the leaves after washing. Sprinkle lightly with salt. Cook over very low heat for about 5 minutes. Drain in a sieve and press out excess water. Place it in a saucepan.

Trim the artichokes and cut them into quarters, removing the fuzzy part of the choke. Blanch them in boiling salted water for 3 minutes, drain them, and add them to the Swiss chard in the saucepan, together with the green peas and the fava (broad) beans. Season with salt and pepper. Mix well and add the butter and the olive oil. Simmer over medium heat for about 5 minutes, stirring frequently.

Beat the cream cheese until it is soft. Separate the remaining 3 eggs and beat the yolks, one at a time, into the cream cheese. Then beat in the Swiss cheese. Beat the egg whites until stiff and fold them into cream-cheese mixture. Season with salt and pepper to taste.

Divide the dough into 2 parts. Roll one out to fit the bottom and sides of a 12-inch pie pan. Line the pie pan with the pastry round and fill it evenly with the vegetables. Top with the cream-cheese mixture, smoothing it on with a spatula. Cover the vegetables and topping with the remaining pastry, pinching the edges together between your thumb and index finger. Paint with the beaten egg yolk. Bake on the lower level of a preheated 350° F. oven for about 1 hour. Serve immediately.

FOR 6 PERSONS:

4 cups flour	Salt
5 whole eggs	Freshly ground black pepper
1 cup lard	3 tablespoons butter
2 tablespoons milk	2 tablespoons olive oil
1 pound Swiss chard	⅓ pound cream cheese
5 very small young artichokes	¼ cup grated Swiss cheese
1½ cups shelled peas	1 extra egg yolk, beaten
1½ cups shelled fava (broad) beans	

/ *Welsh Rabbit with White Wine*

WELSH RABBIT AU VIN BLANC

Cut the Swiss cheese and the Cheddar into tiny dice. Put the cheese into a saucepan, add the beer and the wine, and season with salt and cayenne pepper. Cook over low heat, stirring constantly, until the mixture is smooth, but still on the thin side.

Toast the bread, or sauté it in hot butter and oil. Spread the bread with mustard and place it in a hot serving dish.

Add the ground ham to the cheese mixture and cook, stirring constantly, for 1 minute longer. Pour the mixture over the toasted bread and serve very hot.

FOR 4 PERSONS:

⅓ **pound Swiss cheese**	**Pinch of cayenne pepper**
⅓ **pound Cheddar cheese**	**4 slices of firm white bread**
¼ **cup beer**	**2 teaspoons French mustard**
½ **cup dry white wine**	**2 slices of cooked smoked ham,**
Salt	**ground**

Hot Meat Hors-d'Oeuvre

Hors-d'Oeuvre Chauds de Viandes et Volailles

Brain Fritters / BEIGNETS DE CERVELLES

Separate two of the eggs and beat the yolks together with the remaining whole egg, the flour, oil and beer or milk. Season with salt to taste and beat until the batter is smooth.

Clean the brains by soaking them in salted cold water for 2 hours. Remove the outer membrane and the veins.

Make a *court bouillon* with the water, the vinegar, a little salt and pepper, the thyme and bay leaf. Bring the mixture to the boiling point, cook for 3 minutes, and then add the brains. Simmer over low heat for about 20 minutes.

Drain the brains on a kitchen cloth and cool them. Sprinkle them lightly with salt and pepper and dust them with flour.

Beat the 2 egg whites until stiff and fold them into the batter.

Heat the fat to 375° F. on a frying thermometer.

Spear the brains, one at a time, with a fork, dip them into the batter, and drop them into the hot fat. Cook them until golden, remove them with a slotted spoon, and drain on kitchen paper.

Place the fritters on a hot serving plate and sprinkle with salt.

FOR 4 PERSONS:

3 eggs	⅓ **cup vinegar**
1 cup flour	**Freshly ground white pepper**
1 tablespoon peanut oil	½ **teaspoon dried thyme**
⅔ **cup beer or milk**	**1 bay leaf**
Salt	**Flour**
4 calves' or lambs' brains	**Fat for deep frying**
4 cups water	

Cannelloni / CANNELLONI FARCIS

Heat the butter and the oil in a casserole and cook the minced onions in it until they are golden. Add the sausage meat and the ground chicken livers. Mix well and cook over low heat for 4 to 5 minutes. Pour off excess fat and set the mixture aside.

Make the *cannelloni* dough: Put the flour on a pastry board and make a well in the middle. Put into the well the whole eggs, the extra egg yolks and 1 teaspoon of salt dissolved in 1 tablespoon of lukewarm water. Mix well and then knead the dough for 10 minutes. Shape it into a ball and let it rest for 15 minutes. Roll it out to a thickness of ⅛ inch and cut it into 8-inch squares. There should be enough dough for about 10 squares. Lay these squares side by side on kitchen towels and let them dry for 1 hour.

Cook the pasta squares, a few at a time, in a large quantity of boiling salted water for 10 minutes. Drain them first in a strainer and then on a kitchen cloth; make sure they remain flat.

Place a spoonful of filling on each square and roll it up. Butter a shallow baking dish and put the stuffed *cannelloni* into it, side by side. Top with tomato sauce and sprinkle with the grated Swiss cheese and the bread crumbs. Bake in a preheated 375° F. oven for 20 minutes. Serve immediately.

FOR 5 PERSONS:

3 tablespoons butter	3 whole eggs
1 tablespoon olive oil	6 extra egg yolks
2 onions, minced	Salt
1 pound sausage meat	2 cups Sauce Tomate (p. 769)
6 chicken livers, ground	¼ cup grated Swiss cheese
4 cups sifted flour	¼ cup fine dry bread crumbs

CROQUETTES DE VOLAILLES / *Chicken Croquettes*

Heat the water in a saucepan. Season with salt and pepper and add the carrots, turnip, leeks, onion and, finally, the chicken wings. Bring to the boiling point and simmer, covered, for 1 hour.

Heat the butter in another saucepan and stir in 3 tablespoons of flour. Remove from the heat, cool slightly, and stir the 3 egg yolks into it. Put this *roux* back over low heat and cook it for 2 minutes. Do not let it boil. Season with salt, pepper and nutmeg. Remove from the heat and cool.

When the chicken wings are cooked, drain and bone them. Put the meat through the finest blade of a meat grinder. Add the ground chicken meat to the *roux*.

Heat the frying fat to 375° F. on a frying thermometer.

Make small croquettes, using about 1 tablespoon of the chicken mixture for each. Dust them first with flour, then dip into the beaten whole eggs and coat with bread crumbs. Drop the croquettes into the hot fat and fry until golden. Drain them on paper towels and serve them immediately in a hot serving dish.

FOR 4 PERSONS:

4 cups water	3 tablespoons butter
Salt	Flour
Freshly ground white pepper	3 egg yolks
2 carrots, chopped	Pinch of grated nutmeg
1 turnip, chopped	Fat for deep frying
2 leeks, chopped	2 whole eggs, beaten
1 onion, stuck with 3 whole cloves	1½ cups fresh bread crumbs
12 chicken wings	

Chicken Turnovers / RISSOLES DE VOLAILLE

Prepare the chicken croquette mixture, described in Chicken Croquettes, but do not form it into croquettes.

Divide the puff paste into halves and roll out the 2 pieces into sheets about ⅛ inch thick. Place evenly spaced bits of the chicken mixture about 2 inches apart on one of the sheets of puff paste. Brush the other sheet with water and lay it, wet side down, over the first sheet. Press the dough firmly together around each of the bits of filling and then cut into neat little squares. Drop the squares into deep fat heated to 375° F. on a frying thermometer until puffed and golden. Serve immediately.

Since the dough will absorb some of the frying fat, some cooks prefer to bake the turnovers in a 400° F. oven for about 15 minutes. In this case, paint the tops of the turnovers with beaten egg yolk before baking.

FOR 4 PERSONS:

1 recipe Chicken Croquettes (above)
½ recipe Puff Paste (p. 715)

Fat for deep frying
Optional: 2 egg yolks, beaten

Sautéed Chicken Livers / FOIES DE VOLAILLES SAUTÉS

Cut the chicken livers into thin slices and sauté them in the combined hot butter and oil over fairly high heat for about 3 minutes, turning them frequently. Season them with salt and pepper to taste.

Mince the shallots and the *fines herbes* and add them to the chicken livers. Sauté for about 1 minute longer.

Serve them in a heated serving dish, with a garnish of thin slices of lemon with scalloped edges.

FOR 4 PERSONS:

1 pound chicken livers
3 tablespoons butter
3 tablespoons olive oil
Salt
Freshly ground black pepper

2 shallots
3 tablespoons Fines Herbes (p. 89)
1 lemon

Croque-Monsieur /

Trim the crusts from the bread slices and butter the slices on one side.

The sliced ham and the cheese slices should be about the same size as the bread. On half of the bread slices place the slices of ham and cheese. Top with the remaining bread to make 4 sandwiches. Put them into a buttered shallow baking dish. Dot them with little pieces of butter, sprinkle with grated cheese, and bake in a preheated 400°

F. oven for 15 minutes; or run under the broiler until one side is golden, then turn and brown the other side. Serve immediately.

FOR 4 PERSONS:

8 slices of firm white bread
½ cup butter, softened
4 slices of smoked ham

4 slices of Swiss cheese
¼ cup grated Swiss cheese

/ *Croûte Landaise*

Trim the crusts from the bread slices and sauté the bread in the hot butter until golden on both sides. Put the slices into a buttered shallow baking dish.

Heat the slices of *foie gras* in a 400° F. oven for 2 minutes and place them on the bread. Cover with the *sauce Mornay*. Cook in a 400° F. oven until golden brown and bubbly. Serve very hot.

FOR 4 PERSONS:

4 slices of firm white bread
4 tablespoons butter
4 slices of foie gras, about ¼
    inch thick

1 cup Sauce Mornay (p. 776)

FRITOTS / *Fritters*

You may use sweetbreads, or calf's or lamb's liver.

Trim your choice of meats (sweetbreads will have to be soaked and blanched in the usual manner), cut them into thin slices, and season them with salt and pepper; marinate them in the olive oil, ground thyme and minced *fines herbes* for 2 hours.

Make a batter by combining the flour, vegetable oil, egg yolks, 1 teaspoon of salt, a little pepper and the beer. Beat the egg whites until stiff and fold them into the batter.

Heat the frying oil to 375° F. on a frying thermometer.

Spear the meats with a fork, dip them into the batter, and drop them into the hot oil. When the fritters are golden, remove them with a slotted spoon, drain them on paper towels, and put them on a hot serving dish. Garnish with the lemon quarters and fried parsley.

FOR 4 PERSONS:

1 pound sweetbreads, or lamb's or
    calf's liver
Salt
Freshly ground black pepper
4 tablespoons olive oil
1 teaspoon ground thyme
3 tablespoons Fines Herbes
    (p. 89)

1 cup flour
1 tablespoon vegetable oil
3 eggs, separated
¾ cup beer
Oil for deep frying
1 lemon, cut into quarters
Fried Parsley (p. 130)

Ham and Cheese Beignets /

BEIGNETS SOUFFLÉS AU JAMBON ET AU FROMAGE

Melt the butter in a saucepan and add the water, salt and sugar. When the water has reached the boiling point, add the flour all at once and stir vigorously with a wooden spoon until the batter clears the sides of the saucepan.

Remove from the heat and add the eggs, one at a time; beat well after each addition. Then add the grated cheese and the diced ham.

Heat the frying fat to 375° F. on a frying thermometer, and drop the dough into it by the teaspoons. Fry the *beignets,* a few at a time, until they are golden and have turned upside down.

Remove the *beignets* with a slotted spoon, drain them on paper towels, and serve them in a dish lined with a folded napkin. Keep them hot until all the *beignets* are done.

FOR 6 PERSONS:

½ cup butter	6 eggs
1 cup water	1 cup grated Gruyère cheese
Pinch of salt	1 cup finely diced smoked ham
Pinch of sugar	Fat for deep frying
1¾ cups flour	

Ham Crêpes / CRÊPES AU JAMBON GRATINÉES

First make the *crêpe* batter and chill it in the refrigerator for 2 hours.

Melt 2 tablespoons of the butter in a saucepan and add the flour to it. Stir with a wooden spoon and cook until the mixture is golden. Remove from the heat, cool slightly, and add the lukewarm milk and the nutmeg. Beat well and cook over low heat for 10 minutes, stirring frequently. Beat the egg yolks with the cream and add them, off the heat, to the sauce, together with a pinch of cayenne. Pour off half of the sauce and reserve. Add the minced ham and ⅔ cup of the grated cheese to the sauce in the saucepan.

Make about 24 *crêpes,* and stuff each with a little of the ham and cheese sauce. Roll up the *crêpes* and put them side by side in a buttered shallow baking dish. Top with the remaining sauce (if it seems too thick, thin it with a little heavy cream), sprinkle with the remaining cheese, dot with the remaining butter, and sprinkle with the bread crumbs.

Bake in a preheated 400° F. oven for 15 minutes. Serve immediately.

FOR 6 PERSONS:

1 recipe Crêpes batter (p. 740)	¼ cup heavy cream
6 tablespoons butter	Pinch of cayenne pepper
2 tablespoons flour	1 cup minced smoked ham
1 cup lukewarm milk	1 cup grated Gruyère cheese
Pinch of grated nutmeg	¼ cup fine dry bread crumbs
2 egg yolks	

Ham Rolls / CORNETS DE JAMBON CHAUDS

Blend the cream cheese with the *fines herbes* and the fresh bread crumbs. Season the mixture with salt and pepper to taste.

Cook the asparagus tips in boiling salted water for about 5 minutes, or until barely tender, and drain them well.

Make the *sauce béchamel* and add 2 tablespoons of the grated Swiss cheese to it.

Spread the ham slices out flat. On each, put 2 asparagus tips and a little of the cream-cheese mixture. Roll up the ham slices. Put them side by side in a buttered shallow baking dish. Top with the *béchamel,* dot with little pieces of butter, and sprinkle with the remaining grated Swiss cheese and the dry bread crumbs.

Bake in a preheated 400° F. oven for about 15 minutes, or until the top is brown and bubbly.

FOR 4 PERSONS:

2 ounces cream cheese
4 tablespoons minced Fines
   Herbes (p. 000)
4 tablespoons fresh white
   bread crumbs
Salt
Freshly ground white pepper

8 asparagus tips
1 cup Sauce Béchamel (p. 761)
¼ cup grated Swiss cheese
4 large thin slices of smoked ham
3 tablespoons butter
¼ cup fine dry bread crumbs

SOUFFLÉ AU JAMBON / *Ham Soufflé*

Melt the butter in a saucepan, add the flour, and stir over low heat until the mixture is golden. Stir in 1 cup of the cold milk. Bring to the boiling point and season lightly with salt, cayenne and nutmeg. Be sure to stir the sauce constantly. Remove from the heat and cool slightly.

Beat together the egg yolks and the remaining milk and stir them into the white sauce. Check the seasoning, and add the grated cheese and the ham. Beat the egg whites until stiff and fold them into the ham mixture.

Butter and flour a 1½-quart soufflé dish and pour in the soufflé mixture. Bake in a preheated 375° F. oven for about 30 minutes. Serve immediately.

FOR 4 PERSONS:

3 tablespoons butter
3 tablespoons flour
1 cup plus 2 tablespoons milk
Salt
Pinch of cayenne pepper

Pinch of grated nutmeg
4 eggs, separated
1 cup grated Gruyère cheese
½ cup finely diced smoked ham

TARTE AU JAMBON DE BAYONNE / *Ham Tart*

EDITORS' NOTE: *If Bayonne ham is not available, another well-flavored ham such as Westphalian, prosciutto or smoked Virginian may be substituted.*

Prepare the *pâte brisée,* roll it out ⅛ inch thick, and with it line an 8-inch pie pan or a flan ring placed on a baking sheet. Chill thoroughly, or freeze in a refrigerator.

Put the ham into the pastry shell and bake in a preheated 350° F. oven for 15 minutes.

Beat together the flour and the softened butter, and add the whole egg, the egg yolk, a very little salt (since the ham is salted), the nutmeg and the milk. Pour the mixture over the ham.

Bake for 15 minutes longer and serve hot.

FOR 4 PERSONS:

1 recipe Pâte Brisée (p. 713)
½ pound Bayonne or other well-flavored ham, cut into fine strips or small dice
3 tablespoons flour
¼ cup softened butter

1 whole egg
1 extra egg yolk
Salt
Pinch of grated nutmeg
1 cup milk

Marrow Toast | TOAST À LA MOELLE

Have your butcher cut the marrowbones into 2-inch pieces. Remove the marrow and soak it in salted water to cover for 24 hours. Drain, cut into thick rounds, and simmer them in boiling water for 2 to 3 minutes. Take them out with a slotted spoon and drain on a cloth.

Sauté the bread slices in hot butter and oil until they are golden, and put them in a buttered shallow baking dish. Place 2 or 3 marrow rounds on each slice, season with pepper, and run under a broiler for a moment or two, or just until the marrow begins to spread apart. Serve immediately, very hot.

FOR 4 PERSONS:

2 large marrowbones
Salt
4 slices of firm white bread, trimmed of crusts

3 tablespoons butter
3 tablespoons peanut oil
Freshly ground white pepper

Meat Balls | PETITES BOULETTES DE VIANDE

Heat the butter and the oil in a skillet and cook the onion in it until golden.

Combine the water and the cream and soak the bread crumbs in them. Add the ground beef, the ground pork and the onion. Blend and stir until the mixture is smooth. Season with the salt and a little pepper. Shape the mixture into small balls by using 2 teaspoons dipped into cold water.

Heat the frying fat to 375° F. on a frying thermometer, drop the meat balls into it, and fry them until golden. Serve very hot.

FOR 4 PERSONS:

2 tablespoons butter
2 tablespoons peanut oil
1 small onion, minced
¼ cup water
¼ cup heavy cream
1 cup fresh bread crumbs

¾ pound beef, finely ground
½ pound lean pork, finely ground
1 teaspoon salt
Freshly ground black pepper
Fat for deep frying

RISSOLES DE VIANDE / *Meat Turnovers*

Proceed as in Chicken Turnovers (p. 276), but use the mixture described in Meat Balls (above) for the filling.

QUENELLES DE VIANDE / *Meat Quenelles*

Mince the shallots, crush the garlic cloves, and cut the beef marrow into small dice—there should be about ½ cup. Combine these ingredients with the ground pork and veal, and beat in the whole eggs and 1 tablespoon of flour. Season to taste with salt and pepper.

Shape the mixture into cylindrical *quenelles,* dust them with flour, and poach them in simmering salted water for about 10 minutes. Do not let them boil, or they will disintegrate. (It is well first to make a test with 1 *quenelle;* if it does not hold together during cooking, add a little more flour to the meat mixture.) Drain the *quenelles* on a towel and reserve the cooking liquid.

Sauté the mushrooms in the butter, sprinkle them with 1 tablespoon of flour, and stir in 1 cup of the liquid in which the *quenelles* were cooked. It should be a fairly thin sauce. Carefully add the *quenelles* and let them simmer over the lowest possible heat for about 5 minutes.

At serving time, put the *quenelles* into a heated serving dish and keep hot. Beat the extra egg yolks with the *crème fraîche* and the Madeira and stir the mixture into the *quenelle* sauce to bind it. Simmer it for 2 minutes, but do not let it boil. Pour over the *quenelles* and serve immediately.

FOR 4 PERSONS:

2 shallots	Salt
2 garlic cloves	Freshly ground black pepper
1 beef marrowbone	6 large mushrooms, sliced
⅓ pound lean pork, finely ground	2 tablespoons butter
½ pound veal, finely ground	2 extra egg yolks
2 whole eggs	¼ cup Crème Fraîche (p. 666)
Flour	2 tablespoons Madeira

BOUCHÉES FEUILLETÉES FINANCIÈRE / *Patties Financière*

Put the onions, carrots and celery in a casserole with 4 tablespoons of the butter. Season with salt and pepper. Cook over low heat until the vegetables are golden, and then add 4 cups of water. Bring to the boiling point, add the chicken, and poach it for about 30 minutes, or until the meat is tender.

Take out the chicken, bone it, and cut the meat into dice; return the bones to the casserole. Boil for about 1 more hour. Drain the stock—there should be about 2 cups —and use it for making a *sauce velouté.* First make a *roux* in a saucepan: melt 2 tablespoons of butter, add the flour, and stir for 3 minutes; then stir in the hot chicken stock and cook until smooth.

Beat together 3 egg yolks and the heavy cream. Off the heat, add them to the *velouté.* Return to low heat and stir until the sauce is slightly thickened. Do not boil.

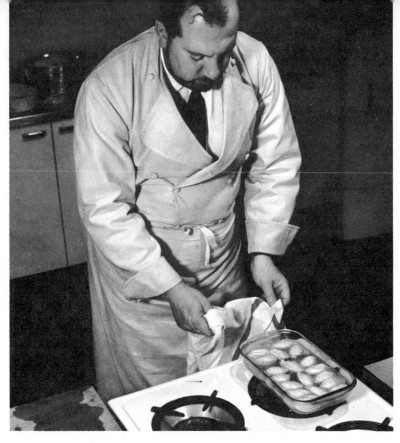

MEAT QUENELLES

The mixture for meat quenelles is made with the following ingredients: veal, pork, beef marrow, shallots, garlic, whole eggs, flour and salt and pepper. The shape of the quenelles may vary, but it should always come as close to a cylinder as possible.

Add the truffle essence and the sherry. Keep warm in the top of a double boiler, over hot water.

Soak the brains in salted cold water for 2 hours and remove the covering membrane and the veins.

Make a *court bouillon* by combining 4 cups of water, the vinegar, thyme, bay leaf and a little salt and pepper. Bring it to the boiling point, simmer for 5 minutes, and add the brains; simmer over low heat for 20 minutes more. Remove the brains with a slotted spoon, cut them into small dice, and add them to the *velouté*. Also add the diced chicken.

Roll out the puff paste to a thickness of ⅛ inch. From it cut 24 rounds 4 inches across. With the remaining butter grease a baking sheet, then dust it with flour. Place 12 rounds on the baking sheet. Brush the outer rims with water. Using a biscuit cutter, press 3-inch circles in the remaining rounds and then place these rounds on top of those on the baking sheet. Brush the tops with the remaining egg yolk, beaten.

Bake the puff-paste rounds in a preheated 375° F. oven for 10 to 12 minutes, or until they are golden and puffed.

When the patties are done, take them out of the oven. With the point of a small knife, remove the cut-out center rounds and scoop out a little of the soft dough in the center. Fill the patties with the hot sauce. Put back into a hot oven for 3 to 4 minutes. Serve immediately, very hot.

FOR 6 PERSONS:

2 onions, minced
2 carrots, minced
1 celery stalk, minced
½ cup butter
Salt
Freshly ground white pepper
Half of a 2-pound chicken
2 tablespoons flour
4 egg yolks
¼ cup heavy cream

1 teaspoon truffle essence, or liquid from canned truffles
1 tablespoon sherry
¾ pound lambs' or calves' brains
6 tablespoons vinegar
½ teaspoon dried thyme
1 bay leaf
1 recipe Puff Paste (p. 715)

PIEDS DE PORC PANÉS / *Breaded Pig's Trotters*

Choose firm white pig's trotters and have them made ready to cook by the butcher; this will save a lot of work.

In a deep kettle, make a well-flavored bouillon with the carrots, onions, celery and the *bouquet garni*; season lightly with salt and pepper; add the pig's trotters and sufficient cold water to cover them. Bring to the boiling point, and simmer over low heat until the trotters are tender. This will take about 4 hours.

Remove them and let them cool in a strainer.

Beat the egg whites until they are foamy. Dip the pig's trotters into the egg whites and coat them on all sides with the bread crumbs. Repeat the process if necessary. There must be enough breading to form a firm crust. Place the breaded trotters on a rack and chill them in the refrigerator for at least 30 minutes.

Arrange the pig's trotters in a baking dish, sprinkle them with oil, and cook them in a 450° F. oven until they are golden, about 15 minutes.

Serve very hot, with *sauce hollandaise* mixed with the mustard.

FOR 4 PERSONS:

4 pig's trotters	1½ quarts water, approximately
2 carrots	4 egg whites
2 onions, each stuck with 3 whole	3 cups fine dry bread crumbs
cloves	4 tablespoons vegetable oil
2 celery stalks	1 recipe Sauce Hollandaise
1 Bouquet Garni (p. 46)	(p. 780)
Salt	3 tablespoons Dijon mustard
Freshly ground black pepper	

Quiche /

Prepare the *pâte brisée* and use it to line a 9-inch pie pan, or a 9-inch flan ring placed on a baking sheet. Chill thoroughly or freeze in the refrigerator.

Cook the bacon in the butter and oil until it is translucent.

Mix the flour with the egg yolks, the *crème fraîche* and the milk. Season lightly with salt and pepper and the nutmeg. Line the bottom of the tart pastry with the cheese and bacon slices, and pour the egg mixture over them. Cook in a preheated 375° F. oven for about 25 minutes, or until the custard is set. Serve immediately.

FOR 4 PERSONS:

1 recipe Pâte Brisée (p. 713)	1 cup milk
½ pound lean bacon slices	Salt
1 tablespoon butter	Freshly ground white pepper
1 tablespoon peanut oil	¼ teaspoon grated nutmeg
2 tablespoons flour	⅓ pound sliced Swiss cheese
4 egg yolks	
1 cup Crème Fraîche (p. 666),	
or heavy cream	

Sausages Tyrolienne / SAUCISSES À LA TYROLIENNE

Coat the sausages lightly with a little oil and broil them until golden. Keep them hot.

Trim the crusts from the bread slices, cut them vertically into halves, and scoop out a little of the center part of each to form *croustades* shaped like *barquettes* (see p. 61). Heat the butter and the remaining oil together in a skillet and sauté the *croustades* until they are golden on all sides. Drain them on paper towels and arrange them in a hot serving dish.

Mix the flour and the beer to a smooth paste and dip the onion rounds into it. If necessary, add a little more butter and oil to the skillet in which the *croustades* were sautéed, and cook the onion rings in it until crisp and golden. Drain on kitchen paper.

Put a little *sauce tomate* in the bottom of each *croustade* and top with a sausage and a few onion rings. Serve immediately, very hot.

FOR 4 PERSONS:

4 large sausages, such as sweet
  Italian sausages
4 tablespoons peanut oil
2 slices of firm white bread,
  about 2 inches thick
4 tablespoons butter

2 tablespoons flour
2 tablespoons beer
2 onions, sliced into rings
¼ cup thick Sauce Tomate
  (p. 769)

/ *Timbale Sabatini*

First make the *timbale*. Put the flour into a bowl, make a well in the center, and put the whole eggs, the lard and milk into this well. Mix together with the fingers to make a dough. Shape it into a ball and let it rest for 15 minutes. Then roll it out to ¼-inch thickness. Butter and flour a 9-inch round springform pan with 3-inch sides and line it with the dough. Line the dough with wax paper and then fill it with dried beans. Bake it in a preheated 350° F. oven for about 20 minutes, or until the pastry is well set. Remove the beans and wax paper carefully, remove the springform sides, and paint the outside with the extra egg yolk beaten with the water. Return the pastry to a 400° F. oven for about 5 minutes. Keep the pastry shell warm.

Put the chicken, veal and pork in a bowl and season with a little salt, pepper and nutmeg; mix well. Shape the mixture into small 2-inch sausages. Broil these sausages for about 5 minutes on each side.

Soak the sweetbreads in ice water for 1 hour and then simmer them in boiling salted water for 10 minutes. Plunge them into ice water and remove the connective tissues and tubes. Cut them into cubes.

Cook the elbow macaroni in a large quantity of boiling salted water until almost tender, about 9 minutes, and drain. In a saucepan, combine the macaroni, the sweetbreads and the meat sausages. Check the seasonings. Add the optional diced truffle and diced *foie gras*.

Add the butter and the *crème* to the saucepan, and shake the mixture (do not *stir* it) until all the ingredients are blended together in the sauce. Fill the warm pastry shell with the mixture and serve immediately.

FOR 6 PERSONS:

For the timbale:

4 cups flour
2 whole eggs
1 cup lard
¼ cup cold milk
1 extra egg yolk, beaten with 1
  tablespoon water

For the filling:
⅓ pound chicken, finely
  ground
⅓ pound veal, finely
  ground

⅓ pound lean pork, finely
  ground
Salt
Freshly ground black pepper
Grated nutmeg
½ pound lamb's sweetbreads
2 cups (½ pound) elbow
  macaroni
Optional: 1 truffle, diced
Optional: ¼ cup diced
  foie gras
½ cup butter, softened
1 cup Crème Fraîche (p. 666)

Frogs' Legs and Snails As Hors-d'Oeuvre

Frogs' Legs à la Crème / GRENOUILLES À LA CRÈME

EDITORS' NOTE: *Frogs' legs in American markets are usually already cleaned, skinned and ready to cook. If, however, you come across whole frogs, or decide to catch your own, they are very simple to clean. Cut off the legs very close to the body so that the legs are still attached to each other, pull off the outer skin, and cut off the feet. Soak the legs in cold water or milk for 2 hours. The frogs' bodies are usually discarded, although some European devotees like to crush the bodies slightly and simmer them in whatever sauce is to accompany the legs; the sauce is strained before serving. The number of frogs' legs to serve per person depends entirely on their size; if small, 6 pairs per person is a good serving; if very large, 3 should be sufficient.*

Put the frogs' legs into a saucepan and add the white wine and the minced shallot and onion. Season lightly with salt and pepper and simmer, covered, over low heat for about 5 minutes. Remove the frogs' legs and set them aside. Reduce the cooking liquid by half, strain it, and return it to the saucepan.

Beat the egg yolks with the heavy cream and stir the mixture into the saucepan off the heat. Add the lemon juice. Stir constantly over the lowest heat until the mixture thickens. Do not let it boil. Return the frogs' legs to the sauce. Reheat gently for 2 minutes, turn out onto a hot serving dish, and sprinkle with the croutons and the parsley.

FOR 4 PERSONS:

16 pairs frogs' legs	**4 egg yolks**
3 cups dry white wine	**½ cup heavy cream**
1 shallot, minced	**Juice of 1 lemon**
½ onion, minced	**1 cup Croutons (p. 62)**
Salt	**2 tablespoons minced parsley**
Freshly ground white pepper	

Frogs' Legs Landaise / CUISSES DE GRENOUILLES LANDAISE

Marinate the frogs' legs in the beer with the thyme for 30 minutes. Drain and dry them. Sprinkle the frogs' legs with salt and pepper and coat them on all sides with flour. Shake off any excess flour. Heat 2 tablespoons of the butter and the oil in a skillet. Sauté the frogs' legs in it, a few at a time, over high heat, adding a little more oil if necessary, until they are golden on all sides.

In another skillet, sauté the pine nuts in the remaining butter until they are golden. Add the lemon juice, garlic and parsley. Sauté gently for 3 minutes.

When the frogs' legs are golden, drain them on kitchen paper and put them into a hot serving dish. Pour the pine-nut mixture over them and sprinkle with the chervil. Decorate the dish with lemon slices. Serve very hot.

FOR 4 PERSONS:

16 pairs frogs' legs	4 tablespoons olive oil
2 cups beer	½ cup pine nuts
1 tablespoon chopped fresh thyme, or 1 teaspoon dried thyme	Juice of 1 lemon
	3 garlic cloves, minced
Salt	2 tablespoons minced parsley
Freshly ground black pepper	2 tablespoons chopped fresh chervil, or parsley
Flour	
5 tablespoons butter	1 lemon, sliced

GRENOUILLES MEUNIÈRE / *Frogs' Legs Meunière*

Soak the frogs' legs in milk or beer to cover for 2 hours. Drain and dry. Coat the frogs' legs on all sides with flour; shake off excess flour. Heat equal amounts of butter and oil in a large skillet. Put in a few of the frogs' legs, side by side. Sauté over fairly high heat until golden, then turn and sauté on the other side until golden. Transfer the legs to a hot platter. Sauté the remaining legs and put them on the platter. Squeeze a little lemon juice over the frogs' legs; sprinkle with a little minced parsley and salt and pepper. Serve immediately.

FOR 4 PERSONS:

16 pairs frogs' legs	Juice of 1 lemon
2 cups milk or beer	2 tablespoons minced parsley
Flour	Salt
3 tablespoons butter	Freshly ground black pepper
3 tablespoons olive oil	

CUISSES DE GRENOUILLES POULETTE / *Frogs' Legs Poulette*

Cook the mushrooms in the butter in a large skillet over medium heat for about 5 minutes, stirring occasionally. Then add the shallots and frogs' legs. Cook for 5 minutes longer, turning the legs once. Sprinkle with the flour; season lightly with salt, pepper and the nutmeg; add the wine and the fish stock. Simmer over low heat for about 10 minutes. Remove the frogs' legs from the skillet.

Beat the egg yolks and the *crème fraîche* together. Add them to the skillet off the heat. Return to very low heat and stir until the mixture thickens slightly. Add the frogs' legs, correct the seasoning, and cook for 2 minutes longer. Turn the frogs' legs and the sauce out into a hot serving dish and sprinkle with the parsley.

FOR 4 PERSONS:

½ **pound mushrooms, thinly
  sliced**
3 tablespoons butter
4 shallots, minced
16 pairs frogs' legs
2 tablespoons flour
Salt
Freshly ground white pepper

¼ **teaspoon grated nutmeg**
¾ **cup dry white wine**
¾ **cup Fish Stock (p. 166)**
4 egg yolks
½ **cup Crème Fraîche (p. 666)
  or heavy cream**
2 tablespoons minced parsley

Frogs' Legs Provençale / GRENOUILLES PROVENÇALE

Proceed generally as in Frogs' Legs Meunière (p. 287). To the skillet in which the frogs' legs were sautéed add 1 minced garlic clove and 3 tomatoes which have been peeled, seeded and chopped. Cook over high heat for 5 minutes and then pour this mixture over the frogs' legs before sprinkling with parsley.

Frogs' Legs Sauté / CUISSES DE GRENOUILLES FRITES

Soak the frogs' legs in beer or milk to cover for 30 minutes. Drain and dry them. Coat the legs on all sides with flour, shaking off any excess.

Beat the eggs in a bowl. Dip the floured frogs' legs into the eggs, coating them well, and coat them with bread crumbs. Shake off any excess crumbs and let stand for 15 minutes.

Heat the butter in a skillet over medium heat and sauté the frogs' legs, a few at a time, in it for about 5 minutes, or until they are golden on all sides. Season them lightly with salt and pepper.

Put the frogs' legs on a heated serving dish, sprinkle with the minced parsley and garlic, garnish the dish with the lemon slices, and serve immediately.

FOR 4 PERSONS:

16 pairs frogs' legs
2 cups beer or milk
Flour
3 eggs
2 cups fine dry bread crumbs
6 tablespoons butter

Salt
Freshly ground black pepper
3 tablespoons minced parsley
1 garlic clove, minced
1 lemon, sliced

ESCARGOTS / *Snails*

EDITORS' NOTE: *Most snails eaten in America are canned. Usually they come with polished shells so that they may be served in the classical fashion. However, fresh snails can be found in the United States, both in nature and in markets. Unless the snails are ready for cooking—and the market should be asked about this—it is best to choose only snails that have sealed themselves in their shells before they hibernate during the winter months. These sealed snails are usually the type found in the markets. Snails feed during the late spring and summer months, often on plants which are good for snails but unwholesome for humans, and thus, if caught during this period, they have to be "purged" before cooking. The simplest way to do this is to store them in a covered basket in a cool place and starve them for 2 weeks. A far better method, however, is to put a generous quantity of lettuce leaves in the basket. The snails will fatten nicely on the lettuce. The lettuce should be changed every few days, before it deteriorates.*

If you are using snails sealed in their shells, the membrane which encloses them must be cut away with a small sharp knife.

Whichever type you are using, they require a long thorough cleaning process. First scrub them thoroughly under running water. Then put them in a large container, cover them with cold water, and add ½ cup salt and ¼ cup of vinegar for about 4 dozen snails. Soak them for 1 hour, occasionally stirring them with a wooden spoon. Remove the snails from the container, and rinse them under running water. Put fresh water, salt and vinegar in the container and soak the snails again. Repeat this process at least one more time, or until the acidulated water is absolutely clear without any trace of slime or dirt. Discard any snails whose heads do not not emerge from their shells.

Now pour boiling water over them in a large pot and boil for 5 minutes. Drain, let them cool, remove them from their shells, and cut off the black ends of their tails. They are now ready for further cooking.

Clean the snails and prepare the snail butter. Scrub and dry the shells.

Make the *court bouillon;* add the unpeeled garlic and the snails. Simmer them very gently for about 3 hours, or until they are tender. Cool them in the *court bouillon.*

Put a little snail butter into each shell, slip the snail back into the shell, and seal it with more snail butter. Put the stuffed shells into a snail dish, or into a shallow baking dish. Heat them thoroughly in a 400° F. oven for about 6 minutes. Serve immediately.

FOR 4 PERSONS:

4 dozen snails, cleaned and parboiled	Court Bouillon for Fish (p. 131) made with white wine
1 cup Snail Butter (p. 795)	2 unpeeled garlic cloves

Hot Fish Hors-d'Oeuvre

Hors-d'Oeuvre Chauds de Coquillages, Crustacés et Poissons

EDITORS' NOTE: *It has often been rumored that the French have larger appetites than ours. A number of these hot fish hors-d'oeuvre, and some of the cold fish hors-d'oeuvre as well, will seem to American cooks to be very hearty fare for a first course. Indeed, many of them are perfectly adequate for a main course, and we urge you to use them as such.*

Anchovy Fritters / ALLUMETTES AUX ANCHOIS

Make a frying batter by beating together the flour and the beer. Wash and dry the anchovies. Or if you are using salted anchovies, cut them into halves and soak them in milk to cover for 3 hours in order to remove the salt.

Heat the fat for deep frying to 375° F. on a frying thermometer.

Dip each anchovy into the batter and fry until golden. Drain on kitchen paper and serve immediately on a hot serving dish.

FOR 4 PERSONS:

½ cup flour
½ cup beer
2 dozen fresh anchovies

Milk
Fat for deep frying

Anchovies au Gratin / ANCHOIS AU GRATIN

Drain the anchovy fillets and soak them in milk for 1 hour in order to remove excess salt.

Sauté the onions in 3 tablespoons of the butter in a skillet over gentle heat for about 10 minutes, or until they are soft.

Butter a baking dish and then make alternate layers of anchovies, onions and potatoes; end with a top layer of potatoes. Sprinkle with a little of the brine in which the anchovies were preserved and dot with the remaining butter. Place the dish in a 375° F. oven.

After 10 minutes, moisten with half of the cream. Return the dish to the oven for another 10 minutes and then add the rest of the cream. Bake for about 20 minutes longer, or until the potatoes are tender.

FOR 6 PERSONS:

2 dozen anchovy fillets,
   preserved in salt brine
Milk
3 onions, minced

½ cup butter
4 medium-sized potatoes, thinly
   sliced
1½ cups heavy cream

FEUILLETÉS D'ANCHOIS / *Anchovy Patties*

Make a puff paste, roll it out to the thickness of ¼ inch, and cut it into 12 rectangles 3 by 4 inches. Make 2- by 3-inch cuts in 6 of these, so that there is a ½-inch edge and the center part will serve as a lid of the patty. Place these rectangles with the incisions on top of the other six and then put them on a buttered and floured baking sheet. Brush the tops with beaten egg and bake them in a preheated 450° F. oven for 10 minutes. Reduce heat to 350° F. and bake for about 15 minutes longer.

Clean the anchovies, remove the bones, and purée them in a blender.

Heat the olive oil and the butter in a saucepan. Stir in the anchovy purée, mix well, season with pepper and nutmeg, and add the *fines herbes*.

Soak the bread crumbs in the milk, squeeze them almost dry, and mix with the anchovy purée. Cook over lowest possible heat for 5 minutes, stirring constantly. Off the heat beat in the egg yolks, one at a time.

Take the patties out of the oven and, with the point of a sharp knife, remove the tops. Scoop out the uncooked dough in the center and fill each patty with a little of the anchovy purée. Cover with the tops and put back into the oven for 10 minutes. Serve very hot.

FOR 4 PERSONS:

1 recipe Puff Paste (p. 715)	Pinch of grated nutmeg
1 egg yolk, beaten	4 tablespoons Fines Herbes
2 pounds fresh anchovies	(p. 89)
2 tablespoons olive oil	1 cup fresh white bread crumbs
3 tablespoons butter	½ cup lukewarm milk
Freshly ground black pepper	3 egg yolks

/ *Swedish or Danish Lumpfish Caviar au Gratin*

CAVIAR SUÉDOIS AU GRATIN

Scald the *crème fraîche* but do not let it boil. Stir in the bread crumbs, caviar, eggs and chives. Mix well. Pour the mixture into a buttered baking dish. Cover with a sheet of buttered parchment paper or aluminum foil and cook in a preheated 350° F. oven for about 20 minutes.

FOR 4 PERSONS:

3 tablespoons Crème Fraîche	½ to ¾ cup Swedish or
(p. 666)	Danish lumpfish caviar
3 tablespoons fresh white bread	3 eggs
crumbs	3 tablespoons minced chives

GRATIN DE CRABE I / *Crabmeat Gratin I*

Spoon a layer of *sauce Mornay* into the bottom of a baking dish. Cover it with the sliced potatoes, hard-cooked egg slices and flaked crabmeat. Season with salt and pepper. Coat with the remaining *sauce Mornay,* sprinkle with the grated cheese, and dot with the butter.

Bake in a preheated 375° F. oven for about 30 minutes.

FOR 4 PERSONS:

2 cups Sauce Mornay (p. 776)	Salt
4 new potatoes, cooked and sliced	Freshly ground white pepper
1 hard-cooked egg, sliced	¼ cup grated Swiss cheese
2 cups flaked crabmeat	3 tablespoons butter

Crabmeat Gratin II / GRATIN DE CRABE II

Cook the crab in a well-seasoned *court bouillion.*

Remove all the meat carefully, reserving the upper shell. Rinse out the shell and simmer it in the Armagnac for 5 minutes. Drain and reserve shell and pan juices.

Carefully pick over the crabmeat and cut it into small pieces. Combine it with the *sauce Mornay,* season it with salt and cayenne, and add the *fines herbes* and a little of the liquid in which the shell was cooked. Fold in the stiffly beaten egg white.

Fill the empty shell with the crabmeat mixture, sprinkle with the cheese, and dot with the butter. Bake in a preheated 375° F. oven for about 15 minutes, or until golden and puffy.

FOR 1 PERSON:

1 large crab	Cayenne pepper
4 cups Court Bouillon for Shellfish (p. 131), made with vinegar	1 teaspoon minced Fines Herbes (p. 89)
¼ cup Armagnac	1 egg white, stiffly beaten
3 tablespoons Sauce Mornay (p. 776)	1 tablespoon grated Swiss cheese
Salt	1 teaspoon butter

Crabmeat with Artichokes / CRABE AUX ARTICHAUTS

Mince the artichoke hearts and cook them in the butter for 15 minutes, or until they are almost tender. Add the flaked crabmeat, mix, and cook over low heat, stirring frequently, for 5 minutes more. Add the potatoes, season with salt and pepper, and simmer until the artichokes are tender and the mixture is very hot.

FOR 4 PERSONS:

4 uncooked artichoke hearts	2 medium-sized potatoes, cooked and minced
3 tablespoons butter	Salt
2 cups flaked crabmeat	Freshly ground white pepper

Grilled Smoked Eels / ANGUILLES FUMÉES SUR LE GRIL

Beat the egg in a bowl and blend it with the water and oil. Season with a little salt, pepper and nutmeg. This is called *anglaise.*

Put the flour into a second bowl and the bread crumbs into yet another.

Cut the eel into 1½- to 2-inch slices. Dip each first into flour, then into the egg mixture, then coat the slices with the bread crumbs. Let stand for 5 to 10 minutes to dry, and then place the eel slices on a very hot broiler rack. Broil under high heat until golden on all sides and serve on a hot serving dish, garnished with lemon quarters.

FOR 4 PERSONS:

1 egg	Grated nutmeg
1 tablespoon water	Flour
1 teaspoon peanut oil	2 cups fine dry bread crumbs
Salt	1 smoked eel (about 1½ pounds)
Freshly ground black pepper	2 lemons, cut into quarters

PIBALES À LA CATALANE / *Pibales Catalane*

EDITORS' NOTE: Pibales *are tiny eels, the size of minnows. They are left whole and eaten as appetizers, with drinks. Elvers, or baby eels, may be used in their stead.*

Wash the *pibales* in beer or in milk, dip them into flour, and fry them in combined hot oil and butter until crisp.

The Spaniards also serve the *pibales* seasoned with garlic and minced parsley, the way we French serve snails.

FOR 4 PERSONS:

2 pounds pibales	¼ cup olive oil
Beer or milk	2 tablespoons butter
Flour	

/ *Fish Pâté with Asparagus Tips*

PÂTÉ DE POISSON AUX POINTES D'ASPERGES

Prepare the whiting *mousseline* (or use another fish, such as pike).

Cook the asparagus tips in boiling salted water for only 5 minutes, or until they are almost tender. Drain them on a kitchen towel.

Choose handsome fish fillets (turbot, John Dory or gray sole).

Line the bottom of a 9- to 10-cup mold with thin sheets of fresh pork fatback, letting it hang over the edges of the mold. Put a sprig of tarragon or a fresh fennel frond on it. Make alternate layers of the *mousseline,* fish fillets and asparagus tips, beginning and ending with the fish *mousseline.* If you wish, you may also put one or more layers of lobster or crabmeat. Cover the pâté with the overhanging sheets of fresh pork fat.

Stand the mold in a baking pan containing 1 inch of water and cook it in a preheated 325° F. oven for 1¼ to 1½ hours. When a knife inserted in it comes out clean, it is done.

At serving time, cut off the pork fat on the top of the mold and unmold the pâté on a warm serving dish. Remove all the remaining pork fat. Serve the pâté, if desired, with melted butter flavored with paprika, *fines herbes* and heavy cream.

FOR 6 PERSONS:

1 recipe Whiting Mousseline (p. 314)	Several sheets of fresh pork fatback
½ pound asparagus tips	1 tarragon sprig, or 1 fennel
2 pounds fish fillets	frond

Fish Soufflé I / SOUFFLÉ DE POISSON I

Melt the butter in a saucepan, stir in the flour and cook, stirring constantly, for 2 to 3 minutes. Add the cold milk. Season with a little salt, cayenne and nutmeg; blend well over low heat.

Beat together the egg yolks and the *crème fraîche*. Stir a little of the sauce into the egg-yolk mixture, and then pour it into the remaining sauce. Check the seasoning.

Poach any of the following fish in a *court bouillon:* hake, John Dory, sole or turbot. When the fish is cooked, remove the skin and the bones. Flake the fish or purée it in a blender and then add it to the sauce.

Beat the egg whites until stiff and fold them into the fish mixture.

Butter and flour an 8-cup soufflé dish and put the soufflé mixture in it.

Cook in a preheated 375° F. oven for about 30 minutes. Serve immediately.

FOR 4 PERSONS:

3 tablespoons butter	4 egg yolks
3 tablespoons flour	1 tablespoon Crème Fraîche (p. 666), or heavy cream
1 cup cold milk	
Salt	1 pound fish
Cayenne pepper	Court Bouillon for Fish (p. 131)
Grated nutmeg	6 egg whites

Fish Soufflé II / SOUFFLÉ DE POISSON II

Cook the fish in a *court bouillon;* skin and bone it, grind or flake it finely and mix it with the mashed potatoes, the onions cooked in butter, the pimientos, garlic, parsley and a little salt and pepper. Beat in the egg yolks, one at a time, and fold in the stiffly beaten egg whites. Pour the mixture into a buttered 8-cup soufflé dish. Sprinkle the soufflé with the bread crumbs and the cheese, and bake it in a preheated 375° F. oven for about 30 minutes.

FOR 4 PERSONS:

1 pound fish (sole, turbot, salmon, etc.)	1 garlic clove, minced
	1 tablespoon minced parsley
Court Bouillon for Fish (p. 131)	Salt
Mashed potatoes made from ½ pound potatoes	Freshly ground white pepper
	4 eggs, separated
2 minced onions, cooked until soft in a little butter	3 tablespoons fine dry bread crumbs
½ cup minced pimientos	3 tablespoons grated Swiss cheese

/ Creamed Fish in Patty Shells

BOUCHÉES FEUILLETÉES DE POISSON À LA CRÈME

Proceed as in Creamed Lobster in Patty Shells (p. 298), and substitute 2 cups of any cooked fish for the lobster.

HARENGS FRITS / *Fried Herring*

Fillet the herrings, trim the fillets, and bread them *à l'anglaise* (see p. 38), that is, first dip them into flour, then into egg beaten with oil and water and seasoned with a little salt and pepper, and finally coat them with bread crumbs. Let the fillets stand for 15 minutes to dry.

Heat the oil and the butter in a skillet, and sauté the fillets in it over fairly high heat for a few minutes, or until they are golden on both sides. Drain the herrings on kitchen paper and serve them in a hot serving dish.

Serve the cream mustard sauce on the side.

FOR 4 PERSONS:

4 herrings (½ pound each)
Flour
1 egg, beaten with 1 tablespoon
    peanut oil and 1 tablespoon water
Salt
Freshly ground black pepper

1 cup fine dry bread crumbs
2 tablespoons peanut oil
3 tablespoons butter
1 cup Cream Mustard Sauce
    (p. 789)

HARENG SALÉ AU GRATIN / *Salt Herring au Gratin*

Clean the salt herrings, cut off their heads, and soak them in a bowl of cold water overnight.

Dry the herrings, remove their skins, and fillet them. Cut the fillets lengthwise into strips.

Mince the onions and potatoes.

Butter a baking dish and put alternate layers of herring and potatoes dotted with butter and onions in it. Season the layers with a little pepper. Sprinkle with bread crumbs and dot with the rest of the butter.

Cook in a preheated 375° F. oven for 30 minutes.

Serve immediately, and very hot.

FOR 4 PERSONS:

1½ pounds salt herring
3 medium-sized onions
6 medium-sized potatoes

½ cup butter
Freshly ground black pepper
½ cup fine dry bread crumbs

HOMARD AU GRATIN / *Lobster au Gratin*

Make a *court bouillon* and cook the lobsters in it for about 15 minutes. Drain and cool them. Cut them lengthwise into halves and shell them. Cut the tail meat into thick slices but keep the meat of the claws whole. Cut the meat from the upper bodies into small dice.

Cut the mushrooms into dice and put them into a casserole with the water, the lemon juice and 2 tablespoons of the butter. Cover the saucepan and simmer for about 8 minutes. Season with salt.

Cut the truffles into very thin slices.

Add the diced lobster meat to the mushrooms, then add 1 cup of the *sauce béchamel* and mix thoroughly.

Line a baking dish with coarse salt and arrange the lobster shells in it; the salt will keep them in place while they are cooking. Or else balance the lobster shells any suitable way to prevent their turning over. Fill the shells with the mushroom-lobster mixture and arrange the meat from the claws on top. Make a small incision in each slice of the tail meat and insert a slice of truffle. Arrange overlapping slices of these truffled rounds on the lobster meat in each shell. Coat with the remaining *sauce béchamel,* sprinkle with the cheese, dot with the remaining butter, and cook in a preheated 350° F. oven for 15 minutes.

Serve the lobster shells on a big serving dish garnished with parsley.

FOR 4 PERSONS:

2 live 1½-pound lobsters
Court Bouillon for Lobster
(p. 243)
¼ pound mushrooms
1 tablespoon water
Juice of 1 lemon
4 tablespoons butter

Salt
2 medium-sized truffles
2 cups Sauce Béchamel (p. 761)
Coarse salt or Kosher salt
¼ cup grated Swiss cheese
Parsley

Lobster Pie | TOURTE DE HOMARD

Prepare the puff paste or *pâte brisée.* If you are using puff paste, prepare two 9-inch rounds, one of which has a narrow strip of puff paste around the edge to serve as a rim. Bake them on a buttered and floured baking sheet in a preheated 450° F. oven for 10 minutes; reduce the heat to 350° F. and bake for about 15 minutes longer. If you are using *pâte brisée,* make and bake 1 single-crust 9-inch tart shell as described on page 714.

Cook the lobster as described on page 381, and remove all the meat from the pieces of shell. Cut the tail meat into slices and the remaining meat into small dice.

Reduce the *sauce à l'américaine* over low heat to 1 cup.

Peel and seed the zucchini and cook them gently in the butter for about 5 minutes. Season lightly with salt and pepper. Fill the baked pastry shell with the zucchini and the slices of lobster. Mix the diced lobster with the truffles and sprinkle over the top.

Combine the *sauce béchamel* with the reduced *sauce américaine* and then strain through a fine sieve. Add the cream, and simmer over low heat for 2 minutes, stirring constantly.

Coat the lobster filling with sauce and heat it through in a preheated 400° F. oven for a few minutes. If you've been using puff paste, cover the pie with the second pastry round. Serve immediately, very hot.

FOR 4 PERSONS:

1 recipe Pâte Brisée (p. 713)
 or ½ recipe Puff Paste
 (p. 715)
1 live 1½-pound lobster, cooked
 as in Lobster à
 l'Américaine (p. 381)
4 small zucchini

3 tablespoons butter
Salt
Freshly ground black pepper
3 medium-sized truffles, finely
 chopped
1 cup Sauce Béchamel (p. 761)
2 tablespoons heavy cream

QUICHE DE HOMARD / *Lobster Quiche*

Make the pastry: pour the flour into a big bowl, make a well in the middle, and put the eggs, lard, milk and salt into the well. Stir with a fork and then knead the dough until smooth. Roll out to the thickness of ⅛ inch.

Cook the lobster in the boiling *court bouillon* for about 15 minutes; then drain and shell it. Cut all the meat into small pieces.

Butter and flour a 9-inch pie dish and line it with the pastry. Arrange the lobster pieces in the pie.

Beat together the whole eggs, the egg yolks, flour and *crème fraîche;* season lightly with salt, pepper and nutmeg. Pour the mixture over the lobster pieces and dot with butter.

Bake in a preheated 350° F. oven for about 35 minutes, or until a knife inserted in the custard comes out clean. Serve in the dish in which the *quiche* was cooked.

FOR 4 PERSONS:

For the pastry:
 2 cups flour
 2 eggs
 ¾ cup lard
 2 tablespoons milk
 1 teaspoon salt
1 live 1½-pound lobster
Court Bouillon for Lobster
 (p. 243)

4 whole eggs
2 extra egg yolks
1 tablespoon flour
2 cups Crème Fraîche (p. 666),
 or heavy cream
Salt
Freshly ground black pepper
Grated nutmeg
2 tablespoons butter

SOUFFLÉ DE HOMARD / *Lobster Soufflé*

When you are preparing certain lobster dishes it can happen that there is too much lobster for the recipe. This is often the case when the shells are to be stuffed with both lobster meat and sauce. In this case, I advise you to save the meat from the claws and the upper body, as well as the coral, and to preserve them in the following manner: Cut the lobster meat into small dice, put them into a container, sprinkle with dry white wine, and cover tightly. Place in the refrigerator.

Mash the lobster coral with the butter and wrap it up in a piece of aluminum foil. Keep it in the refrigerator for even as long as a week.

Then you may want to make the following soufflé.

Melt the butter and stir in the flour. Cook over lowest possible heat until it is smooth but still white; it must not turn golden. Sir in the white wine in which the lobster pieces marinated, and then the milk. Cook for 2 minutes and remove from the heat. Add the egg yolks, one at a time, beating well after each addition to make a very smooth mixture. Season lightly with salt, pepper, nutmeg and cayenne, and stir in the lobster coral.

Stir in all but 2 tablespoons of the cheese and then fold in the stiffly beaten egg whites.

Butter a 2-quart soufflé dish, sprinkle the bottom and sides with the rest of the grated cheese, and pour in the soufflé mixture. Cook in a preheated 375° F. oven for about 30 minutes.

The soufflé should rise by one third and, when done, be very firm inside.

FOR 4 PERSONS:

1 cup (approximately) leftover lobster meat	**1 cup milk**
Coral from the lobster	**4 egg yolks**
¼ cup dry white wine	**Salt**
2 tablespoons butter for the lobster coral	**Freshly ground black pepper**
2 tablespoons butter	**Grated nutmeg**
3 tablespoons flour	**Cayenne pepper**
	½ cup grated Swiss cheese
	6 egg whites, stiffly beaten

Note: If you want to double the amount of this soufflé to serve 8 persons, I would advise you to bake it in 2 soufflé dishes.

Lobster au Gratin with Potatoes /

PETIT GRATIN DE LANGOUSTE

Cook the lobster in the *court bouillon* for about 15 minutes.

Remove all the meat from the shell and cut it into little pieces.

Peel and mince the potatoes and sauté them in the oil combined with 2 tablespoons of the butter. Season them with salt, pepper and nutmeg. Put them into a baking dish with their pan juices and top with the lobster meat. Coat with the *sauce Mornay,* sprinkle with the cheese and bread crumbs, and dot with the remaining butter. Cook in a preheated 375° F. oven for 15 minutes.

FOR 4 PERSONS:

1 live 1½-pound lobster	**Freshly ground black pepper**
Court Bouillon for Lobster (p. 243)	**Grated nutmeg**
4 medium-sized potatoes	**1½ cups Sauce Mornay (p. 776)**
2 tablespoons olive oil	**3 tablespoons grated Swiss cheese**
4 tablespoons butter	**2 tablespoons fine dry bread crumbs**
Salt	

Creamed Lobster in Patty Shells /

BOUCHÉES FEUILLETÉES DE LANGOUSTE

Prepare and bake 4 patty shells as described on page 717.

Cook the lobster in boiling *court bouillon* for about 12 minutes.

When it is cooked, remove all the meat and cut it into small dice. Mix the lobster meat with the *sauce américaine* and bind with the *crème fraîche*.

Fill the patty shells with this mixture, and put them into a preheated 450° F. oven for a few seconds to heat them through. Serve very hot.

FOR 4 PERSONS:

½ recipe Puff Paste (p. 715)
1 live 1-pound lobster
Court Bouillon for Lobster
   (p. 243)

1½ cups Sauce Américaine
   (p. 777)
2 tablespoons Crème Fraîche
   (p. 666), or heavy cream

BARQUETTES DE MOULES | *Mussel Barquettes*

Clean the mussels as described in Mussels in Cream (p. 388), and put them into a large saucepan with the water and the wine. Cook them over high heat for about 5 minutes, or until the shells open. Strain the cooking liquid and reserve.

Drain the mussels thoroughly and remove them from their shells.

Roll out the puff paste to ⅛-inch thickness. Butter and flour 12 *barquette* molds and line them with the puff paste. Press buttered wax paper into the shells and then fill them with dried beans or rice. Bake in a preheated 450° F. oven for 10 minutes, reduce the heat to 350° F., and bake for another 10 minutes. When the *barquettes* are done, turn them over, so that the beans or rice will fall out, and unmold them.

Meantime, make the sauce. Heat 2 tablespoons of the butter in a casserole, stir in the flour and cook, stirring constantly, until the mixture is golden. Stir in about 1¼ cups of the liquid in which the mussels were cooked to make a smooth sauce as thick as heavy cream. Beat the egg yolk with the *crème fraîche* and stir it into the sauce. Season with salt, if necessary, and a little pepper and nutmeg.

Fill each of the *barquettes* with 2 mussels and coat with a generous tablespoon of the sauce. Sprinkle with the cheese and dot with the remaining butter. Run under the broiler until the cheese is melted. Serve very hot.

FOR 4 PERSONS:

24 mussels (about 1½ pounds
   large mussels)
1 cup water
½ cup dry white wine
½ recipe Puff Paste (p. 715)
Dried beans or uncooked rice
4 tablespoons butter

2 tablespoons flour
1 egg yolk
¼ cup Crème Fraîche (p. 666)
Salt
Freshly ground black pepper
Grated nutmeg
½ cup grated Swiss cheese

| *Mussel and Shrimp Crêpes*

CRÊPES FOURRÉES AUX MOULES ET CREVETTES

Make the *crêpe* batter as described on page 740 and from it prepare about 24 *crêpes* in the usual manner.

Clean the mussels as described in Mussels in Cream (p. 388). Put them into a saucepan with the water and the wine. Heat, but do not bring to the boiling point. Simmer the mussels without boiling them for about 15 minutes, or until the shells open.

Melt 3 tablespoons of the butter in a saucepan, stir in the flour and cook, stirring constantly, until the mixture is golden. Remove from the heat, cool, and stir in 2 cups of the liquid in which the mussels were cooked (the mussels will have released some liquid of their own).

Beat the sauce with a wire whisk and cook over lowest possible heat, stirring frequently, for about 10 minutes. Beat together the egg and ½ cup of the *crème fraîche* and stir it into the sauce. Simmer for 5 minutes longer, but do not boil.

Shell the mussels and put them into the top part of a double boiler. Add 1 cup of the sauce and the shelled shrimp.

Fill each *crêpe* with a shrimp and a mussel, roll them up, and put them side by side into a buttered baking dish.

Add the remaining ¼ cup of *crème fraîche* to the remaining sauce and coat the *crêpes* with it.

Sprinkle with the grated cheese and dot with the remaining butter. Brown under a broiler and serve immediately.

FOR 6 PERSONS:

1 recipe Crêpes batter (p. 740)
24 mussels (about 1½ pounds large mussels)
½ cup water
1 cup dry white wine
6 tablespoons butter

3 tablespoons flour
1 egg yolk
¾ cup Crème Fraîche (p. 666)
24 cooked shelled small shrimp
½ cup grated Swiss cheese

Mussels au Gratin | MOULES GRATINÉES

Clean the mussels as described in Mussels in Cream (p. 388). Cook them with 2 tablespoons of the shallots, the wine, parsley sprigs and a little pepper over high heat until they open.

Drain the mussels, shell, and reserve them.

Make this stuffing: Cook the remaining 2 tablespoons of the shallots together with the mushrooms in 3 tablespoons of the butter in a saucepan over low heat for about 10 minutes. Purée them in a blender.

Cook the *fines herbes* (there should be the same amount as mushroom purée) and the bread crumbs in the remaining butter over high heat and blend them with the mushrooms. Season very lightly with cayenne.

Add the mussels to this mixture and put them in a shallow baking dish. Pour the *crème fraîche* over the mussels, sprinkle with the cheese, and brown under the broiler.

FOR 4 PERSONS:

2½ pounds mussels
4 tablespoons minced shallots
1 cup dry white wine
2 parsley sprigs
Freshly ground black pepper
6 medium-sized mushrooms, sliced
6 tablespoons butter

½ cup minced Fines Herbes (p. 89)
4 tablespoons fresh white bread crumbs
Cayenne pepper
1 cup Crème Fraîche (p. 666)
¼ cup grated Swiss cheese

QUICHE AUX MOULES / *Mussel Quiche*

Clean 2½ pounds large mussels as described in Mussels in Cream (p. 388). Cook them over low heat with a little water until the shells open, shell, and reserve them.

Substitute these mussels for the cooked lobster in Lobster Quiche (p. 297), and proceed as described in that recipe.

MOULES À LA VILLEROY / *Mussels Villeroy*

Steam open any desired quantity of mussels in the usual manner and remove them from their shells. Coat them first in Sauce Villeroy (p. 777), and then coat them *à l'anglaise* (p. 38). Fry them in deep fat heated to 375° F. on a frying thermometer until they are golden.

HUÎTRES GRATINÉES / *Oysters au Gratin*

Shuck the oysters and reserve their liquid. Combine the oyster liquid and the wine in an enamelware or glass saucepan (you must never use a metal one), add the oysters, and heat them through *without boiling* for about 5 minutes, or until they plump. Drain the oysters and strain the liquid through a fine sieve or a triple layer of cheesecloth into another saucepan. Reduce over high heat to 1 cup and stir into the *sauce Mornay*.

Clean and wash half of the oyster shells. Cook the mushrooms in the hot butter until they are soft. Line the bottom of the oyster shells with a little of the mushrooms, coat them with a little of the sauce, top with the oysters, and cover with the remaining sauce. Sprinkle with the grated cheese and run very briefly under a broiler until the tops are bubbly.

FOR 4 PERSONS:

24 large oysters
1 cup dry white wine
1 cup very thick Sauce Mornay
   (p. 776)

½ pound mushrooms, minced
3 tablespoons butter
½ cup grated Swiss cheese

BROCHETTES DE HUÎTRES / *Oysters en Brochette*

Count on 8 oysters for each person, and choose only the biggest ones possible. Open the oysters and save the liquid.

Strain the oyster liquid through a very fine sieve or a triple layer of cheesecloth into a casserole. Add the white wine and the oysters and bring to the boiling point.

Place the oysters on a kitchen towel and reduce the pan liquid by two thirds. Beat together the *crème fraîche* with 1 egg yolk, the cornstarch, a little salt and pepper and a pinch of cayenne. Add this mixture to the reduced pan liquid, stir over low heat until it thickens, and strain it into a shallow dish. Let it cool.

OYSTERS AU GRATIN

Poach the oysters without boiling them, reduce their cooking liquid, and stir it into the sauce Mornay.

Put a little sauce into each oyster shell, top it with an oyster and more sauce to cover, and sprinkle with grated cheese. Run them briefly *under* a broiler.

Cut the bacon so that there are about 36 strips about 2 inches long. Sauté these strips in a skillet for a few minutes until they are transparent.

Thread the oysters and pieces of bacon alternately on wooden skewers, beginning and ending with a piece of bacon. Use 8 oysters for each skewer.

Roll each skewer on all sides in the sauce, dust them with flour, and then coat them *à l'anglaise* (see p. 38), using the remaining egg yolks, the water and oil. Finally cover generously with the fresh bread crumbs, taking care that they stick on the oysters.

Fry in deep fat heated to 360° F. on a frying thermometer until golden on all sides. Serve garnished with parsley.

FOR 4 PERSONS:

32 very large oysters	½ pound sliced bacon
1 cup dry white wine	Flour
¼ cup Crème Fraîche (p. 666)	3 tablespoons water
4 egg yolks	3 tablespoons peanut oil
1 teaspoon cornstarch	2 cups fresh white bread crumbs
Salt	Fat for deep frying
Freshly ground black pepper	Parsley sprigs
Cayenne pepper	

Note: Skewered mussels are prepared in the same manner. The proportions of the ingredients remain the same, but count on 2 mussels for each oyster, that is, 2 mussels, a piece of bacon, 2 mussels, etc.

/ *Oysters en Brochette à l'Anglaise*

BROCHETTES D'HUÎTRES À L'ANGLAISE

Open the oysters and put them into a dish. Save their juices and strain them through a triple layer of cheesecloth into a saucepan. Add the oysters and the wine.

Heat the mixture, but do not let it boil. Then remove the oysters when they are plump and put them on a kitchen towel.

Cut the bread into slices the length of the skewers, and the width of the oysters. Sauté the slices in the combined hot oil and 3 tablespoons of the butter until they are golden.

Cut the slices of bacon into halves and sauté them in a skillet until soft and golden.

Wrap half a slice of bacon around each oyster and skewer them, 6 oysters on each of 4 skewers.

Top each slice of sautéed bread with a skewer of oysters, put them on a serving dish, and keep them hot in a preheated 200° F. oven.

Heat the remaining butter in a skillet, and sauté the fresh bread crumbs in it until golden.

Just before serving, pour the hot buttered crumbs over the oysters, sprinkle with cayenne, and serve immediately, very hot.

FOR 4 PERSONS:

24 oysters	½ cup butter
2 cups dry white wine	12 slices of bacon
4 thick slices of white bread	1 cup fresh white bread crumbs
2 tablespoons peanut oil	Cayenne pepper

OYSTERS OR MUSSELS EN BROCHETTE (I)

While the oysters or mussels are cooking, cut the bacon into small pieces. When the shellfish are cooked, thread them on wood skewers alternately with the bacon. Always begin and end with a piece of bacon.

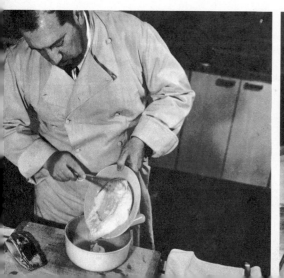

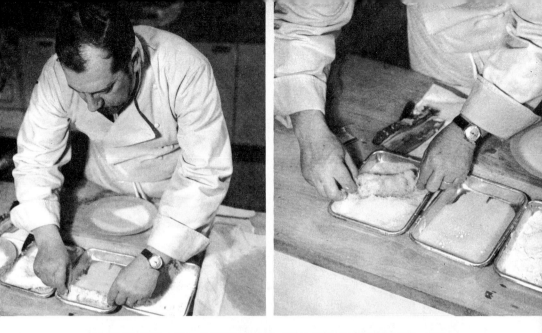

OYSTERS OR MUSSELS EN BROCHETTE (II)

Bread the skewers by first dipping them into the sauce, then into the flour and the anglaise, and finally coating them with the fresh white bread crumbs.

Oysters Villeroy / HUÎTRES À LA VILLEROY

Proceed as in Mussels Villeroy (p. 301), substituting oysters for the mussels. The oysters should first be gently poached in their own liquid for a minute or two.

Pike Mousse / MOUSSE DE BROCHET

Clean the pike; remove the backbone and, if whole, the head, the tail and finally the skin. You should have about a pound of boneless pike flesh. Purée the fish in a blender or in a mortar. Season lightly with salt and white pepper and work in two of the egg whites.

If the purée is not entirely smooth, force it through a fine sieve.

Put the purée into a bowl set into another bowl filled with ice cubes, and stir vigorously. Gradually add the *crème fraîche,* a little at a time, beating constantly. Beat the remaining egg whites until stiff and fold them into the fish mixture.

Butter a 7- to 8-cup savarin or ring mold, spoon the fish mousse into it, and set the mold in a baking pan containing boiling water; the water should reach halfway up the sides of the mold. Cover the top with buttered brown paper and cook in a pre-heated 375° F. oven for 25 minutes.

Remove the mousse from the oven and let it stand for 8 or 9 minutes. Only then unmold on a serving dish. Coat the mousse with a little cream sauce, seasoned with a little fish stock, or *sauce Nantua.*

Serve immediately, with the remaining sauce on the side.

FOR 4 PERSONS:

1 pike (2 pounds)	**2 tablespoons butter**
Salt	**2 cups Cream Sauce (p. 775),**
Freshly ground white pepper	**or Sauce Nantua (p. 778)**
4 egg whites	
2 cups Crème Fraîche (p. 666),	
or heavy cream	

Curried Prawns au Gratin /

GRATIN DE LANGOUSTINES AU CURRY

Make a *court bouillon* and simmer the prawns in it for 5 minutes. Remove them and set them aside. Strain the *court bouillon.*

Peel and mince 1 onion, and sauté it gently in 2 tablespoons of the oil and 1 tablespoon of the butter in a saucepan. Sprinkle with the flour and the curry. Add the thyme, bay leaf and a little salt and pepper. Mix well and simmer, covered, over low heat for 15 minutes. Add 1½ cups of the strained *court bouillon* and simmer for another 10 minutes.

Now cook the rice: Mince the other onion and sauté it in 2 tablespoons each of the remaining oil and butter in a casserole. Add the rice and stir to coat all the grains. Add 2¼ cups of *court bouillon,* bring to the boiling point, cover the casserole very tightly, reduce the heat to very low, and cook until the rice is tender, about 20 minutes.

Shell the prawns, devein them, and sauté them, together with the shallots, in 3 tablespoons of the remaining butter over low heat. Season very lightly with salt and cook only until the shallots are golden.

Line the bottom of a buttered deep baking dish with the rice, arrange the prawns and their pan juices over the rice, and strain the curried sauce over the prawns. Sprinkle with bread crumbs and dot with the remaining 2 tablespoons of butter.

Brown under a broiler and serve very hot.

FOR 4 PERSONS:

2 quarts Court Bouillon for
  Fish (p. 131)
24 prawns or large shrimp
2 onions
4 tablespoons olive oil
½ cup butter
1 tablespoon flour
1 to 2 tablespoons curry powder

Pinch of ground thyme
1 bay leaf, crumbled
Salt
Freshly ground black pepper
1½ cups uncooked rice
2 shallots, minced
1 cup dried bread crumbs

LANGOUSTINES FRITES / *Fried Prawns*

Thread 6 prawns on each of 2 wooden skewers, serving 2 skewers to each person.

Dip the skewered prawns into milk seasoned with a little salt and pepper, and then coat them with flour.

Fry them in deep fat heated to 375° F. on a frying thermometer until golden. Drain and serve on a hot dish lined with a napkin, with *sauce tartare* or *sauce choron* on the side.

FOR 1 PERSON:

12 raw prawns, shelled and
  deveined
Milk
Salt
Freshly ground black pepper

Flour
Fat for deep frying
½ cup Sauce Tartare (p. 785),
  or Sauce Choron (p. 780)

QUICHE DE SAUMON FUMÉ / *Smoked Salmon Quiche*

Proceed as in Lobster Quiche (p. 297), but use about 12 thin slices of smoked salmon instead of lobster.

Use the same quantity of other ingredients and bake in the same manner.

SARDINES FRAÎCHES AU FOUR / *Baked Fresh Sardines*

Clean the sardines, remove their bones, and fillet them. Wash the fish in cold water and dry them.

Cut the anchovy fillets into pieces.

Season the sardines lightly with salt, put a piece of anchovy fillet on each, and roll up the fish.

Butter a baking dish generously and put the rolled fish in it side by side. Sprinkle with half of the bread crumbs, dot with butter and a little of the anchovy oil, and sprinkle with the remaining bread crumbs.

Bake in a preheated 375° F. oven for about 15 minutes.

FOR 4 PERSONS:

2 pounds fresh sardines (sea herrings or pilchards)
12 anchovy fillets, preserved in oil

Salt
4 tablespoons butter
1 cup fresh bread crumbs

Sardines à la Béchamel /

Peel the potatoes and cook them in boiling salted water for 20 minutes, or until tender.

Clean the sardines and sauté them quickly in 3 tablespoons each of the oil and butter over fairly high heat. Season lightly with salt and pepper, remove the fish from the pan, and keep them hot.

Add more oil to the pan, heat it, and sauté the bread strips until golden; they should be about the same size as the sardines.

Drain the potatoes and purée them. Beat in the scalded milk and the remaining butter. Add salt, pepper and nutmeg to taste.

Line a baking dish with the potato purée, arrange the sautéed bread strips and the sardines on top, and coat them with the hot *sauce béchamel*. Sprinkle with the *fines herbes* and serve immediately.

FOR 4 PERSONS:

4 medium-sized potatoes
12 sardines
6 tablespoons olive oil
6 tablespoons butter
Salt
Freshly ground black pepper
12 narrow strips of firm white bread, trimmed of crusts

¼ cup scalded milk
Grated nutmeg
1 cup Sauce Béchamel (p. 761)
4 tablespoons minced Fines Herbes (p. 89)

Fried Sardines with Bacon / SARDINES FRITES AU BACON

Clean the sardines and fillet them.

Roll a thin slice of bacon around each fillet and tie it with a thread.

Heat the oil to 375° F. on a frying thermometer and fry the sardines in it until they are golden.

Remove the fish with a slotted spoon, discard the threads, and keep the sardines hot in a hot dish.

Fry the bread in the same oil until golden, drain it on kitchen paper, and place it in a hot serving dish. Put a few of the sardine fillets on each of the bread slices.

Sprinkle with *fines herbes* and serve immediately.

FOR 4 PERSONS:

12 sardines	4 large slices of bread
12 slices of bacon, halved	3 tablespoons minced Fines
Oil for deep frying	Herbes (p. 89)

COQUILLES SAINT-JACQUES AU NATUREL / *Scallops Naturel*

If the scallops are not already shelled, open the shells, remove the scallops, and wash them in several changes of water (see p. 96). Soak them in milk for 10 minutes.

Drain and dry the scallops. Put them into a baking dish and cook them as is, without any other ingredient, in a preheated 375° F. oven for about 15 minutes.

The scallops may be served by themselves, in the dish in which they were cooked, or dotted with a little butter and sprinkled with lemon juice.

FOR 4 PERSONS:

20 or more sea scallops	Butter
Milk	Lemon juice

SOUFFLÉ D'OURSINS / *Sea Urchin Soufflé*

Open the shells of the sea urchins carefully, following the method described on page 97, keep the bottom portions of the shells in one piece as you will use the shells for tiny soufflé dishes. Discard the liquid as described and remove the coral. Mash the coral and blend it with the *crème fraîche*. Add the *sauce béchamel,* mix well, and season with salt, cinnamon and saffron. Beat the egg white until stiff and fold it into the mixture at the last moment.

Scrub out the empty shells of the sea urchins and dry them thoroughly. Spoon a little of the soufflé mixture into each shell and bake in a preheated 375° F. oven for about 10 minutes, or until the soufflé mixture is puffed up in the shells.

FOR 4 PERSONS:

8 sea urchins	Salt
1 tablespoon Crème Fraîche	Pinch of ground cinnamon
(p. 666)	Pinch of ground saffron
4 tablespoons Sauce Béchamel	1 egg white
(p. 761)	

CRÊPES AUX FRUITS DE MER ET AUX POISSONS / *Seafood Crêpes*

Put the mussels and cockles or clams with a little water into a saucepan and steam them over low heat for about 5 minutes, or until the shells open.

Discard the shells and set the shellfish aside in a bowl. Strain the liquid in which they were cooked and their own juices through a fine sieve or a triple layer of cheese-cloth and reserve it. Cut off the head and tail of the sole and fillet the fish.

Make a fish stock with the liquid in which the shellfish were cooked, the head, tail and bones of the sole, the wine, ½ cup of water, the thyme, onion, peppercorns and whole cloves; cook it for 30 minutes. Strain it into a saucepan, add the fillets of sole and, without letting the fish stock boil, poach them over low heat for about 12 minutes.

Remove the sole fillets and reserve the fish stock.

Make the *crêpe* batter and from it prepare 12 large *crêpes,* about 8 inches in diameter. Keep the *crêpes* hot.

Cook the minced shallots in the butter until they are soft and golden; add the shellfish, the sole lightly flaked and the shrimp. Mix very gently and remove from the heat.

Reduce the fish stock over high heat to 2 cups. Beat together the egg yolks and the *crème fraîche,* beat it into the fish stock off the heat, and then stir over low heat until thickened. Season to taste with salt and pepper. Pour half of this sauce over the seafood and mix well, but very lightly.

Stuff each *crêpe* with a little of the seafood mixture, roll it up, and put the stuffed *crêpes* side by side into a buttered baking dish. Spoon the remaining sauce over them and brown quickly under the broiler, but use care as the sauce will curdle if left too long.

FOR 4 PERSONS:

24 mussels (about 1 pound small mussels), scrubbed
24 cockles or small clams
1 gray or lemon sole (2 pounds)
1 cup dry white wine
Pinch of dried thyme
1 onion, sliced
4 peppercorns
2 whole cloves

1 recipe Crêpes batter (p. 740)
2 shallots, minced
2 tablespoons butter
½ pound shelled shrimp
4 egg yolks
½ cup Crème Fraîche (p. 666)
Salt
Freshly ground white pepper

Seafood Roulade / CHAUSSON FEUILLETÉ AUX FRUITS DE MER

Roll out the puff paste ⅛ inch thick into an oblong about 12 by 18 inches.

Shell the oysters, mussels and scallops, and simmer them in the fish stock for 3 minutes, without boiling them.

Remove the seafood with a slotted spoon. Reduce the pan liquid by half, and stir in the *crème fraîche.* Continue simmering until the sauce is very thick. Add the sea-food and season lightly with salt and generously with pepper and cayenne. Remove from the heat and cool.

Spoon the mixture into the middle of the pastry rectangle. Fold the 2 long ends of the pastry over the filling, pinching it firmly together, and seal tightly at both ends. Put the roll, seam side down, on a buttered and floured baking sheet. Paint with the beaten egg yolk and bake in a preheated 400° F. oven for about 25 minutes. Serve very hot.

FOR 4 PERSONS:

½ recipe Puff Paste (p. 715)
12 large oysters
24 mussels (about 1 pound small mussels), scrubbed
12 large sea scallops
2 cups Fish Stock (p. 166)

1 cup Crème Fraîche (p. 666), or heavy cream
Salt
Freshly ground white pepper
Cayenne pepper
1 egg yolk, beaten

COQUILLAGES GRATINÉS / *Shellfish Gratiné*

Traditional in a shellfish *gratiné* are mussels, cockles or clams, periwinkles, etc., which are removed from their shells, blended with Snail Butter (p. 795) and fine white bread crumbs, put back into their shells, and browned under the broiler or in a hot oven.

The shells may also be stuffed with minced mushrooms cooked in butter or a mushroom purée made from mushrooms cooked in butter. This mixture should be bound with an egg yolk or a little Sauce Béchamel (p. 761). Put a little of the mushroom mixture into each shell, top it with the shellfish, and coat with a little *sauce béchamel*. Sprinkle with grated cheese and brown under a broiler.

What is important is to use only very fresh and live shellfish. Don't use any shellfish that are not firmly closed.

GRATIN DE FRUITS DE MER I / *Gratin of Seafood I*

Make a well-seasoned *court bouillon* with the water, carrots, onion, thyme, bay leaf, garlic, parsley and peppercorns.

Cook the crabs in this *court bouillon* for 15 minutes. Drain them and pick out all the meat. Reserve it in a large casserole.

Scrub and wash the quart of mixed shellfish, put them into a saucepan with the wine, and cook over high heat for 6 to 8 minutes, or until the shells are opened.

Drain the shellfish, remove them from their shells, and add them to the crabmeat. Strain the liquid in which they were cooked through a fine sieve or a triple layer of cheesecloth twice and add it to the casserole.

Open the oysters and strain their liquid through a fine sieve or a triple layer of cheesecloth into a saucepan. Open and drain the sea urchins (see p. 97), and scoop out the coral. Add the oysters and the coral from the sea urchins to the saucepan of strained oyster liquid, and simmer them without boiling for 2 minutes, or until the oysters plump. Drain and reserve them. Add the liquid to the casserole with the crabmeat and shellfish.

Shell the prawns, and then wash and dry them carefully. Do the same for the scallops and add both to the casserole with the seafood, with very little salt and pepper, 3 tablespoons of the butter and the lemon juice.

Bring the casserole to the boiling point, lower the heat, and simmer for 3 minutes. Remove from the heat. Be careful, for seafood, if overcooked, becomes rubbery.

Drain off the liquid in which the seafood was cooked and reserve. Make a *liaison* by beating together the egg yolks and the *crème fraîche*.

Heat the *sauce béchamel* in a saucepan and stir in the seafood liquid, beating constantly with a wire whisk to make a smooth sauce. Stir in the *liaison*, or cream and egg mixture, and cook over lowest possible heat, stirring constantly, until the sauce is thickened and smooth. Check the seasoning and add a pinch of cayenne.

Line the bottom of a buttered baking dish with one third of the sauce and put all of the seafood in it with the oysters and sea urchins on top. Coat with the remaining sauce. Sprinkle with the cheese and dot with the remaining butter. Cook in a preheated 375° F. oven for about 5 minutes, or run briefly under a hot broiler until the top is brown and bubbly. Serve very hot.

FOR 6 PERSONS:

For the court bouillon:	
4 cups water	6 large oysters
2 carrots	15 sea urchins
1 onion	12 prawns, or large shrimp
Pinch of dried thyme	1 pound scallops
1 bay leaf	Salt
1 garlic clove	Freshly ground black pepper
Parsley sprigs	5 tablespoons butter
4 peppercorns	Juice of 1 lemon
6 medium-sized crabs	5 egg yolks
1 quart mixed shellfish, such	⅓ cup Crème Fraîche (p. 666),
as clams, mussels,	or heavy cream
periwinkles, etc.	2 cups Sauce Béchamel (p. 761)
1 cup dry white wine	Cayenne pepper
	¼ cup grated Swiss cheese

Gratin of Seafood II / GRATIN DE FRUITS DE MER II

Make a *court bouillon* with the thyme, bay leaf, onion, carrot, wine and water. Bring it to the boiling point, cook for 20 minutes, and let it cool.

Put the sole and dab fillets into the cold *court bouillon* and heat it up, almost to the boiling point, but do not boil the fish. Remove from the heat and drain the fish in a strainer.

Clean the mussels as described in Mussels in Cream (p. 388). Put them into a saucepan with the wine and cook until the shells open. Shell them and add them to the fish fillets.

Shell the shrimp and prawns, simmer them for 5 minutes in a little *court bouillon*, and add them to the other fish, reserving the shells.

Cook the mushrooms in 3 tablespoons of the butter in a saucepan for about 8 minutes, or until they are soft.

Crush the shells of the shrimps and prawns in a mortar with a pestle. Put the crushed shells in a saucepan and add 2 tablespoons of butter and sprinkle with the flour. Stir over medium heat for a minute, and then add the *crème fraîche,* the brandy, a pinch of cayenne and gradually enough *court bouillon* to make a sauce with the consistency of cream.

Butter a baking dish and line it with the mushrooms and their pan juices. Top it with the fish fillets first, the mussels next and, finally, the shrimps and prawns. Strain the sauce over the fish and sprinkle with the bread crumbs. Cook in a preheated 400° F. oven for 5 minutes.

FOR 5 PERSONS:

For the court bouillon:
  Pinch of dried thyme
  1 bay leaf
  1 onion, chopped
  1 carrot, chopped
  1 cup dry white wine
  2 cups water
1 fillet of gray sole (½ pound)
1 fillet of dab or lemon sole
  (½ pound)
1½ pounds mussels

1 cup dry white wine
⅓ pound shrimp
⅓ pound prawns
½ pound mushrooms, minced
6 tablespoons butter
2 tablespoons flour
¼ cup Crème Fraîche (p. 666),
  or heavy cream
¼ cup brandy
Cayenne pepper
¼ cup fine dry bread crumbs

BROCHETTES DE FRUITS DE MER / *Shellfish en Brochette*

Open and clean the scallops according to the method described on page 96; or buy ready-to-cook scallops; in that case you will have no coral. Put the white muscles and any coral in the milk seasoned with a little salt and pepper for 2 to 3 hours.

Shell the prawns without tearing them, add them to the scallops, and soak them in the milk also.

Thread alternately 1 scallop, 1 piece of coral and 1 prawn on 4 wooden or metal skewers.

Dip the skewers into milk, sprinkle them with the dried *fines herbes,* and then roll in the flour.

Heat the oil and the butter in a deep skillet and sauté the skewers in it over high heat until they turn golden. Remove from the heat and continue cooking them in a baking dish in a preheated 350° F. oven for about 10 minutes.

Serve immediately in the baking dish, with a garnish of parsley and lemon quarters.

FOR 4 PERSONS:

16 large sea scallops
2 cups milk
Salt
Freshly ground white pepper
12 prawns or large shrimp
2 tablespoons mixed dried herbs
  (thyme, chervil, tarragon,
  parsley, etc.)

Flour
¼ cup peanut oil
¼ cup butter
Parsley sprigs
2 lemons, cut into quarters

CROQUETTES DE CREVETTES / *Shrimp Croquettes*

Mince the shelled shrimp and put them into a casserole with the *sauce Mornay.* The mixture should be a thick paste. Bring to the simmering point and stir over high heat for about 5 minutes. Season to taste with cayenne and nutmeg. Pour the mixture into a buttered plate and chill it in the refrigerator.

Then shape into croquettes the size of pigeons' eggs.

Take 3 deep plates. Put the flour into one; in another, make an *anglaise,* that is, beat together the egg with the oil and water, and season with a little salt and pepper; put the bread crumbs into the third plate.

Dip the croquettes first into the flour, then into the egg mixture, and finally into the bread crumbs.

Fry them in deep fat heated to 375° F. on a frying thermometer.

Drain the croquettes on paper towels, and then pile them up in the shape of a pyramid on a hot serving plate lined with a napkin. Surround with lemon quarters and serve very hot.

FOR 4 PERSONS:

1 **pound raw shrimp, shelled and deveined**
¾ **cup very thick Sauce Mornay (p. 776)**
Cayenne pepper
Grated nutmeg
Flour
1 **egg**

1 **tablespoon peanut oil**
1 **tablespoon water**
Salt
Freshly ground white pepper
1½ **cups fine dry bread crumbs**
Fat for deep frying
2 **lemons, cut into quarters**

Whiting Mousseline au Gratin /

MOUSSELINE DE MERLAN AU GRATIN

Ask your fish dealer to fillet the whiting for you since this is a rather complicated thing to do and would take up too much of your time.

Cut the fillets into little pieces and run them through the finest blade of the meat grinder to purée them. Put the fish purée into a bowl and set this bowl in a larger one filled with cracked ice. Work the egg whites into the fish and season lightly with salt and cayenne. Stir well with a wooden spoon to get a very smooth mixture.

Gradually beat in the *crème fraîche*.

Butter a large shallow baking dish and put the fish *mousseline* in it by the rounded spoonful to make even mounds spaced about 2 inches apart. If necessary, use 2 baking dishes.

Very carefully add boiling water to cover the fish mounds. Put the baking dish over low heat and poach for 8 to 10 minutes. The water must on no account boil; it should barely simmer. Remove the *mousselines* with a slotted spoon and drain them on a kitchen towel.

Butter another shallow baking dish and place the drained *mousselines* in it. Sprinkle with the cheese, dot with butter, and brown lightly in a preheated 400° F. oven for 5 minutes. Serve immediately.

FOR 4 PERSONS:

4 **whiting fillets (½ pound each)**
2 **egg whites**
Salt
Cayenne pepper

2 **cups Crème Fraîche (p. 666), or heavy cream**
3 **tablespoons butter**
¼ **cup grated Swiss cheese**

3
EGGS
Les Oeufs

The various methods of cooking eggs are described, with illustrations, beginning on page 115.

Baked Eggs Lorraine / OEUFS COCOTTE À LA LORRAINE

Put ½ teaspoon of butter into each of 4 small individual baking or custard dishes. Put half a slice of bacon in each. Cook in a preheated 375° F. oven until the bacon is transparent, about 5 minutes. Break an egg into each dish and season lightly with salt and a good deal of pepper. Return to the oven and cook for 6 minutes. Serve immediately.

FOR 4 PERSONS:

2 teaspoons butter
2 slices of bacon, cut into halves
4 eggs

Salt
Freshly ground black pepper

Baked Eggs Provençale / OEUFS COCOTTE À LA PROVENÇALE

Rub the bottom of 4 individual baking or custard dishes with the garlic. Put ½ teaspoon butter and 1 tablespoon of the *sauce tomate* into each and then break an egg into each dish. Set the dishes in a pan containing 1 inch of boiling water and bake in a preheated 350° F. oven for 6 to 8 minutes. Serve immediately.

FOR 4 PERSONS:

1 garlic clove
2 teaspoons butter
4 tablespoons Sauce Tomate à la
  Provençale (p. 770)

4 eggs

Eggs in Macaroni Nests / OEUFS MOULÉS AU MACARONI

Use 4 individual baking dishes or *dariole* molds. Butter their bottoms and sides generously. Chill the molds in the refrigerator. Cook the macaroni in salted boiling water until almost but not quite tender. Drain and cool; line the bottom and sides of each mold with macaroni, placing the strands close together to make a nest. Chill again in the refrigerator until the macaroni stick together. Place a spoonful of ham mousse in each mold and break an egg into each. Set the molds in a baking dish containing 1 inch of boiling water, and bake in a preheated 350° F. oven for about 8 minutes, or until the eggs are set. Unmold on a hot serving dish and serve hot with a *sauce tomate*, or cold with any desired cold sauce such as a *mayonnaise tyrolienne*.

FOR 4 PERSONS:

2 tablespoons butter
⅛ pound long thick macaroni
¼ cup Ham Mousse (p. 224)

4 eggs
1 cup Sauce Tomate (p. 769), or
  Mayonnaise Tyrolienne (p. 785)

EGGS IN MACARONI NESTS

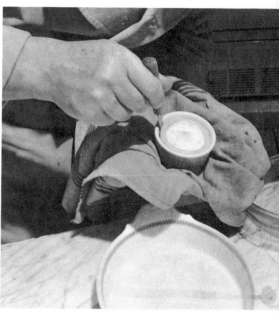

In order to be successful with this original but delicate dish, the macaroni must not be overcooked; it should still be quite firm. To make the macaroni stick to the butter, chill the molds in the refrigerator.

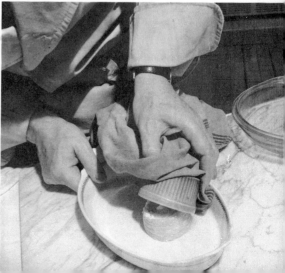

Molded Eggs with Ham | OEUFS MOULÉS AU JAMBON

Butter 4 small individual timbale or custard molds. Cut the ham into rounds the size of the bottom of the molds. Put a round of ham into each of the molds and sprinkle half of the minced *fines herbes* over the ham. Break an egg into each mold and season with salt and pepper to taste. Set the molds in a baking dish containing 1 inch of boiling water. Bake in a preheated 350° F. oven for 6 minutes, or until the whites of the eggs are set. Unmold the eggs on a hot serving dish. Coat the eggs with hot *sauce Aurore*. Sprinkle with the remaining *fines herbes* and serve immediately.

FOR 4 PERSONS:

2 tablespoons butter
4 small slices of ham
2 tablespoons minced Fines
  Herbes (p. 89)

4 eggs
Salt
Freshly ground black pepper
1 cup Sauce Aurore (p. 772)

Eggs Louis Oliver | OEUFS AU PLAT LOUIS OLIVER

Heat 1 tablespoon of the butter in a baking dish or skillet that is presentable enough to go to the table. Cook the *foie gras* in it briefly on both sides. Season it with salt and cayenne to taste. Push the *foie gras* to the middle of the skillet, add the remaining butter and, when it is hot, break the eggs into it, one at each side of the *foie gras*. Cook until the whites of the eggs are set. Cover the *foie gras* with the *sauce velouté*, which must be very hot, and spoon the *sauce Périgueux* around the eggs. Serve immediately.

FOR 2 PERSONS:

4 tablespoons butter
1 slice of foie gras (4 ounces)
Salt
Cayenne pepper
2 eggs

2 tablespoons Sauce Velouté for
  Chicken (p. 762)
2 tablespoons Sauce Périgueux
  (p. 765), heavily truffled

La Pipérade |

There are as many recipes for this Basque specialty as there are Basque cooks, each claiming that his own version is the most orthodox one.

And indeed, a *pipérade* is made with traditional ingredients: eggs, sweet red and green peppers, tomatoes, onions, Bayonne ham and a *bouquet garni*.

Cut the ham into fine dice. Heat 2 tablespoons of the goose fat, ham fat, or lard in a skillet and cook the ham in it until it is beginning to turn brown. Add the onion and the whole garlic clove and cook over low heat, stirring frequently, until the onions are very tender. They must not brown. Mince the peeled pepper and add to the onions. Cook them over low heat for another 5 minutes. Drop the tomatoes first into boiling water and then into cold water, peel them, cut them into halves, and squeeze the halves to remove the seeds and excess juice. Chop them and add them to the skillet, together with the *bouquet garni*. Season with salt and pepper to taste.

Simmer the vegetables over low heat until they are extremely tender, 15 to 20 minutes. Uncover and cook, stirring constantly, until they are very thick and smooth and have the consistency of a very thick tomato sauce. Discard the *bouquet garni* and the garlic clove.

Beat the eggs with 1½ tablespoons cold water. Stir them into the vegetable mixture and check the seasoning.

Heat the remaining goose fat, ham fat, or lard in a shallow earthenware, copper or enamelware casserole, or in a deep skillet. Add the egg mixture. Cook over low heat, stirring with a wooden spoon, until the mixture is set. Remove from the heat and serve immediately in a casserole or skillet.

Here are two variations:

1. Prepare and cook the vegetables for the *pipérade* as described above but omit the ham. Instead, sauté 4 rather thick slices of Bayonne or smoked ham or prosciutto in a little butter. Transfer the ham slices to a hot plate and keep hot. Add 2 garlic cloves to the pan juices and sprinkle 2 tablespoons of vinegar over the garlic. Cook until the garlic turns golden. Cook the *pipérade* as described, put it on a hot serving dish, garnish with the ham slices and the garlic, and sprinkle with the juices in which ham and garlic were cooked.

2. Cook the ham and the vegetables as described above but cook them somewhat longer, or until they are almost dry. Separate the eggs. Off the heat, stir the yolks into the vegetable mixture. Beat the egg whites until stiff and fold them into the mixture. Pour it into a buttered 1½-quart soufflé dish. Stand the dish in a pan containing 1 inch of boiling water, and bake in a preheated 350° F. oven for 45 minutes, or until puffed and cooked in the center. Serve immediately.

FOR 4 PERSONS:

2 ounces Bayonne or smoked ham or prosciutto	2 large tomatoes
5 tablespoons goose fat or ham fat, cut into slivers, or lard	1 Bouquet Garni (p. 46)
1 small onion, minced	Salt
1 garlic clove	Freshly ground black pepper
1 sweet red or green pepper, charred, peeled and seeded (see p. 619)	9 eggs

/ Eggs Scrambled with Tarragon

OEUFS BROUILLÉS À L'ESTRAGON

Beat the eggs with salt and pepper to taste and add a few drops of tarragon vinegar. Melt the butter, but do not let it get very hot. Add the eggs and stir with a wooden spoon. Cook over low heat, stirring constantly, until the eggs are set. Halfway through the cooking time, stir in the minced tarragon. Serve immediately in a hot bowl.

FOR 2 PERSONS:

6 eggs	Tarragon vinegar
Salt	3 tablespoons butter
Freshly ground black pepper	3 tablespoons minced fresh tarragon

Eggs Scrambled with Scallops /
OEUFS BROUILLÉS AUX COQUILLES SAINT-JACQUES

Trim and wash the scallops, plunge them into the boiling *court bouillon* for 3 minutes, and drain them. Crush the coral if there is any, and force it through a fine sieve. Leave the muscles whole.

Beat the eggs with salt and pepper to taste and the sieved coral. Stir in the scallop muscles. Melt the butter in a skillet, but do not let it get very hot. Add the egg mixture and stir with a wooden spoon until the eggs are set. Pour them into a hot serving dish and serve immediately.

FOR 2 PERSONS:

12 small scallops
2 cups Court Bouillon for
   Fish (p. 131)
6 eggs

Salt
Freshly ground white pepper
3 tablespoons butter

Eggs Scrambled with Truffles /
OEUFS BROUILLÉS AUX TRUFFES

Proceed as in Eggs Scrambled with Scallops (above), but substitute 2 fresh or canned truffles, minced, for the scallops.

Scrambled Eggs with Lobster /
OEUFS BROUILLÉS AU HOMARD

Prepare a small lobster *à l'Américaine* with very little sauce. Discard the shells, cut the meat into small pieces, and keep it hot in the sauce.

Beat the eggs with salt and pepper to taste. Melt the butter in a casserole and add the eggs. Stir them constantly with a wooden spoon and cook until they are set. Pour the eggs into a hot serving dish, make a well in the middle, and pour the lobster and sauce into the well. Serve very hot.

FOR 2 PERSONS:

¼ recipe Lobster
   à l'Américaine (p. 381)
6 eggs

Salt
Freshly ground black pepper
3 tablespoons butter

Eggs with Caviar / OEUFS AU CAVIAR

Whip the *crème fraîche* until it is stiff. Beat in the minced onion and the caviar. Put the mixture in the middle of a serving dish and surround with the egg slices. Garnish the dish with the toasted bread slices.

FOR 2 PERSONS:

⅔ cup **Crème Fraîche (p. 666),**
   or heavy cream
2 **tablespoons minced onion**
3 **tablespoons Swedish (or other)**
   caviar

2 **hard-cooked eggs, sliced**
4 **thin slices of toasted bread**

OEUFS AUX CREVETTES / *Eggs with Shrimps*

Cut the eggs into halves horizontally or vertically, as you please. Place them in the middle of a serving dish. Peel the shrimp, devein them, and arrange them around the eggs.

Whip the cream until stiff and combine it with the mayonnaise. Season with a little salt and pepper. Pour the mixture over eggs and sprinkle with the minced chives.

FOR 4 PERSONS:

4 **hard-cooked eggs, shelled**
1 **pound cooked shrimp**
½ **cup heavy cream**
½ **cup Mayonnaise (p. 782)**

Salt
Freshly ground white pepper
2 **tablespoons minced chives**

OEUFS FARCIS AUX ANCHOIS / *Eggs Stuffed with Anchovies*

Cut the eggs into halves horizontally or vertically, as you please. Remove the yolks and mash them or force them through a fine sieve. Using a wooden spoon, beat the butter and the mashed anchovies into the yolks until the mixture is smooth. Season to taste with salt and pepper.

Stuff the eggs with this mixture. You may do this with a spoon or a pastry bag fitted with a small tube. Arrange the salad greens on a platter, place the eggs on top of the greens, and sprinkle them with the minced parsley. Garnish with tomatoes or lemons cut into quarters.

FOR 4 PERSONS:

4 **hard-cooked eggs**
5 **tablespoons butter, at room**
   temperature
10 **anchovy fillets, drained**
   and mashed

Salt
Freshly ground white pepper
4 **lettuce leaves**
3 **tablespoons minced parsley**
2 **tomatoes or lemons, quartered**

OEUFS À LA TRIPE / *Eggs à la Tripe*

Cut the onion into thin rounds, blanch it in boiling water for 3 minutes, and drain. Heat the butter in a casserole and add the onion and thyme or tarragon. Cook, covered, until the onion is soft but still white. Add the *sauce béchamel* and the eggs. Mix well. Bring to the boiling point and cook for 2 to 3 minutes. Serve from the casserole.

FOR 4 PERSONS:

1 large onion	**1 cup Sauce Béchamel (p. 761)**
2 tablespoons butter	**4 hard-cooked eggs, cut into rounds**
Pinch of dried thyme or tarragon	

Note: Excellent egg croquettes may be prepared with this mixture.

Gratin of Eggs with Fines Herbes /

GRATIN D'OEUFS AUX FINES HERBES

Cut the eggs into halves. Remove the yolks and mash them in a bowl with the *crème fraîche,* the vinegar, and salt and pepper to taste. Fill the egg-white halves with this mixture and place them in a well-buttered baking dish. Sprinkle the *fines herbes* over the eggs and cover each with a spoonful of *sauce Mornay.* Sprinkle with the grated cheese and drizzle with a little of the melted butter. Brown slowly under a low broiler flame. Serve very hot.

FOR 4 PERSONS:

8 hard-cooked eggs	**½ cup minced Fines Herbes (p. 89),**
6 tablespoons Crème Fraîche (p. 666),	**made from fresh parsley, chervil,**
or heavy cream	**tarragon and chives**
2 tablespoons vinegar	**1 cup Sauce Mornay (p. 776)**
Salt	**¼ cup grated Swiss cheese**
Freshly ground white pepper	**2 tablespoons butter, melted**

Egg Croquettes / CROQUETTES D'OEUFS

Mince the eggs and combine them with the *béchamel.* Season with salt, pepper and nutmeg. Bring the mixture to the boiling point and cook for a few seconds. Put the mixture in a bowl and chill.

When cold, shape the mixture into 4 large or 8 small egg-shaped croquettes. Dust them with flour, dip them into the well-beaten *anglaise* mixture, and roll them in the bread crumbs, taking care that the bread crumbs cover them on all sides. Chill in the refrigerator again for at least 15 minutes.

Heat the fat to 375° F. on a frying thermometer and fry the croquettes until golden on all sides. Drain them on paper towels and then put them on a hot serving dish lined with a folded napkin. Sprinkle the croquettes with a little salt and the minced parsley. Serve very hot.

FOR 4 PERSONS:

4 hard-cooked eggs	**Anglaise:**
¾ cup thick Sauce Béchamel (p. 761)	**1 egg**
Salt	**1 tablespoon peanut oil**
Freshly ground black pepper	**1 tablespoon water**
Grated nutmeg	**½ teaspoon salt**
Flour	**Pinch of freshly ground black pepper**
	Dry bread crumbs
	Fat for deep frying
	2 tablespoons minced parsley

OEUFS MORNAY AU GRATIN / *Eggs Mornay au Gratin*

Put the poached eggs on a buttered baking dish. Season them with salt and pepper to taste. Coat them with the hot *sauce Mornay*. Sprinkle with the grated cheese and drizzle with the melted butter. Brown quickly under a broiler and serve immediately.

FOR 4 PERSONS:

8 poached eggs
Salt
Freshly ground white pepper

¾ cup Sauce Mornay (p. 776)
4 tablespoons grated Swiss cheese
3 tablespoons butter, melted

OEUFS BORGIA / *Eggs Borgia*

Cut off the stem end of the tomatoes, cut them horizontally into halves, and put them in a baking dish. Sprinkle them with salt and pepper and bake them in a preheated 375° F. oven for 12 to 15 minutes.

Poach the eggs and keep them warm.

Put 2 baked tomato halves in each of 2 small individual baking dishes and top each tomato half with a poached egg. Coat each with *sauce béarnaise* and serve immediately.

FOR 2 PERSONS:

2 large firm tomatoes
Salt
Freshly ground black pepper

4 poached eggs
½ cup Sauce Béarnaise (p. 779)

/ *Poached Eggs with Beef Marrow*

OEUFS POCHÉS À LA MOELLE

Make 4 large croutons: heat the butter in a skillet and fry the bread slices on both sides until golden. Poach the eggs in the usual manner and drain them on a towel. Simmer the marrow in barely boiling salted water for 5 minutes and drain on kitchen toweling.

Put the croutons into a baking dish, top each with a poached egg, and place 2 slices of marrow on each egg. Season with salt and pepper to taste. Heat very quickly under a broiler and serve immediately.

FOR 4 PERSONS:

¼ cup butter
4 slices of firm white bread,
  crusts removed
4 eggs

8 slices of beef marrow, about
  ¼ inch thick
Salt
Freshly ground black pepper

Poached Eggs Bretonne | OEUFS POCHÉS À LA BRETONNE

Gently sauté the ham in 2 tablespoons of the butter for 5 minutes. Remove it to a hot plate and keep it warm. Add the remaining butter to the pan juices, heat it, and sauté the cooked artichoke hearts in it until they are golden and very hot. Put the artichoke hearts into a hot serving dish; top each with a slice of ham and a poached egg. Sprinkle with the melted butter and the minced *fines herbes* and serve at once.

FOR 4 PERSONS:

4 **small slices of boiled ham**	2 **tablespoons butter, melted**
4 **tablespoons butter**	2 **tablespoons minced Fines Herbes**
4 **cooked artichoke hearts (see p. 549)**	**(p. 89)**
4 **poached eggs**	

Poached Eggs Haut-Brion | OEUFS POCHÉS HAUT-BRION

1. Cut the white part of the leeks into fine julienne strips, blanch them in boiling water for 3 minutes, and drain them. Heat the butter in a heavy saucepan; add the leeks and simmer them, covered, over low heat until they are tender, about 15 minutes. They must remain white. Add the wine; season with salt, pepper and nutmeg to taste; add the *bouquet garni.* Simmer, covered, for 40 minutes. Take the sauce off the heat, discard the *bouquet garni,* and thicken the sauce by stirring in small pieces of the *beurre manié.* Simmer the sauce until it is of a good consistency. Poach the eggs in water seasoned with the vinegar, but do not add salt to the liquid. Drain the poached eggs on a towel, put them into a hot serving dish, and coat them with sauce. Garnish with the croutons immediately.

2. Another way is to proceed as above, but do not prepare any croutons. Instead, make 4 very small potato cakes, as described in Potatoes Darphin (p. 635). Sauté a generous amount of small 1-inch rounds of ham in a little butter. Put the potato cakes into a hot serving dish, top each with an egg, sprinkle with the ham rounds, and coat everything with the sauce. Serve immediately.

FOR 4 PERSONS:

2 **leeks, white part only**	1 **Bouquet Garni (p. 46)**
2 **tablespoons butter**	2 **tablespoons Beurre Manié (p. 41)**
1½ **cups Haut-Brion, or another**	4 **eggs**
good red Bordeaux wine	2 **tablespoons vinegar**
Salt	½ **cup small Croutons (p. 62),**
Freshly ground black pepper	**fried in butter**
Grated nutmeg	

Eggs Pancho Villa | PANCHO VILLA

Soak the beans in cold water overnight, drain them, put them in a saucepan, and cover with water. Season with salt and bring to the boiling point over high heat. Reduce the heat and cook the beans until they are tender, about 25 minutes; drain. Heat the butter in a casserole and cook the onions and the garlic in it until they are soft and golden. Add the beans and the *sauce tomate* and simmer for 10 minutes.

Poach the eggs.

Put the beans into a baking dish and top them with the poached eggs. Sprinkle with the cheese and the melted butter. Heat in a preheated 400° F. oven for 3 minutes. Serve immediately.

FOR 4 PERSONS:

½ **pound dried white beans**
Salt
4 **tablespoons butter**
2 **onions, minced**
1 **garlic clove, minced**

1 **cup Sauce Tomate (p. 769)**
4 **eggs**
3 **tablespoons grated Swiss cheese**
2 **tablespoons butter, melted**

OEUFS POCHÉS PARMENTIER / *Poached Eggs Parmentier*

Cut the potatoes into very thin julienne strips. Heat the oil and the butter in a skillet until very hot and put the potatoes in it in 4 mounds. Cook them until they are golden and while they are cooking shape the mounds into *barquettes* by pressing a spoon in the middle of each mound. When the potatoes keep their shape and are golden on one side, turn them over carefully and cook them until barely golden on the other side. Turn them over again, reshaping them if necessary. Cook until golden brown and crisp.

When the potato *barquettes* are cooked through, put them into a hot serving dish. Place a poached egg into each *barquette* and top the egg with the mashed poatoes. Serve immediately.

The mashed potatoes may be replaced with Sauce Velouté (p. 762), a thick *jus,* or simply with a little heavy cream.

FOR 4 PERSONS:

2 **large potatoes, peeled**
3 **tablespoons peanut oil**
4 **tablespoons butter**

4 **poached eggs**
4 **tablespoons mashed potatoes**

/ *Poached Eggs with Roquefort Cheese*

OEUFS POCHÉS AU ROQUEFORT

Cut the hard rolls into halves and remove the soft crumbs. Use 2 tablespoons of the butter to spread the hollowed-out pieces lightly, then sprinkle with the grated Swiss cheese. Toast the rolls in a preheated 375° F. oven for about 8 minutes, or until the interiors of the rolls are golden.

Mix together the Roquefort cheese and the remaining butter. Heat this mixture lightly in a little casserole for about 2 minutes.

Put the toasted rolls on a baking dish, fill each with a little of the heated Roquefort mixture, and top each with a hot poached egg. Serve immediately.

FOR 4 PERSONS:

4 small hard rolls	3 tablespoons Roquefort cheese,
3 tablespoons butter	crumbled
2 tablespoons grated Swiss cheese	4 poached eggs

Jellied Eggs / OEUFS EN GELÉE

Melt one third of the aspic stock until it is barely liquid and line the bottoms of six ½-cup cocottes or custard dishes with a thin layer of it. Chill in the refrigerator until set.

Cut the ham into 6 rounds the same size as the bottom of the cocottes. On the set jelly, place 1 tarragon leaf, 1 ham round and 1 cold poached egg. Melt the remaining aspic in a small saucepan until it is barely liquid and fill the cocottes with it. Chill in the refrigerator for at least 1 hour, or until the aspic is well set. Unmold only at serving time.

FOR 6 PERSONS:

3 cups Brown Stock for Aspics (p. 166), heavily flavored with port, Madeira and fines herbes	3 slices of ham
	6 tarragon leaves
	6 poached eggs, chilled

Eggs à la Périgourdine / OEUFS À LA PÉRIGOURDINE

Poach the eggs and cool them. Chill a serving dish and place the eggs on it. Coat them with the *chaud-froid* sauce and place a slice of truffle on each egg. Spoon a layer of aspic over each egg. Chop the remaining aspic and place it around the eggs.

FOR 4 PERSONS:

4 eggs	4 slices of truffle
½ cup White Chaud-Froid Sauce (p. 776), flavored with Madeira	2 cups Brown Stock for Aspics (p. 166), flavored with Madeira

Sparrows' Nests / NIDS DE MÉSANGES

This dish may be served either on individual plates or on a large platter. In the case of the latter, the person who is first served stirs and mixes the whole dish.

Place little mounds of anchovies, onions, capers, chives, pickles, and potatoes on a flat plate. Place an egg yolk in the middle. Mix with a fork before eating.

FOR EACH PERSON:

2 anchovy fillets, drained and chopped	1 teaspoon minced pickles
	1 tablespoon diced potatoes, cooked and dressed with a little oil
2 tablespoons minced onion	
1 teaspoon capers	1 egg yolk
1 teaspoon minced chives	

/ *Plovers' and Lapwings' Eggs*

OEUFS DE PLUVIERS ET DE VANNEAUX

Plovers' and lapwings' eggs may be cooked like chicken eggs, but usually they are served hard-cooked and cold. They should be brought to the table in their shells, so that each diner shells his own. If they are to be served shelled, they should be placed on a serving dish, coated with a white *chaud-froid sauce* (p. 776) flavored with sherry, topped with a slice of truffle, and then coated with a thin layer of aspic.

Hard-cooked plovers' and lapwings' eggs may be placed in baked tartlet shells (p. 715) which have been lined with a layer of asparagus tips and a little French dressing. They are then garnished with a little chopped aspic around each egg.

Omelets

Omelettes

An illustrated description of making omelets will be found on page 120.

OMELETTE AUX AVOCATS / *Avocado Omelet*

Peel the avocados. Remove the seeds and cut the flesh into thin slices. Season with salt and cayenne to taste.

Heat the butter in a skillet, put the avocado slices in it, and sprinkle with the *fines herbes*. Cook quite gently until the slices are just heated through, no more. Beat the eggs with a little salt, a little pepper and the water. Pour them over the avocado slices. Make a flat omelet, like a *crêpe*, turning it over with a large spatula to cook the second side when the eggs begin to set. Slide it onto a hot serving plate and serve immediately.

FOR 4 PERSONS:

2 firm avocados	9 eggs
Salt	Freshly ground black pepper
Cayenne pepper	3 teaspoons cold water
3 tablespoons butter	
3 tablespoons minced Fines Herbes (p. 89)	

OMELETTE AU FROMAGE / *Cheese Omelet*

Beat the eggs with the water, salt and pepper to taste, the cream and the grated cheese. Heat the butter in a skillet and cook the omelet in the usual manner. Slide it onto a hot serving dish. Score the top with the point of a sharp knife and coat the omelet with the tomatoes. Serve immediately.

FOR 2 PERSONS:

5 eggs
1 tablespoon cold water
Salt
Freshly ground white pepper
1 tablespoon heavy cream

¼ cup grated Swiss cheese
3 tablespoons butter
¼ recipe Tomatoes in Butter
    (p. 647)

Omelet aux Fines Herbes / OMELETTE AUX FINES HERBES

Proceed as in Cheese Omelet (above), but substitute 3 tablespoons minced Fines Herbes (p. 89) for the cheese and omit the tomatoes.

Chicken-Liver Omelet / OMELETTE AUX FOIES DE VOLAILLES

Cut the pork fat into small dice and sauté them with 1 tablespoon of the butter in a skillet for about 3 minutes. Add the whole chicken livers, the thyme, bay leaf, and salt and pepper to taste. Sauté the livers over high heat until they are golden. Sprinkle them with the minced shallots, reduce the heat, and cook for about 4 minutes longer. Pour into a strainer; discard the pan juices, thyme (unless dried thyme was used) and bay leaf; reserve the chicken livers and what remains of the shallots. Marinate the livers in the port in a bowl for 1 hour. Drain the livers and cut them into thin slices.

Make the omelet in the usual manner, using the liver slices as a filling. Roll it up, slide it onto a hot serving dish, and serve immediately.

FOR 4 PERSONS:

2 ounces fresh pork fat
4 tablespoons butter
⅓ pound chicken livers
1 small sprig of fresh thyme,
    or ½ teaspoon dried thyme
1 bay leaf

Salt
Freshly ground black pepper
1 tablespoon minced shallots
½ cup port wine
9 eggs
2 tablespoons cold water

Mushroom Omelet / OMELETTE AUX CHAMPIGNONS

Sauté the mushrooms in 2 tablespoons of the butter until they are slightly browned but still firm. Season them with salt and pepper to taste. Beat the eggs with the water and a little salt and pepper. Add the mushrooms to the mixture. Heat the remaining butter in a skillet, pour in the egg mixture, and make the omelet in the usual manner. Roll it up and serve it immediately on a hot serving dish.

FOR 2 PERSONS:

¼ pound mushrooms, thinly sliced
5 tablespoons butter
Salt

Freshly ground black pepper
5 eggs
1 tablespoon cold water

OMELETTE AUX FRUITS DE MER / *Seafood Omelet*

There are various ways of making this omelet; here are two, of which the second one seems to me the better.

1. Heat the butter in a skillet, cook the shellfish in it for 2 minutes to heat it, then pour the eggs over the shellfish and make the omelet as usual.

2. Cook the seafood with the *béchamel, velouté* or *américaine* sauce. Make a separate omelet, and use the sauced shellfish mixture as a filling before rolling it up.

FOR 2 PERSONS:

3 tablespoons butter
½ cup cooked mixed shellfish,
  such as mussels, lobster, shrimp,
  crab, etc.
5 eggs

¼ cup Sauce Béchamel
  (p. 761), Sauce Velouté for Fish
  (p. 761), or Sauce Américaine
  (p. 777)

OMELETTE AUX CREVETTES / *Shrimp Omelet*

Heat the butter in a skillet and sauté the shrimp in it over high heat for about 3 minutes. Reserve a few of the shrimp for garnish.

Beat the eggs with the water and salt and pepper to taste. Add the sautéed shrimp to the mixture. Make the omelet in the usual manner, roll it up, and put it on a hot serving dish. Score the top of the omelet with the point of a sharp knife and coat the whole surface with the stewed tomatoes. Garnish with the reserved shrimp. Serve immediately.

FOR 2 PERSONS:

3 tablespoons butter
12 small shrimp, shelled and deveined
5 eggs
1 tablespoon water

Salt
Freshly ground black pepper
½ cup very hot Tomatoes in
  Butter (p. 647)

OMELETTE À LA FLORENTINE / *Spinach Omelet*

Trim the spinach, wash it, and shake it as dry as possible in a strainer. Heat 3 tablespoons of the butter in a big enamelware saucepan; add the spinach and a little

SEAFOOD OMELET

Here is the second way of making this omelet.
The sauced shellfish is used as a filling.

salt. Simmer, covered, over low heat for 3 minutes, and then raise the heat. When the spinach is wilted and has sunk to the bottom of the saucepan, remove the lid and let the pan liquid evaporate completely. Remove it from the heat and let it cool to lukewarm.

Beat the eggs with the water and salt and pepper to taste. Heat the remaining butter in a skillet and add the eggs. When they are beginning to set, top them with the spinach. Roll up the omelet, slide it onto a hot serving dish, and serve immediately.

FOR 2 PERSONS:

½ pound spinach	5 eggs
6 tablespoons butter	1 tablespoon cold water
Salt	Freshly ground black pepper

OMELETTE AUX TOMATES / *Tomato Omelet*

Put the tomatoes, with salt and pepper to taste, into a saucepan and simmer them, covered, for 5 minutes. Uncover and cook over high heat, stirring constantly, until the pan liquid has evaporated. Remove from the heat and stir in 1 tablespoon of the butter.

Beat the eggs with the water, salt and pepper to taste, and 3 tablespoons of the *sauce tomate*. Make an omelet in the usual manner in the remaining butter and use the cooked tomatoes and 1 tablespoon of the *fines herbes* as a filling. Slide the rolled omelet onto a hot serving dish. Spoon the remaining *sauce tomate* around the omelet and sprinkle with the remaining *fines herbes*. Serve at once.

FOR 2 PERSONS:

2 tomatoes, peeled, seeded and chopped	5 eggs
Salt	1 tablespoon cold water
Freshly ground black pepper	½ cup Sauce Tomate (p. 769)
4 tablespoons butter	2 tablespoons minced Fines Herbes (p. 89)

/ *Asparagus Omelet au Gratin*

OMELETTE GRATINÉE AUX ASPERGES

Beat the eggs with the milk or cream and season with salt and pepper to taste. Butter a shallow baking dish generously and pour in the egg mixture. Cook in a preheated 350° F. oven for about 25 minutes, or until the eggs are just set and the top is golden. Cover with the creamed asparagus tips and serve immediately.

You may also make the omelet in the usual manner and use creamed asparagus as a filling. Or the asparagus may be replaced with creamed spinach, mushrooms, shrimp or lobster; the omelet will then take the name of its stuffing.

FOR 2 PERSONS:

4 eggs	1 tablespoon butter
1 cup milk or light cream	½ recipe Asparagus in Cream
Salt	(p. 552), using only the tips
Freshly ground white pepper	

Omelet aux Fines Herbes au Gratin /
OMELETTE GRATINÉE AUX FINES HERBES

This omelet is made like the Asparagus Omelet au Gratin (p. 331), but instead of asparagus or any of the other stuffings, 3 tablespoons of minced Fines Herbes (p. 89) are beaten right into the eggs. It is served without any garnish.

Bacon Omelet au Gratin / OMELETTE GRATINÉE AU LARD

Cut the bacon into small dice, blanch them in boiling water for 2 minutes, and drain. Heat the butter in a skillet and cook the bacon dice in it until they are transparent. Beat the eggs with the water and a little salt and pepper to taste, pour them over the bacon, and make the omelet in the usual manner. Roll it up when still very soft and slide it onto a buttered baking dish. Coat the omelet with the hot *sauce béchamel*, sprinkle it with the grated cheese and the melted butter, and brown it quickly under the broiler.

FOR 2 PERSONS:

4 slices of lean bacon	Freshly ground black pepper
2 tablespoons butter	½ cup Sauce Béchamel (p. 761)
5 eggs	1 tablespoon grated Swiss cheese
1 tablespoon water	2 tablespoons butter, melted
Salt	

Mussels Omelet / OMELETTE AUX MOULES

Scrub the mussels, put them into a big saucepan with the wine, and cover tightly. Cook over high heat for 5 minutes, shaking the saucepan from time to time. When the mussels are open, drain them and reserve the pan liquid. Remove the mussels from the shells. Strain the pan liquid through a cloth or a very fine sieve.

Reduce the pan liquid over high heat until there are about 3 tablespoons left. Stir in 2 tablespoons of the *sauce béchamel, sauce américaine* or *sauce velouté* for fish. Add the mussels, taste, and season with salt and pepper if necessary.

Beat the eggs with the water and a little salt and pepper. Make the omelet in the usual manner, using the mussels as a filling. Roll it up, slide it onto a buttered baking dish, and coat with the remaining sauce. Sprinkle with the grated cheese and brown quickly under the broiler. Serve immediately.

FOR 2 PERSONS:

18 mussels (about 1 pound)	Salt
½ cup dry white wine	Freshly ground white pepper
½ cup Sauce Béchamel (p. 761), Sauce Américaine (p. 771), or Sauce Velouté for Fish (p. 761)	5 eggs
	1 tablespoon water
	2 tablespoons grated Swiss cheese

OMELETTE SURPRISE GRATINÉE / *Omelet Surprise au Gratin*

Cook the sorrel in 3 tablespoons of the butter in exactly the same manner as the spinach in the recipe for Spinach Omelet (p. 329). When cooked, strain it through a food mill or purée it in a blender.

Beat two of the eggs with 1 teaspoon water, salt and pepper to taste, and the puréed sorrel. Make an omelet with this mixture in 2 tablespoons of the butter, roll it up, and keep it warm on a plate. It is a good idea to set the plate over a pan of simmering water.

Beat the remaining 6 eggs with 1 tablespoon of water, salt and pepper to taste, the cream and the tomato purée. Cook this omelet as usual in 3 tablespoons of the butter in a large skillet. Before rolling it up, stuff it with the little omelet. Slide the large omelet onto a buttered baking dish. Coat it with the hot *sauce Mornay* and sprinkle it with the grated cheese and the melted butter. Brown the omelet quickly under the broiler and serve immediately.

FOR 4 PERSONS:

⅓ **pound sorrel, or spinach**
8 tablespoons butter
Salt
8 eggs
Freshly ground black pepper

2 tablespoons heavy cream
2 tablespoons thick Tomato Purée
  (p. 157)
½ **cup Sauce Mornay (p. 776)**
3 tablespoons grated Swiss cheese
2 tablespoons butter, melted

4

FISH AND SHELLFISH

Poissons et Crustacés

THE COOKING OF FISH

Cuisson des Poissons

Fish Cooked au Bleu | POISSON AU BLEU

Take a live fish and kill it by striking it sharply on the head. Clean it quickly but do not scale it. The protective coating on the scales is essential for *au bleu* fish cooking. Prepare a *court bouillon* for fish (p. 131), using wine, *not* vinegar, in sufficient quantity to cover the fish in a fish cooker, and let it cool to lukewarm. Boil ½ cup of vinegar separately.

Put the fish on the rack in the fish cooker; sprinkle it with the boiling vinegar first and then add the lukewarm *court bouillon.* Bring barely to the boiling point, and then simmer the fish over low heat for about 8 minutes per pound; the *court bouillon* should just barely simmer.

If the fish is to be served cold, let it cool gradually in the *court bouillon,* in a place that is cool but not cold. The fish may be served with one or with several cold sauces: Mayonnaise (p. 782), Mayonnaise Tyrolienne (p. 785), Horseradish (p. 790), etc.

Braised Fish | POISSON BRAISÉ

Take a large whole fish (salmon, a large trout, etc.) or simply a big piece of any fish. You may, with the help of a small sharp knife, insert into the fish strips of truffle, bacon, or carrot, or a few tarragon leaves; and you may bard it, that is, wrap the fish with thin slices of fresh pork fat. Tie well and season lightly with salt and pepper.

Heat butter and oil in a deep skillet and add a generous quantity of vegetables: carrots, onions, celery and turnips, cut into big dice. Cook them over low heat for about 20 minutes; they should be very tender.

Put the fish into a casserole or any ovenproof dish suited to its size, cover it with the vegetables, and add very little water. Cook the fish in a preheated 400° F. oven for about 15 minutes. Baste it frequently with the pan liquid to prevent scorching the vegetables; turn the fish once. Then add sufficient dry white or red wine, or a light Fish Stock (p. 166), to almost cover the fish; also add a sprig of tarragon or thyme. Return the fish to the oven, bring to the boiling point, lower the heat to 350° F., cover, and simmer gently for a total cooking time of about 8 minutes per pound, or until the fish flakes when tested with a fork. Remove it from the oven and keep it hot.

Strain the liquid in which the fish has been cooked and remove the fat with a bulb baster or a spoon. Pour the strained liquid into a heavy saucepan and bring it to the boiling point. Then remove the saucepan from the heat and add, bit by bit, several tablespoons of butter kneaded with minced *fines herbes,* shaking the saucepan to melt the butter after each addition. There should be enough butter to make the sauce thicken slightly. If necessary to help melt the butter, put the saucepan back on very low heat for a moment or two.

/ *Fish Cooked in a Court Bouillon*

POISSON AU COURT-BOUILLON

Clean the fish. Make a *court bouillon* (p. 131) in a fish cooker. The amount of *court bouillon* should be tailored to the size of the fish to be cooked in it; there should be just barely enough to cover the fish. In the event that there is not enough to cover the fish, do not add water, but cover the fish with a cloth or with celery leaves to prevent its drying out.

Once the fish has been placed on the rack in the fish cooker, you can do one of two things. Either bring the *court bouillon* barely to a boiling point and lower the fish on the rack into it, letting it simmer until done; or put the fish on the rack into a cold *court bouillon* and bring it quickly to a boiling point, letting the fish just simmer until cooked. Poach for about 8 minutes to the pound after the *court bouillon* comes to a boil.

POISSONS FRITS / *Fish Fried in Deep Fat*

Clean the fish. If they are small, leave them whole. If they are large and thick, cut them into thick slices. If they are large but flat, you can also cut them into slices, or fry them whole after removing the main bones. Put the fish, raw, of course, into cold salted milk, let it soak for a few minutes, drain it, and coat it thoroughly with flour. Plunge it immediately into fat heated to 375° F. on a frying thermometer. When the fish are golden on all sides, drain them on paper towels, then pile them high on a heated serving dish lined with a napkin. Sprinkle them with salt and minced parsley, and decorate the dish with lemons cut into quarters. Serve immediately and very hot.

POISSONS GRILLÉS / *Broiled Fish*

Take a whole fish that is gutted but not scaled, or a piece of any big fish. Note that red mullet is different from other fish, inasmuch as it is not gutted. Coat the fish with flour, and sprinkle it with melted butter or oil if it is a lean fish. Put the fish on a very hot oiled broiler rack, and broil it for 5 to 15 minutes, depending on the thickness. Turn it frequently and carefully so that it will not burn. When the fish is cooked, put it on a hot serving dish, bone it very quickly and serve it hot, with parsley, lemon slices and melted butter, or with a Sauce Hollandaise (p. 780), served separately in a sauceboat.

POISSONS RÔTIS / *Roast Fish*

First of all, you must have a suitable oven and roasting pan.

Take a large whole fish, or else the center cut of a large thick fish. Season it lightly with salt and pepper. Prepare the fish for roasting by barding it with thin slices of fresh pork fat which you tie with string. Line the pan with carrots and onions cut into thick slices; add a sprig of thyme, a bay leaf and a dash of water. Lay the fish over the vegetables and roast it in a preheated 400° F. oven for about 8 minutes per pound, basting only occasionally. The exact roasting time depends on the thickness of the fish; it must be cooked through and on no account underdone.

Fish Sautéed à la Meunière / CUISSON DITE "MEUNIÈRE"

Clean the fish, season it, soak it in salted cold milk, and coat it with flour.

Heat oil and a little butter in a saucepan. Put in the fish and sauté it over medium heat until golden on both sides. Flat fish, such as sole, when they are skinned on one side only, are put down skin side first. Coat a heated serving dish with a little melted hot butter and serve the fish in this dish, decorated with lemons cut into quarters.

Poached Fish / POISSONS POCHÉS

Clean the fish. Put it into a deep baking dish, season with salt and pepper, and add enough dry white wine to come up to three quarters of the thickness of the fish. Also add a little Fish Stock (p. 166).

Cover the baking dish with a sheet of buttered parchment paper or brown paper. Poach in a 375° F. oven for about 10 minutes per pound. When the fish is cooked, drain off the cooking liquid and reserve it. Bone the fish and put it on a hot serving dish. Reduce the cooking liquid over high heat by half; add a little heavy cream and reduce further. Rectify the sauce's seasoning if necessary, add a little lemon juice, and cover the fish with the sauce. Serve immediately.

SALTWATER FISH

Poissons de Mer

Brill with Bananas / BARBUE AUX BANANES

EDITORS' NOTE: *Brill is a European fish with a white, tender flesh. Gray or lemon sole may be substituted for it.*

Clean the brill, put it with the black-skin side down into a buttered baking dish, and surround it with half of the banana slices.

Sprinkle with the wine and the water. Season lightly with salt and pepper and cover the dish with a sheet of buttered parchment paper. Cook the fish in a preheated 375° F. oven for about 30 minutes (or 10 minutes less, if using gray or lemon sole).

When the fish is half cooked make a deep incision with a sharp knife the whole length of the fish just above the backbone. Return the fish to the oven for 5 minutes. Take it out again and put the remaining banana slices in the pocket. When the fish is fully cooked, remove the liquid with a bulb baster, reduce it over high heat to ½ cup, and pour it back over the fish.

At the last moment, sprinkle the brill with the bread crumbs sautéed in the butter. Serve very hot, preferably in the dish in which the fish was cooked.

FOR 6 PERSONS:

1 brill or other white firm-fleshed fish (4 pounds)	3 tablespoons butter
4 firm bananas, sliced	Salt
1 cup dry white wine	Freshly ground white pepper
2 cups water	1 cup fine dry bread crumbs
	6 tablespoons butter

BARBUE FARCIE / *Stuffed Brill*

Gut the brill and remove the gills and backbone (see p. 79). Certain culinary practicians say, and not without reason, that it is not necessary to bone a brill, that boning it is even an error, since the fish will taste better if cooked wih its bones. This is true, but leaving the bone takes away the pleasure and comfort of eating a boneless fish, and what's more, a fish well seasoned with stuffing. Thus I have chosen to bone the brill.

When the fish is ready, season it inside with salt, pepper and thyme leaves; let it stand for a few minutes.

Make the stuffing: fillet the whitings (reserving the heads and bones), remove the skins, and put two of the fillets through the fine blade of a meat grinder. Reserve the other 2 fillets. Cook the shallots in 3 tablespoons of the butter; add the mushrooms to the shallots, and cook both without a cover until all the liquid in the pan has evaporated; this liquid comes from the mushrooms while they are cooking. Cool the mixture and combine it with the ground whiting fillets.

Season with salt and cayenne, beat in the egg, and blend thoroughly. If you think that this amount of stuffing will not be sufficient for the brill, stretch it with the bread crumbs which you have first moistened with the cream. Beat in 2 tablespoons of the *fines herbes*.

Make a fish stock with the bones of the brill and the bones and heads of the whitings in this manner: sauté the onion, carrot and parsley in 2 tablespoons of the butter; add the wine and the water and simmer the mixture for 30 minutes. Strain it through a fine sieve into another saucepan and reserve.

Choose an ovenproof serving dish, one that is presentable enough to go to the table. Stuffed fish are rather difficult to transfer from a baking to a serving dish, being very fragile, and it is much better to serve the fish from the dish in which it was cooked.

Butter this dish generously, and put in the fish, black-skin side down. Open up the fish and stuff it. Lay the remaining 2 whiting fillets on the stuffing, in order to give the brill its original shape.

Add the fish stock and cover with a sheet of very well-buttered parchment or brown paper. Cook in a preheated 375° F. oven for about 30 minutes. The fish should be basted frequently. It may also be necessary to change the paper which covers it.

At the end of the cooking time, the fish ought to be glazed, that is, the liquid should cling to it like a glaze. Sprinkle the dish generously with the remaining *fines herbes* and serve very hot.

FOR 6 PERSONS:

1 brill or other white firm-fleshed fish (4 pounds)	1 egg
Salt	Optional: 1 cup fresh white bread crumbs
Freshly ground white pepper	Optional: ¼ cup heavy cream
Fresh thyme leaves, or ½ teaspoon dried thyme	4 tablespoons minced Fines Herbes (p. 89)
2 whitings (1 pound each)	1 onion, minced
2 shallots, minced	1 carrot, minced
6 tablespoons butter	3 parsley sprigs, minced
½ pound mushrooms, minced	1 cup dry white wine
Cayenne pepper	2 cups water

Brill en Chaud-Froid | BARBUE EN CHAUD-FROID

Gut the brill and remove the backbone, but leave the fish whole (see p. 79). Season it inside and out with salt and pepper.

Make a stuffing by mixing together the bread crumbs, cream and *fines herbes*, and season lightly with salt and pepper.

Stuff the brill with this stuffing, giving it back its original shape.

Put the fish on a generously buttered baking dish and add enough fish stock to reach halfway up the sides of the fish. Cover with a well-buttered sheet of parchment or brown paper and cook in a preheated 375° F. oven for about 30 minutes.

When the brill is cooked, transfer it carefully to a rack, let it cool, and then chill in the refrigerator.

Prepare the white *chaud-froid* sauce with the liquid in which the brill was cooked. If necessary, add a little more fish stock to it to make 4 cups.

When the *chaud-froid* sauce is about to jell, coat the fish on all sides. If necessary, give it several coatings to have it well covered.

Chill the fish again in the refrigerator. Then you may decorate it, if you wish, with small slices of truffles or tarragon leaves. Then coat the entire fish with the aspic.

Put the fish on a handsome serving dish. Chill it again. At serving time, surround the fish with a ring of chopped aspic.

FOR 6 PERSONS:

1 brill or other white firm-fleshed fish (4 pounds)	4 cups Fish Stock (p. 166)
Salt	1 recipe White Chaud-Froid Sauce (p. 776)
Freshly ground white pepper	Truffles
	Tarragon leaves
For the stuffing:	4 cups Fish Stock for Aspics (p. 167)
2 cups fresh white bread crumbs	
¼ cup Crème Fraîche (p. 666), or heavy cream	
2 tablespoons minced Fines Herbes (p. 89)	

CABILLAUD RÔTI / *Roast Fresh Cod*

Clean and scale the cod. Put it into a baking dish, sprinkle it with the oil and the lemon juice, and season it with salt and pepper. Let the fish marinate in a cool place for 1 hour and then drain it.

Coat the fish with the melted butter.

Roast the fish in a preheated 400° F. oven for about 30 minutes, basting several times as it roasts.

When the fish is done, transfer it to a heated serving dish. Serve very hot, with any desired sauce: plain melted butter, or a sauce made with lemon juice, *fines herbes,* butter and a little heavy cream, just barely melted together.

FOR 4 PERSONS:

1 cod (4 pounds)	**Salt**
4 tablespoons peanut oil	**Freshly ground white pepper**
Juice of 1 lemon	**3 tablespoons butter, melted**

/ *Poached Salt Cod with Sauce Hollandaise*

MORUE POCHÉE SAUCE HOLLANDAISE

Soak the cod in cold water for 12 hours or overnight. Drain it, cut it into pieces, and poach it in boiling water flavored with thyme and bay leaf for 15 minutes. Drain the salt cod and remove the skin and bones. Put it into a heated serving dish and sprinkle the fish with minced parsley. Serve immediately, with a sauceboat of *sauce hollandaise.*

FOR 4 PERSONS:

2 pounds salt cod	**2 tablespoons minced parsley**
1 sprig of fresh thyme, or	**2 cups Sauce Hollandaise**
a pinch of dried thyme	**(p. 780)**
1 bay leaf	

FILETS DE MORUE À LA PROVENÇALE / *Salt Cod Provençale*

Soak the salt cod in cold water for 12 hours or overnight. Drain, dry, and check to remove any bones. Stuff the fillets with the following filling.

On a chopping board mince together the onion, tomatoes, garlic, parsley, capers and anchovy fillets. Put a little of the stuffing on each fillet, roll them up, and tie with string. Put the fish into a baking dish, sprinkle with the oil, and cook in a 350° F. oven for 1 hour, basting frequently with the olive oil.

Put the fish into a hot serving dish and keep it hot. Pour the tomato sauce into the baking dish, and stir over high heat until the tomato sauce is well blended with the pan juices. Pour the sauce over the cod fillets.

FOR 4 PERSONS:

4 fillets of salt cod	**1 garlic clove**
(½ pound each), or 4 small cod	**2 tablespoons minced parsley**
steaks	**1 tablespoon capers**
1 large onion	**4 anchovy fillets, drained**
2 medium-sized tomatoes, peeled,	**½ cup olive oil**
seeded and chopped	**2 cups Sauce Tomate (p. 769)**

Brandade of Salt Cod / BRANDADE DE MORUE

The true *brandade* of salt cod is that of the Camargue and the Rhône; it emphatically does not contain potatoes. One only adds potatoes to a *brandade* to stretch it. And one does not remove the fish's skin for a *brandade;* it makes the fish incomparably smooth.

Soak the salt cod in cold water for 48 hours, and drain it. Brush the fish to get rid of any scales; this precaution is necessary since you are using the skin. Cut the fish into pieces, and poach these in gently boiling water flavored with the thyme, bay leaf and parsley for about 20 minutes, or until the fish can easily be flaked. Drain the fish and let it cool. Flake the fish and remove all the bones.

Put a tablespoon of the olive oil into a large casserole, heat it gently (the oil must not smoke), add the fish, and mix with a wooden spoon or a wooden pestle until the mixture is smooth.

Heat the remaining oil and the milk separately just until they are warm, and keep them nearby. Alternately pour a tablespoon of the oil and of the milk on the fish, beating well after each addition to make a purée with the consistency of fluffy mashed potatoes. Check the seasoning and beat in the garlic.

Pile the *brandade* into a large baking dish and dot it with butter. Cook in a preheated 500° F. oven for 5 minutes, or run under a broiler until the top is golden.

The *brandade* may also be served surrounded with croutons fried in hot butter and oil.

You may also add chopped truffles, preferably those from Vaucluse, to the *brandade* at the same time as you are adding the garlic.

FOR 4 PERSONS:

1 pound salt cod	1 cup milk
3 sprigs of fresh thyme, or	1 garlic clove, mashed
½ teaspoon dried thyme	3 tablespoons butter
1 bay leaf	Optional: 1 cup Croutons
3 parsley sprigs	(p. 62)
1 cup olive oil	Optional: 2 truffles

Note: One can make a *brandade* in a mortar with a pestle, and that too is an excellent method.

Salt Cod à l'Orange / MORUE À L'ORANGE

Soak the salt cod in cold water for 12 hours or overnight. Put it into a casserole with water to cover and the thyme, bay leaves, rosemary and crushed peppercorns. Simmer for about 15 minutes and then remove the cod to a corner of the stove to keep warm.

In a heavy casserole make a blond caramel by melting 1 teaspoon of the sugar and a few drops of water. When the sugar has colored, add the orange and lemon juices. Mix well and keep hot.

Pare the orange zest from two of the oranges, cut it into tiny julienne strips, and blanch them in boiling water with the remaining sugar and a pinch of salt for 10 minutes.

Peel all of the oranges completely, divide them into sections, and remove the seeds.

Drain the salt cod and reserve the water. Remove the skin and all the bones. Flake the fish and put it into the casserole containing the orange and lemon juice. Add the orange zest, drained, and the orange sections. Add a little of the water in which the orange zest was blanched and a little of the liquid in which the fish was cooked so that the flaked fish is very moist. Keep the fish hot, but do not let it boil.

Make a *coulis,* or tomato sauce: heat the olive oil in a casserole and cook the garlic in it over low heat until golden. Add the tomatoes and a little of the liquid in which the fish was cooked. Season with salt and pepper. Stir with a wooden spoon until the sauce is very thick.

Pour the cod on a hot serving dish, arranging the orange sections on top. Surround it with the tomato sauce. Serve immediately.

FOR 4 PERSONS:

2 pounds salt cod
Pinch of dried thyme
2 bay leaves
Pinch of dried rosemary
4 peppercorns, crushed
2 teaspoons sugar
½ cup orange juice
Juice of 1 lemon

4 oranges
Salt
2 tablespoons olive oil
4 garlic cloves, minced
4 tomatoes, peeled, seeded and
chopped
Freshly ground black pepper

PILAW DE MORUE / *Pilaf of Salt Cod*

Soak the salt cod in cold water for 12 hours or overnight. Drain the fish and cut it into pieces. Poach the fish in boiling water flavored with thyme, bay leaf and parsley for 10 minutes. Let it cool to lukewarm, drain, and remove the skin and bones. Reserve the water in which the fish was cooked.

Make a rice pilaf in the usual manner: Mince a big onion, melt 3 tablespoons of the butter in a large casserole, and cook the onion in it until golden. Add the rice and cook, stirring constantly, until it begins to turn golden. Add 1½ cups of the water in which the fish was cooked. Do not season with salt. Add the *bouquet garni,* cover tightly, and cook over very low heat for 20 minutes.

Sauté the salt cod pieces in the remaining butter until golden and sprinkle with parsley.

Spread half of the rice in the bottom of a buttered 8-inch round mold, top the rice with the fish, and cover with the other half of the rice. Bake in a preheated 375° F. oven for 10 minutes. Unmold on a hot serving dish and serve immediately, with paprika sauce on the side.

FOR 4 PERSONS:

1½ pounds salt cod
Pinch of dried thyme
1 bay leaf
2 parsley sprigs
1 large onion

6 tablespoons butter
1 cup uncooked rice
1 Bouquet Garni (p. 46)
3 tablespoons minced parsley
2½ cups Paprika Sauce (p. 769)

Salt Cod with Portets Wine / MORUE AU VIN DE PORTETS

EDITORS' NOTE: *Portets is a commune of the Graves district, near Bordeaux, where much red and white wine is grown.*

Soak the salt cod in cold water for 12 hours or overnight. Drain it and cut it into pieces. Poach the fish in boiling water flavored with thyme and bay leaf for 10 minutes. Let it cool to lukewarm, drain, and remove the skin and bones. Reserve the cooking liquid. Shred the fish while it is still lukewarm.

Heat the oil and 1 tablespoon of the butter in a casserole, add the onions, and cook them until they are golden. Stir in the flour and cook, stirring constantly, for 2 minutes. Stir in the wine and 1 cup of the water in which the cod cooked. Add the *bouquet garni* and the garlic. Simmer over low heat, without a cover, for 20 minutes. Remove the *bouquet garni* and the garlic cloves.

Butter a deep baking dish, put the fish into it, and top it with the sauce. Cook in a preheated 350° F. oven for 10 minutes. Dot the fish with the remaining butter, garnish with the croutons, and serve very hot.

FOR 4 PERSONS:

2 pounds salt cod
1 sprig of fresh thyme, or
   a pinch of dried thyme
1 bay leaf
2 tablespoons olive oil
2 tablespoons butter
2 onions, minced

3 tablespoons flour
2 cups young red Bordeaux wine
1 Bouquet Garni (p. 46)
2 garlic cloves
1 cup Croutons (see p. 62)
   fried in hot oil

Conger Eel en Brochette / CONGRE GRILLÉ EN BROCHETTES

Clean and skin the eel and cut it into 3-inch pieces. Thread them on 4 skewers alternately with lemon slices.

Sprinkle with the oil and marinate for 1 hour, turning them occasionally.

Season the pieces of eel with salt and pepper, dust them with flour, dip them into the beaten eggs, and coat with the bread crumbs. Broil under a high broiler flame on all sides until golden brown.

FOR 4 PERSONS:

1 eel (3 pounds)
4 lemons, sliced
½ cup peanut oil
Salt

Freshly ground black pepper
Flour
2 eggs, beaten
1 cup fine dry bread crumbs

/ *Goujonnettes*

EDITORS' NOTE: *The name comes from* goujon, *a tiny and popular French freshwater fish.*

A julienne of fish is prepared with fillets of any flat fish such as sole, turbot, flounder or brill.

The fish fillets are cut into small strips and seasoned with salt and pepper. They are dipped into milk, dusted with flour, and fried in deep hot fat. After being drained on kitchen paper, the julienne of fish is piled in the shape of pyramid on a hot dish lined with a napkin. The fish are sprinkled with salt and fried parsley and surrounded with lemons cut into quarters.

They are served hot, with any of the mayonnaise sauces, beginning on page 782.

GRATIN DE HADDOCK / *Gratin of Haddock*

Soak the fillets of haddock in the cold milk for 1 hour. Drain the milk into a saucepan, bring it to the boiling point, and add the fish. Lower the heat and poach the fish over low heat for about 12 minutes. The fish must barely simmer and under no circumstances boil. Drain the fish and keep it hot. Reserve the milk.

Melt the butter in a saucepan, stir in the flour, and cook, stirring constantly, over medium heat until golden. Gradually stir in the reserved milk. Cook, stirring all the time, until the sauce is smooth and thickened. Stir in the cream and reduce the sauce by about one third. Check the seasoning. Prepare the rice *à la Créole* and have it very hot.

Butter a baking dish, line it with the creole rice, and put the haddock on the rice. Pour the sauce over the fish. Sprinkle with the grated cheese and dot with the butter. Bake in a 450° F. oven for about 5 minutes, or run under the broiler until the top is brown and bubbly.

FOR 4 PERSONS:

4 haddock fillets (½ pound each)	¼ cup heavy cream
2 cups milk	1 recipe Rice à la Créole (p. 658)
3 tablespoons butter	¼ cup grated Swiss cheese
2 tablespoons flour	3 tablespoons butter

SAINT-PIERRE / *John Dory*

EDITORS' NOTE: *John Dory, in French* Saint-Pierre *or* Dorée, *is a flat, oval, oddly shaped fish with a large spines jutting from its body. The skin is very thick and covered with small scales. On each flank of the fish there is a large blackish mark, called the "thumbmarks of St. Peter," which gives the fish its French name.*

The flesh is white, firm, with an excellent flavor reminiscent of turbot or the best sole, and it is highly prized in France. The John Dory may be used whole, but it is best filleted.

John Dory does not live in American waters. Sole or even porgy may be used as a substitute.

John Dory may be used in all the recipes for sole and turbot. It is also a traditional part of a French bouillabaisse.

Baked John Dory / SAINT-PIERRE AU FOUR

Put the ready-to-cook John Dory fillets into a buttered baking dish and sprinkle with the onion, tomatoes, parsley and wine, and season with salt and pepper. Bake in a preheated 375° F. oven for about 12 minutes.

Transfer the fillets to a hot serving dish and keep warm.

Strain the pan juices into a saucepan, stir in the lemon juice, and reduce over high heat until there are about 4 generous tablespoons of sauce left. Remove from the heat and stir in the butter, bit by bit. Check the seasoning and pour the sauce over the fish. Serve immediately.

FOR 4 PERSONS:

4 John Dory fillets (½ pound each), or sole or porgy fillets
1 onion, minced
2 tomatoes, peeled, seeded and chopped
1 tablespoon minced parsley

½ cup dry white wine
Salt
Freshly ground black pepper
1 tablespoon lemon juice
3 tablespoons butter, at room temperature

Fillets of John Dory Amandine /

FILETS DE SAINT-PIERRE AUX AMANDES

Take 2 deep plates and fill one with milk or beer and the other with flour.

First dip the fish fillets into milk or beer and then coat them with flour. Cook them *à la meunière* (see p. 338) in the combined hot oil and butter. Season with salt and pepper.

Transfer the fillets to a hot serving dish and keep them hot. Add the slivered almonds and the lemon juice to the pan juices and cook them, stirring constantly, until golden. Pour almonds and pan juices over the fish, sprinkle with the parsley, and garnish with the lemon slices.

FOR 2 PERSONS:

Milk or beer
Flour
2 fillets of John Dory (½ pound each), or sole or porgy fillets
2 tablespoons peanut oil
3 tablespoons butter
Salt

Freshly ground black pepper
¼ cup slivered blanched almonds
1 tablespoon lemon juice
2 tablespoons minced parsley
1 lemon, completely peeled and cut into thin slices

/ Fillets of John Dory with Mushrooms

FILETS DE SAINT-PIERRE AUX CHAMPIGNONS

Fillet the fish and remove the skins. Make a very light and very simple *court bouillon* of water, lemon juice and salt, just enough to cover the fish generously. Bring the *court bouillon* barely to the simmering point and poach the fish in it over lowest possible heat for 6 to 10 minutes, depending on the thickness of the fillets. When done the fish should flake at the touch of a fork. Do not overcook.

Remove the fillets from the *court bouillon,* put them on a hot serving dish, and keep warm.

Separate the mushroom caps and stems. Cook them with a tablespoon or so of water, the lemon juice, the butter and a little salt in a saucepan for 10 minutes. Drain the mushrooms and purée the stems in a blender, or press them through a fine sieve. Add 2 or 3 tablespoons of the cucumber sauce to the mushroom purée, blend, and fill each mushroom cap with a little of this mixture. Arrange the mushroom caps on the serving dish around the fish fillets. Serve immediately, with a sauceboat of cucumber sauce.

FOR 4 PERSONS:

4 fillets of John Dory (½ pound each), or sole or porgy fillets	Juice of 1 lemon
	3 tablespoons butter
Court Bouillon, made with water, a little lemon juice and salt	Salt
12 medium-sized mushrooms	2 cups Cucumber Sauce (p. 789)

/ Fillets of John Dory en Croûte

FILETS DE SAINT-PIERRE EN CROÛTE

Because of its simplicity, I have chosen a *pâte brisée* for this dish, but any good-quality pastry dough may be used, such as *brioche* or puff paste. However, you have to bear in mind that these doughs cook in different amounts of time. Puff paste is more delicate and fragile and it cooks in less time than a *brioche*.

For the pastry shell: Prepare 1½ recipes of *pâte brisée* as described on page 713. Let it rest in the refrigerator for 30 minutes before using.

The fish: Cut each fish fillet into 3 or 4 thin slices. Put these into a deep dish and sprinkle them with the oil, the peppercorns and the *fines herbes*. Let stand in a cool place for about 1 hour.

3 fillets of John Dory (½ pound each), or sole or porgy fillets	½ teaspoon peppercorns
1 cup olive oil	2 tablespoons minced Fines Herbes (p. 89)

For the stuffing: Mince the mushrooms. Sauté them in the butter over high heat for 5 or 6 minutes and season them with salt and pepper. Put them into a bowl and let them cool. Then add the *fines herbes* and just enough bread crumbs to bind the stuffing and to make it smooth.

½ **pound mushrooms**	4 **tablespoons minced Fines**
3 **tablespoons butter**	**Herbes (p. 89)**
Salt	½ **cup (approximately) fresh**
Freshly ground black pepper	**white bread crumbs**

For the sauce: Make a concentrated and well-seasoned fish stock with the fish skin, bones and trimmings, the carrots, onion, *bouquet garni,* water, wine, butter and oil. Boil for about 30 minutes and then strain the stock through a very fine sieve into a saucepan. Reduce over high heat to obtain 1 cup of strong stock. Set this stock aside until about 5 minutes before serving. Then stir in the *crème.* Cook for 2 or 3 minutes, remove from the heat, and stir in the butter and the *fines herbes.* Check the seasoning.

Skin, bones and trimmings of	1 **cup Crème Fraîche (p. 666),**
the filleted fish	**or heavy cream**
2 **carrots, sliced**	½ **cup butter, cut into pieces,**
1 **large onion, sliced**	**at room temperature**
1 **Bouquet Garni (p. 46)**	2 **tablespoons minced Fines**
4 **cups water**	**Herbes (p. 89)**
1 **cup dry white wine**	**Salt**
2 **tablespoons butter**	**Freshly ground black pepper**
1 **tablespoon peanut oil**	

To assemble the dish: Roll out the *pâte brisée* into 2 rounds the thickness of ⅛ inch. One round should be about 9 inches in diameter and the other about 2 inches wider. Put the smaller round on a buttered and floured baking sheet. Spread a layer of half the stuffing in the center, about 1 inch from the edge of the pastry. Top with the fish fillets and cover these with the remaining stuffing. Moisten the edge of the pastry with water. Place the second, larger round of *pâte brisée* over the first, covering the filling. Pinch the 2 edges of dough together firmly. Cut a ½-inch opening in the center to allow the steam to escape. Paint the top with the beaten yolk of 1 egg. Cook in a preheated 350° F. oven for about 35 minutes.

This *croûte* is served hot, accompanied by a sauceboat of the hot sauce. It will serve 4 persons generously.

Sailors' Stew of Small John Dory /

MATELOTE DE PETITS SAINT-PIERRE

Cut the fish into crosswise slices and set the better slices aside. Put the other slices and the head into a saucepan with the parsley sprigs, onion, water and wine to make a condensed *court bouillon.* Simmer for 30 minutes and strain it through a fine sieve. Season to taste with salt and pepper.

Using a rather flat wide casserole, cook the shallots and the garlic in the combined hot oil and butter until they are golden. Add the reserved slices of fish, the *court bouillon* and, depending on taste, the white or red wine, as well as the *bouquet garni.* Cook over medium heat for 15 minutes, or until the fish flakes at the touch of a fork.

Make the *beurre manié,* that is, knead together the butter and the flour. Stir it a little at a time into the hot sauce, but do not let the sauce boil. Sprinkle with the fried croutons and minced parsley.

FOR 4 PERSONS:

2 **John Dory (2 pounds
    each), or sole or porgy**
4 **parsley sprigs**
1 **onion, sliced**
2 **cups water**
½ **cup dry white wine**
Salt
Freshly ground black pepper
2 **tablespoons minced shallots**
1 **garlic clove, minced**

2 **tablespoons peanut oil**
3 **tablespoons butter**
2 **cups dry white or dry red wine**
1 **Bouquet Garni (p. 46)**
**Beurre Manié (see p. 41), made
    from 3 tablespoons butter and 3
    tablespoons flour**
1½ **cups Croutons (p. 62),
    fried in butter**
3 **tablespoons minced parsley**

MAQUEREAUX À LA CRÈME / *Mackerel à la Crème*

Clean the mackerel, and wash and dry them both inside and out. Season the cavity with salt and pepper and roll the fish in flour.

Mince the onions and sauté them in the butter in a casserole or skillet large enough to take the fish. Cook the onions until golden, stirring with a wooden spoon, and then put the mackerel in the casserole.

Cover the casserole and simmer for about 10 minutes. Turn the fish and cook them on the other side for another 5 minutes, or until they flake when tested with a fork. Sprinkle with the minced parsley.

At serving time, pour the *crème fraîche* over the mackerel, heat for a minute longer, and check the seasoning. Transfer the fish to a hot serving dish, pour the sauce over them, and serve immediately.

FOR 4 PERSONS:

4 **small mackerel**
Salt
Freshly ground black pepper
Flour
2 **onions**

4 **tablespoons butter**
3 **tablespoons minced parsley**
1 **cup Crème Fraîche (p. 666),
    or heavy cream**

ROUGETS GRILLÉS / *Broiled Red Mullet*

EDITORS' NOTE: *The French are fond of eating red mullet
without gutting it. Its liver is particularly prized. There is a variety of reddish mullet available in the United States, but it is not
commonly found in fish markets, and gray mullet may be substituted.*

Scale the mullets, but do not gut them, and make 2 crosswise incisions about ½ inch deep on each side of the fish.

Dip them into milk or beer, coat them with flour, and brush them with oil, using a sprig of thyme or rosemary as a pastry brush. Broil them on a hot broiler rack under medium heat for 8 to 10 minutes on each side.

While the fish are cooking, brush them repeatedly with a little more oil, using the thyme or rosemary sprig as the pastry brush. Season the fish with salt and serve them as is, or accompanied by a *sauce béarnaise* or a *sauce choron.*

In the fashion of Provence, the red mullet may also be broiled without even being scaled, and without salt. They must be eaten as soon as cooked.

FOR 4 PERSONS:

2 red mullets (2 pounds each)	**Thyme or rosemary sprigs**
Milk or beer	**Salt**
Flour	**1½ cups Sauce Béarnaise (p. 779),**
1 cup olive oil	**or Sauce Choron (p. 780)**

Red Mullet Grilled Over Dry Fennel Stalks /

ROUGETS GRILLÉS AU FENOUIL

Red mullet (or gray mullet) may be grilled in the same manner as Sea Bass Grilled Over Dry Fennel Stalks (p. 352), but being smaller they should cook for a shorter time.

Red Mullet en Papillotes / ROUGETS EN PAPILLOTES

Scale the red mullet, but do not gut it. Broil it as described (p. 349), but cook only until it is barely three-quarters done.

Cut a piece of parchment paper into the shape of a heart large enough to wrap the fish in. Paint one side of the paper with oil. Spread one side of the ham slice with the *duxelles,* lay the broiled mullet on this side, and roll the ham around the fish. Lay the fish on the oiled paper and top it with the broiled tomato slices. Season with salt and pepper. Fold the paper in half, enclosing the fish, and crimp the edges securely. Heat about 1½ inches of oil in a large deep skillet. Put the wrapped fish into the hot oil. When the *papillote,* that is the fish package, begins to puff out, transfer the skillet to a preheated 400° F. oven and cook them for 4 minutes longer.

Serve the fish as it is, *en papillote.*

FOR 1 PERSON:

1 very small red mullet (about	**1 tablespoon Duxelles (p. 602)**
½ pound)	**3 slices of tomato, broiled**
Olive oil	**Salt**
1 slice of cooked ham	**Freshly ground black pepper**

Red Mullet in Port Wine / ROUGETS AU PORTO

Butter a baking dish. Put the shallot and the tomato on the bottom. Scale the red mullet and remove the guts but leave the liver, which is considered a delicacy. Make 2 crosswise incisions on each side of the fish. Season the mullet with salt and pepper and lay it on the shallot and tomato. Add the port wine, cover with a buttered sheet of parchment paper, and cook in a preheated 400° F. oven for about 10 minutes, or until the fish flakes when tested with a fork.

Spoon out the sauce into another saucepan and keep the fish hot in the baking dish. Put the saucepan with the sauce over high heat, reduce it by one fourth, and stir in the cream and the lemon juice. Correct the seasoning. Remove the saucepan from the heat and stir in the butter. Pour the sauce over the fish and sprinkle with parsley.

FOR 1 PERSON:

1 tablespoon butter	¾ cup tawny port
1 large shallot, minced	¼ cup heavy cream
1 large tomato, peeled, seeded and chopped	Juice of ½ lemon
1 red mullet (1 pound)	1 tablespoon butter, at room temperature
Salt	1 tablespoon minced parsley
Freshly ground black pepper	

ROUGETS FARCIS / *Stuffed Red Mullet*

Remove the backbone from the mullets, as described on page 79, and gut them from this opening. Reserve their livers. Season them inside with salt and pepper.

Mash the livers and blend them with the *sauce béchamel*. Put a little of this mixture into each red mullet. Dip the fish into milk and then coat them with flour. Heat the butter and the oil in a frying pan and cook the fish until golden on their uncut sides. Baste the cut sides with butter and oil from the pan and place the frying pan under a high broiler flame until the cut sides are golden. Season with salt and pepper while they are cooking.

Transfer the fish to a hot serving dish, garnish with lemon quarters, and sprinkle with the parsley.

FOR 4 PERSONS:

4 small red mullets (1 pound each)	Flour
Salt	5 tablespoons butter
Freshly ground white pepper	3 tablespoons peanut oil
¾ cup Sauce Béchamel (p. 761)	2 lemons, cut into quarters
Milk	2 tablespoons minced parsley

CIVET DE BAUDROIE / *Stewed Rockfish*

EDITORS' NOTE: *The baudroie is a European fish not native to American waters. The English call it rockfish, frogfish, angler, monk fish and a variety of dogfish names. The several types of American rockfish have little in common with baudroie and, in fact, our rockfish have a flavor similar to crabmeat. However, they are quite suitable in this recipe.*

Cook the onion, carrots and celery in 2 tablespoons of the butter and the oil in a heavy saucepan. Stir frequently to keep the vegetables from browning. Cook until they are golden.

Fillet the rockfish and cut each fillet into 3 pieces. Coat them with flour, put them into a skillet with 4 more tablespoons of the butter, and cook them over high heat until golden on both sides. Flame the fish with the Armagnac and keep it warm.

Sprinkle the vegetables, when they are golden, with 2 tablespoons of flour and stir in the hot wine. Add the *bouquet garni,* the chocolate, the pieces of fish and the lump of sugar; season with salt and pepper. Cover the saucepan and simmer over very low heat for 5 minutes.

Cut the pork fat into dice, parboil in water for 5 minutes, and drain. Sauté the dice gently in 1 tablespoon of butter in a casserole. Add the shallots and the mushrooms and simmer gently for about 5 minutes, stirring frequently.

Take the fish pieces out of the sauce in which they cooked and put them into the mushroom mixture. Strain the sauce in which the fish cooked and add it to the fish. Simmer for a few minutes.

While the fish is simmering, make the croutons by frying fresh white bread cubes in hot butter.

Pour the fish stew into a hot deep serving dish and surround it with the croutons. Serve very hot.

FOR 4 PERSONS:

1 onion, chopped	1 ounce unsweetened baking
2 carrots, chopped	chocolate
1 celery stalk, chopped	1 lump of sugar
7 tablespoons butter	Salt
2 tablespoons peanut oil	Freshly ground black pepper
3 rockfish (1½	¼ pound fresh pork fat, or salt pork
pounds each)	parboiled for 10 minutes
Flour	4 shallots, minced
¼ cup Armagnac	12 small mushrooms, quartered
2 cups dry red wine, heated	1 cup Croutons (p. 62),
1 Bouquet Garni (p. 46)	fried in butter

Sardines Grilled Over Dry Fennel Stalks /

SARDINES GRILLÉES AU FENOUIL

Fresh sardines may be grilled in the same manner as Sea Bass (below) over dried twigs of fennel, but being much smaller they should be grilled for only a very few minutes.

Sea Bass Grilled Over Dry Fennel Stalks /

LOUP GRILLÉ AU FENOUIL

EDITORS' NOTE: *Dry fennel twigs can be bought in France, but they are difficult to find in the United States. Any dry aromatic twigs may be substituted.*

This is a spectacular dish simply because sea bass is a rather insipid fish and has been much overrated. Grilling it over fennel greatly enhances its flavor.

Sea bass should be grilled the moment it comes out of the water, without being scaled, just gutted.

Put a generous layer of dried fennel stalks in a charcoal grill and light them. Keep adding more fennel until there is a good bed. Lay the fish on the grill when the flames subside but the fire is still very hot.

For a sea bass weighing 3 pounds, you should count on 20 minutes of cooking time, about 10 minutes on each side. The fish may also be stuffed with fennel fronds before broiling.

The fish is served with a simple sauce, such as melted butter or a French dressing flavored with *fines herbes*.

The fish may be served in a very eye-catching way. Place the grilled fish on a rack placed over a fireproof dish containing a few ignited fennel stalks. Finally the fish may also be flambéed by sprinkling it with Cognac, marc, anisette or any other spirit.

DAURADE BERCY / *Sea Bream Bercy*

EDITORS' NOTE: *Bream is a European fish, not available in the United States. Sea bass or fluke may be substituted.*

First of all, gut the sea bream, scale it, wash it, and dry it very carefully with a kitchen towel. Make 2 crosswise incisions about ½ inch deep on each side of the fish. Season the cavity with salt, pepper, thyme leaves and crumbled bay leaf, and stuff it with the fennel. Butter a baking dish generously and sprinkle it with the minced shallots. Put the fish on the shallots and add the olive oil and the wine. Cook in a preheated 375° F. oven for about 30 minutes, basting frequently.

When the fish is done, remove it from the oven and dot it with the herb butter; serve it immediately in the dish in which it was cooked.

FOR 4 PERSONS:

1 sea bream (3 pounds)	2 fennel stalks (finocchio)
Salt	2 tablespoons minced shallots
Freshly ground black pepper	¼ cup olive oil
2 thyme sprigs, or ½	1 cup dry white wine
teaspoon dried thyme	¼ cup Fines Herbes Butter
1 bay leaf, crumbled	(p. 792)

DAURADE POCHÉE / *Poached Sea Bream*

Small sea bream are best broiled or cooked *à la meunière* in a frying pan, whereas the larger sea bream should be poached in a *court bouillon*, or roasted in the oven, in the manner described at the beginning of this section.

Poached sea bream can be served hot or cold accompanied by a sauce, such as melted butter, Sauce Hollandaise (p. 780), Mayonnaise (p. 782), Mayonnaise Tyrolienne (p. 785), or Horseradish Sauce I (p. 790).

ALOSE FARCIE À L'OSEILLE / *Shad Stuffed with Sorrel*

Scale and gut the shad. Make several crosswise incisions about ½ inch deep on both sides. If there is roe in the shad, reserve it; if there is milt, discard it. You can make a marvelous omelet with the shad roe.

Wash and dry the fish carefully inside and out. Put it into a deep dish, pour the oil over it, add the thyme, and marinate in a cool place for 30 minutes.

Clean the sorrel, pluck the leaves, and remove the central vein in each leaf. Wash it, drain it, and wring it dry in a kitchen towel. Melt the butter in a saucepan, add the plucked sorrel, and simmer, covered, for about 6 minutes, or until it is soft and limp.

Uncover the pan and raise the heat to evaporate the pan juices. Season lightly with salt, but do not pepper.

Soak the bread crumbs in the milk and squeeze them dry with your hands or in a kitchen towel.

Combine the bread crumbs, the *fines herbes* and the sorrel in a bowl and mix well. Season with salt and a little pepper and nutmeg. Add 1 or 2 eggs to bind the stuffing, as well as a little brandy or Armagnac.

Put the shad in a baking dish. Stuff the fish and sprinkle with salt and pepper. Add the wine and the oil in which it marinated. Bake in a preheated 375° F. oven for about 30 minutes, basting frequently.

Serve in the dish in which the shad was cooked.

Note that there is another method for this recipe: it consists of broiling the shad and serving it on a bed of sorrel purée. The sorrel should first be mixed with minced *fines herbes* and minced shallots sautéed in butter until soft but still white. Then the sorrel may be strained through a fine sieve or puréed in a blender.

FOR 6 PERSONS:

1 shad (3 pounds)	2 tablespoons minced Fines
½ cup olive oil	Herbes (p. 89)
3 sprigs of fresh thyme, or	Freshly ground black pepper
1 teaspoon dried thyme	Grated nutmeg
2 pounds sorrel	1 or 2 eggs
2 tablespoons butter	2 tablespoons brandy or
Salt	Armagnac
2 cups fresh white bread crumbs	1 cup dry white wine
½ cup lukewarm milk	

Lemon Sole / LIMANDE

All the recipes for sole (below) are suitable for lemon sole.

Sole with Pine Nuts / SOLE SAUTÉE AUX PIGNONS

Remove the black skin only of the sole and let the fish marinate in the beer and anisette for about 30 minutes. Drain the fish, dip it into the flour, season it with salt and pepper, and sauté it very quickly in the combined hot oil and butter until golden on both sides.

Add the pine nuts (if necessary, add a little more butter) and cook the fish over low heat for about 7 more minutes.

Put the sole on a hot serving dish and pour the pan juices and pine nuts over it, as well as the lemon juice and parsley. Serve very hot.

FOR 2 PERSONS:

1 sole (2 pounds)
1 cup beer
1 tablespoon anisette
Flour
Salt
Freshly ground black pepper

2 tablespoons olive oil
3 tablespoons butter
¼ cup pine nuts
1 tablespoon lemon juice
1 tablespoon minced parsley

FILETS DE SOLE AUX AMANDES / *Fillets of Sole Amandine*

Proceed as for Fillets of John Dory Amandine (p. 346).

/ *Sole au Vin Blanc*

Remove the black skin from the soles. With a very sharp knife make a deep horizontal incision just above the backbone, going the whole length of the fish. Then run the knife just under the backbone so that it can be loosened. Using a pair of scissors, cut through the backbone but leave it in the fish. This way it is easy to remove the backbone from the cooked fish.

Season the soles inside and out with salt and pepper, dip them into flour and then into the *anglaise* mixture, and coat with the bread crumbs. Shake off any excess bread crumbs. Fry in deep fat heated to 360° F. on a frying thermometer until the fish are golden, and drain on paper towels. Remove the backbone with a small pointed knife, removing as little of the flesh as possible, and fill the backbone cavity with *maître d'hôtel* butter.

Put the fish on a hot serving plate and garnish with lemon slices.

FOR 4 PERSONS:

2 soles (2 pounds each)
Salt
Freshly ground white pepper
Flour
Anglaise mixture made by beating
   together 2 eggs, 2 tablespoons
   peanut oil, 2 tablespoons water,
   ½ teaspoon salt and a little freshly
   ground white pepper

2 cups fine dry bread crumbs
Fat for deep frying
½ cup Maître d'Hôtel Butter
   (p. 794)
2 lemons, sliced

/ *Sole au Vin Blanc*

Gut the sole, remove the skin on both sides, and put the fish into a baking dish. Dot it with 2 tablespoons of butter and sprinkle it with the shallots. Season with salt and pepper and add the wine. Cover the dish with buttered parchment or brown paper.

Cook the fish in a preheated 350° F. oven or on top of the stove for about 20 minutes.

When the fish is cooked, leave it in the dish, but remove the cooking liquid to a saucepan. Reduce it over high heat to about ½ cup. Stir in the *crème* and bring to the boiling point, beating with a wire whip. Correct the seasoning.

Remove from the heat and stir the remaining butter into the sauce, bit by bit.

Remove the backbone of the sole and then reform the fish in its original shape on a hot serving dish. Garnish the sole with the shrimp and coat it with the hot sauce. Serve immediately.

FOR 2 PERSONS:

1 sole (2 pounds)	**1 cup dry white wine**
6 tablespoons butter	**¼ cup Crème Fraîche (p. 666),**
2 tablespoons minced shallots	**or heavy cream**
Salt	**¼ pound cooked small shrimp,**
Freshly ground white pepper	**shelled and deveined**

Fillets of Sole à la Crème / FILETS DE SOLE À LA CRÈME

Peel and fillet the soles; trim the fillets and cut them into uniform shapes and sizes.

Make a fish stock: First, cook the onion and the carrots in the combined hot oil and butter until they are soft. Add the fish heads, bones and trimmings, the *bouquet garni,* water, wine and a little salt. Simmer for 30 minutes and then strain.

Leave the fillets of sole flat, or roll them up, or split them lengthwise and tie them into a knot. Season them lightly with salt and pepper and put them on a generously buttered baking dish. Add the wine, the lemon juice, and enough of the fish stock to not quite cover them. Cover the dish with buttered parchment or brown paper and cook over medium heat, or in a preheated 350° F. oven, for about 10 minutes.

When the fillets are cooked, keep them in their dish, but remove the cooking liquid. Keep the fillets warm. Put the liquid into a saucepan and reduce it over high heat to about ½ cup. Stir in the *crème fraîche* and cook for 5 more minutes, stirring constantly. Correct the seasoning. Remove from the heat and gradually stir in the butter. Here is the trick of the trade: the butter must be neither too hard nor too soft and there must be enough of it to thicken the sauce slightly and to make it very smooth. This technique, in French, is called *monter une sauce,* and it is a *liaison,* that is, a binding.

Put the fillets of sole on a hot serving dish and spoon the sauce over the fish. Serve very hot. If you want, you may also "glaze" this dish, that is, put it for a few seconds into a preheated very hot oven but keep the oven door open. In that case, don't forget to dish up the fish on an ovenproof serving plate. You may also beat 2 egg yolks into the *crème fraîche* before stirring it into the sauce. This will help glaze the dish.

FOR 4 PERSONS:

2 soles (2 pounds each)	**Salt**
For the Fish Stock:	**Freshly ground white pepper**
1 large onion	**1 cup dry white wine**
2 carrots, minced	**Juice of 1 lemon**
1 tablespoon peanut oil	**½ cup Crème Fraîche (p. 666)**
1 tablespoon butter	**4 tablespoons butter, cut into**
Heads, bones and trimmings	**pieces, at room temperature**
from the soles	
1 Bouquet Garni (p. 46)	
4 cups water	
1 cup dry white wine	
Pinch of salt	

Roll up the fillets of sole (as on the left) or tie them into a knot. Put them into a buttered baking dish.

Below: *The ingredients needed for the fish stock: onion, carrot, bouquet garni, salt, pepper, etc.*

FILLETS OF SOLE À LA CRÈME

Fillet of Sole Dieppoise / SOLE DIEPPOISE

The quality of this dish depends a great deal on the quality of the fish stock that you will be using. If it is well seasoned and flavored with a great deal of fish, you'll have no problems about making this dish successfully.

Remove all the skin from the sole, remove the fillets, and trim them. Reserve the bones, skin, trimmings and head. Shell the cooked shrimp and save the shells.

Make the fish stock in the usual manner. Cook the carrots and onion slowly in the combined hot oil and butter until they are very soft, add the sole and shrimp trimmings, the *bouquet garni,* wine and water. Simmer for about 30 minutes and then strain through a very fine sieve.

Make the sauce: Melt the butter, stir in the flour and cook, stirring constantly, until golden. Stir in gradually 2 cups of the fish stock and make a thick smooth sauce. Reduce it slightly and stir in the cream. Reduce again until it is slightly thickened and beat with a wire whisk until the sauce is very smooth. Season lightly with salt and pepper.

Put the soles into a buttered baking dish. Season with salt and pepper. Add the wine and the remaining fish stock. Cover with a sheet of generously buttered parchment or brown paper. Cook in a preheated 350° F. oven for about 12 minutes.

Drain off the pan juices and use them to thin the sauce, if it is necessary. Pour the sauce over the fish and arrange the shrimp in a circle around the soles. Sprinkle with the bread crumbs and brown quickly under the broiler. Serve very hot.

FOR 2 PERSONS:

1 sole (2 pounds)	For the Sauce:
½ pound cooked shrimp	2 tablespoons butter
For the stock:	2 tablespoons flour
2 carrots, minced	2 cups fish stock (above)
1 large onion, minced	1 cup heavy cream
1 tablespoon peanut oil	Salt
2 tablespoons butter	Freshly ground white pepper
Trimmings from the sole	1 cup dry white wine
and the shrimp shells	1 cup fish stock (above)
1 Bouquet Garni (p. 46)	2 tablespoons fine dry
1½ cups dry white wine	bread crumbs
2½ cups water	

Sole Dominique /

The stuffing: grind the fillets of whiting or hake, using the finest blade of the meat grinder. Cook the mushrooms in hot butter in an uncovered skillet for 5 minutes. Mix the ground fish, mushrooms and *sauce Mornay* together in a bowl to make a light stuffing. Set the bowl with the stuffing into another bowl filled with cracked ice, and beat the cream into the stuffing gradually, stirring constantly with a wooden spoon, as if you were making a *mousseline.* Season with salt and pepper. Add the *fines herbes* and the stiffly beaten egg white.

Slit the soles open along the sides and remove the backbone without separating the fillets (see p. 80). Season the cavities lightly with salt and pepper.

Place a little of the stuffing into the cavity of each sole and cover with the split top fillet. Put the stuffed soles into a generously buttered baking dish and add the wine and the fish stock. Sprinkle with the lemon juice and season lightly with salt and pepper. Cover with a sheet of buttered parchment or brown paper and cook in a preheated 350° F. oven for about 20 minutes.

Drain off the pan liquids into another saucepan. Keep the fish hot in the dish in which they were cooked. Reduce the pan liquid to about ½ cup, stir in the *crème fraîche,* bring to the boiling point, remove from the heat, and stir in the butter. Coat the soles with the sauce and sprinkle with parsley.

FOR 4 PERSONS:

For the Stuffing:
1 pound boned whiting or hake
¼ pound mushrooms, minced
3 tablespoons butter
2 tablespoons Sauce Mornay (p. 776)
4 tablespoons Crème Fraîche (p. 666)
Salt
Freshly ground white pepper
4 tablespoons minced Fines Herbes (p. 89)
1 egg white, stiffly beaten

2 soles (2 pounds each)
Salt
Freshly ground white pepper
2 cups dry white wine
2 cups Fish Stock (p. 166)
4 tablespoons lemon juice
1 cup Crème Fraîche (p. 666), or heavy cream
6 tablespoons butter, cut into pieces, at room temperature
½ cup minced parsley

SOLE AU PLAT TANTE MARIE / *Sole Tante Marie*

Remove all the skin from the soles. Choose a large skillet, so that the fish will have plenty of room, and butter it. Put in the fish and add the lemon juice, wine, fish stock and a little salt and pepper. Cover with a buttered sheet of parchment or brown paper and cook over medium heat for about 20 minutes.

Make *duxelles*: Heat the oil and 2 tablespoons of the butter in a small saucepan and add the shallots and the thyme. Cook until the shallots are golden, add the mushrooms, mix thoroughly, and cook for 5 minutes.

When the soles are cooked, drain them and remove the backbones, but leave the head and fillets intact. Put two of the fillets in a buttered large baking dish, spread half of the mushroom mixture over each, and place the other 2 fillets on top. They should resemble the original soles in shape. Keep hot.

Reduce the liquid in which the fish was cooked over high heat to about 1 cup and strain it through a fine sieve. Return it to a saucepan, add the *crème,* and boil until reduced and slightly thickened. Remove the sauce from the heat when it is very smooth, correct the seasoning, and beat in a parsley butter made from the remaining butter kneaded with parsley. Coat the soles with the sauce and sprinkle with the grated cheese. Brown very quickly under the broiler and serve immediately.

FOR 4 PERSONS:

2 soles (2 pounds each)
Juice of ½ lemon
1 cup dry white wine
2 cups Fish Stock (p. 166)
Salt
Freshly ground white pepper
1 tablespoon peanut oil
6 tablespoons butter

2 shallots, minced
Pinch of dried thyme
¼ pound mushrooms, minced
1 cup Crème Fraîche (p. 666), or heavy cream
2 tablespoons minced parsley
2 tablespoons grated Swiss cheese

Sole Stuffed with Foie Gras / SOLE FARCIE AU FOIE GRAS

Follow the directions for Sole Tante Marie (p. 359), but substitute 2 thick slices of *foie gras* for the mushrooms.

Sole Hermitage /

Remove all the skin from the soles and remove the backbones as described on page 80.

Make this stuffing: combine and mix well the bread crumbs, butter, shallots, egg and *fines herbes*. Season with salt and cayenne.

Stuff the soles, forming them again into their original shape. Put them into a buttered large baking dish, with the fish stock and 4 tablespoons of the *crème*. Cover with a buttered sheet of parchment or brown paper and cook in a preheated 350° F. oven for about 20 minutes.

Remove the cooking liquid to a casserole and reduce it to 1 cup. Stir in the remaining *crème,* bring to the boiling point, and cook for 1 minute. Remove from the heat and stir in the butter, shaking the casserole gently until the sauce is slightly thickened.

Coat the fish with the sauce and serve very hot.

FOR 4 PERSONS:

2 soles (2 pounds each)
For the stuffing:
  2 cups fresh white
    bread crumbs
  2 tablespoons butter, at
    room temperature
  2 tablespoons minced
    shallots
  1 egg
  2 tablespoons minced
    Fines Herbes (p. 89)
Salt
Cayenne pepper

2 cups Fish Stock (p. 166)
½ cup Crème Fraîche (p. 666)
6 tablespoons butter, cut into
    pieces, at room temperature

Fillets of Sole Marguery I / FILETS DE SOLE MARGUERY I

Fillet the sole and trim the fillets. Reserve the head, trimmings, bones and skin.

Make a fish stock: In a saucepan combine the fish head, trimmings, bones and skin with the wine, water, onion, carrot, parsley and bay leaf. Simmer for 30 minutes and then strain through a fine sieve.

Put the sole fillets into a buttered deep ovenproof dish, add the fish stock, and season with salt and pepper. Poach over low heat for about 8 minutes.

Drain the fish and put it into a buttered baking dish. Pour the liquid in which the fish were cooked into a saucepan. Reduce it over high heat to about 1 cup. Remove from the heat. Beat in the egg yolks, butter and parsley to make a thick smooth sauce.

Coat the soles with the sauce. Glaze them quickly under the broiler. Arrange the mussels and shrimps in a circle around the sole.

FOR 2 PERSONS:

1 sole (2 pounds)	Freshly ground white pepper
1 cup dry white wine	2 egg yolks
2 cups water	3 tablespoons butter, cut into
1 large onion, sliced	pieces, at room temperature
1 carrot, sliced	2 tablespoons minced parsley
1 parsley sprig	18 mussels (about 1 pound),
½ bay leaf	steamed and shelled
Salt	½ pound cooked shrimp, shelled
	and deveined

FILETS DE SOLE MARGUERY II / *Fillets of Sole Marguery II*

Remove all the skin from the sole and put the fish into a buttered baking dish. Season the fish with salt and pepper. Add the wine and water. Cover with a sheet of buttered parchment or brown paper and poach in a preheated 350° F. oven for about 20 minutes.

Drain the sole and bone it. Reserve the head, bones and trimmings. Arrange the fillets one on top of the other, in more or less the original shape of the fish, on a buttered ovenproof dish.

Pour the liquid in which the fish was cooked into a saucepan and add the fish head, bones and trimmings, as well as the onion and carrot. Simmer for 10 minutes to make a concentrated fish stock.

Steam the scrubbed mussels until they open and shell them, or poach the shucked oysters in their own liquor for 3 minutes.

Cook the mushrooms in 3 tablespoons of the butter with the lemon juice and a pinch of salt over low heat for 10 minutes. Keep the saucepan covered.

Melt the remaining butter and stir in the flour. Stir in 1½ cups of the hot fish stock and cook, stirring vigorously, for 5 minutes. Remove from the heat and beat in the egg yolks mixed with the *crème*. Season with salt, pepper and nutmeg. Return the sauce to very low heat and stir until it thickens slightly, but do not let it boil.

Arrange the mushrooms in a circle around the sole. Make another circle with the mussels or oysters. Coat the fish with sauce and brown quickly under the broiler.

FOR 2 PERSONS:

1 sole (2 pounds)	8 large mushroom caps
Salt	5 tablespoons butter
Freshly ground white pepper	Juice of ½ lemon
1 cup dry white wine	2 tablespoons flour
1 cup water	2 egg yolks, beaten with
1 onion, sliced	½ cup Crème Fraîche (p. 666),
1 carrot, chopped	or heavy cream
12 mussels (about ⅔ pound),	Pinch of grated nutmeg
or oysters	

Note: One can decorate the platter also with little flowers made of butter puff paste, one for each person. At the Marguery these little flowers are baked twice a day.

Sole en Chaud-Froid /

Proceed generally as for Brill en Chaud-Froid (p. 340), except that sole is usually smaller than brill and thus you may use two 2-pound soles, and bake them for only about 20 minutes.

Turbot in Champagne / TURBOT AU CHAMPAGNE

EDITORS' NOTE: *The turbot is a large flat European fish not found in American waters. Its flesh is very delicate and highly prized. There is, perhaps, no perfect substitute for its firm texture and distinctive flavor, but since only very few American fish markets carry it, you may substitute in these recipes the best available sole or even, in a pinch, halibut steaks.*

Clean the turbot, put it into a buttered baking dish, season it with salt and pepper, and add the champagne. Cook, covered, in a preheated 375° F. oven, or on top of the stove, for about 25 minutes. Transfer the fish to a serving dish and keep hot while you make the sauce.

Reduce the pan liquid over high heat to about ¾ cup and stir in the fish *velouté*. Remove from the heat and stir in the butter. Check the seasoning. Coat the fish with this sauce and brown it very quickly under the broiler. Serve immediately.

FOR 4 PERSONS:

1 turbot (2½ pounds)	1 cup thick Sauce Velouté
Salt	for Fish (p. 761)
Freshly ground white pepper	4 tablespoons butter, cut
½ bottle dry champagne	into pieces, at room temperature

Turbot with Sauce Hollandaise /

TURBOT POCHÉ SAUCE HOLLANDAISE

Gut the turbot and remove the black skin. Poach in the *court bouillon* for about 20 minutes. Drain it and put it on a hot serving dish. Garnish with parsley.

Serve immediately with a sauceboat of *sauce hollandaise*.

FOR 4 PERSONS:

1 turbot (2 pounds)	Parsley sprigs
4 cups Court Bouillon	2 cups Sauce Hollandaise
for Fish (p. 131)	(p. 780)

Turbot à la Grecque /

Fillet the turbot, or leave it whole, after gutting it.

Heat the olive and the peanut oils in a casserole and cook the onions and the julienne-cut carrots in it until they are golden. Add the wine, lemon juice, tomatoes, *bouquet garni,* white peppercorns and coriander seeds. Season with salt.

Simmer without a cover over low heat for 20 minutes. If necessary, add a little water, but very little, since the sauce must be concentrated. Put the turbot into a suitable saucepan; pour the hot sauce over it and a small amount of water if necessary, so that the liquid comes halfway up the sides of the fish.

Simmer, covered, for 12 minutes for fillets, or about 20 minutes for a whole fish.

Remove the *bouquet garni,* put the fish and the sauce into a deep serving dish, and cool completely before serving. At serving time, if desired, sprinkle with a tablespoon or so of olive oil.

FOR 4 PERSONS:

1 turbot (2 pounds)	3 tomatoes, peeled
2 tablespoons olive oil	seeded and chopped
2 tablespoons peanut oil	1 Bouquet Garni (p. 46)
24 very tiny white onions	10 white peppercorns
3 carrots, cut into julienne	½ teaspoon coriander seeds
1 cup dry white wine	Salt
Juice of 1 lemon	

/ *Roast Turbot with Spring Vegetables*

TURBOT RÔTI AUX PRIMEURS

When turbots are very large, they may be roasted in the oven; it is even preferable to cook a large turbot this way, when an oven and a baking dish large enough to hold the fish are available. We must remember that turbot range in size up to 32 inches.

However, it is not necessary to have a whole fish. A good thick centerpiece will have all the qualities to make a delectable roast.

Bard the fish with the slices of fresh pork fat and tie with a string. Strew the carrots and onion in the bottom of a baking dish and sprinkle with a little of the melted butter. Lay the fish on top, put the *bouquet garni* on one side, season with salt and pepper, and pour the remaining butter over the fish. Roast in a 400° F. oven for about 50 minutes. The exact time will depend on the thickness of the fish. Baste frequently with the juices.

Generally, the vegetables used for roasting are discarded.

The fish is served on a hot large serving dish, surrounded by attractively arranged glazed vegetables such as carrots, turnips, leeks, onions, *noisette* or boiled potatoes, and it is accompanied by a sauceboat of hot melted butter.

FOR 8 PERSONS:

1 turbot (6 pounds)	Vegetables for garnishing,
4 or more thin sheets of	cooked and glazed:
fresh pork fatback	1 pound baby carrots
3 carrots, chopped	1 pound baby turnips
1 large onion, chopped	10 small leeks, white part only
½ cup melted butter	1 pound tiny onions
1 Bouquet Garni (p. 46)	2 pounds tiny new potatoes
Salt	Sauce: 1½ cups melted butter
Freshly ground black pepper	

Turbot Soufflé /

Gut the turbot and remove the backbone as described on page 80. Season the inside cavity with salt and pepper and fill it with the fish *mousseline* mixed with the *fines herbes*. Pull up the split top fillet to partially cover the filling. Lay the stuffed fish in a generously buttered baking dish.

Make the fish stock in the usual manner, but without using any wine. The wine, a Sauternes preferably, is added to the dish when the fish is being put into the oven to cook.

Add enough fish stock to reach halfway up the sides of the fish and add the wine; cover with a piece of buttered parchment or brown paper. Cook in a preheated 375° F. oven for about 40 minutes.

Transfer the cooked fish to a hot serving dish and keep it hot. Drain the pan liquid into a casserole and reduce it over high heat to about ½ cup. Stir in the *crème fraîche* and bring to the boiling point, beating constantly with a wire whisk to make a smooth sauce.

Remove the sauce from the heat and stir in the lobster or the paprika butter.

Pour the sauce over the fish and serve very hot.

FOR 10 PERSONS:

1 turbot (4 pounds)
Salt
Freshly ground white pepper
2 cups of fish mousseline, made
  from ½ recipe Pike Mousse
  (p. 306)
¼ cup minced Fines Herbes
  (p. 89)
3 cups Fish Stock (p. 166),
  made without wine or vinegar

1 cup Sauternes or white Bordeaux
  wine
For the Sauce:
  2 cups Crème Fraîche
    (p. 666)
  ½ cup Lobster Butter (p. 793),
    or Paprika Butter (p. 794)

Turbot Soufflé Admiral / TURBOT SOUFFLÉ AMIRAL

This is a way of presenting a turbot soufflé which is a little difficult, but most spectacular and sumptuous.

When the fish is cooked, put it on the hot serving dish and, using a soft paint brush, paint it with a coat of Lobster Butter.

Surround the fish with oysters Villeroy, mussels Villeroy, puff-paste *barquettes* filled with tiny cooked shrimp, sliced truffles, cooked mushrooms and lobster medallions.

Serve very hot, with the sauce separate in a sauceboat.

Note: The Lobster Butter may be replaced by Paprika Butter. I prefer to use Lobster Butter.

TURBOT SOUFFLÉ

Gut the turbot and remove the backbone; season the fish with salt and pepper and stuff it with the fish mousseline. *You may also, as shown on the left, sprinkle a little parsley into the cavity of the fish before stuffing it.*

Once the fish is stuffed, close it by pulling up the 2 fillets to cover the stuffing and pressing them down gently to distribute the stuffing well in the interior of the fish.

FOR 10 PERSONS:

All ingredients listed for Turbot Soufflé (p. 364)	40 tiny cooked shrimp
½ cup Lobster Butter (p. 793)	3 truffles, sliced
20 Oysters Villeroy (p. 306)	1 pound mushrooms, cooked in butter
20 Mussels Villeroy (p. 301)	1 large cooked lobster tail, cut into medallions
10 puff-paste barquettes (see p. 40)	

Whiting en Colère / MERLANS FRITS EN COLÈRE

EDITORS' NOTE: *The* en colère *in the title of this dish, meaning enraged, refers to the fish biting their own tails, as if in a rage.*

Clean and gut the fish, but keep their heads on. Soak them in milk or beer to cover for 10 minutes. Drain them, put them on a plate, season them with salt and pepper, and coat them with flour. Put their tails into their mouths, fastening them with the fish's teeth, so that the fish form a circle and won't come undone during frying.

Fry the fish in deep fat heated to 375° F. on a frying thermometer. Turn them over with a slotted spoon to make certain they turn golden on both sides. Drain them on paper towels and serve them in a hot dish lined with a napkin.

Sprinkle the fish with salt and fried parsley. Decorate them with lemon quarters. Serve very hot, with a sauceboat of *sauce tartare.*

FOR 4 PERSONS:

4 whiting (1 pound each)	Fat for deep frying
2 cups milk or beer	Fried Parsley (p. 130)
Salt	2 lemons, cut into quarters
Freshly ground black pepper	2 cups Sauce Tartare (p. 785)
Flour	

Fillets of Whiting à la Grecque /
FILETS DE MERLAN À LA GRECQUE

These are prepared in the same manner as fillets of John Dory à la Grecque (p. 241).

Whiting Hermitage / MERLANS HERMITAGE

Prepare in the same manner as Sole Hermitage (p. 360), substituting two 2-pound whiting for the 2 soles.

Stuffed Whiting / MERLANS FARCIS

Prepare in the same manner as Omble Chevalier Willi Prager (p. 373), substituting a 2-pound whiting for the *omble chevalier.*

/ *Fillets of Whiting with Mayonnaise Tyrolienne*

FILETS DE MERLAN PANÉS SAUCE TYROLIENNE

Using 2 soup plates, put the flour into one and make the *anglaise* (see p. 38) in the other by beating together the egg, oil, water and a little salt and pepper.

Coat the fish fillets, freed of their skins and any bones, first with the flour and then with the egg mixture. Drop them immediately into deep fat heated to 375° F. on a frying thermometer and cook until golden on both sides; or you may sauté them in very hot oil and butter in a skillet.

Dish up the fish on a hot serving dish, sprinkled with fried parsley. Serve immediately, with a sauceboat of *mayonnaise tyrolienne* on the side.

FOR 4 PERSONS:

Flour | 8 whiting fillets
For the Anglaise: | (⅓ pound each)
  1 egg | Fat for deep frying, or ½
  1 tablespoon peanut oil | cup butter combined with ¼ cup
  1 tablespoon water | olive oil
Salt | Fried Parsley (p. 130)
Freshly ground white pepper | 2 cups Mayonnaise Tyrolienne
 | (p. 785)

FRESHWATER FISH

Poissons d'Eau Douce

/ *Stuffed Carp the Old-Fashioned Way*

CARPE FARCIE À L'ANCIENNE

Choose a live carp and, if possible, one with soft roe. If you have to kill it yourself, you can stun it or plunge it into boiling water, though the best way is to take an icepick or a fine-bladed knife and stick it into the rounded part of the fish's head, the part called *rocher* in French. Gut and wash the carp, and remove the skin on one side only. If you find these operations too tedious, ask your fish dealer to do them for you.

Now lard the carp with the strips of salt pork on the skinned side; the pork strips should be chilled, for easier insertion. Then, lard it with the truffle strips.

Make the following stuffing: In a large bowl, combine the bread crumbs, previously soaked in the lukewarm milk and squeezed dry, the ground whiting or pike, one of the eggs and the carp's roe, if any, blanched and cut into small pieces. (You may, however, want to save the roe for an omelet.) To blanch the roes, soak them first in a solution of water and vinegar (about 1 tablespoon of vinegar for 1 quart of water) for 2 to 3 minutes and then put them into a saucepan with cold water and lemon juice (about 1 tablespoon lemon juice for 1 quart water). Bring to the boiling point and immediately remove the roes, draining them in a strainer.

Season the stuffing with a little salt, pepper and nutmeg and the brandy. Press it through a fine sieve if you don't have a blender, and mix it energetically. Beat in the soft butter, the yolks of the remaining 2 eggs and the heavy cream, beating constantly. It is best to work this stuffing over a bowl filled with cracked ice, as in the making of a fish *mousseline* (see p. 314); it should, in fact, have the consistency of a *mousseline*. If it seems too thick, add a little more cream.

Fill the carp's cavity with this stuffing. Lay the carp, skin side up (the side that is not larded) on a triple layer of cheesecloth. Wrap it so that the edges of the cloth overlap on the carp. If the carp is properly wrapped, it won't be necessary to tie it; but if you have any doubts in the matter, tie it a few times with thread, but loosely, so the stuffing will puff during cooking.

Oil a baking dish the size of the fish, line it with the remaining salt-pork strips, if any, and the onion slices, and dot it with the 4 tablespoons of butter. Lay the fish in the baking dish, skin side down—that is, the side where the cheesecloth ends overlap should face the bottom of the baking dish. This way of wrapping and placing the carp will make it easy to remove the cloth when the fish is done, leaving the larded and truffled side up.

Cook the fish in a preheated 400° F. oven for 10 minutes. Then add the water, the wine and the *bouquet garni;* season lightly with a little salt and pepper. Reduce the oven heat to 300° F. and bake the fish for about 1 hour, or until it yields to the touch of a finger. Baste frequently and check the pan liquid, allowing for evaporation; if necessary, add a little more wine and water. The liquid should come halfway up the sides of the fish.

Strain the pan liquid into a saucepan. Keep the fish in the dish in which it was cooked and keep it hot. Reduce the pan liquid over high heat to about 1½ cups.

Now make the sauce: Melt the butter, stir in the flour, and cook, stirring constantly, until just golden. Do not brown. Stir in the hot reduced liquid and cook, stirring all the time, for 3 to 4 minutes longer. Remove from the heat and stir in the beaten egg yolks and the lemon juice.

Remove the cheesecloth from the fish, coat it with the sauce, and brown it very quickly under the broiler. Serve immediately.

If you want to serve this dish cold, do not make any sauce. Let the fish cool in the cheesecloth, remove the cloth, and place the fish on a rack. Glaze the carp with the liquid in which it was cooked. The carp is a rather gelatinous fish, especially when cooked in this manner.

There is another version of Stuffed Carp the Old-Fashioned Way. I won't give you the details of how to make it because it is practically impossible to do this in one's own home. In this version, the fish must be completely boned, without damaging the skin, and then stuffed back to its original shape with a *quenelles* stuffing and pieces of carp flesh sautéed in butter.

Fish Grilled over Vine Cuttings

Poissons Grillés aux Braises de Vignottes

Fish Grilled over Vine Cuttings

Poissons Grillés aux Braises de Vignottes

SCALE AND GUT the fish.

Make a series of parallel incisions on both sides of the fish. Season the fish with salt and pepper, cover them with the bay leaves, sprinkle with the olive oil, and let them marinate in a cool place for 1 hour before grilling.

Prepare a very hot fire in a charcoal grill with a generous quantity of vine twigs. Before placing the fish on the grill, the fire should be on the wane, beginning to go to ash and with no flame, but still very hot.

Remove the bay leaves and lay the fish on the grill. After 3 minutes, turn the fish and grill them on the other side for 3 minutes more. Turn the fish over again carefully, using 2 forks; sprinkle them with a little marinade and grill them for another 3 minutes on each side.

If, during the grilling, the oil on the fish drips into the fire and produces a flame, move the fish quickly around on the grill so that they will not blacken. Test the fish for doneness with a fork; they should flake easily.

Put the fish on a hot serving dish and serve any desired well-seasoned sauce with it, or lay the fish on a bed of tomatoes stewed with onions and seasoned with salt and pepper. Garnish with lemon slices.

For 1 person:

1 or 2 small fish (brook trout, red mullet, etc.)
Salt
Freshly ground black pepper
6 or 7 bay leaves
¼ cup olive oil
Lemon slices

Note: Of course it is possible to grill the fish over a conventional fire, and today it is not easy to find the cuttings from vinestocks; however, they do give to the dish a very unusual flavor and bouquet.

Whiting Baked in the Shape of Dolphins

Merlans Pochés en Dauphins

Whiting Baked in the Shape of Dolphins

BONE THE WHITING through the back (see p. 79), and season the cavities with salt and pepper.

Combine the bread crumbs, the ground whiting and the *crème fraîche* in a bowl. Season with salt and pepper, blend well, and beat in one of the egg whites. The mixture should be quite thick. Stuff the cavity of each fish with some of the mixture and sew it closed.

Score 4 tracks in the slice of bread, beginning at each corner and going to within an inch of the center; the tracks should be about ½ inch deep and about 2 inches wide. Sauté the slice in the oil and butter until golden on both sides; drain on kitchen paper. Make a paste with the flour and the remaining egg white. Warm an ovenproof platter which is about 10 inches square. Spread the bottom with the paste and glue the bread on it to form a base.

Put each of the stuffed whiting into one of the tracks in the bread *"en dauphin,"* that is, with the tail in the air and the head at the corner of the bread slice. Fasten the tails securely together with food picks or skewers so that the fish will stay in position as they bake. Sprinkle the fish with half of the melted butter.

Bake in a preheated 375° F. oven for about 15 minutes. Baste frequently with the remaining melted butter. A few minutes before removing the fish from the oven, sprinkle them with the lemon juice. Cool and then chill.

Chill the aspic stock in a shallow dish; when jellied, chop it. Fill the spaces between the fish with the chopped aspic. The platter may be decorated with an *attelet* (a decorative skewer) stuck between the tails and anchored in the bread slice. Or you may fasten a bunch of greens to the top of the tails, using a skewer, and decorate the greens with small pieces of raw carrots held by food picks or skewers.

For 4 persons:

4 whiting (1 pound each)	1 slice of firm white
Salt	crustless bread, 1 inch
Freshly ground black	thick and 8 inches square
pepper	3 tablespoons peanut oil
1 cup fresh white bread	3 tablespoons butter
crumbs	2 tablespoons flour
1 pound whiting fillets,	½ cup butter, melted
finely ground	Juice of ½ lemon
2 tablespoons Crème Fraîche	2 cups Fish Stock for
(p. 666)	Aspics (p. 167), clarified
2 egg whites	

Fish Pâté Guillaume Tirel

Pâté de Poisson à la Guillaume Tirel

Fish Pâté Guillaume Tirel

GRIND THE POUND of fish, using the fine blade of a meat grinder. Work in two of the egg whites and season lightly with salt and cayenne. Force the mixture through a very fine sieve into a bowl. Set the bowl in another one filled with cracked ice in order to keep the fish mixture very cold. Gradually beat in the heavy cream, reserving 2 tablespoons of the cream. When this first stuffing, which may be called a *mousseline,* is ready, make the other one. Put the bread crumbs into another bowl, and blend them into a smooth paste with the whole eggs, the tarragon, parsley, chives and a little salt and pepper. Whip the reserved 2 tablespoons of heavy cream and stir into the mixture.

Beat the remaining 2 egg whites lightly and reserve them.

Season the 4 fillets with salt and pepper.

Line a large (about 10-cup) rectangular loaf pan or pâté mold first with fennel fronds and then with sheets of fresh pork fatback; the pork fat should hang over the long sides of the mold. Spread half of the first stuffing, or *mousseline,* over the pork fat. Brush two of the John Dory, or sole, fillets with beaten egg white and lay them on the *mousseline.* Spread about half of the second stuffing over the fillets and top it with the asparagus tips dipped into more beaten egg white. Now spread the remaining half of the second stuffing over the asparagus tips, coat it with more beaten egg white, lay the remaining 2 fillets on it, and paint these too with beaten egg white. Now spread the remaining *mousseline* over the fillets and cover the top with the overlapping slices of the pork fat. Make sure that the pâté is well covered by the pork fat.

Set the mold or loaf pan into a baking dish containing 2 inches of water and cook in a preheated 350° F. oven for about 1½ hours.

This pâté may be eaten warm or cold.

For 12 persons:

1 pound raw fish (hake,
    John Dory, sole or pike)
4 egg whites
Salt
Cayenne pepper
2 cups heavy cream
4 cups fresh white bread
    crumbs
2 whole eggs
2 tablespoons minced fresh
    tarragon

4 tablespoons minced
    parsley
1 tablespoon minced chives
Freshly ground white
    pepper
4 raw ⅓-pound fillets of
    John Dory or gray sole
Fennel fronds
Large thin slices of fresh
    pork fatback
8 asparagus tips

Stuffed Salmon Brillat-Savarin

Saumon Farci Brillat-Savarin

Stuffed Salmon Brillat-Savarin

BONE THE SALMON as described on page 80.

Make the stuffing: in a bowl, combine the whiting, the chopped mushrooms cooked in butter, and the *sauce béchamel* made thick with the egg yolk. Set the bowl in a larger bowl filled with crushed ice, and gradually beat ½ cup of the *crème fraîche* into the mixture. Add 2 tablespoons of the *fines herbes* and fold in the stiffly beaten egg white. Season with salt and pepper.

Stuff the salmon with this mixture and lay it in a generously buttered deep baking dish. Add equal quantities of dry white wine and fish stock to reach halfway up the fish. Cover with a sheet of buttered parchment or brown paper. Cook in a preheated 375° F. oven for about 45 minutes or longer, depending on the thickness of the fish. Put the salmon on a large serving platter, let it cool, and then chill in the refrigerator.

Reduce the cooking liquid to about 2 cups. Season it with the lemon juice, a little cayenne and the remaining *fines herbes*. Let the mixture cool completely and then blend it with the remaining cup of *crème fraîche,* whipped. Serve the sauce on the side, in a sauceboat.

Decorate the platter with a few of the chilled cooked asparagus tips and a generous amount of chopped aspic. Prepare little aspic molds of peeled and seeded tomatoes and asparagus tips in small custard cups filled with liquid aspic, chilled, and then unmolded on the platter.

For 6 persons:

1 whole salmon (6 pounds)
¼ pound ground whiting
6 mushrooms, chopped and cooked in 1 tablespoon butter until tender
¼ cup Sauce Béchamel (p. 761), thickened with 1 egg yolk
1½ cups Crème Fraîche (p. 666), or heavy cream
5 tablespoons minced Fines Herbes (p. 89)
1 egg white, stiffly beaten

Salt
Freshly ground white pepper
3 or more cups dry white wine
3 or more cups Fish Stock (p. 166)
Juice of 1 lemon
Cayenne
36 asparagus tips, cooked
8 cups Fish Stock for Aspics (p. 167)
6 small tomatoes

Coulibiac of Salmon Colette
Coulibiac de Saumon Colette

Coulibiac of Salmon Colette

LIGHTLY SPRINKLE THE fillets of salmon with flour. Top each with a little of the following mixture: mix together the diced lobster, the *sauce Mornay* and the chives. Fold the salmon fillets over to contain the stuffing, secure them with food picks, and sauté them in 3 tablespoons of the butter over medium heat for about 10 minutes, turning frequently. Remove the picks and set aside fillets and pan juices.

Make a pilaf with the rice and the fish stock. You'll need very little rice, about a dessert spoon of uncooked rice per person. Put rice and stock in a saucepan with the *bouquet garni,* the salt and a little pepper. Cover the pan very tightly and bring to a boil. Reduce the heat to very low and cook for 20 minutes, or until the rice is tender.

Add the salmon pan juices to the rice after it has cooled slightly. Add the minced hard-cooked egg as well.

Line a 6-cup buttered baking dish or a pie pan with a thin layer of half of the *brioche* dough, letting it hang over the edge of the pan by ½ inch. Brush the dough with a little melted butter and top it with a sheet of buttered baking parchment or aluminum foil. Fill it with dried beans or raw rice to keep it down while baking. Bake the *brioche* dough and unmold it to see if it is firm enough. If necessary, put it upside down on a baking sheet and return it to the oven to let it turn golden. Butter the baking dish again, replace the *brioche* shell, and arrange the salmon cutlets in it. Fill with the rice mixture and drizzle the remaining 3 tablespoons of melted butter mixed with 2 tablespoons of fish stock over the pan's contents to keep them moist.

Cover with a round of the remaining *brioche* pastry; it should completely hide the filling. Set the dish in a warm place for about 30 minutes to allow the *brioche* dough to rise. Paint the cover with beaten egg yolk and decorate it with little gashes made with a sharp knife. Make a small round hole in the middle and insert in it a small funnel made by rolling a piece of aluminum foil over a pencil. Bake in a preheated 400° F. oven for about 25 minutes, or until the *brioche* top is baked through. Unmold the *coulibiac* or, if this is too difficult, serve it in the dish in which it was baked. In this case, polish up the dish with a cloth dipped into a little vinegar, taking care not to touch the pastry. Serve with horseradish sauce or with melted butter and lemon juice.

For 4 persons:

4 fillets of salmon (¼ pound each)

Flour

¼ pound raw lobster meat, cut into small dice

¼ cup Sauce Mornay (p. 776)

1 tablespoon minced chives

6 tablespoons butter

¼ cup uncooked rice

¾ cup Fish Stock (p. 166)

1 Bouquet Garni (p. 46)

Pinch of salt

Freshly ground white pepper

1 hard-cooked egg, minced

½ recipe Brioche dough (p. 695), risen twice

2 tablespoons Fish Stock (p. 166)

1 egg yolk

1 recipe Horseradish Sauce II (p. 791), or ½ cup melted butter and juice of 2 lemons

Sole en Chaud-Froid Curnonsky

Sole en Chaud-Froid Curnonsky

CHOOSE A FINE firm sole. Poach it in a fish stock made with heads and bones of saltwater fish for about 20 minutes. Drain the fish, reserving the stock, and fillet the fish. Strain the reserved stock and reduce it to about 3 cups. Test to see if it will jell (see p. 166), and add unflavored gelatin if necessary. Clarify the stock (see p. 53), pour it into a shallow pan, and chill until firm.

Put one fish fillet on a serving platter and spread it with the mushroom *duxelles;* top with the other fillet, like a sandwich. Chill, then coat the fish with a generous amount of white *chaud-froid* sauce. Decorate the top with truffles cut into the shapes of diamonds and crescents, and surround the fish with the aspic chopped into fine cubes. Chill again until serving time.

For 2 persons:

1 sole (2 pounds)
4 cups Fish Stock (p. 166)
1 cup Duxelles (p. 602)
2 cups White Chaud-Froid Sauce (p. 776)
2 truffles

Smoked Haddock à l'Anglaise

Haddock à l'Anglaise

Smoked Haddock à l'Anglaise

Haddock à l'Anglaise

PUT THE FISH into a greased casserole and add sufficient milk and water to cover the fillets completely. Bring just to the boiling point. Lower the heat to the lowest possible and simmer the haddock for 10 to 15 minutes. The fish must be poached, not boiled. There is no need to season with salt since the fish is sufficiently salty.

While the haddock is poaching, prepare the butter sauce. Put the lemon juice and a small spoonful of the poaching liquid into a casserole and heat them over very low heat. Stir in the butter, a little at a time, beating thoroughly after each addition.

Remove the haddock with a slotted spoon and drain it on kitchen toweling.

Place it on a serving dish and surround it with the boiled potatoes. Serve the butter sauce on the side in a sauceboat. You may also garnish the plate with lemon quarters and parsley sprigs.

The usual practice is to poach 1 egg for each person and add it to the dish at serving time.

For 4 persons:

2 pounds smoked haddock fillets
2 cups milk (approximately)
2 cups water (approximately)
Juice of ½ lemon
**¾ cup butter, softened to room temperature and cut
   into small pieces**
8 medium-sized potatoes, boiled

Zarzuela

Zarzuela

WASH THE CODFISH, mullet and eel and cut them into thick pieces.

Shell the cooked crayfish and set them aside in a dish. Scrub the mussels and cook them in a tightly covered pot over high heat until their shells open. Remove the mussels from the shells and add them to the bowl of crayfish. Reserve all of the mussel liquid in a separate bowl. Wash the squid and cut them into pieces.

Heat half of the oil and all of the butter in a large skillet and sauté the onions in it until they are soft. Add the pieces of eel and squid, the tomato purée, the wine and the rum. Bring to a boil and cook over high heat for about 10 minutes. Pour the contents of the skillet into a large casserole over low heat. Add half of the reserved mussel liquid and mix well.

Add the remaining oil to the skillet and cook the pieces of codfish and mullet in it for about 3 minutes, or just until their flesh begins to firm. Season them with salt and pepper and then add them to the casserole. Simmer, covered, over low heat for 20 minutes, but avoid actual boiling.

Mix together the garlic, bread crumbs, saffron and half of the parsley in a bowl. Add the remaining mussel liquid and mix until smooth. Add this mixture and the almonds to the casserole. Blend them in carefully, so as not to break the pieces of fish. Finally add the mussels and the crayfish. Cook for 2 minutes longer and correct the seasoning.

Serve directly from the casserole or in a deep hot serving dish. Sprinkle with the remaining parsley and decorate with the triangles of fried bread.

For 6 persons:

1 pound codfish
1 pound freshwater mullet,
    or any similar fish
¾ pound eel
6 large crayfish, cooked
1 pound mussels
4 small squid
6 tablespoons olive oil
2 tablespoons butter
2 onions, thinly sliced
¾ cup Tomato Purée
    (p. 157)
4 cups dry white wine

1 tablespoon rum
Salt
Freshly ground black
    pepper
1 garlic clove, minced
½ cup fresh white bread
    crumbs
⅛ teaspoon ground saffron
½ cup minced parsley
12 blanched almonds
12 triangles of white bread,
    fried in hot oil
    until golden

FOR 10 PERSONS:

1 live carp (4 pounds),
   preferably with roe
¼ pound salt pork, blanched
   and cut into strips ¼ by 4 inches
4 truffles, cut into julienne strips
3 cups fresh white bread crumbs
1 cup lukewarm milk
⅓ pound whiting or
   pike fillets, finely ground
3 eggs
Salt
Freshly ground white pepper
Grated nutmeg
¼ cup brandy
½ cup butter, at room temperature

2 tablespoons (or more)
   heavy cream
Oil
2 onions, thinly sliced
4 tablespoons butter,
   cut into small pieces
2 cups water
2 cups dry white wine
1 Bouquet Garni (p. 46)
For the Sauce:
   1½ tablespoons butter
   1½ tablespoons flour
   1½ cups reduced liquid in
      which the fish was cooked
   2 egg yolks
   Juice of ½ lemon

CARPE À LA JUIVE / *Carp in the Jewish Manner*

Kill the fish, as described in the preceding recipe. Gut it, scale it, and cut it into 2-inch slices. If all this seems too difficult, get your fish dealer to do it for you.

Heat ½ cup of the olive oil in a large deep skillet or saucepan and cook the onions and shallots in it until they are soft. Before they start turning golden, sprinkle them with the flour, mix well, and cook for 30 seconds longer. Add the wine and about 2 cups of water. Stir for a minute and add the carp pieces; the liquid should cover the fish. Season with salt and pepper; add the garlic cloves and the *bouquet garni*. Bring to the boiling point, cover the skillet or saucepan, and simmer over lowest possible heat for about 20 minutes.

When the fish is flaky to the touch of a fork, remove the pieces from the liquid and put them on an oblong serving dish in the shape of the original fish; let them cool.

Strain the pan liquid into a saucepan, reduce it over high heat by two thirds and, off the heat, beat in the remaining oil, stirring constantly. Cool the sauce and then coat the fish with it. Chill in the refrigerator until the sauce has jelled. At serving time, sprinkle with parsley.

FOR 6 PERSONS:

1 live carp (3 pounds)
3 cups olive oil
2 onions, minced
5 shallots, minced
4 tablespoons flour
2 cups dry white wine

Salt
Freshly ground black pepper
5 garlic cloves, crushed
1 Bouquet Garni (p. 46)
¼ cup minced parsley

/ *Carp in the Jewish Manner Orientale*

CARPE À LA JUIVE À L'ORIENTALE

Proceed as in Carp in the Jewish Manner (above), but add 1 teaspoon of ground saffron to the sauce while it is still hot.

Carp in the Jewish Manner with Parsley /
CARPE À LA JUIVE AU PERSIL

Proceed as in Carp in the Jewish Manner (above), but add ½ cup minced parsley at the same time as you are adding the *bouquet garni.*

Carp in the Jewish Manner with Raisins /
CARPE À LA JUIVE AUX RAISINS

Proceed as in Carp in the Jewish Manner (above), but add to the sauce while it is still hot 1 tablespoon of sugar, 2 tablespoons of wine vinegar, ½ cup seedless raisins and ½ cup dried currants. Both raisins and currants should be plumped in lukewarm water for 10 minutes and drained before being used.

Broiled Eel Tartare / ANGUILLES GRILLÉES TARTARE

Cut the eel into 3-inch pieces. Do not skin the eel, but discard the head. Score either side of each piece lightly with a sharp knife and broil, turning the pieces frequently, for 7 or 8 minutes.

Put the broiled eel into a serving dish. Serve very hot, with *sauce tartare.*

FOR 2 PERSONS:

1 pound eel   1 cup Sauce Tartare (p. 785)

Eel Fricassee / FRICASSÉE D'ANGUILLES

Cook the garlic and the shallots in the combined hot oil and butter in a casserole until they are golden; add the eel pieces and cook for 3 to 4 minutes. When the fish is golden on all sides, season it with salt and pepper and add the *bouquet garni,* the clove, wine and water. Bring to the boiling point, cover the casserole, and simmer over low heat for 20 minutes. This is the amount of time necessary to cook young eels, but if they are not tender by that time, cook them a little longer.

Make a *liaison:* beat together the egg yolks and the *crème fraîche.*

When the eel is cooked, stir a few spoonfuls of the liquid into the egg mixture and then add the egg mixture to the casserole. Blend thoroughly and stir over low heat until slightly thickened, but do not allow it to boil. Check the seasoning.

The fricassee is best served in a large heated bowl. Decorate it with butter-fried croutons.

A garnish of cooked vegetables is very well suited to this fricassee: tiny onions, carrots, celery, the white part of leeks, finocchio or fennel and potatoes. The vegetables should be cut into suitable pieces and cooked until barely tender. They are added to the fricassee when it is three-quarters done, so that the flavors will have nicely blended by the time the eel is fully cooked. If some of the vegetables are not suited to more cooking (potatoes, for instance), add them just a minute or so before serving.

Here is another garnish. Take twice as many mushroom caps as there are eel slices. Sauté them in butter over high heat until they have turned golden, season lightly with salt and pepper, and add the mushrooms to the eel fricassee when it is three-quarters done.

Add the butter-fried croutons at serving time.

FOR 4 PERSONS:

1 garlic clove, minced
2 shallots, minced
2 tablespoons olive oil
2 tablespoons butter
2 pounds eel, skinned, cleaned, and cut into 2-inch pieces
Salt
Freshly ground black pepper

1 Bouquet Garni (p. 46)
1 whole clove
1 cup dry white wine
1 cup water
4 egg yolks
½ cup Crème Fraîche (p. 666)
Croutons (p. 62), fried in butter

ANGUILLES AU VERT / *Eel au Vert*

EDITORS' NOTE: *Fresh herbs are essential for the correct flavor of this outstanding dish. It may be served either hot or cold.*

Skin and gut the eels and cut them into medium slices, or ask your fish dealer to do this for you.

Heat the oil and the butter in a large casserole. Season the eel slices with salt and pepper and cook them over high heat until they are golden on all sides, turning them over with a wooden spoon.

Add the shallots and cook, stirring constantly, for 2 or 3 minutes longer. Add the thyme, and cut the bay leaves into fine strips with scissors, right into the casserole.

Lower the heat and add the sorrel, parsley, chervil, tarragon and sage. All the herbs must be finely minced. Cook, stirring constantly with a wooden spoon, until the herbs are soft and tender.

When the herb mixture is well blended, add the anisette, the burnet or vermouth, the lemon juice, fish stock and wine. Bring to the boiling point, cover the casserole, and cook for about 15 minutes, or until the eel slices are tender.

The sauce should be thick; if necessary, uncover the casserole for the last few minutes of the cooking time, and cook over high heat to reduce it.

Beat together in a bowl the cornstarch, the egg yolks and the *crème fraîche*.

When the fish is tender, cool it somewhat. Stir a few spoonfuls of the hot sauce into the egg mixture and then stir the egg mixture into the sauce in the casserole. Mix well and heat until the sauce is slightly thickened, but do not let it boil. Serve in a heated big serving dish.

FOR 6 PERSONS:

3 pounds eel
3 tablespoons olive oil
4 tablespoons butter
Salt
Freshly ground black pepper
10 shallots, minced
3 sprigs of fresh thyme
4 bay leaves
1 pound sorrel
1 cup minced parsley
1 cup minced chervil

1 tablespoon minced fresh tarragon
1 teaspoon minced fresh sage
1 teaspoon anisette
1 teaspoon burnet extract
   or sweet vermouth
Juice of 2 lemons
1 cup Fish Stock (p. 166)
½ cup dry white wine
1 teaspoon cornstarch
4 egg yolks
1 cup Crème Fraîche (p. 666)

Lamprey à la Bordelaise / LAMPROIE À LA BORDELAISE

EDITORS' NOTE: *Lampreys are not eels, though they resemble them in their general appearance, though not in the details such as skin color, dorsal fins, etc. There are 3 different edible kinds of lampreys and they live in the Atlantic and the Mediterranean, migrating to the mouths of rivers in the spring. Their flesh is delicate, but on the rich side. The following recipe is one of the classics of the cuisine of Bordeaux.*

I suppose that the way of dealing with the lamprey in this dish may appear to you a little on the cruel side. It is certainly not very pleasant for the fish, but if you work quickly and skillfully, the lamprey won't have a worse fate than the slow choking to death to which it is almost always condemned after coming out of the water.

First of all, put the live lamprey into a rough wooden box with no top. Take some very hot, *but not boiling,* water and put it into a spouted pitcher. Pour a slow steady stream of water—not too much at a time—over the lamprey. The lamprey will squirm vigorously, rubbing itself against the rough sides of the box, and in doing so, removing the film that covers its skin.

Continue with this operation until the lamprey has been warmed on all sides. Then, and very quickly, douse it with cold water to prevent its dying boiled; the lamprey comes back to life very quickly. If the film of the skin is not completely removed, scrape it off with a knife and rinse the fish under cold water.

When the lamprey is totally free of the film, tie it to a hook just below its head, over a casserole containing the Sauternes. Cut off about 6 inches of the lamprey's tail, reserving it, so that the lamprey's blood, which is essential for the correct preparation of this dish, will mingle with the wine. Stir the mixture constantly with a wooden spoon to blend.

When the lamprey has been bled, remove the cartilage which serves as its backbone: make a number of vertical incisions in the fish, just below the cartilage, and pull the latter out in one piece.

Cut off the fish's head at the eyes and throw it away. Cut the body into 6 to 8 even slices. Remove the guts. Marinate the pieces in the wine and lamprey-blood mixture for 3 hours.

Heat 4 tablespoons of the oil in a saucepan and cook the green parts of the leeks, the onions, garlic, shallots, carrots and celery in it until they are soft. Stir in the flour, cook for 1 minute, and add the lamprey's tail, the wine, *bouquet garni,* ham, some pepper and a very little salt. Bring to the boiling point, cover, and cook in a preheated 300° F. oven for 2 hours.

Add the lamprey and the marinade to this sauce, stirring constantly. Put the casserole over low heat and continue to stir constantly until the sauce reaches the boiling point. Simmer for 5 minutes.

Remove all the pieces of lamprey from the sauce; throw away the tail which merely flavored the sauce; keep the rest in a cool place.

Cover the saucepan again and put it back into the slow oven for 7 hours.

Cut the white part of the leeks into 5-inch strips. Heat the remaining oil and the butter in a casserole and cook the leeks until they are golden. Add the lamprey slices, sprinkle with the Armagnac, and flame. Strain the sauce over the fish and stir carefully so that the fish slices won't break.

Cover the saucepan and simmer over lowest possible heat for 1 more hour. Check occasionally; the fish pieces must remain whole and not be overcooked.

Pour the fish and the sauce carefully into a heated deep serving dish. Arrange a border of fried croutons sprinkled with parsley around it. Serve accompanied by boiled potatoes.

FOR 4 PERSONS:

1 live 2-pound lamprey
1 cup Sauternes or sweet
    white Bordeaux wine
6 tablespoons olive oil
8 leeks, divided into the
    white and green parts and sliced
3 medium-sized onions, chopped
8 garlic cloves, minced
4 shallots, minced
2 carrots, diced
4 celery hearts, sliced
2 tablespoons flour

3 cups dry red wine
1 Bouquet Garni (p. 46)
1 piece of smoked ham
    or prosciutto (¼ pound)
Freshly ground black pepper
Salt
2 tablespoons butter
¼ cup Armagnac
Croutons (p. 62),
    fried in butter
Chopped parsley

/ *Omble Chevalier Willi Prager*

EDITORS' NOTE: *The* omble chevalier, *or red char, is a very fine fish that resembles a salmon trout. It is found in Switzerland's lakes, notably Lake Geneva.*

Remove the hard core from the carrots and cut the red part only into fine julienne strips. Cook them very slowly, seasoned with a little salt, in 2 tablespoons of the butter in a covered saucepan until they are tender.

Cut the celery into fine julienne strips and cook slowly also in 2 tablespoons of the butter, seasoned with a little salt, in another covered saucepan until it is tender.

If the carrots and the celery are not absolutely fresh, blanch them before cooking them. The reason that these 2 vegetables are cooked separately is that their cooking times differ.

Bone the fish along the back, removing the backbone, as described on page 80.

When the vegetables are tender, let them cool a little, mix them, and bind them with 2 tablespoons of the *crème fraîche*. Season suitably with salt and pepper.

Stuff the fish with the vegetables and pull the fillets over the stuffing. Wrap the fish in a triple layer of cheesecloth and place it on a very generously buttered baking dish.

Melt the remaining butter and douse the fish with it. Cook in a preheated 375° F. oven for about 20 minutes. Remove the cheesecloth, and at serving time drizzle the remaining *crème fraîche* over the fish. If you know how to use *fines herbes* judiciously, sprinkle some over the fish, otherwise use a little minced parsley. Serve in the dish in which the fish was cooked, and very hot.

FOR 2 PERSONS:

2 carrots
Salt
½ cup butter
1 celery heart
1 omble chevalier
    (2 pounds)

1 cup very thick Crème
    Fraîche (p. 666)
Freshly ground white pepper
1 tablespoon minced Fines
    Herbes (p. 89), or parsley

Cold Loaf of Pike / PAIN DE BROCHET FROID

First of all, you must very carefully remove all the bones and skin from the pike. Secondly, put the fish through a food mill or a meat grinder into a bowl, and work it with a wooden spoon until it is a very smooth paste.

Beat in alternately the liquid fish stock and the *sauce Mornay*, a little at a time.

Taste the fish and season generously with salt, pepper and nutmeg; it should be well seasoned. Place the bowl over ice and stir until the mixture begins to thicken. Whip the *crème fraîche* until it is very stiff and fold it into the fish mixture.

Oil a 6-cup charlotte mold and spoon the fish mixture into it. Chill it for at least 2 hours in the refrigerator. Unmold only just before serving time. Serve with the mayonnaise, or *mayonnaise tyrolienne*, separately.

FOR 4 PERSONS:

1 pound boned and skinned pike	Freshly ground white pepper
1½ cups Fish Stock for	Grated nutmeg
Aspic (p. 167)	2 cups Crème Fraîche (p. 666)
¼ cup Sauce Mornay (p. 776)	2 cups Mayonnaise (p. 782), or
Salt	Mayonnaise Tyrolienne (p. 785)

Pike Quenelles / QUENELLES DE BROCHET

There are two methods of making pike *quenelles*:
1. With a *panade*, or *lyonnaise*.
2. With a thick pastry cream, but naturally not a sweetened one.

It is easier to be successful with the first method. The second method also gives good results, but it is more delicate to carry out.

In any case, for both methods, the fish must first be skinned and boned, crushed in a mortar with a pestle, and forced through a fine sieve. Then it must be weighed, before you start the *panade* or the pastry cream, for you will need equal quantities of fish and *panade*, or fish and pastry cream.

To make the panade: Combine the liquid, salt, nutmeg and butter in a large saucepan and bring the mixture to the boiling point. When the butter has completely melted, add the flour all at once and stir until the mixture clears the sides of the saucepan.

To make the pastry cream: Melt the butter in a saucepan, stir in the flour and cook, stirring constantly, until the mixture is golden. Stir in the liquid, season with salt and nutmeg, and cook for 2 to 3 minutes over high heat, stirring constantly.

Take equal weights of fish and *panade,* or fish and pastry cream, and mix thoroughly with a wooden spatula. Beat in the eggs, and check the seasoning. If using the pastry cream, use 1 or 2 less eggs if the mixture seems too thin. It must be thick enough to be shaped.

Using 2 spoons dipped into water, shape the *quenelles;* they should look like little sausages. Poach them in barely simmering lightly salted water for 10 minutes; the water must not boil. Drain the *quenelles* on a kitchen cloth and refrigerate them until they are used.

To serve the *quenelles à la Lyonnaise,* sauté them gently in clarified butter until golden, or cook them for 4 or 5 minutes, depending on size, in barely simmering salted water. Drain them and put them into a buttered baking dish. Coat the *quenelles* with *sauce Mornay,* or any other appropriate sauce, sprinkle them with the cheese, and dot with the butter. Brown under the broiler.

FOR 4 PERSONS:

2 pounds pike
For the panade:
  1 cup liquid—water,
    milk, or Fish Stock (p. 166)
  1 teaspoon salt
  Pinch of grated nutmeg
  6 tablespoons butter
  1¾ cups flour

For the pastry cream:
  3 tablespoons butter
  4 tablespoons flour
  1 cup liquid—water,
    milk, or Fish Stock (p. 166)
  Salt
  Grated nutmeg
6 eggs
6 tablespoons clarified butter
  (p. 666), or boiling salted water
3 cups Sauce Mornay (p. 776)
½ cup grated Swiss cheese
3 tablespoons softened butter

/ Salmon Braised with Château Guiraud

SAUMON BRAISÉ AU VIN DE CHÂTEAU GUIRAUD

EDITORS' NOTE: *Château Guiraud is one of the best white Sauternes.*

Use a whole baby salmon or a center cut weighing 4 pounds. With the point of a very sharp, small knife, make a lengthwise incision along the backbone of the fish. Skin the salmon on either side of the incision, without piercing the skin or detaching it from the fish; it should be 2 loose flaps.

Using the point of the knife, make small cuts in the skinned flesh and push the truffle strips and the tarragon leaves into these cuts. Season lightly with salt and pepper.

Cover the skinned flesh of the salmon with thin slices of fresh pork fat, pull back the skin to cover it, and sew the 2 pieces of skin back together with a fine needle and thread. Put the fish into a large deep casserole.

Heat the oil and the butter in a saucepan and cook the onions and carrots in them until they are soft. Add them to the salmon in the casserole along with the water and cook without a cover in a preheated 425° F. oven for about 15 minutes. Baste the vegetables to avoid scorching. Add the wine and the tarragon. Bring to the boiling point, lower the heat to 375° F. and simmer, covered, for about 25 minutes. Transfer the fish to a hot serving dish, sprinkle it with a little wine to keep it moist, and keep it hot.

Strain the pan liquid into a saucepan, degrease it with a bulb baster, and reduce it over high heat to 2 cups.

Beat together the egg yolks, the cream and the lemon juice. Stir this mixture off the heat into the reduced fish liquid. Stir over low heat until slightly thickened, beating constantly with a wire whip. Correct the seasoning and strain it through a fine sieve into a hot sauceboat.

At the table, cut the fish's skin along the backbone and remove it before slicing the salmon for serving.

FOR 6 PERSONS:

4 pounds salmon
4 truffles, cut into small
  thin strips
12 leaves of fresh tarragon
Salt
Freshly ground white pepper
4 thin slices of fresh
  pork fat
2 tablespoons olive oil
2 tablespoons butter
2 large onions, chopped
4 carrots, chopped

1 cup water
1 bottle Château Guiraud, or
  any good white Bordeaux wine
3 sprigs of tarragon
For the sauce:
  4 egg yolks
  1 cup heavy cream
  Juice of ½ lemon
  Salt
  Freshly ground
    white pepper

Salmon Cutlet | CÔTELETTE DE SAUMON

Soak the bread crumbs in the lukewarm milk until they are thoroughly drenched, and squeeze them dry.

Grind the fish through a meat grinder, using a fine blade. Blend the ground fish with the bread crumbs and the ¼ cup of *crème fraîche*. Shape the mixture into cutlets.

Bread the fish cutlets: coat them with flour, then dip them into an *anglaise* (the egg beaten with the water, oil, salt and pepper until the mixture is frothy). Coat the cutlets on all sides with bread crumbs. Cook the fish cutlets in the combined hot oil and 2 tablespoons of the butter in a skillet over fairly high heat until they are golden brown.

Make a sauce: Mince the onion very finely and cook with the remaining butter and the thyme in a saucepan over low heat until it is golden.

Blend in the 2 cups of *crème fraîche* and season with a little salt, cayenne and nutmeg.

Bring the mixture to the boiling point and reduce it by about one fourth, or until it is slightly thickened. Strain through a fine sieve and check the seasoning.

When the cutlets are golden on all sides, place them on a hot serving dish. Serve the sauce in a sauceboat on the side, and accompany the cutlets with steamed potatoes.

FOR 4 PERSONS:

4 cups fresh white bread crumbs
1 cup lukewarm milk
1 pound boned and skinned
  salmon
¼ cup very thick Crème
  Fraîche (p. 666)
For breading the cutlets:
  Flour
  Anglaise made with 1 egg,
    1 tablespoon water, 1 tablespoon
    peanut oil, a little salt and freshly
    ground white pepper
  1½ cups fresh white
    bread crumbs

2 tablespoons olive oil
5 tablespoons butter
1 large onion
½ teaspoon dried thyme
2 cups Crème Fraîche (p. 666)
Salt
Cayenne pepper
Grated nutmeg

GALANTINE DE SAUMON / *Galantine of Salmon*

Bone a fine center slice of salmon and lay it on a triple thickness of cheesecloth. The fish will be poached in the cheesecloth, therefore make sure that the ends of the cloth will overlap sufficiently to make a tight wrapping.

Lard the salmon with truffle strips, rosemary leaves and small strips of blanched salt pork. Stuff the fish with the uncooked fish *quenelles* mixture and, if you would like to, garnish this stuffing with chopped hard-cooked eggs and chopped sour pickles. Form the stuffed salmon into the shape of a thick cylinder. Wrap the fish tightly in the cheesecloth and tie it at both ends.

Poach the fish in a *court bouillon* well seasoned with *fines herbes,* thyme, bay leaf, crushed peppercorns and salt. Cook the fish over medium heat; a galantine weighing 3 to 4 pounds will take about 1 hour. Keep the fish in its cooking liquid until the latter has cooled to lukewarm. Drain the galantine, tighten the wrapping, and let it cool. Remove the cheesecloth and serve the galantine of salmon as is, or cover it with a fish aspic.

FOR 6 PERSONS:

3 pounds center cut of salmon
2 truffles, cut into julienne
   strips
3 or 4 fresh rosemary sprigs
⅛ pound salt pork, cut into
   julienne strips and blanched
¼ recipe Pike Quenelles (p. 374)

2 hard-cooked eggs, chopped
2 or more sour pickles, chopped
3 quarts Court Bouillon for Fish (p.
   131)
Optional: 3 cups Fish Stock
   for Aspic (p. 167)

TRUITES AUX AMANDES / *Trout with Almonds*

Gut the trout, wash them, and dry them with a kitchen cloth. Dip them into the milk first and then into the flour. Heat the butter in a skillet and sauté the fish over fairly high heat until they are golden on both sides. Season with salt and pepper. Put the trout on a hot serving dish and keep them warm.

Sauté the almonds in the butter in the skillet until they, too, are golden. Add more butter to the pan if it seems necessary.

Pour the almond-butter mixture over the trout. Garnish with lemon slices and serve very hot.

FOR 2 PERSONS:

2 trout (1 pound each)
1 cup milk
1 cup flour
6 or more tablespoons butter
Salt

Freshly ground black pepper
⅓ cup slivered blanched
   almonds
1 lemon, cut into slices

TRUITES AU BLEU / *Trout Cooked au Bleu*

Prepare a well-seasoned *court bouillon* (see p. 131). Kill and gut the trout just before cooking it, taking care not to disturb the film on its skin that, in cooking, will give the fish its blue color (see p. 336). Simmer the trout for about 10 minutes, but do not let it boil. Drain the fish and put it on a hot serving plate. Serve very hot with melted butter, or a Sauce Hollandaise (p. 780).

SHELLFISH

Crustacés

Crab Pilaf / PILAW DE CRABE

EDITORS' NOTE: *While small crabs can be used in this recipe, it will be more difficult to pick out the crabmeat after they are cooked.*

Make a rice pilaf, using preferably a good fish stock rather than water.

Prepare a crab ragout: Wash the crab, remove the back, and cut the crab into several pieces. Crack the claws.

Sauté the pieces in the combined hot oil and 4 tablespoons of the butter over high heat for about 5 minutes. Drain off the butter and oil, season the crab with salt and pepper, sprinkle with the brandy, and flame.

In another skillet heat the remaining butter and cook the garlic, onion and shallots in it until they are golden. Add the crabmeat and its pan juices, the wine, tomatoes, sweet pepper and *bouquet garni*. Cook without a cover for 12 minutes. Cool a little, remove the crab, and remove very carefully all the shells and tendons.

Discard the *bouquet garni* and strain the sauce through a fine sieve. Blend it into the *béchamel* to obtain a smooth mixture. Combine half of the sauce with the picked crabmeat; the mixture should be fairly thick. Check and rectify the seasoning.

Butter a deep 6- to 8-cup charlotte mold or baking dish and line it with two thirds of the rice pilaf. Smooth out the rice. Add the crab ragout and cover the crab ragout with the remaining rice. Bake in a 350° F. oven for about 15 minutes to heat through. Unmold on a hot serving dish and drizzle the remaining sauce around the pilaf. Serve immediately.

FOR 4 PERSONS:

Rice Pilaf (p. 659), made with
   1 cup rice and fish stock
1 large crab (3 pounds)
4 tablespoons olive oil
6 tablespoons butter
Salt
Freshly ground black pepper
¼ cup brandy
1 garlic clove, minced
1 large onion, minced

4 shallots, minced
½ cup dry white wine
4 tomatoes, peeled,
   seeded and chopped
1 sweet pepper, charred, scraped,
   seeded and chopped (see p. 619)
1 Bouquet Garni (p. 46)
½ cup very thick Sauce
   Béchamel (p. 761)

ÉCREVISSES À LA NAGE / *Crayfish in Court Bouillon*

Prepare the *à la nage,* that is, *court bouillon* in which the crayfish will swim. Take care with the appearance of the vegetables in the *court bouillon* since they will be served at the table; for instance, it might be desirable to score the carrots before slicing them. Put in a large pot the carrots, onions, shallots, thyme, parsley sprigs, the crumbled bay leaf, the wine, fish stock, a little salt and the peppercorns. Simmer for about 30 minutes.

Wash the crayfish and remove the intestinal tracts by making an incision with a sharp knife along the backs and lifting out the intestines. Plunge them immediately into the *court bouillon.* Add a little cayenne and simmer, covered, over low heat for 5 to 8 minutes, or until they turn red.

Serve the crayfish in their cooking liquid, as you would serve soup.

FOR 2 PERSONS:

3 carrots, thinly sliced
2 onions, chopped
3 shallots, chopped
½ teaspoon dried thyme
4 parsley sprigs
1 bay leaf, crumbled

2 cups dry white wine
2 cups Fish Stock (p. 166)
Salt
4 peppercorns, crushed
16 live crayfish
Pinch of cayenne pepper

ÉCREVISSES À LA BORDELAISE / *Crayfish Bordelaise*

Wash and clean the crayfish as described in the preceding recipe. Heat the oil and the butter in a large deep skillet and sauté the crayfish in it over medium heat until their shells turn red. Season them with salt, pepper and cayenne. Cover the skillet and cook the crayfish over lowest possible heat for 5 minutes. Drain off the butter and oil. Sprinkle the crayfish with the brandy and flame them. Add the wine, onion, carrot, tomato, shallot and the *bouquet garni,* as well as a little more salt, pepper and cayenne. Cover the crayfish and simmer over lowest possible heat for 10 minutes. Take out the crayfish, put them on a hot serving plate, and keep warm.

Press the sauce through a very fine sieve, return it to the skillet, bring to a boil, and stir in the *beurre manié.* Simmer the sauce for 5 minutes and check the seasoning. Pour it over the crayfish, sprinkle with parsley, and serve very hot.

FOR 2 PERSONS:

16 live crayfish
2 tablespoons olive oil
3 tablespoons butter
Salt
Freshly ground black pepper
Cayenne pepper
¼ cup brandy
1 cup dry white wine
1 onion, minced

1 carrot, minced
1 tomato, peeled, seeded and
   chopped
1 shallot, minced
1 Bouquet Garni (p. 46)
1 tablespoon Beurre Manié (p. 41)
   (1 tablespoon each of flour and
   butter)
2 tablespoons minced parsley

Crayfish in Cream / ÉCREVISSES À LA CRÈME

Shell the raw crayfish and remove the intestinal tracts. Coat them with flour and sauté them in the combined hot oil and butter over high heat until they turn red. Season with salt and pepper and simmer over low heat for 5 minutes.

Drain off the pan juices. Sprinkle the crayfish with the brandy and flame them. Add the wine and the fish stock. Cook, uncovered, for 8 minutes. Transfer the crayfish to a hot serving dish and keep them warm. Reduce the pan juices by half and stir in the cream. Cook, stirring constantly, for about 5 minutes, or until the sauce is slightly thickened and smooth. Check the seasoning. Strain the sauce through a fine sieve onto the crayfish. Serve very hot.

FOR 2 PERSONS:

16 live crayfish	**Freshly ground white pepper**
Flour	**¼ cup brandy**
2 tablespoons olive oil	**½ cup dry white wine**
3 tablespoons butter	**1 cup Fish Stock (p. 166)**
Salt	**¾ cup heavy cream**

Flamed Crayfish / ÉCREVISSES FLAMBÉES

Shell the crayfish and remove the intestinal tracts. Sauté them in the combined hot oil and butter over high heat for 10 minutes.

When the crayfish have turned red, sprinkle them with the Armagnac and flame them. Season with salt and pepper, cover, and simmer over lowest possible heat for 10 minutes. Sprinkle with the *crème fraîche*. Bring to the boiling point and cook over high heat for a few minutes, shaking the pan so that the *crème* and the pan juices will blend. Pour into a hot serving dish and serve very hot.

FOR 2 PERSONS:

16 live crayfish	**Salt**
2 tablespoons olive oil	**Freshly ground white pepper**
3 tablespoons butter	**½ cup Crème Fraîche (p. 666)**
¼ cup Armagnac	

Ragout of Crayfish / RAGOÛT D'ÉCREVISSES

Shell the crayfish and remove the intestinal tracts. Dip any coral from the crayfish into flour and sauté it and the shelled crayfish in the combined hot oil and 2 tablespoons of the butter for about 10 minutes. Transfer them to a hot serving dish and keep warm. Bring the crayfish stock to the boiling point, reduce it by half, and add the *crème fraîche*. Reduce again, beating constantly with a wire whip. Remove from the heat, stir in the remaining butter, and shake the pan to make it melt. Pour the sauce over the crayfish and sprinkle with parsley. Serve very hot.

FOR 2 PERSONS:

16 live crayfish	1 cup crayfish stock, or
Flour	Fish Stock (p. 166)
2 tablespoons olive oil	1 cup Crème Fraîche (p. 666)
5 tablespoons butter	2 tablespoons minced parsley

HOMARD GRILLÉ / *Broiled Lobster*

Take a live lobster; split it open lengthwise and remove the sac behind the head and the intestinal tract. Broil it, claws and feelers included, under a hot broiler. Season with salt, cayenne and paprika.

First broil the lobster shell side up; turn it on the other side and broil the meat. A 1½-pound lobster will need about 10 minutes of cooking time.

Put the lobster halves on a hot serving dish and garnish the dish with parsley. Serve with a *sauce béarnaise* or with melted butter.

FOR 2 PERSONS:

1 live 1½-pound lobster	Parsley sprigs
Salt	½ cup Sauce Béarnaise (p. 779),
Cayenne pepper	or melted butter
Paprika	

HOMARD À L'AMÉRICAINE I / *Lobster à l'Américaine I*

There are so many different opinions about lobster *à l'Américaine* that one doesn't dare to say anything without documentary proof. However, it is not my intention to tell you tales, but to give you a good solid recipe; I have chosen father's.

Remove the claws from the lobster and crack them. Separate the tail from the body and cut the tail into 4 or 5 crosswise slices. Cut the upper body into halves and discard the sac behind the head and the intestinal tract. Reserve all the coral and the rich inside liquid that some people call the lobster's "blood." Or, if your fishmonger will cut up the live lobster for you, ask him to save you the coral and this liquid.

Heat the oil and 3 tablespoons of the butter in a large deep skillet. Cook the lobster pieces in it over high heat until the shells turn red. Drain the pan juices into a bowl.

Sprinkle the lobster with the Armagnac and flame it. Transfer it to a china dish. Return the pan juices to the skillet, add the shallots, and cook until they are golden, but do not let them brown. Add the wine and return the lobster and its juices to the skillet, together with the rich lobster liquid or "blood." If you have it handy, add also a little fish stock; but this is not essential. Add the tomatoes and season with salt and very little cayenne pepper as well as the tarragon. It's wrong to think that lobster *à l'Américaine* should be very hot; it should be well seasoned but not such as to burn the roof of your mouth.

Bring to the boiling point. Cook over medium heat, stirring occasionally, for 15 minutes.

Remove the lobster pieces from the sauce and put them into a hot serving dish and keep them hot. Bring the sauce to a quick boil and stir in the remaining butter

LOBSTER À L'AMÉRICAINE

(Above) *Sauté the lobster pieces until the shells turn red. Transfer them to a hot dish and add the vegetables to the pan juices.*

(Below) *Cook the vegetables until they are golden and then add a young, non-vintage wine. Put the lobster pieces back into the pan and cook over fairly high heat for a few minutes.*

mashed with the lobster coral. Cook for a couple of seconds longer and pour the sauce over the lobster. Serve immediately. You may sprinkle the lobster with minced parsley, but only if it is very fresh and crisp; do not bother otherwise.

FOR 2 PERSONS:

1 live 2-pound lobster	4 medium-sized tomatoes,
2 tablespoons olive oil	peeled, seeded and chopped
6 tablespoons butter	Salt
¼ cup Armagnac	Cayenne pepper
12 shallots, minced	1 tablespoon minced tarragon
¾ cup dry white wine	1 tablespoon minced parsley
Optional: ½ cup Fish Stock	
(p. 166)	

HOMARD À L'AMÉRICAINE II / *Lobster à l'Américaine II*

Here is another, more classical recipe.

Cut up the lobster as described in the preceding recipe and remove the intestinal tract and the sac behind the head. Put the coral into a bowl.

Season the lobster pieces with salt and pepper, and cook them over high heat in the very hot oil and 2 tablespoons of the butter in a large deep skillet. When the shells turn red, transfer them to a china plate.

Add another 2 tablespoons of the butter to the skillet and add the garlic, the onion and the shallots. Cook until the onion is golden, stirring frequently with a wooden spoon. Return the lobster pieces to the saucepan and add the *bouquet garni*, the tomatoes and the wine. Season lightly with salt and cayenne. Cover and cook over high heat for 5 minutes, stirring frequently.

On a plate, mash together the lobster coral with the remaining butter.

Transfer the lobster to a hot serving dish and keep warm. Bring the sauce to the boiling point and add the brandy and the sherry. Reduce the sauce by one third. Remove from the heat and gradually beat in the coral butter. Pour the sauce over the lobster and sprinkle with the parsley.

Note that sometimes the lobster is served with a Rice à la Créole (p. 658) on the side. At other times, it is dished up with little fried bread Croutons (p. 62), placed in a circle around the lobster.

FOR 2 PERSONS:

1 live 2-pound lobster	1 Bouquet Garni (p. 46)
Salt	4 tomatoes, peeled, seeded
Freshly ground black pepper	and chopped
3 tablespoons olive oil	1 cup dry white wine
½ cup butter	Cayenne pepper
1 garlic clove, mashed	¼ cup brandy
½ medium-sized onion, minced	¼ cup sherry
3 large shallots, minced	2 tablespoons minced parsley

Lobster Newburg I / HOMARD NEWBURG I

Prepare the lobster *à l'Américaine I* (p. 381). Before adding the coral butter, drain the pieces, remove the meat from the pieces of shell, and keep the meat warm in a hot serving dish.

Reduce the sauce in which the lobster was cooked over high heat by one third and force it through a fine sieve into another saucepan. Gradually stir in the *sauce béchamel* first, then the eggs and cream beaten together, the lemon juice and the sherry; stir constantly over low heat until the sauce thickens slightly. Remove from the heat and check the seasoning.

Pour the sauce over the lobster meat.

Obviously, this is a marvelous and very handsome way of preparing lobster.

FOR 2 PERSONS:

1 **live 2-pound lobster and all the ingredients for Lobster à l'Américaine I (p. 381)**
2 **cups Sauce Béchamel (p. 761)**
2 **egg yolks, beaten with ½ cup heavy cream**

2 **tablespoons lemon juice**
¼ **cup sherry**
Salt
Cayenne pepper

Lobster Newburg II / HOMARD NEWBURG II

Here is another recipe, and one quite close to American cooking.

Your lobster should be newly cooked for about 25 minutes in a *court bouillon* and still warm. Shell the tail only. Save the upper body and claws for another dish.

Using a large enamelware saucepan, melt 2 tablespoons of the butter and add the lobster tail, sherry, brandy, fish stock, tarragon and a little salt and cayenne. Cover and simmer over low heat for 10 minutes.

Take out the lobster tail, cut it into thick slices, and keep them hot.

Reduce the liquid in the saucepan by one quarter. Stir in the *sauce béchamel,* reduce it again by one quarter, and beat in the egg yolks beaten with the cream and the lemon juice. Stir over low heat until slightly thickened.

Remove from the heat and stir in the remaining butter to make a smooth sauce. Shake the saucepan gently to melt the butter. Pour the sauce over the lobster. Serve very hot, with rice *à la Créole.*

FOR 4 PERSONS:

1 **live 3-pound lobster**
Court Bouillon for Lobster (p. 243)
5 **tablespoons butter**
4 **tablespoons sherry**
2 **tablespoons brandy**
½ **cup Fish Stock (p. 166)**
1 **sprig of tarragon**

Salt
Cayenne pepper
2 **cups Sauce Béchamel (p. 761)**
2 **egg yolks, beaten with ½ cup heavy cream**
2 **tablespoons lemon juice**

HOMARD THERMIDOR / *Lobster Thermidor*

Plunge the live lobster into the boiling *court bouillon*. Poach it for 15 minutes. The *court bouillon* must barely simmer and on no account boil.

As soon as the lobster is cooked, drain it. Cut it lengthwise into halves; remove the meat from the tail and the claws. Reserve the shell halves. Cut the lobster meat into small dice and simmer it in the sherry or the brandy in a saucepan for 3 minutes. Set it aside.

Make the following sauce: Combine the fish stock and the wine. Reduce them over high heat by two thirds. Stir the mustard into the hot *sauce béchamel* and add it to the reduced stock. Cook for 2 to 3 more minutes, stirring constantly with a wire whip. Check the seasoning and season strongly with cayenne.

Brush the insides of the lobster shells with the sauce. Place the diced lobster meat on it and cover it with the remaining sauce. Sprinkle with the grated cheese and the melted butter and brown under the broiler.

FOR 2 PERSONS:

1 live 1½-pound lobster	**¼ teaspooon dry mustard**
Court Bouillon for Lobster (p. 243)	**½ cup Sauce Béchamel (p. 761)**
¼ cup sherry or brandy	**Cayenne pepper**
½ cup Fish Stock (p. 166)	**3 tablespoons grated Swiss cheese**
1 cup dry white wine	**2 tablespoons melted butter**

CURRY DE LANGOUSTE / *Curried Rock Lobster*

EDITORS' NOTE: *Rock lobster or spiny lobster is found only in southern waters in the United States. However, New England lobsters may be substituted for it in this and the other recipes for rock lobster.*

Cut up the lobster into pieces as in Lobster à l'Américaine (p. 381).

Cook the pieces in the hot olive oil in a large wide skillet until the shells turn red, and then add the onions and the garlic. Cook, stirring constantly, until the vegetables are golden and then add the apples and the *bouquet garni*. Stir in the curry powder as if it were flour. Season with salt and pepper. Add the fish stock or the wine, cover the saucepan and cook, stirring occasionally, for about 15 minutes longer.

Take out the lobster pieces and put them into a hot serving dish. Reduce the sauce by half and add the *crème* or coconut milk. Simmer for a few minutes and strain the sauce through a fine sieve onto the lobster. Serve the dish with a rice *à la Créole,* or with a rice pilaf.

ROCK LOBSTER GRATIN IN THE CORSICAN MANNER

The cooking is done in 2 steps: first (above) in the hot oil on top of the stove and then (right) in the oven. When you are cooking the rock lobster on top of the stove, be sure to have a hot baking dish ready into which you'll put the 2 halves to bake in the oven.

FOR 4 PERSONS:

1 rock lobster (2 pounds)	Salt
¼ cup olive oil	Freshly ground black pepper
2 onions, minced	1 cup Fish Stock (166)
3 garlic cloves, mashed	or dry white wine
3 tart apples, peeled,	¾ cup Crème Fraîche (p. 666),
cored and minced	or coconut milk (see below)
1 Bouquet Garni (p. 46)	Rice à la Créole (p. 658),
2 (or more) tablespoons curry	or Rice Pilaf (p. 659)
powder	

Note: To make the coconut milk, crack a coconut and save the inside water. Grate the white parts of the flesh and combine them with the saved liquid; if there is not sufficient liquid, make up the difference with milk. Let stand for 2 hours and strain.

/ *Rock Lobster Gratin in the Corsican Manner*

LANGOUSTE GRILLÉE À LA CORSE

> EDITORS' NOTE: *New England lobster may be substituted for the rock lobster.*

Cut the rock lobster lengthwise into halves and reserve the coral. Discard the sac behind the head and the intestinal tract. Heat the oil in a large skillet and sauté the lobster halves on both sides until the shells turn red. Remove them to a baking dish and cook, shell side up, in a preheated 375° F. oven for 10 minutes.

Season the lobster halves with salt and cayenne.

A short time before serving time, mash the coral until it is very smooth. Blend it with about twice its volume of mayonnaise. Spread the rock lobster halves with this mixture and brown quickly under a hot broiler.

FOR 2 PERSONS:

1 rock lobster (2 pounds)	Cayenne pepper
¼ cup olive oil	4 tablespoons Mayonnaise (p. 782)
Salt	

LANGOUSTE À L'AMÉRICAINE / *Rock Lobster à l'Américaine*

Rock lobster may be used in Lobster à l'Américaine (p. 381), but it is never quite as flavorful.

LANGOUSTE À LA BROCHE / *Lobster on the Spit*

This way of cooking crustaceans is best suited to large animals.

Take a living rock lobster and kill it by plunging it into boiling water for a short moment.

Thread it on a spit and brush it with olive oil. Roast it over a lively fire, with a dripping pan underneath, for about 15 minutes.

Put the wine and the butter into the dripping pan; they will refine the taste of the lobster juices which will drip into the pan. Baste the rock lobster frequently with the pan juices.

Split the rock lobster on a large serving dish and serve it with the pan juices on the side.

FOR 2 PERSONS:

1 live 2-pound lobster	**¾ cup dry white wine**
¼ cup olive oil	**6 tablespoons butter**

Lobster Stew / CIVET DE LANGOUSTE

Cut up the lobster as in Lobster à l'Américaine (p. 381).

Discard the intestinal tract and the sac behind the head. Crack the claws. Save all the liquid that will ooze out during this process, and reserve it in a cup. Save also any coral and put it into another cup.

Heat the oil and 2 tablespoons of the butter in a large wide casserole and sauté the lobster pieces in it over high heat until the shells have turned red. Sprinkle them with the Armagnac and flame. Remove the lobster pieces to the casserole.

Add the onion, shallots, garlic, carrot, and celery to the pan juices. Cook them over high heat until they are golden, adding a little butter if necessary to prevent sticking. Then add the wine, the liquid saved from cutting up the lobster, the tomatoes and the *bouquet garni.* Return the lobster pieces to this mixture and season with a little salt and cayenne. Cover and cook over medium heat for 15 minutes, stirring frequently.

Remove the lobster pieces from the sauce and keep them hot in a hot serving dish. Cook the sauce for 15 minutes longer, force it through a fine sieve into a saucepan, and bring it back to the boiling point. Mash the coral together with an equal quantity of butter into a smooth paste. Stir this coral butter into the sauce off the heat and then pour over the lobster pieces.

Circle the dish with butter-fried croutons sprinkled with parsley.

FOR 4 PERSONS:

1 live 2-pound lobster	**4 tomatoes, peeled, seeded**
3 tablespoons olive oil	**and chopped**
6 tablespoons butter	**1 Bouquet Garni (p. 46)**
¼ cup Armagnac	**Salt**
1 large onion, minced	**Cayenne pepper**
4 shallots, minced	**8 large Croutons (see p. 62),**
1 garlic clove, mashed	**fried in butter and sprinkled**
1 carrot, chopped	**with minced parsley**
1 celery stalk, chopped	
½ bottle strong young white	
Bordeaux wine	

Mussels in Cream / MOULES À LA CRÈME

Wash and clean the mussels. Put them into cold water as soon as they arrive in the kitchen, and keep them in cold water throughout the cleaning process. Throw away all the open and broken mussels and any that are not firmly closed. Scrub the shells with a stiff brush, remove all slime and dirt, and cut off the "beard," that is the heavy substance that sticks to the shell. Wash the mussels in several changes of cold water until the water is free from grit and sand.

Put them into a large kettle with the wine, the onion, parsley and a little pepper. Cook them, covered, over high heat until they just open, lower the heat to lowest possible, and simmer for 4 minutes. Drain the mussels and reserve the pan liquid. Discard any mussels which have not opened.

Shell the mussels, adding any juices in the shells to the pan liquid. Rinse the shelled mussels in the pan liquid to remove any possible trace of grit. Put them into a hot serving dish and keep them warm.

Strain the pan liquid through a very fine sieve or a triple layer of damp cheese-cloth and reduce it in a saucepan over high heat by one third. There should be 2 generous cups. Beat together the flour, the egg yolk and the cream. Stir a few tablespoons of the reduced mixture into this *liaison* and then pour it into the saucepan. Bring just to the boiling point and remove from the heat. Stir in the butter to bind the sauce. Strain it over the mussels and serve immediately.

FOR 4 PERSONS:

2½ **pounds mussels**
1½ **cups dry white wine**
1 **tablespoon minced onion**
1 **parsley sprig**
Freshly ground white pepper

3 **tablespoons flour**
1 **egg yolk**
½ **cup heavy cream**
3 **tablespoons butter**

MOULES MARINIÈRES / *Mussels Marinières*

Clean the mussels as described in the preceding recipe.

Put the cleaned mussels into a large kettle with the shallots, the wine, 1 tablespoon of the butter and the parsley. Season generously with pepper. Cook over high heat, covered, for about 5 minutes, or only until the shells open. Transfer the mussels to a hot deep serving dish, cover it, and keep hot. Strain the pan liquid through a fine sieve or through a triple layer of damp cheesecloth to catch any sand. Reduce the pan liquid over high heat by half. Remove from the heat, stir in the remaining butter and the parsley, and pour over the mussels. Serve immediately.

FOR 4 PERSONS:

2½ **pounds mussels**
2 **tablespoons minced shallots**
1 **cup dry white wine**
3 **tablespoons butter**

2 **parsley sprigs**
Freshly ground black pepper
2 **tablespoons minced parsley**

/ *Mussels in the Southwestern Fashion*

MOULES À LA FAÇON SUD-OUEST

Clean the mussels as described in Mussels in Cream (above).

Put them into a deep kettle with the onion, shallots, *bouquet garni,* celery, anisette, wine and a little pepper. Cover the kettle and put over high heat. When the steam begins to pour out, cook for 1 minute; take off the lid and turn the mussels over. Cover again and repeat this process twice more.

Transfer the mussels to a hot serving dish. Pour the hot *crème fraîche* over them and sprinkle with more pepper and the parsley. Serve very hot.

FOR 4 PERSONS:

2½ pounds mussels
1 large onion, chopped
2 shallots, chopped
1 Bouquet Garni (p. 46)
1 celery stalk, minced

¼ cup anisette
1 cup dry white wine
Freshly ground white pepper
1 cup hot Crème Fraîche (p. 666)
2 tablespoons minced parsley

Prawns à la Valencienne | LANGOUSTINES À LA VALENCIENNE

Cook the rice according to package directions, drain, and stir in the oil.

Cut the ham into dice. Scorch the outer skin of the peppers over high heat and peel it off under cold running water; remove the stems and seeds and cut the peppers into thin strips.

Cook the prawns in a *court bouillon* for about 5 minutes, cool them in their cooking liquid, and shell them.

Combine the rice, ham, peas and half of the pepper strips in a bowl and mix well. Butter a 9-inch ring mold, fill it with the rice mixture, and unmold it on a hot serving dish. Set the prawns astride the rice, alternately with the remaining pepper strips.

Serve very hot, with a sauceboat of horseradish sauce.

FOR 4 PERSONS:

1 cup uncooked rice
2 tablespoons peanut oil
¼ pound smoked ham
2 sweet red peppers
12 prawns or very large shrimp

Court Bouillon for Shellfish
   (p. 131), made with vinegar
¼ cup peas, cooked in butter
2 cups Horseradish Sauce II
   (p. 791)

Scallops Landaise | COQUILLES SAINT-JACQUES LANDAISE

EDITORS' NOTE: *This and the other scallop recipes which follow are preparations for scallops in the shell, which the cook will open at home. As a reward for the extra work, there will be coral as well as the white muscle. The coral, which is the roe of the scallop, is delicate in flavor and adds color to the dish. In American markets the ready-to-cook scallop, the white muscle alone, is sold without any coral. These recipes will work as well without any coral.*

Open and clean the scallops according to the method described on page 96; or buy ready-to-cook scallops; in that case you will have no coral. If the scallops are large, cut them into bite-size pieces.

Marinate them in the seasoned beer in a cool place for 10 minutes. Drain the scallops. Dust them with flour and shake off any excess.

Heat the oil and 3 tablespoons of the butter in a large skillet. Sauté the scallops in it until they are just golden on all sides. Season lightly with salt and pepper; add the pine nuts and the remaining butter. Sauté over the lowest possible heat for 3 more minutes. At the last moment, add the parsley and the vinegar. Serve immediately.

FOR 2 PERSONS:

12 large scallops	6 tablespoons butter
1 cup beer, seasoned with salt and freshly ground black pepper	Salt
	Freshly ground black pepper
	2 tablespoons pine nuts
Flour	1 tablespoon minced parsley
2 tablespoons olive oil	1 tablespoon wine vinegar

COQUILLES SAINT-JACQUES PROVENÇALE / *Scallops Provençale*

Open and clean the scallops as described on page 96; or buy ready-to-cook scallops; in that case you will have no coral.

Dip the scallops and coral first into the beer, then coat them with flour, and sauté them in the combined hot oil and butter over high heat until they are golden. Season with salt and pepper. Add the garlic, lower the heat, cover the pot, and simmer for about 5 minutes.

Drain the scallops and put them into a hot serving plate. Spoon the pan juices and the lemon juice over them. Put a mound of the hot tomatoes at each end of the dish and garnish with the parsley sprigs.

Sprinkle the dish with the minced parsley and serve very hot.

FOR 2 PERSONS:

12 large scallops	Freshly ground black pepper
1 cup beer	2 garlic cloves, mashed
Flour	2 tablespoons lemon juice
2 tablespoons olive oil	4 tomatoes, stewed in butter
3 tablespoons butter	Parsley sprigs
Salt	2 tablespoons minced parsley

/ *Scallops Cooked with Saffron*

COQUILLES SAINT-JACQUES AU SAFRAN

Open and clean the scallops as described on page 96; or buy ready-to-cook scallops. Put them into a saucepan with the shallot, saffron, wine and lemon juice, and season very lightly with salt and pepper. Cover the saucepan and poach the scallops for 10 minutes.

Drain the scallops and put them into a baking dish. Reduce the pan liquid over high heat by half. Knead together the butter and the flour and stir it into the liquid. Stir in the *crème fraîche* and simmer for 6 minutes longer.

Coat the scallops with the sauce, sprinkle them with the cheese, and brown quickly under the broiler. Serve very hot.

FOR 2 PERSONS:

12 large scallops	Freshly ground black pepper
1 tablespoon minced shallot	1 tablespoon butter
¼ teaspoon ground saffron	1 teaspoon flour
¾ cup dry white wine	1 tablespoon Crème Fraîche
1 tablespoon lemon juice	(p. 666)
Salt	3 tablespoons grated Swiss cheese

Scallops Cooked with Spices /

COQUILLES SAINT-JACQUES AUX ÉPICES

You will need a piece of puff paste about the size of an egg. Roll it out and line 2 identical scallop shells. They must be generously buttered before being lined with the puff paste. Place a piece of buttered wax paper over the pastry and fill the unbaked shells with dry beans. Bake in a preheated 450° F. oven for 10 minutes. Reduce the heat to 350° F. and bake for 10 minutes longer. Remove the paper and beans and bake for about 5 minutes longer. Remove from the oven and unmold. Or follow the method for making puff-paste shells described on page 56.

Open and clean the scallops as described on page 96; or buy ready-to-cook scallops; in that case you will have no coral. Cook them, together with the coral, in the wine, shallots, lemon juice and 1 tablespoon of the butter over medium heat; season very lightly with salt and pepper. Simmer for about 10 minutes.

Drain the scallops and keep them hot. Strain the pan liquid through a very fine sieve or a triple layer of cheesecloth and reduce it over high heat to 4 tablespoons. Stir in the *crème* and the finely ground *quatre épices*. Beat thoroughly with a wire whisk and simmer for 5 minutes.

Remove from the heat, check the seasoning, and in order to make the sauce smoother and thicker, stir in the egg yolk and the remaining butter.

Fill the pastry shells with the scallops, coat with the sauce, sprinkle with the grated cheese, and brown under the broiler. Serve very hot.

FOR 2 PERSONS:

Puff Paste (p. 715)	Salt
12 large scallops	Freshly ground black pepper
½ cup dry white wine	4 tablespoons Crème Fraîche
1 tablespoon minced shallots	(p. 666)
1 tablespoon lemon juice	1 teaspoon Quatre Épices (p. 667)
3 tablespoons butter, at	1 egg yolk, beaten
room temperature	3 tablespoons grated Swiss cheese

Scallops with Truffles /

COQUILLES SAINT-JACQUES AUX TRUFFES

Open and clean the scallops as described on page 96; or buy ready-to-cook scallops. Put them into a casserole with the shallot, the wine, the fish stock or water and the lemon juice. Season very lightly with salt and pepper. Poach them over high heat for 7 minutes. Drain the scallops and put them in a baking dish; keep hot.

Strain the pan juices through a fine sieve or a triple layer of damp cheesecloth. Add the truffle strips and return to high heat. Reduce until there are only 4 tablespoons of liquid left in the pan.

Beat together the egg yolk and the *créme*. Remove the sauce from the heat and beat in the egg-cream mixture. Check the seasoning. Return it to low heat and stir until it is slightly thickened.

Remove from the heat and swirl in the butter until the sauce is thick and smooth. Coat the scallops with the sauce and sprinkle them with the cheese. Brown quickly under the broiler and serve very hot.

FOR 2 PERSONS:

12 large scallops
1 tablespoon minced shallot
½ cup dry white wine
1 cup Fish Stock (p. 166), or water
1 tablespoon lemon juice
Salt
Freshly ground white pepper

1 truffle, cut into thin julienne strips
1 egg yolk
4 tablespoons Crème Fraîche (p. 666)
2 tablespoons butter, at room temperature
2 tablespoons grated Swiss cheese

CALAMARES À LA BISCAÏENNE / *Squid Biscaïenne*

Cut the cleaned squid into pieces. In a casserole heat together 3 tablespoons of the oil and 2 tablespoons of the butter and cook the pieces in it until golden. Season lightly with salt, pepper and cayenne; sprinkle with the brandy and ignite. Pour the squid and the pan juices into a bowl and reserve.

Put the remaining oil and butter into the casserole with the shallots, onion, carrots, sweet pepper and garlic. Cook the vegetables over lowest possible heat until they are so tender as to be almost a purée. Add the tomatoes, the *bouquet garni* and the squid with the pan juices. Cover and simmer over low heat for 20 minutes. (*Note:* if the squid is not very young, it will require longer simmering.)

Butter a ring mold and fill it with the hot rice. Unmold the rice on a hot serving dish and fill the center with the squid pieces. Spoon the sauce around the outer edge of the rice ring and garnish the top of the rice with pimiento strips.

FOR 4 PERSONS:

2 pounds very small young squid, cleaned
5 tablespoons olive oil
4 tablespoons butter
Salt
Freshly ground black pepper
Cayenne pepper
¼ cup brandy
3 shallots, minced
1 onion, minced

3 carrots, minced
1 sweet pepper, charred, scraped and minced (see p. 619)
1 garlic clove, minced
6 tomatoes, peeled, seeded and chopped
1 Bouquet Garni (p. 46)
3 cups hot cooked rice
Pimiento strips

5
MEATS
Les Viandes

BEEF

Boeuf

Rib Roast of Beef / CÔTE DE BOEUF RÔTIE

To facilitate carving, have the butcher saw through the ribs of a rib roast of beef, both at the end joint and in the middle. This makes it easier to remove them when the meat is done.

The beef is cooked in a preheated 300° F. oven for 18 to 22 minutes a pound, according to taste. It should not be overcooked, and it is a good idea to let it stand for 30 minutes before carving. The heat inside the meat will cook it evenly throughout. Also, the meat will be much easier to carve.

The roast can also be coated before roasting with a paste of coarse salt (Kosher salt) mixed with a little flour so as to have a suit of armor around it. The heat of the oven will harden and brown this protective coating.

Braised Ribs of Beef / CÔTE DE BOEUF À L'ÉTOUFFÉ

First heat the oil and butter in a very large skillet and brown the meat in it. Flame it with the Armagnac and season with salt and pepper.

Line the bottom of a large casserole with the slices of fresh pork fat or ham fat. Add the celery, onion, shallots, carrot and garlic. Transfer the meat to the casserole and cook over medium heat until it sizzles. Add the wine and the *bouquet garni*. Season with salt and pepper. Bring to a boil, cover the casserole, and simmer over low heat for 3 to 4 hours. When you judge the meat almost tender, add the artichoke hearts and the tomato sauce. Put the artichokes around the meat and the tomato sauce on top of it. Cover again and cook until the artichokes are tender, about 30 minutes.

Remove the *bouquet garni* and serve the meat in the casserole with the baked potatoes on the side.

FOR 6 PERSONS:

3 tablespoons peanut oil
3 tablespoons butter
1 two-rib roast of beef (about 5 pounds)
¼ cup Armagnac
Salt
Freshly ground black pepper
3 slices of fresh pork fat or ham fat
1 celery stalk, sliced

1 large onion, chopped
3 shallots, chopped
1 carrot, sliced
1 garlic clove, mashed
1 bottle Sauvignon, muscadet or similar dry white wine
1 Bouquet Garni (p. 46)
8 raw artichoke hearts
1 cup Sauce Tomate (p. 769)
6 small potatoes, baked

FILET DE BOEUF EN CROÛTE / *Beef Fillet en Croûte*

Lard the fillet with the lardoons of fresh pork fat and roast it in a 450° F. oven for about 20 minutes. Remove the meat from the oven and cool it to room temperature.

Roll out the *brioche* dough to the thickness of ⅛ inch. Place the fillet in the middle and completely encase it in the pastry. Seal the edges tight. Place the wrapped beef on a baking sheet and let it rest in a warm place for about 30 minutes. Paint the top with the egg yolk and bake in a preheated 400° F. oven for 15 to 20 minutes.

Serve as soon as the pastry is golden, accompanied by a sauceboat of the *sauce Périgueux.*

As a variation, before wrapping the meat in the pastry, you may also coat it with a layer of puréed mushrooms, or a layer of *foie gras,* or puréed onions.

FOR 4 PERSONS:

1 **fillet of beef (2½ to 3 pounds)**
¼ **pound fresh pork fat, cut into narrow strips (lardoons)**
½ **recipe Brioche dough (p. 695)**

1 **egg yolk**
2 **cups Sauce Périgueux (p. 765)**

FILET DE BOEUF RÉGENCE / *Beef Fillet Régence*

Lard the fillet with some of the lardoons of fresh pork fat and brown it quickly on all sides in the oil in a large skillet.

Line the bottom of a casserole with the remaining lardoons, the sliced carrot and onion. Place the browned fillet on the vegetables, season it with salt and pepper, and add the brandy. Cover and cook in a preheated 350° F. oven for about 40 minutes, basting it frequently with the pan juices.

Transfer the fillet to a hot serving platter. Strain the sauce through a fine sieve and serve it separately, in a sauceboat.

FOR 4 PERSONS:

1 **fillet of beef (about 3 pounds)**
¼ **pound fresh pork fat, cut into narrow strips (lardoons)**
4 **tablespoons peanut oil**
1 **carrot, sliced**

1 **onion, sliced**
Salt
Freshly ground black pepper
½ **cup brandy**

FILET DE BOEUF SARLADAISE / *Beef Fillet Sarladaise*

Lard the fillet with some of the lardoons of fresh pork fat and the truffles. Brown the fillet quickly on all sides in the hot oil in a skillet.

Line a baking dish with the remaining fresh pork fat and the carrot slices. Lay the browned fillet on top and season with salt and pepper. Add the Madeira. Cook, covered, in a preheated 350° F. oven for about 40 minutes, basting frequently with the pan juices.

Transfer the fillet to a hot serving platter and strain the pan juices over it. Serve with a sauceboat of *sauce Périgueux* on the side.

FOR 4 PERSONS:

1 **fillet of beef (about 3 pounds)**	1 **carrot, sliced**
4 **slices of fresh pork fat, cut into narrow strips (lardoons)**	**Salt**
	Freshly ground black pepper
2 **truffles, cut into strips**	1 **cup Madeira**
4 **tablespoons peanut oil**	2 **cups Sauce Périgueux (p. 765)**

Boiled Beef / BOEUF À LA FICELLE

In a large pot combine 6 quarts of water, the beef bones, stock vegetables and a little salt. Bring to the boiling point and simmer for 2 to 3 hours. Be sure to put the beef bones into cold water, so as to extract their flavor to make a good stock. Strain the stock, return it to the pot, and bring it back to a boil.

Put the rump of beef into the boiling stock and simmer over low heat for about 2 hours. Then add the carrots, turnips, the white part of leeks tied into a bundle, the celery, the onion stuck with the clove, and the marrowbone, which should be sealed at either end with rounds of carrots and tied with string to keep the marrow from coming out. Simmer for about 1 hour longer.

About 30 minutes before the beef and vegetables are tender, put some of the stock in another saucepan and cook the potatoes in it.

Slice the raw beef marrow and poach it in boiling salted water for 5 minutes. Drain the marrow and spread it on the slices of toasted bread and season generously with pepper. Brown the marrow toast under the broiler for a moment.

Slice the meat and put it on a large hot serving platter. Surround it with the vegetables and the marrow from the beef bone; pour some of the stock over all. Serve the marrow toast separately.

FOR 6 PERSONS:

For the stock:	6 **leeks, white part only**
4 **pounds beef bones**	4 **celery stalks, cut into 3-inch pieces**
2 **carrots, sliced**	
2 **turnips, sliced**	1 **onion, stuck with 1 clove**
6 **leeks, green part only**	1 **beef marrowbone, the ends sealed with carrot slices**
1 **onion, stuck with 1 clove**	
Salt	12 **small new potatoes**
4 **pounds rump of beef**	¼ **pound raw beef marrow**
4 **carrots, scraped and halved**	6 **slices of bread, toasted**
2 **turnips, quartered**	**Freshly ground black pepper**

Boiled Beef with Coarse Salt / BOEUF GROS SEL

Prepare boiled beef as described above and, on the side, serve sour pickles, Dijon-style mustard and a bowl of coarse salt (Kosher salt).

BOEUF MIROTON / *Beef Miroton*

This dish is especially useful in using leftover boiled beef.

Heat the oil and the butter in a skillet; add the onions, three fourths of the sour pickles, the vinegar and the tomato paste. Season with salt and pepper and cook over high heat for 3 minutes.

Slice the meat, put it in a buttered baking dish, and top it with a few more pickle slices. Coat the meat with the onion and pickle mixture and sprinkle with the cheese. Brown under the broiler and serve in the baking dish.

FOR 4 PERSONS:

1½ pounds Boiled Beef (above)
2 tablespoons peanut oil
3 tablespoons butter
2 onions, minced
1 cup sliced sour pickles

½ cup wine vinegar
1 tablespoon tomato paste
Salt
Freshly ground black pepper
½ cup grated Swiss cheese

BOEUF À LA BOURGUIGNONNE / *Boeuf Bourguignon*

Cut the meat into 1½- to 2-inch cubes and marinate in a mixture of the sliced onions, carrots, peppercorns, parsley, thyme, bay leaf and half of the wine for 12 hours. Turn the meat occasionally.

Heat the oil and the butter in a casserole, add the tiny onions, and cook them until golden. Add the bacon strips and stir until they are golden. Remove the onions and the bacon and reserve.

Remove the meat from the marinade, pat it dry with kitchen towels, and brown it, a few pieces at a time, in the fat in the casserole.

Bring the marinade to a boil in a saucepan, reduce it slightly, and strain it.

Put all of the cubes of browned meat in the casserole, sprinkle with the flour, and stir over high heat for 2 or 3 minutes. Add the garlic cloves, the reduced marinade, the remaining wine, the reserved onions and bacon, the mushrooms and the *bouquet garni*. Season with salt and pepper and simmer, covered, over low heat for 2 hours.

When the meat is very tender, transfer it and the vegetables to a big hot serving dish and keep it hot. Boil the sauce for a few minutes and add the brandy. Boil for 2 more minutes. Strain the sauce through a fine sieve over the meat. Garnish with the croutons and serve with boiled potatoes on the side.

FOR 4 PERSONS:

3 pounds rump of beef
2 onions, sliced
2 carrots, sliced
6 peppercorns
3 parsley sprigs
Pinch of dried thyme
1 bay leaf
1 bottle dry red wine
4 tablespoons peanut oil
2 tablespoons butter
20 tiny white onions

¼ pound blanched bacon, cut into strips
2 tablespoons flour
3 garlic cloves
10 small mushrooms
1 Bouquet Garni (p. 46)
Salt
Freshly ground black pepper
¼ cup brandy
1 cup Croutons (p. 62)
Boiled potatoes

Daube of Beef / BOEUF EN DAUBE

Cut the beef into large cubes. Cut the salt pork into lardoons, or short strips, and roll them in a mixture of the minced parsley and garlic. Lard the cubes of beef with these strips and season with salt and pepper.

Put the meat into a bowl (do not use aluminum) with the shallots, the red wine and the *bouquet garni*. Marinate for 2 hours. Line a casserole or a *daube* pot with the sheets of fresh pork fat.

Drain the meat cubes and sauté them in the lard in a skillet. When they are browned on all sides, put them into the casserole lined with the pork fat and add the marinade.

Seal the lid on the casserole hermetically with a flour and water paste. Cook in a preheated 325° F. oven for 4 hours.

Serve from the same casserole.

FOR 6 PERSONS:

3 pounds rump of beef	**4 tablespoons minced shallots**
¼ pound salt pork	**1 bottle dry red wine**
4 tablespoons minced parsley	**1 Bouquet Garni (p. 46)**
1 garlic clove, minced	**2 thin sheets of fresh pork fat**
Salt	**4 tablespoons lard**
Freshly ground black pepper	**Flour and water paste**

Beef Stroganoff / BOEUF STROGANOFF

EDITORS' NOTE: *M. Oliver's version of this recipe differs somewhat from the standard one for this originally Russian dish.*

Heat the butter in a casserole and brown the meat in it rapidly. Season with salt and paprika and stir with a wooden spoon. Add the onions and cook for 2 minutes. Then add the tomatoes and the tomato paste. Mix with the wooden spoon, cook over low heat for about 3 minutes, and add the consommé. Check the seasoning and cook, covered, in a preheated 350° F. oven for about 45 minutes.

Serve in a hot deep dish, with boiled potatoes on the side.

FOR 2 PERSONS:

6 tablespoons butter	**2 tomatoes, peeled, seeded and**
¾ pound fillet of beef, cut	**chopped**
into thin strips	**1 teaspoon tomato paste**
Salt	**1 cup Beef Consommé (p. 167)**
Paprika	**Boiled potatoes**
1 tablespoon minced onion	

Broiled Steak / STEAK GRILLÉ

Marinate the steak in a mixture of the oil, a little salt, the peppercorns, parsley, bay leaves, chives and shallots in a cool place for at least 12 hours.

Pour steak and marinade into a large skillet over high heat until the marinade is very hot. Remove the steak and broil it on both sides under a high flame, timing it according to taste. Strain the marinade through a fine sieve over the cooked steak.

FOR 4 PERSONS:

1 beefsteak (sirloin,
   porterhouse, etc.), 3 pounds
½ cup peanut oil
Salt
4 peppercorns, crushed

5 parsley sprigs
4 bay leaves
2 tablespoons minced chives
4 shallots, minced

ENTRECÔTE GRILLÉE À L'AILLOLI / *Broiled Steak with Ailloli*

Coat the steak with oil, season with salt and pepper, and broil it according to taste under a high broiler flame. Spread a serving dish with the *ailloli* and place the steak on it.

FOR 4 PERSONS:

1 beefsteak (sirloin,
   porterhouse, etc.), 3 pounds
Olive oil

Salt
Freshly ground black pepper
½ cup Ailloli (p. 787)

/ *Steak with Anchovy Butter*

STEAK GRILLÉ AU BEURRE D'ANCHOIS

Brush the steak with oil and broil it according to taste under a high flame. Season the steak with salt and pepper and place it on a serving dish. Spread anchovy butter over the steak.

FOR 4 PERSONS:

1 beefsteak (sirloin,
   porterhouse, etc.), 3 pounds
Olive oil
Salt

Freshly ground black pepper
4 tablespoons Anchovy Butter
   (p. 792)

ENTRECÔTE MARCHAND DE VIN / *Steak Marchand de Vin*

Broil a steak in the usual manner and accompany it with Marchand de Vin butter, made as follows:

Cook the shallot and the wine together until the mixture is almost dry. Then stir in the meat glaze and the butter. Season with a little pepper only.

At serving time, add the minced fresh parsley and the lemon juice.

MARCHAND DE VIN BUTTER FOR 1 PERSON:

1 shallot, minced
½ cup dry red wine
1 teaspoon meat glaze
2 tablespoons butter, at room
   temperature

Freshly ground black pepper
1 tablespoon minced parsley
Juice of 1 lemon

Steak Bordelaise | ENTRECÔTE BORDELAISE

This steak is very much like a steak *marchand de vin* or *chasseur*. There are two ways of making it, and each has its partisans. Some cooks (from Bordeaux, for instance) broil the steak, whereas others sauté it in a skillet. Personally I have no preferences. Only the sauce matters.

For each person, put ½ cup of a good red Bordeaux wine and 1 finely minced shallot in a saucepan. Bring to the boiling point and then reduce by two thirds. Add 2 generous tablespoons of Sauce Demi-Glace (p. 766) or, if you don't have any, use pan juices from a roast of beef, or very strong consommé. Season to taste and reduce slightly. Prepare a tablespoon of Beurre Manié (p. 41) and stir it into the sauce to thicken it. Simmer for a few minutes. At the last moment add a few rounds of beef marrow which have been poached in boiling salted water for about 5 minutes. Finally add 1 tablespoon of finely minced, very fresh parsley. This is all for 1 serving. Coat the steak with this sauce and serve it with French fried potatoes.

Steak Bruce Matern |

Since I don't want to hurt anybody's feelings, I won't say much about Australian cooking, except to observe that the Australians' idea of gastronomy is a steak large enough to hold 6 fried eggs. Thus, this is a steak that I shall dedicate to my friends Bruce Matern and Chef Chenevier, a man of fine qualities.

With the point of a knife, the kind used for filleting a sole, cut a deep horizontal slit in each of the steaks. Fill these pockets with the onion purée, or more simply with minced onions sautéed in butter. The stuffing should be very well seasoned. Fasten the opening with poultry skewers and string. Broil the steak or sauté it in a skillet, timing it according to taste. If you like the meat well done, you may spread the steak with a little butter and finish cooking it in a preheated 350° F. oven for a few minutes longer.

Serve the steak on a wooden platter with potato croquettes and the fried eggs.

FOR 4 PERSONS:

4 steaks (each about 1 pound)
1 cup Onion Purée, Soubise, (p. 611), or 2 minced onions, sautéed in butter

4 Potato Croquettes (p. 640)
4 fried eggs

Steak Maubeuge |

Trim off the crusts from the bread slices and scoop out the centers so that they are hollowed out. Fry them in hot oil or lard until golden brown. Drain them and keep hot.

Season the steaks with salt and pepper and sauté them quickly in a little hot oil in a skillet, timing them according to taste. When they are golden on both sides, drain them and keep them hot.

Sauté the mushrooms in the pan juices, and season them with salt, pepper and a little thyme. Cook them over fairly high heat, stirring with a wooden spoon, until they are golden. Remove them with a slotted spoon and keep them hot.

Return the steaks to the skillet. Heat them through, add the brandy, and flame. Stir in the port. Cook for about 1 minute longer. Place the steaks on a serving platter and arrange the mushrooms around them. Top each steak with a slice of fried bread.

Add the mustard, the *crème fraîche* and the *sauce béchamel* to the skillet, bring to the boiling point, and cook, stirring constantly, until the sauce is thick and smooth. Spoon a little of this sauce into each of the fried bread slices. Serve immediately.

FOR 4 PERSONS:

4 slices of stale white bread, cut about 1 inch thick
Peanut oil or lard
4 small steaks (each ½ to ¾ pound)
Salt
Freshly ground black pepper

½ pound mushrooms, minced
Pinch of dried thyme
¼ cup brandy
¼ cup port
1 tablespoon Dijon-type mustard
¼ cup Crème Fraîche (p. 666)
¼ cup Sauce Béchamel (p. 761)

/ Steak au Poivre

Spread the peppercorns on a chopping board and crush them with a rolling pin. You'll need about a tablespoon of crushed pepper, called *mignonnette*, for each steak. Season steaks with salt. Rub the crushed peppercorns into both sides of each steak.

Make sauce I: Heat the oil and the butter for the sauce in a casserole and cook the carrots and onions in it until they are golden. Stir in the flour and mix well; add the tomatoes, *bouquet garni,* water and wine, and season lightly with salt; there is no need to pepper the sauce since it will be served with the steak *au poivre.* Cover the casserole and simmer for 1 hour. Then remove the cover and reduce until the sauce is thick. Force this sauce through a fine sieve and keep it hot.

Heat the 2 tablespoons each of oil and butter in a skillet over high heat and then add the steaks. Sauté them according to taste: very rare, rare, medium, or as you wish.

Put the steaks on a serving dish and keep them hot. Add the port to the skillet in which the steaks were sautéed and reduce by half. Stir in sauce I.

Add the *crème fraîche* and the brandy. Bring to the boiling point, remove from the heat, and stir in the softened butter. Pour this sauce over the steaks.

Make sauce II: Add the white wine to the skillet and reduce by half. Add the *crème fraîche* and reduce again. Stir in the brandy and season with a little salt. Remove from the heat and stir in the butter. Pour this sauce around the steaks.

FOR 4 PERSONS:

¼ cup whole peppercorns
4 steaks (each ½ to ¾ pound)
Salt
For Sauce I:
   1 tablespoon peanut oil
   2 tablespoons butter
   3 carrots, minced
   3 onions, minced
   1 tablespoon flour
   2 tomatoes, peeled, seeded and chopped
   1 Bouquet Garni (p. 46)
   2 cups water
   1 cup dry white wine
   Salt

2 tablespoons peanut oil
2 tablespoons butter
1 cup port
1 tablespoon Crème Fraîche (p. 666)
1 teaspoon brandy
2 tablespoons butter, softened
For Sauce II:
   ½ cup dry white wine
   ¼ cup Crème Fraîche (p. 666)
   ¼ cup brandy
   Salt
   3 tablespoons butter, softened

Steak Porteneuve | ENTRECÔTE PORTENEUVE

Broil the steak over a good fire made from vine twigs or the wood of old wine barrels, timing it according to taste.

At serving time, the steak may be covered with minced shallots and dotted with butter. This method, however, does not appeal to delicate palates.

My method is to cook blanched minced shallots in half of the butter until they are soft. Then, the shallots should be removed with a slotted spoon from the cooking butter and the remaining butter added to them. Spread this mixture over the steak and serve the *sauce béarnaise* and souffléed potatoes on the side.

FOR 4 PERSONS:

1 beefsteak (sirloin, porterhouse, etc.), 3 pounds
4 shallots, blanched and minced
8 tablespoons butter

2 cups Sauce Béarnaise (p. 779)
1 recipe Souffléed Potatoes (p. 628)

Steak with Truffles | STEAK AUX TRUFFES

The flavor of a steak may be varied by sprinkling it as it cooks with herbs, such as wild thyme, finocchio, marjoram or rosemary. But these are strong flavorings.

Another variation is to flavor a steak with truffles. One inserts little truffle sticks into the lean part of the meat. It is perhaps best when the steak is broiled over an open fire of vine twigs. The steak should be buttered first and seasoned with a little salt and pepper. Then a layer of raw truffles, spread on the steak, while the underside is broiling, will flavor it fully.

When the steak is done on the underside, scrape off the truffles, but save them. Turn the steak and spread the broiled side with the truffles. Finish broiling it to taste and serve immediately.

Tournedos (or Steak) Chasseur |

TOURNEDOS OU STEAK CHASSEUR

If one were to ask: "What is a tournedos?", the answer might be "a small steak that is cooked before you can turn your back." From this you'll gather that its cooking time is very short. Actually, tournedos are slices cut from the tail section of a fillet of beef. Sometimes, a steak, a sirloin for instance, may be cooked in the same way as tournedos, for instance, *à la chasseur*.

Heat half of the butter and all of the oil in a casserole over high heat and quickly sauté the tournedos on both sides. Time the cooking according to taste, but they should not be overdone. Put them on a serving dish and keep hot. Add the remaining butter to the pan juices, together with the shallots and the mushrooms. Sauté for about 5 minutes, or until golden. Add the wine, bring to the boiling point, and reduce by two thirds. Then add the consommé and the tomato paste. Stir in the *beurre manié* and simmer for 5 minutes longer.

Check the seasoning. Return the tournedos or steaks to the casserole and turn them in the sauce without letting them cook further. Put them back on the serving

STEAK PORTENEUVE
WITH SAUCE BÉARNAISE

This steak is broiled over a fire made from vine twigs or the staves from old wine casks. Cooking the steak hardly presents any difficulties, but the sauce béarnaise *requires careful attention. This sauce is especially appropriate with broiled dishes like this.*

You'll find the recipe for sauce béarnaise *on page 779.*

dish and coat with the sauce. Sprinkle with the minced parsley and garnish with the croutons.

FOR 4 PERSONS:

4 tournedos, ¼ pound each (slices cut from the rib end of a fillet of beef), or small boned sirloin steaks
6 tablespoons butter
3 tablespoons peanut oil
4 shallots, minced
¼ pound mushrooms, minced
1 cup dry white wine

¾ cup Beef Consommé (p. 167)
1 tablespoon tomato paste
1½ tablespoons Beurre Manié (see p. 41)
Salt
Freshly ground black pepper
2 tablespoons minced parsley
1 cup Croutons (see p. 62), fried in butter or goose fat

Tournedos with Herbs from Provence /
TOURNEDOS GRILLÉ AUX HERBES DE PROVENCE

Ask your butcher to bard the sides of the tournedos with slices of fresh pork fat and to tie them. Rub the top and bottom of each tournedos with the herbs. Brush them with oil and broil on both sides under a high flame. Time the broiling according to taste, but they should not be overdone. Season with salt and pepper and serve immediately.

FOR 4 PERSONS:

4 tournedos (¼ pound each), wrapped with fresh pork fat
1 tablespoon mixed dried thyme, basil, marjoram and a little crumbled bay leaf

Olive oil
Salt
Freshly ground black pepper

Beef Rolls / PAUPIETTES

Put the slices of beef between 2 sheets of wax paper and flatten them with a meat mallet or the flat side of a cleaver. Season with salt and pepper and put a spoonful of the following stuffing on each slice: chiffonade of lettuce, chopped blanched spinach and cooked rice, all mixed together. Season again with salt, pepper and nutmeg. Roll up the meat slices, fasten them with food picks, and coat them with oil. Broil the rolls under a high broiler flame, turning them until browned on all sides.

FOR 4 PERSONS:

8 slices of sirloin or top round of beef, cut about ½ inch thick
Salt
Freshly ground black pepper
⅓ cup cooked Chiffonade of Lettuce (p. 599)

⅓ cup Blanched Spinach (p. 644), chopped
½ cup cooked rice
Grated nutmeg
¼ cup peanut oil

ESTOUFFAT CATALAN / *Catalan Stew*

Heat the oil and butter in a casserole and quickly brown the meat in it on both sides. Remove the meat and keep hot. Add the onions and the carrots and cook them until they are soft.

Return the meat to the casserole and add the wine, tomato paste and *bouquet garni*. Season with salt and pepper. Top with the potatoes and cover the casserole. Simmer over low heat for about 1 hour.

Remove the *bouquet garni* and serve in the casserole.

FOR 4 PERSONS:

4 tablespoons olive oil
2 tablespoons butter
4 small beefsteaks, cut ½ inch thick
2 onions, minced
2 carrots, minced

1 cup dry white wine
4 tablespoons tomato paste
1 Bouquet Garni (p. 46)
Salt
Freshly ground black pepper
4 large potatoes, minced

CHACHLIK / *Shashlik*

Cut the meat into 2-inch cubes and marinate the cubes in a mixture of the wine, onion, carrot, shallots, peppercorns, a little coarse salt, the thyme, bay leaf, cloves and brandy for 48 hours.

Drain the meat and dry each piece carefully. Thread the meat on a skewer and broil under a high flame, turning the skewer until the meat is brown on all sides.

Serve the skewer with the rice *à la créole* and with grated onion and carrot on the side.

FOR 1 PERSON:

⅓ pound beefsteak (sirloin, fillet, etc.)
1 cup dry red wine
1 onion, chopped
1 carrot, chopped
2 shallots, chopped
6 peppercorns
Coarse (Kosher) salt

Pinch of dried thyme
1 bay leaf
3 cloves
2 tablespoons brandy
¼ recipe Rice à la Créole (p. 658)
1 onion, grated
1 carrot, grated

/ *Steak Tartare*

The dish of ground raw steak that we call *américaine* or "cannibal," is a first cousin to the dish of ground raw fillet of our fathers. In those days it was a convenient use for the tail end of the fillet, but today steak tartare is made from any cut of good lean beef without gristle.

Everybody thinks he has the best of all recipes for steak tartare but there are no recipes for it. The raw meat must be well salted and peppered, far more heavily so than cooked meat. Then egg yolks and a variety of seasonings may be added to the meat.

Here is a basic recipe, though the amounts depend on individual tastes.

To serve 1 person, combine 1 egg yolk, mustard (1 tablespoon or more of Dijon-style), 1 teaspoon of lemon juice, a generous amount of salt and pepper, and a table-spoon of oil to make a smooth sauce. Stir this mixture into ½ pound of good ground raw beef. Add 1 tablespoon each of capers and *fines herbes* and all the oil the mixture can absorb while still remaining firm. Serve with very hot French fried potatoes.

Sautéed Hamburger / STEAK HACHÉ OU HAMBURGER

Hamburger has the advantage of being tender and quickly cooked, since the cooking time for ground beefsteak is shorter than for an ordinary steak of the same size and weight.

Season the meat with salt and pepper before forming into patties, or season the hamburger at cooking time. Sauté it in a skillet over high heat according to taste.

Serve the hamburger spread with Dijon-type mustard and it becomes *bourguignon,* or top it with a slice of pineapple which makes it "Hawaiian." It becomes *espagnol* with a garnish of sweet peppers, *portugaise* with one of tomatoes, or *flamand* with Belgian endives. Or the hamburger may be heavily seasoned with pepper, or served with a *sauce Bercy* or a Sauce Béarnaise (p. 779). It calls itself *tyrolienne* when it is garnished with fried parsley, fried onion rings, chopped tomato and a few Potatoes Allumette (p. 627). With a fried egg topping the hamburger, it becomes *à cheval* and a strictly classic dish.

Hamburger Boulangère / HAMBURGER À LA BOULANGÈRE

Peel the potatoes and cut them into thin slices. Heat the lard in a very large skillet. Add the potatoes and season with salt and pepper.

Push the potatoes to one side and add the onions. Sauté for 4 to 5 minutes and push the onions to one side. Add the hamburgers, season the meat with salt and pepper, and brown it on both sides. While the hamburgers are cooking, put the onions on top of the meat so that they won't brown too much. Transfer the cooked hamburgers and the onions to a hot serving dish and keep hot. Fry the eggs in the skillet; the eggs and potatoes should be ready at the same time.

Spoon the potatoes around the hamburgers, top each with a fried egg, and serve immediately.

FOR 2 PERSONS:

1 **pound potatoes**	2 **onions, chopped**
6 **tablespoons lard**	2 **hamburger patties (each**
Salt	⅓ **pound)**
Freshly ground black pepper	2 **eggs**

Grilled Oxtail / QUEUE DE BOEUF GRILLÉ

Cut the oxtail into pieces and cook it in boiling salted water for about 2 hours, or until it is tender. Cool the meat, dip the pieces into the melted butter, and coat with

the bread crumbs. Broil under a high broiler flame until golden on all sides.
Serve immediately with a *sauce piquante*.

FOR 4 PERSONS:

1 oxtail	**1½ cups fine dry bread crumbs**
½ cup melted butter	**2 cups Sauce Piquante (p. 765)**

QUEUE DE BOEUF EN HOCHEPOT / *Hodgepot of Oxtail*

Cut the oxtail into bite-size pieces. Heat half of the oil and half of the butter in a casserole and brown the oxtail pieces in it.

Remove the meat and keep it hot. Stir the flour into the fat in the casserole and add the stock. Cook, stirring constantly, until the sauce is smooth and slightly thickened. Season with salt and pepper, add the *bouquet garni* and the garlic, and put the meat back into the casserole. Simmer, covered, for about 1½ hours, or until the meat is tender.

Sauté the turnips slowly in the remaining oil and butter until they are golden and add them to the casserole about 20 minutes before the oxtail is done. Serve very hot in the casserole.

Note: The turnips may be replaced by potatoes or carrots.

FOR 4 PERSONS:

1 oxtail	**Salt**
4 tablespoons peanut oil	**Freshly ground black pepper**
4 tablespoons butter	**1 Bouquet Garni (p. 46)**
1½ tablespoons flour	**1 garlic clove**
1½ cups Brown Stock (p. 164)	**1 pound small turnips, quartered**

COEUR DE BOEUF EN MATELOTE / *Beef Heart Matelote*

Cut the beef heart into halves, wash thoroughly in several changes of water, and remove all the gristle and nerves.

Cut the meat into bite-size pieces and marinate in the vinegar with the thyme, bay leaves, cloves, and a little salt and pepper for 7 hours. The meat should be covered by the marinade.

Drain the meat and pat it dry with kitchen paper. Heat the butter and half of the bacon dice in a casserole and cook until they are golden. Add the pieces of beef heart and stir for 1 minute. Stir in the flour with a wooden spoon and then add enough wine to cover the meat. Season with salt and pepper, add the *bouquet garni* and the garlic, and simmer, covered, over low heat for about 4 hours.

Half an hour before the meat is ready, add the remaining bacon, the onions and the mushrooms.

Remove the *bouquet garni* before serving the beef heart and vegetables in a large hot dish.

FOR 6 PERSONS:

1 beef heart (4 pounds)	1 tablespoon flour
2 cups wine vinegar	2 cups (approximately) dry red
Pinch of dried thyme	wine
4 bay leaves	1 Bouquet Garni (p. 46)
4 cloves	1 garlic clove
Salt	12 tiny white onions
Freshly ground black pepper	12 small mushrooms
3 tablespoons butter	
1 pound bacon, blanched and cut into small dice	

Broiled Beef Liver / FOIE DE BOEUF GRILLÉ

Season the slices of meat with salt and pepper. Broil them quickly on both sides under a high broiler flame. Quickly spread four of the slices with the parsley butter and top each with one of the other slices. Serve immediately, sprinkled with the combined minced parsley and garlic.

FOR 4 PERSONS:

8 thin slices of beef liver	2 tablespoons minced parsley
Salt	1 garlic clove, minced
Freshly ground black pepper	
½ cup butter mixed with 4 tablespoons minced parsley	

Braised Beef Tongue / LANGUE DE BOEUF BRAISÉE

Soak the tongue in several changes of water for 5 to 6 hours. Blanch it in boiling water for 1½ hours and let it cool. Remove the skin and the gristle and bones at the thick end. Lard the tongue with the strips of fresh pork fat. Line a casserole with the slices of bacon and ham, the carrots and onions. Place the tongue on top. Season lightly with salt and pepper and add the *bouquet garni.*

Add the consommé, wine and brandy. Cover the casserole and simmer over very low heat for about 2 hours.

Put the tongue on a hot serving platter and garnish it with the bacon and ham slices. Strain the pan juices through a fine sieve over the tongue.

FOR 4 PERSONS:

1 fresh beef tongue	3 onions, minced
¼ pound fresh pork fat, cut into narrow strips (lardoons)	Salt
	Freshly ground black pepper
¼ pound sliced bacon, blanched	1 Bouquet Garni (p. 46)
4 slices of Bayonne or smoked ham or prosciutto	1 cup Beef Consommé (p. 167)
	1 cup dry white wine
2 carrots, minced	¼ cup brandy

LANGUE DE BOEUF AUX HERBES / *Beef Tongue with Herbs*

Proceed as in the preceding recipe and add to the casserole before braising 3 minced shallots, 1 tablespoon minced parsley, 1 tablespoon minced chives, 10 minced small mushrooms, 3 minced sour pickles, 1 crumbled bay leaf and a pinch of dried thyme.

GRAS-DOUBLE À LA LYONNAISE / *Gras-Double Lyonnaise*

EDITORS' NOTE: Gras-double *is the fat smooth part of beef belly, known in the United States as one of the several kinds of tripe. It is not honeycombed as are the other types of tripe.*

Scrape and clean the tripe carefully and blanch it for a few minutes each in 3 changes of boiling water. Soak it in cold water for 24 hours, changing the water several times. Finally, simmer it in a casserole with the whole onions, the garlic, a little salt and pepper, and water to cover for 6 hours.

Drain the tripe and cut it into 2-inch pieces.

Sauté the onion rings in the combined hot oil and butter in a casserole until golden. Remove them with a slotted spoon. Add the tripe pieces to the casserole and cook them over low heat until golden. Add the onion rings, the vinegar or the wine, the water and the *bouquet garni*. Simmer, covered, over low heat for 30 minutes. Check the seasoning and, if necessary, add a little salt and pepper.

Remove the *bouquet garni* before serving and stir in the hot tomato sauce.

FOR 4 PERSONS:

2 **pounds smooth fat tripe**	2 **tablespoons peanut oil**
2 **onions, each stuck with 2**	3 **tablespoons butter**
cloves	¼ **cup vinegar, or** ½ **cup dry**
1 **whole garlic head**	**white wine**
Salt	1 **cup water**
Freshly ground black pepper	1 **Bouquet Garni (p. 46)**
4 **onions, sliced into rings**	1½ **cups Sauce Tomate (p. 769)**

TRIPES À LA MODE DE CAEN / *Tripe à la Mode de Caen*

Prepare the tripe as described in Gras-Double Lyonnaise (above), simmering it with the whole onions and garlic in salted water for 6 hours.

Heat the oil and butter in a casserole, add the minced carrots and onions, the bacon, *bouquet garni,* the minced garlic, the cloves and the veal knuckle. Add the tripe, cut into bite-size pieces, and wine to cover. Top the tripe with the fresh pork fat, cover the casserole, and simmer over very low heat for 7 to 8 hours.

When the tripe is done, remove the *bouquet garni,* skim the fat off the pan juices, and thicken them with the cornstarch. Serve very hot.

FOR 4 PERSONS:

2 pounds honeycomb tripe
2 onions, each stuck with 1 clove
1 whole garlic head
Salt
4 tablespoons peanut oil
3 tablespoons butter
2 carrots, minced
2 onions, minced
¼ pound blanched bacon, cut
  into small dice

1 Bouquet Garni (p. 46)
2 garlic cloves, minced
3 cloves
1 veal knuckle, cut into pieces
2 (or more) cups dry white wine
4 thin sheets of fresh pork fat
1 tablespoon cornstarch, mixed
  with a little water

Tripe Espagnole / TRIPES À L'ESPAGNOLE

Clean, blanch, soak, and then simmer the tripe with the whole onions and garlic in salted water for 6 hours. This process is described in Gras-Double Lyonnaise (above).

Cut the tripe into bite-size pieces and sauté them with the diced bacon in the combined hot oil and butter in a casserole. When golden, sprinkle the tripe with the flour, stir, and add the tomato paste and the wine. Mix well and add the minced onion and garlic, the *bouquet garni* and brandy. Season with salt and pepper. Cover the casserole and simmer over low heat for about 40 minutes.

FOR 4 PERSONS:

2 pounds honeycomb tripe
2 onions, each stuck with 1 clove
1 whole garlic head
Salt
¼ pound blanched bacon, cut
  into small dice
4 tablespoons olive oil
2 tablespoons butter

2 tablespoons flour
2 tablespoons tomato paste
2 cups dry white wine
1 onion, minced
1 garlic clove, minced
1 Bouquet Garni (p. 46)
¼ cup brandy
Freshly ground black pepper

LAMB AND MUTTON

Agneau et Mouton

EDITORS' NOTE: *French cuts of lamb are quite similar to United States cuts, although there are, of course, some differences. The French make exact distinctions between the different types of lamb, according to the age at which the lamb is slaughtered. Greatly prized is true baby or milk-fed lamb,* agneau de lait. *These tiny creatures are not yet weaned, only a few weeks old and never more than 2 months. A whole* agneau de lait *can weigh as little as 10 pounds and the meat is almost white and of exceptional tenderness. Real baby lamb of this kind is rarely found in American markets. Next comes what we would call spring lamb, which is between 3 and 5 months old and still milk fed. Then* agneau pré-salé, *which is between 5 months and usually less than 1 year old. The best of these have fed on the pré-salés, or salt meadows, along the northern coast and hence their name. All lamb over 1 year of age is mutton. While the meat industry in the United States theoretically makes closely similar distinctions, retail markets tend to be somewhat indiscriminate in the use of the terms spring lamb, genuine spring lamb, or milk-fed lamb.*

Lamb

Agneau

/ *Leg of Lamb en Chevreuil*

GIGOT D'AGNEAU EN CHEVREUIL

Lard the leg of lamb with the fatback lardoons, and marinate it in the vinegar, wine, carrots, onions, the *bouquet garni,* garlic, shallots and a little salt and pepper for 12 hours.

Drain the leg of lamb, dry it, and season it with salt and pepper. Brush it with oil and roast it in a 400° F. oven for about 1 hour, or according to taste.

Put the leg of lamb on a hot serving dish and serve it with a sauceboat of hot *sauce poivrade.*

Note: Some of the marinade liquid may be substituted for red wine in preparing the *sauce poivrade;* or the sauce may be prepared in the usual way, a little of the marinade added to it, and then reduced to the proper consistency.

FOR 6 PERSONS:

1 **leg of lamb (5 pounds)**	1 **Bouquet Garni (p. 46)**
¼ **pound fresh pork fatback,**	1 **garlic clove, chopped**
cut into thin strips (lardoons)	2 **shallots, chopped**
2 **cups vinegar**	**Salt**
4 **cups dry white wine**	**Freshly ground black pepper**
2 **carrots, chopped**	**Peanut oil**
2 **onions, sliced**	2½ **cups Sauce Poivrade (p. 765)**

/ *Leg of Lamb with Spring Vegetables*

GIGOT D'AGNEAU AUX PRIMEURS

Season the leg of lamb with salt and pepper, spread the butter over it, and roast it in a 400° F. oven for about 45 minutes, or according to taste. It should be not quite done.

Combine the *fines herbes* with the bread crumbs and moisten with a little oil. Coat the leg of lamb with the mixture. Return it to the oven for 10 to 15 minutes, or until the topping is crisp. Serve the leg of lamb on a hot platter, surrounded by a garnish of spring vegetables. Serve immediately.

FOR 6 PERSONS:

1 leg of lamb (5 to 6 pounds)	**½ cup Fines Herbes (p. 89)**
Salt	**2 cups fresh white bread crumbs**
Freshly ground black pepper	**Peanut oil**
4 tablespoons butter, softened	

Stuffed Leg of Lamb / GIGOT D'AGNEAU FARCI RÔTI

Bone the leg of lamb, or ask your butcher to do it, and lay it out flat.

Make the stuffing: Mix the veal, pork and chicken livers with the bread crumbs and season with salt and pepper.

Season the lamb with a little salt, pepper and cayenne and sprinkle it with thyme, finocchio and rosemary. Spread the filling over the meat.

Roll up the meat and tie it or fasten it with poultry skewers, so that none of the filling will ooze out during the cooking.

Sprinkle the garlic, carrots and onion in the bottom of a casserole. Put the meat into it, add a very little water, and cook it in a preheated 375° F. oven for about 1 hour, or according to taste. Let the cooked meat stand in a warm place for at least 10 minutes before serving it on a hot serving platter.

FOR 6 PERSONS:

1 leg of lamb (5 pounds)	**Cayenne pepper**
¼ pound boneless veal, ground	**Pinch of dried thyme**
¼ pound lean boneless pork, ground	**2 tablespoons chopped finocchio leaves**
6 chicken livers, chopped	**1 teaspoon dried rosemary**
1 cup fresh white bread crumbs	**1 garlic clove, minced**
Salt	**3 carrots, chopped**
Freshly ground black pepper	**1 onion, chopped**

Roast Saddle of Lamb Mirabelles /

SELLE D'AGNEAU RÔTIE MIRABELLES

EDITORS' NOTE: *A French saddle of lamb,* selle d'agneau, *is the upper part of the leg, extending from just above the aitch bone to the tail end of the loin. Thus it is a fairly small cut. An American saddle is entirely different, comprising both sides of the loin, unseparated.*

Season the French saddle of lamb with salt and pepper and roast it in a 375° F. oven for about 40 minutes, or according to taste.

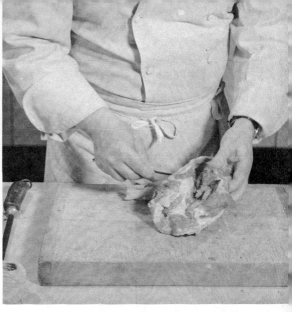

STUFFED LEG OF LAMB EN BALLON
Le Gigot d'Agneau Farci en Ballon

Here, the leg of lamb makes an appearance en ballon. *Bone the leg of lamb and spread it with the stuffing. Then, tie it up.*

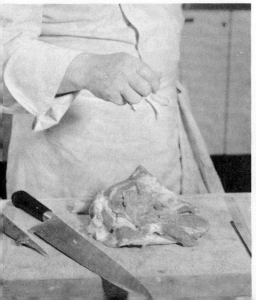

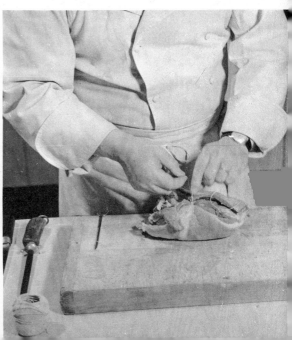

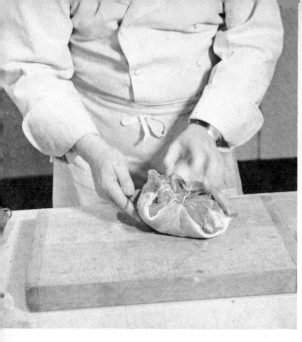

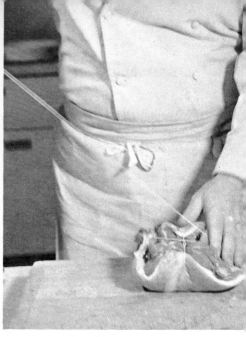

To tie the leg of lamb securely, do this:
Above: *First tie it in the shape of a cross with the string at right angles.*

Below: *Then tie it on the bias, crossing the strings. Notice how the fingers keep the meat in shape, without crushing it.*

Lobster Moscovite

Langouste ou Homard Moscovite

Lobster Moscovite

Langouste ou Homard Moscovite

COOK THE LOBSTERS in the *court bouillon* for about 15 minutes and let them cool in it. Remove the tail meat from the lobsters without damaging the shells. Slice the lobster meat into rounds (including the claw meat, if using New England lobster) and decorate the rounds with small strips of pimiento and sliced black olives (see illustration). Cut the hard-cooked eggs lengthwise into halves. Take out the yolks and mash them with the anchovies. Beat in enough mayonnaise to make a smooth paste.

Mix the vegetable *macédoine* with 1 cup of the mayonnaise and season the mixture with salt and pepper. Stuff the egg whites with the tunafish and decorate with watercress leaves. Slice the cucumbers as thin as possible and sprinkle them generously with salt. Let stand for 1 hour, rinse under running cold water, and squeeze dry. Toss the cucumbers with the French dressing and sprinkle with the *fines herbes*.

Place the lobster shells on a large serving platter and top them with overlapping rows of the garnished rounds of lobster meat. Surround with a circle of the *macédoine* of vegetables and place the stuffed eggs around the edge of the platter. Put the egg-yolk and anchovy mixture in a pastry bag fitted with a fluted tube and pipe decorative mounds around the eggs.

Serve the cucumbers and the remaining mayonnaise on the side.

For 12 persons:

2 lobsters (4 pounds each)
Court Bouillon for Lobster (p. 243)
Pimiento strips
6 black olives, sliced
8 hard-cooked eggs
8 anchovies
6 cups Mayonnaise (p. 782)
6 cups cooked Macédoine of Vegetables (see p. 111)
Salt

Freshly ground black pepper
1 cup tunafish canned in olive oil, drained and flaked
5 sprigs of watercress
6 cucumbers
½ cup Simple French Dressing (p. 787)
2 tablespoons minced Fines Herbes (p. 89)

Congolese Peppersteak
Steak au Poivre Congolais

Congolese Peppersteak
Steak au Poivre Congolais

SEASON THE STEAK with salt and rub it with the green peppercorns. Heat the oil and butter in a deep skillet and cook the steak in it on both sides. Transfer it to a hot serving dish and keep hot. Pour off the pan juices, add the Armagnac to the skillet, and scrape up all the brown bits in the bottom. Heat and then flame. Stir in the *crème fraîche*, bring to the boiling point, and reduce by half. Coat the steak with the sauce and serve very hot.

For 1 person:

1 beefsteak (sirloin, porterhouse, etc.), ¾ pound
Salt
1 tablespoon green peppercorns, coarsely crushed
2 tablespoons peanut oil
2 tablespoons butter
¼ cup Armagnac
½ cup Crème Fraîche (p. 666)

Rib Roast of Beef with Potatoes and Mushrooms
Côte de Charolais Forestière

Rib Roast of Beef with Potatoes and Mushrooms

Côte de Charolais Forestière

ROAST THE BEEF in the manner described in the recipe for Rib Roast of Beef (p. 396).

Bake the potatoes with the meat, basting them occasionally with half of the butter.

Sauté the mushrooms in the remaining butter and season them with salt.

Put the meat on a hot serving platter and garnish it with the potatoes and mushrooms.

For 6 persons:

1 rib roast of beef (approximately 5 pounds)
6 large potatoes, parboiled for 10 minutes and drained
½ cup butter
1 pound girolles, or other mushrooms
Salt

Rib of Beef Grilled over Vine Cuttings

Côte de Boeuf Grillée au Feu de Sarments

Rib of Beef Grilled over Vine Cuttings

Côte de Boeuf Grillée au Feu de Sarments

PREPARE THE BRAISED lettuce.

While the lettuce is cooking, season the meat with salt and pepper and brush it with oil. Prepare a good fire of vine cuttings in an open grill and grill the meat for about 10 minutes on each side, or more to taste.

While the beef is cooking, sauté the potatoes Darphin. Put the grilled meat on a hot serving platter and garnish with the lettuce and the potatoes.

For 4 persons:

1 recipe Braised Lettuce (p. 598)
1 rib of beef (approximately 3 pounds)
Salt
Freshly ground black pepper
3 tablespoons peanut oil
1 recipe Potatoes Darphin (p. 635)

Steak Tartare Tarass Boulba

Steak Tartare Tarass Boulba

PUT THE GROUND steak into a bowl and season it with salt and pepper. Blend in 1 egg yolk, the mustard, oil, lemon juice, cayenne, 2 tablespoons of the minced onion, 1 tablespoon of the capers, 1 tablespoon of the parsley, the ketchup and the Worcestershire sauce.

Shape the ground steak into a mound and put it on a serving plate. Press an egg-shell half, filled with the other egg yolk, into the ground steak, and put the remaining capers, onion and parsley around it.

For 1 person:

⅓ pound ground beefsteak
Salt
Freshly ground black
    pepper
2 egg yolks
1 teaspoon Dijon-type
    mustard
1 tablespoon olive oil

Juice of 1 lemon
Pinch of cayenne pepper
¼ cup minced onion
¼ cup capers
¼ cup minced parsley
1 teaspoon ketchup
Dash of Worcestershire
    sauce

Stuffed Shoulder of Lamb Landaise

Épaule d'Agneau Farcie Landaise

Stuffed Shoulder of Lamb Landaise

Épaule d'Agneau Farcie Landaise

BONE THE SHOULDER of lamb, leaving only the center bone to project from the meat. Or, if this is too difficult, simply bone the meat completely.

Mince or grind together the veal, pork and chicken livers. Add the bread crumbs, the parsley and the brandy. Season with salt and pepper and mix well. Spread the lamb out, stuff it, and roll it up. Tie it securely with kitchen string so that none of the filling will ooze out during cooking. Brown very quickly in the combined oil and butter on top of the stove and then roast in a preheated 400° F. oven for about 45 minutes. Baste frequently, and turn the meat to cook evenly on all sides. When it is three-quarters done, put the tomatoes around the meat and baste them.

Before serving, remove the string, put the meat on a large hot serving platter, and spoon the pan juices over the meat. Surround the meat with mounds of buttered spinach and top each mound of spinach with a tomato. Garnish the platter with the potatoes browned in butter. Lay a few blanched tarragon leaves over the meat.

For 4 persons:

1 boned shoulder of lamb
    (3 pounds)
4 ounces boneless veal
4 ounces boneless lean pork
4 ounces chicken livers
1 cup fresh bread crumbs
2 tablespoons minced
    parsley
1 teaspoon brandy
Salt

Freshly ground black
    pepper
3 tablespoons peanut oil
3 tablespoons butter
4 firm tomatoes
1 recipe Spinach in Butter
    (p. 644)
16 small new potatoes,
    boiled and browned in butter
Tarragon leaves, blanched

Breast of Veal Gascogne
Poitrine de Veau Farcie Gascogne

Breast of Veal Gascogne

Poitrine de Veau Farcie Gascogne

HAVE THE BUTCHER cut a large pocket in the breast of veal.

Prepare the stuffing: combine the sausage meat, bread crumbs, eggs, *crème fraîche* and the *fines herbes*. Mix well and season with salt and pepper. Stuff the breast of veal with this filling and sew it closed. Then tie the veal with string so that it will hold its shape.

With a knife score the top lightly in the shape of a cross. Season with salt and pepper and rub with the thyme.

Heat the lard in a large casserole over high heat and quickly brown the veal in it. Add the onion, carrot, celery and a little water, about 1 cup. Cover the casserole and simmer over low heat for about 3 hours, or until the veal is tender.

About 30 minutes before the veal is fully cooked, boil the elbow macaroni in a large quantity of boiling salted water until almost tender, and then drain it. Put it in a saucepan with the *sauce Mornay* and simmer for a few minutes.

At serving time, put the meat on a large hot serving platter and garnish it with fresh crisp lettuce. If the platter allows, put the macaroni on either side of the veal. Serve the veal pan juices, strained, in a sauceboat.

For 6 persons:

1 breast of veal (4
    pounds)
For the stuffing:
    ½ pound sausage meat
    3 cups fresh white bread
      crumbs
    2 eggs
    2 tablespoons Crème
      Fraîche (p. 666)
    3 tablespoons minced Fines
      Herbes (p. 89)

Salt
Freshly ground black pepper
1 teaspoon dried thyme
3 tablespoons lard
1 onion, minced
1 carrot, minced
2 celery stalks, minced
1 pound elbow macaroni
3 cups Sauce Mornay
    (p. 776)
Lettuce leaves

Shish Kebab Orientale

Chiche Kebab à l'Orientale

Shish Kebab Orientale

Chiche Kebab à l'Orientale

CUT THE LAMB into 2-inch cubes. Brush them with oil, season with pepper, and sprinkle with the crumbled bay leaf and the thyme. Let stand for 30 minutes or longer.

Prepare the rice, peas, tomatoes, peppers and zucchini; keep them warm. The quantity of each vegetable will depend on the number of persons to be served.

Drain the meat and skewer the cubes alternately with the bacon squares, whole bay leaves, pepper squares and mushrooms caps. All the skewer ingredients should be of approximately the same size. Season with salt and pepper and brush with oil. Brown on all sides under a high broiler flame or over a fire of live coals. They should take about 10 minutes.

Spread the rice on a platter, sprinkle with the peas, and lay the skewered meat on top. Garnish the platter with the tomatoes, peppers and zucchini.

For each skewer:

4 cubes of lamb (2-inch size)
½ cup olive oil
Freshly ground black pepper
2 bay leaves, crumbled
1 teaspoon dried thyme
Rice Cooked in Consommé (p. 657)
Peas in Butter (p. 614)
Tomatoes in Butter (p. 647)

Roasted Peppers (p. 619)
Zucchini, blanched and buttered
4 squares of thickly sliced bacon (2-inch size)
4 bay leaves
4 squares of sweet red peppers (2-inch size)
4 mushroom caps
Salt

While the meat is roasting, prepare the carrots, tomatoes, artichokes, green beans, peas, and potatoes.

When the saddle of lamb is ready, put it on a large serving dish and keep it hot. Remove the fat from the roasting pan, add the water and the wine, and deglaze the pan over high heat, scraping up the brown bits in the bottom of the pan with a wooden spoon. Strain the sauce through a fine sieve and pour it over the lamb. Garnish the lamb with the vegetables. Serve immediately, very hot.

FOR 4 PERSONS:

1 French saddle of lamb (2½ to 3 pounds)	½ recipe Boiled Green Beans in Butter (p. 556)
½ recipe Glazed Carrots (p. 576)	½ recipe Peas in Butter (p. 614)
½ recipe Tomatoes in Butter (p. 647)	½ recipe Rissolé Potatoes (p. 625)
4 Braised Artichoke Hearts (p. 545)	1 cup water
	1 cup dry white wine

CARRÉ D'AGNEAU RÔTI / *Roast Rack of Spring Lamb*

Line a baking dish with slices of fresh pork fat. Put the rack of lamb on it, season it with salt and pepper, and sprinkle a little oil over the meat. Roast it in a preheated 400° F. oven for about 35 minutes, or according to taste, basting occasionally.

Remove the lamb when it is golden on all sides. Put it on a large hot serving dish and surround it with a garnish of cooked vegetables, such as carrots, green snap beans and artichoke hearts filled with peas.

FOR 4 PERSONS:

5 or 6 thin slices of fresh pork fat	Salt
1 rack of spring lamb (about 4 pounds)	Freshly ground black pepper
	Peanut oil

/ *Roast Rack of Spring Lamb with Braised Lettuce*
CARRÉ D'AGNEAU RÔTI AUX LAITUES BRAISÉES

Roast a rack of lamb as described in the preceding recipe. Remove the lamb and keep it hot on a serving dish. Remove the fat from the roasting pan, add ¾ cup each of dry wine and water and, over fairly high heat, scrape up all the brown bits at the bottom of the pan with a wooden spoon. Bring to the boiling point, reduce slightly, and strain the sauce through a fine sieve into a sauceboat.

Garnish the lamb with little bundles of watercress and Braised Lettuce (p. 598).

RACK OF SPRING
LAMB

Le Carré d'Agneau

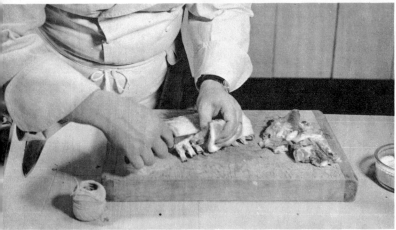

This is the way to p..
pare a rack of lamb.
With a small point..
sharp knife, start cutti..
back the skin from the e..
bones of the chops.

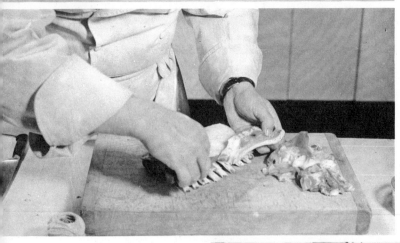

Pull back the skin
expose about 1 inch of t..
bones.

*Trim by cutting off most
of the fat, and arrange the
rack in an attractive shape.*

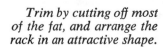

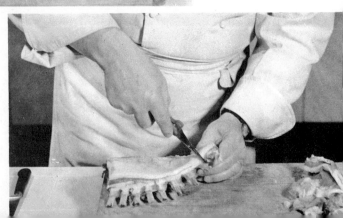

/ Crown Roast of Lamb with Spring Vegetables
COURONNE DE CÔTELETTES RÔTIES AUX PRIMEURS

Tie 2 racks of lamb into a crown shape, or ask your butcher to do it for you. Season it with salt and pepper, brush it with oil, and roast in a preheated 400° F. oven. The cooking time will depend on the thickness of the meat and, of course, your own taste.

At serving time, untie the roast and put it on a large hot serving dish. Garnish with any desired spring vegetables, such as carrots, green peas, or artichoke hearts filled with green peas or diced turnips.

FOR 6 TO 8 PERSONS:

1 crown roast of lamb	Freshly ground black pepper
Salt	Peanut oil

/ Stuffed Shoulder of Lamb with Rosemary
ÉPAULE D'AGNEAU FARCIE AU ROMARIN

Heat the oil and the butter in a deep casserole over fairly high heat and lightly brown the carrots and onions in it. Then add the tomatoes and the unpeeled garlic. Lower the heat, season with salt and pepper, and simmer gently for 20 minutes.

Bone the shoulder of lamb, or ask your butcher to do it. Lay it out flat and stuff it with the following mixture: combine the veal and pork and mix them with the brandy, thyme, parsley, chervil and a little salt and pepper.

Roll up the meat and spread it with the soft butter. Sprinkle the rosemary over the meat and season it with salt. Wrap it in the pig's caul or in the blanched pork slices. Tie the meat with string or fasten it with skewers. Put it on top of the vegetables in the casserole. Cover the casserole and seal it with a paste made by mixing the flour, the egg whites and a little water.

Cook in a preheated 375° F. oven for 1½ hours. Serve it in the casserole.

FOR 4 PERSONS:

2 tablespoons peanut oil	1 tablespoon fresh thyme leaves, or ½ teaspoon dried thyme
3 tablespoons butter	1 tablespoon minced parsley
3 carrots, chopped	1 tablespoon chopped fresh chervil, or ½ teaspoon dried chervil
3 onions, chopped	
3 tomatoes, peeled, seeded and chopped	3 tablespoons softened butter
1 garlic clove, unpeeled	2 tablespoons fresh rosemary leaves, or 1 teaspoon dried rosemary
Salt	
Freshly ground black pepper	Optional: 1 pig's caul or blanched salt pork, sliced paper thin
1 lamb shoulder (4 pounds)	
¼ pound veal, ground	2 cups flour
¼ pound lean pork, ground	2 egg whites
1 tablespoon brandy	

Roasted Whole Baby Lamb / AGNEAU DE LAIT ENTIER RÔTI

> EDITORS' NOTE: *The idea of buying and roasting a whole lamb may seem somewhat gargantuan to American tastes, but it must be remembered that a French baby lamb can be small indeed and may weigh only 10 to 12 pounds. Thus, a whole roasted lamb makes an excellent party dish.*

If you want to stuff the lamb's cavity, proceed as in Stuffed Suckling Pig (p. 457).

A stuffed 10-pound lamb takes about 2 hours to roast in a 375° F. oven, or about 1½ hours when it is not stuffed. In the latter case, let the lamb rest in a hot place for 30 minutes before carving it.

One small milk-fed lamb will serve 10 persons. To stuff a lamb this size with a simple filling, you will need about 3 pounds of stuffing made with fresh white bread crumbs, whole eggs, minced *fines herbes,* and the heart, lungs and liver of the lamb ground fine.

If you want to make a rich filling, the stuffing should include sausage meat, ground ham, truffles, etc. This rich filling should be somewhat precooked before being used to stuff the lamb, since its cooking time is longer than that of the meat.

Stuffed Baby Lamb / AGNEAU DE LAIT FARCI

There is an amusing way to roast a whole lamb without having a single unappealing piece. Separate the legs, French saddle, shoulders, rack and loins, and trim them into attractive-looking pieces. Take care to leave as much fell as possible on the shoulders and loins. Bone all the remaining pieces and trimmings and then grind the meat. Mix the ground meat with a generous quantity of bread crumbs and season with crumbled rosemary and a little salt.

Depending on your taste and the amount of available stuffing, bone several of the reserved lamb cuts, choosing the ones suitable for roasting, such as the shoulders or the legs. Stuff them with the filling, thus replacing the bones, and wrap each piece in lamb's caul or wafer-thin slices of fresh pork fat. Then roast all of the cuts in the usual manner in a good hot oven, 375° F. to 400° F.

Potatoes cooked in the pan juices from the meat are marvelous.

Broiled Lamb Chops /

CÔTELETTES D'AGNEAU GRILLÉES PANÉES

Brush the lamb chops with the oil, season with salt and pepper, and coat with the bread crumbs. Broil the chops on both sides under a hot broiler, timing them according to taste. Put the chops on a hot serving dish, garnish them with watercress, and serve them with the *maître d'hôtel* butter on the side.

FOR 4 PERSONS:

4 large rib lamb chops	½ cup fine dry bread crumbs
2 tablespoons peanut oil	1 small bunch of watercress
Salt	¾ cup Maître d'Hôtel Butter
Freshly ground black pepper	(p. 794)

CÔTELETTES D'AGNEAU À L'ITALIENNE / *Lamb Chops Italienne*

Brush the lamb chops with the hot melted butter and coat them on all sides with the combined bread crumbs and grated cheese, seasoned with salt and pepper. Then dip them into the eggs and then coat them again with the bread-crumb mixture.

Put the lamb chops under a hot broiler flame and broil them on both sides until brown and done to taste.

Serve them on a hot serving dish, with the tomato sauce on the side.

FOR 4 PERSONS:

8 small rib lamb chops	Salt
¼ cup hot melted butter	Freshly ground black pepper
½ cup fine dry bread crumbs	2 eggs, beaten
1 cup grated Swiss cheese	1 recipe Sauce Tomate (p. 769)

/ *Lamb Chops Provençale*

CÔTES D'AGNEAU À LA PROVENÇALE

Brush the lamb chops with a little of the oil and broil them under a very hot broiler flame until done to taste. Season with salt and pepper.

Heat the remaining oil and the butter in a casserole and add the bacon, onion, tomato paste, *bouquet garni* and consommé. Season with salt and pepper. Cook over low heat for 15 minutes and discard the *bouquet garni*.

Put the chops on a hot serving dish, decorate with the green and black olives, and coat with the sauce; if you prefer, serve the sauce on the side.

FOR 4 PERSONS:

4 large rib lamb chops	1 onion, minced
4 tablespoons olive oil	2 tablespoons tomato paste
Salt	1 Bouquet Garni (p. 46)
Freshly ground black pepper	½ cup Beef Consommé (p. 167)
2 tablespoons butter	8 green olives
¼ pound smoked bacon, blanched and cut into small dice	8 black olives

CÔTES D'AGNEAU CHAMPVALLON / *Lamb Chops Champvallon*

Heat half of the oil and half of the butter in a casserole and cook the tomatoes in it until they are very soft. Then add the potatoes, thyme and bay leaf.

Season with salt and pepper and add just enough boiling water to barely cover the potatoes. Cover the casserole and simmer over low heat for about 20 minutes. When the potatoes are done, the water should be absorbed by them. If it is not, uncover and boil the liquid away.

Heat the remaining oil and butter in a skillet; season the chops with salt and pepper and brown them quickly on both sides. Add the onions and cook until golden. Continue cooking until the chops are done to taste. Put the chops on top of the potatoes, pour the onions and pan juices over them, and cover the casserole. Simmer for 2 more minutes. Serve very hot.

FOR 2 PERSONS:

4 tablespoons peanut oil
4 tablespoons butter
3 tomatoes, peeled, seeded and chopped
3 potatoes, thinly sliced
1 sprig of fresh thyme, or ½ teaspoon dried thyme

1 bay leaf
Salt
Freshly ground black pepper
2 large rib lamb chops
2 onions, minced

Lamb Cutlets Bruxelloise | CÔTELETTES À LA BRUXELLOISE

Bone the lamb chops and put them between 2 sheets of wax paper. Flatten them slightly with a mallet or the flat side of a meat cleaver. Season the cutlets with salt and pepper and spread them on one side with a layer of truffled sausage meat. Wrap each completely with a piece of pig's caul, or alternatively, wrap them with very thin slices of salt pork, but this is more difficult.

Broil the cutlets under a hot broiler for about 3 minutes on each side. Serve them on a hot serving dish.

FOR 4 PERSONS:

8 thin rib lamb chops
Salt
Freshly ground black pepper
½ pound sausage meat

1 small truffle, diced
1 whole pig's caul, or 8 paper-thin slices of salt pork

Blanquette of Lamb | BLANQUETTE D'AGNEAU

Cut the lamb into 2-inch cubes. Heat the oil and butter in a casserole over fairly high heat and cook the cubes of lamb in it until golden on all sides. Season the pieces with salt and pepper. Sprinkle with the flour, stir for a minute, and then add the stock. Add the onions, mushrooms and *bouquet garni*. The liquid in the casserole should barely cover the meat. Add a little more stock if necessary. Cover the casserole and bring it to a boil. Then simmer over low heat for about 1 hour, or until the pieces of lamb are tender.

Transfer the meat to a hot serving dish and keep it hot. Remove the casserole from the heat and discard the *bouquet garni*. Beat the egg yolks in a bowl with a little of the liquid in the casserole and then pour this *liaison* into the casserole. Return to low heat and stir until slightly thickened. Do not boil. Off the heat, stir in the softened butter and the lemon juice. Pour the sauce over the meat, sprinkle with the parsley, and serve immediately.

FOR 4 PERSONS:

2 **pounds boneless breast of lamb**
2 **tablespoons peanut oil**
2 **tablespoons butter**
Salt
Freshly ground white pepper
2 **tablespoons flour**
2 **(or more) cups White Stock**
   (p. 165)

12 **small white onions, peeled**
½ **pound small mushrooms**
1 **Bouquet Garni (p. 46)**
4 **egg yolks, beaten**
3 **tablespoons butter, at room**
   temperature
Juice of 1 lemon
2 **tablespoons minced parsley**

CURRY D'AGNEAU / *Curry of Lamb*

Heat the lard in a casserole and add the onions. Cook, stirring with a wooden spoon, until the onions are very soft. Remove them with a slotted spoon.

Brown the meat on all sides in the fat remaining in the casserole over high heat and then return the onions to the casserole. Sprinkle with the curry powder. Mix well and sauté for about 3 minutes. Add the apples. Mix well and simmer until the apples are soft, about 10 minutes. Add the tomato juice and the water. Season with salt and pepper and add the bay leaf. Cover and simmer over low heat for 1½ hours.

Serve the curry in a hot dish, with the rice *à la créole* on the side.

FOR 4 PERSONS:

3 **tablespoons lard**
2 **large onions, minced**
2 **pounds shoulder of lamb, cut**
   into 1-inch pieces
3 **tablespoons curry powder**
½ **pound apples, peeled, cored**
   and chopped
1½ **cups tomato juice, made**
   from fresh tomatoes

1 **cup water**
Salt
Freshly ground black pepper
1 **bay leaf**
1 **recipe Rice à la Créole**
   (p. 658)

/ *Lamb Stew with Spring Vegetables*

RAGOÛT D'AGNEAU AUX PRIMEURS

Heat the oil and the butter in a large casserole and brown the pieces of lamb in it on all sides. Season with salt and pepper and sprinkle with the flour. Stir to blend and add the water or consommé, the *bouquet garni,* the garlic and the onion stuck with cloves. Cover and simmer over low heat for about 1 hour.

Add the white onions, the carrots, turnip, broad beans, peas, green snap beans and new potatoes. Check the seasoning and simmer very, very slowly for 1 more hour. Remove the *bouquet garni* and pour the stew into a very hot serving dish.

FOR 4 PERSONS:

2 tablespoons peanut oil
3 tablespoons butter
2 pounds boned shoulder of lamb,
    cut into 1-inch pieces
Salt
Freshly ground black pepper
2 tablespoons flour
2 cups water or Beef Consommé
    (p. 167)
1 Bouquet Garni (p. 46)
1 garlic clove

1 onion, stuck with 2 cloves
8 tiny white onions
4 carrots, diced
1 turnip, diced
½ cup shelled broad beans
½ cup shelled peas
¼ pound green snap beans,
    blanched in boiling salted
    water for 5 minutes
8 tiny new potatoes

Easter Birds / ALOUETTES PASCALINES

Another cut of lamb may be used for this dish, but it is shoulder that I prefer.

Put the lamb cutlets between 2 sheets of wax paper and flatten them with a mallet or the flat side of a cleaver. Season them with salt and pepper.

Make a stuffing by soaking the bread crumbs in the milk, squeezing them almost dry, and combining them with a goodly amount of *fines herbes,* the egg and the rosemary. Season with salt and pepper.

Put a generous tablespoon of this stuffing in the center of each lamb cutlet and roll it up, fastening the ends with food picks or threads.

Heat the oil and the butter in a casserole over high heat and sauté the mushrooms in it until they are slightly golden. Spoon them into a baking dish and lay the lamb birds on top. Cover the baking dish and cook the birds in a preheated 375° F. oven for about 25 minutes.

At serving time, blend the curry powder with the *crème fraîche.* Heat the mixture without boiling it.

Pour the curry sauce over the lamb birds and serve them immediately in the same dish.

FOR 4 PERSONS:

8 slices of lamb, cut ½ inch
    thick from the shoulder
Salt
Freshly ground white pepper
2 cups fresh white bread crumbs
Milk
¼ cup minced Fines Herbes
    (p. 89)
1 egg

2 tablespoons chopped fresh
    rosemary, or 1 tablespoon
    dried rosemary
2 tablespoons olive oil
2 tablespoons butter
½ pound mushrooms, sliced
1 tablespoon curry powder
1 cup Crème Fraîche (p. 666)

Fried Lambs' Brains / CERVELLE FRITE

Soak the lambs' brains in several changes of cold water for 2 hours. Pull off the thin outer skin and soak for another hour. Blanch the brains for 15 minutes in simmering salted water, acidulated with 1 tablespoon of vinegar per quart of water. Drain thoroughly.

Slice the brains into bite-size pieces. Mix together the batter ingredients and coat the brains with it. Fry them in deep hot fat heated to 360° F. on a frying thermometer until golden. Drain them and serve them on a hot serving dish lined with a folded napkin. Sprinkle with salt and the parsley.

FOR 4 PERSONS:

4 lambs' brains	**Frying batter:**
Salt	1 cup flour
Vinegar	1 teaspoon salt
	1 tablespoon peanut oil
	2 egg yolks
	⅔ cup beer
	Fat for deep frying
	3 tablespoons minced parsley

/ *Lamb Kidneys en Brochette*

ROGNONS D'AGNEAU EN BROCHETTES

Soak the kidneys in cold water for 5 minutes. Remove their thin skins and cut them halfway through. Thread them on skewers, so that they are spread open.

Season the kidneys with salt and pepper and brush them with oil. Broil them under a medium broiler flame or over an open fire for about 10 minutes. When the kidneys are golden, remove the skewers and place the kidneys on a very hot serving dish. Coat the kidneys with the *maître d'hôtel* butter and garnish with the watercress.

FOR 4 PERSONS:

8 lambs' kidneys	1 cup Maître d'Hôtel Butter
Salt	(p. 794)
Freshly ground black pepper	Watercress
Peanut oil	

/ *Lamb Sweetbreads en Brochette*

RIS D'AGNEAU GRILLÉS EN BROCHETTES

Soak the sweetbreads in several changes of cold water for 2 hours. Pull off as much of the outer skin as possible and then soak for 2 or more hours in cold water acidulated with a tablespoon of vinegar per quart of water. Trim the sweetbreads by separating the 2 lobes, discarding the connecting tubes.

Cut the sweetbreads into halves, making 8 pieces. Season them with salt and pepper and sprinkle them with the crumbled dried thyme. The sweetbreads are naturally very bland, so that they have to be well seasoned.

Cut the bacon into 1½-inch slices. Thread on skewers, in this order, a piece of bacon, a mushroom cap, a piece of bacon, a bay leaf, a slice of sweetbread, a bay leaf, etc. Bay leaves should be on both sides of the sweetbread.

Roll the skewers first in flour and then in oil. Broil them under a medium broiler flame for about 10 minutes, turning them to brown on all sides.

FOR 2 PERSONS:

2 pairs lamb sweetbreads	2 slices of bacon
Vinegar	8 mushroom caps
Salt	16 bay leaves
Freshly ground white pepper	Flour
1 teaspoon dried thyme	Peanut oil

Mutton

Mouton

Broiled Breast of Mutton | POITRINE DE MOUTON GRILLÉE

Put the breast of mutton into a casserole with just enough water to cover, and season with salt and pepper. Add a *bouquet garni* of parsley, chives, thyme and bay leaf.

Bring to a boil and then simmer gently for about 1½ hours, or until the mutton is almost tender. Drain it well. Brush it with oil, sprinkle it with the minced parsley and chives, and season it with salt and pepper. Coat it generously with bread crumbs and put it under a high broiler flame until golden brown. Turn it over and brown the other side.

Put in a hot serving dish and serve the *sauce piquante* on the side.

FOR 4 PERSONS:

3 pounds breast of mutton	1 tablespoon minced parsley
Salt	1 tablespoon minced chives
Freshly ground black pepper	2 cups fine dry bread crumbs
1 Bouquet Garni (p. 46)	2 cups Sauce Piquante (p. 765)
Peanut oil	

Mutton Chops as a Sandwich |

CÔTELETTES DE MOUTON EN SANDWICH

Sprinkle the mutton chops with salt and pepper and sandwich each of the thick chops between 2 thin ones, tying them together. Broil them under a medium broiler for about 20 minutes. Turn the chops over very frequently so that the chop in the middle will receive all the juices. Remove them from the broiler and serve only the 4 thick chops which you may garnish with paper frills.

FOR 4 PERSONS:

4 thick rib mutton chops	Salt
8 thin loin mutton chops	Freshly ground black pepper

HARICOT DE MOUTON / *Haricot of Mutton*

Cut the meat into 1-inch pieces and sauté them in the combined hot oil and butter until they are golden. Season with salt and pepper, sprinkle with flour, and stir with a wooden spoon until the flour browns lightly. Add the water, the *bouquet garni,* the garlic and one of the onions. Simmer, covered, over very low heat for 2 hours.

Cook the flageolet or haricot beans in boiling salted water with the remaining onion, the bay leaf and the thyme. When the beans are almost tender, remove the onion, bay leaf and thyme and add the beans to the meat to simmer for the last 30 minutes together. Remove the *bouquet garni.* Pour the *haricot* of mutton into a hot dish and serve immediately.

FOR 4 PERSONS:

2 pounds boned breast or shoulder
  of mutton
2 tablespoons peanut oil
3 tablespoons butter
Salt
Freshly ground black pepper
2 tablespoons flour
2 cups hot water
1 Bouquet Garni (p. 46)

1 garlic clove
2 onions, each stuck with 2
  cloves
1 pound dried flageolet or white
  beans, soaked overnight in
  cold water
1 bay leaf
1 sprig of thyme, or ½ teaspoon
  dried thyme

NAVARIN DE MOUTON / *Navarin of Mutton*

Cut the carrots and the onions into small pieces, and sauté them in hot lard in a casserole until they are golden.

Cut the meat into 1-inch pieces and brown it lightly in the combined hot oil and butter in a skillet. Add the meat to the carrots and onions. Sprinkle with the flour, stir for a minute, and add the wine and enough water to barely cover the mixture. Season with salt and pepper. Add the *bouquet garni,* the unpeeled garlic clove and the tomatoes. Simmer, covered, over low heat for 1½ hours.

Add the potatoes and simmer for 20 more minutes.

When the meat is very tender, remove the *bouquet garni* and serve in a hot serving dish.

FOR 4 PERSONS:

2 carrots
2 onions
3 tablespoons lard
2 pounds boned shoulder of mutton
2 tablespoons peanut oil
2 tablespoons butter
2 tablespoons flour
1 cup dry white wine

Salt
Freshly ground black pepper
1 Bouquet Garni (p. 46)
1 garlic clove, unpeeled
3 tomatoes, peeled, seeded and
  chopped
12 new small potatoes, peeled

/ *Cassoulet*

Cut the shoulder of mutton into pieces and brown the pieces in the goose fat or the lard in a large casserole. Add the sausages, pork rind and pig's hock. Simmer, covered, for 20 minutes, then add enough hot consommé to not quite cover the meats. Simmer, covered, over low heat for 1 hour. Cook the beans with the onion and the *bouquet garni* in boiling salted water until the beans are half tender, about 30 minutes. Then drain them and add them to the meats. Season with a little salt and pepper. Simmer, covered, over low heat for 1 more hour. After 30 minutes, add the tomato paste and check the seasoning. Serve in the same dish, very hot.

FOR 4 PERSONS:

1½ pounds shoulder of mutton
3 tablespoons goose fat or lard
½ pound garlic sausages
½ pound scraped fresh pork rind, cut into small pieces
1 pig's hock
3 (or more) cups Beef Consommé (p. 167)

½ pound dried white beans, soaked overnight in cold water
1 onion, stuck with 1 clove
1 Bouquet Garni (p. 46)
Salt
Freshly ground black pepper
1 tablespoon tomato paste

Roast Leg of Kid / GIGOT DE CHEVREAU

Have the leg boned by the butcher. Flatten out the meat on a board, sprinkle with the brandy, season it with salt and pepper to taste, and rub it with the herbs.

Roll up the meat and tie it in its original shape.

Rub the outside of the meat with salt and pepper and brush with the oil. Roast over a spit or in a preheated 350° F. oven for about 30 minutes. Baste it occasionally.

FOR 3 PERSONS:

1 leg of young kid (3 pounds)
3 tablespoons brandy
Salt
Freshly ground black pepper

3 tablespoons dried Fines Herbes (thyme, basil, bay leaf, etc., p. 89)
3 tablespoons olive oil

VEAL

Veau

Loin of Veal Bourgeoise / LONGE DE VEAU BOURGEOISE

Put the loin of veal with the bacon, oil and butter into a casserole over high heat. Cook until the veal is golden on all sides and then season with salt and pepper. Add the water, the *bouquet garni,* the carrots, onions and turnip, and bring to a boil. Cover the casserole, reduce the heat, and simmer for about 2 hours.

Put the meat on a serving plate. Skim the fat off the sauce and strain it over the meat.

FOR 4 PERSONS:

1 loin roast of veal (4 pounds)	Freshly ground black pepper
½ pound bacon, blanched and cut into small dice	1 cup water
	1 Bouquet Garni (p. 46)
2 tablespoons peanut oil	3 carrots, chopped
3 tablespoons butter	3 onions, chopped
Salt	1 turnip, chopped

/ *Braised Veal Shank with Lemon*

JARRET DE VEAU AU CITRON

Heat the oil and the butter in a large casserole and sauté the meat in it until it is golden on all sides. Add the onion, carrots, turnip, celery and, if you like, a piece of ham fat. Cover and simmer over low heat for 10 minutes. Then add the tomatoes, the *bouquet garni,* the wine and slivered lemon rind. Season with salt and pepper and simmer, covered, for 1 hour.

Peel 4 small potatoes for each person, add them to the casserole, and add a little water, if necessary, to keep the potatoes partially submerged in liquid. Cook for about 25 minutes longer.

Put the meat on a large hot serving platter. Garnish with the potatoes. Keep hot.

Strain the pan juices through a fine sieve, put them back into the casserole, and add the lemon juice. Bring to the boiling point, check the seasoning, and pour over the meat. Sprinkle with the parsley.

FOR 2 PERSONS:

2 tablespoons peanut oil	1 Bouquet Garni (p. 46)
2 tablespoons butter	1½ cups dry white wine
1 veal hind shank	Rind of 1 lemon, slivered
1 onion, stuck with 1 clove	Salt
2 carrots, chopped	Freshly ground black pepper
1 turnip, chopped	8 small new potatoes
1 heart of celery, chopped	Juice of 1 lemon
⅛ pound ham fat	2 tablespoons minced parsley
3 tomatoes, peeled, seeded and chopped	

QUASI DE VEAU / *Quasi of Veal*

Lard the veal with the lardoons of pork fat and then brown it on all sides in the hot olive oil in a casserole over high heat. Add the water and the bay leaf. Reduce the heat, cover, and simmer for about 1½ hours.

In another casserole cook the onions in the butter over medium heat until they are turning golden. Sprinkle them with the sugar and cook them for a few minutes longer, until they are a rich gold. Add 1 or 2 tablespoons of the pan juices of the meat, and the wine. Add the mushrooms, cover the casserole, and simmer until the mushrooms and onions are tender, about 15 minutes.

Put the meat on a serving platter and spoon the onions and mushrooms around it. Combine the meat juices and the liquid from the onions and mushrooms. Bring to a boil, stir in the cornstarch, and heat until slightly thickened. Coat the meat with the sauce and serve very hot.

FOR 4 PERSONS:

3 **pounds veal sirloin**	3 **tablespoons butter**
⅓ **pound fresh pork fat, cut into thin strips (lardoons)**	1 **tablespoon sugar**
4 **tablespoons olive oil**	½ **cup dry red wine**
½ **cup water**	15 **small mushrooms, trimmed**
1 **bay leaf**	1½ **tablespoons cornstarch, dissolved in 2 tablespoons water**
12 **small white onions**	

Boned Ribs of Veal with Mushrooms /

CARRÉ DE VEAU AUX GIROLLES

Have the butcher bone, roll, bard, and tie the ribs of veal and give you the bones. Heat the lard in a casserole over medium heat and add the bones and the meat.

Cook for 30 minutes, then turn the meat and cook for 30 minutes more. Season with salt and pepper. Spoon out most of the fat and add the mushrooms and the wine. Cover the casserole and simmer for about 30 minutes.

When the veal is tender, put it in a hot serving dish and spoon the mushrooms around it. Discard the bones. Add the lemon juice to the juices in the casserole, correct the seasoning, and pour over the veal. Sprinkle with the parsley.

FOR 4 PERSONS:

1 **boned rib roast of veal (3 pounds)**	2 **pounds girolles, or other mushrooms**
4 **tablespoons lard**	¾ **cup dry white wine**
Salt	**Juice of 1 lemon**
Freshly ground white pepper	2 **tablespoons minced parsley**

Jellied Veal / CARRÉ D'AGNEAU EN GELÉE

Have the butcher save the bones and any small bits of meat trimmings from the boned rib roast of veal. Make a deep incision in the meat so that it can be spread out and then flatten it slightly with a meat mallet or the flat side of a cleaver.

Prepare the stuffing: cut the meat trimmings into very fine dice and mix them with the bacon, ham and tongue. Season with salt, pepper and nutmeg. Add the parsley, chives, crumbled bay leaf and thyme. Mix together well and then stir in the eggs. Spread this stuffing on the meat, roll it up, and tie it securely with kitchen string. Wrap it in a pig's caul or very thinly sliced fresh pork fat. Sprinkle in the bottom of a casserole the bacon, pork rind, carrots, onions, *bouquet garni* and cloves. Add the veal bones and the tied meat, season with a little salt, and add the stock and wine. Bring to a boil and then simmer, covered, over low heat for 1½ hours, or until the meat is tender.

Remove the meat, allow it to cool completely, and then chill.

Strain the pan juices through a fine sieve and degrease them completely. Beat the egg whites until almost stiff. Pour the pan juices over the egg whites in a saucepan and put the pan over medium heat, stirring constantly until the mixture has reached the boiling point. Simmer for about 5 minutes and add the lemon juice. Allow it to stand for about 10 minutes and then strain it through several thicknesses of damp cheesecloth into a bowl. When the veal is cold, remove the strings and place it on a rack. Stir the bowl of clarified meat juices over ice until they thicken slightly and then coat the veal with this jelly on all sides. Transfer the meat to a serving dish and chill it for several hours.

FOR 4 PERSONS:

1 boned rib roast of veal
  (3 pounds)
For the stuffing:
  Trimmings from the boned
    veal
  ⅛ pound bacon, blanched
    and finely diced
  ⅓ cup finely minced ham
  ⅓ cup finely minced
    cooked tongue
  Salt
  Freshly ground black pepper
  Grated nutmeg
  1 tablespoon minced parsley
  1 tablespoon minced chives
  1 bay leaf, crumbled
  2 sprigs of thyme, crumbled,
  , or ½ teaspoon dried thyme
  2 eggs

1 pig's caul, or very thinly
  sliced fresh pork fat
2 strips of bacon, blanched
1 piece of scraped pork rind
  (¼ pound), cut into small pieces
2 carrots, minced
2 onions, minced
1 Bouquet Garni (p. 46)
3 cloves
Salt
1 cup White Stock (p. 165)
2 cups dry white wine
2 egg whites
Juice of 1 lemon

CARRÉ DE VEAU BIGARADE / *Rib Roast of Veal Bigarade*

On page 490 I've given you a recipe for Duck Bigarade. Follow that method generally for a rib roast of veal. Roast the veal. Make the Sauce Espagnole (p. 760) with veal bones. All the other ingredients are the same—the oranges, currant jelly and so on.

/ *Roast Rump of Veal with Onions*

RÔTI DE VEAU AUX OIGNONS

Line a roasting pan with a variety of chopped vegetables: celery, carrots, onions, finocchio, turnips, garlic and shallots. Lay the barded meat on it, spread it with the lard or butter, and season with salt and pepper. Add the water to the pan. Roast the meat in a preheated 350° F. oven for about 35 minutes, or until it is about half cooked. Turn the veal over once during this first roasting. Remove the meat from the roasting pan. Strain the pan juices and skim off the fat. Return these juices to the roasting pan. Stick about one third of the little onions with cloves and then add all of the onions to the roasting pan, together with the meat. Finish roasting the meat for about another 35 minutes, basting and turning meat and onions several times to let them cook evenly.

Serve in the same dish or on an earthenware platter.

FOR 4 PERSONS:

1 celery stalk, chopped	2 pounds rump of veal, barded
3 carrots, chopped	6 tablespoons lard or butter
2 large onions, chopped	Salt
½ finocchio bulb, chopped	Freshly ground black pepper
3 turnips, chopped	1 cup water
1 garlic clove, chopped	24 tiny white onions
2 shallots, chopped	8 cloves

Braised Rump of Veal with Prunes /

NOIX DE VEAU AUX PRUNEAUX

Stone the prunes and soak them in the Madeira overnight.

Heat 4 tablespoons of the butter in a casserole over high heat and brown the veal in it on all sides. Add the carrots and celery to the casserole. Season with salt and pepper, reduce the heat and, without adding any liquid at all, cover the casserole and simmer for 45 minutes. Remove the meat from the casserole and let it cool. Discard the vegetables but save the pan juices. Cut a ½-inch slice from the flattest side of the meat. This slice will serve as a lid for the stuffing.

With a very sharp knife, remove the center part of the meat, leaving about a 1-inch core on the bottom and sides. Mince together the meat from the cavity and the bacon. Put this mixture into the casserole with the pan juices. Add the remaining butter and season the minced meat with pepper and a very little salt. Stuff the cavity of the meat with the drained prunes. Cover the prunes with the reserved slice of veal and fasten it with food picks. Let the picks stick out a little so that they will be easy to remove.

Lay the meat on the minced veal and bacon in the casserole, cover, and simmer over low heat for about 1 hour. Remove the picks and serve the meat in the same dish.

If desired, you may add peeled very small new potatoes to the casserole when you are adding the stuffed meat and cook them with it. The combination is excellent.

Also, you may heat a little prune brandy, such as Quetsch or Mirabelle, add it to the meat at serving time, and flame it.

FOR 6 PERSONS:

1 pound prunes	Salt
3 cups Madeira	Freshly ground black pepper
½ cup butter	2 slices of bacon
3 pounds rump of veal	Optional: 18 tiny new potatoes
3 carrots, sliced	Optional: ⅓ cup prune brandy,
1 celery stalk, sliced	such as Quetsch or Mirabelle

/ *Carbonnade of Veal Southwest Fashion*

CARBONNADE À LA FAÇON DU SUD-OUEST

Marinate the veal in the oil and thyme for 12 hours. Drain it and brown it on all sides in half of the butter and 2 tablespoons of the marinade in a casserole over high heat. Season with salt and pepper, cover the casserole, and simmer over low heat for about 1½ hours, or until the meat is tender.

Put the meat on a serving dish and keep it hot.

Add the shallots and the ham to the pan juices in the casserole and cook them for about 5 minutes. Remove them with a slotted spoon and place them on the meat.

Add the remaining butter and the spinach to the casserole and cook for 5 to 8 minutes, or until the spinach is barely tender. Correct the seasoning, but it will need little or no salt. Garnish the veal with the spinach.

FOR 6 PERSONS:

4 **pounds rump of veal**	4 **shallots, chopped**
1 **cup olive oil**	½ **pound Bayonne or smoked ham**
8 **sprigs of thyme, or 2**	**or prosciutto, cut into small**
tablespoons dried thyme	**dice**
6 **tablespoons butter**	2 **pounds fresh spinach,**
Salt	**thoroughly washed**
Freshly ground black pepper	

/ *Old-Style Blanquette of Veal*

BLANQUETTE DE VEAU À L'ANCIENNE

Heat the oil and 3 tablespoons of the butter in a casserole over high heat, add the veal pieces, and sauté them very quickly on all sides without letting them actually brown. Remove the pieces with a slotted spoon and reserve them.

Add the pork fat to the casserole. Stir for a minute and then add the carrots, onions, celery, turnip, leeks and garlic. Cook, stirring frequently, until the vegetables are soft. Add the *bouquet garni,* the lemon rind and the meat. Add just enough boiling water to barely cover the meat. Season with salt and pepper. Bring to the boiling point, lower the heat, and cover the casserole. Simmer for 1 to 1½ hours, or until the meat is just tender.

Put the meat in another casserole with the carrots, onions and mushrooms, all cooked in butter. Keep the casserole warm.

Strain the veal cooking liquid through a fine sieve and degrease it. There should be about 4 cups.

Heat the remaining 4 tablespoons of butter in a saucepan, stir in the flour, and cook until barely golden. Stir the veal cooking liquid into the flour mixture and cook, stirring occasionally, until the sauce is somewhat thickened and smooth. Add the tarragon and simmer over low heat, stirring frequently, for about 20 minutes. Beat together the egg yolks, the *crème fraîche,* the lemon juice and the cayenne. Remove the sauce from the heat and beat in the egg-yolk mixture. Return the sauce to low heat and simmer very slowly until it is slightly thicker. Do not boil.

Add the veal and the vegetables and just heat through. Correct the seasoning and pour the *blanquette* into a hot serving dish.

FOR 4 PERSONS:

2 tablespoons peanut oil
7 tablespoons butter
3 pounds breast of veal, cut into
   2-inch pieces
¼ pound fresh pork fat, diced
3 carrots, diced
2 onions, diced
2 celery stalks, sliced
1 turnip, diced
2 leeks, white parts only, thinly
   sliced
2 garlic cloves, minced
1 Bouquet Garni (p. 46)
Grated rind of 1 lemon

Salt ·
Freshly ground white pepper
24 tiny Carrots in Butter
   (p. 575)
20 Glazed Onions (p. 610)
24 small Mushrooms Braised in
   Butter (p. 603)
4 tablespoons flour
2 tablespoons minced fresh tarragon
4 egg yolks
1 cup Crème Fraîche (p. 666)
Juice of 1 lemon
Pinch of cayenne pepper

Veal Sauté with Eggplant /

SAUTÉ DE VEAU AUX AUBERGINES

Brown the meat lightly on all sides in the combined hot oil and butter in a large casserole over high heat. Add the onions and cook until they are golden. Stir in the flour and then add the wine, garlic, tomatoes and eggplant. Mix well, season with salt and pepper, reduce the heat, and simmer, covered, over low heat for 1 hour and 15 minutes, or until the meat is tender.

Serve immediately in a hot serving dish.

FOR 4 PERSONS:

2 pounds shoulder of veal, cut
   into 1-inch pieces
2 tablespoons olive oil
3 tablespoons butter
2 onions, minced
1 tablespoon flour
1 cup dry white wine

2 garlic cloves, minced
3 medium-sized ripe tomatoes,
   peeled, seeded, and chopped
1 small eggplant, peeled and cut
   into 1½-inch cubes
Salt
Freshly ground black pepper

Veal Sauté Marengo / SAUTÉ DE VEAU MARENGO

Heat the olive oil in a casserole over medium heat, add the garlic and the meat, and sauté and turn the meat until browned on all sides. Stir in the flour and season with salt and cayenne. Add the wine, the *bouquet garni,* the shallots, mushrooms, tomatoes and onions. Season again, cover the casserole, and simmer over low heat for about 1 hour and 15 minutes.

Add the olives when the meat is almost tender and discard the *bouquet garni* before serving.

Cook the crayfish or shrimp in a wine *court bouillon* and fry the eggs in a little olive oil.

This is the way to dish up veal Marengo: Pour all of the casserole contents into a hot, deep serving dish and top them with the crayfish and the fried eggs. Serve immediately, and very hot.

FOR 4 PERSONS:

5 tablespoons olive oil
1 garlic clove, minced
2 pounds breast of veal, cut
   into 1-inch pieces
1 tablespoon flour
Salt
Cayenne pepper
1½ cups dry white wine
1 Bouquet Garni (p. 46)
2 shallots, chopped

¼ pound mushrooms, chopped
4 tomatoes, peeled, seeded and
   chopped
10 tiny white onions
1 cup pitted green olives
12 crayfish or shrimp, cooked in
   a wine Court Bouillon for
   Fish (p. 131) and shelled
4 eggs, fried in olive oil

/ *Veal Sauté with Spring Vegetables*

SAUTÉ DE VEAU PRINTANIER

Lard the slices of veal with the pork fat lardoons and brown them quickly on both sides in the combined hot oil and butter in a casserole over high heat. Season with salt and pepper, add the onion, cover, reduce the heat, and simmer for 10 minutes.

Put the meat on a large hot serving platter and garnish it with spring vegetables, each cooked separately in butter, such as new carrots cut into the shape of olives, peas, turnips, cauliflower, artichoke hearts, green snap beans and asparagus tips.

Pour the pan juices over meat and vegetables.

FOR 4 PERSONS:

2 pounds boned loin of veal, cut
   into ½-inch slices
¼ pound fresh pork fat, cut
   into thin strips (lardoons)
2 tablespoons peanut oil
3 tablespoons butter

Salt
Freshly ground black pepper
1 onion, minced
Fresh spring vegetables, cooked
   in butter (see index)

/ *Tendrons of Veal à l'Orange*

TENDRONS DE VEAU À L'ORANGE

Cut the veal into strips about 4 inches long and ¾ inch thick. Season the strips with salt and pepper, dust them with flour, and brown them quickly in the combined hot oil and butter in a large skillet or casserole. Reduce the heat, cover the casserole, and simmer very slowly for about 1 hour, or until the pieces are tender.

Peel the orange part only of the oranges and the yellow part only of the lemon. Cut these peelings (zest) into slivers and blanch them, using cold water, bringing it to a boil, and boiling for 5 minutes. Drain the slivers and reserve them. Peel the white skin off the oranges and the lemon, holding them over a bowl to catch any juice, and then slice them.

Put the sugar into a casserole and melt it over low heat, stirring with a wooden spoon, until the sugar is golden. Stir in the reserved juices, the vinegar and the white stock. Bring to a boil and simmer for a few minutes.

When the veal is tender, transfer it to a serving dish and keep hot. Pour the sauce into the pan in which the veal cooked and blend the sauce with the pan juices. Mix the cornstarch with the Curaçao and add it to the mixture, together with the currant jelly. Simmer over low heat for about 5 minutes, or until thickened. Correct the seasoning and pour it over the veal. Arrange the sliced fruit and the slivered orange and lemon rinds on top of the veal and serve very hot.

FOR 4 PERSONS:

2 pounds boned veal, cut from the short ribs	1 lemon
Salt	2 tablespoons sugar
Freshly ground black pepper	3 tablespoons vinegar
Flour	1 cup White Stock (p. 165)
2 tablespoons peanut oil	1 tablespoon cornstarch
3 tablespoons butter	2 tablespoons Curaçao
2 oranges	1 tablespoon currant jelly

Rouelle of Veal / ROUELLE DE VEAU

Remove the bone from the meat and flatten the meat somewhat with a mallet or the flat side of a cleaver. Lard the meat with the anchovy fillets and season it with salt and pepper. Put it into a bowl (do not use aluminum), add the vinegar, and marinate for 4 hours, turning it occasionally.

Dry the meat with a kitchen towel and dust it with flour. Heat the olive oil in a large casserole and sauté the veal for 7 to 10 minutes on each side, according to the thickness of the meat.

Serve the meat on a hot serving platter. Sprinkle with the pan juices and the lemon juice and serve immediately.

FOR 4 PERSONS:

1 round slice of veal (about 1½ inches thick, about 2 pounds), cut from the upper leg	Freshly ground black pepper
	1 cup wine vinegar
	Flour
8 anchovy fillets, drained	4 tablespoons olive oil
Salt	Juice of 1 lemon

Veal Chops Maréchal / CÔTES DE VEAU MARÉCHAL

Have the butcher cut the rib chops about ½ inch thick. Season them with salt and pepper, dip them into the beaten eggs, and coat with bread crumbs. Heat the oil and butter in a skillet over high heat and sauté the chops in the hot fat until golden on both sides. Serve very hot.

FOR 4 PERSONS:

8 thin veal rib chops	1½ cups fine dry bread crumbs
Salt	2 tablespoons peanut oil
Freshly ground white pepper	3 tablespoons butter
2 eggs, beaten	

CÔTES DE VEAU EN COCOTTE / *Veal Chops en Cocotte*

Brown the rib chops on both sides in the combined hot oil and butter in a casserole over high heat. Add the onions, season with salt and pepper, and add the *bouquet garni*. Cover the casserole and simmer over very low heat for 30 minutes. Add the carrots, turn the veal chops, and cook for about 30 minutes longer.

Put the chops in a hot serving dish and surround them with the onions and carrots. Skim the fat off the pan juices and pour them over the veal chops.

The bones of the chops may be dressed with paper frills.

FOR 4 PERSONS:

4 large veal rib chops	Salt
2 tablespoons peanut oil	Freshly ground white pepper
3 tablespoons butter	1 Bouquet Garni (p. 46)
12 tiny white onions	1 pound tiny new carrots

CÔTES DE VEAU GRAND-MÈRE / *Grandmother's Veal Chops*

Season the veal chops with salt and pepper and dust them with flour. Heat the oil and half of the butter in a casserole and quickly brown the chops on both sides.

In another casserole, sauté the mushrooms and the bacon together in the remaining butter for about 5 minutes. Add them to the veal chops and mix. Cover the casserole and simmer over low heat for about 25 minutes. Add the glazed onions and the Madeira, mix lightly, and simmer for about 5 minutes longer. Serve in the same dish.

FOR 4 PERSONS:

4 large veal rib chops	6 tablespoons butter
Salt	12 small mushroom caps
Freshly ground black pepper	12 small strips of blanched bacon
Flour	1 recipe Glazed Onions (p. 610)
2 tablespoons peanut oil	⅓ cup Madeira

CÔTES DE VEAU PROVENÇALE / *Veal Chops Provençale*

Sauté the rib chops in 4 tablespoons of the hot oil in a casserole over medium heat until they are browned on both sides and cooked through. Season them with salt and pepper.

Transfer the meat to a serving dish and keep it hot. Add the remaining oil to the casserole and cook the onions in it until they are soft and golden. Stir in the vinegar and the garlic. Simmer, covered, for 5 minutes. Pour the sauce over the veal chops and serve very hot.

FOR 4 PERSONS:

4 large veal rib chops	4 onions, minced
6 tablespoons olive oil	2 tablespoons vinegar
Salt	1 garlic clove, minced
Freshly ground black pepper	

Veal Chops with Artichokes /

CÔTES DE VEAU AUX ARTICHAUTS

Season the rib chops with salt and pepper, dust them with flour, and sauté them quickly in the combined hot oil and half of the butter in a casserole over high heat until they are golden on both sides but not entirely cooked through. Remove the chops and keep them warm.

Melt the remaining butter in the casserole and then add the artichoke hearts. Cook, stirring with a wooden spoon, for about 10 minutes, or until they are golden. Add the rib chops, season with a little salt, cover the casserole, and simmer for 10 to 15 minutes. When chops and artichokes are cooked through, put the artichokes in the middle of a hot serving dish. Top the artichokes with the rib chops and keep hot.

Pour the cream into the casserole, blend it with the pan juices, and bring to the boiling point. Cook, stirring constantly, until it is somewhat thickened and smooth. Correct the seasoning. Coat the meat with the sauce and serve immediately, very hot.

FOR 2 PERSONS:

2 large veal rib chops	**2 tablespoons peanut oil**
Salt	**6 tablespoons butter**
Freshly ground white pepper	**4 large artichoke hearts, minced**
Flour	**1 cup heavy cream**

Veal Chops with Mushrooms /

CÔTES DE VEAU AUX GIROLLES

Slice the mushrooms thickly and sauté them in 2 tablespoons of the oil and 2 tablespoons of the butter in a casserole. Season with salt and pepper and add the garlic and the parsley. Cover the casserole and simmer over low heat for 15 minutes.

Season the rib chops with salt and pepper and dust them with flour. Heat the remaining oil and 3 tablespoons of the butter in a skillet and sauté the chops rather slowly until they are golden brown and cooked through.

At the same time, cook the potatoes in the remaining butter in a casserole, shaking the pan frequently to prevent sticking.

Pour the mushrooms into the middle of a hot deep serving dish and lay the veal chops on top. Surround them with the potatoes and keep hot.

Make the sauce: Add the wine and the brandy to the skillet in which the chops were cooked, scraping up all the brown bits at the bottom. Bring to the boiling point and reduce by about half. Stir in the *crème fraîche* and boil until the sauce is slightly thickened and smooth. Correct the seasoning and coat the meat with the sauce.

FOR 4 PERSONS:

1 pound girolles, or other mushrooms	**2 tablespoons minced parsley**
4 tablespoons peanut oil	**4 large veal rib chops**
8 tablespoons butter	**Flour**
Salt	**12 tiny new potatoes**
Freshly ground white pepper	**1 cup dry white wine**
1 garlic clove, minced	**2 tablespoons brandy**
	½ cup Crème Fraîche (p. 666)

CÔTES DE VEAU EN PAPILLOTES / *Veal Chops en Papillotes*

Have the butcher cut off the ends of the bones so that the chops are fairly compact. Brown the chops quickly on both sides in very hot oil in a large skillet and then remove them from the heat.

Make a stuffing by combining the bread crumbs, bacon, parsley, chives and mushrooms. Spread a little on both sides of the veal chops. Season with salt and pepper. Wrap each veal chop in a piece of buttered parchment cut in the shape of a heart, and crimp the edges securely together. Bake the wrapped chops in a buttered baking dish in a 375° F. oven for about 25 minutes. Transfer them to a hot platter and serve immediately.

FOR 4 PERSONS:

4 veal rib chops	3 tablespoons minced chives
4 tablespoons peanut oil	4 mushrooms, minced
2 cups fresh white bread crumbs	Salt
¼ pound bacon, blanched and minced	Freshly ground white pepper
2 tablespoons minced parsley	4 large sheets of kitchen parchment

/ *Veal Scallops with Herbs*

ESCALOPES DE VEAU AUX FINES HERBES

Sauté the veal scallops quickly on both sides in the combined very hot oil and butter until they are golden. Season them with salt and pepper. Add the consommé and the wine. Simmer for 5 minutes.

Add the minced *fines herbes* and shallots and the lemon juice. Simmer for 2 minutes longer. Put the cutlets on a hot serving dish and pour the sauce over them.

FOR 4 PERSONS:

8 slices of veal (⅜ inch thick), cut from the upper leg and pounded flat	1 tablespoon Beef or Chicken Consommé (p. 167)
3 tablespoons peanut oil	½ cup dry white wine
3 tablespoons butter	4 tablespoons minced Fines Herbes (p. 89)
Salt	4 tablespoons minced shallots
Freshly ground black pepper	Juice of 1 lemon

ESCALOPE DE VEAU FLAMBÉE / *Veal Scallops Flambéed*

Heat the oil and the butter in a deep skillet over fairly high heat, dust the veal slices with flour, and sauté them quickly until golden brown on both sides. Season with salt and pepper. Transfer them to a serving dish and keep hot.

Add the shallots to the pan juices and cook them for about 5 minutes, or until they are soft. Return the veal slices to the skillet, add the Armagnac, and flame it.

Transfer the veal back to the serving dish and keep hot. Stir the *crème fraîche* into the pan juices, together with the white stock (or a good meat juice), and reduce until thick and smooth. Pour the sauce over the veal and sprinkle with chopped parsley.

FOR 1 PERSON:

1½ tablespoons peanut oil
1½ tablespoons butter
2 slices of veal (⅜ inch thick),
cut from the upper leg and
pounded flat
Flour
Salt

Freshly ground white pepper
1 tablespoon minced shallots
2 tablespoons Armagnac
½ cup Crème Fraîche (p. 666)
2 tablespoons White Stock
(p. 165)
2 tablespoons minced parsley

Veal Piccata with Marsala | PICCATAS AU MARSALA

Have the butcher cut small scallops from a leg of veal, the size of a silver dollar but a little less than ½ inch thick. There should be 4 or 5 per person.

Season the scallops with salt and pepper, dust them with flour, and sauté them quickly in the combined hot oil and butter in a skillet over high heat for about 2 minutes on each side.

Put them on a serving dish and keep them hot. Add the wine, reduce the sauce slightly, and pour it over the meat. Sprinkle with the lemon juice, melted butter and parsley. Garnish the dish with lemon slices.

FOR 1 PERSON:

5 very small slices of veal
(⅜ inch thick), cut from the
upper leg
Salt
Freshly ground black pepper
Flour
1 tablespoon peanut oil

1 tablespoon butter
¼ cup Marsala
Juice of ¼ lemon
1 tablespoon butter, melted
1 tablespoon minced parsley
Lemon slices

Saltimbocca |

Top each slice of veal with a slice of prosciutto somewhat smaller than the veal. Sprinkle with the Parmesan. Put a tablespoon of chopped tomato on each piece of meat, and top with a sage leaf or sprinkle with a little dried sage. Season lightly with pepper.

Plac the *saltimbocca* in a baking dish generously brushed with olive oil and cook in a preheated 375° F. oven for about 15 minutes.

FOR 1 PERSON:

2 slices of veal (⅜ inch thick),
cut from the upper leg and
flattened with a mallet or
cleaver
2 slices of prosciutto
2 tablespoons grated Parmesan
cheese

2 tablespoons peeled, seeded
and chopped tomato
2 sage leaves, or ½ teaspoon
dried sage
Freshly ground black pepper
Olive oil

/ *Veal Birds with Tarragon*

PAUPIETTES DE VEAU À L'ESTRAGON

Flatten the veal slices between sheets of wax paper with a mallet or the flat side of a cleaver. Season the slices with salt and pepper. Mix the sausage meat with the tarragon and spread a little of the mixture on each of the veal slices. Roll them up and tie securely with string.

Heat the butter in a casserole, add the veal fat, and brown the veal rolls quickly over high heat on all sides. Sprinkle with the flour, stir for a minute, and add the wine. Bring to the boiling point and add the onion and the *bouquet garni*. Season with salt and pepper and then simmer, covered, over low heat for about 20 minutes.

Remove the strings from the veal birds before serving. Put them on a hot serving dish and strain the sauce over the meat.

FOR 4 PERSONS:

8 slices of veal (¼ inch thick), cut from the upper leg
Salt
Freshly ground black pepper
1 pound sausage meat
4 tablespoons minced fresh tarragon

3 tablespoons butter
2 tablespoons minced veal fat
1 tablespoon flour
¾ cup dry white wine
1 onion, quartered
1 Bouquet Garni (p. 46)

/ *Veal Birds with Cucumbers*

PAUPIETTES DE VEAU AUX CONCOMBRES

Make a stuffing by combining the ground veal, the bread crumbs, ½ cup of the *crème fraîche* and the egg yolk. Season the mixture with salt and paprika. Flatten the veal slices between sheets of wax paper with a mallet or the flat side of a cleaver, and season the slices with salt and pepper. Put a little stuffing on each of the veal slices, roll them up, and tie them securely with string.

Heat the oil and the butter in a casserole and sauté the veal birds quickly over high heat until they are golden on all sides. Add the cucumbers, reduce the heat, cover, and simmer slowly for about 20 minutes.

If the veal birds and the cucumbers have yielded a large amount of pan juices, drain these off into another saucepan and reduce them. Then pour them back on the meat. At serving time, add the remaining *crème fraîche* and a goodly amount of minced chervil or parsley.

FOR 4 PERSONS:

¾ pound boneless veal, ground
½ cup fresh white bread crumbs
1½ cups Crème Fraîche (p. 666)
1 egg yolk
Salt
Paprika
8 slices of veal (¼ inch thick), cut from the upper leg

Freshly ground white pepper
3 tablespoons peanut oil
3 tablespoons butter
2 cucumbers, peeled, cubed, and blanched in salted water for 10 minutes
3 tablespoons minced chervil or parsley

Veal Croquettes / CROQUETTES DE VEAU

Mince the veal into very small dice and sauté them quickly in the oil and half of the butter in a casserole. Remove the meat as soon as it is lightly browned.

Add the remaining butter to the same casserole and sauté the mushrooms for about 5 minutes. Stir in the flour and cook, stirring constantly, until golden. Season with salt, pepper and nutmeg. Add the parsley, the *crème fraîche* and the consommé. Stir until the sauce is very thick. Add the meat, mix well, and let the mixture cool completely.

Shape the mixture into small croquettes, dust them with the flour, dip them into the eggs, and coat with the bread crumbs. Chill in the refrigerator for 1 hour or longer.

Heat the fat to 360° F. on a frying thermometer and fry the croquettes in it until they are golden. Drain them and serve them on a hot serving dish, lined with a napkin. Garnish them with fried parsley.

FOR 4 PERSONS:

1½ pounds boneless veal
2 tablespoons peanut oil
3 tablespoons butter
3 large mushrooms, minced
3 tablespoons flour
Salt
Freshly ground black pepper
Grated nutmeg
4 tablespoons minced parsley

1 cup Crème Fraîche (p. 666)
½ cup Beef or Chicken Consommé (p. 167)
Flour for dusting the croquettes
2 eggs, beaten
2 cups fine dry bread crumbs
Fat for deep frying
Fried Parsley (p. 130)

Calf's Head Poulette / TÊTE DE VEAU POULETTE

Basic Preparation: Wash the calf's head in several changes of water, scrape the skin, and let it stand in cold water for 12 hours, changing the water several times. Drain the calf's head and rub it thoroughly with half a lemon. Put it into a deep kettle, cover it with cold water, season with salt and pepper, and add the onion and the *bouquet garni*. Bring to the boiling point and simmer for about 2 hours, or until the meat on the head is tender. As the water evaporates in cooking, replenish it with more boiling water so that the calf's head is always completely covered. This is important to keep the meat from darkening on contact with the air. When the calf's head is done, remove it from the kettle, bone it, and cut the meat into bite-size pieces. Keep the pieces warm.

Melt the butter in a casserole, stir in the flour, blend well, and stir in the stock and 1 cup of the liquid in which the head was cooked. Add the minced onions, mushrooms, parsley and chives. Season with salt, pepper and nutmeg and simmer for about 30 minutes. Then blend a little of the sauce with the egg yolks and lemon juice, add this mixture to the sauce, and stir over low heat until slightly thickened. Add the reserved calf's-head pieces and just heat through.

Serve in a hot serving dish.

FOR 4 PERSONS:

½ calf's head
½ lemon
Salt
Freshly ground white pepper
1 onion, stuck with 1 clove
1 Bouquet Garni (p. 46)
4 tablespoons butter
3 tablespoons flour
2 cups hot strong White Stock
   (p. 165)

2 onions, minced
¼ pound mushrooms, minced
2 tablespoons minced parsley
1 tablespoon minced chives
Grated nutmeg
2 egg yolks
Juice of 1 lemon

TÊTE DE VEAU VINAIGRETTE / *Calf's Head Vinaigrette*

Prepare the calf's head as described in the basic preparation of Calf's Head Poulette (above). Put the pieces into a big hot serving dish and sprinkle with parsley. Serve the following sauce on the side: Combine the shallot, tarragon, chervil, pickles, salt, capers, pepper, oil, vinegar and hard-cooked egg.

½ cooked calf's head, boned and
   cut into pieces
2 tablespoons minced parsley

For the sauce:
2 tablespoons minced shallot
1 tablespoon minced fresh tarragon
1 tablespoon minced fresh chervil
2 small pickles, finely chopped
2 teaspoons salt
2 tablespoons capers
Freshly ground black pepper
¾ cup olive oil
6 tablespoons vinegar
1 hard-cooked egg, minced

TÊTE DE VEAU RAVIGOTE / *Calf's Head Ravigote*

Prepare and cook the calf's head as described in the basic preparation of Calf's Head Poulette (above); keep the pieces hot.

Put the vinegar and the shallots into a saucepan and reduce the vinegar by half. Add the chervil, tarragon, thyme, bay leaf and 2 cups of liquid in which the calf's head was cooked. Simmer for 30 minutes. Blend a few tablespoons of this sauce with the egg yolks, then stir this mixture into the sauce. Stir over very low heat until slightly thickened. Season with salt and pepper and strain the sauce through a fine sieve into a casserole. Add the reserved calf's-head meat and the parsley. Heat very carefully to avoid curdling the sauce. Off the heat, stir in the butter and serve in the casserole.

FOR 4 PERSONS:

½ cooked calf's head, boned
and cut into pieces
1 cup vinegar
4 shallots, minced
2 tablespoons minced fresh
chervil, or 1 teaspoon
dried chervil
2 tablespoons minced fresh
tarragon, or 1 teaspoon
dried tarragon
2 tablespoons minced fresh
thyme, or 1 teaspoon dried
thyme

1 bay leaf
2 cups liquid in which the calf's
head was cooked
3 egg yolks
Salt
Freshly ground white pepper
3 tablespoons minced parsley
4 tablespoons butter

Veal and Sausage Pie / PIE DE PIEDS DE VEAU

Add to a big kettle of salted water the parsley and tarragon, the flour blended with the vinegar, the kidney fat and the scraped pork rind. Put the calf's feet into this liquid and simmer them, uncovered, for about 4 hours, or until they are tender. Remove the calf's feet and the pork rind and cool. Bone the calf's feet and discard any gristle.

Line a 9-inch pie dish with the slice of pork rind. Spread the sausage meat and the boned meat from the calf's feet on top. Top with the mushrooms, season with the spices, and add a bay leaf. Roll out the *brioche* dough to a shape slightly larger than the pie dish. Cover the dish with the dough, crimping the edges to seal tightly, as you would any pie. Set the pie in a warm place for about 30 minutes for the dough to rise. Bake on the lower rack of a preheated 350° F. oven for about 1 hour. Serve in the pie dish.

FOR 6 PERSONS:

Salt
1 bunch of parsley
1 bunch of fresh tarragon, or 2
tablespoons dried tarragon
3 tablespoons flour
½ cup vinegar
3 tablespoons kidney fat
1 large slice of scraped pork rind

3 calf's feet
⅓ pound sausage meat
¼ pound mushrooms, chopped
½ teaspoon Quatre Épices
(p. 667)
1 bay leaf
½ recipe Brioche dough
(p. 695), risen once

Stuffed Veal Heart / COEUR DE VEAU FARCI

Soak the veal heart in cold water for 4 to 5 hours, changing the water several times. Drain and dry the heart.

Make the following stuffing: mix together the onion, garlic, parsley and sausage meat. Stir in the egg, season with salt and cayenne, and blend until the mixture is smooth.

Stuff the cavity of the heart with this filling. Wrap the heart in a pig's caul or with very thinly sliced fresh pork fat.

Put the heart into a casserole with the oil and the butter, place the carrots, sliced onion and *bouquet garni* around it, season with salt and pepper, and add the wine. Simmer, covered, over low heat for about 2 hours.

Serve the heart on a hot serving dish, and strain the pan juices over it.

FOR 2 PERSONS:

1 **veal heart**	1 **tablespoon peanut oil**
1 **onion, chopped**	1 **tablespoon butter**
1 **garlic clove, minced**	3 **carrots, chopped**
2 **tablespoons chopped parsley**	1 **onion, sliced**
½ **cup sausage meat**	1 **Bouquet Garni (p. 46)**
1 **egg**	**Freshly ground white pepper**
Salt	1 **cup dry white wine**
Cayenne pepper	
1 **pig's caul or very thinly sliced fresh pork fat**	

ROGNONS DE VEAU À LA CRÈME / *Veal Kidneys in Cream*

Season a trimmed veal kidney with salt and pepper and sauté it in 2 tablespoons of butter in an uncovered casserole over medium heat for about 10 minutes, turning it often. Put the kidney on a chopping board. Discard the fat in the casserole. Mince the kidney and return it to the casserole. Add about ¼ cup of Crème Fraîche (p. 666) and heat, but do not let the *crème* boil. Season with a little cayenne. If the sauce is too thin to your taste, add about ½ teaspoon cornstarch blended with a little Madeira, port or brandy. Serve immediately.

Count on 1 large kidney or 2 small ones for 2 persons.

ROGNONS SAUTÉS / *Sautéed Veal Kidneys*

Trim and mince the mushrooms and cook them in 3 tablespoons of the butter in a skillet over low heat for about 10 minutes, shaking the skillet frequently.

Cut the excess fat and outer membrane off the kidneys and slice them. Heat the remaining butter in another skillet over high heat until it is very hot and sauté the kidney slices in it until barely golden, about 5 minutes. Season with salt and pepper, remove the kidney slices with a slotted spoon, and keep them warm. Add the mushrooms to the skillet, sprinkle with the flour, and cook for 1 minute. Add the veal stock and the Madeira, blend thoroughly, and then stir in the *crème fraîche*. Simmer over low heat for 15 minutes. Return the kidney slices to the skillet and heat for 1 minute. Check the seasoning and serve immediately in a hot serving dish.

FOR 4 PERSONS:

½ **pound mushrooms**	1 **tablespoon flour**
½ **cup butter**	½ **cup Brown Veal Stock (p. 165)**
2 **large veal kidneys**	2 **tablespoons Madeira or sherry**
Salt	½ **cup Crème Fraîche (p. 666)**
Freshly ground black pepper	

Veal Kidneys Bordelaise / ROGNONS DE VEAU BORDELAISE

Trim the kidneys of their excess fat and their outer membranes. Cut the kidneys into slices and season them with salt and pepper. Heat half of the butter in a casserole over high heat until it is very hot and sauté the kidney slices in it very quickly, for 4 or 5 minutes only. The butter must be very hot, but not burning.

Combine the wine, shallots, crushed peppercorns, thyme and bay leaf in a small saucepan, and reduce the mixture by half. Stir the mixture into the casserole in which the kidneys were cooked. Boil until the sauce is again reduced by half. Strain it through a fine sieve and add the lemon juice, the remaining butter and the sliced marrow. Sprinkle with the parsley.

Spoon the mushrooms over the kidneys and then pour the sauce over both. Serve immediately.

FOR 4 PERSONS:

2 large veal kidneys
Salt
Freshly ground black pepper
6 tablespoons butter
1½ cups red Bordeaux or other dry red wine
2 shallots, minced
½ teaspoon peppercorns, crushed
2 sprigs of fresh thyme, or ½ teaspoon dried thyme

½ bay leaf
Juice of ½ lemon
1 piece of veal marrow (2 inches), poached in salted water for 3 minutes and then sliced
2 tablespoons minced parsley
½ recipe Mushrooms Braised in Butter (p. 603)

Veal Kidneys Madeira / ROGNONS DE VEAU AU MADÈRE

Trim the excess fat and membrane off the kidneys and cut them into rather thick slices. Season with salt and pepper. Heat the oil and the butter in a skillet over high heat until it is very hot and sauté the kidney slices quickly, about 5 minutes in all.

Transfer them to a hot plate and keep warm. Sauté the mushrooms in the same skillet for about 8 minutes, shaking the pan often. Transfer them to the same plate with the kidneys. Finally, sauté the shallots for about 5 minutes, remove them, and keep them hot with the kidneys and mushrooms.

Add the Madeira and the sugar to the skillet and reduce the mixture by half. Check the seasoning and stir in the brandy. Return the kidneys, mushrooms and shallots to the same sauce and heat for 1 minute.

Place the fried bread in a hot serving dish, top with the sauced kidneys and mushrooms, and sprinkle them with the parsley.

FOR 4 PERSONS:

2 large veal kidneys
Salt
Freshly ground black pepper
2 tablespoons peanut oil
6 tablespoons butter
½ pound mushrooms, thickly sliced

4 shallots, minced
1 cup Madeira
1 lump of sugar
2 tablespoons brandy
4 slices of firm white bread, fried in butter
2 tablespoons minced parsley

/ *Veal Kidneys Flambéed*

ROGNONS DE VEAU FLAMBÉS À L'ARMAGNAC

This recipe can be made with any type of kidneys, but there is no question that veal kidneys are best.

First remove some of the fat from a veal kidney, leaving a little to render itself as the kidney cooks. Season the kidney with salt and pepper. Put a tablespoon each of oil and butter into a small saucepan and cook the kidney in it over high heat for about 10 minutes, turning it frequently. This method of cookery is called *à la coque*.

Drain off all the fat from the saucepan, and flame the kidney with ¼ cup of a young quality Armagnac.

Put the kidney on a hot plate and add ½ cup Madeira or sherry to the pan juices. Reduce them by half. Cut the kidney into thin slices and add any juices it releases to the sauce.

Blend 3 tablespoons of softened butter with 2 tablespoons of Dijon, Champagne or Bordeaux mustard or, if you prefer, with a mixture of all three.

Add the sliced kidney to the sauce and keep it in a hot place, such as over the pilot light of the stove. The mixture must not boil again. Add the mustard-butter, a little piece at a time, shaking the saucepan so that the butter will melt and the sauce be thick and smooth. This step, the most important, must be done away from direct heat.

This kidney dish is usually served with potatoes browned in butter.

One small kidney will serve 1 person, or a large one will serve 2.

/ *Veal Kidneys with Juniper Berries*

ROGNONS DE VEAU AU GENIÈVRE

This is a dish of kidneys *à la coque*.

Leave quite a lot of fat on the kidneys when you trim them and put them in a baking dish in a preheated 400° F. oven, for about 10 minutes. Transfer the kidneys to a casserole without any of the fat which they have rendered in the oven. Crush 1 tablespoon of juniper berries for each kidney. Add the juniper berries to the kidneys, together with ¼ cup dry white wine for each kidney and a spoonful of any good stock, if you have any around. Season with salt and pepper, lower the oven heat to 350° F., and cook for 10 minutes. Stir in 2 tablespoons of butter and return the kidneys to the oven for 3 more minutes. Serve in the same dish.

Count on 1 small kidney for each serving, or a large one will serve 2.

FOIE DE VEAU AUX HERBES / *Calf's Liver with Herbs*

Season the slices of liver with salt and pepper and dust them with the combined flour and half of the thyme.

Heat the butter in a skillet until almost brown and cook the liver slices in it until golden on both sides. Do not turn the liver with a fork; use a spatula to avoid piercing it.

Transfer the sliced liver to a hot serving dish and keep hot. Stir the lemon juice into the pan juices and sprinkle with the parsley, the remaining thyme and the bay leaf. Pour the sauce over the liver and serve immediately.

FOR 4 PERSONS:

4 slices of calf's liver (½ inch thick)
Salt
Freshly ground black pepper
1 cup flour

2 teaspoons ground thyme
6 tablespoons butter
Juice of 1 lemon
1 tablespoon minced parsley
1 bay leaf, crumbled

Calf's Liver Venetian Style / FOIE DE VEAU VÉNITIENNE

Combine the bacon, parsley, shallots and mushrooms. Line a buttered baking dish with half of this mixture, top with the sliced liver, and season with salt and pepper. Top the liver with the remaining ground bacon mixture and dot with butter. Cook in a preheated 350° F. oven for about 20 minutes.

When the liver is half cooked, sprinkle with the bread crumbs and finish cooking. Just before serving, brown quickly under the broiler. Serve in the same dish.

FOR 4 PERSONS:

¼ pound bacon, blanched and ground
4 tablespoons minced parsley
2 shallots, minced
4 large mushrooms, minced
4 slices of calf's liver (½ inch thick)

Salt
Freshly ground black pepper
4 tablespoons butter, cut into small pieces
½ cup fresh white bread crumbs

Braised Calf's Liver / FOIE DE VEAU BRAISÉ

Lard the calf's liver with the lardoons of pork fat, season it with salt and pepper and, if desired, wrap it in the pig's caul.

Heat the oil and the butter in a casserole over high heat and sauté the liver quickly on both sides until golden brown. Transfer it to a serving dish and keep hot.

Put the onions, carrots and bacon in the same casserole. Season with salt and pepper and cook for 3 minutes. Return the liver to the casserole and add the wine and the *bouquet garni*. Simmer, covered, over very low heat for about 1 hour, or until the liver is very tender.

Return the calf's liver to the serving dish and surround it with the onions and carrots. Reduce the sauce to a good strong flavor and skim off the fat. Strain it through a fine sieve over the liver.

FOR 4 PERSONS:

1 calf's liver (2 pounds)
¼ pound fresh pork fat, cut into thin strips (lardoons)
Salt
Freshly ground black pepper
Optional: 1 pig's caul
2 tablespoons peanut oil

2 tablespoons butter
2 onions, chopped
8 medium-sized carrots, sliced
¼ pound bacon, diced
½ bottle dry white wine
1 Bouquet Garni (p. 46)

/ *Calf's Liver Pâté Lyonnaise*

PÂTÉ DE FOIE DE VEAU À LA LYONNAISE

Soak the bread crumbs in the lukewarm milk and squeeze them dry when they are soft. Grind, but not too finely (with the medium knife of the meat grinder), the onions, garlic, liver and pork fat. Put everything into a bowl and mix well. Season generously with salt and pepper and add the eggs and the rendered chicken fat.

Line a baking dish with the pig's caul or the slices of fresh pork fat, spoon in the liver mixture, and then fold the caul or pork fat over the liver mixture, so that it is securely encased in the form of a roll. Sprinkle the sliced carrots on top. Cook in a preheated 350° F. oven for about 1½ hours. Baste frequently with the hot consommé.

Add the Madeira about 5 minutes before the pâté is removed from the oven and baste with it. Remove the carrots and serve the pâté hot or cold.

FOR 12 PERSONS:

4 cups fresh white bread crumbs
Lukewarm milk
3 onions
1 garlic clove
2 pounds calf's liver (or you may use pork liver)
⅓ pound fresh pork fat
Salt
Freshly ground black pepper

6 eggs
4 tablespoons rendered chicken fat
1 pig's caul, or several thin slices of fresh pork fatback
2 carrots, sliced
1 cup Chicken Consommé (p. 168)
¼ cup Madeira

RIS DE VEAU / *Veal Sweetbreads*

Basic Preparation: Wash any desired number of sweetbreads in running cold water and then soak them in several changes of cold water for 2 hours. Gently pull off as much as possible of the thin skin which encases both of the lobes. Soak again in acidulated water (1 tablespoon vinegar per 4 cups of water) for 2 hours and again pull off as much of the covering skin as you can. Separate the two lobes and discard the connecting tube. They are now ready to be braised.

If the sweetbreads are to be sautéed, they must first be blanched: Place the trimmed sweetbreads in a saucepan of lightly salted water and add 1 tablespoon of lemon juice per quart of water. Bring to a boil and then simmer for 15 minutes. Drain and then soak them in cold water for a few minutes. They are now ready for sautéing.

RIS DE VEAU BRAISÉS / *Braised Veal Sweetbreads*

Soak and trim the sweetbreads as described in the basic preparation (above).

Dust the sweetbreads with flour and sauté them in half of the oil and half of the butter in a casserole over medium heat until they are golden. Season with salt and pepper, add the brandy, and flame. Add the port and the white wine. Simmer over very low heat for about 20 minutes.

Heat the remaining oil and butter in another casserole and add the onion and the carrot. Cook for about 10 minutes, stirring occasionally. Stir in the 2 tablespoons flour, cook for about 2 minutes, and then add the sweetbreads and their pan juices, the tomato paste and about ½ cup of water; mix well. Place the casserole, uncovered, in a preheated 325° F. oven for about 25 minutes. Baste the sweetbreads several times.

Place the sweetbreads on a hot serving dish. Strain the sauce through a fine sieve, stir in the softened butter, and pour it over the sweetbreads.

FOR 2 PERSONS:

2 pairs veal sweetbreads	**1 cup dry white wine**
Flour	**1 medium-sized onion, minced**
4 tablespoons peanut oil	**1 carrot, minced**
4 tablespoons butter	**2 tablespoons flour**
Salt	**1 tablespoon tomato paste**
Freshly ground white pepper	**3 tablespoons butter, at room**
¼ cup brandy	**temperature, cut into little pieces**
1 tablespoon port	

Veal Sweetbreads in Cream / RIS DE VEAU À LA CRÈME

Soak and trim the sweetbreads as described in the basic preparation (p. 449). Lard them with the pork fat lardoons.

Heat the butter in a casserole over medium heat and cook the sweetbreads in it until golden on all sides. Add the onions and season with salt and pepper. Add the *bouquet garni* and the mushrooms. Cover the casserole and simmer over very low heat for about 30 minutes.

Beat together the egg yolks and the cream.

Put the cooked sweetbreads on a serving dish with the onions and mushrooms. Take the casserole off the heat. Discard the *bouquet garni* and stir the lemon juice into the pan juices. Then gradually stir in the egg-yolk mixture. Return the casserole to very low heat and stir until the juices have thickened slightly. Pour the sauce over the sweetbreads. Serve immediately.

Note: You may add truffle trimmings to the sauce, and you may also adorn the sweetbreads with a few truffle slivers.

FOR 4 PERSONS:

2 pairs veal sweetbreads	**Freshly ground white pepper**
¼ pound fresh pork fat, cut	**1 Bouquet Garni (p. 46)**
into thin strips (lardoons)	**4 mushrooms, cut into quarters**
3 tablespoons butter	**2 egg yolks**
8 small white onions	**½ cup Crème Fraîche (p. 666)**
Salt	**Juice of 1 lemon**

Veal Sweetbreads Florentine / RIS DE VEAU FLORENTINE

Soak, trim, and blanch the sweetbreads as described in the basic preparation (p. 449).

Slice the sweetbreads. Sauté the slices in the combined hot oil and butter in a skillet over medium heat until barely golden on both sides; season them with salt and pepper.

Line a buttered baking dish with the spinach and top it with the sliced sweetbreads. Coat the sweetbreads with the *sauce Mornay* and sprinkle with the cheese, bread crumbs and melted butter. Brown quickly under the broiler.

Serve with a thin tomato sauce on the side.

FOR 4 PERSONS:

2 **pairs veal sweetbreads**
2 **tablespoons peanut oil**
3 **tablespoons butter**
Salt
Freshly ground white pepper
1 **recipe Spinach in Butter**
   (p. 644)

2 **cups Sauce Mornay (p. 776)**
4 **tablespoons grated Swiss cheese**
2 **tablespoons fine dry bread**
   crumbs
4 **tablespoons melted butter**
2 **cups Sauce Tomate (p. 769)**

RIS DE VEAU AUX RAISINS / *Veal Sweetbreads with Grapes*

Soak and trim the sweetbreads as described in the basic preparation (p. 449).

Lard the sweetbreads with the truffle slivers and the tongue slivers. Season them with salt and pepper, dust them with flour, and sauté them in the combined hot oil and half of the butter in a casserole over medium heat until golden on all sides. Cover the casserole and cook in a preheated 325° F. oven for about 30 minutes, basting and turning the sweetbreads frequently.

Put the cooked sweetbreads in a hot serving dish and keep hot.

Add the grapes, the fresh grape juice and the Madeira to the pan juices and reduce them over high heat by half. Remove from the heat and add the remaining butter; shake the casserole until the butter is melted. Pour the sauce over the sweetbreads and serve very hot.

FOR 2 PERSONS:

2 **pairs veal sweetbreads**
2 **truffles, cut into tiny slivers**
2 **slices of cooked tongue, cut into**
   tiny slivers
Salt
Freshly ground white pepper
Flour

2 **tablespoons peanut oil**
3 **tablespoons butter**
1 **cup white muscatel grapes,**
   peeled and seeded
½ **cup fresh grape juice**
½ **cup Madeira**

/ *Veal Sweetbreads Maréchal*

ESCALOPES DE RIS DE VEAU MARÉCHAL

Soak, trim, and blanch the sweetbreads as described in the basic preparation (p. 449).

Slice the sweetbreads. Season with salt and pepper, dust with flour, and dip into the beaten egg yolk and then coat with the bread crumbs. Heat the clarified butter in a skillet over fairly high heat. Sauté the sliced sweetbreads in it until golden on both sides, then lower the heat and cook for 10 minutes longer.

Arrange the asparagus tips in the middle of a hot serving dish and surround them with the sliced sweetbreads. Place the truffle slices on top of the sweetbreads and drizzle the Madeira sauce over them.

FOR 4 PERSONS:

2 **pairs veal sweetbreads**
Salt
Freshly ground white pepper
Flour
3 **egg yolks, beaten**
1½ **cups fine dry bread crumbs**

5 **tablespoons Clarified Butter**
(p. 666)
1 **recipe Asparagus in Butter**
(p. 552)
2 **truffles, sliced**
2 **cups Madeira Sauce (p. 764)**

Skewered Veal Sweetbreads | RIS DE VEAU EN BROCHETTES

Soak, trim, and blanch the sweetbreads as described in the basic preparation (p. 449).

Cut them into 1½-inch cubes and cut the bacon into 1½-inch squares. Marinate both sweetbreads and bacon in a mixture of the oil, the thyme, and a little salt and pepper for 10 minutes.

Thread 4 skewers with a square of bacon, a cube of sweetbread, and a bay leaf, repeating this combination until all are used, and ending with a bacon square.

Broil the skewers under a hot broiler flame or grill them over live coals, turning them until golden on all sides. Serve with a garnish of parsley.

FOR 4 PERSONS:

2 **pairs veal sweetbreads**
8 **(or more) slices of bacon**
1 **cup olive oil**
3 **sprigs of fresh thyme, or 1 teaspoon dried thyme**

Salt
Freshly ground white pepper
12 **(or more) bay leaves**
Parsley sprigs

Veal Sweetbreads in Pastry | RIS DE VEAU EN PÂTE

Soak, trim, and blanch the sweetbreads as described in the basic preparation (p. 449).

Cut the sweetbreads into slices and sauté them, together with the onion, in the combined hot oil and butter in a skillet over medium heat until just golden. Season with a little salt and pepper and remove from the heat.

Grind together the chicken and the pork fat. To this mixture add the eggs, a little salt and pepper, the truffles and the brandy. Blend thoroughly; it must be smooth.

Divide the *pâte brisée* into 2 portions, one slightly larger than the other. Roll both portions into rounds about ⅛ inch thick. Line a 9-inch pie pan with the larger round. Spread the mushrooms in the bottom, arrange the sliced sweetbreads around the edge, and fill the center with the chicken filling. Cover with the other round of pastry and seal the edges. Make a cylinder from stiff white paper or foil and insert it through a hole in the top crust to allow steam to escape. Bake on the lower rack of a preheated 350° F. oven for about 1 hour.

FOR 4 PERSONS:

2 pairs veal sweetbreads
1 onion, minced
2 tablespoons peanut oil
3 tablespoons butter
Salt
Freshly ground white pepper

For the filling:
¾ pound boneless chicken meat
¾ pound fresh pork fat
2 eggs
Salt
Freshly ground white pepper
2 truffles, minced
¼ cup brandy
1 recipe Pâte Brisée (p. 713)
¼ pound mushrooms, minced

RIS DE VEAU TAILLEVENT / *Veal Sweetbreads Taillevent*

Soak and trim the sweetbreads as described in the basic preparation (p. 449).

Cut the carrots and mushrooms into very fine julienne strips and simmer them in the combined hot oil and butter in a covered casserole over medium heat for 5 minutes. Stir occasionally. Add the sweetbreads and turn them in the butter and oil for 2 minutes. Add the truffle, the wine and, should you be using canned truffle, any juice from the can. Season lightly with salt and pepper. Simmer, covered, over low heat for 30 minutes. Remove the sweetbreads and the vegetables with a slotted spoon and reserve them. Reduce the juices in the casserole by one third, add the *crème fraîche,* and reduce again until slightly thickened and smooth.

Prepare and bake an 8-inch square or round patty shell from the puff paste in the manner described on page 717. Remove it from the oven, lift off the lid, and scoop out the uncooked dough in the center. Slice the sweetbreads, return them and the vegetables to the sauce to heat through, and then pour them into the patty shell. If necessary, reheat briefly in a preheated 400° F. oven. Serve very hot.

FOR 4 PERSONS:

2 pair veal sweetbreads
4 carrots
4 large mushrooms
2 tablespoons peanut oil
3 tablespoons butter
1 large truffle, cut into small dice

1 cup dry white wine
Salt
Freshly ground white pepper
2 cups Crème Fraîche (p. 666)
½ recipe Puff Paste (p. 715)

PORK

Porc

CARRÉ DE PORC AUX LENTILLES / *Loin of Pork with Lentils*

Season the loin of pork with salt and pepper and roast it in a preheated 325° F. oven for 2½ hours.

Put the lentils in a casserole, add cold water to cover, bring to the boiling point, and drain. Heat the lard in the casserole and add the onion, shallot, carrots and turnip. Cook, stirring frequently, until the vegetables are golden. Stir in the flour and mix well. Add the lentils, celery, garlic, bacon, the *bouquet garni,* a little salt and pepper, and just enough water to barely cover the lentils. Cover the casserole and simmer very slowly for 1½ hours.

After the pork has cooked for 2½ hours, carve it into slices and add them to the lentils. Continue cooking for another 30 minutes and serve in the casserole.

FOR 4 PERSONS:

1 loin of pork (4 pounds)	2 carrots, minced
Salt	1 turnip, minced
Freshly ground black pepper	2 tablespoons flour
2 cups dried lentils	1 celery stalk, minced
3 tablespoons lard	1 garlic clove, minced
1 onion, minced	1 piece of bacon (¼ pound)
1 shallot, minced	1 Bouquet Garni (p. 46)

Pork Shoulder with Chestnuts /

PALETTE DE PORC AUX MARRONS

Line the bottom of a deep roasting pan with the unpeeled garlic cloves and the chopped onions, carrots, celery and finocchio. Lay the pork shoulder on the vegetables. Season with a little salt and add the water.

Roast, uncovered, in a 325° F. oven for 2 hours, adding a little more water if necessary.

Remove the meat, strain the pan juices, and degrease them. Put the meat back in the pan with the strained pan juices. Add the chestnuts and the butter. Roast for 1 more hour, adding a little more water from time to time to keep the chestnuts moist.

Serve the roast on a glazed earthenware dish surrounded by the chestnuts.

FOR 4 PERSONS:

4 garlic cloves, unpeeled	Salt
2 onions, chopped	1 cup water
3 carrots, chopped	2 pounds chestnuts, shelled and
1 celery stalk, chopped	blanched for 20 minutes
1 small head of finocchio, chopped	(see p. 582)
1 shoulder butt of pork (3 pounds)	3 tablespoons butter

Skewered Pork / BROCHETTES DE PORC

Cut the meat into 1½-inch cubes and marinate the cubes in a mixture of the oil, brandy, onion, garlic and a little salt and pepper for 2 hours. Turn the meat occasionally. Drain the meat and thread it on skewers.

Put the skewers under a medium broiler flame or over live coals and broil them slowly, turning and basting them occasionally with the marinade. They will take about 20 minutes. The pork should be well cooked.

Serve the pork skewers on a bed of *rice à la créole* and with it serve a salad of raw vegetables.

FOR EACH SKEWER:

⅓ pound pork tenderloin
½ cup peanut oil
1 tablespoon brandy
1 medium-sized onion, minced
1 garlic clove, minced

Salt
Freshly ground black pepper
¼ recipe Rice à la Créole
   (p. 658)

/ *Choucroûte Garnie au Riesling*

CHOUCROÛTE AU RIESLING

Heat the lard in a large casserole, add the fresh ham fat, and stir over medium heat for a few minutes. Then add the chopped onion and carrots, the thyme, bay leaf, peppercorns, juniper berries and chopped parsley. Stir with a wooden spoon and cook over low heat until the mixture is very soft. Remove the vegetables and herbs with a slotted spoon and tie them in a triple layer of cheesecloth, fastening it securely. Return the wrapped vegetables to the casserole. Add the drained sauerkraut, the Riesling, the water, bacon and sausage. Cover the casserole and simmer over low heat for about 1½ hours, either in a preheated 325° F. oven or on top of the stove. If necessary add a little more wine and water during cooking time. After the first hour, add the frankfurters and the ham.

Season the pork tenderloin with salt and pepper and put it in a roasting pan with a spoonful of water, the sliced onion and carrot and the parsley sprigs. Roast in a preheated 325° F. oven for about 1 hour and 15 minutes. From time to time, pour the pan juices of the meat into the sauerkraut. The roast and sauerkraut should be ready at the same time. Slice all the meats.

At serving time, place the sauerkraut in the middle of a large hot serving platter. Surround the sauerkraut with the sliced meats, and add 2 small boiled potatoes for each serving.

FOR 6 PERSONS:

6 tablespoons lard
½ cup chopped fresh ham fat
1 onion, chopped
2 carrots, chopped
1 sprig of fresh thyme, or ½
   teaspoon dried thyme
1 bay leaf
4 peppercorns
10 juniper berries
½ cup chopped parsley
2 pounds sauerkraut, blanched
   in boiling water for 1 minute
   and drained
2 cups Riesling or other dry
   white wine

1 cup water
1 piece of bacon (¼ pound)
1 Lyonnaise sausage, or any
   boiling sausage
6 frankfurters
6 small slices of cooked ham
   (about ½ inch thick)
1 tenderloin of pork (2 pounds)
Salt
Freshly ground black pepper
1 onion, sliced
1 carrot, sliced
3 parsley sprigs
12 new potatoes, boiled

Broiled Pork Chops with Herbs /

CÔTES DE PORC GRILLÉES AUX HERBES

Marinate the pork chops in the olive oil, sage, thyme, bay leaf, rosemary and garlic for 12 hours.

Drain the chops and season them with salt and pepper. Broil them under a medium broiler flame or over live coals until they are golden and well done, about 10 minutes on each side.

Serve the pork chops with a garnish of watercress.

FOR 2 PERSONS:

2 large loin pork chops
½ cup olive oil
2 tablespoons chopped fresh sage, or 2 teaspoons dried sage
1 tablespoon chopped fresh thyme, or ½ teaspoon dried thyme
1 bay leaf, crumbled

1 tablespoon chopped fresh rosemary, or ½ teaspoon dried rosemary
1 garlic clove, minced
Salt
Freshly ground black pepper
Watercress

Pork Chops Limousine / CÔTES DE PORC À LA LIMOUSINE

Season the pork chops with salt and pepper and sauté them in the hot lard in a skillet over medium heat until they are golden on both sides and well cooked through. Put the pork chops in a serving dish and garnish with the red cabbage.

FOR 4 PERSONS:

4 large loin pork chops
Salt
Freshly ground black pepper

6 tablespoons lard
1 recipe Braised Red Cabbage Limousine (p. 566)

Pork Chops Miroton / CÔTES DE PORC MIROTON

Marinate the pork chops in the combined oil, salt, peppercorns, sliced onions, parsley and bay leaf for 3 days.

Turn them once a day. Heat a little oil from the marinade in a casserole. Drain and dry the pork chops and sauté them over moderate heat until they are brown on both sides and are well cooked through. Add the minced onion and simmer over low heat for 10 more minutes. Put the chops in the middle of a hot serving dish and garnish with the braised onions.

FOR 2 PERSONS:

2 large loin pork chops
½ cup peanut oil
Salt
6 peppercorns, crushed
2 onions, cut into thick slices

2 tablespoons chopped parsley
1 bay leaf, crumbled
1 onion, minced
1 recipe Braised Onions (p. 610)

LE COCHON DE LAIT FARCI / *Stuffed Suckling Pig*

Buy a suckling pig ready to cook.

Put the thyme, bay leaves, basil and finocchio in the cavity of the suckling pig and let it stand in a cool place, or refrigerate it, for 24 hours.

Grind the pig's heart, liver and lungs. Put the ground meat in a bowl, add the salt pork, and season this stuffing with salt, pepper and spices. Add the chicken livers, the prosciutto, the *fines herbes* and enough brandy to moisten the mixture. You may also add minced truffles or minced shallots, but not both. Remove the herbs from the pig's cavity and reserve them, leaving those which cling to the sides, and season the cavity with salt and pepper. Fill the pig with the stuffing, and then skewer and lace the opening to close it. Protect the ears and tail with shields of kitchen parchment or aluminum foil.

Line a deep baking pan with a variety of vegetables (carrots, turnips, onions and celery, all coarsely chopped) and add the reserved herbs and the water. Lay the pig on the bed of vegetables and coat the pig with the lard. Roast the pig in a preheated 350° F. oven for 3½ hours, counting on about 20 minutes for each pound. Baste frequently. The pig's skin must be golden and very crisp.

When the pig is half done, remove it. Strain the pan juices through a fine sieve and discard the vegetables. Put the pig back in the baking dish and add the strained pan juices. Spread the pig with the butter and finish roasting it.

FOR 12 PERSONS:

1 small suckling pig (about 10 pounds)
4 sprigs of thyme, or 2 teaspoons dried thyme
4 bay leaves
4 sprigs of basil, or 2 teaspoons dried basil
2 tablespoons chopped finocchio leaves
¼ pound blanched salt pork, finely chopped
Salt
Freshly ground black pepper
½ teaspoon Quatre Épices (p. 667)

10 chicken livers, coarsely chopped
½ pound prosciutto, diced
4 tablespoons minced Fines Herbes (p. 89)
¼ cup brandy
Optional: 2 truffles or shallots, minced
Carrots, turnips, onions, celery
1 cup water
6 tablespoons lard
½ cup butter

PIEDS DE PORC TRUFFÉS / *Truffled Pigs' Trotters*

Put the pigs' trotters into a kettle and cover them with cold water. Bring to the boiling point and skim off any scum. Add the carrots, turnips and onion. Bring to the boiling point once more and skim again. Season with salt and pepper. Simmer over low heat for 7 hours. Let the pigs' trotters cool in the liquid and then remove them.

Grind the chicken or the veal very fine. Mix it with the fresh bread crumbs soaked in lukewarm consommé and squeezed dry, the truffles, egg yolks and *crème fraîche*. Season the stuffing with a little salt, pepper and nutmeg.

Remove the meat and bones from the pigs' trotters, but keep the skins whole. Cut the meat into small dice. Put the skins on a baking dish and split each lengthwise.

Stuff each with some of the filling and top the filling with a little of the diced meat. Roll the skins over the stuffing in the original shape of the trotters and tie them securely.

Sprinkle them with the melted butter and the dry bread crumbs. Put them under a medium broiler flame and broil until they are golden on all sides. Serve very hot.

FOR 4 PERSONS:

4 pigs' trotters
1 pound carrots, sliced
2 turnips, quartered
1 onion, stuck with 3 cloves
Salt
Freshly ground black pepper
½ pound boneless chicken or veal
2 cups fresh white bread crumbs

1 cup Beef Consommé (p. 167)
3 truffles, minced
3 egg yolks
2 tablespoons Crème Fraîche (p. 666)
Grated nutmeg
½ cup melted butter
1 cup fine dry bread crumbs

Baked Ham with Pineapple / JAMBON BRAISÉ À L'ANANAS

Scrub the ham and soak it according to the packer's directions. Put it in a deep kettle, cover it with cold water, and bring to the boiling point. Lower the heat and simmer the ham for 2½ hours; the water must do no more than barely simmer.

Drain the ham and cool it a little. Remove the skin, leaving about a ¼-inch layer of fat. Stick the ham with the cloves, put it into a baking dish, and sprinkle it with half of the sugar. Bake the ham in a preheated 400° F. oven for about 40 minutes, basting frequently with the pan drippings.

Caramelize the remaining sugar in a saucepan.

Crush the peppercorns and add them to the vinegar in a saucepan. Bring to the boiling point and boil until the vinegar has almost completely evaporated. Add the hot consommé, cook for about 5 minutes, and strain the mixture into the saucepan of caramelized sugar. Stir in the sherry, reduce by one third, and pour the sauce into a sauceboat.

Put the ham in a large serving dish and surround it with the pineapple slices. Serve the sauce on the side.

FOR 10 PERSONS:

1 smoked ham (8 pounds)
20 whole cloves
1 cup sugar
20 peppercorns
1 cup wine vinegar

1 cup hot Beef Consommé (p. 167)
½ cup sherry
12 slices of pineapple, fresh or canned

Ham en Croûte / JAMBON EN CROÛTE

Have the butcher remove the bone from the ham. Soak the ham in cold water for 24 hours.

Prepare a *court bouillon* with the turnips, carrots, celery, onion and enough water to cover the ham. Season with pepper, bring to the boiling point, simmer for 5 minutes, and add the ham. Poach the ham over low heat for about 1 hour.

Meantime, make the *brioche* dough and let it rise.

Drain the ham, remove the skin and most of the fat, and put it into a large casserole with the butter and the oil. Cover the casserole and cook the ham over medium heat for about 5 minutes. Then add the port, cover again, bring to the boiling point, and simmer gently for 30 minutes. Add the *crème fraîche* and continue simmering for about 1 hour, or until the ham is tender. Season with a little pepper and nutmeg, and salt to taste. Remove the ham from the sauce and let it cool until the surface of the meat is just warm.

Divide the *brioche* dough into halves and roll out the halves on a floured pastry board. Each half should be somewhat larger than the shape of the pan in which the ham will be baked.

Butter and flour the baking pan, line it with half of the dough, and lay the ham in it. Spoon a little of the sauce over the ham. Or else, you may slice the ham, coat each slice with some of the sauce, and then re-form the ham in its original shape. Cover the ham with the remaining dough, and pinch the edges together to seal tightly. Let the pan rest in a warm place for about 30 minutes to let the *brioche* rise and then paint the top with the beaten egg yolk.

Bake in a preheated 400° F. oven for about 25 minutes. Serve immediately, very hot, with any remaining sauce in a sauceboat.

FOR 10 PERSONS:

1 smoked ham (8 pounds)	3 tablespoons butter
2 turnips	2 tablespoons peanut oil
2 carrots	1 cup port
3 celery stalks	2 cups Crème Fraîche (p. 666)
1 onion, stuck with 3 cloves	Grated nutmeg
Freshly ground black pepper	Salt
1 recipe Brioche dough (p. 695)	1 egg yolk, beaten

JAMBON AUX ÉPINARDS / *Ham Slices with Spinach*

Put the ham slices into a large skillet so that they overlap each other.

Sprinkle the ham with the Madeira. Cover the skillet and simmer over low heat for 20 minutes, or until the ham is tender.

Transfer the ham to a serving dish and keep hot.

Bring the pan juices to the boiling point and reduce them to about 2 tablespoons. Then add the *crème fraîche*. Bring to the boiling point once more and cook, stirring constantly, until the sauce is thick and smooth.

Season the sauce with a little cayenne and pour it over the ham slices. Serve very hot, with a side dish of hot buttered spinach.

FOR 4 PERSONS:

4 slices of tenderized ham (½ inch thick)	Cayenne pepper
1 cup Madeira	1 recipe Spinach in Butter (p. 664)
2 cups Crème Fraîche (p. 666),	

6
POULTRY
Les Volailles

CHICKEN

Poulardes et Poulets

EDITORS' NOTE: *More of the chickens sold in American markets are male, or roosters, than female. Logically a lot of hens are reserved for the sensible business of laying eggs. Many of the hens that do find their way to market are fairly old and only fit for the stewpot. This is not the case in France where fattened hens, or* poulardes, *are widely available. They are considered very choice, and the choicest of these come from Bresse in southern France. We would rarely find a* poularde *of this quality in America, although some years ago caponettes, or altered hens, were fairly common. We need make no apologies for American chickens, however, which are among the finest in the world. We have contented ourselves in these recipes of M. Oliver's with specifying the type of chicken to be used by weight and/or type (frying, roasting, stewing, etc.) without reference to their sex.*

Roast Chicken Chalosse / POULET RÔTI COMME EN CHALOSSE

Season the cavity of the chicken with salt, and then truss and bard it, that is, wrap it in the slices of fresh pork fat and tie them securely. Roast the chicken in a preheated 450° F. oven for 15 minutes, reduce the heat to 350° F., and continue roasting for 1 hour, or 18 to 20 minutes of cooking time for each pound of chicken.

When the bird is three-quarters done, remove the fresh pork fat and let the bird turn golden brown, basting occasionally with the juices in the pan.

Test for doneness by inserting a small skewer in the thickest part of the leg. If the juice that spurts out is clear, and not pink, the chicken is done.

FOR 6 PERSONS:

1 roasting chicken (4 pounds)	Thin sheets of fresh pork fat
Salt	

Chicken Tarragon / POULET À L'ESTRAGON

Brown the chicken on all sides in the combined oil and 4 tablespoons of the butter in a casserole. Transfer the chicken to a hot plate and keep it warm.

Add the shallots and the remaining butter to the casserole and cook until the shallots are soft. Return the chicken to the casserole, sprinkle with the brandy, and flame. Add the wine and the sprigs of tarragon and season with salt and pepper. Simmer, covered, over low heat for about 45 minutes.

Transfer the chicken to a hot serving platter.

Beat together the *crème fraîche* and the egg yolks, and add them to the pan juices; heat slowly and stir until slightly thickened. Correct the seasoning. Pour the sauce over the chicken. Sprinkle it with the combined minced tarragon and chervil.

FOR 4 PERSONS:

1 **roasting chicken (3 pounds)**	**Salt**
1 **tablespoon peanut oil**	**Freshly ground white pepper**
6 **tablespoons butter**	¾ **cup Crème Fraîche (p. 666)**
4 **shallots, minced**	4 **egg yolks**
3 **tablespoons brandy**	2 **tablespoons combined minced**
½ **cup dry white wine**	**fresh tarragon and chervil**
4 **large sprigs of tarragon**	

POULE AU POT | *Chicken in the Pot*

Truss the chicken. Roast the big onion in a 450° F. oven until it is almost black, and stick the little onion with the cloves.

Put the trussed chicken in a casserole and add cold water to cover. Bring to the boiling point and skim. Add all of the vegetables, bring to the boiling point, and skim again. Add the *bouquet garni*. Season with a little coarse salt. Simmer, covered, over low heat for about 1 hour.

When the chicken is fully cooked, put it on a hot serving plate and surround it with the carrots, celery and leeks. Discard the onions and the *bouquet garni*. Sprinkle the chicken and vegetables with a little of their cooking liquid. Serve with coarse salt and sour pickles.

FOR 6 PERSONS:

1 **roasting chicken (4 pounds)**	6 **celery stalks, cut into 3-inch**
1 **large onion**	**lengths**
1 **small onion**	1 **Bouquet Garni (p. 46)**
3 **cloves**	**Coarse (Kosher) salt**
12 **small carrots, trimmed**	**Sour pickles**
6 **leeks (white part only), cut**	
into halves	

POULARDE AU BLANC | *Chicken in Cream*

Season the bird's cavity with salt and pepper and bard, that is, wrap it in the sheets of fresh pork fat and tie them with string.

Put the chicken into a deep casserole. Add enough stock to cover the chicken by about three quarters. Cover, bring to the boiling point, and cook over medium heat for about 1 hour. Check if the chicken is done by pricking the thickest part of the leg with a skewer. If the juice that spurts out runs clear, the bird is done; if not, continue cooking it for a few minutes longer. Remove the fresh pork fat, put the chicken on a hot serving platter, and keep it warm.

Make a *sauce velouté* (see p. 762) with the butter, flour and 2 cups of the liquid in which the chicken was cooked; bind it with the egg yolks and *crème fraîche* beaten together. Correct the seasoning of the sauce and strain it over the chicken. Serve very hot.

FOR 6 PERSONS:

1 roasting chicken (4 pounds)	**3 tablespoons butter**
Salt	**3 tablespoons flour**
Freshly ground white pepper	**3 egg yolks**
Thin sheets of fresh pork fat	**½ cup Crème Fraîche (p. 666)**
3 quarts (approximately) White Poultry Stock (p. 165)	

Chicken with Cucumbers | POULARDE AUX CONCOMBRES

Proceed as in the preceding recipe and garnish the chicken with Cucumbers in Butter (p. 585).

Chicken in Curried Cream | POULARDE AU CURRY

Proceed as Chicken in Cream (above), and add 1 tablespoon of curry powder, or more to taste, to the butter and flour *roux* when making the *velouté* sauce.

Chicken Demi-Deuil | POULARDE DEMI-DEUIL

Season the cavity of the chicken lightly with salt and pepper and put the thyme and crumbled bay leaf in it. Grind the ham and the boneless chicken meat, using the finest blade of a meat grinder, and season the mixture with salt and pepper. Add the *foie gras* dice and about two thirds of the truffle slices. Stuff the cavity with this mixture. Sew the cavity closed with string, or secure it with poultry skewers and string. Insert about half of the remaining truffle slices under the skin of the chicken, spacing the slices evenly all over the bird. Truss the legs and wings and then bard, that is, wrap the chicken in the slices of fresh pork fat and tie them with string.

Put the bird into a deep casserole and add enough stock to come about three quarters of the way up its sides. Bring to the boiling point. Cook, covered, over medium heat for about 1 hour. When the chicken is almost cooked, remove the fresh pork fat and test for doneness by pricking the thickest part of the leg. If the juices are still rosy, cook it a little longer. Transfer it to a hot serving platter and keep warm.

Reduce the cooking liquid over high heat to about 3 cups. Use this liquid to make a *sauce velouté* (see p. 762) by adding it to a *roux* of the butter and flour, and thicken it with the egg yolks and *crème fraîche* beaten together. Add the remaining truffle slices to the *velouté*.

Coat the chicken with about one third of the sauce and serve the rest separately in a sauceboat. Serve very hot.

Veal Birds Brumaire

Alouettes sans Tête à la Brumaire

Veal Birds Brumaire

Alouettes sans Tête à la Brumaire

MAKE THE STUFFING by combining the ground veal, ham and pork. Flatten the veal cutlets with a mallet or the flat side of a cleaver, season with salt and pepper, and put a little of the stuffing on each. Roll up the meat and tie securely with string. Dust the veal birds with flour and sauté them in the combined hot oil and butter over high heat until they are golden on all sides, turning them frequently. Reduce the heat and simmer, covered, for about 15 minutes.

Stir the lemon juice into the caramel powder and put the mixture in a saucepan over low heat.

Transfer the veal birds to a heated serving dish and keep hot. Stir the Madeira into the pan juices and add the caramel and lemon juice. Boil for a few minutes and then stir in the cornstarch and cook until the sauce is thickened and smooth. Correct the seasoning.

Coat the veal birds with the sauce and serve them garnished with the carrots, onions and mushrooms.

For 4 persons:

For the stuffing:
  ⅓ **pound boneless veal, ground**
  ⅓ **pound fat Bayonne or smoked ham or prosciutto, ground**
  ⅓ **pound boneless pork, ground**
8 slices of veal (¼ inch thick), cut from the upper leg
Salt
Freshly ground black pepper
Flour

3 tablespoons peanut oil
3 tablespoons butter
Juice of 1 lemon
1 teaspoon caramel powder
1 cup Madeira
1 tablespoon cornstarch, blended with 2 tablespoons water
1 recipe Carrots in Butter (p. 575)
1 recipe Glazed Onions (p. 610)
1 recipe Mushrooms Braised in Butter (p. 603)

Stuffed Breast of Veal Niçoise

Poitrine de Veau Farcie Niçoise

Stuffed Breast of Veal Niçoise

Poitrine de Veau Farcie Niçoise

ASK YOUR BUTCHER to bone the breast of veal for stuffing and give you the bones as well as the meat.

Heat 1 tablespoon of the oil in a casserole, add the rice, and stir until the rice becomes translucent. Add ¾ cup of water and a little salt. Bring to a boil, cover tightly, and simmer for about 18 minutes, or until the rice is tender.

Soak the bread crumbs in lukewarm milk (or in pan juices from roasted meat, if you have any). Squeeze them dry.

Mince together the salt pork and the chicken livers. Mix them with the cooked rice, the bread crumbs, the spinach, grated cheese, egg yolks and basil. Season to taste with salt, pepper and nutmeg.

Stuff the breast of veal with this mixture and sew the opening closed.

Put the chopped vegetables into a casserole with the remaining oil and the veal bones. Top with the stuffed veal breast and cook over high heat for 7 to 8 minutes. Turn the meat and cook it on the other side for 7 to 8 minutes.

Cover the casserole and transfer it to a preheated 350° F. oven. Cook for about 2½ hours.

After 1 hour of cooking time, pierce the meat in 3 places with a needle. Baste and turn the meat occasionally.

Drain the cooked meat and place it on a large serving dish. Skim the fat off the pan juices and strain the juices over the meat. Chill until serving time. Serve cold, garnished with tomato slices and black olives.

For 6 persons:

1 breast of veal
6 tablespoons olive oil
½ cup uncooked rice
Salt
2 cups fresh bread crumbs
Lukewarm milk
¼ pound salt pork, finely
    diced and blanched
½ cup chicken livers
½ pound spinach,
    blanched and finely
    chopped

¼ cup grated Swiss cheese
2 egg yolks
1 teaspoon minced fresh
    basil
Freshly ground black
    pepper
Grated nutmeg
1 large onion, chopped
2 carrots, chopped
1 leek, white and green
    part, chopped

Pork Chops Charcutière

Côtes de Porc Charcutière

Pork Chops Charcutière

Côtes de Porc Charcutière

HEAT THE LARD in a skillet over medium heat. Season the pork chops with salt and pepper to taste and sauté them in the hot lard until they are thoroughly done and golden brown on both sides.

Transfer them to a hot serving dish and keep warm.

Pour off the fat from the skillet, add the vinegar, and boil until the vinegar has almost evaporated. Scrape up all the little brown bits at the bottom of the skillet. Add the wine, the *bouquet garni,* the shallot, tomato paste and stock. Simmer until reduced by one quarter. Remove the *bouquet garni,* check the seasoning, and stir in the sugar, mustard and pickles. Mix well and coat the pork chops with this sauce.

For 4 persons:

4 tablespoons lard
4 loin pork chops, cut ¾
    inch thick
Salt
Freshly ground black
    pepper
2 tablespoons vinegar
½ cup dry white wine
1 Bouquet Garni (p. 46)

1 shallot, minced
1 tablespoon tomato paste
½ cup Brown Stock (p. 164)
1 lump of sugar
¼ teaspoon prepared
    mustard
¼ cup thinly sliced sour
    pickles

Glazed Ham Doulce France

Jambon Glacé Doulce France

Glazed Ham Doulce France

Jambon Glacé Doulce France

SCRUB AND SOAK the ham according to the packer's directions. Poach it in the Meursault wine for about 2½ hours. Drain and cool it. Remove the skin and the fat, leaving a smooth surface. Slice the ham thinly. Spread one side of each slice with a little truffled *foie gras*. Put the slices back together to re-form the original shape of the ham and then chill.

Coat the ham with the *chaud-froid* sauce and chill again.

To decorate the ham with a floral pattern, cut the green parts of blanched leeks into the shapes of fronds and leaves, and use hard-cooked eggs and tomatoes to make flower petals (see illustration).

Finally, coat the ham with a thin layer of clear aspic and, if desired, garnish the platter with aspic cut-outs. Keep very cold until the moment of serving.

For 10 persons:

1 smoked ham (8 pounds)
3 bottles Meursault wine
1 pound truffled foie gras
4 cups (approximately) White Chaud-Froid Sauce (p. 776)
    made with chicken stock and flavored with a little port wine
4 cups (approximately) Brown Stock for Aspics (p. 166)

Veal Cutlets Pojarski

Côtes de Veau Pojarski

Veal Cutlets Pojarski

Côtes de Veau Pojarski

BONE THE CHOPS but reserve the bones. Grind the meat, using the finest blade of a meat grinder. Weigh the meat, and then beat into the ground meat the same weight of soft butter and fresh white bread crumbs which have been soaked in milk and squeezed dry. Season with salt, pepper and nutmeg to taste.

Divide the mixture into fourths and form each part into the shape of the original chop pressed against one of the bones. Dust lightly with flour and sauté in the hot butter in a skillet until golden brown on both sides.

Place on a hot serving dish and surround with the braised fennel. Garnish with lemon slices and the mushrooms.

For 4 persons:

4 loin or rib veal chops,
    cut 1 inch thick
Softened butter the weight
    of the boned chops
Fresh white bread crumbs,
    soaked in milk and
    squeezed dry, also
    the same weight as
    the boned chops
Salt

Freshly ground black
    pepper
Grated nutmeg
Flour
6 tablespoons butter
1 recipe Braised Finocchio
    or Fennel (p. 595)
1 lemon, sliced
12 mushroom caps, sautéed
    in butter

Ragout of Pigs' Trotters à la
Canadienne

Ragoût de Pattes à la Canadienne

Ragout of Pigs' Trotters à la Canadienne

Ragoût de Pattes à la Canadienne

CUT THE PIGS' trotters lengthwise into halves. Put them into a pot and cover with hot or cold water (it does not matter which). Add the onion stuck with cloves and season with salt and pepper. Simmer, covered, for 3 to 4 hours and then let the trotters cool in the cooking liquid. When they are cool, drain and bone them. Strain and reserve the cooking liquid.

Heat the butter in a casserole and stir in the flour. Add 2 cups of the cooking liquid and the wine. Stir until it comes to a boil and then add the boned trotters, the garlic, the carrots and the broad beans. Season with the *quatre épices*. The sauce will be thin at the beginning, but it will thicken during cooking time. Simmer for 45 minutes and then correct the seasoning.

Serve with mashed potatoes.

Note: If dried broad beans (available at stores featuring Mediterranean groceries) are used, soak them in cold water overnight.

For 4 persons:

4 pigs' trotters	½ bottle dry white wine
1 large onion, stuck with 4 cloves	2 garlic cloves, minced
Salt	4 carrots, sliced
Freshly ground black	1 pound fresh or dried
pepper	broad beans
4 tablespoons butter	½ teaspoon Quatre Épices
4 tablespoons flour	(p. 667)

Fried Chicken with Bananas

Poulet Frit aux Bananes d'Israël

Fried Chicken with Bananas
Poulet Frit aux Bananes d'Israël

CUT THE CHICKEN into 8 pieces for frying.

Prepare the *anglaise* (see p. 38). Put the flour into one bowl and the bread crumbs into another. Dip the chicken pieces first into the flour, then into the *anglaise,* and finally into the bread crumbs. Heat the fat to 360° F. on a frying thermometer. Put the chicken pieces in the fat and fry for about 20 minutes, adjusting the heat so that the bread crumbs won't burn. Transfer the chicken to a hot serving platter lined with a napkin, and keep hot in the oven.

Peel the bananas and season them with salt. Bread and fry them like the chicken. Keep the bananas hot with the chicken pieces.

Throw the bunch of parsley into the frying fat, fry it for only a few seconds, and drain it on kitchen paper.

Sprinkle the fried parsley over the chicken and bananas and serve very hot.

For 4 persons:

1 frying chicken (2½ to 3 pounds)
Anglaise:
 2 eggs
 2 tablespoons water
 2 tablespoons peanut oil
 Salt
 Freshly ground white pepper

Flour
2 cups fine dry bread crumbs
Fat for deep frying
4 firm bananas, not too ripe
1 small bunch of parsley, washed and thoroughly dried

Chaud-Froid of Chicken à l'Ancienne

Chaud-Froid de Volaille à l'Ancienne

Chaud-Froid of Chicken à l'Ancienne
Chaud-Froid de Volaille à l'Ancienne

To MAKE THE chicken stock, combine the calf's foot, the veal knuckle, the *couenne*, the carrots, turnip, leeks, the onion with cloves, the parsley roots, chicken feet, neck and wing tips in a deep kettle. Add cold water to cover, bring to the boiling point, and skim. Add a little salt and pepper and simmer, covered, for 3 hours. Strain the stock, reserving the strained matter. Pour the stock over the chicken in another deep pot; it should cover the chicken completely. Simmer, covered, for about 45 minutes, or until the chicken is tender.

Remove the chicken and let it cool. Return the strained vegetables and bones to the broth. Simmer, covered, for 1 more hour, strain again, and degrease. Use the strained meats for a salad or hors-d'oeuvre on another occasion.

Make the *sauce velouté:* melt the butter, stir in the flour and cook, stirring constantly, until the mixture begins to turn golden. Stir in 3 cups of the stock and cook until the sauce is thickened and smooth. Beat together the egg yolk and cream. Remove the sauce from the heat and stir in the egg-yolk mixture. Season with salt and pepper. Cut the chicken into serving pieces and coat each with some of the sauce. Cool and chill. Garnish the chicken pieces with tarragon leaves. Serve with potatoes Darphin, sprinkled with julienne slivers of truffle.

For 4 persons:

For the stock:
  1 calf's foot, blanched
  1 veal knuckle
  ½ pound piece of couenne
    (fresh pork rind)
  2 carrots, sliced
  1 turnip, sliced
  2 leeks, sliced
  1 large onion, stuck with
    5 cloves
  Several parsley roots
  2 chicken feet
  The neck and wing tips of
    the chicken
  Salt
  Freshly ground black pepper

1 chicken (3 pounds)
For the Sauce Velouté:
  4 tablespoons butter
  4 tablespoons flour
  1 egg yolk
  ½ cup heavy cream
  Salt
  Freshly ground white
    pepper
A few tarragon leaves
1 recipe Potatoes
  Darphin (p. 635)
Julienne slivers
  (bâtonnets) of truffle

FOR 6 PERSONS:

1 roasting chicken (4 pounds)
Salt
Freshly ground white pepper
3 sprigs of fresh thyme, or ½
   teaspoon dried thyme
1 bay leaf, crumbled
¼ pound smoked ham
¼ pound boned white chicken
   meat
¼ pound foie gras, cut into
   small dice

¼ pound truffles, sliced
Thin sheets of fresh
   pork fat
3 quarts (approximately)
   unseasoned White Poultry Stock
   (p. 165)
3 tablespoons butter
3 tablespoons flour
3 egg yolks
½ cup Crème Fraîche (p. 666)

COQ À LA BIÈRE / *Chicken Braised in Beer*

Truss the chicken and cook it in 4 tablespoons of the butter in a casserole over fairly high heat, turning it until it is golden brown on all sides. Season it with salt and pepper, reduce the heat and simmer, covered, for 30 minutes. Remove the chicken to a hot dish and keep it warm.

Cook the shallots in the pan juices until they are golden; then return the chicken to the casserole, sprinkle it with the Holland gin, and flame it. Add 2 tablespoons of the remaining butter, half of the *crème fraîche,* the mushrooms and the beer. Season with salt, pepper and cayenne. Bring to a boil, cover the casserole, and simmer for about 25 minutes.

When the chicken is fully cooked, cut it into 4 parts, put them on a hot serving platter. and keep them warm.

Add the remaining *crème fraîche* to the casserole, bring the sauce to the boiling point, and cook over high heat until reduced and slightly thickened. Check the seasoning. Remove from the heat and stir in the remaining 2 tablespoons of butter, letting it melt without putting the sauce back on the heat. Coat the chicken with the sauce. Sprinkle with the parsley and serve very hot.

FOR 4 PERSONS:

1 roasting chicken (3 pounds)
8 tablespoons butter
Salt
Freshly ground black pepper
1 tablespoon minced shallots
2 tablespoons Holland gin

½ cup Crème Fraîche (p. 666)
½ pound mushrooms, chopped
2 cups dark beer
Pinch of cayenne pepper
2 tablespoons minced parsley

POULET AU XÉRÈS / *Chicken with Sherry*

Season the cavity of the chicken with salt and pepper. Truss and then bard it, that is, wrap it in the fresh pork fat and tie it with string.

Heat the oil and 4 tablespoons of the butter in a casserole and sauté the chicken on all sides in it. Place the casserole in a preheated 350° F. oven for 45 minutes. Remove the pork fat from the chicken, return it to the oven, and roast for about 20 minutes longer, basting it occasionally.

Transfer the chicken to a plate and skim the fat off the pan juices. Return the chicken to the casserole, sprinkle it with the Armagnac, flame it, and add the sherry. Cover the casserole and put it back into the oven for 5 minutes.

Now put the chicken on a hot serving platter and keep hot.

Add the *crème fraîche* and the *sauce espagnole* to the pan juices. Bring to the boiling point and cook for 2 minutes, beating with a wire whisk. Season with salt and pepper. Remove from the heat and stir in the remaining butter. Strain the sauce and serve it in a sauceboat.

FOR 4 PERSONS:

1 roasting chicken (3 pounds)	3 tablespoons Armagnac
Salt	3 tablespoons sherry
Freshly ground black pepper	½ cup Crème Fraîche (p. 666)
Thin sheets of fresh pork fat	½ cup Sauce Espagnole
1 tablespoon peanut oil	(p. 760)
6 tablespoons butter	

Chicken Flamed with Whisky /

POULET FLAMBÉ AU WHISKY

Truss the chicken and slice the vegetables thin.

Heat the oil and 4 tablespoons of the butter in a casserole over fairly high heat, add the chicken, and cook it until golden on all sides. Add the vegetables and the *bouquet garni,* season with salt and pepper, and cover the casserole. Simmer over low heat for about 45 minutes. Then transfer the chicken to a heated serving platter and keep very hot.

Add the remaining butter and the shallots to the casserole and cook until they are soft and golden. Add the brandy, the Madeira and the *crème fraîche*. Bring to the boiling point and stir with a wire whisk until the sauce has thickened slightly. Season with salt and pepper and strain the sauce through a fine sieve into a sauceboat.

At serving time sprinkle the chicken with the hot whisky and flame it. Serve the sauce separately.

FOR 4 PERSONS:

1 chicken (3 pounds)	Salt
2 onions	Freshly ground white pepper
2 carrots	3 tablespoons minced shallots
2 celery stalks	2 tablespoons brandy
1 tablespoon peanut oil	¼ cup Madeira
6 tablespoons butter	1 cup Crème Fraîche (p. 666)
1 Bouquet Garni (p. 46)	¼ cup Scotch whisky, heated

Broiled Chicken American Style /

POULET GRILLÉ À L'AMÉRICAINE

Split the chicken along the backbone. Flatten it, season with salt and pepper, brush with oil, and broil for about 10 minutes on each side. Quite often the chicken is broiled until barely golden, then spread with mustard and sprinkled with bread crumbs and melted butter, and then finished broiling. It may be served with broiled mushrooms, broiled or baked tomatoes, or bacon and French fried potatoes.

FOR 2 PERSONS:

1 broiling chicken (2 pounds)	**Optional: 1 tablespoon Dijon**
Salt	**mustard**
Freshly ground black pepper	**3 tablespoons dry bread**
2 tablespoons olive oil	**crumbs**
	3 tablespoons melted butter

POULET AUX AROMATES / *Aromatic Chicken*

Cut the chicken into 8 pieces for frying and force into the flesh of each piece 2 tarragon leaves, 1 basil leaf and 2 rosemary sprigs. Season the pieces with salt and pepper and lightly brown them in the combined hot oil and 2 tablespoons of the butter in a casserole over fairly high heat until they turn golden. Remove the pieces and keep hot.

Add the remaining butter to the casserole, together with the onions and mushrooms. Simmer for about 5 minutes, then add the chicken pieces. Cover the casserole and simmer for about 25 minutes. When the chicken is tender, transfer the pieces to a hot serving dish.

Serve immediately, very hot.

If you want to vary this recipe, you may add a few garlic cloves along with the onions. But have a light hand with the garlic or it will overpower the taste of the herbs.

You may also add a few thickly sliced potatoes when the chicken is about one-third cooked; in this case, add a little water, but not too much, since all the water must have evaporated when the potatoes are done.

FOR 4 PERSONS:

1 frying chicken (2½ to 3	**Freshly ground black pepper**
pounds)	**1 tablespoon peanut oil**
16 tarragon leaves	**4 tablespoons butter**
8 basil leaves	**20 tiny white onions**
16 tiny rosemary sprigs	**12 small mushroom caps**
Salt	

POULET CHASSEUR / *Chicken Chasseur*

Cut the chicken into 8 pieces for frying.

Dip the tomatoes into boiling water for 2 minutes, rinse them in cold water, peel and seed them. Cut them into coarse pieces. Chop the tarragon leaves and slice the mushrooms.

Heat the oil and the butter in a casserole over fairly high heat and cook the chicken pieces on both sides until they are golden. Remove the pieces to a warm dish.

Add the mushrooms to the casserole, cook them for about 3 minutes, and then add the minced shallots. Stir with a wooden spoon and simmer, covered, over low heat for about 5 minutes. Sprinkle with the flour, stir well, and add the wine and the stock (or water, if you don't have anything else). Add the *bouquet garni,* the tomatoes and half of the chopped tarragon leaves. Return the chicken pieces to the casserole and bring to a boil. Season with salt and pepper and simmer, covered, over low heat for about 25 minutes.

Put the chicken and vegetables in a deep hot serving dish. Serve with the steamed potatoes sprinkled with the remaining tarragon.

FOR 4 PERSONS:

1 frying chicken (2½ to 3 pounds)
1 pound ripe tomatoes
2 tablespoons tarragon leaves
¾ pound mushrooms
2 tablespoons peanut oil
3 tablespoons butter
2 tablespoons minced shallots
2 tablespoons flour

1 cup dry white wine
½ cup White or Brown Poultry Stock (p. 164)
1 Bouquet Garni (p. 46)
Salt
Freshly ground black pepper
1 recipe Steamed Potatoes (p. 621)

Chicken Curry /

Cut the chicken into 8 pieces for frying. Heat the oil and the butter in a casserole over fairly high heat and brown the chicken pieces on both sides in it. Sprinkle with the curry powder and the flour and turn the pieces until the flour is golden. Add the onions, apples and garlic. Season with salt and pepper and simmer, covered, over low heat for about 30 minutes.

Stir in the *crème fraîche,* heat for a few minutes, correct the seasoning, and serve very hot.

Note: Grated coconut or bananas may be used instead of apples and the *crème fraîche* may be diluted with a little coconut milk.

FOR 4 PERSONS:

1 frying chicken (2½ to 3 pounds)
2 tablespoons peanut oil
3 tablespoons butter
2 tablespoons curry powder
1 tablespoon flour
1 pound onions, minced

2 apples, peeled, cored and minced
1 garlic clove, mashed
Salt
Freshly ground black pepper
¾ cup Crème Fraîche (p. 666)

Chicken Emmanuel Berl / POULET EMMANUEL BERL

Cut the chicken into 8 pieces for frying.

Heat the oil and 4 tablespoons of the butter in a casserole over fairly high heat; add the chicken pieces and brown them lightly on all sides. Season them with salt and pepper.

Mince the celery, the fennel and the leeks. Transfer the chicken to a hot plate and keep it warm.

Add 2 more tablespoons of the butter to the casserole. Add the celery and cook until it is turning golden. Return the chicken pieces to the casserole and add the fennel, leeks, *bouquet garni,* garlic and parsley. Season with salt and pepper.

Add enough water to cover the chicken, bring to a boil and simmer, covered, over low heat for about 30 minutes.

Make a *liaison:* beat together the *crème fraîche,* the egg yolks and the cornstarch. Season with a little cayenne. Take the parsley sprigs out of the chicken liquid, mash them, and add them to the *liaison.* Mix well.

When the chicken is fully cooked and tender, transfer the pieces to a serving dish. Reduce the cooking liquid over high heat to 1 generous cup and discard the *bouquet garni.* Stir a few spoonfuls of the cooking liquid into the *liaison* and pour this mixture into the casserole. Stir over low heat until it is thickened. Correct the seasoning, spoon a little of the sauce over the chicken pieces, and pour the remaining sauce into a sauceboat.

Fry the bread slices in the remaining butter until golden. Serve them on the side.

FOR 4 PERSONS:

1 frying chicken (2½ to 3 pounds)	1 Bouquet Garni (p. 46)
1 tablespoon peanut oil	3 garlic cloves, mashed
8 tablespoons butter	3 parsley sprigs
Salt	1 cup Crème Fraîche (p. 666)
Freshly ground white pepper	4 egg yolks
2 celery stalks	1 teaspoon cornstarch
2 fennel stalks, white part only	Cayenne pepper
3 leeks, white part only	4 slices of French bread

POULET À L'AIL / *Chicken with Garlic*

Cut the chicken into 8 pieces. Season the pieces with salt and pepper and cook them in the oil and 4 tablespoons of the butter in a casserole until golden on all sides. Cover the casserole, reduce the heat, and simmer for 10 minutes.

Peel the garlic heads and crush them.

Transfer the chicken to a hot plate and keep hot. Add the remaining butter to the casserole, together with the garlic. Stir with a wooden spoon. Cook over low heat, stirring constantly, until the garlic is so soft that it will cling to the spoon.

Stir in the wine, bring to the boiling point, and cook for 3 to 4 minutes. Return the chicken to the casserole. Pour the hot milk over the chicken, cover the casserole, and simmer for 15 minutes, or until the chicken is tender.

Prepare the *liaison:* blend together the *crème fraîche* and the cornstarch.

When the chicken is fully cooked, stir a few spoonfuls of its cooking liquid into the *liaison,* mix well, and pour this mixture into the casserole to thicken the sauce. Bring to the boiling point and cook over high heat for about 3 minutes. Correct the seasoning.

Place the chicken pieces in a hot serving dish, reshaping them in the form of a chicken if desired, and strain the sauce over the chicken. Serve immediately.

FOR 4 PERSONS:

1 frying chicken (2½ to 3 pounds)	2 heads of garlic
Salt	½ cup dry white wine
Freshly ground white pepper	2 cups milk, scalding hot
1 tablespoon peanut oil	¼ cup Crème Fraîche (p. 666)
5 tablespoons butter	1 tablespoon cornstarch

Chicken Père Lathuile | POULET DU PÈRE LATHUILE

Cut the chicken into 8 pieces for frying and season with salt and pepper.

Trim the artichoke hearts and blanch for 10 minutes in the manner described in Artichoke Hearts in Butter (p. 545).

Heat 1 tablespoon of the oil and 4 tablespoons of the butter in a casserole, and lightly brown the chicken pieces in it on all sides. Sprinkle them with the thyme and bay leaf. Remove from the heat and keep warm.

Slice two of the potatoes thin and sauté them in the remaining oil and 2 tablespoons of the butter in a skillet until the slices are golden on both sides. Season them with salt. Remove the potato slices carefully so as not to break them and drain them on kitchen paper.

Add 3 tablespoons of butter to the same skillet. Mince the remaining 3 potatoes and the artichoke hearts. Season them with salt and pepper and cook them in the butter until they are golden.

Heat the remaining 3 tablespoons of butter in a casserole. Line the bottom with the sautéed potato slices in overlapping rows; do this carefully with your fingers. Top the potato slices with half of the combined minced potatoes and artichoke hearts. Top the vegetables with the chicken pieces, cover the chicken with the remaining minced potatoes and artichoke hearts, and sprinkle with all the pan juices. Cover the casserole and cook in a preheated 375° F. oven for about 40 minutes.

Be sure to use a casserole that is rather small, so that all the contents lie close together, to form a cake. Unmold it on a hot serving platter and garnish with fried parsley. Keep hot while you prepare the shallot sauce.

Heat the oil and the butter in a casserole, and cook the shallots until they are golden. Pour the mixture into the casserole in which the chicken was cooked, stirring up all the brown bits at the bottom of the casserole. Stir in the wine and the stock. Cook over high heat unil the sauce is reduced to a good strong flavor. Serve separately in a sauceboat.

FOR 4 PERSONS:

1 frying chicken (2½ to 3 pounds)
Salt
Freshly ground black pepper
3 artichoke hearts
2 tablespoons peanut oil
12 tablespoons butter
2 tablespoons chopped fresh thyme, or 1 teaspoon dried thyme
1 bay leaf, crumbled

5 medium-sized potatoes
1 small bunch of parsley, deep fried

For the sauce:
1 tablespoon peanut oil
3 tablespoons butter
¼ cup minced shallots
½ cup dry white wine
1 cup Brown Poultry Stock (p. 164)

Chicken Sauté Paysanne | POULET SAUTÉ PAYSANNE

Cut the chicken into 8 pieces for frying.

Heat the ham fat and the lard together in a casserole over fairly high heat, add the chicken pieces, and cook them until they are golden on all sides. Add the big onion, the white onions and the potatoes. Stir with a wooden spoon and cook until golden.

Season with salt and pepper; add the thyme, the bay leaf and the unpeeled garlic cloves. Simmer, covered, over low heat for about 25 minutes.

When the chicken is done, discard the bay leaf and garlic cloves. Pour the chicken and the vegetables into a deep hot serving dish and sprinkle with the parsley. Serve very hot.

FOR 4 PERSONS:

1 **frying chicken (2½ to 3 pounds)**	**Salt**
¼ **cup chopped ham fat**	**Freshly ground black pepper**
2 **tablespoons lard**	1 **sprig of fresh thyme, or ½ teaspoon dried thyme**
1 **large onion, cut into 6 pieces**	1 **bay leaf**
24 **tiny white onions**	4 **unpeeled garlic cloves**
4 **medium-sized potatoes, cut into quarters**	2 **tablespoons minced parsley**

/ *Chicken Sautéed with Riesling*

POULET SAUTÉ AU RIESLING

Cut the chicken into 8 pieces for frying.

Heat the oil and the butter in a casserole over fairly high heat. Add the chicken pieces and cook them until golden on all sides. Add the mushrooms and the tomatoes, reduce the heat slightly, and cook for 5 minutes. Add the wine, the brandy, and the meat juice if you use it. Season with salt and a little cayenne. Bring to a boil, cover the casserole, and simmer for 25 minutes.

Transfer the chicken to a hot serving dish and keep warm.

Skim the fat off the pan juices and add the parsley and the garlic. Bring to the boiling point and cook over high heat until the sauce has reduced slightly. Pour it over the chicken and serve very hot.

FOR 4 PERSONS:

1 **frying chicken (2½ to 3 pounds)**	2 **tablespoons brandy**
1 **tablespoon peanut oil**	2 **tablespoons strong clear meat juice (optional)**
4 **tablespoons butter**	**Salt**
¼ **pound mushrooms, sliced**	**Cayenne pepper**
3 **ripe tomatoes, peeled, seeded and chopped**	3 **tablespoons chopped parsley**
½ **bottle Riesling or dry white wine**	1 **garlic clove, minced**

POULARDE JOINVILLE / *Chicken Joinville*

Bone the chicken, splitting it down the back, but leave in the wing and leg bones. Make a *mousseline* forcemeat with the ground chicken meat by pounding the egg whites into the meat in a mortar, or by blending briefly in a blender. Place this mixture in a bowl over cracked ice and gradually work in the *crème fraîche*. Season with salt and white pepper.

Soak the cocks' combs in cold water, beat them against a chopping board to make them softer, soak them again in cold water, and then blanch them in boiling salted water for 5 minutes. Drain them and cut them into halves.

Soak and blanch the sweetbread as described on page 449 and cut it into small dice. Combine the chicken *mousseline,* cocks' combs and sweetbread dice, mixing well.

Spread the chicken out flat on a board, skin side down. Season the cavity lightly with salt and pepper, spread it with the *mousseline* mixture, and place the truffles in the center of the filling. Roll up the bird in its original shape, sew the back and cavity closed, and bard, that is, wrap it in the fresh pork fat and tie it with string.

Heat the butter in a casserole and lightly brown the bird on all sides. Add the ham. Cover the casserole and simmer over moderate heat for 45 minutes. Add the onions and cook for 45 minutes longer. About 25 minutes before the end of the cooking time, remove the fresh pork fat and lightly brown the bird by turning it on all sides. Then transfer the chicken, onions and ham to a hot serving platter and keep warm.

Skim the fat off the pan juices and stir in the brandy and the verbena, scraping up all the brown bits at the bottom of the casserole. Add the stock, bring to the boiling point, and boil for 5 minutes. Strain the sauce into a sauceboat, and serve it with the chicken, very hot.

FOR 6 PERSONS:

1 chicken (4 pounds)
1 pound boned white chicken
  meat, ground
2 egg whites
1 cup Crème Fraîche (p. 666)
Salt
Freshly ground white pepper
6 cocks' combs
1 veal sweetbread
Freshly ground black pepper

6 black truffles
Thin sheets of fresh pork fat
6 tablespoons butter
¼ pound Bayonne or smoked ham
  or prosciutto, chopped
12 small white onions
2 tablespoons brandy
2 tablespoons verbena liqueur
1 cup Brown Poultry Stock
  (p. 164)

Chicken Marceron | POULET MARCERON

Bone the chicken, splitting it down the back, but do not remove the wing and leg bones. Reserve the rest of the bones.

Using the finest blade of a meat grinder, grind together the ham and the boneless chicken meat. Put them into a bowl and season lightly with salt, depending on the saltiness of the ham, and a pinch of cayenne. Stir in the brandy. Blend well to obtain a very smooth mixture. Add the *foie gras.*

Add the optional kidneys and cocks' combs, prepared in the manner described in Chicken Joinville (above). Spread the chicken out flat on a chopping board, skin side down. Season lightly with salt, pepper, thyme and bay leaf. Spread the filling over the chicken and place the truffles in the center.

Roll up the chicken, reshaping it in its original shape. Sew the back and cavity closed and truss and bard the bird, that is, wrap it in the fresh pork fat and tie it with string.

Line a baking pan with the reserved chicken bones, the onions, carrots and celery. Lay the chicken on the vegetables and add the water. Cook in a preheated 350° F.

oven for 1½ hours, basting frequently. Add more water as it becomes necessary.

Remove the fresh pork fat for the last 20 minutes and raise the temperature of the oven to 400° F. to let the chicken turn golden. Transfer the chicken to a hot serving platter and strain the juices over it. Let it stand in a hot place for 5 minutes before serving.

FOR 4 PERSONS:

1 roasting chicken (3 pounds)	Freshly ground black pepper
¼ pound raw ham	½ teaspoon dried thyme
¼ pound boneless white chicken meat	1 bay leaf, crumbled
Salt	4 truffles
Cayenne pepper	Thin slices of fresh pork fat
2 tablespoons brandy	2 onions, chopped
½ pound foie gras, diced	2 carrots, chopped
Optional: 12 cocks' combs and 24 cocks' kidneys, cut into halves	2 celery stalks, chopped
	½ cup water

POULARDE NANTUA / *Chicken Nantua*

Remove the intestines of the crayfish with the aid of a sharp knife and sauté the crayfish in the oil and 3 tablespoons of the butter in a skillet for about 5 minutes, or until they are red. Sprinkle with the brandy, flame and simmer, covered, for 3 to 5 minutes.

Remove the crayfish and shell them, reserving the shells. Put all the shells into a mortar and crush them finely with a pestle.

Add 2 more tablespoons of butter to the pan juices and cook the shallot in it until it is golden; then add the crushed shells. Simmer for 5 minutes and add the tomatoes, the wine and the *bouquet garni*. Season with salt and pepper and simmer, covered, for 20 minutes. Strain through a fine sieve into a saucepan and reduce the mixture to approximately 6 tablespoons.

Prepare a *mousseline* forcemeat as described in Chicken Joinville (p. 471).

Bone the chicken, splitting it down the back, but leave in the wing and leg bones. Or, if this seems difficult, ask your butcher to do it for you. Spread the chicken out on a board, skin side down. Season very lightly with salt and pepper. Place the chicken forcemeat in the center and cover with the crayfish and the truffle slices. Roll up the bird to give it its original shape. Sew all the openings closed, truss it, and wrap it in the fresh pork fat, securing it with string.

Put the chicken into a deep casserole and cover it with the stock. Bring to the boiling point and simmer, covered, for about 1½ hours. When the chicken is done, remove the fresh pork fat, put the chicken on a hot serving platter, and keep warm.

Make the *sauce suprême:* melt the butter, stir in the flour, and cook until barely golden. Stir in 2 cups of the stock in which the chicken was cooked. Beat together the egg yolks, the *crème fraîche* and the 6 tablespoons of reserved crayfish sauce. Stir this mixture into the sauce; heat slowly and stir until the sauce is thickened. If the sauce becomes too thick, add a little more of the chicken stock. Correct the seasoning. Strain about one third of the sauce over the chicken and the rest into a sauceboat. Serve both very hot.

FOR 6 PERSONS:

24 small crayfish
2 tablespoons peanut oil
5 tablespoons butter
2 tablespoons brandy
1 shallot, minced
2 tomatoes, peeled, seeded and
   chopped
½ cup dry white wine
1 Bouquet Garni (p. 46)
Salt
Freshly ground black pepper

Mousseline Forcemeat made from:
½ pound boneless white
   chicken meat
2 egg whites
1 cup heavy cream
Salt
Freshly ground white pepper

1 roasting chicken (4 pounds)
¼ pound truffles, sliced
Thin sheets of fresh pork fat
3 quarts (approximately) White
   Poultry Stock (p. 165)

For the sauce suprême:
3 tablespoons butter
3 tablespoons flour
6 eggs yolks
1 cup Crème Fraîche
   (p. 666)

Chicken Pierre Anthonioz / POULET PIERRE ANTHONIOZ

Bone the chicken completely, splitting it down the back. Make a stuffing with the beef, which must be very tender; if you are not sure of the tenderness, use tenderloin of beef. Mix together the meat, the eggs, the *fines herbes* and the bacon.

Spread the chicken out on a board, skin side down. Spread it with the stuffing and form it into the shape of a roll, or big sausage. Sew it securely closed. Sauté the roll in the combined hot oil and butter in a casserole over high heat until it is golden. Add the onions and cover the casserole, sealing it with a band of flour and water paste. Simmer over very low heat for 2 hours. Remove the cover and transfer the chicken roll to a hot serving dish. Pour the pan juices over the roll.

Shortly before the chicken is done, tie the bananas together with soft kitchen string. The bananas should be firm and not overripe. Poach them in boiling salted water for about 6 minutes and serve them in their skins, as a garnish for the chicken.

FOR 4 PERSONS:

1 roasting chicken (3 pounds)
½ pound ground beef sirloin
   or tenderloin
3 hard-cooked eggs, chopped
2 tablespoons minced Fines
   Herbes (p. 89)
¼ pound bacon, cut into small
   dice

2 tablespoons peanut oil
4 tablespoons butter
2 large onions, each stuck with
   1 clove
Flour and water paste
4 bananas

/ *Chicken Stuffed with Vegetables*

POULARDE FARCIE AUX PETITS LÉGUMES

Bone the chicken, leaving it whole and leaving in the wing and leg bones. Season the cavity very lightly with salt, pepper, thyme and bay leaf. Blanch the leeks in boiling salted water for 3 minutes, drain them, and then gently sauté them in the butter with the carrots, onions, celery, and peas. Season lightly with salt and pepper.

Slice two of the truffles and cut the other two into small dice.

When the vegetables are not quite tender, remove them from the heat and add the diced truffles; stuff the chicken with this mixture. Loosen the chicken skin a little and insert the truffle slices. Sew the cavity closed. Truss the chicken and bard, that is, wrap it in the fresh pork fat.

Put the chicken into the pig's caul with the Armagnac and tie it with string, to seal the caul completely. Put the chicken into a kettle with enough well-seasoned stock to cover it and simmer over low heat for 1¾ hours.

Take the cooked chicken out of the pig's caul, remove the fresh pork fat, and keep the bird hot on a hot serving dish.

Measure 2 cups of the stock in which the chicken was cooked and strain it through a very fine sieve into a casserole. Bring to the boiling point and reduce by one third.

Beat together the egg yolks with the *crème fraîche* and season with a little salt and cayenne. Stir in a little of the reduced stock and then pour it into the casserole. Heat very slowly, beating the sauce constantly with a wire whisk until it is thickened slightly. Correct the seasoning. Pour the sauce through a sieve into a sauceboat.

Serve the chicken very hot, with the sauce on the side.

FOR 6 PERSONS:

1 roasting chicken (4 pounds)
Salt
Freshly ground black pepper
2 tablespoons chopped fresh thyme, or 1 teaspoon dried thyme
1 bay leaf, crumbled
2 leeks, white part only, sliced lengthwise
4 tablespoons butter
½ pound carrots, cut into small dice
½ pound onions, chopped
¼ pound celery, stalk and leaves, cut into small dice
1 cup shelled peas
4 truffles
Thin sheets of fresh pork fat
1 pig's caul
3 tablespoons Armagnac
3 (or more) quarts White Poultry Stock (p. 165)
4 egg yolks
¼ cup Crème Fraîche (p. 666)
Cayenne pepper

PAIN DE VOLAILLE CHAUD / *Chicken Loaf*

Completely bone the chicken and crush the meat in a mortar with a pestle, or put it through the finest blade of a meat grinder. Season with salt, pepper and cayenne to taste. Blend it with one and one quarter times its volume of *sauce béchamel*. Force the purée through a fine sieve into a bowl.

Beat in the eggs and 1 cup of the *crème fraîche*. Mix well. Pour the mixture into a deep 6- to 8-cup buttered mold, stand the mold in a pan containing 1 inch of hot water, and cook in a preheated 350° F. oven for about 45 minutes. When a skewer plunged in the center comes out clean, it is done.

Serve with the *sauce Mornay* to which you've added the remaining *crème fraîche* and which you have cooked until the sauce is somewhat reduced and very smooth.

FOR 4 PERSONS:

1 chicken (3 pounds)	**2 eggs**
Salt	**2 cups Crème Fraîche (p. 666)**
Freshly ground white pepper	**2 cups Sauce Mornay (p. 776)**
Cayenne pepper	
2 to 3 cups Sauce Béchamel	
(p. 761)	

Chicken-Liver Loaf Lyonnaise /

GÂTEAU DE FOIES DE VOLAILLES À LA LYONNAISE

Grind the chicken livers, using the finest blade of a meat grinder, and put them in a bowl. Beat in the egg yolks. Soak the bread or the *brioche* crumbs in lukewarm milk and then squeeze them almost dry. Mix them with the chicken-liver mixture. Season with salt and pepper to taste. Beat the egg whites until stiff and fold them ino the mixture. Pour it into a well-buttered 6-cup charlotte mold. Set the mold in a baking pan containing 1 inch of hot water and cook in a preheated 350° F. oven for about 40 minutes. It is done when a skewer plunged in the middle comes out clean.

Unmold on a hot serving dish and garnish with mushrooms sautéed with green and black olives. Coat the loaf with very hot *sauce tomate*.

FOR 4 PERSONS:

½ pound chicken livers	**Freshly ground black pepper**
4 eggs, separated	**½ pound mushrooms, sautéed in**
3 cups fresh white bread crumbs	**butter with a few green and**
or brioche crumbs	**black olives**
Lukewarm milk	**2 to 3 cups Sauce Tomate**
Salt	**(p. 769)**

Coq en Pâte /

There are numerous recipes for this dish, but here is an amusing one.

Have the puff paste ready. Cook the chicken any way you fancy: roast, sauté or poach it.

Cut the cooked chicken into appropriate-sized pieces and let them cool.

Divide the puff paste into 3 parts. Roll two of them out to the thickness of ⅛ inch in a rectangular shape, but make one rectangle 1 inch larger on all sides. Put the smaller rectangle on a baking sheet and lay the chicken pieces closely together in the middle. Moisten the edges of the pastry with water and cover with the second larger piece. Crimp the edges to seal thoroughly. Paint with the egg mixture and cut a funnel in the top. Bake in a preheated 375° F. oven for about 25 minutes.

Roll the third piece of puff paste out to the thickness of ⅛ inch. With the point of a knife, score a stylized design of a cock's wings, tail and head.

Cut out the pieces. Paint them with the egg mixture and bake them in a pre-heated 375° F. oven for 15 to 20 minutes.

When the pastry-wrapped chicken is golden, take it out of the oven, put it on a serving platter, and garnish it with the pastry wings, tail and head. Serve immediately, with a sauce that suits the way you cooked the chicken, that is a Sauce Velouté (p. 762) for a poached bird, or a Madeira sauce (p. 764) for a roast one, etc.

FOR 5 TO 6 PERSONS:

1 recipe Puff Paste (p. 715)	1 egg, beaten with 1 tablespoon
1 chicken (3 pounds)	water

POULE EN PIE / *Chicken Pie*

Put the chicken and the beef bone into a kettle, add enough water to cover, and bring slowly to the boiling point. Skim. Add the carrots, turnips, celery, onion and garlic. Bring again to the boiling point and skim. Season very lightly with coarse salt. Simmer, covered, for 45 minutes, or until the chicken is not quite tender.

Remove the chicken from the kettle; let it cool. Skin and bone it and cut the meat into bite-sized pieces. Put the chicken meat into a small saucepan with the port, brandy or Armagnac, and let it simmer, covered, over very low heat for 10 minutes.

Add the chicken bones to the liquid in the kettle and reduce over high heat to a broth of strong flavor; strain. Prepare a *sauce velouté,* as described on page 762, using 2 cups of the chicken broth, the flour and butter, and binding the sauce with three of the egg yolks beaten with the *crème fraîche.* Season with salt and pepper. Simmer slowly until thick and smooth.

Put the chicken meat into a 9-inch pie dish and coat it with the sauce. Let it cool completely. Roll out the *brioche* dough into a round slightly larger than the pie dish and cover the chicken meat. Press the edges firmly to make a tight seal. Make a chimney in the middle. Put the dish in a warm place for 30 minutes to allow the dough to rise. Paint with the remaining egg yolk. Bake in a preheated 375° F. oven for about 25 minutes. Serve very hot.

FOR 6 PERSONS:

1 roasting chicken (4 pounds)	3 tablespoons flour
1 beef marrowbone	3 tablespoons butter
1 pound carrots, chopped	4 egg yolks
½ pound turnips, chopped	½ cup Crème Fraîche (p. 666)
1 small bunch of celery, chopped	Salt
1 onion, stuck with 3 cloves	Freshly ground white pepper
1 garlic head, unpeeled	⅓ recipe Brioche dough
Coarse (Kosher) salt	(p. 695)
¼ cup port, brandy or Armagnac	

CAPILOTADE DE VOLAILLE / *Capilotade of Chicken*

This dish is often made with a whole boiled chicken cut into pieces, or it may be made with just chicken necks, backs, gizzards and wing tips.

Mince the onion and the shallots and cook them in the combined hot oil and butter until they are soft and golden. Add the whole garlic cloves, sprinkle with the flour, and stir in the tomato paste, wine, stock and *bouquet garni*. Season with salt, pepper and cayenne to taste. Bring to a boil and add the chicken pieces.

Simmer, covered, over very low heat for 30 minutes. Serve in a hot deep serving dish, surrounded with Cornmeal Cakes or Cornmeal Crêpes (p. 584).

FOR 6 PERSONS:

1 boiled chicken (4 pounds), cut into pieces, or about 3 pounds boiled chicken necks, gizzards, wing tips and backs
1 large onion
4 shallots
2 tablespoons peanut oil
2 tablespoons butter
2 whole garlic cloves

3 tablespoons flour
3 tablespoons tomato paste
1 cup dry white wine
2 cups White Poultry Stock (p. 165)
1 Bouquet Garni (p. 46)
Salt
Freshly ground white pepper
Cayenne pepper

Chicken Bouillabaisse | BOUILLABAISSE DE POULET

Cut the chicken into 8 pieces for frying, reserving the liver, and marinate the pieces in the combined saffron, Pernod and 3 tablespoons of the olive oil for 30 minutes. Season with salt and pepper and turn the pieces occasionally.

Heat 3 tablespoons of olive oil in a casserole and add the onions and garlic. Cook them until barely golden. Add the tomatoes and cook for 5 minutes, stirring frequently. Add the fennel, parsley, the chicken pieces and their marinade. Add enough boiling water to cover the chicken. Season with salt, cover the casserole, and cook over low heat for 10 minutes. Add the potatoes and simmer, covered, for 15 minutes longer, or until chicken and potatoes are almost cooked through. Uncover the casserole and cook until the liquid has reduced and slightly thickened.

Line a soup tureen with the sliced bread, sprinkle the remaining 2 tablespoons of olive oil over it, and pour chicken, vegetables and sauce over the bread. Keep hot.

Now make a *sauce rouille:* In a blender or with mortar and pestle, blend together the garlic cloves, the hot peppers and the olive oil. Sauté the chicken liver quickly in a little butter, mash it, and add it to the mixture. Add 2 slices of the potatoes from the *bouillabaisse*. Blend or mash until the mixture is smooth. Stir in 6 tablespoons of the *bouillabaisse* sauce and blend again. Serve the sauce separately in a bowl.

FOR 4 PERSONS:

1 frying chicken (2½ pounds)
⅛ teaspoon ground saffron
2 tablespoons Pernod
8 tablespoons olive oil
Salt
Freshly ground black pepper
2 onions, chopped
4 garlic cloves, mashed
6 tomatoes, peeled, chopped and seeded
1 small head of fennel, white part only, chopped

6 parsley sprigs, chopped
4 potatoes, thickly sliced
4 slices of French bread

For the sauce:
1 garlic clove, mashed
4 small hot red peppers
¼ cup olive oil
1 chicken liver
1 tablespoon butter

/ *Cold Chicken Fricassee à l'Ancienne*

FRICASSÉE DE POULET À L'ANCIENNE

Cut the legs, thighs, wings and breasts off the chickens. Reserve the backs and the giblets.

Put the calf's foot and the veal knuckle in a large pot with the chicken backs and giblets. Add the onion and the *bouquet garni*. Cover with cold water, season with salt and pepper, bring to a boil and simmer, covered, for 2 hours.

Heat the oil and 3 tablespoons of the butter in a heavy saucepan. Add the chicken pieces and season with salt and pepper. Sauté over high heat until the pieces are golden on all sides and then transfer them to a plate.

Poach the mushroom caps just covered with water together with the lemon juice, the remaining butter and a pinch of salt in a small saucepan for 5 minutes. Then remove from the heat.

Strain the broth through a fine sieve into a large pot. Add the liquid in which the mushrooms were cooked and reserve the mushrooms. Add the sautéed chicken pieces. Simmer, covered, over low heat until the chicken is just tender, about 20 minutes.

Beat together the *crème fraîche* and the egg yolks.

Remove the chicken pieces and place them in a deep serving dish. Surround them with the mushroom caps and keep warm. Reduce the broth over high heat to about 4 cups. Remove from the heat and stir the egg-yolk mixture into the broth. Bring slowly just to the boiling point, beating with a wire whisk until the sauce is slightly thickened and smooth. Correct the seasoning. Pour it over the chicken and mushrooms. Cool, then chill in the refrigerator and serve very cold.

FOR 6 PERSONS:

2 chickens (2½ pounds each)	3 tablespoons peanut oil
1 calf's foot, blanched	4 tablespoons butter
1 veal knuckle	8 mushroom caps
1 onion, stuck with 3 cloves	Juice of ½ lemon
1 Bouquet Garni (p. 46)	½ cup Crème Fraîche (p. 666),
Salt	or heavy cream
Freshly ground white pepper	4 egg yolks

CHAUD-FROID DE VOLAILLE / *Chaud-Froid of Chicken*

Make a well-seasoned stock with the chicken parts, the calf's foot, the veal knuckle, the *couenne,* the carrots, turnip, celery, leeks, onions, the *fines herbes* (parsley, chervil, tarragon), about 4 quarts of water and a little salt. Simmer it for about 3 hours.

Put the fresh whole truffles into the cavity of the chicken and truss it. Bard it with thin sheets of pork fat and then put it into a pig's caul that is either very fresh or has been soaked in lukewarm water. Tie the bladder tightly closed with string.

Put the wrapped chicken into a deep kettle and strain the stock over it, reserving all the meats, bones, and vegetables. Bring to the boiling point and then simmer the chicken for about 45 minutes, or until tender. Transfer the chicken to a dish and let it cool in the pig's caul.

Put the reserved meats and vegetables back into the kettle of stock and simmer for 1 more hour. Strain through a fine sieve and degrease completely. Discard the meats and vegetables.

When the stock is cool, drizzle a few spoonfuls on a plate and chill to see if it will jell very firmly. If not, add an appropriate amount of unflavored gelatin in the manner described on page 166 and test again.

Make a light *sauce velouté,* using 4 cups of the chicken stock in the manner described on page 762. Cool the sauce completely and then stir it over cracked ice until it becomes very thick and is almost at the point of jelling.

While the sauce is cooling, remove the chicken from the pig's caul and reserve the truffles from the cavity. Cut off the legs, thighs and breasts. Remove all the skin and bone the pieces. Cool and then chill them. Put the pieces on a rack placed over a dish (to catch the excess sauce) and coat them generously with, if necessary, several layers of the sauce which should be just beginning to jell, but still liquid. Chill the coated pieces again. Slice the truffles and decorate the chicken pieces with them. Drizzle the rest of the sauce onto a silver platter and chill. When it is set, place the decorated chicken pieces on the platter. Chill the dish until serving time.

You may also refine this dish in the following manner:

When you have removed the truffles from the chicken's cavity, slice all of the meat of the chicken into long thin strips, but leave the carcass intact. Cut the truffles into thick slices.

Make a purée of the *foie gras* and blend it with the equal amount of softened butter. Season with salt and pepper to taste.

Blend thoroughly and put the mixture into a pastry bag fitted with a thin flat tube. Build up the chicken in its original shape, alternating meat and truffle slices and using the *foie gras* purée to hold them together. Chill until very cold.

Put the rebuilt chicken on a rack and coat it with the sauce. Chill it and decorate it as you wish. Then place it on the silver platter lined with *sauce velouté.*

FOR 4 PERSONS:

2 pounds chicken backs, necks, giblets, or other parts
1 calf's foot
1 veal knuckle
½-pound piece couenne (fresh pork rind)
2 carrots, sliced
1 turnip, sliced
2 celery stalks, sliced
3 leeks, sliced
3 onions, each stuck with 3 cloves
2 tablespoons minced Fines Herbes (p. 89)
Salt
¼ pound fresh truffles, or canned truffles

1 chicken (3 pounds)
Several thin sheets of fresh pork fatback
1 pig's caul

For the Sauce Velouté:
4 tablespoons butter
4 tablespoons flour
6 egg yolks
1 cup heavy cream
Salt
Freshly ground white pepper

Optional: 1 cup foie gras
1 cup butter, softened to room temperature

EDITORS' NOTE: *A final touch of elegance in the preparation of a* chaud-froid *is to give the chicken a final coating of clear aspic which, like the* velouté-chaud-froid *sauce, should be just at the point of jelling but still liquid as it is spooned over the chicken. About 2 cups of the chicken broth in the above recipe should be sufficient and it should be clarified (see p. 53) to make it crystal clear before using.*

CHAUD-FROID OF
CHICKEN

Coat the boned thighs, legs and breasts with several layers of sauce. Decorate with the sliced truffles.

You may coat the chicken a second time with aspic.

The success of this dish depends on proper attention and skill. Here you see only the final stages, that is, coating the cold chicken with sauce.

Chicken in Aspic | POULET À LA GELÉE

Combine the blanched calf's foot, the beef knuckles, the carrots, celery, turnip and onion in a large pot and cover with cold water. Bring to the boiling point and skim. Lower the heat, season with salt and simmer, covered, for 3 hours, skimming as needed. Put the chicken into a deep kettle and strain the hot broth over it. Add the bunch of tarragon and the *bouquet garni*. Bring to the boiling point and then simmer, covered, for 45 minutes, or until the chicken is tender.

Remove the chicken and let it cool to lukewarm. Carve it into neat slices. Cool the broth and then chill it. Remove all the fat from the surface. Put the broth in a large saucepan and heat it to lukewarm. Beat together the egg whites, the chopped green part of the leeks and the chopped tarragon leaves. Stir the mixture into the broth. Bring slowly to the boiling point. Simmer over low heat (the liquid should shudder, to use the French expression) for 45 minutes. Strain it through a triple layer of cheesecloth.

Place the sliced chicken in a deep serving dish or terrine, garnish with tarragon sprigs, and cover with the stock. Chill until set. Unmold on a chilled platter, or serve from the dish.

FOR 4 PERSONS:

1 calf's foot, blanched	1 chicken (3 pounds)
2 beef knuckles	1 bunch of tarragon
2 carrots, sliced	1 Bouquet Garni (p. 46)
2 celery stalks, sliced	2 egg whites
1 turnip, sliced	Green parts of 2 leeks, finely
1 large onion, stuck with 5	chopped
cloves	10 tarragon leaves, chopped
Salt	A few tarragon sprigs

EDITORS' NOTE: *The calf's foot and beef knuckles in the broth should be more than gelatinous enough to make it jell very firmly. To be on the safe side, however, before clarifying it chill a large spoonful on a plate; if it does not jell very firmly, add an appropriate amount of unflavored gelatin, diluted in water, to the broth when clarifying it (see p. 166).*

Chicken Galantine | GALANTINE DE VOLAILLE

Split the chicken down the back and bone it completely. Remove the skin in one piece, being careful not to tear or pierce it.

Cut all the white meat into julienne strips. Marinate them in the brandy with the ham, tongue and truffles in a bowl.

Grind all of the dark meat of the chicken together with the blanched salt pork, using the fine blade of the meat grinder. Season this stuffing with salt and pepper to taste. Mix in the minced truffles.

Spread the chicken skin out on a cloth. Put a layer of stuffing in the middle of the skin. Top the stuffing with a thin layer of marinated white meat, ham, tongue and truffles. Repeat the layers until all the ingredients are used up. The last layer should be one of stuffing.

Cover with the skin, shaping it into a roll, and sew it closed. Wrap it in sheets of fresh pork fatback and tie them with string. Wrap the galantine in the cloth and tie it at both ends. Weigh the galantine and then put it into a deep wide kettle. Add enough white poultry stock to cover it completely. Bring to the boiling point and then simmer the galantine for 25 minutes for each pound of its weight. If necessary, add more hot stock as it cooks so that the galantine remains covered.

When the galantine is done, remove it from the liquid and let it cool to luke-warm. Remove the napkin covering and wash it thoroughly, squeezing it as dry as possible. Roll the galantine again in the napkin but not too tightly. Weight it by placing a board lengthwise on top and weighing down the board with any convenient ½-pound weight. The weight is necessary to make the galantine's ingredients hold together. If the galantine is wrapped too tightly in the napkin or weighted too heavily the juices will escape and the galantine will be dry and without flavor.

When the galantine is thoroughly cooled, remove the napkin and the sheets of fresh pork fat. Chill it and then coat it with aspic in the usual manner. Put it on a long serving dish and surround it with more chopped aspic and aspic cut-outs. Chill until serving time.

Note: You may grind the ham and tongue together with the salt pork and trimmings and blend them into the stuffing rather than using them for layering. In this case, add ⅓ pound freshly shelled pistachio nuts to the stuffing.

FOR 4 PERSONS:

1 chicken (3 pounds)
½ cup brandy
⅛ pound lean ham, cut into julienne strips
⅛ pound cooked tongue, cut into julienne strips
¼ pound truffles, cut into quarters
¼ pound salt pork, blanched
Salt

Freshly ground black pepper
2 truffles, minced
Several thin sheets of fresh pork fatback
4 or more quarts White Poultry Stock (p. 165)
4 to 6 cups Brown Stock for Aspics (p. 166)
Optional: ⅓ pound shelled pistachio nuts

D U C K

Canards

EDITORS' NOTE: *There is a considerable difference between French and American ducks. The two most popular French types, the nantais and rouennais, are usually quite small, of an average weight of 2½ pounds, which is about half the average size of our ducks. French ducks are also quite lean, without any of the heavy casing of fat that our own ducks have, and thus it is the French practice to bard ducks before roasting or to roast them with butter or other fat much in the same manner as roasting any lean type of bird. Obviously this method would be absurd with our ducks, since part of the objective of the cooking technique is to rid them of as much of their fat as possible. We have therefore adapted all of these recipes to our own larger and much, much fatter ducks.*

Roast Duck à l'Anglaise | CANARD RÔTI À L'ANGLAISE

Bake the unpeeled onions in a preheated 400° F. oven for about 20 minutes. When they are tender, peel and mince them. Soak the bread crumbs in milk, squeeze them almost dry, and mix them with the onions. Season with salt and pepper to taste and then with the sage. Mix well.

Stuff the duck with this mixture and sew it closed. Truss it and prick the lower breast and thighs with a fork to allow grease to escape. Roast in a preheated 350° F. oven for 1 hour and 40 minutes, or until the juices run clear when the thigh is pricked with a fork.

Put the duck on a hot serving platter and accompany it with a side dish of applesauce.

FOR 4 PERSONS:

4 large onions
4 cups fresh white bread crumbs
Milk
Salt
Freshly ground black pepper

2 tablespoons minced fresh sage,
  or 1 teaspoon ground sage
1 duck (5 pounds)
Applesauce

Stuffed Duck Rouennaise | CANARD FARCI ROUENNAISE

Heat 2 tablespoons of the butter and the fresh pork fat in a skillet. Add half of the minced onions, the duck livers and the parsley. Sauté for about 5 minutes. Remove the mixture from the heat, let it cool, and season with salt and pepper.

Stuff the duck with this mixture, truss the bird, and prick the lower breast and thighs with a fork to allow grease to escape.

Heat the remaining butter in a very large deep casserole. Brown the duck on all sides. It will release a good deal of fat during this process; remove all of the fat from the casserole. Then add the remaining minced onion, the carrot and the celery. Reduce the heat, cover the casserole, and cook for about 1¼ hours, or until the juices run clear when the thigh is pricked with a fork.

When the duck is done, remove it from the casserole and put it on a hot serving platter. Skim the fat from the juices and add the Madeira. Simmer the sauce for a few minutes and then serve it on the side in a sauceboat.

FOR 4 PERSONS:

6 tablespoons butter
¼ cup chopped fresh pork fat
2 large onions, minced
1 pound duck livers, chopped
2 tablespoons chopped parsley
Salt

Freshly ground black pepper
1 duck (5 pounds)
1 carrot, sliced
1 celery stalk, sliced
¼ cup Madeira

Duck in the Swedish Manner | CANARD À LA SUÉDOISE

Using a 5-pound duck, follow the recipe for marinating in Goose in a Pot (p. 495), and poach it in the manner described in Chicken in the Pot (p. 463).

CANARD AUX CERISES / *Duck with Cherries*

Season the cavity of the duck with salt and pepper and truss it. Roast it in a preheated 350° F. oven for about 1 hour; the duck's flesh must be pink and slightly underdone.

Cut the duck into serving pieces. Melt the butter in a large skillet, add the duck pieces, and turn them briefly in the butter. Add the Armagnac and flame. Add the consommé, wine, sugar and cinnamon. Bring to the boiling point, add the cherries, cover, and simmer for 5 minutes. Put the duck pieces on a hot platter and spoon the cherries and sauce over them.

FOR 4 PERSONS:

1 duck (5 pounds)	⅓ cup dry white wine
Salt	3 lumps of sugar
Freshly ground black pepper	¼ teaspoon ground cinnamon
3 tablespoons butter	2 cups sweet cherries, pitted
¼ cup Armagnac	
¾ cup Chicken Consommé (p. 168)	

CANARD AUX LENTILLES / *Duck with Lentils*

Cook the lentils with a good deal of care. This is how you do it: first blanch the lentils in boiling water for 5 minutes and drain them; then you make a *mirepoix* in a very large casserole by gently sautéing the goose fat and the diced bacon with the minced onion, garlic, shallots, celery and carrot until they are soft and golden. Stir in the flour and then add the blanched lentils and the *bouquet garni;* season with salt and freshly ground pepper. Add enough water to just cover the lentils; bring to the boiling point, cover, and cook on a low rack in a preheated 350° F. oven for 1 hour, or until the lentils are not quite tender.

Season the cavity of the duck with salt and pepper, truss it, and prick the lower breast and the thighs with a fork to allow grease to escape. Roast the duck on an upper rack of the oven for about 1 hour, leaving it underdone and pink. Cut the duck into serving pieces, saving the juices as it is carved.

Add the duck pieces to the lentils, together with the juices. Simmer, covered, for about 20 minutes. Sprinkle with very fresh minced parsley and serve in the casserole.

FOR 4 PERSONS:

2 cups dried lentils	1 carrot, minced
3 tablespoons goose fat or butter	2 tablespoons flour
4 strips of bacon, diced and blanched	1 Bouquet Garni (p. 46)
1 onion, minced	Salt
1 garlic clove, minced	Freshly ground black pepper
2 shallots, minced	1 duck (5 pounds)
1 celery stalk, minced	4 tablespoons minced parsley

Duck with Green Peppers / CANARD AUX POIVRE VERT

Make a stuffing with the rice cooked in the creole manner, the cooked sausage meat and diced green pepper. Stuff the duck with this mixture and truss it. Prick the thighs and lower breasts with a fork to allow fat to escape.

Roast the duck in a preheated 350° F. oven for about 1 hour and 40 minutes, or until the juices run clear when the thigh is pricked with a fork.

FOR 4 PERSONS:

⅓ recipe Rice à la Créole (p. 658)
¼ pound sausage meat, sautéed, crumbled, and drained of fat

2 large green peppers, diced
1 duck (5 pounds)

Lacquered Duck / CANARD LAQUÉ

Make a sauce by blending the *quatre épices,* the soy sauce and the sugar, or better still, honey.

Season the cavity of the duck with salt and pepper and truss it. Prick the lower breast and thighs with a fork to allow grease to escape. Roast it in a preheated 350° F. oven for 30 minutes. Remove all the fat from the roasting pan. Brush the duck on all sides with the sauce. Put it back into the oven to roast for another 45 minutes, basting it with the sauce every 5 minutes.

Cool the duck a little before carving it in the usual manner.

Serve immediately with soy sauce.

FOR 4 PERSONS:

1 tablespoon Quatre Épices (p. 667)
2 tablespoons soy sauce
2 tablespoons sugar or honey

1 duck (5 pounds)
Salt
Freshly ground black pepper

Duckling à la Normande / CANETON À LA NORMANDE

Season the cavity of the duck with salt and pepper and truss it. Prick the lower breast and thighs with a fork to allow grease to escape. Roast in a preheated 350° F. oven for 1¼ hours, or until the juices run clear when the thigh is pricked with a fork.

Put the cooked duckling on a hot plate and keep it warm.

Pour off all of the fat from the roasting pan and then add the Muscadet. Bring to the boiling point and cook until the wine has evaporated. Stir in the Calvados and the *crème fraîche.* Bring to the boiling point again, stirring constantly, and cook until the sauce is thick and smooth. Remove it from the heat, and stir in 2 tablespoons of the butter. Do not reheat the sauce. Quickly sauté the apple pieces in the remaining butter in a skillet until they are golden but not too soft.

Carve the duck, put it into a deep hot serving dish, and coat it with the sauce. Surround it with the sautéed apples.

FOR 4 PERSONS:

1 duck (5 pounds)
Salt
Freshly ground black pepper
1 cup Muscadet
¼ cup Calvados or applejack

1½ cups Crème Fraîche
(p. 666), or heavy cream
6 tablespoons butter
4 apples, peeled, cored, and cut
into quarters

Note: The flavor of this dish depends on the Muscadet and Calvados. It is not advisable to make substitutes for these ingredients. Both Muscadet wine and Calvados are available at good wine stores.

CANARD À L'ORANGE / *Duck à l'Orange*

Season the cavity of the duck with salt and pepper and truss it. Prick the lower breast and thighs with a fork to allow grease to escape. Roast it in a preheated 350° F. oven for 1¼ hours, or until the juices run clear when the thigh is pricked with a fork.

Peel the zest (the yellow skin without any white) from two of the oranges and one of the lemons. Squeeze the juice from these 2 oranges and 1 lemon and combine in a bowl. Cut the zest into fine julienne strips, blanch them in boiling hot water for 5 minutes, and drain. Peel and cut the sections from the remaining 4 oranges and 1 lemon.

Make a caramel: stir the sugar in a saucepan over low heat until it is melted; when it is beginning to turn golden, add the wine vinegar and the orange and lemon juice. Reduce it by half and then stir in the *sauce espagnole.* Simmer gently over low heat.

Make a *liaison* by stirring the cornstarch with the Curaçao and then add the kümmel and the red-currant jelly to the mixture.

When the duck is cooked, put it on a hot platter and keep it warm. Pour off all the fat from the roasting pan and then add the wine to the pan. Place over high heat, scraping up all the brown bits at the bottom, and boil until reduced by half. Strain through a fine sieve into the simmering sauce.

Sprinkle the duck with the blanched orange and lemon strips. Surround the duck with the orange and lemon sections. Stir the *liaison* into the hot sauce, cook until the sauce has slightly thickened, and spoon it over the duck.

FOR 4 PERSONS:

1 duck (5 pounds)
Salt
Freshly ground black pepper
6 oranges
2 lemons
¼ cup sugar
¼ cup wine vinegar

2 cups Sauce Espagnole
(p. 760), made with Brown
Poultry Stock (p. 164), duck
trimmings if possible, and
about half the usual
amount of flour
1 tablespoon cornstarch
¼ cup Curaçao
2 tablespoons kümmel
1 tablespoon red-currant jelly
¼ cup dry white wine

Note: This dish may be made without the red-currant jelly, sugar and vinegar and by simply pouring the fruit juices into the *sauce espagnole,* but the dish becomes less interesting. As a matter of fact, the recipe given above is really not difficult at all, and it yields brilliant results.

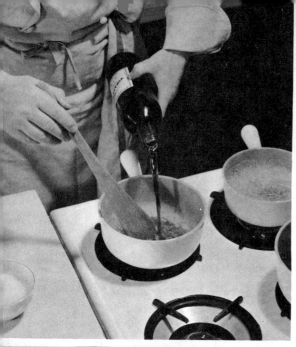

DUCK À L'ORANGE

Above, from left to right: *Preparing th* *sauce. First stir the vinegar into the ca* *amel, and then the orange and lemon juice* *Reduce the mixture and then add th* *sauce espagnole.*

Left and below: *Preparing the* liaison *Blend the cornstarch with the Curaçao an* *stir in the red-currant jelly.*

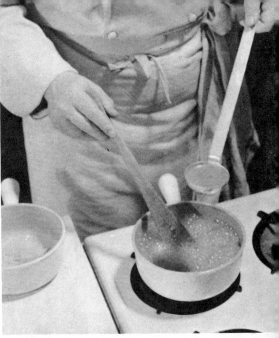

Right and below: *Put the duck on a hot serving dish, sprinkle the orange and lemon strips over it, surround with the orange and lemon quarters, and coat with the thickened sauce.*

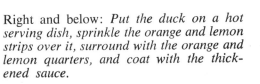

Duck Bigarade / CANARD BIGARADE

Prepare in the same manner as Duck à l'Orange (p. 487), using *bigarades,* that is, bitter or sour Séville oranges. In this case it is not necessary to add lemons to the oranges.

Duck with Pineapple / CANARD AUX ANANAS

Season the cavity of the duck with salt and pepper and truss it. Prick the lower breast and thighs with a fork to allow grease to escape. Place it in a pan lined with the vegetables and sprinkled with the thyme, the bay leaf and 2 tablespoons of water. Roast in a preheated 350° F. oven for 1¼ hours, or until the juices run clear when the thigh is pricked with a fork.

When the duck is roasted "pink," that is, neither bleeding nor overdone, remove all the fat from the pan and then tilt into the pan the juice that has formed in the duck's cavity during roasting. Put the duck on a hot plate and keep it warm.

Add the white wine, or consommé if you have it, to the pan juices. Put the pan over high heat and scrape up all the brown bits in the bottom. Reduce by half and strain through a fine sieve.

Cut the pineapple slices into halves and put them in a saucepan with the juice from the can. Add the kirsch and simmer, covered, over low heat just until very hot.

Stir the sugar in a saucepan over low heat until it is melted; when it becomes golden, stir in the vinegar, the pineapple juice and the juices from the roasting pan. Simmer over low heat for 5 minutes.

Carve the duck into serving pieces, place them on a hot serving platter, and garnish it with the hot pineapple slices. Coat it with the sauce and serve.

FOR 4 PERSONS:

1 duck (5 pounds)	1 bay leaf, crumbled
Salt	1 cup dry white wine or Chicken
Freshly ground black pepper	Consommé (p. 168)
1 onion, sliced	6 slices of canned pineapple
1 carrot, sliced	2 tablespoons kirsch
1 celery stalk, sliced	2 tablespoons sugar
Pinch of dried thyme	1 tablespoon wine vinegar

Duck with Mangoes / CANARD AUX MANGUES

Proceed as in Duck with Pineapple (above), but use 2 mangoes instead of the pineapple.

Choose mangoes that are not too ripe. Peel and seed them and slice them over a bowl, retaining all of their juice. Put the fruit and the juice with a little apricot or peach brandy into a saucepan and simmer, covered, until the mangoes are very tender. Garnish the duck with the mango slices and use the hot juice in the sauce.

SALMIS DE CANARD / *Salmi of Duck*

Cut the duck into serving pieces, reserving the heart, liver and gizzard.

Heat the lard in a large casserole until it is very hot and brown the duck pieces on both sides. Remove all the fat from the casserole. Season the pieces with salt and pepper, sprinkle with the Armagnac, and flame.

Remove the duck pieces and the pan juices from the casserole. Add the ham fat to the casserole and cook until the fat is rendered. Add the shallots and the onions. Cook over low heat until the onions are golden. Sprinkle with the flour and stir well. Add the salt-pork dice and the *bouquet garni*. Stir in all but 1 tablespoon of the wine and bring to a boil. Add the duck pieces and their juices. Season with salt and pepper to taste, cover the casserole, and simmer over very low heat for 1 hour.

Mince the liver, heart and gizzard of the duck very fine. Add the reserved tablespoon of wine and the rum to them and season with salt, pepper and nutmeg. Stir and blend until the mixture is smooth.

Fry the bread slices in the butter or lard in a skillet until golden. Rub the bread slices on both sides with the garlic clove; spread them with a layer of the liver mixture and sauté again very quickly in the skillet.

When the duck is cooked, put the pieces in a hot deep dish and strain the sauce over the meat. Garnish the dish with the fried bread slices.

FOR 4 PERSONS:

1 duck (5 pounds)	4 tablespoons flour
8 tablespoons lard	¼ pound salt pork, blanched and
Salt	finely diced
Freshly ground black pepper	1 Bouquet Garni (p. 46)
¼ cup Armagnac	4 cups dry red wine
¼ cup minced fat from a Bayonne	1 tablespoon rum
or smoked Virginia ham or	Pinch of grated nutmeg
prosciutto	8 slices of French bread
6 shallots, minced	6 tablespoons butter or lard
20 tiny white onions, 4 of them	1 garlic clove, peeled
stuck with cloves	

CIVET DE CANARD / *Stewed Duck*

Cut the duck into pieces and set aside the more attractive pieces. Make a sauce with the less attractive pieces and the vegetables in the following manner:

Heat 4 tablespoons of butter and the ham fat in a casserole and then add the carrots, turnip, celery, leeks, parsley roots, onions, thyme and bay leaf. Cook gently, stirring often, until the vegetables are soft. Add the duck pieces and cook until they are golden. Stir in the wine and add the garlic, sugar, tomatoes and the ham and veal bones. Bring to the boiling point, skim, and season with pepper. Simmer for 2 hours and then strain through a fine sieve.

Sauté the reserved duck pieces in the remaining butter in a large casserole over high heat until golden brown on both sides. Add the strained sauce and the *bouquet garni*. Season to taste with salt. Simmer, covered, over very low heat for about 1 hour. When the duck is thoroughly cooked, skim all of the fat off the sauce. Put the duck into a hot serving dish and strain the sauce over the meat.

FOR 4 PERSONS:

1 duck (5 pounds)
12 tablespoons butter
¼ cup minced ham fat
2 carrots, sliced
1 turnip, sliced
2 celery stalks, sliced
2 leeks, sliced
2 parsley roots, minced
2 onions, sliced
¼ teaspoon dried thyme
1 bay leaf

1 bottle dry red wine
1 garlic clove
2 lumps of sugar
2 tomatoes, peeled, seeded and
chopped
1 small ham bone
1 small veal bone
Freshly ground black pepper
1 Bouquet Garni (p. 46)
Salt

Duck in Aspic with Prunes /

CANARD EN GELÉE AUX PRUNEAUX

EDITORS' NOTE: *We have had, of necessity, to take liberties with this recipe of M. Oliver's which calls for a very small boned rouennais duck, which is stuffed with prunes and the duck's liver before being roasted, then cooled and coated with aspic. We feel that the very large quantity of prunes necessary to stuff our much larger ducks would be excessive and have suggested augmenting the prunes with a like quantity of chestnuts, enough to restore the duck to its original unboned shape. An alternative to the chestnuts might be to use a similar quantity of foie gras.*

Soak the prunes in cold water overnight if necessary or, if they are the tenderized variety, soak them in hot water for 5 minutes. Pit them and then marinate them in the Madeira for 12 hours.

Partly bone the duck, removing all of the bones except the wing, thigh and leg bones. Prepare the aspic stock, adding the bones from the duck and, after the stock is clarified, half of the Quetsch or Slivovitz.

Put the wine, sugar and a little salt in a saucepan. Mix well; add the drained prunes and enough water to cover the prunes. Bring to a boil, simmer for about 5 minutes, or until the prunes are tender, and drain.

Heat the butter in a skillet together with the bacon until the bacon begins to color. Add the duck's liver, the shallots, thyme and bay leaf. Season with salt and pepper to taste and cook for about 5 minutes. Remove from the heat and mash the mixture thoroughly with a fork. In a bowl combine the liver mixture, half of the cooked prunes, the boiled chestnuts (which may be slightly mashed) and the remaining Quetsch or Slivovitz. Taste and season if necessary with salt and pepper. Moisten with a little of the stock if the mixture seems dry.

Stuff the duck's cavity with this mixture and sew the cavity closed. Truss the duck and prick the lower part of the breast and the thighs in several places with a fork to allow excess fat to escape. Roast it in a preheated 350° F. oven for 1½ hours, or until the juices run clear when the thigh is pricked with a fork.

Cool the cooked duck, chill it, and then put it on a rack over a deep dish to catch any aspic which runs off the duck. Arrange a few of the prunes on the duck and coat it with cold but still barely liquid aspic. Chill until the aspic is set and, if necessary, cover with more aspic until it is evenly coated. Chill.

Place the duck on a silver platter; surround it with the remaining prunes; coat duck and prunes again with aspic. Chill until serving time.

FOR 4 PERSONS:

1 **pound dried prunes**	2 **tablespoons butter**
1 **cup Madeira**	¼ **pound bacon, finely diced and**
1 **duck (5 pounds)**	**blanched**
4 **cups Brown Stock for Aspics**	**The duck liver, chopped**
(p. 166), adding the bones	1 **tablespoon minced shallots**
from the duck to the other	**Pinch of dried thyme**
ingredients	1 **bay leaf, crushed**
¼ **cup Quetsch or Slivovitz**	**Freshly ground black pepper**
2 **cups dry red wine**	2 **cups (about 1 pound) Boiled**
4 **tablespoons sugar**	**Chestnuts (p. 582)**
Salt	

/ *Chaud-Froid of Duck Montmorency*

CHAUD-FROID DE CANARD MONTMORENCY

Prepare the *chaud-froid* sauce, using a brown poultry stock and, if possible, a few duck bones or trimmings in the *sauce espagnole* base. Add half of the kirsch to the finished *chaud-froid*.

Pit the cherries and cook them in the wine with the remaining kirsch, the dissolved gelatin and the sugar for about 10 minutes. When they are just tender, drain the juice into the *chaud-froid* sauce. Drain the cherries thoroughly and stuff each with half a fresh blanched almond.

Truss the duck, prick the lower breast and thighs with a fork to allow grease to escape, and season the cavity with salt and pepper. Roast it in a preheated 350° F. oven for about 1¼ hours, or until the juices run clear when the thigh is pricked with a fork. Remove it from the oven, let it cool to lukewarm, and cut off the breast meat in long thin strips.

Make a paste by mashing together in a mortar the *foie gras* and the cooked duck's liver. Add the softened butter and the *crème fraîche* to this mixture. Season with salt and cayenne and flavor with a little brandy.

Mix thoroughly and use the mixture to stick the strips of the duck's breast back onto the breast bone, re-forming it into its original shape. Chill the re-formed duck until very cold. Place the duck on a rack over a dish to catch any sauce which drips off the duck, and coat with a layer of cold but still liquid *chaud-froid* sauce. Chill and coat with the sauce again. Repeat until all of the sauce has been used and the duck is completely covered. Place on a serving platter, surround with the cherries, and chill until serving time.

FOR 4 PERSONS:

2 cups Brown Chaud-Froid Sauce (p. 764), using a Brown Poultry Stock (p. 164), in the Espagnole base
¼ cup kirsch
4 cups sweet cherries
2 cups red Bordeaux wine
1 tablespoon unflavored gelatin, dissolved in a little water
2 tablespoons sugar
⅓ cup (approximately) freshly blanched almonds, cut into halves

1 duck (5 pounds)
Salt
Freshly ground black pepper
2 ounces foie gras
The duck liver, minced and sautéed in a little butter for 5 minutes
2 tablespoons butter, at room temperature
2 tablespoons Crème Fraîche (p. 666), or heavy cream
Cayenne pepper
1 teaspoon brandy

Chaud-Froid of Duck with Oranges /

CHAUD-FROID DE CANARD À L'ORANGE

Prepare in the same manner as in the preceding recipe, using the sections from 4 oranges in place of the cooked cherries. Substitute 2 cups of orange juice to be added to the *chaud-froid* sauce in place of the red wine. The orange juice should be heated with the dissolved gelatin before adding it to the sauce. Substitute Cointreau for the kirsch to flavor the sauce.

GOOSE

Oies

Roast Goose with Sage / OIE RÔTIE À LA SAUGE

Season the cavity of the goose with salt and pepper.

Make a stuffing in the following manner: Roast the unpeeled onions in a preheated 400° F. oven for about 30 minutes, or until they are tender, and let them cool. Peel the onions and mince them. Soak the bread crumbs in the milk and squeeze them dry. Combine the onions, bread crumbs and sage. Season with salt, pepper and nutmeg to taste. Stuff the goose with this mixture. Sew it closed or fasten it with poultry skewers. Roast the goose in a preheated 350° F. oven for about 2½ hours, or until the juices run clear when the thigh is pricked with a fork.

Put the cooked goose on a hot serving platter and serve with a side dish of applesauce. The drippings in the roasting pan may be deglazed with a little water and poured over the goose.

FOR 6 PERSONS:

1 goose (8 pounds)	4 cups crumbled white bread
Salt	Lukewarm milk
Freshly ground black pepper	2 tablespoons dried sage
1 pound large onions	Grated nutmeg

OIE AUX MARRONS / *Goose with Chestnuts*

Cut the goose into serving pieces.

Heat the goose fat or the oil and butter in a very large casserole; add the garlic, onions, carrots and celery.

Mix with a wooden spoon and cook until the vegetables are turning golden. Add the goose and sauté it until golden on all sides. Add the wine, the tomato paste, the *bouquet garni* and enough boiling water to barely cover the bird.

Season with salt, cover the casserole, and simmer over low heat for 2 hours; then add the peeled chestnuts. Simmer for 40 minutes longer.

When goose and chestnuts are tender, put the goose in a deep hot serving dish and surround with the chestnuts. Pour a little of the broth over them and serve immediately.

FOR 6 PERSONS:

1 goose (8 pounds)	1 celery stalk, minced
4 tablespoons goose fat, or 2 tablespoons each of peanut oil and butter	1 cup dry white wine
	2 tablespoons tomato paste
	1 Bouquet Garni (p. 46)
2 garlic cloves, mashed	Salt
2 large onions, minced	2 pounds chestnuts, with outer and inner skins peeled off
4 carrots, minced	

OIE AU POT / *Goose in a Pot*

Mix 1 tablespoon of the coarse salt together with the saltpeter, the sugar and the *fines herbes*. Put this mixture in the cavity of the goose. Put half of the remaining coarse salt in a deep stoneware dish with the juniper berries, cloves, bay leaves, thyme and nutmeg. Place the goose on this mixture, cover it completely with the remaining coarse salt, and cover the dish with a board. Let the goose lie in this brine for 5 days, turning it over every 24 hours.

Rinse the goose under running cold water to remove every trace of the brine. Poach it as in Chicken in the Pot (p. 463), increasing the poaching time to about 2½ hours.

FOR 6 PERSONS:

1 pound coarse (Kosher) salt	20 juniper berries
1 tablespoon saltpeter	12 cloves
1 cup sugar	2 bay leaves
1 cup minced Fines Herbes (p. 89)	1 sprig of fresh thyme, or 1 teaspoon dried thyme
1 goose (8 pounds)	1 teaspoon grated nutmeg

Preserved Goose | CONFIT D'OIE

Clean a goose and cut it into 4 pieces. Cut and pull off as much of the fat as possible.

Put the goose fat into a casserole and melt it over low heat. Add the goose pieces and simmer without a cover over the lowest possible heat for 2 hours. Remove from the heat and cool without stirring.

When the fat has settled, but before it is stiff, spoon about ½ inch of goose fat into a stone crock. Lay one of the goose quarters on the fat, cover with more fat, top with another piece of goose and so on, ending with ¼ inch of goose fat completely covering the top piece of goose. Be very careful not to use any meat juices that may be at the bottom of the casserole, only the pure fat.

Let the fat cool until it is firm and cover the pot with a round of sturdy paper tied with a string. Keep in a cool place and wait for 5 months before using.

Quite aside from the numerous dishes that require preserved goose, here is a way of serving it on its own: Remove all the fat from the goose quarters, reserving it for later use. Put the goose pieces into a skillet and heat them slowly. Cook them until they are golden on both sides and put them on a hot plate. Serve the meat with Cèpes Bordelaise (p. 601), or green peas cooked in goose fat, or with a dish of lentils. Or, you might prefer a simple salad with it.

Stuffed Goose Neck | COU D'OIE FARCI

Remove the skin from the goose neck, including with it a little of the skin of the breast. Be careful not to tear it.

Remove all of the meat from the neck and grind it with the other goose meat, using the finest blade of a meat grinder. Mix it with the sausage, goose livers, minced truffle, brandy, and salt and pepper to taste.

Stuff the goose neck skin with this mixture and sew it closed or tie securely.

Put the stuffed neck in a heavy casserole, together with enough goose fat to cover the neck completely once the fat is melted. Heat gently and simmer, without bringing to the boiling point, for 2 hours. Put the stuffed goose neck into an earthenware pot, cover it with the goose fat, and tie a piece of sturdy paper over the crock. Store in a cool place and wait for 5 months before using it.

Here are two ways of serving the goose neck: Cook it gently in a little goose fat until golden on all sides. Cut the neck into thick slices and serve it with Cornmeal Cakes (p. 584).

Heat the goose neck in a preheated 325° F. oven. Drain it when all the fat around it has melted. Encase it in a sheet of Puff Paste (p. 715). Pinch the puff-paste edges together. Paint the top with a beaten egg yolk and bake in a preheated 400° F. oven for about 20 minutes, or until the puff paste is golden. Serve with a little Sauce Périgueux (p. 765).

FOR 2 PERSONS:

1 goose neck	1 tablespoon brandy
¼ pound minced goose meat	Salt
¼ pound sausage meat	Freshly ground black pepper
¼ pound fresh goose livers	Goose fat
1 truffle, minced	

GOOSE LIVERS

Foies d'Oies

EDITORS' NOTE: *A few specialty butcher shops in larger American cities import from Europe goose livers weighing 1 pound or more. While the preparation of livers of this size will be of only academic interest to most readers, we include these recipes of M. Oliver's for those of you fortunate enough to have access to them.*

FOIE D'OIE AU FOUR / *Baked Goose Livers*

Sprinkle a 1-pound goose liver with coarse (Kosher) salt and keep it in a cool place or in the refrigerator for 24 hours. Rinse it under running cold water and marinate it in 1 cup of Armagnac seasoned with 1 teaspoon each of paprika and Quatre Épices (p. 667) for 48 hours.

Put the goose liver in a baking dish and pour over it sufficient hot goose fat to reach halfway up its sides. Bake in a preheated 325° F. oven, turning the liver several times.

It is impossible to give the accurate baking time, for it depends on the thickness of the liver. Test for doneness after about 15 minutes by piercing the liver with a skewer, a cake tester or a knitting needle. If the juice that spurts out is no longer red, but barely pink, the liver is ready.

FOIE GRAS D'OIE AU PORTO / *Goose Liver in Port Wine*

Prepare a good Brown Stock for Aspics as described on page 166.

Clean the goose liver carefully, sprinkle it with coarse (Kosher) salt on all sides, and let it stand in a cool place for 24 hours. Rinse it under running cold water to remove the salt, dry it with a kitchen cloth, and marinate it in 1 cup of Armagnac seasoned with a little paprika and Quatre Épices (p. 667) for 48 hours.

Lard the liver with truffle pieces dipped into *quatre épices* and wrap it in a pig's caul. Put it in an enamelware casserole, add ½ bottle of port wine, and cook it in a preheated 350° F. oven, basting it frequently. Test the liver with a thin skewer or knitting needle after about 20 minutes; if the juice that spurts out is no longer red, but barely pink, it will be cooked.

Remove the liver from the casserole, take off the pig's caul, and place the liver in a handsome deep silver dish. Add 2 cups of the aspic stock to the casserole, bring to the boiling point, and skim off the fat. Clarify (see p. 53) the stock, adding enough gelatin to make it jell, and pour it over the liver. Let it jell in the refrigerator until serving time.

Goose Liver in Port-Wine Aspic /

FOIE GRAS FRAIS AU PORTO EN GELÉE

Marinate a whole fresh goose liver in 1 cup of port seasoned with a little paprika, cayenne and Quatre Épices (p. 667) for 48 hours.

Rinse a kitchen cloth or table napkin in cold water, spread it on the kitchen table, and put the goose liver in the middle. Roll it up, but not too tightly. Fasten the roll at both ends with string. Poach the goose liver in a well-flavored Brown Poultry Stock (p. 164) to which you have added the marinade. Bring the liquid slowly to a boil and then simmer it for about 15 minutes for each pound of weight. Be sure that the liquid just barely trembles since the goose liver must not boil. Tighten the cloth around the goose liver and let it cool in its own liquid for 12 to 18 hours. Remove it from the liquid, take it out of the cloth, wrap it in aluminum foil, and chill.

To serve, cut the goose liver into thick slices. Coat these slices with an excellent aspic (p. 166) flavored with port wine.

Goose Liver with Raisins / FOIE D'OIE AUX RAISINS

Cook the goose liver in the oven as described in Baked Goose Livers (p. 497), but bake it for only 5 to 6 minutes.

Mince 1 onion and cook it in goose fat until it is soft. Sprinkle with 1 tablespoon of flour, cook for about 2 minutes longer, and add 1 cup of dry white wine, 1 tablespoon tomato paste, a *bouquet garni* and a little consommé or water. Simmer, covered, for 30 minutes and then strain.

Plump ½ cup of raisins in a little lukewarm Madeira for 1 hour.

Put the goose liver, the sauce and the raisins into a casserole, check the seasoning and simmer, covered, over very low heat for 20 minutes.

Serve with large croutons fried in goose fat.

Goose Liver "Sous-Bois Landais" /

FOIE GRAS "SOUS-BOIS LANDAIS"

This is an outstanding country specialty of the Landes, a district in the southwest of France, between the Atlantic and the river Garonne.

Bake the goose liver as described in Baked Goose Livers (p. 497) and keep it hot.

Barely roast a snipe—it must still be rare, and of course, not drawn. Make a *farce* by mixing together a few minced chicken livers and a little minced fat of Landes ham or prosciutto. Cook them together until golden.

Bone the snipe, saving its juices, and mince its meat and innards with a knife. Blend them with the chicken-liver mixture. Season with salt, pepper, nutmeg and a little old Armagnac. Fry thick slices of country bread in goose fat and spread them with the *farce*.

Heat a little goose fat in a large skillet and put the bread in it, spread side down. Sauté until the spread is crusted over. Transfer the slices to a baking sheet and bake them in a preheated 350° F. oven for 5 minutes.

Put the bread slices on a hot serving dish, and top each with a thick slice of goose liver.

Make a simple sauce by boiling the snipe juices and a little Madeira in the skillet in which the bread slices were sautéed. Serve this sauce separately in a sauceboat.

GUINEA HEN

Pintades et Pintadeaux

/ *Braised Guinea Hen with Mushrooms*

PINTADEAU AUX MORILLES

Season the cavity of the guinea hen with salt and pepper and then put the mushrooms and 2 tablespoons of the butter in the cavity. Truss the bird and bard it, that is, wrap it in the sheets of fresh pork fat and tie them.

Heat the oil and the remaining butter in a casserole and sauté the guinea hen until golden on all sides. Add the brandy and flame. Transfer the bird to a hot plate and keep it warm.

Put the unpeeled garlic, the *bouquet garni,* the carrots and onions in the casserole. Cook them gently until they are golden. Return the bird with its juices to the casserole, add the wine and the water, and season with salt. Simmer, covered, for about 45 minutes. About 15 minutes before the bird is done, remove the pork fat to let the bird color on all sides.

Put the cooked bird on a hot serving dish and garnish with the bread slices; or cut it into 4 serving pieces, put each piece on a crouton, and garnish each with one of the mushrooms from the bird's cavity.

Strain the sauce through a fine sieve and spoon over the guinea hen pieces. Serve with a side dish of morels or other mushrooms cooked in butter.

FOR 2 PERSONS:

1 guinea hen (2½ pounds)	1 Bouquet Garni (p. 46)
Salt	3 carrots, chopped
Freshly ground black pepper	3 onions, chopped
4 large morels or other mushrooms	1 cup dry white wine
5 tablespoons butter	½ cup water
Thin sheets of fresh pork fat	4 slices of bread, trimmed of
3 tablespoons peanut oil	crusts, fried in butter
2 tablespoons brandy	½ recipe Mushrooms Braised in
3 garlic cloves, unpeeled	Butter (p. 603)

PINTADEAU AUX LENTILLES / *Guinea Hen with Lentils*

Proceed as in Duck with Lentils (p. 485), using 2 guinea hens each weighing about 2 pounds. The guinea hens should be barded before roasting and they should be roasted for a shorter time than the duck, about 45 minutes.

Roast Stuffed Guinea Hen / PINTADEAU FARCI

Soak the bread crumbs in the milk, squeeze them dry, and mix them with the *fines herbes* and the sausage meat. Add a little of the beaten egg to bind the mixture. Stuff the bird, sew the opening closed, and truss it. Put the brandy and the Armagnac in a bowl with the oil and the thyme. Marinate the guinea hen in this mixture in a cool place for 24 hours, turning the bird every few hours.

Rub the bird with salt and pepper and spread it with the lard. Roast in a preheated 400° F. oven for 15 minutes. Transfer it to a casserole, add the sherry or the port, bring to a boil, and then simmer, covered, for about 40 minutes. Serve from the casserole.

FOR 2 PERSONS:

2 cups fresh white bread crumbs	½ cup Armagnac
Milk	2 tablespoons peanut oil
2 tablespoons minced Fines Herbes (p. 89)	½ teaspoon dried thyme
	Salt
¼ pound sausage meat	Freshly ground black pepper
1 egg, beaten	4 tablespoons lard
1 guinea hen (2 pounds)	½ cup sherry or port wine
½ cup brandy	

Roast Guinea Hen with Truffle Stuffing /

PINTADEAU TRUFFÉ

Heat 1 tablespoon of the butter in a casserole; add the bacon, the minced shallot and the rice. Mix and cook, stirring constantly, until the rice is opaque, 3 to 5 minutes.

Add ⅓ cup of water and simmer, covered for 15 minutes. Remove the casserole from the heat and add the *foie gras* and the truffles.

Stuff the bird with this mixture, sew it closed, and truss it. Heat the oil and the remaining butter in a casserole and brown the guinea hen on all sides. Season it with salt and pepper.

Transfer the casserole to a preheated 375° F. oven and cook, covered, for about 45 minutes.

FOR 2 PERSONS:

6 tablespoons butter	2 truffles, cut into small dice
3 slices of bacon, diced and blanched	1 guinea hen (2 pounds)
1 shallot, minced	1 tablespoon peanut oil
¼ cup uncooked rice	Salt
¼ cup foie gras, cut into small dice	Freshly ground black pepper

SQUAB

Pigeons

PIGEON CRAPAUDINE / *Broiled Squab*

Split a small squab down its back into halves. Flatten the squab with the flat side of a cleaver or with the bottom of a thick plate. Rub the bird with salt and pepper and brush with melted butter. Broil it, skin side down, for about 12 minutes, turn it over, baste with butter, and broil for about 10 minutes longer.

Serve immediately with a little *sauce diable*.

FOR 1 PERSON:

1 squab (1 pound)
Salt
Freshly ground black pepper

4 tablespoons butter, melted
½ cup Sauce Diable (p. 770)

PIGEON GRILLÉ AUX HERBES / *Broiled Squab with Herbs*

Proceed as in the preceding recipe but sprinkle the bird with crumbled dried herbs, such as marjoram and thyme, before broiling.

/ *Squab Broiled with Mustard*

PIGEON GRILLÉ À LA MOUTARDE

Proceed as in Broiled Squab (above), but before broiling coat the bird with 2 tablespoons of Dijon-type mustard, dip it into fresh bread crumbs, and then sprinkle it with melted butter.

PIGEON CHASSEUR / *Squab Chasseur*

Heat the oil and butter in a small casserole and brown the squab in it on all sides. Transfer it to a plate and keep hot.

Cook the shallots in the pan juices until they are soft and add the mushrooms. Cook for 3 minutes.

Add the tomato and cook for 5 minutes longer. Return the pigeon to the casserole, add the wine, the *bouquet garni,* and salt and pepper to taste. Bring to a boil and then simmer, covered, for about 35 minutes. Remove the *bouquet garni,* sprinkle with the parsley, and serve in the casserole.

FOR 1 PERSON:

2 tablespoons peanut oil
2 tablespoons butter
1 squab (1 pound), trussed
2 tablespoons minced shallots
6 small mushrooms, cut into
   quarters

1 small tomato, peeled, seeded
   and chopped
½ cup dry white wine
1 Bouquet Garni (p. 46)
Salt
Freshly ground black pepper
1 tablespoon minced parsley

Squab with Grapes / PIGEON AUX RAISINS

Truss the squab. Heat the oil and butter in a casserole and brown the squab on all sides. Season with salt and pepper, lay the sheet of pork fat over the breast of the squab, and add the wine and the *bouquet garni.* Simmer, covered, over low heat for 25 minutes.

Remove the pork fat from the squab. Crush half of the grapes or push them through a food mill. Strain this juice and add it to the casserole, together with the brandy and the remaining grapes. Cover the casserole and simmer for 5 to 8 minutes, or until the grapes are heated through. Serve from the casserole.

FOR 1 PERSON:

1 squab (1 pound)
2 tablespoons peanut oil
2 tablespoons butter
Salt
Freshly ground white pepper

1 thin sheet of fresh pork fat
½ cup dry white wine
1 Bouquet Garni (p. 46)
1 cup white seedless grapes, peeled
1 tablespoon brandy

Squab Prince Rainier III / PIGEON PRINCE RAINIER III

Bone the squab, splitting it down the back.

Make a stuffing. Combine the pork and veal; season with salt, pepper and cayenne to taste; stir in half of the brandy.

Put the squab, skin side down, on a board. Sprinkle it with very little salt and pepper and with the thyme and bay leaf. Spread with half of the stuffing, sprinkle with the truffle and *foie gras,* place the squab's heart and liver in the center, and cover with the remaining stuffing. Tie and reshape the squab in its original shape. Truss and bard it, that is, wrap it in the sheet of fresh pork fat. Heat the butter in a casserole and brown the squab on all sides. Cover and simmer over low heat for 30 minutes. Then remove the pork fat. Continue cooking, covered, for another 30 minutes. Put the fried bread slice on a hot serving platter and top with the squab.

Degrease the juices in the casserole and then add the wine, scraping up all the brown bits at the bottom. Bring to the boiling point, reduce by half, and stir in the remaining brandy and the *sauce demi-glace.* Bring once more to the boiling point and pour over the squab.

FOR 1 PERSON:

1 squab (1 pound)
2 ounces ground lean pork
2 ounces ground veal
Salt
Freshly ground black pepper
Cayenne pepper
1 tablespoon brandy
Pinch of dried thyme
½ bay leaf, crumbled

1 truffle, diced
2 ounces foie gras, diced
1 thin sheet of fresh pork fat
4 tablespoons butter
1 slice of bread, fried in butter
¼ cup dry white wine
2 tablespoons Sauce Demi-Glace
  (p. 766)

PIGEONS AU SANCERRE / *Squabs au Sancerre*

EDITORS' NOTE: *Sancerre wine, from the upper Loire in Central France, is one of the most pleasant of France's light wines, fruity and with a good bouquet. In this recipe, the wine determines the taste of the dish; failing Sancerre, we suggest using a California wine made from Sauvignon Blanc grapes.*

Heat the oil and the butter together in a casserole, add the onions, and cook until they are beginning to turn golden. Then add the salt-pork dice and cook until golden. Remove the onions and salt-pork dice with a slotted spoon and reserve them.

Put the squab pieces in the casserole and turn them until they are golden on all sides. Remove and reserve them. Remove all but 2 tablespoons of the fat from the casserole. Put the onions and the salt-pork dice back into the casserole, stir in the flour, and then add the wine and the stock. Bring to a boil and add the mushrooms, the *bouquet garni* and the squab pieces. Season with salt and pepper and simmer, covered, for about 30 minutes.

Discard the *bouquet garni* and then pour the contents of the casserole into a hot deep serving dish.

FOR 2 PERSONS:

2 tablespoons peanut oil
3 tablespoons butter
24 tiny white onions
¼ pound salt pork, diced and
  blanched
2 squabs (1 pound each),
  quartered
1½ tablespoons flour

¾ cup Sancerre wine
¾ cup Brown Poultry Stock
  (p. 164)
¼ pound small mushrooms
1 Bouquet Garni (p. 46)
Salt
Freshly ground black pepper

/ *Squab Sautéed with Truffles*

SAUTÉ DE PIGEONS AUX TRUFFES

Cut the squab into 4 pieces. Rub the pieces with salt and pepper and sauté them in the combined hot oil and butter in a deep skillet until golden on all sides. Cover and simmer for about 25 minutes. Transfer the meat to a hot serving dish.

Degrease the juices in the skillet and then stir in the white wine, scraping up all the brown bits at the bottom of the skillet. Bring to the boiling point and cook until the wine has evaporated. Stir in the Armagnac, the *sauce demi-glace* and the truffles. Bring to the boiling point again and pour over the squab.

FOR 1 PERSON:

1 squab (1 pound)	½ cup white wine
Salt	2 tablespoons Armagnac
Freshly ground black pepper	½ cup Sauce Demi-Glace
1 tablespoon peanut oil	(p. 766)
2 tablespoons butter	2 truffles, minced

TURKEY

Dindes et Dindonneaux

Roast Stuffed Young Turkey / DINDONNEAU FARCI

Marinate the truffle slices in the brandy and port for 8 hours.

Loosen the turkey's skin and push the truffle slices under the skin at regular intervals.

Heat the fresh pork kidney fat until it is melted and gently sauté the whole truffles, seasoned with a little salt and pepper and the *quatre épices,* for 10 minutes. Cool, chill, and grind, using the fine blade of a meat grinder. Add the diced goose liver. Season lightly with salt.

Stuff the cavity with this mixture and let the bird stand in the refrigerator for 24 hours. Sew the cavity closed; truss the turkey. Bard, that is, wrap it in the sheets of fresh pork fat, and tie them securely. Roast in a preheated 350° F. oven for about 30 minutes for each pound of meat, about 2½ hours. Turn it over several times and baste the bird frequently. About 30 minutes before the end of the roasting time, remove the pork fat and let the bird brown. Put it on a hot serving platter. Skim the fat off the pan juices, add the wine, bring to the boiling point, remove from the heat, and stir in the butter. Serve this sauce in a sauceboat.

FOR 6 TO 8 PERSONS:

½ cup sliced truffles	½ teaspoon Quatre Épices
½ cup brandy	(p. 667)
2 cups port	½ pound uncooked goose liver,
1 turkey (5 pounds)	cut into dice
1 pound fresh pork kidney fat	Thin sheets of fresh pork fat
1 pound fresh truffles	1½ cups dry white wine
Salt	3 tablespoons butter
Freshly ground black pepper	

/ Roast Young Turkey with Cranberries

DINDONNEAU AUX AIRELLES

Season the turkey's cavity with salt and pepper. Truss the bird and bard, that is, wrap it in sheets of fresh pork fat, tying them securely. Roast it on a bed of the carrots, onions, celery, thyme and bay leaf in a preheated 375° F. oven for about 1 hour and 30 minutes. Turn it and baste frequently as it roasts. About 30 minutes before the bird is done, remove the pork fat and let the bird brown.

Put the turkey on a hot serving platter and keep it hot. Skim the fat off the pan juices, add the wine, bring to the boiling point, and add the stock and the *crème fraîche.*

Bring the sauce again to the boiling point and reduce by half. Correct the seasoning. Strain it into a sauceboat and serve it with the turkey and the cranberry sauce.

FOR 4 PERSONS:

1 turkey (4 pounds)	3 sprigs of fresh thyme, or 1
Salt	teaspoon dried thyme
Freshly ground black pepper	1 bay leaf, crumbled
Thin sheets of fresh pork fat	1 cup dry white wine
2 carrots, chopped	1 cup White Stock (p. 165)
2 onions, chopped	1 cup Crème Fraîche (p. 666)
1 celery stalk, chopped	2 cups canned cranberry sauce

/ Truffled Turkey with Chestnut Stuffing

DINDONNEAU TRUFFÉ FARCI AUX MARRONS

Marinate the truffle slices in the brandy and port for 8 hours.

Loosen the turkey's skin with the point of a knife or the fingers and push the truffle slices under the skin at regular intervals. Let stand in the refrigerator for 24 hours. Stuff the bird with the following mixture: Combine the chestnuts with the ground pork and the minced truffles and season with salt and pepper.

Stuff the turkey and sew it closed. Bard it, that is, wrap it in the sheets of fresh pork fat and tie them securely. Line a greased baking pan with the carrots, onions and celery and lay the turkey on top of the vegetables. Roast it in a preheated 375° F. oven for about 2 hours. Turn and baste it frequently as it roasts. About 30 minutes before the end of the roasting time, remove the pork fat to allow the turkey to brown. Turn the oven off and let the turkey stand for 30 minutes before serving it.

FOR 6 PERSONS:

6 truffles, sliced	Stuffing:
½ cup brandy	½ pound Boiled Chestnuts
½ cup port	(p. 582), mashed
1 turkey (5 pounds)	⅔ pound lean pork, finely
Thin sheets of fresh pork fat	ground
2 carrots, chopped	¼ pound truffles, minced
2 onions, chopped	Salt
2 celery stalks, chopped	Freshly ground black pepper

Turkey au Chocolat / DINDE AU CHOCOLAT

Rub the cavity of the turkey with the thyme, bay leaf, basil and fennel. Wrap it loosely and let it stand in the refrigerator for 24 hours.

Grind the turkey's liver with the pork fat. Add the whole chicken livers to this mixture, together with the ham, brandy, *fines herbes* and truffles. Season lightly with salt and pepper.

Remove the herbs from the cavity of the turkey (reserve them) and stuff the bird with the liver mixture. Sew the cavity closed, truss the turkey and bard, that is, wrap it in the fresh pork fat. Line a baking pan with the carrots, onions and celery and the reserved herbs from the turkey. Smear the vegetables with the butter. Place the turkey on its side over the vegetables and roast in a preheated 375° F. oven for 1 hour, turning it on its other side after 30 minutes. Take the turkey out of the oven and remove the pork fat. Strain the pan juices and put them back into the roasting pan. Return the turkey to the pan, placing it on its side. Finish roasting for about another 45 minutes, turning it on its other side after 15 minutes and then breast side up for the last 15 minutes. Baste frequently with the pan juices.

Transfer the turkey to a hot serving platter and keep it hot. Skim the fat off the pan juices, add the wine, bring to the boiling point, and add the white stock and the cocoa, which you have blended with the *crème fraîche*. Bring again to the boiling point and reduce the sauce by half. Correct the seasoning.

Carve the turkey and strain the sauce over the pieces.

FOR 4 PERSONS:

1 turkey (4 pounds)	**4 truffles, minced**
3 sprigs of fresh thyme, or 1 teaspoon dried thyme	**Salt**
	Freshly ground black pepper
1 bay leaf	**Thin sheets of fresh pork fat**
3 sprigs of fresh basil, or 1 teaspoon dried basil	**2 carrots, chopped**
	2 onions, chopped
6 fresh fennel leaves	**2 celery stalks with leaves, chopped**
¼ pound fresh pork fat	
⅓ pound chicken livers	**6 tablespoons butter, softened**
¼ pound prosciutto or smoked ham, finely diced	**1 cup dry, white wine**
	1 cup White Stock (p. 165)
¼ cup brandy	**4 tablespoons cocoa**
2 tablespoons minced Fines Herbes (p. 89)	**2 cups Crème Fraîche (p. 666)**

Breast of Turkey Dalmau Costa /

ESCALOPES DE DINDE DALMAU COSTA

My Mexican friends are Catalans who have become fiercely Mexican since 1939. Among them, Dalmau Costa is one of the most attractive personalities.

Make a very thick *sauce béchamel*. Add the hard-cooked eggs and the corn to the sauce. Bring to the boiling point and cook for 3 to 5 minutes, stirring constantly with a wooden spoon to prevent sticking. Pour the mixture into a large shallow dish; cool and chill it thoroughly, because it is then easier to bread. Shape the mixture into croquettes of any desired shape, such as 3-inch cylinders. Dip them first into flour, then into the *anglaise,* and finally coat them with the fresh white bread crumbs. Chill the croquettes until cooking time. Then sauté them in half of the butter over low heat so that they will be golden brown and cooked through.

Cut the turkey breast lengthwise into 4 pieces, one for each person. Lard each piece generously with the pork fat and the tongue strips. Season with salt and pepper.

Heat the oil and the remaining butter and sauté the pieces of turkey breast for a minute or two on each side, or until golden. Reduce the heat and simmer, covered, over low heat for 10 to 15 minutes. Test for doneness by pressing the pieces with a finger. If they feel slightly spongy, rather than firm, they are done. Place them in a deep hot dish. Stir the sherry into the pan juices, bring to the boiling point, and pour over the meat. Garnish with the corn croquettes.

FOR 4 PERSONS:

2 **cups thick Sauce Béchamel (p. 761)**	**Fresh white bread crumbs**
4 **hard-cooked eggs, minced**	½ **cup butter**
1 **cup cooked corn**	1 **breast of turkey (1 pound)**
Flour	¼ **pound fresh pork fat, cut into short strips**
Anglaise:	¼ **pound cooked tongue, cut into short strips**
2 **egg yolks**	**Salt**
2 **tablespoons water**	**Freshly ground black pepper**
2 **tablespoons peanut oil**	1 **tablespoon peanut oil**
Salt	¾ **cup sherry**
Freshly ground white pepper	

/ Breast of Turkey with Ginger Sauce

SUPRÊME DE DINDE AU GINGEMBRE

First make the sauce in this fashion: cook the onions in 3 tablespoons of the butter until they are soft and golden. Sprinkle them with the curry powder and cook, stirring constantly, for 2 minutes longer. Add the chopped apple, the *bouquet garni,* the unpeeled garlic and the stock. Season with salt and pepper and simmer, covered, over low heat for 45 minutes.

Strain the sauce through a fine sieve into a casserole; stir in the *crème fraîche,* the lemon juice and the ginger. Check the seasoning. Bring to the boiling point, cook for 2 minutes and, at serving time, pour into a sauceboat.

Sauté the 4 pieces of turkey breast in the combined hot oil and 3 tablespoons of the butter in a casserole until golden. Season with salt and pepper, cover the casserole, reduce the heat, and simmer for about 15 minutes. Test for doneness by pressing the pieces with a finger. If they feel spongy, rather than firm, they are done.

Sauté the banana slices and the apple quarters in the remaining butter in a skillet for about 5 minutes. Place the turkey breasts on a hot serving platter and garnish them with the bananas and the apples.

Serve with the sauce, the rice *à la Créole* and chutney.

FOR 4 PERSONS:

3 medium-sized onions, minced
½ cup butter
2 tablespoons curry powder
1 tart apple, peeled, cored and
  chopped
1 Bouquet Garni (p. 46)
1 garlic clove, unpeeled
2 cups White or Brown Poultry
  Stock (p. 164)
Salt
Freshly ground black pepper
½ cup Crème Fraîche (p. 666)
Juice of ½ lemon

¼ cup chopped drained preserved
  ginger
1 boned turkey breast (1½
  pounds), cut lengthwise into
  4 pieces
1 tablespoon peanut oil
2 bananas, sliced
2 tart apples, peeled, cored and
  quartered
1 recipe Rice à la Créole
  (p. 658)
Chutney

Chaud-Froid of Turkey / CHAUD-FROID DE DINDE

Proceed as in Chaud-Froid of Chicken (p. 479), poaching a small turkey of 4 to 5 pounds for about 20 minutes per pound.

RABBIT

Lapins et Lapereaux

EDITORS' NOTE: *Rabbit is not of course poultry, but M. Oliver follows the French practice of classifying the domestic rabbit in the same category as barnyard fowl.*

Rabbit Morvandelle / LAPIN MORVANDELLE

Cut the rabbit into pieces for frying and sauté them quickly in the combined hot oil and butter in a casserole over fairly high heat. Remove them to a hot plate when they are golden and keep them hot.

Add the ham fat and the onions to the casserole and cook until golden. Add the tomatoes, mustard, wine and the *bouquet garni*. Season with salt and cook, covered, over low heat for about 20 minutes. Strain the sauce through a fine sieve. Return the sauce to the casserole and add the rabbit. Cover and simmer over low heat until the meat is tender, about 25 minutes. Pour it into a hot serving dish and garnish with fried croutons.

FOR 4 PERSONS:

1 rabbit (2½ to 3 pounds)
1 tablespoon peanut oil
4 tablespoons butter
¼ pound ham fat
4 onions, minced
6 tomatoes, peeled, seeded and
   chopped

2 tablespoons Dijon mustard
1 cup dry white wine
1 Bouquet Garni (p. 46)
Salt
Croutons (p. 62)

LAPEREAU À LA MOUTARDE / *Rabbit with Mustard*

1. Spread the inside of the rabbit with mustard and thyme and season with salt and pepper. Wrap the rabbit in sheets of fresh pork fat and tie securely. Roast the rabbit in a preheated 450° F. oven for 15 minutes. Reduce the heat to 350° F. and roast for about 1 hour longer. Turn the rabbit and baste it occasionally as it roasts. Remove the pork fat about 20 minutes before the rabbit is done to let it brown. Serve with French fried potatoes.

2. Or follow this method: Cut the rabbit into pieces for frying and brown them in the oil and butter in a casserole over fairly high heat. Reduce the heat and add the onion, the *bouquet garni* and salt and pepper. Simmer, covered, for about 30 minutes, or until the pieces are tender.

When the rabbit is done, discard the onion and the *bouquet garni.*

Blend the Dijon mustard with the *crème fraîche,* add a little cayenne, the egg yolks and the lemon juice. Mix well and pour the sauce over the cooked rabbit. Simmer slowly over low heat for about 10 minutes, or until the sauce has thickened slightly. Correct the seasoning.

FOR 4 PERSONS:

First Method:
1 rabbit (3 pounds)
3 tablespoons Dijon mustard
1 tablespoon chopped fresh thyme,
   or ½ teaspoon dried thyme
Salt
Freshly ground black pepper
Thin sheets of fresh pork fat

Second method:
1 rabbit (3 pounds)
1 tablespoon peanut oil

4 tablespoons butter
1 onion, stuck with 2 cloves
1 Bouquet Garni (p. 46)
Salt
Freshly ground black pepper
3 tablespoons Dijon mustard
½ cup Crème Fraîche (p. 666)
Cayenne pepper
2 egg yolks, beaten
Juice of ½ lemon

LAPIN AUX PRUNEAUX / *Rabbit with Prunes*

Cut the rabbit into pieces for frying and marinate them in a mixture of the thyme, bay leaf, carrot, onion, ½ bottle red wine and 2 tablespoons of the oil for 24 hours. Reserve the rabbit's liver and, if possible, the blood.

Pit the prunes, soak them in lukewarm water for 3 hours, and then cook them in the remaining wine until tender, about 15 minutes.

Heat the remaining oil and the butter in a casserole, and cook the bacon and the onions in it until golden. Transfer them to a plate.

Drain the rabbit and dry carefully with a kitchen cloth; sauté the pieces in the fat remaining in the casserole until golden on all sides. Stir in the flour, mix, and return the bacon to the casserole. Strain the marinade over the meat in the casserole. Add the mushrooms, season with salt and pepper, cover the casserole, bring to a boil, and simmer for 45 minutes. About 10 minutes before the rabbit is done add the prunes and the onions.

Blend any reserved blood with the vinegar. Mince the rabbit's liver. Add blood and liver to the casserole, together with the currant jelly. Simmer for 2 to 3 minutes; when everything is well blended, pour into a deep hot serving dish. Serve immediately.

FOR 4 PERSONS:

1 rabbit (3 pounds)	2 tablespoons butter
1 tablespoon chopped fresh thyme, or ½ teaspoon dried thyme	4 slices of bacon, diced
	10 tiny white onions
1 bay leaf	1 tablespoon flour
1 carrot, chopped	½ pound small mushrooms
1 onion, chopped	Salt
1 bottle dry red wine	Freshly ground black pepper
3 tablespoons olive oil	½ tablespoon vinegar
1 pound prunes	2 tablespoons currant jelly

Rabbit en Croûte | LAPIN EN CROÛTE

Bone the rabbit completely, but keep the loin meat whole. Remove all gristle and tendons from the remaining meat, cut it into small dice, and grind it, together with the rabbit liver and the ham, using the fine blade of a meat grinder. Season with salt, pepper, the *quatre épices, fines herbes* and the brandy.

Make 2 round and rather thick patties with this mixture, and cook them in the combined hot oil and butter until golden on both sides. Remove the patties and let them cool. Sauté the rabbit loins in the fat remaining in the pan until the meat is golden; season with salt and pepper.

Reserve about one quarter of the pastry and roll out the remainder in an oval shape to the thickness of ⅛ inch. Place the meat patties and the loin meat in the center, leaving a wide empty border all around. Paint this border with egg yolk. Fold the pastry over the rabbit filling and press the edges firmly together. Put the roll on a battered baking sheet, sealed side up, and paint it with egg yolk.

Roll out the remaining pastry into a strip and lay this strip on the seam of the roll; this will keep it sealed. Paint again with egg yolk. Put 2 funnels (a pastry tube with a plain round hole will do) in the top of the roll to allow steam to escape. Bake in a preheated 350° F. oven for about 25 minutes.

FOR 4 PERSONS:

1 rabbit (3 pounds)	2 tablespoons minced Fines Herbes (p. 89)
The rabbit liver	
⅓ pound Bayonne or smoked ham or prosciutto	2 tablespoons brandy
	2 tablespoons peanut oil
Salt	3 tablespoons butter
Freshly ground black pepper	1 recipe Pâte Brisée (p. 713), made with lard instead of butter
½ teaspoon Quatre Épices (p. 667)	
	2 egg yolks

/ *Sautéed Rabbit with Bread Crumbs*

LAPIN SAUTÉ À LA MIE DE PAIN

Cut the rabbit into pieces for frying. In a casserole, heat half of the walnut or peanut oil and all of the olive oil; put the rabbit pieces into it. Cook the pieces until they are golden on all sides. Lower the heat, cover the casserole, and simmer for about 25 minutes. Transfer the meat to a hot plate and keep it warm.

Cook the mushrooms in the pan juices until they are golden. Add the shallots, and season with salt and pepper. Transfer both the mushrooms and shallots to a hot plate and keep them warm.

Return the rabbit to the casserole, add the wine, and season with salt and pepper. Simmer, covered, for 10 minutes. Then add the minced garlic and parsley.

Put the rabbit pieces and the casserole juices into a deep serving dish and arrange the mushrooms and shallots around the meat. Fry the bread crumbs in the remaining walnut or peanut oil in a skillet; when the crumbs are crisp and golden, sprinkle them over the rabbit. Serve very hot.

FOR 4 PERSONS:

1 **rabbit (3 pounds)**	**Salt**
8 **tablespoons walnut or peanut oil**	**Freshly ground black pepper**
	¾ **cup dry white wine**
4 **tablespoons olive oil**	4 **garlic cloves, minced**
1 **pound small mushrooms**	2 **tablespoons minced parsley**
3 **shallots, minced**	2 **cups fresh white bread crumbs**

LAPIN SAUTÉ À LA CRÈME / *Sautéed Rabbit in Cream*

Cut the rabbit into pieces for frying. Season each piece with salt and pepper and sauté in the combined oil and butter in a casserole over fairly high heat until the meat is golden on all sides. Transfer the meat to a hot dish, add the hot brandy, and flame it.

Add the shallots to the casserole and cook until they are golden. Add the rabbit and its juices, the wine, bay leaf and thyme. Cover the casserole and simmer for about 30 minutes, or until the pieces are tender.

Put the pieces in a hot deep serving dish. Stir the *crème fraîche* into the pan juices. Discard the bay leaf. Bring to the boiling point and cook until the sauce is slightly reduced. Check the seasoning. Coat the rabbit pieces with the sauce and serve immediately.

FOR 4 PERSONS:

1 **rabbit (3 pounds)**	6 **shallots, minced**
Salt	½ **cup dry white wine**
Freshly ground black pepper	1 **bay leaf**
1 **tablespoon peanut oil**	1 **tablespoon chopped fresh thyme,**
4 **tablespoons butter**	**or ½ teaspoon dried thyme**
3 **tablespoons brandy, heated**	1 **cup Crème Fraîche (p. 666)**

Rabbit Stew / GIBELOTTE DE LAPIN

Proceed as in Coq au Vin (see index), but use a 3-pound rabbit instead of chicken.

Rabbit Stew Provençale /

GIBELOTTE DE LAPIN À LA PROVENÇALE

Proceed as in Chicken Bouillabaisse (p. 478), but use a 2½- to 3-pound rabbit instead of chicken.

Stuffed Rabbit Alsatian Style /

LAPIN FARCI À L'ALSACIENNE

Season the inside of the rabbit with salt and pepper and spread it with half of the mustard. Put the cooked pig's trotter also into the rabbit's cavity. Close the rabbit by pulling the skin over the pig's trotter, and sew it closed. Fasten the hind legs to the body with skewers.

Spread the whole rabbit with the remaining mustard. Wrap it in the sheets of fresh pork fat and tie securely. Oil the bottom of a large roasting pan and put the rabbit in it.

Roast the rabbit in a preheated 450° F. oven for about 15 minutes. Reduce the heat to 350° F. and roast for about 1 hour longer. Turn the rabbit and baste occasionally as it roasts. About 20 minutes before the end of the roasting time remove the barding fat.

Cook the noodles according to package directions, drain them, and keep them hot.

Transfer the rabbit to a hot serving platter. Put the noodles into the roasting pan and coat them well with the pan juices. Place the noodles around the rabbit on the serving platter and serve very hot.

FOR 4 PERSONS:

1 rabbit (3 pounds)	**1 cooked pig's trotter**
Salt	**Thin sheets of fresh pork fat**
Freshly ground black pepper	**1 pound noodles**
6 tablespoons Dijon mustard	

Terrine of Rabbit in Aspic / TERRINE DE LAPIN EN GELÉE

Cut the rabbit into bite-size pieces and marinate it in a mixture of the thyme, bay leaf, diced onions and carrots, a little salt, the peppercorns and vinegar in a cool place for 24 hours. Turn the pieces occasionally.

Drain the meat and dry with a kitchen towel. Brown the pieces in the oil and butter in a casserole over fairly high heat. Transfer the meat to a plate. Cook the

Chicken Ballottines Curnonsky

Ballottines de Volaille Curnonsky

Chicken Ballottines Curnonsky

CUT THE CHICKEN into 4 sections. Bone the sections and remove all tendons, but leave in the leg bones. Marinate the meat in the combined brandy, port wine, thyme, bay leaf and tarragon for 4 hours. Season the marinade with salt and pepper to taste.

Crush the chicken bones in a mortar with a pestle. Heat the butter and goose fat in a casserole (goose fat is not essential, but it gives the dish a better flavor). Add the chicken bones, carrots, onions, turnip and *fines herbes*. Stir with a wooden spoon and cook until light brown.

While the bones and vegetables are cooking, grind the raw chicken or pork, the ham and the veal, using the fine blade of a meat grinder. Put the mixture into a bowl. Season well with salt and pepper and mix well to make a smooth stuffing.

Remove the chicken pieces from the marinade; drain and dry them. Put them, skin side down, on a board and spread each piece with a little stuffing, a slice of *foie gras* and a slice of truffle. Roll up each piece, enclosing the stuffing and shaping it into a small *ballottine,* or roll. Wrap each in a sheet of fresh pork fat and tie crosswise. Put the *ballottines* on the browned vegetables and bones and cook them over high heat until the pork fat is turning golden. Add the wine and consommé, which should come about three quarters up the sides of the *ballottines*. Bring to a boil, lower the heat and simmer, covered, for about 25 minutes, basting frequently. After the first 15 minutes, remove the strings and the pork fat from the *ballottines* and continue cooking them until tender. When they are tender, place each on a crouton which is slightly larger than the *ballottine* and keep it hot.

To make the sauce, strain the cooking liquid through a fine sieve and degrease it. Put it in a saucepan, bring to the boiling point over high heat, and reduce to about ½ cup. Stir in the *crème fraîche,* bring to the boiling point once more, and reduce until thickened. Remove from the heat and stir in the soft butter, bit by bit. Check the seasoning, adding, if you wish, a little brandy, cayenne pepper and salt, but be discreet about it. Coat the *ballottines* with the sauce. Garnish the serving dish with the artichoke hearts and the rissolé potatoes.

Editors' Note: The illustration on the obverse side shows a serving for 2 persons.

For 4 persons:

1 chicken (3 pounds)
½ cup brandy
½ cup port wine
½ teaspoon dried thyme
1 bay leaf
1 teaspoon dried tarragon
Salt
Freshly ground black pepper
2 tablespoons butter
2 tablespoons goose fat
3 carrots, sliced
2 onions, sliced
1 turnip, diced
2 tablespoons minced Fines
    Herbes (p. 89)
⅛ pound raw chicken meat
    or boneless lean pork

⅛ pound prosciutto, or
    smoked ham, with fat
⅛ pound boneless veal
4 thin slices of foie gras
4 slices of truffle
4 thin sheets of fresh
    pork fatback
2 cups dry white wine
1 cup Chicken Consommé
    (p. 168)
4 large Croutons (see p. 62)
¼ cup Crème Fraîche
    (p. 666), or heavy cream
2 tablespoons soft butter
½ recipe Artichoke Hearts
    in Cream (p. 546)
1 recipe Rissolé Potatoes (p. 625)

Roast Chicken in Aspic
Poulet Rôti en Gelée

Roast Chicken in Aspic

Poulet Rôti en Gelée

ROAST THE CHICKEN in the usual manner, let it cool, and then chill
it.

Cut it into 4 sections. Decorate the sections with the truffle slices
and coat with aspic as described on page 114. Garnish with little
bunches of fresh tarragon and surround with the remaining aspic,
chopped.

For 4 persons:

1 roasting chicken (3 pounds)
4 truffles, sliced into decorative shapes
3 cups Brown Stock for Aspics (p. 166)
A few sprigs of fresh tarragon

Coq au Vin de Pomerol

Coq au Vin de Pomerol

HEAT HALF OF the oil and half of the butter in a casserole, cook the onions in it until they are about to turn golden, and add the bacon strips. Mix with a wooden spoon and cook over low heat until the onions are tender and the bacon is transparent.

Cut the chicken into 8 pieces.

Remove the onions and the bacon with a slotted spoon and reserve them. Put the chicken pieces into the casserole and brown them on all sides. Season with salt and pepper. Sprinkle with the brandy and flame. Heat the wine with the sugar in a separate saucepan. Sprinkle the flour over the chicken and then add the hot wine to the casserole, along with the garlic and the *bouquet garni*. Simmer, covered, over low heat for about 40 minutes.

Sauté the mushrooms in the remaining butter and oil in a skillet for about 5 minutes. Reserve them with the onions and bacon.

When the chicken is fully cooked, add the mushrooms, onions and bacon. Discard the *bouquet garni*.

Transfer the chicken, vegetables and sauce to a hot serving platter. Sprinkle with the *fines herbes*. Garnish the platter with the fried slices of bread.

For 6 persons:

2 tablespoons peanut oil	1 bottle Pomerol
4 tablespoons butter	3 lumps of sugar
20 tiny white onions	4 tablespoons flour
¼ pound bacon, cut into thin strips	2 garlic cloves, mashed
1 chicken (4 pounds)	1 Bouquet Garni (p. 46)
Salt	10 mushroom caps
Freshly ground black pepper	2 tablespoons minced Fines Herbes (p. 89)
¼ cup brandy	6 slices of French bread, fried in butter

Couscous

Couscous

Editors' Note: Couscous is a national dish in Algeria and other North African states. The grain, resembling a fine semolina, is cracked wheat. It gives its name to the whole dish.

Soak the chick-peas in cold water overnight. Change the water, bring them to a boil in a saucepan, and cook them for 1 hour (or use precooked canned chick-peas, drained).

Grind the sirloin, using the fine blade of a meat grinder, and combine it with the *fines herbes* and the shallot. Season it with salt and pepper; mix well. Stuff the chicken with this mixture.

Fill a large kettle with water and put the stuffed chicken and the beef bone into it. Both must be covered by the water. Bring slowly to the boiling point. Skim. Add the carrots, turnips, celery, onion, tomatoes, the unpeeled garlic, the chick-peas and the hot peppers. Bring again to the boiling point and skim. Season lightly with coarse salt. Skim again and simmer, covered, for about 1 hour. Remove the chicken and keep it hot in a little of the broth. Boil the zucchini in the kettle for 5 minutes. Remove all of the vegetables from the kettle and reserve them.

Strain the broth into the bottom part of a couscous pot or into a kettle. Bring to the boiling point. Put the couscous into the top part of the couscous pot or into a colander lined with cheesecloth. Put the top part over the bottom and steam the couscous over the boiling broth until steam begins to come through the grains. Put the couscous on a plate, sprinkle it with ½ cup of cold water, let it cool a little, and return it to the pot or the colander to steam again. Repeat this operation three times. It will take about 40 minutes in all.

Pour the cooked couscous into a bowl and sprinkle it lightly with the fat from the surface of the broth and the melted butter. Toss it lightly with the raisins. Keep hot.

Carve the chicken and arrange the pieces on a serving dish; surround them with the meat stuffing and the reserved vegetables.

Serve with the following sauce: Cook the minced onions in the butter until they are soft and golden. Stir in ½ cup of the broth and the *sauce tomate*. Bring to the boiling point and cook for 2 or 3 minutes. Season heavily with red pepper. This sauce should have the consistency of a thick broth.

For 4 persons:

¼ pound dried chick-peas
1 pound boneless sirloin,
    well marbled
2 tablespoons minced Fines
    Herbes (p. 89)
1 shallot, minced
Salt
Freshly ground black pepper
1 chicken (3 pounds)
1 large beef bone
2 carrots, sliced
2 small turnips, sliced
2 celery stalks, sliced
1 onion, stuck with 2 cloves

4 tomatoes, peeled, seeded
    and chopped
1 unpeeled garlic clove
3 hot peppers
Coarse (Kosher) salt
4 small zucchini squash, sliced
1 pound couscous
4 tablespoons butter, melted
¼ cup raisins, plumped in hot water
For the sauce:
    2 tablespoons minced onions
    2 tablespoons butter
    2 cups Sauce Tomate (p. 769)
    Red pepper

Duck à la Margaux

Canard à la Margaux

Duck à la Margaux

Canard à la Margaux

HEAT HALF OF the oil and half of the butter in a kettle that will comfortably hold the 2 ducks. Add the onions, carrots, shallots, garlic, thyme and bay leaf, as well as the wing tips, necks and gizzards of the ducks. Mix well and cook over low heat, stirring constantly, until the vegetables are very soft.

Rub the ducks inside and out with salt and pepper and truss them. Prick the lower breasts and thighs several times with a fork and then brown them quickly in the remaining butter and oil over high heat. They must be golden brown on the outside and should have drained off much of their fat, but still be *sanglant* (bleeding) on the inside.

Put the ducks into the kettle with the vegetables; add the Château Margaux and enough stock so that the ducks are barely covered. Bring to the boiling point and check the seasoning. Cover the kettle and simmer for about 1 hour.

Remove the ducks and put them in a bowl or casserole that will just hold them. Strain the cooking liquid over them. Chill overnight.

Remove all the fat from the surface and remove the ducks from the casserole. If the cooking liquid has not jellied, add sufficient gelatin to make it jell (see p. 166); then clarify it with the egg whites in the usual way (see p. 53).

Set aside the more handsome of the ducks. Carve all of the breast meat from the other duck into thin slices and set them aside. Remove all the rest of the meat from the second duck. Grind this meat with the duck livers, using the finest blade of a meat grinder, and then force the mixture through a sieve. Stir in the softened butter and beat until the mixture is light and has the consistency of a mousse of *foie gras*. Season with salt and pepper.

Fill the cavity of the whole duck with about half of the meat and liver mousse. Using a little more of the mousse as a glue, fasten some of the breast meat on top. Using a pastry bag fitted with a fluted tube, pipe decorative swirls of the mousse around the slices of meat. Place the decorated duck on a platter and chill in the refrigerator until cold.

Pour about half of the clarified stock into a shallow dish and chill in the refrigerator. Stuff the olives with some of the mousse and chill.

When the duck is cold, decorate the top with a few of the olives and then spoon cold but still liquid stock over it. Surround the duck with the remaining breast slices decorated with swirls of mousse. Coat these with a little more of the aspic stock. Chill in the refrigerator.

Unmold the dish of jellied stock onto a board and cut out crescents from it. Garnish the platter with these crescents, the remaining olives and the watercress. Chill until serving time.

Beat the *crème fraîche* until stiff and mix it with the remaining cold liquid stock. Add enough paprika to color it pink and serve this sauce separately in a sauceboat.

For 6 persons:

4 tablespoons peanut oil
6 tablespoons butter
2 onions, minced
2 carrots, minced
3 shallots, minced
2 garlic cloves
½ teaspoon dried thyme
1 bay leaf
2 ducks (5 pounds each)
Salt
Freshly ground black pepper
1 bottle Château Margaux

4 cups (or more) White
    Stock (p. 165)
Unflavored gelatin
3 egg whites
1 pound duck livers,
    cooked in butter
1 cup butter, softened
2 dozen green olives,
    pitted
1 bunch of watercress
1½ cups Crème Fraîche (p. 666)
Paprika

Duck à la Vasco da Gama

Canard Vasco da Gama

Duck à la Vasco da Gama

Canard Vasco da Gama

SEASON THE CAVITY of the duck with salt and pepper, and truss it. Prick the lower breast and thighs with a fork to allow fat to escape. Roast the duck in a preheated 350° F. oven for 1¼ hours, or until the juice runs clear when the thigh is pricked with a fork.

While the duck is roasting, make the sauce: Using a heavy saucepan, make a blond caramel with the sugar by stirring it over low heat until it melts. When it turns golden, add the vinegar and the poultry stock, boiling hot. Simmer for 3 minutes, then stir in the cornstarch diluted in water. Simmer for 5 minutes and then stir in the red-currant jelly, the orange juice and the Curaçao. Keep hot over very low heat.

Prepare the oranges: peel the zest from four of the oranges (there must be no white membrane), cut it into tiny julienne strips, blanch them in boiling water to cover for 2 to 3 minutes, and drain. Using a very sharp knife, cut off all of the white part from these 4 oranges and cut out the sections so that they are skinless. Set aside both the orange strips and sections until the duck is ready.

Use the remaining 2 oranges to make baskets as shown in the illustration.

When the duck is fully cooked, place it on a hot serving dish; arrange the orange sections around it and put an orange basket at each end. Sprinkle the orange rind over the bird and coat everything with the sauce. Serve very hot.

For 4 persons:

1 duck (5 pounds)
Salt
Freshly ground black
    pepper
⅓ cup sugar
¼ cup vinegar
2 cups Brown Poultry Stock
    (p. 164), made if
    possible with duck
    backs, necks, giblets, etc.

2 tablespoons cornstarch,
    diluted in 2 tablespoons
    water
2 tablespoons red-currant
    jelly
Juice of 1 orange
2 tablespoons Curaçao
6 oranges

Guinea Hen Jean Cocteau

Pintadeau Farci Jean Cocteau

Guinea Hen Jean Cocteau

Pintadeau Farci Jean Cocteau

FINELY CHOP OR grind the guinea hen's liver and gizzard and reserve them. Make a stuffing: Soften the bread crumbs in a little warm milk and squeeze them dry; beat in the whole egg, add the hard-cooked egg, and season with salt and pepper to taste. Add the nutmeg, cinnamon, tarragon, chives, chervil and the reserved liver and gizzard. Mix thoroughly until the stuffing is smooth.

Stuff the guinea hen with the mixture, sew it closed, truss it, wrap it in sheets of fresh pork fat, and tie them on with string. Heat 2 tablespoons of the oil and 4 tablespoons of the butter in a large casserole; add the bird and brown it on all sides. Add the brandy and flame it. Remove the guinea hen from the casserole.

Add the carrots, onions and garlic to the casserole, cook them until they are soft, and then return the guinea hen to the casserole. Add the wine, cover the casserole, bring to a boil, lower the heat, and simmer for 35 minutes.

Puncture the sausages with a fork and sauté them in 1 tablespoon of oil in a skillet. Cook them until crisp. Peel, core, and quarter the apples; cook them in the remaining butter until they are tender but still firm. Season them very lightly with salt.

When the guinea hen is cooked, place it on a hot serving dish. Reduce the pan juices to a good flavor and pour over the bird. Garnish with the sausages, each on top of a crouton, and the apples. If desired the sausages may be decorated with tiny strips of pimiento.

For 2 persons:

1 guinea hen (2 pounds)
2 cups fresh white
    bread crumbs
Lukewarm milk
1 whole egg
1 hard-cooked egg, minced
Salt
Freshly ground black
    pepper
¼ teaspoon grated nutmeg
⅛ teaspoon ground cinnamon
1 tablespoon chopped fresh
    tarragon, or 1 teaspoon
    dried tarragon
1 teaspoon chopped chives
1 tablespoon chopped
    fresh chervil, or ½
    teaspoon dried chervil

Several thin sheets of
    fresh pork fat
3 tablespoons peanut oil
7 tablespoons butter
¼ cup brandy
3 carrots, chopped
3 onions, chopped
2 garlic cloves, mashed
1 cup dry white wine
4 white and 4 dark
    blood sausages
    (boudins blancs et
    noirs), or substitute any
    link sausages
4 tart apples
8 Croutons (see p. 62),
    about the size of the sausages
A few strips of pimiento

Chartreuse of Young Partridge

Perdreaux en Chartreuse

Chartreuse of Young Partridge

Perdreaux en Chartreuse

TRIM THE CABBAGE and separate the leaves. Blanch them in boiling salted water for 10 minutes and then soak in running cold water for another 10 minutes. Heat the goose fat in a deep casserole and cook the onion and carrots in it until they are golden.

Cover the vegetables with half of the cabbage leaves and top the cabbage leaves with the sliced bacon. Put the old partridge on the bacon and top it with the remaining cabbage. Add the stock. Season lightly with salt and pepper. Cook in a preheated 325° F. oven for 3 hours.

About 45 minutes before the end of the cooking time truss the young partridges and roast them in a 375° F. oven, turning them occasionally and basting with the butter.

Broil the tomatoes.

At serving time, transfer the cabbage to a hot serving dish and top it with the roast partridges, the bacon and the tomatoes. Strain the pan juices, degrease them, and pour over the birds.

The braised old partridge should be eaten cold, with mustard and pickles, at another occasion.

For 4 persons:

1 head of green cabbage (about 2 pounds)	4 cups Game Stock (p. 165)
¼ pound goose fat	Salt
1 large onion, sliced	Freshly ground black pepper
3 carrots, sliced	2 young partridges
1 pound sliced bacon	4 tablespoons butter
1 old partridge	4 tomatoes

chopped onions and carrots in the same casserole until they are golden. Stir in the flour and then add the calf's foot, the *bouquet garni* and the wine. Return the rabbit pieces to the casserole and add just enough water to cover. Season with salt and pepper, bring to a boil, cover the casserole, and simmer over very low heat for about 2 hours.

Add the sliced carrots after the rabbit has cooked for 1 hour.

Place the cooked rabbit in a terrine; discard the pieces of calf's foot and the *bouquet garni*. Pour the sauce and vegetables into the terrine. Chill and serve very cold.

FOR 4 PERSONS:

1 rabbit (3 pounds)
For the marinade:
  1 tablespoon chopped fresh
    thyme, or ½ teaspoon dried
    thyme
  1 bay leaf, crumbled
  2 onions, diced
  2 carrots, diced
Salt
  6 peppercorns, crushed
  ¾ cup wine vinegar

1 tablespoon peanut oil
4 tablespoons butter
3 onions, chopped
2 carrots, chopped
1 tablespoon flour
1 calf's foot, blanched, cut into 4
  pieces
1 Bouquet Garni (p. 46)
1 cup dry white wine
1 pound carrots, sliced

7

GAME
Les Gibiers

FEATHERED GAME

Gibiers à Plumes

EDITORS' NOTE: *Game birds are much sought after as a deli-cacy in French cookery. In addition to more familar game such as quail, partridge and pheasant, the French prize such song birds as larks and thrushes on their tables. In the United States, song birds are protected by the law; quite apart from that, it is not our custom to cook and eat them. However, since they are an integral part of France's cuisine and Monsieur Oliver's culinary repertoire, these recipes have been included in this edition of his book.*

As with all game, cooking time depends essentially on the age and condition of the birds, and it is therefore misleading to specify it exactly. While a few persons prefer their game birds on the rare side, generally speaking, the tests for doneness are similar to those for domestic fowl: the juice that spurts from a leg, when pricked with a fork, should be clear and not red, and the leg should move fairly easily at the joints.

It might also be pointed out that, generally speaking, rec-ipes for game birds of the same general kind and size are fairly interchangeable.

Cock Grouse with Raisins | COQ DE BRUYÈRE AUX RAISINS

Pluck and draw the bird. Season the cavity generously with salt and pepper and with the thyme and savory. Lard the breast meat of the bird with half of the ham lardoons.

Marinate the bird in the wine and Armagnac in a china, earthenware or stain-less-steel bowl in a cool place for 2 to 3 days; do not use an aluminum container. Drain the grouse, strain the marinade, and reserve it. Remove any of the herbs that cling to the grouse; dry and truss the bird. Brown it lightly on all sides in the butter in an enamelware casserole. Remove it and keep it hot. In the same casserole, cook to-gether until golden the remaining lardoons, the onions, carrot, garlic and parsley. Add the grouse and the marinade and season with salt and pepper. Bring to a boil, cover the casserole, and simmer over low heat; the cooking time may be only 45 minutes or, if the bird is very old, as long as 2 hours.

When the bird is almost tender, add the raisins or currants and finish cooking. Serve in the same dish, preferably with a few fried croutons.

FOR 2 PERSONS:

1 **cock grouse**	¼ **cup Armagnac**
Salt	5 **tablespoons butter**
Freshly ground black pepper	6 **to 8 tiny white onions**
3 **sprigs of fresh thyme,**	1 **carrot, sliced**
or ½ **teaspoon dried thyme**	1 **garlic clove, mashed**
3 **sprigs of fresh savory,**	1 **small bunch of parsley**
or ½ **teaspoon dried savory**	½ **cup raisins or dried currants,**
½ **cup fat ham, cut into**	**plumped in ¾ cup dry white wine**
strips or lardoons	**and drained**
¾ **cup dry red wine**	½ **cup Croutons (p. 62)**

GROUSE RÔTIE AU VIN ROUGE / *Roast Grouse in Red Wine*

Pluck and draw the grouse. Season the cavity with salt and pepper and put the celery and 2 tablespoons of the butter in it. Cover the breast with the pork fat and tie it on with kitchen string. Roast the grouse in an oiled baking pan in a preheated 450° F. oven for 10 minutes. Reduce the heat to 350° F. and roast for about 35 minutes, or longer if the bird is very large. Remove the pork fat and brown the breast quickly by basting and increasing the oven temperature to 400° F.

Heat the oil and the remaining butter in a casserole and cook the carrot, onion, celery leaves, thyme and bay leaf in it until the vegetables are golden. Add the wine, brandy and stock and simmer, covered, over low heat for 15 minutes.

Put the roast grouse on a hot serving platter and add the pan juices to the sauce. Boil, uncovered, until reduced and of a good flavor. Correct the seasoning and strain the sauce over the bird; serve very hot.

FOR 2 PERSONS:

1 **grouse**	1 **small onion, minced**
Salt	1 **tablespoon minced celery leaves**
Freshly ground black pepper	1 **tablespoon chopped fresh thyme,**
1 **celery stalk, minced**	or ½ **teaspoon dried thyme**
5 **tablespoons butter**	1 **bay leaf**
2 **thin slices of fresh pork fat**	1 **cup dry red wine**
1 **tablespoon peanut oil**	2 **tablespoons brandy**
1 **small carrot, minced**	1 **cup Game Stock (p. 165)**

GROUSE À L'ÉCOSSAISE / *Scotch Grouse*

Pluck, draw, and truss the bird. Bard, that is, wrap it in sheets of fresh pork fat. On top of the stove, heat the butter in a baking pan and brown the grouse in it. Remove from the heat, season with salt, and scatter the pieces of carrot, celery and onion around the grouse. Roast it in the manner described in the preceding recipe, reducing the time slightly if the grouse is very small. Transfer the bird to a hot dish.

Skim the fat off the pan juices and return the grouse to the baking pan. Add the brandy and the whisky and flame. Cover the pan, return it to the oven, and cook for 5 minutes longer.

At serving time, put the fried bread slice in a hot serving dish and lay the grouse on it. Keep hot.

Add the stock to the baking pan, bring it to the boiling point, and boil for 2 minutes; pour the sauce over the bird. Serve immediately with a small sauceboat of bread sauce.

FOR 1 PERSON:

1 small grouse
Thin sheets of fresh pork fat
6 tablespoons butter
Salt
1 small carrot, chopped
1 celery stalk, chopped

1 small onion, chopped
½ cup brandy and whisky combined
1 large slice of bread, fried in butter
½ cup Game Stock (p. 165)
½ recipe Bread Sauce (p. 791)

Roast Larks ./ ALOUETTES RÔTIES

Pluck the larks and truss them without drawing them.

Sauté them in the butter and the fresh pork fat in a casserole over fairly high heat. When they are golden on all sides, remove the trussing strings. Put them in a 350° F. oven and roast them gently until they are done, about 15 minutes. Place them on the fried bread in a hot serving dish.

Skim the fat off the pan juices, stir in the Cognac, bring to the boiling point, and pour over the birds.

FOR 1 PERSON:

4 to 6 larks
1 tablespoon butter
3 tablespoons pork fat

2 slices of bread, fried in butter
2 tablespoons Cognac

Stuffed Roast Larks / ALOUETTES FARCIES RÔTIES

Pluck and draw the larks and stuff them with the following filling: Combine the ground livers, the shallots, parsley, pork and veal; season the mixture with salt, cayenne, nutmeg and 1 tablespoon of the brandy.

Bard the larks, that is, wrap them in the sheets of fresh pork fat and tie them securely. Put them into a baking dish with the butter. Cook them in a preheated 450° F. oven for about 10 minutes and then remove the barding fat. Cook the birds for about 10 minutes longer, or until they are done. Add the wine, meat glaze and remaining brandy; cook for 2 more minutes.

Place the birds on the fried slices of bread in a hot dish and strain the sauce over them.

FOR 6 PERSONS:

24 larks
The livers of the larks, ground fine
3 tablespoons minced shallots
3 tablespoons minced parsley
¾ pound lean pork, ground fine
¼ pound veal, ground fine
Salt

Cayenne pepper
Grated nutmeg
2 tablespoons brandy
Thin sheets of fresh pork fat
1 tablespoon butter
½ cup dry white wine
1 teaspoon meat glaze
6 slices of bread, fried in butter

ORTOLANS AUX PIGNONS / *Ortolans with Pine Nuts*

Season the ortolans with salt and pepper. Bard the birds, that is, wrap each in a slice of fresh pork fat and tie securely. Put them into a buttered baking dish and roast them in a 450° F. oven for about 10 minutes.

Sprinkle the brandy over the birds. Cover the dish, reduce the heat slightly, and roast for a few minutes longer, until done.

Melt the butter and sauté the pine nuts in it until they are golden. Place the ortolans on a hot serving dish and sprinkle the pine nuts over them. Serve at once.

FOR 2 PERSONS:

4 ortolans	1 tablespoon brandy
Salt	3 tablespoons butter
Freshly ground black pepper	30 pine nuts
Thin slices of fresh pork fat	

ESTOUFFADE DE PERDRIX / *Braised Partridge*

Pluck, draw, and truss the birds. Cook the diced pork fat with the butter in a casserole until soft. Add the partridges and sauté them until they are golden on all sides. Add the onions, carrots, garlic, the *bouquet garni,* wine, and game stock. Season with salt and pepper, cover the casserole, and simmer for about 2½ hours.

When the birds are well done, transfer them to a deep skillet. Skim the fat off the sauce, and strain it over the partridges. Simmer for another few minutes before serving.

FOR 2 PERSONS:

2 old partridges	1 Bouquet Garni (p. 46)
¼ pound fresh pork fat, diced	½ bottle dry white wine
2 tablespoons butter	1 cup Game Stock (p. 165)
3 onions, chopped	Salt
3 carrots, chopped	Freshly ground black pepper
1 garlic clove, minced	

/ *Partridge Braised with Cabbage*

PERDRIX AUX CHOUX

Trim the cabbage, cut it into quarters, and blanch it in boiling salted water for 5 minutes. Remove the quarters with a slotted spoon, plunge them into cold water, and drain them in a strainer.

Truss the partridges, rub them with salt and pepper, and put them side by side in a buttered and oiled baking pan. Roast them in a preheated 450° F. oven for 10 minutes. Turn them once during the roasting, so that they may turn golden on all sides.

Transfer the birds to an ovenproof platter, turn off the oven, and keep the birds warm on the platter in the oven, leaving the oven door open so that the birds will not cook further.

Stir the wine and stock into the pan in which the birds were roasted and scrape up any brown bits that may be in the bottom of the pan.

Heat the lard in a large casserole; add the onions, carrots and bacon. Mix and cook for 5 minutes, or until golden. Add the cabbage quarters and the *bouquet garni*. Season with salt and pepper. Pour the pan juices—the wine and stock mixture—over the cabbage and cook, covered, over medium heat for 1½ hours. Stir from time to time; you do not have to be especially careful about this, since the cabbage will become very soft during cooking. After the first hour, add the birds and cover them with part of the cabbage.

At the end of the cooking time, remove the partridges and cut them into halves. Return them to the casserole, let them heat through, and serve them any time you want to.

FOR 4 PERSONS:

1 medium-sized cabbage	½ cup lard
2 young partridges	2 onions, minced
Salt	2 carrots, minced
Freshly ground black pepper	¼ pound bacon, diced
¾ cup dry white wine	1 Bouquet Garni (p. 46)
1½ cups Game Stock (p. 165), or Brown Poultry Stock (p. 164)	

Roast Young Partridge / PERDREAUX RÔTIS

Season the birds with salt and pepper, truss them, wrap each in a sheet of pork fat, and tie the fat on securely. Put the birds into a roasting pan. Sprinkle them with the oil and dot them with the butter. Cook them in a preheated 350° F. oven for about 30 minutes. Remove the strings and the pork fat and keep the birds hot. Fry the bread in the juices remaining in the roasting pan. Put the bread on a hot serving dish and top each slice with a bird.

FOR 4 PERSONS:

4 young partridges	2 tablespoons peanut oil
Salt	2 tablespoons butter
Freshly ground black pepper	4 slices of firm white bread, crusts trimmed off
4 thin sheets of fresh pork fat	

Escabeche of Young Partridge /
PERDREAUX EN ESCABÈCHE

This is a cold dish.

Pluck, draw, and truss the birds. Heat the peanut oil and 3 tablespoons of the olive oil in a casserole, and cook the onions and carrots in it until golden. Add the wine, lemon juice, water, the *bouquet garni*, tomatoes, coriander and peppercorns. Season with salt and cook without a cover for 20 minutes.

Place the birds in a large casserole and pour the hot mixture over them; it should barely cover them. Simmer, covered, for 25 minutes and remove the *bouquet garni*.

Pour birds and pan liquid into a deep serving dish. The birds should be just covered with the liquid. Sprinkle with the remaining olive oil. Chill in the refrigerator for 6 days.

At serving time, remove the birds from their marinade, put them on a platter, and arrange the marinated vegetables around them.

FOR 4 PERSONS:

4 young partridges	1 cup water
3 tablespoons peanut oil	1 Bouquet Garni (p. 46)
6 tablespoons olive oil	4 tomatoes, peeled, seeded and
40 tiny white onions	chopped
1 pound carrots, diced	2 tablespoons coriander seeds
¾ bottle dry white wine	10 peppercorns
Juice of 2 lemons	Salt

PERDREAU MARINÉ / *Marinated Young Partridge*

Draw and clean the bird and split it along the backbone. Spread it open and flatten it with a meat mallet.

In a bowl, combine the garlic, bay leaf, parsley and oil; season with salt and pepper. Marinate the bird in the mixture for 20 minutes.

Drain the bird, and broil or grill it over high heat until golden brown on both sides. Place it in a hot serving dish and sprinkle with the lemon juice. Serve with a sauceboat of *sauce poivrade* or *maître d'hôtel* butter. The dish may be garnished with scored lemon slices.

FOR 1 PERSON:

1 young partridge	Freshly ground black pepper
1 garlic clove, minced	Juice of ½ lemon
1 bay leaf	½ cup Sauce Poivrade (p. 765), or
1 parsley sprig	¼ cup Maître d'Hôtel Butter
½ cup olive oil	(p. 794)
Salt	

PERDREAU À LA NORMANDE / *Partridge Normande*

Season the bird with salt and pepper and truss it. Sauté it in 4 tablespoons of the butter in a skillet over fairly high heat until golden on all sides. Split the bird lengthwise into halves.

Heat the remaining butter in a casserole and cook the apple in it until golden. Top with the partridge halves and sprinkle with the *crème fraîche* and the Calvados.

Cover the casserole and cook in a preheated 350° F. oven for about 30 minutes.

FOR 1 PERSON:

1 young partridge	1 large tart apple, cored and minced
Salt	2 tablespoons Crème Fraîche (p. 666)
Freshly ground black pepper	¼ cup Calvados
7 tablespoons butter	

FAISAN AUX POMMES / *Pheasant with Apples*

Truss and bard the pheasant, that is, wrap it in the sheets of fresh pork fat.

Heat the butter in a casserole over fairly high heat and brown the pheasant in it on all sides. Season the bird with salt and pepper, reduce the heat, cover, and simmer for 25 minutes. Add the apples, and cook until the apples are golden. **Then add the** *crème fraîche*. Simmer, covered, for 25 more minutes. A few minutes before the bird is done remove the fresh pork fat.

Add the Calvados at serving time and serve the pheasant in the same dish.

FOR 4 PERSONS:

1 pheasant	Freshly ground black pepper
Thin sheets of fresh pork fat	1 pound tart apples, peeled and sliced
4 tablespoons butter	1 cup Crème Fraîche (p. 666)
Salt	¼ cup Calvados

Braised Pheasant / FAISAN EN COCOTTE

Season the pheasant with salt and pepper and truss it. Bard it, that is, wrap it in the fresh pork fat, and brown it on all sides in the butter in a casserole over fairly high heat. Reduce the heat, cover the casserole, and simmer for about 45 minutes.

After 30 minutes of cooking time, remove the barding fat and add the onions, the mushrooms and the truffles. Serve in the casserole.

FOR 4 PERSONS:

1 pheasant	20 tiny white onions, browned in
Salt	butter
Freshly ground black pepper	½ pound mushrooms, browned in
Thin sheets of fresh pork fat	butter
4 tablespoons butter	3 truffles, diced

Casserole of Pheasant / FAISAN EN CASSEROLE

Draw, clean, and truss the pheasant; season it with salt and pepper and bard it, that is, wrap it in the sheets of fresh pork fat. Sauté it in 4 tablespoons of the butter in a casserole over fairly high heat until golden on all sides.

Cover the casserole, reduce the heat, and simmer for about 45 minutes. About 10 minutes before the bird is cooked remove the barding fat.

Remove the bird and skim the fat off the pan juices. Return the pheasant to the casserole, add the Cognac, and flame. Add the sherry, cover the casserole, and simmer for about 5 minutes.

Put the pheasant on a hot serving dish. Add the stock to the pan juices and bring to the boiling point; cook for 2 minutes. Stir in the remaining butter; when it **is** melted, pour the sauce over the pheasant.

FOR 4 PERSONS

1 pheasant	¼ cup Cognac
Salt	¼ cup sherry
Freshly ground black pepper	½ cup Game Stock (p. 165), or
Thin sheets of fresh pork fat	Brown Stock (p. 164)
6 tablespoons butter	

FAISAN EN DAUBE EN GELÉE | *Daube of Pheasant in Aspic*

Bone the pheasant completely, saving the bones and trimmings for the stock.

Prepare the stock in the usual way (see p. 165). There should be about 8 cups.

Spread the pheasant out on a chopping board, skin side down. Season it with a little salt and pepper and the thyme and crumbled bay leaf.

Make the stuffing by combining the ground pork, pork fat and veal. Season the mixture with salt, cayenne and brandy. Spread this filling on the pheasant and dot with the truffles and *foie gras*. Roll up the bird, reshaping it in its original form, and sew it closed with string. Put it into an oval casserole with the veal knuckles and add the stock. The stock should barely cover the pheasant. Cover the casserole and seal the cover with a band of flour and water paste. Cook in a preheated 325° F. oven for about 2 hours. Remove the cover and discard the veal knuckles.

Cool the pheasant in the cooking liquid and refrigerate for 12 hours. Unmold it on a cold platter at serving time.

FOR 4 PERSONS:

1 pheasant
For the stock:
  The bones and trimmings of
    the pheasant
  2 veal knuckles, cracked
  2 carrots, sliced
  2 onions, sliced
  2 celery stalks, sliced
  1 Bouquet Garni (p. 46)
  5 juniper berries
  1 cup dry white wine
  2 quarts water
Salt
Freshly ground black pepper

1 tablespoon chopped fresh thyme,
  or ½ teaspoon dried thyme
1 bay leaf, crumbled
¼ pound lean pork, finely ground
⅛ pound fresh pork fat, finely
  ground
¼ pound veal, finely ground
Cayenne pepper
1 tablespoon brandy
4 truffles, cut into small dice
¼ pound foie gras, cut into
  small dice
2 veal knuckles
Flour and water paste

FAISAN À LA MODE DE GASCOGNE | *Pheasant à la Gascogne*

Draw the bird and, if desired, remove the breast bone.

Sauté the chicken livers in half of the butter over medium heat for about 5 minutes. Season them with salt and pepper, drain them, and put them into a bowl with ½ cup of the port wine. Let them stand for 20 minutes, then force both chicken livers and port through a fine sieve, or purée in a blender. Cut three of the truffles into small dice and add them to the mixture.

Stuff the bird with the mixture, truss it, and put it into a deep bowl with the remaining port. Let it marinate in a cool place for 3 days, turning it occasionally.

Drain the pheasant, reserving the marinade, and dry it with a kitchen cloth. Bard it, that is, wrap it in the sheets of fresh pork fat, and brown it in the remaining butter in a casserole until golden on all sides. Season the bird with salt and pepper, reduce the heat and simmer, covered, for 1 hour. Reduce the port of the marinade by half and pour it over the pheasant when it has cooked for 30 minutes, At the same time, add the remaining truffles.

About 15 minutes before the pheasant is done, remove the barding fat. Serve the pheasant in the casserole.

FOR 4 PERSONS:

1 pheasant	**Freshly ground black pepper**
1 pound chicken livers	**½ bottle dry port wine**
½ cup butter	**6 truffles, minced**
Salt	**Thin sheets of fresh pork fat**

Salmi of Plover / SALMIS DE VANNEAUX

Plucked and drawn, a plover is the size of a pretty turtle dove.

The bony sinewy wing tips of a plover are usually trimmed off and discarded. The innards are also usually discarded, although one may keep the heart and the liver, but they will not add much to this dish. The bird is usually drawn and the neck and the feet removed. It cannot be trussed.

First heat 4 tablespoons of the lard in a shallow casserole and, over high heat, brown the birds in it for a minute or two. Transfer them to a preheated 375° F. oven and roast for about 20 minutes. Flame the birds with the Armagnac and set aside. (There is always the risk that the birds may have a fishy taste; flaming with Armagnac helps eliminate this taste.)

Now make the sauce: Heat the oil and butter in a casserole and cook the onion, carrot, leek, celery and turnip in it until they are golden. Stir in the flour and cook for 2 minutes; add the wine, the sugar and the *bouquet garni*. Cook for about 1 hour, or until well reduced and of a good flavor.

Heat the remaining lard in a casserole and add the bacon strips, the tiny onions and mushroom caps (4 or 5 of each for each bird); stir until they are golden. Lower the heat and simmer, covered, for about 5 minutes, or until they are soft, and then season with salt and pepper.

Put the birds in the casserole and strain the sauce over them. Bring to the boiling point and simmer, covered, over low heat until the birds are almost overcooked, that is, when a leg will come off easily when pulled.

If you kept the livers, mash them with the softened butter and the vinegar. Stir this mixture into the sauce just before serving. If you did not keep the livers, use 3 chicken livers.

FOR 1 PERSON:

2 or 3 plovers	**1 bottle dry red wine**
6 tablespoons lard	**3 lumps of sugar**
2 tablespoons Armagnac	**1 large Bouquet Garni (p. 46)**
1 tablespoon peanut oil	**4 slices of bacon, cut into small**
2 tablespoons butter	**strips and blanched**
1 medium-sized onion, chopped	**12 to 16 tiny white onions**
1 carrot, chopped	**12 to 16 small mushroom caps**
1 leek, white and green part,	**Salt**
chopped	**Freshly ground black pepper**
1 celery stalk with leaves,	**The 3 plover livers, or 3 chicken**
chopped	**livers**
½ turnip, chopped	**2 tablespoons butter, softened**
2 tablespoons flour	**1 teaspoon vinegar**

CAILLES CHASSEUR / *Quail Chasseur*

Season the quails with salt and pepper and truss them; sauté them in the butter in a casserole over high heat until golden on all sides. Sprinkle the birds with the flour and turn them for 1 more minute. Reduce the heat and add the bay leaf, thyme, stock and wine. Bring to a boil.

Simmer, covered, for 10 minutes. Put the birds on a hot serving dish and pour the pan juices over them. Serve very hot.

FOR 2 PERSONS:

4 quails
Salt
Freshly ground black pepper
6 tablespoons butter
1 tablespoon flour
½ bay leaf, crumbled

1 tablespoon chopped fresh thyme,
  or ½ teaspoon dried thyme
½ cup Game Stock (p. 165), or
  Brown Stock (p. 164)
½ cup dry white wine

CAILLES GRILLÉES / *Grilled Quail*

Split the birds open, and flatten them a little.

Heat the oil and the butter in a casserole and brown the birds in it. Add the bay leaf, season with salt and pepper, cover the birds with the sheets of pork fat, and simmer for about 5 minutes.

Remove the quails. Dip them into the bread crumbs, broil or grill them for about 3 minutes on each side, and put them on a hot serving dish. Add the stock to the pan juices in the casserole, bring to the boiling point, and strain the sauce into a sauceboat.

FOR 1 PERSON:

2 quails
1 tablespoon peanut oil
3 tablespoons butter
½ bay leaf
Salt

Freshly ground black pepper
Thin sheets of fresh pork fat
1 cup bread crumbs
½ cup Game Stock (p. 165), or
  Brown Stock (p. 164)

CAILLE EN CAISSE / *Potted Quail*

Pluck, draw, and bone the quails, reserving the bones. Marinate the meat in a mixture of the thyme, a little salt and pepper, 2 tablespoons of the brandy and the port for 1 hour; the marinade should cover the meat.

Heat the butter and the goose fat in a casserole and add the bones of the quails, the onion, carrot, celery, leek, parsley and tarragon; cook until the vegetables are golden.

Make a stuffing with the ground pork, ham and veal and season it with salt, cayenne and the remaining brandy.

Drain the quails, dry them with a kitchen cloth, and stuff them. Re-form them into their original shape and sew them closed. Wrap them in sheets of fresh pork fat and tie with string.

Put the birds on the vegetables in the casserole. Add the stock and the wine and bring to a boil.

Cook over high heat, basting frequently, for about 15 minutes. After about 10 minutes of cooking time, remove the pork fat and let the birds turn golden.

Cool the quails in the casserole. Then put them into a little porcelain casserole. Strain the pan liquid and clarify it with the egg white. Pour the liquid over the quails and chill.

FOR 1 PERSON:

2 quails
1 tablespoon chopped fresh thyme, or ½ teaspoon dried thyme
Salt
Freshly ground black pepper
4 tablespoons brandy
1 cup port
2 tablespoons butter
1 tablespoon goose fat
1 onion, chopped
1 carrot, chopped
1 celery stalk, chopped

1 leek, chopped
3 parsley sprigs
3 tarragon sprigs
⅛ pound lean pork, ground fine
⅛ pound fat ham, ground fine
⅛ pound veal, ground fine
Cayenne pepper
Thin sheets of fresh pork fat
1 cup Game Stock (p. 165), or Brown Stock (p. 164)
1 cup Sauternes
1 egg white

Snipe with Champagne / BÉCASSE AU CHAMPAGNE

Pluck the snipe without drawing it and bard it, that is, wrap it completely in the sheets of fresh pork fat and tie securely. Season with salt and pepper and cook it in a deep skillet over high heat for 10 minutes, turning it frequently. Carve off the meat and keep it warm on a hot plate.

Remove the gizzard from the bird's innards and discard it. Put the innards on a plate and mash them with a fork. Crush the bones in a press or with a meat mallet and strain the resulting juices through a sieve. In a small saucepan, reduce the champagne by half and add the mashed innards, the juices from the bones, the butter, *foie gras* and truffles.

Season the sauce with salt, pepper and a little paprika. Simmer it over low heat for 5 minutes, stirring constantly. When the sauce is smooth, pour it over the meat.

You may serve the meat on a bread crouton fried in goose fat or butter and spread with *foie gras*.

FOR 1 PERSON:

1 snipe
1 or more sheets of fresh pork fat
Salt
Freshly ground black pepper
1 cup champagne
2 tablespoons butter

2 tablespoons foie gras, diced
2 truffles, diced
Paprika
Optional: A fried bread crouton, spread with foie gras

Snipe Pie / TOURTE DE BÉCASSES

Skin the snipe and remove all of the meat from the bones, keeping the breast meat separate. Mince all the other meat, the innards, the veal and the pork and grind them, using the fine blade of a meat grinder. Season with salt, pepper and cayenne to taste and add the brandy.

Prepare the piecrust by rolling out 2 rounds of puff paste about ⅛ inch thick. One round should be ½ inch larger than the other.

Put the smaller round of puff paste on a baking sheet. Put half of the ground meat stuffing in the middle. Sandwich each pair of breast halves with truffle slices and a slice of *foie gras*. Lay the breasts on top of the stuffing; cover them with the remaining stuffing and then with the remaining pastry round. Wet the pastry edges and pinch them together.

With the point of a sharp knife, score an outline of diamonds on the top and cut out a small round in the center. Paint with the beaten egg yolk. Bake in a preheated 350° F. oven for 35 minutes.

Serve very hot, with the *sauce Périgueux* on the side.

FOR 4 PERSONS:

6 snipe	1 teaspoon brandy
¼ pound boneless veal	½ recipe Puff Paste (p. 715)
¼ pound lean boneless pork	2 truffles, sliced
Salt	6 slices of foie gras
Freshly ground black pepper	1 egg yolk
Cayenne pepper	1 cup Sauce Périgueux (p. 765)

BÉCASSE À LA BROCHE / *Spitted Snipe*

Do not draw the plucked snipe, but bard it, that is, wrap it in the sheets of fresh pork fat and tie them. Fry the bread slices in the goose fat and then rub each slice with the garlic.

Roast the snipe on a spit over a good fire, or use a rotisserie. Place a dripping pan under the spit, and put the two bread slices into the dripping pan, so that the juices from the roasting bird will fall on the bread.

The snipe is cooked when its interior juices start flowing, that is, in about 15 minutes. Remove it from the spit. Remove the pork fat and the innards. Throw away the gizzard, but mince the other innards and spread them on the fingers of toasted bread fried in butter or goose fat. Season them with salt and pepper. Fry these bread slices again, spread side down, in a little butter or goose fat. Put the snipe on a very hot dish, and flame it with the rum. Cut it into halves and put each half on a slice of the bread that absorbed the bird's cooking juices. Garnish with the bread fingers and serve immediately.

FOR 1 PERSON:

1 snipe	6 fingers of toasted bread, fried
1 or more sheets of fresh pork fat	in butter or goose fat
2 thick slices of bread, trimmed free	Salt
of crusts	Freshly ground black pepper
2 tablespoons goose fat	3 tablespoons butter, or goose fat
1 garlic clove	2 tablespoons rum

BÉCASSE FARCIE / *Stuffed Snipe*

Pluck and draw the snipe. Discard the gizzard; mince the rest of the innards and combine them with the salt pork, the parsley, chives, egg yolk, and salt and pepper to taste. Stuff the bird with this mixture, sew it closed, and truss it.

Line the bottom of a casserole with a sheet of fresh pork fat and put the bird in the middle. Cover the bird with another sheet of pork fat. Cook it over medium heat for 15 minutes.

Add the stock and the wine; season with salt and pepper, bring to a boil and simmer, covered, for 10 minutes.

Put the snipe on a hot serving plate. Remove the pork fat from the casserole, skim the fat off the pan juices, and add the vinegar. Bring to the boiling point and cook for about 5 minutes. Strain the sauce over the bird.

FOR 1 PERSON:

1 snipe	Freshly ground black pepper
2 ounces salt pork, minced and blanched	2 or more thin slices of fresh pork fat
1 tablespoon minced parsley	¾ cup Game Stock (p. 165)
1 teaspoon minced chives	¼ cup dry white wine
1 egg yolk	2 tablespoons wine vinegar
Salt	

Thrush Canapé / GRIVE SUR CANAPÉ

Truss and bard the bird, that is, wrap it in the fresh pork fat. Sauté the bird in the hot butter in a skillet over high heat until it is golden on all sides. Reduce the heat and sauté for another 5 to 10 minutes.

Mince the bird's liver with the *foie gras* and blend them together. Season with salt and pepper and add the brandy. Spread the fried bread with this mixture and broil for about 2 minutes. Lay the thrush on the bread and serve immediately.

FOR 1 PERSON:

1 thrush	Freshly ground black pepper
Thin slices of fresh pork fat	1 teaspoon brandy
3 tablespoons butter	1 slice of firm white bread, fried in butter
2 tablespoons foie gras	
Salt	

Salmi of Wild Doves / SALMIS DE PALOMBES

Pluck, draw, and truss the doves. Reserve the hearts and livers. Heat the fresh pork fat in a casserole and turn the doves in it until they are golden on all sides. Season them with salt and pepper to taste; sprinkle with the Armagnac and flame. Transfer the doves to a hot dish and keep them warm.

Put the salt-pork or the ham-fat dice into the casserole and cook them until they are very soft and transparent. Then add the shallots, the onions and the garlic. Stir with a wooden spoon and cook until golden. Remove most of the liquid fat from the casserole and stir in the flour. Add the wine, stir well, and bring to a boil. Add the doves and the *bouquet garni*. Season with salt and pepper, cover the casserole, and simmer for 1½ hours.

Mince the raw hearts and livers; season them with salt, pepper and nutmeg and stir in the rum.

Fry the bread slices in the oil and butter or in goose fat. Spread them with the minced hearts and livers. Cook them, spread side down, in the hot fat for about 2 minutes to crust them, or run them under a hot broiler. Cut the slices into halves.

When the doves are ready, split them into halves. Put the fried bread slices on a hot serving platter and top each with half a dove. Remove the *bouquet garni* from the sauce and sprinkle the sauce over the doves. Serve very hot.

FOR 4 PERSONS:

2 wild doves
¼ pound fresh pork fat, chopped
Salt
Freshly ground black pepper
2 tablespoons Armagnac
¼ pound salt pork, blanched and diced, or prosciutto fat, diced
6 shallots, minced
20 tiny onions, 4 of them stuck with 1 clove each
1 garlic clove, minced

2 tablespoons flour
½ bottle dry red wine
1 Bouquet Garni (p. 46)
Grated nutmeg
1 tablespoon rum
2 slices of firm white bread, trimmed of crusts
2 tablespoons each of peanut oil and butter, or 4 tablespoons goose fat

CANARD SAUVAGE AUX POMMES / *Wild Duck with Apples*

Make a good applesauce, flavoring it with nutmeg, cinnamon and just a pinch of sugar. It must be very thick, with most of its liquid evaporated. Stuff the duck with the applesauce and sew it closed so that the applesauce won't ooze out during cooking. Rub the bird with salt and pepper. Roast the bird in a preheated 375° F. oven, allowing 12 to 15 minutes a pound.

Combine the vinegar, butter, ½ teaspoon sugar and the crushed peppercorns in a saucepan. Bring the mixture to the boiling point and use it to baste the duck frequently while it is roasting.

Put the cooked bird on a hot serving dish. Stir the apple jelly into the pan juices and coat the bird with this sauce. Serve immediately with a side dish of the apples sautéed in butter.

FOR 2 PERSONS:

2 (or more) cups applesauce
Grated nutmeg
Ground cinnamon
Sugar
1 wild duck
Salt
Freshly ground black pepper

3 tablespoons vinegar
3 tablespoons butter
½ teaspoon sugar
4 peppercorns, crushed
½ cup apple jelly
½ recipe Apples Sautéed in Butter (p. 542)

SALMIS DE CANARD SAUVAGE / *Salmi of Wild Duck*

Season the cavities of the ducks with salt and pepper. Truss the birds and put them in a casserole with 2 tablespoons each of the oil and butter. Brown them on all sides and then cook them, covered, over low heat for 30 minutes. The meat should still be *saignant,* or rare.

Carve the meat off the birds and chop up the carcasses. Add 1 more tablespoon each of oil and butter to the casserole in which the birds were cooked, together with the onion, shallots and carrot. Stir and cook until golden; then add the chopped carcasses. Mix well and add the white wine, water and Madeira. Season lightly with salt and pepper and add the parsley, thyme and bay leaf.

Cook over high heat, without a cover, for 30 minutes, so that the pan juices are well reduced. Make a brown *roux* (see p. 151), that is, heat the remaining 2 tablespoons of butter in a casserole until it turns brown and stir in the flour. Cook until the flour is brown and then strain the pan juices into the *roux*. Blend thoroughly and simmer for 15 minutes. Check the seasoning; add the minced duck livers and the sliced duck meat.

Simmer over very low heat for about 10 minutes, without allowing it to boil, until the meat is heated through. Serve in a hot dish and garnish with the fried croutons.

FOR 6 PERSONS:

2 **wild ducks**	3 **tablespoons Madeira**
Salt	1 **parsley sprig**
Freshly ground black pepper	1 **thyme sprig, or ½ teaspoon**
3 **tablespoons peanut oil**	**dried thyme**
5 **tablespoons butter**	½ **bay leaf**
1 **onion, minced**	2 **tablespoons flour**
3 **shallots, minced**	**The duck livers, minced and mixed**
1 **carrot, minced**	**with 3 tablespoons Madeira**
1½ **cups dry white wine**	6 **large Croutons of white bread**
1½ **cups water**	**(p. 62), fried in butter**

FURRED GAME

Gibiers à Poil

Roast Hare à l'Anglaise | LIÈVRE RÔTI À L'ANGLAISE

Skin the hare, split it open lengthwise, remove the innards, and cut off the head, tail and tips of the paws.

Make a stuffing by combining the salt pork, the fresh pork and the mushrooms. Put this stuffing into a casserole and cook it over low heat for about 5 minutes. Beat in the egg and cream mixture off the heat. Season with salt and pepper to taste, mix thoroughly, and cool.

Stuff the hare with the mixture and sew the cavity closed. Rub the hare with salt and pepper and wrap it in a pig's caul. Roast it on a spit over coals or in a rotisserie for about 1 hour, or roast in a preheated 350° F. oven for about 1½ hours, or until tender. Serve it with red-currant jelly.

FOR 4 PERSONS:

1 young hare	1 egg, beaten with 2 tablespoons
⅓ pound salt pork, diced	Crème Fraîche (p. 666)
and blanched	Salt
⅓ pound lean fresh pork, ground	Freshly ground black pepper
¼ pound mushrooms, cooked briefly	1 large pig's caul
in 3 tablespoons butter and then	1 cup red-currant jelly
minced	

LIÈVRE GRILLÉ À LA BROCHE / *Hare Roasted on a Spit*

Cut off the front part of the hare, leaving only the saddle and the thighs. Reserve the front section for another use.

Marinate the meat with the onion, carrot, thyme, bay leaves, parsley, a little pepper, the salt and the vinegar in a bowl (do not use aluminum) for 24 hours. Drain the hare, dry it, and lard it with the lardoons of salt pork. Truss it and then roast on a spit over live coals or in a rotisserie for about 45 minutes.

Serve with the horseradish sauce.

FOR 4 PERSONS:

1 young hare	Freshly ground black pepper
1 onion, sliced	1 teaspoon salt
1 carrot, sliced	1 cup wine vinegar
1 sprig of fresh thyme, or	¼ pound salt pork, cut into strips or
½ teaspoon dried thyme	lardoons
2 bay leaves	1 cup Horseradish Sauce I (p. 790)
1 parsley sprig	

CIVET DE LIÈVRE SAINT-HUBERT / *Jugged Hare Saint-Hubert*

Skin a freshly killed hare, draw it, and reserve the blood and the liver, but do not forget to remove the gall pocket from the liver. Mince the liver and mix it with the blood and ¼ cup of the white wine to keep the blood from coagulating. Cut the hare into pieces and marinate them in a marinade composed of the sliced onions and carrots, the peppercorns, cloves, shallots, parsley, thyme, rosemary, bay leaf, a little coarse salt, the remaining white wine and the marc or brandy for 24 hours.

Drain the hare pieces and dry them. Reserve the marinade. Heat the oil and butter in a large skillet and sauté the hare pieces over high heat until golden brown on all sides. Flame them with the brandy and remove them from the heat.

Bring the marinade to a boil in a large saucepan.

Heat the bacon pieces in a large enamelware casserole, and add the tiny onions. Stir until they begin to turn golden and then stir in the flour. Add the red wine, the hot strained marinade, the sugar and the *bouquet garni*. Bring to a boil and add the hare pieces. Season with salt and pepper. Simmer, covered, over low heat for 2½ hours.

Remove the *bouquet garni* and add the mushrooms and the blood with the minced liver. Mix gently. Simmer, covered, over the lowest possible heat for 1 more hour.

FOR 8 PERSONS:

1 large hare	3 tablespoons peanut oil
1½ cups dry white wine	3 tablespoons butter
2 onions, sliced	¼ cup brandy
2 carrots, sliced	6 slices of bacon, cut into pieces
25 peppercorns	50 tiny white onions
3 whole cloves	2 tablespoons flour
4 shallots, minced	1 cup dry red wine
2 parsley sprigs	1 teaspoon sugar
½ teaspoon dried thyme	1 Bouquet Garni (p. 46)
1 teaspoon dried rosemary	Salt
1 bay leaf	Freshly ground black pepper
Coarse (Kosher) salt	50 small mushroom caps, sautéed
½ cup marc or brandy	in butter

Jugged Hare Bordelaise / CIVET DE LIÈVRE À LA BORDELAISE

Proceed as in Jugged Hare Saint-Hubert (above), but add to the sauce 1 cup Crème Fraîche (p. 666) about 3 minutes before serving time. Serve with Cèpes Bordelaise (p. 601).

Hare Cutlets in Cream / CÔTELETTES DE LIÈVRE À LA CRÈME

Remove all of the meat from the bones of the hare, keeping the loin meat separate. Cut each loin into 2 cutlets. Flatten the cutlets slightly with the flat side of a cleaver or a meat mallet and marinate them with the onions, carrots, peppercorns, cloves, half of the minced shallots, the thyme, parsley, rosemary, bay leaf, a little coarse salt, the wine and the marc or brandy in a bowl (do not use aluminum) for 24 hours.

Grind the remaining meat together with half of the *foie gras* and all of the pork, using the finest blade of a meat grinder. Mix well, and season this stuffing with salt and pepper to taste.

Drain and dry the cutlets. Spread out the 4 pieces of pig's caul and fill the center of each with a thin layer of stuffing. Top the stuffing with one of the cutlets, a thin slice of the remaining *foie gras*, and a slice of truffle; cover with another thin layer of stuffing. Roll up each sheet of pig's caul and tie securely.

Heat the oil and butter in a casserole and, over high heat, sauté the wrapped cutlets until they are golden on all sides. Transfer the casserole to a preheated 325° F. oven for 45 minutes. Remove the casserole from the oven, put the cutlets on a hot dish, and keep them warm.

Add the remaining minced shallots to the casserole and sauté until they are soft. Return the cutlets to the skillet and flame them with the brandy. Remove them again to a hot serving dish, discard the strings, and keep them warm. Stir the *crème fraîche*, the *sauce poivrade* and the remaining *foie gras*, diced, into the casserole. Check the seasoning and strain the sauce over the cutlets. Serve with a purée of chestnuts.

FOR 4 PERSONS:

1 small young hare	½ pound foie gras
2 onions, sliced	¼ pound lean boneless pork
2 carrots, sliced	Salt
6 peppercorns	Freshly ground black pepper
3 whole cloves	4 pieces of pig's caul
4 shallots, minced	4 truffle slices
½ teaspoon dried thyme	2 tablespoons peanut oil
2 parsley sprigs	2 tablespoons butter
1 teaspoon dried rosemary	2 tablespoons brandy
1 bay leaf	1 cup Crème Fraîche (p. 666)
Coarse (Kosher) salt	1 cup Sauce Poivrade (p. 765)
½ bottle dry red wine	1 recipe Chestnut Purée (p. 582)
2 tablespoons marc or brandy	

LIÈVRE À LA ROYALE I / *Hare à la Royale I*

Marinate the fresh goose livers in the brandy, port wine, *quatre épices* and cayenne in a deep bowl (do not use aluminum) for 8 days. Turn the livers each day and baste them. The livers must not have been trimmed free of the sinews nor soaked in salted water.

Take a young hare which has been killed in a suitable manner, that is, through the head or the rib cage. Skin it, cut it open lengthwise, and remove the insides. Reserve the liver (discard the gall bladder) and the heart. Save the blood and pour it into a bowl with the vinegar to keep the blood from coagulating. Wash out the hare's cavity with dry red wine.

Cut off the head, the tail and the paws. Bone the hare with a fine sharp knife, keeping the body in one piece. Be careful not to pierce the skin, and you may leave a little meat on the bones.

Spread out the boned hare, back side down, on a board. Season lightly with salt, pepper, nutmeg and the thyme. Sprinkle with the Cognac. Roll up the meat and chill in the refrigerator for 12 to 18 hours.

Make a *sauce poivrade*: heat the ham fat and the butter; add the hare's bones, venison bones, onion, carrots and celery; cook them until they are golden. Stir in the Pomerol and the Sauternes wines. Add also a ham bone and simmer, covered, for 3 hours.

Make the following stuffing: using the finest blade of the meat grinder, grind together the chicken livers, the prosciutto and the pork; season the mixture with salt and cayenne and just enough of the marinade from the goose livers to make a loose mixture. Chill the mixture in an uncovered bowl in the refrigerator.

On the day on which the hare is to be eaten, heat the goose fat in a casserole and in it sauté the onion stuck with 3 cloves until it is golden on all sides. Add the goose livers and the marinade; season with salt, cover, and cook in a preheated 400° F. oven for 7 to 8 minutes. Remove from the oven, cool, and then skim off the fat.

Put a good-sized linen cloth rinsed in cold water (to remove any trace of soap or detergent flavor) on a board. Lay the sheets of pork fat (or even better, use ham fat) in the center of the cloth and then lay the boned hare on top.

Place the truffles and the goose livers on the hare, and cover them with the stuffing.

Roll up the hare in the shape of a *ballottine* (or large sausage), completely cover with the sheets of fresh pork fat, and then roll in the linen cloth. Tie both ends with string.

Put the roll into a large casserole and strain the *sauce poivrade* over it. Add sufficient game stock to cover the *ballottine* completely. Bring to the boiling point and then simmer, covered, for 2½ hours. Drain it and cool it; remove the linen cloth and wash it out in lukewarm water. Roll up the hare in the cloth once more and tie it, and put it on a long serving dish. Top it with a board of the same length, weigh down the board with a ½-pound weight, and let it cool like this for 1 to 2 hours, or until shortly before serving time.

Skim the fat off the sauce, strain the sauce twice, and put it into a casserole. Reduce it slowly to about 4 cups. Check the seasoning. Mash the hare's heart and liver and add them to the reserved hare's blood. Stir this mixture into the reduced sauce. Strain the sauce again twice and keep it warm.

Remove the hare from its cloth wrapping and heat it gently in the Madeira and brandy in a big casserole.

While the hare is heating, force the *foie gras* through a fine sieve. Add the *crème fraîche* and stir the mixture into the strained sauce. Reheat gently and keep hot.

When the hare *ballottine* is heated through, remove the sheets of fresh pork fat and put the roll into a deep hot serving dish. Skim the fat off its pan juices and strain them into the sauce. Bring the sauce to the boiling point and pour it over the hare.

Carve the *ballottine* into thick slices, serve 1 slice to each person, and coat generously with the sauce.

FOR 8 PERSONS:

2 fresh 1-pound goose livers
¼ cup brandy
½ bottle port wine
½ teaspoon Quatre Épices (p. 667)
Pinch of cayenne pepper
1 young hare
2 tablespoons vinegar
1 cup dry red wine
Salt
Freshly ground black pepper
Grated nutmeg
½ teaspoon dried thyme
1 tablespoon Cognac

For the Sauce Poivrade:
  ¼ cup ham fat, minced
  2 tablespoons butter
  2 pounds venison bones
  1 medium-sized onion, minced
  2 carrots, minced
  2 celery hearts, minced
  3 bottles Pomerol, or another
    good dry red wine
  1 bottle Sauternes
  1 ham bone

For the stuffing:
  ½ cup chicken livers
  ⅓ pound prosciutto, fat and lean
  ⅓ pound loin of pork without fat
  Salt
  Cayenne pepper

¼ cup goose fat
1 onion, stuck with 3 cloves
Several sheets of fresh pork fat, or
  ham fat
½ pound truffles, thickly sliced
1 quart (or more) Game Stock
  (p. 165)
½ cup Madeira, mixed with 2
  tablespoons brandy
½ pound foie gras
1 cup Crème Fraîche (p. 666)

LIÈVRE À LA ROYALE II / *Hare à la Royale II*

Here is another way of preparing hare *à la royale,* simpler than the first method.

Skin and draw the hare. Reserve the blood and put it into a bowl with the vinegar to keep it from coagulating; reserve the heart, liver, lungs and kidneys; cut off the tail, the head and the tips of the paws, and reserve them.

Bone the hare completely, splitting it along its underside, but being careful not to pierce the skin.

Make a stuffing by mincing together half of the hare's liver, heart and lungs, and all of the veal, pork, ham fat, chicken livers and *foie gras.* Grind the mixture, using the finest blade of a meat grinder, and season it lightly with salt and pepper, the *quatre épices* and half of the brandy.

Lay the hare out flat, skin side down, on a board and put the hare's kidneys in the center. Spread the stuffing evenly over the exposed meat and then form the whole thing into a long roll, or *ballottine.* Wrap the roll in the sheets of fresh pork fat so that it is completely covered. Tie it securely so that it will hold its shape and no stuffing can escape.

Put the hare into a large casserole spread with the goose fat. Arrange around the hare the coarsely chopped onions, the whole carrots, the garlic cloves, the peeled whole shallots, the *bouquet garni,* the celery heart, the hare's bones as well as its head (split lengthwise), the tail and the tips of the paws. Season lightly with salt. Add the remaining brandy and enough red wine to cover the roll completely. Cover the casserole and simmer over low heat for 2 hours.

Remove the roll from the casserole and discard the string and the sheets of pork fat. Put it into another casserole or terrine, cover it, and keep it warm over the lowest possible heat.

Strain the sauce first through a colander and then through a very fine sieve. Pour it into a saucepan and reduce it to about 3 cups. Mash the remaining liver, heart and lungs of the hare and mix together with the reserved blood. Add 2 tablespoons of the boiling sauce and then stir the mixture into the sauce. Bring back to the boiling point and simmer for about 3 minutes. Correct the seasoning. Pour the sauce over the roll, cover the casserole, and simmer over very low heat for 30 minutes. Serve from the casserole.

FOR 6 PERSONS:

1 young hare	Several thin sheets of fresh pork fat
1 tablespoon vinegar	3 tablespoons goose fat or lard
⅓ pound boneless veal, ground	4 onions, chopped
⅓ pound boneless lean pork, ground	4 carrots
⅓ pound prosciutto (or smoked Virginia ham) fat, minced	20 whole garlic cloves
¼ pound chicken livers	40 whole shallots, peeled
¼ pound foie gras	1 Bouquet Garni (p. 46)
Salt	1 celery heart
Freshly ground black pepper	8 (or more) cups dry red wine
½ teaspoon Quatre Épices (p. 667)	
¼ cup brandy	

Saddle of Hare Sauce Poivrade /
RÂBLE DE LIÈVRE SAUCE POIVRADE

Prepare generally in the same manner as Saddle of Venison Grand Veneur (p. 537), but roast the saddle of hare for a shorter time, since it will naturally be much smaller.

Saddle of Hare Saupiquet / RÂBLE DE LIÈVRE SAUPIQUET

Mince the hare's liver, combine it with the blood, and stir in the lemon juice.

Rub the saddle of hare with salt and pepper and wrap it in the sheets of fresh pork fat. Heat the oil and half of the butter in a casserole over high heat and cook the saddle of hare in it until it is golden on all sides. Cover the casserole and place it in a preheated 425° F. oven for about 15 minutes. Remove the sheets of pork fat to let the meat brown and continue roasting for another 5 minutes.

Cook the shallots in the remaining butter in another casserole, until they are very soft but still white. Stir in the vinegar. Bring to the boiling point and cook until the vinegar has evaporated. Season with a little salt and a good amount of pepper; add a *bouquet garni* and the wine. Simmer for 15 minutes. Add the reserved blood and liver and cook for 1 minute longer. Remove from the heat and stir in the softened butter.

The sauce should be ready at the same time as the meat. Put the roasted saddle on a hot serving dish, pour the sauce over it, and serve immediately.

FOR 2 PERSONS:

The liver and blood from a hare	**4 tablespoons butter**
1 teaspoon lemon juice	**2 tablespoons minced shallots**
1 small saddle (loin) of hare	**½ cup wine vinegar**
Salt	**1 Bouquet Garni (p. 46)**
Freshly ground black pepper	**½ cup dry red wine**
Thin sheets of fresh pork fat	**2 tablespoons softened butter**
2 tablespoons peanut oil	

Stuffed Hare Legs Saint-Hubert /
CUISSES DE LIÈVRE FARCIES SAINT-HUBERT

Cut off the hares' legs, bone them, but leave in the very tip end of the bones. Be careful to remove all the sinews. Marinate the legs with the sliced onions and carrots, the peppercorns, cloves, shallots, thyme, parsley, rosemary, bay leaf, a little coarse salt, 1 cup of wine and the marc or brandy in a bowl (do not use aluminum) for 24 hours.

Mince the hare livers, season them with *quatre épices,* and add the blood. Add the lemon juice and set aside.

Make a stuffing by grinding through the finest blade of a meat grinder the remainder of the boned meat from the hares' hindquarters, the ham fat, pork, *foie gras* and the truffle. Season with salt, pepper and half of the brandy.

Drain the legs, dry them, and spread them out on a board. Put a little stuffing on each, roll it up, wrap it in a sheet of fresh pork fat, and tie securely.

Heat half of the oil and half of the butter in a deep skillet and cook the legs in it until they are golden on all sides. Flame with the remaining brandy and keep hot. In another skillet, heat the remaining oil and butter and cook the bacon and the minced onion in it until they are barely golden. Stir in the flour, mix well, and then add the remaining wine, the sugar, the *bouquet garni* and the strained marinade. Season with salt and pepper to taste. Bring to a boil, add the hares' legs, cover, and simmer gently for 2 hours.

Remove the *bouquet garni*. Stir in the reserved hare livers and blood and simmer, covered, over the lowest possible heat for another hour.

Fry the bread slices in hot goose fat or lard, and put them on a hot serving dish. Top each with 1 stuffed leg, and put a paper frill on the bone of each leg. Strain the sauce through a fine sieve and serve it separately in a sauceboat.

FOR 4 PERSONS:

The hindquarters of 2 hares	¼ **pound ham fat**
For the marinade:	¼ **pound lean pork**
2 **onions, sliced**	2 **ounces foie gras**
2 **carrots, sliced**	1 **truffle**
6 **peppercorns**	**Salt**
4 **whole cloves**	**Freshly ground black pepper**
3 **shallots, minced**	4 **tablespoons brandy**
½ **teaspoon dried thyme**	4 **sheets of fresh pork fat**
2 **parsley sprigs**	3 **tablespoons peanut oil**
1 **teaspoon dried rosemary**	3 **tablespoons butter**
1 **bay leaf**	4 **slices of bacon, blanched and dried**
Coarse (Kosher) salt	1 **large onion, minced**
1 **cup dry red wine**	2 **tablespoons flour**
2 **tablespoons marc or brandy**	1 **cup dry red wine**
The hares' livers	½ **teaspoon sugar**
1 **pinch of Quatre Épices (p. 667)**	1 **Bouquet Garni (p. 46)**
The hares' blood	4 **slices of firm white bread**
1 **teaspoon lemon juice**	4 **tablespoons goose fat or lard**

/ Saddle of Venison Grand Veneur

SELLE DE CHEVREUIL GRAND VENEUR

Marinate the meat with the onions, carrots, peppercorns, cloves, shallots, parsley, thyme, rosemary, bay leaf, a little coarse salt, the red wine and brandy for 24 hours.

Make the *sauce poivrade*.

Remove the saddle from the marinade and dry it carefully. Heat the oil and butter in a casserole and brown the saddle on all sides. Transfer it to a preheated 375° F. oven and roast for about 30 minutes.

Strain the marinade and add it to the *sauce poivrade*. Reduce over high heat to about half its quantity and then add the *crème fraîche*. Carve the meat, coat it with the sauce, and serve with a purée of chestnuts.

FOR 6 PERSONS:

1 saddle of venison (4 pounds)	Coarse (Kosher) salt
2 onions, sliced	2 cups dry red wine
2 carrots, sliced	2 tablespoons brandy
6 peppercorns	2 cups Sauce Poivrade (p. 765)
4 whole cloves	3 tablespoons peanut oil
4 shallots, minced	3 tablespoons butter
2 parsley sprigs	1 cup Crème Fraîche (p. 666),
½ teaspoon dried thyme	or heavy cream
1 teaspoon dried rosemary	1 recipe Chestnut Purée (p. 582)
1 bay leaf	

Shoulder of Venison with Three Purées /

ÉPAULE DE CHEVREUIL AUX TROIS PURÉES

Bone and trim the shoulder of venison. Reserve the bones. Season the meat with salt, pepper, nutmeg, the thyme and the brandy.

Roll up the meat and let it rest in a cool place or in the refrigerator for 18 hours.

Make a stuffing by combining the minced bacon, the ground venison meat and the minced wild mushrooms. Cook the stuffing in a skillet over low heat for about 10 minutes. Remove from the heat and stir in the egg-cream mixture.

Unroll the meat and spread it with the mixture. Roll it up again, sew it closed, wrap it in the sheets of fresh pork fat, and tie securely.

Heat the butter in a casserole and cook the onions and carrots in it until they are tender. Add the reserved venison bones, cook for a few more minutes, and then add the rolled and tied shoulder. Sauté the meat until it is golden on all sides. Add the *bouquet garni*, salt and pepper to taste, ½ cup water and the wine. Cook in a preheated 350° F. oven for about 2 hours, basting frequently.

Transfer the meat to a hot deep serving dish. Skim the fat off the sauce, correct the seasoning, and strain over the meat. Serve with puréed chestnuts, puréed celery and puréed lentils.

FOR 4 PERSONS:

1 shoulder of venison (3 to 4 pounds)	⅓ pound wild mushrooms, minced
Salt	1 egg, beaten with ½ cup Crème Fraîche (p. 666)
Freshly ground black pepper	Thin sheets of fresh pork fat
Grated nutmeg	3 tablespoons butter
½ teaspoon dried thyme	2 onions, sliced
1 tablespoon brandy	2 carrots, sliced
4 slices of bacon, minced	1 Bouquet Garni (p. 46)
½ pound lean venison meat, ground	½ cup dry white wine

Noisettes of Venison with Grapes /

NOISETTES DE CHEVREUIL AUX RAISINS

Heat the oil and the butter in a casserole over high heat and sauté the venison slices for about 3 minutes on each side. Season with salt and pepper. Add the grape

juice, the brandy and the peeled and seeded grapes. Simmer for 5 more minutes.
When the grapes are heated through, serve in a hot dish.

FOR 4 PERSONS:

2 tablespoons peanut oil
2 tablespoons butter
4 slices (1 inch thick) from a
   venison fillet
Salt

Freshly ground black pepper
1 cup fresh grape juice
2 tablespoons brandy
1 cup grapes, peeled and seeded

NOISETTES DE MARCASSIN SAUTÉES / *Wild Boar Steaks*

Marinate the steaks with the onions, carrots, peppercorns, cloves, shallots, parsley, thyme, rosemary, bay leaf, a little coarse salt, the red wine and marc or brandy for 24 hours.

Drain the steaks and dry them thoroughly. Sauté them in the oil and butter in a deep skillet over high heat for about 3 minutes on each side. Season with salt and pepper to taste. Transfer the meat to a hot plate and keep warm.

Cook the 2 tablespoons of shallots in the oil and butter remaining in the skillet until they are soft and golden. Return the steaks to the skillet and flame with the brandy. Put the steaks in a hot serving dish and keep hot. Add the sherry to the skillet and reduce the liquid by half. Stir in the *crème fraîche* and reduce again until the sauce is thickened and smooth. Strain the sauce over the steaks and serve immediately.

FOR 4 PERSONS:

8 slices (¾ inch thick), cut
   from the loin of a wild boar
For the marinade:
   2 onions, sliced
   2 carrots, sliced
   7 peppercorns
   2 whole cloves
   2 shallots, minced
   1 parsley sprig
   ½ teaspoon dried thyme
   1 teaspoon dried rosemary
   1 bay leaf
   Coarse (Kosher) salt
   1 cup dry red wine
   2 tablespoons marc or brandy

2 tablespoons peanut oil
4 tablespoons butter
Salt
Freshly ground black pepper
2 tablespoons minced shallots
½ cup brandy
1 cup sherry
¾ cup Crème Fraîche (p. 666)

/ *Sweet-Sour Leg of Wild Boar*

JAMBON DE MARCASSIN À L'AIGRE-DOUCE

Remove the rind and layer of fat from the boar's leg. Marinate the meat in the wine, vinegar, oil, onions, carrots, shallots, garlic, parsley, thyme, bay leaf, a little coarse salt, the peppercorns and 4 cloves in a large bowl (do not use aluminum) for 4 days. Turn the leg frequently.

Make the stock in the usual way, using the trimmings and the bones of wild boar.

Drain the meat and brush off the vegetables. Stick the leg with the 6 cloves and put it into a large deep casserole with the bacon, about half of the marinade, strained, and the white wine. Cover the casserole and cook it in a preheated 350° F. oven for about 2 hours.

Put the leg on an ovenproof dish and sprinkle a few spoonfuls of the braising liquid over it. Then sprinkle with 1 tablespoon of the sugar. Increase the oven temperature to 500° F. and glaze the leg for about 10 minutes.

Melt the remaining sugar in a heavy saucepan to make a light caramel, stir in the vinegar, and bring to a boil. Let the vinegar almost evaporate and add the game stock. Bring to the boiling point and then simmer for 5 minutes. Add the raisins and simmer for 2 more minutes. Serve the sauce separately in a sauceboat.

FOR 4 PERSONS:

1 leg of young wild boar
For the marinade:
    4 cups dry white wine
    1 cup wine vinegar
    1 cup peanut oil
    2 onions, sliced
    2 carrots, sliced
    2 shallots, minced
    2 garlic cloves, minced
    6 parsley sprigs
    ½ teaspoon dried thyme
    1 bay leaf
    Coarse (Kosher) salt
    4 peppercorns
    4 whole cloves

2 cups strong Game Stock (p. 165)
6 whole cloves
½ pound bacon, blanched and diced
1 cup dry white wine
3 tablespoons sugar
1 tablespoon wine vinegar
¼ cup raisins, plumped in hot water

8

VEGETABLES
Les Légumes

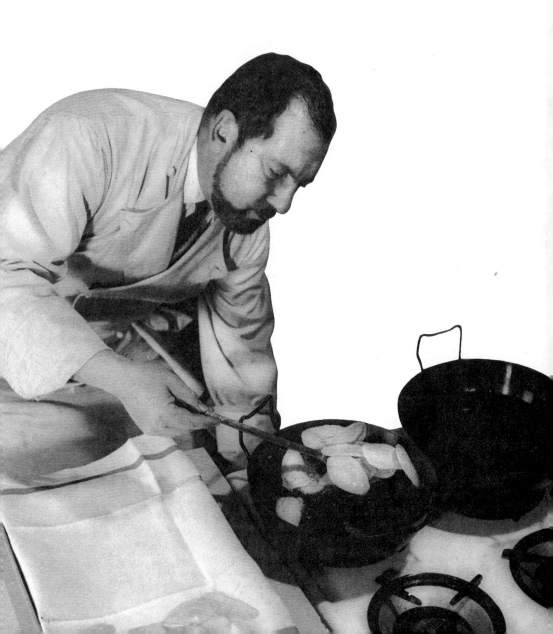

EDITORS' NOTE: *The French take great pains in the preparation of vegetables. It is rare to find, in France, a watery overcooked vegetable. Green vegetables are nearly always first blanched in a large quantity of boiling water until they are just barely tender. They are then very thoroughly drained—in the case of spinach, for instance, all the cooking liquid is squeezed or pressed out—and then finished off simply by gently sautéing them in butter, seasonings and herbs. Or, more elaborately, after the blanching and draining process, they are dressed with an appropriate sauce.*

It perhaps should also be noted that the French, more often than not, serve green vegetables as a separate course. Thus, the quantities suggested in this section may seem somewhat generous to American tastes.

APPLES

Pommes

Buttered Apples / POMMES AU BEURRE

Peel the whole apples and remove the cores with an apple corer.

Heat the butter in a casserole. Add the apples and a little water. Simmer, covered, over very low heat for about 12 minutes, or until the apples are tender. Do not overcook, or the apples will lose their shape.

Season lightly with salt and sugar.

Use the apples as a garnish for poultry, game or roast meats.

FOR 4 PERSONS:

4 firm tart apples	Salt
6 tablespoons butter	1 tablespoon sugar
¼ cup water	

Apples Sautéed in Butter / POMMES SAUTÉES AU BEURRE

Cut the apples into halves; peel and core them. Dust the halves with flour.

Heat the butter in a skillet, add the apples, and sauté them until they are golden on all sides, about 8 minutes. Keep the heat low, so that the apples will not color too quickly. If necessary, add a little water.

Use the sautéed apples as a garnish for a roast or poultry.

FOR 4 PERSONS:

4 firm tart apples	6 tablespoons butter
Flour	1 tablespoon water

ARTICHOKES

Artichauts

ARTICHAUTS ENTIERS BOUILLIS / *Boiled Artichokes*

Trim the artichokes, cut off the stems at their bases, and cut off the spiky leaf tops. Round off each leaf with scissors. Wash the artichokes and put them into a large saucepan full of boiling salted water. There must be plenty of water for the artichokes to float in.

Cook at a rolling boil. Cooking time depends on the size and the quality of the artichokes; you may count from 25 to 45 minutes. You can check whether the artichokes are cooked by putting a fork into the bottom of one of them. If the fork meets no resistance and the leaves are easily torn off, the artichokes are done.

Remove the artichokes with a slotted spoon and put them into a strainer so that they may drain thoroughly. If necessary, squeeze them a little with your hands to remove the water, the way you'd squeeze the juice from an orange.

FOR 4 PERSONS:

**4 or 8 artichokes, depending on
    size**

Note: The artichokes may be served hot or cold, with Simple French Dressing (p. 787).

CARCIOFIONI À L'INFERNO / *Artichokes à l'Inferno*

Cook the artichokes as described in Boiled Artichokes (above). Meantime, mince the garlic, capers and parsley as fine as possible and mix them with the bread crumbs. Add 1 tablespoon of the olive oil to bind the mixture. Season with salt and pepper.

When the artichokes are cooked, drain them thoroughly. Open up the leaves and remove the center choke with a sharp knife or spoon. Fill each cavity with a little of the stuffing.

Put the artichokes into a buttered casserole or baking dish. Mix together the remaining oil and the water and sprinkle the artichokes with the mixture. Cook the artichokes in a preheated 350° F. oven for 15 minutes, basting frequently.

Serve very hot, in the dish in which the artichokes were cooked.

FOR 4 PERSONS:

**4 large artichokes
4 garlic cloves
1 tablespoon capers
1 tablespoon minced parsley
½ cup fresh white bread crumbs**

**½ cup olive oil
Salt
Freshly ground black pepper
½ cup water**

Small Artichokes Petit Salé /

PETITS ARTICHAUTS NOUVEAUX AU PETIT SALÉ

EDITORS' NOTE: *This and the following dish require the very small tender artichokes that are common in France; in the United States they may be found in markets catering to Italian and other Mediterranean peoples. If they are not available, we suggest that large artichokes, quartered and with the chokes removed, may be substituted.*

Cut the bacon into small dice and cook them with the oil in a casserole until they are transparent. Add the trimmed artichokes. Cook over low heat for about 15 minutes, stirring very frequently to prevent scorching.

Mince the onions, shallots and garlic and add them to the artichokes. Mix, cook for 5 minutes, and sprinkle with the flour. Add a cup of water and the *bouquet garni*.

Season lightly, since the bacon will be salty. Cover the casserole and simmer for 15 to 20 minutes. Remove the *bouquet garni* and serve, very hot, in a vegetable dish.

FOR 4 PERSONS:

4 slices of bacon or salt pork	2 garlic cloves
4 tablespoons olive oil	1 tablespoon flour
20 small tender artichokes, trimmed	1 Bouquet Garni (p. 46)
	Salt
4 onions	Cayenne pepper
2 shallots	

Small Artichokes en Ragoût /

PETITS ARTICHAUTS ENTIERS EN RAGOÛT

Trim the artichokes and cut off the stems at their bases.

Heat the oil and the butter in a casserole, add the artichokes, and sauté them until they are golden. Add the peas and the hearts of romaine. Mix well and add the water or consommé. Season with salt, pepper and the sugar. Cover the casserole, and simmer over low heat for about 20 minutes. Shake the casserole occasionally to prevent sticking; do not stir with a spoon or the artichokes and the hearts of lettuce may break.

Serve the vegetables from the dish in which they were cooked, or put them into a vegetable dish. Sprinkle with the *fines herbes* and serve very hot.

FOR 4 PERSONS:

20 small tender artichokes	Salt
3 tablespoons olive oil	Freshly ground black pepper
3 tablespoons butter	2 lumps of sugar, crushed
2 cups shelled peas	2 tablespoons minced Fines Herbes (p. 89)
4 hearts of romaine lettuce	
1 cup water, or Chicken Consommé (p. 168)	

/ *Artichoke Hearts in Butter*

FONDS D'ARTICHAUTS AU BEURRE

Cut off the stems of the artichokes·even with their bases and rub the bottoms with the cut side of a lemon. Snap off all of the leaves and rub again with lemon. Scoop out the choke with a thin spoon or a knife (alternatively, the chokes may easily be removed after cooking) and rub again with lemon.

Beat the flour into a little of the water in an enamelware saucepan. (Never use aluminum.) Add the rest of the water, half of the lemon juice, a little salt and the artichoke hearts. The flour and lemon juice help to keep the artichokes from turning gray. Simmer, covered, over medium heat for about 20 minutes, or until not quite tender.

Heat the butter in an enamelware casserole and add the drained artichoke hearts. Season with salt and pepper, add the remaining lemon juice, and simmer over low heat for 15 to 20 minutes.

Put the artichoke hearts in a hot vegetable dish with the juices in the casserole and sprinkle with the *fines herbes*.

FOR 4 PERSONS:

8 large artichokes	Salt
1 lemon	6 tablespoons butter
¼ cup flour	Freshly ground black pepper
3 (or more) cups water	¼ cup minced Fines Herbes
Juice of 2 lemons	(p. 89)

FONDS D'ARTICHAUTS ÉTUVÉS / *Braised Artichoke Hearts*

Trim the artichokes as described in Artichoke Hearts in Butter (above), and put them into an enamelware casserole with the lemon juice, oil, butter and salt. Cover the casserole and simmer over low heat for about 30 minutes, or until tender. Turn them over occasionally as they cook.

FOR 4 PERSONS:

8 artichoke hearts	3 tablespoons butter
Juice of ½ lemon	½ teaspoon salt
2 tablespoons olive oil	

/ *Braised Stuffed Artichoke Hearts*

FONDS D'ARTICHAUTS BRAISÉS FARCIS

Prepare the artichoke hearts as described in Artichoke Hearts in Butter.

Meantime, cook the rice in boiling salted water. Mince the shallots and cook them in the combined hot oil and butter until they are very tender.

Drain the rice and add it to the shallots. Mix well, add the ham, and bind the mixture with the *crème fraîche* and the egg yolk beaten together. Season with salt and pepper and stir in 1 tablespoon of the grated cheese.

Put the artichoke hearts in a buttered baking dish and stuff them with the rice mixture. Sprinkle with the remaining cheese mixed with the bread crumbs. Brown under the broiler for a few minutes and serve immediately, very hot.

FOR 4 PERSONS:

8 **Artichoke Hearts in Butter** (p. 545)	1 **tablespoon Crème Fraîche** (p. 666)
¼ **cup uncooked rice**	1 **egg yolk**
2 **shallots**	**Salt**
2 **tablespoons olive oil**	**Freshly ground black pepper**
1 **tablespoon butter**	¼ **cup grated Swiss cheese**
2 **slices of Bayonne ham (or prosciutto or Virginia ham), finely chopped**	1 **tablespoon fine dry bread crumbs**

Artichoke Hearts Clamart | FONDS D'ARTICHAUTS CLAMART

Prepare the artichoke hearts as described above.

Heat the butter in a casserole and gently cook the peas in it until they are tender. Season them with a little salt and sugar. When the artichoke hearts are ready, put them into a hot serving dish and fill them with the cooked peas. Sprinkle with the *fines herbes*.

Artichokes cooked in this manner are especially suited as a garnish for roast lamb.

FOR 4 PERSONS:

8 **Artichoke Hearts in Butter** (p. 545)	**Salt**
4 **tablespoons butter**	**Sugar**
1½ **cups shelled green peas**	¼ **cup minced Fines Herbes** (p. 89)

Artichoke Hearts in Cream |

FONDS D'ARTICHAUTS À LA CRÈME

Prepare the artichoke hearts as described above. When they are cooked, keep them warm in the casserole in which they were cooked.

Pour the *crème fraîche* into a small saucepan, bring it to the boiling point, and reduce it by half. Season lightly with salt, pepper and nutmeg.

Lift the artichoke hearts into a hot serving dish, coat them with the *crème fraîche,* and serve very hot.

FOR 4 PERSONS:

8 **Artichoke Hearts in Butter** (p. 545)	**Salt**
2 **cups Crème Fraîche (p. 666)**	**Freshly ground white pepper**
	Grated nutmeg

Artichoke Hearts Hollandaise |

FONDS D'ARTICHAUTS À LA HOLLANDAISE

Prepare artichoke hearts as described above.

Put them into a hot vegetable dish and coat them with *sauce hollandaise.* **Serve** very hot.

FOR 4 PERSONS:

8 Artichoke Hearts in Butter
(p. 545)

2 cups Sauce Hollandaise
(p. 780)

FONDS D'ARTICHAUTS MORNAY / *Artichoke Hearts Mornay*

Prepare artichoke hearts as described above and put them into a buttered baking dish. Coat them with the *sauce Mornay*. Sprinkle them with the grated cheese mixed with the bread crumbs, and dot with butter. Brown quickly under a broiler.

Serve immediately in the same dish.

FOR 4 PERSONS:

8 Artichoke Hearts in Butter
(p. 545)
1½ cups Sauce Mornay
(p. 776)
¼ cup grated Swiss cheese

2 tablespoons fine dry bread crumbs
4 tablespoons butter, cut into tiny pieces

FONDS D'ARTICHAUTS LANDAIS / *Artichoke Hearts Landais*

Prepare the artichoke hearts as described above and put them into a buttered baking dish.

Put into each artichoke heart a small slice of *foie gras* and a slice of truffle. Coat with the *sauce Mornay* and sprinkle with the grated cheese.

Dot with the butter and brown under the broiler. Serve immediately in the same dish.

FOR 4 PERSONS:

8 Artichoke Hearts in Butter
(p. 545)
8 slices of foie gras
8 slices of truffle

1½ cups Sauce Mornay (p. 776)
4 tablespoons grated Swiss cheese
4 tablespoons butter, cut into tiny pieces

/ *Ragout of Artichoke Hearts Portugaise*

FONDS D'ARTICHAUTS EN RAGOÛT À LA PORTUGAISE

Trim the artichokes into hearts as described in Artichoke Hearts in Butter (p. 545). Cut the hearts into quarters, and sauté them in the hot butter for about 12 minutes, or until half tender. Add the onion, tomatoes, garlic and parsley. Season with salt and pepper. Cover the saucepan and simmer for another 10 minutes, or until tender.

Serve the cooked ragout in a vegetable dish and decorate it with the olives. Serve very hot.

FOR 4 PERSONS:

8 large artichokes	1 garlic clove, minced
4 tablespoons butter	3 tablespoons minced parsley
1 onion, minced	Salt
4 very ripe tomatoes, peeled, seeded and minced	Freshly ground black pepper
	½ cup pitted green olives

Souffléed Artichoke Hearts / FONDS D'ARTICHAUTS SOUFFLÉS

Prepare the artichoke hearts as described above, but sauté them in the butter for only about 5 minutes, so that they are only about three-quarters done.

Cut the ham into thin julienne strips and add the strips to the lukewarm *sauce Mornay*. Beat the egg whites until stiff and fold them into the mixture. Season lightly with salt and pepper.

Put the artichoke hearts into a buttered baking dish. Spoon a little of the ham mixture on each, sprinkle with the grated cheese, and cook in a preheated 375° F. oven for about 15 minutes. Serve very hot.

FOR 4 PERSONS:

8 Artichoke Hearts in Butter (p. 545)	2 egg whites
⅓ pound boiled ham	Salt
¾ cup lukewarm Sauce Mornay (p. 776)	Freshly ground white pepper
	4 tablespoons grated Swiss cheese

Stuffed Artichoke Hearts Niçoise /

FONDS D'ARTICHAUTS FARCIS NIÇOISE

Prepare the artichoke hearts as described above, but sauté the hearts for only 5 minutes, or until they are about three-quarters done.

Mince the ham, the fresh pork fat and the onion. Put all three into a casserole with the tomatoes. Add the parsley and garlic. Stir the mixture over medium heat until it is a smooth thick paste. Check the seasoning, but add salt very lightly, since the ham will be salty.

Put the cooked artichoke hearts into a buttered baking dish. Stuff them with the ham mixture, sprinkle with the bread crumbs, and dot with the butter. Bake in a 375° F. oven for 15 minutes. Serve very hot, in the same dish.

FOR 4 PERSONS:

8 Artichoke Hearts in Butter (p. 545)	2 tablespoons minced parsley
2 slices of Bayonne ham or Virginia ham or prosciutto	1 garlic clove, minced
	Salt
2 thin slices of fresh pork fat	½ cup fine dry bread crumbs
1 onion	2 tablespoons butter, cut into tiny pieces
4 very ripe tomatoes, peeled, seeded and chopped	

FONDS D'ARTICHAUTS POCHÉS / *Poached Artichoke Hearts*

Trim 24 small or 12 large artichokes into hearts, as described in Artichoke Hearts in Butter (p. 545), and rub them with a cut lemon to prevent their discoloring. Bring the *court bouillon* (below) to a boil and plunge the artichoke hearts into it. Poach them for 20 to 30 minutes, or until tender. Cool them and keep them in the *court bouillon* until needed.

COURT BOUILLON FOR 24 ARTICHOKE HEARTS:

4 cups water	**2 teaspoons salt**
½ cup olive oil	**Juice of 1 lemon**

PURÉE D'ARTICHAUTS / *Purée of Artichoke Hearts*

Prepare the artichoke hearts as in the preceding recipe. Drain them when they are cooked and purée them in a blender.

Heat the butter in a saucepan, add the puréed artichokes, season with salt and pepper, and mix well. Serve in a vegetable dish, or as a garnish.

FOR 4 PERSONS:

8 Poached Artichoke Hearts (above)	**Salt**
6 tablespoons butter	**Freshly ground white pepper**

/ *Artichoke Hearts with Sausage Meat*

FONDS D'ARTICHAUTS AUX CHIPOLATAS

Prepare the poached artichoke hearts as described above, but cook them for only 10 minutes.

Make the filling: heat 3 tablespoons of the butter in a saucepan and add the garlic and parsley. Cook them over low heat until soft and then add the sausage meat.

Put the cooked artichoke hearts into a casserole and stuff them with the sausage filling. Add the remaining butter and the onions to the casserole. Cook over low heat for 2 to 3 minutes and then add the wine and the *bouquet garni*. Bring to a boil. Cover the casserole and cook in a preheated 325° F. oven for about 20 minutes.

Remove the *bouquet garni* and the onion quarters, put the artichoke hearts into a hot serving dish, and reduce the sauce in which they were cooked by half. Season only if necessary. Pour the sauce over the artichokes and serve at once.

FOR 4 PERSONS:

8 Poached Artichoke Hearts (above)	**2 onions, cut into quarters**
5 tablespoons butter	**2 cups dry white wine**
5 garlic cloves, minced	**1 Bouquet Garni (p. 46)**
1 tablespoon minced parsley	**Salt and freshly ground black pepper, if necessary**
½ pound sausage meat	

CHINESE ARTICHOKES

Crosnes

EDITORS' NOTE: *Chinese artichokes, sometimes called Japanese artichokes or knotroot, are not easy to find in the United States, except in Chinese or Japanese markets, where they may be known as* chorogi.

Chinese Artichokes in Butter / CROSNES AU BEURRE

Wash the Chinese artichokes in running water, drain them, and put them into a thick kitchen towel. Sprinkle them generously with coarse salt and twist the towel, rubbing them against each other to remove their fine skins. If the skins do not come off readily, scrape the artichokes with a knife, as you would a radish, removing as little of the root as possible in the process. Wash them again in several changes of cold water and drain them in a sieve.

Blanch them in boiling salted water for 5 or 6 minutes. Remove them with a slotted spoon and dry them in a kitchen cloth.

Heat the butter in a casserole, add the blanched artichokes, and cook them over low heat for 5 to 10 minutes or until tender, without letting them turn golden. Season with salt and pepper, and add the garlic and half of the parsley. Put them into a vegetable dish and sprinkle with the pan juices and remaining parsley; or serve them as a garnish on a platter of roasted meats.

FOR 4 PERSONS:

1 pound Chinese artichokes	Freshly ground white pepper
Salt	1 garlic clove, minced
4 tablespoons butter	2 tablespoons minced parsley

Chinese Artichokes in Cream / CROSNES À LA CRÈME

Clean the Chinese artichokes as in the preceding recipe, but do not blanch them.

Combine the water, lemon juice, flour and oil in a saucepan and bring the mixture to the boiling point. Add the artichokes and cook for 10 minutes; drain.

Heat the butter in a saucepan; add the artichokes and 3 tablespoons of the *crème fraîche*. Bring to the boiling point and, stirring constantly, reduce the *crème fraîche* by half. Season with salt and add the remaining *crème fraîche*, heat briefly, and pour into a hot serving dish. Serve hot.

FOR 4 PERSONS:

1 pound Chinese artichokes	2 tablespoons olive oil
2 cups water	3 tablespoons butter
Juice of 1 lemon	½ cup Crème Fraîche (p. 666)
1 tablespoon flour	Salt

ASPARAGUS

Asperges

Basic Preparation: Peel the outer skin from 2 pounds of asparagus stalks with a rotary vegetable peeler or with a very sharp knife. Trim off only the very tough bottom ends. Tie into bundles of 5 or 6 spears each. Tying the bundles at both ends makes removal from the cooking liquid much easier.

Bring about 8 quarts of water to boil in a large pot and season it generously with salt. Add the asparagus bundles and cook, uncovered, for about 8 minutes. Test one of the spears for doneness and, if necessary, cook for a minute or two longer. Leaving 1 asparagus spear loose in the pot makes this testing simpler.

When the asparagus is just tender, remove the bundles with 2 forks or with kitchen tongs and drain on a rack for 1 minute. If the asparagus is to be served with a separate sauce, transfer the bundles to a hot serving dish lined with a napkin, remove the strings, and serve as quickly as possible.

ASPERGES SAUCE CHANTILLY / *Asparagus Chantilly*

Cook asparagus as described in the basic preparation (above). Serve Sauce Chantilly (p. 773) separately in a sauceboat.

ASPERGES SAUCE HOLLANDAISE / *Asparagus Hollandaise*

Put the cooked asparagus on a hot serving dish lined with a folded napkin, or into a special asparagus serving dish which has a rack.

Serve the *sauce hollandaise* on the side in a sauceboat. The sauce should be thick, in order to coat the asparagus completely.

FOR 4 PERSONS:

2 **pounds asparagus, cooked according to the basic preparation (above)**	2 **cups Sauce Hollandaise (p. 780)**

/ *Asparagus with Sauce Mousseuse*

ASPERGES SAUCE MOUSSEUSE

Cook 2 pounds of asparagus as described in the basic preparation (above), and serve 2 cups of Sauce Mousseuse (p. 781) separately in a sauceboat.

/ *Asparagus with Fines Herbes French Dressing*

ASPERGES SAUCE VINAIGRETTE AUX FINES HERBES

Cook 2 pounds of asparagus as described in the basic preparation (above).
Prepare about ¾ cup French Dressing with Fines Herbes (p. 788), and pour it

over the hot asparagus on a hot serving dish. Or cool and chill the asparagus before pouring the sauce over it.

Asparagus Polonaise / ASPERGES À LA POLONAISE

Heat the butter and warm the cooked asparagus in it. Transfer the asparagus to a serving dish.

Heat the butter in which the asparagus was warmed until it begins to color. Add the bread crumbs and cook until browned. Add the hard-cooked egg and the *fines herbes* and pour the mixture over the asparagus. Sprinkle with the parsley and serve very hot.

FOR 4 PERSONS:

½ cup butter
2 pounds asparagus, cooked according to the basic preparation (p. 551)
⅓ cup fine dry bread crumbs

1 hard-cooked egg, minced
¼ cup minced Fines Herbes (p. 89)
2 tablespoons minced parsley

Asparagus in Butter / ASPERGES AU BEURRE

Choose asparagus that is very fresh, peel it well, and cook it in boiling salted water as described in the basic preparation (p. 551), but cook it for only 5 or 6 minutes, or until it is not quite tender. Drain the asparagus carefully and put into a casserole with the butter, and a tablespoon or two of the asparagus water.

Cover the casserole and simmer over very low heat for about 10 minutes, or until the asparagus is very tender.

Note: The asparagus may be cooked entirely in the butter, without blanching. It will be less green and handsome to look at than if previously cooked in water, but if it is very fresh, the flavor will be outstanding.

FOR 4 PERSONS:

2 pounds asparagus
Salt

4 tablespoons butter

Asparagus in Cream / ASPERGES A LA CRÈME

Cook the asparagus as described in Asparagus in Butter (above).

When it is tender, add the *fines herbes* and the *crème fraîche,* and season with a little salt and nutmeg. Heat through and serve.

FOR 4 PERSONS:

2 pounds asparagus
Salt
4 tablespoons butter
2 tablespoons minced Fines Herbes (p. 89)

4 tablespoons Crème Fraîche (p. 666)
Grated nutmeg

ASPERGES MILANAISE / *Asparagus Milanaise*

When the asparagus is cooked and drained, put it into a little hot butter and let it heat through. Butter a warm baking dish generously and in it put layers of the hot asparagus, sprinkled with the grated cheese. Sprinkle with the browned butter and brown under the broiler. You may also garnish the dish with as many oil-fried eggs as there are diners.

Note: Asparagus Milanaise is usually made with grated Parmesan cheese. I prefer grated Swiss.

FOR 4 PERSONS:

2 pounds asparagus, cooked
  according to the basic
  preparation (p. 551)
3 tablespoons butter

¾ cup grated Swiss cheese
¼ cup hot browned butter
Optional: 4 eggs, fried in oil

ASPERGES AU GRATIN / *Asparagus au Gratin*

This preparation resembles Asparagus Milanaise (above), except it uses a *sauce Béchamel.*

Arrange a few asparagus spears in a baking dish and cover with a little sauce. Make layers in this fashion with all the asparagus and sauce. Sprinkle the top with the cheese. Brown under a medium broiler flame, but brown more slowly than Asparagus Milanaise, so that the vegetable will be heated through thoroughly.

Grated cheese is more interesting when it made from various cheeses. To my mind, the best combination is ¼ grated Parmesan, ¼ grated Dutch or Edam cheese, and ½ grated Swiss cheese.

Note: One does not serve fried eggs with an asparagus au gratin, but it is perfectly permissible to arrange layers of hard-cooked eggs cut into quarters over the top and to cover the eggs with a layer of sauce. Also, instead of the *sauce Béchamel,* any similar sauce may be substituted in this recipe, even a brown sauce, such as a Madeira.

FOR 4 PERSONS:

2 pounds asparagus, cooked
  according to the basic
  preparation (p. 551)

3 cups Sauce Béchamel (p. 761)
½ cup mixed grated cheeses
Optional: 4 hard-cooked eggs

/ *Ragout of Asparagus and Green Peas*

RAGOÛT D'ASPERGES AUX PETITS POIS

Mince the onions and sauté them in the oil and the butter in a casserole (or use goose fat, if you have any).

When the onions are beginning to turn golden, add the peas and the asparagus pieces. Mix well and cook over low heat for 1 minute. Season with a little salt and pepper and the sugar. Add enough consommé to barely cover the vegetables, and simmer over low heat for about 10 minutes. When the vegetables are tender, put the ragout into a vegetable dish and serve very hot.

FOR 4 PERSONS:

4 small white onions	Salt
2 tablespoons peanut oil	Freshly ground white pepper
2 tablespoons butter	2 lumps of sugar, crushed
1 pound green peas, shelled	1½ cups (about) Chicken
1 pound asparagus, peeled and cut	Consommé (p. 168)
into 1-inch pieces	

Asparagus and Artichokes au Gratin /

ASPERGES ET ARTICHAUTS AU GRATIN

Cook the asparagus tips and the artichokes separately until they are just barely tender. Drain on a kitchen towel and keep warm.

Heat the milk in a saucepan and keep it warm.

Sauté the onions in the combined hot oil and 2 tablespoons of the butter until they are soft. Sprinkle with the flour and gradually stir in the hot milk to make a smooth sauce. Season with a little salt, pepper and nutmeg; add a pinch of cayenne. Spoon out several tablespoons of the sauce and blend with the egg yolk. Return this mixture to the remaining sauce, blend well, and add the remaining butter.

Spoon a little of the sauce on the bottom of a baking dish. Arrange the artichoke hearts on the sauce, and on the center of each place three of the asparagus tips. Coat with the remaining sauce, and sprinkle with the grated cheese.

Brown under the broiler or heat in a preheated 450° F. oven until brown and bubbly. Serve immediately, in the same dish.

FOR 4 PERSONS:

24 asparagus tips, cooked according to the basic preparation (p. 551)	2 tablespoons flour
	Salt
	Freshly ground white pepper
8 poached Artichoke Hearts (p. 549)	Grated nutmeg
2 cups milk	Cayenne pepper
2 onions, minced	1 egg yolk, beaten
1 tablespoon olive oil	⅓ cup grated Swiss cheese
4 tablespoons butter	

Asparagus Tips in Aspic / POINTES D'ASPERGES EN ASPIC

You will need for this dish 4 individual small baking dishes, custard cups or molds, in which individual aspics may be molded. They should be of about 1-cup capacity.

Trim the asparagus stalks into even-sized 2- to 3-inch pieces, cut to the size of the dishes in which the aspics will be molded. Cook the pieces in boiling salted water in the usual manner, drain them thoroughly on a rack or a kitchen cloth, and then chill them.

Coat the bottoms and the sides of the molds with the liquid aspic, as described on page 38. Place the molds in the refrigerator to firm the gelatin. Then stand a suitable number of asparagus pieces in each mold, tip down, and fill the interior of the molds with a little of the purée of *foie gras*. Coat with the remaining gelatin. Chill the molds until the aspics are set and firm.

At serving time, dip the bottoms of the molds into hot water, and unmold the aspics alongside the meat they are to garnish. Or you may use the aspics to garnish a *chaud-froid* of chicken.

FOR 4 PERSONS:

16 asparagus tips, cooked
   according to the basic
   preparation (p. 551)

2 (or more) cups Brown Stock for
   Aspics (p. 166)
1 cup canned purée of foie gras

ASPERGES FROIDES EN BUISSON / *Asparagus and Ham Rolls*

Drain the cooked asparagus thoroughly on a rack or on a kitchen towel and let it cool completely.

Place the ham slices side by side. Put a few asparagus stalks on each slice. The tops and ends of the stalks should overlap the ham slices by about 1 inch. Roll up each ham slice with the asparagus inside and place these rolls side by side in a large oblong serving dish.

Coat the rolls with the jellied mayonnaise. Blend the butter with the spinach juice (or use a few drops of green food coloring) and decorate these bundles with a pattern of lines resembling the veins of a leaf. Chill until the mayonnaise is set.

FOR 4 PERSONS:

2 pounds asparagus, cooked
   according to the basic
   preparation (p. 551)
8 slices of boiled ham
2 cups Jellied Mayonnaise
   (p. 784), still liquid

½ cup butter at room
   temperature
2 tablespoons spinach juice

BEANS

Haricots

EDITORS' NOTE: *Several varieties of fresh beans, still in their shells, are widely used in French cookery. In the United States, different kinds of fresh beans can be found in vegetable markets catering to people of Mediterranean origin.*

The white beans available in America which correspond most closely to the immensely popular French haricots blancs *are Great Northern beans and the smaller Navy beans. However, the other two popular American varieties of white beans, the large marrow beans and the small pea beans, can also be used in French recipes that call for fresh or dried beans. Of course, their cooking time has to be adjusted.*

Very often the fresh beans sold in America are of the same varieties as those of France, Spain or Italy.

Boiled Green Beans in Butter / HARICOTS VERTS BOUILLIS

Trim the ends from the beans; they should be tender and stringless.

Heat a great deal of water in a kettle, at least 6 quarts. Bring to the boiling point, add the green beans, and season with a tablespoon or so of salt. Turn up the heat so that the water will not cease to boil after the beans are added. This will guarantee the good green color of the beans.

Cook without a cover for about 8 minutes and then begin testing for doneness. They should be just tender, but still crisp.

When the beans are done, remove them with a slotted spoon and drain them in a colander. Or you may run cold water over them to stop the cooking process and they may wait for several hours before being finished off in butter.

Heat the butter in a casserole, add the beans, mix, and sauté without a cover for 3 to 4 minutes. Shake the casserole, so that they reheat evenly. Put the beans into a hot serving dish and serve very hot.

FOR 4 PERSONS:

2 pounds green snap beans　　　　　　**6 tablespoons butter**
Salt

Green Beans With Herbs /

HARICOTS VERTS AUX FINES HERBES

Proceed as in Boiled Green Beans in Butter (above), but add 2 tablespoons minced Fines Herbes (p. 89) to the beans.

Green Beans Provençale / HARICOTS VERTS À LA PROVENÇALE

Proceed as in Boiled Green Beans in Butter (above), but add 2 minced garlic cloves to the beans with the butter. At the last minute sprinkle with 2 tablespoons minced parsley.

Green Beans with Tomatoes /

HARICOTS VERTS À LA TOMATE

Proceed as in Boiled Green Beans in Butter (above), but add 4 tablespoons well-seasoned Sauce Tomate (p. 769), to the beans with the butter. At the last minute sprinkle with 2 tablespoons minced parsley.

Mixed Green Beans / HARICOTS VERTS PANACHÉS

EDITORS' NOTE: *This recipe calls for flageolet beans, which are green beans the size of pea beans. They are shelled for eating and are sold fresh or dried. Flageolets have a delicate taste, and they are the classic accompaniment for lamb dishes. In the United States, they may be bought in gourmet shops, imported from France, dried or canned. Dried flageolets are prepared like any other dried beans.*

In the recipe that follows, we suggest that canned flageolets be preferably used. They should be drained, and heated together with the green beans.

Boil the green beans and the fresh flageolet beans as described in Boiled Green Beans in Butter (above), and drain them thoroughly. Or boil the green beans alone and drain a can of flageolet beans.

Heat the butter in a casserole, and add both kinds of beans. Mix carefully and simmer for 3 to 5 minutes. Sprinkle with the parsley and serve in a hot vegetable dish.

FOR 4 PERSONS:

1 pound green snap beans
1 pound shelled flageolet beans,
  or 1 large can (about 2 cups)
  cooked flageolet beans

8 tablespoons butter
4 tablespoons minced parsley

/ Kidney Beans Bourguignonne

HARICOTS ROUGES À LA BOURGUIGNONNE

Soak dried red kidney beans for about 12 hours; if fresh kidney beans are available, merely wash them.

Put the drained kidney beans into a casserole and add the wine and the water, as well as the *bouquet garni,* the garlic, onion, fresh pork or ham fat and bacon. Season lightly with salt and pepper.

Simmer over low heat until the beans are tender. Drain and discard the *bouquet garni,* the garlic and onion. Remove the bacon, cut it into dice, and sauté it with the butter in a skillet. Add the beans, mix well, and serve at once.

FOR 4 PERSONS:

2 pounds shelled fresh kidney
  beans, or 1½ pounds dried
  kidney beans
2 cups dry red wine
2 cups water
1 Bouquet Garni (p. 46)
1 garlic clove

1 onion, stuck with 1 clove
⅛ pound fresh pork or ham fat
⅛ pound lean bacon
Salt
Freshly ground black pepper
3 tablespoons butter

HARICOTS BLANCS FRAIS BOUILLIS / Boiled Fresh White Beans

Put the shelled beans into a casserole and cover them with lukewarm water. Add the onion, the blanched salt pork or fresh ham fat, the garlic and the *bouquet garni.* Season lightly with salt and pepper. Put over low heat and bring to the boiling point. Simmer, covered, over low heat for about 25 minutes. The exact cooking time will depend on the freshness of the beans; they can take as long as an hour. They should be tender but still retain their shape.

Check the beans during cooking time, stirring frequently to prevent their sticking to the bottom of the casserole. Add a little more water if necessary. At serving time, remove the onion and the *bouquet garni*, drain if desired, and serve the beans in a vegetable dish.

FOR 4 PERSONS:

1½ pounds shelled fresh white beans	1 garlic clove
1 onion, stuck with 1 clove	1 Bouquet Garni (p. 46)
¼ pound blanched salt pork or fresh ham fat, diced	Salt
	Freshly ground white pepper

Fresh White Beans in Butter /

HARICOTS BLANCS FRAIS AU BEURRE

Proceed as in Boiled Fresh White Beans (above), but add 6 tablespoons butter to the beans at serving time.

Fresh White Beans in Cream /

HARICOTS BLANCS FRAIS À LA CRÈME

Proceed as in Boiled Fresh White Beans (above), but add 1 cup of Crème Fraîche (p. 666) to the drained beans, and let it reduce by half.

Fresh White Beans with Fines Herbes /

HARICOTS BLANCS FRAIS AUX FINES HERBES

Proceed as in Boiled Fresh White Beans (above), but add 4 tablespoons minced Fines Herbes (p. 89) and 6 tablespoons of butter to the beans at serving time.

Fresh White Beans Normande / HARICOTS NORMANDE

Proceed as in Boiled Fresh White Beans, (above), and add 2 cups Sauce Normande (p. 779) to the drained beans and summer for 3 to 4 minutes. Sprinkle with 2 tablespoons minced parsley.

Braised Fresh White Beans /

ESTOUFFAT DE HARICOTS BLANCS

Blanch the fresh white beans in a very large pot of boiling salted water for 25 to 45 minutes, or until they are not quite tender, and drain them.

Cut the salt pork or the fresh fat into small dice and blanch them in boiling water for 5 minutes. Drain the dice and put them into a casserole with the butter and the lard. Cook over low heat for about 1 minute and add the onions. Cook, stirring constantly, until the onions are soft and golden.

Peel the tomatoes, cut them into pieces, and add them to the onions together with the garlic. Add the blanched beans. Tie the strips of blanched bacon into a bundle and add it to the beans. Season with salt and pepper, cover the casserole, and simmer for about 20 minutes, stirring constantly. When the beans are cooked, untie the strips of bacon, cut them into small dice, and return them to the beans. Pour the beans into a vegetable dish and serve very hot.

FOR 4 PERSONS:

1½ pounds unshelled fresh
    white beans
½ pound salt pork or fresh
    ham fat
3 tablespoons butter
2 tablespoons lard
2 onions, minced

2 tomatoes
1 garlic clove
⅓ pound fat bacon, cut into
    strips and blanched
Salt
Freshly ground black pepper

HARICOTS BLANCS SECS BOUILLIS / *Boiled Dried White Beans*

Wash the beans and let them soak in cold water for 8 to 12 hours. Drain the beans and put them into a casserole with fresh cold water to cover. Bring to the boiling point, season with salt and pepper, and add the onion, *bouquet garni,* garlic, and the fresh pork or ham fat or bacon. Cover the saucepan and simmer over low heat until the beans are tender, about 40 minutes or longer.

Remove the onion and the *bouquet garni,* drain, and serve hot in a vegetable dish.

FOR 4 PERSONS:

1 pound dried white beans
Salt
Freshly ground white pepper
1 onion, stuck with 1 clove

1 Bouquet Garni (p. 46)
1 garlic clove, mashed
¼ pound fresh pork or ham fat
    or blanched bacon

/ *Dried White Beans au Gratin*

HARICOTS BLANCS SECS AU GRATIN

Proceed as in the preceding recipe. When the beans are tender, put them into a buttered baking dish. Dot them with 2 tablespoons butter and sprinkle with 4 tablespoons grated Swiss cheese and 4 tablespoons fine dry bread crumbs. Bake in a preheated 375° F. oven for 20 minutes.

/ *Dried White Beans with Tomatoes*

HARICOTS BLANCS SECS À LA TOMATE

Proceed as in Boiled Dried White Beans (above), but add ½ cup Tomato Purée (p. 157) and 2 tablespoons butter to the cooked beans and sprinkle 2 tablespoons minced Fines Herbes (p. 89) over them.

FAVA BEANS

Fèves

Boiled Fava or Broad Beans / FÈVES BOUILLIES

Shell the broad beans and remove the hard skin that covers each bean. If the beans are young and tender, this need not be done.

Blanch the broad beans in boiling salted water for about 10 minutes. The exact time will depend on the age and size of the beans. Test the beans for readiness by pressing one with your fingers; it should mash.

Drain the broad beans and use them for garnishing roast meats; sprinkle the meat pan juices over the beans.

FOR 4 PERSONS:

3 pounds unshelled fava beans

Fava or Broad Beans in Butter / FÈVES AU BEURRE

Cook the beans as in Boiled Fava or Broad Beans (above).

Heat the butter in a casserole and add the beans. Simmer very gently for about 10 minutes, or until the beans are coated with the butter and are well heated through. Put the beans into a vegetable dish and sprinkle with the *fines herbes*.

FOR 4 PERSONS:

3 pounds unshelled fava or broad beans
6 tablespoons butter

4 tablespoons minced Fines Herbes (p. 89)

Fava or Broad Beans in Cream / FÈVES À LA CRÈME

Proceed as in Fava or Broad Beans in Butter (above), but add ½ cup Crème Fraîche (p. 666) to the cooked beans. Simmer for 3 minutes longer.

Fava or Broad Beans with Savory /
FÈVES À LA SARRIETTE

Proceed as in Fava or Broad Beans in Butter (above), but add a bunch of fresh savory to the water in which the beans are cooked.

Noisettes of Venison Duchesse d'Uzès

Noisettes de Biche Duchesse d'Uzès

Noisettes of Venison Duchesse d'Uzès

Noisettes de Biche Duchesse d'Uzès

SEASON THE VENISON slices, or *noisettes,* with salt and pepper to taste and sauté them in the combined hot oil and butter in a skillet just as you would a *tournedos,* for about 3 minutes on each side. They should be slightly rare. Remove them from the skillet and keep them hot. Stir the vinegar into the pan juices, scraping up all the brown bits at the bottom, and then stir in the *sauce poivrade.*

Place the croutons on a hot serving plate and put a *noisette* on each crouton; coat with the sauce. Garnish the plate with the chestnuts and potato patties. Serve immediately, and very hot.

For 4 persons:

4 slices (1½ inches
    thick) from a fillet of
    venison (preferably a doe)
Salt
Freshly ground black
    pepper
2 tablespoons peanut oil
2 tablespoons butter
2 tablespoons vinegar

1 cup Sauce Poivrade
    (p. 765)
4 Croutons (p. 62), about the
    size of the venison slices
½ recipe Chestnuts in
    Butter (p. 582)
1 recipe Duchess Potato
    Patties (p. 625)

Salmi of Pheasant Laguipière

Salmis de Faisan à la Laguipière

Salmi of Pheasant Laguipière

Salmis de Faisan à la Laguipière

WRAP THE PHEASANT in the sheets of fresh pork fat. Season it with salt and pepper and put it in a buttered roasting pan. Roast in a pre-heated 450° F. oven for 15 minutes. Remove the barding fat. Cut off the bird's breast meat and both legs. Cut the carcass into small pieces and then crush them with a meat mallet.

Cut the ¼ pound of pork fat into dice and put it in a casserole with the onions. Sauté gently until the onions are soft; add the white wine, the Madeira, stock, meat juices, and crushed bones. Simmer, covered, over low heat for 45 minutes. Remove the diced pork fat, reserve it, and strain the sauce. Return the sauce to the casserole and add the mushrooms and the pheasant pieces. Simmer, covered, over moderate heat for 15 minutes.

Heat the oil and the butter in a casserole over high heat. Add the pheasant's liver and crush it with a fork while it cooks. Add the liver and the pork-fat dice to the casserole. Season with salt and pepper and mix well. Toast the bread.

Line the bottom of a hot serving dish with the toast and spoon pheasant and sauce on it. Serve immediately.

For 4 persons:

1 pheasant	½ cup Madeira
Thin sheets of fresh pork fat	½ cup White Stock (p. 165)
Salt	¼ cup meat juices, from a roast
Freshly ground black pepper	½ pound mushrooms, quartered
¼ pound fresh pork fat, preferably breast or belly fat	1 tablespoon peanut oil
	2 tablespoons butter
3 onions, minced	The pheasant liver
¾ cup dry white wine	4 slices of firm white bread

Duck in Port-Wine Aspic

Canard de Barberie à la Gelée de Porto

Duck in Port-Wine Aspic

Canard de Barberie à la Gelée de Porto

MAKE A STUFFING: Sauté the blanched bacon gently in the butter in a casserole and add the minced duck livers and onion. Season with salt and pepper and sprinkle with the thyme and bay leaf. Cook for about 5 minutes and then force through a sieve or grind, using the fine blade of a meat grinder. Stuff the duck with this mixture and sew it closed. Truss the duck and prick the lower breast and thighs in several places to allow fat to escape. Roast it in a 350° F. oven for about 1¼ hours, or until the juices run clear when the thigh is pricked with a fork.

When the duck is done, cool it, chill, and then put it on a rack over a deep dish. Coat the whole bird with cold but still liquid aspic. Take your time. The jelly must cling well; you'll have to repeat the coating operation several times, if necessary using any jelly that dripped into the dish.

When you've finished, place the duck on a serving platter and chill it. Chill the remaining aspic in a small deep mold. Unmold it, cut it into thin slices, and surround the duck with them.

For 4 persons:

¼ pound bacon, minced
    and blanched
3 tablespoons butter
1 pound duck livers,
    minced
1 onion, minced
Salt
Freshly ground black
    pepper

Pinch of dried thyme
1 bay leaf, crushed
1 duck (5 pounds)
4 cups Brown Stock for
    Aspics (p. 166), seasoned
    with ½ cup port wine

Galantine of Turkey

Galantine de Dinde

Galantine of Turkey

Galantine de Dinde

FIRST MAKE THE stuffing: Grind, using the fine blade of a meat grinder, the veal, the fresh pork fat and the ham. Mix well and beat in the *quatre épices,* the egg yolks, the *fines herbes* and the minced truffle. Season with salt and pepper and mix again.

Bone the turkey, splitting it down the back, and reserve the bones. Lay it out, skin side down, on a board. Slice off some of the leg and breast meat where it is thickest and use these slices to pad spots where the meat is thin.

Season with salt and pepper. Spread about a third of the stuffing on the meat, top it with the quartered truffles, half of the strips of tongue and half of the salt-pork strips. Repeat this procedure and finally cover with the remaining stuffing. Roll up the meat into a galantine, or oval roll, enclosing it tightly in the turkey skin. Sew it closed. Wrap it completely in the sheets of fresh pork fat and wrap it again tightly in a napkin. Tie it at the ends and in several places along its length.

Line the bottom of a casserole with 4 thin sheets of pork fat. Put the galantine in the casserole and around it place the onions, carrots, *bouquet garni,* cloves, the reserved turkey bones and the calf's feet or veal knuckle. Add enough chicken or turkey stock to cover the galantine completely. Add the Madeira and the brandy. Cover with more sheets of fresh pork fat or with a heavily buttered sheet of paper. Bring to a boil and then simmer over extremely low heat for 3 hours.

Remove the casserole from the heat. Let it stand for 1 hour.

Remove the galantine from the liquid. Put it into a large oval bowl, top it with a board, and weigh down this board with a 1-pound weight until the galantine is cold. When the galantine is cold, remove the napkin and chill the roll on a platter in the refrigerator.

Strain and degrease the poaching liquid. Test it for its jellying properties and, if necessary, add a little unflavored gelatin (see p. 166). Clarify it with the egg whites (see p. 53).

Garnish the top of the galantine with tarragon leaves and carrot slices in a floral pattern. Spoon cold but still liquid stock over it and chill again in the refrigerator. Chill the remaining stock until it jells, cut it into slices, and surround the galantine with these slices.

For 8 persons:

For the stuffing:
  1 pound boneless veal
  1 pound fresh pork fat
  ½ pound Bayonne ham
    or prosciutto
  2 teaspoons Quatre
    Épices (p. 667)
  2 egg yolks
  2 tablespoons minced
    Fines Herbes (p. 89)
  1 truffle, minced
  Salt
  Freshly ground black
    pepper
1 turkey (6 pounds)
Salt
Freshly ground black pepper
½ pound truffles, cut
    into quarters

½ pound tongue, cut
    into strips
½ pound salt pork,
    cut into strips (lard gras)
Thin sheets of fresh pork fat
4 onions, sliced
4 carrots, sliced
1 Bouquet Garni (p. 46)
3 whole cloves
1 small veal knuckle or
    2 small calf's feet
3 (or more) quarts White
    Poultry Stock (p. 165)
1 cup dry Madeira
2 tablespoons brandy
Unflavored gelatin
3 egg whites
Tarragon leaves, blanched
Thin carrot slices

Braised Young Turkey
Dindonneau Braisé

Braised Young Turkey

Dindonneau Braisé

SEASON THE TURKEY inside and out with salt and pepper and truss it. Heat the lard in a large casserole and brown the turkey on all sides. Remove it to a hot plate and keep it warm. Put the carrots, turnip, celery and onions into the casserole, and add a little more lard if necessary. Cook until the vegetables are soft and golden. Season with salt and pepper, add the garlic, and mix well. Remove the vegetables from the casserole with a slotted spoon.

Line the bottom and sides of the casserole with the sheets of fresh pork fat and put the turkey in the casserole. Add the vegetables, the *bouquet garni,* the tomatoes and the stock. Cover the turkey with another sheet of fresh pork fat.

Cover the casserole, bring the liquid to a boil, and then put the casserole in a preheated 350° F. oven for about 1¾ hours.

Remove the bird and put it on a hot serving dish. Keep hot.

Skim the fat off the braising liquid, strain through a fine sieve, let it stand for 5 minutes, and again skim free of all fat. Return the sauce to low heat and stir in the *beurre manié.* You should use 1 tablespoon of *beurre manié* for each cup of braising liquid. Simmer for at least 5 minutes and correct the seasoning.

Garnish the turkey platter with the braised endives and watercress. Serve the sauce separately in a sauceboat.

For 6 persons:

1 young turkey (5 pounds)
Salt
Freshly ground black
    pepper
4 (or more) tablespoons lard
3 carrots, minced
1 small turnip, minced
2 celery stalks, minced
2 onions, minced
1 garlic clove, minced
Thin sheets of fresh
    pork fat

1 Bouquet Garni (p. 46)
2 tomatoes, cut into
    quarters
3 cups White Poultry
    Stock (p. 165)
3 tablespoons Beurre
    Manié (p. 41)
1½ recipes Braised Belgian
    Endives (p. 593)
1 bunch of watercress

Guinea Hen Marco Polo

Pintadeau Marco Polo

Guinea Hen Marco Polo

Pintadeau Marco Polo

SEASON THE CAVITY of the birds with salt and pepper and truss them. Heat half of the oil and half of the butter in a very large casserole and brown the birds in it on all sides. Remove them, cut off the breast from each bird, and cut each breast into halves, making 8 pieces. Reserve the remainder of the carcasses for a stock or any other desired use. Pour the fat out of the skillet. Add the port wine and scrape up all the little brown bits at the bottom of the casserole. Return the breasts to the casserole and season lightly with salt. Bring to a boil, reduce the heat, cover the casserole tightly, and simmer them over low heat for 15 minutes, or until they are tender.

Meantime, fry the bread slices in the remaining hot oil and butter. Place them on a hot serving platter and top them with the guinea hen breasts. Coat each with a spoonful of the sauce and surround with the noodles dressed with the melted butter and cheese. Garnish the platter with the watercress.

For 8 persons:

4 guinea hens (2 pounds
    each)
Salt
Freshly ground black
    pepper
6 tablespoons peanut oil
6 tablespoons butter
¾ cup port wine

8 slices of French
    bread
1 pound noodles, cooked
½ pound butter,
    melted
4 tablespoons grated
    Swiss cheese
Watercress

Bresse Squab à la Lucien Tendret

Pigeons de Bresse à la Lucien Tendret

Bresse Squab à la Lucien Tendret

Pigeons de Bresse à la Lucien Tendret

SEASON THE CAVITIES of the birds with salt and pepper and truss them. Heat 6 tablespoons of the butter in a casserole and brown the squabs on all sides. Reduce the heat, cover the casserole, and cook the squabs gently for about 40 minutes, turning them over occasionally.

Sauté the bread slices in the remaining butter and the oil until they are golden brown on both sides.

Prepare the potatoes and asparagus so that they are ready at the same time as the squabs are done.

Place the bread slices on a hot serving platter, top each with a squab, sprinkle the birds with the pan juices, and garnish the dish with the asparagus tips and the potatoes.

For 2 persons:

2 squabs (1¼ pounds each)
Salt
Freshly ground black
    pepper
10 tablespoons butter
2 thick slices of
    French bread

2 tablespoons peanut oil
½ recipe Potatoes
    Dauphine (p. 623)
½ recipe Asparagus in
    Butter (p. 552), using
    only the asparagus
    tips

Leg of Venison à la Princess Palatine
Gigue de Chevreuil Princesse Palatine

Leg of Venison à la Princess Palatine

Gigue de Chevreuil Princesse Palatine

TRIM THE VENISON, reserving the trimmings, and season the leg with salt and pepper. Mince the marinade vegatables and line the bottom of a very large bowl (not an aluminum one) with them. Lay the venison leg over the vegetables. Sprinkle with the minced herbs and the spices, and add the wine, the vinegar and the oil. Marinate in a cool place for 2 days, turning occasionally. Drain the meat and strain and reserve the marinade.

Prepare the *sauce poivrade,* adding the trimmings from the meat, and use the strained marinade in place of the red wine and the *sauce espagnole.* Simmer the sauce, covered, over low heat for 3 hours if possible. Add the crushed peppercorns just before straining the sauce through a fine sieve. Keep the sauce hot.

Dry the venison leg with kitchen paper and wrap the sheets of pork fat around it and tie them. Place the meat on a rack in a roasting pan and roast in a preheated 450° F. oven for 15 minutes. Reduce the heat to 325° F. and roast for about 1¼ hours longer, or for a total cooking time of about 15 minutes per pound. Remove the sheets of pork fat from the meat for the last 20 minutes of roasting so the leg will brown. Transfer the meat to a hot serving platter and coat it with the hot sauce.

Serve with chestnut purée, or with potato croquettes, and with a garnish of red-currant clusters and olive halves filled with red currants.

For 8 persons:

1 leg of venison (6 pounds)	½ cup vinegar
Salt	½ cup peanut oil
Freshly ground black	1½ recipes Sauce
pepper	Poivrade (p. 765)
For the marinade:	1 tablespoon peppercorns,
2 carrots	crushed
2 onions	Several thin sheets of
2 celery stalks	fresh pork fat
2 shallots, minced	1 recipe Chestnut Purée
2 garlic cloves, minced	(p. 582), or 1 double
2 parsley roots, minced	recipe Potato
1 teaspoon dried thyme	Croquettes (p. 640)
5 whole cloves	1 quart fresh red
2 teaspoons juniper berries	currants
4 cups dry white wine	1 dozen green olives, pitted

/ *Purée of Fresh Fava or Broad Beans*

PURÉE DE FÈVES FRAÎCHES

Proceed as in Boiled Fava or Broad Beans (above).

Purée the cooked beans in a blender. Put them into a saucepan, add the butter, and cook over low heat for about 5 minutes, stirring constantly. Season with salt, pepper and nutmeg.

If desired, the juices from a roast of veal, pork, or even a chicken may be added to the puréed beans.

FOR 4 PERSONS:

3 **pounds unshelled fava or broad**	**Salt**
beans	**Freshly ground black pepper**
6 **tablespoons butter**	**Grated nutmeg**

/ *Ragout of Fresh Fava or Broad Beans*

RAGOÛT DE FÈVES FRAÎCHES

Shell the broad beans and remove their tough outer skins.

Heat the lard or the goose fat in a casserole and add the onions. Cook until the onions are barely golden. Stir in the flour and cook for 1 minute. Add the broad beans, the *bouquet garni,* the mint and the basil. Season with salt and pepper and add the water. Simmer, covered, over low heat until the beans are tender, for about 10 to 20 minutes.

When the broad beans are ready, take out a ladle full and mash them. Return the mashed beans to the casserole, mix well, and simmer for 2 to 3 minutes longer.

Sauté the bread slices in the hot butter until golden.

Dish up the broad beans in a vegetable dish and garnish them with the bread croutons.

FOR 4 PERSONS:

3 **pounds unshelled fava or broad**	1 **sprig of fresh basil**
beans	**Salt**
2 **tablespoons lard or goose fat**	**Freshly ground black pepper**
2 **onions, cut into quarters**	1 **cup water**
1 **tablespoon flour**	4 **slices of bread, crusts removed**
1 **Bouquet Garni (p. 46)**	3 **tablespoons butter**
1 **sprig of fresh mint**	

JARDINIÈRE DE LÉGUMES AU BEURRE / *Mixed Vegetables*

Prepare the peas, green snap beans, fresh white beans, turnip and carrots. Cook them in boiling salted water until they are tender. They may be cooked separately, or cooked together, timing the addition of each to the salted water so that they will all finish cooking at the same time.

Drain the cooked vegetables in a colander.

Heat the butter in a casserole, add the vegetables, season with salt and pepper, and mix carefully. Simmer for 3 to 4 minutes and sprinkle with the *fines herbes*. Put them in a hot vegetable dish and serve hot.

FOR 8 PERSONS:

1 cup shelled peas
½ pound green snap beans
1 cup shelled fresh white beans
1 turnip, diced
4 medium-sized carrots, diced

½ cup butter
Salt
Freshly ground black pepper
4 tablespoons minced Fines
  Herbes (p. 89)

Mixed Vegetables in Cream /
JARDINIÈRE DE LÉGUMES À LA CRÈME

Proceed as in th epreceding recipe. Add 1 cup of Crème Fraîche (p. 666) to the cooked vegetables in the casserole and simmer until the *crème* is somewhat reduced.

LENTILS

Lentilles

Lentils with Salt Pork or Bacon / LENTILLES AU LARD

Wash the lentils in several changes of cold water.

Put them into a casserole with a great deal of cold water. Season with salt and pepper, add the onion, and bring to the boiling point. Add the bacon. Simmer, covered, over low heat for about 1½ hours.

At serving time, drain the lentils, put them into a vegetable dish, and remove the onion. Serve hot.

FOR 4 PERSONS:

2 cups dried lentils
Salt
Freshly ground pepper

1 onion, stuck with 1 clove
¼ pound slab bacon, blanched
  and cut into small dice

Lentils Ménagère / LENTILLES À LA MÉNAGÈRE

Wash the lentils and put them into a large saucepan with plenty of cold water. Bring to the boiling point and drain immediately.

Mince the carrots, onion, turnip, celery, garlic and shallot and put them into a casserole with the lard. Cook the vegetables over medium heat until they are soft and barely golden. Stir in the flour and mix well. Add the lentils, bacon, *bouquet garni*, pepper and very little salt. Add just enough boiling water to barely cover the lentils. Cover the casserole and simmer over low heat for 1½ hours, stirring occasionally.

When the lentils are tender, cut the bacon into slices. Discard the *bouquet garni*. Put the lentils into a serving dish and garnish with the sliced bacon.

You may also garnish the dish with little sausages cooked in a mixture of butter and oil or in lard in a skillet.

FOR 4 PERSONS:

2 **cups dried lentils**	1 **tablespoon flour**
2 **carrots**	½ **pound slab bacon**
1 **onion**	1 **Bouquet Garni (p. 46)**
1 **turnip**	**Freshly ground black pepper**
1 **celery stalk**	**Salt**
1 **garlic clove**	**Optional: 8 small sausages,**
1 **shallot**	**sautéed**
3 **tablespoons lard**	

CHICK-PEAS

Pois Chiches

POIS CHICHES BOUILLIS / *Boiled Chick-Peas*

Soak the chick-peas in cold water overnight.

Drain them, and put them into a large saucepan. Barely cover with cold water and season with salt and pepper. Add the onion, carrot, *bouquet garni,* and the ham or salt pork. Bring to a boil and simmer over low heat for about 1 hour. Add a little more water from time to time to keep the vegetables covered. When the chick-peas are tender, remove the *bouquet garni* and the onion and drain the peas. Dice the ham or salt pork. Put vegetables and diced meat into a hot serving dish, dot with butter, and sprinkle with the *fines herbes*.

FOR 4 PERSONS:

1 **pound dried chick-peas (or**	1 **Bouquet Garni (p. 46)**
garbanzos)	¼ **pound Bayonne ham, prosciutto**
Salt	**or lean salt pork**
Freshly ground black pepper	3 **tablespoons butter**
1 **onion, stuck with 1 clove**	3 **tablespoons minced Fines**
1 **carrot, minced**	**Herbes (p. 89)**

POIS CHICHES À LA CATALANE / *Chick-Peas Catalan*

Prepare the vegetable in the same manner as in the preceding recipe, except cook the Spanish sausages with the peas and add the olive oil and the sweet pepper at the same time.

When the chick-peas are about half done, remove the *bouquet garni* and the onion, add the tomato paste, mix, and remove the sausages. Cut the sausages and the ham into small dice and return the meats to the saucepan. Add the garlic, and a little more water if necessary. Check the seasoning and simmer very slowly for 1 more hour. Serve the chick-peas in a hot vegetable dish, and very hot.

FOR 4 PERSONS:

1 recipe Boiled Chick-Peas (p. 563)
4 Spanish or garlic sausages
2 tablespoons olive oil

1 sweet pepper, charred, scraped and minced (see p. 619)
3 tablespoons tomato paste
1 garlic clove

BRUSSELS SPROUTS

Choux de Bruxelles

Blanched Brussels Sprouts /

CHOUX DE BRUXELLES CUITS AU BLANC

Trim the bottoms off the Brussels sprouts and wash them under running water. Bring 6 to 8 quarts of water to a boil and season well with salt. Add the Brussels sprouts and cook until tender, about 10 minutes. Drain them thoroughly and use as desired.

FOR 4 PERSONS:

2 quarts Brussels sprouts   Salt

Brussels Sprouts in Butter /

CHOUX DE BRUXELLES AU BEURRE

Blanch the Brussels sprouts as described above, but cook them for only about 6 minutes, or until they are about three-quarters done.

Heat the butter in a casserole, add the Brussels sprouts, and cook, covered, over low heat for 3 to 4 minutes. Season with salt, pepper and nutmeg; serve very hot.

FOR 4 PERSONS:

2 quarts Brussels sprouts
6 tablespoons butter
Salt

Freshly ground white pepper
Grated nutmeg

CHOUX DE BRUXELLES AU JUS **/ *Brussels Sprouts au Jus***

Proceed as in Brussels Sprouts in Butter (above), but omit the nutmeg. Stir in the pan juices of roast chicken or roast wild birds.

/ *Brussels Sprouts au Gratin*

CHOUX DE BRUXELLES AU GRATIN

Blanch the Brussels sprouts as described above but cook them for only about 6 minutes.

Butter a baking dish and put the Brussels sprouts into it. Dot them with the butter and season with salt and pepper. Coat with the *sauce béchamel*. Sprinkle with the grated cheese and the bread crumbs. Cook in a preheated 350° F. oven for about 20 minutes.

FOR 4 PERSONS:

2 **quarts Brussels sprouts**
3 **tablespoons butter**
Salt
Freshly ground white pepper

2 **cups Sauce Béchamel (p. 761)**
¼ **cup grated Swiss cheese**
2 **tablespoons fine dry bread crumbs**

CABBAGE

Choux

CHOU CUIT AU BLANC **/ *Blanched Cabbage***

Remove the wilted outer leaves from the cabbage and cut off the stem. Wash the cabbage and drain it. If using small cabbages, leave them whole; larger cabbages may be halved or quartered.

Put the cabbage into cold salted water to cover, bring to the boiling point, and simmer for 8 to 10 minutes, depending on size. Drain the cabbage in a sieve and let cold water run over it. Drain again and twist it dry in a kitchen towel. Use as desired.

FOR 4 PERSONS:

1 **large cabbage (2 pounds), or**
  2 **small cabbages**

Salted water

Braised Green Cabbage / CHOU VERT BRAISÉ

Blanch the cabbages as described above.

Heat the butter or the lard in a saucepan. Add the carrots, onion, *bouquet garni* and cabbages. Season with salt and pepper, and add enough well-flavored consommé, or water, to cover. Top with the slices of fresh pork fat, or with buttered kitchen parchment or aluminum foil.

Bring to the boiling point, cook for 2 minutes over high heat, lower the heat to the lowest possible, and simmer the cabbages until tender. Begin testing for doneness after 15 minutes. The cabbages may also be cooked in a preheated 325° F. oven.

When the cabbages are done, serve them in a hot serving dish or use them as a garnish for meats.

FOR 4 PERSONS:

4 very small cabbages, or 1 large
   cabbage, quartered
4 tablespoons butter or lard
2 small carrots, sliced
1 onion, stuck with 1 clove
1 Bouquet Garni (p. 46)

Salt
Freshly ground white pepper
3 cups (about) Beef Consommé
   (p. 167), or water
4 slices of fresh pork fat

Braised Red Cabbage Limousine /

CHOUX ROUGES BRAISÉS À LA LIMOUSINE

Separate the leaves of the red cabbage, trim off the ribbed stalks, and cut the leaves into thin julienne strips.

Heat the lard in a casserole; add the cabbage and the chestnuts. Add enough consommé to cover. Season lightly with salt and pepper and, if necessary, add a little more lard. Cover the casserole and simmer over low heat for 40 minutes. Serve very hot.

FOR 6 PERSONS:

1 red cabbage (3 pounds)
6 tablespoons lard
1 pound raw chestnuts, outer
   shells and inner skins removed
   (see p. 582)

3 (or more) cups Beef Consommé
   (p. 167)
Salt
Freshly ground black pepper

Note: Small peeled and cored apples may be put on top of the chestnuts and cooked along with the dish, to serve as its garnish.

Braised Red Cabbage Flemish Style /

CHOUX ROUGES BRAISÉS À LA FLAMANDE

Trim the cabbage, cut it into quarters, remove the ribbed stalks, and cut the leaves into thin julienne strips.

Heat the oil in a casserole, add the cabbage, sprinkle with the vinegar, and dot with the butter. Season with salt and pepper. Cover the casserole and cook over low heat for about 40 minutes.

Peel, core, and slice the apples. Add them to the cabbage together with the sugar and mix well. Simmer, covered, for about 5 minutes longer. Serve very hot.

FOR 6 PERSONS:

1 **red cabbage (3 pounds)**	**Salt**
4 **tablespoons olive oil**	**Freshly ground black pepper**
1 **teaspoon vinegar**	3 **tart apples**
3 **tablespoons butter**	2 **tablespoons sugar**

DOLMAS DE CHOU / *Cabbage Dolmas*

Blanch the whole cabbage as described above (p. 565).

Cook the rice and drain it. Cut the meat into small pieces and mince it, using the fine blade of a grinder. Combine the cooked rice and meat. Season with salt, pepper and nutmeg.

Put the cabbage on a kitchen towel and separate the leaves. Remove the ribbing in the stalks. Line the larger leaves with the smaller ones and put a little of the stuffing in the middle of each leaf.

Roll up each leaf into the shape of a sausage and fasten with food picks, or tie with soft string. Put the oil into a casserole, place the stuffed cabbage leaves in it side by side, and sprinkle with the lemon juice. Cook, covered, over moderate heat for about 30 minutes, basting occasionally. Serve very hot.

FOR 4 PERSONS:

1 **cabbage (2 pounds)**	**Freshly ground black pepper**
½ **cup uncooked rice**	**Grated nutmeg**
½ **pound boneless shoulder of**	3 **tablespoons olive oil**
lamb	**Juice of 1 lemon**
Salt	

FRICASSÉE DE CHOU VERT / *Fricassee of Cabbage*

Trim and wash the cabbage and mince it. Twist it in a kitchen towel to remove excess moisture.

Heat the oil and the lard in a casserole, add the cabbage, season with salt and pepper, and mix well. Simmer, covered, for about 20 minutes. Stir frequently.

Serve the cabbage as a garnish for a roast, such as a roast of pork.

FOR 4 PERSONS:

1 **cabbage (2 pounds)**	**Salt**
1 **tablespoon olive oil**	**Freshly ground white pepper**
4 **tablespoons lard**	

Cabbage Roll | GÂTEAU AU CHOU VERT

Shred a cabbage into fine strips and sauté it in the hot lard in a casserole for 5 minutes. Add the sugar. Simmer, covered, over low heat for 20 minutes, stirring frequently.

Put the flour and the salt in a bowl. Combine the vinegar, lukewarm water, 2 tablespoons of the oil, the whole egg and the egg yolk. Add this mixture to the flour and stir with a fork until the mixture clears the bowl. Knead it for about 5 minutes and shape it into a ball. Let the dough stand in a warm place for 30 minutes. Roll out the dough as thin as possible on a floured cloth, coat it with a little oil, and then stretch it with both hands to make it even thinner, but do not make any holes in this sheet of dough. The simplest way to do this is to place your hands underneath the dough and use a hand over hand motion to stretch it. If the edges are too thick, trim them off. Brush the surface of the dough with more oil.

Spread the cabbage evenly on the dough, up to 1 inch from the edge on all sides. Shape into a roll by lifting the pastry cloth at one end so that the dough rolls over and over itself into a fairly tight roll.

Oil a baking sheet and put the cabbage roll, seam side down, on it. Paint the roll with more oil and bake in a preheated 350° F. oven for 25 to 30 minutes.

FOR 4 PERSONS:

1 cabbage (1½ pounds)
3 tablespoons lard
1 tablespoon sugar

For the pastry:
3 cups flour
Pinch of salt
1 teaspoon vinegar
⅔ cup lukewarm water
¼ cup (or more) vegetable oil
1 whole egg
1 extra egg yolk

Stuffed Green Cabbage | CHOU VERT FARCI

Blanch the cabbage as described above (p. 565).

Remove six of the cabbage's large outer leaves and put them side by side on a kitchen towel. Remove all the other leaves, trim off the ribbed stems, and line each large leaf with several of the smaller ones to give them more body.

Cut the meat into small pieces, remove the tendons and gristle, and mince the meat and the pork fat together, using the fine blade of a meat grinder. Season with salt and pepper; add the *fines herbes* and a tablespoon of the wine. Mix well. Spoon a little of this filling into each cabbage leaf and roll each leaf into a tight ball. Put each cabbage ball separately into a kitchen towel, and twist it to extract all possible moisture from the cabbage ball and to mold it firmly into a round shape. Put the stuffed cabbage balls on a plate.

Mince the shallots, garlic and onion and cook them in the hot lard in a saucepan until they are soft and golden.

Remove the shallots, garlic and onion and put them into the bottom of a baking dish. Stir the remaining wine into the saucepan in which the vegetables were cooked, add the tomato purée, mix well, and bring to the boiling point.

Put the stuffed cabbage balls into the baking dish, on top of the shallots, garlic and onion. Cover each ball with a thin slice of fresh pork fat or ham fat and coat them with the wine and tomato mixture. Cook in a preheated 350° F. oven for 30. minutes, or until the cabbage balls are golden.

Remove the cabbage balls from the oven, and garnish with slice of fried bread next to each cabbage ball. Serve very hot.

FOR 6 PERSONS:

1 cabbage (2½ pounds)
¼ pound lean pork
¼ pound boneless shoulder of veal
¼ pound fresh pork fat or ham fat
Salt
Freshly ground black pepper
2 tablespoons Fines Herbes (p. 89)

½ cup dry white wine
3 shallots
2 garlic cloves
1 onion
3 tablespoons lard
2 tablespoons Tomato Purée (p. 157)
6 thin slices of pork fat or ham fat
6 slices of firm white bread, fried in lard

/ Ballottine of Stuffed Cabbage

CHOU VERT FARCI EN BALLOTTINE

Blanch the cabbage as described above (p. 565).

Separate the leaves of the cabbage and put them on a kitchen towel.

Make the stuffing. Cut the meat and fresh pork fat into small pieces, remove gristle and tendons, and mince, using the fine blade of a meat grinder. Season with salt and pepper and stir in the *fines herbes.*

Put the large sheet of fresh pork fat on the kitchen table. Put 2 or 3 of the cabbage leaves on it, top them with a little of the stuffing, and cover with more cabbage leaves. Continue the layers, ending with cabbage leaves. There should be 3 to 4 inches of overlapping pork fat on all sides. Wrap the overlapping fat tightly over the stuffing, forming it into a rectangular shape, and tie the *ballottine* with firmly drawn string, to prevent its coming apart during the cooking.

Heat the oil in a casserole, put the *ballottine* in it, cover, and cook in a preheated 300° F. oven for 1½ hours.

Remove the pork fat and cut the *ballottine* into thick slices for serving. Serve hot.

FOR 4 PERSONS:

1 cabbage (2 pounds)
¼ pound lean pork
¼ pound boneless shoulder of veal
¼ pound fresh pork fat
Salt

Freshly ground black pepper
4 tablespoons Fines Herbes (p. 89)
1 large sheet of fresh pork fatback
4 tablespoons olive oil

CAULIFLOWER

Chou-fleurs

Blanched Cauliflower | CHOU-FLEUR CUIT AU BLANC

Snap or cut the flowerets from the head of cauliflower and cut a slit in the stem of each floweret to insure even cooking.

Bring a very large kettle of water to a boil and season it generously with salt. Drop the flowerets into the water and boil for 9 to 12 minutes to cook them completely. They are done when a knife will easily pierce one of the stems.

If the cauliflower is to receive further cooking, boil it for only 6 to 9 minutes, so that it will not be overdone after the further cooking.

Generally it is wiser not to blanch a whole head of cauliflower, since the top flowers will be overcooked by the time the thick stem is tender.

FOR 4 PERSONS:

1 large head of cauliflower	**Salt**

Cauliflower in Butter | CHOU-FLEUR AU BEURRE FONDU

Blanch the cauliflower as described above.

Put the flowerets into the serving dish and coat with the hot melted butter. Sprinkle with the parsley and serve immediately.

FOR 4 PERSONS:

1 large head of cauliflower	**2 tablespoons minced parsley**
4 tablespoons hot melted butter	

Cauliflower Hollandaise | CHOU-FLEUR SAUCE HOLLANDAISE

Blanch the cauliflower as described above.

Put the flowerets into a hot serving dish and coat them with the *sauce hollandaise*. Serve immediately, very hot.

FOR 4 PERSONS:

1 large head of cauliflower	**2 cups Sauce Hollandaise (p. 780)**

Cauliflower Sautéed in Butter |
CHOU-FLEUR SAUTÉ AU BEURRE

Blanch the cauliflower as described above, but cook it for only 6 to 9 minutes, or until it is three-quarters done.

Heat the butter in a casserole, add the flowerets, and cook until golden, turning them frequently.

Put the cauliflower into a hot serving dish and sprinkle with the pan juices and the *fines herbes*. Serve hot.

FOR 4 PERSONS:

1 large head of cauliflower	2 tablespoons minced Fines
6 tablespoons butter	Herbes (p. 89)

CHOU-FLEUR SAUCE CRÈME / *Cauliflower in Cream*

Blanch the cauliflower as described above.

Pour the *crème fraîche* into a saucepan and bring it to the boiling point. Season lightly with salt, pepper and nutmeg, and reduce it by half.

Put the cooked cauliflower into a hot serving dish. Dot with the butter and coat with the cream, which should be very hot.

FOR 4 PERSONS:

1 large head of cauliflower	Grated nutmeg
1 cup Crème Fraîche (p. 666)	2 tablespoons butter, cut into
Salt	small pieces
Freshly ground white pepper	

CHOU-FLEUR AU GRATIN / *Cauliflower au Gratin*

Blanch the cauliflower as described above.

Make the *sauce béchamel* or the *sauce Mornay*. Put the flowerets into a buttered baking dish.

Sprinkle the cauliflower with the grated cheese, dot with the butter, and coat with the sauce. Sprinkle with the bread crumbs.

Brown quickly under a broiler and serve very hot.

FOR 4 PERSONS:

1 large head of cauliflower	2 tablespoons butter, cut into
3 cups Sauce Béchamel (p. 761),	small pieces
or Sauce Mornay (p. 776)	3 tablespoons fine dry bread
3 tablespoons grated Swiss cheese	crumbs

PURÉE DE CHOU-FLEUR / *Cauliflower Purée*

Blanch the cauliflower as described above (p. 570).

Purée it in a blender. Put the purée into a saucepan over low heat, add the butter, mix well, and bring to the boiling point. Cook, stirring constantly, for 3 to 4 minutes, or until the purée is beginning to look dry. Add the *crème fraîche,* and season with salt, pepper and nutmeg.

Serve in a vegetable dish or as a meat garnish.

FOR 4 PERSONS:

1 large head of cauliflower	Salt
3 tablespoons butter	Freshly ground white pepper
¼ cup Crème Fraîche (p. 666)	Grated nutmeg

Cauliflower Loaf / PAIN DE CHOU-FLEUR

Prepare the cauliflower as described above.

Purée the flowerets in a blender or force them through a food mill. Beat in the egg yolks. Season to taste with salt, pepper and nutmeg.

Butter a 4-cup charlotte mold and pour the cauliflower purée into it. Set the mold in a pan containing 1 inch of water and cook in a preheated 375° F. oven for 25 minutes. If necessary, add more water to the pan.

Unmold on a hot serving dish and coat the cauliflower loaf with the hot cream sauce. Serve immediately.

FOR 4 PERSONS:

1 recipe Cauliflower in Butter (p. 570)
4 egg yolks, beaten
Salt

Freshly ground white pepper
Grated nutmeg
2 cups Cream Sauce (p. 775)

C A R D O O N S

Cardons

EDITORS' NOTE: *A cardoon is a silvery green, prickly plant which resembles an overgrown bunch of celery, with an average height of 4 to 5 feet. It is closely related to the globe artichoke. The edible parts of the cardoon are the midribs of the plant, which are fleshy and tender. The flavor of a cardoon is delicate and reminds one of that of the oyster plant or the artichoke. It is delicious.*

Cardoons are among the favorite French and Italian winter vegetables. In the United States, they are mostly grown in California for markets catering to people of Italian descent, where they are found during the winter months.

Smaller cardoons are more tender than the big ones. One or two 4-foot cardoons will, generally speaking, produce about 2 pounds of edible parts, sufficient for 4 to 6 helpings.

Cardoons, however they are to be used in a recipe, must be boiled first. Their basic preparation resembles that of celery.

Basic Preparation: Remove all the tough outer and wilted stalks, but beware of the prickles. Strip the tender inner stalks free of all leaves. Cut them into 2- to 3-inch pieces (or the size indicated by the recipe) and remove the stringy parts. Drop each piece immediately into acidulated water (1 quart water to 3 tablespoons lemon juice or vinegar) to prevent the cardoons turning black. Trim the heart and cut it into pieces and drop them into the acidulated water. Cook in boiling salted water over moderate heat and drain thoroughly. If the vegetable is to be served with a sauce, cook it until tender, about 1½ hours. If it is to be cooked further in a recipe, cook it only until three-quarters done; the further cooking will make it completely tender.

CARDONS AU BEURRE / *Cardoons in Butter*

Prepare the cardoons and boil them as described above.

Heat the butter in a casserole. Add the cardoons, season with salt and pepper, and heat through.

Serve very hot, in a vegetable dish, as a garnish for roasts.

FOR 4 PERSONS:

2 pounds (approximately) edible part of cardoons	**Salt**
	Freshly ground white pepper
6 tablespoons butter	

CARDONS AUX FINES HERBES / *Cardoons aux Fines Herbes*

Proceed as in Cardoons in Butter (above) and at serving time add 2 tablespoons of minced Fines Herbes (p. 89).

CARDONS À LA CRÈME / *Cardoons in Cream*

Prepare the cardoons as described above.

Just before serving time, add the *crème fraîche* to the cardoons, bring to the boiling point, and simmer until the *crème* has been reduced by half. Season with salt and pepper.

FOR 4 PERSONS:

1 recipe Cardoons in Butter (above)	**Salt**
	Freshly ground white pepper
1 cup Crème Fraîche (p. 666)	

CARDONS AU NATUREL / *Cardoons Nature*

Prepare the cardoons as in the basic preparation (above), and use them as a garnish for roast meats. Dress them with the pan juices from the meat.

CARDONS AU GRATIN / *Cardoons au Gratin*

Prepare the cardoons as in the basic preparation (above).

Butter a deep baking dish and line it with half of the cardoons. Sprinkle with half of the grated cheese, dot with half of the butter, and top with the remaining cardoons. Cover with the remaining cheese and butter and sprinkle with the bread crumbs. Cook in a preheated 375° F. oven for 15 minutes.

FOR 4 PERSONS:

2 pounds (approximately) edible part of cardoons
½ cup grated Swiss cheese

6 tablespoons butter, cut into little pieces
¼ cup fine dry bread crumbs

Note: The cardoons may also be arranged in alternate layers with Sauce Béchamel (p. 761), sprinkled with fine dry bread crumbs, and cooked in the oven, as above.

Cardoons in Madeira / CARDONS AU MADÈRE

Prepare the cardoons as in the basic preparation (p. 572).

Heat the butter in a casserole; add the cardoons, Madeira sauce and white wine. Season very lightly with salt and pepper. Simmer, covered, until the cardoons are tender, about 10 minutes.

Remove the cardoons with a slotted spoon and put them into a hot serving dish; keep them hot.

Reduce the sauce in which the cardoons were cooked by half and add the Madeira. Coat the cardoons with the sauce and serve them very hot.

FOR 4 PERSONS:

2 pounds (approximately) edible part of cardoons
3 tablespoons butter
¼ cup Madeira Sauce (p. 764), or 2 tablespoons tomato paste diluted with 2 tablespoons Beef Consommé (p. 167)

1 cup dry white wine
Salt
Freshly ground black pepper
½ cup Madeira

Cardoons with Marrow / CARDONS À LA MOELLE

Prepare the cardoons as described above.

Remove the marrow from the bone with the point of a knife. Poach it in simmering salted water for 5 minutes; drain. Cut the marrow into thin rounds.

Put the cardoons into a hot serving dish and top them with the marrow. Serve very hot.

FOR 4 PERSONS:

1 recipe Cardoons in Butter (p. 573)

Marrow of 1 large beef bone

Note: This dish may be improved by coating the cardoons with Madeira Sauce (p. 764) before topping with the beef marrow.

Cardoons Piémontaise / CARDONS PIÉMONTAISE

Prepare the cardoons as in the basic preparation (p. 572).

Heat the oil and the butter in a casserole and add the anchovies and the garlic.

Simmer over lowest possible heat, stirring constantly, but do not let the garlic color. Add the truffle.

Put the cardoons into a hot serving dish, and coat them with the sauce.

FOR 4 PERSONS:

2 pounds (approximately) edible part of cardoons

For the sauce:
½ cup olive oil
½ cup butter
6 anchovy fillets, mashed
4 garlic cloves, mashed
1 small truffle, minced

Note: Very fresh, young and tender cardoons may be used raw in this dish. Cut the tender parts and the heart of the vegetable into 2-inch slices, remove the stringy part, and sprinkle the slices with lemon juice, to prevent discoloring. Put them into a serving dish and serve the hot sauce separately, in a sauceboat.

CARROTS

Carottes

CAROTTES AU BEURRE / *Carrots in Butter*

EDITORS' NOTE: *For carrots braised gently in butter in the French manner one assumes the carrots are absolutely fresh. If the carrots are not very fresh, you may prefer to blanch them first in salted water for 10 minutes.*

Wash and scrape or peel the carrots and cut them into thin rounds.

Heat the butter in a casserole and gently sauté the carrots in it. Season with a little salt and the sugar. Stir frequently to prevent scorching. The exact time will depend on the size and the freshness of the carrots. Begin testing for doneness after 15 minutes.

When the carrots are tender, either dish them up in a serving dish or use them for garnishing a roast.

FOR 4 PERSONS:

2 pounds new carrots
6 tablespoons butter

Salt
1 teaspoon sugar

CAROTTES AUX FINES HERBES / *Carrots with Fines Herbes*

Proceed as in Carrots in Butter (above) and add ¼ cup Fines Herbes (p. 89) just before serving.

Carrots with Sauce Béchamel / CAROTTES À LA BÉCHAMEL

Prepare the carrots as in Carrots in Butter and take care that they do not brown. Make the *sauce béchamel* and pour it boiling hot on the carrots. Mix carefully so as not to crush the vegetable. Serve very hot in a vegetable dish.

FOR 4 PERSONS:

2 pounds Carrots in Butter (p. 575)

2 cups Sauce Béchamel (p. 761)

Carrots in Cream / CAROTTES À LA CRÈME

Proceed as in the preceding recipe, but substitute 2 cups Crème Fraîche (p. 666) for the *sauce béchamel.* Add the *crème fraîche* to the carrots after they have cooked for 10 minutes, so that it can reduce by half before serving the vegetable.

Glazed Carrots / CAROTTES GLACÉES

Scrape or peel the carrots; cut them into even pieces and put them into a casserole with cold water to cover. Bring the water quickly to the boiling point and cook for 2 minutes. Drain the carrots and return them to the casserole. Season lightly with salt, add the sugar and butter, and add cold water barely to cover. Simmer until all the cooking liquid has evaporated and the carrots are tender and glazed with a coat of the butter. Shake the casserole frequently to prevent sticking.

FOR 4 PERSONS:

2 pounds carrots
Salt

2 tablespoons sugar
4 tablespoons butter

Carrot Purée / PURÉE DE CAROTTES

Scrape or peel the carrots and cook them in boiling salted water until very tender, 30 to 40 minutes.

Drain the carrots and mash them as you would mash potatoes. Put the carrot purée back into a saucepan and cook it, stirring constantly, over low heat until the moisture has somewhat evaporated and the purée is thick and smooth. Stir in the butter and season with salt and pepper.

Dish up in a vegetable dish and serve very hot.

FOR 4 PERSONS:

2 pounds carrots
6 tablespoons butter

Salt
Freshly ground white pepper

/ *Carrot Purée with Cream*

PURÉE DE CAROTTES À LA CRÈME

Proceed as in the preceding recipe, using only half of the butter. Add ¾ cup Crème Fraîche (p. 666) and let the mixture reduce slowly to make a thick smooth purée.

/ *Carrot and Potato Purée*

PURÉE DE CAROTTES AUX POMMES DE TERRE

Proceed as in Carrot Purée (above). Add 4 large mashed potatoes to the purée and blend well. Stir 3 additional tablespoons of butter into the purée. Serve in a hot serving dish or as a garnish for roast meats.

BEIGNETS AUX CAROTTES / *Carrot Fritters*

Scrape or peel the carrots and cut them into very fine julienne strips with a vegetable grater.

Make the batter: combine the flour, oil, salt, egg and milk, and beat well. Beat in the carrots.

Heat the fat for frying to 375° F. on a frying thermometer. Scoop up the carrot batter with 2 forks, shaping it into little bundles, and drop them into the hot fat. Fry until golden on all sides, turning with a slotted spoon. Do not be surprised by the shape of the fritters: they will not be round and even, but resemble a spider's web. Drain on kitchen paper and serve in a hot serving dish lined with a folded napkin. Serve very hot.

FOR 4 PERSONS:

8 medium-sized carrots	1 egg
4 tablespoons flour	¼ cup milk
2 tablespoons peanut oil	Fat for deep frying
Salt	

C E L E R Y

Céleri

EDITORS' NOTE: *Bunch celery, in France, is frequently used as a hot vegetable.*

Basic Preparation: Trim the root. Remove the tough or wilted outer stalks and the leaves (save leaves for soups, stews, etc.). Scrub the stalks with a vegetable brush or peel with a vegetable peeler. Wash under running water. Dice or cut into small pieces the prepared stalks and heart. Cook, covered, in 1 inch of boiling water until the celery is just tender. Depending on the size and type of celery, the time may be from 8 to 20 minutes. Drain and serve with a sauce. If the celery is to be cooked further, cook the celery only three-quarters done, so that the further cooking will not make it mushy.

Allow 1 large bunch of celery for 4 servings.

Celery in Butter / CÉLERI AU BEURRE

Prepare the celery as in the basic preparation (above).

Put the cooked celery into a casserole with the butter. Cover and simmer over low heat for 3 to 4 minutes, stirring occasionally with a fork. Season with salt and pepper.

Serve in a hot serving dish or as a garnish for roast meats.

FOR 4 PERSONS:

1 large bunch of celery	Salt
6 tablespoons butter	Freshly ground white pepper

Celery in Cream / CÉLERI À LA CRÈME

Prepare the celery as in the basic preparation (above), but cook it only three-quarters done.

Put the drained celery into a casserole with 4 tablespoons of the butter and add enough chicken consommé to not quite cover the celery. Cover the casserole, bring to the boiling point, and simmer over very low heat for 10 minutes. Or let it simmer in a preheated 325° F. oven.

Remove the celery with a slotted spoon, put it into a hot serving dish, and keep it hot.

Reduce the pan juices by half, add the *crème fraîche,* bring to the boiling point, and reduce the sauce until smooth and slightly thickened. Stir in the remaining butter and check the seasoning. Pour the sauce over the celery and serve very hot.

FOR 4 PERSONS:

1 large bunch of celery	1 cup Crème Fraîche (p. 666)
6 tablespoons butter	Salt
2 cups hot Chicken Consommé (p. 168)	Freshly ground white pepper

Celery au Gratin / CÉLERI AU GRATIN

Prepare the celery as described above.

Make the *sauce béchamel.*

Put the cooked celery into a buttered baking dish, together with the pan juices. Coat with the *sauce béchamel,* check the seasoning, and sprinkle with the grated cheese and the bread crumbs. Brown quickly under the broiler and serve immediately.

FOR 4 PERSONS:

1 recipe Celery in Butter (above)
2 cups Sauce Béchamel (p. 761)
Salt
Freshly ground white pepper

3 tablespoons grated Swiss cheese
2 tablespoons fine dry bread
    crumbs

/ *Celery au Gratin with Cheese*

CÉLERI AU FROMAGE GRATINÉ

Prepare the celery as described above.

Butter a baking dish and make layers of celery sprinkled with grated cheese. Dot each layer with butter. Sprinkle the top layer with bread crumbs.

Cook in a preheated 375° F. oven for 15 minutes.

FOR 4 PERSONS:

1 recipe Celery in Butter (above)
½ cup grated Swiss cheese
6 tablespoons butter, cut into
    little pieces

3 tablespoons fine dry bread
    crumbs

CÉLERI À LA MOELLE / *Celery with Marrow*

Prepare the celery as described above.

Remove the marrow from the bone with the point of a knife. Poach in simmering salted water to cover over low heat for 5 minutes. Drain the marrow and cut it into rounds.

Put the celery into a hot serving dish and top with the marrow. Season lightly with salt and pepper.

Place under the broiler until the marrow begins to melt. Remove the dish and sprinkle with the parsley. Serve very hot.

FOR 4 PERSONS:

1 recipe Celery in Butter (above)
Marrow from 1 large beef bone
Salt

Freshly ground white pepper
2 tablespoons minced parsley

BEIGNETS DE CÉLERI / *Celery Fritters*

Prepare the celery as in the basic preparation (above), but cook it until it is only three-quarters done. Or, if the celery is very tender, it need not be parboiled at all, merely cut into pieces.

Make the fritter batter by thoroughly beating together all the ingredients; dip the celery pieces into it, coating them well.

Heat the fat to 375° F. on a frying thermometer. Fry the celery pieces in it until they are golden on all sides. Drain on kitchen paper. Serve in a hot serving dish lined with a folded napkin, with a sprinkling of salt and minced parsley.

FOR 4 PERSONS:

1 large bunch of celery	**Fat for deep frying**
For the fritter batter:	**Salt**
1 cup flour	**Minced parsley**
3 eggs	
¾ cup beer	
1 tablespoon peanut oil	
1 teaspoon salt	

KNOB CELERY, CELERY ROOT, CELERIAC

Céleri-Rave

> EDITORS' NOTE: *This European variety of celery is a dark root, with a crown of stemmed leaves; only the root is eaten. It is much used in continental Europe, especially in France, in hors-d'oeuvre, salads and hot dishes, and as a flavoring for soups and stews. Knob celery has a strong flavor, and it is eaten raw only when very young and tender. It is a winter vegetable. In the United States it can be found in markets catering to people of European descent.*

Basic Preparation: Scrub the knob celery with a vegetable brush. Cut off the top of the root.

If small, cook whole, without peeling, in boiling salted water. Then peel, slice, dice, or cut into julienne.

If large, have ready a bowl of acidulated water (3 tablespoons lemon juice or white vinegar for 1 quart water). Peel, and slice or dice the celery, or cut into julienne strips, and drop the prepared pieces immediately into the acidulated water to prevent discoloring. Then cook in about 1 inch of boiling salted water for 5 to 10 minutes, or until barely tender. Or, if the pieces are larger, cook slightly longer. Drain; plunge into cold water and drain again. If the knob celery is to be cooked further, cook only until half done.

To prepare raw knob celery: cut off the tops, peel, and slice, dice, or cut into julienne. Drop the prepared pieces immediately into acidulated water.

Old and big knob celery may have a spongy core. Use the firm parts of the vegetable only and throw away the spongy core.

Knob Celery Braised in Butter /

CÉLERI-RAVE ÉTUVÉ AU BEURRE

Prepare and cook the knob celery as in the basic preparation (above), having cut it into slices ¼ inch thick.

Put the vegetable into a saucepan with the butter, and sauté over low heat for 5 to 6 minutes. Season with salt and pepper, and mix carefully so as not to break the slices.

Serve the knob celery in a hot vegetable dish, with the pan juices and a sprinkling of parsley.

FOR 4 PERSONS:

2 **pounds knob celery (about 4 medium-sized roots)**	**Salt**
6 **tablespoons butter**	**Freshly ground white pepper**
	1 **tablespoon minced parsley**

CÉLERI-RAVE AU GRATIN / *Knob Celery au Gratin*

Prepare and cook the knob celery as in the basic preparation (above), having cut it into ⅛-inch-thick slices.

Butter a baking dish and fill it with layers of knob celery, sprinkling each layer with a little melted butter and a little of the cheese.

Pour the *sauce béchamel* over the top and finally sprinkle with a little more grated cheese and the bread crumbs.

Bake in a preheated 400° F. oven for 10 minutes.

Serve in the same dish, as soon as you take it out of the oven.

FOR 4 PERSONS:

2 **pounds knob celery (about 4 medium-sized roots)**	1 **cup Sauce Béchamel (p. 761)**
6 **tablespoons melted butter**	4 **tablespoons fine dry bread crumbs**
¾ **cup grated Swiss cheese**	

/ *Braised Knob Celery with Ham*

CÉLERI-RAVE BRAISÉ AU JAMBON

Prepare the knob celery as in the basic preparation (above), having cut it into ¼-inch slices, and boil it for only 5 minutes. Drain.

Line the bottom of a heavy casserole with half of the slices of ham or ham fat and top this with the onion, carrots, turnips, garlic and tomatoes. Season with a little salt and pepper.

Add the knob celery and cover with the remaining ham or ham fat. Add a little water, about ⅓ cup. Cover the casserole and cook in a preheated 300° F. oven for 1 hour.

Dish up the knob celery in a hot serving dish, and pour the pan juices over the vegetable. Sprinkle with the parsley and serve very hot.

FOR 4 PERSONS:

2 **pounds knob celery (about 4 medium-sized roots)**	2 **to 3 garlic cloves, minced**
¼ **pound sliced ham or ham fat**	3 **medium-sized tomatoes, peeled, seeded and chopped**
1 **onion, minced**	**Salt**
2 **carrots, minced**	**Freshly ground black pepper**
2 **turnips, minced**	3 **tablespoons minced parsley**

CHESTNUTS

Marrons

Boiled Chestnuts / MARRONS BOUILLIS

With a sharp-pointed knife, make a small slit in the flat side of each chestnut. Place them in a saucepan and cover with cold water. Bring to a boil and cook for 1 minute. Remove them from the heat. Take 3 or 4 chestnuts at a time from the hot water and peel the outer and inner skins from them while they are still warm. If the skins do not come off easily from some of them, set them aside, then cover them briefly again with boiling water and peel.

Put the peeled chestnuts in a saucepan with the stock, pieces of celery and the *bouquet garni.* Bring to a boil and then simmer for 40 to 50 minutes, or until they are just tender. Drain thoroughly and use as desired.

FOR 4 PERSONS:

1 pound chestnuts	**2 celery stalks, cut into pieces**
4 cups Brown or White Stock (p. 164)	**1 Bouquet Garni (p. 46)**

Note: The cooking liquid for the chestnuts may be flavored with fennel seeds instead of the *bouquet garni* and celery.

Chestnuts in Butter / MARRONS ÉTUVÉS AU BEURRE

Prepare the boiled chestnuts and drain them.

Heat the butter in a casserole, add the chestnuts, and simmer for a few minutes, or until the chestnuts are heated through thoroughly.

FOR 4 PERSONS:

1 pound Boiled Chestnuts (above)   **6 tablespoons butter**

Chestnut Purée / PURÉE DE MARRONS

Prepare the boiled chestnuts as described above and add a few pieces of fennel to the cooking liquid for added flavor.

Discard the fennel pieces, *bouquet garni* and the celery. Drain the chestnuts, reserving the liquid, and mash them with a potato masher or force them through a food mill. Beat in the butter and a very little of the cooking liquid. Put the purée over medium heat and beat in enough milk to achieve the consistency of mashed potatoes. Keep hot until serving time.

FOR 2 PERSONS:

1 pound Boiled Chestnuts (above)	**5 tablespoons butter**
Slices of fennel	**½ cup milk**

RAGOÛT DE MARRONS / *Ragout of Chestnuts*

Peel the chestnuts as described in Boiled Chestnuts (above).

Put the butter in a casserole together with the diced bacon. Cook over medium heat for 1 minute, stirring constantly, then add the shallots, onions, garlic and carrots. Mix well and simmer without a cover for 10 minutes. Stir in the flour and add the consommé, chestnuts and whichever herb you are using. Cover and simmer for about 40 minutes.

FOR 4 PERSONS:

1 pound chestnuts	**2 garlic cloves, mashed**
3 tablespoons butter	**2 carrots, sliced**
¼ pound lean bacon, diced	**1 tablespoon flour**
2 or 3 shallots, minced	**2 cups Chicken or Beef Consommé**
6 tiny onions, each stuck with 1	**(p. 168)**
clove	**1 sprig of tarragon, parsley or**
12 tiny onions without cloves	**fennel**

Note: Two Belgian endives, or chunks of zucchini or pumpkin, may be cooked with the chestnuts. Place these vegetables under the chestnuts.

MARRONS GRILLÉS / *Roast Chestnuts*

Score the flat side of each chestnut with the point of a sharp knife or cut out a little of the outer skin. Put the chestnuts into an old skillet, or better still, on a baking sheet or other metal plate in which you have punched holes. Roast the chestnuts over high heat, shaking their container to prevent sticking, until the chestnuts are almost black. Peel them and serve as desired.

FOR 4 PERSONS:

1 pound chestnuts

CORN

Maïs

EDITORS' NOTE: *Contrary to what many Americans think, both fresh and canned corn are known and eaten in France, although corn is by no means as popular a vegetable as in the United States. The French recipes for boiled, grilled, buttered* and creamed corn, as well as for corn fritters, are in no way different from their counterparts in America.

Cornmeal, on the other hand, is a staple in some parts of France.

Corn Croquettes / CROQUETTES DE MAÏS

Add the corn to the *sauce béchamel* and bring to the boiling point. Cook, stirring constantly, until the mixture is very thick. Remove from the heat. Beat together the egg yolks and the cream and beat this into the corn mixture.

Return to low heat and cook, stirring constantly, until the mixture is very thick and smooth. Pour it into a buttered plate. Cover with buttered aluminum foil, cool, and then chill in the refrigerator.

Shape the mixture into little flat cakes, dust with flour, dip them into an Anglaise (see p. 38), and coat with bread crumbs. Fry them quickly in deep fat heated to 375° F. on a frying thermometer. Drain and serve very hot in a hot dish lined with a folded napkin.

FOR 6 CROQUETTES:

2 cups cooked corn kernels
¾ cup Sauce Béchamel (p. 761)
2 egg yolks
6 tablespoons heavy cream
Flour

Anglaise made from:
  2 egg yolks
  2 tablespoons peanut oil
  2 tablespoons water
  ½ teaspoon salt

1 cup bread crumbs

Cornmeal Cakes / CRUCHADE

Heat together in a large saucepan the water, milk, salt and sugar, and bring the mixture to the boiling point. Gradually add the cornmeal, stirring constantly to prevent lumping. Cook until the mixture is very thick and smooth, stirring frequently. Remove from the heat and stir in 3 tablespoons of the butter, piece by piece. Cool to lukewarm.

Shape the mixture into 12 round flat cakes. Chill the cakes and then sauté them in the remaining butter, or simply warm them in a buttered pan over hot water.

FOR 12 CAKES:

2 cups water
2 cups milk
1 teaspoon salt
Pinch of sugar

1 cup cornmeal
6 tablespoons butter, cut into
  small pieces

Cornmeal Crêpes / CRÊPES DE MAÏS

Bring the milk to the boiling point, remove it from the heat, and beat in the butter and the salt. Mix, using a wire whip, until the butter has melted.

Sift together the cornmeal and the cornstarch and put them into a large bowl.

Make a well in the middle and put the oil and the eggs into the well. Stir with a fork to blend and then, stirring constantly, add the hot milk. Beat in enough beer to make a batter with the consistency of a thick *crêpe* batter. Beat with the wire whisk until the mixture is very smooth. Chill in the refrigerator for 2 hours and then sauté the *crêpes* in the usual manner.

FOR 12 CRÊPES:

1 cup milk
2 tablespoons butter
Pinch of salt
⅔ cup cornmeal

1 cup cornstarch or potato starch
1 tablespoon peanut oil
4 eggs
½ cup (approximately) beer

CUCUMBERS

Concombres

Basic Preparation: Peel the cucumbers and cut them lengthwise into halves. Scrape out the seeds, split the halves lengthwise, and cut into 1-inch pieces.

Drop the pieces into a very large quantity of boiling salted water for 5 minutes. Drain them, drop them into cold water, and then drain again very thoroughly in a colander. Use as desired.

CONCOMBRES SAUTÉS AU BEURRE / *Cucumbers in Butter*

Blanch the cucumbers as described in the basic preparation (above).

Put them into a casserole with the butter, season with salt and pepper, and simmer, covered, for about 40 minutes, or until they are tender.

Put the cucumbers in a hot serving dish, and sprinkle with the *fines herbes*.

FOR 4 PERSONS:

2 cucumbers (1 pound each)
6 tablespoons butter
Salt

Freshly ground pepper
2 tablespoons minced Fines
Herbes (p. 89)

CONCOMBRES SAUTÉS À LA CRÈME / *Cucumbers in Cream*

Proceed as in the preceding recipe.

When the cucumbers are about half cooked, add the *crème fraîche,* bring to the boiling point, and reduce by half. Check the seasoning. Serve in a hot vegetable dish, very hot.

FOR 4 PERSONS:

1 recipe Cucumbers in Butter
  (above)
1 cup Crème Fraîche (p. 666)

Salt
Freshly ground white pepper

Cucumbers de Boissoudy / CONCOMBRES À LA DE BOISSOUDY

Peel the cucumbers and cut them lengthwise into halves. Blanch the halves for 5 minutes in a large quantity of boiling salted water. Drain, plunge them into cold water, and drain again.

Soak the bread crumbs in the beer. Mince the pork, using the fine blade of a meat grinder. Squeeze the bread crumbs dry with your hands and mix them with the ground meat, together with the *fines herbes* and the mushrooms. Season with salt and pepper. Blend the stuffing thoroughly.

Scoop the seeds from the cucumbers and put the hollowed-out halves into a buttered baking dish. Fill the cavities with the stuffing and cover the dish with buttered kitchen parchment or aluminum foil. Cook in a preheated 350° F. oven for 30 minutes.

Beat the cream cheese with the eggs. Add the milk, mix well, and add a little nutmeg. Remove the paper from the baking dish and pour the sauce over the cucumbers. Sprinkle with the grated cheese. Return the baking dish to the hot oven and cook until the top is golden and bubbly. Serve very hot, in the same dish.

FOR 4 PERSONS:

2 cucumbers (1 pound each)	Salt
3 cups fresh white bread crumbs	Freshly ground black pepper
¾ cup beer	4 ounces cream cheese
¼ pound lean pork	3 eggs
4 tablespoons minced Fines Herbes (p. 89)	2 tablespoons milk
	Grated nutmeg
4 large mushrooms, minced	¼ cup grated Swiss cheese

Cucumbers Smothered in Butter /

CONCOMBRES ÉTUVÉS AU BEURRE

Peel the cucumbers, cut them lengthwise into halves, and remove the seeds with a spoon. Using a round measuring teaspoon or a small melon scoop, shape the cucumbers into small balls.

Heat 6 tablespoons of the butter in a casserole, and add the cucumbers and the lukewarm water. Simmer, covered, over low heat for 30 minutes. Season with salt and pepper. At serving time, stir in the remaining butter and sprinkle with the *fines herbes.*

FOR 4 PERSONS:

2 cucumbers (1 pound each)	Freshly ground white pepper
10 tablespoons butter	4 tablespoons minced Fines Herbes (p. 89)
4 tablespoons lukewarm water	
Salt	

Stuffed Cucumbers / CONCOMBRES FARCIS

Peel the cucumbers and blanch them in a large quantity of salted boiling water for 5 minutes. Drain them, plunge them into cold water, and drain again.

Cut the cucumbers crosswise into halves and scoop out the seeds with a vegetable corer, leaving a center cavity. Fill the cavities with the sausage meat.

Butter a baking dish, line it with the fresh pork fatback, and top the pork fat with the carrot and onion. Place the cucumber halves upright on the vegetables and add enough stock to reach halfway up the cucumbers. Cover the dish and cook in a preheated 350° F. oven for 30 minutes.

Put the stuffed cucumbers into a hot serving dish and keep hot. Reduce the sauce by half, add the butter, and strain the sauce through a fine sieve directly over the cucumbers. Serve very hot.

FOR 4 PERSONS:

2 cucumbers (1 pound each)
⅓ pound sausage meat
1 sheet of fresh pork fatback
1 carrot, minced

1 onion, minced
4 cups Brown Stock or Brown
  Poultry Stock (p. 164)
3 tablespoons butter

CORNICHONS AU VINAIGRE / *Pickled Cucumbers*

Here are two ways of preserving cucumbers.

The hot method: Take very fresh small pickling cucumbers, sprinkle them heavily with coarse salt (Kosher salt), and rub them between kitchen towels until they shed their excess moisture. Then spread a kitchen towel with more coarse salt, and put the cucumbers into the salt; tie the 4 corners of the cloth and put it into a colander, over the kitchen sink. Keep it there overnight.

The next day, dry the cucumbers with another kitchen towel. Bring a quart (or more) of vinegar to the boiling point in a stainless-steel or enamelware saucepan. Put the cucumbers into a large bowl (do not use aluminum) and cover them with the boiling vinegar. Let the mixture stand for 24 hours in a cool place, but do not refrigerate.

Then, drain the cucumbers over a saucepan and bring the same vinegar to the boiling point again. Put the cucumbers back into their bowl and pour the boiling vinegar over them to cover. Let stand again for 24 hours.

Repeat this procedure the next day, and add small pickling onions, pimiento strips, fresh tarragon and whole peppercorns to the cucumbers.

The cucumbers will be ready to eat in 3 weeks. They should be green and crisp.

The cold method: Treat the cucumbers with salt as described above. Put them into a large bowl (do not use aluminum) with small pickling onions, fresh tarragon, bay leaves and whole peppercorns. Cover with vinegar. The cucumbers will be ready to eat in 6 weeks.

/ *Russian Pickled Cucumbers*

CORNICHONS FRAIS SALÉS À LA RUSSE

Trim small pickling cucumbers and wash in lukewarm water; rinse them under running cold water. Drain them and dry with a kitchen cloth. Using a large wide-mouthed pot or jar, make alternate layers of cucumbers and sliced fennel, both white and green parts. Top the last layer with small pieces of peeled fresh horseradish and cover everything with boiled salted water which has cooled. Seal the pot to make it airtight and let it stand in a cool place for at least 24 hours.

EGGPLANT

Aubergines

Basic Preparation: Eggplant usually should be peeled if the skin is either very thick or tough.

It should be drained of its excess moisture before cooking. To do this, cut the eggplant lengthwise into halves or slice it, depending on the recipe. Sprinkle the eggplant with salt. Let it stand at room temperature for about 20 minutes. Drain the eggplant and pat it dry with paper towels. Then proceed as indicated in the recipe.

Be careful in salting a dish using an eggplant thus prepared since some of the salt may still cling to it.

Another method of checking eggplant's moisture is to coat its exposed surfaces with flour before sautéing it.

Eggplant in Butter / AUBERGINES SAUTÉES AU BEURRE

Peel the eggplants and cut them into cubes or into ¾-inch slices. Then salt or flour them as described in the basic preparation (above).

Heat the butter in a casserole if the eggplants are cubed, or in a large skillet if cut into slices. Add the pieces and cook them over fairly high heat until golden. Season with salt and pepper and sprinkle with parsley. Use the eggplant as a garnish for roast meats or poultry.

FOR 4 PERSONS:

2 medium-sized eggplants
6 tablespoons butter
Salt

Freshly ground black pepper
1 tablespoon minced parsley

Eggplant in Cream / AUBERGINES À LA CRÈME

Prepare the eggplants as in the preceding recipe. When the eggplant pieces have turned golden, add the *sauce béchamel* and cook over low heat, stirring constantly, for 2 to 3 minutes.

Check the seasoning and serve in a vegetable dish.

FOR 4 PERSONS:

1 recipe Eggplant in Butter
  (above)
2 cups Sauce Béchamel (p. 761)

Salt
Freshly ground black pepper

AUBERGINES FRITES / *Fried Eggplant*

Peel the eggplants and cut them into cubes, slices or strips, and salt or flour them as described in the basic preparation (above).

Heat the fat for frying to 375° F. on a frying thermometer. Fry the eggplant pieces until golden on all sides.

Remove them with a slotted spoon, drain on kitchen paper, and place them on a hot serving dish lined with a folded napkin. Season lightly with salt and sprinkle with fried parsley. Serve very hot.

FOR 4 PERSONS:

2 medium-sized eggplants   **Salt**
Fat for deep frying   **Fried Parsley (p. 130)**

BEIGNETS D'AUBERGINES / *Eggplant Fritters*

Peel the eggplants and cut them into ½-inch slices, and salt or flour them as described in the basic preparation (above).

Mix the fritter batter ingredients thoroughly together. Dip each slice of eggplant into the batter and fry in the deep fat heated to 375° F. on a frying thermometer until golden on all sides.

Drain on kitchen paper and pile into a hot serving dish lined with a folded napkin. Sprinkle with salt and fried parsley.

FOR 4 PERSONS:

2 medium-sized eggplants   **Fat for deep frying**
Fritter batter: **Salt**
  1 cup flour   **Fried Parsley (p. 130)**
  1 tablespoon peanut oil
  3 eggs
  1 teaspoon salt
  ½ cup beer

/ *Eggplant Gratin from the Languedoc*

GRATIN LANGUEDOCIEN

Peel the eggplants and cut them into thick slices. Coat the slices with flour and sauté them in about ½ cup oil in a casserole over fairly high heat. Season with salt and pepper.

Sauté the tomatoes in 2 tablespoons of the oil in a separate skillet for about 10 minutes.

Butter a baking dish and make alternate layers of eggplant and tomatoes, ending with a layer of eggplant.

Combine the bread crumbs and the parsley and sprinkle the mixture over the vegetables. Sprinkle generously with olive oil and cook in a preheated 400° F. oven for 15 minutes.

FOR 4 PERSONS:

2 medium-sized eggplants	8 tomatoes, peeled, seeded and
Flour	chopped
1 cup olive oil	½ cup fresh white bread crumbs
Salt	¼ cup minced parsley
Freshly ground black pepper	

Eggplant Sautéed with Garlic and Parsley /

AUBERGINES SAUTÉES À L'AIL ET AU PERSIL

Prepare the eggplant as described above. Shortly before the eggplant is done, sprinkle with the combined minced garlic and parsley and cook until done, turning the pieces several times.

FOR 4 PERSONS:

1 recipe Eggplant in Butter (p. 588)	3 garlic cloves, minced
	2 tablespoons minced parsley

Sautéed Eggplant Provençale /

AUBERGINES SAUTÉES PROVENÇALE

Peel the eggplants and cut them into ¾-inch slices. Coat the slices with flour.

Cook the onions in 6 tablespoons of the peanut oil and 2 tablespoons of the olive oil, combined. When they are golden and very soft, add the eggplant slices, a few at a time, and cook over medium heat until golden on both sides, shaking the pan frequently to prevent sticking. Transfer the slices to a hot serving dish as they are browned and continue in this manner until all the slices are sautéed. Season with salt and pepper.

Heat the remaining peanut and olive oils in a skillet and fry the tomato halves in it for about 10 minutes, or until they begin to soften but still hold their shape. Season them with salt and pepper and arrange them around the eggplant slices. Combine the minced garlic and parsley and sprinkle the mixture over the vegetables.

FOR 4 PERSONS:

2 medium-sized eggplants	Freshly ground pepper
Flour	2 large firm tomatoes, halved
2 onions, minced	and seeded
½ cup peanut oil	2 garlic cloves, minced
¼ cup olive oil	1 tablespoon minced parsley
Salt	

Stuffed Eggplant Charcutière /

AUBERGINES FARCIES CHARCUTIÈRE

Cut the eggplants lengthwise into halves but do not peel them. Cut several slashes in the cut side of each half and sprinkle with salt. Let them rest for 30 minutes, then brush off the salt, and scoop out the insides of the halves but leave the shells intact. Mince the scooped-out portion.

Mix together the minced eggplant, sausage meat, onions, garlic and the fresh bread crumbs. Beat in the egg; season with a little salt, pepper and nutmeg; blend thoroughly.

Stuff the eggplant shells with this stuffing, and put them side by side into a large buttered baking dish. Sprinkle with the dry bread crumbs, dot with the butter, and cook in a preheated 375° F. oven for 30 minutes. Serve very hot.

FOR 4 PERSONS:

2 medium-sized eggplants	Salt
½ pound sausage meat	Freshly ground black pepper
2 onions, minced	Grated nutmeg
1 garlic clove, minced	½ cup fine dry bread crumbs
1 cup fresh white bread crumbs	4 tablespoons butter, cut into
1 egg	small pieces

/ *Eggplant Stuffed in the Italian Manner*

AUBERGINES FARCIES À L'ITALIENNE

Prepare eggplant halves as described in the preceding recipe. Scoop out the insides, leaving the shells intact, and mince the scooped-out portion.

Cook the rice in boiling salted water for 20 minutes, drain it, and add it to the minced eggplant. Stir in the tomato paste or purée. Season with salt, pepper and cayenne, and add the garlic and parsley.

Stuff the eggplant shells with this filling, put them into a large buttered baking dish, sprinkle with the bread crumbs, and dot them with the butter.

Cook in a preheated 375° F. oven for about 30 minutes. Serve very hot.

FOR 4 PERSONS:

2 medium-sized eggplants	Cayenne pepper
4 tablespoons uncooked rice	1 garlic clove, minced
2 tablespoons tomato paste, or	2 tablespoons minced parsley
Tomato Purée (p. 157)	½ cup fine dry bread crumbs
Salt	4 tablespoons butter
Freshly ground black pepper	

/ *Eggplant Stuffed in the Oriental Manner*

AUBERGINES FARCIES À L'ORIENTALE

Prepare eggplant halves as described in Stuffed Eggplant Charcutière (p. 590), without peeling them. Scoop out the insides, leaving the shells intact. Mince the scooped-out portion.

Cook the rice in boiling salted water for 20 minutes and drain it thoroughly. Put the lamb through the finest blade of the meat grinder and mix it with the minced eggplant, the rice, parsley and garlic. Season with salt, pepper and cayenne.

Stuff the eggplant shells with this filling, dot with the butter, and put them side by side into a buttered large baking dish. Cook in a preheated 375° F. oven for 30 minutes.

At serving time, coat the eggplant halves with a thick and well-seasoned tomato sauce.

FOR 4 PERSONS:

2 medium-sized eggplants
4 tablespoons uncooked rice
½ pound cooked boneless lamb
1 tablespoon minced parsley
2 garlic cloves, minced
Salt

Freshly ground black pepper
Cayenne pepper
4 tablespoons butter
1½ cups well-seasoned Sauce
  Tomate (p. 769)

Stuffed Eggplant Provençale /
AUBERGINES FARCIES À LA PROVENÇALE

Prepare eggplant halves as described in Stuffed Eggplant Charcutière (p. 590), without peeling them. Scoop out the insides, leaving the shells intact. Mince the scooped-out portion.

Sauté the chopped tomatoes in the hot olive oil over medium heat. Season with salt, pepper and nutmeg, and add the bouquet of dried herbs. Cook, stirring frequently, for about 15 minutes, or until the sauce is thick. Strain the sauce.

Mix the minced eggplant with the tomato sauce and add the garlic and parsley.

Stuff the eggplant shells with this filling and put them side by side into a large buttered baking dish. Sprinkle them with the cheese and dot with the butter. Bake in a preheated 375° F. oven for about 30 minutes.

Serve very hot, in the same dish.

FOR 4 PERSONS:

4 eggplants
6 large tomatoes, peeled, seeded
  and chopped
3 tablespoons olive oil
Salt
Freshly ground pepper
Grated nutmeg

1 small Bouquet Garni of dried
  herbs from Provence (thyme,
  rosemary, orégano, basil)
2 garlic cloves, minced
2 tablespoons minced parsley
½ cup grated Swiss cheese
4 tablespoons butter, cut into
  pieces

BELGIAN ENDIVES

Endives

Belgian Endives in Butter / ENDIVES ÉTUVÉES AU BEURRE

Bring a large pot of water to the boiling point and add the whole endives. Cook them for 5 minutes, remove them with a slotted spoon, and drain them in a sieve. If necessary, squeeze them dry with your hands. Heat half of the butter in a casserole, add the endives, dot with the remaining butter, and season lightly with salt. Cover the saucepan and simmer over low heat for about 40 minutes, turning the endives occasionally, so that they may acquire a slight golden color on all sides. Serve in a hot serving dish.

FOR 4 PERSONS:

12 Belgian endives	**Salt**
6 tablespoons butter	

ENDIVES À LA CRÈME / *Belgian Endives in Cream Sauce*

Proceed as in Belgian Endives in Butter (above). Put the cooked endives in a hot serving dish and coat them with 2 cups Cream Sauce (p. 775).

ENDIVES AU GRATIN / *Belgian Endives au Gratin*

Prepare the endives as described above.

Put the endives in a baking dish side by side, coat with the *sauce béchamel,* and sprinkle with the cheese and the bread crumbs. Cook in a preheated 400° F. oven for 10 minutes, or until the top is golden and bubbly.

FOR 4 PERSONS:

1 recipe Belgian Endives in	**¼ cup grated Swiss cheese**
Butter (above)	**¼ cup fine dry bread crumbs**
2 cups Sauce Béchamel (p. 761)	

ENDIVES MEUNIÈRE / *Belgian Endives Meunière*

Trim, wash, and dry the Belgian endives, and put them into a casserole with the butter. Cook them over low heat for about 40 minutes, turning them occasionally, until they are golden on all sides and very tender.

Put the endives into a hot serving dish, sprinkle them with the lemon juice, season with a little salt, and pour the brown butter in the casserole over them. Serve very hot.

FOR 4 PERSONS:

12 Belgian endives	**Juice of 1 lemon**
6 tablespoons butter	**Salt**

ENDIVES BRAISÉES / *Braised Belgian Endives*

Trim and wash the Belgian endives and dry them.

Butter a deep skillet and place the endives in it, side by side. Add the water, half of the butter, the lemon juice and a pinch of salt. Cover the skillet and bring to the boiling point, then simmer over low heat for 15 minutes.

Add the blanched salt pork, the ham and the stock. Simmer for another 30 minutes. Put the Belgian endives into a hot serving dish and keep hot.

Reduce the pan juices by three quarters, remove from the heat, and stir in the remaining butter. Coat the Belgian endives with the sauce and serve very hot.

FOR 4 PERSONS:

12 **Belgian endives**
½ **cup water**
6 **tablespoons butter**
Juice of ½ lemon
Salt
¼ **pound salt pork, or slab bacon, blanched and cut into dice**

¼ **pound lean ham, diced**
½ **cup Brown Stock or Brown Poultry Stock (p. 164)**

Belgian Endives with Ham | ENDIVES AU JAMBON

Prepare in the same manner as Braised Belgian Endives (above), except instead of diced salt pork and ham, use 4 slices of Bayonne ham or prosciutto, about ¼ inch thick. Add these slices to the casserole about 10 minutes before the endives are fully cooked.

Put the ham slices into a hot serving dish and top them with the Belgian endives.

Ragout of Endives and Chestnuts |

RAGOÛT D'ENDIVES AUX MARRONS

Trim the endives, cut them into 1- to 1½-inch pieces, wash and dry them. Peel off both the outer and inner skin of the chestnuts, as described on page 582.

Heat the lard in a saucepan and add the endives and chestnuts. Add water to cover. Season with salt and pepper. Cover the saucepan and simmer over low heat for about 40 minutes, or until both endives and chestnuts are tender.

Drain and serve in a hot serving dish. Dot with the butter and sprinkle with parsley.

FOR 4 PERSONS:

12 **Belgian endives**
½ **pound chestnuts**
2 **tablespoons lard**
Salt

Freshly ground black pepper
3 **tablespoons butter, at room temperature**
4 **tablespoons minced parsley**

FINOCCHIO OR FENNEL

Fenouil

EDITORS' NOTE: *This vegetable, a staple of French and Italian cooking, has crisp, overlapping leafstalks (like celery) in the shape of a hand. The tops of the stalks have lacy leaves, which resemble dill. The taste resembles that of aniseed. The white part of the stalks is eaten both raw and cooked.*

Finocchio, to give the vegetable its Italian name by which it is best known in the United States, has become increasingly popular during the last few years, and during its season, the late fall and winter, it can be found in many vegetable markets, and in all of those catering to people of Mediterranean origin.

Basic Preparation: Cut off all the green shoots at their bases. Cut off the bottom part of the woody stem. Remove wilted and tough outer leaves. If the finocchio are small, leave whole. Cut large ones into halves, quarters or even eighths, or slice them. As an appetizer, finocchio may be eaten as is, with just salt; or as a salad with a sprinkling of olive oil and lemon juice.

If fennel is to be cooked, it should first be blanched in boiling salted water to cover for 3 or 4 minutes, depending on size. Drain and then use as desired.

/ *Finocchio or Fennel in Butter*

FENOUIL ÉTUVÉ AU BEURRE

Trim and blanch the finocchio as described in the basic preparation (above).

Heat the butter in a casserole, add the finocchio, and season with salt and pepper. Cover and simmer over low heat for about 20 minutes, or until the vegetable is thoroughly tender.

Put the finocchio into a hot vegetable dish, add the pan juices, and sprinkle with the *fines herbes*.

FOR 4 PERSONS:

8 small or medium-sized finocchio	**Freshly ground black pepper**
6 tablespoons butter	**4 tablespoons minced Fines**
Salt	**Herbes (p. 89)**

FENOUIL À LA CRÈME / *Finocchio or Fennel in Cream*

Prepare in the same manner as Finocchio in Butter (above), but add ½ cup Crème Fraîche (p. 666) to the cooked finocchio and let it reduce slightly before serving.

FENOUIL BRAISÉ / *Braised Finocchio or Fennel*

Trim and blanch the finocchio as described in the basic preparation (above).

Heat the butter in a casserole, add the blanched salt pork or bacon dice, the carrots, onions and beef marrow. Put the fennel on top, season with salt and pepper, and add the stock and oil. Cover the casserole and simmer gently over low heat for about 20 minutes.

When the finocchio are very tender, put them into a hot serving dish and pour the pan juices over them. Sprinkle with the *fines herbes* and serve very hot.

FOR 4 PERSONS:

8 small or medium-sized finocchio	Salt
6 tablespoons butter	Freshly ground black pepper
⅓ pound blanched salt pork or slab bacon, diced	½ cup Brown Stock or Brown Poultry Stock (p. 164)
2 carrots, minced	2 tablespoons olive oil
2 onions, minced	4 tablespoons minced Fines Herbes (p. 89)
¼ pound beef marrow, sliced	

GARLIC

Ail

Roasted Fresh Garlic | AIL FRAIS RÔTI

Only very fresh garlic cloves should be used, and they must be peeled.

Heat together the butter, peanut oil and olive oil in a casserole over medium heat. Put in the garlic cloves, side by side, and see that they are well coated with the cooking fat. Bake in a 350° F. oven for about 20 minutes. Baste from time to time and season with salt and pepper to taste.

FOR 4 PEOPLE:

12 large garlic cloves	1 tablespoon olive oil
2 tablespoons butter	Salt
1 tablespoon peanut oil	Freshly ground white pepper

LEEKS

Poireaux

Boiled Leeks | POIREAUX BOUILLIS

Trim off the wilted or tough outer leaves from the leeks and cut off the roots. Trim off the green tops, so that the trimmed leeks are 6 or 7 inches long. Wash them in several changes of cold water to remove every trace of sand. Tie the leeks into bundles.

Bring the salted water to the boiling point in a large saucepan and add the leeks. Cook for 15 minutes, or until the white part is easily pierced with a knife.

Remove the leeks with a slotted spoon and drain them in a colander. Untie them and put them on a hot serving plate; serve them simply with butter, or with a sauce, or use them for a gratin (see below).

FOR 4 PERSONS:

8 to 12 leeks   **Salted water**

POIREAUX À LA CRÈME / *Leeks in Cream*

Trim and cook the leeks as described in the preceding recipe.

Put the cooked leeks into a deep oblong serving dish and keep hot.

Bring the *crème fraîche* to the boiling point and pour it over the leeks. Sprinkle with *fines herbes* and serve immediately, very hot.

FOR 4 PERSONS:

8 to 12 leeks   **¼ cup Fines Herbes (p. 89)**
2 cups Crème Fraîche (p. 666)

Note: Another way of preparing this dish is to put the boiled leeks into a casserole with a little hot butter, and add enough *crème fraîche* to barely cover the vegetables. Let the *crème fraîche* reduce by half, check the seasoning, and serve very hot.

POIREAUX À LA BÉCHAMEL / *Creamed Leeks*

Trim and cook leeks as in Boiled Leeks (above).

Drain the leeks, untie them, and put them into a hot serving dish. Coat the leeks with 2 cups Sauce Béchamel (p. 761), and serve immediately.

POIREAUX À LA BÉCHAMEL GRATINÉS / *Leeks Gratin*

Trim and cook the leeks as in Boiled Leeks (above).

Put the leeks side by side in a buttered baking dish. Coat the leeks with the *sauce béchamel,* sprinkle with grated cheese, dot with the butter, and sprinkle with the bread crumbs. Brown quickly under a broiler.

FOR 4 PERSONS:

8 to 12 leeks   **2 tablespoons butter**
2 cups Sauce Béchamel (p. 761)   **¼ cup fine dry bread crumbs**
4 tablespoons grated Swiss cheese

LETTUCE

Laitues

> EDITORS' NOTE: *In France, lettuce, such as Boston, romaine, or escarole, is frequently used as a cooked vegetable. The crisper varieties are better suited for cooking (with the exception of iceberg lettuce, which is rarely cooked), but any firm, sound head of lettuce will do.*

Braised Lettuce / LAITUES BRAISÉES

Trim and thoroughly wash the heads of lettuce. They must be very firm and very fresh.

Bring a large pot of salted water to the boiling point. Plunge the lettuce heads into the boiling water for 2 minutes, remove them with a slotted spoon, and plunge them into cold water. Drain the lettuce in a colander and press out all surplus water with the hands.

Put the lettuces side by side on a kitchen towel. Spread the leaves open (if necessary, cut partway through the base so that the leaves will lie flat) and stuff each cavity with a little of the sausage meat. Pull the leaves over the filling, enclosing it completely, and roll them up.

Heat the oil and the butter in a casserole; add the carrot, onion, celery and *bouquet garni*. Stir the vegetables and cook them over low heat until they are soft and golden. Then top them with a sheet of fresh pork fatback. Place the lettuces on the pork fat and top them with another sheet of pork fat.

Add the stock and cover the casserole tightly. Cook in a preheated 325° F. oven for about 45 minutes.

Put the lettuces into a hot serving dish, and sprinkle with the pan juices. Serve very hot.

FOR 4 PERSONS:

4 firm heads of lettuce	2 celery stalks, minced
Salt	1 Bouquet Garni (p. 46)
½ pound sausage meat	2 thin sheets of fresh pork
2 tablespoons olive oil	fatback or fresh ham fat
1 tablespoon butter	1 cup Brown Stock or Brown
1 carrot, minced	Poultry Stock (p. 164)
1 onion, minced	

Braised Lettuce with Beef Marrow /

LAITUES À LA MOELLE

Braise the lettuce as described in the preceding recipe.

Fry the bread slices in the combined hot oil and butter until they are golden on both sides. Place them side by side in a hot serving dish. Top each slice with a braised lettuce, and top each lettuce with 2 slices of beef marrow poached in boiling salted water for 5 minutes and well drained.

Deglaze the pan juices with a piece of butter and coat the lettuces and marrow with it. Serve very hot.

FOR 4 PERSONS:

1 recipe Braised Lettuce (above)	2 tablespoons butter
4 slices of white bread, crusts removed	8 slices (¼ inch thick) of beef marrow
3 tablespoons peanut oil	4 tablespoons butter

LAITUES BRAISÉES À LA CRÈME / *Lettuce Braised in Cream*

Proceed as in Braised Lettuce (above), but do not stuff the lettuces.

A few moments before serving time, add ½ cup Crème Fraîche (p. 666). Bring it to the boiling point over fairly high heat and let it reduce by half. Arrange the lettuces in a hot serving dish and spoon the hot sauce over them.

LAITUES EN CHIFFONADE / *Chiffonade of Lettuce*

Wash the lettuce in cold clear water. Discard any wilted leaves, cut off the stems, separate the leaves, and cut them into julienne strips.

Heat 3 tablespoons of the butter in a casserole and add the lettuce. Season with salt and pepper, add the stock, and cover the casserole. Simmer for 5 to 20 minutes, depending on the type of lettuce used.

Put the lettuce in a vegetable dish and dot with the remaining butter. Serve hot.

FOR 4 PERSONS:

4 firm heads of lettuce	Freshly ground white pepper
5 tablespoons butter	4 tablespoons White Poultry
Salt	Stock (p. 165)

LAITUES À LA HOLLANDAISE / *Lettuce Hollandaise*

Braise the lettuce as described above. The heads may be stuffed or not, as desired.

Fry the bread slices in the combined hot oil and butter until they are golden on both sides. Put them side by side into a hot serving dish. Top each slice with a braised lettuce head and coat with the hot *sauce hollandaise*. Serve immediately.

FOR 4 PERSONS:

1 recipe Braised Lettuce (above)	2 tablespoons butter
4 slices of firm white bread, crusts removed	1 cup Sauce Hollandaise (p. 780)
3 tablespoons olive oil	

Stuffed Lettuce | LAITUES FARCIES

Wash the lettuce carefully and remove any wilted leaves. Plunge the heads into a large pot of boiling salted water for 2 minutes, remove them, and plunge them into cold water. Drain the lettuce thoroughly, press out excess water with the hands, and spread open the leaves of each head. Season the cavities with salt and pepper and stuff them with the filling. Turn the leaves back over the filling to enclose it completely and roll them up. Put the stuffed lettuces side by side in a buttered baking dish, top them with the beef marrow, add the water, and cover with a sheet of buttered kitchen parchment or brown paper. Cook in a preheated 375° F. oven for about 45 minutes.

FOR 4 PERSONS:

4 firm heads of lettuce
Salt
Freshly ground black pepper
½ pound stuffing, made from
equal parts of ground veal
and pork

6 slices of beef marrow
½ cup water

MUSHROOMS

Champignons

EDITORS' NOTE: *Mushrooms are a basic staple of French cooking, and are very often served as a course by themselves. The French use many more varieties of mushrooms than we do, especially wild ones, such as* cèpes *(edible* Boletus*),* mousserons (Tricholoma *or blewits) and others. These are greatly prized for their different flavors. The cultivated mushrooms familiar to Americans are called* champignons de Paris.

Several of the wild mushrooms found in France can be found in American woods and fields. However, edible and poisonous wild mushrooms often resemble each other very closely, so that only those who are thoroughly acquainted with mushrooms should attempt to gather wild ones. We cannot sufficiently warn against the folly, often lethal, of the picking of wild mushrooms by anyone not an expert.

Generally speaking, the various mushrooms are cooked in very similar ways in France, the flavor of the dish being determined by the flavor of the mushrooms.

CÈPES À LA BORDELAISE / *Cèpes (Boletus) Bordelaise*

Rub the *cèpes* clean with a damp kitchen cloth, separate the caps from the stems, and chop the stems. Combine the chopped stems with the garlic and parsley.

Heat the oil in a skillet, add the mushroom caps, and sauté them over high heat for about 3 minutes. Season with salt and pepper.

Heat the goose or duck fat in a casserole. Add the chopped mushroom stems with the garlic and parsley, the whole garlic cloves, and the *bouquet garni*. Top with the ham and with the mushroom caps.

Cook over low heat for 15 minutes.

Put the ham slices and the mushrooms in a hot serving dish; discard the *bouquet garni* and the garlic cloves; and pour the pan juices and chopped mixture over the mushrooms. Serve very hot.

FOR 4 PERSONS:

8 large cèpes, or other mushrooms
2 garlic cloves, minced
1 tablespoon minced parsley
4 tablespoons olive oil
Salt
Freshly ground black pepper

½ cup goose or duck fat
2 unpeeled garlic cloves
1 Bouquet Garni (p. 46)
4 thin slices of Bayonne ham, smoked ham, or prosciutto

CÈPES À LA PROVENÇALE / *Cèpes (Boletus) Provençale*

Choose very small firm *cèpes* and rub them clean with a damp kitchen cloth. They need not be washed.

Slice the mushrooms and sauté them in the combined hot oil and butter in a skillet. Season with salt and pepper and cook, stirring frequently, until golden, about 10 minutes.

Put the mushrooms into a hot serving dish and sprinkle them with the parsley, garlic, onion and thyme. Serve very hot.

FOR 4 PERSONS:

1 pound cèpes
3 tablespoons olive oil
3 tablespoons butter
Salt
Freshly ground black pepper
1 tablespoon minced parsley

1 garlic clove, minced
1 tablespoon minced onion
Pinch of ground thyme, or 1 sprig of fresh thyme, crumbled

/ *Mousserons Sautéed with Garlic*

MOUSSERONS SAUTÉS À L'AIL

EDITORS' NOTE: Mousserons *belong to the* Tricholoma *species of wild mushrooms of which there are several varieties. The best known of these are called blewits, or sometimes marked* Tricholoma, *in English.*

Use very fresh mushrooms and do not wash them but simply wipe off any soil that may cling to their stems.

Heat the oil and the butter in a saucepan, add the mushrooms, and shake the pan to coat them with the cooking fat. Do not use a spoon or a fork since this would crush the mushrooms. Season with salt and pepper.

When the mushrooms are tender, sprinkle them with the garlic and the parsley. Put the mushrooms into a hot serving dish and serve immediately.

FOR 4 PERSONS:

1 pound mousserons, or other mushrooms	Salt
	Freshly ground black pepper
1 tablespoon olive oil	4 garlic cloves, minced
3 tablespoons butter	1 tablespoon minced parsley

Duxelles /

Wipe the mushrooms clean and mince them as fine as possible, but do not use a meat chopper or a blender. Put the minced mushrooms in a kitchen towel, and twist the towel to extract as much of the mushrooms' moisture as possible.

Mince the shallots equally fine. Heat all but 1 tablespoon of the butter in a casserole, add the shallots, and cook them, stirring constantly, until they are soft. Add the remaining tablespoon of butter and the mushrooms and stir the mixture with a wooden spoon. Add the *bouquet garni,* season with salt and pepper, and cook over low heat, without a cover, until all the pan liquid has evaporated. Remove from the heat and stir in the *crème fraîche.*

FOR 4 PERSONS:

12 large mushrooms	Salt
6 large shallots	Freshly ground black pepper
6 tablespoons butter	¼ cup Crème Fraîche (p. 666)
1 Bouquet Garni (p. 46)	

Blanched Mushrooms /

CHAMPIGNONS DE PARIS CUITS AU BLANC

Wash and dry the mushrooms, and separate the caps from the stems. Frequently only the heads will be used in a given recipe, and the stems may be refrigerated for later use.

Put the mushroom caps into a casserole with the butter, lemon juice, water and a little salt. Cook, covered, over high heat for about 5 minutes.

Drain the mushrooms and reserve the liquid for a *sauce béchamel* or a *sauce suprême.* Use the mushrooms as desired.

FOR 4 PERSONS:

1 pound mushrooms	½ cup water
3 tablespoons butter	Salt
Juice of ½ lemon	

/ *Ragout of Mushrooms in Cream*

RAGOÛT DE CHAMPIGNONS À LA CRÈME

Blanch the mushrooms as described above and reserve the cooking liquid.

Heat the butter in a casserole, stir in the flour, and let the mixture cool.

Combine the liquid in which the mushrooms were cooked with the *crème fraîche*. Season with salt, pepper and a little cayenne. Stir this mixture into the flour and butter and simmer over low heat for about 10 minutes. Add the blanched mushrooms and simmer for 3 minutes longer. Serve very hot.

FOR 4 PERSONS:

1 recipe Blanched Mushrooms (above)	Salt
2 tablespoons butter	Freshly ground white pepper
2 tablespoons flour	Cayenne pepper
6 tablespoons Crème Fraîche (p. 666)	

/ *Mushrooms Braised in Butter*

CHAMPIGNONS ÉTUVÉS AU BEURRE

Wash the mushrooms and pat them dry, or wipe them clean with damp paper towels. Cut them into slices and put them into a casserole with the butter. Season with salt and pepper.

Cook the mushrooms over high heat for 2 minutes, stirring them with a wooden spoon. Lower the heat, cover the casserole, and simmer for about 6 or 7 minutes longer.

When the mushrooms are cooked, put them into a hot serving dish and pour the pan juices over them. Serve very hot.

FOR 4 PERSONS:

1 pound mushrooms	Salt
3 tablespoons butter	Freshly ground white pepper

CHAMPIGNONS À LA CRÈME / *Mushrooms in Cream*

Proceed as in Mushrooms Braised in Butter (above).

When the mushrooms are half cooked, add all but 1 tablespoon of the *crème fraîche* and bring to the boiling point, uncovered. Cook over high heat, stirring constantly, until the *crème fraîche* has almost evaporated.

Reduce the heat and stir in the remaining spoonful of *crème*. Check the seasoning. Serve the mushrooms and their sauce in a hot serving dish.

FOR 4 PERSONS:

1 pound mushrooms	1 cup Crème Fraîche (p. 666)

Mushrooms with Vermouth |

CHAMPIGNONS DE PARIS AU VERMOUTH

Prepare a recipe of Mushrooms in Cream (above), and add a tablespoon of dry vermouth just before serving.

Mushrooms Poulette | CHAMPIGNONS À LA POULETTE

Braise the mushrooms and keep them hot in the casserole in which they were cooked.

Make the sauce: Put the egg yolks into a heavy saucepan. Gradually stir in the *sauce velouté* and the white poultry stock. Add the diced mushrooms and the butter.

Cook the sauce over low heat, stirring constantly, until thick and smooth, then strain it through a fine sieve. Season with salt, pepper and nutmeg, and add the parsley and lemon juice. Pour the sauce over the braised mushrooms and blend gently. Serve in a hot dish.

FOR 4 PERSONS:

- 1 recipe Mushrooms Braised in Butter (above)
- 3 egg yolks
- 2 cups Sauce Velouté (p. 761)
- 1¼ cups White Poultry Stock (p. 165)
- ¼ cup finely diced mushrooms, or mushroom peelings

- 3 tablespoons butter
- Salt
- Freshly ground white pepper
- Grated nutmeg
- 2 tablespoons minced parsley
- Juice of ½ lemon

Mushrooms Sautéed in Butter |

CHAMPIGNONS SAUTÉS AU BEURRE

Clean the mushrooms: wash them very briefly and pat them dry with kitchen paper; or wipe them with damp paper towels.

Separate the caps of the mushrooms from the stems. If the caps are small or medium sized, leave them whole; if large, quarter them. Slice the stems. Sprinkle with the lemon juice in a bowl to prevent darkening.

Heat the oil and the butter in a casserole and add the mushrooms. If the caps are much larger than the sliced stems, cook them first for a couple of minutes and then add the sliced stems. Season with salt and pepper. Mix well and cook over medium heat until golden, about 5 minutes. Stir gently with a two-pronged fork to avoid crushing the mushrooms.

When the mushrooms are cooked, put them into a hot serving dish, or use them as a garnish for poultry or game. Sprinkle with the parsley and the thyme.

FOR 4 PERSONS:

- 1 pound mushrooms
- Juice of 1 lemon
- 2 tablespoons peanut oil
- 3 tablespoons butter
- Salt

- Freshly ground white pepper
- 2 tablespoons minced parsley
- Pinch of ground thyme, or 1 sprig of fresh thyme, minced

/ *Mushrooms Sautéed with Fines Herbes*

CHAMPIGNONS SAUTÉS AUX FINES HERBES

Proceed as in the preceding recipe, but substitute 2 tablespoons minced Fines Herbes (p. 89) for the minced parsley and the thyme.

CROÛTE AUX CHAMPIGNONS DE PARIS / *Mushroom Toast*

Wash the mushrooms and dry them thoroughly on a kitchen cloth. Mince them fine.

Heat the oil and the butter in a skillet over medium heat and add the mushrooms. Cook them, stirring constantly with a wooden spoon, for about 8 minutes, or until they are golden. Season with salt and pepper.

Scoop out a little of the center of each bread slice to make a hollow. Fry the bread on both sides in hot goose fat or lard. Put the fried bread into a buttered baking dish and spoon a little of the cooked mushroms into each. Coat each slice with a little *sauce Périgueux* or *sauce Mornay* and sprinkle with grated cheese.

Brown under the broiler and serve in the same dish.

FOR 4 PERSONS:

1 pound mushrooms	8 thick slices of firm white
1 tablespoon peanut oil	bread, crusts removed
3 tablespoons butter	4 tablespoons goose fat or lard
Salt	1 cup Sauce Périgueux (p 765),
Freshly ground black pepper	or Sauce Mornay (p. 776)
	¼ cup grated Swiss cheese

Note: Instead of mincing the mushrooms, you may also use their caps only, whole if they are small, or quartered if they are big. But big mushrooms should be blanched first (p. 602). The liquid from the blanching may be used for a *sauce béchamel.* You may also combine the mushrooms and a *sauce béchamel* and garnish the fried bread with this mixture.

CHAMPIGNONS DE PARIS FARCIS / *Stuffed Mushrooms*

Wash and dry the mushrooms and separate the caps from the stems.

Heat 3 tablespoons of the butter in a saucepan; add the lemon juice and the mushroom caps. Season lightly with salt and add the water. Bring to the boiling point and cook for 2 minutes. Drain the mushroom caps and reserve the cooking liquid.

Chop the stems fine. Cut the shallots and the ham into minute dice.

Heat the remaining butter and the oil in a saucepan. Add the shallots and cook them, stirring constantly, until they are soft and turning golden. Add the chopped mushroom stems and mix well with a wooden spoon. Season with salt and very little pepper. Simmer for 5 or 6 minutes and then add the minced ham. Beat the egg yolk with the *crème fraîche* and bind the mushroom mixture with this thickening. Simmer for 2 or 3 minutes, but do not boil.

Place the mushroom heads, round sides down, in a buttered baking dish and stuff the cavities with the filling. Sprinkle with the reserved liquid in which the heads were cooked and then with the cheese. Cook in a preheated 375° F. oven for 5 minutes. Serve very hot, in the same dish.

FOR 4 PERSONS:

16 large mushrooms
6 tablespoons butter
Juice of 1 lemon
Salt
¼ cup water
6 shallots
2 slices of Bayonne or smoked ham or prosciutto

1 tablespoon peanut oil
Freshly ground black pepper
1 egg yolk
¼ cup Crème Fraîche (p. 666)
3 tablespoons grated Swiss cheese

Mushroom Croquettes /

CROQUETTES DE CHAMPIGNONS DE PARIS

Wash the mushrooms, dry them carefully, and mince them.

Heat 3 tablespoons of the butter in a skillet, add the mushrooms. and sauté them over high heat for about 5 minutes. Season with salt and pepper.

Cook the noodles in boiling salted water according to package directions and drain them.

Heat the remaining butter in a casserole and add the mushrooms and the drained noodles. Beat the egg yolks with the *crème fraîche* and add the mixture to the mushrooms and noodles to bind them.

Cook over very low heat, stirring constantly, until the mixture is smooth and rather thick. Season with salt and pepper, add the grated cheese, remove the casserole from the heat, and let it cool completely.

Shape the mixture into 12 balls and flatten these out to resemble thick *crêpes*. Dip them into the *anglaise* mixture and then coat with the bread crumbs. Heat the fat to 375° F. on a frying thermometer, and fry the croquettes in it until they are golden on both sides.

Remove them from the fat with a slotted spoon, drain well on kitchen paper, and serve them, very hot, in a hot serving dish lined with a napkin.

FOR 4 PERSONS:

1 pound mushrooms
½ cup butter
Salt
Freshly ground black pepper
⅓ pound fine noodles
4 egg yolks
½ cup Crème Fraîche (p. 666)
½ cup grated Swiss cheese

Anglaise composed of:
2 egg yolks
2 tablespoons peanut oil
2 tablespoons water
Pinch of salt

2 cups bread crumbs
Fat for deep frying

Mushroom Pannequets /

PANNEQUETS DE CHAMPIGNONS DE PARIS

Pannequets and *crêpes* are really the same thing, but custom decrees that *pannequets* are smaller and slightly thicker than *crêpes*.

Mushroom *pannequets* can be made like Potato Crêpes (p. 640), substituting minced mushrooms for the potatoes. I would like to give you a recipe that is a little different.

Peel the potatoes and grate them. Put them into a kitchen cloth and twist them to extract as much juice as possible. Mince the mushrooms, twist them dry in the same manner, and mix them with the potatoes. Add the egg and blend in a blender. Season with salt, pepper and nutmeg. If the mixture is too thick, add a little *crème fraîche* to achieve the consistency of a thick *crêpe* batter.

Cook the *pannequets* in the usual manner in combined hot oil and butter in a skillet. Drain on kitchen paper and serve in a hot serving dish.

FOR 4 PERSONS:

½ **pound potatoes**	**Grated nutmeg**
½ **pound mushrooms**	¼ **cup Crème Fraîche (p. 666)**
1 **egg**	¼ **cup peanut oil**
Salt	¼ **cup butter**
Freshly ground black pepper	

/ *Mushroom Tart*

TOURTE FEUILLETÉE AUX CHAMPIGNONS DE PARIS

Make the puff paste and from it prepare and bake an 8-inch patty shell, as described on page 717.

Cook the mushrooms as in Blanched Mushrooms (p. 602). Drain them, reserving the cooking liquid, and keep them hot.

Put the egg yolks into a heavy saucepan and beat in the reserved mushroom liquid. Using a wire whisk, beat in the white poultry stock, the mushroom peelings and the butter. Season with salt, pepper and nutmeg. Stir over very low heat until slightly thickened. Add the parsley, lemon juice and blanched mushrooms to the sauce. Mix well and keep hot.

With the point of a knife, loosen and remove the top inner round from the baked patty shell. Scoop out any soft pastry from the bottom shell and fill the cavity with the mushroom mixture. Cover with the top pastry round.

Place the mushroom tart on a serving dish and serve immediately, very hot.

FOR 4 PERSONS:

½ **recipe Puff Paste (p. 715)**	2 **tablespoons butter**
1 **pound mushrooms**	**Salt**
4 **egg yolks**	**Freshly ground white pepper**
1 **cup White Poultry Stock**	**Grated nutmeg**
(**p. 165**)	2 **tablespoons minced parsley**
1 **tablespoon mushroom trimmings,**	**Juice of** ½ **lemon**
finely diced	

/ *Mushroom Tartlets*

TARTELETTES DE CHAMPIGNONS DE PARIS À LA CRÈME

Prepare and bake the tartlet shells, as described on page 715.
Wash and dry the mushrooms and cut them into small dice.

Cook the mushrooms in the hot butter in a covered casserole over low heat for about 2 minutes, then remove the cover and cook until all the liquid has evaporated. Stir frequently with a wooden spoon.

Stir in the cornstarch and the *crème fraîche*. Mix well and let the liquid reduce by half. Season with salt, pepper and nutmeg. Stir in the lemon juice.

Spoon a little of the mushroom mixture into each tartlet, sprinkle with the grated cheese, and brown under the broiler. Serve immediately, very hot.

FOR 4 PERSONS:

4 **baked tartlet shells (5-inch size) made from Pâte Brisée (p. 713)**	½ **cup Crème Fraîche (p. 666)**
	Salt
	Freshly ground black pepper
¾ **pound mushrooms**	**Grated nutmeg**
3 **tablespoons butter**	**Juice of ½ lemon**
1 **teaspoon cornstarch**	4 **tablespoons grated Swiss chesse**

Mushroom Timbale / TIMBALE DE CHAMPIGNONS DE PARIS

Cook the macaroni according to package directions, drain it, and keep it hot in a casserole. Stir half of the butter into it.

Blanch the mushrooms as described on page 602. Instead of draining the mushrooms, cook them, uncovered, over high heat until the cooking liquid has almost completely evaporated. Keep them hot.

Broil the sausages and drain them. Add the mushrooms and the sausages to the macaroni and mix well. Add the grated cheese and the remaining butter and toss the mixture. Check the seasoning.

Pile the mixture in the shape of a dome on a hot serving plate and serve very hot.

FOR 4 PERSONS:

⅓ **pound small elbow macaroni**	¼ **cup grated Swiss cheese**
6 **tablespoons butter**	**Salt**
¾ **pound mushrooms**	**Freshly ground black pepper**
12 **tiny sausages**	

OKRA

Gombos

Okra in Butter / GOMBOS ÉTUVÉS AU BEURRE

Cut off the stems and tips of the okra.

Add the lemon juice to a large pot of boiling salted water and cook the okra in it for 5 minutes. Drain in a colander.

Heat the butter in a casserole and add the okra. Sauté gently for 5 to 6 minutes and dish up in a hot serving dish.

Boiled Beef La Villette

Boeuf à la Ficelle La Villette

Boiled Beef La Villette

Boeuf à la Ficelle La Villette

IT'S IMPORTANT TO have an excellent stock made with beef shin, the usual soup greens and seasonings for this dish.

Trim the celery stalks, the leeks, carrots, turnips and potatoes neatly so that they will look well when they are served; needless to say, their quality must also be excellent. Tie each kind of vegetable in a piece of cheesecloth so that it may easily be removed without breaking as soon as it is done. Also tie the beef with a string so that it too can be easily removed from the pot after it is cooked.

It is best to cook this dish in separate steps: cook the vegetables in simmering stock, timing each so they are just barely tender; they may be reheated briefly in the stock at serving time. Cook the beef in barely simmering stock for about 3½ hours, or until it is tender. Put the beef in a large deep serving dish, reheat the vegetables in the stock, and then surround the beef with them. Pour a generous amount of stock over the meat and vegetables. Serve with sour pickles.

For 8 persons:

1 triple recipe Brown Stock (p. 164), made with shin of beef	16 medium-sized carrots
	2 turnips, quartered
	8 potatoes, peeled
8 celery stalks	5 pounds rump of beef
8 leeks, white part only	Sour pickles

Editors' Note: Other cuts of beef can be used for this dish, but remember to adjust the cooking time according to the cut of beef used. The cut in the photograph is the French cut called aiguillette, *a special cut of the sirloin; if you use a cut similar to the* aiguillette, *it will not need to be cooked for longer than 1 hour.*

Quail with Muscat Grapes
Cailles de Vignes aux Raisins Muscats

Quail with Muscat Grapes

Cailles de Vignes aux Raisins Muscats

DRAW AND CLEAN the birds and truss them. Season them with salt and pepper. Heat 2 tablespoons of the oil and 3 tablespoons of the butter in a casserole over high heat and sauté the quails in it until golden on all sides. Add the brandy and flame, then add the wine. Cover the casserole and simmer over low heat for 10 minutes, or until tender.

Peel and seed the grapes. Heat 2 tablespoons of the butter in a small saucepan. Add the grapes and cover the saucepan. Simmer over low heat for 5 minutes.

Scoop out the center of the bread slices, forming slight hollows, and sauté them in the remaining oil and butter until they are golden on all sides. Place them in a hot serving dish. Put a quail on each slice of fried bread and add a few grapes. Sprinkle with the pan juices and serve immediately, very hot.

For 2 persons:

4 quails
Salt
Freshly ground white
    pepper
6 tablespoons peanut oil
½ cup butter

2 tablespoons brandy
½ cup dry white wine
1 cup white muscat grapes
4 thick slices of firm
    white bread

Rack of Lamb Cecilia

Carré d'Agneau Rôti Cécilia

Rack of Lamb Cecilia

Carré d'Agneau Rôti Cécilia

HAVE YOUR BUTCHER shorten the rib bones and scrape the meat and fat off the ends. Rub the roast with salt, put it in a roasting pan, and place it in a preheated 500° F. oven for 10 minutes. Then lower the heat to 325° F. and roast for about 20 minutes longer; the exact time will depend on the thickness of the loin.

Set the meat on a heated large serving platter. Deglaze the drippings in the pan with a little water and pour over the roast. Garnish with some of the potatoes, carrots, green beans, braised endives, baked tomatoes and artichoke hearts filled with peas. Arrange any remaining vegetables on another hot serving dish.

For 4 persons:

1 rack (loin) of baby lamb (8 inches long)
Salt
¼ recipe Rissolé Potatoes (p. 625)
¼ recipe Carrots in Butter (p. 575)
¼ recipe Boiled Green Beans in Butter (p. 556)

4 Braised Belgian Endives (p. 593)
4 small Baked Tomatoes (p. 646)
4 Artichoke Hearts in Butter (p. 545)
1 cup Peas in Butter (p. 614)

Cassoulet of Castelnaudary
Cassoulet de Castelnaudary aux Genêts

Cassoulet of Castelnaudary

Cassoulet de Castelnaudary aux Genêts

SOAK THE BEANS in cold water overnight, blanch them in boiling salted water for 2 minutes, and drain them.

Heat the 4 tablespoons of butter in a big casserole and add the fresh pork lardoons and the minced onions and garlic. Cook, stirring frequently with a wooden spoon, until the mixture is soft and blended. Stir in the flour and mix well. Add the drained beans, the ham bone, Lyonnaise sausages, ham butt, pork rind, pork shoulder, tomato juice, *bouquet garni,* cloves, peppercorns and a little salt. Add enough hot consommé to not quite cover the mixture. Cover tightly and simmer over low heat for about 2 hours; if necessary, add a little more hot consommé.

Meantime, put the loin of pork, the loin of mutton, the Toulouse sausages and the preserved goose in a large roasting pan and add the sliced onions, the carrots and a little water. Roast them all together in a preheated 400° F. oven until each is tender. The goose will take very little time, the pork well over an hour. As the different meats are cooked, remove them and put them into a large heavy casserole; cover the casserole, keeping the meats hot. Save the pan juices. Roasts kept hot in this manner can easily stand for an hour or two.

After the beans have cooked for 2 hours, remove the pork shoulder, the sausages, ham butt, ham bone and *bouquet garni* from the beans. Cut the meat on the ham bone into small pieces and return these pieces to the beans. Also add the pan juices from the roasted meats. Put the pork shoulder, ham butt and sausages into the same casserole with the roasted meats and keep them all hot together. Cook the beans very slowly for 1 more hour. Cut all of the meats into appropriate slices.

Take a very large deep baking dish (or use several smaller baking dishes) and spread the cooked beans over the bottom. Arrange all of the sliced meats on top of the beans in an orderly fashion. Sprinkle the top with the bread crumbs and dot with the softened butter. Bake in a hot oven until the top is brown and crisp. Serve very hot in the same dish.

For 10 persons:

1½ pounds dried white beans
Salt
4 tablespoons butter
¼ pound fresh pork fat,
    cut into thin strips
    (lardoons)
4 onions, minced
6 garlic cloves, minced
2 tablespoons flour
1 raw ham bone, blanched
2 truffled Lyonnaise
    sausages, or any large
    boiling-type sausages
1 smoked ham butt (2
    pounds), soaked, and
    parboiled for 15 minutes
½ pound scraped fresh
    pork rind, cut into pieces
1 pound boneless fresh
    pork shoulder

1 cup tomato juice, made
    from fresh tomatoes
1 big Bouquet Garni (p. 46)
4 whole cloves
8 peppercorns, crushed
6 cups hot Beef Consommé
    (p. 167), or more
2 pounds loin of pork
    (4 to 6 chops)
1½ pounds loin of mutton
1 pound Toulouse sausages,
    or any small well-
    seasoned sausages
10 pieces of preserved
    goose (confit d'oie)
2 onions, sliced
3 carrots, chopped
1½ cups fine dry bread
    crumbs
6 tablespoons soft butter

Pig's Knuckle with Lentils

Jarret de Porc aux Lentilles

Pig's Knuckle with Lentils

Jarret de Porc aux Lentilles

WASH THE LENTILS in water. Put them in a casserole with a large amount of water. Season with salt and pepper, add the onion, and bring to a boil. Add the pig's knuckle and cook for about 1 hour. Put the sausages and the duck's wings in a roasting pan and roast briefly in a preheated 375° F. oven until they are golden brown. Add them to the casserole after the lentils have cooked for an hour. Remove the pig's knuckle from the casserole, place it in the roasting pan, and brown it in the 375° F. oven for about 15 minutes. Return the knuckle to the lentils, simmer for a few minutes longer, and then put everything on a hot platter. Serve with a side dish of mustard.

For 2 persons:

½ pound dried lentils
Salt
Freshly ground black pepper
1 onion, peeled
1 pig's knuckle (the bottom
    end of the hind leg)

2 chipolata sausages
2 duck's wings
Dijon-style mustard

Chicken à la Queen of Houdan

Poulet Reine de Houdan Germinal

Chicken à la Queen of Houdan

Poulet Reine de Houdan Germinal

EACH OF THE vegetables for this dish should be cooked separately. The potatoes must be cut to the same size and weight so that they will cook uniformly, and the carrots also should be trimmed to equal-sized pieces. Trim the beans and shell the peas.

First braise the lettuce as described on page 598.

Cook the chicken, spread with the softened butter, on a spit or rotisserie for about 45 minutes. While the chicken is roasting, cook the other vegetables.

Blanch the potatoes and then cook them in a small casserole as described on page 625. Keep them hot.

Blanch the carrots, put them into a casserole with butter and water, and cook them until they are tender and glazed. Keep them hot.

Blanch the peas with a few sprigs of fresh mint and then cook them in butter in another casserole until tender. Keep hot.

Boil the beans and then cook them in a fourth casserole with some butter. Keep hot.

Drain the braised lettuce when it is fully cooked, put it on a hot serving dish, and garnish with poached marrow. Keep hot.

Bake the tomatoes in a 350° F. oven, then put them on a hot serving dish.

Arrange the roasted chicken on a hot platter surrounded by the peas, carrots, potatoes and beans.

For 4 persons:

¼ recipe Rissolé
    Potatoes (p. 625)
½ recipe Glazed
    Carrots (p. 576)
½ recipe Boiled Green
    Beans in Butter
    (p. 556)
½ recipe Peas with
    Mint (p. 617)

1 recipe Braised Lettuce
    with Beef Marrow
    (p. 598)
1 roasting chicken
    (3 pounds)
4 tablespoons butter,
    softened
1 recipe Baked Tomatoes
    (p. 646)

Spaghetti with Mussels

Spaghetti aux Moules

Spaghetti with Mussels

Spaghetti aux Moules

COOK THE MUSSELS *à la marinière*: Put the shallots, onion, garlic and parsley into a kettle with the wine and the crushed peppercorns. Add the mussels, cover tightly, and cook over high heat until the mussel shells open, about 5 minutes. Remove from the heat and cool to lukewarm. Drain the mussels and reserve all the liquid. Shell the mussels, being careful to save all of the liquid that drains from the shells, and keep them barely warm.

Boil the cooking liquid over moderate heat for 5 minutes. Strain it twice through a very fine sieve or a triple layer of damp cheesecloth.

Heat the butter in a saucepan, stir in the flour, and cook until golden. Stir in the strained liquid and simmer for 10 minutes. Beat together the *crème fraîche* and the egg yolks and stir into the sauce off the heat. Return it to low heat, but do not let it boil or it will curdle.

Cook the spaghetti *al dente*. Drain carefully and toss quickly with the sauce. Add the reserved mussels and serve immediately with the grated Parmesan cheese on the side.

For 4 persons:

3 dozen mussels, scrubbed
4 shallots, minced
1 onion, minced
1 garlic clove, mashed
2 parsley sprigs, minced
1 cup dry white wine
3 peppercorns,
    crushed

2 tablespoons butter
2 tablespoons flour
½ cup Crème Fraîche
    (p. 666)
2 egg yolks
1 pound spaghetti
1 cup grated Parmesan
    cheese

Polish Koldouny

Koldouny Polonais

Polish Koldouny

Koldouny Polonais

COMBINE THE FLOUR, the whole egg, the egg yolks and the water and salt. Stir together with a fork, and then knead until the dough is smooth and elastic. Shape it into a ball and let it rest for 1 hour.

Grind together, using the finest blade of a meat grinder, the beef, the kidney fat and the fresh chervil. Season this stuffing with the marjoram and a little salt and cayenne. Stir it with a wooden spoon until the mixture is very smooth. Shape it into balls the size of hazelnuts.

Divide the dough into halves and roll each half out into a thin rectangle about ⅛ inch thick. Arrange the tiny meat balls, spaced evenly about 2 inches apart, on one half of the dough. Brush the other rectangle of dough with water and lay it, wet side down, on top of the first one. Firmly press the dough together around each little mound of filling. Cut the dough with a sharp knife into 2-inch squares, each square enclosing one of the balls of meat filling. Dust the squares lightly with flour and let them dry for about 2 hours.

Cook the *koldouny* in boiling water for 10 minutes. Turn them once during the cooking time, using a slotted spoon rather than a fork, which might damage the fragile dough.

Cook the onion rings in the butter in a skillet over high heat until they are golden. Do not let them get very brown.

Remove the *koldouny* from the boiling water with a slotted spoon and put them on a hot serving dish. Surround them with the onion rings and spoon the butter over them. Spoon the *sauce tomate* over them and garnish with the parsley.

Koldouny are not eaten with a fork, but with a spoon, so that each remains whole and juicy.

For 4 persons:

For the dough:
2¼ cups sifted all-
   purpose flour
1 whole egg
3 egg yolks
1 tablespoon water
1 teaspoon salt
For the stuffing:
½ pound tender beef
   (top round, sirloin, etc.)
½ pound fresh kidney fat

2 tablespoons minced fresh
   chervil
2 teaspoons ground marjoram
Salt
Cayenne pepper
Flour
2 large onions, sliced
   and broken into rings
½ cup butter
1 cup Sauce Tomate (p. 769)
Parsley sprigs

FOR 4 PERSONS:

2 pounds okra	**Salt**
Juice of 1 lemon	**6 tablespoons butter**

GOMBOS ÉTUVÉS À LA CRÈME / *Okra in Cream*

Proceed as in the preceding recipe but add ½ cup Crème Fraîche (p. 666) to the cooked okra. Let the *crème fraîche* reduce by half, and then add 1 more tablespoon *crème fraîche.*

GOMBOS AUX FINES HERBES / *Okra with Fines Herbes*

Proceed as in Okra in Butter (above) and add 4 tablespoons minced Fines Herbes (p. 89) to the cooked okra.

GOMBOS À LA TOMATE / *Okra with Tomatoes*

Blanch the okra in boiling salted water with the juice of ½ lemon added for 6 minutes. Drain thoroughly.

Heat the oil and the butter in a casserole. Add the onions and cook them until they are soft and golden. Add the tomatoes and the bay leaf and season with salt, pepper and nutmeg. Mix well and simmer, covered, over low heat for about 15 minutes.

Add the blanched okra to the sauce, mix, and simmer for about 5 minutes longer. Sprinkle with the thyme and serve, very hot, in a vegetable dish.

FOR 4 PERSONS:

1½ pounds okra	**4 tomatoes, peeled, seeded and**
Salt	** chopped**
Juice of ½ lemon	**½ bay leaf**
2 tablespoons olive oil	**Freshly ground black pepper**
2 tablespoons butter	**Grated nutmeg**
2 onions, minced	**1 sprig of thyme, chopped**

GOMBOS EN BEIGNETS / *Okra Fritters*

Blanch the okra in boiling salted water with the juice of ½ lemon added for 5 minutes. Drain the okra in a colander and pat it dry with a kitchen towel.

Make the batter: Combine the flour, oil, salt, eggs and milk in a large bowl. Beat thoroughly and let stand for 15 minutes.

Heat the fat for frying to 375° F. on a frying thermometer.

Put the okra into the frying batter, coat every piece well on all sides, and take it out with a fork. Drop the okra into the hot fat and fry until golden on all sides. Drain well on kitchen paper and serve in a hot dish lined with a folded napkin. Sprinkle with salt before serving and serve very hot.

FOR 4 PERSONS:

1½ pounds okra	1 teaspoon salt
Salt	2 eggs
Juice of ½ lemon	¼ cup milk
½ cup flour	Fat for deep frying
1 tablespoon peanut oil	

ONIONS

Oignons

Braised Onions / OIGNONS RISSOLÉS

Mince the onions; put them into a casserole with oil and butter. Cook them over low heat, stirring constantly, until they are soft and golden, but do not let them brown. Season lightly with salt and add a pinch of sugar. Use as a garnish.

If you are using the tiny onions, called *grelots* in France, peel them and keep whole. Cook them as described above.

The casserole may be covered for 10 minutes or so to intensify the heat slightly.

FOR 4 PERSONS:

1½ to 2 pounds onions	Salt
3 tablespoons olive oil	Pinch of sugar
3 tablespoons butter	

Onions in Cream / OIGNONS À LA CRÈME

Peel the onions and slice them.

Heat half of the butter in a casserole, add the onions, and cook them gently until they are soft and golden. Season with salt and pepper. Heat the *crème fraîche* over medium heat and let it reduce by half. Add it to the onions and, off the heat, stir in the remaining butter. Mix well and serve hot, in a hot serving dish.

FOR 4 PERSONS:

1½ pounds onions	Freshly ground white pepper
6 tablespoons butter	1 cup Crème Fraîche (p. 666)
Salt	

Glazed Onions / OIGNONS GLACÉS

Choose very small and very round onions. Peel them, but leave them whole.

Heat the butter in a casserole, add the onions, season them lightly with salt, add the sugar, and cook them over medium heat until they begin to turn golden. Add the stock, reduce the heat, cover the casserole, and cook the onions, without stirring them, but occasionally shaking the pan to prevent sticking, for about 20 minutes. The stock will be almost completely absorbed by the onions. Use as a garnish.

FOR 4 PERSONS:

1½ pounds tiny white onions	Pinch of sugar
4 tablespoons butter	½ cup Brown Stock (p. 164)
Salt	

OIGNONS AU GRATIN / *Onions au Gratin*

Peel the onions and mince very fine.

Heat 3 tablespoons of the butter in a casserole. Add the onions, mix well, and cook them over low heat until they are soft and golden; do not let them brown. Season with salt, pepper and nutmeg.

Butter a baking dish, add the onions and their pan juices, coat with the *sauce tomate,* dot with the remaining butter, and sprinkle with the bread crumbs. Cook in a preheated 375° F. oven for 10 minutes, or brown quickly under a broiler.

Serve very hot, in the same dish.

FOR 4 PERSONS:

1½ pounds onions	Grated nutmeg
5 tablespoons butter	1 cup Sauce Tomate (p. 769)
Salt	¼ cup fine dry bread crumbs
Freshly ground black pepper	

/ *Onion Purée (Purée Soubise)*

PURÉE D'OIGNONS (PURÉE SOUBISE)

> EDITORS' NOTE: *A* soubise *generally calls for a thickening of cooked rice. It isn't absolutely necessary, however, and M. Oliver prefers to thicken it with a little* sauce béchamel.

This dish is often called *soubise,* though the correct name is simply an onion purée.

Peel the onions, mince them, and blanch them in boiling salted water for 5 minutes. Remove them with a slotted spoon. Drain them thoroughly and then cook them in 3 tablespoons of the butter in a little saucepan over low heat for about 10 minutes, or until they are very soft. Add the *sauce béchamel,* season with salt and pepper, and add the sugar. Strain the purée through a fine sieve or blend in a blender. Return to low heat and stir in the remaining butter and the *crème fraîche.* Simmer until the desired consistency is reached and use as desired.

FOR 4 PERSONS:

1 pound onions	Freshly ground white pepper
6 tablespoons butter	¼ teaspoon sugar
2 cups very thick Sauce Béchamel (p. 761)	6 tablespoons Crème Fraîche (p. 666)
Salt	

Stuffed Onions | OIGNONS FARCIS

Choose large onions, peel them, and scoop out the centers. Mince the scooped-out centers very fine. Put the onion shells into a buttered baking dish.

In a casserole heat half of the butter and add the minced onions, the sausage meat and the bread crumbs. Season lightly with salt, pepper, and nutmeg. Mix well and stir in the *fines herbes*. Cook over low heat, stirring constantly, for 10 to 15 minutes.

Stuff the onions with this filling. Dot them with the remaining butter. Pour the stock around the onions and cover the baking dish with a sheet of buttered kitchen parchment or brown paper. Cook in a preheated 350° F. oven for about 30 minutes.

Put the onions into a serving dish, keep them hot, reduce their cooking liquid by three fourths, and pour it over the onions. Serve hot.

FOR 4 PERSONS:

4 large onions	Salt
6 tablespoons butter	Freshly ground black pepper
¼ pound sausage meat	Grated nutmeg
1 cup fresh white bread crumbs, soaked in milk and squeezed dry	1 tablespoon Fines Herbes (p. 89)
	1½ cups Brown Stock (p. 164)

OYSTER PLANT

Salsifis

EDITORS' NOTE: *Oyster plant is a winter root vegetable highly prized in France and Italy. It is white, with a delicate flavor somewhat reminiscent of an oyster. In the United States, the roots can be found in vegetable markets catering to people of Mediterranean origin.*

Basic Preparation: Prepare a bowl with acidulated water (3 tablespoons lemon juice or vinegar to 1 quart water). Scrape or peel the roots and drop them immediately into the acidulated water to prevent darkening.

Taking out 1 oyster plant at a time, cut it into 3-inch sticks. Drop the prepared sticks into a casserole containing salted cold water and the juice of ½ lemon. Cover the casserole, bring to the boiling point, and cook until the vegetable is almost tender, about 7 minutes. Cooking time depends on the age of the roots. Test them for doneness with a knife or a fork.

Drain the oyster plant in a colander and use them as indicated in the recipes.

Oyster Plant in Butter | SALSIFIS ÉTUVÉS AU BEURRE

Prepare the oyster plant as described in the basic preparation (above).

Heat 3 tablespoons of the butter in a casserole and add the blanched oyster plant.

Season with salt and pepper and simmer over very low heat for about 10 minutes.

Serve the oyster plant in a hot vegetable dish and dot with the remaining butter. Serve very hot.

FOR 4 PERSONS:

2 pounds oyster plant	**Salt**
6 tablespoons butter	**Freshly ground white pepper**

/ *Oyster Plant with Fines Herbes*

SALSIFIS AUX FINES HERBES

Proceed as in Oyster Plant in Butter (above), and add 4 tablespoons minced Fines Herbes (p. 89) to the oyster plant at serving time.

SALSIFIS PROVENÇALE / *Oyster Plant Provençale*

Prepare in the same manner as Oyster Plant in Butter (above), and just before serving sprinkle with ¼ cup minced parsley and 2 minced garlic cloves.

SALSIFIS ÉTUVÉS À LA CRÈME / *Oyster Plant in Cream*

Prepare the oyster plant as described in the basic preparation (above).

Heat the butter in a casserole, add the oyster plant, mix, and add enough *crème fraîche* to barely cover the vegetable. Cover the casserole and cook over low heat until the *crème fraîche* is greatly reduced and partly absorbed by the oyster plant. Season with salt, pepper and nutmeg.

Put the oyster plant into a hot serving dish and sprinkle with 2 more tablespoons *crème fraîche*.

FOR 4 PERSONS:

2 pounds oyster plant	**Grated nutmeg**
5 tablespoons butter	**2 (or more) cups Crème Fraîche**
Salt	**(p. 666)**
Freshly ground white pepper	

SALSIFIS FRITS / *Fried Oyster Plant*

Prepare the oyster plant as described in the basic preparation (above).

Put the drained pieces of oyster plant into a bowl and sprinkle them with the oil and the lemon juice, coating them on all sides. Season with salt and pepper and sprinkle with the parsley. Let the vegetables stand for 30 minutes.

Thoroughly blend together the batter ingredients in a bowl and heat the frying fat to 375° F. on a frying thermometer.

Drain the marinated oyster plant and drop it into the frying batter, coating well on all sides. Shake off any excess batter. Fry the pieces in the deep fat until they are golden on all sides.

Drain them on kitchen paper and serve them in a hot serving dish lined with a folded napkin.

FOR 4 PERSONS:

2 pounds oyster plant
4 tablespoons olive oil
Juice of 1 lemon
Salt
Freshly ground white pepper
1 tablespoon minced parsley

Batter for Frying:
1 cup flour
1 teaspoon salt
1 tablespoon peanut oil
2 eggs
½ cup milk
Fat for deep frying

Oyster Plant Fritters | BEIGNETS DE SALSIFIS

Prepare the oyster plant as described in the basic preparation (p. 612).

Purée the drained oyster plant in a blender, or force it through a food mill. Beat in the butter and season with salt and pepper. It should be very thick. If the purée is too thin, put it into a casserole and cook it over low heat, stirring constantly, until it is thick and dry. Let the mixture cool.

Shape the mixture into round balls the size of walnuts, dust them with flour, and fry them in deep fat, preheated to 375° F. on a frying thermometer, until they are golden.

Drain the fritters on kitchen paper and serve them in a hot serving dish lined with a folded napkin.

FOR 4 PERSONS:

2 pounds oyster plant
6 tablespoons butter
Salt

Freshly ground white pepper
Flour
Fat for deep frying

PEAS

Petits Pois

Peas in Butter | PETITS POIS ÉTUVÉS AU BEURRE

Shell the peas, and while you're shelling them heat a good deal of water in a big saucepan. Bring it to the boiling point, season with salt and the sugar, and add the peas. Cook without a cover for 5 to 15 minutes, depending on the size and age of the peas. They should be almost tender. Drain them in a colander.

Heat the butter in a saucepan, add the peas, and simmer gently for about 5 minutes. Put the peas into a vegetable dish and sprinkle with the *fines herbes*.

FOR 4 PERSONS:

3 pounds unshelled peas
Salt
1 teaspoon sugar

6 tablespoons butter
2 tablespoons minced Fines
  Herbes (p. 89)

PETITS POIS AUX ASPERGES / *Peas with Asparagus*

Shell and blanch the peas as described in the preceding recipe.

Peel the asparagus stalks and blanch them in boiling salted water for about 8 minutes, or until they are almost tender. Remove them with a slotted spoon and drain them on a kitchen towel. Cut the asparagus into 1-inch pieces.

Put the peas and the asparagus into a casserole with the butter.

Mix well, check the seasoning, and simmer over low heat for about 5 minutes. If necessary, add a tablespoon of hot water to prevent sticking. Serve hot in a hot vegetable dish.

FOR 4 PERSONS:

2 pounds unshelled peas
1 pound asparagus
Salt

6 tablespoons butter
Freshly ground black pepper

PETITS POIS ÉTUVÉS AU LARD / *Peas with Bacon*

Shell and blanch the peas as described in Peas in Butter (above).

Drain the peas in a colander and reserve the cooking liquid.

Heat the butter in a casserole and add the minced onion and the diced bacon. Cook, stirring constantly, for about 5 minutes, or until the onion is soft, and then add the peas and the sugar.

Mix well and simmer over low heat for another 5 minutes. If necessary, add a little of the liquid in which the peas were cooked.

Serve the peas and the bacon in a vegetable dish, sprinkled with the *fines herbes*.

FOR 4 PERSONS:

3 pounds unshelled peas
Salt
6 tablespoons butter
1 onion, minced
½ cup diced blanched bacon or
  fresh pork fat

½ teaspoon sugar
2 tablespoons minced Fines
  Herbes (p. 89)

PETITS POIS À LA CRÈME / *Peas in Cream*

Prepare a recipe of Peas in Butter (above). At the same time that you put the peas and butter in the casserole, add 1 cup of hot Crème Fraîche (p. 666), and simmer until the *crème* is well reduced. Season with salt, pepper and nutmeg.

Peas à la Française / PETITS POIS À LA FRANÇAISE

Shell the peas. Heat the butter in a casserole and put the peas into it, together with the lettuce and the *bouquet garni*. Season with salt and pepper and the sugar. Add the lukewarm water to moisten the vegetables. Mix well, bring to the boiling point, and simmer over very low heat for about 20 minutes, or as long as 40 minutes if the peas are older and larger.

You may also add small white onions, either left whole or sliced, to the peas.

When the peas are cooked, remove the *bouquet garni* and stir the *beurre manié* into the pan juices to thicken them. Simmer for another 5 minutes. Put the peas into a vegetable dish and serve hot.

FOR 4 PERSONS:

3 pounds unshelled peas
6 tablespoons butter
1 head of lettuce, cut into
   julienne strips
1 Bouquet Garni (p. 46)
Salt

Freshly ground black pepper
½ teaspoon sugar
½ cup lukewarm water
Optional: 4 small white onions
1 tablespoon Beurre Manié
   (p. 41)

Peas with Ham / PETITS POIS AU JAMBON

Shell the peas. Mince the onion and cook it in the butter in a casserole until it is soft. Add the ham and the peas. Season very lightly with salt, a little pepper and the sugar. Mix well and simmer over low heat for 2 minutes. Add the *bouquet garni* and the water. Cover the casserole and simmer over very low heat for 20 to 40 minutes, depending on the age and size of the peas.

At serving time, remove the *bouquet garni* and put the peas into a hot vegetable dish. Sprinkle with the *fines herbes*.

FOR 4 PERSONS:

3 pounds unshelled peas
1 onion
3 tablespoons butter
¼ pound Bayonne or smoked ham
   or prosciutto, diced
Salt

Freshly ground black pepper
½ teaspoon sugar
1 Bouquet Garni (p. 46)
½ cup water
2 tablespoons minced Fines
   Herbes (p. 89)

Peas with Lettuce / PETITS POIS AUX LAITUES

Shell the peas. Heat half of the butter in a casserole, add the peas, season with salt and pepper, and add the sugar. Add the *bouquet garni*.

Trim the lettuce and remove the outer leaves; you'll use only the hearts. Tie each of the hearts with string and add them to the peas, together with the water. Cover the casserole and simmer, covered, for 20 minutes to 40 minutes, depending on the size and age of the peas.

Remove the *bouquet garni* when the peas are tender. Stir in the remaining butter off the heat and untie the lettuce.

Put the peas into a hot vegetable dish and surround them with the lettuce. Serve very hot.

FOR 4 PERSONS:

3 pounds unshelled peas	**½ teaspoon sugar**
6 tablespoons butter	**1 Bouquet Garni (p. 46)**
Salt	**4 hearts of lettuce**
Freshly ground black pepper	**½ cup water**

PETITS POIS À LA MENTHE / *Peas with Mint*

Shell the peas and blanch them and the mint in boiling salted water for 5 minutes. Drain the peas and mince the sprigs of mint.

Heat half of the butter in a casserole and add the peas and the minced mint.

Simmer over low heat for 5 to 15 minutes, depending on the size of the peas. Check the seasoning; add a little more salt and a little sugar, if desired.

When the peas are tender, put them in a hot vegetable dish and dot them with the remaining butter.

FOR 4 PERSONS:

3 pounds unshelled peas	**6 tablespoons butter**
Salt	**Sugar**
2 or 3 sprigs of fresh mint	

PURÉE DE POIS FRAIS / *Purée of Fresh Peas*

Shell the peas and put them into a large saucepan of boiling salted water. Cook for 10 to 15 minutes, or until they are very tender. Drain the peas in a colander.

Purée the peas in a blender or force them through a food mill. The purée must be very smooth; put it into a saucepan with the butter and cook it over low heat, stirring constantly, until it is thick. Season with salt and a little sugar.

Serve the purée as is, or as a garnish for a roast or for roast chicken. Decorate it with croutons fried in butter.

FOR 4 PERSONS:

3 pounds unshelled peas	**Sugar**
Salt	**½ cup Croutons (p. 62),**
6 tablespoons butter	**fried in butter**

POIS CASSÉS BOUILLIS / *Boiled Split Peas*

Soak the dried peas in cold water for 2 or 3 hours. Drain them, put them into a saucepan, and cover them with a large quantity of cold water. Add the onion, carrot, ham and *bouquet garni,* and season with salt and pepper. Cover the pan and let the peas cook gently for about 1 hour.

FOR 4 PERSONS:

1 pound dried split peas	**1 Bouquet Garni (p. 46)**
1 onion, minced	**Salt**
1 carrot, minced	**Freshly ground black pepper**
⅓ pound Bayonne ham, diced	

Purée of Split Peas / PURÉE DE POIS CASSÉS

Soak and then cook the split peas, but mince the ham.

When the peas are cooked, remove the *bouquet garni* and purée the peas in a blender, or force them through a food mill. If the purée is too liquid, put it into a casserole with the butter, and cook over low heat to the desired consistency. Stir constantly.

Serve the peas in a hot vegetable dish and garnish with the fried bread.

FOR 4 PERSONS:

1 recipe Boiled Split Peas (above)	**4 slices of white bread, crusts**
4 tablespoons butter	**removed, fried in butter**

SNOW PEAS

Haricots Mange-tout

EDITORS' NOTE: Mange-tout, *as these peas are familiarly called in France, are a type of pea with a tender pod which is eaten along with the tiny peas. In the United States, they are found in Chinese markets under the name of snow peas. Frozen snow peas are also commercially available.*

Snow Peas in Butter /
HARICOTS MANGE-TOUT ÉTUVÉS AU BEURRE

String the snow peas and blanch them in boiling salted water for about 5 minutes. Drain them in a colander.

Heat the butter in a casserole and add the snow peas. Mix well, cover the casserole, and simmer very gently for 10 minutes, stirring occasionally.

Put the snow peas in a hot serving dish and sprinkle with the parsley and garlic. Serve hot.

FOR 4 PERSONS:

1½ pounds snow peas	**2 tablespoons minced parsley**
6 tablespoons butter	**1 garlic clove, minced**

Snow Peas Sautéed in Lard /
HARICOTS MANGE-TOUT SAUTÉS AU LARD

String the snow peas and blanch them in boiling salted water for about 5 minutes. Drain them in a colander.

Cut the fresh pork or ham fat into small dice. Heat the lard in a casserole, add the pork or ham fat, and sauté for 2 to 3 minutes without letting the fat turn golden. Add the snow peas, mix, and simmer over low heat for about 10 minutes.

Pour the snow peas into a vegetable dish and sprinkle with minced parsley. Serve hot.

FOR 4 PERSONS:

1½ pounds snow peas
¼ pound fresh pork or fresh
    ham fat

1 tablespoon lard
2 tablespoons minced parsley

PEPPERS

Poivrons

GARNITURE DE POIVRONS / *Roasted Peppers*

Brush red or green sweet peppers on all sides with oil and put them into a preheated 500° F. oven.

Take them out when they are well scorched. Remove the scorched outer skin under running cold water; it will come off easily.

Cut the peppers lengthwise into halves. Remove the membranes and seeds.

You may now use the peppers in various ways: in a ragout, or stewed in butter, or as a garnish for roasts or poultry.

POIVRONS FRITS / *Pepper Fritters*

Skin the peppers as described in the preceding recipe. Cut off the stems, remove the membranes and seeds, and slice the peppers crosswise into rounds. Season with salt and pepper.

Prepare the frying batter. Beat together the flour, oil, egg yolk, beer and salt. Beat the egg white until stiff and fold it into the mixture.

Heat the fat to 375° F. on a frying thermometer. Dip the pepper rounds into the batter and fry them in the hot fat until golden. Drain them on kitchen paper and serve them on a hot serving dish lined with a folded napkin. Serve very hot.

FOR 4 PERSONS:

4 sweet peppers
Salt
Freshly ground black pepper

Fritter batter:
½ cup flour
1 tablespoon peanut oil
1 egg, separated
¼ cup beer
½ teaspoon salt

Fat for deep frying

Omelet Soufflé with Peppers /

OMELETTE SOUFFLÉE AUX POIVRONS

Skin the peppers as described above and then cut them lengthwise into halves. Remove the seeds and membranes.

Cut 2-inch diamonds out of each pepper half and cut the remaining parts into thin strips.

Heat the oil and the butter in a skillet. Cook the diamond-shaped pepper pieces in it until they are barely golden. Keep them flat by pressing them down with the back of a spoon. Take them out with a slotted spoon and reserve them.

Cook the thin pepper strips in the same skillet, then take them out and reserve them separately.

Lightly beat together the 5 egg yolks and the 2 whole eggs. Season with salt and pepper. Beat the egg whites until stiff and fold them carefully into the beaten yolks, so that the mixture will be light and airy. Fold the pepper strips into the egg mixture. Reheat the oil and butter in the skillet, adding a little more if necessary, and pour the egg mixture into it. Cook the omelet on one side, turn it over with a wide spatula, and let it cook until golden on the other side, shaping it into the usual omelet shape.

Put the omelet soufflé on a hot serving dish and decorate it with the diamond-shaped peppers. Sprinkle the pan juices over the omelet and serve immediately.

FOR 4 PERSONS:

6 large sweet peppers	**2 whole eggs**
2 tablespoons olive oil	**Salt**
2 tablespoons butter	**Freshly ground black pepper**
5 eggs, separated	

Peppers Stuffed with Rice / POIVRONS FARCIS AU RIZ

Cut off the stem ends of the peppers. Remove the seeds from this opening with a spoon or knife, but keep the shell intact.

Blanch the peppers in boiling salted water for 15 minutes. Remove them with a slotted spoon and drain them on a kitchen cloth.

Heat half of the butter in a casserole and cook the onion in it until it is soft but still white. Season with salt and pepper.

Cook the rice in boiling salted water for 20 minutes. Drain it and add it to the onions. Sprinkle the mixture with the thyme. Add the sausage meat and simmer, stirring constantly, for about 5 minutes.

Stuff the peppers with the filling and put them side by side into a buttered baking dish. Dot with the remaining butter, sprinkle with the bread crumbs and brown under a broiler. Serve hot, in the same dish.

FOR 4 PERSONS:

4 large sweet peppers	**¼ cup uncooked rice**
Salt	**¼ teaspoon ground thyme**
6 tablespoons butter	**¼ pound sausage meat**
1 onion, minced	**¼ cup fine dry bread crumbs**
Freshly ground black pepper	

POTATOES

Pommes de Terre

POMMES DE TERRE VAPEUR / *Steamed Potatoes*

Choose small potatoes, peel and wash them, and put them into a metal vegetable basket that fits into a saucepan, or on the rack of a steamer.

Put cold salted water into the saucepan or steamer. Bring it to the boiling point and cook the potatoes in the steam. When they are done, put them into a hot serving dish and serve melted butter on the side.

FOR 4 PERSONS:

1½ **pounds small new potatoes**
Salt

½ **cup butter, melted**

POMMES DE TERRE AU BASILIC / *Boiled Potatoes with Basil*

Boil the peeled potatoes in salted water, but add a sprig of fresh basil, or a little dried basil to the water.

Put the boiled potatoes into a serving dish and sprinkle them with minced fresh or dried basil.

FOR 4 PERSONS:

8 **medium-sized potatoes**
Salt

Fresh or dried basil

/ *Boiled Potatoes with Mint*

POMMES DE TERRE À LA MENTHE

Proceed as in Boiled Potatoes with Basil (above), but substitute fresh or dried mint for the basil.

POMMES DE TERRE FONDANTES / *Potatoes Fondant*

Choose small potatoes, peel them, and cut them into the shape of small drops, like bonbons.

Heat the butter in a casserole and add the potatoes. Season the potatoes lightly with salt, cover the casserole, and cook over medium heat.

Shake the casserole frequently, so that the potato bonbons will turn golden on all sides.

Serve the potatoes in a hot serving dish. Pour the pan juices over them and sprinkle them with *fines herbes*.

FOR 4 PERSONS:

2 pounds potatoes	2 tablespoons minced Fines
6 tablespoons butter	Herbes (p. 89)
Salt	

Potatoes in Cream | POMMES DE TERRE À LA CRÈME

Cook the potatoes in their skins in boiling water for about 15 minutes. Peel them and cut them into thin slices. Put them into a casserole and add just enough *crème fraîche* to cover them. Bring to the boiling point and season with salt, pepper and nutmeg.

Cook over low heat until the *crème fraîche* is well reduced and mostly absorbed by the potatoes. Be careful not to scorch the potatoes.

Put the potatoes into a hot serving dish, and add a few more spoonfuls *crème fraîche* to the dish at serving time.

FOR 4 PERSONS:

1½ pounds potatoes	Salt
2 cups (or more) Crème Fraîche	Freshly ground white pepper
(p. 666)	Grated nutmeg

Potatoes Maître d'Hôtel |

POMMES DE TERRE MAÎTRE D'HÔTEL

Peel the potatoes and boil them in salted water for about 10 minutes. Drain them and cut them into slices. Put the potatoes into a casserole and add the butter and enough scalding hot milk to barely cover. Then season with salt and pepper.

Cook the potatoes until they are creamy and the milk has been almost absorbed by the potatoes.

Put the potatoes into a hot vegetable dish and sprinkle them with the *fines herbes*.

FOR 4 PERSONS:

1½ pounds potatoes	Freshly ground white pepper
6 tablespoons butter	3 tablespoons minced Fines
2 (or more) cups hot milk	Herbes (p. 89)
Salt	

Mashed Potatoes | PURÉE DE POMMES DE TERRE

Peel the potatoes and cut them into quarters. Put them into a casserole with cold salted water. Bring to the boiling point and cook for about 20 minutes, or until the potatoes are soft.

Drain them in a colander, return them to the saucepan over low heat, and dry them out slightly.

Force them through a food mill or ricer, or mash them with a masher. Beat in the butter and hot milk and season with nutmeg. Continue to beat until the potatoes are fluffy. Serve hot in a vegetable dish.

FOR 4 PERSONS:

2 pounds potatoes
Salt
6 tablespoons butter

½ cup (approximately) scalded
    milk
Grated nutmeg

POMMES DE TERRE DAUPHINE / *Potatoes Dauphine*

Prepare the mashed potatoes and the *choux* paste. There should be about equal quantities of mashed potatoes and *choux* paste.

Season with salt and pepper and mix them together well. Shape into croquettes. Heat the frying fat to 375° F. on a frying thermometer and fry the croquettes until they are golden on all sides. Remove them with a slotted spoon and drain them on a kitchen cloth. Sprinkle with salt. Serve very hot.

FOR 4 PERSONS:

½ recipe Mashed Potatoes
    (above)
½ recipe Pâte à Choux
    (p. 710)

Salt
Freshly ground white pepper
Fat for deep frying

SOUFFLÉ DE POMMES DE TERRE / *Potato Soufflé*

Prepare the mashed potatoes. Beat in the egg yolks. Beat the egg whites until stiff and fold them into the potato mixture.

Butter a 6-cup soufflé dish, spoon in the mashed potatoes, and bake in a pre-heated 375° F. oven for 25 to 30 minutes.

FOR 4 PERSONS:

1½ cups Mashed Potatoes
    (above)

4 eggs, separated

POMMES DE TERRE MOUSSELINE / *Potatoes Mousseline*

Boil the potatoes in their skins. Peel the potatoes and mash them very smooth with a potato masher, or force them through a food mill or ricer. Beat in the ½ cup butter and the egg yolks. Season with salt, pepper and nutmeg. Mix well and beat in enough *crème fraîche* so that the potatoes are very smooth but still thick enough to hold their shape.

Butter a baking dish and pile the potatoes in it in the shape of a dome. Sprinkle with the melted butter. Cook in a preheated 400° F. oven for 10 minutes, or until the potatoes are golden.

FOR 4 PERSONS:

2 pounds potatoes
½ cup butter
4 egg yolks
Salt
Freshly ground white pepper

Grated nutmeg
6 tablespoons Crème Fraîche
    (p. 666)
4 tablespoons melted butter

POTATOES DAUPHINE
LES POMMES DE TERRE DAUPHINE

Above, left: *The mashed potatoes.* Right: *The* choux *paste. The mashed potatoes must be on the dry side.*

Below, left: *Combine equal parts of mashed potatoes and* choux *paste.* Right: *Blend thoroughly.*

POMMES DE TERRE DUCHESSE / *Duchess Potatoes*

Peel the potatoes and cook them in salted water for about 20 minutes.

Drain the potatoes and mash them until they are very smooth. Put them into a casserole over low heat and, stirring with a wooden spoon, cook until the mashed potatoes are dry. Add the butter and season with salt, pepper and nutmeg.

Remove from the heat and beat in the egg yolks and the whole egg. Whip until very smooth and fluffy. Serve immediately.

FOR 4 PERSONS:

1½ pounds potatoes	Grated nutmeg
4 tablespoons butter	2 egg yolks
Salt	1 whole egg
Freshly ground white pepper	

Note: These potatoes are usually squeezed through a pastry tube into decorative shapes and lightly browned in a hot oven. *Duchesse* potatoes are frequently used as a garnish.

/ *Duchess Potato Patties*

GALETTES DE POMMES DE TERRE DUCHESSE

Prepare the *duchesse* potatoes.

Shape the potatoes into even-sized, thick, round patties and coat them with flour.

In a bowl, beat together the eggs and the oil; season with salt, pepper and nutmeg. Dip the floured patties into this mixture.

Heat the oil and the butter in a skillet and sauté the patties in it until they are golden on both sides. Drain them and serve them immediately in a hot serving dish.

FOR 4 PERSONS:

1 recipe Duchess Potatoes (above)	Salt
Flour	Freshly ground white pepper
2 eggs	Grated nutmeg
2 tablespoons peanut oil	3 tablespoons each of peanut oil and butter for sautéing

POMMES DE TERRE NOISETTE (RISSOLÉES) / *Rissolé Potatoes*

Peel the potatoes. With a round melon scoop or similar tool, cut out small balls from the potatoes. Cook the potato balls in boiling salted water for about 10 minutes, or until they are three-quarters done. Drain them.

Heat the butter in a casserole, add the potatoes, and cook them until they are golden on all sides. Shake the pan frequently to prevent sticking. Season with salt. Serve very hot.

FOR 4 PERSONS:

2 pounds potatoes	Salt
6 tablespoons butter	

Potatoes Sautéed in Goose Fat /
POMMES DE TERRE SAUTÉES À LA GRAISSE D'OIE

Prepare as in the preceding recipe, substituting goose fat for the butter.

Sautéed Potatoes Lyonnaise /
POMMES DE TERRE SAUTÉES À LA LYONNAISE

Peel the potatoes, cut them into fine slices, wash them, and dry them in a kitchen cloth.

Heat the lard in a casserole and add the potatoes. Season with salt and pepper and simmer, covered, over low heat for about 10 minutes.

Heat the butter in another casserole and cook the onions in it until they are soft.

Add the onions and their pan juices to the potatoes and toss lightly. Cover the casserole and continue to simmer over low heat until the potatoes are tender, about 10 minutes longer. Serve in a hot serving dish.

FOR 4 PERSONS:

1½ pounds potatoes	Freshly ground white pepper
4 tablespoons lard	3 tablespoons butter
Salt	4 onions, minced

Potatoes Sarladaise / POMMES DE TERRE SARLADAISE

Peel the potatoes and cut them into thin rounds. Wash and dry them in a kitchen cloth. Heat the goose fat or the lard in a casserole, add the potatoes, and season with salt and pepper. Simmer, covered, over medium heat for about 10 minutes, or until the potatoes are halfway cooked. Add the truffles, mix well, cover the casserole, and continue to simmer until the potatoes are tender.

Serve in a hot serving dish, or as a garnish.

FOR 4 PERSONS:

1 pound potatoes	Freshly ground black pepper
3 tablespoons goose fat or lard	4 truffles, minced
Salt	

Potatoes Sautéed with Bacon /
POMMES DE TERRE SAUTÉES AU LARD

Peel the potatoes, cut them into thin slices, wash them, and dry them in a kitchen cloth.

Heat the lard in a skillet, add the bacon, and cook for 2 to 3 minutes, but do not let the bacon turn golden. Add the potatoes and season with salt and pepper. Mix well and simmer, covered, over low heat until the potatoes are golden on the bottom. Turn them out onto a hot serving dish and sprinkle with the parsley.

FOR 4 PERSONS:

1½ pounds potatoes	Salt
4 tablespoons lard	Freshly ground black pepper
¼ pound slab bacon, blanched and cut into small dice	4 tablespoons minced parsley

/ *Sautéed Potatoes with Fines Herbes*

POMMES DE TERRE SAUTÉES AUX FINES HERBES

Boil the potatoes in boiling salted water for about 15 minutes. Peel them, cut them into slices, and let them cool.

Heat the butter in a casserole and add the potatoes. Season with salt and pepper, mix well, and cook until the potatoes are golden, turning them frequently.

Sprinkle the potatoes with the *fines herbes* and serve them in a hot serving dish. Pour the pan juices over them.

FOR 4 PERSONS:

1½ pounds potatoes	Freshly ground black pepper
6 tablespoons butter	4 tablespoons minced Fines
Salt	Herbes (p. 89)

/ *Sautéed Potatoes Provençale*

POMMES DE TERRE SAUTÉES À LA PROVENÇALE

Proceed as in Sautéed Potatoes with Fines Herbes (above), and add 2 minced garlic cloves to the potatoes at serving time, with the *fines herbes*.

POMMES DE TERRE FRITES / *French-Fried Potatoes*

Peel the potatoes and cut them into even strips about ½ inch thick. Wash them and then dry them in a cloth.

Heat the frying fat to 360° F. on a frying thermometer and fry the potatoes until they are golden on all sides.

Drain them on kitchen paper and sprinkle them with salt. Serve very hot.

FOR 4 PERSONS:

1½ pounds potatoes	Salt
Fat for deep frying	

POMMES DE TERRE ALLUMETTES / *Potatoes Allumette*

Prepare like French-Fried Potatoes (above), but cut the potatoes into strips the size of kitchen matches.

Fried Potato Chips / POMMES DE TERRE CHIPS

Prepare like French-Fried Potatoes (above), but cut the potatoes into large very thin rounds.

French-Fried Potato Pennies / POMMES DE TERRE EN LIARDS

Prepare like French-Fried Potatoes (above), but cut the potatoes into small thin rounds, the size of pennies.

Souffléed Potatoes / POMMES DE TERRE SOUFFLÉES

Here are the rules for successful souffléed potatoes.

Choose very large potatoes (not new potatoes, but if at all possible, not very old ones either) and cut them into even-sized slices. Any other shape is of no importance and only reeks of unsuitable fantasy. The ideal thickness of the potato slices is a little less than ⅛ inch.

Do not wash the potatoes. Wipe them dry after peeling them and wipe them dry again after slicing them.

Heat the frying fat to 275° F. on a frying thermometer. Test a potato slice or two; the oil should not boil up. Plunge in quite a lot of potatoes, that is, enough to equal about one third of the volume of the frying fat.

The temperature of the fat must remain steady during the first cooking period. There are two ways of ensuring this. You may use an electric, thermostatically controlled deep fryer, or if you have the usual frying utensils, make sure that the temperature will come back as fast as possible to 275° F. after you've put the potatoes into the fat, and stay there. To achieve this, you increase or lower heat under the kettle.

Stir the potatoes so that they will be coated with fat on all sides and not stick together.

Be patient, for the cooking time will be about 10 minutes. When all the potatoes have been fried for the first time, you'll see that one or two will puff up somewhat. Prepare more frying fat; this time it must be hotter, 375° F. on the frying thermometer. Remove the potatoes from their first frying fat and put them immediately into the second, hotter one; all of them must puff up.

If you are ready to serve the potatoes now, fry them all until they are golden and dry. If you will be serving them later, take them out of the fat when they have puffed up but are not yet golden. Drain them on kitchen paper. The potatoes will collapse. Lay them side by side on a baking board or a baking sheet lined with a kitchen cloth, and take care that the potatoes do not touch each other. When you are about to serve them, put them back into the hot fat until they are golden. They will puff up immediately.

FOR 4 PERSONS:

2 pounds potatoes	**Fat for deep frying**

Potatoes Boulangère / POMMES DE TERRE BOULANGÈRE

Peel and mince the onions and cook them in the combined hot oil and butter until they are slightly golden. Drain the onions and keep them hot.

Peel the potatoes and cut them into thin slices.

Butter a baking dish. Make alternate layers of potatoes and onions, beginning and ending with a layer of potatoes. Season each layer with salt and pepper.

Add enough water to barely cover and add the pan juices from the onions. Cook in a preheated 350° F. oven for 30 minutes, or until all the water has evaporated. Serve very hot.

FOR 4 PERSONS:

4 medium-sized onions	2 pounds potatoes
2 tablespoons olive oil	Salt
3 tablespoons butter	Freshly ground black pepper

POMMES DE TERRE MACAIRE / *Potatoes Macaire*

Bake the potatoes in a 375° F. oven for about 45 minutes, or until tender. Scoop out the potato pulp, season with salt and pepper, and stir in 2 tablespoons of the butter, making a smooth mixture.

Heat the oil and the remaining butter in a large skillet. Put the potatoes in a flattened shape in the skillet and cook until they are golden on the bottom. Turn them and cook them until golden on the other side. Serve very hot.

FOR 4 PERSONS:

1 pound potatoes	½ cup butter
Salt	2 tablespoons olive oil
Freshly ground white pepper	

POMMES DE TERRE ROBERT / *Potatoes Robert*

Bake the potatoes in a 375° F. oven for about 45 minutes, or until tender.

Cut the baked potatoes lengthwise into halves and scoop them out. Put the scooped-out potato pulp into a bowl, season with salt and pepper, blend with a fork, and beat in half of the butter and all the eggs and chives.

Heat the oil and the remaining butter in a large skillet. Spread the potatoes smoothly on the bottom of the skillet. Cook over low heat until golden and crusty on the bottom. Turn the potatoes and cook them on the other side in the same manner.

Put them into a hot serving dish and serve hot.

FOR 4 PERSONS:

1 pound potatoes	2 eggs
Salt	2 tablespoons minced chives
Freshly ground white pepper	2 tablespoons olive oil
6 tablespoons butter	

POMMES DE TERRE BYRON / *Potatoes Byron*

Prepare the Potatoes Robert (above).

Put the potato cake, which must be very crisp, into a buttered baking dish. Heat

SOUFFLÉED

POTATOES

Cut the potatoes into very thin slices wth a slicer. Their average thickness should be less than ⅛ inch.

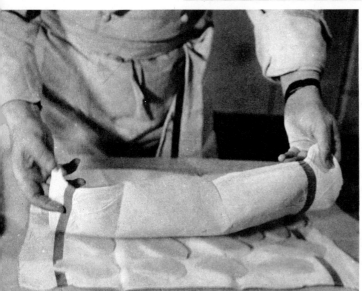

Dry the potatoes carefully between kitchen towels. Do not wash them under any circumstances.

Drop the potato slices, one by one, into the hot oil. The temperature of the oil must remain constant, or you won't be successful with this recipe.

Fry the potatoes in the hot fat, shaking the pan or stirring so that the potatoes will not stick to each other.

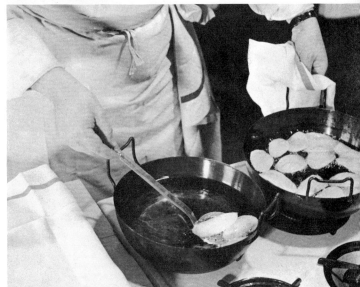

Prepare another kettle of frying fat, hotter than the previous one. When the potatoes begin to puff, after 10 minutes or so, transfer them immediately and as fast as possible into the second kettle with the hotter fat.

If you are going to serve the potatoes immediately, fry them until golden. Else, remove the potatoes from the fat as soon as they have puffed up and lay them on a kitchen cloth.

the *crème fraîche* in a saucepan and season it with salt, pepper and nutmeg. Pour it over the potatoes, sprinkle them with the grated cheese, and brown under a broiler. Serve immediately.

FOR 4 PERSONS:

1 recipe Potatoes Robert (p. 629)	Freshly ground white pepper
¾ cup Crème Fraîche (p. 666)	Grated nutmeg
Salt	3 tablespoons grated Swiss cheese

Potato Cake / GÂTEAU DE POMMES DE TERRE

Peel the potatoes and mince them. Heat the oil and 1 tablespoon of the butter in a round casserole. Add the potatoes, season with salt and pepper, and toss once or twice to blend the potatoes with the cooking fats. Dot with the remaining butter and put the casserole into a preheated 450° F. oven for 10 minutes without stirring the potatoes. Reduce the heat to 300° F. and bake for about 10 minutes longer. Remove from the oven, let them rest for a minute, and then unmold them on a hot round serving dish.

The potato cake must be very crisp and golden on the bottom and the sides. Serve immediately, very hot.

FOR 4 PERSONS:

2 pounds potatoes	Salt
4 tablespoons peanut oil	Freshly ground white pepper
4 tablespoons butter	

Potato Cake with Avocados /
GÂTEAU DE POMMES DE TERRE ET D'AVOCATS

Peel the avocados, cut them into halves, remove the stones, and mince the pulp.

Heat 4 tablespoons of the butter in a skillet, add the avocados, and sauté them over high heat for 2 minutes. Remove them with a slotted spoon and keep them hot.

Peel and mince the potatoes. Sauté them in the same skillet, adding the oil if necessary. Season with salt and pepper and cook for about 10 minutes, or until three-quarters done.

Butter a 6-cup charlotte mold and make alternate layers of potatoes and avocados, beginning and ending with potatoes. Melt the remaining butter and sprinkle it over the top. Bake in a preheated 375° F. oven for 20 minutes.

When the cake is done, unmold it on a hot serving dish. Serve immediately, and very hot.

FOR 4 PERSONS:

4 large avocados	3 tablespoons olive oil
7 tablespoons butter	Salt
2 pounds potatoes	Freshly ground white pepper

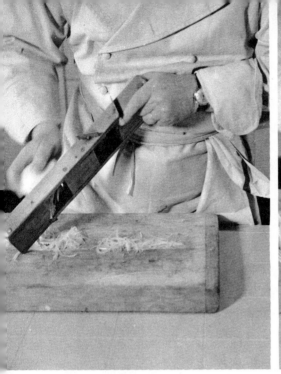
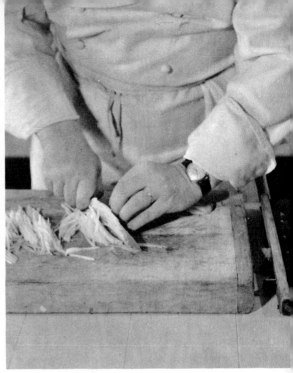

POTATO NESTS
LES NIDS EN POMMES PAILLE (1)

Above: *With the help of a shredder, called a* mandoline *in France, or by hand, cut the potatoes into julienne strips.*

Below: *Shape the julienne potatoes into a nest with the help of a special double frying basket. Or use 2 strainers, one slightly larger than the other. Plunge them into hot fat heated to 360° F. on a frying thermometer.*

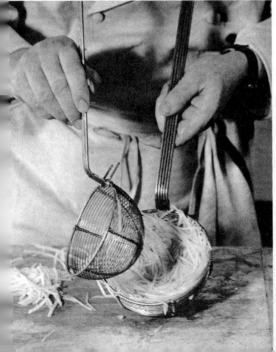

Fry in hot fat, without separating or loosening the two strainers.

When the potatoes are beginning to turn golden, remove from the fat and unmold the nest.

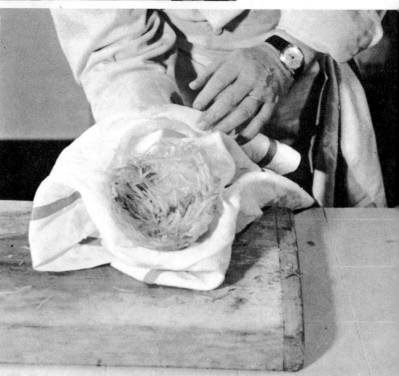

POTATO

NESTS

LES NIDS EN
POMME PAILLE

(2)

Plunge the potato nest back into the hot fat and proceed as in French-Fried Potatoes (p. 627), taking care that the potato nest turns golden on all sides. Keep it down in the fat with a slotted spoon.

POMMES DE TERRE DARPHIN | *Potatoes Darphin*

Peel the potatoes and cut them into very thin julienne strips, or shred them.
Wash and dry them, put them into a dish, and sprinkle with salt.
Heat the oil and butter in a skillet and add the potatoes. Cook them, without stirring, until golden on the bottom, about 10 minutes. Turn them and cook them in the same manner on the other side.
Serve in a hot serving dish.

FOR 4 PERSONS:

1½ pounds potatoes	2 tablespoons peanut oil
Salt	3 tablespoons butter

POMMES DE TERRE VOISIN | *Potatoes Voisin*

Peel the potatoes and mince them. Season them with salt and pepper.
Heat half of the butter in a skillet and make several layers of potatoes in it, sprinkling each with grated cheese. Top with a final layer of potatoes and dot with the remaining butter.
Cook over medium heat, shaking the pan occasionally to prevent sticking. When the potatoes are crisp and golden on the bottom, turn them over and cook until golden on the other side. Serve in a hot serving dish.

FOR 4 PERSONS:

1½ pounds potatoes	6 tablespoons butter
Salt	¾ cup grated Swiss cheese
Freshly ground white pepper	

GRATIN DU BUGEY | *Potato Gratin Bugey*

Peel the potatoes and mince or grate them. Season them with salt and pepper.
Butter a baking dish and make layers of potatoes sprinkled with grated cheese. Sprinkle with the chicken fat and add enough stock to barely cover the potatoes.
Bring to the boiling point over high heat and then bake in a preheated 325° F. oven for 45 minutes. Serve in the same dish.

FOR 4 PERSONS:

1½ pounds potatoes	½ cup chicken fat, cut into
Salt	small pieces
Freshly ground white pepper	1½ cups (approximately) White
1 cup grated Swiss cheese	Poultry Stock (p. 165)

GRATIN DAUPHINOIS | *Potato Gratin Dauphinois*

Peel the potatoes and grate them. Season with salt and pepper. Rub the bottom of an earthenware baking dish with a cut clove of garlic. Butter the baking dish.
Put the potatoes in the baking dish, making several layers. Sprinkle each layer

with a little thyme. Mix the milk, the *crème fraîche* and the eggs. Pour over the potatoes and lift them gently, so that the mixture will be well distributed.

Cook in a preheated 375° F. oven for about 30 minutes. Serve in the same dish.

FOR 4 PERSONS:

1½ pounds potatoes	½ teaspoon ground thyme
Salt	1 cup milk
Freshly ground black pepper	¼ cup Crème Fraîche (p. 666)
1 garlic clove	2 eggs

Potato Gratin Savoyard / GRATIN SAVOYARD

Prepare in the same manner as the preceding recipe but substitute 1¼ cups White Poultry Stock (p. 165) for the milk and the *crème fraîche*.

Hungarian Potatoes / POMMES DE TERRE À LA HONGROISE

Peel and mince the onions. Heat the butter in a casserole. Add the onions and cook them until they are soft and golden. Add the tomato and the paprika. Mix and cook over low heat for 10 minutes.

Peel the potatoes and cut them into thin rounds. Add them to the sauce in the casserole and season with salt. Add enough stock to barely cover the potatoes. Cook, covered, over low heat for about 30 minutes, or until the potatoes are tender.

At serving time, sprinkle with the parsley.

FOR 4 PERSONS:

2 medium-sized onions	1½ pounds potatoes
3 tablespoons butter	Salt
1 tomato, peeled, seeded and chopped	2 (or more) cups Brown Stock (p. 164)
1 tablespoon paprika	4 tablespoons minced parsley

Potatoes Landaise / POMMES DE TERRE À LA LANDAISE

Peel the potatoes and cut them into large dice.

Heat the lard or the goose fat in a casserole. Add the onions and cook them until they are soft and golden. Then add the ham and the potatoes. Season with very little salt (since the ham may be salty) and some pepper, and add enough water to barely cover the potatoes.

Cover the casserole and cook in a preheated 375° F. oven for about 30 minutes, or until the potatoes are tender. Do not stir while the potatoes are cooking.

At serving time, stir in the garlic and the parsley.

FOR 4 PERSONS:

1½ pounds potatoes	Salt
4 tablespoons lard or goose fat	Freshly ground black pepper
2 onions, minced	2 garlic cloves, minced
⅓ pound Bayonne or smoked ham or prosciutto, diced	2 tablespoons minced parsley

POMMES DE TERRE FARCIES | *Stuffed Potatoes*

Bake the potatoes in a 375° F. oven for about 45 minutes, or until tender. Cut a slice from the top of each potato. Scoop out the potato pulp, taking care not to break the skins. Mash the pulp and force it through a sieve or a ricer. Save the potato shells.

Cook the onion in the hot lard until it is soft; do not let it brown. Add the onion and the sausage meat to the potato purée. Season with salt, pepper and nutmeg. Stir in the *sauce béchamel.*

Stuff the potato shells with the filling, and put them side by side into a buttered baking dish. Sprinkle with the grated cheese and bake in a preheated 375° F. oven for about 20 minutes.

FOR 4 PERSONS:

4 large baking potatoes
1 onion, minced
2 tablespoons lard
¼ pound sausage meat
Salt

Freshly ground black pepper
Grated nutmeg
½ cup Sauce Béchamel (p. 761)
4 tablespoons grated Swiss cheese

| *Stuffed Potatoes Florentine*

POMMES DE TERRE FARCIES FLORENTINE

Bake the potatoes and purée the pulp, as described in Stuffed Potatoes (above).

Cook the spinach. Using roughly equal quantities of mashed potatoes and spinach, mix together thoroughly and season with salt, pepper and nutmeg.

Stuff the potato shells with this stuffing, coat with the *sauce Mornay,* and sprinkle with the grated cheese and the bread crumbs. Cook in a preheated 375° F. oven for about 15 minutes, or brown slowly under the broiler. Serve in the same dish.

FOR 4 PERSONS:

4 baking potatoes
1 recipe Spinach in Butter
   (p. 644)
Salt
Freshly ground black pepper

Grated nutmeg
½ cup Sauce Mornay (p. 776)
4 tablespoons grated Swiss cheese
¼ cup fine dry bread crumbs

| *Stuffed Potatoes Provençale*

POMMES DE TERRE FARCIES À LA PROVENÇALE

Bake the potatoes and purée the pulp, as described in Stuffed Potatoes (above). Put the potato skins side by side in a buttered baking dish.

Combine the hard-cooked egg yolks, the tomato purée, anchovy fillets, olives and tunafish. Mix well until the filling is smooth. Check the seasoning and then beat in the mashed potatoes.

Stuff the potato skins with this filling. Sprinkle the potatoes with a little olive oil and cook in a preheated 375° F. oven for about 15 minutes. At serving time, sprinkle with the *fines herbes.* Serve in the same dish.

FOR 4 PERSONS:

4 baking potatoes	1 tablespoon tunafish in oil,
2 hard-cooked egg yolks, mashed	mashed
2 tablespoons Tomato Purée (p. 157)	2 tablespoons olive oil
4 anchovy fillets, mashed	4 tablespoons minced Fines
8 green olives, pitted and minced	Herbes (p. 89)

Stuffed Potatoes Soubise /

POMMES DE TERRE FARCIES SOUBISE

Bake the potatoes and purée the pulp, as described in Stuffed Potatoes (p. 637). Put the potato skins side by side in a buttered baking dish.

Blend the onion purée with the potato purée. Check the seasoning. Stuff the potato skins with this filling. Brown slowly under a broiler, or heat in a preheated 375° F. oven for 10 minutes.

FOR 4 PERSONS:

4 baking potatoes	1½ cups Onion Purée (p. 611)

Potatoes Stuffed with Ham /

POMMES DE TERRE FARCIES YORKAISE

Bake the potatoes and purée the pulp, as described in Stuffed Potatoes (p. 637). Put the potato skins side by side in a buttered baking dish.

Mince together the ham, mushrooms and onion.

Heat the oil and 2 tablespoons of the butter in a casserole, add the minced ham mixture, cover the casserole, and cook, stirring frequently, for 4 to 5 minutes. Add the *crème fraîche* and season with a little salt and pepper and the paprika. Add the mashed potatoes and mix well.

Stuff the potato shells with the filling. Sprinkle with the bread crumbs and the remaining butter, melted, and bake in a preheated 375° F. oven for about 15 minutes, or brown slowly under the broiler.

FOR 4 PERSONS:

4 baking potatoes	2 tablespoons Crème Fraîche
3 slices of ham (about ⅛ pound)	(p. 666)
4 large mushrooms	Salt
1 onion	Freshly ground black pepper
2 tablespoons peanut oil	1 teaspoon paprika
6 tablespoons butter	¼ cup fine dry bread crumbs

Potatoes Stuffed with Bacon /

POMMES DE TERRE FARCIES AU LARD

Peel the potatoes and cut a thick slice off the top of each. Scoop out the center part of each with a sharp-sided spoon or a grapefruit knife, leaving the hollowed-out potatoes in the shape of a basket. Put these side by side in a buttered baking dish.

Boil the scooped-out potato pulp in salted water for about 18 minutes. Drain and mash it until very smooth.

Heat the lard in a skillet. Add the bacon and the onion and cook until both are soft, but do not let them turn golden. Drain and mix with the mashed potatoes. Stir in 3 tablespoons of the butter. Season with salt, pepper, cayenne, nutmeg and the *fines herbes.*

Stuff the potatoes with this filling, sprinkle with the remaining butter, melted, and bake in a preheated 350° F. oven for about 35 minutes. Add a little water or stock to the dish as they bake to keep the potatoes from sticking. Serve in the same dish.

FOR 4 PERSONS:

4 baking potatoes	Salt
2 tablespoons lard	Freshly ground black pepper
¼ pound slab bacon, blanched and minced	Cayenne pepper
	Grated nutmeg
1 onion, minced	2 tablespoons minced Fines
5 tablespoons butter	Herbes (p. 89)

/ *Stuffed Potatoes Basquaise*

POMMES DE TERRE FARCIES À LA BASQUAISE

Prepare the potatoes as described in the preceding recipe; cook and mash the pulp and reserve it. Put the potato shells in a buttered baking dish.

Cook the onions in the combined hot oil and 2 tablespoons butter in a casserole until they are turning golden. Add the ham, peppers and tomatoes. Mix well and cook over low heat, stirring constantly, until the mixture is thick and smooth. Stir in the mashed potatoes and blend well. Season with a little salt and pepper.

Stuff the potato shells with the filling and sprinkle with some of the melted butter. Cook in a preheated 375° F. oven for about 35 minutes, or until the potato shells are tender. Baste occasionally with more of the melted butter. Serve in the baking dish.

FOR 4 PERSONS:

8 medium-sized baking potatoes	2 tomatoes, peeled, seeded and chopped
2 onions, minced	
2 tablespoons olive oil	Salt
2 tablespoons butter	Freshly ground black pepper
¼ pound Bayonne or smoked ham or prosciutto, diced	4 tablespoons (or more) melted butter
2 small sweet peppers, charred, scraped, and cut into thin slices (see p. 619)	

/ *Stuffed Potatoes Chasseur*

POMMES DE TERRE FARCIES CHASSEUR

Prepare the potatoes as described in Potatoes Stuffed with Bacon (above); cook and mash the pulp, and put the potato shells in a buttered baking dish.

Sauté the chicken livers in the combined hot oil and butter in a casserole for about 3 minutes. Season with salt and pepper. Drain and keep hot.

Put the shallots into the same casserole, adding a little more butter if necessary. Cook until they are soft, then add the mushrooms. Mix well, season with salt and pepper, and cook for about 5 minutes over low heat, stirring frequently. Add the mashed potatoes, the chicken livers and the tomato purée. Mix well. Check the seasoning and add a little cayenne and nutmeg. Stuff the potatoes with this filling and sprinkle with the bread crumbs. Cook in a preheated 375° F. oven for about 35 minutes. Add a little water during cooking time to keep the potatoes from sticking.

Serve hot, in the same dish.

FOR 4 PERSONS:

4 baking potatoes
¼ pound chicken livers, minced
2 tablespoons olive oil
2 tablespoons butter
Salt
Freshly ground black pepper

2 shallots, minced
4 mushrooms, minced
2 tablespoons thick Tomato Purée
   (p. 157)
Cayenne pepper
Grated nutmeg
2 tablespoons fine dry bread
   crumbs

Potato Crêpes / CRÊPES DE POMMES DE TERRE

Peel the potatoes and shred them fine.

In a bowl combine the flour, eggs, milk, a little salt, pepper and nutmeg, and a dash of cayenne. Beat well with a wire whisk, add the beer, oil and melted butter, and beat again.

Strain the batter through a fine sieve. Add the shredded potatoes and mix well. If the mixture seems too thick, add a little more beer.

Heat some of the oil and butter in a skillet. Pour in ¼ cup of the batter. Cook it until golden, turn with a spatula, and cook on the other side. Continue frying the *crêpes* and put them on a hot serving dish as they are cooked.

Add a little more butter and oil to the skillet with each *crêpe*.

FOR 4 PERSONS:

3 large potatoes
1 cup flour
3 eggs
½ cup milk
Salt
Freshly ground black pepper
Grated nutmeg

Cayenne pepper
¼ cup (or more) beer
1 tablespoon peanut oil
3 tablespoons melted butter
4 tablespoons each of peanut oil
   and butter for sautéing

Potato Croquettes / CROQUETTES DE POMMES DE TERRE

Peel the potatoes and grate them fine. Put them into a bowl and add the egg. Season with salt, pepper and nutmeg. Mix well.

Heat the oil and the butter in a skillet. Shape the mixture into small croquettes with 2 spoons. If the mixture is on the dry side and the croquettes don't hold together well, add an egg yolk to them. Sauté them in the hot fat until they are golden on all sides. As the croquettes are done, put them on a hot serving dish and keep them hot.

FOR 4 PERSONS:

3 large potatoes
1 egg
Salt
Freshly ground white pepper

Grated nutmeg
3 tablespoons each of peanut oil
and butter for sautéing

/ *Potato Croquettes with Cheese*

CROQUETTES DE POMME DE TERRE AU FROMAGE

Proceed as in Potato Croquettes (above), and add ¼ cup of grated Swiss cheese to the potato mixture.

/ *Potato Croquettes with Ham*

CROQUETTES DE POMMES DE TERRE AU JAMBON

Proceed as in Potato Croquettes (above), and add ½ cup minced cooked ham to the potato mixture.

/ *Potato Croquettes with Hazelnuts*

CROQUETTES DE POMMES DE TERRE AUX NOISETTES

Proceed as in Potato Croquettes (above), and add ½ cup grated hazelnuts to the potato mixture.

/ *Potato Croquettes with Mushrooms*

CROQUETTES DE POMMES DE TERRE AUX CHAMPIGNONS

Proceed as in Potato Croquettes (above), and add 2 large mushrooms, minced and cooked in butter, to the potato mixture.

/ *Potato Croquettes Niçoise*

CROQUETTES DE POMMES DE TERRE NIÇOISE

Proceed as in Potato Croquettes (above), and add ¼ cup of very thick, garlic-flavored tomato paste to the potato mixture.

/ *Potato Croquettes with Onions*

CROQUETTES DE POMMES DE TERRE AUX OIGNONS

Proceed as in Potato Croquettes (above), and add 2 large onions, minced and cooked in butter until soft, to the potato mixture.

Potato Croquettes Périgourdine /

CROQUETTES DE POMMES DE TERRE PÉRIGOURDINE

Proceed as in Potato Croquettes (p. 640), and add 2 grated truffles to the potato mixture.

Potato Gnocchi Parmentier / GNOCCHI PARMENTIER

Peel the potatoes, boil in salted water for about 20 minutes, and drain them. Mash them very smooth. Beat in 3 tablespoons of the butter and the *crème fraîche*. Put the potatoes into a saucepan over low heat and, stirring constantly, cook them until they are dry. Off the heat beat in the egg and the egg yolks and ¼ cup of the grated cheese. Season with salt and pepper and nutmeg. The mashed potatoes must be very thick. Allow the mixture to cool.

Shape the mixture into small balls or cylinders. Roll them in flour and lay them on a rack to dry out.

Bring a large pot of water to the boiling point and add the potato gnocchi, a few at a time. Reduce the heat and simmer for about 5 minutes. Remove the gnocchi with a slotted spoon and drain them on a kitchen towel. Continue until all are cooked. Put them in a hot serving dish and sprinkle with the remaining butter, melted, and the remaining cheese. If necessary, heat them briefly in a 375° F. oven or under a broiler.

FOR 4 PERSONS:

1 pound potatoes	2 egg yolks
Salt	¾ cup grated Swiss cheese
7 tablespoons butter	Freshly ground white pepper
¼ cup Crème Fraîche (p. 666)	Grated nutmeg
1 whole egg	Flour

EDITORS' NOTE: *Different potatoes absorb moisture differently so that it could happen that the gnocchi might be too soft, which would cause them to disintegrate during cooking. It is best to cook a few gnocchi first to see if they will hold up. If not, add a little flour to the mixture, 1 tablespoon at a time, to firm it. Do not add any more flour than necessary since it affects the taste of the dish.*

PUMPKIN

Potiron

Pumpkin Soufflé / SOUFFLÉ DE POTIRON

Peel the pumpkin and remove the seeds and membranes. Cut into pieces and cook, uncovered, in boiling salted water until tender. Drain the pumpkin, force it through a food mill, and drain again. There should be about 1 generous cup. Blend the pumpkin with the *sauce béchamel* and season with salt and pepper. Beat in the egg yolks and the grated cheese. Beat the egg whites until very stiff and fold them into the mixture.

Pour the mixture into a 6-cup soufflé mold, filling it about three-quarters full.

Bake it in a preheated 350° F. oven for 20 minutes. Then increase the heat to 375° F. and bake for 5 to 10 minutes longer.

FOR 4 PERSONS:

½ small pumpkin
½ cup thick Sauce Béchamel (p. 761)
Salt

Freshly ground white pepper
4 eggs, separated
¼ cup grated Swiss cheese

SORREL

Oseille

CHIFFONADE D'OSEILLE / *Chiffonade of Sorrel*

Wash the sorrel thoroughly and cut the leaves into fine julienne strips.

Heat the butter in an enamelware casserole and add the sorrel. Cover the casserole and cook until almost tender, about 10 minutes. Stir occasionally. Remove the cover, season lightly with salt, and evaporate all the cooking liquid.

Put the sorrel chiffonade into a hot serving dish and serve at once.

FOR 4 PERSONS:

2 pounds sorrel
6 tablespoons butter

Salt

PURÉE D'OSEILLE / *Sorrel Purée*

Cook 2 pounds of sorrel as described in the preceding recipe.

Purée it in a blender or force it through a food mill. Serve hot, as a garnish.

PURÉE D'OSEILLE À LA CRÈME / *Sorrel Purée with Cream*

Add ½ cup of Crème Fraîche (p. 666) to a sorrel purée (above), and simmer gently until slightly thickened.

At serving time, stir in another 3 tablespoons of butter. Put into a hot serving dish and serve immediately.

SPINACH

Épinards

Blanched Spinach / ÉPINARDS BLANCHIS

Trim 2 pounds of spinach and remove the thicker stems. Wash in several waters to remove every trace of sand.

Bring a large quantity of salted water to the boiling point, add the spinach, and cook for about 2 minutes after the water comes back to a boil.

Drain the spinach in a colander and squeeze it dry, using a spatula or the back of a spoon to press it against the sides of the colander. Use as desired.

Spinach Purée / PURÉE D'ÉPINARDS

Blanch the spinach and drain it as described in Blanched Spinach (above). Purée it in a blender or force it through a food mill.

Add the *sauce béchamel* and the heavy cream. Season with the sugar and a little salt and nutmeg. Serve with fried croutons.

FOR 4 PERSONS:

2 pounds spinach	Salt
¼ cup Sauce Béchamel (p. 761)	Grated nutmeg
¼ cup heavy cream	1 cup Croutons (p. 62),
Pinch of sugar	fried in butter

Spinach in Butter / ÉPINARDS AU BEURRE

Blanch and drain the spinach as described in Blanched Spinach (above). Chop it fine or force it through a food mill.

Heat the spinach with the butter, check for salt, and add a little sugar and nutmeg. Serve the spinach in a hot serving dish, sprinkled with croutons fried in butter.

FOR 4 PERSONS:

2 pounds spinach	Pinch of sugar
4 tablespoons butter	Grated nutmeg
Salt	1 cup Croutons (p. 62),
	fried in butter

ÉPINARDS À LA CRÈME / *Spinach in Cream*

Prepare the spinach as described in the preceding recipe, but add 4 tablespoons of Crème Fraîche (p. 666) to the hot spinach just before serving and mix well. Do not sprinkle with croutons.

ÉPINARDS AU GRATIN / *Spinach au Gratin*

Prepare the spinach as described above.

Butter a baking dish, spread the spinach in it, and coat it with the *sauce béchamel*. Dot with the butter and sprinkle with the grated cheese and the bread crumbs.

Brown under the broiler or cook in a preheated 500° F. oven for about 5 minutes.

FOR 4 PERSONS:

1 recipe Spinach in Butter (above)
1 cup Sauce Béchamel (p. 761)
3 tablespoons butter, cut into small pieces

2 tablespoons grated Swiss cheese
¼ cup fine dry bread crumbs

ÉPINARDS EN BOUILLABAISSE / *Spinach Bouillabaisse*

Blanch and drain the spinach as described in Blanched Spinach (above). Purée it in a blender.

Heat the oil in a casserole and add the onion, potatoes and spinach purée. Season with salt and pepper and add a pinch of saffron.

Add the water and the garlic. Bring to a boil, cover the casserole, and simmer over low heat for about 15 minutes, stirring occasionally. Then, with a spoon, shape the spinach and potatoes into 4 nests and break 1 egg into the cavity of each nest. Cover the casserole again and simmer for about 3 minutes, or until the eggs are poached.

Meantime, fry the bread in the butter, and insert the fried bread slices between the spinach nests. Serve in the casserole.

FOR 4 PERSONS:

2 pounds spinach
4 tablespoons olive oil
1 onion, minced
2 medium-sized potatoes, peeled and sliced fine
Salt
Freshly ground black pepper

Pinch of ground saffron
4 cups water
2 garlic cloves, minced
4 eggs
4 slices of bread, crusts removed, fried in butter

PAIN D'ÉPINARDS / *Spinach Roll*

Blanch and drain the spinach as described in Blanched Spinach (above). Purée it in a blender and put it in a bowl. The purée should be quite dry.

Beat in the egg yolks and 4 tablespoons of the butter. Stir in the flour and then the *crème fraîche*. Season with salt and nutmeg. Beat the 2 egg whites until stiff and fold them into the mixture.

Butter an 8-inch-square baking dish and spread it with the spinach mixture, making a layer about ½ inch thick. Bake in a preheated 375° F. oven for about 15 minutes; the spinach should be still soft but puffed slightly.

Heat the remaining 2 tablespoons of butter in a skillet. Beat the 4 whole eggs lightly with a little salt and scramble them in the butter, leaving them very soft.

Remove the baking dish from the oven, pour the scrambled eggs over the spinach, roll up the mixture like a jelly roll, and put it on a hot serving dish.

Tint the *sauce béchamel* a pale pink with the tomato purée, and drizzle it around the spinach roll. Serve very hot.

FOR 4 PERSONS:

1 **pound spinach**	**Salt**
2 **eggs, separated**	**Grated nutmeg**
6 **tablespoons butter**	4 **whole eggs**
2 **tablespoons flour**	2 **cups Sauce Béchamel (p. 761)**
6 **tablespoons Crème Fraîche**	1 **tablespoon Tomato Purée (p. 157)**
(p. 666)	

T O M A T O E S

Tomates

Baked Tomatoes / TOMATES GRILLÉS

Choose ripe, firm, even-sized tomatoes. Slice off the tops and put them into a baking dish. Sprinkle with oil and season generously with salt and pepper. Bake in a preheated 350° F. oven for 15 to 20 minutes. Put the baked tomatoes on a hot serving dish.

FOR 4 PERSONS:

8 **medium-sized tomatoes**	**Salt**
4 **tablespoons olive oil**	**Freshly ground black pepper**

Baked Tomatoes Provençale / TOMATES PROVENÇALE

Slice off the tops of the tomatoes.

Butter a baking dish and put the tomatoes in it, side by side. Season generously with salt and pepper.

Mix together the bread crumbs, garlic and parsley, and moisten the mixture with the olive oil. Coat the tomatoes with this mixture and brown slowly under a low broiler flame, or bake in a preheated 350° F. oven for 15 minutes.

FOR 4 PERSONS:

4 large tomatoes	4 garlic cloves, minced
Salt	4 tablespoons minced parsley
Freshly ground black pepper	4 tablespoons olive oil
⅓ cup fine dry bread crumbs	

TOMATES ÉTUVÉES AU BEURRE / *Tomatoes in Butter*

Choose ripe and even-sized tomatoes. Slice off the tops and put them into a casserole with the combined oil and butter. Season generously with salt and pepper. Cover the casserole and simmer the tomatoes over low heat for about 15 minutes, basting occasionally with the fat in the casserole.

When the tomatoes are cooked, transfer them to a hot serving dish and sprinkle with the pan juices and the parsley. Serve hot.

FOR 4 PERSONS:

8 medium-sized tomatoes	Salt
4 tablespoons olive oil	Freshly ground black pepper
3 tablespoons butter	2 tablespoons minced parsley

FONDUE DE TOMATES (COULIS) / *Melted Tomatoes*

Peel and mince the onions and put them into a casserole with the combined hot oil and butter. Cook the onions over low heat until they are tender, but do not let them turn golden.

Add the tomatoes. Season with salt and pepper and mash the tomatoes lightly with a fork. Cook for about 20 minutes, or until the tomatoes have become a thick sauce. Stir in the garlic.

Serve in a vegetable dish or as a garnish for meat, eggs, fish, rice or pasta.

FOR 4 PERSONS:

2 onions	Salt
1 tablespoon olive oil	Freshly ground black pepper
3 tablespoons butter	1 garlic clove, minced
2 pounds tomatoes, peeled, seeded and chopped	

FONDUE DE TOMATES À LA NIÇOISE / *Tomatoes Niçoise*

Prepare Melted Tomatoes (above).

At serving time add 4 chopped anchovy fillets and 1 tablespoon each of minced chervil, tarragon and capers.

GRATIN PROVENÇAL / *Tomato Gratin Provençale*

Prepare the melted tomatoes and the sautéed eggplant.

Butter a baking dish and make alternate layers of tomatoes and eggplant, beginning and ending with tomatoes. Sprinkle with the grated Parmesan, bread crumbs and olive oil. Cook in a preheated 375° F. oven for about 15 minutes. Serve hot, in the same dish.

FOR 4 PERSONS:

1 recipe Melted Tomatoes (above)	¼ cup fine dry bread crumbs
1 recipe Eggplant Sautéed with Garlic and Parsley (p. 590)	2 tablespoons olive oil
4 tablespoons grated Parmesan cheese	

Basque Tomatoes / FONDUE DE TOMATES BASQUAISE

Cut the ham into dice and cook it in the hot oil in a casserole for 2 to 3 minutes. Add the whole peeled garlic cloves, the onion, peppers and tomatoes. Season lightly with salt and pepper and sprinkle with the thyme. Cover and simmer over low heat for about 25 minutes, stirring frequently.

Uncover, bring to the boiling point, and reduce the cooking liquid. Remove the garlic cloves. Use the tomatoes as desired.

FOR 6 PERSONS:

¼ pound Bayonne or smoked ham or prosciutto, diced	2 pounds tomatoes, peeled, seeded and chopped
3 tablespoons olive oil	Salt
4 garlic cloves, peeled	Freshly ground black pepper
1 large onion, minced	1 sprig of thyme, chopped
6 sweet peppers, charred, scraped, seeded and cut into julienne strips (see p. 619)	

Sautéed Tomatoes / TOMATES SAUTÉES

Slice off the tops of the tomatoes and squeeze them lightly to remove the seeds and the juice. Cut them into quarters or thick slices.

Heat the oil and butter in a skillet, add the tomatoes, and season with salt and pepper. Sauté over fairly high heat until golden on both sides. Remove the tomatoes and serve them as a garnish.

FOR 4 PERSONS:

8 medium-sized tomatoes	Salt
3 tablespoons olive oil	Freshly ground black pepper
2 tablespoons butter	

Sautéed Tomatoes Provençale /

TOMATES SAUTÉES PROVENÇALE

Sauté tomatoes as described in the preceding recipe.

Put the tomatoes in a hot serving dish and sprinkle with 2 tablespoons minced parsley, 1 garlic clove, minced, ¼ cup dry bread crumbs, and the pan juices.

TOMATES FARCIES AU MAIGRE / *Stuffed Tomatoes*

Cut off the tops of the tomatoes and scoop them out. Sprinkle the cavities with salt.

Sprinkle the fresh bread crumbs with the milk and mix with a fork. Stir in the beaten eggs. Season with salt, pepper and nutmeg; add the *fines herbes,* onion and garlic.

Turn the tomatoes upside down to drain them and then put them in a buttered baking dish. Stuff them with the filling, and sprinkle with the cheese, the dry bread crumbs and the oil. Cook in a preheated 300° F. oven for about 30 minutes. Serve in the same dish.

FOR 4 PERSONS:

4 large ripe tomatoes	4 tablespoons minced Fines
3 cups fresh white bread crumbs	Herbes (p. 89)
½ cup lukewarm milk	1 onion, minced
2 eggs, beaten	1 garlic clove, minced
Salt	4 tablespoons grated Swiss cheese
Freshly ground black pepper	¼ cup fine dry bread crumbs
Grated nutmeg	4 tablespoons olive oil

TOMATES FARCIES MÉNAGÈRE / *Stuffed Tomatoes Ménagère*

Prepare the tomatoes as in the preceding recipe, but stuff them with a filling made by combining:

⅓ pound veal, ground	Freshly ground black pepper
⅓ pound lean pork, ground	4 tablespoons minced Fines
⅓ pound chicken livers, ground	Herbes (p. 89)
Salt	2 tablespoons port or brandy

/ *Tomatoes Stuffed with Sausage*

TOMATES FARCIES CHARCUTIÈRE

Prepare like Stuffed Tomatoes (above), but stuff them with a filling made by combining:

½ pound sausage meat	Salt
2 cups fresh white bread crumbs, sprinkled with 4 tablespoons lukewarm milk	Freshly ground black pepper
	Grated nutmeg
2 eggs	4 tablespoons minced Fines
	Herbes (p. 89)

TRUFFLES

Truffes

EDITORS' NOTE: *So much has been written about truffles, about their incomparable aroma and flavor, about the fantastic methods of gathering them with pigs or dogs, and above all about their price, that we hesitate to add to an already overburdened literature. Suffice it to say that fresh truffles are imported to the United States when they are in season in the fall and winter. Their price is naturally even more astronomical here than in France, and the thought of buying a pound or so, as some of these recipes call for, is fairly staggering. However, perhaps you have an oil well or two in your background or you don't mind ruining yourself momentarily for a very, very rare treat. If so, try to make sure that the truffles are really fresh; they should not be more than a week old.*

Canned truffles have their very distinctive uses and add greatly to the savor of a dish. They may be used in these recipes of M. Oliver's, but naturally fresh truffles are greatly to be preferred.

We might also point out that white Italian truffles are also imported by air to the United States, and indeed many people find them superior to French truffles.

Sautéed Truffles | TRUFFES SAUTÉES

Chop the truffles.

Heat the goose fat in a casserole and add the truffles. Season with salt and pepper. Cook over medium heat for 5 minutes, without letting the truffles brown. Remove the truffles with a slotted spoon and put them into a hot serving dish. Stir the Madeira into the pan juices, scraping up any brown bits in the bottom of the casserole. Reduce the sauce slightly and coat the truffles with it. Serve hot.

FOR 4 PERSONS:

¾ pound truffles	Freshly ground black pepper
4 tablespoons goose fat	1 cup Madeira
Salt	

Truffles in Cream | RAGOÛT DE TRUFFES À LA CRÈME

Cut the truffles into thick slices.

Heat half of the butter in a casserole and add the truffles. Season with salt and pepper and add the brandy. Cover the casserole and simmer gently for 5 minutes if the truffles are canned, or about 15 minutes if fresh.

Add the *sauce béchamel* and the *crème fraîche* to the casserole. Simmer over low heat for about 3 minutes. Mix well and check the seasoning. Off the heat stir in the remaining butter. Serve very hot, in a hot serving dish.

FOR 4 PERSONS:

1 pound truffles	**2 tablespoons brandy**
½ cup butter	**1 cup Sauce Béchamel (p. 761)**
Salt	**½ cup Crème Fraîche (p. 666)**
Freshly ground black pepper	

RAGOÛT DE TRUFFES AU PORTO / *Truffles in Port*

Mince the ham, veal and fresh pork fat and put them into a casserole with the oil and butter. Mix well and cook over low heat for about 3 minutes.

Add the celery, carrot, onion, parsley, thyme, bay leaf, basil, garlic and cloves. Mix thoroughly and cook until the vegetables are beginning to turn golden. Season with salt, pepper and nutmeg. Add the truffles and the port.

Simmer, covered, over low heat for 16 minutes.

Remove the truffles from the casserole with a slotted spoon and keep them hot. Strain the sauce through a fine sieve or purée it in a blender. Return the sauce to the casserole and simmer, covered, over low heat for 10 more minutes. Mix the truffles and the sauce and serve hot, in a hot serving dish.

FOR 4 PERSONS:

⅓ pound Bayonne or smoked ham or prosciutto	**1 sprig of fresh thyme**
¼ pound lean veal	**½ bay leaf, crumbled**
¼ pound fresh pork fat	**1 sprig of basil**
2 tablespoons olive oil	**1 garlic clove, minced**
3 tablespoons butter	**2 cloves**
2 celery stalks, minced	**Salt**
1 carrot, minced	**Freshly ground black pepper**
1 onion, minced	**Grated nutmeg**
1 tablespoon minced parsley	**¾ pound truffles**
	½ bottle of good port

TRUFFES EN TIMBALE / *Timbale of Truffles*

Prepare the truffles in port and the *pâte brisée*. Roll out the pastry to ⅛-inch thickness and divide it into halves.

Line an 8-inch pie pan with half of the pastry and then with the fresh pork fat. Spoon the truffle mixture into the pie and cover with the remaining pastry. Pinch the pastry edges together, paint the top with the egg yolk, and make a few slits in the top. Bake the timbale on a lower rack in a preheated 350° F. oven for about 45 minutes.

Serve very hot.

FOR 4 PERSONS:

1 recipe Truffles in Port (above)	**4 thin sheets of fresh pork fat**
1 recipe Pâte Brisée (p. 713)	**1 egg yolk, beaten**

Truffles Baked in Puff Paste | TRUFFES EN CHAUSSON

Wash the truffles under running cold water if they are fresh, or drain them thoroughly if they are canned, and dry them.

Prepare the puff paste and roll it out to ⅛-inch thickness. From it cut 4 rectangles, each 6 by 8 inches.

First cover each truffle with a slice of *foie gras* and then wrap with a slice of ham. Put one of these bundles on each piece of puff paste and roll it up, pinching the edges firmly to enclose the bundle. Paint with the beaten egg yolk and put on a buttered baking sheet.

Bake in a preheated 375° F. oven for 10 minutes. Reduce the heat to 350° F. and bake for 5 or 6 minutes longer.

When the rolls have puffed up and are golden, put them on a hot serving dish. Serve the *sauce Périgueux* on the side.

FOR 4 PERSONS:

4 large truffles	**4 small slices of boiled ham**
¼ recipe Puff Paste (p. 000)	**1 egg yolk, beaten**
¼ pound foie gras	**1 recipe Sauce Périgueux (p. 765)**

TURNIPS

Navets

Boiled Turnips à l'Anglaise | NAVETS À L'ANGLAISE

Peel the turnips and cut them into large dice.

Put them into a saucepan and cover them with salted cold water. Bring to the boiling point and cook for 15 to 20 minutes, or until they are tender.

Drain the turnips, put them into a serving dish, and dot them with the butter. Serve hot.

FOR 4 PERSONS:

1 pound turnips	**6 tablespoons butter**
Salt	

Glazed Turnips | NAVETS GLACÉS

Peel the turnips and cut them into large dice, or choose very small young turnips which need only be peeled.

Heat the butter in a casserole and add the turnips. Season lightly with salt and pepper and sprinkle with the sugar. Cook the turnips over low heat for about 20 minutes, or until they are soft and glazed.

Serve them as a garnish for a roast.

FOR 4 PERSONS:

1 pound turnips	**Freshly ground white pepper**
6 tablespoons butter	**Pinch of sugar**
Salt	

NAVETS À LA CRÈME / *Turnips in Cream au Gratin*

Peel the turnips and cut them into small cubes.

Bring a large quantity of salted water to the boiling point. Add the turnips and cook for 15 to 20 minutes. Drain in a colander.

Season the milk with a little salt, pepper and nutmeg; scald it in a saucepan.

Blend the flour with a little water to a smooth paste and beat it into the scalded milk. Stir in half of the butter. Keep hot.

Put the turnips in a buttered baking dish, coat them with the sauce, sprinkle with the grated cheese, dot with the remaining butter, and sprinkle with the bread crumbs.

Bake in a preheated 375° F. oven for about 10 minutes, or until the top is golden and bubbly. Serve very hot.

FOR 4 PERSONS:

1 pound turnips	**1 tablespoon flour**
Salt	**4 tablespoons butter**
1 cup milk	**3 tablespoons grated Swiss cheese**
Freshly ground white pepper	**¼ cup fine dry bread crumbs**
Grated nutmeg	

ZUCCHINI

Courgettes

/ *Sautéed Zucchini Niçoise*

COURGETTES SAUTÉES À LA NIÇOISE

Scrub the zucchini and cut them into thick slices. Season with salt and pepper and dust with flour. Sauté the slices in the combined hot oil and butter in a skillet until they are golden on both sides. Remove them with a slotted spoon, put them on a serving dish, and keep hot.

Sauté the tomato halves in the fat remaining in the skillet, adding more oil if necessary. Sprinkle with salt and the sugar, cook them until they are barely tender, and put them on the serving dish with the zucchini.

If necessary, add a little more oil to the skillet, add the garlic and the parsley, and sauté them until barely golden.

Pour this sauce over the zucchini and the tomatoes. Check the seasoning, garnish with the olives, and serve immediately, very hot.

FOR 4 PERSONS:

4 zucchini	**4 tomatoes, cut into halves**
Salt	**Pinch of sugar**
Freshly ground black pepper	**4 garlic cloves, minced**
Flour	**4 tablespoons minced parsley**
4 tablespoons (or more) olive oil	**Green or black olives, pitted**
4 tablespoons butter	

Sautéed Zucchini Provençale /

COURGETTES SAUTÉES À LA PROVENÇALE

Scrub the zucchini and cut into thick slices. Season with salt and pepper, dust them with flour, and sauté them in the combined hot oil and butter in a skillet.

Add the tomatoes and season with salt and the sugar.

Cook both vegetables over low heat for about 10 minutes, turning the zucchini slices and the tomato halves carefully so as not to break them. Put them on a serving dish and sprinkle with the garlic and parsley and with the pan juices.

FOR 4 PERSONS:

4 zucchini	**2 tablespoons butter**
Salt	**4 tomatoes, cut into halves**
Freshly ground black pepper	**Pinch of sugar**
Flour	**2 garlic cloves, minced**
4 tablespoons olive oil	**4 tablespoons minced parsley**

Stuffed Zucchini / COURGETTES FARCIES

Wash the zucchini and cut them lengthwise into halves. Scoop out the zucchini pulp with a spoon. Put the pulp into a bowl and the hollowed-out zucchini shells in a buttered baking dish.

Heat 3 tablespoons of the butter in a saucepan; add the shallots, parsley and tomatoes. Cook over low heat until the tomatoes are soft. Add the zucchini pulp, raise the heat slightly, and cook for about 5 minutes.

Soak the fresh bread crumbs in milk and squeeze them dry. Add them to the tomatoes and zucchini pulp, mix well, and season with salt and pepper. Stuff the zucchini shells with this filling, sprinkle them with the dry bread crumbs, and dot with the remaining butter. Bake in a preheated 375° F. oven for about 15 minutes.

If desired, you may also add a little ground cooked chicken, veal or beef to the stuffing.

FOR 4 PERSONS:

4 **zucchini**	**Milk**
7 **tablespoons butter**	**Salt**
3 **shallots, minced**	**Freshly ground black pepper**
1 **tablespoon minced parsley**	½ **cup fine dry bread crumbs**
3 **tomatoes, peeled, seeded and**	**Optional:** ½ **cup ground cooked**
chopped	**beef, veal or chicken**
1 **cup fresh white bread crumbs**	

/ *Stuffed Zucchini Niçoise*

COURGETTES FARCIES À LA NIÇOISE

Wash the zucchini and cut them lengthwise into halves. With a small spoon scoop out the flesh, leaving the hollowed-out shells. Put the flesh into a bowl and the shells into an oiled baking dish.

Purée the zucchini flesh. Put the purée in a bowl and add the bread crumbs, the egg, half of the cheese, the *fines herbes* and the garlic to the mixture. Season with salt and pepper and mix thoroughly.

Stuff the shells with the filling. Sprinkle the zucchini with the oil and the remaining cheese, and cook them in a preheated 375° F. oven for about 15 minutes.

You may serve the stuffed zucchini either hot or cold.

FOR 4 PERSONS:

4 **zucchini**	1 **garlic clove, minced**
1 **cup fresh white bread crumbs**	**Salt**
1 **egg, beaten**	**Freshly ground black pepper**
6 **tablespoons grated Swiss cheese**	2 **tablespoons olive oil**
2 **tablespoons minced Fines Herbes**	
(p. 89)	

/ *Stuffed Zucchini Provençale*

COURGETTES FARCIES À LA PROVENÇALE

Prepare the zucchini as in the preceding 2 recipes. Purée the zucchini pulp and put the hollowed-out zucchini shells in a buttered baking dish.

Purée the tomatoes in a blender or in a food mill.

Combine the puréed zucchini and tomatoes and add the egg, *fines herbes* and garlic. Season with salt, pepper, nutmeg and a sprinkling of thyme.

Stuff the shells with this filling and sprinkle with the cheese, bread crumbs and oil. Cook in a preheated 375° F. oven for about 15 minutes.

FOR 4 PERSONS:

4 zucchini	Freshly ground black pepper
4 tomatoes, peeled, seeded and	Grated nutmeg
drained	2 sprigs of thyme, chopped, or ½
1 egg, beaten	teaspoon dried thyme
2 tablespoons minced Fines	4 tablespoons grated Swiss cheese
Herbes (p. 89)	½ cup fine dry bread crumbs
2 garlic cloves, minced	4 tablespoons olive oil
Salt	

Zucchini Stuffed with Spinach /

COURGETTES FARCIES AUX ÉPINARDS

Prepare the zucchini as in the preceding recipes. Purée the zucchini pulp, and put the hollowed-out zucchini shells in a buttered baking dish.

Gently cook the blanched spinach in 3 tablespoons of the butter for 5 minutes and then purée it in a blender.

Combine the puréed spinach and zucchini, mix well, and add the egg, half of the grated cheese, the *fines herbes* and garlic. Season with salt and pepper.

Stuff the zucchini shells with this filling. Sprinkle with the remaining cheese and the bread crumbs. Dot with the remaining butter and bake in a preheated 375° F. oven for about 15 minutes.

FOR 4 PERSONS:

4 zucchini	2 tablespoons minced Fines
1 pound spinach, blanched	Herbes (p. 89)
(see p. 644)	2 garlic cloves, minced
6 tablespoons butter	Salt
1 egg	Freshly ground black pepper
½ cup grated Swiss cheese	¼ cup fine dry bread crumbs

Ratatouille Niçoise /

Peel the zucchini, tomatoes, eggplant and onions, and cut all the vegetables into thick slices.

Trim the finocchio and slice it. Remove the seeds and membranes from the peppers and slice them also. Cut the artichoke hearts into small pieces.

Heat the olive and the peanut oils in a deep skillet or in a casserole. Add the artichoke pieces, sauté them for 2 minutes, and then add all the other vegetables. Mix well and season with salt, pepper and nutmeg. Sprinkle with the thyme. Cover the skillet or the casserole, and cook over the lowest possible heat for about 30 minutes. The vegetables must be stewed, and not fried.

Serve the *ratatouille* hot or cold.

FOR 4 PERSONS:

3 zucchini	3 tablespoons olive oil
4 tomatoes	3 tablespoons peanut oil
1 small eggplant	Salt
2 onions	Freshly ground black pepper
1 head of finocchio or fennel	Grated nutmeg
2 sweet peppers	2 sprigs of thyme, chopped
3 artichoke hearts	

RICE

Riz

EDITORS' NOTE: *In France, rice is generally bought loose, rather than packaged, and thus requires more careful washing than is our custom in the United States. Also some French rice is not as polished as our rice, and thus French cooks have the habit of first blanching rice in a large quantity of water, to rid it of its excess starch, before cooking it further. This is a perfectly sound practice and will give excellent results with our own rice.*

The French use long-grain, medium-grain, and the stubbier short-grain rice. In these recipes, we recommend that ordinary long-grain rice, readily available in the United States, be used.

RIZ AU GRAS / *Rice Cooked in Consommé*

Wash the rice thoroughly under running cold water. Put it into a large saucepan containing plenty of boiling salted water. Cook for 3 minutes. Drain the rice in a colander.

Heat the butter in a casserole and stir in the rice, coating it well. Add the consommé and bring to the boiling point. Cover the casserole and cook in a preheated 350° F. oven for about 18 minutes. If the rice has not completely absorbed the consommé, remove the cover and cook for a few minutes longer.

FOR 4 PERSONS:

1 cup uncooked rice	1½ cups Beef or Chicken
Salt	Consommé (p. 167)
4 tablespoons butter	

CROQUETTES DE RIZ / *Rice Croquettes*

Cook the rice and cool it slightly. It should be slightly on the dry side.

Blend the egg yolks into the rice. Shape into croquettes and dip them into the beaten whole eggs and then dust with the flour.

Sauté the croquettes in the combined hot oil and butter in a skillet, or deep fry them in very hot fat preheated to 375° F. on a frying thermometer.

Drain, put on a hot serving dish lined with a napkin, and serve hot, with fried parsley.

FOR 4 PERSONS:

1 recipe Rice Cooked in Consommé (p. 657)	4 tablespoons each of butter and olive oil, or fat for deep
3 egg yolks	frying
2 whole eggs, beaten	Fried Parsley (p. 130)
Flour	

Rice à la Créole / RIZ À LA CRÉOLE

Wash the rice thoroughly in cold water and then put it into a large saucepan containing plenty of boiling salted water. Cook for about 12 minutes.

Drain the rice in a colander, rinse it under running cold water, and then pour boiling water over it to heat it up.

Put the rice into a casserole and cook it, uncovered, in a preheated 325° F. oven for 10 to 15 minutes longer.

If desired, scrape off the surface crust and then fluff up the rice with a 2-pronged fork.

FOR 4 PERSONS:

1½ cups uncooked rice	Salt

Creole Rice à la Provençale / RIZ CRÉOLE À LA PROVENÇALE

Prepare the rice as described in the preceding recipe.

Cook the onions in the olive oil until they are golden. Add the tomatoes and season with salt and pepper. Add the ginger and the peppers and simmer, covered, over low heat. Add the cooked rice and mix well. Put the rice mixture into a hot serving dish.

Garnish the rice with the anchovies, eggs, capers, pickle and olives. Sprinkle with the *fines herbes*. Serve immediately.

FOR 4 PERSONS:

1 recipe Rice à la Créole (above)	4 anchovy fillets, drained
2 onions, minced	2 hard-cooked eggs, sliced
4 tablespoons olive oil	1 tablespoon capers
2 large tomatoes, peeled, seeded and chopped	1 sour pickle, sliced
Salt	8 green olives, pitted
Freshly ground black pepper	2 tablespoons minced Fines Herbes (p. 89)
½ teaspoon ground ginger	
4 small sweet peppers, charred, scraped and minced (see p. 619)	

RIZ À L'INDIENNE / *Indian Rice*

Wash the rice thoroughly under running cold water. Put it into a large saucepan with a great deal of salted water. Bring to the boiling point and cook for 15 minutes. Stir the rice occasionally with a wooden spoon.

Drain the rice in a colander and then rinse it under running cold water. Put the rice into a kitchen towel and wrap it up as a parcel so that it is completely covered. Put the wrapped rice into a casserole and cook it in a preheated 350° F. oven for 15 minutes.

FOR 4 PERSONS:

1 cup uncooked rice	**Salt**

/ *Indian Rice with Curry Sauce*

RIZ À L'INDIENNE AU CURRY

Prepare the rice as in the preceding recipe. Make the curry sauce and combine with the cooked rice. Mix well and serve immediately.

FOR 4 PERSONS:

1 recipe Indian Rice (above)	**1 recipe Curry Sauce (p. 777)**

Note: If desired, the rice and the sauce may be served separately.

/ *Timbale of Rice with Mushrooms*

TIMBALE DE RIZ AUX CHAMPIGNONS

Cook the rice as in Indian Rice (above).

Cut the mushrooms into quarters and put them into a casserole with the lemon juice and half of the butter. Cover the casserole and cook over low heat for about 3 minutes. Remove the cover and continue cooking the mushrooms until all the pan juices have evaporated; be careful not to brown the mushrooms too much. Add the sausages and cook until they are golden.

Put the rice in a hot large serving dish, toss with the mushrooms and sausages, stir in the remaining butter, and sprinkle with the cheese. Shape the rice into a dome and serve hot.

FOR 4 PERSONS:

1 cup uncooked rice	**6 tablespoons butter**
½ pound mushrooms	**4 small link sausages**
Juice of 1 lemon	**¼ cup grated Swiss cheese**

RIZ PILAW / *Rice Pilaf*

Wash the rice under running cold water and drain it.

Sauté the onion in the combined hot oil and 4 tablespoons of the butter in a casserole until it is golden. Add the rice, mix well, and cook, stirring occasionally, until the rice is golden.

Add the hot consommé or fish stock. Season with salt and pepper and add the *bouquet garni*. Cover the casserole tightly and cook over very low heat for 20 minutes.

Remove the *bouquet garni* and stir in the remaining butter, using a 2-pronged fork to keep the rice fluffy.

FOR 4 PERSONS:

1 cup uncooked rice	Salt
1 onion, minced	Freshly ground white pepper
1 tablespoon olive oil	1 small Bouquet Garni (p. 46)
6 tablespoons butter	
1½ cups Beef or Chicken Consommé (p. 167), or Fish Stock (p. 166)	

Curry Risotto / RISOTTO AU CURRY

Prepare the rice as in Rice Pilaf (above), but add 3 tablespoons tomato paste, 1 tablespoon curry powder and a pinch of ground saffron to the rice when adding the consommé or fish stock.

Risotto with Saffron / RISOTTO AU SAFRAN

Prepare the rice as in Rice Pilaf (above), and add ¼ teaspoon of ground saffron when adding the consommé or fish stock. Stir ½ cup of grated Swiss cheese into the rice just before serving.

Risotto with Ham / RISOTTO AU JAMBON

Heat the oil and 4 tablespoons of the butter in a casserole and add the onion and the ham. Cook until they are golden. Add the rice, mix well, and cook until the rice is well coated with the butter and oil. Add the consommé. Season very lightly with salt and pepper and add the *bouquet garni*. Bring to a boil, cover the casserole tightly, and cook in a preheated 325° F. oven for about 20 minutes. Remove the *bouquet garni* and dot the rice with the remaining butter. Serve in a hot serving dish.

FOR 4 PERSONS:

1 tablespoon peanut oil	1½ cups Beef or Chicken Consommé (p. 167)
6 tablespoons butter	Salt
1 onion, minced	Freshly ground white pepper
⅓ pound Bayonne or smoked ham or prosciutto, diced	1 small Bouquet Garni (p. 46)
1 cup uncooked rice	

RIZ À L'ESPAGNOLE / *Spanish Rice*

Cook the rice in boiling salted water for about 20 minutes. Drain in a colander, cover the colander with a damp towel, and put it in a 300° F. oven for about 15 minutes to dry.

Heat the olive oil in a casserole, add the onion and the chicken livers, and cook until golden. Take out the onion and chicken livers with a slotted spoon and reserve them. Put the peas and the tomatoes into the same casserole and season with a little salt and pepper and the sugar. Cook for 5 to 7 minutes, or until the peas are half tender. Add the mushrooms and the peppers, check the seasoning, and simmer, covered, over low heat until the peas are tender.

Cook the green snap beans in boiling salted water until they are tender, drain them, and cut them into pieces.

Put the rice in a big hot serving dish; add the onions and chicken livers and all the vegetables. Mix well and serve hot.

FOR 4 PERSONS:

1 cup uncooked rice	Salt
2 tablespoons olive oil	Freshly ground black pepper
1 onion, minced	Pinch of sugar
2 large chicken livers, cut into pieces	¼ pound mushrooms, blanched
1 cup shelled tiny peas	4 small sweet peppers, charred, scraped and sliced (see p. 619)
6 tomatoes, peeled, seeded and chopped	½ pound green snap beans

NOODLES

Nouilles

NOUILLES FRAÎCHES / *Homemade Noodles*

Put the flour on a baking board and make a well in the center. Put the eggs and the dissolved salt into the well. Work the dough with your hands, kneading it until it is very smooth. Let the dough rest for 1 hour.

Divide the dough into halves and roll out each half as thin as possible, about 1/16 inch. Fold the dough over on itself several times and then cut it into strips of any desired width.

Spread the noodles on a floured cloth and let them dry for 4 to 5 hours. Cook in a large quantity of boiling salted water from 5 to 10 minutes, or until tender but still firm.

FOR 4 PERSONS:

3 cups flour	1 teaspoon salt dissolved in 1
4 eggs	tablespoon water

Noodles with Tomatoes and Cheese /

NOUILLES À LA TOMATE AU FROMAGE

Prepare homemade noodles as described above and let them dry.

Heat half of the butter in a saucepan and cook the onion in it until it is golden. Add the tomatoes, season with salt, pepper and nutmeg, and simmer, covered, for 10 minutes, stirring frequently. If the sauce is too thin, remove the cover and reduce it to the desired consistency.

Cook the noodles in a very large quantity of boiling salted water and drain them. Heat the remaining butter in a casserole and add the noodles to it, mixing well. Strain the tomato sauce through a sieve onto the noodles. Mix well and stir in the cheese. Serve immediately.

FOR 4 PERSONS:

1 recipe Homemade Noodles (above)	Salt
6 tablespoons butter	Freshly ground white pepper
1 onion, minced	Grated nutmeg
6 tomatoes, peeled, seeded and chopped	¼ pound grated Swiss cheese

Basque Noodle Croquettes /

CROQUETTES DE NOUILLES BASQUAISE

Prepare the homemade noodles and let them dry. Make a very thick *sauce béchamel.*

Cook the noodles in boiling salted water and drain them. Combine the sauce, the noodles and the egg in a saucepan. Season with salt, pepper and nutmeg. Simmer over low heat for a few minutes until very thick. Remove from the heat and cool completely. If necessary, chill briefly in the refrigerator.

Take generous spoonfuls of the mixture and shape it into little croquettes. Dip them into the *anglaise,* coat with bread crumbs, and fry in deep fat heated to 360° F. on a frying thermometer.

Serve very hot with the Basque tomatoes on the side.

FOR 6 PERSONS:

1 recipe Homemade Noodles (above)	Anglaise:
2 cups Sauce Béchamel (p. 761)	3 egg yolks
1 egg	3 tablespoons water
Salt	3 tablespoons peanut oil
Freshly ground white pepper	1 teaspoon salt
Grated nutmeg	
	2 cups bread crumbs
	Fat for deep frying
	½ recipe Basque Tomatoes (p. 648)

/ *Macaroni and Cheese au Gratin*

MACARONI AU FROMAGE GRATINÉS

Cook the macaroni in a large quantity of boiling salted water until it is almost but not quite tender, about 8 minutes. Drain and mix with 6 tablespoons of the butter and 1 cup of the cheese.

Put the macaroni into a buttered baking dish, dot with the remaining butter, and sprinkle with the remaining cheese and the bread crumbs.

Bake in a preheated 375° F. oven for about 15 minutes. Serve hot.

FOR 4 PERSONS:

½ pound macaroni	1½ cups grated Swiss cheese
½ cup butter	¼ cup fine dry bread crumbs

/ *Macaroni à la Béchamel with Ham*

MACARONI À LA BÉCHAMEL ET AU JAMBON

Cook the macaroni in a large quantity of boiling salted water until almost but not quite tender, about 8 minutes. Drain it and mix with 4 tablespoons of the butter.

Make the *sauce béchamel,* add the ham to it, and blend the sauce with the macaroni. Stir in 6 tablespoons of the grated cheese.

Put the macaroni into a buttered dish, sprinkle with the remaining cheese, dot with the remaining butter, and sprinkle with the bread crumbs.

Bake in a preheated 375° F. oven for about 15 minutes.

FOR 4 PERSONS:

½ pound macaroni	⅓ pound cooked ham, cut into
6 tablespoons butter	small pieces
1½ cups Sauce Béchamel	½ cup grated Swiss cheese
(p. 761)	¼ cup fine dry bread crumbs

MACARONI À LA MILANAISE / *Macaroni Milanaise*

Cook the macaroni in a large quantity of boiling salted water until tender, about 12 minutes. Drain and mix with the butter, cheese, *sauce tomate* and a little nutmeg. Add the ham, tongue, mushrooms and truffle. Check the seasoning.

Serve the macaroni, very hot, in a hot serving dish.

FOR 4 PERSONS:

½ pound macaroni	2 slices of cooked tongue, diced
6 tablespoons butter	2 large mushrooms, minced and
½ cup grated Swiss cheese	sautéed in butter
2 cups Sauce Tomate (p. 769)	1 small truffle, minced
Grated nutmeg	Salt
1 slice of boiled ham, diced	Freshly ground black pepper

9

DESSERTS
Les Desserts

EDITOR'S NOTE: *French cakes and desserts, and the attitude of the French to their cakes and desserts, are different from ours. Far more fruit is eaten as a dessert in France than in America, and far fewer desserts are made at home. Cakes, and pastries especially, are usually bought in a good* pâtisserie *rather than being home baked, and no French home cook is expected to be the equal of a* pâtissier.

French cakes, generally speaking, are not the light and fluffy confections cakes are in America, but richer, more substantial ones. They are also made with techniques that differ from ours quite frequently, and they may call for ingredients not easily found in the United States. The following hints are given to bridge matters.

Clarified Butter /

Place any desired quantity of sweet butter (do not use salt butter)in a saucepan and place over low heat until the butter becomes very clear, particles of sediment sink to the bottom of the pan, and foam stops rising to the surface. Skim off the foam from the surface as the butter heats. One half pound of butter will take 15 to 20 minutes; a larger quantity can take as long as an hour. Remove it from the heat and strain it through an extremely fine sieve or through several thicknesses of cheesecloth, leaving any excess sediment in the bottom of the pan. Allow the butter to cool to lukewarm before using it in cakes, such as *génoise.* Clarified butter may be stored in the refrigerator for several weeks, or it may be frozen and can be stored frozen for a very long time.

Crème Fraîche /

American heavy cream is considerably thinner than French heavy cream, which is known as *crème fraîche* or *crème double.* This is because French heavy cream is allowed to mature and a natural fermentation takes place which thickens the cream and gives it a slightly nutty flavor. A simple way to achieve a comparable cream is to allow American heavy cream and a tiny amount of buttermilk to stand at room temperature until the cream thickens.

Use 1 teaspoon of buttermilk for each cup of heavy cream. Heat it in a saucepan until it is lukewarm (about 85° F.), pour it into a glass container, and allow it to stand at room temperature until it thickens. Preferably the temperature should not be lower than 60° F., nor higher than 85° F. In very hot weather it can thicken in as little as 6 hours; in cold weather it can take as long as 36 hours. *Crème fraîche* can be stored in the refrigerator for at least a week.

Sugar Syrup /

Fruits are frequently poached in a sugar syrup until they are tender, before using them in a wide variety of desserts. Generally a medium-thick syrup is preferred, that is, one that is not too thick or too thin. A good proportion to use is twice as much sugar as water. Stir the sugar and water in a saucepan over medium heat until the sugar begins to dissolve. Raise the heat and boil without stirring for about 10 minutes, or until a candy thermometer registers about 220° F. (the temperature need not be exact in this instance). Two cups of sugar and 1 cup of water will produce slightly less than 2 cups of syrup. It may be used immediately or stored in a covered jar on the kitchen shelf. There is no need to refrigerate it.

COMPOTE AUX FRUITS / *Fruit Compote*

Fruit compotes may be made with one or several kinds of fruit. Generally speaking, it is better to cook the fruits separately and combine them afterwards. However, if the fruits will cook tender in the same amount of time, they may be cooked together. Fruit compotes may be flavored with any desired spices, such as cinnamon, cardamom, ginger, cloves, etc. Vanilla is much used in French cookery to flavor apple, pear, apricot and peach compotes. Fruit compotes, such as those made from apples, pears and peaches, benefit from being made with equal parts of water and dry red or white wine.

BASIC METHOD FOR MAKING FRUIT COMPOTES

For each pound or quart of fruit, use, generally speaking, 1 cup sugar and 1 cup water plus the flavoring of your choice. Make a syrup by boiling together the sugar, water and flavoring in a covered saucepan for 5 to 10 minutes. Add the washed fruit, a few pieces at a time, and poach over medium heat until done. Remove the fruit with a slotted spoon, put it into a glass or silver dish, and repeat until all the fruit is used. If the syrup is too thin, boil it rapidly until the right consistency for making a sauce is achieved. Pour the syrup over the fruit and serve hot or chilled, with or without heavy, plain, or whipped cream.

/ *Jams, Jellies, or Preserves as Glazes*

Boil any desired quantity of jam, jelly, or fruit preserves over medium heat, stirring constantly, until the quantity is reduced slightly. If you are using preserves, mash the fruit with a fork as it boils. Remove from the heat and immediately press through a fine sieve. Use this glaze while still hot, as it tends to harden slightly as it cools.

/ *Quatre Épices*

Literally "Four Spices," this is a spice mixture frequently used in French cookery and which in France is sold premixed. There used to be different formulas for *quatre épices,* according to the maker. One of the most common follows, as taken from the *Larousse Gastronomique.*

1⅛ cups (125 grams) ground white pepper	3½ tablespoons (30 grams) ground ginger
1½ tablespoons (10 grams) ground cloves	4 tablespoons ground nutmeg

Combine the spices and mix thoroughly. Use in quantities specified by recipe.

If *quatre épices* is not available, ground allspice may be substituted. This has been done, even in France.

FROSTINGS

Glaçages

Basic Fondant Frosting |

EDITORS' NOTE: *Fondant, which is an ingredient in several of the frostings that follow, may be made in several ways. M. Oliver gives two methods on page 90, but these methods require the skill of an experienced hand. This recipe, supplied by the editors, is somewhat more detailed and makes use of the exact temperature on a candy thermometer, a method easier for and more familiar to American cooks.*

Put sugar, water and corn syrup in a heavy saucepan and stir constantly with a wooden spoon over very low heat until the sugar is completely dissolved and the mixture is clear. This will take 10 to 15 minutes. Wash down the sides of the pan with a brush dipped into cold water. Cover the pan tightly and continue cooking for 5 minutes so that steam forms on the inside of the pan and dissolves any sugar crystals that have formed. Remove the cover, raise the heat, and cook without stirring until a candy thermometer registers 240° F. The temperature must be exact. Remove from the heat and pour the syrup onto a wet marble slab, an enameled surface, or a large heat-proof plain dish. Allow it to cool to lukewarm and then work it with a wooden spoon by lifting from the edges toward the center. Work very quickly. When it becomes opaque, cover it with a damp towel. Now, take a small amount at a time and knead it with the palms of the hands until it is very smooth and creamy. Repeat until all of it has been kneaded. Store in a covered bowl.

Usually, 2 cups of fondant are enough to frost a 9-inch layer cake generously. Heat the fondant with any desired flavoring over hot but not boiling water just until it is warm; if it becomes actually hot, it will lose its characteristically shiny gloss. If the warm fondant seems too thick to be spread easily, add about 1 teaspoon of egg white per cup of fondant, mixing it in thoroughly.

FOR ABOUT 4 CUPS:

6 cups granulated sugar
2 cups water

3 tablespoons light corn syrup
Optional: 1 egg white

Caramel Glaze | GLAÇAGE AU CARAMEL

Put the sugar and water in a heavy saucepan and stir with a wooden spoon over low heat until the sugar is almost dissolved. Raise the heat and cook until the caramel is light brown, or a candy thermometer registers about 310° F. Remove immediately from the heat.

FOR ABOUT 3 CUPS:

4 cups granulated sugar   **1 cup water**

GLAÇAGE AU CHOCOLAT | *Chocolate Frosting*

Put the fondant into the top part of a double boiler and heat it over hot, but not boiling, water. Melt the chocolate over low heat in another pan. When the fondant has softened, stir in the chocolate. Blend thoroughly. It is important that the fondant never becomes actually hot or it will lose its characteristically shiny gloss.

2 cups Fondant (above)   **3 ounces sweet cooking chocolate**

GLAÇAGE AU CAFÉ | *Coffee Frosting*

Heat the fondant in the top part of a double boiler over hot, but not boiling, water. Combine the instant coffee with the boiling water and stir the liquid into the softened fondant.

2 cups Fondant (above)   **2 tablespoons boiling water**
1 tablespoon instant coffee powder

GLAÇAGE COLORÉ | *Colored Frosting*

Heat the fondant in the top part of a double boiler over hot, but not boiling, water. When it has softened, stir in a few drops of food coloring of any desired color.

2 cups Fondant (above)   **Vegetable food coloring**

GLAÇAGE AUX LIQUEURS | *Liqueur-Flavored Frosting*

Heat the fondant in the top part of a double boiler over hot, but not boiling, water. Stir in any desired liqueur (kirsch, Curaçao, etc.) when it has softened.

2 cups Fondant (above)   **2 tablespoons liqueur**

GLAÇAGE À LA ROYALE | *Royal Frosting*

Combine the egg whites and the sugar in a bowl. Blend them with a wooden spoon until the mixture is very smooth, soft and white. Blend in the lemon juice.

FOR ABOUT 1½ CUPS:

2 egg whites   **Juice of ½ lemon**
2 cups confectioners' sugar

DESSERT SAUCES

Les Sauces pour Entremets

Apricot Sauce | SAUCE ABRICOT

1. *With fresh apricots:* Use very ripe apricots, pit them, and force them through a fine sieve with a pestle, or purée them in a blender. Weigh the purée, and add the same weight in sugar. Cook over very low heat, stirring frequently, until the purée reduces somewhat and coats the back of a spoon.

Flavor with vanilla, rum, kirsch, or Curaçao just before serving time.

2. *With apricot preserves:* Put the preserves into a heavy saucepan and cook them over very low heat, stirring constantly.

Strain the preserves through a fine sieve, or purée them in a blender. Weigh the purée, and add a quarter of its weight of a light sugar and water syrup (p. 666) which has been cooked to about 230° F. Flavor as above, just before serving time.

Caramel Sauce | SAUCE CARAMEL

Put any desired quantity of sugar into a very heavy saucepan, moisten it slightly with water, and stir it over very low heat until it is completely dissolved. Raise the heat and cook, without stirring, until it is golden in color. If the sugar is heating too rapidly, cool it by plunging the saucepan into a bowl of cold water.

Add a little boiling water or hot heavy cream to thin the caramel to the pouring consistency of a thick pancake batter. Cool.

Pour the caramel sauce over ice cream or pastries just before serving them.

Chocolate Sauce | SAUCE AU CHOCOLAT

Melt the chocolate with the water over hot water. Add the *crème fraîche* and sweet butter. Then add the sugar and the vanilla. Stir thoroughly until the butter has been completely blended into the mixture and the sauce is very smooth.

FOR ABOUT 2½ CUPS:

8 ounces sweet cooking chocolate
1 cup water
¼ cup Crème Fraîche (p. 666)

¼ cup butter
1 tablespoon sugar
2 teaspoons vanilla extract

SABAYON AU CHOCOLAT / *Chocolate Sabayon*

Combine the egg yolk and the sugar in the top part of a double boiler. Heat the mixture over simmering water (the water must not touch the top of the double boiler or the egg will curdle), beating it constantly and energetically until it is light and foamy; it should about triple its volume. Add the chocolate and continue beating until the mixture drops from a spoon in broad ribbons. Serve warm.

FOR EACH SERVING:

1 egg yolk
1 tablespoon sugar

½ ounce sweet cooking chocolate, melted

SABAYON AU CAFÉ / *Coffee Sabayon*

Proceed as in Chocolate Sabayon (above), but omit the chocolate and add 1 tablespoon of very strong prepared coffee at the beginning before beating the egg yolk and sugar together.

SABAYON AU PORTO / *Port-Wine Sabayon*

Proceed as in Chocolate Sabayon (above), but omit the chocolate and add 1 tablespoon of port wine at the beginning before beating the egg yolk and sugar together.

Note: All *sabayons* may be flavored in this manner with liqueurs or wines. The most frequently used ones are: maraschino, Triple Sec, kirsch, framboise, champagne, Sauternes, sherry, muscat. You may also use very finely minced or grated orange or lemon rind.

SAUCE AUX FRAMBOISES / *Raspberry Sauce*

Strain the raspberries through a fine sieve or purée them in a blender. Pour the boiling sugar syrup over the purée, and flavor the sauce with any desired liqueur.

FOR ABOUT 2½ CUPS:

1 quart ripe raspberries
1 cup Sugar Syrup (p. 666)

2 tablespoons maraschino or kirsch

SAUCE AUX GROSEILLES / *Red-Currant Sauce*

Melt the red-currant jelly over hot water, and then stir in the kirsch.

1 cup red-currant jelly

2 tablespoons kirsch

CREAMS AND CUSTARDS

Crèmes

Crème Chantilly /

Dilute the *crème fraîche* with the light cream in a bowl and set this bowl into another filled with cracked ice. Beat until the cream is stiff but not yet buttery, and then gradually add the sugar, beating until very stiff. Blend in the vanilla.

FOR ABOUT 4 CUPS:

2 cups very cold Crème Fraîche (p. 666)
½ cup cold light cream

½ cup superfine sugar
1 teaspoon vanilla extract

Chocolate Crème Chantilly /

CRÈME CHANTILLY AU CHOCOLAT

Proceed as in plain Crème Chantilly (above), but beat gently into the finished cream 4 ounces of sweet cooking chocolate, melted with 4 tablespoons water and cooled.

Coffee Crème Chantilly / CRÈME CHANTILLY AU CAFÉ

Proceed as in plain Crème Chantilly (above), but beat gently 1 tablespoon instant coffee powder, or more to taste, into the finished cream.

Strawberry Cream / CRÈME AUX FRAISES

Purée the strawberries in a blender; stir in the sugar and the vanilla. Just before serving, mix with the whipped cream.

FOR 4 TO 6 SERVINGS:

4 cups fresh strawberries
1½ cups superfine sugar

1 teaspoon vanilla extract
2 cups heavy cream, whipped

Crème Anglaise /

A *crème anglaise,* or light custard sauce, is sweeter than a *crème pâtissière,* being made, as a rule, with 1¾ cups of sugar and 7 egg yolks to 4 cups of milk. Whole eggs or flour are never used in a *crème anglaise.*

It is desirable to use 2 heavy enamelware saucepans, since they are very important for the success of the custard.

In one saucepan, scald the milk with the vanilla bean.

In another saucepan, beat the egg yolks energetically with the sugar until they are well blended and form a ribbon when dropped from a spoon. Heat the mixture over very low heat, stirring constantly. Add the scalding hot milk gradually to this mixture and cook over low heat, still stirring constantly with a wooden spoon. The *crème* is done when it coats the back of the spoon, and when any trace of froth has disappeared from its surface. Remove it from the heat.

Set a bowl over a larger vessel of crushed ice or ice cubes and immediately strain the custard through a fine sieve into the bowl. Stir it slowly until it has cooled completely.

This kind of custard was used in my childhood as a dessert in itself. Nowadays, it serves more usually as a sauce for *oeufs à la neige* (p. 736), Floating Island (p. 736), and pastries, as well as a base for frozen desserts. It may be perfumed with many other flavors beside vanilla.

Cooling the custard rapidly and stirring constantly until it is cooled adds considerably to its fine, smooth quality.

FOR ABOUT 5 CUPS:

4 cups milk	7 egg yolks
1 piece of vanilla bean, 6 inches long, halved lengthwise	1¾ cups sugar

CRÈME D'AMANDES / *Almond Crème Anglaise*

Prepare a *crème anglaise* as described above. Blend the finely ground almonds and the butter into a smooth paste. Beat in the sugar and blend thoroughly. If desired, the mixture may be made completely smooth by puréeing in a blender for a few minutes.

When the *crème* has cooled, beat in the almond mixture, a little at a time, until thoroughly blended.

FOR 3½ TO 4 CUPS:

½ recipe Crème Anglaise (above)	½ cup butter, softened
⅔ cup blanched almonds, very finely ground	½ cup sugar

CRÈME AU CARAMEL / *Caramel Crème Anglaise*

Prepare a *crème anglaise* as described above.

Make a caramel by putting ¾ cup (5 ounces) of crushed lump sugar and 1 tablespoon of water in a heavy saucepan and stirring it over low heat until the sugar is dissolved and light brown in color. Remove from the heat and very gradually stir in 2 tablespoons boiling water. Allow the caramel to cool for about 10 minutes, or until the saucepan is cool enough to touch. Then gradually blend the *crème* into the caramel and mix thoroughly.

Cool the cooked *crème* over a bowl of crushed ice, stirring constantly until it is cold.

Chocolate Crème Anglaise / CRÈME ANGLAISE AU CHOCOLAT

Proceed as in plain *crème anglaise* (p. 672), but scald the milk with 6 ounces of sweet cooking chocolate before adding it to the other mixture.

Coffee Crème Anglaise / CRÈME ANGLAISE AU CAFÉ

Proceed as in plain *crème anglaise* (p. 672), but stir 2 tablespoons of instant coffee powder into the egg and sugar mixture before adding the scalded milk.

Liqueur-Flavored Crème Anglaise /

CRÈME ANGLAISE AUX LIQUEURS

Proceed as in plain *crème anglaise* (p. 672), but add 4 tablespoons of kirsch, Curaçao or rum to the strained *crème* before cooling it over ice.

Crème Anglaise Collée /

Soften 2 envelopes of unflavored gelatin in ¼ cup water and heat over boiling water until thoroughly dissolved. Proceed as in plain *crème anglaise* (p. 672), and stir the gelatin into the strained custard before cooling it over ice.

Crème Brûlée /

Blend the egg yolks with the granulated sugar and the cornstarch in a saucepan over low heat and, stirring constantly with a wooden spoon, immediately add the heavy cream, a little at a time.

Flavor the custard with the cinnamon, lemon rind and pistachios. Cook it over low heat, stirring constantly, for about 10 minutes, or until the custard is smooth and thickened. Pour it into an 8-inch shallow glass serving dish, allow it to cool, and then chill it in the refrigerator until it is set.

Put the lump sugar and water in a saucepan over medium heat, stir until the sugar is dissolved, and then boil until the mixture turns golden brown and caramelizes. Pour this caramel immediately over the surface of the set custard.

FOR 4 SERVINGS:

4 egg yolks	**Grated rind of 1 lemon**
¼ cup granulated sugar	**1 tablespoon minced pistachios**
1 tablespoon cornstarch	**1 cup lump sugar, crushed**
2 cups heavy cream	**¼ cup water**
½ teaspoon ground cinnamon	

CRÈME AU BEURRE AU SIROP / *Buttercream*

Put the sugar and the water in a saucepan and stir over very low heat until the sugar is completely dissolved. Wash down the sides of the pan with a brush dipped into cold water to dissolve any sugar crystals that have formed. Cover the pan tightly and continue cooking for 5 minutes. Remove the cover, raise the heat, and cook without stirring until a candy thermometer registers 238° F. Remove from the heat.

Meanwhile, beat the egg yolks thoroughly until they are pale and fluffy.

Pour the hot syrup very slowly into the yolks, beating constantly. Continue beating until the mixture is cool and thick. Add the vanilla and fold in the softened butter.

FOR ABOUT 3 CUPS:

1¾ cups sugar	1 teaspoon vanilla extract
½ cup water	1 cup butter, softened
4 egg yolks	

CRÈME AU BEURRE AU CHOCOLAT / *Chocolate Buttercream*

To 1 recipe of Buttercream (above) add 4 ounces of sweet cooking chocolate, melted with 3 tablespoons of water, immediately after adding the hot syrup.

CRÈME AU BEURRE AU CAFÉ / *Coffee Buttercream*

To 1 recipe of Buttercream (above) add 1 tablespoon instant coffee powder mixed with 1 tablespoon of boiling water.

CRÈME AU BEURRE À L'ANGLAISE / *Custard Buttercream*

Prepare ½ recipe of Crème Anglaise (p. 672). Beat 2 cups of softened sweet butter into the *crème,* a little at a time, after the *crème* has been cooked and then cooled to lukewarm. Beat until the mixture is very smooth and then cool it completely over a bowl of ice, stirring it gently but constantly.

/ *Liqueur-Flavored Buttercream*
CRÈME AU BEURRE AU KIRSCH OU AUTRES LIQUEURS

To 1 recipe of Buttercream (above) add 1 tablespoon, or more to taste, of kirsch, rum, Curaçao or any other desired liqueur. Omit the vanilla.

CRÈME AU BEURRE À LA MERINGUE / *Meringue Buttercream*

Beat the egg whites until they form soft peaks and then beat in the sugar, a little at a time. Continue beating until they form stiff peaks. Gradually beat in the softened butter, a small piece at a time. Continue beating the mixture until the butter has been completely absorbed.

FOR ABOUT 4 CUPS:

4 egg whites   1½ cups butter, softened
1¼ cups sugar

Orange or Lemon Buttercream /

CRÈME AU BEURRE À L'ORANGE, AU CITRON

To 1 recipe of Buttercream (p. 675) add the juice of 1 lemon or of ½ orange plus 1 tablespoon of the grated rind of either. Omit the vanilla.

Simple Buttercream / CRÈME AU BEURRE SIMPLE

Beat together the sugar and the egg yolks until the mixture is white and fluffy. Stir in the vanilla and beat in the softened butter, a little at a time. Beat for 5 minutes, until the mixture is very smooth.

FOR ABOUT 2 CUPS:

1¼ cups superfine sugar   1 teaspoon vanilla extract
6 egg yolks   1 cup butter, softened

Note: This buttercream may be flavored with very strong coffee, melted sweet cooking chocolate, or liqueurs, in the same manner as the basic Buttercream on page 675.

Crème Pâtissière /

This pastry cream is frequently used and is very easy to make. However, it very often happens that the *crème* is not sufficiently smooth and that it has been scorched.

First of all, let us speak about the ingredients and their proportions to each other.

The amount of sugar depends largely on the use to which you will put the cream. Whether it is to be added to an already sweetened dish, or on the other hand, if it has to supply all the sweetening in a dish, the sugar content in the cream may be varied as much as ½ cup, more or less. That is, the minimum amount of sugar will be 1¼ cups, and the maximum amount 1¾ cups for the proportions listed below.

The same applies to the amount of the flour, which varies depending on whether the cream is to stretch a dish, or whether it will be used as is. We also must consider if the cream will have to cook further inside a tart or a puff-paste pastry, etc., because in this case, the cream has to be thicker than if used as is. In any case, the flour in the cream has to be cooked thoroughly to avoid a raw taste. The flour content may be as little as ½ cup or as much as 1 cup. However, if the cream is well cooked through, the larger amount of flour will give better results.

The number of egg yolks largely determines the quality of the cream. There are minimum and maximum amounts here too, and we must find a just middle. Let us settle that the ideal number of egg yolks might be seven, 5 egg yolks being the minimum and 10 the maximum. Frequently 1 or 2 whole eggs may substitute for a portion of the egg yolks, but this method is not advisable when the cream will be used in soufflés.

Here is the way to achieve a cream that is completely smooth and that has not been scorched:

Use 2 saucepans. One should be heavy, preferably of enamelware. Never use aluminum as the use of a whisk in an aluminum pan can discolor the cream. Any saucepan will serve for the other since it will only be used to boil the milk. Off the heat put the sugar and the 5 egg yolks into the heavy-bottomed saucepan. Better still, add 1 egg yolk at a time to the sugar, beating the mixture with a whisk or a wooden spoon after each addition until the sugar has been gradually absorbed by the egg yolks. If this is not done by gradual beating, the egg yolks will become burnt and red in color in the cooking, and lose their quality as well. When the egg yolks have absorbed all the sugar, the mixture has to be beaten energetically until white, very thick and creamy. Add the flour, together with 1 whole egg.

Beat until the mixture is smooth and homogenized, and then beat in the second whole egg.

Place the saucepan over low heat to warm up the contents slightly, beating constantly. Pour the boiling milk all at once into the mixture and stir rapidly to blend. Continue cooking and stirring, scraping the bottom of the saucepan constantly.

When the mixture begins to bubble, cook it for 3 minutes longer. Pour the cream into a bowl and add the vanilla. Butter the top surface of the cream immediately, either by rubbing the surface with a tablespoon of butter, or dotting it with bits and spreading these around with the back of a spoon. This will prevent a crust forming on the surface.

This cream will keep extremely well in a refrigerator.

Note: This cream may be enriched by beating in the optional ½ cup sweet butter when it is lukewarm.

FOR ABOUT 6 CUPS:

1¼ cups granulated sugar
5 egg yolks
¾ cup sifted all-purpose flour
2 whole eggs
4 cups milk, brought to a boil

4 teaspoons vanilla extract
1 tablespoon butter, softened
Optional: ½ cup butter, softened

/ Chocolate Crème Pâtissière

CRÈME PÂTISSIÈRE AU CHOCOLAT

Proceed as in Crème Pâtissière (above), but add 6 ounces of sweet cooking chocolate melted over hot water, immediately after removing the *crème* from the heat. Reduce the quantity of vanilla extract to 1 tablespoon.

CRÈME PÂTISSIÈRE AU CAFÉ / Coffee Crème Pâtissière

Proceed as in Crème Pâtissière (above), but sift 2 tablespoons of instant coffee powder with the flour and omit the vanilla extract.

CRÈME PÂTISSIÈRE AU CITRON / Lemon Crème Pâtissière

Proceed as in Crème Pâtissière (above), omitting the vanilla extract and adding the juice of 2 lemons to the eggs and sugar before cooking. For a stronger lemon flavor, 1 tablespoon of grated lemon rind may be added to the milk before it is brought to a boil; it should then be strained before adding it to the egg-sugar-flour mixture.

Orange Crème Pâtissière | CRÈME PÂTISSIÈRE À L'ORANGE

Proceed as in Lemon Crème Pâtissière (above), but substitute the juice of ½ orange for the lemon juice and 1 tablespoon of grated orange rind for the lemon rind.

Liqueur-Flavored Crème Pâtissière |

CRÈME PÂTISSIÈRE AUX LIQUEURS

Proceed as in Crème Pâtissière (p. 676), and add 2 tablespoons of any desired liqueur (kirsch, Curaçao, etc.) after removing the *crème* from the heat.

Crème Saint-Honoré |

Prepare the *crème pâtissière* and, while it is still hot, stir in the gelatin which has been completely dissolved with 1 tablespoon of water in the top part of a double boiler over boiling water. Cool the mixture slightly.

Beat the egg whites until very stiff and fold them into the lukewarm *crème*.

This is the classic filling for a *Gâteau Saint-Honoré*.

FOR 7 TO 8 CUPS:

1 recipe Crème Pâtissière (p. 676)	1 envelope unflavored gelatin
	8 egg whites

Frangipane Cream | CRÈME FRANGIPANE

Combine the egg yolks and the sugar in a heavy enamelware saucepan and beat them together with a whisk until the mixture drops in broad ribbons from a spoon. Beat in the softened butter, the salt and the sifted flour. Then, gradually, stir in the boiling milk and continue to stir until the cream is smooth.

Bring the cream to a boil over low heat, stirring constantly with a whisk. Boil slowly for 3 to 4 minutes, being very careful it does not scorch on the bottom. Remove from the heat and continue stirring for 2 minutes.

Grind the macaroons very finely, put them into a bowl, and slowly pour the cream over them, stirring all the time. Stir in the vanilla and mix thoroughly.

FOR ABOUT 5 CUPS:

8 egg yolks	4 cups milk, brought to a boil
1¼ cups granulated sugar	¼ pound Macaroons Oliver
¼ cup butter, softened	(p. 689)
½ teaspoon salt	2 teaspoons vanilla extract
1 cup sifted all-purpose flour	

CRÈME DE MARRONS / *Chestnut Cream*

Make a gash in the flat side of each chestnut. Place the nuts in a saucepan, cover with cold water, and add the salt. Bring to a boil, cook for 1 minute, and remove from the heat. Take only a few chestnuts out of the hot water at a time, since they are easier to peel when warm, and peel off the outer and inner skins. Put aside any that are hard to peel and cover them with boiling water again to soften their skins.

Put the peeled chestnuts in a saucepan, cover with cold water, and cook for about 1 hour, or until the chestnuts are tender. Cut the vanilla bean lengthwise into halves and add it and the sugar to the chestnuts. Stir until the sugar is dissolved and cook for 5 minutes longer.

Remove from the heat, take out the vanilla bean, and drain, reserving the liquid. Purée the chestnuts in a blender or press them through a food mill. Add enough of the cooking liquid, a little at a time, to make a very fine paste. Stir in the rum.

Beat in the *crème anglaise* (it may be either warm or cold) and chill in the refrigerator. Beat in the *crème Chantilly* just before serving time.

FOR ABOUT 6 CUPS:

1 **pound chestnuts**	3 **tablespoons rum**
1 **teaspoon salt**	2 **cups (about ½ recipe) Crème**
1 **piece of vanilla bean, 5 inches**	**Anglaise (p. 672)**
long	2 **cups Crème Chantilly**
1½ **cups sugar**	**(p. 672)**

CRÈME AU CHOCOLAT / *Chocolate Cream*

Blend the sugar and the *crème fraîche* together in a heavy saucepan. Simmer the mixture over low heat, stirring frequently, until it has been reduced by one fourth; there should be a little less than 2 cups of cream. Remove it from the heat and let it cool. Beat in the egg yolks, one at a time, beating well after each addition. Melt the chocolate over hot water and add it to the cream. Return the saucepan to very low heat and cook until it has thickened, stirring constantly. Do not allow it to boil. Chill before serving if using the cream as a dessert by itself.

FOR ABOUT 2 CUPS:

¾ **cup sugar**	3 **egg yolks**
2 **cups Crème Fraîche (p. 666)**	2 **ounces sweet cooking chocolate**

CRÈME AU THÉ / *Tea Cream*

Put the cream into a heavy saucepan over low heat, bring it to the boiling point, and let it reduce by half. There should be about 1 cup of cream. Put the sugar into a bowl and beat in the egg yolks, one at a time; then the whole eggs, one at a time also. Beat well after each addition. Then beat in the tea. Pour the reduced cream gradually into the mixture, mix well, and pour it back into the saucepan. Then stir it over low heat until it thickens. Do not allow it to boil.

Strain the cream through a very fine sieve into a 3-cup mold or 4 individual custard cups and set in a pan containing about 2 inches of hot water. Bake in a preheated 300° F. oven for about 1 hour.

FOR ABOUT 3 CUPS:

2 cups Crème Fraîche (p. 666)	2 whole eggs
1 cup sugar	1 cup very strong cold tea
3 egg yolks	

Almond Custard / CRÈME D'AMANDES CUITES

Put the *crème fraîche* in a saucepan and bring it to the boiling point. Stir in the sugar, the ground almonds and the almond extract. Mix well and bring the mixture again to a simmer. Let it simmer for 5 minutes, stirring constantly.

Beat the egg yolks with the milk and orange-flower water in a bowl and gradually add the hot almond cream. Pour the mixture into the top part of a 2-quart double boiler and stir over simmering water for about 20 minutes. Strain the custard into a bowl set in ice and stir until cooled.

FOR 4 TO 6 SERVINGS:

4 cups Crème Fraîche (p. 666)	½ teaspoon almond extract
1½ cups sugar	4 egg yolks
½ cup blanched almonds, finely ground	2 tablespoons milk
	1 tablespoon orange-flower water

Almond Custard for Pithiviers /

CRÈME D'AMANDES POUR PITHIVIERS

Grind the almonds very finely, combine them with the sugar, and beat in two of the egg yolks. Then blend in the softened butter and beat in the remaining 2 egg yolks. Beat and blend this mixture energetically until it is smooth. If desired, the mixture may be made completely smooth by blending a little of it at a time in an electric blender.

Cut the vanilla bean lengthwise into halves and scald the pieces with the milk. Stir the milk gradually into the almond paste. Cook the mixture over low heat, stirring constantly, until the custard is thickened and smooth. Strain it through a fine sieve into a bowl set in ice, and stir it gently but constantly until it is cooled.

FOR ABOUT 3 CUPS:

½ cup blanched almonds	1 piece of vanilla bean, 4 inches long
1 cup sugar	
4 egg yolks	2 cups milk
¼ cup butter, softened	

Caramel Custard / CRÈME RENVERSÉE AU CARAMEL

Boil the lump sugar and the water in an 8-cup mold until the caramel is slightly browned. Immediately dip the mold into cold water for 2 seconds to cool it. Turn the mold in all directions until the entire inside is filmed with the caramelized sugar. Dip again into cold water, if necessary, until the caramel stops running.

Boil the milk with the vanilla bean halved lengthwise, cool it, and remove the vanilla bean.

Beat together the whole eggs, the extra egg yolks and the sugar until very light. Gradually add the milk and stir until well blended. Pour the custard into the mold and set the mold in a pan of simmering water. Bake it in a preheated 325° F. oven for about 50 minutes, or until a knife inserted in the custard comes out clean.

Cool the custard in the mold and then unmold it on a serving dish.

FOR 6 SERVINGS:

1 cup lump sugar, crushed	**4 whole eggs**
¼ cup water	**8 extra egg yolks**
4 cups milk	**1 cup granulated sugar**
1 piece of vanilla bean, 6 inches long	

CRÈME RENVERSÉE À LA VANILLE / *Vanilla Custard*

Proceed as in Caramel Custard (above), omitting the caramel lining of the mold. If desired, the custard may be flavored with 1 tablespoon of grated orange rind.

CRÈME RENVERSÉE AU CAFÉ / *Coffee Custard*

Bring the milk to a boil and let it cool.

Beat together in a large bowl the whole eggs, the extra egg yolks, the sugar and the instant coffee. Stir in the milk, a little at a time.

Coat the inside of a 6-cup mold with melted butter, and pour the custard into it. Set the mold in a pan of simmering water and bake in a preheated 325° F. oven for about 40 minutes, or until a knife inserted in the custard comes out clean. Replenish the boiling water as it evaporates during the baking.

Cool the custard in its mold and then unmold it on a serving dish.

FOR 6 SERVINGS:

4 cups milk	**1¼ cups sugar**
4 whole eggs	**1½ tablespoons instant coffee powder**
8 extra egg yolks	

CRÈME RENVERSÉE AU CHOCOLAT / *Chocolate Custard*

Proceed as in Coffee Custard (above), but omit the coffee and gradually stir the hot milk into 4 ounces of melted sweet cooking chocolate.

Let it cool slightly before adding it to the eggs and sugar. If desired, add 1 tablespoon of rum.

CRÈME SURPRISE / *Surprise Custard*

Soak the prunes in lukewarm water for 1 hour, and then cook them in boiling water for about 30 minutes, or until tender. Bake a vanilla-flavored custard.

Drain and pit the cooked prunes and purée them with the sugar in a blender. Spread the purée in the bottom of a compote dish. Unmold the custard over the purée and chill the dish before serving.

At serving time, sprinkle the top with glacéed fruits or glacéed nuts cut into halves.

FOR 6 TO 8 SERVINGS:

1 pound dried prunes	**1 recipe Vanilla Custard (p. 681)**
½ cup superfine sugar	**Glacéed fruits or nuts**

Chocolate Mousse | MOUSSE AU CHOCOLAT

Melt the chocolate in the water, beat it into the *crème anglaise,* and chill the mixture. At serving time, beat in the whipped cream.

FOR 4 TO 6 SERVINGS:

16 ounces sweet cooking chocolate	**1 cup Crème Anglaise (p. 672)**
½ cup water	**1½ cups heavy cream, whipped**

CAKES AND PASTRIES

Les Gâteaux et les Pâtisseries

Except where otherwise noted, all of the cakes and pastries in this section will provide 8 to 10 normal servings.

Almond Cake | PAIN DE GÊNES

Grind the almonds to a very fine powder in a mortar and mix them with the sugar. Beat in the eggs, one at a time, then the melted butter and the Curaçao. Fold in the cornstarch and blend thoroughly. If desired, the mixture may now be blended in an electric blender, a little at a time, to give it a very smooth texture.

Butter and flour an 8-inch round layer-cake pan and pour the batter into it. Bake it in a preheated 325° F. oven for 1 hour and 15 minutes, or until the center of the cake is well puffed and a knife inserted in the center comes out clean.

3 cups blanched almonds, finely ground	**⅔ cup butter, melted**
1¾ cups superfine sugar	**2 tablespoons Curaçao**
5 eggs	**1 cup sifted cornstarch**

/ Génoise

Break up the eggs with the sugar lightly with a fork in a large bowl. Place the bowl over, but not touching, simmering water and beat with a wire whisk until the mixture feels hot to the finger. Remove from the heat and beat with a rotary or an electric beater for about 15 minutes until the mixture is completely cool, has tripled in bulk, and forms a ribbon when dropped from a spoon. Beat in the vanilla.

Very gently fold in the flour alternately with the liquid, but cooled, clarified butter, adding a little of each at a time. Use immediately.

Génoise may be baked in pans of various sizes, but the most common are either 9-inch round layer-cake pans or jelly-roll pans (11 by 16 inches). The pans should be buttered and lightly dusted with flour. The ingredients in this recipe are sufficient for two 9-inch round layers or 1 sheet of jelly-roll size. Bake on the second rack from the bottom of a preheated 350° F. oven for 20 to 25 minutes for 9-inch layers, or slightly less for the jelly-roll size. They are done when the cake springs back if lightly touched with the finger. Turn the cakes out of the pans onto a wire rack to cool immediately after removing them from the oven.

7 eggs
1 cup granulated sugar
1 teaspoon vanilla extract

1¾ cups sifted all-purpose
flour
½ cup clarified butter

GÉNOISE À L'ANIS / *Anise Génoise*

Prepare and bake a *génoise* in a jelly-roll pan (11 by 16 inches), as described above, substituting 1 tablespoon anisette liqueur for the vanilla extract.

Meantime, prepare the anisette-flavored frosting.

When the *génoise* is done, remove it from the pan, allow it to cool completely, and frost on all sides.

1 recipe Génoise (above)

1 recipe Liqueur-Flavored
Frosting (p. 669), made with
2 tablespoons anisette liqueur

Note: This cake may be decorated with little anise-flavored bonbons.

GÉNOISE AU CHOCOLAT / *Chocolate Génoise*

Melt 4 ounces of sweet cooking chocolate with 3 tablespoons of water in a saucepan and allow it to cool. Proceed as in plain *génoise* (above), adding the chocolate to the eggs and sugar after they have been beaten until tripled in bulk.

/ Chocolate Génoise with Cream

GÉNOISE AU CHOCOLAT À LA CRÈME

Prepare and bake a chocolate *génoise* in a jelly-roll pan as described above.

Prepare the *crème Chantilly*. Flavor half of this *crème* with the cooled chocolate in a separate bowl.

When the *génoise* is done, remove it from the pan and cool it on a cake rack.

Cut the cake into 2 pieces (8 by 11 inches) and then cut each piece horizontally into halves. Spread 3 slices with the chocolate *crème Chantilly* and place them one on top of another. Top with the fourth slice and frost the whole cake with the chocolate frosting. Put the remaining plain *crème Chantilly* into a pastry bag fitted with a small star tube and pipe decorative swirls on top of the frosting.

Keep the cake in the refrigerator or in a cold place until serving time.

1 recipe Chocolate Génoise (above)	4 ounces sweet cooking chocolate, melted with 3 tablespoons water and cooled
1 recipe Crème Chantilly (p. 672)	1 recipe Chocolate Frosting (p. 669)

Coffee Génoise / GÉNOISE AU CAFÉ

Prepare and bake a *génoise* in 2 round 9-inch layers as described above.

Meantime, prepare a walnut buttercream filling, as described in Hungarian Nut Cake (p. 687).

When the cake is done, remove the layers from their pans, allow them to cool completely, and cut each layer horizontally into halves. Spread 3 layers with walnut buttercream and place them one on top of another. Top with the fourth layer and frost the whole cake with coffee frosting.

1 recipe Génoise (p. 683)	For the walnut buttercream: 6 tablespoons milk
1 recipe Coffee Frosting (p. 669)	1½ cups ground walnuts ¾ cup butter, softened ¾ cup superfine sugar ¼ cup rum 1 egg

Lemon or Orange Génoise /

GÉNOISE AU CITRON OU À L'ORANGE

Proceed as in a plain *génoise* (p. 683), substituting the grated rind of 1 orange or 1 lemon and the juice of ½ orange or 1 lemon for the vanilla extract.

Liqueur-Flavored Génoise / GÉNOISE AUX LIQUEURS

Proceed as in a plain *génoise* (p. 683), substituting ¼ cup of any desired liqueur (Curaçao, rum, Triple Sec, etc.) for the vanilla extract.

Old-Fashioned Génoise / GÉNOISE À L'ANCIENNE

Prepare and bake a *génoise* in 2 round 9-inch layers, as described above.

Cook the apricot jam in a saucepan over high heat for 3 minutes, stirring constantly, and then purée it through a sieve. Prepare the Italian meringue.

When the *génoise* is done, remove the layers from their pans and allow them to cool on a cake rack. Cut each layer horizontally into halves and spread the 4 layers with hot apricot purée. Pile the layers one on top of another.

Spread the top and the sides of the cake with the Italian meringue and decorate the top with the apricot halves. Bake the cake in a 500° F. oven for 3 minutes.

Serve immediately, or keep in a cool place for a short time.

1 recipe Génoise (p. 683)
1 cup apricot jam

1 recipe Italian Meringue
(p. 694), flavored with 1
teaspoon vanilla extract
6 canned apricot halves

PAVÉS AUX NOISETTES / *Hazelnut Pavés*

Prepare and bake a liqueur-flavored *génoise* in a jelly-roll pan (11 by 16 inches), as described on page 683.

Meantime, prepare the coffee buttercream and the coffee frosting.

When the cake is done, remove it from the pan and cool on a cake rack.

Cut the cake into 20 squares, 3-inch size. Spread five of the squares with coffee buttercream and five with half of the ground hazelnuts mixed with plain buttercream. Top them with the remaining squares. Frost the *pavés* on all sides with the coffee frosting and sprinkle them with the remaining ground hazelnuts. Keep the *pavés* in a cool place until serving time.

1 recipe Liqueur-Flavored
Génoise (above), using ¼
cup orange or apricot liqueur
½ recipe Coffee Buttercream
(p. 675)

1 cup ground hazelnuts
1 cup Buttercream (p. 675)
1 recipe Coffee Frosting
(p. 669)

GÂTEAU MARBRÉ / *Marble Cake*

Butter and flour a 9-inch tube pan with high sides. Pour into the pan alternate layers of plain *génoise* and chocolate *génoise* batter, making 2 layers of each.

Bake in a preheated 350° F. oven for about 35 minutes.

½ recipe Génoise (p. 683)
½ recipe Chocolate Génoise
(p. 683)

BISCUIT AU CHOCOLAT / *Chocolate Cake*

Sift the flour and the cocoa together.

As in making a *génoise* (p. 683), combine the eggs and the sugar in a bowl and beat them together over hot water until the mixture feels hot to the touch. Remove from the heat and beat the mixture until it is very light and tripled in bulk. Gradually fold in the flour-cocoa mixture alternately with the lukewarm clarified butter.

Butter and flour 2 round 9-inch layer-cake pans and distribute the batter equally into them. Bake the cake in a preheated 350° F. oven for about 25 minutes. Turn the layers out onto a cake rack to cool.

Make the chocolate cream as follows: Melt the chocolate with the butter and then cool it. Whip the *crème fraîche,* gradually adding the sugar, and fold in the chocolate-butter mixture.

Cut each layer horizontally into halves and spread three of the thin layers with the chocolate cream filling. Stack them up, top with the 4th layer, and frost the whole cake with the chocolate frosting. Chill the cake for 3 hours before serving.

For the cake:
- 1½ cups sifted all-purpose flour
- ½ cup cocoa powder
- 7 eggs
- 1¼ cups sugar
- ½ cup clarified butter, melted and cooled

For the cream filling:
- 2 ounces sweet cooking chocolate
- ¼ cup butter
- 1 cup Crème Fraîche (p. 666)
- ¼ cup sugar

For the frosting:
- 2 cups Chocolate Frosting (p. 669)

Honey Cake | PAIN D'ÉPICE

Combine the honey and the sugar in a bowl. Pour the boiling water over them and blend thoroughly with a wooden spoon until the mixture is smooth. Stir in the anisette liqueur and then the flour sifted with the baking powder.

Spoon the batter into a buttered loaf pan (4½ by 8 inches) and bake it in a preheated 350° F. oven for about 45 minutes.

When the cake is done, take it out of the oven and let it cool in the pan. Unmold it on a long dish. Serve it with a sauceboat full of *sabayon.*

- ⅓ cup honey
- ⅔ cup superfine sugar
- ¾ cup boiling water
- 1 teaspoon anisette liqueur
- 2½ cups sifted all-purpose flour

- 3 teaspoons double-acting baking powder
- 2 cups Port-Wine Sabayon (p. 671)

Honey Cookies | SABLÉS AU MIEL

Let the butter stand at room temperature until it is softened and has about the same consistency as the honey. Combine the two in a bowl and stir them long and hard, so that they are thoroughly blended.

Put half of the flour on a pastry board, make a well in the center, and put the whole egg into it. Stir a little flour into the egg. Then add the butter-honey mixture and ¾ cup of the confectioners' sugar. Blend everything and then stir in the remaining flour and the allspice. Work and knead the dough until it is thoroughly smooth.

Roll out the dough to the thickness of ¼ inch. Cut it into any desired shapes and put the cookies on a buttered and floured baking sheet.

Mix the egg white with the remaining 1¼ cups of the sugar and frost the cookies with it, or decorate them with any desired patterns. Bake them in a preheated 350° F. oven for about 15 minutes.

FOR ABOUT 50 COOKIES:

1 cup butter	2 cups confectioners' sugar
¼ cup honey	2 teaspoons ground allspice or
4 cups sifted all-purpose flour	Quatre Épices (p. 667)
1 whole egg	1 extra egg white

SABLÉS / *Sugar Cookies*

Combine the flour, the softened butter and the sugar in a bowl and mix well. Force the hard-cooked egg yolks through a sieve and add them, the salt and the cinnamon to the mixture. Continue mixing until the dough is a smooth paste.

Roll out the dough between 2 sheets of wax paper to the thickness of ¼ inch. Chill in the refrigerator until the dough is firm, remove the wax paper, and cut with cookie cutters into any desired shapes.

Put the cookies on a buttered and floured baking sheet and bake them in a preheated 400° F. oven for 10 to 12 minutes.

FOR ABOUT 20 COOKIES:

2 cups sifted all-purpose flour	6 hard-cooked egg yolks
¾ cup butter, slightly softened	½ teaspoon salt
½ cup granulated sugar	½ teaspoon ground cinnamon

Note: You may also make these cookies with raw egg yolks rather than hard-cooked ones. If the dough is too soft, add enough flour to make a dough that is firm enough for rolling out.

GÂTEAU HONGROIS AU NOIX / *Hungarian Nut Cake*

Beat the egg whites until they form soft peaks, slowly add the sugar, and continue beating until they form stiff peaks. Mix the egg yolks with the water and vanilla, and fold the mixture into the egg whites. Sift the flour with the baking powder and the cocoa and then very gently fold them into the other mixture.

Butter and flour the bottom only of a 9-inch tube pan with high sides, fill it with the batter, and bake the cake in a preheated 325° F. oven for 40 minutes.

While the cake is baking, make the walnut buttercream filling. Bring the milk to a boil, add the ground nuts, and cook the mixture slowly for 5 minutes, stirring constantly. Remove from the heat, strain through a sieve, and cool. Cream together the butter and the sugar and add it to the nut mixture. Beat until the mixture is smooth and gradually add the rum. Beat in the egg.

Remove the cake from the oven, invert the pan on a cake rack, and cool completely. Cut it horizontally into 3 slices.

Spread the slices thinly with some of the buttercream filling, pile them on top of each other, and frost the cake on all sides with the remaining cream. Smooth the frosting with a metal spatula and keep the cake in a cool place until ready to serve.

6 eggs, separated
¾ cup superfine sugar
1 tablespoon water
1 teaspoon vanilla extract
¾ cup sifted all-purpose flour
1 teaspoon double-acting baking
   powder
½ cup cocoa powder

For the walnut buttercream:
6 tablespoons milk
1½ cups ground walnuts
¾ cup butter, softened
¾ cup superfine sugar
¼ cup rum
1 egg

Note: The cake may be decorated with nuts or glacéed cherries, if desired.

Jam Cookies / BISCUITS DE CONFITURE

Let the lemon rind steep in the orange-flower water for several minutes. Strain the apricot jam through a fine sieve and mix it with the lemon rind.

Beat the egg yolks with ½ cup of the sugar until the mixture is almost white and drops off the spoon in broad bands. Blend in the apricot jam and the lemon rind. Beat the egg whites until they form peaks, gradually add the remaining ¼ cup of sugar, and beat until they form stiff peaks. Gently fold the egg whites into the other mixture.

Put the mixture into a pastry bag fitted with a ½-inch round tube and squeeze out 1-inch mounds onto a baking sheet lined with unglazed white or brown paper. Space the mounds 2 inches apart as they will spread as they bake.

Bake in a preheated 325° F. oven for 10 minutes.

FOR ABOUT 24 COOKIES:

2 teaspoons grated lemon rind
1 tablespoon orange-flower water
2 tablespoons apricot jam

4 eggs, separated
¾ cup superfine sugar

Ladyfingers / BISCUITS À LA CUILLER

Beat the egg yolks and 1 cup of the superfine sugar together in a bowl until the mixture is almost white and will drop from a spoon in broad bands. Stir in the orange-flower water and then blend in the flour.

Beat the egg whites until they form soft peaks. Gradually beat in the remaining superfine sugar, continuing to beat until the egg whites form stiff peaks. Fold the egg whites into the batter.

Fill a pastry bag fitted with a ½-inch round tube with the batter. Line 2 large baking sheets with white or brown unglazed paper and pipe strips of the batter about 4 inches long and 1 inch wide. The strips should be spaced 1 inch apart so that they won't stick together during the baking.

Sift confectioners' sugar lightly over the ladyfingers. Bake in a preheated 350° F. oven for about 8 minutes, or until the ladyfingers are just turning golden.

FOR ABOUT 5 DOZEN LADYFINGERS:

8 eggs, separated
1⅓ cups superfine sugar
1 tablespoon orange-flower water

1¾ cups sifted all-purpose
   flour
1 cup confectioners' sugar

GÂTEAU AU CITRON / *Lemon Cake*

Beat the eggs and the sugar with an electric beater until the mixture is white and fluffy. Stir in the lemon rind and the melted butter. Sift the flour with the baking powder and fold it into the batter. Beat again with the electric beater until thoroughly blended.

Butter and flour 2 round 8-inch layer-cake pans and divide the batter into the pans. Bake in a preheated 350° F. oven for about 30 minutes. When done, remove the layers from the pans and cool on a cake rack.

Cut each layer horizontally into halves and spread each with lemon buttercream, placing them one on top of the other. Coat the top and the sides with more buttercream and then sprinkle them with finely chopped toasted almonds.

3 eggs
1 cup superfine sugar
2 teaspoons grated lemon rind
½ cup butter, melted
1¾ cups sifted all-purpose flour

2 teaspoons double-acting baking powder
1 recipe Lemon Buttercream (p. 676)
¾ cup chopped toasted almonds

MACARONS OLIVER / *Macaroons Oliver*

Grind the almonds very fine (in an electric blender, if desired) and mix them with the confectioners' sugar. Stir in the unbeaten egg whites to form a stiff paste.

Dissolve the granulated sugar in the water very slowly over very low heat. Brush any sugar crystals that form on the sides of the pan down into the syrup with a brush dipped into cold water. Cover the pan tightly for 2 minutes. Uncover, raise the heat, and cook the syrup to the thread stage, 234° F. on a candy thermometer. Pour the syrup in a thin stream over the stiffly beaten egg whites, beating constantly with a rotary or electric beater. Continue beating until the mixture is cool and very stiff. Beat the almond extract into the mixture and then fold it as gently as possible into the ground-almond mixture.

Put the mixture into a pastry bag fitted with a plain round ½-inch tube and squeeze out 2-inch mounds onto a baking sheet lined with unglazed white or brown paper. Space the mounds 1 inch apart. Bake in a preheated 300° F. oven for 25 minutes. Cool completely and remove from the paper, if necessary, by moistening the paper from the underside.

FOR ABOUT 4 DOZEN MACAROONS:

2½ cups blanched almonds
3½ cups sifted confectioners' sugar
4 egg whites, unbeaten

2 cups granulated sugar
½ cup water
5 egg whites, stiffly beaten
1½ teaspoons almond extract

MACARONS AU CHOCOLAT / *Chocolate Macaroons*

Proceed as in Macaroons Oliver (above), adding ⅔ cup unsweetened cocoa powder to the ground-almond and confectioners'-sugar mixture. Add 1 additional unbeaten egg white if the mixture seems too dry.

Madeleines I /

Cream the softened butter and the sugar together in a bowl. Beat in the eggs, one at a time. Stir in the vanilla and beat in the flour and the baking powder. The batter must be extremely smooth. Butter generously two 12-*madeleine* molds and spoon the batter into them. Bake in a preheated 350° F. oven for 20 minutes. Remove from the molds onto a wire rack immediately.

FOR ABOUT 24 MADELEINES:

½ cup butter, softened
½ cup sugar
4 eggs
1 teaspoon vanilla extract

1 cup sifted all-purpose flour
½ teaspoon double-acting baking
    powder

Madeleines II /

Cream the softened butter and the sugar together in a bowl. Beat in the egg yolks, one at a time, then the vanilla and the flour. Gently fold in the stiffly beaten egg whites. Bake in the same manner as in the preceding recipe.

FOR ABOUT 24 MADELEINES:

¼ cup butter, softened
½ cup superfine sugar
3 eggs separated

1 teaspoon vanilla extract
1 cup sifted all-purpose flour

Mousseline Spongecake / BISCUIT MOUSSELINE

Beat the egg yolks and 1 cup of the sugar together in a bowl until the mixture is almost white and drops off a spoon in broad bands. Add the vanilla and then blend in the flour and the cornstarch sifted together. Beat the egg whites with the salt until they form soft peaks. Gradually add the remaining sugar, continuing to beat until they form stiff peaks. Fold them into the batter, lifting it to incorporate as much air as possible.

Grease and dust with flour the bottoms only of 2 round 9-inch layer-cake pans. Distribute the batter evenly into the pans. Bake in a preheated 350° F. oven for 20 to 25 minutes. Allow the cake to cool completely in the pans. Then loosen the sides with a sharp knife and remove the cakes from the pans.

If desired, this cake may be baked in a high 9-inch tube pan. The baking time should be increased to 35 to 40 minutes.

6 eggs, separated
1⅓ cups superfine sugar
1 teaspoon vanilla extract

⅔ cup sifted all-purpose flour
⅔ cup sifted cornstarch
1 pinch of salt

Savoy Spongecake / BISCUIT DE SAVOIE

Beat the egg yolks and ¾ cup of the sugar together in a bowl until the mixture is almost white and drops off a spoon in broad bands. Add the vanilla and then blend in the flour and cornstarch sifted together.

Beat the egg whites until they form soft peaks. Gradually add the remaining sugar, continuing to beat until they form stiff peaks. Fold them into the batter, lifting it to incorporate as much air as possible.

Butter and flour the bottom only of an 8-cup ring mold. Pour the batter into the mold and bake in a preheated 350° F. oven for 35 minutes.

5 eggs, separated	**½ cup sifted all-purpose flour**
1 cup granulated sugar	**¾ cup sifted cornstarch**
1 teaspoon vanilla extract	

PÂTE À QUATRE-QUARTS / *Poundcake*

Soften the butter slightly. Cream the butter and the sugar by beating vigorously with a wooden spoon or with an electric beater. Beat in the eggs, one at a time, and then stir in the vanilla. Sift the flour and baking powder over the mixture, and fold it in gently to obtain a smooth batter.

Butter and dust lightly with flour a loaf pan (8 by 4½ inches). Pour the batter into the pan and bake in a preheated 350° F. oven for about 1 hour. Allow the cake to cool in the pan.

6 eggs	**Their weight in sifted all-**
Their weight in butter (about	**purpose flour (about 1¾ cups)**
¾ cup)	**2 teaspoons double-acting baking**
Their weight in superfine sugar	**powder**
(about 1 cup)	**1 teaspoon vanilla extract**

TARTE SACHER / *Sachertorte*

Probably more than any other restaurant in Vienna, the Sacher has captured the popular imagination. Though its rank as the best in the Austrian capital has been disputed, there isn't a chef in the world who doesn't know the famous *Sachertorte*. I myself have at least 3 authentic recipes, which were given to me by Sacher's chefs, ex-chefs, patrons and ex-patrons.

One of the chefs at the Sacher gives the following recipe: Mix butter, sugar, chocolate, flour, egg yolks and vanilla; fold in the stiffly beaten egg whites. This cake, when baked, is covered first with an apricot glaze and then with a chocolate frosting. Obviously, this is a dry cake that will keep well and which is easy to pack and mail. As a matter of fact, a great part of the activities of the Restaurant Sacher consists of a mail-order business of this cake—a very well-organized one.

In another recipe, almonds are added to the cake dough, and in yet another, dried bread crumbs. Thinking of these recipes, here is a chocolate cake with an unmistakably Viennese character; it was inspired by Sacher, the Prater and the beautiful Blue Danube (which is not blue at all, but still beautiful).

Combine the eggs and the sugar in the top part of a double boiler or in a heavy saucepan, and beat them thoroughly over hot water, just as if you were making a *génoise* (p. 683), until they feel very warm to the touch. Remove from the heat and beat very energetically for about 15 minutes, or until the mixture is cool and has tripled in bulk. Sift together the grated chocolate and the flour, and fold it into the mixture gradually, alternately with the clarified butter. Add the vanilla bean.

Bake the cake in 2 buttered and floured 10-inch springform pans in a preheated 350° F. oven for about 30 minutes. Unmold the cake onto a cake rack, cool it, and sandwich the 2 layers with the following cream: Beat the cream until stiff, gradually adding the sugar and grated chocolate. Then frost the cake with the chocolate frosting.

Chill the cake in the refrigerator for 24 hours. This cake is not 'a true *Sachertorte,* though it resembles one, but it has merits of its own, and it is certainly a Viennese kind of cake.

For the cake batter:
- **8 eggs**
- **1¼ cups sugar**
- **6 ounces sweet cooking chocolate, very finely grated**
- **2 cups sifted all-purpose flour**
- **½ cup butter, clarified and cooled**
- **The scraped inside of 1 vanilla bean**

For the filling:
- **1 cup heavy cream**
- **¼ cup sugar**
- **2 ounces sweet cooking chocolate, finely grated**
- **2 cups Chocolate Frosting (p. 669)**

Yule Log with Chestnuts | BÛCHE DE NOËL AUX MARRONS

Remove the inner and outer skins of the chestnuts as described in Chestnut Cream (p. 679).

Cook the chestnuts with the milk, the cubes of sugar and the vanilla bean in a saucepan over medium heat for about 45 minutes, or until they are tender.

While the chestnuts are cooking, prepare the cake. Beat together the egg yolks and 1¼ cups of the superfine sugar until the mixture is very creamy. Add the cold water and vanilla extract and then fold in the flour which has been sifted with the baking powder. Gently fold in all the egg whites, stiffly beaten.

Butter a jelly-roll pan (11 by 16 inches), line it with wax paper, butter it again, and dust with flour. Pour the batter into it, smooth the top with a metal spatula, and bake in a preheated 325° F. oven for 20 minutes.

Drain the chestnuts when they are tender. Purée them through a food mill or a sieve and cool. Weigh the purée and beat in the same weight of softened butter. Blend thoroughly, stir in 2 tablespoons of the rum, and season to taste with the remaining cup of superfine sugar.

Combine the sugar syrup and the remaining 2 tablespoons of rum.

When the cake is baked, take it out of the oven and sprinkle it immediately with the syrup. Roll it up at once and place it on a serving dish.

Put the chestnut butter into a pastry bag fitted with a fluted tube. Pipe decorative swirls over the cake and surround it with *marrons glacés.*

- **1 pound chestnuts, peeled**
- **3 cups milk**
- **10 cubes of sugar**
- **1 piece of vanilla bean, 4 inches long**
- **3 eggs, separated**
- **2¼ cups superfine sugar**
- **¼ cup cold water**
- **2 teaspoons vanilla extract**

- **2¼ cups sifted all-purpose flour**
- **2 teaspoons double-acting baking powder**
- **1 extra egg white**
- **1 to 2 cups butter, softened**
- **¼ cup rum**
- **½ cup hot Sugar Syrup (p. 666)**
- **12 marrons glacés**

YULE LOG

WITH

CHOCOLATE

LA BÛCHE DE NOËL AU CHOCOLAT

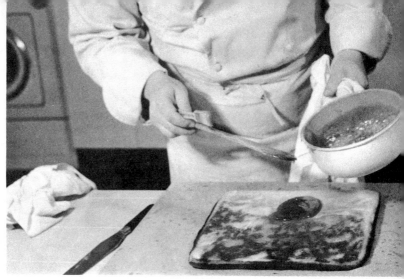

This is a variation of the Yule Log with Chestnuts (692).

When the cake is baked, take it from the oven and spread it with Chocolate Cream (p. 679). Roll up the cake at once to form the log and cover it with more of the cream.

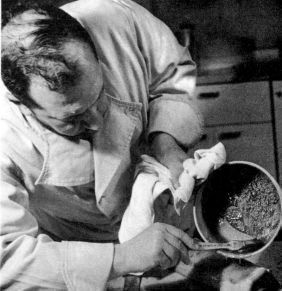

Meringues /

Beat the egg whites until they form soft peaks. Gradually add the sugar by generous spoonfuls, beating constantly for about 15 minutes, or until the mixture is extremely stiff.

Put the mixture into a pastry bag fitted with a ½-inch round tube and squeeze out 2-inch mounds onto a baking sheet lined with unglazed white or brown paper. Space the mounds about 1 inch apart.

Meringues should be slowly dried, rather than actually baked. This is a long process. Preheat the oven to 200° F., place the meringues in it, and turn the oven off. After 1 hour turn the oven on to 200° F. for 10 minutes and then turn it off. Repeat this process 4 to 6 times, or until the meringues are completely dry but still snow white.

FOR 20 MERINGUES, 2-INCH SIZE:

4 egg whites   **1 cup superfine sugar**

Italian Meringue / PÂTE À MERINGUE À L'ITALIENNE

Put the egg whites and the sugar in the top part of a double boiler, preferably not aluminum, and beat over hot water until the mixture forms soft peaks, about 7 minutes. Remove from the heat and beat until it forms stiff peaks.

4 egg whites   **1¼ cups superfine sugar**

Italian Coffee Meringue /

PÂTE À MERINGUE À L'ITALIENNE AU CAFÉ

Proceed as in Italian Meringue (above), adding 3 tablespoons instant coffee powder before beating.

Italian Chocolate Meringue /

PÂTE À MERINGUE À L'ITALIENNE AU CHOCOLAT

Proceed as in Italian Meringue (above), adding 4 tablespoons unsweetened cocoa powder before beating.

Meringue Spongecake / BISCUIT MERINGUÉ

Bake a spongecake in 2 round 9-inch layer-cake pans. Cut each layer horizontally into halves and sprinkle each slice lightly with kirsch.

Spread the first slice with raspberry jam, the second with *crème pâtissière,* and the third with more raspberry jam. Top with the fourth slice and cover the whole cake with Italian meringue. Springle it lightly with confectioners' sugar and then with toasted slivered almonds.

Place the cake on a board and bake it in a preheated 500° F. oven for about 3 minutes, or until the meringue is golden brown.

1 **Mousseline Spongecake (p. 690)**	1 **recipe Italian Meringue**
½ **cup kirsch**	**(above)**
½ **cup raspberry jam**	½ **cup confectioners' sugar**
½ **cup Crème Pâtissière**	¼ **cup blanched almonds,**
(p. 676)	**slivered and toasted**

/ *Brioche*

Have all ingredients at room temperature.

Place ¾ cup of the flour in a bowl and make a well in the center. Mix the compressed yeast with ¼ cup of lukewarm water (80° to 90° F.), or use ⅓ cup of warmer water (105° to 115° F.) if using dry yeast, and pour the mixture into the flour well. Stir the flour into the yeast mixture to make a fairly firm dough and knead it into a ball. In French, this is called a *levain,* or sponge. Place the sponge in a bowl and cover it completely with lukewarm water. Set the bowl in a warm place until the sponge expands and rises to the surface of the water. Then remove it. Do not allow it to remain too long or it will disintegrate.

Place the remaining flour on a marble slab or pastry board and make a well in the center. Put in this well the salt, sugar, milk, whole eggs and extra egg yolks and half of the butter. Blend the flour into the other ingredients and then knead in the sponge.

Knead for about 15 minutes in order to get a smooth and elastic dough. Then knead in the remaining butter, which should be of the same consistency as the dough. To do this, flatten out the dough, spread the butter over half of it, and cover with the other half. If the butter breaks out, the dough will become very sticky, but do not add more flour. Simply continue kneading until the dough no longer clings to the board or marble and it is completely smooth and homogenized.

Grease a large bowl with butter and put the dough in it. Cover the bowl with a kitchen towel and keep in a warm place for about 2 hours, or until the dough has doubled in bulk. An oven with only the pilot lighted is excellent, provided the temperature is not above 95° F.

When doubled in bulk, turn the dough out on the marble slab or pastry board and punch it down. Return it to the bowl to rise again in a warm place until doubled in bulk and then punch it down again.

Place the dough in the refrigerator overnight to mellow, punching it down once after the first 2 hours.

To bake a single large *brioche,* pull off a piece of dough about the size of a plum and roll the remaining dough into a ball. Place the ball in a lightly greased round 5- to 6-cup fluted mold. It should fill the mold about two thirds full. Roll the smaller piece into a ball, punch a small depression in the larger ball with the forefinger, and insert the smaller ball. Place the mold in a warm place until the dough has doubled in bulk and then brush the top with the egg beaten with heavy cream. Bake on the second rack from the bottom of a preheated 400° F. oven for 45 minutes. Remove the *brioche* from the mold immediately.

Small individual *brioches* may be baked in greased 3-inch fluted molds or in muffin tins. They are formed in the same way as a large *brioche,* reserving about one fifth of the dough to form the knobs at the top. If exact uniformity of size is desired, weigh out 2-ounce pieces of dough to form the larger balls. The baking time should be decreased to 15 minutes.

The ingredients below will make 1 large or about 16 small *brioches*.

5 cups sifted all-purpose flour	2 whole eggs
1 ounce compressed yeast, or 2 packages active dry yeast	6 extra egg yolks
	1 cup sweet butter, softened
1 tablespoon salt	1 egg, beaten with 1 tablespoon
3 tablespoons sugar	heavy cream
½ cup lukewarm milk	

Raisin Brioche | BRIOCHE AUX RAISINS SECS

Prepare a plain *brioche* dough as described above, mixing in a generous cup of mixed raisins and dried currants after the dough has risen for the second time. Allow the dough to mellow in the refrigerator and bake in the same way as a plain *brioche*.

Crown Brioche | BRIOCHE EN COURONNE

After the *brioche* dough has mellowed overnight in the refrigerator, shape it into a ball and flour it on all sides. Place your index fingers in the middle to make a hole. Gradually pull the dough apart with both hands, shaping it into a large ring about 10 inches in diameter. Using a pointed knife, decorate the top of the ring with crisscross patterns.

Put the ring on a buttered baking sheet, flatten it lightly, and let it rest in a warm place until nearly doubled in bulk.

Paint the top with egg beaten with cream and sift the sugar over it. Bake in a preheated 400° F. oven for 30 minutes.

1 recipe Brioche dough (above)	½ cup superfine sugar

Crown Brioche with Glacéed Fruits |

BRIOCHE EN COURONNE AUX FRUITS CONFITS

Soak the glacéed fruits in the lukewarm rum for 1 hour and drain thoroughly, reserving the rum.

Pull off about one fifth of the *brioche* dough and knead the drained fruits into it. Form this smaller piece into 6 small balls.

Form a large ring with the remaining dough, as described in the preceding recipe, and place it on a buttered baking sheet. Make 6 evenly spaced indentations around the top of the ring with the forefinger and insert one of the smaller balls in each. Place the ring in a warm place until nearly doubled in bulk.

Crush the lumps of sugar in the reserved rum. Paint the ring with egg beaten with cream and then brush it lightly with the crushed sugar. Bake in a preheated 400° F. oven for 30 minutes.

¾ cup mixed glacéed fruits, chopped fine	1 recipe Brioche dough (above)
	6 lumps of sugar
¼ cup lukewarm rum	

BRIOCHE MOUSSELINE / *Mousseline Brioche*

Butter a 5- to 6-cup round mold with straight tall sides. You can make it even taller by generously buttering a piece of strong paper and tying it to the mold an inch from its upper edge.

Fill the mold two-thirds full with *brioche* dough after the dough has mellowed in the refrigerator overnight. Let the dough rise in a warm place for about 2 hours, or until doubled in bulk. Brush the top with egg beaten with cream and bake on the second rack from the bottom of a preheated 400° F. oven for 45 minutes.

1 recipe Brioche dough (p. 695)

GÂTEAU BRIOCHÉ / *Brioche Cake*

Dissolve the compressed yeast in ½ cup of lukewarm water (80° to 90° F.), or use ⅔ cup warmer water (105° to 115° F.) if using dry yeast.

Put 1½ cups of the flour in a bowl and make a well in the center. Pour the yeast mixture into this well and mix to make a soft dough, which is the sponge. Knead the sponge into a ball and allow it to rest in a warm place until doubled in bulk.

Mix the whole eggs and the salt into the remaining flour, kneading until the dough is smooth.

Make a syrup with the sugar, orange-flower water and rum. Mix this syrup into the dough, together with the softened butter, and then knead in the sponge. Add the orange and lemon rinds and knead the dough for about 15 minutes until it is very smooth and elastic.

Let the dough rest in a warm place until doubled in bulk.

Shape the dough into a large ring, as in Crown Brioche (above), and place it on a buttered and floured baking sheet. Cut notches in the top with a knife and sprinkle pieces of candied citron into the notches. Brush the top of the cake with the extra egg yolk and bake it in a preheated 400° F. oven for about 40 minutes.

FOR 12 TO 16 SERVINGS:

**2 ounces compressed yeast, or 4
   packages active dry yeast
10 cups sifted all-purpose flour
7 eggs
1 tablespoon salt
1 cup granulated sugar
½ cup orange-flower water**

**½ cup rum
1¾ cups butter, softened
1 tablespoon grated orange rind
1 teaspoon grated lemon rind
1 cup chopped candied citron
1 extra egg yolk**

KOUGLOF / *Kugelhupf*

Place ¾ cup of the flour in a bowl and make a well in the center. Mix the compressed yeast with ¼ cup of lukewarm water (80° to 90° F.), or use ⅓ cup warmer water (105° to 115° F.) if using dry yeast. Pour this mixture into the well and stir to make a soft dough. Roll into a ball and cut a cross in the top. Put this sponge into 3 cups of the lukewarm milk in a bowl until it rises to the surface of the milk.

Put the remaining flour on a pastry board and make a well in the center. Dissolve the salt in 2 tablespoons of warm water and pour it into the well. Add the sugar, then the eggs and the remaining 1 cup of milk.

Blend the flour into the other ingredients and knead in the drained sponge.

Knead the dough in the same manner as a *brioche* by folding it back on itself so that it will absorb as much air as possible and keep kneading until it clears the fingers and the pastry board. It will take about 15 minutes to obtain a smooth and elastic dough. Then knead in the butter which should have the same consistency as the dough. The dough will become quite sticky, but do not add more flour. Simply continue kneading until the dough is perfectly smooth.

Dust a bowl with flour, and also dust the dough with flour. Put the dough into the bowl, cover it with a kitchen towel, and let it stand in a warm place until the dough is doubled in bulk, about 2 hours.

Turn the dough out onto the pastry board and punch it down. Knead in the currants. Allow the dough to rise twice more, punching it down each time. Butter a Kugelhupf pan, or a 9-inch tube pan with high sides, and line the inside with almonds. Fill the pan about halfway full with the dough. Bake it in a preheated 350° F. oven for about 50 minutes. Allow the cake to cool in the pan for about 5 minutes and then unmold it.

4 cups sifted all-purpose flour	½ cup superfine sugar
1 ounce compressed yeast, or 2 envelopes active dry yeast	4 eggs
	¾ cup butter, softened
4 cups lukewarm milk	½ cup dried currants
2 teaspoons salt	1½ cups blanched almonds, halved

Panettone /

Put ¾ cup of the flour in a bowl and make a well in the center. Mix the compressed yeast with ¼ cup of lukewarm water (80° to 90° F.), or use ⅓ cup warmer water (105 to 115° F.) if using dry yeast, and pour the mixture into the well. Mix the flour into the yeast mixture to make a soft dough, knead it into a ball, and let it rise in a warm place until doubled in bulk.

Mix the rest of the flour with the salt, the 3 whole eggs, half of the granulated sugar dissolved in 2 tablespoons lukewarm water and half of the softened butter. Then add the sponge.

Knead the dough as for *brioche,* that is, until it clears the fingers. Roll it out smoothly and sprinkle the top with the remaining granulated sugar. Spread the remaining softened butter and two of the extra egg yolks over it and top it with the raisins and chopped citron.

Knead again for about 15 minutes until the dough is smooth and elastic. Roll it into a ball and put it in a buttered and floured bowl. Let it rise in a warm place until doubled in bulk. This will take longer than usual because of the dried fruits.

Form the *panettone* into a round loaf and place it on a buttered and floured baking sheet. Beat the remaining 2 egg yolks with a tablespoon of water and the confectioners' sugar and spread the mixture on the top of the cake. Score the top decoratively with a knife and sprinkle with the crushed cube sugar.

Bake in preheated 350° F. oven for about 50 minutes.

5 cups sifted all-purpose flour	⅔ cup butter, softened
1 ounce compressed yeast, or 2 packages active dry yeast	4 extra egg yolks
	½ cup raisins
2 teaspoons salt	½ cup chopped candied citron
3 whole eggs	1 tablespoon confectioners' sugar
⅔ cup granulated sugar	4 sugar cubes, crushed

/ *Christmas Pudding*

Plump the raisins and currants in lukewarm water until they are soft and drain them.

Combine the suet with the raisins and currants. Add the bread crumbs, flour, salt and sugar; then beat in the milk and the eggs.

Beat the mixture until thoroughly mixed and let it rest in the refrigerator overnight. The next morning, stir in the lemon juice and ¼ cup of the rum. Shape the dough into a ball and let it rest overnight once more.

The day after, add the chopped glacéed fruits, the nutmeg, cinnamon and allspice. Blend everything together, and put the pudding into a well-buttered 12-cup pudding mold. Let it rest in the refrigerator for 3 or 4 days.

Put a clean napkin or cloth over the pudding and fasten it to the mold by tying it firmly with string. Set the pudding mold into a large deep saucepan partially full of boiling water; the water should come three quarters of the way up the sides of the mold. Take care that the water does not reach the edge of the bowl, or it may seep into the pudding.

Cook the pudding for 5 to 6 hours, replenishing the boiling water as it evaporates during the cooking time.

When the pudding is ready, unmold it on a warm serving plate. At serving time, sprinkle it with the remaining rum, heated, and flame it. Serve the *crème anglaise* in a sauceboat.

1½ cups seedless golden raisins	6 eggs
1½ cups seedless dark raisins	Juice of 2 lemons
3 cups dried currants	¾ cup rum
1 cup beef suet, minced fine	1 cup glacéed fruits, finely chopped
2 cups fine dry bread crumbs	1 tablespoon grated nutmeg
2 cups sifted all-purpose flour	1 tablespoon ground cinnamon
1 teaspoon salt	1 teaspoon ground allspice
¾ cup sugar	3 cups Crème Anglaise (p. 672)
½ cup milk	

PUDDING RAPIDE / *Quick Christmas Pudding*

Soak the raisins in lukewarm water for several hours, or until they are softened, and drain them.

Combine the beef marrow with the sugar in a bowl and beat them together thoroughly. Beat in the eggs, one at a time, and then gradually add the flour, alternately with the milk. Add the raisins. Squeeze the bread crumbs dry and beat them, ¼ cup of the rum, the nutmeg and lemon rind into the mixture.

The batter should be well blended. Put it into a piece of clean linen or a triple thickness of cheesecloth, shape it into a ball, and tie it solidly with string. Cook it in a big pot full of boiling water for 4 hours; the water must be boiling before you put in the pudding. Turn the ball of dough at regular intervals so that it will cook on all sides.

After 4 hours, remove the pudding with a ladle, drain it well, take it out of its cloth, and cut it into slices. Place the slices on a serving dish, sprinkle them with the rest of the rum, heated, and flame the pudding.

3 cups seedless raisins or dried
  currants
1 cup beef marrow
⅓ cup sugar
6 eggs
4 cups sifted all-purpose flour

½ cup milk
1 cup fine dry bread crumbs,
  soaked in milk
¾ cup rum
1 tablespoon grated nutmeg
Grated rind of 1 lemon

Fruitcake I /

Soak the glacéed fruits, raisins and currants in the rum and vanilla for 1 hour, stirring occasionally. Drain the fruits, reserving the liquid.

Cream the softened butter with the sugar and then beat in the eggs, one at a time.

Sift together the flour and the baking powder, and add it alternately with the rum, a little of each at a time, to the butter and egg mixture, Fold in the drained fruits.

Butter and flour 2 loaf pans (5½ by 9½ inches) and then line the bottom and the longer sides with unglazed brown paper, allowing the paper to hang over the sides by about 4 inches. Butter the paper generously.

Pour the batter into the 2 pans and bake in a preheated 350° F. oven for about 1 hour. After the first half hour, fold the overhanging paper over the tops of the cakes so that they will not brown too much. After baking, allow the cakes to cool for 20 minutes before removing them from the pans.

1 cup mixed glacéed fruits, finely
  chopped
1 cup raisins
1 cup dried currants
1 cup rum
1 teaspoon vanilla extract
2 cups butter, softened

2½ cups superfine sugar
10 eggs
4½ cups sifted all-purpose
  flour
1 tablespoon double-acting baking
  powder

Note: This dough may also be baked in *baba* molds to make small individual cakes. The baking time should be decreased to about 25 minutes.

Fruitcake II /

Soak the lemon and orange rinds, the raisins and currants in the rum for 12 hours, stirring occasionally, and drain, reserving the rum.

Cream the softened butter with the sugar and then beat in the eggs, one at a time. Sift the flour with the baking powder and stir it into the other mixture alternately with the reserved rum, a little at a time, and blend thoroughly. Then stir in the drained fruits.

Butter and flour a loaf pan (5½ by 9½ inches) and then line the bottom and the longer sides with unglazed brown paper, allowing it to hang 4 inches over each side. Butter the paper generously.

Pour the batter into the pan and bake in a preheated 350° F. oven for about 1 hour. After the first half hour fold the overhanging paper over the top so that the cake will not brown too quickly. After baking allow the cake to cool for 20 minutes before removing from the pan.

2 teaspoons grated lemon rind
1 tablespoon grated orange rind
1 cup raisins
1 cup dried currants
¾ cup rum
½ cup butter, softened

1¼ cups superfine sugar
4 eggs
2¼ cups sifted all-purpose
flour
2 teaspoons double-acting baking
powder

CROISSANTS GLACÉS AUX CERISES / *Cherry Croissants*

Put ¾ cup of the flour in a bowl and make a well in the center. Mix the compressed yeast with ¼ cup of lukewarm water (80° to 90° F.), or use ⅓ cup of warmer water (105° to 115° F.) if using dry yeast, and pour the mixture into the well. Mix the flour into the yeast mixture to make a fairly soft dough and then knead the dough into a ball; set the ball to rise in a warm place until doubled in bulk.

Put the remaining flour on a baking board and make a well in the middle. Put the salt, sugar, milk and ¼ cup of the softened butter in it. Mix thoroughly and knead in the sponge. Shape the dough into a ball, put it in a bowl, and let it rest in the refrigerator overnight.

Soften the remaining butter slightly so that it has about the consistency of the dough and form it into a flat cake about 4 by 5 inches.

Roll out the dough on a floured pastry board into a rectangle about 15 inches long and 8 inches wide. Place the butter crosswise in the center of the dough. Fold the upper extending flap of dough over the butter, pressing the edges together firmly, and then fold the lower flap over the upper, forming an oblong about 5 by 8 inches. Again press all the edges together firmly so that the butter is securely enclosed. Turn the dough over with one of the shorter sides facing you. Roll it out into an oblong about 15 by 8 inches. Fold it again into thirds as you did when enclosing the butter, roll it out into an oblong again, again fold into thirds, and chill in the refrigerator for 30 minutes.

Each folding and rolling out of the dough is called a "turn." Make 2 more turns and chill again for 30 minutes.

Now cut the dough into halves and roll out each half into long strips about 5 inches wide and ⅛ inch thick. Cut the strips into triangles. Form each triangle into a *croissant* by rolling the widest side toward the opposite point and then curling the ends slightly toward each other.

Butter a baking sheet. Arrange the *croissants,* spaced well apart, on the baking sheet and brush them with the egg-yolk and milk mixture. Let them stand at room temperature for 30 minutes and bake in a preheated 475° F. oven for 10 to 12 minutes.

When the *croissants* are half done, put 2 or 3 cherry halves on top of each and finish baking.

Remove the *croissants* from the oven when they are golden brown, let them cool, and spread them with the royal frosting.

FOR 24 TO 36 CROISSANTS, DEPENDING ON SIZE:

4 cups sifted all-purpose flour
1 ounce compressed yeast, or 2
packages active dry yeast
2 teaspoons salt
2 tablespoons sugar
1 cup milk

1½ cups butter, softened
2 egg yolks, mixed with 2
tablespoons milk
1 cup glacéed cherries
1 double recipe Royal Frosting
(p. 669)

Frosted Caramel Croissants /

CROISSANTS GLACÉS AU CARAMEL

Proceed as in Cherry Croissants (above), but omit the cherries and glaze the *croissants* with a Caramel Glaze (p. 668), instead of the Royal Frosting.

Frosted Fruit Croissants /

CROISSANTS GLACÉS AUX FRUITS CONFITS

Proceed as in Cherry Croissants (above), but substitute mixed glacéed or preserved fruits such as oranges, apricots, prunes, peaches, pears, figs, etc., for the cherries. The fruits should be cut into small dice and soaked in rum. Use a Royal Frosting, as indicated, or a Liqueur-Flavored Frosting (p. 669).

Frosted Nut Croissants / CROISSANTS GLACÉS AUX NOIX

Proceed as in Cherry Croissants (above), but substitute 2 cups of nutmeats for the cherries. You may also lightly color the Royal Frosting with a little vegetable coloring.

Savarin / PÂTE À SAVARIN

Place ¾ cup of the flour in a bowl and make a well in the center. Mix the compressed yeast with ¼ cup of lukewarm water (80° to 90° F.), or use ⅓ cup of warmer water (105° to 115° F.) if using dry yeast, and pour the mixture into the well. Mix the flour into the yeast mixture to make a fairly soft dough and then knead it into a ball. This ball will act as a *levain* or sponge. Place the sponge in a bowl containing 3 cups of the lukewarm milk (80° to 90° F.). Set the bowl in a warm place until the sponge expands and rises to the surface of the milk; then drain it.

Place the remaining flour in a large bowl and beat the eggs into it, one at a time, beating well after each addition. Stir in the salt, the sugar, the remaining ⅓ cup of the milk and the melted butter. Mix together thoroughly and then knead in the drained sponge. Knead in the bowl for about 15 minutes until the dough is completely smooth and elastic. It should be quite soft and rather sticky. Allow the dough to rise in a warm place until it is doubled in bulk and then punch it down.

Butter a 6-cup ring mold and distribute the dough evenly in the mold. It should fill it about halfway. Place the mold in a warm place and allow the dough to rise for about 1 hour, until slightly puffed above the sides of the mold. Care should be taken not to let it rise too much, as the dough is delicate and can fall easily.

Bake on the middle level of a preheated 375° F. oven for about 30 minutes. Allow it to cool for 5 minutes until barely warm and then remove it from the mold to cool.

Meanwhile, prepare the sugar syrup: Put the cubed sugar and water in a saucepan and stir over low heat until the sugar is completely dissolved. Raise the heat and boil for about 5 minutes, or until a candy thermometer reads 230° F. Cool to lukewarm and stir in the rum.

Place the *savarin* in a shallow dish, prick the top all over with a fork, and pour some of the syrup over it. Let it stand for about 30 minutes, using more syrup and basting as necessary to soak the *savarin* thoroughly. Glaze the top lightly with the apricot jam purée. Remove any excess syrup in the dish with a bulb baster before serving.

2 cups sifted all-purpose flour	2 tablespoons superfine sugar
1 ounce compressed yeast, or 2 packages active dry yeast	½ cup butter, melted
	½ pound cubed sugar
3⅓ cups lukewarm milk	1 cup water
4 eggs	½ cup rum
1 teaspoon salt	½ cup apricot jam, puréed

SAVARIN AUX CERISES / *Cherry Savarin*

Proceed as for Savarin (above), but substitute cherry brandy for the rum in the sugar syrup and scatter 1 cup of glacéed cherries over the apricot glaze.

/ *Babas au Rhum*

Prepare the *savarin* dough and allow it to rise in a bowl until doubled in bulk. Distribute the dough evenly in 12 buttered *baba* molds or in 12 muffin cups. They should be about half filled. Allow them to rise again in a warm place until the dough is slightly puffed over the edges of the molds. Bake immediately in a preheated 375° F. oven for about 15 minutes, or until the tops are lightly browned. Remove the *babas* from the molds and allow them to cool to lukewarm.

To make the syrup: Put the cubed sugar and the water into a saucepan. Stir over low heat until the sugar is completely dissolved. Raise the heat and boil for 5 to 10 minutes, or until a candy thermometer reads 235° F. Let it cool to lukewarm and stir in the rum.

Prick the tips of the lukewarm *babas* with a fork and put them fairly close together in a shallow dish. Pour the syrup over them and let them stand for 30 minutes, basting occasionally. Spread a little of the apricot jam on the top of each and transfer them to a serving dish.

1 recipe Savarin dough (p. 702)	½ cup rum
½ pound cubed sugar, crushed	½ cup thick apricot jam, puréed
1 cup water	

Note: Kirsch may be substituted for the rum, if desired.

STRUDEL AUX POMMES / *Apple Strudel*

Put the flour on a pastry board, make a well in the center, and pour in the oil, salt, eggs, lemon juice and enough of the water to make a fairly soft dough. Knead until the dough is smooth.

Shape the dough into a ball and let it rest for 30 to 40 minutes.

Spread a clean tablecloth over a table (it should be at least 30 inches square) and rub flour evenly into the cloth. Put the ball of dough in the middle of the floured cloth. With a lightly floured rolling pin, roll the dough in all directions to make as perfect a round as possible. Lift the dough and put the backs of your hands under it. With very gentle hand-over-hand movements, stretch the dough in all directions until it is almost paper thin and it extends to the edges of the table. Be careful not to tear the dough. If it becomes too dry before it is sufficiently stretched, brush it very lightly with oil. Cut off the thick edges with scissors.

Prepare the filling: Sauté the bread crumbs in the butter until golden and spread them out on the dough. Peel, core, and slice the apples very thinly and spread them over the bread crumbs. Sprinkle with the sugar, the cinnamon and the raisins. Keep the edges free of the filling. Blend together the egg yolk and the melted butter, and paint a little of it on the edges of the pastry.

Roll up the dough by lifting the tablecloth so that the strudel rolls over and over itself. Paint the whole strudel with the remaining egg-yolk and butter mixture and place it on a buttered baking sheet.

Bake the strudel in a preheated 350° F. oven for about 50 minutes, or until golden brown. Sprinkle immediately with the confectioners' sugar.

For the strudel dough:	For the filling:
4 cups sifted all-purpose flour	2 cups fine dry bread crumbs
½ cup peanut oil	½ cup butter
1 teaspoon salt	6 to 8 tart cooking apples
2 eggs	1¼ cups sugar
Juice of 1 lemon	2 teaspoons ground cinnamon
¾ to 1 cup warm water	1 cup seedless raisins, plumped in ½ cup rum
	1 egg yolk
	2 tablespoons butter, melted
	½ cup confectioners' sugar

Cream Strudel / STRUDEL À LA CRÈME

Prepare a strudel dough, following the directions for Apple Strudel (above), and spread it with the following cream filling:

Beat the butter until it is light and fluffy. Beat in the sugar, egg yolks, lemon rind and juice, *crème fraîche,* bread crumbs and seedless raisins. Beat the egg whites until very stiff and fold them into the mixture.

Roll up the strudel and bake it in a preheated 350° F. oven for about 50 minutes.

As it is baking, prepare a basting cream: Combine the milk, whole eggs and extra egg yolks, sugar and vanilla in the top part of a double boiler, and beat them together energetically.

Pour half of this cream over the strudel after it has baked for 25 minutes. Baste once or twice more as it finishes baking. Cook the remaining cream over simmering water, stirring constantly with a wooden spoon, until it is slightly thickened.

When the strudel is baked, serve it on a warm platter, and pour the thickened cream over it.

The Prior's Chocolate Cake
Gâteau au Chocolat du Prieur

The Prior's Chocolate Cake

Gâteau au Chocolat du Prieur

BAKE THE CHOCOLATE *génoise* batter in 2 buttered and floured 9-inch-square cake pans in a preheated 350° F. oven for about 30 minutes.

Prepare the coffee and the chocolate buttercreams.

When the cake is baked, unmold the layers on a cake rack and let them cool. Cut each layer into 3 very thin slices and spread the slices alternately with the 2 buttercreams. Stack the slices and frost the cake with chocolate frosting. Refrigerate it until serving time.

1 recipe Chocolate Génoise (p. 683)
1½ cups Coffee Buttercream (p. 675)
1½ cups Chocolate Buttercream (p. 675), flavored with 2
    tablespoons rum
2 cups Chocolate Frosting (p. 669)

Cherry Génoise Montmorency

Génoise aux Cerises de Montmorency

Cherry Génoise Montmorency

Génoise aux Cerises de Montmorency

PREPARE AND BAKE a *génoise* in 2 round 9-inch layer-cake pans. Cool the layers on a cake rack.

Make the buttercream and the Italian meringue.

Spread one layer with the buttercream, arrange the glacéed cherries over it, and spread a little of the Italian meringue on top. Top with the other layer. Frost the whole cake with the remaining Italian meringue and garnish with the candied violets.

1 recipe Génoise (p. 683)
1 cup Liqueur-Flavored Buttercream (p. 675),
  made with kirsch
1 recipe Italian Meringue (p. 694)
2 cups glacéed cherries
½ cup candied violets

Charlotte à la Valentin

Charlotte à la Valentin

PUT THE RASPBERRY preserves in a heavy saucepan and cook over low heat, stirring constantly, for about 20 minutes, or until they are very thick. Make a round cake, about 7 inches in diameter, by over-lapping layers of ladyfingers, sticking them together with the preserves. Leave an empty space in the center and pour some of the preserves carefully into this space. Top with a few ladyfingers and then coat the cake with the remaining preserves.

Put the cake on a gold-foil doilie on a small round cake tin. Beat the egg whites and gradually add the sugar. Beat until very stiff. Pipe the meringue in decorative swirls onto the top of the cake and around the bottom. Bake it in a preheated 500° F. oven just long enough to turn the meringue barely golden. Remove from the oven, cool, and chill it.

For 6 persons:

3 cups raspberry preserves
3 dozen (approximately) Ladyfingers (p. 688)
4 egg whites
¾ cup superfine sugar

The Queen of Sheba's Mocha Cake
Moka de la Reine de Saba

The Queen of Sheba's Mocha Cake
Moka de la Reine de Saba

BAKE THE *génoise* batter in 2 buttered and floured 9-inch round lay-er-cake pans in a preheated 350° F. oven for about 30 minutes. Or, for a more decorative effect, bake one of the layers in a 9-inch pan with the bottom molded in a pattern (see illustration).

Unmold the layers on a cake rack and let them cool. Cut each hori-zontally into 2 slices and spread the slices with coffee buttercream. Frost the cake on all sides with coffee frosting and decorate the top with glacéed cherries and angelica cut into the shape of leaves. Sprin-kle the almonds around the base of the cake. Refrigerate it until serv-ing time.

1 recipe Génoise (p. 683)
2 cups Coffee Buttercream (p. 675)
2 cups Coffee Frosting (p. 669)
¼ cup glacéed cherries
¼ cup green angelica leaves
⅔ cup toasted slivered blanched almonds

Strawberry Génoise Lucullus

Génoise aux Fraises Lucullus

Strawberry Génoise Lucullus

Génoise aux Fraises Lucullus

BAKE 2 ROUND 9-inch layers of *génoise,* unmold the layers on a cake rack, and allow them to cool.

Purée the raspberries in a blender or through a food mill and put them in a saucepan with the sugar and two thirds of the strawberries. Bring slowly to a boil and simmer for 3 minutes; the strawberries should retain their shape. Drain the fruit, reserving the juice, and cool.

Prepare the royal frosting.

Put the cooled strawberries between the 2 layers and then frost the top and the sides of the cake with the royal icing. Decorate with the uncooked strawberries and dribble the reserved fruit juice over the cake.

1 recipe Génoise (p. 683)
2 cups raspberries
½ cup superfine sugar
1 quart small fresh strawberries
2 cups Royal Frosting (p. 669)

Venetian Chestnut Gâteau

Gâteau de Marrons à la Vénitienne

Venetian Chestnut Gâteau

Gâteau de Marrons à la Vénitienne

COOL THE *crème anglaise*. Prepare the chestnut cream, using only 1 cup of *crème anglaise* so that it will be very thick. Mix both creams together and chill. The mixture must be thick enough to hold its shape when cold. Turn it out onto a round ovenproof serving platter and form it into a cake shape about 10 inches in diameter.

Prepare a meringue by beating the egg whites until they form soft peaks, gradually adding the sugar, and continuing the beating until they form stiff peaks. Pipe the meringue over the cake in thick decorative wedges so that it is very generously covered. Sprinkle the sides with the slivered almonds. Place the dish on a board and bake in a 500° F. oven for about 4 minutes, or until the meringue is golden brown.

This will serve 12 people.

1 recipe Crème Anglaise (p. 672), made with 1 additional egg yolk
1 recipe Chestnut Cream (p. 679)
8 egg whites
2½ cups sugar
1 cup slivered blanched almonds

Grandmother Chanart's Crêpes au Gratin

Crêpes Gratinées de Grand-Mère Chanart

Grandmother Chanart's Crêpes au Gratin

Crêpes Gratinées de Grand-Mère Chanart

THIS IS NOT a dessert, but an entrée.

Prepare the *crêpe* batter and fry 12 large *crêpes* about 8 inches in diameter. Keep them warm.

Make the *béchamel*. Beat together the egg yolks and the *crème fraîche* and incorporate the mixture in the *béchamel*, beating vigorously. Season with the nutmeg and the cayenne. Cut the ham and the sliced Gruyère into thin julienne strips and add about three quarters of them to the *béchamel*. Spoon a little of the sauce on each *crêpe* and roll it up. Place the *crêpes* side by side in 1 large or 2 smaller buttered shallow baking dishes, and spoon the remaining *béchamel* over them. Sprinkle with the grated cheese and the melted butter. Then sprinkle the remaining strips of ham and cheese over the top. Bake in a preheated 400° F. oven for about 10 minutes. Serve very hot.

For 4 persons:

1 recipe Crêpes (p. 740)
3 cups Sauce Béchamel
    (p. 761)
2 egg yolks
¼ cup Crème Fraîche
    (p. 666)
¼ teaspoon grated nutmeg

Pinch of cayenne pepper
¼ pound cooked ham,
    sliced
¼ pound Gruyère cheese,
    sliced
1 cup grated Gruyère
¼ cup butter, melted

Crêpes Flambées au Grand Marnier

Crêpes Flambées au Grand Marnier

MAKE ABOUT 24 *crêpes*, as described on page 740. Sprinkle them with sugar, fold them into quarters, and put them into a chafing dish. Sprinkle them generously with the Grand Marnier. Heat the *crêpes* and flame them.

For 6 persons:

1 recipe Crêpes (p. 740)
¼ cup sugar
¾ cup Grand Marnier

Note: You may add the grated rind of 1 or 2 oranges to the *crêpe* batter to accentuate the orange flavor.

duce the heat to 350° F. and bake for about 25 minutes longer. When done, sprinkle with confectioners' sugar.

4 tart cooking apples	**½ recipe Puff Paste (p. 715)**
½ cup water	**1 egg yolk, beaten**
¼ cup sugar	**¼ cup confectioners' sugar**
1 piece of vanilla bean, 4 inches long	

Frangipane Dartois / DARTOIS À LA FRANGIPANE

Proceed as in Dartois with Apples (above), but substitute 1½ cups of Frangipane Cream (p. 678) for the apple compote.

Jam Dartois / DARTOIS AUX CONFITURES

Proceed as in Dartois with Apples (above), but substitute 1 cup of any desired jam for the apple compote.

Gâteau Pithiviers /

Roll out the puff paste to the thickness of ⅛ inch. Cut it into 2 equal rounds, about 9 inches in diameter. Put one of the rounds on a buttered and floured baking sheet.

Spread the almond custard on the puff-paste round on the baking sheet, keeping it about 1 inch from the edge. Brush the edge with water. Top the custard with the second puff-paste round and pinch the edges of the 2 rounds together firmly.

Brush the top of the cake with the beaten egg yolk. Using a sharp knife, score the top with arc-lines radiating from the center. Bake the cake in a preheated 400° F. oven for 20 minutes. Reduce heat to 325° F. and bake about 20 minutes longer.

½ recipe Puff Paste (p. 715)	**1 egg yolk**
1½ cups Almond Custard for Pithiviers (p. 680)	

Mille-Feuilles au Kirsch / MILLE-FEUILLES AU KIRSCH GLACÉ

Roll out the puff paste on a floured pastry board to a thickness of about ⅛ inch. Cut it into rectangles about 2 inches wide and 4 inches long. Put them on buttered baking sheets and cook them in a preheated 450° F. oven for about 12 minutes. Reduce heat to 350° F. and bake for 15 minutes longer.

Cool them on a cake rack. Put 3 rectangles together with kirsch-flavored *crème pâtissière*, sandwich fashion, and repeat until all are used.

Glaze them with the kirsch frosting.

For the dough:
>   4 cups sifted all-purpose
>   flour
> ½ cup peanut oil
> 1 teaspoon salt
> 2 eggs
>   Juice of 1 lemon
> ¾ to 1 cup warm water

For the filling:
> 1 cup butter, softened
> 1¼ cups sugar
> 7 eggs, separated
>   Grated rind and juice of 1
>   lemon
> 1¼ cups Crème Fraîche
>   (p. 666)
> 1 cup fine dry bread crumbs
> ½ cup seedless raisins,
>   plumped in rum

For the basting cream:
> 4 cups milk
> 2 whole eggs
> 3 extra egg yolks
> ½ cup sugar
> 1 teaspoon vanilla extract

CORNETS À LA CRÈME / *Cream Horns*

To successfully make pastry horns, or *cornets,* it is necessary to have horn molds. These are available in kitchen equipment shops which specialize in French or other European utensils.

Roll out the puff paste on a floured pastry board to a thickness of about ⅛ inch. Cut it into very long strips about ¾ inch wide and roll the strips around 12 buttered horn molds so that they slightly overlap. Chill for several hours or freeze completely. Brush them with the beaten egg yolk and put the horn molds on a buttered baking sheet. Bake the horns in a preheated 400° F. oven for about 15 minutes.

When they are ready, slide the horns off the molds and let them cool before filling them with the cream.

As they are cooling, beat the egg whites until very stiff and fold them into the *crème pâtissière.* Fill a pastry bag fitted with a large round tube with the pastry cream and pipe it into the baked horns.

> 1 recipe Puff Paste (p. 715)   3 egg whites
> 2 egg yolks, beaten
> 2½ cups Crème Pâtissière
>   (p. 676)

DARTOIS AUX POMMES / *Dartois with Apples*

Peel and core the apples and cut them into slices. Cook the slices with the water, sugar and vanilla in a saucepan over fairly low heat for about 10 minutes. They should make a very thick compote.

Divide the puff paste into 2 equal parts and roll each into a 9-inch round, about ⅛ inch thick.

Put the first round on a buttered and floured baking sheet. Spread the apple compote over it and cover it with the second puff-paste round. Press the edges together lightly so that the compote will not escape during the baking. Brush the top with the beaten egg yolk and bake the cake in a preheated 450° F. oven for 10 minutes. Re-

FOR ABOUT 6 MILLE-FEUILLES:

½ recipe Puff Paste (p. 715)
1½ cups Liqueur-Flavored Crème
Pâtissière (p. 678), made
with kirsch

1 cup Liqueur-Flavored Frosting
(p. 669), made with Kirsch

MILLE-FEUILLES AU CAFÉ / *Coffee Mille-Feuilles*

Proceed as in Mille-Feuilles au Kirsch (above), but substitute Coffee Crème Pâtissière (p. 677), and Coffee Frosting (p. 669), for the kirsch-flavored ones.

MILLE-FEUILLES AUX CONFITURES / *Jam Mille-Feuilles*

Proceed as in Mille-Feuilles au Kirsch (above), but substitute a generous quantity of any desired jam for the kirsch-flavored *crème pâtissière,* and sprinkle the tops with confectioners' sugar instead of frosting them.

/ *Strawberry or Raspberry Mille-Feuilles*
MILLE-FEUILLES AUX FRAISES OU AUX FRAMBOISES

Proceed as in Mille-Feuilles au Kirsch (above), but instead of using kirsch-flavored *crème pâtissière,* spread 1 layer of each cake with strawberry or raspberry jam and the other with Crème Chantilly (p. 672). You'll need about ½ cup of strawberry jam and about 1 cup of the *crème.* Do not frost the tops, but sprinkle with confectioners' sugar.

Note: You can make *mille-feuilles* cakes filled in any desired way with creams or fruit jams. The tops may be finished as you like with a frosting, a meringue, or confectioners' sugar.

PALMIERS / *Palm Leaves*

Step by step illustrated instructions are on pages 708 and 709.

For about 2 dozen palm leaves, roll out ½ recipe of Puff Paste (p. 715) into a long rectangle ⅛ inch thick.

Brush the whole surface with a little water. Fold the 2 long edges of the dough lengthwise toward the center so that they just touch each other. Brush again with water and fold the 2 edges again toward the center, as before. Repeat the process a third time to obtain a long thin roll of folded-over puff paste. Cut the roll into ¼-inch slices; brush each slice with beaten egg yolk and sprinkle lightly with sugar. Place the slices on a buttered and floured baking sheet and bake in a preheated 400° F. oven for about 15 minutes.

PALM LEAVES

LES PALMIERS

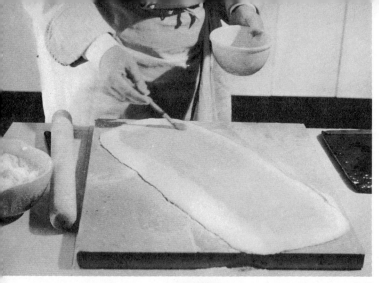

Roll out the puff paste into a rectangle and brush it with water.

Fold the long sides toward the center so that the edges come together along the whole length.

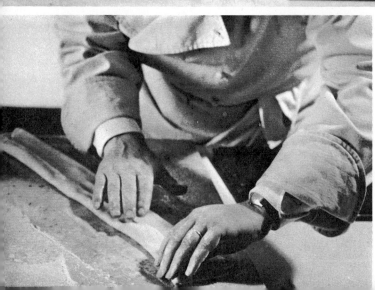

Don't squash the pastry, but press it together gently with the fingertips.

Brush it again with water. This light moistening helps the folds to stick together.

Again fold the two sides together lengthwise. Notice the shape of the folded pastry.

Press the two sides together, but gently. Cut the strip of pastry into slices. Brush the slices with egg yolk so they will become golden brown as they cook. Bake them on a buttered and floured baking sheet.

Braids | TRESSES

This recipe utilizes leftover puff-paste scraps.

Roll out any leftover puff paste and cut it into long strips about 4 inches wide. Leave a 1-inch edge on the end of each strip and cut the remaining length into narrow strips about ¾ inch wide. Braid the strips loosely and brush them with beaten egg yolk. Bake them on a buttered and floured baking sheet in a preheated 400° F. oven for about 15 minutes.

When they are half done, sprinkle them with crushed sugar lumps. Finish baking the braids until they are golden brown.

Apple Turnovers | CHAUSSON AUX POMMES

Roll out the puff paste about ⅛ inch thick and from it cut out 4-inch rounds (or make them smaller, if you wish). Moisten the edge of each round with water. Prepare a thick apple compote with the apples, water, granulated sugar and vanilla bean, as described on page 667. Spread half of each round with a little of the compote and fold the other half over. Pinch the edges together to keep them tightly closed. Put the turnovers on a buttered baking sheet and brush the tops with beaten egg yolks. Bake them in a preheated 400° F. oven for 12 to 15 minutes. Sprinkle them with confectioners' sugar after removing them from the oven.

FOR ABOUT 12 TURNOVERS:

½ recipe Puff Paste (p. 715)
4 tart cooking apples
½ cup water
¼ cup granulated sugar

1 piece of vanilla bean, 4 inches long
2 egg yolks, beaten
½ cup confectioners' sugar

Pâte à Choux |

Heat the milk or water in a saucepan, and let the butter, salt and sugar melt in it. Bring to a boil and add the flour all at once.

Stir briskly with a wooden spoon, until the mixture comes away from the sides of the pan and is perfectly smooth. Turn the paste out into a bowl and let it cool for 15 minutes.

Add the eggs, two at a time, and beat until the mixture is smooth and glossy after each addition. The finished batter should be fairly solid and just able to hold its own shape. The drier the paste, the better it will absorb the eggs; the more eggs you use, the better the cream puffs will puff up during baking.

FOR 12 TO 16 LARGE CREAM PUFFS, THE SAME NUMBER OF ÉCLAIRS, OR ABOUT 3 DOZEN PROFITEROLES:

1 cup milk or water
½ cup butter
1 teaspoon salt
1 tablespoon sugar

1¾ cups sifted all-purpose flour
6 to 7 eggs

To bake fairly large cream puffs:

Fill a pastry bag fitted with a ¾-inch round tube and squeeze out mounds about 2 inches in diameter, spaced about 2 inches apart, onto an ungreased baking sheet. Use 2 baking sheets if necessary, rather than spacing the mounds too closely together. Bake in a preheated 400° F. oven for 20 minutes, reduce the heat to 375° F., and bake for 10 minutes longer. Remove the puffs from the oven and make a slit in the side of each puff to allow the steam to escape. Return them to a turned-off oven with the door slightly ajar for another 10 minutes to dry. Allow them to cool completely before filling.

To bake *éclairs:*

Fill a pastry bag fitted with a ½-inch round tube and squeeze out strips 1 inch wide and 4 inches long onto the baking sheet. Bake and dry in the same manner as cream puffs.

To bake *profiteroles:*

Fill a pastry bag fitted with a ½-inch plain round or star tube and squeeze out small mounds about 1 inch in diameter spaced 2 inches apart on the baking sheet. Bake and dry in the same manner as cream puffs, but reduce the baking time to 20 minutes at 400° F.

/ Cream Puffs Filled with Crème Pâtissière

CHOUX À LA CRÈME PÂTISSIÈRE

Prepare and bake about a dozen cream puffs, as described above.

Cool the cream puffs on cake racks. With a sharp knife, make a hole into the side of each. Fill a pastry bag fitted with a small round tube with the *crème pâtissière*. Fill the cream puffs with the *crème* and sprinkle with confectioners' sugar.

1 recipe Pâte à Choux (above), made with 1 cup water	2 cups Crème Pâtissière (p. 676) ½ cup confectioners' sugar

/ Cream Puffs Filled with Chestnut Cream

CHOUX À LA CRÈME AUX MARRONS

Proceed as in the preceding recipe, but substitute Chestnut Cream (p. 679) for the *crème pâtissière*.

Note: Cream puffs may be filled with Chocolate or Coffee Crème Pâtissière (p. 677), or Crème Chantilly (p. 672).

ÉCLAIRS AU CHOCOLAT / Chocolate Éclairs

Prepare and bake about a dozen *éclairs* as described in the recipe for *pâte à choux*.

Cool the *éclairs* on cake racks. Cut them lengthwise into halves and fill them with chocolate *crème pâtissière*. Frost the top with warm chocolate frosting.

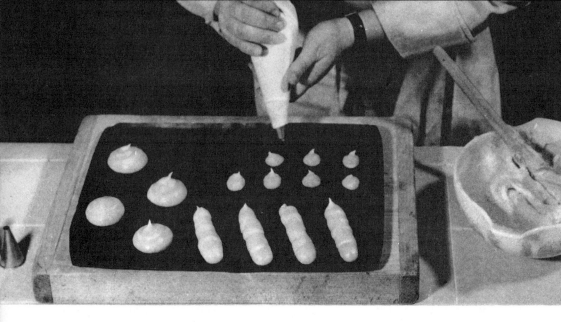

CREAM PUFFS, ÉCLAIRS AND PROFITEROLES

CHOUX, ÉCLAIRS ET PROFITEROLES

Use a pastry bag to squeeze out the cream puffs, éclairs *and* profiteroles. Profiteroles ar[...] *tiny cream puffs.*

Above at the left, *notice that tubes of various sizes are adaptable to the pastry bag. A[...]* the right *the bowl of smooth rich batter.*

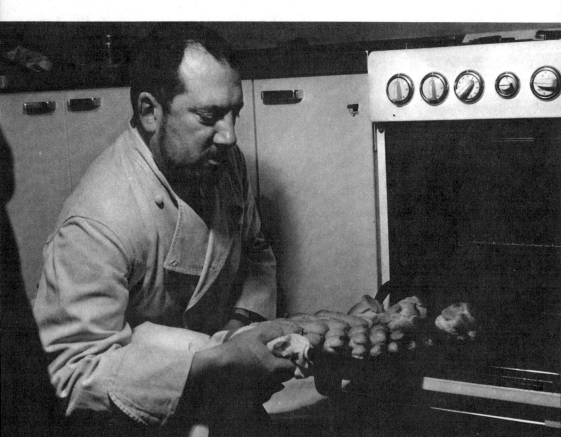

1 recipe Pâte à Choux (p. 710),
made with 1 cup water
2 cups Chocolate Crème
Pâtissière (p. 677)

1 cup Chocolate Frosting
(p. 669)

ÉCLAIRS AU CAFÉ GLACÉS / *Coffee Éclairs*

Proceed as in Chocolate Éclairs (above), but substitute 2 cups of Coffee Crème
Pâtissière (p. 677) and Coffee Frosting (p. 669) for the chocolate-flavored ones.

PROFITEROLES AU CARAMEL / *Caramel Profiteroles*

Prepare and bake about 36 *profiteroles* as described in the recipe for Pâte à
Choux (p. 710).

Profiteroles may be filled with any of the fillings suggested for cream puffs. Or
else, they may be unfilled and plunged into a Caramel Glaze (p. 668). Only about 1
cup of glaze will be needed.

PROFITEROLES AU CHOCOLAT / *Chocolate Profiteroles*

Prepare and bake about 36 *profiteroles* as described in the recipe for Pâte à
Choux (p. 710), and fill them with Crème Pâtissière (p. 676), or Crème Chantilly (p.
672). About 2 cups of either *crème* will be needed.

Just before serving time, put the *profiteroles* into a deep bowl and cover them
with about 2 cups of hot Chocolate Sauce (p. 670). Serve immediately.

TARTS AND TARTLETS

Tartes et Tartelettes

All of the tarts in this section will make 8 normal servings.

/ *Pâte Brisée*

Place the flour in a large bowl and make a well in the center. Put the whole egg,
the salt, cream and butter into it. Gradually blend the flour into the other ingredients.
Knead the pastry until smooth. Chill in the refrigerator for 2 hours before rolling out.

Tartlet shells, as well as *barquettes* or other small pastry shells, generally require
more handling than large tart shells, and hence they should be made firmer by substituting water for the heavy cream and by adding 1 additional egg white to the other
ingredients.

SUFFICIENT PASTRY FOR ONE 9-INCH TART WITH A LATTICE TOP, OR ABOUT 8 TART-LETS, 3-INCH SIZE:

2 cups sifted all-purpose flour	3 tablespoons heavy cream, or
1 whole egg	water (for tartlets)
1 extra egg white (for tartlets)	⅔ cup sweet butter
½ teaspoon salt	

Pâte à Sablé /

Warm a bowl slightly over low heat. Put in the softened butter and stir in the sugar and the salt, blending thoroughly. Gradually stir in the flour, mixing well after each addition so that it will be completely absorbed. Blend in the eggs and knead the pastry thoroughly. Chill in the refrigerator for 2 hours before rolling out.

FOR ONE 9-INCH TART WITH A LATTICE TOP, OR ABOUT 8 TARTLETS, 3-INCH SIZE:

½ cup butter, softened	2 cups sifted all-purpose flour
¼ cup superfine sugar	2 eggs
½ teaspoon salt	

Cinnamon Sablé Pastry / PÂTE À SABLÉ À LA CANNELLE

Proceed as above, but add ½ teaspoon of ground cinnamon when adding the flour.

BAKING DIRECTIONS FOR PÂTE BRISÉE OR PÂTE À SABLÉ

To Bake an Unfilled Tart:

The pastry is easier to handle if well chilled before rolling out; then roll it out between 2 sheets of wax paper.

Using two thirds of the pastry, reserving the remainder for a lattice topping, roll it out into a round and to a thickness of slightly less than ¼ inch. It should be slightly larger than the flan ring or tart pan which you are using. Remove the top layer of wax paper, invert the pastry over the tart pan, or the flan ring placed on a baking sheet, and peel off the other piece of wax paper. With the fingers fit the pastry into the pan, leaving it slightly thicker at the top edge. Trim off excess pastry neatly and then make a decorative edge with the blunt end of a knife, with the fingers, or in any desired manner.

Freeze the pastry thoroughly before baking. The freezing will help keep the sides from falling during the baking, particularly when using a flan ring or a tart pan with straight sides.

Prick the bottom of the unbaked pastry several times with a fork. Bake on the middle level of a preheated 350° F. oven for about 18 minutes for a partially baked shell, or about 25 minutes for a completely baked shell. During the first 10 minutes of baking, prick the bottom again with a fork if the pastry tends to bubble and, if the sides fall slightly, simply push them back up with the back of a fork or spoon. Cool the shell before removing it from the pan or flan ring. Great care must be taken in removing the shell from a tart pan as the pastry is extremely delicate and will break easily. Hence it is considerably easier to use a flan ring placed on a baking sheet, if a free-standing tart is desired.

Alternate Method:

If there is insufficient time to freeze the unbaked shell, it may be lined with a lightweight foil and filled with dried peas or beans or uncooked rice. The foil should extend about 2 inches above the edge of the shell for easy removal. This weight will keep the sides from falling and the bottom from puffing up. Bake the pastry as described above, except remove the foil and dried beans immediately after the pastry is set and when there is no longer any danger of the sides falling. This will usually take about 10 minutes. After removing the beans, prick the bottom with a fork and then complete the baking as described above.

To Bake Unfilled Tartlets:

Proceed generally as in baking pastry for a large tart. Use all of the pastry, unless a lattice topping is desired. The unbaked tartlets may be frozen or filled with dried beans, whichever is more convenient. Since tartlet pans have sloping sides, an even simpler way of keeping the pastry sides from falling during the baking process is to press a second buttered tartlet mold lightly down into the one lined with the pastry; put a few dried beans into the mold to weight it slightly. Tartlets will take slightly less time than a large tart to bake completely, 15 to 18 minutes for a completely baked shell. Hence the foil or second tartlet-mold lining should be removed after about 8 minutes.

Note: Since tartlet shells are always removed from their molds before serving, and thus require considerable handling, it is recommended that water be substituted for the heavy cream in the ingredients for *pâte brisée* in order to make the dough somewhat less fragile. Also, 1 additional egg white may be mixed with the pastry for greater firmness.

To Bake Filled Tarts or Tartlets:

Line a tart pan, flan ring, or tartlet molds with pastry as described above. If possible, freeze the shaped pastry before baking, or chill thoroughly. Fill with any desired filling and bake on the lowest rack of a preheated 350° F. oven. Fruit tarts should be baked for 1 hour to 1 hour and 15 minutes, or until the filling bubbles and the pastry is lightly browned. Fruit tartlets will take less time, 35 to 45 minutes. Custard fillings will require 25 to 30 minutes; bake just until the filling is set and the pastry lightly browned.

PÂTE FEUILLETÉE / *Puff Paste*

Allow ¼ cup of the butter to stand at room temperature until quite soft. Knead the remaining cold butter until it is smooth, waxy, and free of excess water. If it becomes very soft during this process, chill it briefly in the refrigerator. It is important that this portion of the butter be neither ice cold and hard nor really soft. It should have roughly the same consistency as the dough.

Blend the ¼ cup of softened butter with the flour in a bowl until it is evenly distributed. Turn the flour out onto a pastry board and make a well in the center. Put the salt and cold water into the well and blend them with the flour until a medium-firm dough is formed. Knead the dough thoroughly for about 15 minutes, until it becomes very soft and elastic. If the room temperature is above 70° F., chill the dough in the refrigerator for 15 minutes.

Roll out the dough, preferably on a well-floured pastry cloth, into an oblong roughly 15 inches long and 8 inches wide. Form the kneaded butter into a flat cake about 5 by 4 inches and place it crosswise in the center of the dough. Fold the upper extending flap of dough over the butter, pressing the edges together firmly, and then fold the lower flap over the upper, forming an oblong about 5 by 8 inches. Again press all the edges together firmly so that the butter is securely enclosed. Turn the dough over with one of the shorter sides facing you and roll it out into an oblong abut 15 by 8 inches. Fold it again into thirds in the same manner used when the butter was enclosed; roll it out into an oblong, again fold into thirds, and chill in the refrigerator for 30 minutes.

Each folding and rolling out of the dough is called a "turn." Make 2 more turns and chill again for 30 minutes. Repeat this operation twice more, making 8 turns in all.

It is very important that the butter not break through the dough at any time during the rolling out.

It is extremely difficult to make puff paste when the room temperature is much above 80° F., since the butter softens too quickly and is likely to break through the dough. It is helpful in warm weather if not only the flour and butter are somewhat chilled, but also the rolling pin, pastry board and cloth.

SUFFICIENT FOR TWO 9-INCH TARTS* OR ABOUT 2 DOZEN 3-INCH TARTLETS:

2 cups sweet butter	**1 teaspoon salt**
4 cups sifted all-purpose flour	**1¼ cups cold water**

Baking Directions:

Roll out the prepared puff paste about ⅛ inch thick and into rounds slightly larger than the tart pan or tartlet molds. Line the inside of the tart pan or the backs of the tartlet molds with the pastry. Chill thoroughly or, if possible, freeze the shaped pastry. Bake in a preheated 450° F. oven for 10 minutes. Reduce heat to 350° F. and bake for 15 to 20 minutes longer for a large tart shell, or 10 to 15 minutes longer for individual tartlet shells.

*Puff paste is an elastic pastry and it is difficult for some cooks to gauge the thickness of rolled-out pastry with absolute accuracy. Thus, the recipe above is somewhat generous for two 9-inch tarts, but any leftover scraps can always be put to good use.

EDITORS' NOTE: *Puff paste may be used for tart and tartlet shells, as indeed the French frequently do. Our inclination, however, is always to prebake the shell so that the puff paste will rise to its full flaky glory; if a filling is placed on top of puff paste before baking it, it will not rise properly and the bottom at least will tend to be soggy. It should also be noted that baked puff paste will not retain its prebaked shape as well as* pâte brisée *or* pâte à sablé; *that is, the sides of a tart shell will tend to fall during the baking. A pie pan with sloping sides will work better than a tart pan with straight sides, and freezing the shaped pastry before baking will also help. Another, slightly more complicated method, but one that will give splendid results, is to cut out a 9-inch round of puff paste about ⅛ inch thick, place it on a baking sheet, moisten the outer edge with water, and then build up 2 or 3 layers of very narrow strips of puff paste around the edge to serve as sides; moisten each strip with water before placing another on top, and be careful that the strips lie flat and are not twisted as they are placed.*

It is also recommended when using puff paste for tartlet shells that rounds of the pastry be fitted over the backs of the tartlet molds and that they then be baked upside down on a baking sheet. While it is possible to prebake a puff-paste shell by lining it with dried peas or beans, and indeed M. Oliver suggests this method for certain hors-d'oeuvre, it is better to bake these small pastry shells upside down, because the weight of the dried legumes keeps the pastry from rising properly.

If any scraps are left over, make Braids (710), or roll out the scraps, cut them into any desired shapes, brush with beaten egg yolk, sprinkle with cinnamon and sugar, and bake in a preheated 400° F. oven for 15 minutes. These make delicious little tea cookies.

Whenever rolling out leftover puff-paste pieces, always try to keep the pieces from turning sideways, that is, keep the pieces flat on the board as they were originally rolled out. This allows the pastry to rise up as it should and not spread sideways during the baking.

Puff paste freezes very well. Wrap it in an airtight, plastic container. Thaw before rolling out according to recipe directions.

Halving a puff-paste recipe:
  Some of the recipes that follow call for ½ recipe of puff paste. Depending on the recipe, there might be some scraps of puff paste left over. Use them for braids or for tea cookies, as above.

BOUCHÉES OU VOL-AU-VENTS / *Patty Shells*

Roll out puff paste to a thickness of ¼ inch and from it cut 2 rounds of any desired diameter. Place one of the rounds on a baking sheet lightly moistened with water. On the other round cut an inner circle with a very sharp knife, using an appropriately sized round pan as a guide; on large rounds of pastry this inner circle should be about 1 inch from the edge, on smaller ones it should be about ½ inch from the edge. Moisten with water the outside circumference of the round of pastry on the baking sheet and then place the second round on top. Brush the top with beaten egg or with an egg yolk diluted with 1 or 2 tablespoons of milk, but be careful not to let the egg drip down the sides of the pastry, as this will impair its rising. Bake in a preheated 450° F. oven for 10 minutes, reduce the heat to 350° F., and bake for about 20 minutes longer for a large patty shell, or about 15 minutes longer for a small one. Remove from the oven and carefully take out the inner top circle of pastry. You may at this point scoop out a little of the dough from the center of the shell which looks undercooked, being very careful not to break through to the bottom; this isn't really necessary, but it does make slightly more room for whatever filling you will put in the shell. In any case, now return the shell and the center round, which will serve as a lid, to the oven for about 10 minutes. This final baking will fully cook the underdone center.

Almond Tartlets / TARTELETTES AUX AMANDES

Line 8 tartlet pans, 3-inch size, with the pastry as described on page 715, reserving one fourth of it for lattice topping. Freeze the pastry or chill it thoroughly.

Mix the ground almonds with the sugar and partially fill the pastry-lined molds with the mixture. Roll out the reserved pastry, cut it into ½-inch strips, and arrange these strips lattice-fashion on the tops of the tartlets.

Paint both the edges of the tartlets and the lattices with the egg yolk. Bake the tartlets on the bottom level of a preheated 350° F. oven for about 40 minutes.

When they are baked, cool them and then fill the spaces between the lattices with jam.

1 recipe Pâte Brisèe (p. 713), or Pâte à Sablé (p. 714)	½ cup superfine sugar
	1 egg yolk, beaten
1½ cups blanched almonds, finely ground	½ cup any desired jam

Honeyed Nut Tartlets / TARTELETTES AUX NOIX ET AU MIEL

Proceed as in Almond Tartlets (above), using preferably a *pâte à sablé*. Substitute ground walnuts for the almonds. When the tartlets are baked, and still very hot, fill the spaces between the lattices of each tart with honey.

Apple Tart / TARTE AUX POMMES

Prepare and prebake a 9-inch tart shell as described on page 714.

Cut the apples into thick slices and poach them in the sugar syrup for about 5 minutes.

Melt the apple jelly over low heat and stir in the kirsch.

When the tart shell has cooled, unmold it onto a serving dish and spread the bottom with half of the kirsch-flavored apply jelly. Arrange the drained apple slices decoratively in the shell and spread them lightly with the remaining apple jelly.

1 recipe Pâte à Sablé (p. 714), or Pâte Brisée (p. 713)	1½ cups Sugar Syrup (p. 666)
	¾ cup apple jelly
4 to 5 tart cooking apples, peeled and cored	2 tablespoons kirsch

Peach Tart / TARTE AUX PÊCHES

Proceed as for Apple Tart (above), using, if you like, Puff Paste (p. 715). Substitute 4 to 5 very ripe peaches for the apples. Peel and pit them, cut them into halves and arrange them, round side up, in the baked shell. If the peaches are not quite ripe, they may be poached in sugar syrup for a few minutes, in the same manner as the apples. Substitute apricot jam for the apple jelly.

TARTE TATIN / *Apple Tart à la Tatin*

Roll out the pastry into a 9-inch round ¼ inch thick. Butter and sprinkle with sugar the bottom of a 9-inch tart pan with straight sides. Peel, core, and quarter the apples, and arrange them neatly in the pan. Sprinkle the apples with the remaining sugar and dot with the butter. Cover the apples with the pastry, and paint the pastry with the egg yolk.

Bake on the middle level of a preheated 400° F. oven for about 20 minutes.

Unmold the tart upside down on a serving plate.

½ recipe Pâte Brisée (p. 713)	½ cup butter, softened
½ cup sugar	1 egg yolk, beaten
4 to 5 tart cooking apples	

TARTE TUTTI-FRUTTI / *Tutti Frutti Tart*

Proceed as in Apple Tart à la Tatin (above), but substitute 3 to 4 cups of mixed pitted fruits, such as cherries, plums, apricots, etc., for the apples.

/ *Applesauce Tart*
TARTE GRILLÉE À LA MARMELADE DE POMMES

Roll out three quarters of the pastry to the thickness of about ¼ inch, and line a 9-inch tart pan or flan ring with it as described on page 715. Chill it thoroughly or freeze.

Peel the apples, core them, and cut them into fine slices. Cook them with the sugar over low heat until they make a thick applesauce; flavor with the vanilla and cool.

Put the applesauce into the unbaked pastry. Roll out the remaining pastry and cut it into long strips about ½ inch wide. Make a lattice with these strips on top of the applesauce. Paint the lattice with the egg yolk. Bake on the lowest level of a preheated 350° F. oven for about 1 hour and 15 minutes.

1 recipe Pâte Brisée (p. 713)	½ teaspoon vanilla extract
5 to 6 tart cooking apples	1 egg yolk
½ to ¾ cup sugar	

TARTE AUX REINES-CLAUDES / *Greengage-Plum Tart*

Proceed as in Applesauce Tart (above), but substitute about a dozen greengage plums, pitted and cut into halves, for the apples and cook them with the sugar for only about 5 minutes before placing them in the tart shell. Spread the interstices of the lattice topping lightly with red-currant jelly after baking.

Apricot Tartlets / TARTELETTES AUX ABRICOTS

Prepare and prebake 8 tartlet shells with the pastry of your choice as described in the recipe for the pastry.

When they are done, take them out of the oven, cool them slightly, and unmold them on a cake rack. Fill each with about 2 tablespoons of *crème pâtissière.*

Place an apricot half, round side up, on top of the *crème,* spread with the apricot glaze, and top each with a few slivered almonds.

1 recipe Pâte Brisée (p. 713), Pâte à Sablé (p. 714), or about ⅓ recipe Puff Paste (p. 715)	4 large fresh apricots, peeled, pitted and halved, or use 8 canned apricot halves
2 cups Crème Pâtissière (p. 676)	¾ cup apricot glaze (see p. 667) ½ cup slivered blanched almonds

Raspberry Tartlets / TARTELETTES AUX FRAMBOISES

Proceed generally as in Apricot Tartlets (above).

Fill the baked tartlets with a little *crème pâtissière,* top with a neatly arranged layer of fresh raspberries, and spoon a little raspberry jelly over the berries.

1 recipe Pâte Brisée (p. 713), Pâte à Sablé (p. 714), or ⅓ recipe Puff Paste (p. 715)	2 cups Crème Pâtissière (p. 676) 2 to 3 cups fresh raspberries ¾ cup raspberry jelly, melted

Strawberry Tartlets / TARTELETTES AUX FRAISES

Proceed as for Raspberry Tartlets (above), but substitute strawberries and strawberry jelly for the raspberries and the raspberry jelly.

Alsatian Apricot Tartlets /

TARTELETTES AUX ABRICOTS À L'ALSACIENNE

Prepare and prebake 8 puff-paste tartlet shells as described on page 716. Cool the tartlets and unmold them.

Put the dried apricots in a saucepan with the sugar and water and simmer for about 8 minutes. Let the apricots cool in the syrup.

Place a drained apricot in each tartlet shell and then fill each with *crème pâtissière.*

⅓ recipe Puff Paste (p. 715) 8 dried apricots ¼ cup sugar	½ cup water 2 cups Crème Pâtissière (p. 676)

Note: In the same fashion you can make tartlets with prunes, plums, apples and cherries.

TARTELETTES AUX BANANES / *Banana Tartlets*

Prepare and prebake 8 tartlet shells from the pastry of your choice, as described in the recipe for the pastry (pp. 713 to 717).

Peel the bananas and cut them lengthwise into halves. Sauté them gently in the butter for 2 or 3 minutes, but they must keep their shape. Sprinkle the bananas with half of the sugar.

When the tarts are ready, take them out of the oven and let them cool. Partially fill them with *crème pâtissière* and garnish each with half a banana cut into appropriate pieces. Sprinkle the tops with the remaining sugar and put them back into a preheated 400° F. oven for a few seconds, until the sugar is melted.

1 recipe Pâte Brisée (p. 713) Pâte à Sablé (p. 714), or ⅓ recipe Puff Paste (p. 715)	⅓ cup superfine sugar 2 cups Crème Pâtissière (p. 676), flavored with 2 tablespoons rum
4 bananas	
3 tablespoons butter	

TARTE AUX MYRTILLES / *Blueberry Tart*

Prepare and prebake a 9-inch tart shell with the pastry of your choice, as described in the recipe for the pastry (pp. 713 to 717).

When the shell is baked and has cooled, fill it with the *crème pâtissière* and spread the blueberries over the top.

Cover the berries with a thin glaze of red-currant jelly.

1 recipe Pâte Brisée (p. 713), Pâte à Sablé (p. 714), or about ½ recipe Puff Paste (p. 715)	2 to 3 cups Crème Pâtissière (p. 676) ½ cup red-currant-jelly glaze (see p. 667)
2 cups fresh blueberries	

Note: You may omit the pastry cream. Use another cup of blueberries and sweeten them to taste with superfine sugar.

TARTE AUX CERISES / *Cherry Tart*

Line a 9-inch tart pan or flan ring with the pastry, as described on page 715. Freeze or chill the pastry thoroughly.

Sprinkle the pastry with sugar, spread the cherries in it, and sprinkle with more sugar. Cover the cherries with the *crème pâtissière*. Bake the tart on the lowest rack of a preheated 350° F. oven for about 50 minutes. After baking, spread a thin layer of cherry-jelly glaze over the *crème pâtissière*.

1 recipe Pâte Brisée (p. 713), or Pâte à Sablé (p. 714)	2 cups Crème Pâtissière (p. 676) ½ cup cherry-jelly glaze (see p. 667)
¼ to ½ cup superfine sugar	
2 cups fresh cherries, pitted	

Fresh Pineapple Tart / TARTE À L'ANANAS

Proceed as in Cherry Tart (above), substituting thin slices of fresh pineapple for the cherries, and apricot glaze for the cherry-jelly glaze.

Yellow Plum Tart / TARTE AUX MIRABELLES

Proceed as in Cherry Tart (above), substituting about a dozen pitted and sliced yellow plums for the cherries.

Cherry Gâteau / GÂTEAU AUX CERISES

Put the pitted cherries into a bowl and sprinkle them with the granulated sugar, cinnamon and rum. Let them marinate for 30 minutes.

Line a 9-inch tart pan or flan ring with the *pâte à sablé, as* described on page 715, and chill thoroughly. Place the cherries with their juices in the pastry-lined pan.

Cream the butter with the superfine sugar and add the ground almonds and the 2 eggs. Beat thoroughly until smooth. Cover the cherries with this mixture.

Bake the tart on the bottom rack of a preheated 350° F. oven for about 1 hour.

Cool the tart, paint the surface with the red-currant jelly, and then cover with the kirsch frosting. Decorate with the glacéed cherries. Let it stand for 30 minutes before serving to allow the frosting to harden.

4 cups sweet cherries, pitted	**¾ cup blanched almonds, ground**
1½ cups granulated sugar*	**2 eggs**
¼ teaspoon ground cinnamon	**¼ cup red-currant-jelly glaze**
2 tablespoons rum	**(see p. 667)**
1 recipe Pâte à Sablé (p. 714)	**1 cup Liqueur-Flavored Frosting**
½ cup butter, softened	**(p. 669), made with kirsch**
½ cup superfine sugar	**12 glacéed cherries**

* If the cherries are very sweet, reduce the amount of sugar accordingly, to ¾ to 1 cup.

Cranberry Gâteau / GÂTEAU AUX AIRELLES

Proceed as in Cherry Gâteau (above), but substitute cranberries for the cherries.

Cherry Tartlets / TARTELETTES AUX CERISES

Prepare and prebake 8 tartlet shells, 3-inch size, with the puff paste as described on page 716.

While the tarts are baking, prepare the buttercream and poach the pitted cherries in the sugar syrup for 5 minutes. Let the cherries cool in the syrup. When the tartlets are baked, unmold them and let them cool on a cake rack.

Partially fill them with kirsch-flavored buttercream. Drain the cherries, place them on the buttercream, and cover them with a little red-currant-jelly glaze.

⅓ recipe Puff Paste (p. 715)	2 to 3 cups fresh cherries, pitted
2 cups Liqueur-Flavored Butter-cream (p. 675), made with kirsch	1½ cups Sugar Syrup (p. 666)
	¾ cup red-currant-jelly glaze (see p. 667)

/ *Millas*

Line a 9-inch tart pan with the pastry and partially bake it, for about 15 minutes at 350° F., as described on page 714.

Beat together the egg yolks and the sugar until the mixture is very thick and white. Beat in the softened butter, the flour, the salt and the whole egg. Flavor with the orange-flower water and the anisette and gradually add the milk, beating constantly.

Pour this mixture into the pastry shell. Bake on the lowest rack of a preheated 325° F. oven for about 30 minutes, or until the custard is set.

1 recipe Pâte Brisée (p. 713)	½ teaspoon salt
4 egg yolks	1 whole egg
½ cup sugar	2 teaspoons orange-flower water
½ cup butter, softened	2 teaspoons anisette liqueur
⅓ cup sifted all-purpose flour	2 cups milk

/ *Cherry or Plum Millas*

MILLAS AUX CERISES OU AUX PRUNES

Line a 9-inch tart pan with the *pâte à sablé* or *pâte brisée* and prick the bottom of the pastry with a fork.

Put the cherries or plums into the pastry and sprinkle them lightly with 2 tablespoons of the sugar.

Beat together the egg yolks and the remaining sugar. Beat in the softened butter, the flour and the whole egg. Stir in the milk gradually and beat until very smooth. Pour the mixture over the cherries. Bake in a preheated 350° F. oven for about 30 minutes.

1 recipe Pâte Brisée (p. 713), or Pâte à Sablé (p. 714)	2 egg yolks
4 cups sweet cherries, pitted, or pitted plum halves	¼ cup butter, softened
6 tablespoons sugar	¼ cup sifted all-purpose flour
	1 whole egg
	1 cup milk

TARTELETTES AUX MARRONS / *Chestnut Tartlets*

Blend the chestnut cream with the *crème pâtissière*.

Prepare and prebake 8 tartlet shells, 3-inch size, as described on page 715. Brush them with egg yolk before baking. When they are done, let them cool and then un-mold them on a cake rack.

Partially fill the tarts with the chestnut and pastry-cream mixture, reserving ½ cup of it. Fold this remaining ½ cup into the kirsch-flavored *crème Chantilly*. Pile a little of this *crème* on each tartlet and top it with a few candied violets and chopped *marrons glacés*.

1½ cups Chestnut Cream (p. 679)	1 cup liqueur-flavored Crème Chantilly (p. 672), made with kirsch
1½ cups Crème Pâtissière (p. 676)	
1 recipe Pâte Brisée (p. 713)	½ cup chopped marrons glacés
2 egg yolks, beaten	¼ cup candied violets

Chestnut Vacherin / VACHERIN AUX MARRONS

First of all, make the chestnut ice cream. Slash the flat side of the chestnuts with the point of a sharp knife, cover them with water in a saucepan, bring to a boil, and boil for 2 minutes. Since the chestnuts are more easily peeled when still warm, take only a few at a time out of the water, and remove the shells and inner skins. Cook the peeled chestnuts in the milk, covered, over low heat for 45 more minutes.

Press the chestnuts with their cooking liquid through a fine sieve or a food mill and cool them. Beat the 3 egg whites until very stiff. Stir the rum into the chestnut purée, and gradually fold in the egg whites, the melted butter and the *marrons glacés* pieces. Freeze the chestnut cream in the refrigerator or in a freezer in the usual manner.

To make the *vacherin,* beat the egg whites until they form soft peaks, gradually add the sugar, and continue beating until they form stiff peaks. Fold in the vanilla. Mix the ground almonds with the flour and fold them into the egg whites.

Butter and flour a large baking sheet and spread out three quarters of the mixture into a rectangle about 8 by 12 inches. Make 6 rounds, 3 inches across, on the baking sheet with the remaining mixture. If possible, bake in the same slow manner suggested for meringues (p. 694), but halfway through the baking period, before the mixture dries, quickly roll the rectangle around a hollow buttered and floured cylindrical tin (an empty can will do) about 8 inches long and 4 inches in diameter. Work very quickly so that the pastry does not cool. Roll the small rounds around 6 small buttered and floured *cornet* molds to form cornucopias. Return the shaped pastry to the oven to complete drying. When completely dry, like a meringue (it should still be white and not have colored at all), remove from the oven, cool, and then chill.

Roll the *pâte à sablé* into a neat 9-inch round about ¼ inch thick. Place the round on a baking sheet, prick it several times with a fork, and bake it in a preheated 350° F. oven for about 20 minutes, or until nicely browned. Cool and then chill.

Using the caramel glaze as a glue, fasten the almond-meringue cylinder on the baked *pâte à sablé* round. Glue the cornucopias to the pastry round so that their tips touch the top edges of the almond-meringue cylinder.

Chill the *vacherin* in the refrigerator for at least 1 hour. At serving time, fill the almond-meringue cylinder with the chestnut ice cream. Top it with 6 *marrons glacés*.

Using a pastry tube, fill the cornucopias with *crème Chantilly*. If any is left over, use it for decorating the outside of the cornucopias.

For the chestnut ice cream:
- ½ pound chestnuts
- 2 cups milk
- 3 egg whites
- ¼ cup rum
- 2 tablespoons butter, melted
- ½ cup chopped marrons glacés

For the vacherin:
- 5 egg whites
- ¾ cup superfine sugar
- 1 teaspoon vanilla extract
- ¾ cup blanched almonds, finely ground
- ½ cup sifted all-purpose flour
- ¾ recipe Pâte à Sablé (p. 714)
- ½ cup Caramel Glaze (p. 668)
- 6 whole marrons glacés
- 1 cup Crème Chantilly (p. 672)

TARTELETTES AU CHOCQLAT / *Chocolate Tartlets*

Prepare and prebake 8 tartlet shells, 3-inch size, as described on page 715, and allow them to cool.

Fill a pastry bag fitted with a large star tube with the rum-flavored *crème Chantilly* and fill the cooled tartlets with it.

- 1 recipe Pâte à Sablé (p. 714)
- 2 cups Chocolate Crème Chantilly (p. 672), flavored with 3 tablespoons rum

TARTELETTES AU CAFÉ / *Coffee Tartlets*

Proceed as in Chocolate Tartlets (above), but substitute 3 cups Coffee Buttercream (p. 675) for the chocolate *crème Chantilly* and decorate each tartlet with a walnut half.

TARTE AU CITRON / *Lemon Tart*

Peel the yellow zest from the lemons and chop it fine. Peel off the white part from the lemons and discard. Cut the lemons into very thin rounds and remove the seeds.

Line a 9-inch tart pan, or a flan ring placed on a baking sheet, with the pastry as described on page 715. Freeze the shaped pastry or chill it thoroughly. Sprinkle the pastry with the sugar and the chopped lemon rind. Arrange the lemon rounds in 2 layers in the pastry. Cover with the *crème pâtissière* and bake on the lowest rack of a preheated 350° F. oven for about 40 minutes.

When the tart is ready, cover it with the Italian meringue, taking care that the meringue completely covers the *crème*. Return it to a very hot 500° F. oven for 3 or 4 minutes, or until the meringue is pale golden in color.

- 6 to 8 lemons
- 1 recipe Pâte Brisée (p. 713)
- ½ cup sugar
- 2 cups Crème Pâtissière (p. 676)
- 1 recipe Italian Meringue (p. 694), flavored with 1 tablespoon lemon juice

Lemon Tartlets | TARTELETTES AU CITRON

Prepare and prebake 8 tartlet shells, 3-inch size, as described on page 715.

Remove the entire peel from the lemons and either cut the pulp into very thin rounds or mince with a very sharp knife. Beat the granulated sugar and the whole eggs together until they are pale and form a ribbon when dropped from a spoon. Blend in the melted butter and then fold in the lemon rounds or pulp; blend thoroughly. Partially fill the baked shells with the mixture.

Beat the egg whites until they form soft peaks, add the superfine sugar gradually, and beat until they form stiff peaks. Cover the filled tarts with this meringue. Bake them on a lower rack of a preheated 325° F. oven for about 30 minutes, or until the meringue is of a light gold color.

Cool the tarts for a few moments before serving them.

1 recipe Pâte Brisée (p. 713)	⅓ cup butter, melted
6 lemons	4 extra egg whites
¾ cup granulated sugar	½ cup superfine sugar
4 whole eggs	

Pear Tart à la Bourdaloue |

TARTE AUX POIRES BOURDALOUE

Line a 9-inch tart pan, or a flan ring placed on a baking sheet, with the pastry as described on page 715. Freeze the shaped pastry or chill it thoroughly. Spoon half of the frangipane cream into the pastry. Bake the tart on a lower rack of a preheated 350° F. oven for about 35 minutes.

Peel and core the pears and cut them into thin slices. Poach the pears in the sugar syrup over low heat for about 5 minutes, or until just tender; they should keep their shape. Drain the pears and cool them.

When the tart is baked and cooled, put the remaining frangipane cream into it. Arrange the pear slices in overlapping rows on the frangipane cream, spread them with the apricot preserves, and sprinkle the tart with the macaroon crumbs.

1 recipe Pâte Brisée (p. 713)	2 cups Sugar Syrup (p. 666)
3 cups Frangipane Cream	½ cup apricot preserves
(p. 678)	6 macaroons, crumbled
6 pears	

Deep-Dish Pear Pie | PIE AUX POIRES

Peel and core the pears and cut them into thin slices. Pile the pear slices in the shape of a pyramid in a deep 8-inch pie plate and sprinkle them with sugar. Roll out a 9-inch round of puff paste to the thickness of ¼ inch and cover the pears with it, taking care not to pull the pastry. Wet the edges of the pie plate and the under edge of the pastry, and pinch them together. Paint with the egg yolk. Make a few slashes in the pastry with the point of a knife. Bake in a preheated 425° F. oven for about 25 minutes.

Serve the *crème anglaise* or port-wine *sabayon* separately in a sauceboat.

6 large pears
½ cup sugar
½ recipe Puff Paste (p. 715)
1 egg yolk, beaten

2 cups Crème Anglaise (p. 672)
or Port-Wine Sabayon
(p. 671)

/ *Deep-Dish Apple or Rhubarb Pie*

PIE AUX POMMES OU DE RHUBARBE

Proceed as for Deep-Dish Pear Pie (above), but substitute 6 peeled, cored and sliced apples, or about 4 cups of rhubarb cut into 1½-inch pieces, for the pears.

TARTE DE FRUITS À L'ANGLAISE / *English Fruit Tart*

Line a 9-inch tart pan, or a flan ring placed on a baking sheet, with the pastry as described on page 715. Freeze the pastry or chill it thoroughly. Partially fill the pastry with a good thick vanilla-flavored fruit compote and top it with the sliced apples arranged in a decorative pattern and sprinkled with the sugar. Bake the tart on the lowest rack of a preheated 350° F. oven for about 45 minutes.

Cool the tart and cover the top with the apricot glaze.

Any variety of fruits may be used in the compote. You may substitute Crème Pâtissière (p. 676) for the fruit compote, or mix 2 or more fruits such as, for instance, apples and blueberries or blackberries, or apples and rhubarb, or apples and red or black currants, etc. Serve these fruit tarts with a sauceboat of *crème fraîche*.

1 recipe Pâte à Sablé (p. 714),
   or Pâte Brisée (p. 713)
3 cups vanilla-flavored fruit
   (blackberry, raspberry,
   rhubarb, etc.) compote
   (see p. 667)

4 tart cooking apples, peeled,
   cored and sliced
½ cup sugar
½ cup apricot glaze (see p. 667)
2 cups Crème Fraîche (p. 666)

TARTELETTES À L'ANANAS / *Pineapple Tartlets*

Prepare and prebake 8 tartlet shells, 3-inch size, as described on page 715.

When the tartlets are baked, cool them before unmolding them. Then fill them with the kirsch-flavored *crème pâtissière*. Top each with a slice of pineapple, and place a cherry in its center. Coat the tops of the tarts with apricot glaze.

1 recipe Pâte Brisée (p. 713)
2 cups Liqueur-Flavored Crème
   Pâtissière (p. 678), made
   with kirsch

8 small thin slices of fresh
   pineapple
8 glacéed cherries
¾ cup apricot glaze (see p. 667)

TARTE À LA RHUBARBE / *Rhubarb Tart*

Wash and peel the rhubarb stalks and cut them into 2-inch pieces. There should be about 3 cups. Put the pieces into a bowl, sprinkle with the sugar, and let them stand at room temperature for 2 to 3 hours. If desired, add the dissolved cornstarch to thicken the fruit juice as the pie bakes.

Line a 9-inch tart pan, or a flan ring placed on a baking sheet, with three quarters of the pastry, as described on page 715. Freeze the pastry or chill thoroughly. Put the rhubarb pieces and their juices into the pastry.

Roll out the remaining pastry and cut it into long ½-inch strips. With these strips make a lattice over the rhubarb. Paint the lattice with egg yolk. Bake on the lowest rack of a preheated 350° F. oven for about 1 hour.

8 to 12 stalks of rhubarb	1 recipe Pâte Brisée (p. 713)
1 cup sugar	1 egg yolk, beaten
Optional: 2 tablespoons cornstarch mixed with 2 tablespoons water	

Strawberry Tart / TARTE AUX FRAISES

Prepare and prebake a 9-inch tart shell as described on page 715. Cool and then unmold the tart shell on a cake rack. Cover the bottom with half of the kirsch-flavored red-currant jelly. Arrange the strawberries on top, sprinkle with the sugar, and cover with the remaining jelly. Or you may partially fill the tart with 1 cup of Crème Pâtissière (p. 676), arrange the strawberries on top, and cover the berries with kirsch-flavored red-currant jelly.

1 recipe Pâte Brisée (p. 713), or Pâte à Sablé (p. 714)	4 cups strawberries, stemmed
1 cup red-currant jelly, melted with 2 tablespoons kirsch	½ cup sugar

Vanilla Tart / TARTE À LA VANILLE

Line a 9-inch tart pan, or a flan ring placed on a baking sheet, with the pastry as described on page 715. Freeze the pastry or chill it thoroughly. Fill the pastry with the *crème pâtissière* and bake it on a lower rack of a preheated 350° F. oven for about 40 minutes.

Remove it from the oven, cool, and then chill it.

Put the *crème Chantilly* into a pastry bag fitted with a star tube and garnish the top with decorative swirls.

1 recipe Pâte à Sablé (p. 714)	1 cup Crème Chantilly (p. 672)
3 cups Crème Pâtissière (p. 676)	

Clafoutis /

In 1964, the Académie Française turned its mind on the origins of the word *clafoutis*. After accepting the definition that a *clafoutis* is a fruit *flan*, the Académie decided that it was really a cherry *flan*. Let us add that the cherries must be sweet and very ripe.

If one is to believe the people of the Limousin, this recipe is strictly their own, though the people of the Auvergne make the same claim. A long time ago, this cake was cooked very simply in a skillet. The cherries (with their pits but without their stems), were added to a simple, unflavored *crêpe* batter, and cooked in a heavily buttered skillet. Since then, the recipe has changed considerably. We must admit that a *crêpe* batter goes well with black cherries that are full of flavor and sufficiently acid to give this dish its unmistakable and very pleasant flavor.

Today, the dish is often made with a pastry base in a *flan* mold, but I would advise against it. Even a puff-paste lattice put on the cherries would mean little more than a decoration.

Use very ripe cherries and pit them carefully without tearing them apart.

For the batter, beat together the sugar and the egg yolks and, when they are well blended, beat in the whole egg. Gradually add the butter, beat again, and stir in the flour. Then beat some more, energetically. Stir in the rum, almond extract and, finally, the milk. The batter must be very smooth.

Put the cherries into a heavily buttered 8- to 9-inch baking dish. Pour the batter over the cherries. Bake immediately on a lower rack of a preheated 400° F. oven for about 40 minutes.

3 **cups dark sweet ripe cherries**	1 **cup flour**
½ **cup sugar**	2 **tablespoons rum**
2 **egg yolks**	¼ **teaspoon almond extract**
1 **whole egg**	1 **cup milk**
½ **cup butter, softened**	

/ *Clafoutian*

This word is a compromise between *clafoutis* and *tian*. But perhaps I'd better explain the *tian;* it is a vegetable tart traditional in Nice. Originally these tarts, as so many others, were made with homemade clabbered milk. Only in modern times has this clabbered milk disappeared from among the ingredients of our cakes. One of the etymological interpretations of the word *brioche* takes this milk into account. It makes a certain amount of sense when we remember that, in those days, the problem of preserving milk had not been solved by pasteurization or refrigeration. I, in associating the two words, have also associated the cooking techniques; I am talking now of the vegetable tart.

The method of making it is the same as making *clafoutis,* except the vegetables are cooked just until crisp and firm before the batter is added. Naturally, the sugar in a vegetable *clafoutian* is omitted, in favor of a little discreet spicing.

CLAFOUTIAN AUX FRUITS / *Fruit Clafoutian*

Pit or do not pit the cherries, as you like. Peel and core the pear, and cut it into thin slices.

Mix the flour with the sugar and the softened butter, add the salt, and beat in the egg yolks and the whole egg. Gradually beat in enough milk to give the batter *crêpe* consistency, and stir in the rum or kirsch. Put the cherries and the pear slices into a well-buttered 8- to 9-inch skillet and pour the batter over the fruit.

Cook over low heat. When one side is browned, as in a pancake, turn carefully and cook until the other side is equally done.

2 cups sweet dark ripe cherries
1 pear
½ cup flour
¼ cup sugar
¼ cup butter, softened

½ teaspoon salt
2 egg yolks
1 whole egg
1 cup milk
1 tablespoon rum or kirsch

Vegetable Clafoutian | CLAFOUTIAN AUX LÉGUMES

Trim the green beans and cut them into 1-inch pieces. Shell the broad beans and the peas. There should be about ½ cup of each. Chop the artichoke hearts into little pieces. Put the broad beans and artichoke hearts into a vegetable steamer and steam them over lightly salted boiling water for about 10 minutes. Add the green beans and peas and continue steaming for about another 10 minutes, or until all the vegetables are tender.

Meantime, mix the flour with the softened butter and blend in the eggs. Stir in the salt, cayenne pepper, nutmeg and sufficient milk to make a batter of *crêpe* consistency.

Put the vegetables into a buttered 8- to 9-inch skillet, pour the batter over them, and cook over low heat. When one side is browned, turn carefully and cook until the other side is equally done.

¼ pound green snap beans
½ pound broad beans, or lima beans
½ pound peas
2 artichoke hearts
½ cup sifted all-purpose flour
¼ cup butter, softened

2 egg yolks
1 whole egg
½ teaspoon salt
⅛ teaspoon cayenne pepper
¼ teaspoon grated nutmeg
1 cup milk

SWEETS

Entremets

All of the desserts in this section will make 6 to 8 servings, unless otherwise noted.

Baked Apples | POMMES AU FOUR

Peel the tart apples, core them, and cut them into very thin slices. Sprinkle them with the sugar and cook until they have become a very thick applesauce. Stir in the vanilla.

Put this applesauce into a 9-inch shallow baking dish and spread it with the apricot preserves.

Core but do not peel the baking apples. Poach them in the sugar syrup until half tender, about 10 minutes. Drain the apples and arrange them on the applesauce. Stuff each one with a small piece of butter and pour 1 teaspoon of kirsch into each apple.

Bake in a preheated 350° F. oven for about 20 minutes, or until the apples are cooked and golden brown. Put a glacéed cherry into each.

6 tart apples	**4 cups Sugar Syrup (p. 666)**
¼ cup sugar	**½ cup butter**
½ teaspoon vanilla extract	**2 tablespoons kirsch**
½ cup apricot preserves, heated and strained	**6 large glacéed cherries**
6 baking apples, such as Courtlands, Winesaps, Rome Beauties or Baldwins	

BANANES AU FOUR / *Baked Bananas*

Make a cut with a sharp knife down the length of each banana so that the skin may be removed in one piece. Carefully take the bananas out of their skins without breaking them and reserve the skins.

Put the bananas into a deep dish, sprinkle them with the sugar, pour the rum over them, and let them stand for 2 to 3 hours. The bananas may also be cut into slices, but the slices are much harder to put back into the skins.

Drain the bananas, reserving the rum, and carefully put them back into their skins. If necessary, tie them with string so that the skins will not open as they bake. Put them side by side into a buttered baking dish. Pour the rum over them and bake them in a preheated 375° F. oven for about 15 minutes. Remove the strings and serve immediately.

6 bananas	**1 cup rum**
1 cup sugar	

BANANES FLAMBÉES / *Bananas Flambé*

Make a syrup with the sugar and the water and let it simmer for 5 to 10 minutes. Peel the bananas and poach them in the syrup for about 5 minutes.

Drain the bananas carefully without breaking them, put them on a hot serving dish, and pour the rum or any other desired spirit over them. Flame them and serve them immediately.

3½ cups sugar	**½ cup very hot rum, kirsch or Calvados**
2 cups water	
6 bananas	

BANANES GRILLÉES FLAMBÉES / *Broiled Bananas Flambé*

Peel the bananas, put them into a baking dish, and brush them with the melted butter. Broil them under a medium broiler flame for about 8 minutes, or until they are golden brown. Sprinkle them with sugar about 2 minutes before they are done. Pour the hot rum or any other desired spirit over them, flame them, and serve them immediately.

6 bananas	**½ cup very hot kirsch, rum or**
½ cup butter, melted	**Calvados**
½ cup sugar	

Souffléed Bananas | BANANES SOUFFLÉES

Combine the milk, sugar and vanilla bean, and bring to the boiling point. Mix the cornstarch and the salt with the water into a smooth paste and gradually add it to the milk, stirring constantly with a wooden spoon so that the mixture won't lump. Cook over low heat, stirring all the while, until thickened and smooth. Remove from the heat, discard the vanilla bean, and cool.

Lay the bananas on a flat surface and make a cut with a sharp knife down the whole length of each without cutting through the ends.

Carefully take the bananas out of their skins, leaving each of the skins in one piece. Mash the bananas into a smooth purée. Mix the banana purée with the egg yolks and the softened butter. Blend this purée with the thickened milk mixture.

Fold the stiffly beaten egg whites into the mixture and generously stuff the banana skins with it. Put them side by side into a buttered baking dish and bake them in a 375° F. oven for about 12 minutes, or until they are well puffed.

6 tablespoons milk	**2 tablespoons water**
3 tablespoons sugar	**6 ripe bananas**
1 piece of vanilla bean, 3 inches long	**2 egg yolks**
1 tablespoon cornstarch	**1 tablespoon sweet butter, softened**
⅛ teaspoon salt	**3 egg whites, stiffly beaten**

Basic Bavarian Cream | APPAREIL À BAVAROISE

Put the egg yolks into a saucepan, add the sugar, and beat the mixture until it is fluffy and almost white. Place the saucepan over low heat and, stirring constantly with a wooden spoon, immediately add the boiling milk. Cook, stirring constantly, until the mixture thickens, being careful not to let it lump. Remove the saucepan from the heat before the mixture starts boiling.

Strain the custard through a very fine strainer into a bowl and stir in the softened gelatin. Set the bowl into another full of cracked ice and cool the custard until it is no longer warm, stirring it all the while. Beat the egg whites until they form stiff peaks and fold them into the custard.

Keep the bowl of custard over the cracked ice, stirring occasionally, until it is quite cold and just on the point of setting. Fold in the *crème Chantilly*.

Rinse an 8-cup Bavarian mold with cold water, pour in the cream, and chill it for 6 hours before unmolding it at serving time.

4 eggs, separated	**2 envelopes unflavored gelatin, softened in ¼ cup cold water**
¾ cup sugar	
2 cups boiling milk	
	2 cups Crème Chantilly (p. 672)

BAVAROISE AU CAFÉ / *Coffee Bavarian*

Bake a Basic Bavarian Cream (above), and add 2 tablespoons instant coffee powder to the egg-yolk and sugar mixture before heating it.

BAVAROISE À L'ANANAS / *Pineapple Bavarian*

Proceed as in Basic Bavarian Cream (above), but soak 2 cups of crushed pineapple in 1 cup of rum, drain the mixture, and add it to the chilled custard. Use a slightly
larger mold and, if desired, line it with 25 to 30 ladyfingers.

BAVAROISE À LA VANILLE / *Vanilla Bavarian*

Make a Basic Bavarian Cream (above), but add a 6-inch piece of vanilla bean,
halved lengthwise, to the milk before boiling it. Remove it when the milk has boiled.

BAVAROISE AUX FRAISES / *Strawberry Bavarian*

Put the strawberries into a saucepan and add the sugar. Let them stand for 15
minutes, until their juice begins to run, and cook them over low heat for about 15
minutes, or until they form a very thick purée. Cool the purée.

Make a vanilla Bavarian cream and remove the vanilla bean before adding the
milk to the egg yolks and sugar. Add the cooled strawberry purée at the same time as
adding the *crème Chantilly*. Use a slightly larger mold and, if desired, line it with
ladyfingers.

Another method is to make alternate layers of Bavarian cream and strawberry
purée in the mold, ending with a layer of Bavarian cream.

2 cups strawberries	**18 to 24 Ladyfingers (p. 688)**
½ cup sugar	
1 recipe Vanilla Bavarian	
(above)	

BAVAROISE AUX FRAMBOISES / *Raspberry Bavarian*

Proceed as in Strawberry Bavarian (above), but substitute 2 cups of raspberries
for the strawberries.

DIPLOMATE / *Diplomat Pudding*

Make a Bavarian cream, but do not allow it to set.

Soak the ladyfingers in the kirsch and plump the raisins and currants in lukewarm
water.

Oil the bottom of a 10-cup mold and then rinse the mold in cold water. Arrange the glacéed fruits in the bottom and then fill the mold with alternate layers of Bavarian, ladyfingers, a few raisins and currants and apricot preserves, ending with a layer of ladyfingers. Chill the pudding for several hours before serving time. Serve it with a fruit sauce.

1 recipe Vanilla Bavarian (p. 733)
25 to 30 Ladyfingers (p. 688)
½ cup kirsch
1 cup mixed raisins and dried currants

¾ cup mixed glacéed fruits
2 tablespoons thick apricot preserves
3 cups any desired fruit sauce (pp. 670, 671)

Apple Charlotte | CHARLOTTE AUX POMMES

Make an apple compote in this way: peel and core the apples, cut them into small pieces, put them in a saucepan with ¼ cup of the butter, and cook them over low heat until they are soft. Stir them frequently to keep them from sticking. Add the sugar, cinnamon and the vanilla bean, halved lengthwise.

Cook slowly for about 15 minutes, until the compote is very thick and reduced. Remove the vanilla bean. Add the apricot-jam purée and mix thoroughly.

Melt the remaining butter and quickly sauté the slices of bread on both sides until golden. Line a 6- to 8-cup charlotte mold with the slices of bread, reserving a few for the top. Spoon the apple compote into the mold and cover the top with the remaining bread slices. Bake the charlotte in a 300° F. oven for 30 minutes. Cool it, chill, and then unmold before serving.

10 medium-sized apples
¾ cup butter
½ cup sugar
¼ teaspoon ground cinnamon
1 piece of vanilla bean, 6 inches long

4 tablespoons apricot preserves, heated and puréed
12 slices of white bread, crusts removed

Apricot Charlotte | CHARLOTTE AUX ABRICOTS

Simmer the pitted apricots in the sugar syrup for about 15 minutes, or until they are very soft, and then purée them in a blender. Add the lemon juice and the softened gelatin and let the fruit cool. Add the kirsch.

Place the purée over cracked ice and stir until it is just on the point of setting. Blend in the *crème Chantilly*.

Meanwhile, cut the *génoise* layer into 2 thin horizontal slices and line a buttered 8-cup charlotte mold with the *génoise*, reserving some for the top.

Spoon the apricot purée into the mold, cover the fruit with the remaining *génoise*, and chill in the refrigerator for 6 hours.

4 cups pitted apricots
2 cups Sugar Syrup (p. 666)
Juice of 1 lemon
2 envelopes unflavored gelatin, softened in ¼ cup cold water

2 tablespoons kirsch
2 cups Crème Chantilly (p. 672)
1 baked layer of Liqueur-Flavored Génoise (½ recipe, p. 684), made with kirsch

/ *Charlotte à la Chantilly*

Chill the *crème fraîche* thoroughly. Beat it, adding the sugar gradually, until very stiff, and add the vanilla.

Line a 6-cup charlotte mold with the ladyfingers and fill it with the whipped *crème.*

Cover a serving dish with a paper doily and unmold the charlotte on it immediately.

2 cups Crème Fraîche (p. 666)	**1 teaspoon vanilla extract**
¾ cup sugar	**25 to 30 Ladyfingers (p. 688)**

CHARLOTTE AUX FRAMBOISES / *Raspberry Charlotte*

Proceed as in Apricot Charlotte (above), but substitute 4 cups raspberries for the apricots and white framboise liqueur for the kirsch.

/ *Charlotte Russe*

Make a Vanilla Bavarian cream (p. 733). Line an 8-cup charlotte mold with 18 to 24 Ladyfingers (p. 688). Pour the Bavarian cream into it and chill the charlotte in the refrigerator for 6 hours.

CHARLOTTE RUSSE AU CAFÉ / *Coffee Charlotte Russe*

Proceed as in Charlotte Russe (above), using a Coffee Bavarian (p. 733) instead of one flavored with vanilla.

GÂTEAU AUX MARRONS / *Chestnut Cake*

Remove the inner and outer skins from the chestnuts as described in Chestnut Cream (p. 679). Cook them in water to cover for 1 hour, or until very tender. Purée them in a blender or by pressing them through a ricer or food mill.

Put the chestnut purée in the top part of a double boiler, stir in the softened butter, the sugar, vanilla and rum. Mix well. Stir over simmering water for 10 minutes and cool completely.

Make a caramel with the lump sugar and water, as described in Caramel Custard (p. 680), in a 4- to 5-cup fluted mold. Fill the mold with the chestnut cream and chill in the refrigerator for 2 hours. Unmold at serving time and serve with the *crème anglaise* in a sauceboat.

1 pound chestnuts	**½ cup lump sugar, crushed**
½ cup butter, softened	**2 tablespoons water**
½ cup sugar	**2 cups (about ½ recipe) Crème**
1 teaspoon vanilla extract	**Anglaise (p. 672)**
2 tablespoons rum	

Chestnut Mont Blanc / MONT-BLANC AUX MARRONS

Remove the inner and outer skins of the chestnuts as described in Chestnut Cream (p. 679). Cook them in water to cover 1 hour, or until very tender, and then purée them in a blender or by pressing them through a ricer or food mill. Add the sugar and the vanilla and cook over low heat until the sugar has melted. Cool.

Put the purée in a pastry bag fitted with a very small plain round tube and make a 9-inch circle of very fine spaghetti-sized ribbons on a round serving platter. Chill the shaped purèe and fill the center of the ring with *crème Chantilly*.

1 pound chestnuts	2 teaspoons vanilla extract
1 cup sugar	3 cups Crème Chantilly (p. 672)

Meringue Chestnut Cake / GÂTEAU DE MARRONS MERINGUÉ

The *crème anglaise* and the chestnut cream in this confection are mixed together and should be thick enough to hold their own shape in a pyramid form when they are chilled. Thus, it is advisable to use 2 additional egg yolks for the *crème anglaise*.

Fill a pastry bag with the meringue and, using a large round tube, decorate the mounded mixture of the creams with vertical meringue ridges. Sprinkle the cake with the slivered almonds, and put it into a 500° F. oven for 2 minutes, or until the meringue is golden in color. Place the glacéed cherry on the cake's summit.

2 cups Crème Anglaise (p. 672)	1 cup slivered blanched almonds
4 cups Chestnut Cream (p. 679)	1 glacéed cherry
1 recipe Meringue batter (p. 694)	

Floating Island I / ÎLE FLOTTANTE

Cut the Savoy spongecake horizontally into 3 slices. Sprinkle the slices with kirsch and maraschino. Spread each slice with apricot jam and sprinkle with half of the slivered almonds and currants. Re-form the cake's original shape and put it on a deep serving dish. Cover it with the *crème Chantilly*. Decorate it with the remaining slivered almonds and currants.

Pour the cold *crème anglaise* around and in the center of the cake so that the *crème* comes halfway up the sides.

1 baked ring of Savoy Sponge-cake (p. 690)	¾ cup slivered blanched almonds
½ cup kirsch	1 cup dried currants, plumped in lukewarm water and drained
½ cup maraschino	2 cups Crème Chantilly (p. 672)
1 cup apricot jam, puréed	4 cups Crème Anglaise (p. 672)

Floating Island II / OEUFS À LA NEIGE

Beat the egg whites with the superfine sugar until they are very stiff.
Boil the milk with the granulated sugar and the vanilla bean halved lengthwise.

Reduce the heat so that the milk barely simmers. Shape the egg whites into ovals with 2 tablespoons and poach them, a few at a time, in the barely simmering milk for 2 minutes. Turn them over and poach on the other side for 2 minutes. When they are cooked, remove them with a slotted spoon, drain them well on a towel, and then place them in a deep serving dish.

Beat the egg yolks until thick and pale. Gradually add the hot milk, stirring constantly. Stir over very low heat until the mixture thickens enough to coat the back of a spoon. Do not allow to boil. Pour the custard around the poached egg whites, and serve either lukewarm or chilled.

8 eggs, separated	1¾ cups granulated sugar
1½ cups superfine sugar	1 piece of vanilla bean, 6 inches
4 cups milk	long

GÂTEAU AUX FRUITS / *Fruit Gâteau*

Soak the fruits in the rum for 2 hours, and drain.

Cut the toasted bread into small cubes.

Put a layer of toast cubes on the bottom of an 8-cup baking dish, top it with a layer of fruits, and continue layering loosely until all are used. The last layer should be of toast.

Put the egg yolks into a bowl and gradually stir in the sugar, milk and vanilla. Fold in the stiffly beaten egg whites. Stir the mixture well into the bread and fruits.

Set the baking dish in a pan of hot water and bake in a preheated 325° F. oven for about 1 hour. Serve with a caramel sauce.

2 cups mixed glacéed fruits,	¾ cup sugar
chopped	2 cups milk
1 cup rum	1 teaspoon vanilla extract
6 slices of bread, lightly toasted	2 cups Caramel Sauce (p. 670)
4 eggs, separated	

PÂTE À BEIGNETS / *Fritter Batter*

Beat together in a bowl the flour, salt, oil, egg yolks and whole egg.

Add the beer and the milk, and beat the mixture with a wire whisk or with an electric beater to form a fairly thick batter. Then fold in the stiffly beaten egg whites.

This batter is used to coat foods before frying them in deep fat.

1¾ cups sifted all-purpose	2 eggs, separated
flour	1 whole egg
1 teaspoon salt	⅔ cup flat beer
1 tablespoon peanut oil	¾ cup milk

BEIGNETS DE POMME / *Apple Beignets*

Peel and core the apples and chop them rather coarsely. Put them into a bowl, sprinkle them with the sugar and the cinnamon, pour the rum over them, and let them marinate for 2 hours, turning them several times.

Make the fritter batter by mixing together the flour, oil, melted butter, salt, eggs and milk. Beat thoroughly until very smooth. Let the batter rest for about 2 hours.

Add the apples and their juice to the batter.

Heat the oil to 375° F. on a frying thermometer and drop the apple batter by generous spoonfuls into it. Fry the *beignets* until golden, take them out with a slotted spoon, and drain them on paper towels. Serve the *beignets,* sprinkled with sugar, on a dish lined with a napkin.

6 tart cooking apples	**For the batter:**
½ cup sugar	**1¾ cups sifted all-**
¼ teaspoon ground cinnamon	**purpose flour**
½ cup rum	**2 tablespoons peanut oil**
	2 tablespoons butter,
6 to 8 cups peanut oil for deep	**melted**
frying	**¼ teaspoon salt**
1 cup confectioners' sugar	**2 eggs**
	¼ cup milk

Banana Beignets I / BEIGNETS DE BANANES

Beat all of the batter ingredients together until very smooth and free of any lumps. Let it rest for 30 minutes.

Peel the bananas and cut them into fairly thick slices. Holding the slices with a fork, dip them into the batter until they are well coated on all sides. Shake off excess batter.

Heat the oil to 375° F. on a frying thermometer, or until a bread cube dropped into the oil browns in 60 seconds. Put a few of the *beignets* into the frying basket, and fry them for about 4 minutes, or until golden brown and puffy. Drain on paper towels and keep hot until all the *beignets* have been deep fried. Sprinkle with confectioners' sugar and serve very hot.

For the batter:	**10 ripe bananas**
2 cups sifted all-purpose	**6 to 8 cups peanut oil for deep**
flour	**frying**
½ teaspoon salt	**1 cup confectioners' sugar**
2 tablespoons butter,	
melted	
1 tablespoon peanut oil	
1 cup lukewarm water	
2 tablespoons sugar	
2 eggs	
1 tablespoon rum	
½ teaspoon vanilla extract	

Banana Beignets II / BEIGNETS DE BANANES FOURRÉS GLACÉS

Peel the bananas and cut them into fairly thick slices. Tear off little pieces of the *brioche* dough the size of a plum. Flatten them on the palm of one hand, put a banana round on each piece of dough, and wrap the dough completely around the banana in the shape of a ball.

Deep-fry the *brioche* balls, a few at a time, in the oil heated to 375° F. on a frying thermometer until they are golden and puffy. Drain on paper towels, and keep the fried ones hot until all have been done. Serve them on a dish lined with a linen napkin and sprinkle them with confectioners' sugar.

1 recipe Brioche dough (p. 695), which has risen once	6 to 8 cups peanut oil for deep frying
10 ripe bananas	1 cup confectioners' sugar

BEIGNETS D'ACACIA / *Acacia Beignets*

Proceed as in Banana Beignets I (above), but substitute for the bananas 30 to 40 very fresh acacia flowers.

BEIGNETS DE CRÈME / *Cream Beignets*

Boil the milk until it is reduced to half its volume, about 2 cups.

Crush the macaroons very finely and blend them with the egg yolks, grated lemon rind and orange-flower water into a smooth paste. Gradually stir in enough of the hot milk to make a mixture that will just hold its shape, and blend thoroughly.

Drop by the teaspoon into the oil heated to 375° F. on a frying thermometer. Fry until puffy and golden, drain on kitchen toweling, sprinkle with confectioners' sugar, and serve very hot.

4 cups milk	1 tablespoon orange-flower water
½ pound almond macaroons	6 to 8 cups peanut oil for deep frying
6 egg yolks	
Grated rind of 1 lemon	1 cup confectioners' sugar

BEIGNETS À LA DAUPHINE / *Beignets Dauphine*

Drop walnut-size pieces of the *brioche* dough into the oil heated to 375° F. on a frying thermometer. Fry them until the *beignets* come to the surface, turn over in the fat, and are golden and puffy. Drain thoroughly, place on a dish lined with a linen napkin, sprinkle with sugar, and serve very hot.

1 recipe Brioche dough (p. 695), which has risen once	1 cup confectioners' sugar
6 to 8 cups peanut oil for deep frying	

/ *Stuffed Beignets Dauphine*

BEIGNETS À LA DAUPHINE FOURRÉS

Divide the *brioche* dough into 2 equal parts.

Roll out each half ¼ inch thick. At 2-inch intervals on half of the *brioche* dough, put teaspoons of *crème pâtissière,* thick jam, or rum-soaked and drained glacéed fruit. Wet with water the edges around each spoonful of filling. Cover with the second half of the *brioche* dough. Firmly press down the edges of the dough around each mound of filling. Cut the dough apart into evenly shaped pieces and let them rest for 15 minutes. Deep-fry the *beignets* in the fat heated to 375° F. on a frying thermometer until they are golden and puffy. Drain them and serve them very hot, sprinkled with the sugar.

1 recipe Brioche dough (p. 695)	6 to 8 cups peanut oil for deep
1 cup cold Crème Pâtissière	frying
(p. 676), or any thick jam,	1 cup confectioners' sugar
or 1½ cups chopped	
glacéed fruits, soaked in	
rum and drained	

Beignets Soufflés /

Make the *pâte à choux* and flavor it with the rum or with the grated rind.

Heat the oil to 375° F. on a frying thermometer and drop the batter by the teaspoon into it. Fry the *beignets* for about 3 minutes, or until golden brown, remove them with a slotted spoon, and drain them on paper towels. Serve them on a dish lined with a linen napkin. Sprinkle the *beignets* with the confectioners' sugar before serving.

1 recipe Pâte à Choux (p. 710)	6 to 8 cups peanut oil for deep
2 tablespoons rum, or the grated	frying
rind of 1 orange or 1 lemon	1 cup confectioners' sugar

Crêpes /

Heat the milk, salt, sugar and butter together in a saucepan, until the butter has completely melted.

Put the flour into a large bowl and make a well in the center. Pour the oil into the well and add the eggs. Mix thoroughly by beating with a wire whisk. Add the milk mixture and then stir in the beer. Strain the batter through a fine sieve, and let it rest in the refrigerator for 2 hours before using it.

To fry the *crêpes,* use a heavy iron skillet with a 6- to 7-inch bottom and sloping sides. The French use a classic *crêpe* pan which comes in varying sizes and, like their omelet pan, is dedicated to a single use. Grease the pan very lightly with butter or oil and heat it over fairly high heat until it is on the verge of smoking. Pour about 2 tablespoons of the batter into the pan, just enough to cover the bottom, and fry for about 1 minute, or until nicely browned. Turn with a spatula and fry for about 30 seconds on the other side; it is more professional and amusing to turn the *crêpe* by giving the pan a sharp bang on the stove to loosen it and toss in the air to land on its other side in the pan. Several skillets may be used at one time. *Crêpes* may be cooked well in advance and stacked one on top of the other.

FOR ABOUT 24 CRÊPES:

1 cup milk	2½ cups sifted all-purpose
1 teaspoon salt	flour
2 tablespoons sugar	1 tablespoon vegetable oil
½ cup butter	4 eggs
	1 cup flat beer

Let the batter rest for 2 hours before using it. The skillet should be only very lightly buttered or oiled.

CRÊPES

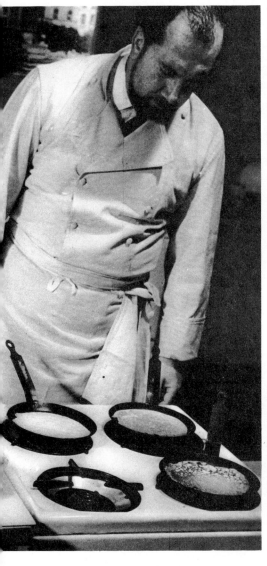

Use several skillets at the same time. With three of them, you can easily keep up the pace, provided that frying crêpes is all you do at this time.

Anise-Flavored Crêpes / CRÊPES À L'ANIS

Prepare a recipe of *crêpes*, as described above, but add 6 ground almonds and 2 tablespoons anisette liqueur to the batter.

Cherry Crêpes / CRÊPES AUX CERISES

Prepare about 2 dozen *crêpes*.

Simmer the cherries in the sugar syrup for about 5 minutes, or slightly longer if they are not wholly ripe. Drain them and then put a generous spoonful on each *crêpe*. Roll up the *crêpes*, put them in a buttered baking dish, sprinkle them with the sugar, and broil them under a medium flame for about 3 minutes, or until the sugar glazes.

1 recipe Crêpes (p. 740)	2 cups Sugar Syrup (p. 666)
3 cups ripe cherries, pitted	½ cup superfine sugar

Chestnut-Stuffed Crêpes /

CRÊPES FOURRÉES À LA CRÈME DE MARRONS

Proceed as in Cherry Crêpes (above), but stuff each *crêpe* with a generous spoonful of Chestnut Cream (p. 679) instead of the cherries. About 2 cups of the chestnut cream will be needed.

Glazed Crêpes / CRÊPES GLACÉES AU SUCRE

Prepare about 2 dozen *crêpes*, as described on page 740. Spoon 1 tablespoon of *crème pâtissière* onto each *crêpe*, roll them up, and put them on a buttered baking dish. Sprinkle them with the sugar and broil them under a medium broiler flame for about 3 minutes, or until the sugar has glazed. Serve immediately, very hot.

1 recipe Crêpes (p. 740)	½ cup superfine sugar
2 cups Crème Pâtissière (p. 676)	

Crêpes Otéro /

Proceed as in Glazed Crêpes (above), but flavor the *crème pâtissière* with 2 tablespoons of Grand Marnier and flame the finished *crêpes* with ¼ cup each of Grand Marnier and Cognac, heated together.

Crêpes Soufflées /

Proceed as in Glazed Crêpes (above), but fold 4 stiffly beaten egg whites into the *crème pâtissière* before stuffing the *crêpes*. Instead of rolling up the *crêpes*, fold them into loose triangles. Put them in a buttered baking dish and bake in a preheated 375° F. oven until they are nicely puffed.

/ Crêpes Suzette

Prepare about 2 dozen *crêpes,* as described on page 740.

Rub the orange rind energetically with the lump sugar, and put the sugar into a large shallow metal serving dish. Mash the sugar together with the butter, add ¼ cup of the Cognac and all of the Grand Marnier, and place the serving dish over an alcohol burner. Mix well until the sugar has dissolved completely. Soak the *crêpes,* a few at a time, in the mixture, fold each in half and then in quarters, and place the folded *crêpes* on one side of the pan until all have been soaked and folded. Sprinkle them with the sugar and flame them with the remaining Cognac, heated, without letting them brown. Serve immediately.

1 recipe Crêpes (p. 740)	**¾ cup Cognac**
1 orange	**¼ cup Grand Marnier**
7 lumps of sugar	**½ cup superfine sugar**
½ cup butter, softened	

GAUFRES / Waffles

Put the flour in a large bowl, make a well in the center, and pour into it the egg yolks, sugar, salt and cinnamon. Mix well to make a smooth paste. Melt the butter without browning it and combine it with the *crème fraîche.* Beat the mixture into the paste, together with the rum and the grated lemon rind. Fold in the egg whites, stiffly beaten. The batter should be smooth and well blended.

Heat a waffle iron and cook the waffles until nicely browned on both sides. Arrange them on a hot dish, and sprinkle them with confectioners' sugar.

1 cup sifted all-purpose flour	**2 tablespoons Crème Fraîche**
2 eggs, separated	**(p. 666)**
½ cup sugar	**2 tablespoons rum**
½ teaspoon salt	**Grated rind of 1 lemon**
½ teaspoon ground cinnamon	**½ cup confectioners' sugar**
¼ cup butter	

OMELETTE / Omelet

Break the eggs into a bowl and beat them with a wire whisk until they are frothy. Beating constantly, add the rum or the kirsch and the sugar.

Heat the butter in a skillet until it stops foaming and is pale gold. Pour in the eggs and make the omelet in the usual manner. Turn half of the omelet over the other half and let it stand for 2 or 3 minutes over very low heat. Turn it onto a serving dish and serve immediately.

FOR 2 TO 3 SERVINGS:

5 eggs	**2 tablespoons sugar**
2 tablespoons rum or kirsch	**¼ cup butter**

Apple Omelet / OMELETTE AUX POMMES

Peel and core 2 small apples and cut them into very thin slices. Soak them in ½ cup rum for 5 minutes and drain. Prepare a basic dessert Omelet (above), using 2 tablespoons of the rum in which the apples soaked. Make the omelet in the usual manner, and fill it with the apple slices before folding it in half.

Jam Omelet / OMELETTE AUX CONFITURES

Make a basic dessert Omelet (above), but spread the finished omelet with 5 tablespoons heated apricot preserves.

Strawberry Omelet / OMELETTE AUX FRAISES

Make a basic dessert Omelet (above), but fill the omelet with a generous cup of sliced strawberries before folding it in half.

Omelet Soufflé / OMELETTE SOUFFLÉE

Beat the egg yolks together with the sugar and stir in the Grand Marnier. Beat the egg whites until stiff and fold them into the other mixture.

There are 2 ways of making this omelet.

1. In the oven: Butter a 9-inch baking dish, put in the egg mixture, and bake in a preheated 325° F. oven for about 20 minutes. Sprinkle with the superfine sugar 1 minute before the omelet has finished baking.

2. In a skillet: Butter two 9-inch skillets very heavily and heat both of them. Pour in the egg mixture and cook, covered, over medium heat for about 5 minutes. Invert the omelet into the other hot skillet and cook for about 3 minutes longer. Turn out onto a serving dish and sprinkle with the sugar.

Serve these omelets very hot.

FOR 2 TO 3 SERVINGS:

5 eggs, separated	**¼ cup butter**
1 cup sugar	**½ cup superfine sugar**
2 tablespoons Grand Marnier	

Oriental Oranges / ORANGES ORIENTALES

Using a vegetable parer, peel the yellow rind only off the oranges. Cut it into fine julienne strips and put them into a saucepan with water to cover. Bring to the boiling point, drain, and rinse in cold water.

Put the orange rind strips into a saucepan, together with the sugar and the water. Dissolve the sugar over low heat and then boil over medium heat for about 10 minutes. Cool the mixture, add the kirsch or the Cointreau, and color with the grenadine.

Meantime, peel the white rind off the oranges, leaving the bare pulp. Cut the oranges horizontally into halves, put them into a deep serving dish, and cover with the sugar syrup.

Chill in the refrigerator for 2 to 3 hours before serving. At serving time, decorate each orange half with a candied violet.

4 large oranges	¼ cup kirsch or Cointreau
3 cups sugar	½ tablespoon grenadine
1 cup water	8 candied violets

ANANAS SURPRISE / *Pineapple Surprise*

Choose a large pineapple with good-looking leaves. Cut off the top and reserve it.

With a sharp knife and spoon, scoop out the flesh of the pineapple, leaving a shell about ½ inch thick. Do not pierce the shell. Cut away the core from the pineapple pulp and cut the pulp into small dice. Pit the apricots, the cherries and the peach; cut them and the strawberries into the same-sized dice as the pineapple. Put all of the fruits into a bowl, sprinkle with the sugar and the kirsch, and add the slivered almonds. Let the fruit marinate for 1 hour.

Stand the pineapple shell in a serving dish filled with ice. Fill the shell with the fruits, replace the top, and chill for about 2 hours before serving.

1 pineapple	½ cup sugar
2 apricots	½ cup kirsch
4 cherries	1 tablespoon slivered blanched
1 peach	almonds
4 strawberries	

FRAISES JEAN COCTEAU / *Strawberries Jean Cocteau*

Put the macaroons into a serving dish, sprinkle them with ½ cup of the kirsch, and let them stand until they have absorbed the kirsch.

Beat the remaining kirsch into the *crème Chantilly*. Cover the macaroons with half of the strawberries, sliced. Spread the *crème Chantilly* over the berries and decorate with the remaining berries and the candied violets.

Set the serving dish into a bowl of cracked ice.

8 Macaroons Oliver (p. 689)	12 large fresh strawberries
¾ cup kirsch	8 candied violets
1 recipe Crème Chantilly (p. 672)	

GÂTEAU DE RIZ / *Rice Gâteau*

Put the rice in a strainer and wash it under running cold water. Cook it, together with the milk, the grated lemon rind and the sugar, tightly covered over low heat for about 40 minutes, or until it is very tender but still moist.

Remove it from the heat and beat in the egg yolks, one at a time. Then gently fold in the stiffly beaten egg whites.

Butter a 6-cup baking dish, pour the mixture into it, and bake it in a preheated 350° F. oven for about 30 minutes.

1 cup uncooked long-grain rice	**½ cup sugar**
2 cups milk	**4 eggs, separated**
Grated rind of 1 lemon	

Rice Gâteau with Apples / GÂTEAU DE RIZ AUX POMMES

Prepare the Rice Gâteau mixture as described in the preceding recipe.

Put the mashed cube sugar and the water in a 6-cup charlotte mold and heat over medium heat until the mixture is golden and forms a light caramel. Remove from the heat and revolve the mold so that the caramel will cover all sides. Line the bottom and the sides of the mold with about two thirds of the rice mixture, put the apple compote in the center, and cover with the remaining rice mixture. Set in a pan of boiling water and bake in a preheated 325° F. oven for about 50 minutes.

½ recipe Rice Gâteau (above)	**2 cups apple compote, flavored**
8 cubes of sugar, mashed	**with vanilla (see p. 667)**
2 tablespoons water	

Basic Dessert Soufflé / SOUFFLÉ

Melt the butter in a saucepan over medium heat, add the flour, and stir until well blended. Add the hot milk all at once and stir until very smooth. Add the sugar and cook for 2 or 3 minutes longer. The mixture should be very thick but perfectly smooth. Remove from the heat and beat for a few minutes longer to cool it. Beat in the egg yolks, one at a time. Beat the egg whites until they form stiff peaks. Gently fold the whites into the other mixture.

Butter a 10- to 12-cup soufflé dish and sprinkle it with superfine sugar. Pour the mixture into it and bake the soufflé in a preheated 375° F. oven for 1 hour and 15 minutes, or slightly longer if a drier soufflé is preferred.

1 cup butter	**1¼ cups sugar**
1 cup sifted all-purpose flour	**2 teaspoons vanilla extract***
4 cups milk, scalded	**8 eggs, separated**

* If desired, a 6-inch piece of vanilla bean may be heated with the milk instead of using vanilla extract. Remove the vanilla bean before using the milk.

EDITORS' NOTE: *The large amounts of flour, milk and butter in proportion to the eggs in M. Oliver's soufflé may surprise the American cook who is accustomed to a soufflé's being a very light airy dish. This soufflé is altogether different, being a much sturdier full-bodied affair.*

SOUFFLÉ AU CHOCOLAT / *Chocolate Soufflé*

Prepare a Basic Dessert Soufflé (above), but add 8 ounces melted unsweetened baking chocolate to the batter, just before folding in the beaten egg whites.

SOUFFLÉ AU CAFÉ / *Coffee Soufflé*

Prepare a Basic Dessert Soufflé (above), but add 2 tablespoons instant coffee powder to the batter, just before adding the sugar.

/ *Soufflé aux Confitures*

Prepare a Basic Dessert Soufflé (above), but reduce the amount of sugar added to the flour and milk mixture to ¼ cup, and add 2 cups heated fruit preserves (any kind you like) to the batter along with the sugar. Use 2 additional egg whites and bake the soufflé in a 3- to 4-quart soufflé dish.

SOUFFLÉ AUX FRUITS / *Fruit Soufflé*

Combine ⅓ cup seedless raisins, 2 tablespoons chopped angelica, 2 tablespoons chopped pineapple, 10 chopped glacéed cherries and 4 chopped glacéed apricots. Soak them in 1 cup of kirsch for 3 hours. Prepare a Basic Dessert Soufflé (above), and add the drained fruits to the batter just before folding in the beaten egg whites.

/ *Soufflé au Grand Marnier*

Prepare a Basic Dessert Soufflé (above), but omit the vanilla and add ¼ cup Grand Marnier to the batter after removing it from the heat.

SOUFFLÉ AU CITRON / *Lemon Soufflé*

Prepare a Basic Dessert Soufflé (above), but heat the milk with the grated rind of 2 lemons; strain the hot milk before using it. Omit the vanilla. Stir the grated rind of 1 lemon into the batter just before folding in the beaten egg whites.

LE SOUFFLÉ SAXON

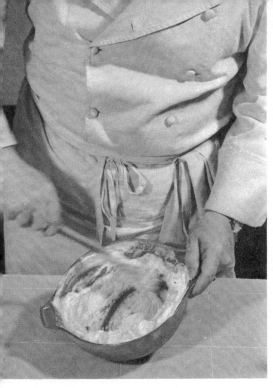 

Above, from left to right: *Beat the egg whites until very stiff, fold them into the batter, and pour the mixture into a soufflé dish.*

Below, from left to right: *Strain the* crème anglaise *through a* chinois *(a metal, cone-shaped, fine-meshed sieve) or through any fine sieve; it should be rather liquid. Unmold the soufflé and cover it with the* crème.

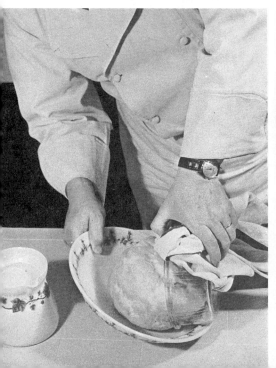 

Orange Soufflé / SOUFFLÉ À L'ORANGE

Prepare a Basic Dessert Soufflé (p. 746), but cook the grated rind of ½ orange with the milk; strain the milk before using it. Omit the vanilla. Add ¼ cup Grand Marnier together with the grated rind of 1 orange to the batter before folding in the stiffly beaten egg whites.

Soufflé Palmyre /

Sprinkle about 18 ladyfingers with ½ cup Grand Marnier, rum or kirsch.

Prepare a Basic Dessert Soufflé (p. 746). Spoon a little of the soufflé mixture into the bottom of a buttered and sugared 12-cup soufflé dish, cover with a few of the ladyfingers, and continue making layers until all is used, ending with a layer of soufflé mixture. Bake in the same manner as the basic soufflé.

Raspberry Soufflé / SOUFFLÉ AUX FRAMBOISES

Prepare in the same manner as a Soufflé aux Confitures (p. 747), but instead of fruit preserves use 3 cups fresh raspberries which have been simmered in 2 cups of Sugar Syrup (p. 666) for 5 minutes and drained. If desired, ¼ cup of raspberry liqueur may be poured over the top of the soufflé after it is baked.

Strawberry Soufflé / SOUFFLÉ AUX FRAISES

Prepare a Basic Dessert Soufflé (p. 746). Spoon the batter and 3 cups ripe strawberries in alternate layers in the soufflé dish, ending with a layer of batter.

Soufflé Saxon /

Heat the milk together with the butter and sugar. Bring to the boiling point and add the flour and cornstarch all at once, stirring briskly and constantly with a wooden spoon. Stir the batter until it clears the sides of the saucepan and until it is very smooth and homogenized. This is called "drying the batter."

Beat in the egg yolks, one at a time, beating well after each addition. Beat the egg whites until very stiff and then fold them into the other mixture.

Butter and flour a 2- to 2½-quart soufflé dish and pour the soufflé mixture into it. Set on a rack in a large pan of simmering water and bake in a preheated 375° F. oven for about 45 minutes.

Dilute the *crème anglaise* with enough of the hot milk to give it pouring consistency.

Unmold the baked soufflé in a deep serving dish, cover it with a little *crème,* and serve the remaining *crème* separately, in a sauceboat.

2 cups milk
½ cup butter
½ cup sugar
½ cup flour, sifted with
  ½ cup cornstarch

6 eggs, separated
3 cups hot Crème Anglaise
  (p. 672)
¼ cup hot milk

FROZEN DESSERTS

Desserts Glacés

EDITORS' NOTE: *The French usually freeze their ice cream in a traditional freezer. However, like all ice cream, it may be frozen in refrigerator trays in the freezing compartment of the refrigerator set at the lowest temperature. However, this ice cream will not be as smooth.*
All of these frozen desserts will provide 6 to 8 servings.

PARFAIT GLACÉ À LA VANILLE / *Vanilla Ice Cream*

Pour the heavy cream into a bowl, set this bowl in another bowl full of ice, and beat until the cream thickens. Gradually add ½ cup of the sugar and continue beating until it is very stiff. Beat the egg yolks and the remaining sugar until the mixture is white and fluffy. Fold in the whipped cream and the vanilla. Pour the mixture into two 1-quart shallow metal pans and freeze until the mixture begins to harden at the edges. Remove from the freezer and beat energetically for 1 minute. Return to the freezer for 2 hours, or until firm.

4 cups heavy cream
¾ cup superfine sugar

4 egg yolks
2 teaspoons vanilla extract

PARFAIT GLACÉ AUX BANANES / *Banana Ice Cream*

Proceed as in Vanilla Ice Cream (above), but add ¼ cup additional sugar, 2 tablespoons banana cordial and 2 cups puréed bananas to the egg yolks before folding in the whipped cream. Omit the vanilla.

PARFAIT GLACÉ AU CHOCOLAT / *Chocolate Ice Cream*

Proceed as in Vanilla Ice Cream (above), and add 5 ounces melted sweet cooking chocolate to the egg yolks before folding in the whipped cream.

Coffee Ice Cream / PARFAIT GLACÉ AU CAFÉ

Proceed as in Vanilla Ice Cream (p. 751), but add ¼ cup additional sugar and 2 heaping tablespoons of instant coffee powder to the egg yolks before folding in the whipped cream.

Cointreau Ice Cream / PARFAIT GLACÉ AU COINTREAU

Proceed as in Vanilla Ice Cream (p. 751), but add ¼ cup additional sugar and ¼ cup Cointreau to the mixture before folding in the whipped cream. Omit the vanilla.

Glacéed Fruit Ice Cream /

PARFAIT GLACÉ AUX FRUITS CONFITS

Soak 1 cup diced glacéed fruits in 1 cup of rum for several hours. Make a Vanilla Ice Cream (p. 751), and add ¼ additional cup of sugar and the drained fruits to the egg yolks before folding in the whipped cream.

Grand Marnier Ice Cream /

GLACE À LA CRÈME AU GRAND MARNIER

Proceed as in Vanilla Ice Cream (p. 751), and add ¼ additional cup of sugar and ¼ cup Grand Marnier to the egg yolks before folding in the whipped cream. Omit the vanilla.

Hazelnut Ice Cream / PARFAIT GLACÉ AUX NOISETTES

Proceed as in Vanilla Ice Cream (p. 751), and add ¼ additional cup of sugar to the egg yolks before folding in the whipped cream. Finally fold 1 cup of ground hazelnuts into the mixture before freezing.

Orange Ice Cream / PARFAIT GLACÉ À L'ORANGE

Proceed as in Vanilla Ice Cream (p. 751), and add ¼ cup additional sugar and ¼ cup Curaçao to the egg yolks before folding in the whipped cream. Finally fold 1 cup very finely diced glacéed orange peel into the mixture before freezing. Omit the vanilla.

PARFAIT GLACÉ À L'ANANAS / *Pineapple Ice Cream*

Proceed as in Vanilla Ice Cream (p. 751), and add ¼ cup pineapple cordial and 1 cup drained canned pineapple, finely diced, to the egg yolks before folding in the whipped cream. Omit the vanilla.

PARFAIT GLACÉ AUX FRAISES / *Strawberry Ice Cream*

Proceed as in Vanilla Ice Cream (p. 751), and add ¼ cup additional sugar, ¼ cup strawberry cordial and 1 cup puréed strawberries to the egg yolks before folding in the whipped cream.

SOUFFLÉS GLACÉS / *Frozen Soufflé*

This is not a recipe, but a way of serving ice cream.

Line the sides of a 6-cup soufflé dish with strong paper so the paper extends an inch or two above the dish. Fill the soufflé dish up to the edge of the paper with the ice-cream mixture after it has been partially frozen and beaten. Decorate the top with ground toasted almonds, chocolate curls, or minced glacéed fruits; the decorations should match the flavor of the ice cream. Freeze until firm. Remove the paper collar before serving.

In this way, you can make soufflés with any kind of ice cream, such as orange, vanilla, chocolate, strawberry, Cointreau, etc.

SOUFFLÉ GLACÉ PALMYRE / *Frozen Soufflé Palmyre*

Cut six of the ladyfingers into small dice and moisten them with three quarters of the kirsch and anisette. Prepare the vanilla ice cream, adding the ladyfinger dice to the mixture before freezing it. Be careful not to crush the pieces. Pour the mixture into a 6-cup soufflé mold with a high paper collar and freeze in the usual manner.

At serving time, remove the paper collar. Crumble the remaining 4 ladyfingers and sprinkle them lightly with the remaining kirsch and anisette. Sprinkle them on the top and the sides of the frozen soufflé.

10 Ladyfingers (p. 688)	**1 recipe Vanilla Ice Cream**
⅓ cup kirsch	**(p. 751)**
⅓ cup anisette liqueur	

SORBET À L'ABRICOT / *Apricot Sherbet*

If the apricots are very ripe, press them through a food mill or purée them in a blender without cooking them. If they are slightly hard, poach them in 2 cups of

Sugar Syrup (p. 666) for 5 minutes. Drain and then purée them.

Dissolve the sugar in the water, boil for 5 minutes, and combine this syrup with the apricot purée. Cool completely and then fold in the egg whites and the lemon juice. Pour the mixture into a 4-cup shallow metal pan and freeze until firm around the edges. Remove from the freezer and beat the mixture energetically for 1 minute. Return to the freezer until firm.

Serve the sherbet in a chilled dish.

½ **pound apricots, pitted**
1¾ **cups sugar**
1 **cup water**

2 **egg whites, stiffly beaten**
Juice of 1 lemon

EDITORS' NOTE: *The temperature of freezing compartments of many home refrigerators is not low enough to completely freeze sherbets. If you are in doubt, add 1 envelope of unflavored gelatin softened in ¼ cup of water to the hot syrup and fruit purée before cooling the mixture.*

Kirsch Sherbet | SORBET AU KIRSCH

Make a syrup with the sugar and water and boil it for 5 minutes. Stir in the lemon juice and cool the syrup completely. Stir in the kirsch and fold in the egg whites. Pour the mixture into a 4-cup shallow metal pan and freeze until the edges are firm. Remove from the freezer, beat energetically for 1 minute, and then return the mixture to the freezer until firm.

1¾ **cups sugar**
1 **cup water**
Juice of 2 lemons

½ **cup kirsch**
2 **egg whites, stiffly beaten**

Lemon Sherbet | SORBET AUX CITRONS

Proceed as in Apricot Sherbet (p. 753), substituting the puréed pulp and grated rind of 3 lemons for the apricot purée. If desired, the sherbet may be flavored with 2 tablespoons of Curaçao before adding the egg whites.

Orange Sherbet | SORBET À L'ORANGE

Proceed as in Apricot Sherbet (p. 753), substituting the puréed pulp and grated rind of 3 oranges for the apricot purée. Add 2 tablespoons of Curaçao before adding the beaten egg whites.

Raspberry Sherbet | SORBET AUX FRAMBOISES

Proceed as in Apricot Sherbet (p. 753), substituting 2 cups of raspberry purée for the apricot purée and 2 tablespoons of kirsch for the lemon juice.

SORBET AUX FRAISES / *Strawberry Sherbet*

Proceed as in Apricot Sherbet (p. 753), substituting 2 cups strawberry purée for the apricot purée.

SORBET AU THÉ / *Tea Sherbet*

Make the tea very strong, strain it, and let it cool.

Dissolve the sugar in the water and add the vanilla bean, halved lengthwise, and the grated orange and lemon rinds. Boil for 5 minutes.

Remove the vanilla bean from this syrup, then add the tea, the orange and lemon juices and the rum. Cool completely. Fold in the beaten egg whites and pour the mixture into a 4-cup shallow metal pan. Freeze until the edges are firm, remove from the freezer, and beat energetically for 1 minute. Return to the freezer.

1 cup very strong tea	Grated rind of 1 orange and 1
1¾ cups sugar	lemon
1 cup water	Juice of 1 orange and 1 lemon
1 piece of vanilla bean, 6 inches	¼ cup rum
long	2 egg whites, stiffly beaten

COUPE GLACÉE AUX ABRICOTS / *Apricot Coupe*

Make an apricot sherbet.

Pit the apricots, cut them into small dice, sprinkle the pieces with kirsch, and chill them for several hours.

At serving time, put half of the diced apricots into a serving dish, top them with the apricot sherbet, and cover the sherbet with the remaining diced apricots. Sprinkle the chopped almonds over the top.

1 recipe Apricot Sherbet	½ cup kirsch
(p. 753)	1 cup finely chopped blanched
5 apricots	almonds

/ *Bananas Glacées à la Norvégienne*

BANANES À LA NORVÉGIENNE

Slit 6 bananas lengthwise and remove the fruit without damaging the banana skins. Reserve the skins and use the banana pulp to make the banana ice cream.

Fill the banana skins with the ice cream. Fill a shallow baking dish with coarsely crushed ice and arrange the filled bananas on it. Put the Italian meringue into a pastry bag with a star tube and pipe decorative swirls over the bananas. Bake the bananas in a preheated 500° F. oven for 3 minutes, or until the meringue is golden. Serve immediately.

6 bananas	2 cups Italian Meringue
½ recipe Banana Ice Cream	(p. 694)
(p. 751)	

Pears Hélène / POIRES HÉLÈNE

Peel the pears, but keep them whole. Poach them in the syrup flavored with the vanilla until barely tender, about 8 minutes. Drain them on a rack until they are completely cool and then chill them. Fill the bottom of a serving dish with vanilla ice cream and stand the pears on it. Decorate with the candied violets. Serve the hot chocolate sauce on the side.

4 pears	8 candied violets
3 cups Sugar Syrup (p. 666)	3 cups hot Chocolate Sauce
1 teaspoon vanilla extract	(p. 670)
½ recipe Vanilla Ice Cream	
(p. 751)	

Pineapple Coupe / COUPE GLACÉE À L'ANANAS

Prepare the vanilla ice cream. Marinate the diced pineapple in the kirsch in a cool place. Drain the pineapple and reserve the kirsch.

At serving time, beat the diced pineapple into the vanilla ice cream. Spoon it into 6 individual coupe dishes. Top each serving with a slice of fresh pineapple and drizzle the kirsch over the top.

½ recipe Vanilla Ice Cream	½ cup kirsch
(p. 751)	6 slices of fresh pineapple
2 slices of canned pineapple,	
finely diced	

Chocolate Meringues Glacées /

MERINGUES GLACÉES AU CHOCOLAT

Prepare the vanilla ice cream, the meringues and the chocolate sauce.

At serving time, fill 6 individual coupe dishes with the ice cream. Put 2 meringues on the ice cream in each coupe and drizzle the chocolate sauce over them.

½ recipe Vanilla Ice Cream	2 cups Chocolate Sauce (p. 670)
(p. 751)	cooled
12 small Meringues (p. 694)	

Meringues Glacées with Raspberries /

MERINGUES GLACÉES AUX FRAMBOISES

Prepare the raspberry sherbet, the meringues and the raspberry sauce.

At serving time, fill 6 individual coupe dishes with the raspberry sherbet. Put 2 meringues on the sherbet in each coupe and drizzle the raspberry sauce over them.

1 recipe Raspberry Sherbet	2 cups Raspberry Sauce (p. 671),
(p. 754)	cooled
12 small Meringues (p. 694)	

/ Pineapple Coupe with Meringues

GLACE À L'ANANAS MERINGUÉE

Prepare the pineapple ice cream, the meringues and the *crème Chantilly*.

At serving time, line the bottom of a serving dish with half of the pineapple ice cream, arrange the meringues on top of it, and cover them with the remaining ice cream. Cover with the *crème Chantilly* and sprinkle with the diced pineapple.

½ recipe Pineapple Ice Cream (p. 753)	2 cups Crème Chantilly (p. 672)
6 Meringues (p. 694)	1 cup canned pineapple, drained and finely diced

CITRONS GIVRÉS / Frosted Lemons

Cut the tops off the lemons and reserve them. Scrape out the pulp without breaking through the lemon rind. Cut a slice off the bottom so that the lemons will stand up. Prepare the lemon sherbet, using the pulp from 3 of the hollowed-out lemons.

At serving time, fill the lemon shells with the sherbet. Put the tops back on, slightly on the slant.

6 large lemons	1 recipe Lemon Sherbet (p. 754)

MANDARINES GIVRÉES / Frosted Tangerines

Proceed as in Frosted Lemons (above), substituting tangerines for the lemons and filling them with a tangerine sherbet made in the same way as Lemon Sherbet (p. 754).

MOUSSE AUX FRAISES / Strawberry Mousse

Purée the strawberries in a blender. Dissolve the sugar in the water and boil for 5 minutes. Mix the purée with this syrup and cool completely.

Fold the beaten egg whites into the mixture.

Pour the mixture into a 6-cup metal container and freeze until firm at the edges. Stir thoroughly and freeze until firm.

1 quart fresh strawberries	1 cup water
1½ cups sugar	3 egg whites, stiffly beaten

Note: Raspberry, apricot or pineapple mousses may be prepared in the same manner, using the same amount of fruit purée.

/ Strawberry Mousse Chantilly

MOUSSE AUX FRAISES CHANTILLY

Proceed as in Strawberry Mousse (above), but substitute 1½ cups Crème Chantilly (p. 672) for the egg whites.

10
SAUCES
Les Sauces

BASIC SAUCES

Grandes Sauces

Sauce Espagnole /

It is hard to be precise in giving a recipe for *sauce espagnole;* what is important is to remember the general way in which it is made. This is a basic sauce from which several other sauces are prepared, such as *Madère, Périgueux, bigarade* and others. *Espagnole* always consists of two parts, one being the basic ingredients which never change (carrots, onions, etc.) and the other, either the additional ingredients which are especially appropriate to the dish in which the *espagnole* will be used, or simply ingredients which are at hand.

Make a *mirepoix* of various vegetables: onion, carrots, leeks and celery, to which you can add a few shallots and a turnip. Use a good-quality fat to cook these vegetables in: goose fat, duck fat, lard or ham fat are excellent. Cook the vegetables gently in the fat over low heat with a *bouquet garni* of parsley leaves and root and some *fines herbes.* Stir about 4 tablespoons of flour into the *mirepoix;* the quantity of the flour depends on how much the *mirepoix* will absorb and how thick you wish the finished sauce to be. Cook the flour a little and then add the wine and the stock, a little at a time. Then add the tomato paste and salt and pepper, and bring the sauce to a boil. Fresh tomatoes may be used instead of tomato paste; you will need a pound and, in this case, use only 3 cups of stock. The tomatoes should be very ripe; just take off the stems before slicing and adding the tomatoes to the sauce.

Then add the veal or the pork bone, the ideal bones for the sauce. They may be first quickly browned in the oven or not, but they must be fresh and cut to yield the maximum amount of flavor. Then add the chicken pieces.

This sauce may be cooked in as little as 1 hour. Let it simmer, covered, for about 45 minutes, then uncover and raise the heat to reduce the sauce to a good flavor. It is better, however, to prepare it 24 hours ahead, letting it cook, partially covered, for 3 to 5 hours and adding a ham bone or a veal tongue. The ham bone adds excellent flavor, but remember to salt the finished sauce very little or not at all.

Skim the sauce when it begins to boil, and keep on degreasing it, if necessary, while it cooks with a ladle or a bulb baster. If the liquid seems to be evaporating too quickly, add a little water from time to time. When the sauce is cooked, strain it first through a sieve and then through a triple layer of cheesecloth. Season it to taste with salt and pepper, or, if it is to be used as the base of another sauce, you may wish to defer the seasoning.

This sauce may be kept in the refrigerator for several days.

Note: The amount of flour used in this recipe should make a medium-thin sauce, depending on how much it reduces and how tightly the pan is covered as it cooks; even a thick sauce tends to thin out if it is simmered tightly covered. If the finished sauce seems too thin, it may be thickened by simmering it with a tablespoon or two of *beurre manié.*

FOR ABOUT 4 CUPS:

1 **large onion, chopped**
3 **carrots, chopped**
2 **leeks, chopped**
1 **celery heart, with leaves**
Optional:
   3 **shallots**
   1 **turnip**
4 **tablespoons lard or goose fat**
1 **Bouquet Garni:**
   parsley leaves
   parsley root
   thyme
   bay leaf
4 **tablespoons flour**
1 **cup dry white wine**

4 **cups Brown Stock (p. 164), or**
   any other stock which is
   appropriate to the dish in
   which the espagnole is to
   be used
2 **tablespoons tomato paste**
Salt
Freshly ground black pepper
1 **large veal or pork bone**
1 **to 2 pounds chicken feet,**
   wings, necks and backs
Optional:
   1 **ham bone**
   1 **small veal tongue**

/ *Sauce Béchamel*

Nowadays, we seldom if ever make a *béchamel* in the old-fashioned way with lean meat of veal and with blanched onions. Here is the way we make it today: Bring the milk to a boil, seasoned with salt, pepper, cayenne, grated nutmeg, and a *bouquet garni* or a *bouquet* of fresh *fines herbes* tied with a string. Simmer the milk for a few minutes.

While it is simmering, prepare a white *roux* (see p. 151) with the butter and flour and then cool the *roux* by plunging the saucepan into another pan full of cold water. Strain the milk through a fine sieve and add it all at once to the *roux*. Bring the mixture to a boil, stirring it constantly, and let it simmer for about 10 minutes. Then, if desired, add enough heavy cream to enrich the sauce and to give it any desired consistency.

If you respect the rule that one moistens a hot *roux* with cold milk, or, vice versa, a cold *roux* with a hot liquid; if you pour the hot liquid all at once onto the cold *roux;* if you use only first-class ingredients; then, nothing will prevent your being successful with this sauce. It is wise to have a cup of unseasoned hot milk at hand (heat a little of it in the saucepan in which the seasoned milk was cooked) so that if your sauce turns out to be too thick, you can thin it slightly.

FOR 4 TO 5 CUPS:

4 **cups milk**
2 **teaspoons salt**
Freshly ground white pepper
Cayenne pepper
Grated nutmeg

1 **Bouquet Garni (p. 46)**
½ **cup butter**
½ **cup flour**
Optional:
   1 **cup heavy cream**

SAUCE VELOUTÉ DE POISSON / *Sauce Velouté for Fish*

If you know how to make a *béchamel* and a fish *fumet* (a good strong fish stock) and if you know how to bind a *sauce Mornay*, a fish *velouté* will have no secrets for you. Thus:

1. Make an excellent fish *fumet*. 2. Prepare a white *roux* with the butter and flour. 3. Moisten the *roux* with a little of the *fumet* and then gradually stir all of it into the *roux*. 4. Let it cook for about 10 minutes. 5. Blend the egg yolks with the cream and, off the heat, stir them into the sauce. 6. Bring the mixture just to a boiling point, stirring constantly. Remove it from the heat. 7. Season to taste with salt and pepper. 8. Then, if you want to, you may add a little lemon juice.

But I wish to impress you with the necessity of a perfect fish *fumet* if you want to make a good *velouté*. You know that a good *fumet* must be carefully skimmed. To make it, you must use only lean fish, and in a generous amount.

FOR ABOUT 5 CUPS:

4 cups Fish Stock (or fumet) (p. 166)	1 cup heavy cream
	Salt
6 tablespoons butter	Freshly ground white pepper
6 tablespoons flour	Optional:
6 egg yolks	Juice of 1 lemon

Sauce Velouté for Chicken | SAUCE VELOUTÉ DE VOLAILLE

Proceed as for a fish *velouté* (above), with the same quantity of ingredients, but instead of the fish *fumet* use an excellent and very concentrated stock made with chicken or other fowl (see p. 165).

Sauce Suprême |

A *sauce suprême* is a *sauce velouté* for chicken (above) with the addition of *crème fraîche*. For 4 cups of chicken *velouté* you'll need 1 cup of *crème fraîche* (p. 666). Add hot *crème fraîche* gradually to the hot *velouté,* stirring constantly. Remove the sauce from the heat.

BROWN SAUCES

Sauces Brunes

Sauce Bigarade |

For meats and braised or roasted fowl. Especially suited for duck with orange.

Cut the yellow zest (without any of the white part) from two of the oranges into fine julienne strips. Blanch them: put them into a saucepan with cold water, bring the water to the boiling point, and boil it for 5 minutes. Drain. Squeeze the juice of the 2 oranges and of 1 lemon. Peel the remaining fruits and divide them into sections.

Crush the lumps of sugar in a saucepan with the water. Simmer the sugar over medium heat until it becomes a blond caramel. Keep the saucepan on the heat and stir into this caramel the vinegar and the juice of the 2 oranges and 1 lemon. Reduce this liquid by half; add the *sauce espagnole* and the blanched orange julienne. Cook gently for a few more minutes. Stir in the red-currant jelly. Mix the Curaçao with 1 tablespoon of cornstarch and stir this mixture into the sauce. The amount of cornstarch should be varied, either more or less, according to the thickness of the sauce; if the *espagnole* was very thick to begin with, you may need less cornstarch.

To serve: When the meat or the fowl for which you are making the sauce is ready, remove it from the pan in which it has been cooked and place it on a heated serving dish. Remove the fat from the pan, add ½ cup of dry white wine, and boil for 5 minutes as you deglaze the drippings in the pan with a wooden spoon. Then add the prepared sauce. Season to taste with salt and pepper. Take the julienne strips of zest out of the sauce and arrange them on top of the meat or the fowl. Arrange the orange and lemon sections around it and pour the sauce over it.

FOR ABOUT 3 CUPS:

6 oranges	1 tablespoon red-currant jelly
2 lemons	½ cup Curaçao
3 pieces of lump sugar	1 tablespoon cornstarch
2 tablespoons water	½ cup dry white wine
¼ cup red-wine vinegar	Salt
2 cups Sauce Espagnole (p. 760)	Freshly ground black pepper

Note: The *sauce espagnole* used in a *bigarade* should be prepared with both stock and parts of the appropriate fowl or meat with which the *bigarade* is to be served. That is, make the *espagnole* with duck stock and parts if it is to be served with duck.

/ *Sauce Bordelaise*

For broiled and grilled meats.

Simmer the shallots gently in the wine, together with a little garlic if desired. Season the liquid with a little cayenne pepper and *mignonnette* (crushed whole peppercorns) and reduce it to half its amount. Add the *sauce espagnole* (the *espagnole* should be fairly thick) and bring again to a boil. Add the brandy and remove the sauce from the heat. To make the sauce shiny, swirl in the butter, letting it melt in the sauce. Cut the poached marrow into small dice or rounds and add it to the sauce just before serving. (To poach the marrow, simmer it in boiling water for 2 minutes.) Season to taste with salt if necessary.

If desired, you may strain the sauce through a fine sieve before adding the butter.

FOR ABOUT 1½ CUPS:

3 shallots, finely chopped	Whole peppercorns, crushed
¾ cup good-quality red Bordeaux wine	1 cup Sauce Espagnole (p. 760)
Optional:	1 tablespoon brandy
½ garlic clove, finely chopped	2 tablespoons butter, softened
Cayenne pepper	¼ pound beef marrow (ask your butcher for this), poached
	Salt

Brown Chaud-Froid Sauce / SAUCE CHAUD-FROID BRUNE

In a saucepan, add the meat glaze to the *sauce espagnole*. Let the mixture reduce by a third over medium heat, stirring it occasionally.

Season to taste with salt and pepper and determine if the sauce is thick enough to use as a coating (a *chaud-froid* is always cooled, then spooned over meat, fish, or vegetables, and then chilled to jell the coating completely). In order to do this, you have to make tests: put a little of the sauce on a small plate and chill it. If the sauce does not jell when cold, reduce it a little further and test it again. Or else, dissolve 1 tablespoon of gelatin in ¼ cup of cold water, add it to the hot sauce, and simmer for a minute or two.

Finish the sauce with the Madeira or port and let it cool completely before spooning it over the food that is to be treated *à la chaud-froid*.

FOR ABOUT 2 CUPS:

3 tablespoons ordinary meat glaze	**Freshly ground black pepper**
3 cups Sauce Espagnole (p. 760)	**1 tablespoon unflavored gelatin**
Salt	**3 tablespoons Madeira or port**

Sauce Lyonnaise /

For broiled or grilled meats.

Cook the onions in the butter over the lowest possible heat, stirring constantly. They should not brown and must remain white and extremely soft, and become almost dissolved. When they are cooked, add the wine and the vinegar. Reduce the liquid slowly by two thirds. Stir in the *sauce espagnole*. Bring the sauce to the boiling point, and cook over low heat for about 5 minutes to make it extremely smooth. Season to taste with salt and pepper. Strain the sauce through a fine sieve and serve it very hot.

FOR ABOUT 3 CUPS:

3 medium-sized onions, minced	**3 cups Sauce Espagnole (p. 760)**
3 tablespoons butter	**Salt**
½ cup dry white wine	**Freshly ground black pepper**
½ cup wine vinegar	

Madeira Sauce / SAUCE MADÈRE

For broiled and grilled meats and roasts.

The preparation of this sauce varies depending on the thickening used. Thickened with cornstarch, Madeira sauce becomes shinier than when it is thickened with butter, and furthermore, it can stand for a while on the kitchen stove before being served. Madeira sauce thickened with butter must be served immediately.

To prepare a Madeira sauce thickened with cornstarch, blend the cornstarch with cold Madeira. Stir the mixture gradually into a boiling hot *sauce espagnole,* stirring constantly with a wooden spoon. Simmer the sauce for a few minutes before serving.

To prepare a Madeira sauce thickened with butter, bring the *sauce espagnole* to the boiling point and stir in the Madeira. Remove the sauce from the heat, and swirl in the butter cut into little pieces. Let it melt by shaking the saucepan. Do not heat the sauce again.

FOR 1 GENEROUS CUP:

1 cup Sauce Espagnole (p. 760)
1 liqueur glass of Madeira
  (about 2 tablespoons)

For thickening:
  1 teaspoon cornstarch, or
  3 tablespoons butter, softened

/ *Sauce Périgueux*

For broiled and grilled meats and roasts.

Sauce Périgueux is prepared like Madeira Sauce (above), but when you are adding the Madeira, add also 1 tablespoon of truffle liquid and 1 tablespoon of chopped truffles for each cup of *sauce espagnole*.

/ *Sauce Piquante*

For broiled, grilled and roast pork; and for boiled beef.

Boil the wine with the vinegar and the shallots over high heat until the liquid is reduced by half. Add the *sauce espagnole,* bring to the boiling point, and simmer the sauce for 10 minutes. Remove it from the heat and add the pickles and *fines herbes.* Season to taste with salt and pepper.

FOR ABOUT 1½ CUPS:

½ cup dry white wine
¼ cup wine vinegar
2 tablespoons chopped shallots
1 cup Sauce Espagnole (p. 760)
1 tablespoon minced sour pickles

2 tablespoons fresh Fines Herbes
  (p. 89)
Salt
Freshly ground black pepper

/ *Sauce Poivrade*

For game.

First, heat the oil and butter together in a saucepan. Add the carrot, onion and parsley, and sauté them gently until the vegetables are tender. Then add the livers, giblets and/or bones of the game, and sauté them until they are golden. Add the crushed garlic, a pinch of salt, the crushed peppercorns and the vinegar. Simmer gently until the vinegar has evaporated, then stir in the flour and the cornstarch. Mix everything with a wooden spoon for 2 minutes. Finally add the wine and the *sauce espagnole.* Cover the sauce and simmer it for 30 minutes. Strain it before using and add the brandy.

FOR ABOUT 2½ CUPS:

1 tablespoon vegetable or olive oil
2 tablespoons butter
1 carrot, thinly sliced
1 medium-sized onion, thinly
  sliced
2 parsley sprigs
1 pound livers, giblets and/or
  bones of game birds
1 garlic clove, crushed

Salt
6 peppercorns, crushed
½ cup wine vinegar
1 teaspoon flour
1 teaspoon cornstarch
½ cup dry red wine
2 cups Sauce Espagnole (p. 760)
1 liqueur glass of brandy (about
  2 tablespoons)

Sauce Grand Veneur /

For venison.

This sauce should be made just before serving time. Add to the boiling *sauce poivrade* the red-currant jelly, the cream, and the cornstarch which you'll have mixed with the brandy. Blend the sauce well with a wooden spoon. Simmer it over low heat for a few minutes, stirring constantly.

FOR 3 CUPS:

2 cups hot Sauce Poivrade (p. 765)
1 tablespoon red-currant jelly

⅔ cup heavy cream
1 teaspoon cornstarch
3 tablespoons brandy

Sauce Robert /

For grilled or roast pork.

Cook the onion in the butter until it is soft and golden. Moisten it with the wine, bring to the boiling point, and reduce the liquid by two thirds. Then add the *sauce espagnole,* cover the saucepan, and simmer the sauce over low heat for 10 minutes. At serving time, remove from the heat and stir in the sugar and mustard.

FOR 1 GENEROUS CUP:

1 large onion, minced
2 tablespoons butter
½ cup dry white wine

1 cup Sauce Espagnole (p. 760)
1 pinch of sugar
1 tablespoon Dijon mustard

Sauce Demi-Glace /

Simmer the *espagnole* and brown stock in a saucepan until they have reduced to 2 cups. If desired, flavor with the sherry or Madeira. Season to taste with salt and pepper; use care, since the sauce is so reduced it will likely need little or no seasoning.

2 cups Sauce Espagnole (p. 760)
2 cups Brown Stock (p. 164)
Optional:
   2 tablespoons sherry or
   Madeira

Salt
Freshly ground black pepper

Sauce Rouennaise /

For duck.

With a mortar and pestle, make a smooth paste of the duck livers. Cook the shallots in the butter until they are golden, and add the wine. Bring to the boiling point, reduce by half, and then add the parsley and the *sauce demi-glace.* At serving time, blend in the duck livers, stir until the sauce is smooth, and add a little more red wine if the sauce seems too thick. Season with salt and pepper if necessary.

FOR ABOUT 2½ CUPS:

¼ **pound duck livers**
2 **tablespoons minced shallots**
2 **tablespoons butter**
1 **cup (or slightly more) dry red wine**

2 **tablespoons chopped parsley**
2 **cups Sauce Demi-Glace (above)**
Salt
Freshly ground black pepper

/ *Sauce Saupiquet*

For venison.

Blend the hare's blood with the lemon juice in a bowl so that it will not coagulate. Cook the shallots in 1 tablespoon of the butter until they are soft, stirring them frequently with a wooden spoon. Add the vinegar and simmer, without a cover, until the vinegar has evaporated. Add the red wine, the *bouquet garni,* a little salt and a good deal of pepper. Simmer, covered, for 15 minutes and then discard the *bouquet garni.* At serving time, add the mashed liver to the hare's blood, stir them into the sauce, and remove the sauce from the heat. Cut the remaining butter into small pieces and swirl them into the sauce, shaking the saucepan so that the butter will blend into the sauce.

FOR 1 GENEROUS CUP:

¼ **cup hare's blood**
1 **tablespoon lemon juice**
1 **tablespoon minced shallots**
3 **tablespoons butter, softened**
½ **cup wine vinegar**

1 **cup dry red wine**
1 **Bouquet Garni (p. 46)**
Salt
Freshly ground black pepper
Liver of 1 hare, mashed

/ *Sauce Bourguignonne*

Sauté the minced shallots gently in 2 tablespoons of the butter. Add the wine, parsley, thyme and bay leaf. Reduce the sauce to half its amount over the lowest possible heat. Knead 2 tablespoons of the butter with the flour to make *beurre manié,* add it to the sauce, and simmer for about 5 minutes. Remove from the heat and swirl in the remaining butter. Season to taste with salt and a little cayenne. Remove the parsley and bay leaf before serving.

FOR ABOUT 1 CUP:

2 **shallots, finely minced**
6 **tablespoons butter, softened**
2 **cups good-quality Burgundy wine**
1 **parsley sprig**

⅛ **teaspoon ground thyme**
½ **bay leaf**
1½ **tablespoons flour**
Salt
Cayenne pepper

/ *Sauce Miroton*

For boiled beef.

Gently sauté the sliced onions and the tarragon in the butter for 10 minutes. Keep the heat low and stir frequently. Add the vinegar and reduce the sauce by half over high heat. Add the pickles, tomato paste, and wine. Season to taste with salt and pepper and then simmer the sauce for about 10 minutes before serving it.

FOR ABOUT 1 CUP:

2 medium-sized onions, sliced
1 tablespoon chopped fresh
   tarragon, or ½ teaspoon
   dried tarragon
3 tablespoons butter
½ cup red-wine vinegar

8 small sour pickles, sliced
2 tablespoons tomato paste
½ cup dry white wine
Salt
Freshly ground black pepper

Sauce Chasseur /

Sauté the minced mushrooms gently in 2 tablespoons of the butter in a saucepan for about 5 minutes. Season them with a little salt and add the minced shallots. Continue cooking for another 5 minutes, or until both the mushrooms and shallots are fairly soft. Remove them from the heat and reserve them in a bowl. Add another 2 tablespoons of butter to the saucepan, add the flour, and stir over medium heat until it is golden. Gradually add the wine, the stock, and then the tomato paste. Stir the mixture with a wooden spoon, bring it to a boil, lower the heat, and let it cook for about 10 minutes. At serving time, add the mushrooms, shallots and *fines herbes*. Keep the sauce on the heat just long enough to heat through, but do not let it boil again. Remove the sauce from the heat and swirl in the remaining butter. Season to taste with additional salt and freshly ground pepper.

FOR ABOUT 2½ CUPS:

¼ pound mushrooms, minced
6 tablespoons butter, softened
Salt
1 tablespoon minced shallots
2 tablespoons flour
½ cup dry white wine

1 cup Brown Stock (p. 164)
1 tablespoon tomato paste
1 tablespoon minced fresh Fines
   Herbes (p. 89)
Freshly ground black pepper

Sauce Nivernaise /

For freshwater fish (pike, trout, carp, salmon, etc.).

Melt 3 tablespoons of the butter in a deep saucepan; add the carrots, onions, thyme, bay leaf and parsley; simmer until the vegetables are tender, stirring frequently with a wooden spoon. Add the fish heads, fish bones and the *mignonnette* (crushed whole peppercorns). Cover the saucepan and simmer over very low heat for 15 minutes. Add 2 cups of the wine. Reduce the sauce by half by simmering it uncovered; then, cover the saucepan and cook the sauce over lowest possible heat for 30 minutes. Strain the sauce through a fine sieve, return it to the saucepan over low heat, and add the remaining wine and the fish stock.

Reduce the sauce again by half, cooking it uncovered. Season to taste with salt. Remove it from the heat and swirl in the remaining butter.

FOR ABOUT 1½ CUPS:

6 tablespoons butter, softened
2 medium-sized carrots, finely
   diced
2 medium-sized onions, finely
   diced
½ teaspoon dried thyme
1 bay leaf

3 parsley sprigs
1 pound fish heads and bones
1 pinch of mignonnette
3 cups dry red wine
1 cup Fish Stock (p. 166)
Salt

SAUCE PAPRIKA | *Paprika Sauce*

This sauce accompanies, or is made for, any number of dishes, including pilafs. As much as possible, it should be made with a base liquid or stock suited to the dish it is meant for. For a pilaf of cod, for instance, the sauce could be made with the liquid in which the cod was cooked.

Cook the onions in the butter until they are just barely golden. Stir in the paprika and the flour and cook the mixture for 2 minutes, stirring it constantly. Gradually add the cold stock and the tomato paste and bring the sauce to the boiling point, stirring it all the while with a wooden spoon. Strain the sauce through a fine sieve. Put it back on the heat, season to taste with salt and pepper, and stir in the cream. Let the sauce heat through.

FOR 1¼ CUPS:

2 medium-sized onions, minced
3 tablespoons butter
1 tablespoon paprika
1 tablespoon flour
1 cup stock (White or Brown
   Stock, p. 165, or any
   appropriate stock)

2 tablespoons tomato paste
Salt
Freshly ground white pepper
2 tablespoons Crème Fraîche
   (p. 666), or heavy cream

| *Sauce Tomate*

Heat the fat in a saucepan and cook the onion in it until it is soft. Stir in the flour and cook the mixture for a few minutes, stirring constantly with a wooden spoon. Peel, seed, and drain the tomatoes; force them through a sieve or purée them in a blender. Add them to the sauce, together with the sugar, about 2 teaspoons of salt, a little pepper, and the *bouquet garni*. Simmer, partially covered, for 1 hour, stirring occasionally.

FOR ABOUT 2 CUPS:

3 tablespoons goose fat, lard, or
   butter
1 large onion, minced
2 tablespoons flour
2 pounds tomatoes

1 teaspoon sugar
Salt
Freshly ground white pepper
1 Bouquet Garni (p. 46)

Sauce Diable /

This sauce is often prepared with Sauce Espagnole (p. 760) or White Stock (p. 165). Here is a way to make it differently.

Combine the vinegar with the minced shallots, and cook the mixture over very low heat, stirring constantly, until the vinegar has evaporated. Then add the wine, tomato sauce and ketchup. Simmer the sauce for 5 minutes. Season it with salt, if necessary, and strongly with cayenne pepper, and strain it through a very fine sieve.

FOR ABOUT 2½ CUPS:

½ cup wine vinegar
¼ cup minced shallots
½ cup dry white wine
1 cup Sauce Tomate (p. 769)

1 cup ketchup
Salt
Cayenne pepper

Sauce Tomate à la Provençale /

Peel, seed, and chop the tomatoes; heat them in a casserole with the oil. Season with salt and pepper. Add the sugar, garlic and parsley. Simmer, partially covered, for 30 minutes. Correct the seasoning before serving.

FOR ABOUT 4 CUPS:

12 large ripe tomatoes
½ cup olive oil
1 tablespoon salt
Freshly ground white pepper

½ teaspoon sugar
1 garlic clove, mashed
3 parsley sprigs

Shrimp Sauce / COULIS D'ÉCREVISSES

Peel and devein the shrimp. Heat the butter and the oil in a skillet and sauté the shrimp for 3 to 5 minutes, or until they have turned a bright red. Drain the butter and oil from the skillet and set aside. Sprinkle the shrimp with the Armagnac and flame them. Drain the pan juices from the skillet and reserve them separately from the butter and oil. Crush the shrimp in a mortar. Put the reserved butter and oil back into the skillet. Add the shallots and sauté them for about 5 minutes, or until they are soft. Then add the crushed shrimp and the reserved Armagnac pan juices. Simmer, covered, for a few minutes. Add the wine, tomatoes and tarragon. Season lightly with salt and pepper, cover, and cook over fairly high heat for 15 minutes. Strain the sauce through a fine sieve or purée it in a blender. Return it to the saucepan and reduce to a good consistency. There should be about 2½ cups. Correct the seasoning before serving.

FOR ABOUT 2½ CUPS:

1½ pounds shrimp
4 tablespoons butter
1 tablespoon vegetable or olive oil
½ cup Armagnac
12 shallots, minced

½ cup dry white wine
3 tomatoes, peeled, seeded and chopped
1 sprig of fresh tarragon
Salt
Freshly ground white pepper

WHITE SAUCES

Sauces Blanches

/ *Sauce Albert*

For braised beef.

Simmer the horseradish and the stock gently for 10 minutes. Stir the butter into the hot *béchamel*. Add to the horseradish mixture the buttered *béchamel*, the *crème fraîche* and the bread crumbs. Blend quickly and reduce over high heat, stirring constantly, for 3 minutes. Strain the sauce through a fine sieve or purée in a blender; add the egg yolk and season to taste with salt and pepper. Soften the dry mustard in the vinegar and add it to the sauce at serving time.

FOR 1½ CUPS:

- **4 tablespoons freshly ground horseradish**
- **¼ cup White Stock or White Poultry Stock (p. 165)**
- **1 tablespoon butter, softened**
- **¼ cup hot Sauce Béchamel (p. 761)**
- **2 tablespoons Crème Fraîche (p. 666)**

- **½ cup very fine fresh bread crumbs**
- **1 egg yolk**
- **Salt**
- **Freshly ground white pepper**
- **½ teaspoon dry mustard**
- **1 teaspoon vinegar**

/ *Sauce Albufera*

Have the *béchamel* very hot on the stove, and add the butter and the veal stock to it. Remove from the heat and swirl in the pimiento butter. Correct the seasoning.

FOR ½ CUP:

- **¼ cup Sauce Béchamel (p. 761)**
- **1 tablespoon butter, softened**
- **2 tablespoons White Stock (p. 165)**

- **1 tablespoon Pimiento Butter (p. 794), softened**
- **Salt**
- **Freshly ground white pepper**

/ *Sauce Allemande*

For variety meats, poultry, vegetables and poached eggs.

Combine the egg yolks and the stock in a saucepan, and if you like the flavor, add the mushroom stock. Stir in the *sauce velouté*. Gently simmer the mixture just below the boiling point for about 5 minutes, stirring constantly with a small wire whisk. Do not allow it to boil. At serving time, add the *crème fraîche*, the lemon juice, and a little grated nutmeg. Season to taste with salt and pepper.

FOR ABOUT 4½ CUPS:

2 egg yolks	4 tablespoons Crème Fraîche
¼ cup White Stock or White Poultry	(p. 666)
Stock (p. 165)	1 tablespoon lemon juice
Optional: 2 tablespoons mushroom	Pinch of grated nutmeg
stock	Salt
4 cups Sauce Velouté for Chicken	Freshly ground white pepper
(p. 762)	

Sauce Poulette /

Especially for mutton.

Bring the mushroom stock to a boil and reduce it by two thirds. Then add the *sauce allemande,* bring to a boil again, and cook, stirring constantly, until the sauce is smooth. Remove the sauce from the heat; then stir in the lemon juice, butter and parsley.

FOR 4½ CUPS:

1 cup mushroom stock	4 tablespoons butter, softened
4 cups Sauce Allemande (above)	and cut into small pieces
Juice of 1 lemon	1 tablespoon minced parsley

Sauce Aurore /

For eggs and poultry.

Have the *velouté* very hot on the stove, and stir in the tomato paste. Bring the sauce just to the boiling point, and cook it gently until it is very smooth, stirring constantly with a wooden spoon or a small wire whisk. Do not let it boil. Remove the sauce from the heat and swirl in the butter, bit by bit. Do not return the sauce to the heat. A *sauce aurore* for fish is made in the same manner, using a Sauce Velouté for Fish (p. 761) instead of the *sauce velouté* for chicken.

FOR ¾ CUP:

½ cup Sauce Velouté for Chicken	1 tablespoon tomato paste
(p. 762)	3 tablespoons butter, softened

Sauce Bretonne /

For eggs, fish, white meats and variety meats.

Heat 4 tablespoons of the butter in a saucepan, add the onion, leeks and celery, and cook the vegetables until they are very tender. Season lightly with salt and pepper. Add the mushrooms and the wine. Cook over high heat, stirring constantly, until all the liquid has evaporated. Stir in the *sauce velouté*. Simmer for 5 minutes longer but do not allow it to boil. Then stir in the *crème fraîche*. Remove the sauce from the heat and stir in the remaining butter, bit by bit.

FOR ABOUT 2 CUPS:

½ cup butter, softened
1 medium-sized onion, cut into
  julienne
2 leeks, white part only, cut
  into julienne
1 celery stalk, cut into julienne
Salt
Freshly ground white pepper

4 medium-sized mushrooms, cut into
  julienne
½ cup dry white wine
1 cup Sauce Velouté for Chicken
  (p. 762)
2 tablespoons Crème Fraîche
  (p. 666)

Note: When using *sauce bretonne* with fish, use Sauce Velouté for Fish (p. 761) in place of the chicken *velouté*.

SAUCE AU BEURRE (SAUCE BÂTARDE) / *Butter Sauce*

For vegetables and boiled fish.

Melt 4 tablespoons of the butter in a saucepan, add the flour, and cook until golden; stir the mixture constantly. Add the boiling salted water and, stirring occasionally with a small wire whip, simmer for about 10 minutes. Remove it from the heat, let it cool a little, and stir in the egg yolks, the *crème fraîche* and the lemon juice. Season to taste with salt and pepper. Return the sauce to the heat, bring it almost to the boiling point, and stir until slightly thickened. Do not boil. Remove it from the heat again and stir in the remaining butter, bit by bit.

FOR ABOUT 4½ CUPS:

1¼ cups butter, softened
4½ tablespoons flour
3 cups boiling salted water
5 egg yolks
2 tablespoons Crème Fraîche
  (p. 666)

2 tablespoons lemon juice
Salt
Freshly ground white pepper

SAUCE AUX CÂPRES / *Caper Sauce*

For boiled fish.

Caper sauce is a Butter Sauce (above), to which a generous tablespoon of drained capers and a little extra lemon juice are added at serving time.

/ *Sauce Chantilly*

For poultry, vegetables and poached eggs.

Have your *sauce suprême* very hot, but not boiling. Stir in the *crème fraîche* off the heat and serve immediately.

FOR ABOUT ¾ CUP:

½ cup very thick Sauce Suprême
  (p. 762)

3 tablespoons Crème Fraîche
  (p. 666), whipped

LE SAUCE CHANTILLY

Have your sauce suprême *very hot, but it should be off the stove. Fold in the whipped* crème fraîche, *preferably over ice.*

SAUCE AU CIDRE / *Cider Sauce*

For broiled and grilled meats.

Heat 2 tablespoons of the butter in a saucepan and cook the onion in it until it is soft. Stir in the cider, salt and paprika. Bring the sauce to the boiling point and cook it until it is reduced to one third. Add the *sauce velouté* and cook for a few minutes longer. Remove from the heat and stir in the remaining butter and the mustard.

FOR 1½ CUPS:

½ cup butter, softened
1 tablespoon minced onion
1 cup cider
½ teaspoon salt

½ teaspoon paprika
1 cup Sauce Velouté for Chicken
   (p. 762)
1 teaspoon Dijon mustard

SAUCE À LA CRÈME / *Cream Sauce*

For fish, vegetables, poultry and eggs.

Make a *béchamel* with 2 tablespoons of the butter, the flour and the milk. Add 2 tablespoons of the *crème fraîche*. Cook the sauce, stirring constantly, until it is thickened and smooth. Remove it from the heat, season to taste with salt and pepper, stir in the remaining butter and *crème,* and add a little lemon juice if desired.

FOR 2 CUPS:

4 tablespoons butter, softened
2 tablespoons flour
1 cup milk
⅔ cup hot Crème Fraîche
   (p. 666)

Salt
Freshly ground white pepper
Optional:
   1 teaspoon lemon juice

SAUCE AUX PIMENTS / *Pimiento Sauce*

For eggs, fish and poultry.

To make the tomato essence, peel, seed, drain, and coarsely chop the pound of very ripe tomatoes. Then press them through a fine sieve or a food mill (or blend them briefly in an electric blender). Bring this purée to the boiling point, reduce it by half, strain it again, and boil it again until of the consistency of a thick sugar syrup. Strain the purée once more.

Heat the butter and cook the flour in it until it is golden. Gradually stir in the stock and blend with a wire whip. Cook slowly for 10 minutes, stirring occasionally, to reduce the sauce slightly. Stir in the tomato essence, the chopped sweet pepper and the parsley. Simmer for 5 minutes. Season to taste with salt and pepper.

FOR 2 GENEROUS CUPS:

¼ cup tomato essence, made from
   1 pound fresh ripe tomatoes
3 tablespoons butter
3 tablespoons flour
2 cups White Stock or White Poultry
   Stock (p. 165)

1 sweet red pepper, charred,
   scraped, seeded and chopped
   (see p. 619)
2 tablespoons chopped parsley
Salt
Freshly ground white pepper

White Chaud-Froid Sauce / SAUCE CHAUD-FROID BLANCHE

For eggs, poultry and fish.

This sauce, based on gelatin or a jellied mixture, is never served by itself, but is used to coat meats, poultry, vegetables or fish that are to be presented *chaud-froid*. It needs a very good consommé or strong stock; for coating fish it should have an excellent fish stock as its base. When the consommé is ready, take a couple of spoonfuls and see if they will jell (see p. 764).

If the consommé jells slightly firmer than a usual meat jelly, make a *béchamel* with the butter, the flour and the consommé; then add the egg yolks which you have beaten together with the cream; stir over gentle heat until slightly thickened.

If the consommé does not jell sufficiently, make the *béchamel* as described above but add an appropriate amount (see p. 764) of unflavored gelatin, no more than 2 tablespoons, which you have softened and dissolved over hot water; then heat with the egg yolks and cream until slightly thickened. Be careful not to boil. If necessary, season with salt and pepper.

Strain the sauce through a very fine sieve. Let it cool, stirring it constantly with a wooden spoon. Spoon the cold sauce generously over the foods you want to present in *chaud-froid* fashion. The foods that will be covered with the sauce must be chilled, or the sauce will not adhere to them. They have to be cooked well in advance and then chilled. Once the dish has been covered with the sauce, chill it until serving time.

In order to make a pink *chaud-froid* sauce, add 4 tablespoons very thick *sauce tomate* (p. 769) to the *béchamel* at the time you are adding the egg yolks, and color the sauce further with a little paprika.

FOR 4 GENEROUS CUPS:

4 cups Chicken or Beef Consommé (p. 168), or Fish Stock (p. 166)
6 tablespoons butter
6 tablespoons flour

7 egg yolks
½ cup heavy cream
Salt
Freshly ground white pepper

Sauce Mornay /

This is a *béchamel*, with the addition of grated Gruyère cheese, egg yolks and *crème fraîche*.

For each 2 cups of *béchamel* you'll need 6 to 8 egg yolks and 1 cup of grated cheese, and 1 tablespoon of *crème fraîche* for each egg yolk. Beat the egg yolks together with the cream, and stir in a little hot *béchamel*. Stir the mixture into the remaining *béchamel*, bring it just under the boiling point, simmer gently for a few minutes, stirring constantly, and then stir in the grated cheese. When the cheese has melted, season to taste with salt and pepper and remove the sauce from the heat. If the sauce is not to be used immediately, *Mornay* as well as *béchamel* may be spread with a little softened butter over the top, to prevent its forming a skin as it cools.

FOR 3 GENEROUS CUPS:

2 cups Sauce Béchamel (p. 761)
6 egg yolks
1 cup grated Gruyère cheese

6 tablespoons Crème Fraîche (p. 666)
Salt
Freshly ground white pepper

EDITORS' NOTE: *M. Oliver's sauce Mornay is a rich one and extremely thick. If a thinner sauce is desired, have an extra cup of heavy cream on hand and use it to thin the sauce to the desired consistency.*

/ Sauce Villeroy

This is a *velouté* which you bring to the simmering point and to which you add the essence of truffles and the optional essence of ham. Then the sauce is removed from the heat, and the *crème fraîche* is stirred into it.

FOR 1 GENEROUS CUP:

1 cup thick Sauce Velouté
   for Chicken (p. 762)
1 tablespoon essence of truffle
   (commercially available) or
   juice from canned truffles

Optional:
1 tablespoon essence of
   ham*
1 tablespoon Crème Fraîche
   (p. 666)

*EDITORS' NOTE: *An essence of ham is commercially available but difficult to find. It is simply a reduced ham stock; since it is quite salty, the* velouté *should* not *be seasoned with salt if you choose to use ham essence in a* sauce villeroy.

SAUCE CURRY / Curry Sauce

Heat the butter and cook the onions in it until they are soft and barely golden. Stir in the curry powder and flour and cook for a few minutes longer, stirring constantly. Add the apple, the *bouquet garni* and the garlic clove. Depending on the dish the sauce will accompany, add fish stock or brown stock. Simmer, partially covered, over low heat for 30 to 45 minutes, stirring frequently. Remove the *bouquet garni* and the garlic clove. Season to taste with salt and pepper and strain the sauce through a fine sieve.

FOR 2 CUPS:

3 tablespoons butter
2 medium-sized onions, minced
1 tablespoon curry powder
1 tablespoon flour
1 tart apple, peeled, cored and
   finely chopped

1 Bouquet Garni (p. 46)
1 garlic clove, unpeeled
2 cups Fish Stock (p. 166), or
   Brown Stock (p. 164)
Salt
Freshly ground white pepper

/ Sauce Américaine

To my mind, there is no *sauce américaine* without shellfish. Prepared with lobster, it becomes the classic dish, lobster *à l'américaine*. It may also be made with crayfish. Here is the way to do it.

Separate the bodies from the tails of the lobsters, cut the tails into 3 crosswise pieces, split the bodies into halves, and discard the sacs behind the heads. (If using crayfish, they may be left whole.) Heat the oil and the butter in a deep skillet, put the lobster pieces in it, and season with salt and pepper. Cook over high heat until the shells are bright red and then remove the lobster pieces with a slotted spoon. Add the shallots and garlic to the skillet and sauté until soft. Now add the wine, fish stock, tomatoes and *bouquet garni*. Simmer for 30 minutes, correct the seasoning, and strain the sauce through a fine sieve. Heat the lobster pieces in another skillet, add the brandy, and ignite. Pour the sauce over the lobster and simmer for 15 minutes. Without the lobster pieces this is simply a *sauce américaine*.

FOR ABOUT 3 CUPS OF SAUCE:

3 lobsters (1½ pounds each), or
  2 pounds crayfish
2 tablespoons peanut oil
2 tablespoons butter
Salt
Freshly ground white pepper
2 shallots, minced
1 garlic clove, mashed

½ cup dry white wine
½ cup Fish Stock (p. 166)
6 ripe tomatoes, peeled, seeded
  and crushed
1 Bouquet Garni (p. 46)
1 liqueur glass of brandy (about
  2 tablespoons)

Sauce Cardinal /

For fish.

Heat the butter in a saucepan, add the flour and, stirring constantly with a wire whisk, cook until barely golden. Gradually add the cold fish stock and simmer for about 5 minutes, stirring all the time, until the sauce is thickened and smooth. Add the *sauce américaine*. Mix well, and simmer until the whole sauce is extremely smooth. Season to taste with salt and pepper.

FOR 2 CUPS:

1½ tablespoons butter
1½ tablespoons flour
1 cup Fish Stock (p. 166)

1 cup Sauce Américaine (above)
Salt
Freshly ground white pepper

> EDITORS' NOTE: *Classically a* sauce cardinal *is made with a* béchamel *or a* velouté *made from fish stock and may or may not contain finely minced lobster or truffles. The above recipe is* M. Oliver's *own version.*

Sauce Nantua /

Have the *béchamel* boiling hot on the stove and stir 1 cup of *crème fraîche* into it. Bring the sauce to the boiling point and reduce it by one third. Strain the sauce through a fine sieve, add the remaining *crème fraîche,* and cook the sauce until it reduces to the desired thickness. Remove it from the heat and season to taste with salt and pepper. Stir in the shellfish butter and the crayfish tails or minced lobster.

FOR ABOUT 4 CUPS:

4 cups Sauce Béchamel (p. 761)
2 cups Crème Fraîche (p. 666)
Salt
Freshly ground white pepper

¾ cup crayfish butter (see
  note below), or Lobster
  Butter (p. 793), softened
20 small cooked crayfish tails, or
  1 cup minced cooked lobster

EDITORS' NOTE: *Crayfish are not often available in most parts of the United States and lobster may easily be substituted for them in a* sauce Nantua. *Whenever crayfish are to be found, for this sauce they should be simmered in a Court Bouillon for Fish (p. 131) for about 5 minutes; the shells are then removed, and the crayfish reserved for adding to the sauce at the last minute.*

A crayfish butter should be prepared well in advance by pounding the shells with ¾ cup of softened sweet butter in a mortar; the butter may then be pressed through a fine hair sieve. More simply, the pounded shells and butter may be boiled with 1 cup of water, the whole mixture strained through cheesecloth, and the strained liquid then chilled for easy removal of the butter from the surface of the water.

/ Sauce Normande

Heat the butter and cook the flour in it until it is golden. Stir in the fish stock gradually. Cook for a few minutes, stirring constantly. Remove the sauce from the heat, beat in the egg yolk mixed with the *crème fraîche,* and season to taste with salt and pepper. Return the sauce to very low heat and stir constantly until slightly thickened. Do not allow it to boil.

FOR ABOUT 1¾ CUPS:

2 tablespoons butter
2 tablespoons flour
1 cup Fish Stock (p. 166)
½ cup Crème Fraîche (p. 666)

1 egg yolk
Salt
Freshly ground white pepper

BÉARNAISE, HOLLANDAISE AND RELATED SAUCES

Sauces Émulsionnées Chaudes

/ Sauce Béarnaise

For broiled and grilled dishes.

Combine the vinegar, shallots, 1 tablespoon of the tarragon, and the peppercorns in a saucepan. Bring the mixture to the boiling point and cook it, stirring constantly, until all the liquid has evaporated. Remove the saucepan from the heat and let it cool for a few minutes. Then add the egg yolks, one at a time, beating constantly with a wire whisk; add the water and blend well; put the saucepan back on very low heat (or over a pan of hot water, double-boiler fashion) and heat the sauce again, beating it all the time. When it has become creamy, remove it again from the heat and let it cool while beating it gently. When the sauce is cool enough so that you can hold the saucepan between your hands, add the clarified butter gradually, beating gently. The butter must be at the same temperature as the egg mixture to be properly incorporated in the sauce. Strain the sauce through a fine sieve. Season it with salt to taste and add the remaining tarragon and the optional chervil. Keep the sauce warm over barely hot water or at room temperature. Do not heat it up again; it is served lukewarm. A well-made *béarnaise* should have the consistency of mayonnaise.

FOR 2 CUPS:

½ cup white-wine vinegar (tarragon vinegar, if possible)
5 shallots, minced
2 tablespoons minced fresh tarragon
½ teaspoon crushed white peppercorns
4 egg yolks

¼ cup boiling water
1 cup barely hot Clarified Butter (p. 666)
Salt
Optional: 1 tablespoon minced fresh chervil

Sauce Choron /

For broiled and grilled meats, and roasts.
Cook the tomato purée until it is well dried out. Let it cool slightly and add it to the *sauce béarnaise*. Keep the sauce at room temperature.

½ cup Tomato Purée (p. 157)   1 recipe Sauce Béarnaise (above)

Sauce Hollandaise /

For fish and boiled vegetables.
Proceed as for *sauce béarnaise* (above), but use only vinegar (about half as much as for *béarnaise*) and crushed peppercorns, without any herbs. The vinegar should be only slightly reduced, not completely evaporated. Beat the sauce vigorously so that it will be very light. Taste and add the optional lemon juice for a more strongly flavored sauce.

FOR 2 CUPS:

¼ cup white-wine vinegar (not tarragon vinegar)
¼ teaspoon crushed white peppercorns
4 egg yolks
2 tablespoons boiling water

1 cup barely hot Clarified Butter (p. 666)
Optional: Juice of ½ lemon
Salt

/ *Sauce Hollandaise with Capers*

SAUCE HOLLANDAISE AUX CÂPRES

For boiled fish.
Mix the well-drained capers into the *sauce hollandaise.*

1 recipe Sauce Hollandaise (above)	**2 tablespoons well-drained capers**

SAUCE CHANTILLY / *Sauce Hollandaise Chantilly*

For fish and boiled vegetables.
At serving time beat the whipped *crème* into the *sauce hollandaise.* This sauce is also called *sauce mousseline.*

1 recipe Sauce Hollandaise (above)	**½ cup Crème Fraîche (p. 666), whipped**

/ *Sauce Mousseuse*

This is the simplest of the emulsified butter sauces. It is not as delicate as a *sauce béarnaise* or a *hollandaise,* but it can be used for adding to other sauces.

Use an enamelware saucepan or a lined copper or glass one, but do not use aluminum because it will discolor the sauce. The saucepan should be wide, so that the sauce can easily be stirred. Put the egg yolks into the saucepan. Add 4 eggshell-halves of water and season with the salt and the cayenne. Put the saucepan over very low heat (or over a pan of hot water, double-boiler fashion). Beat the mixture with a wire whip until it becomes very light, thick and foamy. Beating all the time, remove the sauce from the heat every now and then to prevent its cooking too quickly. When the sauce is thick enough so that you can see the bottom of the pan while you beat it, remove it from the heat and continue beating until it is slightly cooled. Then add the clarified butter, bit by bit, beating constantly. The butter must be well clarified and at the same temperature as the egg mixture. When the sauce is high and fluffy, let it stand until serving time at room temperature since it must not be heated again. It is always served lukewarm. Taste the sauce to see if the seasoning is correct, and at serving time beat in the lemon juice.

FOR 4 CUPS:

7 egg yolks	**2 cups Clarified Butter (p. 666),**
Water equal to 4 eggshell halves	**barely hot**
1 teaspoon salt	**Juice of 2 lemons**
Pinch of cayenne pepper	

BEURRE BLANC / *White Butter*

Especially for pike.
Cook the vinegar and the shallots together until the vinegar has almost com-

pletely evaporated. Season with salt and pepper, and gradually add the softened butter, beating the mixture with a wire whip over very low heat.

¼ cup white-wine vinegar	½ cup butter, softened and cut into small pieces
2 tablespoons minced shallots	

Note: Experts say, not without reason, that the best butter for this sauce is the salty butter from Brittany.

MAYONNAISE AND OTHER COLD EMULSIFIED SAUCES

Sauces Émulsionnées Froides

Mayonnaise /

Put the egg yolks, salt, pepper, cayenne, ¼ cup of vinegar and the mustard into a bowl. Beat the mixture rapidly with a wire whip. Start adding the oil, first by drops, then by teaspoons, and finally by tablespoons, beating all the time. Before adding more oil to the mixture, make sure that the previously added oil has been totally absorbed. A good mayonnaise is not necessarily stiff; on the contrary, it should be soft. Once the mayonnaise is made, stabilize it by rapidly beating in the boiling vinegar.

When the sauce is completed, taste for any additional seasoning: salt, pepper, mustard (add Dijon mustard, if desired), vinegar, etc. If the mayonnaise seems too thick, thin it slightly with spoonfuls of boiling water or vinegar according to its flavor.

You will find it easy to make mayonnaise if you take these elementary precautions:

1. Do not use eggs fresh from the refrigerator or oil that has been standing in a warm place. The two ingredients should be at room temperature.

2. Do not store mayonnaise in the refrigerator. Simply keep it in a cool place.

3. Don't despair if mayonnaise separates. In a separate bowl, blend a generous spoonful of mayonnaise with 1 tablespoon of boiling vinegar and then gradually add the rest of the curdled mayonnaise, beating constantly.

FOR ABOUT 5½ CUPS:

6 egg yolks	¼ cup wine vinegar
1½ teaspoons salt	¾ teaspoon dry mustard
⅛ teaspoon freshly ground white pepper	4 cups oil*
Pinch of cayenne pepper	2 tablespoons boiling wine vinegar

*EDITORS' NOTE: *The type of oil used in a mayonnaise is largely a matter of personal preference. Olive oil naturally gives*

MAYONNAISE

Above, you see all the in-gredients needed: vinegar, oil, egg yolks, salt, pepper, mustard.

Season the egg yolks with salt and pepper, add the vinegar and the mustard, and beat immediately with a wire whip.

It is important to add the oil gradually, first in small quantities and then in larger ones. Make sure that each addition of oil has been absorbed before adding more.

A good mayonnaise must be soft.

a fairly strong flavor and a slightly oily taste, which many cooks prefer. For a lighter flavor, use vegetable oil or a combination of olive and vegetable oils.

Mayonnaise Chantilly /

For cold fish and meats.

Mix the *crème fraîche* with one fourth of its volume of iced milk and then whip it.* In another bowl, blend the mustard with the lemon juice. Beat the mixture gently into the whipped *crème fraîche* and then beat in the mayonnaise. Season to taste with salt and pepper and beat rapidly until the sauce is thick and smooth.

FOR ABOUT 3 CUPS:

½ cup Crème Fraîche* (p. 666)
2 tablespoons milk, iced
½ teaspoon dry mustard
1 teaspoon lemon juice

2 cups Mayonnaise (p. 782)
Salt
Freshly ground white pepper

*EDITORS' NOTE: *French naturally aged* crème fraîche, *or even the cultivated kind on page 666, has a special nutty flavor all its own and we recommend its use in this recipe as elsewhere generally. However, plain heavy cream, whipped, may be substituted here.*

Green Mayonnaise / MAYONNAISE VERTE

For cold fish, especially salmon.

Put the mustard, spinach and *fines herbes* into a bowl. Beat in the mayonnaise with a small wire whip. Or, if desired, the spinach, *fines herbes* and mustard may be blended briefly in an electric blender before combining them with the mayonnaise.

FOR 2½ GENEROUS CUPS:

1 teaspoon Dijon mustard
½ cup finely minced cooked spinach, very well drained

2 tablespoons minced Fines Herbes (p. 89)
2 cups Mayonnaise (p. 782)

Jellied Mayonnaise / MAYONNAISE COLLÉE

This sauce is never used by itself. Like a *sauce chaud-froid,* it is used to coat cold fish, meat or poultry.

Dissolve 1 tablespoon of unflavored gelatin in ⅓ cup of water, wine, or any desired stock. Place this mixture over hot water to liquefy completely and then gradually beat it into 1½ cups lukewarm mayonnaise. Cool until somewhat thickened if it is to be spread over foods, or cool until it is almost firm if it is to be piped through a pastry tube.

/ *Mayonnaise Mousseline*

Fold the beaten egg white into the mayonnaise.

1 egg white, stiffly beaten   **2 cups Mayonnaise (p. 782)**

/ *Mayonnaise Mousquetaire*

For broiled and grilled meats and fish, and fried eggs.
Simmer the shallots in the wine over low heat until all the wine has evaporated.
Cool the shallots, and add them to the mayonnaise with the chives, beating constantly
with a wire whip.

FOR 2 CUPS:

3 shallots, minced   **2 cups Mayonnaise (p. 782)**
½ cup dry white wine   **1 tablespoon minced chives**

/ *Mayonnaise Tartare*

For fish, fried eggs and cold meats.
Mince the pickles and capers and dry them well in a kitchen towel. Put them into
a bowl with the *fines herbes* and the mayonnaise; blend the mixture with a wooden
spoon or small wire whip.

FOR 2 GENEROUS CUPS:

5 small pickles (gherkins or   **1 tablespoon minced fresh Fines**
** any similar pickle)**   ** Herbes (p. 89)**
1 tablespoon capers   **2 cups Mayonnaise (p. 782)**

/ *Mayonnaise Tyrolienne*

For raw vegetables, shrimp and other shellfish, and also for fried fish.
Put the tomato purée, mustard and mayonnaise into a bowl; beat the mixture vigorously with a small wire whip. Add a little vinegar if the sauce is too thick.

FOR 2 GENEROUS CUPS:

2 tablespoons Tomato Purée   **2 cups Mayonnaise (p. 782)**
** (p. 157)**   **1 teaspoon vinegar**
1 teaspoon Dijon mustard

/ *Sauce Tartare*

Often the *mayonnaise tartare* above is called *sauce tartare*. But there is another
kind of *sauce tartare* which is prepared in the following manner:
Take the yolks of 6 hard-cooked eggs, force them through a fine sieve or mash
them, and work them with a wooden spoon until they have become a smooth paste.

Cut the pickles into lengthwise strips and flatten them with the wide side of the knife. Gather the strips together and mince them finely.

Mince the capers. Dry the minced pickles and capers on kitchen toweling.

MAYONNAISE TARTARE

Combine the pickles, capers and fines herbes in a bowl; add the mayonnaise and blend the mixture with a wooden spoon or small wire whip.

Season the eggs with the salt and the pepper and stir in 1 teaspoon of vinegar for each egg yolk. Combine the finely minced chives with the mayonnaise and strain the mixture. Blend in the egg yolks. Then gradually beat in the oil, that is, ½ cup of olive oil for each egg yolk, as if you were making a mayonnaise.

FOR ABOUT 4 CUPS:

6 hard-cooked egg yolks
1 teaspoon salt
¼ teaspoon freshly ground white pepper

2 tablespoons vinegar
3 tablespoons minced chives
4 tablespoons Mayonnaise (p. 782)
3 cups olive or vegetable oil

/ *Ailloli*

This is the name for both the sauce and the dish with which it is served. It is simply a garlic mayonnaise. The best way of making it is to peel the garlic and pound it in a mortar into a smooth paste. Add the egg yolks and seasoning, continue pounding until absolutely smooth, and then beat in the vinegar with a whisk. Then begin adding the oil just as if making a mayonnaise. Taste for seasoning and correct the consistency with a little boiling water or vinegar as you would an ordinary mayonnaise.

As a dish, *ailloli* usually consists of boiled carrots, potatoes, other vegetables, codfish and other fish, and tomatoes, served with the *sauce ailloli* on the side.

FOR ABOUT 3 CUPS:

4 garlic cloves
3 egg yolks
1 teaspoon salt
¼ teaspoon freshly ground white pepper

1 teaspoon Dijon mustard
3 tablespoons wine vinegar
2 cups olive or vegetable oil
2 or more tablespoons boiling water or vinegar

VINAIGRETTE AND OTHER TART SAUCES

Vinaigrette et Sauces Diverses

VINAIGRETTE SIMPLE / *Simple French Dressing*

Put the salt and vinegar in a bowl and let the salt dissolve. Add the oil and the pepper and mix well.

French dressings can be varied ad infinitum. One may use aromatic vinegars with olive, walnut, hazelnut, vegetable or peanut oil. The vinegar may be replaced by another acid, such as lemon, orange or grapefruit juice, and one may use equal quantities of fruit juice and oil. The oil may also be replaced by Crème Fraîche (p. 666).

FOR ¼ CUP:

½ teaspoon salt
1 tablespoon wine vinegar
3 tablespoons oil

⅛ teaspoon freshly ground white pepper

Mustard French Dressing / VINAIGRETTE À LA MOUTARDE

Proceed as in Simple French Dressing (above), but add ½ teaspoon dry mustard.

French Dressing with Fines Herbes /

VINAIGRETTE AUX FINES HERBES

Proceed as in Simple French Dressing (above), but add 1 tablespoon of minced fresh *fines herbes* (p. 89). Dried herbs may be substituted for the fresh; use about 1 teaspoon of mixed dried herbs.

Avocado French Dressing / VINAIGRETTE AUX AVOCATS

Add to the French dressing the minced pepper, the *fines herbes* and, gradually, the mashed avocado. Beat until the dressing is smooth and thick like cream.

FOR ABOUT 1½ CUPS:

1 cup Mustard French Dressing (above)
¼ green pepper, charred, peeled, seeded and minced (see p. 619)

1 tablespoon minced fresh Fines Herbes (p. 89)
1 avocado, peeled and mashed

Sauce Ravigote /

Combine all the ingredients and blend them thoroughly.

FOR ABOUT 1 CUP:

1 teaspoon minced fresh parsley
2 teaspoons minced fresh chervil
1 teaspoon minced fresh tarragon
1 teaspoon minced fresh chives

½ cup Simple French Dressing or Mustard French Dressing (above)
1 small onion, minced
1 tablespoon minced capers, well drained

Shallot Vinegar / VINAIGRE À L'ÉCHALOTE

For oysters and shellfish.
Blend together the salt, pepper and vinegar, and then add the shallots.

¼ cup wine vinegar
Pinch of salt
Pinch of freshly ground white
  pepper

2 tablespoons minced shallots

SAUCE À LA MENTHE / *Mint Sauce*

For roast or boiled lamb *à l'anglaise*.
Combine the mint, sugar, vinegar and water in a bowl, blend well, and season with the salt and pepper.

FOR ABOUT 1 CUP:

½ cup fresh mint leaves, minced
2 tablespoons sugar
½ cup vinegar
¼ cup water

½ teaspoon salt
Pinch of freshly ground white
  pepper

/ *Sauce Rémoulade*

Blend together the mustard, salt and pepper. Gradually beat in the oil with a wire whisk, as if you were making a mayonnaise. Add the vinegar or lemon juice.

FOR ABOUT ¾ CUP:

2 tablespoons Dijon mustard
½ teaspoon salt
Pinch of freshly ground white
  pepper

½ cup olive or vegetable oil
1 tablespoon wine vinegar or
  lemon juice

SAUCE MOUTARDE À LA CRÈME / *Cream Mustard Sauce*

Put the mustard, lemon juice, salt and pepper into a bowl and blend thoroughly. Gradually beat in the *crème fraîche* with a wire whisk, as if you were making a mayonnaise.

FOR ½ CUP:

1 tablespoon Dijon mustard
1 teaspoon lemon juice
½ teaspoon salt

⅛ teaspoon freshly ground white
  pepper
½ cup Crème Fraîche (p. 666)

SAUCE AUX CONCOMBRES / *Cucumber Sauce*

Peel a whole cucumber with a vegetable peeler. Cut it lengthwise into halves, remove the seeds with a coffeespoon, and cut the cucumber into large dice. Blanch the cucumber by plunging it into boiling water for 5 minutes. Drain and plunge into cold water, drain again very thoroughly, and press it through a food mill or a fine sieve.

The cucumber purée will be soft, since cucumber is a watery vegetable. Allow the cucumber purée to rest in a fine sieve over a bowl for 10 minutes, and reserve the drained juice. Season the pulp with salt and a few drops of Tabasco. Thin the *crème fraîche* with a few drops of the reserved juice and whip it; then mix the whipped *crème* with the cucumber purée. The sauce should be served very cold.

FOR 1 CUCUMBER:

½ teaspoon salt
Tabasco

2 tablespoons Crème Fraîche
(p. 666)

Egg Sauce / SAUCE AUX OEUFS

For cold fish and meats.
Mash the hard-cooked egg yolks until they are a smooth paste. Stir in the mustard and add the oil gradually, as if making a mayonnaise. Blend in the vinegar, a little at a time, as the mixture becomes thick. Add the capers, pickles, *fines herbes* and whipped cream. Mix together thoroughly and correct the seasoning.

FOR ABOUT 1¾ CUPS:

3 hard-cooked egg yolks
1 teaspoon Dijon mustard
1 cup olive or vegetable oil
1½ tablespoons wine vinegar

1 tablespoon minced capers and pickles
1 tablespoon minced fresh Fines Herbes (p. 89)
3 tablespoons heavy cream, whipped

Sauce Gribiche /

For fish and cold shellfish.
Mash the hard-cooked egg yolks until they are a smooth paste. Beat in the mustard, salt and pepper. Add the oil, little by little, beating with a wire whisk as if you were making a mayonnaise. As the mixture becomes thick, add a little of the vinegar at a time. Then beat in the *fines herbes,* pickles, capers, and the minced hard-cooked egg whites. Correct the seasoning, and add a little boiling water or vinegar if too thick.

FOR ABOUT 3 CUPS:

6 hard-cooked egg yolks
1 tablespoon Dijon mustard
1 teaspoon salt
⅛ teaspoon freshly ground black pepper
2 cups olive or vegetable oil

3 tablespoons wine vinegar
1 tablespoon fresh Fines Herbes (p. 89)
2 tablespoons minced pickles
2 tablespoons capers
3 hard-cooked egg whites, minced

Horseradish Sauce I / SAUCE RAIFORT I

For cold fish.
If fresh horseradish is not available, you may use drained bottled horseradish. Combine the grated horseradish, lemon juice, salt and pepper. Fold this mixture into the whipped *crème fraîche.*

FOR ABOUT 1 CUP:

4 tablespoons freshly grated
  horseradish
1 teaspoon lemon juice
½ teaspoon salt

⅛ teaspoon freshly ground white
  pepper
½ cup Crème Fraîche (p. 666),
  stiffly whipped

SAUCE RAIFORT II | *Horseradish Sauce II*

For cold asparagus.
Blend all the ingredients, adding salt and pepper to taste, and serve the sauce in a sauceboat.

FOR 1½ CUPS:

4 tablespoons freshly grated
  horseradish
¼ cup Mayonnaise (p. 782)
½ cup Crème Fraîche (p. 666),
  stiffly beaten

Salt
Freshly ground white pepper

SAUCE AU CITRON | *Lemon Sauce*

For cold asparagus.
Blend together the cream cheese, the finely grated black radish, and the *fines herbes*. Then beat in sufficient lemon juice to make a smooth sauce. Season to taste with salt and pepper, and serve in a sauceboat.

FOR ABOUT ¾ CUP:

½ cup cream cheese
1 black radish, grated
2 tablespoons minced Fines
  Herbes (p. 89)

3 tablespoons (or more) lemon
  juice
Salt
Freshly ground black pepper

SAUCE AU PAIN | *Bread Sauce*

Combine milk and veal stock in a saucepan and bring to the boiling point. Beat in the fresh bread crumbs and season to taste with salt and pepper. Simmer the sauce for 15 minutes and then beat it with a wire whisk until smooth and fluffy. Stir in the cream and the lemon juice and heat the sauce again, but do not let it boil. Keep the sauce warm over hot water until serving time.

FOR ABOUT 2½ CUPS:

1 cup milk
1 cup White Stock (p. 165)
1 cup fresh white bread crumbs
Salt

Freshly ground white pepper
¼ cup heavy cream
2 teaspoons lemon juice

COMPOUND BUTTERS

Beurres Composés

Note: Each of the recipes in this section will yield about ½ cup unless otherwise noted.

Almond Butter | BEURRE D'AMANDES

Mash the almonds to a fine paste in a mortar, adding a few drops of water to prevent their becoming oily. Beat the almonds into the butter and strain through a fine sieve. Yields about 1 cup.

½ cup blanched almonds   **½ cup butter, softened**

Anchovy Butter | BEURRE D'ANCHOIS

Mash the anchovy fillets in a mortar (there should be about 3 tablespoons), beat them into the butter, and keep on beating until butter and anchovies form a smooth paste.

3 large anchovy fillets   **½ cup butter, softened**

Black Butter | BEURRE NOIR

Cook the butter in a saucepan until it is dark brown. Then add the parsley, the capers and the hot vinegar.

½ cup butter   **1 tablespoon capers**
2 tablespoons minced parsley   **1 tablespoon hot vinegar**

Caviar Butter | BEURRE DE CAVIAR

Mash the caviar, mix it with the butter, and strain through a fine sieve.

3 tablespoons caviar   **½ cup butter, softened**

Fines Herbes Butter | BEURRE DE FINES HERBES

Beat the cream into the butter with a wire whisk and then beat in the *fines herbes* and the lemon juice. Yields about 1 cup.

½ cup heavy cream
½ cup butter, softened
2 tablespoons minced fresh Fines
   Herbes (p. 89)

1 teaspoon lemon juice

BEURRE D'AIL / *Garlic Butter*

Peel and mash the garlic, beat it into the butter and, if desired, strain through a fine sieve.

3 garlic cloves

½ cup butter, softened

BEURRE VERT / *Green Butter*

Blend the spinach juice with the butter and strain through a fine sieve. To make the spinach juice, mash 2 pounds washed and well-drained spinach in a mortar. Put the spinach into a kitchen towel and squeeze out the juice. Reduce the juice in a saucepan over low heat until it is concentrated.

¼ cup spinach juice

½ cup butter, softened

BEURRE DE NOISETTES / *Hazelnut Butter*

Toast the hazelnuts lightly in a warm oven. Peel them by rubbing them over a coarse sieve or between kitchen towels. Mash them in a mortar, with a few drops of water to prevent their becoming oily. Add the butter and strain through a fine sieve. Yields about 1 cup.

½ cup shelled hazelnuts

½ cup butter, softened

BEURRE AU CITRON / *Lemon Butter*

Beat the lemon rind and the butter together and season with the salt and pepper.

Grated rind of 1 lemon
½ cup butter, softened
½ teaspoon salt

⅛ teaspoon freshly ground white
   pepper

BEURRE DE HOMARD / *Lobster Butter*

Mash the green liver and the raw coral from the lobster and beat in the butter to make a creamy mixture. Yields about ¾ cup.

Green liver and coral from a
   2-pound lobster

½ cup butter, softened

Maître d'Hôtel Butter | BEURRE MAÎTRE D'HÔTEL

Mash the *fines herbes* in a mortar and beat in the butter and the lemon juice. Season with salt and beat until smooth. Yields about ¾ cup.

2 tablespoons minced fresh Fines Herbes (p. 89)
½ cup butter, softened

2 teaspoons lemon juice
½ teaspoon salt

Mustard Butter | BEURRE DE MOUTARDE

Blend together the butter, the mustard and the tarragon.

½ cup butter, softened
1 tablespoon Dijon mustard

1 teaspoon minced fresh tarragon

Paprika Butter | BEURRE DE PAPRIKA

Beat the paprika thoroughly into the butter.

1 teaspoon (or more to taste) paprika

½ cup butter, softened

Pâté Butter | BEURRE DE PÂTÉ DE FOIE

Mash the pâté and beat it into the butter to make a smooth paste.

2 ounces pâté de fois gras

½ cup butter softened

Pimiento Butter | BEURRE DE PIMENT

Mash the chopped pepper in a mortar into a smooth paste. Beat in the butter and season with the salt and cayenne. Yields about ¾ cup.

1 large red or yellow sweet pepper, charred, scraped, seeded and chopped (see (p. 619)

½ cup butter, softened
½ teaspoon salt
Pinch of cayenne pepper

Pistachio Butter | BEURRE DE PISTACHES

Mash the pistachios in a mortar, with a few drops of water to prevent their becoming oily. Beat in the butter and strain through a fine sieve. Yields about 1 cup.

½ cup shelled pistachios

½ cup butter, softened

BEURRE DE SARDINES / *Sardine Butter*

Mash the sardines in a mortar and beat them into the butter to make a smooth paste. Yields about ¾ cup.

1 small can (2 ounces) sardine fillets

½ cup butter, softened

BEURRE D'ESCARGOT / *Snail Butter*

Mash the shallots to a paste in a mortar. Beat in the butter and the parsley and season with salt and pepper. Garlic may be used in place of the shallots, and the butter may also be seasoned with lemon juice.

3 shallots, minced
½ cup butter, softened
1 tablespoon minced parsley

½ teaspoon salt
⅛ teaspoon freshly ground white pepper

BEURRE D'ESTRAGON / *Tarragon Butter*

Mash the tarragon in a mortar. Blend in the butter to make a smooth paste.

3 tablespoons minced fresh tarragon

½ cup butter, softened

BEURRE DE TOMATES / *Tomato Butter*

Mix the tomato purée with the butter to a smooth paste. Yields about ¾ cup.

¼ cup Tomato Purée (p. 157)

½ cup butter, softened

BEURRE DE TRUFFES / *Truffle Butter*

Mash the truffles to a paste in a mortar, mix them with the *béchamel,* and beat in the butter. Yields about ¾ cup.

3 truffles
2 tablespoons cold Sauce Béchamel (p. 761)

½ cup butter, softened

III

WINES

Les Vins

FROM THE VINE TO THE TABLE

Wine is a living product which begins to exist with the fermentation of the sugar inside a fresh grape. It was Pasteur, in 1866, who explained the phenomenon of alcoholic fermentation from the grapes harvested in his vineyard in Arbois. Around 1880, the entire area under vines in France, which then covered about 6,000,000 acres, was completely destroyed in a few years by a parasite whose larvae attacked the roots of the vine: the phylloxera came from North America, where the native vines were resistant to it. The devastation by phylloxera had two consequences:

—To maintain the quality of wines, it has been necessary since then to graft the European vine varieties onto crosses resulting from the hybridization of European varieties and American varieties resistant to phylloxera.

—To put an end to the manufacturing of artificial wines from raisins, sugar and coloring matter (particularly red Bordeaux wines), the French law of August 14, 1889, stipulated that wine must be produced exclusively by the fermentation of fresh grapes or fresh grape juice.

For centuries, man has used his ingenuity to devise all kinds of ingredients to put into wine to stop it going bad or to cover up an unpleasant taste, usually that of vinegar resulting from the oxidation of ethyl alcohol into acetic acid through bacterial action.

Modern methods of vinification make use both of asepsis and a moderate amount of sulfur anhydride, an antiseptic that is also an antioxidant and keeps the wine in good condition. Sulfur anhydride eventually disappears into the wine, combining with potassium sulphate, which is found in grapes in an appreciable quantity, as are organic acids, particularly tartaric acid.

Vinification begins with the picking of the grapes. Except in special cases such as the natural sweet wines of Roussillon and the *vins de paille* of Jura, harvesting should be done when the grapes are at their peak of ripeness. In the Middle Ages, the proclamation that the grapes were ripe produced general gaiety, and carefree merrymaking accompanied the *Ban des Vendanges*. Nowadays, the date of the grape-picking is set scientifically by thrice-weekly samplings from the vines. The juice is analyzed and when the sugar count remains steady and the acidity has gone below a certain level, the harvest is open. Then, briefly, here is how matters progress:

Red wines: The grapes, pressed and macerated, are put into vats to undergo fermentation for one to eight days depending on whether low-alcohol wine is wanted or whether it is to be bottled. The fermentation is "revved up" by making the wine in the vat flow to the bottom and then pumping it back to the top, forcing air into it. The extra oxygen makes the yeast develop prodigiously and the sugar from the must is changed into alcohol.

Once the fermentation is finished, the resulting wine is piped into casks or vats, while what is left behind is the *marc*. This is then taken to the winepress. The wine that has been drawn off slowly throws off its impurities, and two months after the harvesting, in December, the *soutirage* is performed, which means that the clear wine is put into fresh casks for a further rest. In the spring, a second racking is done to separate the pure wine from the sediment or lees. This operation is repeated four times during the year before the wine is considered stable, and ready for drinking or bottling.

White wines: The grapes are pressed as soon as they arrive at the vats. The must that gushes from the winepress is immediately piped into casks or vats; sulfur anhydride is added to sterilize it and to delay fermentation. During this period, the winemaker proceeds with the *débourbage,* the elimination of impurities in the clear must. After this first operation the juice is racked and put to ferment in fresh vats. The performance is repeated several times during the year until the wine is completely clear.

Pink wines are treated sometimes like white, sometimes like red. In the former method, the winemaker can collect the juice from the vat of unpressed black grapes; this "bleeding" is more or less prolonged, depending on the color required. In the latter method, the black grapes are pressed immediately, but the resulting juice is very pale in color. It is of course possible to combine the two methods, but it is still difficult to get a good deep pink color. It all depends on the variety of grapevine, the ripeness of the grapes, and the region.

Champagne is the result of a second fermentation in bottle, the discovery of which, in 1666, is due to Dom Pérignon, the cellar-master at the Abbey of Hautvillers in the district of the Marne.

Two thirds of the vineyards of the province of Champagne are planted with varieties of red wine grapes, principally the Pinot Noir that is responsible also for the great red Burgundies, and with the white wine grape Pinot Chardonnay, equally widespread in Burgundy. The harvesting is done with a great deal of care to eliminate defective grapes. The pressing, carried out right next to the vineyards, produces wine that is absolutely white, even from black grapes. It would therefore be logical to say that there are *champagnes blancs de rouges* in the same way that one says *champagne blanc de blancs,* since the latter comes only from white grapes, cultivated for the most part on the Côte des Blancs, near Épernay, between Cramant and Vertus.

In the spring following the harvest the white wines, to which a sugar syrup is added, are put in bottles; these are put to lie in limestone cellars and kept at a constant temperature. Progressively, the sugar changes to alcohol and carbon dioxide; this second fermentation, in bottle, goes on for at least a year, often for two or three. When the bottle fermentation is completed the bottles are placed, neck down, on perforated inclined racks called *pupitres,* and every day, for three to six months, specialists shake and turn them to make the sediment thrown off by the yeast slide down to the necks of the bottles. When the sediment adheres to the surface of the cork, it is removed and the bottle is finally recorked for shipping. A top-quality champagne should not be drunk until three or four years after the vintage.

Each brand of champagne has its own special taste, the result of blending in varying proportions—before the second fermentation in bottle—white wines made from white grapes and white wines made from black grapes coming from different soils. The cellar-master of each champagne house does his utmost to maintain the level of sweetness or dryness from one year to the next. This is why the vintage year does not count as much for champagne as it does for the wines of Burgundy and Bordeaux. Furthermore, in the greatest champagne years only a certain proportion of the harvest is allowed to carry a vintage label.

The *dosage* of champagne is done by adding syrup. If it has received only a very little syrup or none at all, the wine is "extra dry" or *"brut."* If some syrup is added, it is *"sec."* A more pronounced addition of sugar gives *"demi-sec"* and *"doux."*

To conserve part of the natural sugar of the grape, it has been customary for

Strawberry Cake à la Dacquoise

Gâteau aux Fraises à la Dacquoise

Strawberry Cake à la Dacquoise

Gâteau aux Fraises à la Dacquoise

BAKE 2 ROUND 9-inch layers of *génoise*, unmold the layers on a cake rack, and allow them to cool.

Prepare the kirsch-flavored buttercream and frosting and the *crème Chantilly*.

Spread one layer of the cake with the buttercream and about two thirds of the strawberries; if they are very big, they must be cut into halves. Top with the other cake slice and frost it with kirsch frosting. Dip the remaining strawberries into the strawberry-jam purée and place them on the icing. Put the *crème Chantilly* into a pastry bag fitted with a star tube and pipe decorative swirls on the surface of the cake. Refrigerate the cake until serving time.

1 recipe Génoise (p. 683)
1 cup Liqueur-Flavored Buttercream (p. 675), made with kirsch
1 cup Liqueur-Flavored Frosting (p. 669), made with kirsch
1 cup Crème Chantilly (p. 672)
1 quart fresh strawberries
1 cup strawberry jam, puréed

Normandy Ice Cream

Glace à la Crème de Normandie

Normandy Ice Cream
Glace à la Crème de Normandie

PROCEED AS IN Vanilla Ice Cream (p. 751) and add ¼ cup additional sugar, ¼ cup Grand Marnier and 2 tablespoons of instant coffee powder to the egg yolks before folding in the whipped cream. Omit the vanilla flavoring. If desired freeze the mixture in a decorative mold.

Sausages à la Normande

Boudins à la Normande

Sausages à la Normande

Boudins à la Normande

Editors' Note: The two types of sausages in the illustration for this dish are the famous boudins noirs *and* boudins blancs *(blood sausages). The French dote on blood sausages, but they are, to say the least, an acquired taste for Americans, and certainly they are difficult to find in this country. We suggest you simply substitute country-style sausages, or whatever is your favorite kind.*

PEEL AND CORE the apples. Cut them into thick wedges. Reserve about 8 wedges and cook the remainder with ¼ cup of water in a saucepan over medium heat for about 20 minutes. Drain and mash into applesauce. Season to taste with sugar, but leave very tart. Keep hot.

Sauté the reserved 8 apple wedges in the combined hot oil and butter in a skillet until golden. Remove them and keep them hot. Cook the sausages in the same skillet until done.

Pour the applesauce into a hot serving dish and arrange the sausages in a circle around the edges. Put the apple wedges in the middle and serve immediately.

For 4 persons:

2 pounds tart apples
Sugar
2 tablespoons peanut oil
2 tablespoons butter
8 sausages

Lobster à l'Armoricaine

Homard à l'Armoricaine

Lobster à l'Armoricaine
Homard à l'Armoricaine

PUT THE LOBSTERS into the boiling *court bouillon*. Cook for 10 minutes after the *court bouillon* returns to a boil. Drain the lobsters and cool slightly. Cut the tails into thick slices; split the upper bodies lengthwise into halves; discard the sacs behind the heads and reserve the coral and the tomalley; sever the claws from the bodies and crack them.

Heat the oil in a casserole and sauté the onions and the shallots in it until they are soft. Add all of the lobster pieces, season with salt and pepper to taste, and cook for about 5 minutes. Add the *sauce tomate*. Cook for 5 minutes more and add the brandy. Simmer over low heat for 20 minutes. Transfer the lobster pieces to a hot dish.

Strain the sauce and then return it to the casserole. Stir in the reserved tomalley mashed with the coral. Add the Madeira. Reduce the sauce by about one third and correct the seasoning. Stir in the butter. Return the lobster pieces to the sauce and keep over lowest possible heat until serving time. Serve with plain boiled rice.

For 4 persons:

2 live 2-pound lobsters	**Freshly ground black**
Court Bouillon for	**pepper**
Lobster (p. 243)	**2 cups Sauce Tomate (p. 769)**
3 tablespoons peanut oil	**¼ cup brandy**
½ cup minced onions	**2 tablespoons Madeira**
4 shallots, minced	**2 tablespoons butter**
Salt	

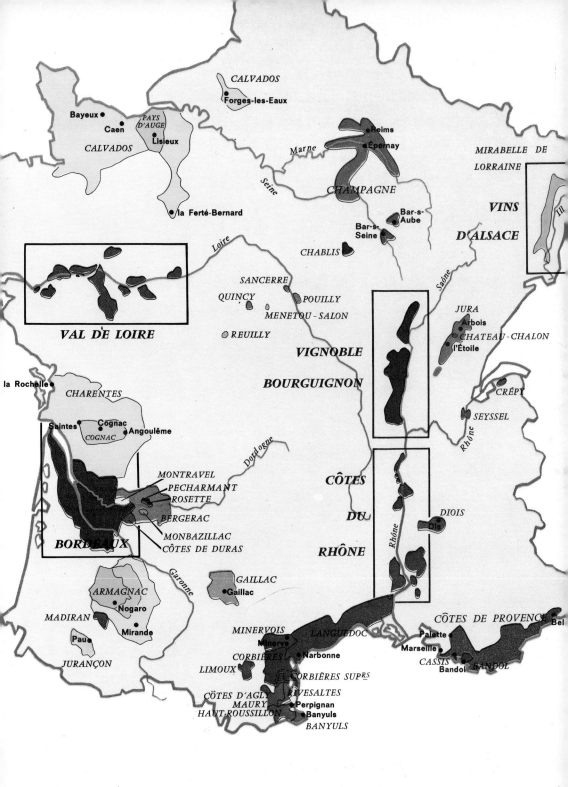

The Vineyards of France

Les Vignobles de France

The Vineyards of France

Les Vignobles de France

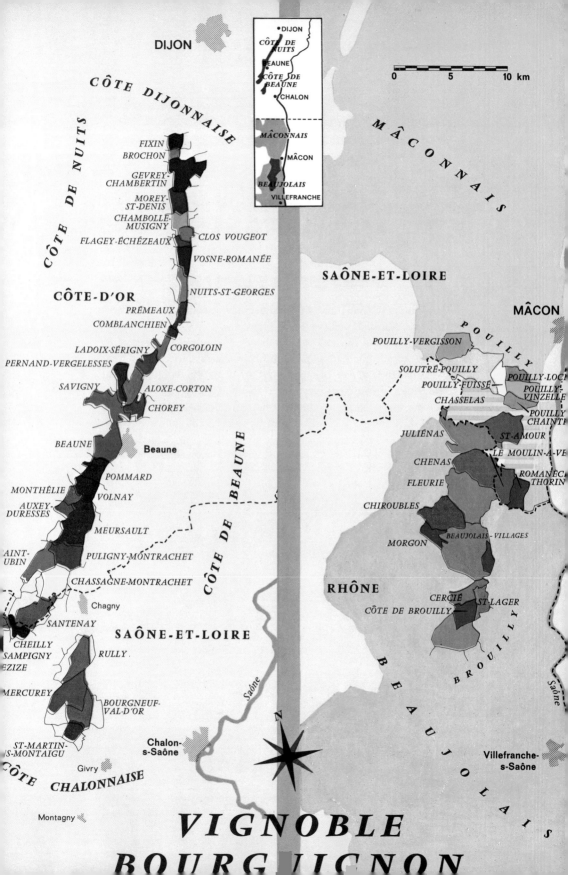

DIJON

CÔTE DIJONNAISE

CÔTE DE NUITS

FIXIN
BROCHON
GEVREY-
CHAMBERTIN
MOREY-
ST-DENIS
CHAMBOLLE-
MUSIGNY
FLAGEY-ÉCHÉZEAUX
CLOS VOUGEOT
VOSNE-ROMANÉE
CÔTE-D'OR
NUITS-ST-GEORGES
PRÉMEAUX
COMBLANCHIEN
LADOIX-SÉRIGNY
CORGOLOIN
PERNAND-VERGELESSES
SAVIGNY
ALOXE-CORTON
CHOREY
BEAUNE
Beaune
POMMARD
MONTHÉLIE
VOLNAY
AUXEY-
DURESSES
MEURSAULT
AINT-
UBIN
PULIGNY-MONTRACHET
CHASSAGNE-MONTRACHET
Chagny
SANTENAY
CHEILLY
SAMPIGNY
EZIZE
RULLY
MERCUREY
BOURGNEUF-
VAL-D'OR
ST-MARTIN-
S-MONTAIGU
Givry
CÔTE
CHALONNAISE
Montagny

CÔTE DE BEAUNE

SAÔNE-ET-LOIRE

Chalon-
s-Saône

Saône

N

DIJON
CÔTE DE
NUITS
BEAUNE
CÔTE DE
BEAUNE
CHALON
MÂCONNAIS
MÂCON
BEAUJOLAIS
VILLEFRANCHE

0   5   10 km

MÂCONNAIS

SAÔNE-ET-LOIRE

MÂCON

POUILLY

POUILLY-VERGISSON
SOLUTRÉ-POUILLY
POUILLY-FUISSÉ
CHASSELAS
POUILLY-LOCH
POUILLY-
VINZELLE
POUILLY
CHAINT

JULIÉNAS
ST-AMOUR
LE MOULIN-A-VE
CHENAS
ROMANÈC
THORIN
FLEURIE
CHIROUBLES
BEAUJOLAIS - VILLAGES
MORGON
RHÔNE
CERCIE
ST-LAGER
CÔTE DE BROUILLY
BROUILLY

BEAUJOLAIS

Saône

Villefranche-
s-Saône

VIGNOBLE
BOURGUIGNON

The Vineyard Districts of Burgundy

THE WINE-PRODUCING area of Burgundy covers four administrative districts: Yonne, Côte-d'Or, Saône-et-Loire, Rhône; each of their wines is made from a single variety of grape: Pinot Chardonnay for the whites, Gamay for the Beaujolais, and Pinot Noir for the red Burgundies.

The wines of Chablis and Montrachet have acquired a worldwide reputation as thoroughbred dry white wines.

The most famous Burgundies are those of Haute-Bourgogne; Côte de Beaune, which one can start to drink in the second or third year; Côte Chalonnaise, which one can start to drink in the fourth year; Côte de Nuits, in the sixth year after the vintage.

The wine lover learns as much as he can about the different vineyards and then makes his choice according to taste and judgment.

The Vineyard Districts of Bordeaux

There are three leading grapevine varieties for white wines, three for red, and forty *appellations d'origine*.

CLASSIFIED GREAT GROWTHS OF SAINT-ÉMILION (1958)

CHÂTEAUX

L'Arrosée
L'Angélus
Balestard-La Tonnelle
Bellevue
Bergat
Cadet-Bon
Cadet-Piola
Canon la Gaffelière
Cap de Mourlin
Chapelle-Madeleine
Chauvin
Corbin (Giraud)
Corbin (Michotte)
Coutet
Croque-Michotte
Curé Bon
Fonplégade
Fonroque
Franc-Mayne
Grand Barrail Lamarzelle-Figeac
Grand-Corbin Despagne
Grand-Corbin Pecresse
Grand-Mayne
Grand-Pontet
Grandes-Murailles
Guadet Saint-Julien
Jean Faure
La Carte
La Clotte
La Clusière
La Couspaude
La Dominique

Larcis-Ducasse
Lamarzelle
Larmande
Laroze
Lasserre
La Tour-du-Pin Figeac (Bélivier)
La Tour-du-Pin Figeac (Moueix)
La Tour Figeac
Le Châtelet
Le Couvent
Le Prieuré
Mauvezin
Moulin-du-Cadet
Pavie-Decesse
Pavie-Macquin
Pavillon Cadet
Faurie de Souchard
Petit Faurie de Soutard
Ripeau
Sansonnet
Saint-Georges Côte-Pavie
Soutard
Tertre-Daugay
Trimoulet
Trois-Moulins
Troplong-Mondot
Villemaurine
Yon Figeac
Clos des Jacobins
Clos de la Madeleine
Clos Saint-Martin

For a listing of the classified first great growths of Saint-Émilion, see page 809.

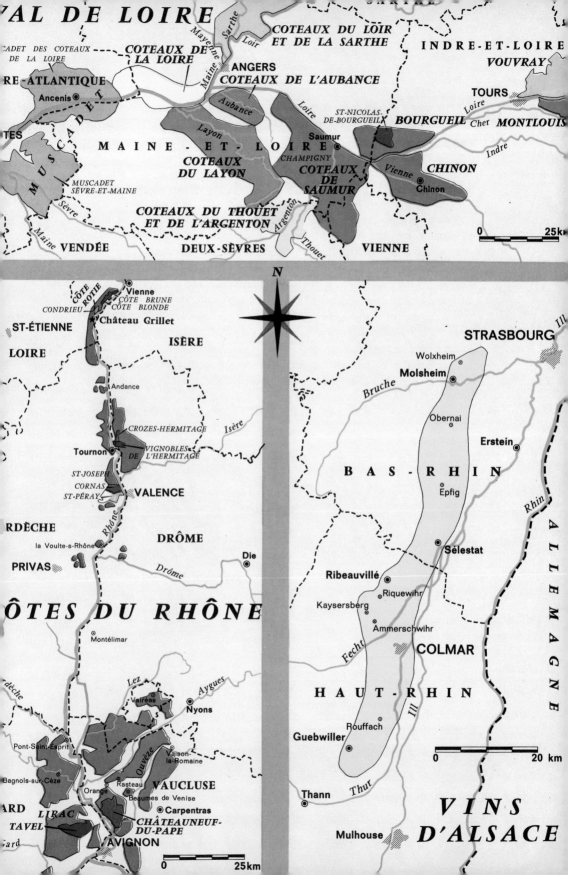

Val de Loire, Côtes du Rhône, Alsace

THE LOIRE VALLEY is well known for its white wines, dry, semi-sweet or sweet, and its rosés. However, the reputation of its white and rosé wines was made by its reds, which are few in number.

In the Côtes du Rhône, wine lovers make a distinction between the northern wines, which grow north of Montélimar and are the product of a single grape variety, and the southern Côtes du Rhône, whose potency comes from strong sunlight and the blending of different varietals.

The wines of Alsace are popular all over France because of their delicacy, and even more because of their very special bouquet, the result of each grape variety undergoing vinification separately.

centuries to add brandy at the beginning of fermentation. This produces *vins doux naturels* such as Banyuls, Muscat de Rivesaltes, Muscat de Frontignan, Muscat de Samos, or *vins de liqueur* like Pineau des Charentes, port, etc.

These are *apéritif* or dessert wines, much appreciated with pastries, desserts and ices. Pineau des Charentes and the Muscat wines are bottled very young in order to keep the taste of the grapes. But Banyuls and the other *vins doux naturels,* such as port, reach their peak after long aging in wooden casks, prolonged by being kept in bottle. Vintage ports, specially selected, are bottled two or three years after the vintage and aged in bottle. It is absolutely necessary to decant them before drinking.

Vins blancs liquoreux, or naturally sweet dessert wines (Sauternes, Barsac, Monbazillac, Vouvray, Anjou), are the result of a natural phenomenon. The vineyards of these regions are in areas that are particularly damp in the fall. A mold develops on the grapes that absorbs the juice and some of the organic acids they contain and withers them. The natural grape sugar becomes even more concentrated by this overripening, and gives highly sweet musts. The fermenting agent turns only part of the natural grape sugar into alcohol; these wines are exceptional in the balance of their chief components: alcohol, sugar and low acidity.

After the alcoholic fermentation comes the *élevage* of the wine. The wine is clarified by the deposit of albuminoid matter, the yeast that started the fermentation, and excess potassium bitartrate, in the bottom of the casks.

Aging brings about various phenomena of oxidization, helping the development of the multiple chemical components that go to make the *bouquet* of the wine.

The knowledge of the *éleveur* is used to bring out the special characteristics that a given wine gets from the soil, the variety of grapevine, and the method of cultivation. A wine has to be carefully watched and guided throughout its life, and beneficent changes in the organism must be found and encouraged. On the other hand, the breeder has to do everything he can to prevent poor conditions that would result in damage and disease and make the wine unfit for drinking. Because of this, the *sommelier* should know precisely where the wines are going to be laid away, and how they should be treated in the wood and in bottle. He should know the conditions required for a good cellar as well. He should be able to keep the equipment in order and carry out all the operations necessary to keep the wines in good condition.

Special equipment is needed because barrels in which wine is stored must always be kept full. If this is not done, air seeps slowly into a pocket underneath the bung and very soon starts a chemical process known as the *"fleur."* This is the precursor of an acid condition in the wine, particularly liable to occur at times when the wine is "working," for instance, at the equinoxes.

Sulfuring the casks, *fining* and *racking* the wines, are all methods used to separate the wine from the lees.

Blending can improve certain wines that are too low in alcohol.

Filtering helps in the clarification of wines.

Bottling. Although nowadays certain producers make themselves responsible for this on the spot, this operation has traditionally been done by wine merchants, and the wine lover should be familiar with it. Many precautions must be taken to insure the cleanliness and hygiene on which depends the keeping of wines and spirits.

The most favorable moment for bottling is at the end of the winter, a few weeks before the sap rises in the spring. It is best to choose dry days, with the wind coming from the north, rather than damp days, in order to avoid a resumption of activity of the yeasts and bacteria when they are inevitably exposed to the air at the moment of bottling; this exposure of the wine to the air should of course be made as brief as possible.

The bottles must be scrupulously clean, thoroughly washed and rinsed; wine can be spoiled if the bottles are dirty or the glass poorly made. Naturally bottles will be chosen that accord with the origin of the wine (Burgundy, Bordeaux, Champagne, etc.).

Corking. The choice and softening of the cork, which is put into boiling water and then soaked in the wine for several hours, are very important. To avoid accidents, such as a wine that tastes of cork, experts have approved the use of corks covered with a light coating of paraffin.

If the wine is to be aged for a long time, the neck of the bottle and the cork are dipped into hot sealing wax to reduce oxidization. The cap that completes the operation, like the sealing wax, is there to prevent air getting to the cork.

Wine very easily gets sick: grease is particularly bad for white wines, making them thick or oily.

Acid turns wine into vinegar; this disease attacks light wines above all and is often due to negligence when filling the casks.

Overfermentation makes wine of a poor year fizzy or sour, at the time when the wine is working.

Mannitol gives wine a cloudy appearance and a bittersweet taste, resulting from too much lactic fermentation.

An off-taste, woody, moldy, a rotten-egg flavor, or whatever, or wine that is bitter, green or grapey, are faults that can be recognized by tasting.

Everyone, and especially the unfortunate city-dweller, cannot own a pretty vaulted cellar, which has a pleasant temperature, like the traditional winecellars of our big country houses. In modern apartment buildings, the wine lover should choose, in the basement, a room as far away as possible from the heating system and free from the vibrations of the street. This cellar should be provided with special racks or, at the very least, shelves where the bottles should be laid away horizontally.

A gentleman's cellar consists of at least a hundred bottles of good-quality wine. The selection covers local wines like Sancerre, Alsace, Beaujolais and Muscadet, and includes champagne and the better wines of Bordeaux and Burgundy.

As soon as a case arrives, the wine lover carefully unpacks the bottles and puts them away in their appointed places; they should rest for at least three weeks, because travel, temperature changes and handling are tiring for wine.

SERVING TEMPERATURES FOR WINES

Wines	Temperatures
Dry whites, medium-dry whites, rosés	Between 45° and 55° F.
Sweet white dessert wines	40° F.
Vins jaunes (Château-Chalon)	Cellar temperature, 60° F.
Champagne	Iced, at just under 40° F.
Sparkling wines	Iced, at 35° F.
Beaujolais	Slightly chilled, or at 60° F.
Côtes du Rhône and Burgundy	Cellar temperature, or just warm at 62° to 65° F.
Red Bordeaux and Touraine	*Chambrés,* from 65° to 68° F.

SERVING WINE

You can have too much of a good thing, and this rule should be remembered by people who feel they should serve a different kind of wine with each course. Such an outpouring of wine often spoils an excellent meal and it can make the guests feel uncomfortable. You should not let yourself be influenced by memories of romantic menus where anywhere from six to ten great bottles accompanied an equal amount of very substantial food!

Today's gastronomy is content with two very good dishes and two great wines, a white for the hors-d'oeuvre and fish course, and a red for the roast and the cheeses. Some connoisseurs prefer a single wine to be served with regional meals consisting of one dish, such as *bouillabaisse, pot-au-feu, cassoulet* and the like. In such instances, wines from Provence and Beaujolais are particularly suitable, and so is champagne.

At elaborate dinners, the range can be extended to include a splendid white Burgundy, for instance, a Montrachet, with the melon and the trout. A delicate red wine, such as Saint-Émilion, with the sweetbreads; with the game and the cheese a Burgundy from the Côte de Nuits. I am not mentioning champagne, which will be served with the dessert, although there are connoisseurs who care for it only *brut,* as an apéritif.

Generally speaking, one should always go up the scale, which means starting with the lightest and finishing with a full-bodied wine.

Cooling: White and rosé wines should be served at a temperature between 40° and 55° F. Some red wines, such as Beaujolais, Côtes du Rhône, Chinon and Bourgueil, should be drunk between 45° and 55° F., although many people prefer them warmer, around 65° F. They can either be cooled outdoors in winter, or left in a mixture of water and ice in a bucket, or refrigerated, so long as the bottle is some distance from the freezing compartment.

Chambrer: To *chambrer* a bottle is to bring it into a moderately warm room forty-eight hours before it is to be drunk. Unfortunately, this principle, enunciated by all experts of the 19th century, became obsolete with the invention of central heating. Our ancestors used to bring their bottles into rooms where the temperature was never higher than 60° F. These days, the bottle is taken from a cold storage vault into an overheated room; the wine drinker should take this fact into consideration and turn off the heat in the room where the wine is to be *chambré.* In any case, this is still the best method of presenting the great wines of Burgundy or Châteauneuf-du-Pape in all their glory.

Decanting is used chiefly in the service of the greatest wines of Bordeaux, for old clarets have a tendency to throw a heavy sediment. Decanting consists of separating the wine from the sediment by pouring the wine into a carafe. This should be done two hours before drinking and is carried out as follows:

Rinse out the carafe with warm water and drain it well.

Rinse out the carafe with wine by pouring into it a liqueurglassful of wine; shake well and pour out the wine.

Uncork the bottle, using a corkscrew with blades.

Put a glass funnel over the carafe and tilt the bottle gently.

Pour gently; the air should not enter the bottle with a rush.

Pour faster when the bottle is horizontal.

Watch the position of the sediment: when it is close to the neck of the bottle, stop pouring and place the bottle upright.

THE VINTAGE YEAR

In certain famous cellars in Bordeaux and Burgundy, there are little alcoves, usually latticed or barred, where some bottles are lying under a layer of dust and a halo of moss. Here you can see bottles of Haut-Brion 1864, Lafite 1869, Latour 1877, Romanée-Conti 1895, Chambertin 1900. For a while, the happy owners explained that they were keeping these bottles for a celebration: a wedding, a birth. We no longer desecrate them, and perhaps it is a good thing, since these centenary wines have little chance of being in perfect drinking condition.

Here is a list taken from the finest years where the wines still have a chance of being in decent condition—not necessarily excellent. They are the oldest wines we are familiar with:

Burgundy

Red: 1895 - 1900 - 1904 - 1906 - 1915 - 1923 - 1926 - 1929 - 1934 - 1945 - 1947 - 1949 - 1952 - 1953 - 1955 - 1959 - 1961 - 1962 - 1964 - 1966.

White: 1898 - 1904 - 1908 - 1911 - 1915 - 1923 - 1929 - 1934 - 1943 - 1945 - 1947 - 1949 - 1952 - 1955 - 1959 - 1961 - 1962 - 1964 - 1966.

Bordeaux

Red: 1893 - 1899 - 1900 - 1904 - 1906 - 1916 - 1918 - 1920 - 1924 - 1928 - 1929 - 1934 - 1943 - 1945 - 1947 - 1948 - 1949 - 1950 - 1952 - 1953 - 1955 - 1959 - 1961 - 1962 - 1964 - 1966.

White: 1893 - 1900 - 1901 - 1904 - 1906 - 1908 - 1914 - 1919 - 1921 - 1929 - 1934 - 1937 - 1945 - 1947 - 1949 - 1952 - 1953 - 1959 - 1961 - 1962 - 1964 - 1966.

Champagne

1901 - 1904 - 1906 - 1911 - 1914 - 1915 - 1918 - 1921 - 1926 - 1928 - 1934 - 1937 - 1959 - 1961 - 1964 - 1966.

It is impossible to discuss vintage years in regard to brandies. Wine is a living thing, which reaches a peak before it begins to "wear out," and this is because it is not distilled. Distillation, which destroys all micro-organisms, stabilizes brandy, and the only changes that can then take place are the result of a mutual exchange between the brandy and the wood of the cask during the aging process.

During this period, which varies in length, brandy acquires its color, loses its original bitterness, and becomes better balanced, more "rounded." Since air can pass through wood, evaporation takes place and it can be of quite considerable proportions. Because of this, 230 quarts of Cognac could completely disappear in less than fifty years if one didn't watch out. To avoid such disagreeable surprises, care is taken to keep the cask absolutely full and this is done by filling it up with Cognac. Each year, the product of the current distillation is carefully added to what has gone before. The only correct name is *"hors d'âge."* One thing is certain: from the moment the brandy is in bottle, keeping it around for years makes absolutely no difference to it. A VSOP label, or better, is a guarantee of the high quality and age of the brandy.

The same thing applies to the white liqueurs which are not aged in cask since their color would be spoiled. Old *marc* acquires color from being in contact with wood, but this has no effect on the flavor. It is better drunk young, but the taste of the drinker is the final arbiter.

The question of the vintage year is equally pointless when it comes to liqueurs, and aging is only relevant at the precise moment they are made. Fruit liqueurs should not be aged; others, made from plants, should be left in cask for several years before being bottled. From this moment on, none of them is improved by keeping.

THE ART OF DRINKING

The **visual test** is the contemplation of wine in a crystal glass or a winetaster's silver cup. Wine should be clear and shining. It should have a beautiful color attesting its race: white, red or rosé. From the quality of the color can be deduced whether it is too old or too young, or more or less oxidized. According to whether it is deep or light-toned, it is termed *"épais"* or *"clairet."* Purple reflections are always a bad sign.

The **olfactory test** prepares the palate: there is a definite relationship between the senses of smell and taste. Among the different kinds of scents emanating from different wines are floral scents (violet, rose, mignonette, jasmine, linden blossom), fruit scents (banana, peach, red currant, raspberry, apricot, apple), and other scents such as amber, resin, Russian leather, musk, mushroom, venison, kirsch and truffle.

The winetaster is capable of distinguishing through his sense of smell the different components of a wine, and this enables him to name its origin precisely.

Biological chemists have already isolated almost a hundred chemical components and it would seem that each variety of grapevine is characterized by one or more specific components.

The **gustatory test** helps to make the final judgment. The wine should be sipped freely, masticated, and then allowed to slip slowly down the throat.

Three specific kinds of reaction are produced:

—The **sensations of touch,** reacting chiefly on the tongue; they show mainly whether the wine is heavy, flat, rounded, thin, piquant, silky, light or sturdy.

—The **physical sensations** resulting from the presence of alcohol and tannic acid are felt mainly in the gums and mucous membranes and denote freshness, potency or astringency.

—The **sensations of taste** are the province of the papillae at the end of the tongue, which detect flavors that are sharp or salty; sweet flavors are transmitted by the middle of the tongue, and bitter ones by the back.

Wine should be seen: throw out your colored glasses and choose plain crystal glasses of a decent size in a simple basic shape, in which you can admire the incomparable colors of your wines.

Wine should be sniffed and breathed in through the sense of smell. A glass should not be filled to the brim. Glasses of balloon or tulip shape help to release the bouquet of the wine.

Wine should be tasted by swallowing it attentively and noticing each subtle effect on your tongue, palate and throat made by a different body, a hidden potency, or a new delicacy of bouquet.

Afterward every guest can "speak" of it.

THE GREAT GROWTHS

THE WINES OF BURGUNDY

Coming from the north, the first famous name we see in Burgundy is **Chablis,** where the hillsides produce an admirable white wine, unfortunately in rather limited quantity.

The **Haute-Bourgogne.** In the year 1110, Cistercian monks dug over the uncultivated soil of the Vougeot hill and planted the Pinot Chardonnay grape there. Their building still stands in the midst of the vines, a sturdy proof of the lasting work of the monks in the vineyard. The riches of Burgundy are divided into three sections, and we have room for only a few of the celebrated names in each area:

1. The **Dijonnais:** south of Dijon, the capital of the Dukes of Burgundy, are to be found light wines such as the rosés of Marsannay, Fixin*, the rather heady Chenôve, and Brochon.

2. The **Côte de Nuits** is celebrated for the most illustrious growths of the province: Napoleon's Chambertin, the legendary Clos de Vougeot, elegant Richebourg, delicate Chambolle-Musigny and the wine of kings, Romanée-Conti, preferred above all others by Mme de Pompadour and described neatly by Gaston Roupnel as "the biggest pearl in the Burgundy necklace." The capital of this section is the village of Nuits-Saint-Georges, seat of the members of the influential Confrérie des Chevaliers de Tastevin.

3. The **Côte de Beaune** has its famous names too: Beaune, Corton, Vergelesses, Pommard, Volnay, Monthélie, Auxey-Duresses, all full-flavored red wines, tasting of the fruit. There are also some dry and full-bodied white wines, like Meursault, Corton-Charlemagne, Montrachet (Puligny-Montrachet and Chassagne-Montrachet).

The **Côte Chalonnaise** takes its name from Chalon-sur-Saône; it produces red Mercurey and Givry, white Buxy, Montagny and Rully, this last being an admirable adjunct to a Burgundian dish called *pauchouse,* made with freshwater fish in a sauce.

The **Mâconnais** has a few red wines, but it is chiefly known for its fragrant and heady whites, such as the golden Pouilly-Fuissé, Viré, Chaintré, Solutré, Vergisson, etc.

The **Beaujolais:** the name means the red wine of friendship; its chief virtue is its youth and freshness. It is admirably suited to the gastronomy of Lyon. All its vineyards are worthy of mention: among them the firm and refreshing Juliénas, subtle and fragrant Fleurie, racy and charming Chiroubles, powerful Chenas and Moulin-à-Vent, Côte-de-Brouilly with its aroma of fruit, Morgon with its characteristic Burgundy taste, and all the wines of Beaujolais-Villages.

---

* *Editors' Note: Fixin has been reclassified and is now the northernmost wine of the Côte de Nuits.*

THE WINES OF BORDEAUX

It is only in the past two or three hundred years that the wines of Bordeaux have come to be really appreciated in France. They were, however, known to the Romans, because the poet Ausonius praised Aquitaine and its wines 1,500 years ago, and he is duly remembered by having a wine of Saint-Émilion named for him. Richard Coeur de Lion fought tooth and nail for this district of France from which more than 20,000 casks of wine were sent yearly to England. It was only in the reign of Louis XIV that the French discovered the wine of Bordeaux. Since then it has had an honorable place in their cellars.

The classification of the wine of Bordeaux has not been changed since it was made in 1855; the greatest are:

In the reds: Lafite-Rothschild, Margaux, Latour, Haut-Brion.

In the whites: Château d'Yquem, which everybody admires.

The other wines are catalogued into first, second, third, fourth, and fifth growths. This classification covers 89 vineyards, and does not include the wines of Pomerol or Saint-Émilion.

Médoc stretches north of Bordeaux, between the estuary of the Gironde River and the Atlantic Ocean. The gravelly hills overlooking the river, covered with stubby Cabernet vines, produce wines with very famous names: Saint-Estèphe, Pauillac (Château Lafite-Rothschild, Château Latour), Saint-Julien, and Château Margaux, the wine which brings to mind the name of Mme Du Barry. The vineyard also produces a dry white wine called Pavillon Blanc de Château Margaux. We should not overlook Château Calon-Ségur, Château Gruaud-Larose and Château Gloria. These ruby-red wines are exceptionally soft and delicate, with a penetrating bouquet, and the older they get, the finer they are.

Graves: the left bank of the Garonne, south of the city of Bordeaux, is probably where the Bordeaux wine district had its origin. The wines of Graves are soft and velvety. The first growth is Château Haut-Brion, which in 1529 was the dowry of the daughter of the nobleman who owned this piece of France. The other growths, in the reds, are Château Bouscault, Château Chevalier, Château Olivier, Château Haut-Lafite, Château Haut-Bailly, etc. There are some very great white Graves, such as Château Malartic-Lagravière. The dry white wines of Graves are Château Carbonnieux, Château Laville, Château Haut-Brion, etc.

Sauternes: this region produces splendid white wines, the most prestigious being Château d'Yquem. Others are Château Coutet, Château Rieussec, Château Guiraud, Château de Malle, Château Filhot, etc.

The **Côtes:** these are the red wines grown around the city of Libourne, the exhilarating Pomerol and its Château Pétrus, Château l'Évangile, etc.

Saint-Émilion: perched on its blue hill, with the ruins of the medieval ramparts standing out against the sky, Saint-Émilion has been the dwelling place of the Compagnie des Jurats for almost a thousand years. Traditionally, these first citizens of the wine trade are empowered to announce the *Ban des Vendanges,* declaring the harvest open. Saint-Émilion gives its name to such full-flavored clarets as Château Ausone, Château Cheval Blanc, Château Cap du Mourlin, Château Belair, etc.

The **Fronsac** district produces the red wines of Château Calon and Château Comte, the reds and whites grown around the towns of Bourg and Blaye and in the district of Entre-deux-Mers, where there are some Premières Côtes de Bordeaux, such as Château du Biac, Château Fauberet, etc.

Classification of the Great Red Wines of Bordeaux (1855)

MÉDOC

Château Haut-Brion, classified in 1855 with the great red wines, is the only one that does not come under the *appellation contrôlée* of Médoc, since it belongs to the district of Graves.

Next to the name of each château is the name of its *commune,* or township.

FIRST GROWTHS

Châteaux	Communes	Châteaux	Communes
Lafite-Rothschild	Pauillac	Latour	Pauillac
Margaux	Margaux	Haut-Brion	Pessac

SECOND GROWTHS

Mouton-Rothschild	Pauillac	Gruaud-Larose-Sarget	Saint-Julien
Rauzan-Ségla	Margaux	Gruaud-Larose-Faure	Saint-Julien
Rauzan-Gassies	Margaux	Brane-Cantenac	Cantenac
Léoville-Las Cases	Saint-Julien	Pichon-Longueville	Pauillac
Léoville-Poyferré	Saint-Julien	Pichon-Longueville-Lalande	Pauillac
Léoville-Barton	Saint-Julien	Ducru-Beaucaillou	Saint-Julien
Durfort-Vivens	Margaux	Cos-d'Estournel	Saint-Estèphe
Lascombes	Margaux	Montrose	Saint-Estèphe

THIRD GROWTHS

Kirwan	Cantenac	Palmer	Cantenac
Issan	Cantenac	La Lagune	Ludon
Lagrange	Saint-Julien	Desmirail	Margaux
Langoa	Saint-Julien	Calon-Ségur	Saint-Estèphe
Giscours	Labarde	Ferrière	Margaux
Malescot-Saint-Exupéry	Margaux	Marquis d'Alesme-Becker	Margaux
Brown-Cantenac	Cantenac	Boyd-Cantenac	Margaux

FOURTH GROWTHS

Saint-Pierre-Bontemps	Saint-Julien	La Tour Carnet	Saint-Laurent
Saint-Pierre-Sevaistre	Saint-Julien	Rochet	Saint-Estèphe
Branaire Ducru	Saint-Julien	Beychevelle	Saint-Julien
Talbot	Saint-Julien	Le Prieuré	Cantenac
Duhart-Milon	Pauillac	Marquis de Terme	Margaux
Pouget	Cantenac		

FIFTH GROWTHS

Pontet-Canet	Pauillac	Le Tertre	Arsac
Haut-Batailley	Pauillac	Haut-Bages Liberal	Pauillac
Batailley	Pauillac	Pédesclaux	Pauillac
Grand Puy Lacoste	Pauillac	Belgrave	Saint-Laurent
Grand Puy Ducasse	Pauillac	Camensac	Saint-Laurent
Lynch-Bages	Pauillac	Cos Labory	Saint-Estèphe
Lynch-Moussas	Pauillac	Clerc-Milon	Pauillac
Dauzac	Labarde	Croizet-Bages	Pauillac
Mouton-baron Philippe	Pauillac	Cantemerle	Macau

Classification of the Great White Wines of Bordeaux (1855)

FIRST GREAT GROWTH

Château d'Yquem, *commune* of Sauternes

FIRST GROWTHS

Châteaux	*Communes*	*Châteaux*	*Communes*
La Tour Blanche	Bommes	Coutet	Barsac
Peyraguey	Bommes	Climens	Barsac
Vigneau	Bommes	Guiraud	Sauternes
Suduiraut	Preignac	Rieussec	Fargues
		Rabaud	Bommes

SECOND GROWTHS

Myrat	Barsac	Caillou	Barsac
Doisy	Barsac	Suau	Barsac
Arche	Sauternes	Malle	Preignac
Filhot	Sauternes	Romer	Fargues
Broustet	Barsac	Lamothe	Sauternes
Nairac	Barsac		

CLASSIFICATION OF THE CHÂTEAUX OF SAINT-ÉMILION (1958)

CLASSIFIED FIRST GREAT GROWTHS

Ausone	La Gaffelière
Cheval Blanc	Naudes
Beauséjour Dufau	Magdelaine
Beauséjour Fagouet	Pavie
Belair	Trottevieille
Canon	Clos Fourtet
Figeac	

For a listing of the Classified Great Growths of Saint-Émilion, see the reverse of the color plate The Vineyard Districts of Bordeaux (opposite).

CLASSIFICATION OF THE RED AND WHITE WINES OF GRAVES (1959)

WHITE WINES

Bouscaut	Cadaujac	Latour-Martillac	Martillac
Carbonnieux, Chevalier,	Léognan	Laville Haut-Brion	Pessac
Malartic-Lagravière,		Couhins	Villenave-d'Ornon
Olivier			

RED WINES

Bouscaut	Cadaujac	Latour-Martillac,	Martillac
Haut-Bailly,	Léognan	Smith-Haut-Lafitte	
Carbonnieux,		Haut-Brion,	Pessac
Chevalier, Fieuzal,		La Mission, Haut-Brion,	
Malartic-Lagravière,		Latour Haut-Brion,	
Olivier		Pape-Clément	

CHAMPAGNE

"There is no Champagne from anywhere but the Champagne country," declared Curnonsky, stressing the fact that all the sparkling wines in the world are but miserable imitations of the laborious method known as the Champagne process, discovered in the reign of Louis XIV at the abbey of Hautvillers in the district of the Marne, by the Benedictine monk Dom Pérignon. Voltaire proclaimed it "the civilizing wine," and Mme de Pompadour declared it to be the only drink that improved her looks.

The whole secret of champagne lies in the selection of the wines that are blended to make the *cuvée*. The Champagne wine district takes up almost the entire administrative district of the Marne. Its grapevines stretch south into the Haute-Marne and the Aube. Champagne is divided into two distinct regions:

The **zone of the Marne:** with Épernay, Ay, Mareuil, Hautvillers, Cumières, etc., and the white grape slopes where the Chardonnay grows, the grape that gives champagne its delicacy. The famous centers are at Avize, Cramant, Oger, Le Mesnil.

The **Mountain of Reims:** with Verzenay, Sillery, Mailly, Ambonnay, and the red wine of Bouzy.

A champagne made from white grapes only is called *blanc de blancs*. A wine from the Champagne district that has not undergone the Champagne process is called *champagne nature*.

Champagne bottles come in various sizes.

split	20 centiliters	Rehoboam	6 bottles
half	40 centiliters	Methuselah	8 bottles
medium	60 centiliters	Salmanazar	12 bottles
bottle	80 centiliters	Balthazar	16 bottles
magnum	2 bottles	Nebuchadnezzar	20 bottles
Jeroboam	4 bottles		

The amount of syrup added to the wine—the *dosage*—determines whether champagne is *brut, sec, demi-sec* or *doux*, that is, on the dry side or on the sweet side. Purists prefer *brut* champagne, where the natural flavor prevails. Champagne should be drunk very cold in a *flûte* glass, or a tulip-shaped glass, never in a shallow *coupe*.

THE WINES OF JURA

Jura is fortunate in possessing white wines, *vins jaunes, vins de paille,* and full-bodied red wines. There are:

Côtes du Jura and **Arbois:** reds, whites and rosés.

Château-Chalon: it has a taste of walnuts and keeps happily in its stumpy bottle for a hundred years. This is the king of the sherrylike *vins jaunes* that are produced also in Pupillin and Arbois.

Vins de Paille of Poligny and Arbois: these are white wines made from the best grape varieties. The grapes are left to semi-raisin on straw mats, in warm airy rooms, until the spring, when they are put in the winepress almost completely dried out. They make unbeatable *vins de liqueur,* generally very expensive, and difficult to market other than locally.

THE WINES OF ALSACE

This is the golden wine of regional gastronomy. It should be drunk on the spot with the soup of frogs' legs, the salmon from the Rhine and, of course, the traditional sauerkraut. In Alsace wines are not named for their native villages but for the grape variety from which they are made. The wine drinker can pick out the delicate bouquet of *Riesling,* the rounded spiciness of *Gewürztraminer,* the ceremonious *Tokay,* the agreeable *Sylvaner,* the straightforward simplicity of *Traminer,* the cool distinction of *Muscat.* Fresh and cheerful, the wines of Alsace should be drunk young, a fact that certainly hasn't stopped the winemakers of Saint-Étienne d'Amerschwihr from keeping in their collection excellent bottles dated 1865 and even 1834: but these are vintages for oenologists only!

THE WINES OF THE LOIRE VALLEY

These wines are the product of the hills overlooking the River of Kings, from the hill on which Sancerre stands, down to the Atlantic.

Sancerre and **Pouilly-Fumé** are produced from the famous Sauvignon Blanc grape. The same grape makes the nearby wines of Quincy and Reuilly.

The princely district of **Orléans** offers the pleasing Gris Meunier (made royal by Louis XI) and the curious Cour-Cheverny.

The **Côteaux de Touraine** give wines praised by Ronsard, Rabelais and du Bellay. They spoke of the golden Vouvray springing from the vines of the Vallée Coquette and nearby Montlouis; Bourgueil tasting of raspberries and Chinon of violets; the full-bodied and generous Jasnières and the Côteaux du Loir.

The wines of **Anjou** and **Saumur** come from vineyards which rise harmoniously, tier upon tier, on the light slopes of the valley of the Loire, the country of the *douceur de vivre.*

The **Côteaux de Saumur** are known for White Parnay, Brézé and Pizay, and red Saumur-Champigny.

The **Côteaux du Layon:** heady Quarts de Chaume, Faye d'Anjou, Rablay-sur-Layon, Beaulieu-sur-Layon.

The **Côteaux de la Loire,** producing wines that are semi-dry and powerful, with breed and character.

The **Côteaux de l'Aubance,** with its delicate wines, tasting of the fruit.

The Cabernet produces vigorous rosé wines called Cabernet d'Anjou and Cabernet de Saumur.

MUSCADET

The ideal wine to accompany shellfish and seafood. It is found in three regions:

Sèvre-et-Maine carries the first growths (districts of Vallet, La Haie-Fouassière and Vertou).

The **Côteaux de la Loire,** giving dry, full-bodied wines from around Saint-Herblain and Ancenis. To these should be added the *gros plant,* an agreeable wine, with less distinction than Muscadet, but pleasant because of its tartness.

Muscadet, by regional application, bordering Muscadet of Sèvre-et-Main and that of the Côteaux de la Loire.

THE WINES OF THE VALLEY OF THE RHÔNE

As soon as the last suburbs of Lyon, the capital of gastronomy, are left behind, the squat vinestocks of the **Côte Rôtie** come into view, holding fast to the bare mountainside. After five years in bottle, Côte Rôtie, made from a blend of the two grape varieties Côte Brune and Côte Blonde, is a wine of great distinction, character and elegance.

The Viognier, the white grape of the Rhône Valley, grows in the steep terraced vineyards overlooking the river, and produces the typical white wines of Condrieu and Château-Grillet. Further south, in the Ardèche region, we find the sturdy wines of Cornas and Saint-Joseph, and the slightly sparkling Saint-Péray.

The legendary hillside of Hermitage offers reds and whites with the full flavor and deep color produced by long sunny hours. The region of Haute-Drôme invites us to drink its sparkling Clairette de Die. The wines of the district of Vaucluse, Gigondas, Vacqueyras and Sainte-Cécile, are sturdy yet soft.

Châteauneuf-du-Pape dominates the landscape of Comtat-Venaissin from its hill. These venerable vines produce a full-flavored wine that is deep crimson in color, with a fine bouquet.

From the district of Gard comes Tavel, and very close to Marcoule a wine called Chusclan is produced.

THE WINES OF PROVENCE, LANGUEDOC AND ROUSSILLON

Rosé de Palette, grown near Aix-en-Provence, and rosé de Bandol are popular with sailors and lovers of bouillabaisse, and so are all the sunny wines of the **Côtes de Provence** (Cavalaire, Pierrefeu, Vallée de l'Argens, Luc, Confaron, etc.). Above Nice, people drink Bellet wine with the local specialty—sea bass flamed with fennel.

The vineyard district that lies between Nîmes and Narbonne produces ordinary table wine that is not unattractive. The chief names are Costières du Gard, Corbières and Minervois.

In the valley of the River Aude there is a sparkling Blanquette de Limoux, and near the wine port of Sète is produced the marvelous Muscat de Frontignan that was the favorite of Rabelais and Voltaire.

Roussillon offers muscats and sweet wines from Côtes d'Agly, Maury and Banyuls. Curnonsky described them as Saracen in their fullness and flavor.

LITTLE-KNOWN LOCAL WINES

Here are just a few of the many regional wines:

In the Yonne district Sauvignon of Saint-Bris and the rosé of Irancy have acquired a good reputation. In Savoy, there are pungent wines like Apremont, Montmélian, Marestel, Seyssel, Arbin, Crépy, Ripaille and Feternes. In the upper Rhône valley are found Montagnieu, wines from the Ain district like Cerdon, and those of Valromay, dear to the heart of Brillat-Savarin.

Then there are the wines grown in the Landes, Entraygues and Marcillac from the Rouergue region, Fel and Chanturgue from the hillsides of Auvergne, Vic-Bilh, Irouléguy, Madiran and Jurançon, which was a favorite of King Henri IV who came from the Béarn region, and the deepest-colored wine of France, Cahors.

We should not miss the excellent wine from Gaillac, dry and frisky, which is beginning to live up to its former reputation since the growers have learned how to work together; the golden wines of Clairac, near Villeneuve-sur-Lot, those from the districts of Jasnières and Côteaux du Loire in the Sarthe region; the wine of Les Riceys in the Aube district, Monbazillac and Bergerac in Périgord, the wines grown around Lyon, and lastly the heady wines of Corsica, Muscat of Patrimonio and Calvi wines.

COOKING WITH WINE

Everyone has heard of *coq au vin!* But this is not the only recipe calling for wine. The very old recipe from the Beaujolais district for *matelote*—a stew of eels and carp from the River Saône—has become popular over the centuries in all the other provinces. Another freshwater fish dish from Burgundy, *pauchouse bourguignonne,* made with pike, eel, tench and perch, in rather the same way as the Mediterranean *bourride* of Sète, has kept its regional identity. Of course it is cooked in the excellent white wines of the Mâconnais, among them Pouilly-Fuissé.

Many typical regional dishes are prepared with wine: the surprising and unique *matelote des tonneliers de Touraine,* which turns out to be a veal stew in red wine, in the manner of the coopers of Touraine, and which resembles a veal stew in white wine made at Sancerre; the *grillade des mariniers du Rhône,* really a beef stew marinated in the sunshiny wine of Côtes du Rhône and cooked by the river bargemen; eggs poached in wine in Burgundy or the Loire Valley; tripe in Riesling or sauerkraut in champagne. The *charbonnée* of central France is a fresh pork stew cooked in red wine. Let us not miss, when they are running, the little fresh mackerel from Dieppe marinated in Muscadet from Nantes, and pike simmered in Santenay or Pommard from Beaune.

We can have a feast of trout from Alsace, cooked *au bleu* and plunged into a *court-bouillon* scented with Sylvaner, or trout caught in the River Loue in Jura and braised in the *vin jaune* of Pupillin. In Guyenne, we can taste lampreys with leeks, bathed in their own juices and Saint-Émilion.

We can eat rabbit braised with cabbage the way our grandmothers cooked it, and the remarkable hare stew in Chambertin, and also the simple rabbit stew from the Île-de-France, cooked on a bed of onions and mushrooms in the local white wine.

WINE AND FOOD AFFINITIES

Several authors have drawn up, more or less successfully, comparative tables of these affinities between food and drink. It is our opinion that the most complete, and the most readable, of these lists is *Les Bonnes Epousailles* by Dr. Paul Ramain, an independent gastronome.

Between each wine and each dish one should drink a little pure fresh water, not the carbonated kind. Any good meal, from the simplest to the most sumptuous, can be accompanied solely by excellent champagnes, differing in body, vintage and taste: *sec, brut, demi-sec, demi-doux, blanc de blancs, blanc de rouges* or *oeil de perdrix* (a very light pink). And a good meal should end in a way that is worthy of it, an excellent choice of liqueurs being the most suitable conclusion.

APÉRITIFS

All the usual apéritifs, according to what is liked. Champagne, either *brut* or *sec*, served iced at 40°F. Also very good dry white wines, or white wine and cassis of good quality, served very cold. Finally, *vins doux naturels,* good Pineau des Charentes, straight or with water. Certain spirits with water and ice.

SOUPS

No wine, or an excellent dry white wine. Sometimes a good-quality rosé. But for bisques and soups thickened with cream or eggs: Meursault, Montrachet, Château-Chalon; for cream soups based on poultry or mushrooms: dry and fruity white wines: Traminer, dry Muscat d'Alsace, Hermitage, Condrieu and Château-Grillet; or excellent rosés: Tavel, Cabernet d'Anjou, Arbois, Beaugency, etc.; for consommés in which wine has been used for flavoring: the same wine used in the preparation of the soup.

BOUILLABAISSE, FISH SOUPS, STEWS

Full-bodied dry white wines and powerful rosés from Provence or Corsica (Cassis-sur-Mer, Cavalaire, Bellet, Mercurol, Tavel, Tholonet, Piana, etc.) and also—yes, really!—red wines with an iodine taste (Châteauneuf-du-Pape), dry white wines from the Atlantic seaboard (Muscadet, Graves, Landes).

HORS-D'OEUVRE

Local white or rosé wines. Dry or semi-dry white wines (Graves, Touraine, Chablis, Quincy, Pouilly-Blanc-Fumé, Sancerre, Pouilly-Fuissé, Mâcon, Rully, Riesling, Sylvaner, Crépy, white Arbois, Gaillac, *champagne nature*). Rosé wines (Lirac, Les Riceys, Cabernet rosé, Arbois, Pagny-sur-Moselle, *vin gris de Lorraine,* etc.).

MELON

Served as is, or with salt and pepper, as an hors-d'oeuvre: Meursault, Montrachet, dry white Muscat d'Alsace, Château-Chalon, dry sherry.

Served as is, or with sugar, as a dessert: Sauternes, Barsac, Sainte-Croix-du-Mont, Jurançon, sweet Anjou, Vouvray, Pineau des Charentes, port.

OYSTERS, CLAMS, ETC.

Local dry white wines, from inland or the shore. Good-quality dry whites: Graves, Muscadet, Chablis, Sancerre, Chavignol, Pouilly-Blanc-Fumé, Saint-Pourçain, Pouilly-Fuissé, Cassis-sur-Mer, dry Touraine, Limeray, Crépy, Riesling, Sylvaner, white Arbois, etc.

SHELLFISH

Fragrant, full-bodied white wines or *vins jaunes:* Meursault, Montrachet, Corton-Charlemagne, white Musigny, white Hermitage, Mercurol, Château-Grillet, Pouilly-Fuissé, very good white Graves (such as white Château Haut-Brion), Traminer, Gewürztraminer, Pupillin, Château-Chalon, and even dry sherry.

Powerful rosés: Chusclan, Tavel, Bellet, Piana.

FISH

In general, all dry or semi-dry white wines: Graves, Muscadet, Gaillac, medium-dry Anjou, dry Touraine, Chablis, Meursault, Montrachet, Corton-Charlemagne, white Beaune, white Mercurey, Pouilly-Fuissé, white Hermitage, Condrieu, Château-Grillet, still Saint-Péray, Pouilly-Blanc-Fumé, Sancerre, Chavignol, Quincy, Saint-Pourçain, Arbois, Étoile, Ménétru, Riesling, Traminer, Gewürztraminer, Crépy, etc.

For fish that is baked or served with a sauce: either the wine used to cook the fish or make the sauce, or else—yes, really!—a good-quality sweet white wine: Barsac, Sauternes, Anjou (Quarts de Chaume, Savennières, etc.), Vouvray, Rochecorbon, etc.

MATELOTES, PAUCHOUSES, MEURETTES
(freshwater fish stews)

The same wine—red or white—that was used in cooking the dish.

FOIE GRAS

When served at the beginning of the meal (as it should be), there are two schools of thought:

Great white wines that are semi-dry, full-bodied and fruity: Meursault, Montrachet, Corton-Charlemagne, white Musigny, Traminer, Gewürztraminer, Tokay d'Alsace, white Muscat d'Alsace, Château-Grillet, white Châteauneuf-du-Pape, white Château Haut-Brion, Pupillin, Château-Chalon. Serve the same wine with the fish course.

or:

Great sweet white wines, sherries, etc.: Sauternes and Barsac, the "Château" wines of Yquem, Rayne-Vigneau, Climens, etc., Vic-Bilh, Pacherenc, Monbazillac, white port, Banyuls, sherry, Amontillado, etc.

When served later in the meal: Great full-bodied red wines with bouquet: Burgundy (Chambertin, Romanée, Musigny, Richebourg, Clos de Tart, La Tâche, Morey, Nuits, Corton), Côte Rôtie, Vieil Hermitage, Châteauneuf-du-Pape, Saint-Émilion (Ausone, Cheval-Blanc), Pomerol (Pétrus). Great Médoc wines with breeding (Haut-Brion, Latour, Lafite, Mouton), and Vieux Cahors. Then serve the same wine with the cheese course.

ENTRÉES

Good-quality rosé wines. Red wines that are light or moderately full-bodied, but they should be fragrant: Beaujolais, Mâcon, Beaune, Médoc, red Graves, Chinon, Bourgueil, Arbois, Irancy from the Yonne, red wines from the Champagne country.

SAUCES

Wine sauces: the same wine used in making the sauce.

Cream or other sauces (except for vinaigrettes and tart sauces): fine sweet white wines: Sauternes, Barsac, Vouvray, Anjou (Layon, Savennières, Faye, Rablay, Thouarcé, etc.), Sainte-Croix-du-Mont, Monbazillac, Jurançon. Also Montrachet and Gewürztraminer.

EGGS

Just plain old water!

WHITE MEAT, CHICKEN, CAPON, RABBIT

Excellent red wines with bouquet but not too full-bodied: Médoc, Graves, Beaujolais, Mâcon, Mercurey, Beaune, Santenay, Monthélie, Volnay, Bourgueil, Chinon, Champigny, Chanturgue, Côte Rôtie and Croze-Hermitage. Red wines from the Champagne country.

DARK MEAT, SQUAB, DUCK, GUINEA HEN

Excellent full-bodied red wines: Moulin-à-Vent, Beaune, Pommard, Corton, Côte Rôtie, Cornas, Hermitage, Châteauneuf-du-Pape, Pomerol, Saint-Émilion, Irouléguy, Madiran, etc.

TRIPE, CHITTERLINGS, BLACK PUDDINGS, SNAILS

Local white wines.

Good-quality rosé wines or light red wines: Beaujolais, Graves, Bourgueil, Chinon, Saint-Jean-de-la-Porte, Savoie, Arbois, Lirac, Touraine rosé de Cabernet, Saumur-Champigny, Irouléguy-Paragabos, Les Riceys, Beaugency, Fel, Chusclan, etc.

Vins jaunes from Jura: Étoile, Ménétru, Pupillin, etc.

BRAISED OR SAUTÉED HAM

Red wines from Burgundy, not too full-bodied. Local red wines: Arbois, Chanturgue, Foye-Montjault, Pécharmant, Figeac, etc.

Local rosé wines: Côtes de Toul, Cabernet of Anjou or of Saumur, Confolens, Brissac, *vin de sables des Landes,* Irouléguy, Les Riceys, Tavel, Chusclan, etc.

Dry sherry, Château-Chalon, good Madeira, pale Malmsey.

GAME

Furred game and venison: great, full-bodied red wines: Nuits, Chambertin, Musigny, Clos de Vougeot, Morey, Richebourg, Romanée, Corton, Bonnes Mares, Côte Rôtie, Hermitage, Châteauneuf-du-Pape, Vieux Cahors, Saint-Émilion, château-bottled Pomerol.

Feathered game and small birds: very good red wines with plenty of bouquet: Beaune, Santenay, Volnay, Fixin, Chambertin, Épineuil, Irancy (yes, really!), Médoc and château-bottled Graves, Bourgueil, Champigny, Croze-Hermitage, and even Côte Rôtie.

VEGETABLES

Noncarbonated water, especially with artichokes and asparagus. Otherwise, local wines and ordinary table wines, whites, rosés or light reds.

MUSHROOMS

Sautéed: local white or rosé wines.

Simmered in a sauce, as an entrée, baked *au gratin,* etc.: any good fruity white wine, from the driest to the sweetest (yes, I mean it!).

Cèpes: any very good red wine; Château-Chalon as well.

Morels: white wines from Jura and Alsace. *Vins jaunes* from Jura. Also Crépy, white Hermitage and Meursault.

FRESH TRUFFLES

Fine old red wines, full-bodied and with plenty of bouquet: all the Burgundies, top-quality Saint-Émilion and Pomerol, Hermitage, Côte Rôtie, Châteauneuf-du-Pape, Vieux Cahors.

Also good *brut* champagne and excellent sweet white wines: Sauternes, Barsac, Monbazillac, Jurançon, port, sherry, Madeira, etc., especially when the truffles have been cooked in one of these wines and are served as a hot hors-d'oeuvre.

SALADS

Water, even carbonated water. However, when the salad is dressed with dry white wine rather than with vinegar or lemon juice, it is permissible to drink the same white wine.

CHEESE

Strong blue cheeses or strong fermented cheeses (Roquefort, Camembert, Maroilles, Livarot, Munster): the best and greatest red wines, the finest vintages in your cellar! Also very good *brut* champagne.

Mild blue cheeses, Swiss-type cheeses, semi-soft cheeses (Port-Salut, Reblochon, Saint-Marcellin): the best dry or semi-dry white wines. *Vins jaunes* from Jura.

SWEETS AND DESSERTS

Semi-dry or semi-sweet champagne. Very good sparkling wines. All the great sweet white wines: Sauternes, Barsac, Jurançon, Vic-Bilh, Monbazillac, Sainte-Croix-du-Mont, very good Anjou wines, *vins de paille* from Hermitage, Jura and Alsace, Muscat, Frontignan, Lunel, Banyuls, Rancio, Agly, port, sherry, Amontillado, Marsala, Zucco, Malmsey, Cape of Good Hope, Cyprus, Samos, etc.

AFTERNOON TEA

Champagne (from *brut* to *doux),* Crémant, port, Frontignan, good-quality Muscat, Samos, Carthage, Cyprus, *vin du Cap,* Málaga, Marsala, Zucco, Agly, Rancio, Banyuls. Also good Sauternes, Monbazillac and Jurançon.

Spirits over ice.

THE IDENTIFICATION OF
WINES AND SPIRITS

EDITORS' NOTE: *In order to protect the consumer, the production and selling of wines and spirits in France is strictly supervised by the government, and French law is very specific as to what claims may be made for a wine or liqueur. The following explanations of the most frequently used terms of the complicated French wine terminology are not literal translations of M. Oliver's remarks, which were written for French consumers, and presume their knowledge of the conditions of the French wine industry. What follows has been adapted to the needs of the American wine lover, to familiarize him with French wine terminology.*

Appellation d'Origine. These words mean that the place name of the wine, which may be the name of the district, the town, the geographical location—such as a river or a château—or the very specific name of a small vineyard where the wine was produced, is guaranteed, and that the wine bearing the name was made in that place. There are three categories. The first, and highest and to be found on the best wines of France, is *Appellation Contrôlée.*

Appellation Contrôlée. These well-known words, found on labels of the better French wines, are an official and legal stamp of approval and mean that the wine is genuine, that is, that it *must* come from the specific district, town or even vineyard indicated by the name it bears, from certain established varieties of grape only, cultivated in certain specific ways, and from grapes that have reached an approved state of ripeness; also that it must have been made according to the ways of the place from where it comes. All of this does not necessarily mean that the wine is good, but since these controls (set up since 1935 to include over 200 different wines) are rigidly and forcefully carried out, the consumer's protection is great.

The second category is known as V.D.Q.S., that is *Vins Délimités de Qualité Supérieure,* and is no less strictly regulated than the first. Though not quite so famous and expensive as the wines of the first category, this second team includes a great many excellent and very desirable wines.

Appellation Simple refers to seldom-exported wines, protected by French law in a general and rather loose way against misrepresentation.

Vins de Pays is a loose term, seldom found on wine labels, which indicates a local or regional wine, drunk mostly where it is made. Often these have a low alcohol content and do not travel well, therefore they are seldom imported. *Vin du Pays* is a similar term, referring to a specific wine made in a specific district. Both terms take their clue from the commonly used words *mon pays,* "my country," which in this connotation mean the place of origin, and neither of them has much legal standing.

Vin Ordinaire. More than half of the wine drunk in France goes under this name, which refers to wine of unknown or nondescript origin. The alcoholic content, however, is specified, such as *Vin Rouge, 12%. Vin ordinaire* can be red, white or rosé, and it can also be sold under a brand name. In other words, this is the table wine drunk day in, day out, by most Frenchmen, and there is nothing wrong with it when it is a good wine of its kind—as it very often is.

Mis en Bouteille au Château. A wine bottled by the vintner who made it, on the place where he made it; this term is used especially for Bordeaux wines. In other areas the term is "estate-bottled," *mis en bouteille au domaine.* The term guarantees the authenticity, but not necessarily the quality, of the wine.

CHAMPAGNE

The word champagne, strictly speaking, applies *only* to a specific wine, made in a specific region of France, by a specific process, from only certain specific varieties of grapes. Many countries have recognized this terminology and have given different names to their wines that are made by the same method, such as Germany (Sekt), and Italy (Spumante). But in the United States, any sparkling wine, white or red, may be called champagne if it is made by the same bottle-fermented process as the original French champagne and bears on its label the region of its origin, such as California, New York State, etc., where the wine was made. Any kind of grapes may be used for American champagne.

All champagne is a blend, and certain official rules and regulations protect the public from a fraudulent wine. Because of the special way in which it is made, champagne is one of the very rare wines for which the brand name is more important than that of the vineyard or district the wine came from. The names used to classify champagne are *vintage champagne, non-vintage champagne* and B. O. B.

Vintage champagne need not be made *entirely* from the wines of a single, especially good year, but it *must* be made *in large part* from these wines, which are blended with wines from other years. No producer is allowed to sell as the champagne of a certain vintage more wine than he produced in that particular year; in other words, he cannot stretch a certain vintage with wine of lesser years. No vintage champagne may be shipped until it is three years old, and before shipping it has to be approved by a special interprofessional committee of experts.

Non-vintage champagne is almost always a blend of the wines of less good plus good years, the latter improving the quality of the first, which, alone, could not be sold. Non-vintage champagne bears the name of the French *shipper,* and this name is your guarantee. In practice, this means that in the case of the dozen-odd best champagne shippers, the wine is very good indeed. There are also smaller houses which produce a most creditable wine.

B. O. B. champagne, which stands for Buyer's Own Brand, is the least expensive kind; it is the champagne sold by a *retailer* under his own brand name. It is as good as the champagne the retailer bought in the first place, and is suitable for large-scale occasions like parties. It can be good, but never great.

Tête de Cuvée is a brand of champagne put out by some houses, which is supposed to be even better than their vintage champagne, usually made only from the first and most delicate pressing of the finest grapes or from special grapes. It is more expensive and sometimes worth the money; other times, not.

Blancs de Blancs are wines made entirely from white grapes, as distinguished from the usual way of making champagne from red grapes or a blend of white and red. (The juice of all grapes is white; the color is in the skin of the grapes.) *Blancs de Blancs* are supposed to be lighter wines, but this is a matter of personal opinion about a rather recent fashionable development in champagne making.

EDITORS' NOTE: *Now we continue with M. Oliver's remarks on spirits and liqueurs.*

SPIRITS AND LIQUEURS

Appellation d'origine contrôlée: three liqueurs in France achieve this status, which means that they are officially recognized and legally defined by governmental decree: Cognac, Armagnac, Calvados from the Pays d'Auge.

Cognac has seven subdivisions or growths: Grande Champagne, Petite Champagne, Borderies, Fins Bois, Bons Bois, Bois Ordinaires and Bois à Terroir.

Fine Champagne is a mixture of the Grande Champagne and Petite Champagne brandies, in which Grande Champagne is responsible for at least half. Grande Fine Champagne contains only brandies classed as Grande Champagne. Commercial sym-

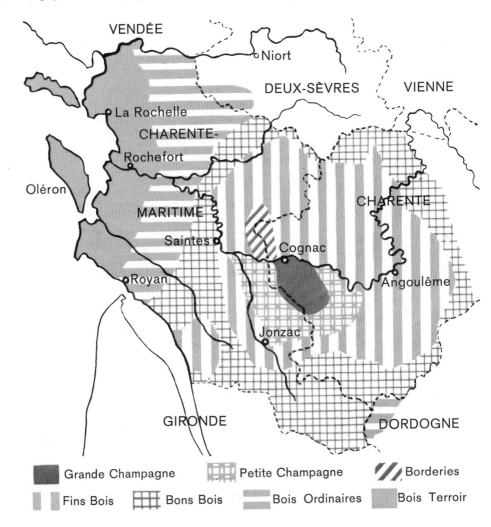

bols are used by producers to denote the different ages of their brandies, and they must honor the following minimum aging requirements:

—*One, two or three stars* for a minimum aging of one year.

—*Cognac superior* for a minimum aging of three years.

—*VO* (very old), *VSO* (very superior old), *VSOP* (very superior old product or pale), *VOP* (very old product), for a minimum aging of four years.

—*VVO* (very very old), *VVSO* (very very superior old), *VVSOP* (very very superior old product), *XO* (x-years old), *Extra, Napoléon, Vieille Réserve, Vieux,* for a minimum aging of six years.

It is forbidden to offer for sale Cognac brandies less than a year old. A *liqueur* based on Cognac or Armagnac must contain at least 51% of these brandies; a liqueur from Cognac must contain at least 30%. *Crème de Cognac* or *Crème d'Armagnac* are based only on those brandies.

For **Armagnac** there are three subdivisions: Bas-Armagnac (which has the highest reputation), Ténarèze and Haut-Armagnac.

Calvados du Pays d'Auge is made by distilling cider from the Pays d'Auge.

Appellation d'origine réglementée, controlled at the place of origin: Liqueurs made from wine of the following regions: Aquitaine, Bugey, Burgundy, Centre-Est, Côteaux de la Loire, Côtes du Rhône, Fougères, Franche-Comté, Languedoc, Marne, Provence.

Liqueurs made from *marc* of the following regions: Aquitaine, Auvergne, Bugey, Burgundy, Centre-Est, Champagne, Côteaux de la Loire, Côtes du Rhône, Franche-Comté, Languedoc, Provence, Savoy.

Calvados: from Avranchin, Calvados, Domfrontais, Mortanais, Pays de Bray, Pays de Merlerault, Pays de la Risle, Perche, Vallée de l'Orne.

Cider liqueurs from Brittany, Maine and Normandy.

Mirabelle (plum brandy) from Lorraine, *Crème de Cassis* (black-currant liqueur) from Dijon and *Vermouth* from Chambéry.

LIST OF APPELLATIONS

Table of Recent Vintage Years (*millésimes*)

MILLÉSIME	BOURGOGNE		BEAUJOLAIS	CHABLIS	BORDEAUX		COTES-DU-RHONE	ALSACE	VAL DE LOIRE	CHAMPAGNE
	Rouges	Blancs			Rouges	Blancs				
1950	1	3		2	3	2	2	2	2	2
1951	—	1		1	1	1	1	1	1	1
1952	3	3		3	3	3	3	2	2	3
1953	3	3		2	3	3	1	2	3	3
1954	1	1		1	1	1	2	1	1	1
1955	3	3		3	3	3	3	3	3	3
1956	1	2	1	1	1	1	2	1	1	1
1957	2	3	2	2	2	3	2	2	1	1
1958	1	2	2	—	1	1	1	2	1	1
1959	4	3	4	3	2	3	1	4	4	4
1960	2	2	1	2	3	2	3	3	2	2
1961	4	4	4	3	4	3	3	4	3	4
1962	3	3	3	3	3	2	4	4	3	3
1963	2	2	2	2	1	1	2	3	2	2
1964	4	3	3	3	4	3	2	4	2	3
1966	4	4	3	4	4	4	4	4	3	4

(1) Fair   (2) Good   (3) Very Good   (4) Exceptional

Wines with *Appellations Contrôlées* (A. C.) are generally found on wine lists under the heading of large wine-producing regions which include the following departments:
—— **Wines of Bordeaux:** Gironde.
—— **Wines of Burgundy:** Yonne, Côte-d'Or, Saône-et-Loire, Rhône.
—— **Wines of the Southwest:** Dordogne, Lot-et-Garonne, Basses-Pyrénées, Tarn.
—— **Wines of the Côtes du Rhône** (south of Lyon): Loire, Drôme, Ardèche, Gard, Vaucluse.
—— **Wines of the Loire Valley:** Loire-Atlantique, Maine-et-Loire, Deux-Sèvres, Indre-et-Loire, Sarthe, Loir-et-Cher, Indre, Cher, Nièvre.
—— **Wines of the Mediterranean South:** Alpes-Maritimes, Var, Bouches-du-Rhône.
Other: Haute-Savoie.
Wines classified as *Vins Délimités de Qualité Supérieure* (V. D. Q. S.) are found under the headings of the following districts: Midi, Sud-Est, Sud-Ouest, Centre-Ouest, Vallée du Rhône, Lorraine, Lyonnais, Savoie-Bugey.

D'ORIGINE CONTRÔLÉES

I. Still Wines

APPELLATION	MEN-TION	RÉGION	BLANC	ROUGE	ROSÉ	NOTES
Alsace cépages Knipperlé et Chasselas	A.C.	Haut-Rhin et Bas-Rhin	●			clairet
Alsace grand cru ou **grand·vin** titrant plus de 11° pour les cépages nobles : Traminer, Gewürztraminer, Riesling, Tokay ou Pinot gris, Klevner, Muscat, Sylvaner	A.C.	Haut-Rhin et Bas-Rhin	●			
Pinot	A.C.	—			●	
Aloxe-Corton	A.C.	Côte de Beaune	●	●		premier cru
Anjou	A.C.	Anjou	●	●	●	
Anjou Coteaux de la Loire	A.C.	Anjou	●			
Arbois	A.C.	Jura	●	●	●	
Arbois (vin jaune)	A.C.	Jura	●			
Arbois (vin de paille)	A.C.	Jura			●	
Auxey-Duresses	A.C.	Côte de Beaune	●	●	●	premier cru
Bandol	A.C.	Var	●	●	●	
Barsac	A.C.	Bordelais	●			crus classés
Bâtard-Montrachet	A.C.	Côte de Beaune	●			premier cru
Beaujolais	A.C.	Rhône	●	●	●	
Beaujolais supérieur	A.C.	Rhône	●	●	●	
Beaujolais-Villages	A.C.	Saône-et-Loire	●	●	●	
Beaune	A.C.	Côte de Beaune	●	●		premier cru
Bellet	A.C.	Alpes-Maritimes	●	●	●	
Bergerac	A.C.	Dordogne	●	●	●	
Bergerac Côtes de Saussignac	A.C.	Dordogne	●			
Bienvenues Bâtard-Montrachet	A.C.	Côte de Beaune	●			premier cru
Blagny	A.C.	Côte de Beaune	●	●		
Blagny Côte de Beaune	A.C.	Côte de Beaune	●	●		
Blanc Fumé de Pouilly	A.C.	Nièvre	●			
Blaye ou **Blayais**	A.C.	Bordelais	●	●		

The words *crus classés* (classified growths) in the column of notes indicate an official classification. For the Côtes de Provence V. D. Q. S., wines from the more renowned vineyards may be sold as *crus classés*.

The words *Premier Cru* (first growth) applicable in Burgundy indicate that certain vineyards (*climats*) have the right to the classification associated or not with the name of that vineyard.

			B	R	r	
Bonnes Mares	A.C.	Côte de Nuits		●		
Bonnezeaux	A.C.	Anjou	●			
Bordeaux	A.C.	Bordelais	●	●	●	
Bordeaux clairet ou **rosé**	A.C.	Bordelais			●	
Bordeaux Haut-Benauge	A.C.	Bordelais	●			
Bordeaux Côtes de Castillon	A.C.	Bordelais		●		
Bordeaux supérieur	A.C.	Bordelais	●	●		
Bourg, Bourgeais	A.C.	Bordelais	●	●		
Bourgogne	A.C.	Yonne, Côte-d'Or Saône-et-Loire et Rhône	●	●	●	
Bourgogne Passe-tout-grain	A.C.	Bourgogne		●	●	
Bourgogne aligoté	A.C.	—	●			
Bourgogne ordinaire	A.C.	—	●	●	●	
Bourgogne clairet ou **rosé**	A.C.	—			●	
Bourgogne grand ordinaire	A.C.	—	●	●	●	
Bourgogne grand ordinaire clairet	A.C.	—			●	
Bourgueil	A.C.	Touraine		●	●	
Brouilly	A.C.	Beaujolais		●		
Cabernet d'Anjou	A.C.	Anjou			●	
Cabernet de Saumur	A.C.	Anjou			●	
Cabrières	V.D.Q.S.	Hérault			●	
Cahors	V.D.S.Q.	Lot		●		
Cassis	A.C.	Bouches-du-Rhône	●	●	●	
Cérons	A.C.	Bordelais	●			
Chablis Grand Cru	A.C.	Yonne	●			
Chablis Premier Cru	A.C.	Yonne	●			premier cru*
Chablis	A.C.	Yonne	●			
Chambertin	A.C.	Côte de Nuits		●		premier cru
Chambertin Clos de Bèze	A.C.	Côte de Nuits		●		premier cru
Chambolle-Musigny	A.C.	Côte de Nuits		●		premier cru
Chapelle-Chambertin	A.C.	Côte de Nuits		●		premier cru
Charlemagne	A.C.	Côte de Beaune	●			premier cru
Charmes-Chambertin	A.C.	Côte de Beaune		●		premier cru
Chassagne-Montrachet	A.C.	Côte de Beaune	●	●		premier cru
Chassagne-Montrachet C. de Beaune	A.C.	Côte de Beaune	●	●		
Château-Chalon	A.C.	Jura	●			vin jaune
Château-Grillet	A.C.	Côtes-du-Rhône	●			
Château Meillant	V.D.Q.S.	Cher		●	●	
Châteauneuf-du-Pape	A.C.	Côtes-du-Rhône	●	●		
Châtillon-en-Diois	V.D.Q.S.	Drôme	●	●	●	
Cheilly-lès-Maranges	A.C.	Côte de Beaune-Villages		●		premier cru
Cheilly-lès-Maranges Côte de Beaune	A.C.	—		●		
Chenas	A.C.	Beaujolais		●		
Chevalier-Montrachet	A.C.	Côte de Beaune	●			premier cru
Chinon	A.C.	Touraine	●	●	●	
Chiroubles	A.C.	Beaujolais		●		
Chorey-lès-Beaune	A.C.	Côte de Beaune	●	●		
Chorey-lès-Beaune Côte de Beaune	A.C.	Côte de Beaune	●	●		
Clairette de Bellegarde	A.C.	Gard	●			
Clairette de Die	A.C.	Drôme	●			
Clairette du Languedoc	A.C.	Hérault	●			
Clos de la Roche	A.C.	Côte de Nuits		●		
Clos Saint-Denis	A.C.	Côte de Nuits		●		
Clos de Tart	A.C.	Côte de Nuits		●		
Clos Vougeot	A.C.	Côte de Nuits		●		
Condrieu	A.C.	Côtes-du-Rhône	●			
Corbières	V.D.Q.S.	Aude	●	●	●	
Corbières supérieures	V.D.Q.S.	Aude	●	●	●	
Corbières du Roussillon	V.D.Q.S.	Roussillon	●	●	●	

*Vineyards with the right to use *Chablis Premier Cru* are Les Vaudésirs, Les Clos, Les Grenouilles, Les Preuses, Bougros, Valmur, Les Blanchots.

			B	R	r	
Corbières supérieures du Roussillon	V.D.Q.S.	Roussillon	●	●	●	
Corbières des Aspres	V.D.Q.S.	Roussillon	●	●	●	
Costières-du-Gard	V.D.Q.S.	Gard	●	●	●	
Cornas	A.C.	Côtes du Rhône		●		
Corton	A.C.	Côte de Beaune	●	●		
Corton-Charlemagne	A.C.	Côte de Beaune	●			
Côte de Beaune	A.C.	Côte de Beaune	●	●		
Côte de Beaune Villages	A.C.	Côte de Beaune		●		
Côte de Nuits Villages	A.C.	Côte de Nuits	●	●		(1)
Coteaux d'Aix-en-Provence	V.D.Q.S.	Bouches-du-Rhône	●	●	●	
Coteaux de l'Aubance	A.C.	Anjou	●			
Coteaux d'Ancenis	V.D.Q.S.	Loire-Atlantique	●	●	●	
Coteaux des Baux-en-Provence	V.D.Q.S.	Bouches-du-Rhône	●	●	●	
Coteaux du Giennois	V.D.Q.S.	Loiret	●	●		
Coteaux du Languedoc	V.D.Q.S.	Hérault et Aude		●	●	(2)
Coteaux du Layon	A.C.	Anjou	●			
Coteaux du Layon Chaume	A.C.	Anjou	●			
Coteaux du Loir	A.C.	Anjou	●			
Coteaux de La Méjanelle	V.D.Q.S.	Hérault	●	●		
Coteaux du Marmandais	V.D.Q.S.	Sud-Ouest	●	●		
Coteaux de Pierrevert	V.D.Q.S.	Basses-Alpes	●	●	●	
Coteaux de Saint-Christol	V.D.Q.S.	Hérault	●	●		
Coteaux de Saumur	A.C.	Anjou		●		
Coteaux du Tricastin	V.D.Q.S.	Vaucluse, Drôme	●	●	●	
Coteaux de Vérargues	V.D.Q.S.	Hérault		●	●	
Côtes d'Auvergne	V.D.Q.S.	Puy-de-Dôme	●	●	●	
Côtes de Bergerac	A.C.	Dordogne	●	●	●	
Côtes de Blaye	A.C.	Bordelais	●			
Côtes de Bordeaux Saint-Macaire	A.C.	Bordelais	●			
Côtes de Bourg	A.C.	Bordelais	●	●		
Côtes de Brouilly	A.C.	Beaujolais		●		
Côtes de Buzet	V.D.Q.S.	Sud-Ouest	●	●		
Côtes de Duras	A.C.	Lot-et-Garonne	●	●		
Côtes du Forez	V.D.Q.S.	Loire		●	●	
Côtes de Fronsac	A.C.	Bordeaux		●		
Côtes de Fronton	V.D.Q.S.	Haute-Garonne		●	●	
Côtes de Canon Fronsac	A.C.	Bordelais		●		
Côtes de Gien	V.D.Q.S.	Loiret	●	●		
Côtes du Jura	A.C.	Jura	●	●	●	vin de paille et vin jaune
Côtes du Lubéron	V.D.Q.S.	Vaucluse	●	●	●	
Côtes de Montravel	A.C.	Dordogne	●			
Côtes de Provence	V.D.Q.S.	Var et Alpes-Maritimes	●	●	●	crus classés
Côtes-du-Rhône	A.C.	Vallée du Rhône	●	●	●	
Côtes-du-Rhône Gigondas	A.C.	Vaucluse	●	●	●	
Côtes-du-Rhône Cairanne	A.C.	Vaucluse	●	●	●	
Côtes-du-Rhône Laudun	A.C.	Gard	●	●	●	
Côtes-du-Rhône Chusclan	A.C.	Gard		●	●	
Côtes-du-Rhône Vacqueyras	A.C.	Vaucluse	●	●	●	
Côtes-du-Rhône Vinsobres	A.C.	Drôme	●	●	●	
Côte Roannaise	V.D.Q.S.	Loire		●	●	
Côtes de Toul	V.D.Q.S.	Lorraine	●	●	●	
Côtes du Ventoux	V.D.Q.S.	Vaucluse	●	●	●	
Côtes du Vivarais	V.D.Q.S.	Ardèche	●	●	●	
Côtes du Vivarais Orgnac	V.D.Q.S.	Ardèche	●	●	●	
Côtes du Vivarais Saint-Montant	V.D.Q.S.	Ardèche	●	●	●	

(1) Same as *vins fins de la Côte de Nuits*.

(2) The Côteaux du Languedoc V. D. Q. S. includes the following thirteen appellations:

(a) in Hérault: Cabrières, Côteaux de Vérargues, Faugères, Côteaux de la Méjanelle, Montpeyroux, Pic Saint-Loup, Saint-Chinian, Saint-Christol, Saint-Drézéry, Saint-Georges d'Orques, Saint-Saturnin.

(b) in Aude: La Clape, Quatorze.

			B	R	r	
Côtes du Vivarais Saint-Remèze	V.D.Q.S.	Ardèche	●	●	●	
Crépy	A.C.	Haute-Savoie	●			
Crozes-l'Hermitage	A.C.	Drôme	●	●		vin de paille
Dezize-lès-Maranges	A.C.	Côte de Beaune-Villages		●		
Dezize-lès-Maranges Côte de Beaune	A.C.	—		●		
Echézeaux	A.C.	Côte de Nuits		●		premier cru
Entre-Deux-Mers	A.C.	Bordelais	●			
Etoile	A.C.	Jura	●			vin jaune
Faugères	V.D.Q.S.	Hérault	●	●		
Fitou	A.C.	Aude, Pyrénées-Orientales		●		
Fixin	A.C.	Côte de Nuits	●	●		premier cru
Fleurie	A.C.	Beaujolais		●		
Fronton	A.C.	Haute-Garonne	●	●	●	
Gaillac	A.C.	Tarn	●			*
Gaillac Premières Côtes	A.C.	Tarn	●			
Gevrey-Chambertin	A.C.	Côte de Nuits		●		premier cru
Givry	A.C.	Châlonnais	●	●		premier cru
Grands Echézeaux	A.C.	Côte de Nuits		●		premier cru
Graves	A.C.	Bordelais	●	●		crus classés
Graves supérieures	A.C.	Bordelais	●	●		crus classés
Graves de Vayres	A.C.	Bordelais	●	●		
Griots Bâtard-Montrachet	A.C.	Côte de Beaune	●			premier cru
Griottes Chambertin	A.C.	Côte de Nuits		●		premier cru
Gros-Plant du Pays Nantais	V.D.Q.S.	Loire-Atlantique	●			
Haut-Comtat	V.D.Q.S.	Vaucluse		●	●	
Haut-Médoc	A.C.	Bordelais		●		
Haut-Montravel	A.C.	Dordogne	●			
Irouléguy	V.D.Q.S.	Basses-Pyrénées	●	●	●	
Jasnières	A.C.	Sarthe	●			
Jurançon	A.C.	Basses-Pyrénées	●			
La Clape	V.D.Q.S.	Aude	●	●	●	
Ladoix-Serrigny	A.C.	Côte de Beaune	●	●		premier cru
Lalande-de-Pomerol	A.C.	Bordelais		●		
La Tâche	A.C.	Côte de Nuits		●		premier cru
Latricières-Chambertin	A.C.	Côte de Nuits		●		premier cru
Lavilledieu	V.D.Q.S.	Tarn-et-Garonne	●	●		
Limoux nature	A.C.	Aude	●			
Lirac	A.C.	Gard	●	●	●	
Listrac	A.C.	Bordelais		●		
Loupiac	A.C.	Bordelais	●			
Lussac Saint-Émilion	A.C.	Bordelais		●		
Lyonnais	V.D.Q.S.	Rhône	●	●	●	
Mâcon	A.C.	Mâconnais	●	●	●	
Mâcon supérieur	A.C.	Mâconnais	●	●	●	
Mâcon Villages	A.C.	Mâconnais	●	●	●	
Madiran	A.C.	Basses-Pyrénées		●		
Margaux	A.C.	Bordeaux		●		crus classés
Mazis Chambertin	A.C.	Côte de Nuits		●		premier cru
Mazoyères Chambertin	A.C.	Côte de Nuits		●		premier cru
Médoc	A.C.	Bordelais		●		crus classés
Menetou-Salon	A.C.	Cher	●	●	●	
Mercurey	A.C.	Châlonnais	●	●		premier cru
Meursault	A.C.	Côte de Beaune	●	●		premier cru
Meursault-Blagny	A.C.	Côte de Beaune	●	●		
Minervois	V.D.Q.S.	Hérault et Aude	●	●	●	
Monbazillac	A.C.	Dordogne	●			
Mont-près-Chambord Cour-Cheverny	V.D.Q.S.	Loir-et-Cher	●			
Montagne Saint-Émilion	A.C.	Bordelais		●		

*Grape variety: *Mauzac bourru* (unfermented).

			B	R	r	
Montagny	A.C.	Châlonnais	●			premier cru
Monthélie	A.C.	Côte de Beaune	●	●	●	premier cru
Montlouis	A.C.	Touraine	●			
Montpeyroux	V.D.Q.S.	Hérault		●	●	premier cru
Montrachet	A.C.	Côte de Beaune	●			premier cru
Montravel	A.C.	Dordogne	●			
Morey-Saint-Denis	A.C.	Côte de Nuits	●	●		premier cru
Morgon	A.C.	Beaujolais		●		
Moselle	V.D.Q.S.	Lorraine	●	●		
Moulin-à-Vent	A.C.	Beaujolais		●		
Moulis ou Moulis-en-Médoc	A.C.	Bordelais		●		
Muscadet	A.C.	Loire-Atlantique	●			
Muscadet des Coteaux de la Loire	A.C.	Loire-Atlantique	●			
Muscadet de Sèvre-et-Maine	A.C.	Loire-Atlantique	●			
Musigny	A.C.	Côte de Nuits	●	●		
Néac	A.C.	Bordelais		●		
Nuits-Saint-Georges	A.C.	Côte de Nuits	●	●		premier cru
Orléanais	V.D.Q.S.	Loiret	●	●		
Pachérenc du Vic-Bilh	A.C.	Basses-Pyrénées	●			
Palette	A.C.	Bouches-du-Rhône	●	●	●	
Parsac Saint-Émilion	A.C.	Bordelais		●		
Pauillac	A.C.	Bordelais		●		crus classés
Pécharmant	A.C.	Dordogne		●		
Pernand-Vergelesses	A.C.	Côte de Beaune	●	●		premier cru
Petit Chablis	A.C.	Yonne	●			
Picpoul de Pinet	V.D.Q.S.	Hérault	●			
Pomerol	A.C.	Bordelais		●		
Pommard	A.C.	Côte de Beaune		●		premier cru
Pouilly-Fuissé	A.C.	Mâconnais	●			
Pouilly-sur-Loire Fumé	A.C.	Nièvre	●			
Pouilly-Fumé	A.C.	Nièvre	●			
Pouilly-Loché	A.C.	Mâconnais	●			
Pouilly-Vinzelles	A.C.	Mâconnais	●			
Premières Côtes de Blaye	A.C.	Bordelais	●	●		
Premières Côtes de Bordeaux	A.C.	Bordelais	●	●		
Premières Côtes de Bordeaux Cadillac	A.C.	Bordelais	●	●		
Puisseguin Saint-Émilion	A.C.	Bordelais		●		
Puligny-Montrachet	A.C.	Côte de Beaune	●	●		premier cru
Quatourze	V.D.Q.S.	Aude	●	●	●	
Quarts de Chaume	A.C.	Anjou	●			
Quincy	A.C.	Cher	●			
Renaison-Côte Roannaise	V.D.Q.S.	Loire		●	●	
Reuilly	A.C.	Indre	●			
Richebourg	A.C.	Côte de Nuits		●		
Romanée	A.C.	Côte de Nuits		●		
Romanée-Saint-Vivant	A.C.	Côte de Nuits		●		
Romanée-Conti	A.C.	Côte de Nuits		●		
Rosé des Riceys	A.C.	Champagne (Aude)			●	
Rosé de Béarn	V.D.Q.S.	Basses-Pyrénées			●	
Rosette	A.C.	Dordogne	●			
Rousselet de Béarn	V.D.Q.S.	Basses-Pyrénées			●	
Roussette du Bugey	V.D.Q.S.	Ain	●			
Roussette de Savoie	V.D.Q.S.	Savoie	●			
Roussillon des Aspres	V.D.Q.S.	Roussillon	●	●	●	
Ruchottes Chambertin	A.C.	Côte de Nuits		●		premier cru
Rully	A.C.	Châlonnais	●	●		premier cru
Sables Saint-Émilion	A.C.	Bordelais		●		
Saint-Amour	A.C.	Beaujolais		●		
Saint-Aubin	A.C.	Côte de Beaune	●	●		premier cru
Saint-Chinian	V.D.Q.S.	Hérault		●		
Sainte-Croix-du-Mont	A.C.	Bordelais	●			
Saint-Drézéry	V.D.Q.S.	Hérault		●		

			B	R	r	
Saint-Émilion						
Premier Grand Cru classé	A.C.	Bordelais		●		crus classés
Saint-Émilion grand cru classé	A.C.	Bordelais		●		crus classés
Saint-Émilion cru classé	A.C.	Bordelais		●		crus classés
Saint-Émilion	A.C.	Bordelais		●		
Saint-Estèphe	A.C.	Bordelais		●		crus classés
Sainte-Foy Bordeaux	A.C.	Bordelais	●	●		
Saint-Georges Saint-Émilion	A.C.	Bordelais		●		
Saint-Georges d'Orques	A.C.	Bordelais		●		
Saint-Joseph	A.C.	Côtes du Rhône	●	●		
Saint-Julien	A.C.	Bordelais		●		crus classés
Saint-Nicolas de Bourgueil	A.C.	Touraine		●	●	
Saint-Péray	A.C.	Côtes du Rhône	●			
Saint-Pourçain-sur-Sioule	V.D.Q.S.	Allier	●	●	●	
Saint-Romain	A.C.	Côte de Beaune	●	●	●	
Sampigny-lès-Maranges	A.C.	Côte de Beaune Villages		●		
Sancerre	A.C.	Cher	●			
Santenay	A.C.	Côte de Beaune	●	●		premier cru
Saumur	A.C.	Anjou	●	●	●	
Saumur Champigny	A.C.	Anjou		●		
Sauternes	A.C.	Bordeaux	●			crus classés
Savennières	A.C.	Anjou	●			
Savigny ou **Savigny-lès-Beaume**	A.C.	Côte de Beaune	●	●		premier cru
Savoie ou **vin de Savoie**	V.D.Q.S.	Savoie	●	●	●	
Seyssel	A.C.	Ain et Savoie	●			
La Tâche	A.C.	Côte de Nuits		●		
Tavel	A.C.	Gard			●	
Touraine	A.C.	Touraine	●	●	●	
Touraine Azay-le-Rideau	A.C.	Touraine	●			
Touraine Mesland	A.C.	Touraine	●	●	●	
Touraine Amboise	A.C.	Touraine	●	●	●	
Tursan	V.D.Q.S.	Landes	●	●	●	
Villaudric	V.D.Q.S.	Haute-Garonne		●		
Vins d'Entraygues et du Fel	V.D.Q.S.	Aveyron	●	●	●	
Vins Fins de la Côte de Nuits ou **Côte de Nuits - Villages**	A.C.	Côte de Nuits		●		
Vin d'Auvergne	V.D.Q.S.	Puy-de-Dôme	●	●	●	
Vin de Béarn	V.D.Q.S.	Basses-Pyrénées	●	●	●	
Vin du Bugey	V.D.Q.S.	Ain	●	●	●	
Vin de Savoie	V.D.Q.S.	Savoie et Isère	●	●	●	
Chignin-Bergeron	—		●			
Marignan et Ripaille	—		●			
Sainte-Marie-d'Alloix	—			●	●	
Volnay	A.C.	Côte de Beaune		●		premier cru
Vosne-Romanée	A.C.	Côte de Nuits		●		premier cru
Vougeot	A.C.	Côte de Nuits	●	●	●	premier cru
Vouvray	A.C.	Touraine	●			

II. Semi-Sparkling or Crackling Wines

			B	R	r	
Anjou	A.C.	Anjou	●		●	
Montlouis	A.C.	Touraine	●			
Saumur	A.C.	Anjou	●	●	●	
Touraine	A.C.	Touraine	●	●	●	
Vouvray	A.C.	Touraine	●			

III. Sparkling Wines

			B	R	r
Anjou mousseux	A.C.	Anjou	●	●	
Arbois mousseux	A.C.	Jura	●	●	
Blanquette de Limoux	A.C.	Aude	●		
Bordeaux mousseux	A.C.	Bordeaux	●	●	
Bourgogne mousseux	A.C.	Yonne, Côte-d'Or, Saône-et-Loire, Rhône	●	●	●
Clairette de Die	A.C.	Drôme	●		
Côtes du Jura	A.C.	Jura	●	●	
L'Étoile	A.C.	Jura	●		
Gaillac	A.C.	Tarn	●		
Montlouis	A.C.	Touraine	●		
Saint-Péray	A.C.	Côtes-du-Rhône	●		
Saumur	A.C.	Anjou	●	●	●
Seyssel	A.C.	Ain et Savoie	●		
Touraine	A.C.	Touraine	●	●	●
Vouvray	A.C.	Touraine	●		

Among the V. D. Q. S., only the sparkling white wine of Savoy is permitted the *appellation d'origine*.

Sweet Dessert Wines and Fortified Wines

			B	R	r	
Banyuls	A.C.	Roussillon	●	●	●	
Banyuls Grand Cru	A.C.	Roussillon	●	●	●	
Côtes d'Agly	A.C.	Roussillon	●	●	●	
Côtes de Haut-Roussillon	A.C.	Roussillon	●	●	●	
Frontignan	A.C.	Hérault	●			
Grand Roussillon	A.C.	Roussillon	●	●	●	*
Maury	A.C.	Roussillon	●	●	●	
Muscat de Beaumes-de-Venise	A.C.	Vaucluse	●			
Muscat de Frontignan	A.C.	Hérault	●			
Vin de Frontignan	A.C.	Hérault	●			
Muscat de Lunel	A.C.	Hérault	●			
Muscat de Mireval	A.C.	Hérault	●			
Muscat de Rivesaltes	A.C.	Roussillon	●			
Muscat de Saint-Jean-de-Minervois	A.C.	Hérault	●			
Pineau des Charentes	A.C.	Charentes	●	●	●	
Rasteau	A.C.	Vaucluse	●	●	●	
Rivesaltes	A.C.	Roussillon	●	●	●	

*The appellations Maury, Rivesaltes, Côtes d'Agly, Côtes de Haut-Roussillon, are encompassed by the region Grand Roussillon.

IV
CHEESE

Les Fromages

CLASSIFICATION OF CHEESES

Cheese is a product of cows' milk and, to a lesser extent, of goats' milk. Traditionally, Roquefort is made from ewes' milk. All cheese is made from curds that have been drained, and usually fermented. The curdling of the milk (whole milk, skim milk, or milk enriched with cream) happens naturally by the action of lactic ferments, or else is caused by using rennet.

Depending on what is to be done with it, the coagulated milk, the curd, is treated and molded. The action of the ferments produces the maturing of the curds.

There are several categories of cheese:

Fresh cheeses are not fermented, or only slightly.

Fromage blanc is the curd of cows' milk, eaten fresh. The *carré demi-sel,* also called simply *demi-sel,* is whole-milk curds, to which are added cream and a very little salt. *Petit-suisse* and cream cheese are made from curds of whole milk beaten up with cream. Others of this type are fresh Boursin, the Vacherin made in the Alps, and double-cream cheese. The last two are very slightly fermented.

Cheeses with a soft crust fall into two types, depending on the crust. With a moldy crust: ripened Boursin, Camembert, Coulommiers, Brie, Carré de l'Est, Petit-Duc and Sainte-Maure (made with goats' milk).

With a washed crust: Pont l'Évêque, Livarot, Munster, Maroilles, Reblochon, certain goat cheeses.

In the category of **cheeses with a semi-hard or pressed crust** are Saint-Paulin, Port-Salut, Cantal, Tomme, Saint-Nectaire, Cheshire, and some goat cheeses, such as Valençay.

Cheeses with a hard rind are Gruyère, Emmenthal, Comté, Beaufort, Parmesan.

Cheeses with a blue mold: bleu d'Auvergne, bleu des Causses, bleu de Bresse, Gex, persillé de Savoie, Roquefort, Gorgonzola, Saingorlon, Stilton.

Cheeses with a melted crust are rarer: Cancoillotte, crème de Gruyère, *fromage fondu au raisin* and processed cheeses.

SERVING CHEESE

If cheese is stored in the refrigerator, it must be taken out at least half an hour before serving, to give it a chance to breathe. Cheese is offered after the meat, vegetable and salad courses, when these are served, and in any event before the dessert. Some people still think that cheese should be served after the dessert; however, this practice has fallen into disuse.

All cheeses are offered unadorned, that is without their boxes or paper, with the single exception of Roquefort. Sometimes the crust is scraped before serving, or the cheese is given a thin coating of bread crumbs, but these practices are frowned on by true cheese lovers.

The best method of serving cheeses, even at family meals, is to put them on a platter: in this way everyone present can serve himself as he wishes.

SAVOY AND THE ALPS

BEAUFORT

This cheese resembles Gruyère, and is made high up in the mountains at altitudes of more than 6,000 feet, where the pastures are exceptionally rich in wild flowers. The fruitgrowers of Beaufortin and the Tarentaise and Maurienne valleys, who are also skilled in cheesemaking, make it in their chalets. A good-quality Beaufort has a smooth elastic texture. This is a cheese without holes, which looks rather like butter. The cheeses weigh anything from 65 to 130 pounds each, and carry a guarantee of their origin and a distinctive label.

Dry, delicate white wines, and very fruity whites such as dry Sauternes.

EMMENTHAL

This is a round cheese weighing about 200 pounds. It is a large-size Gruyère, with the characteristic neat holes that give it, according to some of its admirers, a very special quality.

White, rosé and red wines, which should be young and fruity, dry and light.

REBLOCHON

This is a product of La Clusaz*, at 4,000 feet in the Savoy. Its color can vary from saffron-yellow to dull red and is reminiscent of autumn leaves. It is a small-size round cheese and is bought whole.

Fruity whites, rosés and red wines.

*This is how we say *massif des Aravis* in America!

PERSILLÉ DES ARAVIS

This is made with goats' milk and is cylindrical in shape. It is quietly competing with Reblochon.

Full-bodied rosés and red wines like Beaujolais.

TOMMES

There are several varieties of Tomme, and the best known are the *tomme au marc de raisin,* covered in grape seeds, the *tomme des Beauges* and the *tomme de Savoie.* These are unsophisticated cheeses, rather hard, with good keeping qualities. Their characteristics can vary a good deal, depending on their origin. All of them have a very delicate flavor.

Nearly all the usual table wines, especially those that can be served cool.

PERSILLÉS

Coming from Thônes, Mont-Cenis and Grand-Bornand. Their marbling goes from blue to light green. They are often very highly colored, and typical of cheeses that are made blue by outside agency.

Wines with high alcoholic content, like Côtes du Rhône.

VACHERIN

Vacherin des Beauges is a medium-size round cheese. Since it is very soft, it is usually equipped with a kind of collar made of birch bark. It should be eaten when almost liquid, even with a spoon. As it has a very strong smell, it is sometimes sprinkled with caraway seeds.

Any great red wine.

TRAPPISTES DE TAMIÉ

Toupin, Tignes, Cervin and Beaumont are traditional Alpine cheeses of exceptional quality and flavor. They are little known outside of their own localities.

Mountain wines, such as Seyssel.

FRANCHE-COMTÉ

COMTÉ

This is a cheese of the Gruyère type, and an exceedingly good one. It is made by the fruitgrowers of Franche-Comté. The cattle of the region—Montbéliard and the spotted cows from Eastern France—are excellent breeds. Comté is ivory or butter-colored. It feels oily under the fingers, and there are a few holes in it, no bigger than hazelnuts, appearing at regular intervals. The rind is solid and grainy, and yellowish-brown in color. This cheese keeps very well.

Any good wine.

GEX-SEPTMONCEL

This cheese, which also goes under the name of Bleu du Haut-Jura, is made in the mountains, by tradition at an altitude of more than 2,500 feet. A white cheese with an orange-yellow rind, it is close-textured and streaked with royal blue when ripe. The quantity produced is in inverse proportion to the quality.

Red wines such as Chinon and Bourgueil.

MORBIER

A semi-hard cheese, made in the chalets of the Haut-Jura district. It is streaked with black, coming from the soot of the resinous wood used to "smoke" it. The cheese has a strong smokehouse aroma.

Vins gris of the Clairet type.

CANCOILLOTTE

This is a cooked cheese, to which is added, after careful melting and simmering, white wine and aromatic plants. Each producer has his own recipe.

Full-flavored wines such as Saint-Émilion.

MASSIF CENTRAL

SAINT-NECTAIRE

This is the oldest of the cheeses made in Auvergne. It is made in a vast region spreading from the Dômes to the Cantal hills from milk from the cows of Salers. When ripened, it shows, on cutting, a space between the rind and the cheese, as if the rind were about to fall off; it ready for eating at precisely this moment.

Dry, powerful rosé wines from Provence, and any other wine from the Mediterranean littoral.

MUROLS

It has some resemblance to Saint-Nectaire, as far as flavor goes. But it does not look like it. It is a reddish-colored cheese with a hole in the middle, and looks like a small brick-colored wheel.

Chanturgue wine.

CANTAL

This is one of the oldest cheeses in existence. It is named after the administrative district of Cantal, which makes a great deal of it. The cheeses made at Auban and Gévaudan are the most popular. It has a very special flavor, a compact texture, and is yellow with tiny white spots. As it matures it crumbles very easily, making it a very difficult cheese to imitate. It keeps very well.

Great Bordeaux wines, but not the greatest.

BLUE CHEESES

They are made in the Causses area of Aveyron, in Laqueville in the Puy-de-Dôme, and in Auvergne, Cantal and surrounding districts.

Like the Persillés, their name comes from the blue veins that marble the cheese. They are creamy cheeses, made from cows' milk, and have been made for a long time. The blue veins come from a mold on rye bread and are very rich in penicillin. The breed of cattle raised around Salers gives a creamy, rather strong cheese. Small in size, with good keeping qualities, these blue cheeses are easier to handle than Roquefort, which has a tendency to crumble and is not always dependable in quality.

Full-flavored wines of the Pomerol type, and Pommard.

FOURMES

These cheeses are produced in the Monts du Forez, at Ambert, Montbrison and Pierre-sur-Haute; they have a taste all their own and they keep very well. They are column-shaped.

Great Burgundy.

VACHARD

A rough-and-ready local cheese. It is not sold outside of its district.

Wines from the administrative district of Hérault and, in general, wines from the south of France.

CHAMBERAT

Like Vachard, this is a local cheese that is little known and hard to find away from home.

Wines from the administrative district of Hérault, from Cahors, and from the south of France.

GAPRON

A strong cheese, tasting of pepper and garlic, which is not usually available. It is ripened in the pastures, in the second crop of grass.

Minervois wine, and lots of it.

ROQUEFORT

The cheeses are ripened in the town of Roquefort in the district of Rouergue, but they can be made in different regions and the best probably comes from Corsica. It is made from ewes' milk. This is an extremely well-known cheese, which does not always live up to its reputation.

Narbonne and Minervois wines.

THE NORTHERN AND EASTERN PROVINCES

CARRÉ DE L'EST

A soft cream cheese made in Champagne and Lorraine, with special characteristics of its own, in spite of the fact that it closely resembles Camembert and Brie. It comes in various shapes, but always boxed.

Any wine with a respectable origin and no pretensions to greatness.

MUNSTER

Splendid soft cream cheese, which has been made for more than a thousand years in the Vosges Mountains of Alsace and Lorraine from the milk of the Vosges cattle. The crust, which is often washed, gives off a strong aroma that has nothing to do with the really delicate flavor of the cheese itself. Munster is often eaten with caraway seeds or aniseeds.

Alsatian wine, claret or white Graves.

GÉROMÉ

It takes its name from its place of origin: Gérardmer. A Géromé is bigger than a Munster, but the taste is very much the same.

Alsatian wine or light red wines.

ROCROI

An excellent cheese made in the Forest of Ardennes, little known outside of its region.

Dry rosé wines.

RICEY-CENDRÉ
CENDRÉ DE CHAMPAGNE

Cheeses of the vineyard districts of the Champagne country named after the

cendres, the ashes of the vine shoots and twigs, which give them their gray appearance. They are rough and ready, few and far between.
Corbières wines.

CHAOURCE
Rustic cheese made in the Bar-sur-Seine region. It stays white during the ripening period.
Provence rosé.

LANGRES
Made in the district of Haute-Marne, this is a soft cream cheese, smooth and yellow, with a yellow crust. It is cone-shaped.
Very good red Burgundies.

MAROILLES
This cheese, made in the Thiérache region of Picardy, was the favorite cheese of Charles V of France. Its crust is the color of reddish-brown brick, its aroma is famous, and the cheese itself is golden-yellow. This great cheese comes in several shapes. Sorbais, Mignon and Quart are made on the same lines.

Maroilles ages well, and if it is ripened for purposes of aging, it is described as *"gris"*: Gris de Lille, or Vieux de Lille.
Any very good red wine.

DAUPHIN
A crescent-shaped cheese resembling Maroilles, it is seasoned with herbs—tarragon, parsley and bay leaves—and spices—pepper and cloves.
Great and heady Burgundies.

BOULETTE D'AVESNES
This is a Picardy cheese, from the Thiérache region. There is a version from Cambrai, which resembles Dauphin in that herbs and spices are added, but the cheese is made with buttermilk.
Great Bordeaux wines.

TRAPPISTE DU MONT-DES-CATS
Simple cheese made by monks.
Any good, simple wine.

FRENCH EDAM AND GOUDA
MIMOLETTE
Edam and Gouda are Dutch cheeses. They have been imported into Flanders. Mimolette is the French name for this type of cheese: it is larger and has an orange-red color.
Decent red, rosé and white wines.

NORMANDY

ROLLOT
This is a small cheese in the form of a disk, made in Picardy.
Any good wine.

CAMEMBERT
This cheese is as Norman as Marie Harel, the peasant woman who invented it and thereby became famous. This is the shining example of soft cream cheeses. There are certain Camembert strains that are famous, and the cheesemakers responsible for them are awe-inspiring experts and strict upholders of tradition. Camembert, which has earned a world-wide reputation, is imitated, usually unsuccessfully. It is sold in round boxes.
All the great red wines.

PONT-L'ÉVÊQUE

This is a very good cheese with a firm, elastic texture, although it comes in the category of soft cream cheeses. It is sold in square boxes.

Rather strong red wines.

LIVAROT

In the Pays d'Auge, this cheese is nicknamed "the colonel," because the rushes around it look like a French army colonel's insignia. These rushes, or sedges, give the cheese a very special flavor. It is packed in boxes that are bigger and deeper than those of its neighbors, Camembert and Pont-l'Évêque.

Great red wines.

NEUFCHÂTEL
BONDON

Like Bondard, Coeur, Gournay and Briquette, they come from the Bray country. They are mild velvety cheeses, usually very smooth and creamy.

Light wines with plenty of bouquet, such as Moulin-à-Vent.

ÎLE-DE-FRANCE

BRIE

In shape it is rather like a good-sized pie on a straw mat. It is a great cream cheese, ripening quickly and with a fine, delicate flavor.

All the great red wines.

COULOMMIERS

This is a small Brie. It is eaten at two different stages: fresh, after salting, known as "*mousse,*" when it is smooth and creamy and tastes like fresh cream cheese. Allowed to ripen like Brie, called "*à coeur,*" the cheese becomes even creamier and has a nutty taste. It is sold sometimes in boxes, sometimes without.

Fruity, full-flavored reds and rosés.

BRIE DE MELUN

This is a very creamy cheese that can be eaten fresh, or "*bleu.*" Connoisseurs, however, usually prefer to wait until it is ripe.

Excellent red wines.

MONTEREAU

When eaten fresh, it is exactly like a smaller version of Coulommiers. When kept until ripe it is more like Brie de Melun.

The same wines that go with Coulommiers or Brie.

LA FEUILLE DE DREUX

A very good cheese of the same type as the preceding ones. It is wrapped in a few chestnut leaves.

Any fruity red wine.

BRITTANY

PORT-SALUT, SAINT-PAULIN

Formerly called "Port-du-Salut," Port-Salut should not be confused with Saint-Paulin. Port-Salut has become well known outside Brittany, whereas Saint-Paulin has not. The difference between the two cheeses is in their texture: Saint-Paulin is covered with tiny holes, and Port-Salut is smooth.

For Saint-Paulin, light reds, rosés and whites. For Port-Salut, good respectable reds.

NANTAIS, known as FROMAGE DE CURÉ
An excellent cheese made around Nantes.
Light and fruity red, rosé and white wines.

CHEESES OF MONTAUBAN-DE-BRETAGNE
Like those of Saint-Agathon and Conneré, these cheeses have been rescued from oblivion by the persistence of the Breton dairy farmers.
Vins gris, and good dry cider, draft or bottled.

TOURAINE CAMEMBERT AND CARRÉ
These can be very good. The Carré de l'Est benefits from the milder climate of Touraine and the local Camembert is sometimes sweeter than the original.
Touraine wines, Joué-lès-Tours and Chinon.

VENDÔMOIS
The ashes from the fires of vine twigs are used to cover some of the blue cheeses and goat cheeses of the Vendôme region, and these are called Vendômois *bleus* and Vendômois *cendrés*.
Anjou and Touraine wines.

VALLEY OF THE LOIRE

VILLEBAROU can still be found around Blois.

OLIVET, first made in the Orléans region, is a kind of Vendôme *bleu* or *cendré;* the blue cheese is very delicate in flavor and the *cendré* type keeps marvelously well.

PITHIVIERS is ripened on hay, and this gives it a special flavor.

GIEN, SAINT-BENOÎT (made in Sully-sur-Loire or Jargeau) and PATAY are local cheeses that go well with the local wines.
For all these cheeses, regional wines.

THE OTHER PROVINCES

ÉPOISSES is a well-known cheese made in Burgundy. Like *fromage des Laumes,* which it resembles, Époisses has a very special taste.
The best Burgundies.

SOUMAINTRAIN, also called Saint-Florentin, made in the district of Yonne, looks very much like Coulommiers. It is yellow in color, with a yellowish-orange crust.
Red Burgundies.

BROCCIO is a Corsican cheese made from goats' milk.
Corsican wines or Côtes du Rhône.

CACHAT, made in Provence from ewes' milk, is ripened in vinegar. It has a pleasant aroma.
Châteauneuf wine.

SAINT-MARCELLIN is made in the district of Isère, from goats' milk. SASSENAGE, from the same region near Grenoble, is made from a mixture of cows', goats' and ewes' milk.
Côtes du Rhône and local wines.

INDEX

This index lists each recipe alphabetically under the heading of its principal ingredient, English recipe names appearing under English headings, as Beef, Eggs, Mushrooms, Spinach, and French recipe names appearing under French headings, as *Boeuf, Oeufs, Champignons, Épinards*. In addition recipes are listed under menu categories, as Hors-d'Oeuvre, Salads, Soups, and under the names of specific preparations, as Aspic Dishes, Barquette, Croûte, Fritter, Mousse, Soufflé, and so on; under these headings both French and English names are listed.

The reader should look for a salmon recipe under Salmon rather than under Fish, for a leek recipe under Leek rather than vegetable; under general terms such as Fish or Vegetable are listed only those recipes in which these words are part of the recipe name.

Basic information on preparation and cooking is listed alphabetically as well as with the specific food or kind of preparation to which it applies.

NOTE: *CP* = Color Plate. See List of Color Plates on pages 895-896.

A

C

D

H

I

M

P

Q

R

S

T

V

W